Stephen Birnbaum Travel Guides

Canada
Caribbean, Bermuda, and the Bahamas
Disneyland
Europe
Europe for Business Travelers
Florida for Free
France
Great Britain and Ireland
Hawaii
Italy
Mexico
South America
United States
USA for Business Travelers
Walt Disney World

CONTRIBUTING EDITORS

Burton Anderson
Jeff Davidson
Linda Davidson
Marcia Feltheimer
Dwight V. Gast
Sari Gilbert
Judith Harris
Arline Inge
Theadora Lurie
Diane Melville
Michael Mewshaw

Wendy Owen
Linda Parseghian
Clare Pedrick
Susan Pierres
Peter Rosenwald
Patricia Schulz
Janet Stobart
Phoebe Tait
Robert Tine
David Wickers
Anne Marshall Zwack

MANUSCRIPT EDITOR Barbara G. Flanagan

COVER Robert Anthony

MAPS Andrew Mudryk

SYMBOLS Gloria McKeown

A Stephen Birnbaum Travel Guide

Birnbaum's ITALY 1987

Stephen Birnbaum
EDITOR

Brenda Goldberg
EXECUTIVE EDITOR

Kristin Moehlmann
Barbara Benton
Associate Editors

Kathleen McHugh
Assistant Editor

Eleanor O'Neill
Editorial Assistant

HOUGHTON MIFFLIN COMPANY / BOSTON 1987

For Alex, who merely makes this all possible.

This book is published by special arrangement
with Eric Lasher and Maureen Lasher.

ISBN: 0-395-42333-3
ISSN: 0749-2561 (Stephen Birnbaum Travel Guides)
ISSN: 0890-1139 (Italy)

Printed in the United States of America

Q 10 9 8 7 6 5 4 3 2 1

Contents

GETTING READY TO GO

A compendium of all the practical travel data you need to plan your vacation down to the final detail.

When and How to Go

Preparing

On the Road

Sources and Resources

PERSPECTIVES

A cultural and historical survey of Italy's past and present, its people, politics, and heritage.

THE CITIES

Thorough, qualitative guides to each of the 13 cities most often visited by vacationers and businesspeople. Each section, a comprehensive report of the city's most appealing attractions and amenities, is designed to be used on the spot. Directions and recommendations are immediately accessible because each guide is presented in a consistent form.

DIVERSIONS

A selective guide to more than 20 active and cerebral vacations, including the places to pursue them where your quality of experience is likely to be highest.

For the Body

For the Mind

For the Experience

DIRECTIONS

The most spectacular routes and roads, most arresting natural wonders, and most magnificent palazzos, villas, and gardens — all organized into 18 specific driving tours.

A Word from the Editor

In the course of our roamings around Italy to collect data for this guide, it became increasingly obvious that "Italians" are a rare species. Oh, we found lots of folks who were enthusiastic about describing themselves as Venetian, Milanese, Roman, or Neapolitan, but almost no one who would characterize himself or herself as an Italian. This is hardly inexplicable in a nation that became unified only as recently as 1870 and where regional distinctions are such a source of local pride and delight.

Our guidebook contradicts the fiction that Italy is any sort of homogeneous country, a nation with a single face and similar sensitivities stretching from Sicily to the Swiss border. As anyone who has traveled widely in Italy soon discovers, nothing could be further from the truth. The atmosphere and ambience that thrive across the length of the Italian peninsula are spectacularly varied, and in trying to provide an accurate guide to each distinct region, the travel editor often feels as though at least a dozen distinct countries are demanding attention — not entirely incomprehensible, since about that number of sovereign city-states once occupied the boundaries of what modern maps cavalierly call Italy.

It isn't easy blending these diverse districts into a coherent whole. Making some sense of the relationship between the high-powered citizens of Milanese commerce and their somnolent siblings down on the *fattoria* in Calabria takes some doing. No less trying is the task of relating raucous Romans to the more dour and dignified denizens of Venice's canals.

In the most practical terms, it's just these very broad differences — ones that have existed throughout the spectrum of Italian history — that provide the most compelling motivation to create this detailed guide to Italian life and landscape, for where travelers once routinely visited only Rome — and then said they'd seen Italy — there is now a far broader recognition that Rome is no more an accurate mirror of all of Italy than New York is a perfect image of the many faces of the United States. This new guide to Italy continues our own strong sense of the need to treat the world's most popular travel destinations in substantially greater depth.

Such treatment only reflects the growing trend among travelers to return again and again to favorite foreign countries. Once upon a time, even the most dedicated traveler would visit distant parts of the world no more than once in a lifetime — usually as part of that fabled Grand Tour. But greater numbers of would-be travelers are now availing themselves of the increasingly easy opportunity to visit favored parts of the world as frequently as the impulse strikes.

So where once it was routine to say you'd "seen" a particular country after a very superficial, once-over-lightly encounter, the more perceptive travelers of today recognize that it's entirely possible to have only skimmed the surface of a specific travel destination even after having visited that place more than a dozen times. Similarly, repeated visits to a single site permit true exploration of special interests, whether they be sporting, artistic, or cerebral. Multiple visits also allow an ongoing relationship with foreign citizens sharing similar interests and an opportunity to discover and appreciate different perspectives on a single field of endeavor.

For those of us who spent the last decade working out the special system under which we present information in this series, the luxury of being able to devote nearly as much space as we'd like to just a single country is as close to guidebook heaven as any of us expects to come. But clearly this is not the first guide to the glories of Italy — one suspects that guides of one sort or another have existed at least since Caesar's legions began to develop itchy feet. But if guides to Italy have been available literally for centuries, a traveler might logically ask why a new one is necessary at this particular moment.

Our answer is that the nature of travel to Italy, and even the travelers who now routinely make the trip, have changed dramatically. For the past 2,000 years or so, travel to and through Italy was an extremely elaborate undertaking, one that required extensive advance planning. Even as recently as the 1950s, a person who had actually been to Rome, Venice, Florence, or Milan could dine out on his or her experience for years, since such adventures were quite extraordinary and usually the province of the privileged alone.

With the advent of jet air travel in the late 1950s, however, and of increased-capacity, wide-body aircraft during the 1960s, travel to and around once distant lands became extremely common. In fact, in two and a half decades of nearly unending inflation, air fares may be the only commodity in the world that has actually gone down in price. And as a result, international travel is now well within the budgets of mere middle-class mortals.

Attitudes, as well as costs, have also changed significantly in the last couple of decades. Beginning with the so-called flower children and hippies of the 1960s, international travel lost much of its aura of mystery. Whereas their parents might have been satisfied with a superficial sampling of Florence or Venice, these young people, motivated as much by wildly inexpensive "youth fares" as by the inclination to see the world, simply picked up and settled in various parts of Europe for an indefinite stay. While living as inexpensively as possible, they usually adopted with great gusto the local lifestyle and generally immersed themselves in things European.

Thus began an explosion of travel to and through Italy. And over the years, the development of inexpensive charter flights and packages fueled and sharpened the new American interest in and appetite for more extensive exploration.

Now, as we reach the late 1980s, those same flower children have undeniably aged. While it may be impolite to point out that they are probably well into their untrustworthy thirties and forties (and most firmly entrenched in establishment activities), their original zeal for travel remains unabated. For them it's hardly news that the way to get from western Europe to the Italian Riviera is to head toward the Mediterranean, make a left, and then wait for the pebbled beachfronts to appear. Such experienced and knowledgeable travelers have decided precisely where they want to go and are more often searching for ideas and insights to expand their already sophisticated travel consciousness. And — reverting to their youthful instincts and habits — they are after a deeper understanding and fuller assimilation of Italian consciousness. Typically, they visit single countries (or even cities) several times and may actually do so more than once in a single year.

Obviously, any new guidebook to Italy must keep pace with and answer the real needs of today's travelers. That's why we've tried to create a guide that's specifically organized, written, and edited for this more demanding modern audience, one for whom qualitative information is infinitely more desirable than mere quantities of unappraised data. We think that this book and the other guides in our series represent a new generation of travel guides one that is especially responsive to contemporary needs and interests.

For years, dating back as far as Herr Baedeker, travel guides have tended to be encyclopedic, seemingly much more concerned with demonstrating expertise in geography and history than in any analysis of the sorts of things that more often concern a typical tourist. But today, when it is hardly necessary to tell a traveler where Rome is, it is hard to justify devoting endless pages to historical perspectives. As suggested earlier, it's not impossible that the guidebook reader may have been to Italy nearly as often as the guidebook editor, so it becomes the responsibility of that editor to provide new perceptions and to suggest new directions to make the guide genuinely valuable.

That's exactly what we've tried to do in our series. I think you'll notice a different, more contemporary tone to the text, as well as an organization and focus that are distinctive and more functional. And even a random examination of what follows will demonstrate a substantial departure from the standard guidebook orientation, for we've not only attempted to provide information of a different sort, but we've also tried to present it in a context that makes it particularly accessible.

Needless to say, it's difficult to decide precisely what to include in a guidebook of this size — and what to omit. Early on, we realized that giving up the encyclopedic approach precluded our listing every single route and restaurant, which helped define our overall editorial focus. Similarly, when we discussed the possibility of presenting certain information in other than strict geographical order, we found that the new format enabled us to arrange data in a way we feel best answers the questions travelers typically ask.

Large numbers of specific questions have provided the real editorial skeleton for this book. The volume of mail I regularly receive seems to emphasize that modern travelers want very precise information, so we've tried to address those needs and have organized our material in the most responsive way possible. Readers who want to know the best restaurants around Bologna or the best places to find inexpensive couture in Milan will have no trouble whatever finding that data in this guide.

Travel guides are, above all, reflections of personal taste, and putting one's name on a title page obviously puts one's preferences on the line. But I think I ought to amplify just what "personal" means. I do not believe in the sort of personal guidebook that's a palpable misrepresentation on its face. It is, for example, hardly possible for any single travel writer to visit thousands of restaurants (and nearly as many hotels) in any given year and provide accurate appraisals of each one. And even if it were possible for one human being to survive such an itinerary, it would of necessity have to be done at a dead sprint and the perceptions derived therefrom would probably be less valid than those of any other intelligent individual visiting the same establishments. It is, therefore, impossible (especially in an annually revised and updated guidebook *series* such as we offer) to have only one person provide all the data on the entire world.

I also happen to think that such individual orientation is of substantially less value to readers. Visiting a single hotel for just one night or eating one hasty meal in a given restaurant hardly equips anyone to provide appraisals that are of more than passing interest. No amount of doggedly alliterative or oppressively onomatopoeic text can camouflage a technique that is specious on its face. We have, therefore, chosen what I like to describe as the "thee and me" approach to restaurant and hotel evaluation and, to a somewhat more limited degree, to the sites and sights we have included in the other sections of our text. What this really reflects is a personal sampling tempered by intelligent counsel from informed local sources, and these additional friends-of-the-editor are almost always residents of the city and/or area about which they have been consulted.

Despite the presence of several editors, a considerable number of writers and researchers, and numerous insightful local correspondents, very precise editing and tailoring keep our text fiercely subjective. So what follows is purposely designed to be the gospel according to Birnbaum, and it represents as much of my own taste and insight as is humanly possible. It is probable, therefore, that if you like your cities genteel and your mountainsides uncrowded, prefer small hotels with personality to huge high-rise anonymities, and can't tolerate fresh fish that's been relentlessly overcooked, we're likely to have a long and meaningful relationship. Readers with dissimilar tastes may be less enraptured.

I also should point out something about the person to whom this guidebook is directed. Above all, he or she is a "visitor." This means that such elements as restaurants have been specifically picked to provide the visitor with a representative, enlightening, stimulating, and above all pleasant experience. Since so many extraneous considerations can affect the reception and service accorded a regular restaurant patron, our choices can in no way be construed as a definitive guide to resident dining. We think we've listed all the best places in various price ranges, but they were chosen with a visitor's viewpoint in mind.

Other evidence of how we've tried to tailor our text to reflect changing travel habits is most apparent in the section we call DIVERSIONS. Where once it was common for travelers to spend a foreign visit nailed to a single spot, the emphasis today is more likely to be directed toward pursuing some active enterprise or special interest while seeing the surrounding countryside. So we've selected every activity we could reasonably evaluate and have organized the material in a way that is especially accessible to activists of either an athletic or cerebral bent. It is no longer necessary, therefore, to wade through a pound or two of extraneous prose just to find the very best crafts shop or the quaintest country inn within a reasonable radius of your destination.

If there is a single thing that best characterizes the revolution in and evolution of current holiday habits, it is that most travelers now consider travel a right rather than a privilege. Travel today translates as the enthusiastic desire to sample all of the world's opportunities, to find that elusive quality of experience that is not only enriching but comfortable. For that reason, we've tried to make what follows not only helpful and enlightening but the sort of welcome companion of which every traveler dreams.

Finally, I should point out that every good travel guide is a living enterprise; that is, no part of this text is cast in bronze. In our annual revisions, we refine, expand, and further hone all our material to serve your travel needs even better. To this end, no contribution is of greater value to us than your personal reaction to what we have written, as well as information reflecting your own experiences while using this book. We earnestly and enthusiastically solicit your comments on this book *and* your opinions and perceptions about places you have recently visited. In this way, we will be able to provide the most current information — including the actual experiences of the travel public — and to make those experiences more readily available to others. Please write to us at 60 E 42nd St., New York, NY 10165.

We sincerely hope to hear from you.

STEPHEN BIRNBAUM

How to Use This Guide

A great deal of care has gone into the organization of this guidebook series, and we believe it represents a real breakthrough in the presentation of travel material. Our aim has been to create a new, more modern generation of travel books and to make them the most useful and practical travel tools available today.

Our text is divided into five basic sections in order to best present information on every possible aspect of a vacation in Italy. This organization itself should alert you to the vast and varied opportunities available as well as indicate all the specific, detailed data necessary to plan a trip. You won't find much of the conventional "quaint villages and beautiful scenery" text in this guide; we've chosen instead to use the available space for more useful and purposeful information. Prospective itineraries tend to speak for themselves, and with so many diverse travel opportunities, we feel our main job is to explain them and to provide the basic information — how, when, where, how much, and what's best — to allow you to make the most intelligent choices possible.

What follows is a brief summary of the five sections of this book and what you can expect to find in each. We believe that you will find both your travel planning and en route enjoyment enhanced by having this book at your side.

GETTING READY TO GO

This mini-encyclopedia of practical travel facts is a sort of know-it-all companion that provides all the precise information you need to go about creating a trip. There are entries on more than 30 separate topics, including how to travel, what preparations to make before you leave, what to expect on location, what your trip is likely to cost, and how to avoid problems. The individual entries are specific, realistic, and cost-oriented.

We expect that you will use this section most in the course of planning your trip, for its ideas and suggestions are intended to facilitate the often confusing planning period. Entries are intentionally concise in an effort to get directly at the meat of the matter. This information is further augmented by extensive lists of sources for more specialized information and some suggestions for obtaining travel information on your own.

PERSPECTIVES

Any visit to an unfamiliar destination is enhanced and enriched by understanding the cultural and historical heritage of that area. We have, therefore, provided just such an introduction to Italy, its past and present, politics, architecture, literature, and food and drink.

THE CITIES

Individual reports on the 13 cities most visited by tourists and businesspeople have been researched and written by professional journalists on their own turf. Useful at the planning stage, THE CITIES is really designed to be taken with you and used on the spot. Each report offers a short-stay guide to its city within a consistent format; an essay, introducing the city as a historical entity and a contemporary place to live; *At-a-Glance*, a site-by-site survey of the most important (and sometimes most eclectic) sights to see and things to do; *Sources and Resources*, a concise listing of pertinent tourist information, meant to answer myriad potentially pressing questions as they arise — from the address of the tourist office to where to find the best night spot, to see a show, to play golf, or to get a taxi; and *Best in Town,* our cost and quality choices of the best places to eat and sleep on a variety of budgets.

DIVERSIONS

This very selective guide is designed to help travelers find the very best places in which to pursue a wide range of physical and cerebral activities without having to wade through endless pages of unrelated text. With a list of 26 theme vacations — for the body, the mind, and the experience — DIVERSIONS provides a guide to the special places where the quality of experience is highest. Whether you seek fishing or bicycling, romantic hotels or cooking schools, each entry is the equivalent of a comprehensive checklist of the absolute best in Italy.

DIRECTIONS

Here are 18 itineraries that range all across Italy, along the most beautiful routes and roads, past the most spectacular natural wonders, through the most historic cities and countryside. DIRECTIONS is the only section of the book organized geographically, and its itineraries cover Italy in short, independent journeys of 1 to 7 days' duration that may also be connected for longer trips. Each entry includes a guide to sightseeing highlights; a cost and quality guide to accommodations and food along the road (small inns, castle hotels, country hotels); and suggestions for activities.

Although each of the sections of the book has a distinct format and a special function, they have all been designed to be used together to provide a complete package of travel information. To use this book to full advantage, take a few minutes to read the table of contents and random entries in each section to give you an idea of how it all fits together.

Pick and choose information that you need from different sections. Assume, for example, that you have always wanted to take that typically Italian vacation, an eating tour of the country's temples of gastronomy, but you never really knew how to organize it or where to go. Turn first to the chapter entitled *Dining in Italy* in the PERSPECTIVES section, where you will find a discussion of the food specialties and wines of the various regions and advice on Italian menus, manners, and methods. Next, choose specific restaurants from the selections offered in each city chapter in THE CITIES, in each tour route in DIRECTIONS, and in the roundup of the best in the country called *Buon Appetito: The Best Restaurants of Italy* in the DIVERSIONS section.

In other words, the sections of this book are building blocks to help you put together the best possible trip. Use them selectively as a tool, a source of ideas, a reference work for accurate facts, and a guide to the best buys, the most exciting sights, the most pleasant accommodations, the tastiest food — *the best travel experiences* that you can have.

GETTING READY TO GO

When and How to Go

When to Go

 For North Americans as well as Europeans, the period from mid-May to mid-September has long been — and remains — the most popular travel period, traditionally the peak vacation time. If Italy is the destination, however, there are reasons to depart somewhat from tradition. Travelers who prefer to see Italian cities when they're filled with Italians rather than foreign visitors avoid the month of August (when all Italians who can manage it are out of town); those who prefer not to risk the possibility of a heat wave avoid both July and August. Furthermore, the traditional high-season travel period does not encompass the reality of tourism in Italy, which increases notably just before Easter in many parts of the country, while the weather generally cooperates to make the season endure through October in other parts. Thus, while May, June, and September are ideal times for a visit, April and October are almost as desirable.

Nevertheless, it is important to emphasize that off-season travel — from November to Easter — is a viable alternative to travel at the best of times, and one that can offer substantial advantages. Though some lesser tourist attractions may have shorter hours or be closed for the winter, the major sites stay open and are far less crowded — as is the country in general. During the off-season, Italian life proceeds at its most natural pace, with its ordinary social and cultural seasons energetically under way. But for more and more people, the most convincing argument in favor of off-season travel is the economic one. Simply put, getting there and staying there is less expensive. Air fares drop in the fall and relatively inexpensive package tours become available, benefiting both independent and group travelers. Hotel rates tend to go down and discounts for stays of more than one night are more common. In areas where high- and low-season rates exist, the applicable periods are precisely defined, and although not all hotels in those areas offer two sets of rates, many do — anywhere from 10% to 30% lower during the off-season.

There are, however, some notable exceptions to this rule. Off-season is ski season in the Italian Alps, meaning high prices and crowds across the board. Carnival in Venice occurs during the off-season, but it's hardly a time hoteliers need to drum up business.

What's more, traveling in the dead of winter is not everyone's cup of tea. While most of Italy does not suffer freezing temperatures, the rain, fog, and cold, gray skies in some regions are not conducive to relaxed sightseeing. But Italy has devotees who prefer to visit in each of the seasons, and the matter is clearly one of very personal choice.

CLIMATE: Most people prefer traveling when the weather is likely to be fair. Even though the northern Italian cities of Bolzano and Milan are at approximately the same latitude as Québec and Montréal, respectively, and Palermo in Sicily is only a bit farther north than Richmond or San Francisco, the tendency is to think of Italy as a sunny southern country. True, a Mediterranean climate blesses most of the land with summers that are dry and warm to hot and winters mild enough that precipitation is rain rather than snow. But there is more to the climate than that, given the country's long, narrow bootlike shape, the length of its coastline, and the fact that roughly three-quarters is covered with hills and mountains.

The great barrier of the Alps, which top the boot much like a turned-over, fur-lined cuff, and the Apennines, which run the entire length of the peninsula, are a prime cause of climatic diversity. Alpine winters are long and severe, but at the same time the Alps shield the Lombardy Lake region from the worst rigors of the northern European winter. Both the Alps and the Apennines protect the narrow coastal strip of Liguria from cold north winds and reinforce the influence of its Mediterranean exposure, producing winter temperatures much like those of Naples or Sicily and nurturing winter flowers that are shipped all over Europe. The rest of the north, however, is not similarly favored. Across the Apennines, the vast plain of the Po River has a climate of the Continental type, running to extremes. Winters can be damp, foggy, and penetratingly cold; summers are hot, without the pleasant coolness of the Alps and only partly moderated by proximity to the sea.

The peninsula proper conforms to the Mediterranean type. In general, the farther south one goes, the milder winter temperatures become, although summer temperatures rise only to a limited extent. Summers do become progressively drier; fall and winter, progressively wetter. Snow is a rare and fleeting phenomenon, except in the higher reaches of the Apennines. Instead there is rain, heavier in most areas in October, November, and December than at any other time of the year. Some familiar winds embellish the weather pattern: Cold is colder when the *tramontana,* a cold, dry wind from the north, is blowing; hot is suffocating when the *scirocco* sweeps across the Mediterranean from Africa, heavy with dust and accumulated moisture.

But it bears repeating that the weather in any given spot depends on its position vis-à-vis the mountains and water. At any latitude, winters can be raw in the Apennines and mild along the shore. The coastlines of Naples and Salerno, with steep, rocky promontories at their back, are subtropical sweeps of oranges and lemons, characterized by a mean annual temperature of 62°F or above and by at least five months a year with mean temperatures of 68°F or above. Such readings are more typical of the island of Sicily, which is only 90 miles from North Africa at its closest point and thus comes by its subtropical climate naturally. Both Sicily and Sardinia have long, hot, and dry summers and warm winters. Taormina, with an average winter temperature of 55°F, has been attracting refugees from the cold since the beginning of the century.

In the five large Italian cities most popular with visitors — Venice, Milan, Florence, Rome, and Naples — light, cool clothing is appropriate for summer.

Venice can reach a muggy 90°F in July and August, rendering the aroma from its canals less than agreeable. Although there is rarely extreme cold in winter, precipitation ranges from fine mist to torrential downpour, and when the *bora* blows in from the northeast Adriatic, the effect can be more chilling than Alpine snow. Woolens and sweaters under wind- and raingear are needed, and if the *acqua alta* (high water) comes up over the canal banks, high rubber boots are handy for slogging around.

In Milan, temperatures are generally moderate, although the city sometimes suffers extremes. Summer can be hot and airless, with temperatures as high as the mid-80s; winter can be cold, wet, and foggy, accompanied by below-freezing temperatures and occasional snow.

The weather in Florence, much farther south but set in a bowlful of hills, tends to be rather severe. Temperatures range from 60°F to 90°F from mid-June to mid-September, and summer can be stifling. In winter, the temperature rarely drops below freezing, ranging from 36°F to 52°F from December through mid-March, but the cold is damp, often gripping. Heavy overcoats are advisable, an umbrella a necessity.

In Rome, average July and August temperatures hover around the low to mid-80s, but a heavy *scirocco* can push the maximum above 100°F. A refreshing breeze often provides relief on summer evenings, sometimes making a light wrap advisable. Winters are moderate, with temperatures averaging in the high 40s from December through February. The temperature seldom drops below freezing, and snow is very rare — although in February 1986 Romans were astounded by a snowfall for the second year in a row — but the *tramontana* can be chilly (definitely overcoat weather) and winter rains are heavy.

Summer in Naples is hot, with average highs in the mid-80s. Winter, though milder than in more northern parts of Italy, is rainy. Temperatures stay well above freezing, so a raincoat or light topcoat should be sufficient.

The following chart lists average low and high temperatures for specific cities at different times of the year and provides an idea of what weather conditions to expect and, therefore, what to pack.

AVERAGE TEMPERATURES (in °F)

City	January	April	July	October
Bari	43°–54°	52°–64°	70°–84°	59°–70°
Bergamo	29°–42°	46°–64°	63°–83°	49°–63°
Bologna	30°–41°	50°–64°	68°–86°	54°–68°
Bolzano	23°–41°	45°–66°	61°–82°	45°–66°
Cagliari	45°–57°	52°–66°	70°–86°	59°–73°
Cosenza	39°–52°	45°–66°	64°–90°	54°–72°
Florence	36°–48°	46°–66°	64°–86°	52°–68°
Genoa	41°–52°	52°–63°	70°–81°	59°–68°
Milan	32°–41°	50°–64°	68°–84°	52°–63°
Naples	39°–54°	48°–64°	64°–84°	54°–72°
Olbia	45°–59°	50°–66°	66°–84°	57°–73°
Palermo	46°–61°	52°–68°	70°–86°	61°–77°
Rome	41°–52°	50°–66°	68°–86°	55°–72°
San Marino	36°–45°	46°–61°	64°–82°	52°–64°
San Remo	45°–55°	52°–66°	68°–82°	59°–72°
Siena	37°–45°	46°–61°	64°–82°	54°–59°
Stromboli	50°–59°	54°–66°	70°–88°	63°–77°
Taormina	46°–57°	54°–66°	72°–88°	61°–73°
Taranto	43°–54°	52°–64°	72°–86°	61°–72°
Trieste	37°–45°	50°–63°	68°–82°	55°–64°
Turin	28°–39°	46°–64°	66°–84°	48°–63°
Udine	32°–43°	46°–63°	63°–82°	50°–66°
Venice	34°–43°	50°–63°	66°–81°	52°–66°
Verona	32°–43°	48°–64°	63°–84°	50°–64°

SPECIAL EVENTS: Many travelers may want to schedule a trip to Italy to coincide with some special event. A concert in a great cathedral or in a splendid natural setting may be much more memorable for music lovers than a visit to the same place in the course of a day's sightseeing, while a classical play in an ancient amphitheater may pack a powerful evocative punch for theatergoers — even if they don't understand the language. For history buffs, not to mention dedicated photographers, there are numerous folkloric happenings whose participants look as though they had stepped out of the Middle Ages or the Renaissance.

Italy's special events tend to fall into three categories. Festivals of the performing arts are usually presentations of music, especially opera, although there are also festivals of dance, drama, and film. Religious ceremonies and processions are tied to the liturgical calendar or result from the accumulation of centuries of tradition around a historical fact — often they continue to fulfill a vow of thanksgiving for deliverance from some natural disaster. These occur in towns of all sizes throughout Italy, but they are especially common in the south and in Sicily and Sardinia, where they are among the few remaining occasions to see islanders gloriously turned out in traditional regional costumes.

Historical reenactments or displays of historical pageantry are another type of event, particularly common in central Italy. The focus of the event is usually a medieval or Renaissance game, contest, or mock combat, generally preceded or followed by a parade of citizens in historical costume and by exhibitions of flag throwing, the baton twirling of days long gone. These wondrously photogenic occasions are the delight of visitors, but it's a mistake to think they are put on simply to stimulate tourism. In most cases, the games actually *were* played by the ancestors of the modern Italians, pitting halves, quarters, and smaller sections of a community against each other. Some games are said to commemorate a specific event and can therefore be traced to a particular date, although their origins are usually lost in time. Florence's *Calcio in Costume,* for instance, commemorates a "soccer" match played in defiance of the invading imperial troops of Charles V and dates from 1530; when the time came for the Florentines to show their mettle, they already knew what and how to play.

Thus Italy has *giostre* (jousts), *tornei* (tournaments), *balestrieri* (crossbowmen), and the *palio* (strictly speaking, a banner awarded to the winner of a competition; more broadly, the competition itself, possibly translated as "stakes"). In some cases, they are indeed reenactments; in others, there has been hardly any lapse between the modern revival and the historical counterpart. Of the numerous *palio* contests in Italy, the most famous, that of Siena, has been documented as far back as 1310 and has been a part of Sienese life almost uninterruptedly for centuries. No one who's seen it doubts that for the Sienese, the two midsummer incarnations are the World Series and the Super Bowl, contested in turn.

The events noted in the calendar on the following pages are the major ones, but they are only a sampling. Among the many not mentioned are numerous music festivals that proliferate as spring progresses into summer and numerous festivities for the feast day of the patron saint of a town or city, a day that is also generally a local holiday. A further cause for celebration not exhausted by the list below is the harvesting of the grape. Almost every district that makes wine also makes merry about it. If you see colored lights being strung around a *piazza* in September or October and a bandstand and booths going up, it's likely that a *sagra dell'uva* (feast, or consecration, of the grape) is about to begin, and you'll be in for some festive tasting.

The calendar of special events in Italy is a busy one from Easter through September, but if you're visiting at another time of the year, don't despair. In any city, the regular cultural season is under way from late fall through spring and a great deal is happening. Christmas, too, is a nice time to visit. The first sign of the season is the arrival in town of the *zampognari,* shepherds who roam the streets playing the *zampogna,* a strange bagpipe-like instrument that makes a haunting sound. Christmas decorations are not as ubiquitous or as showy as they are in the US; on the other hand, the tradition of the *presepio* (manger scene) is still strong. Italians always make time to go from church to church comparing the scenes, especially in Naples, where the making of *presepi* reached a state of high art in the 18th century. The season lasts through Epiphany (January 6), when good Italian children receive a second round of gifts from an old witch known as the *Befana* (bad children, should any exist, receive lumps of coal). New Year's celebrations range from spirited to downright dangerous, especially in Rome and in the south. Firecrackers begin to explode in the afternoon and increase as the evening advances, making it imperative for partygoers to be off the streets and at their destinations early. (The next day, newspapers report the number of fingers and eyes lost to this practice, and in recent years, it seems, a good number of gunshots have been added to the traditional fireworks.) At the stroke of midnight, Romans throw open their

windows and throw out the old — plates, bottles, furniture — to make room for the
new, and they do it with a vengeance.

The events in the following list are arranged by month. Since there can be some
variation from year to year, check with the Italian Government Travel Office (see
Tourist Information) for the exact date of anything you don't want to miss. For more
information on major events, see *Italy's Most Colorful Festas* in DIVERSIONS and see
Special Events in respective chapters in THE CITIES.

January/February

Carnevale: Pre-Lenten festivities reviving and rivaling those of the last days of the
Venetian Republic. Masked and costumed merrymakers prowl the city; balls,
parties, and happenings take place indoors and out. Begins 10 days before Ash
Wednesday. Venice.

Carnevale: Pre-Lenten festivities known for parades (usually four) of colorful,
humorous floats featuring larger-than-life caricatures. Viareggio.

Sa Sartiglia: Pre-Lenten festivities with 17th-century origins. Highlight is a race
of horsemen in masquerade jousting at stars. Sunday and Tuesday before Ash
Wednesday. Oristano.

Festival of San Remo: Three days of competition for the best new Italian pop song
— "Volare" was a winner in the late 1950s. February. San Remo.

March/April

Holy Week Processions: Activities include a pilgrimage by hooded penitents and
a procession of the mysteries, when eight groups of statues depicting the Passion
of Christ — the *misteri* — are carried about town. Holy Thursday and Good
Friday. Taranto.

Procession of the Mysteries: Twenty groups of statues are carried on the shoulders
of townsfolk for a grueling 24 hours in this descendant of a medieval Passion
play. Good Friday. Trapani.

Easter Services: Byzantine-rite celebration featuring colorful traditional costume
in a town founded by Albanians in the 15th century. Easter Sunday. Piana degli
Albanesi.

Scoppio del Carro: Traditional explosion of a cartful of fireworks, at the Duomo.
Noon, Easter Sunday. Florence.

Urbi et Orbi: Papal blessing of the faithful in St. Peter's Square. Noon, Easter
Sunday. Rome.

Investiture of the Captains Regent: Twice-yearly ceremony inaugurating this tiny
republic's new rulers, who serve six-month terms. Held in the presence of
foreign diplomats and uniformed armed forces. April 1 and October 1. San
Marino.

Fiera Internazionale di Milano: Italy's biggest international trade fair, held since
1920. April. Milan.

VinItaly: The country's biggest trade fair dedicated to grape growing and winemaking. April. Verona.

May

Sagra di Sant'Efisio: Four-day-long religious procession to and from the shrine of
the saint 18 miles away. Cortege of traditionally costumed islanders and decorated ox carts is most colorful for the departure and the return. May 1–4.
Cagliari.

Miracle of San Gennaro: Twice-yearly gathering of Neapolitans at the Duomo for
the recurrence of the miracle — the liquefying of the saint's blood — that keeps
their city safe. Saturday preceding the first Sunday in May and September 19.
Naples.

Festa del Grillo (Cricket Day): A day in the park for the Florentines, who buy crickets in cages and set them free. Ascension Thursday. Florence.

Corsa dei Ceri (Race of the Candles): Traditional folkloric event, dating from the 12th century or earlier. Three massive wooden shrines are paraded through town and then raced to their year-round resting place near the top of a mountain. May 15. Gubbio.

Cavalcata Sarda (Sardinian Cavalcade): Folk festival drawing men and women from all over the island in spectacular traditional costumes. Next to last Sunday in May. Sassari.

Palio della Balestra: Match in medieval costume between the crossbowmen of Gubbio and Sansepolcro, with flag throwing and a historical procession. Last Sunday in May. Gubbio. (Also held in September in Sansepolcro.)

Maggio Musicale Fiorentino: One of Italy's most important music festivals, with artists of international renown. Festival continues into June. Florence.

June

Infiorata: Religious procession over a street carpeted with flower petals in decorative patterns. A Sunday in mid-June. Genzano di Roma.

Regatta of the Four Ancient Maritime Republics: Colorful, choreographed parade of boats and a race pitting the four old rivals. A Sunday in June. Rotates annually among Pisa (1987), Venice, Amalfi, and Genoa.

Festa del Giglio (Lily Festival): Three-hour procession of eight huge allegorical towers, each with a band playing at its base and each shouldered by forty men. Sunday following June 22. Nola.

Calcio in Costume: Rough and tumble soccer match in 16th-century costume. Three games are played, one usually June 24, the feast of St. John the Baptist. Florence.

Festival of Two Worlds: Gian Carlo Menotti's creation, a celebration of music, dance, theater, painting, and sculpture, in an Umbrian hill town. Late June to mid-July. Spoleto.

Venice Biennale: International exhibition of modern art, begun in the 1890s. Even years only, June through September. Venice.

July

The Palio: The most famous and most popular of Italy's traditional events includes a parade in full 15th-century dress, flag throwing, and a wild bareback horse race around the town square. July 2, repeated August 16. Siena.

Gioco del Ponte (Battle of the Bridge): Parade in medieval costume followed by a pitched battle from north and south of the Arno for possession of the middle of the bridge. First Sunday in July. Pisa.

Umbria Jazz Festival: Italy's most important jazz get-together. A week of daily concerts outdoors and nightly jam sessions in the clubs. Perugia.

International Ballet Festival: More than three weeks of nightly performances by visiting companies. Nervi.

Festa del Redentore (Feast of the Redeemer): Fireworks, all-night picnics afloat, and a cross-canal procession over a bridge of boats to give thanks for the lifting of a 16th-century plague. Third Saturday night and Sunday in July. Venice.

Verona Opera Festival: Three or four operas, a ballet, and concerts outdoors in a 20,000-seat Roman amphitheater. Each night's performance begins with the lighting of 20,000 candles. Early July through August. Verona.

Baths of Caracalla Opera Season: Two months of open-air opera staged in the ruins of 3rd-century Roman baths and noted for elephantine productions of *Aïda.* Early July through August. Rome.

Arena Sferisterio Opera Season: Mostly opera, but also ballet outdoors in a 19th-century arena. Mid-July to mid-August. Mercerata.

Taormina Festival: An international film competition in conjunction with theater, music, and dance performances, some in an ancient Greco-Roman amphitheater. Mid-July through August. Taormina.

August

Torneo della Quintana: Historical pageantry, including jousting and a parade in 15th-century costume. First Sunday in August. Ascoli Piceno.

Li Candelieri (Festival of the Candlesticks): Folkloric happening with secular and religious roots. Representatives of medieval guilds parade huge candlesticks through the old town. August 14. Sassari.

The Palio: Second yearly running of this rousing race (see July). August 16. Siena.

Puccini Opera Season: The composer's operas performed in the open air in the place where he lived and wrote. Torre del Lago.

Sagra del Redentore: Two-part celebration: a religious pilgrimage and a folk festival of Sardinian songs and dances with a parade of thousands in regional costume. August 29 (the pilgrimage) and another day that varies from year to year. Nuoro.

Rossini Opera Festival: A mid-August to mid-September *bel canto* salute to the composer, in the city of his birth. Pesaro.

International Film Festival: Two weeks of screenings, with the international film crowd and plenty of homegrown paparazzi livening the Lido scene. Late August to early September. Venice.

Stresa Musical Weeks: Three or four weeks of symphony, chamber music, and recitals by world-famous soloists and young winners of international competitions. Late August to late September. Stresa.

September

Palio della Balestra: Crossbowmen's contest and parade in Renaissance costume; celebrates the foundation of the world's smallest republic and honors its patron saint. September 3. San Marino.

Living Chess Game: Played with people costumed as chess pieces and the town square as chessboard. Even years only; first Sunday in September and the immediately preceding Saturday. Marostica.

Giostra del Saracino: Reenactment of a medieval joust. Knights in armor representing the town's four quarters attack an effigy of a Saracen and vie for the golden lance. First Sunday in September. Arezzo.

Regata Storica (Historical Regatta): Parade of decorated boats, 15th-century style, and a gondola race on the Grand Canal. First Sunday in September. Venice.

Palio della Balestra: Return match between costumed crossbowmen of Gubbio and Sansepolcro. (Also held in Gubbio in May.) Second Sunday in September. Sansepolcro.

Giostra della Quintana: Historical pageantry, including a day of jousting and a parade in 17th-century costume the night before. Second Sunday in September. Foligno.

Miracle of San Gennaro: Feast day of the city's patron saint and second of the twice-yearly recurrences of the miracle (the first is in May). September 19. Naples.

Festival delle Sagre–Festa del Vino Douja d'Or: A day-long cookout of local food specialties during a week-long wine festival. Asti.

October

Investiture of the Captains Regent: Second of the twice-yearly ceremonies inaugurating the republic's new rulers (the first is held April 1). October 1. San Marino.

November

Fiera del Tartufo (Truffle Fair): Harvest festival celebrating food, wine, the famous local white truffle, and the skill of the truffle dog. First full week of November. Alba.

Marionette Festival: Sicilian *pupi* take center stage, but guest puppets from elsewhere in Europe perform, too. Palermo.

Festa della Madonna della Salute: Another cross-canal pilgrimage on a bridge of boats to give thanks for the lifting of a plague — this time a 17th-century one (see also July). November 21. Venice.

December

Opening Night at La Scala: Beginning of the season at the world's most celebrated opera house. Traditionally held on December 7, feast day of Sant'Ambrogio, patron saint of the city. Milan.

Traveling by Plane

 The air space between North America and Europe is the most heavily trafficked in the world. It is served by dozens of airlines, almost all of which sell seats at a variety of prices under widely different terms. It is not uncommon for passengers sitting side by side on the same wide-body jet to have paid fares varying by hundreds of dollars, and all too often the traveler paying more would have been equally willing to accept the terms regulating a less expensive ticket.

SCHEDULED FLIGHTS: Of the dozens of airlines serving Europe from the United States, those currently offering regularly scheduled flights to Italy are *Alitalia, Pan Am,* and *TWA.*

Gateways – At present, nonstop flights to Italy depart year-round from Boston, Chicago, and New York. Los Angeles has nonstop service during the summer only. Additional direct flights depart from these cities plus some others, such as St. Louis, San Francisco, and Washington, DC. (*Be on your guard:* A direct flight means that there is no change of flight number between the originating and terminating cities, although there is at least one stop en route and in quite a few cases even a change of aircraft, as from a small, short-range plane to a jumbo jet — what's known in the industry as a "change of gauge.") Nonstop or direct, nearly all of these flights land at Milan's *Malpensa Airport* or Rome's *Leonardo da Vinci Airport* at Fiumicino. In summer, Alitalia flies from New York via Rome to Palermo's *Punta Raisi Airport.*

Fares – Perhaps the most common misconception about fares on scheduled airlines is that the cost of the ticket determines how much service you'll receive on the flight. This is true only to a very limited extent. A far more realistic rule of thumb is that the less you pay for your ticket, the more the restrictions and qualifications that will apply before you get on the plane as well as after you get off. These qualifications relate to the months during which you travel, how far in advance you must purchase your ticket, the minimum and maximum amount of time you may or must remain abroad, your willingness to decide on a return date at the time of booking — and your ability to stick to your decision. The ticket you buy will fall into one of several fare categories currently offered by scheduled carriers flying between the US and Italy. From most to least expensive, these are first class, business class, economy, excursion, and advance purchase excursion (APEX).

1. *First Class:* Short of flying your own private jet, this is the most comfort you can buy in the air. In general, first-class fares cost more than double — and sometimes almost triple — economy fares, but a first-class ticket is the price of admission to the

section of the plane with the widest seats, the fewest seats per row, and the most legroom aloft. Sleeper seats, which recline deeply and are accompanied by footrests allowing the body to approximate a horizontal position, are the rule rather than the exception on long-haul routes. Headphones are free, drinks (from cocktails to after-dinner liqueurs) are free, the food is fancier, and there are more selections on the menu. Moreover, because first-class travelers have so few fellow travelers, they can count on being the object of the flight attendants' relatively undivided attention. No advance booking is required, no minimum or maximum stay is required, and there is no cancellation penalty. Unlimited free stopovers are allowed, a very attractive bonus on a long trip. If you're planning to visit countries besides Italy, you can stop in any number of cities en route to your most distant destination, provided that you stay within certain maximum, but generous, mileage limits.

Note: It is not easy to inform yourself about stopover possibilities by talking to most airline reservations clerks. More than likely, an inquiry concerning any projected trip will prompt the reply that a particular route is nonstop aboard the carrier in question, thereby precluding stopovers completely, or that the carrier does not fly to all the places you want to visit. It will take a good travel agent, working with the airline's rate desk (to which the general public doesn't have access), to apprise you fully of stopover privileges. Travelers might be able to squeeze in visits to Lisbon and Madrid or to London and Copenhagen on a first-class ticket to Rome or Milan, for instance, even a one-way ticket; Rome or Milan might only be the first of many free European stopovers possible on a one-way or round-trip ticket to a point beyond Europe. The airline that flies you on the first leg of your trip across the Atlantic issues the ticket, though you may have to use several different airlines to complete your travel. First-class tickets are valid for a full year, so there's no rush.

2. *Business Class:* Not too long ago, there were only two classes of air travel — first class and all the rest, called economy class. But because passengers paying full economy fares — frequently business travelers — sat in the same compartment as passengers flying for considerably less on various promotional or discount fares, the airlines introduced special services to compensate those paying the full price. Thus, business class came into being, one of the most successful of recent airline innovations. At first, business-class passengers were merely curtained off from the other economy passengers. Now a separate cabin, or cabins, usually toward the front of the plane, is the norm. While standards of comfort and service are not as high as in first class, they represent a considerable improvement over conditions in the rear of the plane, with roomier seats, more leg and shoulder space between passengers, and fewer seats abreast. Free liquor and headphones, a choice of meal entrées, and a separate counter for speedier check-in are other inducements. As in first class, you travel on any scheduled flight you wish, you may buy a one-way or round-trip ticket, and the ticket is valid for a year. There are no minimum or maximum stay requirements, no advance booking requirements, and no cancellation penalties, and the fare allows the same unlimited free stopover privileges as first class. Airlines have their own names for their business-class service — such as Clipper Class on Pan Am, Ambassador Class on TWA, and Prima Business Class on Alitalia.

3. *Economy:* Once the standard fare on flights to Europe, this has fewer takers as the years go by, and with good reason. Economy-fare passengers sit in the economy-class compartment of the plane and receive the airline's basic economy-class service, yet they pay a lot more for the ride than do most of the other passengers crowded in tightly around them. Thus, many prospective full-fare economy passengers prefer to upgrade themselves to business class if they need an unrestricted ticket or if comfort is a priority; if not, they buy one of the promotional tickets listed below. The exact terms of economy fare vary slightly from route to route and airline to airline, and an airline occasionally may sell more than one type of economy fare. Whatever the case, economy

fares are substantially less than business fares, the saving effected by limiting the frills (you pay for liquor and headphones, you check in with the masses) and, usually, the stopovers (if they are limited, they may be reduced to one or two, with a charge for each one, or they occasionally may not be allowed at all). But common to all economy fares is their relative convenience. As is the case with the higher-priced tickets, they can be bought for a flight up to the minute of takeoff (if seats are available), and if the ticket is round-trip the return reservation can be made anytime you wish — months before you leave or the day before you return. They are valid for a year, after which they can be renewed if not used (you must pay any price increase that may have occurred in the meantime), and if you ultimately decide not to fly at all, your money will be refunded. Economy (and business-class) tickets cost the same year-round between the US and Italy, though on some transatlantic routes they vary in price from a basic (low-season) price in effect most of the year to a peak (high-season) price in summer.

4. *Excursion:* Excursion fares have long been the traditional bargain fares. They apply to round trips only, and they have minimum and maximum stay requirements, but generous ones — in some cases you can stay away as much as a year. They have "open jaws," meaning that you can fly to one city and depart from another, arranging and paying for your own transportation between the two, and they usually permit one stopover, though not a free one, in each direction. Excursion fares of this type have been discontinued on flights to many European countries, but they still exist on flights between the US and Italy, where they cost about a third less than economy. The ticket is currently good for a minimum of seven days and a maximum of six months abroad and is sold at basic and peak rates. Open returns are permitted; that is, you do not have to reserve the return flight at the time of purchase. If you buy the ticket at high-season prices but return in low season, you are refunded the difference; if the reverse is true, you pay the difference.

5. *Advance Purchase Excursion (APEX):* This is nothing more than an excursion ticket with strings attached. On most transatlantic routes it is the cheapest fare available from the major carriers — about 50% less than economy — and it is certainly the most commonly used fare to Europe. As its name implies, the ticket must be completely paid for a certain number of days (usually 21) in advance of departure, not a difficult condition for most leisure travelers to fulfill. Minimum and maximum stay requirements are still generous: currently seven days to three months in the case of tickets to Italy. The drawback to the APEX is that it penalizes travelers who change their minds. The return flight must be reserved at the time the ticket is purchased, and if for some reason you are forced to change it while abroad, you will pay a penalty. On a few routes, the penalty for changing a return reservation *after* travel has begun is no more than $50 to $100. On other routes, you must pay the difference between the APEX fare and the round-trip cost of the next highest fare category. In the case of tickets between the US and Italy, this amounts to about $200, the difference between an APEX and an excursion, but on other transatlantic routes you may have to pay the difference between an APEX and a full-fare economy round trip — several hundred dollars. There is also a penalty of $50 or $75 or more for canceling or changing a reservation *before* travel begins. No stopovers are allowed, but it is possible to create an open-jaw effect by buying an APEX on a split-ticket basis, for example, flying to Rome and returning from Milan (or some other city). The total price would be half the price of an APEX to Rome plus half the price of an APEX to Milan. APEX tickets to Italy are sold at basic, shoulder, and peak rates (with the price season in effect on the departure date determining the price of the round trip) and may include surcharges for weekend flights.

At present, most airlines flying to Italy offer a variation of the APEX fare as a youth fare for those aged 12 through 24. The maximum stay is extended to a year and the return can be left open.

Other types of promotional or discount fares are sometimes available on scheduled flights. Among these are standby fares, at one time the rock-bottom fares to Europe. Standby fares have most commonly been offered on flights between the US and London; on flights to other European cities, they have proved elusive. At present, the major scheduled airlines do not offer standby to Italy, but because airline fares and their conditions constantly change, bargain hunters should not hesitate to ask if such a fare exists. While the definition of standby varies from airline to airline, it generally means that you make yourself available to buy a ticket for a flight (usually no sooner than the day of departure) and then literally stand by on the chance that a seat will be free. Once aboard, however, you have the same meal service and frills (or lack of them) enjoyed by others in the economy compartment. Also to be said in defense of standby: The fare is a one-way fare; in fact, it is the only way to fly one way on a major scheduled airline short of paying the full economy fare.

Another discount option is the GIT (group inclusive tour) fare. This is for passengers traveling as a group, taking the same flight, and prepurchasing a minimum amount of ground arrangements at their destination. (The tour operator handling the ground arrangements forms the group.) In the past, GIT fares were among the least expensive in the fare schedules of the major carriers, but with the advent of promotional fares, group fares have all but disappeared from some air routes — or their price tags have been made the equivalent of the other promotional fares. Travelers perusing brochures on package tours to Italy will find that in almost all cases, the applicable air fare given as a sample (to be added to the price of the land package to obtain the total tour price) is an APEX fare, the same available to the independent traveler. But very attractive group fares still appear from time to time, often as the applicable air fare for winter ski packages.

Travelers looking for the least expensive air fares should, finally, scan the travel pages of their newspapers for announcements of special promotional fares. These are the airline industry's equivalent of a sale and may be offered not only to encourage travel in slow seasons but also to inaugurate and publicize new routes. Ordinarily, promotional fares — such as the APEX — are capacity controlled; that is, only a certain number of seats per flight are sold at the low price (a number the airline may raise or lower depending on how many seats it expects to sell at higher prices). The seat allocation for a special offer may be very small indeed, and may, therefore, sell out quickly, while the offer itself may come on the market with a set expiration date and may not be available when you want to travel.

Low-Fare Airlines – Still another way to fly to Europe for less is to fly with one of the smaller airlines that consistently manage to offer bargain rates. You will probably note early in your research that there is little, if any, difference in the prices charged by the major carriers for a ticket in the same fare category between the same two cities. In addition to other factors, including bilateral agreements between the US and individual European countries, the economics of the marketplace tend to rule, with airlines rushing to match any new fare proposed by a competitor to avoid being priced out of business. But some airlines, among them a few that were once strictly supplemental, or charter, airlines, can provide a lot for less because of lower overhead, uncomplicated route networks, and other limitations in their service. Some of them sell tickets in one fare category only; others have several fares. Note that even though the difference in price between a ticket on a low-fare airline and an APEX on a major carrier may sometimes be negligible, the former may still be the better buy because the ticket may be governed by fewer restrictions.

Unfortunately, none of these airlines flies to Italy at the moment. *People Express* (phone: 201-596-6000, or see your phone book for a local number), no longer such a "small" airline, flies from Newark to London, and so does *Virgin Atlantic* (phone: 201-623-0500). Virgin Atlantic also flies from Miami to London, and People Express also flies from Newark to Brussels. *Tower Air* (phone: 718-917-8500 in New York State; 800-221-2500 elsewhere) flies from New York to Brussels. *Icelandair* (phone: 800-223-5500), whose low-cost scheduled flights to Europe have been popular with budget travelers for decades, flies from New York, Baltimore/Washington, DC, Chicago, Detroit, and Orlando to Luxembourg, stopping in Iceland on most flights. It offers "thru-fares" aboard Luxembourg's *Luxair* to a number of major cities in Europe, including Rome.

Intra-European Fares – Those who intend traveling by plane to other countries in Europe besides Italy will find that although bargain fares have been introduced between some cities (London and Amsterdam, for instance) and less-impressive promotional fares exist on other routes, flights between European cities are usually quite expensive — especially if you want a one-way ticket. This cost can be avoided by careful use of stopover rights on the higher-priced transatlantic tickets — first class, business class, and full-fare economy. If your ticket doesn't allow stopovers, ask about excursion fares and PEX fares (a type of excursion that must be paid for at the time you make the reservation and that has minimum and maximum stay requirements and cancellation penalties) for round trips only and about Eurobudget fares, which can be bought one way. They are available on many routes between Italy and major European cities, and if the restrictions that govern them allow you to use them, you may save as much as 35% to 45% off full-fare economy. Note that some airlines sell these fares both in the US and in Europe, while others sell them in Europe only. At press time, both legal and diplomatic actions were taking place that might soon lower air fares within Europe. The European Economic Community — the so-called Common Market — was focusing on fares and promising a form of deregulation. This could mean substantially lower costs and free competition.

Domestic service within Italy is provided by *Alitalia* and its subsidiary *ATI* (Aero Trasporti Italiani) and by a few smaller carriers. Full economy fares prevail on their flights; among the few reductions are youth fares, children's fares, and infants' fares, as well as night fares (a reduction of 30% applicable to a limited number of flights). All of these are available whether the ticket is purchased in the US or Italy. Weekend promotional fares, also 30% off, are sold in Italy only.

Reservations – When making plane reservations through a travel agency, ask the agent to give the airline your home phone number as well as a daytime business number. All too often, the airline has only an agency number as the official contact for changes in flight plans. Especially during the winter, weather conditions sometimes hundreds or even thousands of miles away can wreak havoc with flight schedules. The airlines are fairly reliable about getting this sort of information to passengers if they can reach them, but often they can't if the agency is closed for the night or the weekend. Specify to your travel agent that you want a home phone contact provided to the airline, and if you have any doubts, call the airline and do it yourself.

Note: Most return reservations from international destinations are automatically canceled after the required reconfirmation period (usually 72 hours before the flight) has passed. On the back of your airline ticket, the need to reconfirm is specifically spelled out. Don't let yourself be lulled into a false sense of security by the "OK" on your ticket next to the number and time of a returning flight. That only means that a reservation has been entered. *A reconfirmation is still necessary.*

Seating – Airline seats are usually assigned on a first-come, first-served basis when you check in, although some airlines permit you to reserve a seat when you purchase your ticket, and some go a step further by allowing you to visit a ticket office prior to departure to secure a boarding pass for the flight. There are a few basics to consider in choosing a spot. You must decide whether you want to sit in a smoking or nonsmoking section and whether you prefer a window, aisle, or middle seat. A window seat protects you from aisle traffic and gives you a view (unless it is over a wing), while an aisle seat enables you to get up and stretch your legs without disturbing anyone. Middle seats are less desirable for most people, and seats in the last row are the least desirable of all, since they seldom recline all the way.

The amount of legroom you'll have (as well as chest room when the seat in front of you is in a reclining position) is determined by pitch, a measurement of the front to rear spacing between seats. Since airplanes have tracks along which this spacing can be adjusted, the amount of pitch is a matter of airline policy, not of the type of plane you fly. First-class and business-class seats have the greatest pitch, a fact that figures prominently in airline advertising. In economy class, the standard pitch on transatlantic flights is 34 inches, not quite comfortable for most people, and on some low-fare airlines and charter flights it can be as little as 31 or 32 inches — downright cramped. Passengers with long legs are advised to choose a seat directly behind a door or emergency exit, since these seats often have greater-than-average pitch, or a bulkhead seat — a seat in the first row of the cabin. (But steer clear of the first row if you want to watch the movie.) The number of seats abreast, another factor determining comfort, depends on a combination of airline policy and airplane dimensions. First class and business class have the fewest seats per row. Economy class generally has nine seats per row on a DC-10 and an L-1011, making those planes slightly more comfortable than a 747, on which there are up to ten seats per row. However, charter flights on DC-10s and L-1011s can have ten seats per row and be noticeably more cramped than 747 charters, on which the seating remains at ten per row.

Smoking – Regulations regarding smoking on airplanes require that nonsmoking sections be enlarged to accommodate all passengers who want to sit in them, provided the passengers have confirmed reservations and do not arrive late for the flight. Cigar and pipe smoking are banned even from the smoking sections. These rules apply to domestic flights and to flights by US carriers departing from or returning to the US. They do not apply to flights by foreign carriers into or out of the US.

Flying with Children – As a general rule, an infant under 2 years of age (and not occupying a seat) flies to Europe at 10% of whatever fare the accompanying adult is paying. A second infant without a second adult pays the fare applicable to children aged 2 through 11. In most cases, this amounts to 50% of an adult economy fare and two-thirds of an adult APEX fare, but note that on flights to Italy, children pay 50% of an excursion fare whether the accompanying adult is flying on an excursion or an APEX ticket. Comparable fares apply to infants and children on Italian domestic services.

Most airlines make complimentary bassinets available. On some planes they hook into a bulkhead wall (at the front of the cabin); on others they are placed on the floor in front of the adult passenger. Ask about obtaining one when you make your reservation, and when checking in request a bulkhead or other seat that has enough room in front to use it. (On longer flights, the bulkhead seats are usually reserved for families traveling with small children.) Even if you do use a bassinet, babies must be held during takeoff and landing. Do not plan to use your own bassinet aloft until you've checked with the airline. Some airlines prohibit their use during flight; others may require that they be strapped into a seat and that you pay a child's fare rather than an infant's fare. Airline policy regarding infant safety seats also varies widely, although the Federal Aviation Administration has approved the use on planes of infant seats manufactured after January 1, 1981.

Meals – It is possible to order many kinds of special meals for your flight if you give the airline 24 hours' notice. The available cuisines and diets usually include high protein, vegetarian, kosher, Muslim, low calorie, and low sodium.

Getting Bumped – A special problem with scheduled flights occurs when an airline accepts more reservations (and sells more tickets) than there are seats on a given flight. This is entirely legal and is done to make up for passengers who reserve a seat and then don't show up for the flight. If the airline has oversold the flight and everyone does show up — either on a domestic flight or on one going overseas from the US — the airline is subject to stringent rules that protect travelers.

In such cases, the airline first seeks ticketholders willing to give up their seats voluntarily in return for a negotiable sum of money or some other inducement, such as an offer of upgraded seating on the next flight or a voucher for a free trip at some other time. If there are not enough volunteers, the airline may bump passengers against their wishes. Anyone inconvenienced in this way is entitled to an explanation of the criteria used to determine who does and does not get on the flight as well as to compensation if the resulting delay exceeds certain limits. If the airline can put the bumped passengers on an alternate flight that gets them to their destination within one hour of their originally scheduled arrival time, no compensation is owed. If the delay is more than an hour but less than two hours on a domestic flight and less than four hours on an international flight, the bumped passengers must be paid denied-boarding compensation equivalent to the one-way fare to their destination (but not more than $200). If the delay is more than two hours beyond the original arrival time on a domestic flight or more than four hours on an international flight, the compensation must be doubled. The airline may also offer bumped travelers a voucher for a free flight instead of the denied-boarding compensation. The passenger can choose either the money or the voucher (the dollar value of which may be no less than the monetary compensation to which the passenger would be entitled). The voucher is not a substitute for the bumped passenger's original ticket — the airline continues to honor that as well. Note that these rules do *not* apply to inbound flights from abroad, even on US carriers, nor do they apply to flights between foreign cities or to charter flights. Furthermore, no compensation is due if the airline bumps passengers because it substitutes a plane smaller than the one it originally intended to use.

The rules also do not apply if the flight is canceled or delayed due to mechanical problems. In such cases, some airlines provide amenities to stranded passengers, but these are strictly at the individual airline's discretion. Deregulation of the airlines has meant the traveler must find out for himself what he is entitled to receive. A useful booklet, *Air Travelers' Fly Rights,* is available for $2.75 from the Superintendent of Documents, US Government Printing Office, Washington, DC 20402; stock number 003-006-00106-5.

Baggage – The amount of free baggage allowed travelers flying from the US to Europe on a US airline or a major foreign carrier is almost always determined by the piece method. There are variations among airlines in how the method is applied, however, so before you begin to pack, check with your airline for specifics — especially if you don't intend to travel light. In general, the piece method permits each passenger one or more carry-on bags, but the combined dimensions (length, width, and depth) of *all* carry-on luggage must be less than 45 inches and it all must fit easily under a seat of the plane. In addition, each first-class passenger is allowed to check two bags, neither of which may exceed a total of 62 inches (combined length, width, and depth) or, usually, 70 pounds. Economy- and promotional-fare passengers are also allowed two bags in the cargo hold, the total dimensions of *both* not to exceed 107 inches (and usually neither one more than 70 pounds). On some airlines, business-class passengers are given the first-class allowance; on others, the economy-class allowance. Such things as a coat, pocketbook, umbrella, camera, baby food, and a reasonable amount of reading matter are not considered baggage. Children paying 50% or more of an adult fare are entitled to the same baggage allowance as a full-fare passenger, whereas infants traveling at 10% of an adult fare are entitled to one piece of checked baggage the combined dimensions of which may not exceed 45 inches. Charges for additional, oversize, or overweight pieces are assessed at a flat rate.

On many European local or trunk carriers, including Italian domestic services, luggage is subject to weight determination. Each first-class (sometimes business-class) passenger is allowed a total of 66 pounds of luggage without charge. All other passengers are allowed a total of 44 pounds. If you are flying from the US to Europe and connecting to a domestic flight, you will be allowed the same amount of baggage as you had on the transatlantic flight. If you break your trip and then take a domestic flight, the weight rule applies.

To reduce the chances of your luggage going astray, remove all airline tags from previous trips, label each bag inside and out, and lock it. Double-check the tag that the airline attaches to make sure it is coded for your destination: *MXP* for Milan's Malpensa Airport, for instance, *FCO* for Rome's Leonardo da Vinci Airport, better known as Fiumicino. If your bags are not in the baggage claim area after your flight or if they're damaged, report the problem to airline personnel immediately. Fill out a report form about your lost or damaged luggage and keep a copy of it and your claim check. If you must surrender the check to claim a damaged bag, get a receipt for it to prove that you did indeed check baggage on the flight. Most airlines have emergency funds to dispense to passengers stranded away from home without luggage, but if it turns out that your bags are truly lost and not simply delayed, do not immediately sign any paper indicating that you'll accept a settlement offer. Since the airline is responsible for the value of your bags within certain statutory limits, you should take time to assess the extent of your loss (see *Insurance*, GETTING READY TO GO). It's a good idea to keep records indicating the price you paid for the bags and their contents to expedite your claim.

CHARTER FLIGHTS: By actually renting a plane or at least booking a block of seats on a specially arranged flight, charter operators have long been able to offer travelers air transportation — often coupled with hotel rooms, meals, and other arrangements — for less money than most economy and excursion fares on scheduled flights. Charters were once the only bargains available, but no longer. Numerous promotional fares on scheduled flights are often nearly as low as charter prices, especially on the more competitive routes, and their terms are usually more flexible. Nevertheless, after a few lean years, the charter business is staging a strong comeback. The saving possible on a flight varies considerably depending on the country to which it is headed (some governments do not allow charters to land; others allow them to undercut scheduled fares by a wide margin). Among the current offerings, charter flights to Italy are common, a sign that they still represent good value.

Charter travel once required that an individual be a member, of fairly long standing, of an organization, club, or other "affinity" group whose main purpose was not travel. Newer "public charters" are more flexible. Public charters are open to anyone, whether part of a group or not; they have no advance booking requirements; and they have no minimum stay requirements. They allow passengers to book a one-way flight, and charter operators that have flights to several different cities usually allow passengers to "mix and match" flights, that is, fly to one city and come home from another. These are American regulations, however, and they are sometimes more permissive than the charter laws of other countries. For example, Italy does not allow one-way charters, and only in certain circumstances can you fly into an Italian city and return from another European city. The charter operator may offer air-only charters, selling the flight alone, or charter packages, which include the flight and a combination of land arrangements such as accommodations, meals, tours, or car rental.

Bookings – Charter operators rent planes from scheduled airlines or from specialized charter airlines and then offer the flights to the public either directly through advertisements or through travel agents. Passengers buy tickets from the operator or the agent, not from the airline owning the plane. Keep in mind while reading the ads and the brochures that most charters have little of the flexibility of regularly scheduled flights regarding changes of flight dates, cancellations, and refunds; the price you pay for saving money is the risk of losing some or a lot of it if you cannot stick to your plans. Keep in mind, too, that by virtue of the economics of charters, the plane will almost always be full, with all seats taken, including the extra ones that are often squeezed onto charter flights. There is a good chance you'll be crowded and uncomfortable. On the other hand, charters sometimes make up for discomfort with convenience — for instance, by taking off from nearby airports that are otherwise without nonstop service, saving travelers the wear and tear of getting to a major city to begin an overseas trip. If you do decide to take a charter, read the contract carefully and note the following:

1. Stipulations regarding cancellation by the consumer. It cannot be repeated often enough that if you are forced to cancel your trip, you can lose much and possibly all of your money unless you have cancellation insurance, which is a *must* (see *Insurance*, GETTING READY TO GO). Frequently, if you cancel well in advance (often six weeks or more), you may forfeit only a $25 or $50 fee. If you cancel only two or three weeks before the flight, there may be no refund at all unless you or the operator can supply a substitute passenger.

2. Stipulations regarding cancellations and major changes made by the charterer. Charter flights may be canceled by the operator up to ten days before departure for any reason, usually underbooking. If that happens, your money will be returned in two weeks, but that may leave you too little time to make new arrangements. (The charter may *not* be canceled within ten days of departure except for circumstances — such as natural disasters or political upheavals — that make it physically impossible to perform the flight.) Charter operators may also make "major changes," such as in the date or place of departure or return, but if you don't accept these changes you are entitled to cancel and receive a full refund. In addition, operators are permitted to assess a surcharge (for fuel or other rising costs) of up to 10% of the air fare up to ten days before departure. If the price increase is more than 10%, that too is considered a major change, giving you the right to a full refund — though, again, if you cancel, you may have too little time to make alternate plans. Increasing numbers of charter operators are offering "insurance" — for a small fee — against any increase in the charter price. In any event, prices may not be increased at all within ten days of departure.

3. Instructions concerning the payment of the deposit and the balance and to whom the check is to be made payable. Ordinarily, checks are made out not to the charter company but to a bank escrow account. This means that the bank pays the charter airline and any providers of ground arrangements (in the case of a charter package) prior to the flight but does not release the balance of the account to the charter company until after the flight is completed. If the flight is not completed, there is a ready reserve of cash for refunds, but if you or your travel agent makes your check out to the charter company directly, you automatically lose this protection. The charter company is required to furnish further security in the form of a surety bond or trust agreement issued by an insurance company or a bank, and you should know the name of this bonding agent or other securer. If you want to file a claim against a charter company that has gone out of business, the claim should be sent to the securer within 60 days of the date of your intended return flight.

DISCOUNT TRAVEL SOURCES: The APEX fare is an example of a promotional fare offered on regularly scheduled transatlantic flights by most major airlines. Promotional fares are often referred to as discount fares because they are lower in price than what used to be the standard airline fare — full-fare economy. Nevertheless, they cost the traveler the same whether they are bought through a travel agent or directly from the airline. Tickets that cost less if bought from some outlet other than the airline do exist, however. While it is likely that the vast majority of travelers flying to Europe in the near future will be doing so on a promotional fare or charter rather than on a "discount" air ticket of this sort, it is still a good idea for cost-conscious consumers to be aware of the latest developments in the budget air fare scene.

Bucket Shops – Some vendors of travel services can afford to sell tickets to their customers at a discount because the airline has sold the tickets to them at a discount, a practice in which many airlines indulge, albeit discreetly, preferring that the general public not know they are undercutting their own "list" prices. Straight discounting of this sort, long common in the European market and especially on certain routes (such as flights to the Orient), is now becoming more common in the US and not strictly on flights to Asia. Once upon a time, travel agencies specializing in such discounting were known as *bucket shops,* a term fraught with connotations of unreliability. But in today's highly competitive travel marketplace, more and more conventional travel agencies are selling discounted tickets, and the old bucket shops are becoming more respectable too. Agencies that specialize in discounted tickets are located in most large cities and can be found by studying the smaller ads in the travel sections of Sunday newspapers.

Net Fares – These come about through rebating, a very recent twist to the discounting described above. Travel agents ordinarily do not charge for their services, making their money instead from the commissions they receive from their suppliers — traditionally, 8% to 10% of the price of airline tickets. If an agency does a greater-than-average volume of business with a single airline, its commission can be increased substantially, and an agency that has earned an "override" can afford to pass some of it along to the customer in the form of a price reduction. A few agencies take rebating a step further by passing all of their commission along to the customer and making their profit by charging a fixed fee for service. One of the first to practice this type of net fare pricing is *McTravel,* 2335 Sanders Rd., Northbrook, IL 60062 (phone: 312-498-9390), which sells domestic and international tickets, charging one fee for each reservation made and another for each ticket issued. (Travelers residing outside the Chicago area can transact business by phone and pay with a credit card.) The amount saved depends on the cost of the airline ticket being purchased; it may be no bargain for the lowest-priced domestic promotional fare, but it may be significant on a long-haul international itinerary.

Note: Although rebating and discounting are becoming increasingly common, there is some legal ambiguity concerning them. Strictly speaking, it is legal to discount domestic tickets but not to discount international tickets; even when it is legal, an airline can claim that a travel agency practicing rebating is violating agreements governing airline-agency relations. On the other hand, the law that prohibits discounting is not usually enforced, in part because many illegal arrangements are indistinguishable from legal ones (such as entirely legitimate bulk fares, which are seats sold in bulk by an airline, usually to a charter operator, who resells them to the public as though they were charter seats). Since the line separating legal and illegal discounts is so fine that even the authorities can't always tell the difference, it is unlikely that most consumers would be able to do so, and, in fact, it is not illegal to *buy* a discount ticket.

Flexible-Schedule Travel – Another way to take advantage of bargain air fares is to be able to travel with less than the usual amount of advance notice. A number of organizations, usually set up as last-minute travel clubs to which people subscribe as members, routinely keep in touch with travel suppliers to help them dispose of unsold inventory at discounts of between 15% and 60%. Most of the inventory consists of complete tour packages and cruises, but some clubs offer air-only charter seats and, occasionally, seats on scheduled flights. Members pay an annual fee and receive the toll-free number of a telephone hot line to call for information about imminent trips. In some cases, they also receive periodic mailings with information about upcoming trips for which there is more advance notice. Despite the suggestive names of the clubs providing these services, last-minute travel does not necessarily mean that you cannot make plans until literally the last minute. Trips can be announced with as little as a few days' notice or as much as two months' notice, but the average is from one to four weeks' notice. It does mean that your choice at any given time is limited to what is offered and, if your heart is set on a particular destination, you might not find what you want, no matter how attractive the bargains. The following are some last-minute clubs:

Discount Travel International, Ives Building, Suite 205, 114 Forrest Ave., Narberth, PA 19072 (phone: 215-668-2182). Annual fee, $45.

Moment's Notice, 40 E 49th St., New York, NY 10017 (phone: 212-486-0503). Annual fee, $35.

On Call to Travel, PO Box 11622, Portland, OR 97211 (phone: 503-287-7215). Annual fee, $45.

Stand Buys Ltd., 311 W Superior St., Suite 414, Chicago, IL 60610 (phone: 312-943-5737 or 800-972-5858 in Illinois; 800-621-5839 elsewhere). Annual fee, $45.

Worldwide Discount Travel Club, 1674 Meridian Ave., Miami Beach, FL 33139 (phone: 305-534-2082). Annual fee, $45.

Generic Air Travel – Organizations that apply the flexible-schedule idea to air travel only and sell tickets at literally the last minute also exist. The service they provide is sometimes known as "generic" air travel, and it operates somewhat like an ordinary airline standby service except that the organizations running it offer seats on not one but several scheduled and charter airlines. One pioneer of generic flights is *Airhitch,* 2901 Broadway, Suite 100, New York, NY 10025 (phone: 212-864-2000), which arranges flights to Europe from various US cities at very low prices ($160 from the East Coast in 1986, more from points farther west). Precise destinations are not guaranteed, however. Prospective travelers register by paying a fee (applicable toward the ticket purchase) and stipulating a range of acceptable departure dates and the place to which they would prefer to fly, along with alternative choices. A few days before the date range begins, they are notified of flights that *may* be available during the time period, agree on an assignment, and remit the balance of the ticket price to the company. If they do not accept any of the suggested flights, they lose their deposit; if, through no fault of their own, they do not ultimately get on any agreed-on flight, all of their money is refunded. Return flights are arranged the same way. *Airhitch* cautions that, given the number of variables attached to the flights, they are suitable only for travelers willing to accept approximate destinations. The time period will be the one specified by the traveler, however, and a majority of travelers arrive right on target.

CONSUMER PROTECTION: Consumers who feel that they have not been dealt with fairly by an airline should make their complaints known. Begin with the customer service representative at the airport where the problem occurs. If he or she cannot resolve the complaint to your satisfaction, write to the airline's consumer office. In a businesslike, typed letter, explain what reservations you held, what happened, the names of the employees who were involved, and what you expect the airline to do to remedy the situation. Send copies (never the originals) of the tickets, receipts, and other documents that back your claims.

If you still receive no satisfaction and if the problem concerns lost baggage, compensation for getting bumped, smoking rules, charter regulations, or unfair or deceptive practices by an airline, the US Department of Transportation will do what it can to help you. Call Consumer Affairs at 202-755-2220; or, if you prefer, write to the Consumer Affairs Division, Room 10405, Office of Community and Consumer Affairs, US Department of Transportation, 400 Seventh St., SW, Washington, DC 20590. Include a daytime phone number in your letter. The Department of Transportation's consumer booklet *Fly-Rights* is a good introduction to regulations governing the airlines. To receive a copy, send $1 to the Consumer Information Center, Department 165-P, Pueblo, CO 81009.

To avoid more serious problems, charter flights and tour packages should always be chosen with care. When you consider a charter, ask your travel agent who runs it and check out the company. The Better Business Bureau in the company's home city can tell you the number of complaints, if any, lodged against the company in the past. Protect yourself with trip cancellation and interruption insurance (see *Insurance*, GET-TING READY TO GO), which can help safeguard your investment if you or a traveling companion is unable to make the trip and must cancel too late to receive a full refund from the company providing your travel services (this insurance is advisable whether you're buying a charter flight alone or a tour package that includes a charter flight or a scheduled flight). Some travel insurance policies have an additional feature, covering the possibility of default or bankruptcy on the part of the tour operator or airline, charter or scheduled — no longer remote, given estimates that some fifty commercial passenger airlines have ceased operation since the advent of airline deregulation in 1978.

Should this type of coverage be unavailable to you (insurance regulations vary by state, there are wide differences in price, and so on), your best bet is to pay for airline tickets and tour packages with a credit card. The federal Fair Credit Billing Act permits purchasers to refuse payment for credit card charges for which services have not been delivered, so the onus of dealing with a bankrupt airline falls on the credit card company. Do not rely on another airline to honor the ticket you're holding; the days when major carriers subscribed to a program that bound them to do so are long gone. Some airlines may voluntarily step forward to accommodate the stranded passengers of a bankrupt carrier, but this is now an entirely altruistic act.

An excellent source of information about economical travel opportunities is the *Consumer Reports Travel Letter*, published monthly by Consumers Union. It keeps abreast of the air travel scene, including package tours, rental cars, insurance, and more, but it is especially helpful for its coverage of air fares, offering guidance on all the options from scheduled flights on major or low-fare airlines to charters and discount sources. For a year's subscription, send $37 to *Consumer Reports Travel Letter*, Subscription Department, Box 5248, Boulder, CO 80322.

Traveling by Ship

 Alas, the days when steamships reigned as the primary means of transatlantic transportation are gone, when Italy, France, Sweden, Germany, Norway, the Netherlands, England — and the US — had fleets of passenger liners that offered week-plus trips across the North Atlantic. Only one ship continues to offer this kind of service between the US and Europe with any regularity; others make the trip at most a few times a year. At the same time, the possibility of booking passage to Europe on a cargo ship is becoming less practicable. Fewer and fewer travelers, therefore, set foot on Italian soil with sea legs developed during an ocean crossing. A great many do visit Italian ports during a Mediterranean cruise, however, or take a ferry to one of the Italian islands.

TRANSATLANTIC CROSSINGS: One of the largest and most luxurious vessels afloat has long been Cunard's *Queen Elizabeth 2*. Each year, in addition to a full calendar of cruises — Caribbean, Canadian, Alaskan, and European, plus one around the world — the *QE2* is scheduled for approximately a dozen round-trip transatlantic crossings between April and, usually, December. (The ship went out of service for refitting in November 1986 and was scheduled to resume sailing in May 1987.) While the ship normally sets its course from New York to Southampton, England (a five-day trip) and then directly back to the US, on a few of the crossings it proceeds from Southampton to Cherbourg, France, or to Lisbon, Portugal, before beginning the return trip. Similarly, on some crossings the ship calls at Baltimore, Port Everglades, or other US ports in addition to New York, thus giving non-New Yorkers a choice of where to embark or disembark.

Transatlantic crossings do not come cheap. In 1986 the one-way, per-person cost of passage from New York to Southampton ranged from $1,350 (for the least expensive, two-per-cabin, transatlantic-class accommodations at the end of the season) to $7,195 (for one of the grandest travel experiences imaginable). Cunard brings a voyage aboard a luxury liner within reach of the less affluent traveler, however, by offering an air/sea package in conjunction with British Airways. The one-way ticket to Europe by sea includes an allowance toward return air fare from London that — depending on how long you stay, where you live, and your seating on the plane — can amount to a free flight home. If you want to splurge, you can even fly home on British Airways' supersonic Concorde, provided you make up the considerable difference between your air allowance and the Concorde fare. Cunard also has various European tour packages applicable to the basic air/sea offer. For information, contact *Cunard/NAC,* 555 Fifth Ave., New York, NY 10017 (phone: 212-661-7777 in New York State; 800-221-4770 elsewhere).

One other ship, Polish Ocean Lines' *Stefan Batory,* crosses the Atlantic with some frequency, though on a much more modest scale than the *QE2.* The *Stefan Batory* makes roughly a half dozen round trips a year between Montréal and Gdynia, Poland, calling at London and Rotterdam en route. For information, contact *McLean Kennedy Passenger Services,* 410 St. Nicolas St., Montréal, Qué. H2Y 2P5, Canada (phone: 514-849-6111).

Another interesting possibility for those who have two or three weeks to devote solely to crossing the Atlantic is what the industry calls a *positioning cruise.* This is the sailing of a US- or Caribbean-based vessel from its winter berth to the city in Europe from which it will offer summer cruises. Eastbound positioning cruises take place in the spring; westbound positioning cruises return in the fall. Because of the long delay before the ships return to their original US or Caribbean port, most lines offering positioning cruises have some sea/air arrangement that allows passengers to fly home economically — though the cruises themselves are not inexpensive.

Among the ships that have offered positioning cruises for a number of years are Cunard's *Vistafjord,* formerly of Norwegian American Cruises, and the Royal Viking Line's *Royal Viking Sea* and *Royal Viking Sky.* Itineraries and ports of call vary from year to year, and in any given year there may be no positioning cruise allowing passengers to disembark at an Italian port. Typically, the ships set sail from Florida or San Juan, Puerto Rico, and cross the Atlantic to any of a number of European ports — Málaga, Barcelona, Genoa, Naples, Venice, Piraeus, Cherbourg, Le Havre, Southampton — where the trip may be broken before proceeding to cruise European waters (the Mediterranean, the Baltic Sea, the Black Sea, the Norwegian fjords). Passengers usually can elect to stay aboard for the transatlantic segment alone or for both the crossing and the subsequent European cruise. For information, contact *Cunard/ NAC,* 555 Fifth Ave., New York, NY 10017 (phone: 212-661-7777 in New York State; 800-221-4770 elsewhere); *Royal Viking Line,* One Embarcadero Center, San Francisco, CA 94111 (phone: 415-398-8000 in California; 800-422-8000 elsewhere); or a travel agent. Other cruise ships to investigate for possible transatlantic positioning cruises are the *Royal Odyssey* (*Royal Cruise Lines,* One Maritime Plaza, Suite 660, San Francisco, CA 94111; phone: 415-956-7200); the *Mermoz* (*Paquet French Cruises,* represented in North America by *Sun Line Cruises,* One Rockefeller Plaza, New York, NY 10020;

· phone: 212-397-6400 or 800-468-6400); the *Sea Princess* (*P&O Cruises,* 2029 Century Park East, Suite 3000, Los Angeles, CA 90067; phone: 213-553-1770); and the *Stella Solaris* (*Sun Line Cruises,* One Rockefeller Plaza, New York, NY 10020; phone: 212-397-6400 or 800-468-6400).

FREIGHTERS: Some cargo ships take a limited number of passengers (usually about twelve) in reasonably comfortable accommodations. The idea of traveling by freighter has long appealed to romantic souls, but it is likely that in the future, fewer and fewer of those so inclined will be able to turn wishful thinking into reality. Because of increased use of containerization, the number of freighters equipped to cater to passengers is shrinking, and though passenger-carrying cargo ships still sail over many of the world's ocean routes, they are almost a thing of the past across the North Atlantic. Even if you do find a freighter going your way, there are several things to keep in mind before deciding to cast off with it. Accommodations and recreational facilities vary, but freighters were not designed to amuse passengers, so it is important to appreciate the idea of freighter travel itself. Schedules are erratic, and the traveler must fit his or her timetable to that of the ship. Passengers have found themselves waiting as much as a month for a promised sailing, and because freighters follow their cargo commitments, it is possible that a scheduled port could be omitted at the last minute or a new one added. Once upon a time, a major advantage of freighter travel was its low cost, but even this is no longer the case. Though freighters are usually less expensive than cruise ships, the difference is not as great as it once was, and excursion air fares are certainly cheaper.

Anyone contemplating taking a freighter from a US port to an Italian port should be aware that at press time only two freighter lines still carried passengers to the Mediterranean. *Prudential Lines,* with three ships carrying a maximum of five or six passengers each, sailed out of New York to Constantsa, Romania, roughly every eighteen days, with ports of call in Spain, Italy, Egypt, Israel, Greece, and Turkey. Partial trips could not be booked; passengers who wished to disembark at an interim port could do so but were required to pay for the entire round trip at a cost of $3,850 per person, single or double occupancy. Contact *Prudential Lines,* One World Trade Center, Suite 3701, New York, NY 10048 (phone: 212-524-8212 in New York State; 800-221-4118 elsewhere). *Lykes Lines,* with considerably more ships, sailed three or four times monthly from Gulf Coast ports (New Orleans or Houston) to the eastern and western Mediterranean, making stops in various countries depending on cargo commitments (Italy was among the usual stops). The ships carried a maximum of twelve passengers in double cabins only, and either full or partial trips could be booked (a full round trip cost $3,200 per person double occupancy, while the price of a partial trip to a particular port varied according to its placement in the itinerary). Lykes also sailed from the Great Lakes to the Mediterranean once or twice monthly from April through October and from the Gulf Coast to northern Europe (Rotterdam, Bremerhaven) once or twice monthly year-round. For information, contact *Lykes Lines,* Lykes Center, 300 Poydras St., New Orleans, LA 70130 (phone: 504-523-6611 in Louisiana; 800-535-1861 elsewhere). Another line, *Polish Ocean Lines,* sailed from Port Newark, NJ, to northern Europe only (Le Havre, Rotterdam, Bremerhaven). For information, contact *Gdynia America Line* (the general agent for Polish Ocean Lines), 39 Broadway, New York, NY 10006 (phone: 212-952-1280).

Despite the dwindling number of freighters offering space to passengers, specialists still exist who deal only (or largely) in this type of travel. They provide information, schedules, and, when you're ready to sail, booking services for passengers:

Freighter World Cruises: A travel agency specializing in freighters. Publishes *Freighter Space Advisory,* a bimonthly newsletter listing space available on sailings worldwide ($22 a year), and handles customer bookings. 180 S Lake Ave., Suite 335, Pasadena, CA 91101 (phone: 818-449-3106).

Pearl's Freighter Tips: Pearl Hoffman, an experienced hand in freighter travel, finds sailings for her customers and sends them off with all kinds of information and advice. 175 Great Neck Rd., Suite 303, Great Neck, NY 11021 (phone: 516-487-8351).

TravLtips Cruise and Freighter Travel Association: A freighter travel agency and club ($30 a year, $15 during "special offers") whose members receive the bi-monthly *TravLtips* magazine of cruise and freighter travel. PO Box 188, Flushing, NY 11358 (phone: 718-939-2400).

MEDITERRANEAN CRUISES: The Mediterranean Sea is one of the world's most popular and picturesque cruising grounds, busy with ships offering sailings of varying lengths from spring through fall. Unfortunately, terrorism in the area has disrupted many Mediterranean cruise programs. In 1986, more than one cruise company canceled Mediterranean sailings completely, preferring to cruise in northern European waters instead. Even in the best of times, however, few cruises devote a significant portion of their itinerary to exploring Italian territory, although many Mediterranean cruises begin or end in an Italian port and many that begin or end elsewhere include stops in Italy.

Among the cruises especially oriented to Italy in 1986 were *Royal Viking Line*'s 13-day Mediterranean/Adriatic cruises between Venice and Barcelona, calling at Dubrovnik, Catania, Naples, Monte Carlo, Livorno (for visits to Florence and Pisa), and Civitavecchia (for visits to Rome). Except for two days anchored at Civitavecchia, however, the cruises spent at most one day in each of the Italian ports. For information, contact *Royal Viking Line,* One Embarcadero Center, San Francisco, CA 94111 (phone: 415-398-8000 in California; 800-422-8000 elsewhere). *Paquet French Cruises* offered a 14-day Music Festival at Sea cruise in 1986, beginning and ending in Toulon, France, and stopping for two days in Venice, a half day in Ravenna, and a full day in Salerno. Paquet is particularly well known for its concerts at sea, but the Royal Viking Line cruises also featured classical concert artists whose performances provided an added dimension to the usual shipboard entertainment. For information about the Paquet cruises, contact *Sun Line Cruises,* One Rockefeller Plaza, New York, NY 10020 (phone: 212-397-6400 or 800-468-6400).

The 7-day Around Italy cruises operated by *Sun Line Cruises* sailed regularly throughout the summer between Venice and Nice, calling at Dubrovnik, Corfu, and Malta in addition to half-day stops at Messina and Olbia, a half day at Elba, and, weather permitting, an evening at Portofino. Contact *Sun Line Cruises* (address above). Another line with a variety of Mediterranean cruises in 1986 was *Sea Goddess Cruises,* whose 7-, 10-, and 11-night itineraries between Venice and Monte Carlo featured stops at Portofino, Viareggio, Elba, Porto Cervo, Sorrento, Capri, Taormina, and Syracuse, as well as at non-Italian ports, the number and order of the calls depending on cruise length and direction. Contact *Sea Goddess Cruises,* 5805 Blue Lagoon Dr., Miami, FL 33126 (phone: 305-266-8705 or 800-457-9000 in Florida; 800-458-9000 elsewhere). Two other lines that ordinarily visit Italian ports on their Mediterranean cruises, but did not do so in 1986, are *Ocean Cruise Lines,* 1510 SE 17th St., Ft. Lauderdale, FL 33316 (phone: 305-764-5566 or 800-528-8500 in Florida; 800-556-8850 elsewhere), and *Epirotiki Lines,* 551 Fifth Ave., New York, NY 10176 (phone: 212-599-1750 or 800-221-2470).

FERRIES: Numerous ferries link the Italian mainland with Sicily and Sardinia, with the many smaller Italian islands, and with other countries. Most carry both passengers and cars and most of the routes are serviced year-round. Cabins and space for cars should be booked as early as possible, especially for July and August crossings, even though many of the lines schedule more frequent service during the summer.

Italy's largest shipping line, *Tirrenia*, operates most of the car- and passenger-carrying services from the mainland to Sicily and Sardinia and between the two islands, including daily service between Naples and Palermo on Sicily (a 10-hour ride), between Genoa and Porto Torres on Sardinia (12½ hours), between Civitavecchia and Olbia on Sardinia (7 hours), and between Civitavecchia and Cagliari on Sardinia (13 hours). Other Tirrenia services, varying from once a week to three or four times weekly, include connections from Genoa to Palermo (a 23-hour ride, the longest route), from Naples to Catania on Sicily, from Genoa to Cagliari and to Olbia, from Naples and Livorno to Cagliari, and from Livorno to Porto Torres. In addition, there is service once or twice weekly between Palermo and Cagliari and between Cagliari and Trapani on Sicily. All of the above services are overnight, and the least expensive ticket, deck class (*posto ponte*), does not necessarily buy a seat. A reserved armchair (*poltrona*) indoors that reclines airline style costs a bit more; second- and first-class cabins cost still more. In Italy, reservations can be made and tickets purchased at Tirrenia offices in the cities served and through travel agents. Reservations and tickets for cars and first- and second-class cabins (but not *poltrone*) are also available from Tirrenia's representative in the US, *Extra Value Travel*, 437 Madison Ave., New York, NY 10022 (phone: 212-750-8800 in New York State; 800-223-1980 elsewhere), or 689 S Collier Blvd., Marco Island, FL 33937 (phone: 813-394-3384 or 800-282-3922 in Florida; 800-223-2712 elsewhere). Allow plenty of time to make the arrangements — at least three weeks before your trip off-season and two to three months in advance for summer crossings.

Other shipping lines provide additional service between the mainland and Italy's two largest islands. Among these are *Grandi Traghetti*, *Trans Tirreno Express*, and *Italian State Railways* (*Ferrovie dello Stato*), whose car and passenger ferries connect Civitavecchia with Golfo Aranci, Sardinia, and Villa San Giovanni and Reggio Calabria with Messina, Sicily. Sicily is also connected to the mainland by *Aliscafi SNAV* hydrofoils, which make the crossing from Naples to Palermo (summer only, via the island of Ustica) in only 5 hours (compared to 10 hours by ferry) and shorten the crossing from Reggio Calabria to Messina to only 20 minutes.

Ferries operated by the *Siremar*, *Caremar*, and *Toremar* lines make connections with the smaller Italian islands. Siremar car and passenger ferries leave from Naples and Milazzo, Sicily, for the main islands of the Lipari, or Aeolian, group (Lipari, Stromboli, Panarea, Vulcano, Salina, Filicudi, Alicudi) lying north of Sicily. Hydrofoil service from the mainland and Sicily to and between various of the same islands is provided by Siremar and Aliscafi SNAV. The island of Ustica, north of Palermo, is reached by Siremar ferries and hydrofoils from Palermo as well as by Aliscafi SNAV hydrofoils (summer only) from Naples. The Egadi Islands (Favignana, Levanzo, Marettimo), just off the west coast of Sicily, are also served by Siremar ferries and hydrofoils departing from Trapani, and the island of Pantelleria, closer to Tunisia than to Sicily, and the faraway Pelagie Islands (Lampedusa and Linosa) are reached by Siremar ferries only, the former from Trapani and the latter two from Porto Empedocle, Sicily.

Caremar ferries make numerous runs daily year-round to islands in the Bay of Naples, departing from Naples and Sorrento for Capri and from Naples and Pozzuoli for the islands of Ischia and Procida. Equally frequent hydrofoil services for the three islands are provided by Caremar, Aliscafi SNAV, and *Alilauro*. Capri, furthermore, can be reached by the ferries of other lines, and in summer ferries and hydrofoils operate to and from points along the Amalfi Coast and to and from Ischia.

The islands of the Tuscan archipelago (Elba, Capraia, Giglio, and others) are served mainly by *Toremar* ferries and hydrofoils. The most direct service to Elba, the largest island in the group (in fact, the third largest Italian island, after Sicily and Sardinia), leaves from Piombino and arrives in Portoferraio many times daily year-round, taking

1 hour by car and passenger ferry and 30 minutes by hydrofoil. The Livorno to Portoferraio route, also operated daily year-round, takes approximately 3 hours if direct, more with a stop at Capraia. Additional ferries and hydrofoils from Piombino and Portoferraio serve other ports on Elba, while the island of Giglio, farther south, is reached by ferries from Porto Santo Stefano.

An island group in the Adriatic Sea, the Tremiti Islands, off the coast of the Puglia region, is served by *Adriatica,* the major Italian shipping line operating in the Adriatic. Adriatica also operates car ferries to Yugoslavia, with departures from Trieste, Venice, Rimini, Ancona, Pescara, and Bari for Zadar, Split, and Dubrovnik, and is the joint operator, with *Hellenic Mediterranean Lines* of *Sea Bridge Italy-Greece,* the major car ferry service to Greece. All Sea Bridge sailings are overnight, departing from Brindisi at approximately 10:30 PM and calling at Corfu and Igoumenítsa the next day prior to an early evening arrival at Patras. Supplementary summer sailings leave Brindisi earlier and go directly to Patras, arriving at approximately 1 PM the next day. For information or reservations, contact Adriatica's US representative, *Extra Value Travel,* 437 Madison Ave., New York, NY 10022 (phone: 212-750-8800 in New York State; 800-223-1980 elsewhere), or 689 S Collier Blvd., Marco Island, FL 33937 (phone: 813-394-3384 or 800-282-3922 in Florida; 800-223-2712 elsewhere). Reservations are especially advisable for high-season sailings from mid-July to mid-August.

Italy also has ferry links with other countries in and around the Mediterranean. Adriatica sails from Venice via Piraeus to Alexandria, Egypt. Tirrenia sails from Naples, Catania, and Syracuse to Malta, from Naples to Tunis via Palermo, and from Cagliari to Tunis via Trapani. *Miura Line* sails from Genoa to Barcelona. Finally, there are numerous links to Bastia, Corsica, from Genoa, La Spezia, Livorno, and Piombino, by *Corsica Line* and *Navarma* ferries, in addition to summer service from Porto Torres, Sardinia, to Toulon on the French mainland.

Touring by Car

There is almost no place in Italy that cannot be reached by train or bus or a combination of the two, yet many visitors are not in the country long before they wish they had a car. Trains whiz much too fast past the most enticing landscapes, tunnel through mountains rather than climb up and around them for a better view, and frequently deposit passengers in the least appealing part of town. Buses have greater range, but they still don't permit many spur-of-the-moment stops and starts. A car, on the other hand, provides maximum flexibility, allowing visitors to cover large amounts of territory, to visit major cities and sites, or to move from one village to the next while exploring the countryside. A car is obviously not a good idea if you plan to visit only large cities because historic centers are usually full of *zone pedonali* (pedestrian zones) and are so threaded with one-way streets that they drive even the natives wild. Nor will a car always get you inside the walls and to the tops of all those quaint hill towns where the center is a maze of narrow streets better negotiated by man or beast than motorcar. Such towns usually allow residents to park at their doors, if that's possible, but have a parking lot or two midway up where visitors can leave their cars while they proceed on foot.

For the rest, however, Italy is an ideal country to tour by car. Travelers who wish to cover the country from the tip of its snow-capped peaks to the toe of its boot can count on a good system of superhighways to help them make time, including the well-known *Autostrada del Sole* (Highway of the Sun), which connects Milan and Bologna, Florence, Rome, Naples, Salerno, and, finally, Reggio Calabria. (Superhighways are not usually the scenic way to go, but the Autostrada del Sole, as it cuts across the Apennines between Bologna and Florence, is an emphatic exception.) Travelers who wish to explore only one region will find secondary roads in generally good condition and Italy's historical and cultural density such that distances between points of interest are reasonably short.

But driving isn't an inexpensive way to travel. Gas prices are far higher in Europe than in North America, and car rentals are seldom available at bargain rates. Because the price of getting wheels abroad will be more than an incidental expense, it is important to investigate every alternative before making a final choice.

RENTING A CAR: Although there are other options, such as leasing or outright purchase, most people who want to drive in Europe simply rent a car through a travel agent or international rental firm before they go or, once they are in Europe, from a local company. Another possibility, also arranged before departure, is to rent a car as part of a larger package. Arrangements of this sort used to be called fly/drive packages, but increasingly they are now described in tour brochures as self-drive, go-as-you-please, or car tours.

Renting from the US – Travel agents can arrange foreign rentals for clients, but it is just as easy to do it yourself by calling the international division of a familiar car rental firm such as *Hertz* (phone: 800-654-3001), *Avis* (phone: 800-331-2112), *Budget* (phone: 800-527-0700), *National* (known in Europe as *Europcar;* phone: 800-CAR-RENT), or *Dollar Rent a Car* (affiliated in Europe with *InterRent;* phone: 800-421-6878). All of these companies publish directories listing the foreign locations in which they operate and, in most cases, the rates for various types of cars; all quote flat weekly rates based on unlimited mileage with the renter paying for gas. Some also offer time and mileage rates (a basic per-day or per-week charge plus a charge for each mile, or kilometer, driven), which are generally only to the advantage of those who plan to do very little driving — the basic time and mileage charge for a given period of time is lower than the unlimited mileage charge for a comparable period, but the kilometers add up more quickly than most people expect.

It is also possible to rent a car before you go by contacting one of several smaller or less well known US companies that do not operate worldwide but specialize in European auto travel, including leasing and car purchase in addition to car rental; some are actually tour operators with a well-established European car rental program. These firms, some of which are listed below, act as agents for a variety of European suppliers, offer unlimited mileage almost exclusively, and frequently manage to undersell their larger competitors. Comparison shopping is always necessary, however, because the company that has the least expensive rentals in one country may not necessarily have the least expensive in another, and even the international giants offer discount plans whose conditions are easy for most travelers to fulfill. *Hertz*'s Affordable Europe, *Avis*'s Supervalue Rates Europe, and similar plans offered by *Budget, National,* and *Dollar* allow discounts of anywhere from 15% to 50% off their usual rates, provided the car is reserved a certain number of days in advance of departure (usually 7, but it can be less), is rented for a minimum period (5 days or, usually, a week), and, in most cases, is returned to the same location that supplied it or another location within the same country.

No matter which firm you choose, the first factor influencing cost is, naturally, the type and size of car. Rentals are based on a tiered price system, with different sizes of cars — mini, standard subcompact, compact, mid-size, large, and luxury — often listed as A (the smallest and least expensive) through F, G, H, or higher (the largest and most expensive). The typical A car available in Italy is a two-door mini car or subcompact, often a hatchback, seating two adults and one or two small children (examples are Fiat Panda, Ford Fiesta, and Austin Mini or Metro). The typical F, G, or H car is a four-door sedan seating four or five adults (BMW, Fiat Regata, Lancia Prisma) or a minibus. The larger the car, the more it costs to rent and the more gas it consumes, but for some people the greater comfort and extra luggage space of a larger car (in which bags can be locked out of sight) may make it worth the additional expense, especially on a long trip. Be warned that very few European cars have automatic transmission, and those that do are more likely to be in the F group than in the less expensive categories. Cars with automatic transmission must be specifically requested at the time of booking, and, again, they cost more (at least $5 to $10 a day more than the same model with standard shift) and they consume more gas. Similarly, cars with air conditioning are likely to be found in the F group and no lower.

Other costs to be added to the price tag include drop-off charges or one-way service fees. The lowest price quoted by a company may apply only to a car that is returned to the same location from which it was rented. A slightly higher rate may be charged if the car is to be returned to a different city within the same country, and a considerably higher rate may prevail if the rental begins in one country and ends in another. The cost of optional collision damage waiver protection, if you want it, must also be added to the price tag. Rates for rental cars include public liability, property damage, fire, and theft coverage and collision coverage with a deductible — usually no less than $500. In the event of an accident, you are responsible for the deductible amount, but you can dispense with the obligation to pay it by buying the offered waiver at a cost of approximately $5 to $10 a day, depending on the car group. If you opt not to take the waiver, you will probably be required to leave a blank credit card slip or a refundable cash deposit equal to the deductible amount.

A further consideration: Don't forget that car rentals are subject to European value added taxes; in Italy, the rate charged is 18% for all rental cars except those in the highest luxury car group (where the tax is a whopping 38%). This tax is rarely included in the rental price quoted, but it must always be paid, whether you prepay it in the US or pay it when you drop off the car in Italy. Taxes vary a great deal from country to country, and even if you intend to visit only Italy, you still might consider Switzerland, where the tax rate is zero, as the pickup point. The tax rate in France, equally convenient as a pickup point, is unfortunately 33%. Or, because one-way rentals bridging two countries are frequently exempt from tax, consider dropping the car off in another country. If you pick up a car in Italy and drop it off in France, Switzerland, or Austria, you will pay no tax. One-way rentals that begin in France — as well as in Denmark or Sweden — are *not* exempt from tax, however.

Finally, currency fluctuation is another factor to consider. Most brochures quote rental prices in dollars, but these dollar amounts are frequently only guides; that is, they are the foreign currency amount converted to dollars at the rate of exchange prevailing when the brochure was printed. In these cases, when you call to make your booking, the amount you owe will be the foreign currency amount recalculated at that day's rate of exchange. If there has been a significant change in the rate, you may owe more or less than the amount shown in the brochure. Some companies guarantee rates in dollars, but this is not always an advantage. If the dollar is growing consistently stronger overseas, for instance, you would be better off with rates guaranteed in local currency.

You can find legitimate bargains in car rentals if you shop for them. Call all the familiar car rental names (the toll-free numbers are given at the beginning of this section) and ask about their special discount plans, and then call the companies listed below. In the recent past, the regular rates of the latter have tended to be significantly lower than the regular rates of the international giants, though not necessarily lower than their discount plans. It always pays to compare, and it also pays to begin your comparison shopping early because the best deals may be booked to capacity quickly and may require payment 14 to 21 days before pickup.

Auto-Europe, PO Box 500, Yorktown Heights, NY 10598 (phone: 914-962-5252 or 800-942-1309 in New York State; 800-223-5555 elsewhere).

The Cortell Group, 3 E 54th St., New York, NY 10022 (phone: 800-442-4481 in New York State; 800-223-6626 elsewhere).

Europe by Car, 1 Rockefeller Plaza, New York, NY 10020, or 9000 Sunset Blvd.,

Los Angeles, CA 90069 (phone: 212-581-3040 in New York State; 800-252-9401 in California; 800-223-1516 elsewhere).

Foremost Euro-Car, 5430 Van Nuys Blvd., Van Nuys, CA 91401 (phone: 800-272-3299 in California; 800-423-3111 elsewhere).

Kemwel, 106 Calvert St., Harrison, NY 10528 (phone: 800-468-0468).

Maiellano Tours, 441 Lexington Ave., New York, NY 10017 (phone: 212-687-7725 in New York State; 800-223-1616 elsewhere), a tour operator specializing in Italy, also rents cars in Italy and offers many pickup and delivery points within the country.

Note: The minimum age at which Italians may drive a car in Italy is 18 years, but the minimum age to rent a car varies with the company supplying it. Many firms have a minimum age requirement of 21 years. Others raise that to 25 for mid-size cars and to as high as 30 for some luxury models.

Fly/Drive – Airlines, charter companies, car rental companies, and tour operators have been offering fly/drive packages for years, and even though the basic components of the packages have changed somewhat — the rule used to be return air fare, a car waiting at the airport, and perhaps a night's lodging in the gateway city all for one inclusive price — the idea remains the same. You rent a car *here* for use *there* by booking it along with other components of the trip. These days, the minimum arrangement possible is the result of a tie-in between a car rental company and an airline that entitles the customer to a rental car for less than the company's usual rates provided he or she shows proof of having booked a flight on the airline. Slightly more elaborate fly/drive packages can be found listed under various names (go-as-you-please, self-drive, or, simply, car tours) in the independent vacations sections of tour catalogues, and the most common ingredients are the rental car plus some sort of hotel voucher plan, with the applicable air fare listed separately. You set off on your trip with a block of prepaid accommodations vouchers, a list of hotels that accept them (usually members of a hotel chain or association), and a reservation for the first night's stay, after which the staff of each hotel books the next one for you or you make advance reservations yourself. Naturally, the more establishments participating in the scheme, the more freedom you have to range at will during the day's driving and still be near a place to stay for the night. *Hertz*'s Affordable Europe Hotel Program, open to participants in the company's Affordable Europe car rental plan, provides a choice of vouchers at five different price levels in Italy, applicable to stays at a total of approximately 100 Italian hotels as well as many more in surrounding countries.

Less flexible car tours provide a rental car, a hotel plan, and a prearranged itinerary that permits no deviation because the hotels are all reserved in advance. The five 16-day itineraries that make up *Italia Adagio*'s Flying Solo program are of this sort and so are the car tours packaged by *AutoVenture,* which has a 10-day Italian itinerary that can be bought in either a self-drive or a chauffeured version. Book *Italia Adagio* tours directly with the company (162 Whaley St., Freeport, NY 11520; phone: 516-868-7825 or 516-546-5239); *AutoVenture* packages are booked through travel agents.

Local Rentals – It has long been common wisdom that the least expensive way to rent a car is to do it in Europe. This is less true than before. Many medium to large European car rental companies have become the overseas suppliers of stateside companies such as those mentioned above, and often the stateside agency, by dint of sheer volume, has been able to negotiate more favorable rates for its US customers than the European firm offers its own. Lower rates can certainly be found by searching out small, strictly local car rental companies overseas, whether at less than prime addresses in major cities or in more remote areas. But to find them you must be willing to invest a sufficient amount of vacation time comparing prices on the scene. You must also be prepared to return the car to the location that rented it — drop-off possibilities are likely to be limited.

Travelers who intend to rent a car only occasionally in Italy, relying mainly on other means of transportation, should bear in mind that Italian State Railways offers a car rental service — *Treno + Auto* — in conjunction with a number of rental firms in most of the larger cities. Passengers reserve the car before boarding the train and pick it up at their destination. Reservations are made either at the rental company's office or, if there isn't one in that city, at the station. (See *Touring by Train.*)

LEASING: Many travelers who remain in Europe for three weeks or more find that it costs less to lease a car than to rent one for the same period of time. While the money saved by leasing rather than renting for a 22-day (the minimum) or 30-day period may not be great, over the course of a long-term lease — 45, 60, 90 days, or more, for example — a traveler can save hundreds, even thousands, of dollars. Leasing is actually a financed purchase/repurchase plan: You reserve the car by specific make and model rather than by size group, and it is delivered to you fresh from the factory. Part of the money saved by leasing is due to the fact that leased cars are exempt from the stiff taxes applicable to rented cars. In addition, leasing plans provide collision insurance with no deductible amount, so there is no need to add the daily cost of collision damage waiver protection offered as an option by rental companies.

Unfortunately, leasing as described above is offered only in Belgium and France, and the saving it permits can be realized to the fullest only if the cars are picked up and returned in those countries. While leased cars can be delivered to other countries, the charge for this service can be as high as $300 in the case of Italian cities, and the return charge is identical. If you don't intend to keep the car very long, the two charges could nullify the amount saved by leasing rather than renting, so you will have to do some arithmetic. It is possible to lease a car in countries other than Belgium or France, but most of the plans offered are best described as long-term rentals at preferential rates. They differ from true leasing in that tax is not included nor is collision damage waiver protection, and the cars are usually late-model used cars rather than brand new. Some of the car rental firms listed above — *Auto-Europe, Europe by Car, Foremost Euro-Car,* and *Kemwel* — arrange European car leases.

BUYING A CAR: If your plans include both buying a new car of European make and touring Europe in it, you can combine the two ventures and save some money on each. By buying the car abroad and using it to tour during your vacation, you pay quite a bit less for it than the US dealer would charge you and at the same time spare yourself the expense of renting or leasing a car for use during your holiday. There are two basic ways to achieve this end, but one — factory delivery — is far simpler than the other — direct import.

Factory delivery means that you place an order for a car in the US and then pick it up in Europe, often literally at the factory gate. It also means that the car you ultimately take possession of is built to American specifications, complying with all US emission and safety standards. Consequently, cars made by manufacturers who have established a formal program for such sales to American customers can be bought the factory-delivery way. At present, the list includes Audi, BMW, Jaguar, Mercedes, Peugeot, Porsche, Renault, Saab, Volkswagen, and Volvo, among others (whose manufacturers generally restrict their offerings to only those models they ordinarily export to the US), as well as one car of Italian manufacture — Alfa Romeo. The factory-delivery price, set in US dollars, usually runs about 10% to 20% below the sticker price of the same model at a US dealership and includes the costs of shipping the car home, US customs duty, incidentals, and the insurance necessary for driving the car while still in Europe.

One of the few disadvantages of factory delivery is that car manufacturers make available this way only a limited number of cars per year, and for certain popular models you may have to get in line early in the season. Furthermore, you must take your trip when the car is ready, not necessarily when you are. The actual place of delivery can vary; it is more economical to pick up the car at the factory, but arrangements can be made to have it delivered elsewhere for an extra charge. Cars for factory delivery can usually be ordered either through one of the manufacturer's authorized dealers in the US or through companies — *Europe by Car, Foremost Euro-Car,* and *Kemwel* among them — that specialize in such transactions. Alfa Romeos are an exception. They must be ordered through a US dealer and, although manufactured in Italy, must be picked up in Frankfurt. They can, however, be dropped off for shipment home in any of a number of Italian or European cities at no extra charge. For information, write to European Delivery Program, *Alfa Romeo, Inc.,* 250 Sylvan Ave., Englewood Cliffs, NJ 07632.

The other way to buy a car abroad — direct import — is sometimes referred to as "gray market" buying. It is perfectly legal, but not hassle-free. Direct import means that you buy abroad a car that was meant for use abroad, not one built according to US specifications. It can be new or used and may even include — in Great Britain — a steering wheel on the right side. The main drawback to direct import is that the process of modification to bring the car into compliance with US standards is an expensive and time-consuming one that typically costs an estimated $5,000 in parts and labor and takes from three to six months to complete. In addition, the same shipping, insurance, and miscellaneous expenses (another $2,000 to $5,000, according to estimates) that would be included in the factory-delivery price must be added to the purchase price of the car, and the considerable burden of shepherding it from showroom to backyard garage is usually borne by the purchaser. Direct-import dealers do exist (they are not the same as your factory-authorized foreign car dealer, with whom you are now in competition), but even if you use one, you still must do a certain amount of paperwork yourself.

The main advantages of the direct-import method are that it can be used for makes and models not available with factory-delivery programs and that you can save much more money importing an expensive car this way than the factory-delivery way. Just how much you save depends not only on the selling price of the car in the European market but also on the dollar's rate of exchange. Experts advise that a car costing less than $25,000 is a candidate for factory delivery only. Both options are feasible for cars costing more than $25,000, but the potential greater gain by the direct-import method must be weighed against its greater difficulties. The regularly revised *Handbook of Vehicle Importation* ($22.95), published by the Automobile Importers Compliance Association, a trade group of direct importers, modifiers, and others involved in the process, is an invaluable resource for getting a grip on what lies ahead. Order it from *AICA,* at 12030 Sunrise Valley Dr., Suite 201, Reston, VA 22091 (phone: 703-476-1100 in Virginia; 800-862-6666 elsewhere).

DRIVING: According to Italian regulations, a US citizen is required to have an International Driver's Permit in order to drive a rented car in Italy. A US citizen driving his or her own car must have either an International Driver's Permit or a valid US driver's license accompanied by a translation (approved by an Italian consulate in the US) or by a declaration obtained for a small fee from any frontier or provincial *Automobile Club d'Italia (ACI)* office in Italy. Italian regulations are not always enforced, and foreign drivers are known to have driven in Italy without incident using the license of their choice. Nevertheless, it is strongly recommended that American drivers obtain an International Driver's Permit before driving any car in Italy, particularly if they plan to do a lot of driving. The permit can be bought from most branches of the American Automobile Association for $5 (the application should be accompanied by two passport-size photos). Proof of liability insurance is also required to drive in Italy, but it is a standard part of any car rental contract. If you are driving your own car, you must carry an International Insurance Certificate, known familiarly as a Green Card (*Carta Verde*). Your insurance carrier can arrange for a special policy to cover you in Europe and will automatically issue your Green Card with the policy.

Contrary to first impressions, Italians tend to be skillful, if not disciplined, drivers. Also contrary to first impressions, rules of the road do exist. Driving is on the right side of the road, as in most of Europe; passing is on the left. Unless otherwise indicated, those coming from the right at intersections have the right of way, but streetcars have priority over other vehicles, and pedestrians, provided they are on the diagonal stripes at zebra crossings, have priority over all vehicles. On mountain passes, traffic going up has priority over traffic coming down. High-beam lights should not be used in cities and towns, and in many towns the use of the horn is restricted. At night, flash headlights to signal that you are passing. A portable triangular reflector (*triangolo*) must be placed as a warning to other drivers behind any car that is stalled or blocking the road for any other reason. This piece of necessary equipment is provided with rental cars; otherwise, it can be rented from ACI offices. The use of seat belts is not compulsory. Watch out for bicycles and motor scooters — they are everywhere — and do not drive under the influence of alcohol. Police have the power to levy on-the-spot fines for drunken driving and other violations.

As in the rest of Europe, distances are measured in kilometers and are registered as such on the speedometer. Speed limits vary with the size of the car. In a town, the speed limit is 50 kph (31 mph) for all cars. Outside the town, the speed limit is 80 kph (50 mph) for subcompacts up to 600 cc, 90 kph (56 mph) for compacts up to 900 cc, 100 kph (62 mph) for standard cars up to 1,300 cc, and 110 kph (68 mph) for larger cars of 1,300 cc and more. On superhighways (*autostrade*) speed limits are higher: 90 kph (56 mph), 110 kph (68 mph), 130 kph (80 mph), and 140 kph (86 mph), respectively. Italy's *autostrade* are designated by the letter A, with A1, A2, and A3, from Milan to Reggio Calabria, making up the *Autostrada del Sole.* Except for free stretches in the vicinity of cities, most *autostrade* are toll roads, and they are fairly expensive. They save time, gas, and wear and tear on the car, but they are obviously not the roads to take if you want to browse and linger along the way. Other roads are the *strade statali* (state, or national roads), designated by SS and a number and sometimes better known by their ancient names, such as Via Aurelia, Via Flaminia, and Via Cassia; the unnumbered *strade provinciali* (provincial roads); and the *strade comunali* (local roads). Most of these are much more picturesque than the superhighways.

Traffic congestion is at its worst on main roads (particularly those radiating from major cities) on the days before and after public holidays and on the last days of July and the first days of August. In fact, since most Italians take their vacations in August, traffic on roads leading to beaches or mountains is so bad on these latter days that authorities monitoring road conditions have come to refer to them as the annual *grande esodo* (great exodus) and, via the media, begin counseling the nation's drivers well ahead of time as to the best days, hours, and routes to use for departure. Bottlenecks also occur on the days surrounding August 15 (*Ferragosto,* or Assumption Day), the date by which every Italian family that has not already done so will plan to set out on vacation. Weekends at the end of August and the beginning of September tend to be tied up with the traffic of the *grande rientro* (great reentry).

Excellent road maps of Italy are published by the Italian Touring Club, or *Touring Club Italiano* (*TCI*). Several series are available, but the *Carta Automobilistica d'Italia,* which covers the whole country in two maps on a scale of 1:800,000 (1 centimeter equals 8 kilometers), should be sufficient for the needs of most motorists. The *Grande Carta Stradale d'Italia* series of 15 regional maps (1:200,000; 1 centimeter equals 2 kilometers) is useful for those traveling extensively in one region. A road atlas, *Atlante Stradale d'Italia,* uses the latter scale to map the country in three volumes (northern, central, and southern Italy). Besides all the other information that they contain, TCI maps highlight especially scenic stretches in green, making it easy for motorists to pick out the most desirable travel routes. Another source of good road maps of Italy is the *Istituto Geografico De Agostini* (*IGDA*), which publishes a variety of series in a variety of scales, including a series of regional maps on a scale of 1:250,000. Both the TCI and the IGDA maps are readily available throughout Italy and at certain map stores and travel bookstores in the US, but if they prove difficult to find, *Michelin*'s red map 988, published by the French tire company, may suit the driver's purposes equally well. On a scale of 1:1,000,000 (1 centimeter equals 10 kilometers), it covers the country in considerable detail, and it, too, uses a contrasting color to highlight choice travel routes.

Gasoline is called *benzina* in Italy; it's sold by the liter in *normale, super,* and *diesel* grades (diesel fuel pumps normally carry a sign for *gasolio*). A liter is slightly more than 1 quart; 3.75 liters equal one US gallon. Gas prices everywhere rise and fall depending on the world supply of oil, and the American traveler overseas is further affected by changes in the rate of exchange, so it is difficult to say exactly how much fuel will cost when you travel. It is not difficult to predict, however, that it will cost roughly twice as much as you are accustomed to paying in the US. (At press time, *normale* cost 1,230 lire per liter in Italy; *super,* 1,280 lire; *diesel,* 640 lire.) A gasoline discount program for tourists exists, but it may be used only by foreigners driving their own non-Italian-registered cars and not by foreigners driving rental cars. The discount coupons, which can be bought at the border, entitle those eligible to a discount of 15% off 150 liters of *super* bought in northern Italy and off another 200 liters bought in southern Italy (south of Rome). If you're planning a driving tour, you should check the current price of gasoline just before you go and budget accordingly. Rental cars are delivered with a full tank of gas. Remember to fill the tank before you return the car because you will be charged for a full tank in any case, and the rate at the gas station where you fill it is sure to be less than the price you are charged by the rental firm.

Italy's main automobile club, the *Automobile Club d'Italia,* Via Marsala 8, 00185 Rome (phone: 4998), provides emergency service on *autostrade* and other roads throughout the country. In case of a breakdown, call 116 or, on *autostrade,* use the special SOS call boxes. Though it isn't necessary to belong to ACI to qualify for emergency assistance, service is cheaper, and sometimes free, if you are a member. Because of reciprocal arrangements, ACI automatically extends to American Automobile Association (AAA) members the same courtesies and assistance it extends to its own members.

Touring by Train

Perhaps the most economical and often the most satisfying way to see a lot of a foreign country in a relatively short time is by rail. It is certainly the quickest way to travel between two cities up to 300 miles apart (beyond that, a flight would be quicker, even counting commuting time from airport to city center). But time isn't always the only point. Traveling by train is a way to keep moving and seeing at the same time, and with the special discounts available to visitors, it can be an almost irresistible bargain.

TRAINS AND FARES: The government-owned and -operated *Ferrovie Italiane dello Stato* (*FS*) — known to the English-speaking world as *Italian State Railways* — runs a dense network of trains over nearly 10,000 miles of track extending from the tunnels and passes of the Alps to the heel of the boot in Puglia and the toe in Calabria. Nor do the trains stop there, even though the tracks do; the train ferry carries the cars across the water from Villa San Giovanni, Calabria, to Messina, Sicily, where the rails resume, one main line branching south along the coast to Syracuse and the other west along the coast to Palermo. Sicily has only a few secondary lines, and Sardinia's main line, running from Olbia to Sassari, Oristano, and Cagliari, is not much more than a secondary line, but at least on the Italian mainland, there are few places of interest to a visitor that cannot be reached by rail. The rolling stock ranges from the ultramodern, in which passengers speed along between principal cities in quiet, air-conditioned comfort, to the antiquated, in which they clack from stop to local stop on upholstered wooden seats. The trains don't all run on time, even though older Italians are fond of recalling Mussolini's efforts to achieve punctuality, and they are frequently stopped completely by strikes. But kilometer for kilometer they are among the least expensive in Europe. Consequently, they are crowded, especially on weekends and during the summer, and ticket lines can be long.

From most to least direct, trains in Italy are classified as *rapidi,* fast trains connecting major cities; *espressi,* long-distance express trains making stops at main stations; *diretti,* trains stopping at many stations; and *locali,* trains stopping at all stations. Except for the *rapidi,* many of which are first class (*prima classe*) only, and the *locali,* some of which are second class (*seconda classe*) only, all trains have both first-class and second-class cars.

There are three types of *rapido* trains in Italy, but all require payment of a supplement for all departures. At the top of the list are the *Trans-Europ Express* (*TEE*) trains. As their name implies, these are largely international trains operated by several of Europe's national railway companies, including Italian State Railways. The TEE system came into being in the 1950s to provide the emerging European Economic Community with efficient, not to mention luxurious, train service between major Continental cities, and only the fastest and most direct trains, offering the highest standards of comfort and convenience, attained TEE status. Italy's contribution to the network includes four trains that operate entirely within Italian borders — the *Colosseum* and the *Ambrosiano,* which both travel between Milan and Rome; the *Adriatico,* which travels between Milan and Bari; and the *Vesuvio,* between Milan and Naples. A fifth TEE operating on Italian soil is the Swiss-owned *Gottardo,* which makes a daily round trip between Zürich and Milan. All TEE trains are first class only, and the supplement required to ride them includes the price of a reserved seat, which is obligatory on Italian TEE's and on TEE's crossing borders.

Other types of *rapido* trains in Italy are the *rapidi a prenotazione obbligatoria* and the *rapidi ordinari,* the latter including a special group known as *International Intercity* (*IC*) trains. Like the TEE's, *rapidi a prenotazione obbligatoria* are first class only and require a seat reservation, the cost of which is included in the supplement. Ordinary *rapidi,* however, carry first- and second-class cars; seats can be reserved in either class, but since the reservation is not obligatory, the reservation fee is in addition to, not included in, the supplement. A word about International Intercity trains: These are in part a legacy of the TEE system because many of them are former TEE's to which second-class cars have been added to combat a problem of low ridership (TEE's are relatively expensive to operate and thus relatively expensive to ride). Note that if you take an IC between two cities in Italy, the seat reservation is optional just as on any other *rapido ordinario,* but if you take an IC crossing a border (such as the *Ligure* from Milan to Marseille, the *Mont Cenis* to Lyon, the *Lutetia, Cisalpin,* or *Lemano* to Geneva, or the *Mediolanum* to Munich), the seat reservation is obligatory.

Train fares are based on a combination of the distance traveled and the quality of accommodations chosen. A ticket in first class costs approximately 80% more than a ticket in second class. Because of this, first class is usually less crowded. Those electing to travel second class, however — as most Italians do — will probably find it perfectly satisfactory, provided the train is not full and they find a seat. If they don't, and seats are available in first class, they are permitted to upgrade their tickets aboard the train, paying the conductor the difference in classes.

Tickets can be bought at train stations, at offices of the Italian State Railways' own travel agency, *Compagnia Italiana Turismo* (*CIT*), at other travel agencies displaying the FS sign, and, if necessary, on the train, though they cost more that way. They can also be bought at CIT offices in the US (addresses are given under *Further Information* later in this section) where, given fluctuations in the rate of exchange, they may cost more or less than they would at the same time in Italy. (Each August, the various European railways set dollar prices for tickets to be sold overseas using a rate of exchange they anticipate will be valid for the following year and taking into account any price increases they foresee. The resulting Eurailtariff fares go into effect on January 1 and remain in effect until December 31.)

As a rule, a round-trip ticket (*biglietto di andata e ritorno*) costs simply double the price of a one-way (*andata* or *corsa semplice*) ticket. An exception is a round-trip ticket between stations a maximum of 250 kilometers from each other, for which there is a reduction of 15% provided the ticket is bought in Italy and not the US. Many other discounts allow both Italians and foreign visitors to economize on train travel, but they tend to be reserved for special groups of people. For instance, children under 4 travel free on Italian trains as long as they do not occupy a seat, and children aged 4 through 11 travel at half price. In addition, there are the Family Card (*Carta Famiglia*) for families of at least three members traveling together and the Silver Card (*Carta d'Argento*) for senior citizens, both purchased in Italy only and allowing discounts of 30%. Nevertheless, most visitors who plan to do a lot of train travel will find that a rail pass (see *Passes* later in this section) is an equally good bargain. Some rail passes are meant for foreigners only and must be purchased before you go.

RESERVATIONS, DINING AND SLEEPING CARS, OTHER SERVICES: Both first- and second-class seats on most trains can be reserved in advance for a flat fee per seat. Reservations reduce flexibility, but they are advisable during the summer on popular routes, particularly long-distance routes. They are also advisable at holiday times (but note that no reservations except the obligatory ones are accepted for trains departing a few days before Christmas and Easter). In Italy, seats can be reserved as much as two months in advance, with the reservation period closing usually three to six hours before the departure of the train. Reservations for first-class and sometimes second-class seats can also be made before you leave home; in high season it's suggested you do this as early as six weeks and no later than four weeks before your intended train ride. There is a price to pay for making reservations in the US. Whereas the fee per seat is only 2,000 lire in Italy and $2 in the US at present, communications charges for reservations made from this side of the Atlantic add up. It is possible to buy tickets here and make reservations, even those that are obligatory, after your arrival in Italy.

Dining facilities on the trains vary. Only TEE's and long-distance *rapidi* have an actual dining car (*vettura-ristorante*); reservations can be made after boarding. Other trains have self-service or *trattoria* cars, where tray meals are eaten at tables. An even greater number of trains have "mini-bar" service: an ambulatory vendor dispenses beverages and sandwiches from a cart. If you're sure that you'll want to eat en route, it's a good idea to inquire beforehand exactly what meal service is offered on the train you'll be taking. If none is offered, remember that box lunches are for sale at many stations and that when trains pull into larger stations, box lunches, sandwiches, wine, and other drinks can be purchased from vendors with carts on the platform. Purchases are made quickly, money and food passing through the windows.

Sleeping accommodations are found on overnight trains going long distances, such as between Milan and Rome, Naples, Bari, and Brindisi; Rome or Naples and Sicily; Rome and Venice, Turin, and Genoa; and between Italy and other European countries. Two types of arrangements are possible. Couchettes (*cuccette*), available in both first- and second-class versions, are basically the coach seats of a compartment converted to sleeping berths, with pillows, sheets, and blankets. First-class compartments contain four couchettes (an upper and a lower on each side of the aisle); second-class compartments contain six (an upper, middle, and lower on each side). Since couchettes cost only a standard supplement per person (9,500 lire for either class in Italy, $11 plus communications charges in the US) above the first- or second-class fare, they are a relatively inexpensive way to get a night's rest aboard the train. However, they provide privacy only for those traveling with a family or other group that can use the whole compartment; individual travelers are mixed with strangers of either sex and disrobing is not allowed.

A sleeping car (*vettura-letto*) contains actual bedroom compartments providing one to three beds with a mattress, pillow, sheets, and blanket, plus a washbasin with hot and cold water and a mirror. Several kinds of compartments are available, though not on every train. Singles, specials, and doubles are all first-class accommodations. The single and special are individual compartments, with the special being slightly smaller and less expensive; the double is for two people who have booked it together. Tourist compartments (T2 and T3) are second-class compartments for two and three people traveling together or for strangers; unlike couchette accommodations, strangers of the opposite sex are segregated. Sleeping accommodations require payment of the basic first- or second-class fare plus a supplement that varies with the type of compartment and the distance traveled. From the least to the most expensive, sleeping car arrangements can cost anywhere from two or three times the price of a couchette to as much as ten times more.

Passengers are allowed to carry 20 kilos (44 pounds) of baggage free, but since luggage in your possession is not weighed, you could conceivably carry more. Some trains are equipped with a place to put luggage just inside the doors, but otherwise you will have to hoist your suitcase onto an overhead rack. If you have too much luggage to handle yourself, it can be sent as registered baggage (the cost of this service depends on weight and distance), but it does not always travel on the same train as you do. Most stations have a baggage checkroom (*deposito bagagli*) where you can temporarily free yourself of surplus bags.

Other FS services of interest to visitors include *Treno + Auto,* a car rental service offered in cooperation with several rental firms and available in larger cities. Passengers can reserve a car before boarding the train — either directly from one of the companies (*Hertz, Avis, Maggiore, Eurotrans*) if it has an office in the departure city or, if not, at the train station — and find it waiting for them at their destination. Trains that carry cars (*Trasporto a Bagaglio di Auto al Seguito del Viaggiatore*) are another convenience. These operate on international routes or on long-distance national routes — from northern cities such as Genoa, Turin, Milan, Bolzano, and Bologna to southern cities such as Rome, Naples, Bari, Brindisi (connecting with car ferries for Greece), and Villa San Giovanni in Calabria (connecting with car ferries for Sicily) — and allow car owners to take to the rails while their car travels with them on the same train. Book well in advance, especially in summer (the reservation period opens two months in advance of travel and closes two weeks and 24 hours in advance for international routes and national routes respectively. Ferries and buses are also part of the FS network. In addition to the ferry that carries passengers aboard the train across the Strait of Messina to Sicily, Italian State Railways operates conventional car and passenger ferries between the mainland and Sardinia. It also cooperates with the railroad systems of other European countries in running *Europabus,* which offers all-inclusive escorted sightseeing tours geared to the foreign visitor. Itineraries can cover one or more European countries and range anywhere from a few days to two weeks. The five-day tour of Sicily, from Palermo to Agrigento, Syracuse, Catania, and Taormina and back to Palermo, is an example.

Some helpful hints: You can charge tickets to your Visa card at the larger Italian train stations, and if you're buying your ticket on the train you can even pay in foreign currency provided you're traveling on one of the main lines. The *orario ferroviario* (train timetable) on display in stations shows *arrivi* (arrivals) and *partenze* (departures); the *binario* is the track. If the train you're considering taking operates on *giorni festivi*, it operates on Sundays and public holidays only; the other days, including Saturdays, are *giorni feriali*. Large train stations such as those in Rome and Milan have an *albergo diurno* (day hotel) where you can take a bath or shower, have your hair done, get a shave, or even rent a room by the hour to sleep — all a wonderful way to revive yourself if jet lag and rail fatigue have combined to make you look and feel your worst and you have time to kill between trains.

OTHER RAILROADS: Some trains in Italy have nothing to do with FS, although the average first-time visitor is unlikely to encounter them. An exception is the narrow-gauge *Circumvesuviana Railway*, which travels back and forth between Naples and Sorrento and is a handy way to visit Pompeii. The *Orient Express* — although not the Orient Express of old — also passes through Italy. The legendary luxury hotel on wheels that carried tourists and tycoons, kings and conspirators, from London and Paris via Eastern Europe to Istanbul made its final run in 1977 but has since been revived in two forms. One is the *Venice Simplon-Orient-Express*, which leaves London for Paris, Zürich, Innsbruck, Verona, and Venice twice weekly from mid-March to mid-November, giving passengers a taste of the golden age of rail aboard sumptuously restored carriages from the 1920s. From January to mid-March, it makes one trip weekly in each direction with some extra stops en route to provide access to Alpine ski resorts. Information on these deluxe trips, on which the usual fares and tickets do not apply and which can be taken all the way or in part in either direction, is available from *Venice Simplon-Orient-Express*, Suite 1235, One World Trade Center, New York, NY 10048 (phone: 212-938-6830 or 800-524-2420). The other revival, also with original cars, is the *Nostalgic Istanbul Orient Express*, owned by a Swiss company, Intraflug, and operated in the spring and fall on nine- and ten-day trips between Paris and Istanbul by *Society Expeditions*, 723 Broadway E, Seattle, WA 98102 (phone: 206-324-9400 or 800-426-7794). Its itinerary does not include Italy.

PASSES: Rail passes offer unlimited train travel within a set period of time for a flat purchase price. They can save a considerable amount of money for the serious rail traveler, and they frequently include trips on other forms of transportation as extra features. They can also save a considerable amount of time. Once they are validated by a railroad clerk on the day of your first trip, they spare you the trouble of standing in ticket lines — which can be very long in the peak travel season.

The *Eurailpass*, the first and best known of all rail passes, is valid in Italy as well as in fifteen other European countries. It entitles holders to 15 or 21 days or one, two, or three months of unlimited first-class travel plus many extras, including free travel or substantial reductions on Danube and Rhine river trips, lake steamers, ferry crossings such as the Italy–Greece services of certain shipping lines, and transportation by bus and private railroads. Since the Eurailpass is a first-class pass, Eurail travelers can ride TEE and any other trains as they wish, and they are exempt from all supplements. A Eurail pass for children under 12 is half the adult price and includes the same features. The *Eurail Youthpass*, for travelers under 26 years of age, is slightly different. It is available in one- and two-month versions only, is valid for travel in second class only, and does not exempt the holder from all supplements. The newly introduced Eurail Saverpass resembles the basic Eurailpass except that it allows 15 days of unlimited first-class travel for three people traveling together. All three types of passes must be bought before you go, from a travel agent, from a US office of *CIT*, or from one of the other European national railway companies (French National Railroads, Germanrail, or Swiss Federal Railways).

The Eurailpass is a bargain for those who will be traveling widely throughout Europe, but for those who will be traveling strictly within Italy, the less expensive *Italian Tourist Ticket* (*BTLC*, or *Biglietto Turistico di Libera Circolazione*), Italy's own unlimited-mileage pass, is the better alternative. It is issued for either first-class or second-class travel for periods of 8, 15, 21, or 30 days, with children under 12 entitled to their own passes at half the adult price. Holders of the first-class pass are exempt from paying all *rapido* supplements, including the special TEE supplement. Holders of the second-class pass are exempt from paying only the supplement applicable to second-class *rapido* travel. If they decide to travel first class or even on a TEE, they may do so, but they'll be charged both the difference between fares and that between supplements. Holders of either pass are also exempt from paying any reservations fees when reservations are obligatory; they must pay to reserve a seat when the reservation is not obligatory, however. The Italian Tourist Ticket is meant for nonresidents of Italy only and can be bought either before going abroad through CIT offices or travel agents or in Italy at main train stations, CIT offices, and other travel agencies displaying the FS sign.

Another type of ticket, the *Italian Kilometric Ticket* (*Biglietto Chilometrico*) is not truly a rail pass, but it does allow unlimited mileage up to a point. The purchaser is entitled to travel a total distance of 3,000 kilometers (1,875 miles) in as many as 20 trips within a period of two months. This is a generous allowance and one that the average traveler might not exhaust during the course of the typical vacation, but the advantage of the ticket is that it may be used by up to five people, who do not have to be members of the same family. When used by more than one person, the total distance of any trip is multiplied by the number of adults taking the trip (children under 12 are charged for half the distance traveled). The Italian Kilometric Ticket is sold in either first-class or second-class versions, but unlike the Eurailpass or the BTLC it does not exempt holders from paying *rapido* supplements. Reservations fees must be paid when not included in the supplement, and anyone with a second-class ticket wanting to ride in first class must pay the difference in fares as well. The ticket is further unlike a rail pass in that it must be validated before each use rather than before the first use only. It can be bought from CIT offices (addresses below) or travel agents in the US or at main train stations, CIT offices, and travel agencies in Italy.

FURTHER INFORMATION: In addition to its many offices in Europe, the Italian State Railways' own travel agency, *CIT* (*Compagnia Italiana Turismo*), has three offices in the US that make reservations, sell tickets and rail passes, and provide information on all FS services. They distribute a flyer giving the prices of the various rail passes valid in Italy along with sample first-class and second-class fares for point-to-point travel between a number of Italian cities and between the main cities in Italy and the rest of Europe. Ask for the flyer because you can add up the fares of likely trips and judge whether a rail pass would be worth your while. Distances in kilometers are also given between the sample Italian cities, a help in judging the usefulness of the kilometric ticket. *CIT* has offices in the following US locations:

California: 15760 Ventura Blvd., Suite 819, Encino, CA 91436 (phone: 818-783-7245 or 800-CIT-RAIL in California; 800-CIT-TOUR in other western states)

Illinois: 765 Route 83, Bensenville, IL 60106 (phone: 312-860-1090 or 800-558-5678)

New York: 666 Fifth Ave., New York, NY 10103 (phone: 212-397-2667)

The official timetable of the Italian State Railways, *Il Treno,* a bulky tome sold in stations and at newsstands in Italy, contains more than anyone except a railroad clerk needs to know. CIT offices in the US occasionally make available *Principali Treni,* a small booklet that is widely distributed throughout Italy. It contains timetables of the main rail services between towns and cities of any size in Italy, and although it is written in Italian, most of the writing is confined to footnotes and the essential schedule information can be extracted without too much difficulty. If this is not enough to help you plan a rough itinerary, you may want to buy the *Thomas Cook Continental Timetable,* a detailed compendium of European international and national rail services that is the most revered and accurate railway reference in existence. The *Timetable* comes out monthly, but because most European countries switch to summer schedules at the end of May and back to winter schedules at the end of September, the June edition is the first complete summer schedule and October the first complete winter schedule. The *Thomas Cook Continental Timetable* is sold by travel bookstores and by the *Forsyth Travel Library,* PO Box 2975, Dept. TCT, Shawnee Mission, KS 66201 ($15.95 plus $1 for postage; you can also call 913-384-0496 and pay by credit card).

Some other books you may want to consult before embarking on an extensive rail trip in Europe include *Train Guide Europe* by George Pandi ($9.95), which discusses train travel in general and gives details of the fares, supplements, reductions, passes, reservations procedures, and meal, sleeper, baggage, and other services of the railway systems of the 16 Eurail countries plus Great Britain. Two others are the *Eurail Guide* by Kathryn Saltzman Turpin and Marvin Saltzman ($10.95), and *Europe by Eurail* by George Wright Ferguson ($8.95). Both discuss train travel in the Eurail countries (the former also discusses Eastern Europe and the rest of the world), and both suggest numerous sightseeing excursions by rail from various base cities.

Package Tours

 If the thought of buying a package for travel to and through Europe conjures up visions of a race through ten countries in as many days with a busload of frazzled fellow passengers as companions, be aware that packages are not what they used to be. For one thing, a package does not have to include any organized touring at all, nor does it necessarily provide traveling companions. If it does, however, you'll find that people of all sorts — some just like you — are taking advantage of packages today because they are economical and convenient, save the purchaser an immense amount of planning time, and exist in such variety that it's virtually impossible for the Europe-bound traveler not find one that fits most if not all of his or her preferences.

In essence, a package is a combination of travel services that can be purchased as a single booking. It may include any or all of the following: transatlantic transportation, local transportation (and/or car rentals), accommodations, some or all meals, sightseeing, entertainment, transfers to and from the hotel at each destination, taxes, tips, escort service, and a variety of incidental features that might be offered as options at additional cost.

In other words, a package may be any combination from a fully escorted tour offered at an inclusive price to a simple fly/drive booking allowing the purchasers to do exactly as they please. Its principal advantage is that it saves money; invariably the cost of the combined arrangements is well below the price of all the elements purchased separately. An important additional feature is that because all the elements are purchased at the same time, travelers are left free to devote their full attention to the trip — its burdensome details settled.

The lower prices that are possible through package travel result from volume participation. The tour packager negotiates for services in wholesale quantities — blocks of hotel rooms to be used during a given period of time, group meals, busloads of ground transportation, and so on — and thus purchases them at a lower per-person price. Even after markups and commissions are added, the retail tour price is still reasonably below what independent travelers would pay if planning such a trip on their own. Most packages, however, are subject to restrictions governing the duration of the trip and require total payment a certain time before departure.

Packages are put together by tour operators or wholesalers, some retail travel agencies, airlines, charter companies, hotels, and even special-interest organizations, and what goes into them depends on who is organizing them. The most common type, assembled by tour wholesalers and sold through travel agents, can run the gamut from deluxe everything to simple tourist-class amenities or even bare necessities. Fly/drive and fly/cruise packages are usually the joint planning efforts of airlines and, respectively, car rental organizations and cruise line operators. Charter flight programs may range from little more than air fare and a minimum of ground arrangements to full-scale tours. There are also hotel packages organized by hotel chains or associations of independent hotels and applicable to stays at any combination of member establishments; resort packages covering arrangements at a specific hotel; and special-interest tours, which can be once-only programs organized by particular groups through a retail agency or regular offerings packaged by a tour operator. They can feature food, music or theater festivals, a particular sporting activity or event, a commemorative occasion, or even scientific exploration. Since almost all packages are bought through travel agents, a good agent is the best guide to sorting through this abundance. The agent will be able to provide information not only on packages of general interest but also on those more specialized, even though the latter can sometimes be booked through the packager as well, particularly if the program caters to a small number of people and is limited to one or a few departures annually.

To determine whether a package — or, more specifically, which package — fits your travel plans, start by evaluating your interests and needs, deciding how much you want to spend and what you want to see and do. Gather whatever information is available about programs that fit your schedule and read the brochures carefully to determine what is included. Tour brochures almost always highlight — in eye-catching type — the lowest price at which a tour is offered. This price, however, may be available off-season only, at the lowest-priced hotel among several in the program (which nonetheless may be quite satisfactory), or in such limited numbers that it has a waiting list. Note, too, that prices quoted in brochures are almost always based on double occupancy. The rate listed is for each of two people sharing a double room; if you travel alone, the supplement for single accommodations can raise the price considerably (see *Hints for Single Travelers*).

Increasingly, in this age of ever-changing air fares, brochures do not include the price of the airline ticket in the price of the package, though sample applicable fares from various gateway cities are usually listed separately, to be added to the price of the ground arrangements. Get the latest fares from the airline because the samples will invariably be out of date by the time you read them. If the brochure gives more than one category of sample fares per gateway — in the case of flights to Italy, for example, an economy fare, an excursion or APEX fare, or, possibly, a group fare — your travel agent or airline tour desk clerk will be able to tell you which one applies to the package you choose depending on when you travel, how far in advance you book, and other factors. When the brochure does include round-trip transportation in the package price, don't forget to add the round-trip transportation cost from your home to the departure city to come up with the total cost of the package. Finally, read the general information regarding terms and conditions and the responsibility clause (usually in fine print at the end of the descriptive literature) to find out what the tour operator is — and is not — liable for. In reading, ask the following questions:

1. Does the tour include air fare or other transportation, sightseeing, meals, transfers, taxes, baggage handling, tips, or any other services? Do you want all these services?
2. If the brochure indicates that "some meals" are included, does this mean welcoming and farewell dinners, two breakfasts, or every evening meal? It makes a difference.

3. What classes of hotels are offered? If you will be traveling alone, what is the single supplement?
4. Does the tour itinerary or price vary according to the season?
5. Are the prices guaranteed; that is, if costs increase between the time you book and the time you depart, can surcharges be added?
6. Do you get a refund if you cancel? (If not, be sure to obtain cancellation insurance.)
7. Can the operator cancel if too few people join?

Read the responsibility clause very carefully because it is there that the tour operator frequently expresses the right to change services or schedules as long as equivalent arrangements are offered. This clause also absolves the operator of responsibility if circumstances beyond human control affect the operation of the tour.

One of the consumer's biggest problems is finding enough information to judge the reliability of a tour packager since individuals seldom have direct contact with the firm putting the package together. Usually, a retail travel agent is involved between customer and tour operator, and much depends on his or her candor and cooperation. So ask a number of questions about the tour you are considering. For example: Has the agent ever used the packages provided by this tour operator? How long has the tour operator been in business? Which and how many companies are involved in the package? If air travel is by charter flight, is there an escrow account in which deposits will be held; if so, what is the name of the bank?

This last question is very important. The law requires that tour operators deposit every charter passenger's deposit and subsequent payments in a proper escrow account. Money paid into such an account cannot legally be used except to pay for the costs of a particular package or to refund the money if the trip is canceled. To ensure the safe handling of your money, make your check payable to the escrow account — by law, the name of the depository bank appears in the operator-participant contract and is usually found in that mass of minuscule type on the back of the brochure. Write the details of the charter, including the destination and dates, on the face of the check; on the back, print "For Deposit Only." Your travel agent may prefer that you make your check out to the agency, saying that it will then pay the tour operator the fee minus commission. But it is perfectly legal to write your check as we suggest, and the agent should have sufficient faith in the tour operator to trust him to send the proper commission. If your agent objects too vociferously to this procedure, consider taking your business elsewhere; if you don't make your check out to the escrow account, you lose the protection of escrow should the trip be canceled or the tour operator or travel agent fail. Furthermore, recent bankruptcies in the travel industry have served to point out that even the protection of escrow may not be enough to safeguard investment. Increasingly, insurance is becoming a necessity (see *Insurance*).

SAMPLE PACKAGES TO ITALY: There are so many packages available to Italy that it's probably safe to say you can get any arrangement you want for as long as you want it. Travelers seeking the maximum in structure will find that the classic sightseeing tour by motorcoach, fully escorted and all-inclusive (or nearly), has withstood the test of time and is still well represented among the programs of the major tour operators. Typically, these tours last anywhere from 11 or 12 days to as many as 23 or 24 days. At their briefest, they may begin in Milan, move east to Venice, and then travel down the backbone of Italy to Florence and Rome, often with a detour to the Naples area to see Pompeii, Capri, and the Amalfi Drive before returning to Rome for departure. With more time, they may begin and end in Milan or Rome and trace a long, narrow loop around the country, adding a variety of secondary sights to the itinerary. Tours concentrating on the north of Italy or on the south, including the island of Sicily, are also easy to find, although tours exploring a single region in depth are not common. The notable exception is Sicily, which is often packaged on its own.

Hotel accommodations in packages of this kind are usually characterized as first class or better, with private baths or showers in all rooms. Breakfast daily is almost always included, whereas the number of lunches and dinners may vary considerably, and meals include wine only when the tour literature clearly states so. Also included are transfers between airport and hotel, baggage handling, tips to maids and waiters, local transportation, sightseeing excursions and admission fees, as well as any featured evening entertainment — almost everything, in fact, except round-trip air fare between the US and Italy (which is generally shown separately), personal expenses for laundry, incidentals, and souvenirs, and tips to the motorcoach driver and to the tour escort, who remains with the group from beginning to end.

An example of this type of escorted, highly structured program is *Travcoa*'s 24-day Italy and Sicily tour, which goes from Milan to Venice, through Tuscany to Rome and Naples, and then on through Calabria to Sicily, with three meals included every day. The tour is not for the budget traveler, but almost all the well-known tour operators have similar escorted programs of varying length and often with varying categories of hotels, thus creating less expensive alternatives to their standard packages. In addition, there are the packages of the smaller or less well known tour operators specializing in travel to Italy. These include *CIT Tours*, whose parent company, CIT, owned by Italian State Railways, is Italy's largest tour operator. CIT Tours offers a two-week escorted All That Italy program (book it through a travel agent or a CIT Tours office in New York, Chicago, or Los Angeles; see "Further Information," *Touring by Train*, for addresses), as well as a variety of arrangements for independent travelers.

Smaller companies are *Perillo Tours*, 30 N William St., Pearl River, NY 10965 (phone: 212-584-8300 or 914-735-2000 in New York State; 800-431-1515 elsewhere), which has 15-day packages to the north or the south (including Sicily) of Italy and a 10-day Italy Off-Season package; *Donna Franca Tours*, 470 Commonwealth Ave., Boston, MA 02215 (phone: 617-227-3111 in Massachusetts; 800-225-6290 elsewhere), which also has a 15-day package including Sicily among its tours; and *Amelia Tours*, 280 Old Country Road, Hicksville, NY 11801 (phone: 516-433-0640), whose 11-day Just Sicily program is just that. All these packages can be booked through a travel agent, but the 23-day Theme and Variations tour by *Italia Adagio*, 162 Whaley St., Freeport, NY 11520 (phone: 516-868-7825 or 516-546-5239), should be booked directly with the company. It covers the territory from Rome to Venice at a leisurely pace and visits many more small towns than is customary on such tours.

Less restrictive arrangements for travelers who prefer more independence than that found on escorted tours are listed in the semi-escorted and hosted sections of tour catalogues. These may combine some aspects of an escorted tour, such as moving from place to place by motorcoach, with longer stays in one spot, where participants are at liberty but where a host or hostess — that is, a representative of the tour company — is available at a local office or even in the hotel to answer questions and assist in arranging activities and optional excursions.

Many of the very popular city packages to Italy are hosted arrangements. They appeal to travelers who want to be on their own and remain in one place for the duration of their vacation, although it is not unusual to buy more than one package at a time. Basically, they include transfers between airport and hotel, a choice of accommodations (with Continental breakfast) in several price ranges, plus any of a number of other features that may not always be needed or wanted but are time-consuming to arrange when they are. A half-day sightseeing tour of the city is a common feature; others may be anything from a souvenir travel bag to a dinner or a show or some sort of discount card to be used in shops and restaurants. Rome, Florence, and Venice are the most frequent destinations for this type of package, and *American Express* has 4-day or 7-day packages to all three. *TWA* has a 10-day package to Rome, while *CIT Tours* has an 8-day package that includes a full-day excursion to either Florence or Naples. CIT

Tours also has a selection of 2-night city packages (that can be extended by extra nights) to more than two dozen Italian cities. In essence, the packages are much like prepaid hotel stays; travelers with a rental car or a rail pass can pick and choose from the list and string them together to form their own tours.

Another possibility for those who want a degree of independence is a fly/drive package. At its simplest, this can involve no more than a rental car and a block of as many prepaid hotel vouchers as needed for the length of the stay. At its most restrictive, the packager supplies an itinerary that must be followed day by day, with a specific hotel to be reached each night. Often, plans such as the latter are more deluxe as well. Top hotels are a feature of *Italia Adagio*'s Flying Solo program, a series of five 16-day itineraries largely focused on central Italy, especially the hill towns of Umbria and Tuscany but also embracing scenic routes as far north as the Lombardy Lakes and as far south as the Amalfi Coast and Sicily. The 10-day Renaissance Road car tour packaged by *AutoVenture* features stays in hotels that are converted villas or palaces, and the package can be bought in either a self-drive or a chauffeured version (see your travel agent).

Special-interest tours are a growing sector of the travel industry. Not surprisingly, programs that emphasize food and wine are among such packages put together for visitors to Italy. They tend to be quite structured rather than independent, and they are rarely created with the budget traveler in mind. Also note that inclusive as they may be, few food and wine tours include all meals in the package price. This is not necessarily a cost-cutting technique on the part of the packager; rather, because of the lavishness of some of the meals, others may be left to the discretion of the participants, not only to allow time for leisure but also to allow for differing rates of metabolism. Similarly, even on wine tours that spend entire days in practically full-time tasting, unlimited table wine at meals may not always be included in the package price. The brochures are usually clear about what comes with the package and when.

A package that stresses food, particularly the preparation of it, is the 10-day Ruffino's Tuscan Experience package offered by *The World of Oz*, Cortell Group, 3 E 54th St., New York, NY 10022 (phone: 212-751-3250 or 800-442-4481 in New York State; 800-223-6626 elsewhere), which has several departures from May through October. Participants are based in Florence and visit some sights not ordinarily open to tourists, but the highlight of the experience is the five 3-hour cooking demonstrations, which take place at a private estate belonging to the owners of the Ruffino house of wine and are conducted by some of Italy's leading chefs. Two wine-tasting sessions and several meals at select restaurants are included, in addition to the meals prepared at the cooking demonstrations.

Another *World of Oz* package, run from April through September, is the 15-day Castles, Cuisine, and Wine of Italy tour. It moves from Rome to Milan, visiting wine cellars and vineyards in the Frascati, Orvieto, Chianti, and Soave regions, among others, and sampling some of Italy's better restaurants en route. Food markets, an oil-pressing mill, a wine museum, and lunch at a farmhouse that produces all that it serves are other stops, and there is one cooking demonstration. Completely devoted to wine — although the restaurants featured on this tour are among Italy's finest — is the once-a-year, three-week Italian Caprice offered by *Bacchants' Pilgrimages*, 323 Geary St., Suite 514, San Francisco, CA 94102 (phone: 415-981-8518). It pays homage to the wines of Umbria and Tuscany (including Brunello di Montalcino in addition to Chianti) before a trip to Venice and the vineyards of Friuli-Venezia Giulia, and then it backtracks through the Soave region of the Veneto to visit several wine zones of Piedmont — Gattinara, Barolo, and Barbera among them.

Other packages cater to lovers of classical music and opera. The roster of tours offered year-round by *Dailey-Thorp*, 315 W 57th St., New York, NY 10019 (phone: 212-308-1555), is always changing, but the company regularly sends a group to opening night at La Scala in December. At other times, the tours visit various Italian music festivals such as Florence's Maggio Musicale, the Rossini Festival at Pesaro, Stresa's Musical Weeks, and the outdoor opera at the Arena of Verona and take in performances at Venice's Teatro La Venice, Turin's Teatro Regio, Florence's Teatro Comunale, and Rome's Teatro dell'Opera in addition to La Scala. Music-related activities such as backstage tours and visits to sites associated with the composers or their works are part of the itineraries. Another tour packager, marching to a different beat, sends jazz lovers to the Umbria Jazz Festival, Italy's largest such gathering, held in the summer. A package to the Festival of Two Worlds in Spoleto is also available. For information, contact *New York Jazztour,* 2 King St., Suite 5F, New York, NY 10012 (phone: 212-243-0003).

Ski tours are foremost among the special-interest packages of a sporting variety. The foundation of the typical package is usually a week or two of hotel or condominium accommodations at a ski resort (Bormio, Cervinia, Cortina d'Ampezzo, Courmayeur, Madonna di Campiglio, Selva di Val Gardena, and Sestriere are the common destinations), and for those staying in a hotel rather than an apartment the price often includes a meal plan of breakfast and dinner daily. The other features of a ski vacation — round-trip bus, train, or rental car transportation between the airport and the resort, ski passes, baggage handling, taxes, and tips — are included in varying combinations according to the packager. If transatlantic transportation is by charter flight (not unusual on ski packages), air fare, too, will be included in the price. If not, the applicable "group ski" or other fare will be listed separately.

The largest selection of Italian resorts — a baker's dozen from the Valle d'Aosta and Piedmont regions across to the Trentino–Alto Adige and Friuli–Venezia Giulia — is available on the Intermezzo–Ski in Italy program offered by *Central Holiday Tours* in conjunction with *Alitalia* and booked through travel agents. Although there is a minimum stay for some departures, most of the packages are one week long; each comes with a ski pass good for six days of skiing, and discounts of 30% on group ski lessons are possible at all the resorts. Other ski trip packagers with a number of European destinations, including Italy, are *Alpine Skiing and Travel,* 534 New State Hwy., Raynham, MA 02767 (phone: 617-823-7707 or 800-343-9676), and *Steve Lohr's Skiworld,* Cortell Group, 3 E 54th St., New York, NY 10022 (phone: 212-751-3250 or 800-442-2410 in New York State; 800-223-1306 elsewhere). *Club Med,* which operates its own resort villages around the world, has a club hotel in Sestriere; vacation packages there include lessons at the club's private ski school. For membership and details, contact *Club Méditerranée International,* 40 W 57th St., New York, NY 10019 (phone: 800-528-3100).

Special-interest tours for practitioners and spectators of other sports include many bicycle and hiking tours of varying difficulty. For the names and addresses of their organizers, see *Camping and Caravanning, Biking, and Hiking.* Horseback riding holidays in Italy — in the Abruzzo region for one week, for experienced riders only — are arranged by *FITS Equestrian,* 2011 Alamo Pintado Rd., Solvang, CA 93463 (phone: 805-688-9494). The Great Balloon Adventures, one-week programs operated in May and June by the *Bombard Society,* 6727 Curran St., McLean, VA 22101 (phone: 703-448-9407 or 800-862-8537), explore Tuscany — from on high and with feet on the ground. The packages include daily flights via hot air balloon (flown by pilots, not tour participants), sightseeing, hotel accommodations, and meals. Spa packages covering arrangements at various of Italy's thermal resorts are available from a number of sources. They are usually one week long and provide accommodations, some or all meals, and one or two treatments daily (classic spa treatments such as manual or hydromassage, mud baths, and so on), often with the option of a beauty program rather than the basic spa regimen. *Health and Fitness Vacations,* 2911 Grand Ave., Suite 3A, Mayfair in the Grove, Miami, FL 33133 (phone: 305-445-3876), a specialist in spa vacations throughout Europe, has packages to Abano Terme near Venice, to Monte-catini Terme, the well-known spa about 30 miles northwest of Florence, and to the island of Ischia. *Central Holiday Tours* offers packages (through travel agents) to the same three resorts.

Since Italy is a land of pilgrimage, it is also the destination of tours geared to Roman Catholic travelers. One of the largest providers of these is *Faith Tours*, 265 Sunrise Hwy., Rockville Centre, NY 11570 (phone: 516-536-4422 or 718-746-0900 in New York State; 800-428-0006 elsewhere), which offers a 9-day Heart of Italy tour, taking in Siena, Florence, Assisi, and Rome, and an 11-day Pilgrims Route to Rome tour, visiting various shrines. Both tours include a papal audience. For Jewish travelers, the *American Jewish Congress*, 15 E 84th St., New York, NY 10028 (phone: 212-879-4588 in New York State; 800-221-4694 elsewhere) regularly arranges tours to Europe, in-cluding Italy, in addition to its tours to Israel.

Camping and Caravanning, Biking, and Hiking

CAMPING AND CARAVANNING: Italy has about 1,700 campgrounds, or *campeggi*, most on the northern lakes and on the coasts of the Adriatic, Tyrrhenian, and Ligurian seas. They are used by more than 4 million people a year, a third of them foreigners. Italian campgrounds are graded by stars: Degree of organization, quality of accommodations, and rates increase according to the number of stars. Some campgrounds have minimal facilities, and others are quite elaborate, with bungalows, tourist villages, shopping centers, and even hotel accommo-dations on site.

If you want to camp during the peak summer season, you should reserve a site by early May. The *Touring Club Italiano* publishes a paperback book, *Campeggi e villaggi turistici in Italia*, a succinct and specific outline of facilities at sites, organized by localities, which will help you select where you'd like to stay. To obtain the book or make reservations, contact *Touring Club Italiano*, Corso Italia 10, 20122 Milan. You can also make reservations by writing to the Italian national camping organization, *Centro Internazionale Prenotazioni Campeggio* (or *Federcampeggio*), Casella Postale 23, 50041 Calenzano (Florence). Give names of desired localities, dates, and the num-ber of people. Include a deposit of 55,000 lire by International Money Order; this amount will be deducted from your bill. Federcampeggio also publishes a camping map available free from them or from the Italian Government Travel Office. To make reservations after you're in Italy (this will be a chancy venture), contact Federcam-peggio's international reservation headquarters, Via Vittorio Emanuele 11, 50141 Calenzano (phone: 055-882391).

Fees for camping in Italy frequently are not inclusive; the operator of a site should furnish you with information about billing when you check in. At the end of your stay you will be given a "fiscal receipt" or an "invoice" that will itemize tax and surcharges. The average rates are 1,500 to 5,000 lire per person per night depending on the facilities; surcharges for tents and vehicles vary proportionally.

The *International Camping Carnet*, a pass that gives bearers modest discounts and insurance coverage throughout Europe, is required at many Italian campgrounds. It is available in Italy through the *Touring Club Italiano* or the *Federcampeggio* (address above) and in the US from the *National Campers and Hikers Association*, 7172 Transit Rd., Buffalo, NY 14221 (phone: 716-634-5433), for a fee of $20, which includes camp-ing information and membership in the association. If you are already a member of the

American Automobile Association (AAA), you can get the carnet through AAA for $7.50; for $14, you will also receive a copy of the British Automobile Association's *Camping and Caravanning in Europe.* This book, which alone costs $10.50, contains much helpful information on camping in general and a location map and a "gazetteer" of camp sites in each European country. Contact *AAA Travel Agency,* 8111 Gatehouse Rd., Suite 2112, Falls Church, VA 22047 (phone: 703-222-6810).

Although Italian state forests and national parks are off limits to campers, in some communities it is possible to camp free on other public grounds. Ask the city police or local tourist information office about regulations. If you want to camp on private property, you must ask the landowner's permission. Naturally, owners will be inclined to accommodate you if previous campers have been considerate, as they will be inclined toward those who come after you, if you treat their land well.

For warm-weather, sea-level camping in Italy, all you really need is a sleeping bag, a foam pad, and a waterproof tarp; from these items you can expand to as sophisticated and elaborate an outfit as you wish. Most experienced campers (particularly bikers and hikers; see below) prefer to bring their own tried-and-true equipment, but you can buy camping gear in Italy.

Caravans — recreational vehicles or campers — can be rented in Italy, but most people find it preferable to deal with firms that have US offices and are accustomed to serving the American market. Both *Auto-Europe,* PO Box 500, Yorktown Heights, NY 10598 (phone: 800-942-1309 in New York State; 800-223-5555 elsewhere), and *Kemwel,* 106 Calvert St., Harrison, NY 10528 (phone: 800-468-0468 in New York State; 800-431-1362 elsewhere), serve all the major Italian cities, eliminating additional delivery charges. Reservations should be made well in advance, as the supply of caravans is limited and the demand great.

Generally, two types of vehicles are offered: minibuses customized in various ways for camping, often including elevated roofs, and large coach-type vans. US firms do not offer towed vehicles, but these can be rented in Italy. If you plan to caravan all over Europe, make sure that whatever you drive is equipped for electrical and gas standards of all countries on your itinerary. There are differences, for instance, between the bottled gas supplied on the Continent and in Britain. If you're going to both places, you should have either a sufficient supply of the type your camper requires or equipment that can use either type. If you're towing a camper, note that a towed vehicle is not automatically covered by the liability insurance of the primary vehicle; the primary vehicle's Green Card (insurance voucher) must carry a specific endorsement for the towed vehicle.

Whether you are driving a camper or towing one, it is essential to have an experienced driver, especially in northern Italy where the terrain is quite steep. Be aware that mountain passes and tunnels into France, Switzerland, Austria, and Yugoslavia are sometimes closed in the winter, depending on altitude, road grade, and severity of the weather. Listen to Radio Uno (medium wave) at 1:55 PM each day for news on weather, traffic, and road conditions broadcast in four languages. (For more detailed information on driving in Italy, see *Touring by Car.*)

A packaged camping tour abroad is a good way to have your cake and eat it too. The problems of advance planning and day-to-day organizing are left to someone else, yet you reap the saving that shoestring travel affords. These packages are usually geared to the young, with ages 18 to 35 as typical limits. Transfer from place to place is by bus as on other sightseeing tours, but overnights are in tents and meal arrangements vary. Often a general food fund covers meals in restaurants or in the camp; sometimes there is a chef and sometimes the cooking is done by the participants themselves. *Camping Tours of Europe, Ltd.,* 40 Underhill Blvd., Syosset, NY 11791 (phone: 516-496-7400), and *Contiki Travel,* 1432 E Katella Ave., Anaheim, CA 92805 (phone: 714-937-0611 or 800-626-0611), market European camping tours that include Italy.

BIKING: Italians are such cycling enthusiasts that they even have a patron saint for the sport — the Madonna del Ghisallo, whose statue adorns the town of Bellagio on Lake Como! And for young or energetic travelers, the bicycle does offer a marvelous way of seeing Italy. The best biking is in the northern lakes area; grades are steep, but the scenery is worth the effort. Farther south the secondary roads are often in bad condition and clogged with traffic; it's a good idea to travel with a biking tour group for which the best routes have been worked out in advance.

Bikers (and hikers) are not necessarily campers, but the two activities are highly compatible. A freewheeling traveling style can be achieved with a combination of accommodations: campgrounds, inexpensive hotels and *pensioni* (see *Accommodations and Reservations*), and youth hostels.

Membership in the *American Youth Hostels* (*AYH*) organization is a prerequisite for staying in any of the nearly 60 hostels run by the *Italian Youth Hostels Association* (*AIG*). There is no age limit for membership, although many hostels give priority to members under 30 years of age (meaning that in summer and on holidays, there probably will not be space available for older travelers). The *International Youth Hostel Handbook, Volume One: Europe and the Mediterranean,* which can be purchased with an AYH membership, includes a chapter on Italy that describes the hostels and locates them on a map. AIG headquarters are at Palazzo della Civiltà del Lavoro, Quadrato della Concordia 9, 00144 Rome (phone: 06-5913702 or 06-5913758). For those who prefer to travel in groups, AYH and some of its local chapters, or councils, sponsor a number of biking (and hiking) tours of Europe each year. Usually, at least one of these tours includes Italy. Departures are geared to various age groups and levels of skill; overnights are spent in hostels and hotels. For information, contact the national organization, *American Youth Hostels,* 1332 I St., NW, Suite 800, Washington, DC 20005 (phone: 202-783-6161), or your local council. The Metropolitan New York Council of the American Youth Hostels, 132 Spring St., New York, NY 10012 (phone: 212-431-7100) is an affiliate with a particularly broad tour program of its own; its free store catalogue, *Information & Equipment,* is another useful planning aid for cyclists as well as hikers and campers.

One of the attractions of a biking tour is that shipment of your equipment is handled by organizers, and the shipping fee is included in the total tour package. Travelers simply deliver their bikes to the airport, already disassembled and boxed; shipping boxes can be obtained from most bicycle shops. Bikers not with a tour must make their own arrangements with the airline, and there are no standard procedures for this. Some international carriers provide shipping cartons for bikes and charge only a nominal fee. Other airlines don't provide cartons and may charge as much as $50 or more. A further attraction of some tours is the existence of a "sag wagon" to carry extra luggage or you and your bike when you tire.

The *International Bicycle Touring Society* (*IBTS*) is another nonprofit organization that regularly sponsors low-cost bicycle tours around the US and Canada and overseas. Participants must be over 21 and are usually between 30 and 60 years old. A sag wagon accompanies the tour group, and accommodations are in inns and hotels. Contact *IBTS,* 2115 Paseo Dorado, La Jolla, CA 92037 (phone: 619-459-8775). Numerous other organizations, nonprofit and commercial, sponsor bicycle tours of the US and abroad. For an annually published list of sponsors (available each March), send a stamped, self-addressed #10 envelope and $2 to the *League of American Wheelmen,* BICYCLE USA, Suite 209, 6707 Whitestone Rd., Baltimore, MD 21207 (phone: 301-944-3399). You may also want to investigate the tours of Britain and the Continent offered to members of Britain's *Cyclists Touring Club* (*CTC*), Cotterell House, 69 Meadrow, Godalming, Surrey GU7 3HS, England; join early if you decide to participate.

Detailed maps will infinitely improve a biking tour. In addition to those available from the *Touring Club Italiano,* mentioned above, excellent maps are available from *Michelin Guides and Maps,* PO Box 3305, Spartanburg, SC 29304 (phone: 803-599-0850). A number of other maps, not distributed in the US, can be purchased en route in Italy. (For more information on maps, see "Driving" under *Touring by Car.*)

A valuable book for planning a trip is *Bicycle Touring in Europe* by Karen and Gary Hawkins (Pantheon Books; $5.95), which contains information specific to Italy, including a suggested two-week tour of the northern lakes.

HIKING: Walking is a good way to explore any country, and Italy is no exception. By all means, cover as much area as you can by foot; you'll see everything in far more detail than you would from the window of any conveyance. See *Walking* in DIVERSIONS for suggested hikes through the national parks.

The best hiking trails are in the north of Italy, in the Lombardy lake district and in the Dolomites. The terrain here is hilly to mountainous. If you are physically fit — that is, if you can walk a strenuous 5 to 10 miles a day — you will truly enjoy hiking this scenic alpine region. Serious hiking — with backpack and compass — in the south of Italy, however, is less than rewarding. Especially in peak season, from May to October, the weather is hot and the traffic along footpaths, which generally run parallel to roadways, is heavy.

For those intent on getting about on their own steam, the best sources of information are the Italian hiking and mountaineering organizations. The *Club Alpino Italiano,* Via Ugo Foscolo 3, 20121 Milan, owns about 600 huts in the mountain districts and publishes annually a book with a map and information on access, equipment, and tariffs for each site. The club also has highly qualified instructors and guides who assist travelers with itineraries, excursions, and arrangements for any specialized mountain sport. The *Touring Club Italiano,* Corso Italia 10, 20122 Milan, and the *Federazione Italiano Escursionismo,* Via Cibrario 33, 10143 Turin, which is a member of the European Ramblers' Association, also publish detailed maps and other information useful to hikers.

There are no hiking guidebooks specific to Italy, but two good general books on Europe that include Italian trails are *Tramping in Europe* by J. Sydney Jones (Prentice-Hall, 1984; $7.95) and *100 Hikes in the Alps* by Ira Spring and Harvey Edwards (Seattle: The Mountaineers, 1985; $9.95). The latter is particularly informative, containing 16 suggested hikes along the French, Swiss, and Austrian borders.

If you intend to hike on your own, without benefit of a guide or group, be sure you have a map on a scale of 1:50,000 or, better, 1:25,000 (see sources above). Study the map carefully, choose a route in keeping with your physical condition, and stick to the defined path unless you are an experienced mountain hiker and know the area well. Let someone know where you are going and when you expect to be back — if the hike is impromptu, leave a note on your car. Always know your own limits.

All you need to set out on a simple hike are a pair of good hiking shoes that come up over the ankle; heavy socks; long pants to protect your legs; a canteen of water; a hat to protect you from the sun; and a picnic lunch. It is a good idea to dress in layers so that you can peel off a sweater or shirt or two and then put them back on to keep pace with the rising and setting sun. Make sure, too, to wear clothes with pockets or bring a backpack to keep your hands free. Some useful and important pocket or pack stuffers include a jackknife, waterproof matches, and a compass.

If you prefer to travel as part of an organized group, see the January/February issue of *Sierra* magazine for the Sierra Club's annual list of foreign outings, or contact the *Sierra Club Outing Department,* 530 Bush St., San Francisco, CA 94108 (phone: 415-981-8634). Each year the club sponsors at least one two-week mountain "ramble" that includes the Dolomites. Distances are usually traveled in minibuses, and overnights are in alpine hotels from which the group takes day hikes. *Mountain Travel,* a company specializing in adventure trips around the world, offers four 11- to 17-day hikes in Italy, including the northern Alps, Valle D'Aosta, the Dolomites, and the foothills of Piemonte. Travel between areas of interest is by minibus, and accommodations are in small hotels, mountain inns, or refuges. Contact *Mountain Travel,* 1398 Solano Ave., Albany, CA 94706 (phone: 415-527-8100 in California; 800-227-2384 elsewhere). *Wilderness Travel,* 1760 Solano Ave., Berkeley, CA 94707 (phone: 415-524-5111 in California; 800-247-6700 elsewhere), offers similar treks, including Chianti Classico, which emphasizes food and wine.

A variety of both biking and hiking tours is offered by *Butterfield & Robinson,* 70 Bond St., Suite 300, Toronto, Ont. M5B 1X3 Canada (phone: 416-864-1354).

Preparing

Calculating Costs

$ Italy has always been one of the most popular European countries for both the first-time and the seasoned traveler. While it has never been one of Europe's least expensive destinations, it is certainly one where the strong dollar of recent years worked hardest to counteract the effects of inflation and turn a dream into reality for more than a happy few. Exchange rates are no longer as advantageous as they were even a year or two ago, however, and even though other factors continue to make a trip to Europe affordable — discount fares, charter flights, and package tours, all of which can greatly reduce the cost of a European vacation — most travelers still have to plan carefully and marshal their funds prudently while abroad.

Many variables affect the cost of a vacation, but the major expenses are transatlantic transportation, accommodations, and food, the latter two especially affected by fluctuations in the exchange rate — that is, how much of a foreign currency the dollar will buy. A number of other expenses must also be anticipated: local transportation, sightseeing excursions, shopping, and miscellaneous items such as admission tickets, drinks, local taxes, and tips.

The easiest way to put a ceiling on the price of all these expenses is to consider buying a package tour. If it is totally planned and escorted, with nearly all transportation, rooms, meals, sightseeing excursions, local travel, tips, and the like included and prepaid, you will know beforehand almost exactly what the trip will cost; the only surprise will be the one you spring on yourself by succumbing to some irresistible expensive souvenir rather than the trifles you intended. Various packages are discussed above in *Package Tours*, but a few points bear repeating here. Not all packages are package *tours*. Some packages are simply loosely organized arrangements in which some features (transatlantic transportation, rooms, transfers) are taken care of beforehand but others (such as sightseeing and dining) are left to your discretion. More and more, even experienced travelers are being won over by the idea of packaged travel, not only for the convenience and the planning time saved but above all for the money saved. Whatever elements you choose to have in your package, the organizer has gotten them for you wholesale — and they are prepaid.

The possibility of prepaying certain elements of your trip is important to consider even if you intend to be strictly independent, with arrangements entirely of your own making and all bought separately. You may not be able to match the price of the wholesale tour package, but at least you will have introduced an element of predictability into your accounting, thus reducing the risk that some budget-busting expense along the way might put a damper on the rest of your plans.

With the independent traveler in mind, this section presents some suggestions of how to pin down the cost of a trip beforehand. There are two additional variables that will influence the cost of your holiday whether you buy a package or do it all yourself. One is timing. If you are willing to travel during the less trafficked off-season, when air fares are lower, you'll find many hotel rates lower also. Keep in mind those periods between the traditional high and low seasons generally referred to as the shoulder months (approximately late March to mid-May and late September to mid-November). Costs may be only a little lower than in high season, and the weather may not be as balmy, but you won't be bucking the crowds that in peak months can force a traveler without a hotel reservation into the most expensive hostelry in town. Don't forget, however, to find out what is going on in any place you plan to spend a good deal of your vacation — some of the largest public events do not take place during the peak season. Easter, for example, attracts a crowd in Rome; the International Trade Fair, in April, does the same in Milan; and Venice is quite crowded at Carnevale, even if it does take place in the gloom of winter (see *When to Go*). Another factor influencing the cost of your trip is whether you will be traveling alone or with another person. The prices quoted for package tours are almost always based on double occupancy of hotel rooms, and the surcharge — or single supplement — for a room by yourself can be quite substantial. When shopping for a hotel room, you'll find there are many more double rooms than singles. If you ask for a single, however, and are given a double, it cannot, by Italian law, cost more than the maximum price posted for a single. But don't expect singles to cost less than two-thirds the price of doubles.

TRANSPORTATION: Air fare is really the easiest cost to pin down, though the variety of flights and the restrictions that go with them may be confusing initially. A detailed explanation of the various categories is given in *Traveling by Plane*. Essentially, you can choose one of several categories of scheduled flights — ranging in expense from first class, which presumably no vacation traveler needs, to excursion and APEX — or a charter.

Earlier sections of GETTING READY TO GO discuss the most common means of getting from place to place within Italy: by rented car or train. The most important factors in determining which to use are the amount of traveling you plan to do and the length of time you will be abroad. If you intend to move about a great deal between cities, a pass allowing unlimited train travel is likely to be most economical. The *Italian Tourist Ticket* (*Biglietto Turistico di Libera Circolazione,* or *BTLC*) is valid for travel in Italy only; the Eurailpass is valid in Italy and much of the rest of Europe. Both are attractively priced, but if you are traveling strictly in Italy, the BTLC, which costs less and is available in first- and second-class versions for periods of 8, 15, 21, or 30 days, is the one to buy. If driving through the countryside is your object, you should look carefully into fly/drive arrangements versus straight rentals and also compare the rates offered by some of the less familiar US firms specializing in car travel in Europe with those offered by the large, international firms. The latter all have discount plans if the car is booked a certain number of days before departure and the rental is for a minimum period of time (see *Touring by Car*). Always look for the flat rate based on unlimited mileage.

ACCOMMODATIONS: Room costs vary considerably. Most expensive — as high as $150 to $300 for a double room — are the deluxe hotels of the major cities. But there is no sacred edict stating that travelers must put up at deluxe hotels. At the opposite end of the scale are the one- and two-star hotels (rated by to the government's official classification system) that many will find perfectly adequate, if not usually full of charm. Two additional options for anyone staying for an extended period are the "self-catering" rental and the home exchange. In the first case, you rent a furnished apartment or house with kitchen facilities; in the second, you and a foreign family exchange homes for an agreed-upon time. In rural areas, rentals arranged through members of *Agriturist* are being used more and more by tourists. Accommodations can range from a campsite to a furnished apartment or house on or near a working farm, and though surroundings may be homey or Spartan, prices can be as low as $5 a day (a minimum stay requirement is often imposed — anywhere from a few to 30 days).

If you don't want to stay in one spot but still want to eliminate the element of surprise from your accommodations budget, look for hotel voucher schemes that frequently come as part of a fly/drive package. You receive a block of prepaid vouchers and a list of hotels that accept them as total payment for a night's stay, but if you want to upgrade your lodgings from time to time, there is often another set of hotels that accept the same vouchers plus payment of a supplement. (For a detailed discussion of the range and variety of places to stay in Italy, see *Accommodations and Reservations.*)

FOOD: Restaurant dining — particularly in the better establishments of major tourist cities — is going to hit your wallet hardest. If you're an independent traveler eating all of your meals out, allow roughly $30 to $50 per person per day for food. That includes breakfast because the price of the standard Continental breakfast of *caffè latte,* rolls, butter, and jam is usually quoted separately from the price of the room in Italian hotels. That amount should also cover taxes and the service charge and perhaps a carafe of wine at dinner — but you won't be splurging. The estimate is based on meals chosen with a watchful eye on the right-hand column of the menu (no Florentine steaks, no fish sold *al kilo,* no truffles) and on fixed-price meals chosen from the tourist menu, which can at least provide a tasty and occasionally imaginative selection of food, but no cocktails before dinner. If you want to order a dinner of your choice in one of the major cities, be prepared for the tab to rise much higher, and if you're addicted to only the finest restaurants, the sky is the limit. All of this is no reason to forgo your trip, however — remember, it's *dining* that is going to hit your wallet hard. If you stick to picnic lunches of *panini* from the bakery stuffed with cold cuts and cheese from the grocery or delicatessen, snack on fruit, and finish off the day with modest meals at modest *trattorie* and *pizzerie,* alternating with a few stand-up meals at the *tavola calda,* you will do very well indeed.

Our restaurant choices, listed in the *Best in Town* sections in CITIES and in the *Eating Out* sections of each tour route in DIRECTIONS, were selected on the basis of the best value for the money. The restaurants are rated as expensive, moderate, or inexpensive, with approximate price ranges supplied for those labels in each area.

LOCAL TAXES AND SERVICE CHARGES: A sales tax or VAT (value added tax) is added to both goods and services in many European countries. In Italy it's known as IVA (*imposta sul valore aggiunto*). The tax is buried in the prices charged for hotel rooms and restaurant meals, so you won't even notice it. It is also included in the amount shown on the price tag of purchased goods. There is no escaping the tax on services, but for foreigners the tax on purchases — typically 18% — can be reimbursed, although the procedure for obtaining the reimbursement is not as streamlined in Italy as it is in some other European countries. For a full discussion of VAT refunds, see *Shopping.* A service charge of 12% to 18%, usually 15%, is almost universal on restaurant and hotel bills in Italy. Nevertheless, many situations still are not covered by the service charge, and an additional gratuity is sometimes appropriate. For more information, see *Tipping.*

Entry Requirements and Documents

A valid US passport is the only document a US citizen needs to enter Italy, and that same passport is also needed to reenter the US. No visas are necessary. As a general rule, possession of a US passport entitles the bearer to remain in Italy as a tourist for up to 90 days. Those wishing to stay longer can apply at any police station (*questura*) for a one-time extension of an additional 90 days, which is readily granted provided the applicant can prove that he or she is a bona fide tourist with an independent means of support and no intention to work or study in Italy. Resident aliens of the US should inquire at the nearest Italian consulate (see *Tourist Information* for addresses) to find out what documents are needed to enter Italy; similarly, US citizens intending to work, study, or reside in Italy should address themselves to the consulate.

Among the items you may bring into Italy duty-free are two still cameras and 10 rolls of still film, one movie camera and 10 rolls of film for it, 400 cigarettes and 1.1 pounds (500 grams) of cigars or pipe tobacco, two bottles of wine and one bottle of hard liquor (the bottles must have been opened), and personal effects and sports equipment appropriate to a pleasure trip.

Few tourists are aware that they are required to register with the police within three days of their arrival in Italy. If you are staying in a hotel, the staff takes care of this formality for you, using particulars gleaned from your passport. If you are staying in a private home, you are supposed to do it yourself, but since the authorities rely on you to come to them, enforcement is not customary. If, having registered, you then move to another private home in a different town, you are supposed to register again.

Vaccination certificates are required only if the traveler is entering from an area of contagion as defined by the World Health Organization. Because smallpox is considered eradicated from the world, only a few countries continue to require visitors to have a smallpox vaccination certificate. You will not need one to travel to Italy or to return to the US.

New US passports are now valid for ten years from the date of issue (five years for those under age 18). The expired passport itself is not renewable but must be turned in along with your application for a new, valid one (you will get the old one back, voided, when you receive the new one). Delivery can take as little as two weeks or as long as a month, and anyone applying for a passport for the first time should allow at least four weeks for delivery — even six weeks during the high season, from approximately mid-March to mid-September. In an emergency, a passport can be issued in as little time as one business day, but you will have to present an airline ticket with a confirmed reservation for a specific and imminent date to qualify for such handling — which you should resort to, obviously, only in a genuine emergency. Go directly to the nearest passport office to plead your case. For emergencies occurring outside business hours, there is a 24-hour telephone number in Washington, DC (202-634-3600), which can put you in touch with a State Department duty officer who may be able to expedite your application.

Normal passports contain 24 pages, but frequent travelers can request a 48-page passport at no extra cost. Every individual, regardless of age, must have his or her own passport. Family passports are no longer issued.

Passport renewal can be done by mail, but anyone applying for the first time or anyone under 18 renewing a passport must do so in person at one of the following places:

1. The State Department passport agencies in Boston, Chicago, Honolulu, Houston, Los Angeles, Miami, New Orleans, New York City, Philadelphia, San Francisco, Seattle, Stamford, CT, and Washington, DC.
2. A federal or state courthouse.
3. Any of the 1,000 post offices across the country with designated acceptance facilities.

Applications blanks are available at all these offices and must be presented with the following:

1. Proof of US citizenship. This can be a previous passport or one in which you were included. If you are applying for your first passport and you were born in the United States, your birth certificate is the required proof. If you were born abroad,

a Certificate of Naturalization, a Certificate of Citizenship, a Report of Birth Abroad of a Citizen of the United States, or a Certification of Birth is necessary.

2. Two 2-by-2-inch, front-view photographs in color or black and white, with a light, plain background, taken within the previous six months. These must be taken by a photographer rather than by a machine.
3. Cash, a check, or a money order for the $7 execution fee (not required if you are renewing a passport) and the $35 passport fee ($20 for those under 18).
4. Proof of identity. Again, this can be a previous passport, a Certificate of Naturalization or of Citizenship, a driver's license, or a government ID card with a physical description or a photograph. Lacking any of these, you should be accompanied by a friend of at least two years' standing who will testify to your identity. Credit cards or social security cards do not suffice as proof of identity.

A passport can be renewed by mail on a form obtained at one of the locations mentioned above only if the expired passport was issued no more than eight years before the date of application for renewal and if it was not issued before the applicant's eighteenth birthday. Send the completed form with the expired passport, two photos (signed in the center of the back), and $35 (no execution fee required) to the nearest passport agency office.

■ **Should You Lose Your Passport Abroad:** Report the loss to the nearest US consulate immediately. You can get a three-month temporary passport directly from the consulate, but you must fill out a loss of passport form and follow the same application procedure — and pay the same fees — as you did for the original. It's likely to speed things up if you have a record of your passport number and the place and date of its issue.

Planning a Trip

123 For most travelers, any week-plus trip to Europe can be too expensive an undertaking for an "I'll take my chances" type of vacation. Hence a little planning is crucial. Not that you should work out your itinerary to the last detail before you go, but by considering where you want to go, what you want to do, and how much you want to spend, you'll find it much easier to avoid delays, unexpected expenses, and the need to alter your plans because of unforeseen developments. In thinking out your trip, start with the following basics:

1. How much time will you have to spend?
2. Do you want to visit one, a few, or several different places?
3. When do you plan to travel? (It can make a considerable difference in what is open and functioning at your destination as well as in the cost and availability of transportation and accommodations.)
4. Do you want an unstructured trip (in which you'll be on your own when you get to your destination) or would you prefer the company and schedule of an escorted tour?
5. How much money do you have to spend on your trip?

With firm answers to these major questions, start reviewing the literature on the areas in which you're most interested. The *Italian Government Travel Office* has three locations in the US (see *Tourist Information* for addresses); they are ready sources for brochures, maps, and other information about the Italian cities and the countryside. Other good sources of information are airlines, hotel representatives, and travel agents, who should be well supplied with literature from wholesalers and tour operators. In other words, up-to-date travel information is plentiful and you should be able to accumulate everything you want to know, not only about the places you plan to visit but also about the relevant tours and packages that are available (see *Package Tours*).

You can make almost all of your own travel arrangements if you have time to follow through with hotels, airlines, tour operators, and so on. But you'll probably save considerable time and energy if you have a travel agent make the reservations and arrangements for you. The agent also should be able to tell you about other arrangements of which you may not be aware. Only rarely will a travel agent's services cost you money, and they may even save you some (see *How to Use a Travel Agent*). Well before departure (depending on how far in advance you make your reservations), the agent will give you a packet that includes all your tickets and hotel confirmations and often a day-by-day outline of where you'll be, along with a detailed list of whatever flights or trains you're taking.

Before your departure, find out what the weather is likely to be at your destination. Consult *When to Go* for a chart of average temperatures in various Italian cities as well as for a list of special events that may occur during your stay. See *How to Pack* for further details on weather variables and what clothes to take. And if you're visiting Italy for the first time, make a special effort to read up on its cuisine, history, and culture. A good place to begin is our own PERSPECTIVES section, but if you're planning an extended stay in a particular city or region, you'll probably want to add some more specific literature to your reading.

While making vacation arrangements is fun and exciting, don't forget the things that must be done at home to prepare for your absence. Before you leave, attend to these household matters:

1. Arrange for your mail to be forwarded, held by the post office until you return, or picked up at your house daily by a friend or neighbor. Someone should check your door occasionally to collect any unexpected deliveries. Piles of mail, circulars, or packages are an announcement to prospective thieves that no one is home.
2. Cancel all deliveries (of newspapers, for example).
3. Arrange for your lawn to be mowed at regular intervals.
4. Arrange for the care of pets.
5. Etch your social security number in a prominent place on all appliances (television sets, radios, cameras, kitchen appliances). This considerably reduces their appeal to thieves and facilitates identification.
6. Leave a house key and your itinerary with a relative or friend. Notify the police that you are leaving and tell them who has your key and itinerary.
7. Empty the refrigerator and lower its thermostat.
8. Immediately before leaving, check that all doors, windows, and garage doors are securely locked.

To discourage thieves further, set up several variable timers around the house so that lights (and perhaps even a television set or radio) go on and off several times in different rooms each night. Make a list of any valuable items you are carrying with you, including credit card numbers and the serial numbers of your traveler's checks. Put copies in your luggage, purse, and briefcase so that they can be reported quickly in case of loss. Put your name and business address — *but never your home address* — on labels on the inside and outside of your luggage.

Review your travel documents. If you are traveling by air, check to see that your ticket has been filled in correctly. The left side of the ticket should have a list of each stop you will make (even if you're stopping only to change planes), beginning with your departure point. Be sure that the list is correct, and count the number of carbons to see that you have one for each plane you will take. If you have confirmed reservations, be sure that the column marked "status" says "OK" beside each flight. Have in hand vouchers or proof of payment for any reservation for which you've paid in advance; this includes hotels, transfers to and from the airport, sightseeing tours, car rentals, special events, and so on.

How to Pack

The goal is to remain perfectly comfortable, neat, clean, and adequately fashionable wherever you go but actually to pack as little as possible. The main obstacle to achieving this end is habit: Most of us wake up each morning with an entire wardrobe hanging in our closets, and we assume that our suitcase should offer the same variety and selection. Not so; only our anxiety about being caught short makes us treat a suitcase like a mobile closet, and you can eliminate even the anxiety (and learn to travel light) by following two firm packing principles:

1. Organize your travel wardrobe around a single color — blue or brown, for example — that allows you to mix, match, and layer clothes. Holding firm to one color scheme will make it easy to eliminate items of clothing that don't harmonize; and by picking clothes for their adaptability and compatibility with your basic color, you will put together the most extensive wardrobe with the fewest pieces of clothing.
2. Use laundries to renew your wardrobe. Never overpack to ensure a supply of fresh clothing — shirts, blouses, underwear — for each day of a long trip. Business-people routinely use hotel laundries to wash and clean clothes and if these prove too expensive or your hotel is without one, there are laundries (*lavanderie*) or self-service laundromats (*lavanderie automatiche*) in most towns of any size.

CLIMATE AND CLOTHES: Although Rome sits astride latitude 41°53′, about even with Providence, Rhode Island (Milan is approximately even with Montréal), the weather in Italy is milder than at similar latitudes in North America. Residents of the Middle Atlantic states, for instance, will find that the same wardrobe they would be wearing at home will, with a few adjustments, be appropriate for most parts of Italy in the same season. Anyone going to Italy from the late fall through the early spring (November through March) should take into account that central heating exists in Italian hotels, interiors are not usually heated to the same degree they are in the US. Thus, although you do not need to prepare for subzero winters outdoors, you will probably feel more comfortable wearing heavier clothing indoors than you might at home — sweaters rather than lightweight shirts and blouses, wool dresses rather than silks, and leather boots rather than open pumps. Clothes to be worn at night in particular should be of the warmth-retaining variety. This holds true even in the south of Italy because old stone *palazzi* can be chilly and damp inside even while the sun is blazing outside.

The winter overcoat worn by most Italians is not quite as heavy as the one that would be worn in, say, New York or Chicago — no fur or down linings, usually; an unlined loden coat is a classic — but your warmer one will do fine if you are visiting north or central Italy. From Naples south, a lined raincoat should be sufficient, but if your trip will encompass all parts of Italy, opt for the heavier coat or meet the challenge through layering. This means a shirt on top of an undershirt, a sweater (or two) on top of both, topped by a jacket or windbreaker over all. Layering permits you to stay warm while allowing you to remove pieces in response to temperature changes and, provided you have adhered to the principle of dressing according to a single basic color scheme, should not be difficult to achieve. In fact, you will probably be tempted by the great variety of sweaters in shop windows all over Italy to acquire more layers than you really need, so buy only the very basics before departure.

Layering is also a good solution to handling the gradations of temperature encountered in the shoulder seasons. Note that Italians get a good deal of wear out of wool suits — both the spring and fall suit-wearing seasons last comparatively longer than they do in the Middle Atlantic states. Since one characteristic of a Mediterranean climate is rain in the late fall and early winter, an umbrella and a raincoat are needed in most regions, especially in November and December.

For summer, light, loose clothing is desirable everywhere in Italy, except in high mountain areas. Synthetics are immensely practical for a trip, and they have improved immeasurably in appearance lately, but Italians wear cottons and linens, both because they are cooler and because of a taste for 100% natural fabrics. Travelers may find blends to be the best answer. Air conditioning is not the rule, so it's not necessary to pack a sweater against a chilled environment. On the other hand, even as far south as Rome and Naples, a light summer wrap or jacket is sometimes useful in the evening.

Italians dress with care and style. Indeed, they are very fashion conscious. Fortunately, except for very special occasions (such as opening night at La Scala, which is strictly formal), the dress code tends to be informal. In summer, men rarely wear jackets and ties, and women wear stockings even more rarely. However, the dress code is not quite as informal as many tourists interpret it to be, a fact often noted in the Italian press. Travelers who don't mind appearing part of the horde — and possibly making headlines on a slow news day — wear short shorts and bathing suits for sightseeing. Those who prefer to maintain at least a minimum of dignity restrict these items to beachwear.

More than a minimum is suggested for visiting churches. Women are no longer required to cover their heads and wear long sleeves, but in some churches, St. Peter's among them, some sort of sleeve is required. Depending on the mood of the attendant, a capped sleeve may be sufficient, but since nothing could be more heartbreaking than to be turned away from a landmark on the only day your itinerary permits a visit, women are advised to tuck a scarf into their bags to cover bare backs and shoulders in an emergency. Needless to say, tank tops on men and short shorts on either sex also are inappropriate for churches.

Comfortable walking shoes are a must for both sexes, no matter what the season or the fashion. You will do a lot of walking, up and down stairs, up and down hills, to the end of the ruins and back. Even in the evening, when you anticipate walking no farther than to the nearest restaurant, women should avoid spike heels. Cobblestones are ubiquitous, and chunkier heels have a better chance of not getting caught — and ruined.

More information about the climate in Italy, along with a chart of average low and high temperatures for specific cities, is given in *When to Go*.

PACKING: A recommended packing procedure is the so-called layer method, designed to get everything in and out of a bag with as few wrinkles as possible. Put heavy items on the bottom and sides, and stuff the corners with such articles as socks, underwear, shoes, handbags, and bathing suits. Then layer on the more easily wrinkled items, such as shirts and slacks, dresses and skirts, even jackets. Pack them with as few folds as possible. On the top layer put immediate needs, such as pajamas, sweater, raincoat, and the like. Make the layers even and the total contents of your bag as full and firm as possible to keep things from shifting around during transit.

TRAVELING WRINKLE-FREE: While packing, interleave each layer of clothes with plastic cleaning bags, which will help preserve pressed clothes while they are in the suitcase. Unpack your bags as soon as you get to your hotel. Nothing so destroys freshly cleaned and pressed clothes as sitting for days in a suitcase. Finally, if something is badly wrinkled and can't be professionally pressed before you must wear it, hang it overnight in a bathroom where the bathtub has been filled with very hot water; keep the bathroom door closed so the room becomes something of a steam room. It really works miracles.

SOME FINAL PACKING HINTS: Try to pack toiletries and cosmetics that come in plastic containers. Glass bottles containing liquids should be placed in plastic bags. Packing travel-size toilet articles will help to lighten the load. For a free catalogue of popular grooming aids in small sizes, write to *Travel Mini Pack,* 10 South Broadway, Nyack, NY 10960. If traveling overnight, put a few necessary toilet items in a purse, shoulder bag, or some other small, easily carried case. Add an empty airline bag or small tote bag to your suitcase; you'll find it handy for overnight trips, beach outings, or carrying purchases home. Don't ever put necessities such as medicine, travel documents, cash, or credit cards in your checked luggage; keep them in your purse or a piece of hand luggage that you carry.

LUGGAGE: If you already own serviceable luggage, do not feel compelled to buy new bags. If, however, you have been looking for an excuse to throw out that old suitcase that saw you through four years of college and innumerable weekends, this trip to Italy can be the perfect occasion.

Luggage falls into three categories — hard, soft-sided, and soft — and each has advantages and disadvantages. Hard suitcases have a rigid frame and sides. They provide the most protection from the depredations of rough handling, but they are also the heaviest. Wheels and pull straps are available to rectify this problem, but they should be removed before the luggage is turned over at check-in or they may be wrenched off in transit. In addition, hard bags will sometimes pop open, even when locked, so a strap around the suitcase is advised. Soft-sided suitcases have a rigid frame that has been covered with leather, fabric, or a synthetic material. The weight of the suitcase is greatly reduced, but many of the materials used as coverings (except leather, which is also the heaviest) are vulnerable to rips and tears from conveyor machinery. Not surprisingly, the materials that wear better are generally found on more expensive luggage. The third category, seen more and more frequently, is soft luggage. Lacking any rigid structural element, it comes in a wide variety of shapes and sizes and is easy to carry, especially since it often has a shoulder strap. Most carry-on bags are of this type because they can be squeezed to fit under the plane seat. They are even more vulnerable to damage on conveyor equipment than are soft-sided bags, however, and be prepared to find a brand-new set of wrinkles pressed into everything that was carefully ironed before packing.

Whatever type of luggage you choose, remember that it should last for many years. Shop carefully, but be prepared to make a sizable investment. In fact, you might consider putting off the purchase of new luggage until you get to Italy, where some of the world's most impeccably designed and carefully crafted leather goods are to be found.

How to Use a Travel Agent

A reliable travel agent remains your best source of service and information for planning a trip abroad, whether you have a specific itinerary that requires only reservations or need extensive help in sorting through the maze of air fares, tour offerings, hotel packages, and the scores of other arrangements that you may need for a trip to Italy. It is perfectly reasonable to expect your travel agent to be a thorough travel specialist, with information about your destination and, even more crucial, a command of current air fares, package tours, charters, ground arrangements, and other details.

To make the most intelligent use of a travel agent's time and expertise, you should know something of the economics of the industry. As a client, you traditionally pay nothing for the agent's services; with few exceptions, it's all free, from advice on package tours to hotel bookings. Any money that the travel agency makes on the time spent arranging your itinerary — booking hotels, resorts, or flights or suggesting activities — comes from commissions paid to the agency by the suppliers of these services — the airlines, hotels, and so on. The commissions generally run from 8% to 20% of the total cost of the service, although suppliers often reward agencies that sell their services in volume with an increased commission called an override.

Among the few exceptions to the general rule of free service by a travel agency are the limited number of agencies practicing net pricing. In essence, travel agencies operating this way rebate all of their commissions and overrides to their customers and make their income instead by charging a flat fee per transaction (thus adding a charge after the rebate reduction has been made, although you sometimes receive the rebate later, in a check). Net fares and fees are a very recent and not widespread phenomenon, but even a conventional travel agent may sometimes charge you a fee for extras such as long-distance telephone or cable costs incurred in making a booking, for reserving a room in a place that does not pay a commission (such as a small, out-of-the-way hotel), or for special attention such as planning a highly personalized itinerary. In most instances, however, you'll find that travel agents make their time and expertise available to you at no charge, and you do not pay more for an airline ticket, package tour, or other product bought from a travel agent than you would for the same product bought directly from the supplier.

The commission system implies two things about your relationship with any travel agent:

1. You will get the best service when you are requesting commissionable items. Since there are few commissions on camping or driving/camping tours, an agent is unlikely to be very enthusiastic about helping to plan one. Don't expect the agent to spend a lot of time helping you answer such basic questions as where you want to go and what you want to do, especially if the answers to those questions hold out the promise of only minimal income. It's a good idea to arrive at the agency with a rough itinerary already in mind. Then use the agent to advise you on facilities, activities, and alternatives within the limits of that itinerary and above all to make the bookings.
2. There is always the danger that an incompetent or unethical agent will send you to a place offering the best commission rather than the best facilities for your purposes, so be careful.

If you live in a small town, choosing a travel agent may be a simple matter. If you live in a city of any size — where there may be larger and smaller full-service agencies as well as specialists in certain kinds of travel and certain destinations, agencies geared to business travelers and others to leisure travelers, and agencies serving the carriage trade and others the budget market — your choice will be much more difficult. Nevertheless, you should choose a travel agent with the same care with which you would choose a doctor or lawyer because you will be spending a great deal of money on the basis of his or her knowledge and judgment. Unfortunately, at the moment, there aren't many standards within the industry to help you gauge competence, and the quality of individual agents varies enormously. Although several states are in the process of drawing up legislation, only four states (California, Hawaii, Ohio, Rhode Island) at present license agents. One industry organization, the *American Society of Travel Agents,* requires its members — who usually display the ASTA logo on their literature and in their offices — to adhere to its strict Principles of Professional Conduct and Ethics code. If you feel you have been dealt with improperly or unfairly, complaints can be made to *ASTA,* Consumer Affairs Department, 4400 MacArthur Blvd., NW,

Washington, DC 20007 (phone: 202-965-7520). The *Association of Retail Travel Agents* (*ARTA*) is a smaller but highly respected trade organization similar to ASTA, and its member agencies and agents similarly agree to abide by a code of ethics. Complaints about an ARTA member's service can be made to *ARTA,* Grievance Committee, 25 S Riverside Ave., Croton-on-Hudson, NY 10520 (phone: 914-271-9000). More useful is the knowledge that any travel agent who has been in the business for at least five years and has completed the five-part, 18-month course of study conducted by the Institute of Certified Travel Agents in Wellesley, Massachusetts, will carry the initials CTC (Certified Travel Counselor) after his or her name. This indicates a relatively high level of expertise.

Perhaps the best way to find a travel agent is by word of mouth. If the agent (or agency) has done a good job for friends over a period of time, it probably indicates a high level of commitment and concern. But always ask for the name of a specific agent because it is that individual who will serve you, and quality can vary widely even within a single agency. You may still want to contact the Better Business Bureau to find out whether there have been many (or any) complaints about the agency you are considering.

Once you've chosen an agent, be entirely frank and candid. Budget considerations rank at the top of the candor list, and there's no sense in wasting the agent's (or your) time poring over itineraries you know you can't afford. Similarly, if you like a fair degree of comfort, you should not keep that fact a secret from your travel agent, who may assume that you wish to travel on a tight budget when that's not the case. Finally, be prepared. The more vague your plans, the less direction you can expect from most agents. If you walk into an agency and say, "I have two weeks in June, what shall I do?" you will most likely walk out with nothing more than a handful of brochures. So do your homework.

Hints for Handicapped Travelers

Roughly 35 million people in the US alone have some sort of disability. At least half this number are physically handicapped. Like everyone else today, they — and the uncounted disabled millions around the world — are on the move. More than ever before, the disabled are demanding facilities they can use comfortably, and they are being heard. Accessibility is being brought up to more acceptable standards every day, especially in the US and in Western Europe.

Italy, a country of many hills and steps, has been comparatively slow in developing access for the handicapped. Only a few of the best hotels and restaurants are easily accessible to a person in a wheelchair, and, unless you are on a special tour for the handicapped, you will need to rely mostly on taxis for transportation. Nevertheless, with ingenuity and the help of an able-bodied traveling companion, you can get around this fascinating country well enough to thoroughly enjoy its varied delights. What the Italians lack in facilities for the handicapped they more than make up in willingness to help when necessary.

PLANNING: It is essential to make travel arrangements in advance and to specify to all those who will provide you services — the travel agent, airline, hotel, and so on — the degree of your disability or restricted mobility.

Organizations – Some excellent organizations can help you plan for your needs abroad (for general information on medical aid in Italy, see *Medical and Legal Aid and Consular Services*).

> *Rehabilitation International/USA* (*RIUSA*) is a national organization that provides information, employment, and research services to the disabled. Affiliated

with similar organizations in more than 75 countries, RIUSA sponsors *Access to the Skies,* a program that coordinates the efforts of the international air travel industry in providing airport and airplane access for the handicapped. Membership, which costs $40 annually, includes several helpful publications as well as regular notification of conferences on subjects of interest to the handicapped traveler. Contact *RIUSA,* 1123 Broadway, Suite 704, New York, NY 10010 (phone: 212-620-4040). An affiliate organization in England publishes the *Access Guide to Rome and Florence.* Send £3 sterling to *Project Phoenix Trust,* 68 Rochfords, Coffee Hall, Milton Keynes, MK6 5DJ, England.

Mobility International has contacts in 45 countries and offers advice and assistance to the disabled, including information on accommodations, access guides, and organized tours. Write *Mobility International USA (MIUSA),* PO Box 3551, Eugene, OR 97403 (phone: 503-343-1284, voice and TTY).

The *Travel Information Center* at *Moss Rehabilitation Hospital* is designed to help handicapped people plan trips. For a fee of $5, the center will send you information from its files on as many as three cities, countries, or special interests. Write to the *Travel Information Center,* Moss Rehabilitation Hospital, 12th St. and Tabor Rd., Philadelphia, PA 19141 (phone: 215-329-5715).

The Society for the Advancement of Travel for the Handicapped (SATH) is devoted exclusively to promoting and servicing handicapped travelers. Tax-deductible membership is $40 per year ($20 for students) and includes a quarterly newsletter. Contact *SATH,* 26 Court St., Brooklyn, NY 11242 (phone: 718-858-5483). (Mobility Tours, a travel agency associated with SATH, is listed below under *Tours.*)

Publications – Several excellent publications provide information and advice about planning a trip abroad and functioning comfortably once there.

Access to the World: A Travel Guide for the Handicapped by Louise Weiss (Facts on File; $14.95) provides extensive information on transportation and hotels and offers sound tips for the disabled traveler abroad.

A Travel Guide for the Disabled: Western Europe by Mary Meister Walzer (Van Nostrand Reinhold; $11.95) gives a country-by-country listing of hotels and restaurants along with their access ratings and other useful information; it dedicates a section specifically to Italy.

TravelAbility by Lois Reamy (Macmillan; $13.95) offers a step-by-step planning guide.

The Itinerary, a travel magazine for people with disabilities, is published every other month with information on accessibility, listings of tours, news of devices, travel aids, and special services as well as numerous general hints. To subscribe ($7 a year), write to *The Itinerary,* PO Box 1084, Bayonne, NJ 07002 (phone: 201-858-3400). (*Whole Person Tours, Inc.,* a travel agency associated with the magazine, is listed below under *Tours.*)

Almost all of the material published with disabled travelers in mind deals with the chairbound traveler, for whom architectural barriers are a prime concern. For travelers with diabetes, a pamphlet entitled *Your Turn to Fly* is available for 25¢ from the *NY Diabetes Association,* 505 8th Ave., New York, NY 10018 (phone: 212-947-9707). For breathing-disabled persons, the pamphlet *Travel for the Patient with Chronic Obstructive Pulmonary Disease* is available for $2 from *Dr. Harold Silver,* 1601 18th St., NW, Washington, DC 20009.

TRAVEL BY PLANE: Make reservations well in advance and provide the airline with all relevant details about your condition when doing so. Include information on mobility, toileting, and your need for airline-supplied equipment such as a wheelchair or portable oxygen. Be sure that the airline reservations clerk understands fully the degree of your disability. Then, the day before the flight, call the airline to make sure that all arrangements have been made. On the day of the flight, arrive early so that you can board before the rest of the passengers. Carry with you a medical certificate stating your specific disability and the need to carry particular medicines (some airlines require the certificate). In most cases, you can be wheeled as far as the plane, and sometimes right onto it, in your own wheelchair. Some airlines, depending on the degree of your dependency on your wheelchair, will allow you to stow it in the cabin. Airlines that don't allow this provide a boarding chair. Your own wheelchair is folded and put in the baggage compartment; it should be tagged as escort luggage to ensure that it's available at the plane immediately on landing rather than in the baggage claim area.

The Airport Operators Council International publishes *Access Travel: Airports,* a guide to the accessibility of more than 470 airports here and abroad, including information on all Italian airports. For a free copy, write to *Access America,* Washington, DC 20202. (Leonardo da Vinci Airport in Rome has a special waiting lounge with two areas, one for children and one for the handicapped, in the International Transit Hall, next to the 24-hour post office.)

Useful information on every stage of air travel from planning to arrival is provided in the booklet *Incapacitated Passengers Air Travel Guide.* To receive a free copy, write to Senior Manager, Passenger Services, *International Air Transport Association,* 2000 Peel St., Montréal, Qué. H3A 2R4, Canada (phone: 514-844-6311).

TRAVEL BY SHIP: If you will be touring throughout Europe, you might prefer to reach the Continent by ocean liner. Cunard's *Queen Elizabeth 2* is considered the best-equipped ship for the handicapped — all but the top deck is accessible. The *QE2* crosses the Atlantic regularly from April through December between New York and its home port of Southampton, England, sometimes calling at Cherbourg, France, and Lisbon, Portugal. As with travel by plane, you must provide the ship's management with details of your condition and a physician's letter.

TRAVEL BY CAR, BUS, OR TRAIN: The best way for a handicapped person to get around Italy is to hire a chauffeured auto. Another solution is to travel with an able-bodied companion who can drive. As for doing the driving yourself, it is difficult in Italy to find rental cars with hand controls for the disabled; if your timing is right, you may reserve one of the few available at the Rome airport. Bus or train travel in Italy is not recommended for travelers who are totally wheelchair-bound unless they have someone along who can lift them on and off or they are members of a group tour designed for the handicapped and are using a specially outfitted conveyance. If you have some mobility, however, you'll find personnel usually quite happy to help you board and exit.

TOURS: The following travel agencies and tour operators specialize in group tours or independent travel arrangements for the handicapped. Their tour packages are thoroughly researched to make sure that hotels, restaurants, and places of interest present no insurmountable obstacles.

Evergreen Travel Service/Wings on Wheels Tours, 19505 L, 44th Ave. W, Lynnwood, WA 98036 (phone: 206-776-1184 or 800-562-9298). Handles cruises, group tours, and individual arrangements for the physically disabled and the blind.

Flying Wheels Travel, Box 382, Owatonna, MN 55060 (phone: 507-451-5005 or 800-533-0363). Handles tours and individual arrangements for the physically disabled and the elderly.

The Guided Tour, 555 Ashbourne Rd., Elkins Park, PA (phone: 215-782-1370). Arranges tours for both the physically and developmentally disabled.

Handi-Travel, First National Travel Corp., Suite 405, Thornhill Sq. at 300 John

St., Thornhill, Ont. L3T 5W4 Canada (phone: 416-886-2800). Arranges tours and individual trips.

Interpretours, Encino Travel Service, 16660 Ventura Blvd., Encino, CA 91436 (phone: 818-788-4118 or 818-788-4515, voice and TTY). Arranges independent travel, cruises, and tours for the deaf, with an interpreter as tour guide.

Mobility Tours, 26 Court St., Suite 1110, Brooklyn, NY 11242 (phone: 718-858-6021; TTY 212-625-4744). Associated with SATH; arranges tours for both physically and developmentally disabled persons.

Travel Horizons Unlimited, 11 E 44th St., New York, NY 10017 (phone: 212-687-5121). Arranges cruises, group tours, and independent travel for those who require hemodialysis.

Whole Person Tours, Inc., 137 W 32nd St., Bayonne, NJ 07002 (phone: 201-858-3400). Associated with *The Itinerary;* arranges group tours.

Hints for Traveling with Children

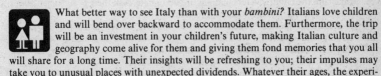 What better way to see Italy than with your *bambini?* Italians love children and will bend over backward to accommodate them. Furthermore, the trip will be an investment in your children's future, making Italian culture and geography come alive for them and giving them fond memories that you all will share for a long time. Their insights will be refreshing to you; their impulses may take you to unusual places with unexpected dividends. Whatever their ages, the experience will be invaluable to them — and to you.

PLANNING: With careful planning, your children's company does not have to be a burden or their presence an excessive expense. It is necessary, however, to take some extra time beforehand to prepare them for travel. Here are several hints for making a trip to Italy with children easy and fun.

1. Children, like everyone else, will derive more pleasure from a trip if they have knowledge of a country before they arrive. Begin their education about a month before you leave, using maps, atlases, travel magazines, and travel books to make clear exactly where Italy is and how far away it is. Part of the excitement of the journey will be associating the tiny dots on the map with the very real places you visit a few weeks later. You can show the children pictures of streets and scenes in Rome, Venice, or Naples, which they will soon see for themselves. Keep lessons age-appropriate, light, and anecdotal. You can find books on Italy written especially for children, such as Miroslav Sasek's *This Is Rome* and *This Is Venice* (Macmillan) or Ronald and Perla Clark's *We Go to Northern Italy* (International Publisher Service). *Welcome to Ancient Rome* (Passport Books, National Textbook Company) is a tiny, but information-packed, book for children in the fourth grade or older. The volumes on Italy in Ernest Raboff's "Art for Children" (Doubleday) and in *Newsweek*'s "Great Museums of the World" (Simon and Schuster) series are very good. Piero Ventura's *Great Painters* and (with Gian Paolo Ceserani) *Grand Constructions* (Putnam's) are good general books with many Italian examples. Most of these books are informative for adults as well. In addition to books, audio cassettes can make Italy come alive; play a language tape, a few Italian operas, or folk songs. However, don't overdo the educational approach. If you simply make materials available and keep Italy and your travel plans a topic of everyday conversation, your children will absorb more than you realize.

2. Children should help to plan the itinerary, and where you go and what you do should reflect some of their ideas. If they know something about architecture and

geography before they go, they will have the excitement of recognition when they arrive and the illumination of seeing how it is or is not like what they expected: The Leaning Tower of Pisa really leans; the Baths of Caracalla do not have faucets!

3. Learn the language with your children — a few basics like *scusi* ("excuse me") and *grazie* ("thank you") and *vorrei avere* ("I'd like to have") will help them fend for themselves; thus armed, they will delight the Italians and help break the ice wherever you go.

4. Familiarize the children with lire (see *Credit and Currency*). Give them an allowance for the trip and be sure they understand just how far it will or won't go.

5. They probably already love pizza and pasta, but your children need to know, too, that Italians eat many other equally delicious foods that they will want to try: *risotto* (rice), *polenta* (cornmeal porridge), *minestrone* (vegetable soup), *gelato* (ice cream). You might sample a few standard dishes ahead of time in a good restaurant here. In Italy, give them every opportunity to experience the delights of the varied cuisine. Restaurants are a treat, but children also enjoy picnics and nutritious snacks on the go. In large cities, milk is pasteurized and water is potable; stick to bottled water for small children and those with sensitive stomachs.

6. Make sure the children's inoculations are up to date. Ask their pediatrician about shots of gamma globulin against infection.

7. Give children specific responsibilities for the trip. When traveling, the job of carrying their own flight bags and looking after their personal things, along with other light tasks, will give them a stake in the journey. Tell them how they can be helpful when you are checking in or out of hotels.

8. Give each child a travel diary or scrapbook to take along. Filling these with impressions, observations, and mementos will pass the time on trains and planes and help the children to assimilate, or "concretize," their experiences.

PACKING: Choose your children's clothes much as you would your own. Select a basic color (perhaps different for each child) and coordinate everything with it. Plan their wardrobe with layering in mind — shirts and sweaters that can be taken off and put back on as the temperature varies. Take only drip-dry, wrinkle-resistant items that they can manage themselves, comfortable shoes — sneakers and sandals — and a few things to keep them warm and dry. Younger children will need more changes, but keep packing to a minimum. No one likes to carry added luggage (remember that *you* will have to manage most of it!).

Take along as many handy snacks as you can squeeze into the corners of your suitcases — things like dried fruit and nut mixes, hard candies, peanut butter, and crackers — and moist towelettes for cleaning. Don't worry if your supply of nibbles is quickly depleted. Airports and train stations are well stocked with such items, and it's fun to try foreign-made snacks.

Pack a special medical kit (see *Medical and Legal Aid and Consular Services*), including children's-strength aspirin or acetaminophen, an antihistamine or decongestant, Dramamine, and diarrhea medication. If you travel in warm weather, take along insect repellent, even if you do not use it yourself. Do not feel you must pack a vacation's worth of disposable diapers. *Assorbenti per bambini* (also called *pannolini di carta*) are available in pharmacies, department stores, and children's stores. Baby food is available in pharmacies and supermarkets, but you'd better bring as much infant formula as you think you will need — in the "ready-to-feed" cans. Disposable nursers are handy. If you breast-feed your baby, there is no reason you can't continue abroad; be sure you get enough rest and liquids.

Good traveling toys for infants are the same things they like at home — high-quality, brightly colored huggables and chewables; for small children, a favorite doll or stuffed animal for comfort, spelling and counting games, and tying, braiding, and lacing activities; for older children, playing cards, travel board games with magnetic pieces, and hand-held electronic games. Softcover books and art materials (crayons, markers, paper, scissors, glue sticks, stickers) ward off boredom for children of most ages, as do radio-cassette players with headphones. Take along a variety of musical and storytelling cassettes, maybe even an extra set of headphones so two children can listen, and extra batteries. *Advice:* Avoid toys that are noisy, breakable, or spillable, those that require a large play area, and those that have lots of little pieces that can be scattered and lost. When traveling, coordinate activities with attention spans; dole out playthings one at a time so you don't run out of diversions before you get where you're going.

GETTING THERE AND GETTING AROUND: Take time to investigate all available discount and charter flights as well as any family-package deals and special rates offered by the major airlines. You may find that charter plans offer no reductions for children or not enough to offset the risk of last-minute delays or other inconveniences to which charters are subject. The major scheduled airlines, however, almost invariably provide hefty discounts for children. (For specific information on fares and in-flight accommodations for children, see *Traveling by Plane.*)

Request seats on the aisle if you have a toddler or if you think you will need the bathroom frequently. (Try to discourage children from being in the aisle when meals are served.) Carry onto the plane all you will need to care for and occupy your children during the flight — diapers, formula, "lovies," books, sweaters, and so on. (Never check as baggage any item essential for a child's well-being, such as prescription medicine.) Have your baby dressed simply, with a minimum of buttons and snaps, because the only place you may have to change a diaper is at your seat. Your flight attendant can warm a bottle for you. For takeoffs and landings, have a bottle or pacifier on hand for an infant and some gum or hard candy for older children. This will keep everyone swallowing properly and ensure against earaches caused by rapid changes in air pressure. (Don't shush a baby who cries during takeoff or landing; he or she may *need* to do so to alleviate ear pain.) Newborn babies, whose lungs may not be able to adjust to the altitude, should not be taken on an airplane. (*Note:* Some airlines refuse to carry pregnant women in their eighth or ninth month for fear that something could go wrong with an in-flight birth. Check with the airline ahead of time. You should also consult your obstetrician about any travel plans.)

If you plan to travel by train, note that on Italian State Railways children under 4 travel free provided they do not occupy a seat; children from 4 through 11 travel at half the adult fare (they get a seat). Depending on how much rail traveling you plan to do in Italy, you might consider buying the discounted *Family Card* (*Carta Famiglia*), the *Italian Tourist Ticket* (*Biglietto Turistico di Libera Circolazione,* or *BTLC*), or the *Italian Kilometric Ticket* (*Biglietto Chilometrico*). If you will be traveling throughout Europe, the Eurailpass is a bargain. (For more specific information, see *Touring by Train.*)

ACCOMMODATIONS AND CONVENIENCES: Children surely are adaptable and, with the right parental example, take easily to the vicissitudes of travel. Most young children, however, do best if they are not moved from hotel to hotel every day or two. Try to find accommodations central to the sites you want to see, and settle in for a while. Use your hotel as the base for several excursions before you move on.

Often you can have a cot or crib placed in your hotel room at little or no extra charge. If you want your children to sleep in a separate room, special rates are sometimes available for families in adjoining rooms. You might look into accommodations along the way that will add to the color of your trip. A reconverted country villa, for instance, a farmhouse, or a well-run *pensione* might be more fun for your children and give them a different view of Italian life than they would have from staying in a conventional hotel. (See *Accommodations and Reservations.*)

For the times you will want to be without the children — for an evening's entertainment or a particularly rigorous stint of sightseeing — you can probably make arrangements for a babysitter at the hotel desk. Whether you hire the person directly or through an agency, be sure she has good references. Unless you or your children are fluent in Italian, make sure the babysitter can speak English.

Knowledge of the probable locations of restrooms is a necessity when you travel with children. In Italy, ask for *il gabinetto.* You will find restrooms in hotels and restaurants, museums, theaters, and other public places you visit as well as near all the major sites, especially in Rome. All airport and railway stations have them. *Leonardo da Vinci Airport* in Rome has a special lounge for children adjacent to the lounge for the handicapped in the International Transit Hall. The *Albergo Diurno,* a day-hotel in Rome's Stazione Termini, has baths and showers as well as toilet facilities.

SIGHTSEEING: In DIVERSIONS, you will find many wonderful things to do with your children in Italy. Remember that a child's attention span is far shorter than an adult's. Children don't have to see every museum (or all of any museum) to learn something from their trip. Watching, playing with, and talking to other children can be equally enlightening experiences. Try to break up the day into short, leisurely segments — no more than a morning or an afternoon dedicated to any one activity, be it travel or sightseeing. Let your children lead the way sometimes — their perspective is different from yours, and they may lead you to things you would never have noticed on your own.

Hints for Older Travelers

Special package deals and more free time are just two of the factors that have helped bring the world closer to the many millions of Americans over age 65. Senior citizens are a growing segment of the travel population, and the trend among them is to travel more frequently and for longer periods. Retired travelers are in a particularly good position to take advantage of off-peak opportunities; they have fewer constraints on vacation time, and they can escape, at least in part, from high-season prices and crowds. In addition, overseas, as in the US, they are frequently eligible for special discounts.

PLANNING: In the US, many hotel and motel chains, airlines, car rental companies, bus lines, and other travel suppliers offer discounts to older travelers. Some of these discounts, however, are extended only to members of certain senior citizens organizations. Because the same organizations frequently offer package tours to both domestic and international destinations, the benefits of membership can be twofold. Those who join can take advantage of discounts as individual travelers and also reap the saving that group travel affords. In addition, because the age requirements for some of these organizations are surprisingly low (or nonexistent), the benefits can begin to accrue early. The following are among the organizations dedicated to helping you see the world:

> *American Association of Retired Persons (AARP):* Travel programs designed exclusively for AARP members cover the globe and include a broad range of escorted motorcoach tours at more than one price level; extended vacations in European cities and resorts with accommodations in apartments; regional tours of rural areas of Europe; and cruises. Membership is open to anyone age 50 and older, whether retired or not; dues are $5 a year or $12.50 for 3 years. Contact *AARP,* 1909 K St., NW, Washington, DC 20049 (phone: 202-872-4700).

> *National Association of Mature People (NAMP):* Membership is $9.95 per year for either an individual or a couple and is open to anyone age 40 and older. NAMP offers a changing schedule of tours every year; inquire about Italy. Contact *NAMP,* PO Box 26792, Oklahoma City, OK 73126 (phone: 405-848-1832).

National Council of Senior Citizens: The roster of tours offered by this organization is also different each year, but the emphasis is always on keeping costs low. The annual membership fee is $8 for an individual or $10 for a couple. There is no age requirement; most members are over 50, however. Contact *National Council of Senior Citizens,* 925 15th St., NW, Washington, DC 20005 (phone: 202-347-8800).

Many tour operators specialize in group travel for older persons. *Grand Circle Travel,* which caters exclusively to the over-50 traveler, packages a large variety (no continent is left untrod) of escorted tours, cruises, and extended vacations in one spot. It offers some packages that include Italy. Contact *Grand Circle Travel,* 347 Congress St., Boston, MA 02210 (phone: 617-350-7500 in Boston; 800-221-2610 elsewhere). Grand Circle publishes a quarterly magazine (which includes a column for the single traveler) and a helpful free booklet entitled "101 Tips for the Mature Traveler Abroad." *Saga International Holidays,* a subsidiary of a British company specializing in the older traveler, has a similarly broad selection of escorted coach tours, cruises, apartment-stay holidays, and combinations thereof open to those 60 and older or to those 50 to 59 traveling with someone 60 or older. Members of the Saga Holidays Club receive the club magazine, which also contains a column aimed at helping lone travelers find suitable traveling companions (see *Hints for Single Travelers*). Saga has no packages strictly to Italy at this time, but it does visit Italy on some of its European tours. A 3-year membership in the club costs $5. Contact *Saga International Holidays,* 120 Boylston St., Boston, MA 02116 (phone: 800-462-3322 in Massachusetts; 800-343-0273 elsewhere). *Gadabout Tours* offers escorted tours to numerous North American destinations and also has tours to Europe, with one that includes Italy. For information, write to *Gadabout Tours,* 700 E Tahquitz Way, Palm Springs, CA 92262 (phone: 619-325-5556), or see your travel agent.

Educational travel is another choice open to older people. *Elderhostel* is a nonprofit organization offering educational programs at a huge number of colleges and universities in the US and Canada as well as at cooperating institutions overseas, a few of which are in Italy. The Italian programs run for two weeks in the spring, summer, and fall in Rome, Verona, Perugia, and Assisi. Mornings are devoted to class lectures on three courses of study, such as art, architecture, history, or contemporary politics and society, and afternoons are reserved for field trips to museums, churches, monuments, and other sites. Elderhostelers usually stay in residence halls and take their meals in student cafeterias, but on the Italian programs the accommodations range from hotels (double occupancy) to small double rooms (with private bath) in a renovated convent. Meals are on the premises or in restaurants. Although participants in Elderhostel's stateside programs are expected to make their own travel arrangements to the campus, travel to the overseas programs is by designated scheduled flights, and arrangements to remain abroad at the end of the program are possible. Groups are limited to about 40 people who must be at least 60 years old (or younger if a spouse or companion qualifies), not in need of special diets, and in good health since the Italian programs require stamina for walking and climbing of steps and slopes. For information, write to *Elderhostel,* 80 Boylston St., Suite 400, Boston, MA 02116 (phone: 617-426-7788).

Interhostel, similar to and the predecessor of Elderhostel, is a program sponsored by the Division of Continuing Education of the University of New Hampshire. It sends travelers back to school at cooperating institutions in various European countries, including Italy. Participants attend lectures on the history, economy, politics, and cultural life of the country, go on field trips to pertinent points of interest, take part in activities meant to introduce them to their foreign contemporaries, and also do some conventional sightseeing. Trips are for two weeks, accommodations are on campus in university residence halls or off campus in modest hotels (double occupancy). Groups are limited to 25 to 35 participants who are at least 50 years old (or younger if a participating spouse is at least 50), physically active, and not in need of special diets. The Italian program takes place in the spring in Florence and concentrates on the study of the city's great art treasures. For further details, contact *Interhostel,* UNH Division of Continuing Education, Brook House, Rosemary La., Durham, NH 03824 (phone: 603-862-1147). For more information on educational travel, see *Hints for Students.*

A word of caution to all travelers, but especially to older ones — don't overdo it. Allow time for some relaxation each day to refresh yourself for the next scheduled event. Traveling across time zones can be exhausting. Plan to spend at least one full day resting after your arrival before you begin touring. If you're part of a group tour, be sure to check the planned itinerary thoroughly. Some package deals sound wonderful because they include all the places you've dreamed of visiting. In fact, they can become so hectic and tiring that you won't enjoy your trip.

An excellent book to read before embarking on any trip, domestic or foreign, is Rosalind Massow's *Travel Easy: The Practical Guide for People over 50,* available for $8.95 from *AARP Books,* 1909 K St., NW, Washington, DC 20049 (phone: 202-872-4700). It discusses a host of travel-related subjects, from choosing a destination to getting set for departure, with chapters on transporation options, tours, cruises (including a rundown on who's who aboard a cruise ship and whom to tip), avoiding health problems, and handling dental emergencies en route.

PACKING: If you are traveling in the fall, winter, or spring, bear in mind that you will not always find central heating in public places in Italy and that even if your hotel has it, it may not warm your room to the temperatures you're accustomed to at home. Museums and old stone *palazzi* can be chilly and damp, so pack accordingly. However, remember that one secret to happy traveling is to *pack lightly.* Most common toilet articles, in familar brands, are available throughout Italy. Be sure to take with you any medication you need to carry you through for the duration of your trip; pack it separately in a carryall in case your luggage is lost or detoured, along with a note from your doctor for the benefit of airport authorities (or a copy of your prescription, which will not only settle disputes at customs but will come in handy in case of emergency). It is also wise to take along a few common medications — aspirin or acetaminophen and upset stomach medication may come in handy. If you are diabetic or have heart problems, carry your medical records with you. Two organizations that provide lists of qualified, English-speaking doctors in Italy (and throughout the world) are the International Association for Medical Assistance to Travelers (IAMAT) and Intermedic. (For addresses and information about these and other medical services, see *Medical and Legal Aid and Consular Services.*)

DISCOUNTS TO AND IN ITALY: TWA's VSP Senior Pass allows people 65 or older a year of unlimited travel (with certain restrictions) on that airline's domestic routes, including Puerto Rico, for a one-time fare of $1,299. For an additional charge, travelers can purchase an International Option, permitting one round-trip per year to an international destination (for most cities the surcharge is $499; for Rome or Milan it is $599). For the same prices, each VSP Senior Pass holder is allowed to purchase a Companion Pass for someone under age 65 — who may not travel without the sponsoring Senior Pass holder, however. The *Carta d'Argento* (*Silver Card*) entitles men over 65 and women over 60 to a 30% discount on rail fares in Italy. The card can be bought in Italy at rail stations, CIT offices, and certain other travel agencies on presentation of a passport. The cost is under $5 and the card is good for a year. Other discounts exist in Italy, but it's not easy for short-term visitors to take advantage of them. Still, wherever you go and whatever you do, it can't hurt to ask if there are special rates for senior citizens. The answer, sometimes, will be *sì.*

Hints for Single Travelers

Just about the last trip in human history in which the participants were precisely and neatly paired was the voyage of Noah's Ark. Ever since, passenger lists and tour groups have reflected the same kind of asymmetry that occurs in real life, as countless individuals set forth to see the world unaccompanied (or unencumbered, depending on your outlook) by spouse, lover, friend, or relative.

There are very significant attractions to traveling alone. It forces you to see more; it requires that you be self-reliant, independent, and responsible. Traveling alone necessitates that you be more outgoing, and, therefore, you tend to meet more people than you would traveling in a pair. But, unfortunately, it also turns you into a second-class citizen.

The truth is that the travel industry is not yet prepared to deal fairly with a person who vacations by him- or herself. Most travel bargains, including package tours, hotel accommodations, resort packages, and cruises, are based on *double-occupancy* rates. This means that the per-person price is offered on the basis of two people traveling together and sharing a double room. For exactly the same package, the single traveler has to pay a surcharge, called the "single supplement," which can add 30% to 55% to the basic per-person rate.

Don't despair, however. Throughout Italy there are scores of inexpensive smaller hotels and former *pensioni* that provide a cozy atmosphere (sometimes including a delicious breakfast) appropriate for the single traveler. A home-stay arrangement, in which the traveler lives for a short time with an Italian family, is another possibility. (For more information on where to stay, see *Accommodations and Reservations* and *Hints for Students* in this section; *Best in Town* in THE CITIES; and *Checking In* in DIRECTIONS.)

If you prefer to have your arrangements made for you, a number of options have emerged. In addition to several tour operators that specialize in the age 18-to-35 market, some travel organizations cater solely to single vacationers of all ages. One example is *Singleworld,* a club joined through travel agents for a yearly fee of $18, paid at the time of booking. Some, such as Singleworld, charge minimal membership fees; others offer their services free. But the basic service offered by all is the same — to match the unattached person with a compatible travel mate. Perhaps the most recent innovation along these lines is the creation of organizations that "introduce" the single traveler to other single travelers, somewhat like a dating service. The better established among these are:

> *Grand Circle Travel,* 347 Congress St., Boston, MA 02210 (phone: 617-350-7500 in Boston; 800-221-2610 elsewhere), arranges escorted tours for "mature" travelers, including singles. Membership, which is automatic when you book a trip through Grand Circle, includes a free subscription to its quarterly magazine, discount certificates on future trips, and other extras. (For more information, see *Hints for Older Travelers.*)
>
> *Saga International,* 120 Boylston St., Boston, MA 02116 (phone: 800-343-0273), is an organization for seniors over 60, including singles. (For more information, see *Hints for Older Travelers.*)
>
> *Travel Companion Exchange,* PO Box 833, Amityville, NY 11701 (phone: 516-454-0080), functions on a membership basis (the fee ranging from $18 for a

three-month trial to $60 a year for full benefits). Members fill out a lengthy questionnaire to establish a personal profile and write a mini-listing much like an ad in a personals column. The listings are circulated among members who, for $1, can request a copy of any complete questionnaire and go on to make contact to plan a joint vacation.

Travel Partners Club, PO Box 2368, Crystal River, FL 32629 (phone: 904-795-1117), is run by and for people over the age of 50. The membership fee, $30 per year, includes biographical listings and a bimonthly newsletter.

The single traveler who is particularly interested in getting to know Italians better than chance encounters in train stations allow may be interested in two very different possibilities. One is *Club Méditerranée,* an organization that heartily welcomes singles. Of Club Med's 104 activity-oriented resorts around the world, 7 are in Italy — and more than 95% of the guests at its Italian resorts are European; French and Italian are spoken predominantly. For details, contact *Club Med Sales, Inc.,* 40 W 57th St., New York, NY 10019 (phone: 800-CLUB MED). The other possibility is the *United States Servas Committee,* which maintains a list of hosts around the world (nearly 400 in Italy) who welcome interested foreigners into their homes. See *Accommodations and Reservations* for information on this nonprofit organization.

A word to the single woman traveler: You need not worry about your personal safety in Italy any more than you would anywhere else, but be forewarned that Italian men like to show their appreciation of women, and sometimes their attentions can be a bit disconcerting. Some women love this direct approach; others find it enraging. As one woman we know put it, "Italian men do things they would be shot dead for back home!" Don't take this remark too literally, but do be prepared to deal with men of the Mediterranean temperament. Remember that any reply you make to an overture will be regarded, in Italian culture, as encouragement. The best defense (if you feel a defense is needed) is always to be with other people when you are in public places, especially off the beaten track. An obvious solution is to travel with a group. Among the organizations catering directly to women travelers is Estilita Grimaldo's *Womantours,* 5314 N Figueroa St., Los Angeles, CA 90042 (phone: 213-255-1115), which can help you arrange either a group or an individual travel program.

Hints for Students

Travel *is* education. Travel broadens your knowledge and deepens your perception of the world in a way no media, or "armchair," experience ever can. In addition, to study a country's language, art, culture, or history in one of its own schools is to enjoy the highest form of liberal education.

By "student" we do not necessarily mean a person who wishes to matriculate at an Italian university to earn an academic degree. Nor do we necessarily mean a younger person, although many of our suggestions are for junior high school, high school, and college-age people. A student is anyone who wishes to include some sort of educational program in a trip to Italy.

For a complete listing of programs administered by Italian institutions, contact the *Italian Cultural Institute,* 686 Park Ave., New York, NY 10021 (phone: 212-879-4242). The following are among the best short-term offerings.

Università Italiana per Stranieri: Founded in 1925 by the Italian government, the "University for Foreigners" is housed in the eighteenth-century Palazzo Gallenga of Perugia. Well run, with a diverse student body and nominally priced courses in subjects as varied as elementary Italian and Etruscology, it puts much of the country's regular university system to shame. Courses of varying lengths

— from two weeks to nine months — are offered throughout the year. Contact *Università Italiana per Stranieri,* Palazzo Gallenga, Piazza Fortebraccio, Perugia, Italy (phone: 075-64344).

Società Dante Alighieri: The Dante is a worldwide organization for the diffusion of Italian culture, with 400 branches teaching Italian to 50,000 students a year. The Rome branch offers courses in art, music, theater, furniture, and interior decoration; it sponsors films, concerts, lecture series, and assorted excursions. There are four two-month terms from October to May plus two-month summer terms in June and July. Fees are quite low and instruction first rate. For information about instruction in Rome and other Italian cities, contact *Società Dante Alighieri,* Piazza Firenze 27, 00186 Rome, Italy (phone: 06-6781105).

Eurocentro: Part of an international foundation with headquarters in Zürich and schools of language and civilization in several other European countries, the Eurocentro branch in Italy is in a Renaissance *palazzo* in the heart of Florence. In addition to providing excellent Italian language instruction, the center emphasizes teaching its students about Italian art and architecture, some of the finest of which can be seen from the school's windows. Contact *Eurocentro,* Piazza Santo Spirito 9, 50125 Florence, Italy (phone: 294605).

If you are already a full-time student, you can take advantage of many travel benefits. Begin your trip by consulting the *Council on International Educational Exchange* (*CIEE*), 205 E 42nd St., New York, NY 10017 (phone: 212-661-1450), or 312 Sutter St., San Francisco, CA 94108 (phone: 415-421-3473). This organization, which is affiliated with nearly 200 North American secondary schools, colleges, and universities, administers a variety of work, study, and travel programs for students. It is the US sponsor of the *International Student Identity Card,* the only internationally recognized student ID. Reductions on trains, air fares, and entry fees to most museums and other exhibits all over the world are only some of the advantages of the card. To apply for it, write to CIEE; the application requires an $8 fee, a passport-size photograph, and proof that you are a full-time student (this means a letter or bill from your school registrar with the school's official seal; junior high school and high school students can use their report cards). There is no maximum age limit, but you must be at least 12 years old. The *ID Discount Guide,* which gives details of the discounts country by country, is free with membership. The student travel office associated with CIEE in Italy is *Centro Turistico Studentesco e Giovanile,* Via Genova 16, 00184 Rome. This office has branches in Florence, Milan, Venice, and other major cities.

The *National Association of Secondary School Principals* (*NASSP*), an affiliate of CIEE, is an association of administrators, teachers, and state education officials. Together these organizations sponsor the *School Exchange Service,* a program in which secondary schools in the US are linked with partner schools abroad for an annual short-term exchange of students and faculty. The Ministry of Foreign Affairs and the Ministry of Public Instruction are the official cosponsors in Italy. For more information, contact the CIEE (address above) or the *NASSP,* 1904 Association Dr., Reston, VA 22091 (phone: 703-860-0200).

You might also consult the *Institute of International Education* (*IIE*), an information resource center, which annually publishes several reference books on study abroad, including *Academic Year Abroad* and *Vacation Study Abroad.* Both volumes are available for $15.95 each from IIE headquarters, 809 UN Plaza, New York, NY 10017 (phone: 212-883-8200).

Another organization specializing in travel as an educational experience is the *American Institute for Foreign Study* (*AIFS*). One particularly enticing AIFS program — based at the University of Florence, Fortman Studios, and the University of Siena — is designed for college students wishing to study art history, studio art, and Italian language and culture. Students can enroll for the full academic year or for any number of semesters. AIFS caters primarily to bona fide high school or college students, but noncredit international learning and continuing education programs are open to independent travelers of all ages. (Approximately 30% of AIFS students are over 25.) Contact *AIFS,* 102 Greenwich Ave., Greenwich, CT 06830 (phone: 203-869-9090).

If you are interested in a home-stay travel program, in which you learn about Italian culture by living with a family in Italy, contact *Experiment in International Living,* Box E-10, Brattleboro, VT 05301-0676 (phone: 802-257-7751 in Vermont; 800-451-4465, ext. 3, elsewhere). The organization aims its programs at high school or college students, but it can also arrange home stays of one to four weeks for adults in more than 40 countries, including Italy.

Elderhostel is a network of schools, colleges, and universities that sponsors week-long study programs for people over 60 years of age on campuses throughout the US and Europe, including Italy. Some of its programs are offered in cooperation with the *Experiment in International Living* and involve home stays. Contact *Elderhostel,* 80 Boylston St., Suite 400, Boston, MA 02116 (phone: 617-426-7788). The University of New Hampshire, the original sponsor of Elderhostel, has its own program for travelers over 50; contact *Interhostel,* University of New Hampshire, Division of Continuing Education, Brook House, Rosemary La., Durham, NH 03824 (phone: 603-862-1147). (For more detailed information about both programs, see *Hints for Older Travelers.*)

Two books that can help you plan your trip are *Work, Study, Travel Abroad: The Whole World Handbook,* available for $7.95 from the Council on International Educational Exchange, 205 E 42nd St., New York, NY 10017 (phone: 212-661-1450); and *Global Guide to International Education* by David Hoopes (Facts on File; $75.00). A vast (and expensive) resource compilation, the latter is widely available in public and campus libraries.

For information on low-cost fares and accommodations, see *Traveling by Plane; Touring by Train; Accommodations and Reservations;* and *Camping and Caravanning, Biking, and Hiking.*

Insurance

It is unfortunate that most decisions to buy travel insurance are impulsive and usually made without any real consideration of one's existing coverage. Too often the result is the purchase of needlessly expensive short-term policies that duplicate existing coverage and reinforce the tendency to buy insurance trip by trip rather than to work out a total, continuing travel insurance package that might be more effective and economical.

The first person with whom you should discuss travel insurance, therefore, is your own insurance broker, not a travel agent or the clerk behind the airport insurance counter. You may well discover that the insurance you already carry — homeowner's policies and/or accident, health, and life insurance — protects you adequately while you travel and that your real needs are in the more mundane areas of excess value insurance for baggage or trip cancellation insurance.

To make insurance decisions intelligently, however, first understand the basic categories of travel insurance and what they are designed to cover. Then decide what you should have in the broader context of your personal insurance needs, and choose the most economical way of getting the desired protection: through riders on existing policies; with one-time short-term policies; through special programs for the frequent traveler; through coverage as part of a travel club's benefits; or with a combination policy sold by insurance companies through brokers, tour operators, and travel agents.

There are five basic categories of travel insurance: baggage and personal effects; personal accident and sickness; trip cancellation and interruption; flight (to cover death or injury); and automobile (for driving your own or a rented car).

BAGGAGE AND PERSONAL EFFECTS INSURANCE: If baggage and personal effects are included in your current homeowner's policy, check with your broker about the necessity for a special floater to cover you for a trip. The object is to protect your bags and their contents in case of damage or theft anytime during your travels, not just while you're in flight and covered by the airline's policy. Furthermore, only limited protection is provided by the airline. For most international flights, including domestic portions of international flights, the airline's liability limit is approximately $20 per kilo ($9.07 per pound) for checked baggage and $400 per passenger for unchecked baggage. (On domestic flights, the limit of liability on most airlines is $1,250 per passenger.) But these limits, which should be specified in the fine print on your ticket, are maximums, and to be awarded even this amount you would have to provide an itemized list of lost property. If you have suffered the loss of any new or expensive items, it may be necessary to back up your claim with sales receipts or other proofs of purchase.

If you are carrying goods worth more than the maximum protection offered by the airline, consider excess value insurance, available from the airlines at an average, currently, of 50¢ per $100 worth of coverage. This insurance can be purchased at the airline counter when you check in, though you should arrive early to fill out the necessary forms and to avoid holding up other passengers checking in. Excess value insurance is also included in some of the combination travel insurance policies discussed below.

■ **WARNING:** Be sure to read the fine print of any excess value insurance policy, or indeed of any baggage insurance policy; there are often specific exclusions, such as money, tickets, furs, gold and silver objects, art, and antiques. And remember that insurance companies ordinarily will pay only the depreciated value of the goods rather than their replacement value. The best way to protect the items you're carrying is to take photographs of them and to keep a record of the serial numbers of such items as cameras, typewriters, radios, and so on. This will establish that you do, indeed, own the objects. If your luggage disappears en route or is damaged, report the situation immediately at the airport, train station, or bus station. If an airline loses your luggage, fill out a Property Irregularity Report before you leave the airport. Claims are accepted if after five days the items reported as lost or stolen have not turned up; settlement is within 30 to 90 days. If your property disappears elsewhere, report it to the police at once.

PERSONAL ACCIDENT AND SICKNESS INSURANCE: This covers you in case of illness on the road (hospital and doctor's expenses, lost income, and so on). It is usually a standard part of existing health insurance policies, but check with your broker to be sure that your policy will pay for any medical expenses incurred abroad.

TRIP CANCELLATION AND INTERRUPTION INSURANCE: Most package tours, cruises, and charter flights require full payment a substantial period of time before departure. Although cancellation penalties vary (they are listed in the fine print on the brochure; before making any purchase you should know exactly what they are), rarely will you get more than 50% of your money back if you are forced to cancel within a week or two of leaving, and rarely will you get any money back at all if you must cancel on the day of departure or during a trip. Any refund of money paid for a charter flight canceled even well in advance may depend on your being able to supply a substitute passenger. Therefore, if you book a package tour or a charter flight, you should have trip cancellation insurance to guarantee a full refund should you, a traveling companion, or a member of your immediate family get sick, forcing you to cancel your trip or *return home early.* The key here is *not* to buy just enough insurance to guarantee full reimbursement in case of cancellation. The proper amount of coverage should be sufficient to reimburse you for the cost of having to catch up with a tour after its departure or having to travel home at the full economy air fare if you have to forgo the return trip of a discounted flight (such as an excursion with advance purchase requirements) and especially if you have to forgo the return portion of a charter flight. There is usually quite a discrepancy between the charter air fare and the amount you would have to pay to travel the same distance on a regularly scheduled flight.

Cancellation insurance is available from travel agents and tour operators in two forms: as part of a short-term, all-purpose travel insurance package sold by the travel agent; or as specific cancellation insurance designed by the tour operator for a specific package tour. Generally, the tour operator's policies are cheaper but less inclusive. Read any policy carefully before you buy it, and be sure the policy you choose provides enough money to get you home from the farthest point on your itinerary should you have to take a scheduled flight. Also be sure to check the specific definition of "family members" and "preexisting medical conditions." Some policies will not pay if you become ill from a condition for which you have received treatment in the past.

DEFAULT AND/OR BANKRUPTCY INSURANCE: Note that trip cancellation insurance usually protects you in the event that you, the traveler, are unable to take — or complete — your trip. A fairly recent innovation is coverage in the event of default and/or bankruptcy on the part of the tour operator, airline, or other travel supplier. In some travel insurance packages, this contingency is included in the trip cancellation portion of the coverage; in others it is a separate feature. Either way, it is becoming increasingly important. Whereas most travelers have long known to beware of the possibility of default or bankruptcy when buying a charter flight or tour, in recent years more than a few respected scheduled airlines have unexpectedly revealed their shaky financial condition, sometimes leaving ticketholders stranded. Moreover, escrow protection of a charter passenger's funds has lately been unreliable. While default /bankruptcy insurance will not ordinarily result in reimbursement in time for you to pay for new arrangements, it can ensure that you will eventually get your money back, and even independent travelers buying no more than an airplane ticket may want to consider it.

Note, however, that because of differing state insurance regulations, default and/or bankruptcy insurance is not universally available. In addition, it can be expensive. In its absence, consider using a credit card to pay for travel arrangements whenever possible. The federal Fair Credit Billing Act permits purchasers to refuse payment for credit card charges where services have not been delivered, so the potential onus of dealing with a bankrupt airline falls on the credit card company. Do not assume that another airline will automatically honor the ticket you're holding on a bankrupt airline since the days when virtually all major carriers subscribed to a default protection program are long gone. Some airlines may voluntarily step forward to accommodate stranded passengers, but this is now an entirely altruistic act.

FLIGHT INSURANCE: Airlines have carefully established limits of liability for the death or injury of passengers. For international flights, these are printed on the ticket: a maximum of $75,000 in case of death or injury. But remember, these limits of liability are not the same as insurance policies; they merely state the *maximum* an airline will pay in the case of death or injury, and every penny of that is usually subject to a legal battle.

This may make you feel that you are not adequately protected. But before you buy last-minute flight insurance from an airport vending machine, as many passengers do, consider the purchase in light of your existing insurance coverage. A careful review of your current policies may reveal that you are already amply covered for accidental death, sometimes up to three times the amount provided by the airport flight insurance.

Be aware that airport insurance, the kind you typically buy from a counter or a vending machine, is one of the most expensive forms of life insurance coverage available anywhere and that even within a single airport, rates for approximately the same coverage can vary. Often the vending machines are more expensive than coverage sold over the counter, even when the policies are with the same national company.

If you pay for your ticket with an American Express, Diners Club, or Carte Blanche card, you are automatically issued accident and accidental death insurance at no extra cost. American Express automatically provides $100,000 of free accidental death insurance; Diners Club and Carte Blanche, $650,000. American Express offers up to $1 million of additional insurance at low cost.

COMBINATION POLICIES: A number of insurance companies offer all-purpose travel insurance packages that include baggage and personal effects, personal accident and sickness, trip cancellation insurance, and, sometimes, default and bankruptcy protection. They cover you for a single trip and are sold by travel agents, insurance agents, and others. The following are a few of the best policies of this type.

> *Access America:* A subsidiary of the Blue Cross/Blue Shield plans of New York and Washington, DC, now available nationwide. Contact *Access America,* 600 Third Ave., PO Box 807, New York, NY 10163 (phone: 800-851-2800).
>
> *Near:* Part of a benefits package offered by a travel service organization, underwritten by the Chubb Group of Insurance Companies. An added feature is coverage for lost or stolen airline tickets. Contact *Near, Inc.,* 1900 North MacArthur Blvd., Suite 210, Oklahoma City, OK 73127 (phone: 800-522-6237 in Oklahoma; 800-654-6700 elsewhere).
>
> *Travel Guard:* Endorsed by the American Society of Travel Agents, underwritten by the Insurance Company of North America. Contact *Travel Guard International,* 1650 Briggs St., Stevens Point, WI 54480 (phone: 715-345-0505 in Wisconsin; 800-826-1300 elsewhere).

AUTOMOBILE INSURANCE: Public liability and property damage (third party) insurance is compulsory in Europe, and whether you drive your own car or a rental you must carry insurance. Car rental rates include public liability, property damage, fire, and theft coverage as well as collision damage coverage with a deductible. Optional collision damage waiver protection, offered at a few dollars extra per day, relieves the car renter of paying the deductible amount in the event of an accident. Keep your rental contract (with the appropriate insurance box ticked off) with you as proof of insurance. To drive your own car in Italy, you should have an *International Insurance Certificate,* or *Green Card* (*Carta Verde*), available through insurance brokers in the US or at the frontier as you enter Italy. (For more information on driving in Italy, see *Touring by Car.*)

Medical and Legal Aid
and Consular Services

 MEDICAL AID IN ITALY: The surest way to return home in good health is to be prepared for common medical concerns en route. So before we describe the health facilities available in Italy, here are some tips to consider while still in the US.

Prepare a compact, personal medical kit that includes Band-Aids, first-aid cream, nose drops, suntan cream, insect repellent, aspirin or acetaminophen, an extra pair of prescription glasses or sunglasses if you wear them, Lomotil or an equivalent to combat diarrhea, Dramamine or an equivalent for motion sickness, a thermometer, and a supply of any medicines you take regularly. In a corner of your kit, keep a list of all the drugs you have brought and their purpose as well as a spare copy of your doctor's prescriptions (or a note from your doctor). This could come in handy if you are ever questioned by police or airport authorities about why you are carrying certain drugs. It is also a good idea to ask your doctor to prepare a medical identification card that includes such information as your blood type, your social security number, any allergies or chronic health problems you have, and your medical insurance number.

Be sure to check with your health insurance company about the applicability of your policy while you're abroad; many policies do not apply, and others are not accepted in Italy. Older travelers should know that Medicare does not make payments out of the country. Fortunately, hospitalization is less expensive in Italy than it is here; it is free in public hospitals if you can prove inability to pay.

If your policy does not protect you while you're traveling, you can take advantage of programs specifically designed to fill such a gap. International Underwriters/Brokers has developed two *HealthCare Abroad* programs that provide comprehensive coverage for travelers. For $1 to $2.50 per day, depending on age, one program includes a $2,000 blanket sickness and accident benefit (with a $50 deductible), a $15,000 major medical benefit, a $5,000 medical evacuation benefit, and more. There is 30-day minimum coverage and an age limit of 70 (no medical examination is required). For $3.00 per day, the second program offers significantly better dollar limits, a minimum-maximum range of 10 to 120 days, and an age limit of 85 (a doctor's certificate is required after age 75). For further information, contact *HealthCare Abroad, International Underwriters/Brokers,* 210 Investment Bldg., 1511 K St., NW, Washington, DC 20005 (phone: 703-255-9800 in Virginia; 800-336-3310 elsewhere). (Also see *Insurance* for information about combination policies.)

Other organizations provide a variety of medical services for travelers:

Assist-Card International provides a number to call — 24 hours a day, 365 days a year — through which complete emergency medical assistance can be arranged, including ambulance or air transportation to the proper treatment facilities, local lawyers for a case resulting from an accident, and up to $5,000 in bail bonds for a judicial proceeding that is the result of an accident. This organization will arrange for a flight home if the traveler is unable to complete the trip because of illness or accident and will pay any necessary fare differential. It will also pay the first $3,000 in medical expenses and $500 in prescriptions. Fees vary according to the length of the trip abroad, ranging from $30 for a 5-day card to $180 for a 90-day itinerary. For information, contact *Assist-Card Corporation of America,* 347 Fifth Ave., New York, NY 10016 (phone: 212-752-2788 in New York; 800-221-4564 elsewhere).

International SOS Assistance also offers a program to cover medical emergencies while traveling. Members are provided with telephone access — 24 hours a day, 365 days a year — to a worldwide, monitored, multilingual network of medical centers. A phone call brings assistance ranging from telephone consultation to transportation home by ambulance or aircraft, and in some cases the transportation of a family member to the place of hospitalization. The service can be purchased for a week ($15; each additional day, $2), a month ($45), or a year ($195) and includes a $1,000 blanket medical expense reimbursement (with a $25 deductible). For more information, contact *International SOS Assistance,* PO Box 11568, Philadelphia, PA 19116 (phone: 215-244-1500 in Pennsylvania; 800-523-8930 elsewhere).

Medic Alert Foundation International sells identification tags that specify that the wearer has a medical condition — such as a heart condition, diabetes, epilepsy, or severe allergies — that may not be readily apparent to a casual observer. These are conditions that, if not recognized when emergency treatment is necessary (and when you may be unable to speak for yourself), can result in tragic errors. In addition to the identification emblems, a central file is maintained (with the telephone number clearly inscribed on the ID), where your complete medical history is available 24 hours a day by telephone. The one-time membership fee of $15 to $38 depends on the type of emblem you select — stainless steel to 10K gold-filled. For information, contact *Medic Alert,* PO Box 1009, Turlock, CA 95381-9986 (phone: 209-668-3333 in California; 800-228-6222 elsewhere).

Unfortunately, you cannot rely on the competence of doctors on call at Italian hotels, so it would be wise to carry with you the names and telephone numbers of English-speaking doctors in the cities you will visit. Two health organizations provide lists of English-speaking doctors abroad:

Intermedic provides a directory of English-speaking doctors in more than 90 countries — in Italy, Florence, Milan, Rome, and Taranto are represented — with telephone numbers. Membership is $6 for an individual, $10 per family. For information, write to *Intermedic,* 777 Third Ave., New York, NY 10017 (phone: 212-486-8900).

International Association for Medical Assistance to Travelers (IAMAT) provides its members with a directory of affiliated medical centers to call for a list of participating English-speaking doctors. More than 100 countries, including 30 Italian cities, are listed. Membership is available for a donation of any amount over $5; for $25, a set of worldwide climate charts detailing weather and sanitary conditions will be included. To join, write well in advance of your trip to *IAMAT,* 417 Center St., Lewiston, NY 14092 (phone: 716-754-4883).

We strongly urge you to give some thought ahead of time to what you will do if you need medical aid in Italy. If you are disabled (see *Hints for Handicapped Travelers*) or have recently been ill, discuss emergency procedures with your doctor before you go. Familiarize yourself with the Italian health care system and decide on your plan of action should you need aid quickly. Take along the telephone numbers of agencies and individuals who will be able to help you.

Although Italian medicine has been nationalized, its administration is carried out on the local level, and private practice continues to flourish. Also, the training and licensing of doctors (*medici*) and health care workers is not strictly regulated. For these reasons, the level of health care in Italy is highly variable from region to region and from hospital to hospital. In general, it is not quite as good as care in the US or in some other European countries. If at all possible, you should return home for complex medical procedures. If you must remain in Italy, however, you can get excellent care — up-to-date and efficiently rendered — in full-service, government-run teaching hospitals associated with universities in major northern cities, as far south as Rome.

■ **IN CASE OF MEDICAL EMERGENCY:** Italian law specifies that seriously injured, ill, or unconscious persons be taken directly to one of the public hospitals. Driving routes are usually marked with the international sign of the white "H" on a blue background (even though the Italian word for hospital is *ospedale*). If you need help, call the Public Emergency Assistance number of the State Police — 113 — or the Immediate Action Service number of the Carabinieri — 112. It is best to explain your problem (or have it explained) in Italian, but if you cannot, ask for an English-speaking operator. The efficiency and speed of the service will be variable. If you require an ambulance, be aware that it will provide transportation only — not medical aid — to the nearest public hospital. After treatment in the emergency room, *pronto soccorso,* a patient in stable condition may transfer to the hospital of his or her choice.

Some of the best public hospitals are:

Bari: Ospedale Regionale Consorziale Policlinico (Regional Polyclinic Hospital), Piazza G. Cesare (phone: 080-221514). Full service. Intensive care unit.

Florence: Arcispedale Santa Maria Nuova (General Hospital of Santa Maria Nuova), Viale Morgagni, Careggi (outside Florence) (phone: 055-27741). Full service except for pediatrics.

Genoa: Ospedale Generale Regionale San Martino (San Martino Regional Hospital), Viale Benedetto XV (phone: 010-54841). Full service.

Milan: Ospedale Ca' Granda Niguarda (Niguarda Hospital), Piazza Ospedale Maggiore 3 (phone: 02-6444). Full service. Good coronary care unit. Also Ospedale Policlinico (Polyclinic Hospital), Via Francesco Sforza 33 (phone: 02-581655). Full service.

Naples: Ospedale Cardarelli (Cardarelli Hospital), Via Cardarelli 9 (phone: 081-258044). Full service except for coronary care. Also Policlinico II (Polyclinic II), Via Servio Pansini 5 (phone: 081-255522). Full service except for emergency care. Also Ospedale San Paolo (San Paolo Hospital), Via Terracina (phone: 081-634161). Twenty-four-hour emergency room.

Rome: Policlinico A. Gemelli (Gemelli Polyclinic), Largo Agostino Gemelli 8 (phone: 06-3383730). Full service.

Venice: Ospedali Civili Riuniti di Venezia (Civil Hospital), Campo S.S. Giovanni e Paolo (phone: 041-705622). Full service, including hemodialysis.

Italy has a number of good private hospitals. They are called *case di cura* ("houses of care" or "cure"), villas, or clinics — to distinguish them from public hospitals. The best of these reputedly is *Salvatore Mundi International Hospital,* Viale Mura Gianicolensi 67, Rome (phone: 06-586041). US military hospitals on bases in Livorno, Vicenza, and Naples will treat seriously injured or ill travelers until their conditions are stabilized and then transfer them to other hospitals.

We do not recommend that you have extensive dental work done in Italy. Have a checkup some weeks before your trip to allow time for any necessary work to be done before you go. If you have a dental emergency while in Italy, call the American consulate for the names of competent dentists. Have only the most necessary and minimal repairs done until you can get to your own dentist.

Italian drugstores, *farmacie,* sell drugs only. Toiletries and cosmetics are sold in *profumerie* (perfume shops) or in stores such as the Standa and Upim chains. Pharmacies are identified by a red cross or a caduceus out front, and there is one open 24 hours a day in every city. Night duty rotates; each *farmacia* has a schedule posted on its door or front window, or you can find listings in your hotel lobby or in the local newspapers. After regular hours, you must ring the night bell. Italian pharmacists, identified by a gold badge on the lapel, will prescribe remedies for minor complaints, and some are not averse to filling a foreign prescription. Nevertheless, to make most effective use of the *farmacia,* it's a good idea to ask your doctor for the generic names of any drugs you use so that you can ask for their equivalents should you need a refill. Americans will also notice that some drugs sold only by prescription in the US are sold over the counter in Italy. Though this can be very handy, be aware that common cold drugs and aspirin that contain codeine or other controlled substances will not be allowed back into the US.

Water is clean and potable in major cities throughout Italy. Still, travelers may want to drink bottled water, at least at the beginning of the trip. This is not because there is something wrong with the water but because any unfamiliar microbes to which the digestive tract has not had time to become accustomed may cause mild stomach or intestinal upsets. Milk is pasteurized in major cities, and milk products (cheese, yogurt, ice cream, and so on) are safe to eat, as are fresh produce, meat, poultry, and fish.

Because of Mediterranean pollution, however, fish and shellfish should be eaten only after being cooked. Raw is a real risk.

For a thorough description of the medical services in seven of Italy's larger cities, see *Traveling Healthy,* by Sheilah M. Hillman and Robert S. Hillman, MD. Unfortunately out of print, it may be found in a library.

LEGAL AID ABROAD: It is often far more alarming to be arrested abroad than at home for an infringement of the law. Not only are you alone among strangers, but the punishment can be harsher. Granted, the US consulate can advise you of your rights and provide a list of lawyers, but it cannot interfere with local due process. The best advice is to be honest and law-abiding. If you get a traffic ticket, pay it. If you are approached by drug hawkers, ignore them. The penalties for possession of hashish, marijuana, cocaine, and other narcotics are generally more severe than in the US.

CONSULAR SERVICES: There is one crucial place to keep in mind when you are outside the US, namely the US consulate. If you are injured or become seriously ill, the consulate will direct you to medical assistance and notify your relatives. If, while abroad, you become involved in a dispute that could lead to legal action, the consulate, again, is the place to turn. And in case of natural disasters or civil unrest, consulates around the world handle the evacuation of US citizens if such a procedure is necessary. Keep in mind, though, that nowhere does the consulate act as an arbitrator or ombudsman on an American citizen's behalf. The consul has no power, authorized or otherwise, to subvert, alter, or contravene the legal processes, however unfair, of the country in which he or she serves. Nor can a consul oil the machinery of a foreign bureaucracy or provide legal advice. The consul's responsibilities do include providing a list of lawyers and information on local sources of legal aid, assigning an interpreter if the police have none, informing relatives in the US, and organizing and administering any defense monies sent from home. If a case is tried unfairly or the punishment seems unusually severe, the consul can make a formal complaint to the authorities. In a case of what is called "legitimate and proven poverty" — of an American stranded abroad without funds — the consul will contact sources of money such as family or friends in the US, apply for aid to agencies in foreign countries, and, as a last resort, arrange for repatriation at government expense.

Do not expect the consulate to help you with trivial difficulties such as canceled reservations or lost baggage. The consulate is primarily concerned with the day-to-day administration of services such as issuing passports and visas; providing notarial services; distributing VA, social security, and civil service benefits to resident Americans; depositions; extradition cases; and reporting to Washington any births, deaths, and marriages of US citizens in its territory. In Rome, the consulate is at Via Vittorio Veneto 121 (phone: 06-46741), next to the US Embassy. The seven other US consulates in Italy are in Florence, Genoa, Milan, Naples, Palermo, Trieste, and Turin (for addresses, see *Sources and Resources* in respective chapters in THE CITIES).

On the Road

Credit and Currency

It may seem hard to believe, but one of the greatest (and least understood) costs of travel is money itself. If that sounds simplistic, consider that you can lose as much as 30% of your dollars' value simply by changing money at the wrong place, at the wrong time, or in the wrong form. So your one objective in relation to the care and retention of your travel funds is to make them stretch as far as possible. And when you do spend money, it should be on things that expand and enhance your travel experience, not on unnecessaries. This requires more than merely ferreting out the best air fare or the most charming budget hotel. It means being canny about the management of money itself. We offer a primer on making travel funds go as far as possible.

TRAVELER'S CHECKS: Most people understand the necessity of protecting travel funds from loss or theft by carrying them in the form of replaceable or refundable traveler's checks rather than in cash. An equally good reason is that traveler's checks invariably get a better rate of exchange than cash does — usually by at least 1%. The reasons for this are rather technical, but it is a fact of travel life that you should not ignore.

That 1% won't do you much good, however, if you have already spent it buying your traveler's checks. Several of the major traveler's check companies charge 1% for the privilege of using their checks; others don't — but the *selling* institution (i.e., the particular bank at which you purchase them) may itself charge a fee. Thomas Cook checks issued in US currency are free if you make your travel arrangements through their travel agency, for example; and if you purchase traveler's checks at a bank in which you maintain significant accounts (especially commercial accounts of some size), you might also find that the bank will absorb the 1% fee as a courtesy to an important customer.

The traveler's checks listed below are readily recognized and convertible in Italy. However, don't assume that restaurants, smaller shops, or other establishments in small towns are going to be able to change checks of large denominations. And don't expect to exchange them for US currency except at banks and international airports.

We cannot overemphasize the importance of knowing how to replace lost or stolen checks. All of the traveler's check companies have agents around the world, both in their own name and at associated agencies (usually, but not necessarily, banks), where refunds can be obtained during business hours. Most of them also have 24-hour toll-free telephone lines, and some will even provide emergency funds to tide you over on a Sunday or holiday. Be sure to make a photocopy of the refund instructions that are given to you by the issuing institution at the time of purchase. Keep the original in your wallet, but keep the copy with other "emergency information," stashed in the bottom of your luggage. This emergency packet should include an accurate list of the serial numbers of your traveler's checks, the purchase receipt, your passport number and date of issue, the numbers of any credit cards you are carrying, and any other bits of information you can't bear to be without. The serial numbers and purchase receipt will certainly facilitate refund arrangements if the checks are lost or stolen. Here is a list of the major companies issuing traveler's checks and the number to call for refunds.

American Express: To report lost or stolen checks in the continental US, 800-221-7282; from Italy, 801-968-8300, collect. In Italy, for fastest service, call any of the 15 American Express travel service offices (check local listings).

BankAmerica: To report lost or stolen checks in the continental US except California, 800-227-3460; elsewhere worldwide, 415-624-5400, collect.

Citicorp: To report lost or stolen checks anywhere in the US, 800-645-6556; from Italy, 813-623-1709, collect. Also from Italy, you can call this London number collect: 438-1414.

Thomas Cook MasterCard: To report lost or stolen checks in the US and from Italy, 212-974-5696, collect. In Italy, you can call the nearest branch of Thomas Cook (check local listings) or this London number collect: 733-502995.

MasterCard: To report lost or stolen checks in the continental US except New York State, 800-223-9920; in New York State and from Italy, 212-974-5696, collect.

Visa: To report lost or stolen checks in the continental US except California, 800-227-6811; in California, 800-632-0520; from Italy, 415-574-7111, collect. Also from Italy, you can also call this London number collect: 937-8091.

TIP PACKS: It's not a bad idea to buy a *small* amount of Italian coins and bank notes before your departure. But note the emphasis on small: Exchange rates for these "tip packs" are uniformly terrible. Their advantages are threefold: You become familiar with the currency (really the only way to guard against being cheated during your first few hours in a new country); you are guaranteed some money should you arrive when a bank or exchange counter isn't open or available; and you don't have to depend on hotel desks, porters, or taxi drivers to change your money. A "tip pack" is the only Italian currency you should buy before you leave. Although foreign currency traveler's checks are available from American Express, Thomas Cook, and Deak-Perera (41 E 42nd St., New York, NY 10017; phone: 212-883-0400), the exchange rates are usually worse than you will get in banks abroad, and it is generally better to carry the bulk of your travel funds in US dollar traveler's checks.

CREDIT CARDS: There are two different kinds of credit cards available to consumers in the US, and travelers must decide which kind best serves their interests. Travel and entertainment cards — American Express, Diners Club, and Carte Blanche are the most widely accepted — cost the cardholder a basic membership fee but put no limit on the amount that may be charged to the card in any month. However, the entire balance must be paid in full at the end of each billing period, so the cardholder is not actually extended any meaningful credit — although deferred payment plans can usually be arranged for some types of purchases.

Bank cards, too, are rarely issued free these days, and certain services they provide (check cashing, for example) can cost extra. But they are real credit cards in the sense that the cardholder has the privilege of paying a minimum amount of the total balance in each billing period. For the privilege, a high annual interest rate (typically, three to four times the going passbook savings rate) is charged on the balance owed. Many banks now charge interest from the purchase date, not from the first billing date as they used to do; consider this when you are calculating the actual cost of a purchase. In addition, a maximum is set on the amount the cardholder can charge, which represents the limit of credit the card company is willing to extend. Major bank cards are Visa and MasterCard.

One of the thorniest problems of using credit cards abroad has to do with the rate of exchange at which the purchase is charged. The exchange rate in effect on the date that you make a foreign purchase has nothing at all to do with the rate of exchange at which your purchase is billed to you when you get the invoice months later in the US. The amount American Express charges is ultimately a function of the exchange rate in effect on the day your charge is received at an American Express service center, and there is a one-year limit on the time a shop can take to forward its charge slips. The rate Visa uses to process an item is a function of the rate the shop's bank used to process it. Thus, although up to 60 days may pass between the date of your purchase and the date Visa converts it, the conversion rate usually varies little from the one prevailing about two weeks after your purchase, assuming the foreign merchant makes deposits weekly and that the merchant's bank processes them in three to five days.

The principle at work in this credit card–exchange rate roulette is simple but very hard to predict. You make a purchase at a particular dollar versus local currency exchange rate. If the dollar gets stronger in the time between purchase and billing, your purchase actually costs you less than you anticipated. If the dollar drops in value during the interim, you pay more than you thought you would. There isn't much you can do about these vagaries except to follow one very broad, clumsy rule of thumb: If the dollar is doing well at the time of purchase, its value increasing against the local currency, use your credit card on the assumption that it will still be doing well when billing takes place. If the dollar is doing badly, assume it will continue to do badly and pay with traveler's checks. If you get stuck, your only recourse is to complain. Cardholders have been pleasantly surprised at the willingness of credit card companies to adjust rates of exchange when justifiable complaints are made very emphatically. Be aware, too, that the credit card issuers regularly charge an unitemized, unannounced 1% for the process of changing foreign currency purchases into US currency billings.

In any case, all types of credit cards are handy additional ways to avoid carrying a lot of cash. However, not all the establishments that you encounter in Italy will honor *all* the major cards. You'll find it helpful to take several different credit cards with you. Following is a list of credit cards that are widely used in Italy, with some of their key features of greatest significance to travelers and a telephone number for further information.

American Express: Emergency personal check cashing at American Express or representatives' offices (up to $200 cash in local currency, $800 in traveler's checks). Emergency personal check cashing for guests at participating hotels and motels (up to $250 in the US and Canada, $100 elsewhere) and, for holders of airline tickets (valid within 48 hours), at participating airlines in the US (up to $50). Extended payment plan for cruises, tours, plane, and Amtrak tickets. $100,000 free travel accident insurance on plane, train, bus, and ship if ticket was charged to card; up to $1 million additional low-cost flight insurance available. Contact *American Express Card,* PO Box 39, Church St. Station, New York, NY 10008 (phone: 800-528-4800).

Carte Blanche: Emergency personal check cashing at participating Hilton hotels in the US (up to $1,000) and for guests at other participating hotels and motels (up to $250 per stay). Extended payment plan for airline tickets. $650,000 free travel accident insurance on plane, train, and ship if ticket was charged to card. Contact *Carte Blanche,* PO Box 5824, Denver, CO 80217 (phone: 800-525-9135).

Diners Club: Emergency personal check cashing at participating Citibank branches worldwide (up to $1,000, with a minimum per check of $50 in the US and $250 overseas); emergency personal check cashing for guests at participating hotels and motels (up to $250 per stay). Extended payment plan for all charges can be arranged. $650,000 free travel accident insurance on plane, train, and ship if ticket was charged to card. Contact *Diners Club,* PO Box 5824, Denver, CO 80217 (phone: 800-525-9135).

MasterCard: Cash advance at participating banks worldwide. Interest charge on unpaid balance and other details are set by issuing bank. Check with your bank for information.

Visa: Cash advance at participating banks worldwide. Interest charge on unpaid balance and other details are set by issuing bank. Check with your bank for information.

SENDING MONEY ABROAD: If you have used up your traveler's checks, cashed as many emergency personal checks as your credit card allows, drawn on your cash advance line to the fullest extent, and still need money, you can have it sent abroad via the *Western Union Telegraph Company.* A friend or relative can go, cash in hand, to any of Western Union's 9,000 offices in the US, where, for a *minimum* charge of $29.95 (it rises with the amount of the transaction), the funds will be transferred to one of Western Union's many correspondent banks in major Italian cities. When the money arrives in Italy, the funds will be turned over to you in local currency based on the rate of exchange in effect on the day of receipt. The US party to this transaction may also use his or her MasterCard or Visa card to send up to $1,000 by phone by dialing Western Union's toll-free number (800-435-7556) anywhere in the US. Allow two to four days for delivery (faster than the conventional form of international bank transfer, a method usually so cumbersome and time-consuming that it is of little use to the average traveler).

If you are literally down to your last few lire, the nearest US consulate (see *Medical and Legal Aid and Consulate Services*) will let you call home collect to set these remedies in motion.

FOREIGN EXCHANGE: There is no limit to the amount of US currency that you can bring into Italy. However, you cannot take out more than you brought in since the country's objective is to prevent an excess of Italian currency from leaving Italy — something that could conceivably happen if unlimited amounts were convertible into dollars by departing tourists. There is likewise no restriction on the amount of traveler's checks (in dollars or lire) that you can bring into Italy, and these usually present no difficulties when you leave the country since their US origin is obvious. To avoid problems anywhere along the line, it's advisable to fill out the V-2 customs form that will be provided on board your flight to Italy, on which you can declare all money you are bringing into the country — cash, traveler's checks, and so on. Although travelers to Italy are seldom actually questioned by officials with regard to currency going into or out of the country, the sensible course is to observe all the regulations just to be on the safe side. You might also note that US law requires that anyone taking more than $10,000 into or out of the US must report this fact on customs form 4790, which is available at all international airports. You must do this *before* leaving the country, and you should include this information on your customs declaration when you return.

Rule number one: Exchange your money *only* at banks, where your dollars always buy the greatest amount of foreign currency. (Save your exchange receipts. When you reconvert lire to dollars at the end of your trip, you will need at least one receipt to show that you exchanged at least the amount of money you are trying to reconvert. But it is better to save them all.) Unless someone holds a gun to your head, never (repeat: *never*) exchange dollars for foreign currency at hotels, restaurants, or retail shops, where you are sure to lose a significant amount of your dollar's buying power. Also, do not buy money on the black market. While the exchange rate is invariably better, it is a common practice to pass off counterfeit bills to unsuspecting foreigners who aren't familiar with the currency. It's usually a sucker's game, and you are almost always the sucker; it also can land you in jail.

Rule number two: Learn the local currency quickly and keep aware of daily fluctuations in the exchange rate. These are listed in the English-language *International Herald*

Tribune daily for the preceding day as well as in every major newspaper in Europe. They are also usually displayed in banks and international airports. Rates change to some degree every day. For rough calculations it is quick and safe to use round figures, but for purchases and actual currency exchanges, you should carry a small pocket calculator so you can use the exact rate.

Rule number three: Estimate your needs carefully; if you exchange too much money, you lose twice — buying and selling back. Every time you exchange money, someone is making a profit, and rest assured it isn't you. Although you are allowed to leave Italy with up to 400,000 lire (nearly $300), that's rather a lot of money to keep tied up as a souvenir (and will cost rather a lot to convert to dollars when you get home). Use up foreign notes before leaving, saving just enough for last-minute incidentals and tips.

CURRENCY: The basic unit of Italian currency is the *lira*. Because the value of the single *lira* is so low — about 1,500 to the dollar — that it is practically nonnegotiable, up to now there has been no one-lira denomination. (It is common in Italy to pay 500 lire for a cup of coffee and tens of thousands for a single meal.) However, as this volume goes to press, the Bank of Italy has announced plans for a new lira worth a thousand times more than the old. This means prices in Italy will soon appear with three fewer zeros on the tag. When activated by Parliament (government ministers continue to "examine the technicalities" of the plan), the new currency will include one-lira coins and bills (equal to 1,000 current lire). During a six-month transition period, both old and new currencies will circulate; then the new currency will be in use exclusively. At this writing, lire are still distributed in coin denominations of 50, 100, 200, and 500 and in bill denominations of 500, 1,000, 2,000, 5,000, 10,000, 50,000, and 100,000.

Accommodations and Reservations

 Whether you stay in an elegant, centuries-old *palazzo,* a modern, functional high-rise, or a modest, inexpensive hostelry carved out of someone's city flat or reconverted country villa, you can be comfortable and well cared for on almost any budget in Italy. There are, admittedly, plenty of deluxe establishments providing expensive services to people with money to burn, but more affordable alternatives have always been available, particularly outside the main tourist centers. It's true that inflation continues unabated in Italy and that the dollar is not quite as strong abroad as it has been in very recent years. Still, if you're shopping for the best, you'll find the price tags of top-of-the-line accommodations no more extravagant than they are in the United States, and if you're watching your budget, you may be pleased to find a larger selection and a greater variety of accommodations within your range than is the case at home. And at the lower end of the price scale, you will not always have to forgo charm. While a fair number of inexpensive establishments are simply no-frills, "generic" places to spend the night, even the sparest room may have the cachet of having once been slept in by a monk or a nun. And some of the most delightful places to stay are the smaller, less expensive, often family-run *pensioni,* a type of accommodation peculiar to Italy and no longer what it once was, but still in existence.

Our accommodations choices are included in the *Best in Town* sections of CITIES and in the *Checking In* sections of each tour route in DIRECTIONS. They have been selected for a variety of traveling budgets, but the lists are not comprehensive; with some diligent searching, before you leave and en route, you will turn up an equal number of "special places" that are uniquely yours.

HOTELS AND PENSIONI: Not too long ago, Italian hotels (*alberghi*) were officially classified according to their quality of service and level of amenities as deluxe, first class, second class, third class, and fourth class. Now they are classified in terms of stars, with five stars or five stars plus "L" corresponding to the former deluxe, the highest rating; four stars corresponding to first class; three stars to second class; two stars to third class; and one star to fourth class. Hotels are placed in categories by the provincial or local tourist boards and are then assigned a range of rates they may charge for different types of rooms (single or double, with or without bath or a view). By law, they are not permitted to charge more than the maximum in their category, and if you are in doubt, a rate card should be available at the reception desk. The maximum rate that may be charged for a particular room is also posted inside the room, usually on the back of the door.

Italy's *pensioni* used to be somewhat like our boardinghouses. Not as large as hotels, with fewer services and a homier atmosphere, they tended to cater to those staying awhile and usually required guests to take one or both of their main meals in the house. Sophisticated travelers prized them because they often offered a good deal more character and intimacy than a hotel in a comparable price range. They, too, were classified, with a first-class *pensione* the equivalent of a second-class hotel, a second-class *pensione* the equivalent of a third-class hotel, and a third-class *pensione* the equivalent of a fourth-class hotel. For some time, however, *pensioni* have been changing. Most no longer discourage one-night stays, many have dispensed with meal requirements, and some have eliminated meal service entirely, turning the dining room into a breakfast room. In fact, there is no longer an official distinction between hotels and *pensioni*, and most accommodations brochures no longer list them separately. You'll still find them among the three-star, two-star, and one-star listings in newer hotel brochures using the star system, but unless an establishment has retained the word in its name, there is no way to tell that it was once a *pensione*.

The simplest hotels in Italy are the *locande*. Roughly translated as "inns," these are modest lodgings indeed, and whether brochures use the star system or class system to list establishments, they will be among the least expensive entries. Quite often, they are found in small towns and rural areas, and it is not uncommon for them actually to be restaurants with no more than a few rooms to rent.

The maximum rates posted in Italian hotel rooms include service charges and value added tax (VAT — 18% in five-star hotels, 9% in others), so receiving the bill at the end of a stay is rarely a cause for shock. If the locality imposes a visitors tax (a minimal amount, called the *imposta di soggiorno*), that, too, is usually included in the posted price. No surcharge may be made for central heating, but a surcharge (often per person) for air conditioning is allowed. The price of breakfast is usually quoted and itemized separately from the room price. Note that breakfast is almost always a Continental one of coffee or tea, bread or rolls, butter, and jam, and, particularly in the more modest establishments, there is an increasing tendency for these items to be cellophane- or foil-wrapped — you may save money and enjoy breakfast more by taking it at the nearest bar.

Many localities have official high- and low-season rates and thus post two sets of prices per room. This is especially true of resort areas, where, at the height of the season, it may be difficult to get a room in either a hotel or a *pensione* unless you stay a certain number of nights and agree to take some meals, on a half-board (*mezza pensione,* that is, breakfast and one other meal per day) or full-board (*pensione completa*) basis. (Speaking of resort hotels, if you are staying at one with a private beach, be sure to clarify at the outset whether there is an extra charge for use of the beach facilities — don't assume that it's all free.) A single room is a *camera singola;* a double room is a *camera doppia.* If you request a single and are given a double, it may not cost more than the maximum price for a single room. If you specify a double, you may be asked whether you prefer a *camera a due letti* (twin-bedded room) or a *camera matrimoniale* (with a double bed). A single room to which an extra bed has been added may not cost more than a double room, and a double room to which an extra bed has been added may not increase in price by more than 35%. If you are traveling on a shoestring, you will be interested to know that a great many rooms that do not have a private bath or shower (*bagno privato* or *doccia privata*) do have a sink with hot and cold running water (occasionally cold water only) and often a bidet. Sometimes there is even a toilet. Thus you can save money by denying yourself the luxury of a private bathroom and still not be totally without convenience.

In the US, the *Italian Government Travel Office* (*ENIT*) distributes a list of hotels in Italy's main cities, giving the class of each, its address, and a few other details (such as the existence of a restaurant, air conditioning, parking facilities, and so on), but no telephone numbers. One-star, or fourth-class, hotels are not listed, and price ranges for individual hotels are not given, but a general range of prices for each of the four hotel categories is included. In addition, ENIT distributes hotel guides published by Italy's regional, provincial, and local tourist boards that list hotels in all categories. In most cases, the listing for each hotel includes its address and telephone number, category, number of rooms, amenities, and minimum and maximum prices, and though the latter are unavoidably out of date by the time of publication, they include service tax and value added tax and can be considered indicative. (For addresses of ENIT offices in major US cities, see *Tourist Information.*)

OTHER ACCOMMODATIONS: More than a few travelers to Italy elect to stay in convents, monasteries, seminaries, and other religious institutions that provide room and board to paying guests. You need not be a pilgrim to take advantage of this economical solution to the problem of where to stay abroad; in fact, a number of such institutions are officially rated in the Italian hotel system, generally as one-star or fourth-class hotels, formerly *pensioni.* Staying in a religious institution is not exactly like staying in a hotel, however. Some are for men only and some for women only, although most accept couples. A great many also observe a curfew, doors closing promptly at 10 or 11 PM. The Italian Government Travel Office can supply a list of institutions offering accommodations in some cities, but if nothing is available for the cities you want to visit, write directly to the archdiocese of each city or town in question. (Address the envelope simply to the Arcidiocesi di Milano, Milan, Italy, for example.)

For a discussion of camping and information about staying in youth hostels, see *Camping and Caravanning, Biking, and Hiking.*

APARTMENT AND VILLA RENTAL: An alternative to hotels for the visitor content to stay in one spot for a week or more is to rent a house or an apartment. A vacation in a furnished rental has both the advantages and disadvantages of living "at home" abroad. It can certainly be less expensive than staying in a top hotel for the same period of time, although very luxurious and expensive rentals are available, too. It has the comforts of home, including a kitchen, which means saving on food. Furthermore, it gives a sense of the country that a large hotel often cannot. On the other hand, a certain amount of housework is involved because if you don't eat out, you have to cook, and though some rentals, especially the luxury ones, come with maid service, most don't.

Most provincial and local tourist boards in Italy have information on companies arranging rentals in their areas. In addition, there are agencies in the US that arrange rentals in Europe. They handle bookings and confirmation paperwork, generally for a fee included in the rental price. Those listed below have many properties in Italy, but to have your pick you should begin to make arrangements for a summer rental at least six months in advance.

At Home Abroad: The choice ranges from apartments to villas and exceptionally stately homes, especially at the sea and in the countryside, in the Veneto region, Tuscany, Umbria, and Sardinia, as well as along the Amalfi Coast and on Capri. The minimum rental period is usually two weeks or a month. Photographs of properties can be requested by mail for a $50 registration fee. 405 E 56th St., Apt. 6H, New York, NY 10022 (phone: 212-421-9165).

RAVE (Rent a Vacation Everywhere): Rentals include apartments in Rome and Florence plus a few in Milan; villas on the Italian Riviera and around Lake Como; and properties in Tuscany ranging from rustic farmhouses and converted barns to the luxurious estates of the landed gentry. Minimum rental period is usually two weeks. 500 Triangle Bldg., Rochester, NY 14604 (phone: 716-454-6440).

Vacanze in Italia: This organization specializes in apartments and houses in the Tuscan countryside, especially in the Chianti Classico area near Siena, but it also has a few properties in Umbria and Puglia and some small apartments in Rome and Florence. Minimum rental period is one week, but two weeks in summer is preferred. 153 W 13th St., New York, NY 10011 (phone: 212-242-2145).

Villas International: Apartments in cities (Rome, Florence, a few in Venice) are a specialty. Elsewhere there are apartments, villas, and chalets in the northern lake district, villas on the Amalfi Coast, and anything from a cottage to a restored farmhouse or a modern villa in Tuscany and Umbria. An illustrated catalogue of properties in the latter two regions costs $5; otherwise, photos of properties that may suit your needs are sent at no charge. Minimum rental period is usually a week, sometimes two weeks in summer. 71 W 23rd St., New York, NY 10010 (phone: 212-929-7585 in New York State; 800-221-2260 elsewhere).

AGRITURISM: Many of the properties for rent through the organizations in the preceding list are converted barns, farmhouses, and other rustic buildings in the countryside. But if the idea of staying in the country, especially the idea of spending time on a working farm, appeals to you, you should know something about *Agriturist.* Founded in 1965, this organization promotes country vacations as a means to several worthy ends, among them bridging the cultural gap between the city and the country, familiarizing urban dwellers with the production of typical local foods and handicrafts, safeguarding the landscape by finding new uses for abandoned rural buildings, and providing farmers in marginal hill and mountain areas with alternative sources of income. The organization is made up of farm families throughout Italy who have some sort of accommodations to let, and although there are many variations, the possibilities are basically three. You rent a furnished room, frequently without private bath, in the family's own living quarters or in an independent structure, on a half- or full-board basis; you rent a furnished apartment, house, or other lodging complete with kitchen and bath; or you camp, on a fully equipped campsite or with acccess to essential services only. Depending on the situation, you may be alone with your hosts or there may be several parties occupying rooms and apartments on the same premises; you may be right on a farm or isolated some distance from it. There is a variety of choice: You can rent an apartment in the mountains of the Valle d'Aosta; stay with a family that grows olives, grapes, and grain in Umbria; or opt to be within striking distance of the sea on land belonging to a fruit farmer in Sicily. Opportunities for swimming, fishing, horseback riding, and other outdoor activities abound.

Prices can be quite moderate, anywhere from $5 to $20 per person per day for the lodging alone, with an additional $10 to $25 and up for full board. (Agriturist rates the accommodations as basic, comfortable, or superior but makes no guarantee that the price charged at any particular place corresponds to its rating.) The major drawback to arranging an Agriturist vacation is the lack of information in English. The *Guida dell'Ospitalità Rurale (Guide to Rural Hospitality)*, a guide to members in all regions, with descriptions of facilities offered by each and an indication of any languages besides Italian spoken, is largely in Italian. It contains approximately 1,700 farm listings, of which about 400 are set off (by asterisks) as being particularly suitable for foreign guests. The guide can be consulted at ENIT offices; otherwise, write to *Agriturist,* Corso

Vittorio Emanuele 101, 00186 Rome, Italy, enclosing an International Money Order for the equivalent of 20,000 lire, which entitles you to a year's membership and a copy of the latest edition of the guide. After that, arrangements are made directly with the proprietors of the properties listed, and in most cases a knowledge of Italian helps.

HOME EXCHANGES: Still another alternative for travelers content to stay in one place while on vacation is a home exchange: The Smith family from Chicago moves into the home of the Rossi family in Milan, while the Rossis enjoy a stay in the Smiths' home. It is an exceptionally inexpensive way to ensure comfortable, reasonable living quarters with amenities that no hotel could possibly offer. Often the trade includes a car; almost always it means living in a new community in a manner the average hotel guest never experiences. Several companies publish directories of individuals and families willing to trade homes with others for a specified period of time. In some cases, you must be willing to list your home in the directory; in others, you can subscribe without appearing in it. Arrangements for the actual exchange take place directly between you and the homeowner. There is no guarantee that you will find a listing in the area in which you are interested, but each of the directories below has Italian homes among many other foreign and domestic listings. Most are for straight exchanges only, but each of the directories also has a certain number of listings placed by people interested in other arrangements such as either exchanging or renting (for instance, if they own a second home); an exchange of hospitality while owners are in residence; or a youth exchange, i.e., an offer to put up your teenager as a guest in return for your putting up their teenager at another time. A few house-sitting opportunities also arise.

> *Holiday Exchanges:* A six-month subscription costs $25, which pays for a listing, 6 back issues, and 6 new ones as they come out; a year's subscription ($32) includes the back issues plus 12 new ones and allows your listing to appear twice. PO Box 5294, Ventura, CA 93003 (phone: 805-642-4879).
>
> *International Home Exchange Service/Intervac US:* The $45 fee includes copies of the three directories published yearly and a listing in one of them (subscribing to the directories without listing your house costs $60). PO Box 3975, San Francisco, CA 94119 (phone: 415-382-0300).
>
> *Vacation Exchange Club:* About 6,000 listings, including several hundred in Italy. A subscription costs $24.70 a year, for which the subscriber receives two directories (a late winter edition and a follow-up edition in early spring) plus a listing in one of them. The directories without the subscriber's own listing cost $16. 12006 111th Ave., Suite 12, Youngtown, AZ 85363 (phone: 602-972-2186).

A fourth organization, *Home Exchange International,* with offices in New York, Los Angeles, London, Paris, and Milan, functions differently in that it publishes no directory and shepherds the exchange process most of the way. Interested parties supply HEI with photographs of themselves and their homes, information on the type of home they want and where, and a registration fee of $40. The company then works with its other offices to propose a few possibilities, and only when a match is made do the parties exchange names, addresses, and phone numbers. For this service, HEI charges a closing fee, which ranges from $150 to $450 for domestic or international switches from two weeks to three months long and from $275 to $525 for switches longer than three months. Contact *Home Exchange International,* 185 Park Row, Suite 14D, New York, NY 10038 (phone: 212-349-5340), or 22458 Ventura Blvd., Woodland Hills, CA 91364 (phone: 818-992-8990).

HOME STAYS: In the absence of any formal "meet the Italians" program arranging for visitors to stay in private homes as guests of Italian families, you may be interested in the *United States Servas Committee,* which maintains a list of hosts throughout the world willing to throw open their doors to foreigners entirely free of charge. The aim of this nonprofit cultural program is to promote international peace and understanding, and every effort is made to discourage freeloaders. Servas will send you an application form and the name of the nearest of about 150 interviewers around the US for you to contact. After the interview, if you're approved, you'll receive documentation certifying you as a Servas traveler. There is a membership fee of $30 for an individual and also a deposit of $15 to receive the host list, refunded on return of the list. The list gives the name, address, age, occupation, and other particulars of the hosts, including languages spoken. From then on, it is up to you to write to them directly, and Servas makes no guarantee that you will be accommodated. If you are, you'll normally stay two nights. Servas stresses that you should choose only people you really want to meet and that for this brief period you should be interested mainly in your hosts, not in sightseeing. It also suggests that one way to show your appreciation once you've returned home is to become a host yourself. The minimum age of a Servas traveler is 18 (however, children under 18 may accompany their parents), and though quite a few are young people who've just finished college, there are travelers (and hosts) in all age ranges and occupations. At present, there are almost 400 listings in Italy. Contact *Servas,* 11 John St., Room 706, New York, NY 10038 (phone: 212-267-0252).

RESERVATIONS: From Easter through fall, the high season for Italian tourism, advance hotel reservations are a must in major tourist destinations such as Rome, Florence, and Venice, and if you want to be sure of finding space in the hotel of your choice in these cities, advance reservations are recommended year-round. A few months before arrival is not too soon to make the booking. During the peak summer travel season, the advice to book ahead extends to provincial cities and popular tourist sites throughout the country. If you plan to spend any time at a beach, lake, or mountain resort, the advice becomes particularly compelling during July and August, when the Italians themselves take to the roads, packing vacation spots and coastlines from border to border, islands included. Advance reservations are also advisable for ski resorts in December, January, and February.

To the extent that you are able to settle on a precise itinerary beforehand, it is best to reserve as many as possible of your accommodations before you go. The simplest way is to leave it all to a travel agent, who will provide this service free if the hotels you or the agent chooses pay commissions. The larger and more expensive ones invariably do, and more and more budget hotels are beginning to follow suit. If the one you pick doesn't, the travel agent may charge a fee to cover costs or you may have to make the reservation yourself.

Reserving rooms yourself is not difficult if you intend to stay mainly in hotels that are members of chains or voluntary hotel associations, whether Italian ones with US representatives or American ones with hotels overseas. Hilton International, Holiday Inn, and Sheraton are some of the well-known non-Italian names with Italian properties. Among the best-known Italian chains, both with US offices to provide information and handle reservations, are *CIGA Hotels,* 745 5th Ave., New York, NY 10151 (phone: 212-935-9540 or 800-221-2340), a group of two dozen luxury hotels (mainly five-star); and *Jolly Hotels,* 501 5th Ave., New York, NY 10017 (phone: 212-557-5116 or 800-221-2626), which has 30 hotels largely in the four-star category. Both offices can supply brochures on the individual hotels or a booklet listing all of them. The approximately 40 *MotelAgip* motels that make up Italy's largest motel chain are also represented in the US. A booklet giving the highway location, phone number, and a description of facilities at each is available from *Affordable Hotels,* 19 W 34th St., Suite 700, New York, NY 10001 (phone: 212-714-2323).

International voluntary hotel groups represented in Italy include the very prestigious Relais et Châteaux, an association of independently owned luxury establishments native to France but with members in other countries. Many Relais et Châteaux hotels are converted castles and one-time patrician villas; while there are some city properties, most are in quiet surroundings in the countryside, frequently graced with parks and gardens, and they all have good restaurants. An illustrated catalogue of all the properties, including the 25 in Italy, comes out yearly and is available for $10 from travel bookshops or the association's North American representative, *David Mitchell and Company*, 200 Madison Ave., New York, NY 10016 (phone: 212-696-1323). More than 50 Italian hotels, also independently owned and mainly in the three-star and four-star categories, are linked to Best Western International. For an illustrated directory, write to *Best Western International*, Travel Guide Dept., PO Box 10203, Phoenix, AZ 85064, requesting the *Best Western International Atlas & Hotel Guide: Europe & Middle East*. For reservations, call 800-528-1234.

Still other hotels are represented individually by various US reservations services. The *Italian Government Travel Office* (see *Tourist Information*) can tell you who in the US represents a particular hotel, but if the answer ultimately is no one, you will have to make the reservation directly. If you choose to write rather than telephone, it's a good idea to leave plenty of time for the answer and to enclose at least two International Reply Coupons (sold at post offices) to facilitate a response. Give full details of your requirements and several alternative dates, if possible. You will probably be asked to send a deposit for one night's lodging, payable by foreign draft or sometimes by personal check; in return, be sure to get written confirmation of the reservation. In the case of most hotels, a letter written in English will present no problems. Be reasonably sure about your plans before paying the deposit, however, because Italian hotels observe stiff rules governing refunds in the event of cancellation. You will get your deposit back if you cancel at least 7 days in advance in the case of a city hotel and 14 days in advance (a month in high season) in the case of a resort hotel.

Some people prefer not to contain their wanderlust by making hotel reservations too far in advance. Although the advice still stands to reserve high-season hotel space in Rome, Florence, and Venice well beforehand and although the traveler must keep an eye on the special-events calendar to avoid arriving *anywhere* blissfully unaware that the place is already bursting at the seams — Siena at Palio time, Venice during Carnevale, and so forth — it is possible to travel in Italy reserving as you go. Naturally, the best method is to call ahead to hotels in the next town on your itinerary before checking out of the one you're in because it allows you to alter your course if you don't turn up any vacancies. (Hotels will usually hold rooms on the strength of a phone call provided you arrive no later than expected.) If even that amount of advance planning cramps your style, you do have further recourse. The provincial or local tourist board in each city or town assists travelers arriving without reservations, usually for no charge. In smaller towns, go directly to the tourist office; in larger cities where the tourist office may have more than one location, the branch that performs this service is generally the one in the train station. Go there as early in the day as possible; at the latest, be there when the office opens for the afternoon. You will probably have to stand in line, and there are no guarantees that you will find anything when your turn comes, but if you are traveling somewhat off the beaten track you should have few really close calls.

Time Zones and Business Hours

 TIME ZONES: The countries of Europe fall into three time zones. Greenwich Mean Time — measured from Greenwich, England, at longitude 0°0′ — is the base from which all other time zones are measured. Areas in zones west of Greenwich have earlier times and are called Greenwich Minus; those to the east have later times and are called Greenwich Plus. For example, New York City (Greenwich Minus 5) is 5 hours earlier than Greenwich, England; when it is noon in Greenwich, it is 7 AM in New York. Italy falls into the Greenwich Plus 1 time zone, so when it is noon in Rome, it is 6 AM in New York and Washington (5 AM in Chicago and Houston, 4 AM in Denver and Phoenix, and 3 AM on the West Coast).

Like most Western European nations, Italy moves its clocks ahead an hour in the spring and back an hour in the fall. However, the Italians make the change slightly earlier than we do in the US. Italy goes on Daylight Saving Time the last Sunday in March, whereas the US, beginning in 1987, does so the first Sunday in April. (Until recent legislation, the US traditionally went on Daylight Saving Time the last Sunday in April.) Italy goes off Daylight Saving Time the last Sunday in September, whereas the US changes its clocks the last Sunday in October (this cutoff date has not changed). Therefore, for a brief period in the spring and during October, there is a 7-hour time difference between the East Coast of the US and Italy (and a 10-hour time difference between the West Coast and Italy).

Italian and other European timetables use a 24-hour clock to denote arrival and departure times, which means that hours are expressed sequentially from 1 AM. For example, the departure of a train at 6 AM will be announced as "0600," whereas one leaving at 6 PM will be noted as "1800." A departure at midnight is "2400."

PUBLIC HOLIDAYS: Italy shuts down more thoroughly on public holidays than does the US. Banks and offices are closed tight, and so are shops — holidays are not considered occasions for clearance sales. Public buildings and museums are usually closed as well.

Italian public holidays are as follows: *New Year's Day, Epiphany* (January 6), *Easter Monday, Liberation Day* (April 25), *Labor Day* (May 1), *Ferragosto or the Assumption of the Virgin* (August 15), *All Saints' Day* (November 1), *Immaculate Conception* (December 8), *Christmas Day,* and *December 26.* Prior to 1977, several more days were considered holidays, but they were abolished in an effort to discourage Italians from constructing *ponti* (bridges) and taking off extra days when a holiday fell close to a weekend. One of the holidays suppressed, *Epiphany,* the day children receive gifts from a witchlike old woman, the *Befana,* has been reinstated recently by popular demand. And a new holiday, *Tricolor* or *National Independence Day,* is under consideration, possibly to be celebrated on the second Sunday in May.

The feast day of a city's patron saint is a local public holiday. Among these are the feast day of St. Mark, celebrated on April 25 in Venice; St. John the Baptist, June 24, Florence; Sts. Peter and Paul, June 29, Rome; St. Janarius (San Gennaro), September 19, Naples; and St. Ambrose, December 7, Milan.

San Marino celebrates most of the Italian public holidays (except Liberation Day), and it adds a few of its own, such as *Liberation Day* (February 5); *Anniversary of the Arengo* (March 25); *Investiture of the Captains Regent* (April 1 and October 1); *Fall of Fascism* (July 28); and *San Marino's Day* (September 3).

BUSINESS HOURS: Travelers who are used to the American workday may be surprised to find that the Italians, like many other Europeans, follow a more eccentric schedule. Banks are usually open Mondays through Fridays from 8:30 AM to 1:30 PM and from 2:45 to 3:45 PM; they are closed Saturdays, Sundays, holidays, and half-holidays. As a *general* rule, businesses (shops and offices) are open from 9 AM to 7 or 8 PM with a generous 3-hour siesta break starting at 12:30 or 1 PM. Among the exceptions to this rule are the many offices in the north of Italy that work straight through the day and close earlier in the evening; shops, too, may take a shorter lunch break and close earlier. In the south, however, including Rome, only bars, newsstands, and the most energetic entrepreneurs operate during the midday break. Another variation on the theme: Shops may be open all day Saturday or Saturday mornings only, depending on the kind of shop (retailer, dry cleaner, grocery, and so on), the season (summer, the rest of the year), and the city, and those that stay open on Saturday afternoons may then close on Monday mornings. The moral to this story is that if you're having some alterations done on a last-minute purchase and are planning to pick up the item on a Saturday afternoon or Monday morning just before taking a cab to the airport, make sure the store will be *open*. Almost all shops are closed on Sundays. Public buildings and museums have relatively short hours and are closed one day a week, usually Mondays. Restaurants have a *riposo settimanale* ("weekly repose"), which entitles them to be closed one day each week; the day varies from restaurant to restaurant. Hours in general tend to be a bit later in summer, and they vary from city to city; check local listings in *Special Places, Best in Town,* and *Eating Out* in CITIES and DIRECTIONS.

Mail, Telephone, and Electricity

 MAIL: The Italian Postal Service maintains about 14,000 post offices throughout Italy, including small outlets such as those in train stations and airports. Most are open until 2 PM Mondays through Fridays and until noon on Saturdays. In larger cities, counters at main post offices are open until 7:30 or 8 PM, although not necessarily for all services. In international airports, they are open 24 hours a day. Mail rates change frequently, following the upward trend of everything else; stamps are bought at the post office and at authorized tobacconists — ask for *francobolli.* Letters can be mailed in the red letter boxes found on the street, but it is better to mail them (and certainly packages) directly from post offices. Be advised that delivery from Italy can be slow (especially if you send something any distance by surface mail) and erratic (postcards, even air-mail ones, seem to be given no priority at all, so don't use them for important messages). Send mail *via aerea* if it's going any distance, and to ensure or further speed delivery of important letters, send them *raccomandata* (registered mail) or *espresso* (express or special delivery). Many travelers prefer not to use the Italian post office at all and hold their mail for international delivery until they leave Italy. Others, at least in Rome (and this includes travelers and natives alike), consider the Vatican post office, just to the side of St. Peter's, much more reliable. (If you're going to use the Vatican post office, don't buy *Italian* stamps — the Vatican has its own.) If you're mailing to an address within Italy, another way to ensure or speed delivery is to use the five-digit postal code, if you know it. It breaks the country down into regions, provinces, towns or cities, and even into districts within cities, and since many small towns in Italy have very similar names, proper delivery of a letter may depend on it. Put it on the envelope immediately before the name of the town or city and on the same line.

You can, if you are brave, have mail sent to you care of the post office in the city you are visiting. Have your correspondents print your last name in big block letters on the envelope (lest there be any doubt as to which is your last name). Tell them to include the full address of the post office, in case there is more than one in town, and the words *Fermo Posta* (General Delivery). Claim your mail in person, with your passport as identification; there may be a small service charge.

American Express offices will hold mail free for clients only (letters only — registered mail and packages are not accepted). You must be able to show an American Express card, traveler's checks, or a voucher proving you are on one of the company's tours to avoid paying for mail privileges. Those who aren't clients must pay a nominal fee each time they ask if they have received mail, whether they actually have a letter or not. There is also a forwarding fee, for clients and nonclients alike. Mail should be addressed to you, care of the American Express office of your choice. Addresses of American Express offices in Italy are listed in the "Services and Offices" pamphlet available from the nearest US branch of American Express.

US consulates in Italy (or anywhere else) do not accept mail for tourists. They will, however, help out in emergencies — if you need to receive important business documents or personal papers, for example. It is best to inform them either by separate letter or cable, or by phone if you are in the country already, that you will be using their address for this purpose.

TELEPHONE: It is easy enough to call Italy: Just dial the international access code (011), the country code for Italy (39), the city code (if you don't know this, ask the international operator), and the local number. For example, to place a call from anywhere in the US to Rome, dial 011+39+6 (city code for Rome)+local number.

To call the US from Italy, usually a more expensive proposition, dial the international access code for Italy (00), the country code for the US (1), the US area code, and the local number. For example, to place a call from anywhere in Italy to New York City, dial 00+1+212+local number. If you need an English-speaking operator to help you, dial 170 to make a call to the US (or dial 15 to reach an English-speaking operator for a call within Europe).

There are several ways to keep down the cost of telephoning from Italy. Leave a copy of your itinerary and telephone numbers in the US so that people can call you instead; or place a quick call home and have the US party call you back. Place your calls during reduced-rate periods — weekdays from 11 PM to 8 AM and all day Sunday. Avoid the shock of an expensive hotel surcharge (up to 500%) by asking the hotel management ahead of time what the policy is (only the Hilton hotels in Rome and Milan subscribe to AT&T's reduced-rate Teleplan); you might decide you would rather place your call from a public telephone.

Pay telephones in Italy can be found in cafés and restaurants (look for the sign outside — a yellow disk with the outline of a telephone or a receiver in black) and, less commonly, in booths on the street. (All too often, however, these are out of order — if you're lucky, a *guasto* sign will warn you.) There are two kinds of pay phones: The old-fashioned kind works with a *gettone* (token) only, which can be bought for 200 lire from the bar or restaurant cashier and at newsstands; newer phones function with either *gettoni* or 200 lire in coin. To use a *gettone,* place it in the slot at the top of the phone. When your party answers — and *not* before — push the button at the top of the phone, causing the token to drop (otherwise the answering party will not be able to hear you). If your party doesn't answer, hang up and simply lift the unused *gettone* out of the slot. In newer phones using either *gettoni* or coins, the coins or *gettoni* drop automatically when you put them in, as in US phones; if your party doesn't answer, you have to press the return button (sometimes repeatedly) to get them back.

Long-distance (*interurbano*) calls, including international ones, can also be made from pay phones. You will need anywhere from several to a fistful of *gettoni* or coins, or magnetic cards (available in 3,000-, 6,000-, or 9,000-lire values at SIP offices — see below). If you have trouble or if you cannot raise a sufficient amount of change, remember that long-distance and international calls can also be made from the Posto Telefonico Pubblico (PTP), literally the "public phone place." In fact, this is perhaps the simplest way to place such a call. In a small town, the PTP may be no more than a booth in the corner of a bar. In larger cities, it will be either the local SIP (Società Italiana per l'Esercizio Telefonico) or ASST (Azienda di Stato per i Servizi Telefonici) office. Go to the telephone counter and explain what kind of call you want to make and to where. (A collect call is a *comunicazione "R"* or *con pagamento a destinazione;* a person-to-person call is a *comunicazione personale* or *con preavviso;* a station-to-station call is a *comunicazione posto a posto.*) You may be assigned a *cabina* (booth) from which to direct-dial the call yourself, or the clerk may put the call through for you, telling you which *cabina* to go to when he or she is about to connect the call. In either case, after you have hung up, return to the counter and pay the clerk for the call. Using the PTP allows you to avoid stiff hotel switchboard surcharges and to dispense with the hassle of pay telephones. The only drawback to their use is that in a city of any size there is usually a line of people waiting for an empty booth.

ELECTRICITY: A useful brochure, "Foreign Electricity Is No Deep Dark Secret," will be mailed to you if you send a stamped, self-addressed envelope to the *Franzus Company,* 352 Park Ave. S, New York, NY 10010. It provides information about converters and adapter plugs for electrical appliances manufactured for use in the US but to be used abroad. The US runs on 110-volt, 60-cycle alternating current; Italy runs on both 115-volt and 220-volt, 50-cycle alternating current. (The voltage is rarely indicated on the outlet or anywhere else in hotel rooms, so it's always best to ask each time you change address. Even though 220-volt current is more common than 115-volt current, some places, such as Rome, use both.) The large difference between US and most European voltage means that without a converter, the motor of a US appliance used overseas would run at twice its intended speed and would quickly burn out. You can solve the problem by buying a lightweight converter to transform foreign voltage into US voltage (there are two types of converters, depending on the wattage of the appliance) or by buying dual-voltage appliances that convert from one to the other at the flick of a switch (hair dryers of this sort are common). The difference between the 50-cycle and 60-cycle currents will cause no problem — the appliances will simply run more slowly — but you will still have to deal with differing socket configurations before plugging in. A standard European plug of two long, round prongs is required in Italy. Sets of adapter plugs for use worldwide can be bought at hardware stores.

Tipping

 Throughout Italy (and most of Europe), a service charge — usually 15% — is almost always added to basic hotel and restaurant bills. This can confuse the North American who is not familiar with the custom. On the one hand, many a traveler, unaware of this policy, has left a superfluous *mancia.* On the other hand, many a traveler, made aware of the policy, has mistakenly assumed that it takes care of everything. It doesn't. While "service included" in theory eliminates any question about how much and whom to tip, in practice there are still occasions when on-the-spot tips are appropriate. Among these are tips to prepare the way for future service (as in the case of a fairly large initial tip to the hotel doorman who will be getting taxis for you during your stay), as well as tips meant to say "thank you" for services rendered. So keep a wad of 1,000-lire notes (about 65¢) ready and hand them out like dollar bills.

For help with suitcases, the doorman and the bellhop each get an on-the-spot tip of no less than 1,000 lire per piece of luggage — 1,500 lire per piece would not be excessive. The concierge need not be tipped if he only hands you your key, but if he has been especially helpful or has performed a particular service, you should give him at least 5,000 lire. Chambermaids are taken care of by the service charge included in the bill, but you might want to leave an additional tip — 1,000 to 1,500 lire for each day of your stay. If you order from room service, 1,000 lire to the waiter for each delivery is sufficient.

In restaurants, the service charge is included, but almost everyone leaves an extra 5% to 10% for the waiter (leave the lesser amount for larger tabs). The maitre d' is rarely tipped, except periodically by regular customers; however, keep in mind that slipping him something in a crowded restaurant may get you a preferred table. The wine steward is not tipped for simply serving the wine, although if he has selected the wine for you, it is customary to leave him 10% of the price of the bottle. When eating or drinking standing up at a *caffè* counter, the procedure is to pay at the cash register first and then take the small receipt (*scontrino*) over to the counter, where you leave it with 100 to 500 lire (depending on what you're having — only a coffee, drinks with sandwiches, pastries, and so on) as you order from the barman. If you're sitting at a *caffè* table, service may or may not be included, and a good rule of thumb is to leave 5% to 10% (depending on your inclination) in either case. The more elegant the establishment, the more likely that service is included, but 5% to 10% extra is still customary; at a corner bar in an ordinary neighborhood, service probably isn't included, but no more than 5% to 10% would be expected.

Tour guides should also be tipped. If you are traveling in a group, decide as a group what you want to give the guide and present it from the group at the end of the tour. If you have been individually escorted, the amount should depend on the degree of your satisfaction, but 15% of the cost of the tour is a safe figure, or 2,000 lire per person for a half-day tour and about 2,500 lire per person for a full-day tour. Museum and monument guides are also usually tipped, and 1,000 or 2,000 lire to the person who unlocks a small church or turns on the lights in a chapel for you in some out-of-the-way town is a nice gesture.

Some miscellaneous tips: At the hairdresser, leave 10% to 15% of the bill. Theater ushers used to be tipped, but the practice is becoming increasingly rare. Washroom attendants are tipped — they usually set out a little plate with a coin already on it suggesting the expected denomination, which is never less than 100 lire, much more in a very exclusive establishment. Taxi drivers get 10% to 15% of the meter. Don't forget service station attendants, for whom about 1,000 lire for cleaning the windshield or other attention is not unusual.

Tipping is always a matter of personal preference. In the situations covered above, as well as in any others that arise where you feel a tip is expected or due, feel free to express your pleasure or displeasure. You should never hesitate to reward excellent and efficient attention or to penalize poor service. If you didn't like the service — or the attitude — don't tip.

Shopping

Browsing through the boutiques, street markets, and craft studios of Italy will undoubtedly be one of the highlights of your trip. You may not be quite as enthusiastic about prices as you might have been a year or two ago, when the dollar was a lot stronger, but there is still plenty of value for the money. In few other countries are the quality of the raw materials, the creativity of the styling, and the craftsmanship that go into the finished product quite as impressive as in Italy, so even when the price is a bit higher than you intended to spend, you will still find many items irresistible. To help steer you in the right direction, several sections of this book are devoted to shopping. Individual city reports (THE CITIES) include a list of specific shops and markets as well as descriptions of special shopping streets where they exist. And DIVERSIONS contains a roundup of where to buy the best merchandise Italy has to offer.

WHAT TO BUY: Unless you're a confirmed customer of the Army-Navy store — and even if you are — you probably don't need to be told that clothing, above all, is the thing to buy in Italy. France and Italy vie as the world's fashion capitals, and each has its partisans, but that hardly matters. One stroll down almost any Main Street, Italian-style, and the desire to acquire hits almost everyone — hard. Clothing for women — from the highest of high fashion (*alta moda*) through ready-to-wear with a striking degree of panache — fills the windows of a greater number of shops, but the menswear available in Italy is sufficiently enticing to coax even the most unworldly dresser out of nondescript duds (while the more sophisticated are being measured for that perfectly tailored Italian suit, made perhaps by the same tailor Yves St. Laurent uses).

On the whole, your own eye and your own fancy will be your guide, but note that Italy is particularly well known for its knitwear, from dresses and ensembles to basic sweaters and bulky knits down to lowly, luxuriously soft cotton T-shirts in myriad vibrant colors that have ripened to maturity in the bright Mediterranean sun. Naturally, you'll find those incomparable Italian shoes everywhere in Italy, so many fashionable styles and in such abundance that it seems a pair and a spare have been made for every foot in creation. Boots may be hard to spot if you visit in summer, but they're such a good buy that it's not a bad idea to ask the storekeeper to pull some out or to have some custom-made if you have time. Furthermore, since the Italians excel in the production of leather goods of all description, it's highly advisable to make a serious list before departure of all the handbags, wallets, belts, and gloves your wardrobe will need in the next few seasons. Of all the Italian cities, Florence is most famous for fine leather, so save the list until you get there, and if your budget is not up to the famous labels, shop at the *bancarelle* (carts) in the San Lorenzo market. They're well stocked and reasonably priced, and many take credit cards. Suede and leather jackets and coats will also be tempting in Florence.

If you're at all handy with a needle, you may want to shop for yard goods — the raw materials of all those wonderful Italian fashions. Italy produces cottons, linens, and incomparable silks. Other articles of adornment that are especially enticing are lingerie, hand-embroidered items, baby clothing, and jewelry — cameos in Naples, examples of the goldsmith's art on Florence's Ponte Vecchio, costume jewelry, antique jewelry.

Articles for the home range from very packable embroidered and appliquéd table linens, bed linens, and bath linens to very unpackable furniture, antique or supermodern in design. Prints, drawings, and reproductions of Italy's famous artworks also make good souvenirs for the home. Venetian glass — anything from a small vase or a heavy paperweight to a ballroom chandelier — is *the* souvenir of Venice, while Florence is known for a variety of handicrafts that result in old-fashioned, handmade paper products, antiqued wooden boxes and trays, mosaic boxes, mosaic picture frames, and, indeed, mosaic pictures. A number of smaller towns specialize in ceramics: You can browse through the *maiolica*, or faïence pottery, in Faenza (from which faïence takes its name) or shop for it in Vietri sul Mare, at the end of the Amalfi Drive. Orvieto and Gubbio are also decked from end to end with plates, pitchers, mugs, and ceramic knickknacks. Volterra is known for alabaster.

Budget travelers need not feel cheated by the limits of their purse. Flea markets abound to delight the poor, the thrifty, the just plain stingy, and the *amatori* of bric-a-brac. Department stores are not as ubiquitous as they are in the US, but two moderately priced chains, *Standa* and *Upim,* are a source of authentic Italian souvenirs — that's where many Italians buy everything from cosmetics and toiletries to household furnishings, kitchenware, tableware, toys, school supplies, and clothing. Food shopping in itself can be an unforgettable experience. Take a string bag and wander from the *panificio* (or *panetteria* — bread bakery) for some *rosette* (one of many types of bread rolls) to the *pizzicheria* (or *salumeria, drogheria,* or *pizzicagnolo* — delicatessen/grocery) for some mortadella or *prosciutto crudo* and a selection of several kinds of cheese, then stop by the *fruttivendolo* for some lusciously sun-kissed tomatoes, peaches, figs, or grapes, and have yourself an authentic epic picnic. Don't expect to bring samples of these home with you because they most likely won't pass US customs (see *Customs and Returning to the US*). For edible (and potable) souvenirs, stick to wine or such specialties as Siena's *panforte* (a kind of fruitcake), a Milanese *panettone,* or perhaps some cellophane packs of dried *porcini* mushrooms or a box of beautifully wrapped *marrons glacés* (candied chestnuts).

A few tips: Stores in Italy very rarely exchange things or take them back. Once you've bought something, it's usually yours forever, even if you try to return it the same day. Don't buy things to be shipped home if you can avoid it. It's always the best policy to take your purchases with you. If you are having clothing custom-made, be sure you have time for enough fittings — three should do it — and pick up the finished piece yourself, if you can, and take it with you. Bargaining has not been the rule in Italy for a long time. Most stores have *prezzi fissi* (fixed prices), although if you do a lot of spending in one place, a *sconto* (discount) is not hard to come by. Real haggling as it used to be practiced is now confined mainly to the used-goods sections of flea markets and to antique shops.

VALUE ADDED TAX: Commonly abbreviated as VAT, this is a tax levied by numerous European countries and added at varying rates to the purchase price of most goods as well as services. In Italy, the tax is known as the *imposta sul valore aggiunto* (IVA), and the rate on merchandise is 18%. The tax is meant to apply only to residents of Italy, but visitors are required to pay it, too. Having done so, visitors are entitled to a refund, provided their purchases exceed a certain amount and provided the articles in question leave the country with them. In several countries, such as France and Great Britain, procedures for obtaining the refund are well established and are used by large numbers of tourists and thus operate smoothly. In Italy, this is not the case, although a VAT-refund scheme exists. First, a refund is granted only if the price of an item is 250,000 lire or more (a higher minimum pertains to residents of Common Market countries), and multiple purchases in a single shop may *not* be grouped to reach the minimum as is frequently allowed in other countries. Second, the store must agree to participate in the tax-refund scheme — paperwork is involved and although stores are obliged to offer the refund when asked, many find a way to circumvent it. Quite often, if you have spent a large amount of money in one shop, the shopkeeper will offer you a discount rather than bother with the forms. On the other hand, if you have already been given a discount, it may disappear if you insist on a tax refund.

To claim the refund, you must ask the store clerk for a refund form (original plus two copies) filled out with your full name, address, passport number, and a description of the purchase. On leaving Italy, you must present this same form with the merchandise (do not pack it in the bottom of your suitcase) to Italian customs officials, who will stamp the original and return it and the copies to you. The stamped original should be sent back to the store by registered mail (from any country other than Italy) within three months of the date of purchase. Stores have 15 days from receipt of the stamped invoice to send out the refund, but since the Italian post office is not known for the speed of its deliveries, there may be a considerable wait. Note that ordinarily the refund arrives in the form of a check in Italian lire, and if the refund is less than a significant amount, conversion charges imposed by US banks — which can run as high as $15 or more — could make the whole exercise hardly worthwhile. (Far less costly is sending the foreign currency check — after endorsing it — to *Ruesch International,* 1140 19th St., NW, Washington, DC 20036; phone: 800-424-2923. Its flat fee for conversion of foreign currency checks to US dollars is only $2.) Occasionally, if the purchase was made by credit card, the refund will be in the form of a credit to your account in the amount of the tax. An even better method of reimbursement is possible if the store agrees to make two credit card charges, one for the price of the goods and the other for the amount of the tax. Then, when the stamped form arrives, the store simply tears up the charge slip for the tax, and the amount never appears on your account.

DUTY-FREE SHOPS: If common sense tells you that it is always less expensive to buy goods in an airport duty-free shop than to buy them at home or in the streets of a foreign city, you'd best be aware of some basic facts. First of all, duty-free does not mean that the goods you buy will be free of duty when you return to the US. Rather, it means that the shop has paid no import tax acquiring goods of foreign make because the goods are not to be used in the country. This is why duty-free goods are available in the restricted passengers-only area of international airports or are delivered to departing passengers on the plane. In a duty-free store, you save money only on goods of foreign make because they are the only items on which import tax would be charged in any other store. There is usually no saving on locally made items, although in countries that impose a value added tax (see above) that is refundable to foreigners, the prices in airport duty-free shops generally do not include this tax. Travelers can therefore avoid paying the tax on inexpensive items that don't qualify for the refund and are spared the cumbersome procedures that must be followed to obtain the refund on expensive items that do. Beyond this, there is little reason to delay buying local souvenirs until you reach the airport. In fact, because airport duty-free shops usually pay high rents, the local goods sold in them may be more expensive than they are in a downtown store.

The real bargains are foreign goods, but — let the buyer beware — not all foreign goods are automatically less expensive in an airport duty-free shop. Spirits, smoking materials, and perfumes are fairly standard bargains, but when buying cameras, watches, clothing, and luxury items, be sure to know what they cost elsewhere. Terrific savings do exist (they are the reason for such shops, after all), but so do overpriced items that an unwary shopper might find equally tempting.

Two of Europe's best-known duty-free shops are at Ireland's Shannon Airport, the oldest, and at Amsterdam's Schiphol Airport, the largest. Rome's *Leonardo da Vinci Airport* at Fiumicino has a number of duty-free and tax-free shops selling everything from liquor and perfumes to clothing, gifts, jewelry, cameras, toys, and food specialties. But its range of style choices and sizes does not approach that of downtown shops, so it's not recommended that you wait to begin your spree at the airport unless you are willing to choose from comparatively slim pickings. Milan's *Malpensa Airport* has a small duty-free shop.

Customs and Returning to the US

Customs allowances for US citizens returning from abroad are revised from time to time, and the most recent change — an increase in the individual duty-free exemption — was in the traveler's favor. You may now bring into the US articles totaling $400 in value (up from $300) without paying duty on them, provided they accompany you and are for personal use. A flat 10% duty based on the "fair retail value in country of acquisition" is assessed on the next $1,000 (up from $600) worth of merchandise brought in for personal use or gifts. Amounts over $1,400 are dutiable at a variety of rates. The average rate for typical tourist purchases is about 12%; you can find rates on specific items by consulting *Tariff Schedules of the United States* in a library or any US Customs Service office.

Families traveling together may make a joint declaration to customs, a procedure that permits one member to exceed his or her duty-free exemption to the extent that another falls short. Families may also pool purchases dutiable under the flat rate. A family of three, for example, is eligible for up to a total of $3,000 at the 10% flat duty rate (after its total duty-free exemption of $1,200) rather than three separate $1,000 allowances. This grouping of purchases is extremely useful when considering the duty on a high-cost item, such as jewelry or a fur coat. Individuals are allowed one carton of cigarettes (200) and 100 cigars regardless of age and one liter of alcohol if they are over age 21. Alcohol above this allowance is liable for both duty and an Internal Revenue tax. Antiques, if they are 100 or more years old and you have proof from the seller of that fact, are duty-free, as are paintings and drawings if done entirely by hand.

Personal exemptions can be used once every 30 days; to be eligible, an individual must have been out of the country for more than 48 hours. If any portion of the exemption has been used once within any 30-day period or if your trip is less than 48 hours long, the duty-free allowance is cut to $25. The allotment for individual "unsolicited" gifts mailed from abroad (no more than one per day per recipient) has been raised to $50 retail value per gift. These gifts do not have to be declared and are not included in your duty-free exemption.

Clearing customs is a simple procedure. Forms are distributed by airline or ship personnel before arrival. If your purchases total no more than the duty-free $400 limit, you need only fill out the identification part of the form and make an oral declaration to the customs inspector. If you are entering with more than $400 worth of goods, you must submit a written declaration. It is illegal not to declare dutiable items; not to do so, in fact, constitutes smuggling, and the penalty can be anything from a stiff fine and seizure of the goods to a prison sentence. It simply isn't worth doing. Nor should you go along with the suggestions of foreign merchants who offer to help you secure a bargain by deceiving customs officials in any way. Such transactions are frequently a setup, using the foreign merchant as an agent of US customs. Another agent of US customs is TECS, the Treasury Enforcement Communications System, a computer that stores all kinds of pertinent information on returning citizens. There is a basic rule to buying goods abroad, and it should never be broken: If you can't afford the duty on something, don't buy it. Your list or verbal declaration should include all items purchased abroad as well as gifts received abroad, purchases made at the behest of others, the value of repairs, and anything brought in for resale in the US.

Do not include in the list items that do not accompany you (i.e., purchases that you have mailed or have had shipped to your home), which are automatically dutiable, even if they are for your own use and even if the items that do accompany your return from the same trip do not exhaust your $400 duty-free exemption. In fact, it is a good idea, if you have accumulated too much while abroad, to mail home any personal effects (made and bought in the US) that you no longer need rather than your foreign purchases to take full advantage of your exemption. These personal effects pass through customs as "American Goods Returned" and are not subject to duty. If you cannot avoid shipping home your foreign purchases, however, the US Customs Service suggests that the packages be clearly marked "Not for Sale" and that a copy of the bill of sale be included. The customs examiner will usually accept this as indicative of the article's fair retail value, but if he or she believes it to be falsified — or feels the goods have been seriously undervalued — a higher retail value may be assigned. Remember, the examiner is empowered to impose a duty based on his or her assessment of the value of the goods. The duty owed is collected by the US Postal Service when the package is delivered. More information on mailing packages home from abroad is contained in the US Customs Service pamphlet *International Mail Imports* (see the list at the end of this section for where to write for this and other useful brochures).

Gold, gold medals, bullion, and up to $10,000 in currency or negotiable instruments may be brought into the US without being declared. Sums over $10,000 must be declared in writing. Drugs are totally illegal, with the exception of medication prescribed by a physician. It's a good idea to travel with no more than you actually need of any medication and to have the prescription on hand in case any question arises — either abroad or when reentering the US.

Customs implements the rigorous Department of Agriculture regulations concerning the importation of vegetable matter, seeds, bulbs, and the like. Living vegetable matter may not be imported without a permit, and everything must be inspected, permit or not. Processed foods and baked goods are usually okay. Regulations on meat products generally depend on the country of origin and manner of processing. As a rule, commercially canned meat, hermetically sealed and cooked in the can so that it can be stored without refrigeration, is permitted, but not all canned meat fulfills this requirement. Do not attempt to bring any sausages or salamis back from Italy because they will not be allowed into the country, and the inevitable confiscation of a Parma ham would be a terrible loss, given its cost. Hard, dry cheeses are acceptable, but soft, runny ones like *ricotta* are not.

Customs also enforces federal laws that prohibit the entry of articles made from the furs or hides of animals on the endangered species list. Beware of shoes, bags, and belts made of crocodile and certain kinds of lizard, and if you're shopping for big-ticket items, beware of fur coats made from spotted cats. All can be found in Europe, but they will be confiscated on your return, and you will receive no refund.

Customs agents are businesslike, efficient, and not unkind. During the peak season, clearance can take time, but this is generally because of the strain imposed by multiple jumbo jets disgorging their passengers at the same time, not because of unwarranted zealousness on the part of the customs people. Efforts to streamline procedures include the Citizens' Bypass Program which allows Americans whose purchases are under $400 to go to the "green line," where they simply show their passports to the customs inspector. This, in effect, completely eliminates the old obligatory inspection, although inspectors still retain the right to search any luggage they choose, so don't do anything foolish or illegal.

The US Customs Service publishes a series of free pamphlets with customs information. It includes *Know Before You Go,* a basic discussion of customs requirements pertaining to all travelers; *International Mail Imports; Travelers' Tips on Bringing Food, Plant and Animal Products into the United States; Importing a Car; GSP and the Traveler; Currency Reporting; Pets, Wildlife, US Customs; Customs Hints for Visitors (Nonresidents);* and *Trademark Information for Travelers.* For the entire series or individual pamphlets, write or call the *US Customs Service,* PO Box 7407, Washington, DC 20044 (phone 202-566-8195), or contact any of the seven regional offices, in Boston, Chicago, Houston, Los Angeles, Miami, New Orleans, and New York. For information about animals on the endangered species list, write the Department of the Interior, US Fish and Wildlife Service, Division of Law Enforcement, PO Box 28006, Washington, DC 20005, and ask for *Facts About Federal Wildlife Laws,* also free. All told, these pamphlets provide great briefing material, but if you still have questions after you're in Italy, you can contact the customs representative at the *US Embassy,* Via Vittorio Veneto 119/A, 00187 Rome (phone: 06-46741, ext. 475 or 533).

Sources and Resources

Camera and Equipment

Vacations are everybody's favorite time for taking pictures. After all, most of us want to remember the places we visit — and show them off to others — through spectacular photographs. Here are a few suggestions to help you get the best results from your travel photography.

BEFORE THE TRIP: If you're just taking your camera out after a long period in mothballs or have just bought a new one, check it thoroughly before you leave to prevent unexpected breakdowns and disappointing pictures.

1. Shoot at least one test roll, using the kind of film you plan to take with you. Use all the shutter speeds and f-stops on your camera, and vary the focus to make sure everything is in order. Do this well before your departure so there will be time to have the film developed and to make repairs if necessary. If you're in a rush, most large cities have custom labs that can process film in as little as 3 hours.
2. Clean your camera thoroughly, inside and out. Dust and dirt can jam mechanisms, spoil pictures, and scratch film. Remove surface dust from the lenses and camera body with a soft camel's-hair brush. Next, use at least two layers of crumpled lens tissue and your breath to clean the lenses and filters. Don't rub hard and don't use compressed air on lenses or filters because they are easily damaged. Persistent stains can be removed by using a Q-tip moistened with liquid lens cleaner. Anything that doesn't come off easily needs professional attention. Once your lens is clean, protect it from dirt and damage with an inexpensive skylight or ultraviolet filter.
3. Check the batteries in the light meter, and take along extra ones in case they wear out during the trip.

EQUIPMENT TO TAKE ALONG: Keep your gear light and compact. Items that are too heavy or bulky to be carried with you will likely stay in your hotel room.

1. Most single-lens reflex (SLR) cameras come with a conventional 50mm lens, a general-purpose lens good for street scenes taken at a distance of 25 feet or more and full-body portraits. You can expand your photographic options with a wide-angle lens, such as a 35mm, 28mm, or 24mm lens. These are especially handy for panoramas, cityscapes, and large buildings or statuary from which you can't step back. For closeups, a macro lens is best, but a screw-on magnifying lens is an inexpensive alternative. Telephoto and zoom lenses are bulky and not really necessary unless you are shooting animals in the wild. If you want one such lens that gives a range of options, try a 35–80mm zoom; it is relatively light, though expensive. Protect all lenses with a 1A or 1B skylight filter, which should be removed for cleaning only. And take along a polarizing filter to eliminate glare and reflection and to saturate colors in very bright sunlight.
2. Travel photographs work best in color. The preferred and least expensive all-around slide films are Kodachrome 64, Fujichrome, and Agfachrome. For very

bright conditions, try slower film, such as Kodachrome 25. In places that tend to be cloudy, or indoors with natural light (as in museums), use a fast film such as Ektachrome 400, which can be "pushed" during development to ASA 800 or 1600. Different films render color in slightly different ways. Kodachrome brings out reds and oranges. Agfachrome mutes bright tones and produces fine browns, yellows, and whites. Fujichrome is noted for its yellows, greens, and whites. Anticipate what you are likely to see, and take along whichever types of film will enhance your result. If you choose film that develops into prints rather than slides, try Kodacolor VR-G 100 for bright, sunny days. For environments without much contrast — in the shade or on dark, overcast days — use Kodacolor 400.

How much film should you take? The rule of thumb, if you are serious about photography, is to pack one role (36 exposures) for each day of your trip, but Italian regulations permit you to enter with only 10 rolls of still film (and 10 of movie film) duty-free. Film is expensive abroad, and if you pack more than you use, the leftovers can be bartered away or brought home and stored in your refrigerator. Processing is also more expensive abroad and not as safe as at home. If you are concerned about airport security X-rays damaging your undeveloped film (X-rays do not affect processed film), store the film in lead-lined bags sold in camera shops. In the US, incidents of X-ray damage to unprocessed film are minimal because low-dosage X-ray equipment is used virtually everywhere. Photo industry sources say that film with speeds up to ASA 400 can go through security machinery in the US five times without any noticeable effect. Overseas, the situation varies from country to country, but at least in Western Europe the trend is also toward equipment that delivers less radiation. On the other hand, the threat of terrorism has resulted in increasingly stringent security measures in most European airports and has increased the possibility of repeated X-ray exposures to both carry-on and checked luggage. While it is doubtful that one X-ray would ruin your pictures, if you're traveling without a protective bag you may want to ask to have your photo equipment inspected by hand, especially on a long trip with several security checks. In the US, Federal Aviation Administration regulations require that if you request a hand inspection, you get it, but overseas the response may depend on the humor of the inspector. Naturally, a hand inspection is possible only if you're carrying your film and camera on board with you; it's a good idea to do so anyway because it helps preclude loss or theft or the possibility that checked baggage will be X-rayed more heavily than hand baggage. Finally, the walk-through metal detector devices at airports do not affect film, though the film cartridges will set them off. *A note of warning:* The new very high speed film with an ASA rating of 1,000 should never be subjected to X-rays, even in the US. If you're taking some of this film overseas, note that there are lead-lined bags made especially for it.

3. A small battery-powered electronic flash unit is handy for very dim light or at night, but only if the subject is at a distance of 15 feet or less. Flash units cannot illuminate an entire scene, and many museums do not permit flash photography, so take such a unit only if you know you will need it. If your camera does not have a hot shoe, you will need a PC cord to synchronize the flash with your shutter.

4. Invest in a broad camera strap if you now have a thin one. It will make carrying the camera much more comfortable. For safety and ease of use, keep the camera strapped around your neck (not on your shoulder) whenever it is out of its bag.

5. A sturdy canvas or leather camera bag — not an airline bag — will keep equipment clean, organized, and easy to find.

6. For cleaning, take along a camel's-hair brush that retracts into a rubber squeeze bulb. Also take plenty of lens tissue and plastic bags to protect cameras and lenses against dust.

7. Pack some extra lens caps — they're the first things to get lost.

PICTURE-TAKING TIPS: For better pictures, remember the following pointers:

1. *Get close.* Move in so your subject fills the frame.
2. *Vary your angle.* Get down, shoot from above, look for unusual perspectives.
3. *Pay attention to backgrounds.* Keep the background simple or blur it out.
4. *Look for details.* Not just a whole building, but a decorative element; not just an entire street scene, but a single remarkable face.
5. *Don't be lazy.* Always carry your camera gear with you, loaded and ready for those unexpected memorable moments.

Weights and Measures

When you are traveling in Italy, you'll find that just about every quantity, whether it is length, weight, or capacity, will be in an unfamiliar figure. In fact, this is true for travel almost everywhere in the world since the US is one of the last countries to resist adopting the metric system.

The following are some specific facts to keep in mind about weights and measures during your trip. Fruits and vegetables at a market are recorded in kilos (kilograms), as is your luggage at the airport and your body weight. (The latter is particularly pleasing to people of large build, who instead of weighing 220 pounds hit the scales at a mere 100 kilos.) A kilo is 2.2 pounds, and 1 pound is .45 kilo. Body temperature is measured in degrees centigrade or Celsius rather than Fahrenheit, so a normal body temperature is 37°, not 98.6°, and freezing is 0° rather than 32°. Gasoline stations sell gas by the liter (approximately four liters to a gallon), and machines measure air for tires in kilograms per square centimeter rather than in pounds per square inch. Highway signs are written in kilometers rather than miles (1 mile equals 1.6 kilometers; 1 kilometer equals .62 mile). And speed limits are in kilometers per hour, so think twice before hitting the gas when you see a speed limit of 100. That means 62 miles per hour.

The tables and conversion factors listed below should give you all the information you will need to understand any transaction, road sign, or map you encounter on your travels.

APPROXIMATE EQUIVALENTS		
Metric Unit	**Abbreviation**	**US Equivalent**
LENGTH		
meter	m	39.37 inches
kilometer	km	.62 mile
millimeter	mm	.04 inch
CAPACITY		
liter	l	1.057 quarts
WEIGHT		
gram	g	.035 ounce
kilogram	kg	2.2 pounds
metric ton	MT	1.1 tons
ENERGY		
kilowatt	kw	1.34 horsepower

CONVERSION TABLES
METRIC TO US MEASUREMENTS

Multiply:	by:	to convert to:
LENGTH		
millimeters	.04	inches
meters	3.3	feet
meters	1.1	yards
kilometers	.6	miles
CAPACITY		
liters	2.11	pints (liquid)
liters	1.06	quarts (liquid)
liters	.26	gallons (liquid)
WEIGHT		
grams	.04	ounces (avoir.)
kilograms	2.2	pounds (avoir.)

US TO METRIC MEASUREMENTS

LENGTH		
inches	25.0	millimeters
feet	.3	meters
yards	.9	meters
miles	1.6	kilometers
CAPACITY		
pints	.47	liters
quarts	.95	liters
gallons	3.8	liters
WEIGHT		
ounces	28.0	grams
pounds	.45	kilograms

TEMPERATURE

$$°F = (°C \times 9/5) + 32 \qquad °C = (°F - 32) \times 5/9$$

Tourist Information

This section contains a list of the Italian government tourist offices in the US. They can provide travel and entry information, and literature is usually free. When requesting brochures and maps, state the regions you plan to visit (Umbria, the Alps) as well as particular interests you wish to pursue (music festivals, hiking, horseback riding) while traveling in Italy. It may also be helpful to specify the type of accommodations you prefer (luxury or budget, in major cities, in the country on farms, and so on). Offices are generally open Monday through Friday. There is no official San Marino government tourist office in the US, but the San Marino consulates listed here handle requests for travel information.

Italian Government Travel Office (Ente Nazionale Italiano di Turismo, ENIT)
  Chicago: 500 N Michigan Ave., Chicago, IL 60611 (phone: 312-644-0990)
  New York: 630 Fifth Ave., Suite 1565, New York, NY 10111 (phone: 212-245-
    4822)
  San Francisco: 360 Post St., Suite 801, San Francisco, CA 94108 (phone: 415-
    392-6206)

If your query cannot be answered by ENIT, you may want to write directly to the
appropriate tourist authorities in Italy. If the area of your interest is one of the country's
20 regions, write to the *Regional Tourist Board* (*Assessorato Regionale per il
Turismo*), which promotes tourism on a regional basis. The following are the 20
Regional Tourist Boards in Italy:

  Abruzzo: Viale G. Bovio, 65100 Pescara (phone: 085-75094)
  Basilicata: Via Crispi, Palazzo ex-Gil, 85100 Potenza (phone: 0971-3590)
  Calabria: Vico 3 Raffaelli, 88100 Catanzaro (phone: 0961-44319)
  Campania: Via Santa Lucia 81, 80132 Napoli (phone: 081-400044)
  Emilia-Romagna: Viale Silvani 6, 40122 Bologna (phone: 051-559-111)
  Friuli-Venezia Giulia: Via San Francesco d'Assisi 37, 34133 Trieste (phone: 040-
    7355)
  Lazio: Via Rosa Raimondi Garibaldi 7, 00145 Roma (phone: 06-54571)
  Liguria: Via Fieschi 15, 16121 Genova (phone: 010-54851)
  Lombardia: Via Fabio Filzi 22, 20124 Milano (phone: 02-67651)
  Marche: Via Gentile da Fabriano, 60100 Ancona (phone: 071-8061)
  Molise: Via Mazzini 94, 86100 Campobasso (phone: 0874-9491)
  Piemonte: Via Magenta 12, 10128 Torino (phone: 011-57173230)
  Puglia: Via Capruzzi 212, 70124 Bari (phone: 080-401111)
  Sardegna: Viale Trento 69, 09100 Cagliari (Phone: 070-650971)
  Sicilia: Via Emanuele Notarbartolo 9, 90141 Palermo (phone: 091-251266)
  Toscana: Via di Novoli 26, 50127 Firenze (phone: 055-439311)
  Trentino–Alto Adige: Provincia Autonoma di Bolzano, Via Raiffeisen 2, 39100
    Bolzano (phone: 0471-993666) for the Alto Adige; Provincia Autonoma di
    Trento, Corso 3 Novembre 132, 38100 Trento (phone: 0461-895111) for the
    Trentino
  Umbria: Corso Vannucci 30, 06100 Perugia (phone: 075-6961)
  Valle d'Aosta: Piazza Narbonne 3, 11100 Aosta (phone: 0165-35653)
  Veneto: Palazzo Balbi Dorsoduro 3901, 30123 Venezia (phone: 041-792111)

In Italy, regions are broken down into provinces, and most cities and larger towns
have a *Provincial Tourist Board* (*Ente Provinciale per il Turismo, EPT*), which supplies
information on both the city and the surrounding provincial area. Furthermore, all
towns with an interest in serving tourists have a *Local Tourist Board* (*Azienda Autonoma di Soggiorno e Turismo, AAST*). Thus, for any given town, the correct office
to write for information may be either the EPT or the AAST (in the case of a large
city or town) or the AAST (in the case of a small one). There are far too many of these
— more than 100 EPT offices and still more AAST offices — to list here, but the Italian
Government Travel Office should be able to supply any address you need. In addition,
you can request information about any major city in Italy from the tourist office cited
(with address and phone number) in *Sources and Resources* in the relevant CITIES
chapter.

The address of the *Ufficio di Stato per il Turismo* (State Tourist Office) in San Marino
is Palazzo del Turismo, Contrada Omagnano, San Marino (phone: 0541-992101).

The Italian government maintains a number of consulates in the US, one of whose
primary functions is to provide visas for certain resident aliens, depending on their
country of origin, and for Americans planning to stay in Italy longer than six months

(holders of US passports may remain in Italy up to 90 days without a visa provided that they do not intend to work or study, and the initial 90-day period can be easily extended to an additional 90 days at any Italian police station). San Marino consulates handle a number of matters for the large San Marinese community in the US, and they are also a source of travel information about San Marino. Note that there are no border formalities between Italy and San Marino, and your US passport is the only document required for a visit of three months or less.

Italian Consulates in the US

Boston: 100 Boylston St., Boston, MA 02116 (phone: 617-542-0483)

Chicago: 500 N Michigan Ave., Chicago, IL 60611 (phone: 312-467-1550)

Detroit: One Kennedy Square Bldg., Suite 2305, 719 Griswold, Detroit, MI 48226 (phone: 313-963-8560)

Houston: 1300 Post Oak Blvd., Suite 660, Houston, TX 77056 (phone: 713-850-7520)

Los Angeles: 11661 San Vicente Blvd., Suite 911, Los Angeles, CA 90049 (phone: 213-826-5998)

New Orleans: 708 Cotton Exchange Bldg., 231 Carondelet St., New Orleans, LA 70130 (phone: 504-524-2271)

New York: 690 Park Ave., New York, NY 10021 (phone: 212-737-9100)

Philadelphia: 421 Chestnut St., Philadelphia, PA 19106 (phone: 215-592-7329)

San Francisco: 2590 Webster St., San Francisco, CA 94115 (phone: 415-931-4924)

Washington, DC: Italian Embassy, 1601 Fuller St., NW, Washington, DC 20009 (phone: 202-797-8842)

San Marino Consulates in the US

New York: 150 E 58th St., New York, NY 10155 (phone: 212-751-7027)

Troy, MI: 1685 E Big Beaver Rd., Troy, MI 48084 (phone: 313-528-1190, Saturdays only)

Washington, DC: 2033 M St., NW, Suite 800, Washington, DC 20036 (phone: 202-223-3517)

The *Italian Cultural Institute* (*Istituto Italiano di Cultura*) is the Italian embassy's cultural arm abroad. It serves as a liaison between the American and Italian people and is an especially good source of information on educational programs in Italy. There are five branches in the US, three of which — in Chicago, Los Angeles, and Washington, DC — are at the same addresses as the consulates in those cities. In New York, the address is 686 Park Ave., New York, NY 10021 (phone: 212-879-4242); in San Francisco, 1 Charlton Court, Suite 102, San Francisco, CA 94123 (phone: 415-922-4177). The New York branch maintains a library of books, periodicals, and newspapers that is open to the public; San Francisco, too, has a small library, open to the public by appointment.

Books and Magazines

Throughout GETTING READY TO GO, numerous books and brochures have been recommended as good sources of further information on a variety of topics. In many cases, these have been publications of the Italian Government Travel Office and are available at its US addresses. Other publications may be found in the travel section of a good general bookstore. If you still can't find something, the following bookstores and mail-order houses specializing in books on travel are a further resource. Their lists are not concentrated in any particular country or continent, but they offer books on Italy along with guides to the rest of the world, and in some cases, even an old Baedeker or two.

> *Book Passage,* 57 Post St., Suite 401, San Francisco, CA 94104 (phone: 415-982-7866 in California; 800-321-9785 elsewhere). Travel guides, maps to all areas of the world. Catalogue available.
>
> *Bradt Enterprises,* 95 Harvey St., Cambridge, MA 02140 (phone: 617-492-8776). Guides and maps, especially for budget travel and special interests (backpacking, mountain climbing, and so on). Mail order only; catalogue available.
>
> *Forsyth Travel Library,* PO Box 2975, 9154 W 57th St., Shawnee Mission, KS 66201 (phone: 913-384-0496). Travel guides and maps, old and new, to all parts of the world. Catalogue available.
>
> *Gourmet Guides,* 176 Stockton St., San Francisco, CA 94133 (phone: 415-391-5903). Travel guides and maps, along with cookbooks. No formal catalogue, but mail orders filled.
>
> *The Travel Suppliers,* 727 N Placentia Ave., Fullerton, CA 92631 (phone: 714-528-2502). Books and maps plus travel paraphernalia from carry-on luggage to voltage converters. Catalogue available.
>
> *Traveller's Bookstore,* 22 W 52nd St., New York, NY 10019 (phone: 212-664-0995). Travel guides and maps, old and new. Catalogue available.

In addition, *Rizzoli Editore,* the Italian publishing company, has several bookstores in the US. They carry a vast array of books of all publishers, a great selection of art books, and numerous travel guides to various countries, as well as newspapers, magazines, and records from Italy and books in Italian — novels, nonfiction, and guides to Italy published by the Italian Touring Club. The largest store is *Rizzoli International Bookstore & Gallery,* 31 W 57th St., New York, NY 10019 (phone: 212-759-2424). A smaller New York store is at 454/A W Broadway, New York, NY 10012 (phone: 674-1616). Other US addresses are Copley Place, 100 Huntington Ave., Boston, MA 02116 (phone: 617-437-0700); Water Tower Place, 835 Michigan Ave., Chicago, IL 60611 (phone: 312-642-3500); 316 North Park Center, Dallas, TX 75225 (phone: 214-739-6633); and South Coast Plaza, 3333 Bristol, Costa Mesa, CA 92626 (phone: 714-957-3331).

Before or after your trip, you may want to subscribe to a publication devoted exclusively to Italy. A very interesting magazine for Italophiles is *Italy Italy,* which comes out 10 times a year, full of beautifully illustrated travel articles bound to whet your appetite for a visit or to provoke nostalgia for a return. Subscriptions are available for $30 a year from *Italy Italy Corp.,* Madison Sq. Sta. Box 1807, New York, NY 10159, or call *Speedimpex,* 45–45 39th St., Long Island City, NY 11104 (phone: 718-392-7477). Another magazine, *Attenzione,* is geared to both Italian-Americans and lovers of Italy. One of the 10 issues a year is dedicated to travel; others keep abreast of events in Italy and what Italians and Italian-Americans are doing in the US. To subscribe, send $21 to *Attenzione,* Subscription Services Dept., PO Box 1917, Marion, OH 43306.

Food is likely to be one of the highlights of your trip, and you will find reading about the subject worthwhile either before you go or after you return. Articles on the foods of Italy, with recipes, regularly appear in *Attenzione* magazine (information and address above). *Gourmet,* a magazine specializing in food, also frequently carries articles on Italian *cucina,* although its scope is much broader than Italy alone. It is available at newsstands throughout the US at $2.50 an issue or for $18 a year from *Gourmet,* PO Box 2980, Boulder, CO 80302. Waverley Root's *The Food of Italy* (Vintage; $9.95, paperback), a companion to his *The Food of France,* is a classic; it treats Italian food region by region, interweaving the discussion with background notes on history, geography, and culture. Burton Anderson's *Vino* (Little, Brown; $19.95) moves from region to region, too — discussing Italian wine and winemakers. Other books on Italian wine are *Burton Anderson's Guide to Italian Wines* (Simon & Schuster; $8.95, paperback) and *Italian Wine* (Knopf; $17.95) by Victor Hazan, whose wife, Marcella Hazan, is the author of *The Classic Italian Cook Book* and *More Classic Italian Cooking.* Both of the latter are available in hardcover (Knopf; $18.95) or paperback (Ballantine; $4.95) and both strive to help the American cook produce authentic Italian results.

More books have been written about the history and culture of Italy than about almost any other country. You probably won't want to plow through Edward Gibbon's multivolume, umpteen-page *The Decline and Fall of the Roman Empire,* but an abridged version of the 18th-century English historian's life work does exist (Penguin Classics; $6.95, paperback) for those so inclined. Histories of the Roman period by writers much closer to the action — Livy, who begins with the story of Romulus and Remus and ends with the 1st century BC; Tacitus, who presents a thorough picture of Roman life in the 1st century AD; Pliny the Younger, whose letters contain an eyewitness account of the eruption of Vesuvius; Suetonius, who wrote biographies of twelve of the Caesars — are all available in the classics department of a good bookstore. Alternatively, *The Romans,* by R. H. Barrow (Pelican; $4.95, paperback), is a slim volume on the statesmanship, religion, philosophy, and literature of ancient Rome and the enduring effect of that civilization on our modern one. For more on Roman artistic achievement, see *Roman Art and Architecture* by Mortimer Wheeler (World of Art Series, Thames and Hudson; $9.95, paperback).

On the next great period in Italian history, there remains Jacob Burckhardt's seminal work *The Civilization of the Renaissance in Italy;* the 19th-century Swiss historian's political-cultural slant on the era, still a best seller after all of these years and still required reading in many college courses, is available in two paperback volumes (Harper Colophon; $4.95 each). Niccolò Machiavelli's *The Prince,* a treatise on Renaissance power politics, is also surprisingly popular considering it's been around since the 16th century. (If you find the subject irresistible, you might also like Baldassare Castiglione's *The Book of the Courtier,* a sort of 16th-century book of etiquette.)

Numerous titles exist on Italian Renaissance art. Millard Meiss and Erwin Panofsky have written very scholarly works, but Frederick Hartt's *History of Italian Renaissance Art: Painting, Sculpture, Architecture* (Abrams; $45) may be more accessible to the general reader willing to pay the price for a basic, comprehensive, and hefty illustrated tome. Linda and Peter Murray, together and separately, have contributed several titles available in paperback, among them *The Architecture of the Italian Renaissance* (Peter Murray; Schocken; $5.95), strictly about Italy, and *The Art of the Renaissance* (Linda and Peter Murray; World of Art Series, Thames and Hudson; $9.95) and *The High Renaissance and Mannerism* (Linda Murray; World of Art Series, Thames and Hudson; $9.95), not strictly about Italy. Other pertinent titles in the World of Art Series: *A Concise Encyclopaedia of the Italian Renaissance,* edited by J. R. Hale, and *A Concise History of Venetian Painting* by John Steer (both $9.95). But you may want to hear some Renaissance men tell it in their own words. Giorgio Vasari's *The Lives of the Most Eminent Italian Architects, Painters, and Sculptors . . . ,* published in 1550 and revised and enlarged in 1568, is *the* source book on Renaissance artists from Cimabue to Vasari's own contemporaries — in fact, poor Giorgio, a painter and architect himself, is remembered more for his book than for the rest of his work. A selection of parts from the whole — *Lives of the Artists* — is available from Penguin Classics at $5.95 (paperback). If that sounds too dry, try Benvenuto Cellini's *Autobiography* (Penguin Classics; $5.95, paperback). It's full of Renaissance gossip and reads like a novel. Irving Stone's *The Agony and the Ecstasy* is a modern biographical novel about Michelangelo (Signet; $4.50).

Italy has inspired much travel writing, some of it outstanding. H. V. Morton's *A Traveller in Italy* (Dodd, Mead; $13.95, paperback), describing a trip through northern

Italy, and *A Traveller in Rome* (Dodd, Mead; $12.95) are fast becoming classics. (His *A Traveller in Southern Italy* may still be found in some bookstores.) Also see Kate Simon's *Italy: The Places In Between* (Harper; $9.95), in which she visits some of the delightful smaller cities of central and northern Italy. Other books, some mentioned in the pertinent CITIES and DIRECTIONS chapters of this book but worth repeating here, are Mary McCarthy's *The Stones of Florence* (Harcourt Brace Jovanovich; $4.95, paperback) and *Venice Observed* (Harcourt Brace Jovanovich; $3.95, paperback) as well as James Morris's *The World of Venice* (Harcourt Brace Jovanovich; $3.95, paperback), Eleanor Clark's *Rome and a Villa* (Atheneum; $8.95, paperback), and Lawrence Durrell's *Sicilian Carousel* (Penguin; $2.95, paperback).

You could read about Italy for a lifetime; in fact, were you to begin with the Etruscans, work your way up to the unexpurgated memoirs of Giacomo Casanova, and continue to modern times without omitting anything ever written about Michelangelo, you could occupy several lifetimes — and never have a chance to travel. Rather than let that happen, curl up with Luigi Barzini's wonderful book *The Italians* (Atheneum; $8.95). It's a wry, perceptive, and affectionate portrait of his people and it's *must* reading!

Useful Words and Phrases

Unlike the French, who have a reputation for being snobbish and brusque if you don't speak their language perfectly, the Italians do not expect you to speak Italian — but are very flattered when you try. In many circumstances, you won't have to, because staffs at most hotels and tourist attractions, as well as at a fair number of restaurants, speak serviceable English, or at least a modicum of it, which they are usually eager to improve — and that means practicing on you. If you find yourself in a situation where your limited Italian proves to be the only means of communication, take the plunge. Don't be afraid of misplaced accents or misconjugated verbs (Italians themselves often lapse into the all-purpose infinitive form of the verb when speaking with a novice) — in most cases you will be understood and will then be advised on the menu or pointed in the right direction. The list on the following pages is a selection of commonly used words and phrases to speed you on your way.

Note that in Italian, nouns are either masculine or feminine as well as singular or plural, and the adjectives that modify them must follow suit. Nouns ending in *o* in the singular are almost always masculine; the *o* becomes an *i* in the plural. Nouns ending in *a* in the singular are feminine; the *a* becomes an *e* in the plural. Nouns ending in *e* in the singular can be masculine or feminine; the *e* becomes an *i* in the plural. Because Italian is very nearly a phonetic language, pronunciation is usually straightforward. Pronounce all syllables clearly and distinctly, with the accent usually on the next to last syllable, and eliminate all indeterminate *uh* sounds from the vowels. The *a* sounds like *ah,* the one the doctor tells you to say. The *e* is pronounced sometimes as in the English *get* and sometimes as the *ai* in *air;* the *i* as in *machine;* the *o* sometimes as in *for* and sometimes as in *know;* the *u* as in *prune.* The consonants *c* or *g* before *a, o,* and *u* have hard sounds, as in the English *car, core, gore, guru.* Before *e* or *i,* they have soft sounds, as in the English *check, chief, general, gee.* But in the latter case, if an *h* is added the soft sound becomes hard again: *Che* (what) and *chi* (who) are pronounced as though they were *kay* and *key* in English, and the Ponte Vecchio in Florence is not "*vetch*-io" but "*veck*-io." Of course, these are only the most basic rules, and even they may seem daunting at first, but they shouldn't remain so for long.

Nevertheless, if you can't get your mouth to speak Italian, try your hands at it: With a little observation, you'll pick it up quickly and be surprised at how often your message will get across.

Greetings and Everyday Expressions

Good morning! *Buon giorno!*
Good evening! *Buona sera!*
Hello! *Ciao!* (familiar) *Pronto!* (on the telephone)
How are you? *Come sta?*
Pleased to meet you! *Molto lieto/a!*
Good-bye! *Arrivederci! Addio!* (final)
So long! *Ciao!* (familiar)
Good night! *Buona notte!*
Yes! *Sì!*
No! *No!*
Please! *Per favore* or *per piacere!*
Thank you! *Grazie!*
You're welcome! *Prego!*
Excuse me! *Mi scusi!* (I beg your pardon) *Permesso!* (May I get by, on a bus or in a crowd)
I don't speak Italian. *Non parlo italiano.*
Do you speak English? *Parla inglese?*
I don't understand. *Non capisco.*
Do you understand? *Capisce?*
My name is . . . *Mi chiamo . . .*
What is your name? *Come si chiama?*
miss *signorina*
madame *signora*
mister *signor(e)*

open *aperto*
closed *chiuso*
  chiuso per ferie (for annual vacation)
  chiuso per riposo settimanale (for weekly day of rest)
  chiuso per restauro (for restoration)
entrance *entrata*
exit *uscita*
push *spingere*
pull *tirare*
today *oggi*
tomorrow *domani*
yesterday *ieri*
Is there a strike? *C'è uno sciopero?*
Until when? *Fino a?*

Checking In

I would like *Vorrei*
I have reserved *Ho prenotato*
  a single room *una camera singola*
  a double room *una camera doppia*
  a quiet room *una camera tranquilla*
  with private bath *con bagno privato*

with private shower   *con doccia privata*
with a sea view   *con vista sul mare*
with air conditioning   *con aria condizionata*
with balcony   *con balcone/terrazzo*
for one night   *per una notte*
for a few days   *per qualche giorno*
for a week   *per una settimana*
with full board   *con pensione completa*
with half board   *con mezza pensione*

Does the price include   *Il prezzo comprende*
breakfast   *la prima colazione*
service charge   *servizio*
taxes   *tasse*

What time is breakfast served?   *A che ora si serve la prima colazione?*
It doesn't work.   *Non funziona.*
May I pay with traveler's checks?   *Posso pagare con traveler's checks?*
Do you accept this credit card?   *Accettate questa carta di credito?*

Eating Out

ashtray   *un portacenere*
bottle   *una bottiglia*
chair   *una sedia*
cup   *una tazza*
fork   *una forchetta*
knife   *un coltello*
napkin   *un tovagliolo*
plate   *un piatto*
spoon   *un cucchiaio*
table   *una tavola*

beer   *una birra*
cocoa   *un cioccolato*
coffee   *un caffè* or *un espresso*
coffee with milk   *un cappuccino* (served in a bar, with steamed milk)
   un caffè latte (usually served at breakfast, with warm milk)
fruit juice   *un succo di frutta*
lemonade   *una limonata*
mineral water (carbonated/not carbonated)   *acqua minerale (gassata/non gassata)*
orangeade   *un'aranciata*
red wine   *vino rosso*
rosé wine   *vino rosato*
tea   *un tè*
water   *acqua*
white wine   *vino bianco*

cold   *freddo/a*
hot   *caldo/a*
sweet   *dolce* or *amabile*
(very) dry   *(molto) secco*

bacon   *la pancetta*
bread/rolls   *il pane/i panini*
butter   *il burro*
eggs   *le uova*
   hard-boiled   *uova sode*
   poached   *uova affogate/in camicia*
   soft-boiled   *uova à la coque*
   scrambled   *uova strapazzate*
   sunny-side up   *uova fritte all'occhio di bue*
honey   *il miele*
jam/marmalade   *la confettura/la marmellata*
omelette   *l'omelette*
orange juice   *la spremuta d'arancia*
pepper   *il pepe*
salt   *il sale*
sugar   *lo zucchero*

Waiter!   *Cameriere!*

I would like   *Vorrei*
   a glass of   *un bicchiere di*
   a bottle of   *una bottiglia di*
   a half bottle of   *una mezza bottiglia di*
   a carafe of   *una caraffa di*
   a liter of   *un litro di*
   a half liter of   *un mezzo litro di*
   a quarter liter of   *un quarto di*

The check, please.   *Il conto, per favore.*
Is the service charge included?   *Il servizio è incluso?*

Shopping

bakery   *il panificio*
bookstore   *la libreria*
butcher shop   *la macelleria*
camera shop   *il negozio d'apparecchi fotografici*
delicatessen   *la salumeria/la pizzicheria*
department store   *il grande magazzino*
drugstore (for medicine)   *la farmacia*
grocery   *la drogheria/la pizzicheria*
jewelry store   *la gioielleria*
newsstand   *l'edicola/il giornalaio*
pastry shop   *la pasticceria*
perfume (and cosmetics) store   *la profumeria*
shoestore   *il negozio di scarpe*
supermarket   *il supermercato*
tobacconist   *la tabaccheria*

cheap   *a buon mercato*
expensive   *caro/a*
large   *grande*
larger   *più grande*
too large   *troppo grande*

small   *piccolo/a*
smaller   *più piccolo*
too small   *troppo piccolo*
long   *lungo/a*
short   *corto/a*
antique   *antico/a*
old   *vecchio/a*
new   *nuovo/a*
used   *usato/a*
handmade   *fatto/a a mano*
washable   *lavabile*
How much does it cost?   *Quanto costa?*
What is it made of?   *Dì che cosa è fatto/a?*
  camel's hair   *pelo di cammello*
  cotton   *cotone*
  corduroy   *velluto a coste*
  lace   *pizzo*
  leather   *pelle/cuoio*
  linen   *lino*
  silk   *seta*
  suede   *pelle scamosciata*
  synthetic material   *materiale sintetico*
  wool   *lana*
  brass   *ottone*
  copper   *rame*
  gold   *oro*
  gold plate   *placcato d'oro*
  silver   *argento*
  silver plate   *placcato d'argento*
  stainless steel   *acciaio inossidabile*
  wood   *legno*

Colors

beige   *beige*
black   *nero/a*
blue   *blu* (navy) *celeste/azzurro/a*
brown   *marrone*
green   *verde*
gray   *grigio/a*
orange   *arancio*
pink   *rosa*
purple   *viola*
red   *rosso/a*
white   *bianco/a*
yellow   *giallo/a*
dark   *scuro/a*
light   *chiaro/a*

Getting Around

north   *nord*
south   *sud*
east   *est*
west   *ovest*

right   *destra*
left   *sinistra*
straight ahead   *sempre diritto*
far   *lontano/a*
near   *vicino/a*
gas station   *la stazione di rifornimento/il distributore di benzina*
train station   *la stazione ferroviaria*
bus stop   *la fermata dell'autobus*
subway   *la metropolitana*
airport   *l'aeroporto*
travel agency   *l'agenzia di viaggi*
map   *una carta geografica*
one-way ticket   *un biglietto di sola andata*
round-trip ticket   *un biglietto di andata e ritorno*
track   *il binario*
in first class   *in prima classe*
in second class   *in seconda classe*
no smoking   *non fumare/divieto di fumare*
gas   *la benzina*
tires   *le gomme/i pneumatici*
oil   *l'olio*
Fill it up, please.   *Faccia il pieno, per favore.*
Where is . . .?   *Dov'è . . .?*
Where are . . .?   *Dove sono . . .?*
How many kilometers are we from . . .?   *Quanti chilometri siamo da . . .?*
Does this bus go to . . .?   *Quest'autobus va a . . .?*
What time does it leave?   *A che ora parte?*

Danger   *Pericolo*
Dead end   *Strada Senza Uscita*
Detour   *Deviazione*
Do Not Enter   *Vietato l'Accesso*
Falling Rocks   *Caduta Massi*
Men Working   *Lavori in Corso*
No Parking   *Divieto di Sosta*
No Passing   *Divieto di Sorpasso*
One Way   *Senso Unico*
Pay Toll   *Pagamento Pedaggio*
Pedestrian Zone   *Zona Pedonale*
Reduce Speed   *Rallentare*
Ring Road   *Raccordo Anulare*
Stop   *Alt*
Use Headlights in Tunnel   *Accendere i Fari in Galleria*
Yield   *Dare la Precedenza*

Personal Items and Services

aspirin   *l'aspirina*
Band-Aids   *i cerotti*
barbershop   *il barbiere*
beauty shop   *l'istituto di bellezza*
dry cleaner   *la tintoria*
hairdresser   *il parucchiere per donna*
laundromat   *la lavanderia automatica*

laundry   *la lavanderia*
post office   *l'ufficio postale*
sanitary napkins   *gli assorbenti igienici*
shampoo   *lo shampoo*
shaving cream   *la crema da barba*
shoemaker   *il calzolaio*
soap   *il sapone*
soap powder   *il sapone in polvere*
stamps   *i francobolli*
tampons   *i tamponi*
tissues   *i fazzoletti di carta*
toilet   *il gabinetto/la toilette/il WC*
toilet paper   *la carta igienica*
toothbrush   *lo spazzolino da denti*
toothpaste   *il dentifricio*

Where is the men's/ladies' room?   *Dov'è il gabinetto?* (The door will say
   Uomini or *Signori* for men, *Donne* or *Signore* for women.)
Is it occupied/free?   *E occupato/libero?*

Days of the Week
Monday   *lunedì*
Tuesday   *martedì*
Wednesday   *mercoledì*
Thursday   *giovedì*
Friday   *venerdì*
Saturday   *sabato*
Sunday   *domenica*

Months
January   *gennaio*
February   *febbraio*
March   *marzo*
April   *aprile*
May   *maggio*
June   *giugno*
July   *luglio*
August   *agosto*
September   *settembre*
October   *ottobre*
November   *novembre*
December   *dicembre*

Numbers
zero   *zero*
one   *uno*
two   *due*
three   *tre*
four   *quattro*
five   *cinque*
six   *sei*
seven   *sette*
eight   *otto*

nine   *nove*
ten   *dieci*
eleven   *undici*
twelve   *dodici*
thirteen   *tredici*
fourteen   *quattordici*
fifteen   *quindici*
sixteen   *sedici*
seventeen   *diciassette*
eighteen   *diciotto*
nineteen   *diciannove*
twenty   *venti*
thirty   *trenta*
forty   *quaranta*
fifty   *cinquanta*
sixty   *sessanta*
seventy   *settanta*
eighty   *ottanta*
ninety   *novanta*
one hundred   *cento*

Genealogy

 Unfortunately for modern-day pretenders to the throne, only a privileged few will find their ancestral roots reverently inscribed in the exclusive *Libro d'Oro della Nobiltà Italiana* (*Golden Book of the Italian Nobility*), published by the Istituto Araldico Romano (Via Santa Maria dell'Anima, 00186 Roma) and available in most genealogical libraries. This is just as well. The monarchy was outlawed in Italy in 1946, and having to see if you're listed in the *Golden Book* is like wanting to know the price of an Alfa Romeo — if you have to ask, it's not for you. Also, be forewarned that there are no proven extant lines of descent extending back to the ancient Etruscans, Greeks, or Romans, despite many impassioned claims to the contrary. (However, if behavior is any indication of kinship, these claims may have some basis. The ancient Romans were so eager to prove that they had descended from the city's founding fathers that they had their *sacra gentilica* — family tree, Roman style — painted on the walls of their homes, and fake ancestor portraits and spurious pedigrees were not unknown even then. Rather than dusty canvases, though, these parvenus proudly displayed phony portrait busts, and Aeneas replaced the *Mayflower* as the preferred point of ancestral departure.)

Happily for contemporary ancestor-worshipers, Italians have kept meticulous records, beginning as far back as the 13th century, and legitimate evidence of Italian forebears — no matter how humble their origins — is usually yours for the searching. With a little digging around, you'll probably at least be able to visit the church where your Great Uncle Sal married your Great Aunt Rosa before leaving for America, or the port where your grandfather waved goodbye to the Old Country, or the cemetery where your mother's family has been resting quietly for centuries.

For those who would rather leave the digging to others, reputable genealogical societies in Italy will do it for you for a fee. Among them are *Istituto Araldico Coccia,* Borgo Santa Croce 6, 50122 Firenze (write for their "international ready reckoner," which lists six programs for heraldic and genealogical research); *Istituto di*

Genealogia e Araldica, Via Antonio Cerasi 5A, 00152 Roma; *Istituto Genealogico Italiano,* Conte Guelfo Guelfi Camaiani, Via Torta 14, 50122 Firenze; and *Istituto Genealogico Italiano,* Largo Chigi 19, 00187 Roma.

But if dig you must, try to do as much preliminary research as possible before your trip. The *US Library of Congress* (Local History and Genealogy Room, Jefferson Building, Washington, DC 20540) and the *New York Public Library* (Division of United States History, Local History, and Genealogy, Room 315N, 42nd St. & 5th Ave., New York, NY 10018) both have extensive facilities for in-person research. Also, the *Genealogical Society of the Church of Jesus Christ of Latter-Day Saints* has more than 3,000 reels of Italian genealogical records on microfilm, available for consultation in person at its headquarters (35 North West Temple St., Salt Lake City, UT 84150; phone: 801-531-2331) or through any of its branch libraries (addresses are available by writing to Mary J. Brown, 254 East 1300 North, Bountiful, UT 84010). Using the Mormons' index reels, you can, for a small fee, order from Salt Lake City the microfilm records of any Italian town. Film should arrive at the branch library in about six weeks, and loans are renewable for two-week periods up to six months. The *Italian Cultural Institute* (686 Park Ave., New York, NY 10021) publishes an information sheet on how to go about researching your Italian ancestry. Further tips can be provided by two other publications: *Italian Genealogist* (published for the Augustan Society, 1510 Cravens Ave., Torrance, CA 90501) and *Italian Family Research* (Summit Publications, PO Box 222, Munroe Falls, OH 44062). Look in your library for T. Beard and D. Demong's *How to Find Your Family Roots* (McGraw-Hill, 1977), which contains an excellent list of genealogical resources available in both Italian and English. In Italy, the *Ministry of Foreign Affairs* (*Ministero degli Affari Esteri,* Piazzale Farnesina 1, 00194 Roma) has an Office for Research and Studies of Emigration (*Ufficio Ricerche e Studi dell'Emigrazione*), which may also be of assistance.

Constructing a family tree is a backward process: You need to start with your parents' dates and places of birth, their parents' dates and places, and so on as far back as your search will take you. It should be a considerable stretch since it's quite possible to trace Italian families to about 1500, when it became obligatory for baptisms to be registered in parish churches. To obtain the relevant documents, make sure you have the exact names of each ancestor (remember, many Italian surnames were irrevocably, if unwittingly, changed through clerical misspellings at Ellis Island and other ports of entry) as well as the names of any family members closely related to the ancestor you are researching. You can request many different types of documents that contain information about a previous generation: for example, birth and death certificates, marriage licenses, emigration and immigration records, and baptism and christening records.

REQUESTING RECORDS: Birth, marriage, and death certificates are available from the civil registration office (*Ufficio di Stato Civile*) in the town where the event took place, if it occurred after about 1860, when the country became officially unified as the Kingdom of Italy. Exact addresses of each office are available from the *National Association of Italian Communes* (*ANCI*), Via dei Prefetti 46, 00186 Roma. While many of the offices have English-speaking personnel, making a request in Italian will usually facilitate matters considerably. The form letter on the following page will be of great use in your research (send a separate letter for each ancestor).

DIGGING DEEPER: Once you've done your basic research, you might want to turn to some older records or even use them as duplicates to verify information you've already accumulated. The following are some of the most readily available records by mail or in person.

Certificates of Family Genealogy – Write the General Records Office (*Ufficio Anagrafe*) in the town where your family member lived (for office addresses, see *ANCI* above) to obtain a certificate of your family genealogy (*certificato di stato di*

Ufficio di Stato Civile
Street Address
Postal Code, City
Italy

Gentilissimi Signori:
Desiderando conoscere la storia della mia famiglia, chiedo se cortesemente potreste inviarmi i seguenti certificati:
(*Check the documents desired.*)

_____ certificato di nascita (*birth certificate*)
_____ certificato di matrimonio (*marriage certificate*)
_____ certificato di morte (*death certificate*)

riguardante la persona seguente:
(*Fill in the appropriate information for your ancestor.*)

(*for a man*) Il Signor: _____*(name of man)*_____
(*for a woman*) La Signora: _____*(name of woman)*___
nato/a a: _____*(place of birth)*_____
il: _____*(date of birth)*_____

RingraziandoVi anticipatamente per la Vostra cortese attenzione, spero di ricevere al più presto notizie.

Distinti saluti,
(*sender's signature*)
(*name of sender*)

This letter states that you wish to know the history of your family and therefore are requesting the document or documents specified regarding the person indicated by name, place of birth, and date of birth; it thanks the addressee in advance for his or her kind attention to your request.

---

famiglia) giving names, relationships, birthdates, and birthplaces of all living family members at the time of recording. These certificates usually date from about the turn of the century and can go back as far as 1869.

Emigration Records – Write to the prefecture of the province of the emigrant's birthplace or port of departure to obtain documentation of an ancestor's emigration from about 1869 to the present. (Addresses of provincial prefectures are available from *Unione delle Province Italiane,* Largo Fontanella di Borghese, 00186 Roma.)

Draft Records – For draft records dating from 1869 to the present, write to the military district in charge of an ancestor's town of residence (*Distretto Militare,* name of town), giving birthdates and birthplaces. Some conscription records go back to the Napoleonic era (as early as 1792).

Clerical Surveys – To obtain Catholic parish records (*status animarum*), write to the *Central Office for Italian Emigration* (UCEI, Via Circonvallazione Aurelia 50, 00165 Roma) for addresses of local parishes. Records of birthdates, marriage dates, and other biographical information date, irregularly, from the beginning of the 18th century.

Protestant Parish Registers – Write to the *Genealogical Society* in Salt Lake City (address above) for the addresses of 16 Waldensian parishes in the Pinerolo district. The parish records include information similar to Catholic clerical surveys and date from 1685.

Roman Catholic Parish Records – Write to the *Vicar-General* of the diocese involved (you can get the address from the *Central Office for Italian Emigration,* above) for permission to consult the records, which are usually written in Latin. Baptism and christening records, as well as marriage records, date from 1545 (1493 in the town of Fiesole) to the present. Death and burial records go back to the beginning of the seventeenth century.

Tax Assessment or Census Registers – Write to the *Istituto Centrale di Statistica* (Via Cesare Balbo 16, 00184 Roma) to locate the old census returns (*catasti*), also called *libri di fuochi* in southern Italy and *libri degli estimi* in the north. Often dating from the 14th century, these contain so-called real estate records (actually tax records — census takers were no fools even then) of heads of households, subtenants, or taxpayers and their residences along with the amount of tax assessed. Most of the records are located in the *Archivio Secreto del Vaticano* in Rome, the *Archivio di Stato* in Florence, and the archives of the *Kingdom of the Two Sicilies* in Naples.

Ecclesiastical Records – For clerical records from the 13th to the 19th century, write to the *Archivio Segreto,* Città del Vaticano.

Notarial Records – Write to the Ispettore Generale (*Archivio Notarile,* Via Flaminia 160, 00196 Roma) for records concerning wills, donations, settlements, and land sales dating from about 1340. For similar records from Waldensian Protestant archives beginning in 1610, write to the Ispettore Generale, *Archivi di Stato di Torino,* Piazza Castello 165, 10122 Torino.

Other Sources – The Italian national archives are located in a central office at Corso Rinascimento 40, 00186 Roma; more complete records are kept in the various former independent states that existed before the unification of Italy. There are substantial archival centers in Bologna, Florence, Genoa, Lucca, Mantua, Milan, Modena, Naples, Palermo, Parma, Siena, and Venice.

With the above information and a little *pazienza* (patience), you should have a firm grasp for a lengthy climb up your Italian family tree.

PERSPECTIVES

History

The nineteenth-century statesman Count Metternich dismissed Italy as no more than a "geographical expression." Although he was politically motivated to say this, as he pressed for Austria's interests in Venetia and Lombardy, his point was well taken. Italy lagged far behind its European neighbors in developing a distinct *national* identity. It was not until 1870 — when its twenty regions were finally brought under one central government — that Italy became a unified political entity. Even into this century, the country has been divided geographically on certain governmental issues. Nevertheless, the Italian *cultural* identity has been in existence since antiquity. In fact, the name *Italy* has been used for more than 3,000 years to define this peninsula, a 1,500-mile-long landspit that stretches from the Alps into the Mediterranean.

Geography is the key to much of Italian history. In ancient times, the country's position in the Mediterranean, much like a bridge joining East and West, made it a logical way station for Greek civilization and later an effective "launching pad" for Roman conquest. On the other hand, Italy's more than 3,000 miles of coastline on the Adriatic, Ionian, and Tyrrhenian seas — as well as its 1,058-mile land frontier with France, Switzerland, and Austria — have made it an almost certain prey for foreign invaders and have contributed to the ethnic diversity of the population. At the same time, the peninsula's geographical structure, divided by the Apennine Mountains, has made possible sharply defined internal regions that developed — linguistically, artistically, politically, economically, and culturally — along noticeably distinct and separate lines. Even until fairly recent times, patriotism in Italy most often connoted loyalty and allegiance to one's home region rather than to the nation as a whole. From a historical point of view, however, Italy has always been a precise entity.

ORIGINS

The earliest known inhabitants of the Italian peninsula and islands were Latin and other Italic tribes who had settled there by 2000 BC. For the most part, these groups had only local influence and appear to have been unable to resist the sway of the Etruscans, whose origins remain controversial but who appeared in Italy about 1200 BC and who dominated vast areas of central Italy until the rise of Latin Rome.

By the second millennium BC, Greek ships and traders had come with their goods, their crafts, and their culture. By the eighth century BC, the first Greek colonies were established in the Italian south, particularly in Calabria and Apulia. Sicily, and to a lesser degree Sardinia, became a battleground for rivalry between the Greeks and Carthage, the Phoenician colony in North Africa that was allied with the Etruscans.

THE ROMANS

Rome was founded in 753 BC, when Latin and other villagers are believed to have settled on the Palatine hill. The ruler they chose was Romulus, said to be a descendant of Aeneas, Prince of Troy. Romulus was followed by three Sabine kings and by three Etruscans who left their mark in the identification they fostered between church and state.

In 509 BC, the city-state's great landowners ended the first monarchy and founded the Roman Republic. For centuries thereafter, Rome was the scene of struggle between the founding patricians and the plebeians, mostly urban artisans, who had been left out of the new power arrangements. The life of the Republic was increasingly disrupted by civil strife and social unrest, which culminated in the civil wars of the first century BC, the rise of Julius Caesar as dictator, his assassination by a group of angry senators in 44 BC, and the eventual establishment in 27 BC of the imperial monarchy under Caesar's nephew, the emperor Augustus.

Although the Roman Republic had been troubled by social problems, corruption, and power feuds among members of the ruling oligarchy, this period of Roman history witnessed the first successes of Roman military and political expansion. Paradoxically, it was probably an invasion by the Gauls into central Italy that led to the defeat and destruction of many Etruscan towns early in the fourth century BC and laid the groundwork for future Roman success.

The defeat of the Etruscans made Roman expansion northward easier in later years, and the Gallic threat also convinced many of the semi-independent Latin city-states to form alliances with Rome. For example, the ruling nobles of Capua, then the capital of the Campania region, enlisted the Romans to help against the marauding Samnite tribes of the Apennine Mountains. The eventual Roman victory, symbolized by the construction of the Appian Way from Rome to Capua, was only the first step in a series of conquests that extended Rome's power throughout the peninsula. The Republic's growing influence eventually led to conflict with some of the Greek colonies in Italy. With the defeat of Tarantum in the south in 272 BC and of the last Etruscan city, Volsinii, in 265 BC, the Romans became masters of the Italian mainland.

However, these conquests made war with Carthage inevitable. From Carthaginian bases in Spain, the great general Hannibal led his army overland through France and the Alps to Italy. He was stopped only by dissension at home. Then, in 202 BC, Carthage was defeated and destroyed by the Roman general Scipio Africanus. This victory also led to Roman rule of Spain and then Greece. The overseas empire had begun.

In the first century BC, Caesar conquered and colonized Gaul, a move designed as much to win him the loyalty of the Roman soldiers as to extend Rome's power further throughout Europe. When Augustus defeated Mark Antony and the Egyptian queen Cleopatra in 31 BC at Actium, Roman supremacy took another step forward.

Augustus's victory over Antony reestablished the Western orientation of the Roman Empire, stretching its frontiers from the Rhine and the Danube in the west to the Syrian Desert in the east. But continuing problems inside Rome threatened the stability of the regime, whose powers remained divided between the Senate and its oligarchs and the emperor. The reigns of Tiberius, Caligula, Claudius, and Nero were fraught with palace intrigues, the only major positive achievement being the conquest of Britain, begun by Claudius in AD 43.

In the second century AD, under such emperors as Trajan, Hadrian, and Marcus Aurelius, periods of peace were interspersed with further territorial expansion. But by the end of Marcus Aurelius's reign, invasions by the barbarians from the north had begun and an outbreak of plague signaled the onset of a new period of chaos. With the death of Commodus, Marcus Aurelius's son, in AD 198, a series of new pretenders made their claims to the throne, and it was not until the accession of Diocletian in AD 284 that order, prosperity, and peace were at least temporarily restored. Diocletian saw that the Empire had become too big and divided its administration among himself and four other leaders. His successor, Constantine, moved the capital eastward, away from the invaders, and established Constantinople, making the split of the Empire into East and West inevitable.

With the sack of Rome in AD 410 by the Visigoths, the death knell of the Empire had inexorably sounded. Marauding German tribes gradually established kingdoms throughout the peninsula, and constant warfare brought influence increasingly into the hands of the army, while the emperors were weak and easily dethroned. The last Roman emperor in the West, Romulus Augustulus, was dethroned by a general of barbarian origin, Odoacer, in 476.

THE MIDDLE AGES

From 488 to 526, Theodoric, king of the Ostrogoths, ruled Italy from Ravenna, where he built beautiful monuments. Subsequently, the Byzantine emperor Justinian defeated the Goths, only to open the way to new invasions by the Lombards, who set up their own dynasty. Meanwhile, the Roman papacy had become more influential, and in 754 Pope Stephen II asked Pepin, king of the Franks, to expel the Lombards. Pepin restored the city and its immediate territory to the papacy, thus establishing the basis of the future Papal States of Italy. A few decades later, Pope Leo II reestablished the form of the Western Roman Empire when he offered an imperial crown to Charlemagne, king of the Franks. However, in the north of Italy and in Rome itself, the authority of the Holy Roman Empire was often nominal, while in the south, there were repeated Saracen incursions, followed by later Norman invasions.

Beginning in the eleventh century, under the formal authority of the German emperors — who were crowned in Rome but generally resided on the other side of the Alps — the towns and communities of northern and central Italy began a spurt of intense economic development and experimentation with self-rule. The major characteristics of life in these city-states, or "communes," as they were called, were government by constitution and by an elected official known variously as a *podestà* or *console* and the emergence of a merchant bourgeoisie and of a skilled urban artisan class. This situation contrasted markedly with that in the south, where the Norman king Roger II ruled Sicily and the southern mainland, and the feudal system became so firmly entrenched that its effects endured even into the twentieth century, accounting for much of the difference between northern Italy and the *mezzogiorno* (south) today.

Thus, in northern and central Italy, civilization continued to mature. Venice was an independent state of international renown, and the cities of Lombardy, Umbria, and Tuscany, as well as others in Venetia, had growing cultural and trading ties with the rest of Europe. The constant conflict between pope and emperor was an unsettling factor at the time, however, reaching a high point when Frederick Barbarossa arrived with a 3,000-man invading force in 1154, seeking — unsuccessfully in the end — to unite Italy under his own authority. During the twelfth and thirteenth centuries, most of Italy's city-states were forced to choose sides, becoming either Guelph (supporters of the papacy) or Ghibelline (allies of the emperor). Nevertheless, they prospered, even though by the middle of the thirteenth century a number of them were no longer democratically governed. They were now under the sway of important local families, or *signorie,* such as the Visconti of Milan (and later the Sforza), the Gonzaga of Mantua, the Malatesta of Rimini, the Este of Ferrara, and, eventually, the Medicis of Florence.

Despite wars, plagues, and famine, the wealth and military strength of these families grew, increasing the power of the city-states they governed. There is no doubt that as the Renaissance gathered momentum two city-states in particular, Florence and Milan, were major players on the chessboard of Italian politics, along with the Papal States (which had recouped losses suffered during the fourteenth-century Babylonian captivity and the Great Schism), the still independent maritime republic of Venice, and Naples. Naples had fallen under the influence of the popes, who supported the unpopular Anjou princes and, until the fifteenth century, helped fend off the Aragonese that were already in control of Sicily.

The city-states were fully autonomous, and the courts of their ruling families often equaled or surpassed those of the great national royal families of Europe. Their courts also sponsored the most skilled and important Italian artists, writers, and scholars of the time. In this respect, none was as eminent as the city-state of Florence, ruled by the financially and politically skilled Cosimo de' Medici and later his grandson Lorenzo the Magnificent; these two were mostly responsible for the Tuscan city's power and prestige. Florence was, in fact, the linchpin in a formal alliance (called the Italian League) of the most powerful Italian states formed in the mid-fifteenth century, largely at the pope's urgings, to protect Italy from foreign intervention. It was successful until the death of Lorenzo in 1492 prompted events that led to its demise.

THE FOREIGN DOMINATIONS

As the alliance among the Italian states disintegrated, the French were encouraged to put forward their long-standing claims to Milan and Naples. In a series of army invasions toward the end of the fifteenth and beginning of the sixteenth centuries, the French succeeded in taking Milan twice and Naples once but were routed after Charles the Fifth, the Hapsburg king of Spain, became Holy Roman Emperor and forged a defensive European alliance to contain the French.

For the next 200 years, the Spanish Hapsburgs were the major dominating force in Italy, with Milan given to the Infant, Don Philip, and Naples still in the hands of the Aragonese. Except for Venice and the Duchy of Savoy-Piedmont, the other Italian states gradually came under Spanish domination. From an artistic and cultural point of view, the level of Italian civilization remained very high.

The War of the Spanish Succession (1701–13) ended with Austria's emergence as the dominant foreign power in Italy. The Duchy of Tuscany gradually gained a reputation as one of the most liberal states in Europe, enforcing policies of free trade and suppressing ecclesiastical tribunals. Joseph II's reign in Milan was also influenced by the Enlightenment, and Naples became a major European intellectual center. However, the new sea routes to America and India led to the economic decline of most of Italy's coastal republics, although Venice's commercial downturn was to an extent hidden by its brilliance as a cultural center.

From the start, the French Revolution won support only from the liberal aristocracy and some segments of the middle class. Opposition was widespread and gradually solidified. Nevertheless, by 1806 Napoleon had annexed large portions of Italy, including Rome, Piedmont, and the Venetian possessions in Dalmatia. He abandoned the 1,200-year-old Venetian Republic to Austria and established the Kingdom of Italy in central and northern Italy under his own control. In hindsight, the Napoleonic period was of great importance to Italy's future development as a modern state: The hegemony of Austria was definitively shattered; French laws and institutions left a decisive influence; trade and industry received a substantial impetus; and the invasion, combined with the intellectual influence of the Enlightenment, stimulated feelings of nationalism.

THE RISORGIMENTO

The Napoleonic period was brought to a close by the Congress of Vienna (1815) and the subsequent restoration of Europe's absolutist monarchies. Shortly thereafter, however, the influence of French ideas took hold in Italy, with the first liberal revolts in Naples (1820) and Turin (1821). The revolts were put down, and there was a general attack, particularly in Lombardy-Venetia, on the Carbonari and other "subversive" secret societies.

The French Revolution of 1830 stimulated another wave of rebellion in Italy, but at this point the nationalist movement gradually came under control of the Young Italy movement, headed by Giuseppe Mazzini, a Republican ideologue from Genoa. From exile in London, Mazzini conducted a campaign for independence that sought to involve an ever greater part of the population.

The 1848 Revolution in Paris sent another shock wave throughout Italy that more or less coincided with the Piedmont king Charles-Albert's decision to take advantage of Austrian political unrest to invade Lombardy, where the population had already risen during the Five Days of Milan, expelling the Austrians from the city. There were other revolts in Rome, where Mazzini established a short-lived republic, as well as in Palermo and Naples. Once again, however, the forces of change were to be defeated. Despite the aid of thousands of volunteers from Tuscany, Modena, Parma, and Lombardy, the Piedmontese troops were unable to defeat the Austrians.

In Rome, French troops intervened to protect the pope, and in Venice the Republicans were forced to surrender to the Austrian army in August 1849 after months of constant bombardment, famine, and plague. However, one bright spot was to have incalculable consequences for the future. Under the pressure of events and the influence of modern ideas, a liberal constitution had been promulgated in Piedmont that transformed that state into a limited monarchy with a strong parliamentary government. The only Italian state with a respectable military establishment of its own and a history of independence, Piedmont emerged as the only political entity capable of providing concrete leadership for the Risorgimento.

Mazzini's influence was as a political thinker. The man who actually forged Italian unity was the prime minister of Piedmont, Count Camillo Cavour. Cavour's first goal was to enlarge the Piedmontese state ruled by the House of Savoy, specifically by King Victor Emmanuel II, who had assumed control from his father, Carlo Alberto, when the latter abdicated after the Italian defeat by the Austrians on March 23, 1849. Diplomatic accords with France meant that after the Austrian-French war of 1859, Piedmont was able to obtain Lombardy in return for ceding Nice and Savoy to France.

New annexations followed rebellions in other Italian states such as Tuscany and Emilia-Romagna. At this point, Cavour put unification on hold, to Mazzini's dismay. But Cavour's hand was forced by freedom fighter Giuseppe Garibaldi and his Thousand Red Shirts, who landed in Sicily in 1860 and moved up through the island and to Naples, deposing the Bourbon monarchy there and proclaiming conquest in the name of Victor Emmanuel. Fearful of international reactions to an attack on Rome, a Piedmontese army was sent to bar Garibaldi's advance. Garibaldi turned over Naples and Sicily to Piedmont, and in 1861 Cavour convened a national parliament that adopted the Piedmontese Constitution as the law of the new nation. Venetia became part of Italy after a third war with Austria in 1866, leaving only Rome outside a united Italy.

Pope Pius IX refused to consider an offer by Cavour for privileges within Italy for the Catholic church in return for a disclaimer to the papacy's temporal claim to Rome. After France's defeat by Prussia in 1870, the French garrison supporting the Pope was withdrawn from Rome, and the situation shifted. Italian troops under General Cadórna entered the city at Porta Pia, and at last Italy became a fully united country. However, the dispute with the Pope was to cast a pall over the first decades of national life; the Pontiff rejected all attempts at reconciliation, excommunicated Italy's new king, and declared himself a prisoner in the Vatican. Catholics were forbidden to vote or take part in political life, and for the most part government was left to the country's anticlericals.

THE CONSTITUTIONAL MONARCHY

The new Kingdom of Italy was faced with a series of grave problems, not least of which was the integration into a single nation of a variety of regions with different cultural and linguistic traditions. There were widespread banditry in the south, particularly in Sicily, turmoil and armed skirmishing (until Rome and Venice were incorporated into the Kingdom), and a huge foreign debt. Extreme poverty was endemic, especially in the south. Over the next half century, several million Italians, most of them from Calabria and Sicily, emigrated — the majority to the US. (In one decade alone — 1900–1910 — two million went to New York City.)

From the start, the new Italian Parliament — an appointed Senate and an elected lower Chamber — was dominated by politicians from Piedmont. The main players in the political system were the Right, in the Cavour tradition, and the Left, which from 1876 was to hold a parliamentary majority and which sought to broaden the electorate and pass several important social reforms, such as compulsory primary school education. However, the Left was so severely split into factions that orderly party government became impossible. *Trasformismo,* a system of political brokerage leading to constantly shifting alliances, dominated the Parliament. Popular disillusionment led gradually to the growth of the Socialist party (founded in 1892), which by 1900 controlled about a quarter of the seats in Parliament. However, fear of socialism, plus a reaction to the anarchist violence that in 1900 took the life of King Umberto I, led to a rapprochement between the Liberals, led by Giovanni Giolitti, and the Catholics, who after 1904 had been allowed by Pope Pius X to return to political action.

The new nation also found itself in need of a foreign policy, especially since the other European countries were at first reluctant to recognize Italy, whose appearance on the diplomatic scene meant an inevitable reshaping of alliances. Seeking a place among the family of nations, the Italian government soon sought to join the race for overseas colonies. The Leftist prime minister Francesco Crispi sent troops to Africa to seize parts of Eritrea and Somalia in 1889. When Crispi's attempt to conquer Ethiopia in 1896 ended in military defeat at Adowa, with 4,000 Italians killed and 2,000 captured, he was driven from office. Colonial expansion was resumed under Giolitti in 1911 and 1912, when the Balkan war with Turkey left Italy in possession of both Libya and the Dodecanese Islands.

In Europe, Italian foreign policy rested primarily on membership in the Triple Alliance with Germany and Austria, although under Victor Emmanuel III and Giolitti closer ties were gradually forged with France and Great Britain. The outbreak of World War I caused great controversy in Italy, with public opinion sharply divided between those favoring neutrality, the government's initial position, and those claiming that Italy was duty-bound to live up to its Triple Alliance obligations and fight on the side of Germany and Austria.

In the end, reasons of national interest prevailed. The government secretly negotiated its entry into the war on the side of France and Britain in return for promises that the Italian-speaking areas of Austria — Trentino, Trieste, and Istria as well as the South Tyrol — would be returned to it along with new colonial concessions. On May 23, 1915, Italy declared war on Austria and, a year later, on Germany.

The decision to go to war proved fatal for Italian democracy. The long conflict took the lives of 600,000 Italians, and deprivation and low morale gripped the home front. Italy's aspirations were only partly satisfied at the Versailles Conference. It gained South Tyrol, Trentino, and Trieste, but Fiume and the Dalmatian coast remained in alien hands, to become the focus of a resurgent Italian nationalism. Italy's claim to share in the parceling out of colonies from the division of the defeated German and Turkish empires was ignored. As a result, embittered, disappointed Italians turned to a nationalistic strongman, Benito Mussolini.

THE FASCIST REGIME

Along with its sense of betrayal and frustration, Italy after World War I was faced with inflation, food shortages, an enormous war debt, and spreading strikes that threatened to further paralyze the economy. Socialist militancy was encouraged by the success of the Russian Revolution, and a Communist party was formed in 1921. Many factories were occupied by workers, and the government's inability to reassert control convinced the frightened middle classes that they would have to turn elsewhere for help.

Against this background rose Mussolini, a former Socialist who had broken with the party when it opposed Italian entry into World War I. A charismatic orator, Mussolini in 1919 had already organized his Blackshirt squads and later, in 1921, a small political party, the Fascists, which won thirty-five seats in Parliament and was included in a coalition government to help form a majority. In October 1922, Mussolini was asked by the king to form his own government, as prime minister, in a coalition with some of the major parties, including the Italian Popular Party, the Popolari, Italy's first mass-based Catholic party and the forerunner of today's Christian Democratic Party.

The Popolari withdrew from the coalition in 1923, but Mussolini revised the electoral law and in the 1924 general election won two-thirds of the seats in Parliament. In June 1924, his government was threatened by a wave of revulsion over the murder of Socialist politician Giacomo Matteotti by Fascist thugs. But when the king refused to support the opposition against him, Mussolini assumed dictatorial powers in January 1925 and thereafter ruled by decree through the Fascist Grand Council. A totalitarian system was quickly established, although both the economy and the Church continued to operate in relative freedom. One of Mussolini's major accomplishments was the 1929 signing of a concordat with the Holy See that ended the church-state breach that had existed for fifty years.

The Lateran Pacts created the Vatican State as an independent entity, restored the Church's role in Italian education, recognized its jurisdiction in ecclesiastical matters, including marriage and divorce, and established Rome as a sacred city. The pacts became part of the Italian Republic's Constitution in 1948, although some aspects of church-state relations as laid out in the concordat were modified by a renegotiation ratified in 1985.

Along with doomed attempts to create a self-sufficient Italian economy, colonial expansionism and imperialism were also important aspects of Fascist policy. In the mid-1930s Mussolini conquered and occupied Ethiopia. The League of Nations' attempt to impose economic sanctions only revived support for Mussolini and created a new wave of bitterness toward Great Britain and Western Europe. Mussolini signed alliances with Hitler's Germany and with Japan.

As in 1915, however, the military was not as well prepared as it looked. Italy suffered military setbacks or defeats in almost all of its World War II campaigns: France, Greece, Africa, and the Soviet Union. Consequently, when the Allies landed in Sicily in July 1943, they were greeted as liberators. Their arrival set off a palace coup by the Fascist Grand Council that forced Mussolini to resign and flee to the rump Fascist Republic of Salò in the Italian north, and power was restored to the undeserving Victor Emmanuel III. The king appointed a military officer, Marshal Pietro Badoglio, as prime minister. An armistice was quickly signed with the Allies, and war was declared on Germany. In the Italian south, which was liberated by the Allies, the Committee of National Liberation was set up by six anti-Fascist parties, ranging from the Christian Democrats and the Socialists to the Republicans and Communists; in the north, Resistance activities were carried on by several groups, particularly the Communists, with some help from the Allies. After the liberation of Rome in June 1944, a six-party government was established by veteran politician Ivanoe Bonomi. The following year, Mussolini was killed by partisans as he tried to flee to Switzerland.

THE ITALIAN REPUBLIC

The end of World War II left Italy with a whole spectrum of problems. The economy was seriously disrupted, many cities were partially destroyed, and hundreds of thousands of people were unemployed and homeless. To make matters worse, when peace negotiations were concluded, the Allies treated Italy as a defeated power rather than as a cobelligerent. The peace treaty limited the size of the Italian armed forces, established reparations payments, and deprived Italy of Istria, Zara, and islands in the Adriatic, all of which were restored to Yugoslavia. The colonial possessions in Africa and the Dodecanese Islands also had to be given up.

These disappointments were somewhat mitigated by the salvaging of Trieste and South Tyrol and by the rejection of French claims on Valle d'Aosta by the other Allies. Italy had few doubts about the direction of its postwar foreign policy. The first few years after the war were characterized by strong neutralist sentiment, somewhat prompted by the emerging East-West tensions that raised fears of another war and that came to a head with the battle over NATO membership in 1948–49. Italy's decision to join NATO has never wavered, and the Italian commitment to the Atlantic alliance has remained one of the strongest in Europe, evidenced by the relatively painless decision by a coalition government in 1979 to accept the installation of cruise missiles on Italian soil.

At the same time that Italy was moving toward close Atlantic relations, Count Carlo Sforza, the chief architect of postwar foreign policy, was laying the foundations for another major tenet of postwar policy: the commitment to European integration. At a very early stage, Sforza and Prime Minister Alcide De Gasperi realized that Italy's fate was inexorably tied up with that of its Western European allies. Thus, Italy was a charter member of the European Coal and Steel Community, the Western European Union, and the European Economic Community (the Common Market), set up in 1956. (Italian foreign policy has never strayed from these two basic and overlapping orientations, and, indeed, in the late 1970s and early 1980s the governments in power became even more active in cooperative foreign policy. For example, Italy was a major participant in the Multinational Peace Force sent to Lebanon in 1982.)

Following the end of the war in 1945, the House of Savoy could possibly have survived if King Victor Emmanuel, whose reputation had been irrevocably sullied by his relations with Mussolini, had abdicated in favor of his son Umberto immediately after the fall of Mussolini. But by the time a popular referendum on the monarchy was held in June 1946, there was so much bitterness toward the royal family that a majority of Italians voted in favor of a republican form of government, and Umberto II, who had become king in May when his father belatedly stepped down, was forced into exile in Portugal.

The June 1946 elections also chose a Constituent Assembly charged with writing a new Italian constitution to replace that of 1848. The voters, including women for the first time, gave 35 percent of the seats in the Assembly to the new Christian Democratic Party, 20 percent to the Socialists, and 19 percent to the Communists. The rest of the seats were divided among smaller Italian parties, including a neo-Fascist group. The new constitution was approved in December 1947 by an overwhelming majority; it called for a popularly elected two-house Parliament and a president, elected by the Parliament, who would have the power to appoint a prime minister and to dissolve Parliament in the event of an insoluble government crisis. The constitution also adopted the 1929 concordat that gave the Catholic church special privileges. The Italian Communists, following their postwar policy of cooperation, went along.

The first national elections under the new constitution took place in April 1948 and were preceded by months of sharp political debate reflecting the country's gradual polarization between the Left and the Right. When the vote was in, the elections had given Alcide De Gasperi's Christian Democrats a clear majority with 48% of the vote (and 305 of the 574 seats in the Chamber of Deputies), compared with the 31% won jointly by the Communists and Socialists. In 1947, De Gasperi had already succeeded in forcing the Marxist parties out of the joint tripartite coalitions that had followed the war, and after April 1948 this trend continued. For years, Italy was to be governed by the Christian Democrats alone or in coalition with smaller centrist parties like the Social Democrats, the Liberals, and the Republicans. But the Christian Democrats, a highly fragmented political group that got both the credit for laying the foundations of postwar economic prosperity and a good part of the blame for the equally present corruption and inefficiency, were never again able to match their 1948 showing. Despite its frequent reliance on anticommunism in its electoral propaganda, the party saw its share of the vote decline gradually to an all-time low of 32.6% in 1982, although there was a slight improvement (to 35%) in the local elections of 1985.

In the early 1960s, a major political shift occurred in Italy: the formation of the first Center-Left government with the participation of Italian Socialists, who over the years had gradually pulled away from an initial postwar alliance with the Communists. The Hungarian uprising of 1956 and the consequent Soviet intervention had led the Socialists to reject dogmatic Marxism and the Soviet Union and to swing around to pro-Western positions. Although the Socialists have never surpassed 12% of the vote in national elections, the increasing weakness of the Christian Democrats, the continued exclusion of the powerful Communists from government, and a major political scandal in 1981 combined to give the Socialists a determining influence. When he resigned in the summer of 1986, the Socialist Bettino Craxi had enjoyed the longest term as prime minister in Italy's postwar history — and at press time was indeed once again prime minister at the head of a new government.

The reduced influence of the Christian Democrats, although they remain Italy's single largest party, reflected both disillusionment with what was viewed by many as unresponsive government and a general change in Italian society after the student movement of 1968, considered by many to be a watershed in recent Italian history. Since 1968, the traditional influence of both the Church and the Christian Democrats has shrunk sharply, as could be seen by the outcomes of the popular referendums on divorce and abortion, in which the yes votes of the progressive side of the political spectrum were victorious, despite an active Church campaign for rejection.

For a while, these winds of change brought huge political benefits to the Italian Communist party, which throughout the postwar period has been Italy's second largest political group. The good government provided by the Communists in many of the cities and regions in their traditional strongholds plus widespread political frustration in 1975 and 1976 led the party to make large electoral gains, bringing it within a few points of overtaking the Christian Democrats and winning a vast amount of influence in the day-to-day decision making of the Italian Parliament. Indeed, in 1978 the Communist party came closer to government participation than at any other time since 1947, when it was forced out of the postwar tripartite alliance. To help deal with the labor and economic situation, as well as with spreading terrorism, the Christian Democrats and Italy's other parties officially asked the Communists to join the parliamentary majority that supported the coalition government, headed by Christian Democrat Prime Minister Giulio Andreotti.

Unfortunately, however, the day of this historic agreement coincided with the kidnaping of former Christian Democrat Premier Aldo Moro. Because of strains within the government and inside the Communist party itself, where hardliners were unhappy with the degree of cooperation now accorded the country's capitalists, this de facto alliance lasted less than two years. The Communists, with their 30% vote, have been consistently excluded from taking part in Italian government. However justified, this exclusion has had profound negative effects on the Italian political system. It means there is never an acceptable alternative to rule by the Christian Democrats and their allies. Government in Italy remains a permanent preserve of the same five parties — the Christian Democrats, Socialists, Social Democrats, Liberals, and Republicans — that have governed it, in one group or another, for the past thirty-five years. Not only does this mean that no substantial change is possible or likely in key government decisions, but it also makes government downright difficult since all five parties agree on little more than Italy's democratic system, its mixed economy, and its pro-Western foreign policy. Everything else is compromise or deadlock.

On the one hand, the changes in Italian society and the frustrations caused by political unresponsiveness led to some sympathy for the Communists as a progressive force operating within the system. On the other, there was recognition of the negative aspects of the party as well. A surge of political radicalism increasingly found an outlet in terrorism or other forms of political violence. The appearance of the Red Brigades in the early 1970s, flanked by several other similar organizations such as Front Line and Communist Fighting Units, was paralleled on the far Right by subversive organizations such as the Armed Revolutionary Nuclei. What the two sides had in common was the goal of fomenting change through terrorism and murder, so that between 1974 and 1982 several hundred people died in terrorist attacks.

In recent years, however, the terrorist phenomenon has abated somewhat. The major terrorist leaders are now almost all behind bars, and the widespread support that once enabled them to operate so efficiently within Italian society has now almost disappeared, drastically isolating the small number of holdouts who have avoided arrest. Unfortunately, however, the decline of home-grown terrorism has been paralleled by an increase in Middle Eastern terrorism. In 1985, there were several murderous terrorist attacks by Palestinians, including the hijacking of the *Achille Lauro* cruise ship and the Christmas holiday massacre at Leonardo da Vinci Airport.

During the entire postwar period, perhaps the most impressive achievement of contemporary Italy has been its remarkable economic recovery from wartime impoverishment to its status as one of the world's ten most industrialized nations.

Although the economy's record has been by no means unblemished, the "economic miracle" that occurred between 1950 and 1964 laid the basis for further expansion and industrial development. Admittedly, Italy's economic development since then has been marked by double-digit inflation that lasted through 1984 and is still higher than elsewhere in the West, by high unemployment, still prevalent in some parts of the Italian south, and by a huge and expanding budget deficit. Also, high labor costs have hurt Italian competition abroad, and the need to import most important raw materials, particularly oil, puts a constant strain on the balance of payments. A poorly functioning bureaucracy and government indecision — not surprising, given the inevitable reliance on coalition governments — has slowed social programs, particularly housing and health care, which lag behind general European levels and which have led to discontent and, until recently, substantial strikes and other labor unrest.

This makes it all the more remarkable that Italy today is an economically thriving country, offering almost all its citizens a better standard of living than ever before. In certain sectors, Italy has made an international name for itself, and companies such as Fiat (automobiles), Olivetti (typewriters and communications), Montedison (chemicals), Augusta (helicopters), Alfa Romeo (automobiles), Pirelli (tires), Perugina (candy), Parmalat (dairy products), Gucci (leather goods), and Benetton (knitwear) are known throughout the world. In recent years, Italy has become one of the world's major producers of robots, while its fashion designers have made *la moda italiana* into a household phrase. Indeed, from cars to shoes, products "Made in Italy" have won wide acclaim for their style, design, craftsmanship, and quality — all characteristics that make modern life in Italy so interesting and pleasant.

Literature

Italy's culture is virtually impossible to understand from the comfort of an armchair, for the secrets of Italy's art, its music, and particularly its literature are locked in the landscape, the climate, and the life of the various corners of the peninsula where they are created. If there is one single key to Italian literature, it is its regional diversity.

From the fall of the Roman Empire to the unification under Garibaldi in 1860, Italy did not exist as a country but was made up of independent mini-states. And the novels of the Sicilian Giovanni Verga are as different from the writings of the Lombard Alessandro Manzoni as the spicy *spaghetti alla napoletana* is from the northern tortellini in cream sauce — all of which gives the person interested in Italy's literary heritage an ironclad excuse to embark on an on-site investigation. It is much easier to appreciate the poetry of Dante after wandering through the streets of Florence, where he first glimpsed his beloved Beatrice more than six centuries ago. Similarly, the dramatic impact of Carlo Levi's *Cristo si è fermato a Eboli* (*Christ Stopped at Eboli*) cannot be fully grasped unless you have visited one of the remote villages in the deep south and witnessed the poverty, the searing hot sunshine, and the people's deep-rooted superstitions and traditions.

During the Middle Ages, Italy, like France, had a strong courtly love tradition that provided the themes for the poems of troubadours — the idolization of woman and the capriciousness of love. The center of activity was Sicily, which had been conquered by the Normans in the eleventh century, and there the tradition had its roots. But there was also a Tuscan school, one of whose most colorful exponents was Cecco Angiolieri of Siena (1260–1312), who adapted the chivalrous style to produce a far more earthy and witty tone. One of his most unforgettable sonnets describes his wife in the morning before she puts on her makeup.

Francesco Petrarca (1304–74), known to moderns as Petrarch, is traditionally considered the father of the European love lyric and the man who invented the sonnet. His poems are dominated by the image of the woman he loved, though the feeling was unrequited. She was Laura, whom he first saw in a church in Avignon on April 6, 1327, and who died on the same day twenty-one years later. One theory contends that Laura never actually existed, but it is more commonly believed that she was Laure de Noves, the wife of Hugues de Sade. Whatever her identity, she provided inspiration for the lovesick poet, whose style and sentiment are far more complex and sophisticated than those of the courtly love poets. His collection, *Rime* (*Rhymes*), broaches subjects previously untouched in Italian love poetry, not least of which is physical love.

Dante Alighieri was a contemporary of Petrarch, but his works eclipsed all of his predecessors — and most of those who followed. Today, he is still regarded as one of Western civilization's most important and influential poets. Although exact details of Dante's life are sketchy, he was born in the late thirteenth century and was brought up in Florence, the city that dominates his works and from which he was exiled for much of his life. He wrote during a time of bitter struggle between church and state in Europe, against the background of an Italy sharply divided by internal warfare between partisans of the pope and of the emperor — Guelphs and Ghibellines. His own Florence, after the expulsion of the Ghibellines, was further rent by rivalry between Black and White Guelphs, and Dante, of the latter faction, was expelled when the Blacks came to power. His writing is highly influenced by his political experiences, especially by his banishment from his birthplace.

Dante is credited with having established Tuscan as the language for all Italy, a measured, conscious decision on his part. Remarkably, it took hold and still endures. Dante's works include *La vita nuova* (*The New Life*), a love poem dedicated to Beatrice, who was to Dante what Laura was to Petrarch, and the political treatises *De monarchia* (*On the Subject of Monarchy*) and *Convivio* (*The Banquet*). But his *Divina commedia* (*Divine Comedy*) dwarfs them all. This is Dante's vision of Hell, Purgatory, and Paradise, charting the poet's odyssey through all three regions, as well as of the political, dynastic, and military convolutions of his time. Dante himself called it simply *Commedia;* posterity supplied the adjective.

Giovanni Boccaccio (1313–75) created Italian literature's first prose monuments. The setting for his major work, the *Decameron,* is only a stone's throw from Dante's Florence — an elegant villa in the Tuscan hill town of Fiesole. But the style and tone of the *Decameron* could not be more different from the somber and spiritual *Divine Comedy.* The *Decameron* is a collection of tales told by a group of lords and ladies seeking refuge in the clean air of Fiesole from the Black Death, which has carried off thousands of their compatriots. To while away their time and distract them from their troubles, they tell stories to one another. Some of the tales are sad, some touching, some even tragic, but many are ribald and earthy accounts of jealous husbands, unfaithful wives, and nuns and priests who are anything but celibate.

The dawning of the fifteenth century brought humanism to Italy, a movement that rejoiced in human dignity, artistry, and the excellence of learning, painting, sculpture, and architecture. The models were classical Greece and Rome, and artists and scholars reveled in digging up the statuary, architecture, and artwork of those periods. Writers cast off the fatalism of medieval times and set out to acquire firsthand knowledge, which they believed to be the key to a new and bright future. The period produced a flourishing literature, particularly in the fields of education, the plastic arts, criticism, philosophy, and history. It also saw the beginning of court literature, with noblemen such as the Medici clan of Florence acting as patrons and sponsors of the arts.

The latter half of the fifteenth century was dominated by characters who were first and foremost personalities and who also wrote. The two most notable were Lorenzo de' Medici (1448–92), prince of the famous banking family that ruled Florence during the Renaissance, and Girolamo Savonarola (1452–98), also in Florence, the fire-and-brimstone monk who preached of doom and destruction in a godless society. The former wrote mainly poetry, though his protégé Angelo Poliziano was far more talented than his master. Savonarola, who hated the Medicis, wrote inflammatory treatises. His major work, *Trionfo della croce* (*Triumph of the Cross*), was completed shortly before he was arrested by the Borgia pope Alexander VI in 1496, to be hanged and then burned.

Niccolò Machiavelli (1469–1527) is known for a view of life that shocks some readers and appeals to others as realistic. His pro-military philosophy of expediency was born of a passionate involvement in the troubled Florentine Republic. Machiavelli served the republic as a diplomat before, like Dante, being banished into exile. His most famous work, *Il principe* (*The Prince*), is a modus operandi for an effective ruler. In it Machiavelli calls on the Medici family to use force to save the Italian city-states from the claims of foreign invaders. Although he preached the famous "end justifies the means" theory, he also outlined the virtues necessary for a good ruler, including love for his subjects and just laws. Machiavelli's *Arte della guerra* (*The Art of War*) laid down the principles on which Italian compulsory military service is still based.

In his *Storia Fiorentina* (*History of Florence*), fellow Florentine and political historian Francesco Guicciardini (1482–1540) disagreed with Machiavelli on almost every point. He believed that things were not ordered, but happened by chance, and he refuted Machiavelli's claim that one could look to history for an example of what to expect in the future. Guicciardini also differed in his lack of optimism; he did not share Machiavelli's belief in a golden future for Italy.

The epic poem was a popular form in Italy throughout the fifteen century, but it was Lodovico Ariosto (1474–1533) who raised it from a rattling tale spattered with blood and guts to the level of literature. This servant's son from Ferrara was attached to the court of the Este family, where he wrote his masterpiece, *Orlando Furioso,* taking thirty years to complete it. Ariosto's characters and their adventures through the world of magic spells and gory battles are the same as those of his predecessors, but they are far more finely drawn and sophisticated.

The most famous member of the Ferrara school of epic poetry was Torquato Tasso (1544–95), who spent twenty years at the court under the patronage of Duke Alfonso d'Este. After Dante, Tasso is generally regarded as the prince of Italian poets, although his life was plagued by misfortune, including seven years spent imprisoned in a mental hospital. His *Gerusalemme liberata* (*Jerusalem Liberated*) is more solemn, more sensuous, and more ornate than Ariosto's poem and is bound by the strict discipline of neoclassicism, which was to become important to the seventeenth-century playwrights in France.

Italian theater has its roots in the medieval mystery plays that acted out the stories of the Church, the martyrdom of saints, and the biblical origins of Christmas and Easter. Examples of these still survive in village processions that commemorate the lives of local saints. Like the religious paintings of the time, the theater was built on ritual, with flat, two-dimensional characters. The late fifteenth and early sixteenth centuries saw further development, as

Italian writers began translating Latin comedies, but in these, too, stock characters went through stock situations. The plays were full of young men in love, helped or thwarted by wily servants, amid much changing of clothes and confusion of identities. In the sixteenth century, Machiavelli, Pietro Aretino (1492–1556), Angelo Beolco (1502–73), and Giangiorgio Trissino (1478–1550) all developed the theatrical technique. But it was Giambattista Giraldi (1504–73) of Ferrara who made the greatest strides. He shifted the focus away from the realm of kings and dukes to real people and introduced what was to become central to the development of modern theater — the concept of tragicomedy.

The seventeenth century was a period less remarkable for the quality of its literature than for the courage of certain notable intellectuals who dared to question principles based on a God-centered world. This century saw the birth of science, the thirst for knowledge in politics and theology, but it was also the age of the Inquisition. Among the largely southern-based writers who broke the mold of flowery poetry that slavishly followed the rules of Plato and Aristotle was Giordano Bruno (1548–1600), who dared to suggest that there were as many poetic styles as there were individual poetic inspirations. His individualism cost him his life — he was burned at the stake as a heretic in Rome in 1600. Galileo Galilei (1564–1642), who typified this age of intellectual discovery, won international fame for his invention of the telescope in 1609. But his attachment to Copernicus's claim that the earth moved around the sun, and not vice versa, condemned him to years in prison and a lonely death in 1642.

Wealthy, carefree Venice of the eighteenth century spawned Carlo Goldoni (1707–93), whose plays are full of lightheartedness, humor, and fast-paced action that often approaches farce. His best-known comedies, *La locandiera* (*The Innkeeper*) and *La bottega del caffè* (*The Coffee Shop*), are both still widely performed. One of the most prolific Italian playwrights, his works are full of social comment, but they contain no tragedy and little soul-searching. Goldoni's world is populated by likable rogues trying to get themselves out of tight corners.

With Ugo Foscolo (1778–1827) came the first glimmerings of the romantic movement, with its themes of human despair, suicide, and the conviction that the only real truth was to be found in the beauty of nature. Foscolo's best-known work, the autobiographical novel *Le ultime lettere di Jacopo Ortis* (*The Last Letters of Jacopo Ortis*), is a study of unhappiness born of his own misery, when his fiancée married another man. Unable to bear the defeat of Napoleon and the return of Austrian domination to Italy, Foscolo left his homeland in 1816 to live in London, where he died in penury eleven years later.

In addition to its cult of individual sentiment and the self-indulgent outpourings of the soul, Italian romanticism was marked by a longing for political freedom. The movement developed against the background of the hated Austrian occupation. The revolutionary and liberal ideas expressed by this school of writers cost some of them their liberty. Silvio Pellico (1789–1854) spent ten years in an Austrian jail, where he wrote *Le mie prigioni* (*My Prisons*).

Alessandro Manzoni (1785–1873) felt the burden of foreign rule particularly strongly since he was from the northern region of Lombardy, which was firmly under Austrian control. His poem *Cinque maggio* (*The Fifth of May*) poignantly laments the death of Napoleon, who had briefly ousted the northern invaders. But Manzoni is best known for his classic novel *I promessi sposi* (*The Betrothed*), the story of young lovers Renzo and Lucia. Manzoni, like his contemporaries, had his moments of despair, but he also possessed a keen eye for humor, and the very human touches, such as the failings of the priest Don Abbondio, have made *I promessi sposi* one of the best-loved works in Italian literature.

Far more pessimistic is the mood of Giacomo Leopardi (1798–1837), the poet who comes closest to the romantics of French and English literature. To Leopardi, humans are an insignificant speck towered over by Nature, which is indifferent to human suffering but nonetheless always magnificent. This conviction gives rise to poetry of great beauty and lyricism. The poet's love-hate relationship with Recanati, the small town in the Marches region where he was born and raised, is central to his works. As a young boy, Leopardi showed a prodigious appetite for knowledge and spent much of his childhood in the library devouring works in Greek and Hebrew. He died at age thirty-nine, after a life plagued by ill health.

The traumatic experience of foreign occupation and the famed victory of Garibaldi and his Thousand, who brought Italy under one rule, produced a crop of patriot poets in the mid-nineteenth century. Some, like Giovanni Prati and Goffredo Mameli, died fighting for freedom. Mameli's *Fratelli d'Italia* (*Brothers of Italy*) became the Italian national anthem after its author was killed in 1849. But the patriot poet par excellence was Giosuè Carducci (1835–1917), whose forceful poems are full of indignation and anger at Italy's humiliation under foreign domination. Carducci went on to become professor of Italian literature at Bologna University as well as a winner of the Nobel Prize in Literature, and his works have a strong classical and historical framework. But in spite of his respectability, Carducci never lost his youthful rebelliousness and the fierce republicanism that dominates the collection *Odi barbare* (*Savage Odes*), familiar to every Italian schoolchild.

With the demise of romanticism, a new school in Italian literature emerged, one more suited to the novel form than to poetry. This was realism — *verismo.* Sicilian-born Luigi Capuana (1839–1915) was one of the first exponents of the new trend, which sought to suppress the personality and presence of the author in favor of a scientific description of characters and events. Fellow Sicilian Giovanni Verga (1840–1922) developed the style, examining social conditions in the impoverished south, depicting in his novels poor and often unlikable wretches whose lives are filled with physical and spiritual suffering. In *Nedda,* the title role is that of a girl who loses her mother, then her lover, and finally her baby. In Verga's most famous novel, *I Malavoglia* (*The Malavoglia Family*), a family in a poor Sicilian fishing community suffers one misfortune after another. Another writer in the *verismo* vein was Grazia Deledda, whose naturalistic novels of peasants set against the background of her native Sardinia won her the Nobel Prize for Literature.

Light years apart from the sordid world of the realists was Gabriele d'Annunzio (1863–1938), one of the most flamboyant characters in Italian literature. His heroic exploits during World War I, his skill as a pilot, his colorful love affair with the actress Eleonora Duse, and his dramatic raid on the Yugoslav border town of Fiume would have earned him a place in history even if he had never written a line. But he was also a prolific author, producing poems and novels that were highly sensual, often to the point of cruelty and sadism, and full of the human life force that was the stamp of the man himself. D'Annunzio's was a philosophy based on self-confidence and a belief in the ability of humans to achieve their aims. He espoused the Nietzschean cult of the Superman, a belief that went hand in hand with his love of fast cars and airplanes. A man of great talents, his best-known works are his poems, notably the Laudi collection, but he also wrote novels and plays. His writings expressed many of the same hopes and ideas as Mussolini's fascism. The two men were friends and intellectual comrades.

The gentle lyricism of Antonio Fogazzaro (1842–1911) could not have been more different from the bombastic style of d'Annunzio. Unlike d'Annunzio, whose raison d'être was passion, Fogazzaro's was the human quality of love. His best novel, Piccolo mondo antico (Little Old World), is the story of a Lombardy community under Austrian domination in the mid-nineteenth century, but the suffering is tempered with a strong sense of comic indulgence for his characters, which makes them very human.

Meanwhile, the spirit of fascism was gaining momentum, and with it grew a school that was to sweep Europe but that had its roots in Italy — futurism. This was the cult of the now, rejecting the past. Its chief proponent was F. T. Marinetti (1878–1944), who in 1909 launched the Futurist Manifesto, which was to have strong repercussions in European literature, freeing it from old naturalist forms and heralding a new, exciting experimental age in art. Futurist poets such as Marinetti and Giovanni Papini (1881–1956) scorned the traditional and praised only what was bizarre, ugly, and discordant. Rhymes were often abolished in favor of versi liberi, or prose poems, and sweet assonances forsaken in favor of jarring, rasping sounds.

But futurism was more important for the barriers it broke down than for the quality of the literature itself. In Italo Svevo (1861–1928) emerged an artist of real stature who used the new freedom of expression but rejected the positive, self-confident attitudes of d'Annunzio and Marinetti. His novels are characterized by purposelessness, full of unremarkable people leading humdrum lives — subjects previously considered too banal for literature. Svevo's major work, La coscienza di Zeno (The Conscience of Zeno), revolves around nothing more exceptional than the hero's attempt to give up smoking.

Any rules and conventions still intact by the time Luigi Pirandello (1867–1936) came on the scene were summarily dismantled by this highly successful revolutionary author. Pirandello, another Nobel Prize winner, tried most literary forms, but in his plays he was most daring. His characters frequently take control of the author, most strikingly in Sei personaggi in cerca d'autore (Six Characters in Search of an Author). Often there is no beginning, middle, or end to his plays, and his characters break off in the middle of a scene to talk to each other, or even to the audience. Gone, too, is the traditional plot. One of Pirandello's recurring themes is the gap that exists between the way we see ourselves and the image other people have of us. His life was deeply influenced by his unhappy marriage, arranged by his father, to a woman who was his cousin. His wife developed a persecution complex, accusing Pirandello of cruelty and unfaithfulness, which was not at all how the author saw himself. In his novel *Uno, nessuno e centomila* (*One, No-One and a Hundred Thousand*), Pirandello describes a man whose wife points out to him that his nose is lopsided. The discovery sparks a chain of uncertainties in the mind of the hero, who had always imagined himself to be a person with a perfectly straight nose.

The Fascist regime took its toll on the artists of Italy, with exile, prison, and sometimes death facing those who expressed antigovernment feelings too emotionally. Some, like Cesare Pavese and the Jewish author Carlo Levi, were banished to remote Italian outposts. Levi used this experience to write his memorable portrait of peasant life in southern Italy, *Cristo si è fermato a Eboli* (*Christ Stopped at Eboli*). Antonio Gramsci (1891–1937), one of the founders of the Italian Communist party, was imprisoned for ten years, which resulted in his death at the age of forty-six. It was only after Mussolini's death that Gramsci's work about this period, *Quaderni del carcere* (*Prison Notebooks*), was published, in 1948. Another young victim of fascism was Pietro Gobetti (1901–26), who died after a series of beatings by Fascist squads.

Nevertheless, this period spawned an abundance of writing talent. The mid-twentieth century literature of Italy is one of the richest in Europe. Three poets especially stand out during this time: Giuseppe Ungaretti (1888–1970), Eugenio Montale (1896–1983), and Salvatore Quasimodo (1901–68). Montale and Quasimodo were both awarded the Nobel Prize for Literature. Collectively, the three are known as the hermeticist poets, a term that refers to the new style they brought to poetry and that has close links with the French symbolists. They worked to concentrate ideas and distill images and associations using a minimum of verbiage. Ungaretti's poetry strongly reflects his experiences on the front line in World War I and the death of his nine-year-old son. But his sense of despair is always expressed in the most sparing style, reducing words to the bare minimum to make maximum effect of their evocative powers. Montale's poetry shows a similar technique but has a marked quality of wry humor, often directed at himself. Sicilian-born Quasimodo interpreted the style in a more approachable manner, but the distillation was still strong. One of his classic poems, *Ed è subito sera* (*And Suddenly It's Evening*), captures in just three short lines a host of ideas and concepts about evening, death, and loneliness.

Meanwhile, the Italian prose tradition was anything but stagnant. One immediate success was Giuseppe Tomasi di Lampedusa's (1896–1957) *Il gattopardo* (*The Leopard*). A novel set in Sicily, it charts the decline of the old order through a portrait of a noble Sicilian family whose young hero, Tancredi, breaks with tradition by marrying into the nouveau riche family of the town's mayor. The book was published largely through the efforts of Giorgio Bassani (b. 1916), whose own novel *Il giardino dei Finzi Contini* (*The Garden of the Finzi Continis*) has also become a modern classic.

Perhaps because of Italy's political traumas during the war, leading to the abolition of the monarchy and the flowering of communism, modern Italian literature and culture have tended to stay freer of intellectual snobbery than those of many other European countries. In Italy, good literature is usually also popular.

One of the best-known and best-loved Italian novelists writing today is Alberto Moravia (b. 1907), whose anecdotal style and portraits of life in Rome are unmistakable. He first made his mark in 1929 with *Gli indifferenti* (*The Indifferent*), which paints a picture of the emptiness of bourgeois life. Since then Moravia has continued to delight his huge readership with his finely drawn characters, often from the working classes and usually up to no good — waiters who plot to steal their friends' wives, servant girls who try to dupe their bosses.

Until his death in 1985, Italo Calvino (b. 1922) was another prolific novelist who obtained considerable recognition during his lifetime. A former partisan fighter during World War II, Calvino had an extraordinarily fertile imagination that produced tales of fantasy and make-believe, such as *Il barone rampante* (*The Baron in the Trees*), the story of an eighteenth-century nobleman who lived in the trees. But Calvino had an equally keen eye for contemporary life and for the plight of the ordinary working class in a bewildering world. Portraits such as that of Marcovaldo, the title character in a collection of his short stories, lost and confused in the concrete jungle of a northern Italian industrial city, have endeared Calvino to a generation of readers, both in Italy and abroad.

The runaway success of Umberto Eco's (b. 1932) first novel, *Il nome della rosa* (*The Name of the Rose*), is proof that Italy still occupies a key place in the ranks of world literature. Eco, a lecturer at the University of Bologna, turned his hand to fiction with the publication in 1980 of what has been described as a medieval whodunit. It is set in a Benedictine monastery, where a series of bizarre murders of monks leads a Franciscan in pursuit of the culprit. The novel became an immediate best seller and was translated into several languages, and it was also hailed by critics in Europe and the United States as a work of great literary merit, winning two major awards, the *Premio Strega* and the *Prix Medici*.

Dining in Italy

Next to losing your way in a foreign city, perhaps the most distressing aspect of traveling is trying to enjoy a meal in a restaurant where the waiters are distant and the menu unintelligible.

Relax. This time you're in Italy, land of the *pizzeria,* the *caffè,* the wine bar, and the ever-satisfying *trattoria.* The art of eating here is an open secret, told in the hiss of the espresso machine and the crackle of spit-roasted meats sizzling over an open fire; in tempting, brilliantly colored ice creams arranged like the paints on Giotto's palette; and in giant platters of *antipasti* with each mushroom, olive, and anchovy curl arranged as carefully as a Venetian mosaic. When your waiter says, *"Buon appetito,"* it is as direct an invitation to the feast as the knife sticking out of the watermelon wedge that he brings to your table in the piazza.

It is really hard to get a bad meal in a country where nature has put a larder of Mediterranean vegetables, wine grapes and tree-ripened fruits, fresh-caught fish, carefully tended animals, and a forest carpeted with mushrooms outside the kitchen window. Centuries have taught cooks here not to "improve" the food too much. Give Italians some fruity olive oil, a fragrant lemon, a basket of ripe tomatoes, garlic, pepper, a few snips of basil, and a slab of Parmesan cheese, and they can dress a pasta you'll remember as long as an afternoon in the Uffizi.

But let's get back to that table in the piazza. This time we'll order some wine and mineral water and study *la lista,* the Italian menu. Even though the traditional three-hour lunch break is losing ground in the larger cities, restaurants still offer full meals at lunch as well as dinner. Since ordering is generally à la carte, it's easy to tailor the meal to suit your own schedule by choosing only the courses you want.

The first items listed are *antipasti,* those irresistible hors d'oeuvres of sliced salami and paper-thin raw beef (*carpaccio*), fresh figs wrapped in rosy ham, *prosciutto,* bits of stuffed zucchini, eggplant and roasted peppers, sweet-and-sour baby onions, seafood salads, and other temptations. Italians go easy on these nowadays, alas, often preferring a simple munch of *crostini,* rounds of toast touched with olive oil and garlic or spread with a purée of chicken livers, while waiting for the first plate, the *primo piatto.*

The *primo* is not just a small starter course but a full partner to the *secondo piatto.* Together these two dishes make up the Italian main course. The first part, also called the *minestra,* is served by itself, typical choices being a half-portion of pasta or a soup with pasta in it. In the north the rice-based specialty *risotto* or a savory cornmeal pudding (*polenta*) is served. During any visit in Italy, a traveler will eat pasta in dozens of widths, lengths, and squiggles matched to various sauces and preparations by culinary tradition, the cook's own estimate of the clinging power of a sauce to its pasta, and personal taste. Some common combinations are *pastini,* little stars and dots in broth, tubular factory-made macaroni and spaghetti with tomato sauces, and fresh, handmade egg noodles and fold-ups (often filled with meats and cheeses) with cream-based sauces.

Only after the first course has been cleared will the waiter bring the *secondo,* or meat course, which explains why spaghetti with meatballs is seldom served in Italy. (If the fresh, crusty bread hasn't appeared yet — Italians don't usually eat bread with pasta — it will come to the table now, but minus butter; that's for breakfast). To say that the *secondo* is the meat course does little to convey the first taste of fork-tender milk-fed veal; spit-roasted baby lamb rubbed with rosemary; roast kid or suckling pig; game meats like boar, venison, partridge, and hare; or sea creatures such as octopus, squid, and skate — less familiar to Americans but to which Italian cooks turn as naturally as we do to fried chicken or filet of sole. *Contorni,* side dishes of steamed green vegetables — spinach, escarole, or asparagus, for instance — can be ordered *al burro* (with butter), *all'olio* (drizzled with olive oil), or *all'agro* (with lemon). Italians also deep-fry vegetables — pieces of zucchini and zucchini blossoms, artichokes, and peppers — which are listed on the menu as *fritti.*

Salads of crisp fresh lettuces and herbs come next, and some diners will end the meal here; most Italians, however, don't feel satisfied without cheese and fruit — a fresh peach or some cherries or berries from the sideboard or, in winter, perhaps a poached pear. The finale is an inch of rich, dark-roast espresso. And if you plan to linger, take some sweet dessert wine, Vin Santo, with little dry biscuits (*biscotti*) for dunking.

And what about the espresso-and-cream-soaked *tiramisù* cake, the *zuppa inglese,* like English trifle, or the *Monte Bianco* chestnut purée creation on the cart in the corner? Go right ahead. But take note that most Italians don't eat dessert with the meal. They usually have their pastries in mid-afternoon or later in the evening at a *caffè* or *pasticceria.*

We use the word *restaurant* to mean a sit-down eating place, but in Italian a *ristorante* means formal dining with a wide selection of food, a full complement of waiters and stewards, and higher prices — the works. For informal meals, a simpler menu (but still excellent food), and a less budget-bending bill, even the chic crowd choose a *trattoria.* In current usage, *ristorante* and *trattoria* sometimes overlap capriciously. The word *osteria* is also seen all over Italy, and it can indicate anything from a neighborhood wine pub to a good *trattoria.* When in doubt, check the menu posted near the door. Remember that an automatic extra charge of about 15% will be added to the posted prices for service (*servizio*), and it is customary to leave an optional tip (5% to 10%) for the waiter on top of that. A charge for *pane e coperto* will most likely also appear on your check: Don't make a fuss that you didn't order this item — it translates as the bread and cover charge. Since fine *ristoranti* and *trattorie* have loyal followings, always call ahead for a table. That's the way to be sure not to arrive on the establishment's weekly closing day or during a summer hiatus.

Keep Italian dining hours in mind, too. Restaurants are generally open from 1 to 3 PM for lunch and from 8 to 10 or 11 PM for dinner. Some open at 7:30, but don't show up that early unless you want to be the only diner.

Not that you'll ever go hungry. There's always a hot roast meat sandwich, a salad, a small pizza, an omelette, sometimes a hamburger, too, or a sweet waiting at a nearby self-service hot table (*tavola calda*), caffè, or espresso bar. Even a wine bar serves sandwiches.

Having a breakfast of cappuccino and pasta at a stand-up espresso bar is a bracing way to start the day — the pasta (literally translated as "dough"), a brioche in this case or perhaps a crescent-shaped cornetto. Here, as in the ice cream shop (*gelateria*), pay the cashier first and then take the stamped receipt to the serving counter to collect your choices. In hotels, continental breakfast is standard, although a few offer ham and eggs — at a staggering price — for unadaptable Americans.

Throughout the day, Italians return to the bar for a quick espresso pick-me-up. If straight coffee is too strong, ask for a *lungo* (diluted with water), and if you want a drop of milk, order it *macchiato*. Spoon in the sugar yourself. Cappuccino comes with the familiar head of steamed milk, and *caffè con panna* is topped with whipped cream. Don't expect lemon peel with your espresso. That's mostly an American custom now, brought over years ago by southern Italians who had used it back home to cut the taste of chicory, which the poor drank instead of coffee. (Early owners of Neapolitan restaurants in America are also credited with introducing the debatable etiquette of twirling spaghetti against the bowl of a soup spoon and promoting the myth that all Italian cuisine is spaghetti with tomato sauce.)

A bar in Italy serves coffee and wine but not hard liquor, which is served in what is called an American bar, easier to find in hotels catering to foreign businesspeople than on the street. Italians simply don't go in for the hard stuff. They are, however, the world's biggest consumers of wine. There is no minimum drinking age, often to the delight of teenage tourists who routinely get a glass of wine set before them. For an *aperitivo*, a glass of white wine or Campari is usual, and after dinner Italians prefer liqueurs and sometimes the strong grape aquavit *grappa*.

Until the spring of 1986, when a number of Italians died from lethal doses of methyl alcohol in ordinary table wine, travelers were advised to order local house wines, always economical, usually adequate, and sometimes wonderful. Italians who can ascertain the integrity of local winemakers can still do so, but prudent strangers should ask the waiter for bottled wines bearing the DOC designation, which ensures a high-quality product that is made under strict supervision.

Here's some good news for off-season visitors. The *gelaterie* (ice cream parlors) now stay open year-round. (Italians used to think only fools would want ice cream cones in winter.) Don't fail to treat yourself to *gelato*, the soft, egg-rich ice cream, or *granite*, tongue-smarting coarse ices. There will be dozens of fanciful flavors, from deadly strong chocolate and coffee to intense fruits and berries. No wonder so many people walk out with triple scoops in a rainbow of flavors. Plan to get your ice cream when you're in the mood for strolling and people-watching around the square.

In general, your cache of lire will go further if you remember that stand-up food is often half the price of table service and that a *caffè* or restaurant table on the Piazza Navona in Rome or Piazza San Marco in Venice is like a front-row-center seat at a street theater performance. You can eat for far less in a place down the street, where you won't have to pay rent for the sidewalk.

Please don't leave Italy without at least one picnic — it's your passport to the fragrant world of the *salumeria,* or consummate delicatessen. The strings of sausages, the hams and salamis and cheeses, in various stages of aging, are sold by the *etto* (100 grams, about one-quarter pound, enough for two sandwiches). Prices are usually marked, so just point and say *un etto* or *due etti* (100 or 200 grams). Then pick up some fruit, bread, and small bottles of wine, soda, and mineral water, also at the *salumeria.* On the *autostrada* without lunch, don't hesitate to stop in a cafeteria-style roadside eatery. They're much better than the US variety, but if you don't find what you want, walk out; the worst the serving women behind the counter will do is grumble.

ON THE ROAD

While driving along the back-country roads, the chances of stumbling across a serendipitous gastronomic treat rise dramatically. Every traveler comes home with his or her own story of walking into a plastic-tablecloth *trattoria* just when the owner's wife is pulling a hot loaf of bread out of the oven and the saucer-size porcini mushrooms she gathered at dawn are drizzled with olive oil, ready for the grill. How about braised rabbit with *polenta?* Some tiny wild strawberries with cream? Discoveries like these make travelers want to eat in Italy forever. In the rich, fertile north, dishes are sauced with cream and butter, and rice and corn dishes often replace pasta. Moving south, tomatoes and olive oil make the sauce, and pasta rules. Cheeses and sausages are different from region to region. It would take a lifetime of traveling to taste the full range of Italy's culinary ingenuity, but the highlights are accessible to even the most casual tourist. The traveler who knows what to look for has the best chance of choosing wisely and eating well.

ROME AND THE NORTHERN CULINARY CIRCUIT

Most of us get our first taste of Italy in Rome. If it's the only stop on your Italian itinerary, you can conduct all your culinary travels right there. Roman restaurants serve the best dishes from all over the country. But if Rome is simply your springboard to a far-ranging Italian tour, when in Rome eat Roman.

Drink the pale dry Frascati wines and enjoy the wondrous little green vegetables such as incredibly sweet peas (*piselli*) and young, chokeless artichokes (prepared with mint, a favorite Roman herb in *carciofi alla romana*). Order tender egg noodles in butter (*fettuccine al burro*) or thick tubular pasta with tomato sauce and unsmoked bacon (*bucatini all'amatriciana*) and *spaghetti alla carbonara,* sauced with egg yolk, or *con vongole,* with tiny clams. More suggestions: peppery grilled chicken (*pollo alla diavola*) and roasted meats, baby lamb (*abbacchio*), and suckling pig (*porchetta*).

Rome's baby lamb comes from the Abruzzo region, which, with its neighbor Molise, makes up a rugged rustic area to the east and southeast of Rome. In the country inns, it's hard to resist the spit-roasted meats, and along the narrow Adriatic coastline shared by these regions, be sure to investigate the various fish soups (*brodetti*). Abruzzo cooks have a distinctive way of cutting pasta into long thin strands for their lamb sauces and soups: they press the dough against a set of taut strings, and out comes *maccheroni alla chitarra.*

The landlocked region of Umbria, north of Rome, is the place to sample mushrooms and truffles. The precious black truffles grow so profusely hereabouts that Umbrians supply them to France. Sauces, stews, and stuffings are lavished with fresh mushrooms all summer, and in the fall with mushrooms and truffles. Two of Umbria's towns are famous for their specialties — Orvieto for its dry white wine and Perugia for luxurious chocolates. The region of the Marches, east of Umbria, best known for the city of Urbino, makes hearty oven-baked pasta specialties such as a rich meat and cheese lasagna known as *pasticcatta.* The string of fishing villages along the coast is a *brodetto* fancier's heaven.

But it is farther north in Tuscany that a visitor begins to understand what is meant by "the glories of Italian cooking." Tuscany is blessed with the finest olive oils and the country's king of wines, Brunello. Tuscans even raise cattle (a rarity in Italy); the white Chianinas produce meat that is so lean that ranchers in the cholesterol-conscious US are starting to breed them. A grilled T-bone steak (*bistecca alla fiorentina*) will come extra rare unless you warn the waiter "*ben cotta.*" Try the succulent Florentine *arista,* roast pork rubbed with rosemary, and for the flavor of Tuscan game, *pappardelle con la lepre,* pasta in hare sauce. The bean and vegetable soup, *ribollita,* thickened with slices of peasant bread, is a favorite *minestra.* Don't miss meaty Tuscan white beans in olive oil. The Chianti Classico wines are tailor-made for Tuscany's hearty cooking. And be sure to treat yourself to a bottle of Brunello di Montalcino, a fitting partner to the richest game and roasts.

North of Tuscany lies the gastronome's heaven, Emilia-Romagna. It has never been decided whether the title "dining room of Italy" should be accorded to the entire region or just to its principal city, Bologna. The difficulty of this dilemma becomes apparent with the first taste of mild, air-dried Parma ham (*prosciutto di Parma*) and fresh *parmigiano-reggiano,* the "real" Parmesan cheese, moister than the aged wheels that are sent abroad.

In the town of Modena, home of the famous barrel-aged herbed balsamic vinegar, try *zampone,* boiled pig's foot stuffed with sausage. It's the star of Bologna's *bollito misto,* the assortment of boiled beef, veal, sausage, chicken, tongue, and more that is offered from a serving cart rolled to the table. Taste the Bolognese *ragù,* the classic meat-and-tomato pasta sauce, and pistachio-studded mortadella sausage. The Emilia-Romagna restaurants stuff their dainty egg noodle rings (*cappelletti* and *tortellini*) with inventive cheese and meat fillings and float them in broth or serve them with butter and cheese. The Lambrusco wines here will be pleasant enough, but they are not the equals of the Emilia-Romagna kitchen. Try the distinctive walnut liqueur called Nocino.

Separating Emilia-Romagna from the Mediterranean is another of Italy's narrow coasts, Liguria, a paradise for seafood lovers. Try the baked seafood pastas. The capital city, Genoa, lays claim to originating *pesto.* This fragrant uncooked sauce of fresh basil, pine nuts, and olive oil (mashed and blended with mortar and pestle) is found in pasta, *gnocchi,* soups, and salad.

North of Liguria is Piedmont, where the prized white truffle (*trifola d'Alba*) hides at the base of old oak trees — and nowhere else in Europe. It's necessary to be in Italy during the autumn to taste the truffles, but you don't have to be in Piedmont. In better restaurants everywhere in Italy, waiters will be shaving precious flakes of the *tartufo* onto pastas. Piedmontese will be shaving them over *fonduta,* fondue of melted Fontina cheese, and they'll add a few crisp truffle slices to their *bagna caôda,* a garlicky, hot olive oil dip for raw vegetables. Even better known than the truffles are the wines of Piedmont — dry reds like Barbera, Barolo, and Barbaresco, and Asti Spumante, sweetly sparkling Italian champagne. The wine-based *aperitivo* commonly known as Vermouth was developed here.

Turn east toward Milan to find Italy's dairy country. This is Lombardy, where the cuisine is recognizable by the sweet taste of butter in the cooking and fork-tender veal prepared in simple ways such as *scaloppine, osso-buco* (braised shanks with marrow), and *costoletta alla milanese,* a breaded chop fried in butter and accompanied with lemon. Milan's signature dish, *risotto alla milanese,* rice golden with saffron, is brought to almost every diner. The local *mascarpone* cheese, more like whipped cream, is the basis for moist, sweet confections, or, topped with sugar and berries, it's a dessert in itself.

Heading still farther north toward the Dolomites and the Austrian border, *polenta* and Teutonic dumplings share the menu. Enjoy the *prosciutto* of nearby San Daniele alongside Austria's smoky ham, called *Speck.* The port city of Trieste, on the Yugoslav border, adds a third ethnic element, Serbo-Croatian cooking, to the Italo-Austrian mix — sauerkraut bean soup, *jota,* and goulash, for instance.

In Venice, order the famous *scampi,* served cold with olive oil and lemon, but don't neglect the local spider crab (*granseola*) or *risotto* blackened by the ink from the cuttlefish, *seppie,* and pungent with ocean flavor. *Pasta e fagioli* (bean and pasta soup) and *polenta* are favored in Venice in place of pasta in heavy sauces. And whether or not you think you like liver, try Venice's signature fork-tender liver and onion dish (*fegato alla veneziana*). The sturdy red lettuce, *radicchio,* which Italians serve grilled as a cooked vegetable as well as raw in salads, flourishes in the Veneto region. You will soon recognize its familiar bitter flavor in many Venetian favorites, including *radicchio risotto.*

LOOKING SOUTH FROM ROME

The Neapolitans invented *pizza,* and they still make it in every conceivable combination in friendly, crowded pizzerias. The thin-crusted, individual-size pizzas are popular here (hungry folks sometimes eat two), and the *pizza Margherita* is the reliable classic — tomato, garlic, olive oil, and basil, with a liberal shower of mozzarella. The Neapolitan specialty, *calzone,* is a thick turnover made from pizza dough and filled with (instead of topped by) the traditional pizza sausages and cheeses.

Another singular local treat is mozzarella made from water buffalo milk. Have it in *carrozza,* a fried sandwich, or in a salad of fresh tomato and basil. Here in the heart of plum tomato country, try an order of spaghetti with plain tomato sauce (*al pomodoro*). By the way, the spaghetti with the salty taste of anchovies and the spicy title *alla puttanesca* (woman of the evening) was invented in Naples.

Save room for afternoon visits to the dazzling pastry shops of Naples for flaky, custard-filled *sfogliatelle* and the cream-and-ricotta-filled cake *pastiera.*

Head south from Naples into Apulia, the heel, or down through Basilicata to Calabria, the toe of Italy. The countryside here quickly explains why the term *la cucina povera* (the cuisine of the poor) is so often used to describe the cooking in these regions. The cooks are inventive, but they have few of the farm-raised meats, dairy foods, and delicate greens of their northern cousins. Expect to find fish, goat, sheep, and pigs (which do not require rich pastures), heat-loving vegetables like eggplants and squashes, and the reliable standby, pasta with tomato-based sauces.

Except in the towns of Brindisi and Bari, where the ferries run between Italy and Greece, travelers are few, as are restaurants. But once a traveler has crossed the Strait of Messina to Sicily — island of oranges, sesame, and almonds — meals take on an exotic new feeling. The conquering Saracens left Sicily a culinary legacy in the Middle Ages, and it endures today. Restaurants serve Arab *couscous.* A famous Sicilian sardine and pasta dish, *pasta con sarde,* combines the sweetness of white raisins and the crunch of pine nuts. Spectacular *trompe l'oeil* candy fruits are made from almond paste (*marzapane*), and towering *cassata* is sponge cake filled with nuts, candied fruits, and ricotta, sometimes with ice cream. Equally popular is the familiar little cream-filled rolled pastries, *cannoli.* We also have Sicily to thank for originating Marsala, one of the greats among fortified wines and an essential ingredient of *zabaione,* a foamy dessert of whipped egg yolks and wine.

The other big island, Sardinia, boasts at least two favorites: roast pig served on a bed of myrtle leaves, and crisp rounds of paper-thin shepherd's bread called *carta da musica* (music paper).

The catalogue of Italian culinary delights is nearly endless, and one of the authentic pleasures of any Italian visit is the opportunity to expand a personal list of gastronomic experiences. It is hard to imagine a nation with a table set with greater diversity and variety, all the more reason to enthusiastically accept the Italian invitation to dine.

Music

MUSIC IN ROMAN TIMES

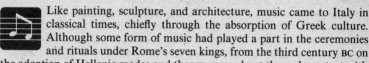 Like painting, sculpture, and architecture, music came to Italy in classical times, chiefly through the absorption of Greek culture. Although some form of music had played a part in the ceremonies and rituals under Rome's seven kings, from the third century BC on the adoption of Hellenic modes and theory came about through contact with Greek drama and recited poetry, which used music as accompaniment. Unfortunately, we have no way of reconstructing how this music sounded, but the historian Livy makes several references to the significant role of music in Roman society. Later, in the first century AD, music assumed even greater importance in the contests sponsored by the emperors Augustus and Nero. Public concerts of instrumental music were given in open-air theaters, while ensembles and soloists performed at more intimate banquets of wealthy patricians. Eventually music would free itself of its dependence on literary associations and become a self-sufficient means of expression.

RELIGIOUS MUSIC OF THE MIDDLE AGES

In early Christian times, music was taken over almost entirely by the needs of religious observance. Embellishment of the sacred word was entrusted to the most perfect instrument, the human voice. The basis for inspirational chant derived from a tradition different from the Greek classics — the Hebrew synagogue service. Its psalter and psalmody were adapted and expanded to suit the needs of the Christian faith. When Christianity became the state religion of the decaying Roman Empire in 315, the liturgy further developed to meet the expanded needs that came with this new status. Antiphonal, or responsive, singing, in which the congregation replies in unison to the invocation of the officiating priest, was a way of actively including the congregation in celebration of the mass. It was very effective. Its purported inventor, St. Ambrose, then bishop of Milan, often felt compelled to confess what he saw as the sinful pleasure derived from music quite apart from the sacred text that it accompanied. Indeed, if music was to continue to serve religion, its role had to be more strictly controlled.

Gregorian chant is named for Pope Gregory the Great (560–604), who was the first great reformer of church music and who standardized the liturgy for the entire Catholic world. The Latin texts and music were meticulously edited and transcribed into a rudimentary notation system for codification. An all-male chorus, the *schola cantorum,* was formed to ensure the correct performance of the mass. Two centuries later, Gregory's reforms were reinforced by Charlemagne, who relied on the monastic organization to carry on the tradition. But music was not to remain monodic forever. The gradual introduction of harmony into religious music started a revolution that affected all Western music, secular as well as religious.

The first step, the movement from the austere Gregorian chant into polyphonic music, was essentially a natural one. The stark, unaccompanied melody, consisting of a reciting note with a final cadence, gradually gave way to variation. First the choir was diversified into parts. The authorized text and melody, the *cantus firmus,* remained inviolate and was performed by the highest male voice, the tenor (so called because it "held" the melody). The text and rhythm of the other parts remained unchanged, thus preserving the intelligibility of the words. But these parts provided the harmony for the *cantus firmus* at a regular interval below the higher pitch, and further experimentation eventually led to even greater divergence. Elaborate disjunctions in intervals and rhythms, and ultimately the introduction of different texts, gave greater weight to the musical play at the expense of textual clarity. Although such a development was frowned on in Italy, where papal authority was strongest, it was allowed to flourish unhindered north of the Alps, particularly in France. French polyphonic innovations were to filter back into Italy later in secular music, thus stimulating even more change. Italy, however, did make a significant contribution to music theory. A Benedictine monk, Guido of Arezzo (995–1050), devised a system of staff notation that established the exact pitches and time values of notes and provided the basis for the system of musical notation that is still in use.

THE RISE OF POLYPHONY

Secular polyphony moved into Italy in the eleventh and twelfth centuries. Pilgrimages and the Crusades stimulated increased mobility throughout Europe. Those passing through Italy on the long route to the Holy Land turned to singing as an important social activity — first religious singing, and then church melodies were put to alternative secular lyrics. The rise of city-states and courts also encouraged secular music, as the troubadours from southern France, with their lutes and recorders, provided accompaniment not only for their Provençal love lyrics but for dance as well. Meanwhile, new forms of religious expression began to undermine the supremacy of liturgical plain chant. The *laude* was a particularly Italian phenomenon. A lyric in the vernacular that arose out of spontaneous popular piety, it was free of the modal and tonal restrictions of official church music. St. Francis of Assisi (1186–1226), who called himself "the Troubadour of Christ," was the author of several *laudi.*

MUSIC OF THE ITALIAN RENAISSANCE

The secularization of music advanced further in the 1300s, paralleling a similar development in the arts and letters. Just as Tuscan painters showed an unprecedented interest in the depiction of the world around them and Dante, Petrarch, and Boccaccio elevated Italian language as a means of literary expression, in music, too, the *Ars Nova* — the new polyphonic art

— was gaining ground. Initially taking its cue from the more elaborate French model, this new polyphony quickly assumed its own Italian characteristics. The main distinction lay in the innate Italian feeling for melody and the predominance of the uppermost vocal line, as opposed to northern practice, in which the various parts were more equitably and abstractly treated. New descriptive forms emerged: the *madrigale* (a vernacular lyric), the *ballata* (a lively dance tune), and the *caccia* (a hunting scene). Padua and Bologna initially vied for the lead, but both were superseded in the fourteenth century by Florence, where the chief exponent of the Ars Nova was the remarkable Francesco Landino (1325–97). Blinded by a childhood disease, Landino nevertheless mastered every instrument, from the voice to the organ. His achievements as poet and composer were recognized when he was crowned with the laurel wreath in Venice in 1346. Most of his work has survived and is an interesting document of the age.

In the fifteenth century, Italy fell behind the rest of Europe in musical development. Polyphony had as yet made no impression on religious music, and it survived mostly in the courts at Milan, Mantua, Ferrara, Naples, and especially Florence, which became an important center under the Medici ruler Lorenzo the Magnificent. A productive exchange of ideas between north and south finally began at mid-century, when significant numbers of Flemish choirmasters were employed at the Italian courts. Inevitably, church music adopted polyphony. The most noteworthy example is provided by Adriano Willaert (1482–1562), who in 1527 became *maestro di cappella* at St. Mark's in Venice. The availability of two organs in the same church enabled him to experiment with more intricate harmonies on a grander scale. Willaert's sojourn in Florence resulted in the founding of a local school that was dominated by Andrea Gabrieli (1510–86) and his nephew Giovanni (1557–1612). The school's chief characteristic was the rich tonal effects achieved through experimenting with the combinations of voice and other instruments. These three men set Venice on its way to becoming an important center in instrumental music.

Polyphony did less well in Rome. Not only was the new form seen as obscuring the all-important text, it smacked of the north, where the papacy had lost so much power in the Protestant Reformation. The Council of Trent drew up strict guidelines for religious music. Had it not been for Giovanni Pierluigi da Palestrina (1525–94), papal patronage of change in music might have disappeared altogether. The greatest composer of the sixteenth century, Palestrina had spent most of his life as a choirmaster in one Roman church or another. In his hundred-odd masses, he outwardly emulated the *a cappella* Gregorian chant while in fact using an exquisitely refined choral harmony. History knows him as the "first musician of the Catholic Church," and his religious works are in their way the musical counterparts of Michelangelo's frescoes in the Sistine Chapel.

THE RISE OF OPERA

The Renaissance search for the classical past that fostered the revival of the visual arts in Italy also prompted the emergence of opera. In the last quarter of the sixteenth century, a group of intellectuals, theoreticians, and musicians in the circle of Count Giovanni de' Bardi sought to re-create the essence of Greek theater. The *Camerata,* as the group was called, believed that ancient drama had been chanted or sung rather than simply recited. But the text was still considered the more important element, and consequently complex polyphony was avoided. Instead, a new kind of supporting harmony developed that favored the individual musical instruments.

Chief theoretician of the Camerata was the lutist Vincenzo Galileo (1533–91), father of the scientist Galileo Galilei. In his 1581 treatise *Dialogue Between Old and New Music,* Galileo devised the principles of the new form. The first concrete efforts in the form were produced by the singers Jacopo Peri (1561–1633) and Giulio Caccini (1550–1618). The earliest *dramma per musica* that still survives was Peri's *Dafne,* with a libretto by the poet Ottavio Rinuccini. Both composers set the librettist's *Euridice* to music. These early operas are largely in a declamatory style, with a bass accompaniment, and contain relatively few moments of song. Their interest is mostly historical. The first giant in the field was Claudio Monteverdi (1567–1643) from Cremona. This singer, viol player, and composer became associated with the Florentine Camerata and then developed his own ideas more fully under the patronage of Duke Vincenzo Gonzaga, the ruler of Mantua. It was for Gonzaga's court that Monteverdi produced the first authentic masterpiece in opera history, *Orfeo* (1607). In this work, Monteverdi respected the *stile recitativo* of the Camerata, but he assigned a greater role to the musical component by demonstrating its expressive potential. His work became central to the development of baroque music in Italy.

This new form of entertainment spread rapidly throughout the peninsula, and each city produced its own style. Rome became the style setter for the rest of the century with the establishment of a school headed by Stefano Landi (1590–1655) and Luigi Rossi (1598–1653). Opera became a favorite form of entertainment with the Roman nobility, and the Barberini family sponsored performances in the family palace as part of the pre-Lenten carnival festivities.

A religious answer to opera was the creation of the *oratorio.* In contrast to opera's mythological subject matter, an oratorio presented a biblical event, in Latin, set to music, without the lavish scenery or costumes of its secular counterpart. Giacomo Carissimi (1605–74) became Rome's outstanding composer of these sacred works, which later reached a high point in England and Germany through the works of Handel and Bach.

In the seventeenth century, Venice superseded Rome as the opera capital of Italy, with Monteverdi's arrival in Venice as choirmaster of St. Mark's in 1613. In his later works for the stage, such as *Il ritorno di Ulisse* (1641) and *L'incoronazione di Poppea* (1642), Monteverdi's style became more elaborate, with the orchestra playing a more significant role. He was succeeded by Francesco Cavalli (1602–76), Antonio Cesti (1623–90), and Alessandro Stradella (1645–82), all of whom were concerned with the musical element of opera, which stimulated composition and performance techniques well into the next century.

It was also in Venice that opera lost its exclusive association with the nobility. The melodrama became a commercial enterprise, and performances were increasingly spectacular. The world's first public opera house opened in Venice in 1627, and by the end of the century Venice had eight such establishments. Other cities followed.

THE EIGHTEENTH CENTURY

In the Age of Reason, conservatories were founded all over Italy to promote what was becoming a local industry. It was a chief export commodity as well, for Italian composers, singers, and soloists were in much demand in the non-Italian capitals of Europe. During this period the entire range of Italian musical terms, from *allegro* to *vivace,* first gained universal acceptance. It was also a time of great experimentation, and although few true masterpieces were produced, opera proved to be the country's main concern. Italy's most illustrious theaters of the time, such as San Carlo in Naples (1737), La Scala in Milan (1778), and La Fenice in Venice (1792), were built to house opera.

Naples supplanted Venice as the operatic center largely through the accomplishments of Alessandro Scarlatti (1660–1725). He wrote more than 115 operas and is alone responsible for the creation of a new kind of opera that enjoyed overwhelming success throughout Europe.

Neapolitan opera reversed the basic tenets of opera's Florentine originators by making music the more important element. The *opera seria* (serious opera) still dealt with themes from ancient history, but its librettos were constructed in ways that separated dramatic and musical components. The heart and soul of Neapolitan opera was the extended piece known as the *da capo* aria, which Scarlatti devised to give freer reign to musical virtuosity. It consisted of a recitative, which related the actual plot, followed by the tripartite aria, which expressed the character's emotional state. The first segment ordinarily would have been complete in itself, but it was followed by a contrast in key, tempo, or mood. The aria closed with a repetition of the initial segment, but it allowed for elaborate improvisations by the singer. Clearly, when the plot was always being interrupted by a series of musical parentheses, dramatic continuity could not be maintained. On the other hand, the succession of beautiful arias sung with great skill was musically satisfying — good show business. For this reason, Italian opera spread across Europe, gaining the interest and support of even non-Italian composers. Its greatest genius was the German composer Handel, who established the tradition in England when he moved there in 1711.

Neapolitan opera made another contribution to the evolution of musical forms in the sprightly instrumental piece known as the overture. Scarlatti is credited with giving the overture a symmetrical structure with three movements — *allegro, adagio, allegro* — providing the basis for what became the orchestral symphony. But the most surprising offshoot of *opera seria* was the *opera buffa* (comic opera). Humorous intermezzos that were performed during the scenery changes of the *opera seria* proved to be the major work's antithesis. The plot was simple, often amusing, dealing with everyday people speaking in local dialect. The short arias were spontaneous and graceful tunes, and there was greater use of duets and closing finales. The two comic scenes were often so popular that they became detached from the *opera seria* and were presented independently as a short continuous comic work. The most famous example of this is *La serva padrona* (*Maid as Mistress*) (1733) by Giovanni Battista Pergolesi (1710–36). His successors Niccolò Piccinni (1728–1800), Giovanni Paisiello (1740–1816), and Domenico Cimarosa (1749–1801) took this Neapolitan invention as far afield as Paris, St. Petersburg, and Berlin.

Overshadowed by Naples, Venice nonetheless produced a variant of *opera seria* that was more balanced and richly orchestrated. While Lotti, Caldara, and Albinoni all wrote works for the stage, only those of Antonio Vivaldi (1675–1743) are currently enjoying a much deserved revival. In the comic vein, Baldassare Galuppi (1706–85) produced a local brand in collaboration with Carlo Goldoni, whose librettos provided for greater character development.

Venice managed to establish a musical sphere of influence in northern Italy, which was far more receptive to the reforming influence of northern composers who revitalized opera later in the century. The most important exponent of the movement against the excesses and abuses of Neapolitan opera was Christoph Willibald Gluck (1714–87). With the help of his librettist Calzabigi, Gluck established a new balance between music and drama in his operas *Orfeo ed Euridice* (1762) and *Alceste* (1767). And while the child prodigy Mozart (1756–91) wrote typical Italian operas for Milan, his masterpieces in collaboration with the notorious Lorenzo da Ponte performed a similar service for the *opera buffa. Le nozze di Figaro, Don Giovanni,* and *Così fan tutte* remain the most enjoyable and satisfying of all operas, with their sublime music and careful blend of dramatic and comic elements.

Despite the eighteenth century's obsession with opera, Italy's most significant advances were made in the field of instrumental music, a fact that is inextricably linked to the new level of perfection attained in the making of the instruments themselves. The evolution of the viol family was complete, culminating in the supreme craftsmanship of the violin in the workshops of Giuseppe Antonio Guarnieri (1687–1745) and Antonio Stradivari (1644–1737) in Cremona. The various keyboard instruments and their treatment underwent improvement and modification. The organ, perfected by the Antegnati family of Brescia, was consequently freed from its role as a mere support for the voice in sacred music. The harpsichord enjoyed a similar liberation, largely due to Domenico Scarlatti (1685–1757), whose 545 compositions showed the full potential of the harpsichord as a solo instrument. It was soon to be eclipsed by the pianoforte, invented by the Paduan Bartolomeo Crisofari in 1711, and its protagonist was to be Muzio Clementi (1752–1832), who provided the new percussion instrument with a series of exercises, *Gradus ad Parnassum,* that are still used today.

The most active center for instrumental music was understandably Venice, given its long-standing tradition dating to the sixteenth century. The champions of the age were now Tommaso Albinoni (1674–1745) and Antonio Vivaldi (1675–1741). The Venetian gift for creativity in contrasting textures was admirably displayed in new forms and combinations, such as the *sonata a tre, concerto,* and *concerto grosso.* Of the two composers, Vivaldi's work has greater appeal. Nicknamed the Red Priest because of his rust-colored hair, he was excused from ecclesiastical duties for health reasons and devoted most of his time to music. His main achievement lies in the mastery of form through his 600 concertos. His inventive nature produced new combinations, such as adding wind instruments to a string ensemble. His ideas concerning the descriptive potential of abstract forms are expressed in his program concerto the *Four Seasons,* which remains his best-known work.

In the latter half of the century, Italy lost some of its natural resources through the emigration of its most gifted composers. Luigi Cherubini (1762–1842) went to Paris in 1788 and quickly learned to adapt his style to French taste and language. His operas showed some of the influence of Gluckian reforms, but in the greater use of the orchestra, substantial chorus, and insertion of the obligatory ballet he became the father of the French style of grand opera. Although Cherubini's operas are somewhat conventional, his overtures are exceptionally powerful, even earning him Beethoven's admiration. His works represented official taste in Napoleonic France, and for the last twenty years of his life he served as the director of the national conservatory. Gasparo Spontini (1774–1851) was active in Paris, where he won the favor of Empress Josephine, and subsequently in Berlin, where he helped forge German opera. Ultimately, however, neither Cherubini nor Spontini was to have any lasting effect on the younger generation of Italian composers.

THE NINETEENTH CENTURY

The romantic era met with an anomaly in Italy. While the rest of Europe was passionately involved with the fuller and freer development of instrumental forms, Italian interests lay elsewhere. Only in the figure of Niccolò Paganini (1782–1840) did the country produce a virtuoso performer and composer of international standing. Born of a musical family and blessed with exceptional talent, Paganini became the prototype of the romantic soloist. Early in his career he found the available repertory for the violin far too limited for his purposes and composed works of incredible technical complexity, which he performed to the astonishment of audiences all over Europe. His success made others possible, most notably that of the virtuoso pianist Franz Liszt.

Opera remained the chief musical concern in Italy, but not, however, as a mere extension of the highly stylized genre of the previous century. Librettists, drawing on the wealth of European literature, provided better texts, and the scores incorporated musical innovations. And unlike the previous century, the nineteenth century produced a steady flow of masterpieces by genius composers, resulting in the golden age of Italian opera.

The outstanding composer of this golden age was Gioacchino Rossini (1792–1868). Born into a musical family, he quickly mastered several instruments, and by the time he was twenty-one he had both tragic and comic masterpieces to his credit. His *Il barbiere di Siviglia* (1816) remains the supreme *opera buffa.* In Rossini's hands the genre evolved fully, as his highly individualized characters, capable of dishing out wit and satire, emerged from the stock figures of the form's Neapolitan origins. Musically, too, opera was considerably enhanced by Rossini's brilliant orchestration and spontaneity. His accomplishments in *opera seria,* which show an exceptional talent for vocal writing, have been a feature of the world's opera houses since his time.

Rossini's popularity took him all over the Continent to oversee the production of his operas. In 1824 he settled in Paris, where he revived earlier successes and wrote *William Tell,* a grand opera in four acts, his last work for the stage. He lived for several more decades, composing little and enjoying the intellectual life in Paris.

In Italy, the operatic tradition was carried on by Vincenzo Bellini (1801–35). Although his career was brief and he had none of Rossini's gaiety or talent for orchestration, Bellini secured a place in operatic history. A gentle strain of melancholy runs through his works, which are characterized by an extremely sensitive talent for vocal writing. In such works as *Norma* and *La sonnambula* (a subject best suited to comic opera), Bellini attained new depths of feeling in the perfect blend of vocal line and text. It is little wonder that Chopin was to fall under Bellini's spell in his elegiac compositions for the piano.

Gaetano Donizetti (1797–1848) brought Italian opera to mid-century. His first popular success was a sentimental comedy, *L'elisir d'amore* (1832), but he was also capable of expressing pathos and profound sentiment. His *Lucia di Lammermoor* (1835) vies with Bellini's *Norma* as the masterpiece of *bel canto,* but Donizetti's work is characterized by a more extensive use of the orchestra and a more subtle fusion of recitative and aria. Success took him to Paris, where he wrote a comic opera after the French fashion, replete with spoken dialogue, called *La Fille du Régiment* (1840), as well as a grand opera, *La Favorite* (1842). A few years later, he was incapacitated by the disease that was to cause his death, but his legacy consists of some seventy works for the stage.

Giuseppe Verdi (1813–1901) was the giant who closed the century. He was as much a national as a musical hero, for many of his works during the 1840s dealt with the plight of the oppressed and became associated with the struggle for freedom from foreign domination and the instinct for Italian unity. Verdi rose to greatness against all odds. Of humble birth, he was denied conservatory training and felt deeply the effects of his initial failures; it was the faith of his friends and his second wife that sustained him. Aware of opera's shortcomings, Verdi demanded better librettos, and in his highly theatrical works based on the dramas of Schiller, Hugo, Dumas, and Shakespeare the human voice became the primary means of dramatic and musical communication.

Between 1851 and 1853, Verdi composed three masterpieces for the Italian repertory, *Rigoletto, Il trovatore,* and *La traviata.* Despite their proximity in date, each opera is distinct, largely through the skillful use of orchestral color that defines the particular setting. Verdi's fame was secure, and, like his predecessors, he responded to the call of Paris; his association with French grand opera is evident in *Un ballo in maschera* (1859) and *Don Carlos* (1867). During a brief political interlude between 1861 and 1865, he became a member of the new Italian parliament. Despite the innovative features of *Aïda* (1871), however, his style was considered anachronistic as Italy began assimilating developments from beyond the Alps, where Wagner's music dramas were creating a stir. Verdi, however, had hardly exhausted his talent, and his last stage works, *Otello* (1887) and *Falstaff* (1893), with the help of Arrigo Boito, saw the evolution of the closed form of the traditional opera into a sung symphonic poem.

Opera felt the impact of changing literary tastes as well. *Verismo* took its cue from the slice-of-life brutality of the real world, and its use in opera was spread through the success of Bizet's *Carmen* (1875). This modern genre swept away the earlier operatic conventions, as arias became short and expressive, and the orchestra was charged with the task of creating the setting and mood.

Cavalleria rusticana (1890), based on a short story about Sicilian honor by Giovanni Verga, can be considered not only the masterpiece of the genre but also that of its composer, Pietro Mascagni (1863–1945). Its only real contender is *I Pagliacci* (1892), whose plot was taken from a real incident, by Ruggiero Leoncavallo (1857–1919). Others who adapted *verismo* to historical dramas included Umberto Giordano (1867–1948), who composed *Andrea Chenier* (1896), and Francesco Cilea (1866–1950), the composer of *Adriana Lecouvreur* (1902). But for all their merits, none of these composers could compete with Giacomo Puccini's consistent gift for the theater.

Puccini (1858–1924) descended from a long line of composers of sacred music, but his interests lay solely in the stage. Despite a slow start, his fresh, impulsive music flowed steadily into operas from the time of his first triumph with *Manon Lescaut* (1893). Few composers have such a large body of their works in the standard repertory, and while *La Bohème* (1896) and *Madame Butterfly* (1904) are often criticized for their sentimentality, both works are remarkable for their balance and superb musicality. *Tosca* (1900), showing a darker side, and *La fanciulla del west* (1910), often denigrated as the first "spaghetti western," are nonetheless incredibly rich scores that give evidence of a receptiveness to the ways of progressive composers and foreign modes. With *Turandot* (1926), incomplete at Puccini's death, the golden age of Italian opera came to a close.

THE TWENTIETH CENTURY

Even after World War I, opera continued to be Italy's chief musical preoccupation. As a result, the country was less responsive to the European revolution in instrumental music. Links with Berlin, Vienna, and Paris were tenuously forged by the number of Italians who studied abroad and returned with new ideas. The case of Ferruccio Busoni (1866–1924) is unfortunately typical. One of the most cultured figures of his age, the composer-pianist-conductor was little appreciated on native soil and spent the better part of his creative life in Germany.

A younger generation including Alfredo Casella (1883–1947), Idelbrando Pizzetti (1880–1968), Ottorino Respighi (1879–1936), and Francesco Malipiero (1882–1973), brought the works of the Continental avant-garde to the attention of the Italian public through the music of Schoenberg and Stravinsky, among others. Under fascism, nationalist sentiment encouraged new music as well as the revival of forgotten masters, most notably Monteverdi and Vivaldi. The end of World War II saw a denationalization of Italian music, and dodecaphony became the medium for the successive generation headed by Luigi Dallapiccola (1904–75) and Goffredo Petrassi (b. 1904). Of the still younger composers, Bruno Maderna (1920–73) and Luciano Berio (b. 1920), in their experiments with electronic music and other media, have brought Italian music to its present status.

Painting and Sculpture

 In spite of the abundance of Italian art in museums around the world, so much art remains where it originated that Italy probably has more fine art per square inch than any other country on earth. Italians live intimately with their art — it's not just in the museums. Churches, chapels, and piazzas bring art into everyday Italian life. The devout burn candles in front of masterpieces of religious painting, children routinely splash around remarkable Baroque fountains, and even the humblest citizens proudly hold forth on artworks major and minor in the most remote country villages. This enthusiasm has been shared by visitors for centuries. In 1666, the French established the Prix de Rome, a fellowship that enables young artists to continue their education in Rome. Many other countries followed suit, offering similar programs that still exist. As they have done for hundreds of years, thousands of artists, students, and visitors still come to Italy each year to observe and absorb works of art firsthand.

ANCIENT ART

Much of what we know about ancient Greek civilization is derived from its influence in Italy. The Greeks left traces of their art in Magna Graecia, the southern part of the Italian peninsula, and in Sicily, which they began colonizing around the eighth century BC. Remnants of Greek art were reverently preserved by the Etruscans, who lived to the north of Magna Graecia at about the same time and who valued Greek vases so highly that they included them in their burial chambers. The Romans collected, copied, and imitated Greek art, bringing back paintings and sculpture by the boatload and using Greek artists to glorify their own empire.

One of the arts the Greeks valued most highly was vase painting. They decorated their terra cotta vessels first with black designs on the reddish clay and later in a more naturalistic red-on-black scheme. Two of the finest such vessels were found at Etruscan sites in Italy: the Chigi vase, an *oenochoe,* or wine pitcher, now on display at the *Museo Nazionale di Villa Giulia* in Rome, and the *krater,* a François vase used for mixing water and wine, which is in Florence's *Museo Archeologico.* Like many Greek vases, these depict lively battle scenes and are considered to be among the best examples of this unique art form.

Archaeological excavations in Italy have revealed much about Greek art. Pompeii and Herculaneum, excavated in the eighteenth century, are the best-known sites, but even more recently other dramatic discoveries have brought to light long-forgotten aspects of Greek art.

One such find occurred in 1968 in a tomb outside Paestum, a Greek colonial town near Naples. Here the supple rendering of figures in vase painting is combined for the first time with landscape and seascape elements in a type of painting on plaster walls called *fresco*. This technique, like many principles of Greek art and philosophy, was revived during the Renaissance.

Another discovery took place not on land but in the Ionian Sea off Riace, a coastal town in southern Italy. In 1972, a diver casually happened on two bronze statues of Greek warriors, now called the Riace bronzes and dated to about the middle of the fifth century BC. Although Italian museums are replete with examples of Greek sculpture, the bronzes on exhibit in the *Museo Archeologico Nazionale*, in Reggio di Calabria, are among the few statues that are not just Roman copies of Greek originals.

While the Greeks were occupying the south of Italy, the Etruscans were building up a network of cities in central Italy. Although the Etruscans were not considered as inventive as their Greek contemporaries, many of their works of art nevertheless show real mastery, especially the terra cotta statues they used as tomb sculptures and temple decorations. The Etruscans were also adept at bronze casting (although much of it was done by Greek artisans) and decorated their tombs with paintings influenced by motifs from Greek vases.

The Romans, likewise, took much from Greek art, including the art itself. Greek painting, sculpture, and objets d'art, much of it intended for religious purposes, were imported for use in Roman homes as decoration. In this respect, the Romans may have been the first art collectors who didn't understand what they were collecting. The insatiable Roman taste for things Greek brought many Greek artists to Rome and created a large market for copies of ancient Greek masterpieces in both Greece and Rome.

The Romans' devotion to their ancestors, coupled with their realistic approach to life, gave rise to a highly developed form of portraiture. From the Etruscans the Romans adopted the practice of making portrait busts (to the Greeks, such sculptures would have looked like severed heads), and they also excelled in painted portraits. The excavations at Pompeii reveal Roman skill at depicting other subjects in painting (still life, landscape, and *trompe l'oeil* architecture) and the masterful use of mosaic as well.

Like Roman architecture, Roman sculpture was meant to glorify the state and was made on a grand scale. Typical subjects were the heroic deeds of Roman generals and emperors, often executed in appropriately colossal proportions.

EARLY CHRISTIAN AND GOTHIC ART

When Christianity effectively became the official state religion with the Edict of Milan in AD 313, artists began to turn their talents toward church subjects. In AD 330 Emperor Constantine transferred the capital of the empire to the Greek town Byzantium, renaming it Constantinople. This brought the influence of Middle Eastern art forms to the provincial Italian peninsula. Sculpture, which had been used by the Romans primarily for monumental purposes, had little place in the humble new religion and was largely replaced by painting, which could be spread out on the flat walls of the new church buildings, as the predominant art form. The Latin dictum of the time, "*Quod legentibus scriptura, hoc idiotibus pictura"* ("Painting is the illiterates' reading of the scriptures"), best explains its use to educate the masses to the ways of the new religion.

Although much early Christian wall decoration was done in the relatively perishable form of fresco, another medium inherited from the Romans proved to be much more durable: mosaics. The *tesserae,* or cubes, the Romans used for floor decoration were adapted to decorate church walls. They were even improved on since for walls they did not have to be hard stone, which limited the colors that could be used. Marble *tesserae* were replaced by colored glass stones, often backed with gold to create a floating, shimmering effect. In Italy, the Adriatic naval town of Ravenna became the capital of the Western Roman Empire in 402, and the Byzantine influence flourished there in mosaics that are the best preserved outside Istanbul and the most intact in the world. The insides of domes and the walls of churches and tombs throughout the city are lined with mosaics that depict religious scenes and naturalistic landscape details such as rocks and plants that were to influence the beginnings of modern painting.

The Romanesque movement made an even briefer appearance in Italy than in most of the rest of Europe, but it is important in the evolution of Italian art because with it came the first of many distinct personalities in the history of Italian art, Wiligelmo da Modena. This sculptor's most important work is a series of reliefs (c. 1099–c. 1106) on the Cathedral of Modena, showing the creation and fall of the Garden of Eden with a sense of movement and pathos that had been disregarded during the Byzantine era. As sculpture gradually regained its prominence in the Gothic period, other masters emerged, notably Nicola (1220–1284) and Giovanni (1245–1314) Pisano in Tuscany, whose works show a keen interest in classical prototypes.

At this time, painting again became important, primarily because of the increased need for large altarpieces in religious ritual. Although the works of early painters such as the Tuscan Cimabue (c. 1240–c. 1302) and the Roman Pietro Cavallini (c. 1250–c. 1330) show a familiarity with contemporary sculpture, it wasn't until the early Renaissance that painters finally began to abandon the Byzantine style, which reached its peak in Italy in the early fourteenth century. The first of these masters was the Sienese painter Duccio (c. 1255–c. 1319).

THE RENAISSANCE

The term "Renaissance" is often used to mean a rebirth of interest in classical civilizations, but since the classical influence persisted all along in Italy, in the Italian context it refers more to a rebirth of the importance of the individual. During this period the great personalities in art history began to emerge. The first painter to completely break with the Byzantine tradition was Giotto (c. 1267–1337), whose paintings are full of ingeniously detailed characterizations. A dominant personality, he was well documented by Renaissance writers. Dante wrote of Giotto's fame in his *Purgatorio,* and according to another contemporary writer, Giovanni Villani, the artist "translated painting from Greek into Latin," that is, from Eastern into Western models. The sixteenth-century writer Giorgio Vasari, considered the world's first art historian, praised Giotto as "a pupil of Nature and no other," and his many fresco paintings throughout Italy have a naturalistic quality that endures brilliantly today. Considered the father of the Renaissance, as well as of modern painting, Giotto dominated early-fourteenth-century painting in Florence, where he worked extensively, and throughout Tuscany.

During the following century, the 1400s or *quattrocento,* sculpture made great strides as artists began to give a new depth to their works. The Florentine Lorenzo Ghiberti (1378–1455) designed bronze reliefs for the doorways of the Florence baptistry, about which, according to Vasari, Michelangelo is supposed to have proclaimed, "O work divine! O door worthy of heaven." Even more influential was Ghiberti's apprentice, Donatello (c. 1386–1466), who, with his friend the architect Filippo Brunelleschi (c. 1377–1446), made extensive studies of ancient Rome. Donatello produced sculptures of a form that had not been attempted since Roman days, notably the freestanding David in Florence and an equestrian monument to Gattamelata in Padua, which served as a model for all northern Italian sculpture. One of the most important sculptures it influenced was the equestrian statue of Colleoni in Venice, executed toward the end of the century by Andrea del Verrocchio (1435–1488), who was also a painter and the teacher of Leonardo da Vinci.

At the same time, the exciting notions of the Renaissance were being expressed in experiments in painting. In Florence, Masaccio's (1401–1428) frescoes in the Carmine chapel were among the earliest to explore volume; Paolo Uccello (1397–1475) became obsessed with perspective; and in the Convent of San Marco, Fra Angelico (1387–1455) made fresh use of color and line, which attained its most poetic expression in the lyrical paintings of Sandro Botticelli (c. 1444–1510). Outside Florence, in Arezzo, Piero della Francesca (c. 1420–1492) brought wonderful new effects of light and color to the fresco tradition. In Mantua in the north, Andrea Mantegna (1431–1506) experimented with foreshortening, and in Venice, Giovanni Bellini (c. 1430–1516) began a long tradition of fascination with color.

The Renaissance reached its peak during the sixteenth century, the *cinquecento,* otherwise known as the High Renaissance. Under the patronage of the Medici family in Florence, the popes in Rome, and the Sforza family in Milan, great geniuses flowered. The best-known names in all of Italian art were the great artists of this period: Leonardo da Vinci (1452–1519), Raphael (1483–1520), and Michelangelo (1475–1564). Leonardo did his painting, with its characteristic *sfumato* (mist), mostly in Milan; Raphael and Michelangelo painted in Florence and Rome, where Michelangelo also produced his famous sculptures. At the same time, another school of painting was developing in Venice: Giorgione (c. 1478–1511), Titian (1477–1576), Jacopo Tintoretto (1518–1594), and Paolo Veronese (1528–1588) — all masters of the rich coloration that characterized Venetian painting.

As Renaissance artists became increasingly sophisticated, they began to break their own rules in a deliberate attempt to demonstrate their courage; bodies became more attenuated and set in distorted poses, scale and perspective were treated irreverently, and colors became harsh. Even in its own time, the work was considered stylized or "mannered"; hence the term Mannerism.

Many of the precepts of Mannerism were laid down by the High Renaissance artists (Raphael, Michelangelo, Tintoretto), and although certain artists achieved fame in this tradition — Giulio Romano (1499–1546), Jacopo Pontormo (1494–1557), Rosso Fiorentino (1494–1540), Francesco Parmigianino (1503–1540) — it was short-lived and soon gave way to the splendor of the Baroque. Just before that happened, however, decorative painting reached new heights in the unique works of the Bolognese artists Ludovico Carracci (1555–1619) and his cousins Annibale (1560–1609) and Agostino (1557–1602) Carracci.

Baroque art began in Rome as political and economic power began to centralize there under the popes. As a reaction to Mannerism, forms became simpler and more direct. Caravaggio (c. 1565–1609), with his strong *chiaroscuro,* or contrasting light and shadow, was the primary exponent of Mannerism in painting, while Gianlorenzo Bernini's (1598–1680) exuberant sculpture and playful fountains were its counterparts in three-dimensional works of art. Baroque was primarily a Roman phenomenon in Italy and lasted there and in the south of the country well into the eighteenth century, while the decorative schemes of Giovanni Battista Tiepolo (1696–1770) dominated the salons of Venice.

THE MODERN WORLD

In 1748, Herculaneum and Pompeii were dug out of the lava of Vesuvius, which had buried them for millennia. The discoveries there revived an interest in the classical past. Combined with a gradual tiring of Baroque excesses, this caused the birth of a new art movement in Rome, Neoclassicism. Unlike previous classical revivals, this time there was physical contact with the relics of ancient civilizations, which were examined firsthand from the excavations, and great pains were taken to reproduce them in the most scientific way possible. Antonio Canova (1757–1822) was the greatest champion of Neoclassical sculpture in Rome, where Giovanni Battista Piranesi (1720–1778) also produced hundreds of etchings showing both the ancient and contemporary city. In Milan to the north, Andrea Appiani (1754–1817), Napoleon's court painter in Italy, painted extensively in this style.

During the nineteenth century, a group of Italians working mainly in Tuscany revolted against the prevailing academic style, much as the Impressionists were doing in France. Some of these painters produced realistic, usually outdoor scenes built up from blobs, or *macchie,* of color (hence the name *macchiaioli*). Others, paralleling Romantic movements in northern Europe, preferred indoor historical scenes that reflected the prevailing taste for patriotism, as the peninsula of Italy was gradually being united for the first time in its history.

At the beginning of the twentieth century, certain Italian artists, such as Amedeo Modigliani (1884–1920), emigrated to Paris. However, independent movements started up within Italy as well, notably Futurism — championed by Umberto Boccioni (1882–1916), Carlo Carrà (1881–1966), Giacomo Balla (1871–1958), and Gino Severini (1883–1966) — and Metaphysical painting — Giorgio de Chirico (1888–1978) and Carlo Carrà. Subsequent twentieth-century movements followed the course of international art history (realist painting during the war years, abstract painting in the postwar period, minimalist and conceptualist art more recently). During the past few years, however, Italian painting has again taken a leading role with the so-called neoexpressionist painters, many of whom reside in New York, making a tremendous splash in galleries and collections throughout the world.

Architecture

For centuries, Italian architects have built and embellished cities in their own country and throughout the world. With their formidable skill as engineers, the ancient Romans established or expanded settlements not only on the Italian peninsula but all over Europe, the Middle East, and Africa. Almost every major architectural style since ancient times originated in Italy before exerting considerable influence outside the country, often at the direct invitation of foreign rulers who recognized the Italians' preeminence in the field. Italian genius gave birth to the Renaissance in Florence and, encouraged by the French king François I, was spread to France. Austrian architecture was influenced by the northern Italian Renaissance and, later, by the Baroque, a style that originated in Rome. As far away as Russia, Ivan III employed Italian engineers in Moscow during the fifteenth century; three centuries later the son of an Italian ballerina laid out St. Petersburg in a neoclassical style inspired by Rome, while the neoclassicism of Palladio influenced architecture in England and even in the United States. Indeed, Italy has served as the inspiration for lovers of architectural beauty virtually since the beginning of Western civilization, and architects and students have traditionally gone to Italy to complete their studies. Even for the nonspecialist, the rich architectural heritage of Italy is one of the best reasons for visiting the country.

MAGNA GRAECIA

As early as the eighth century BC, the Greeks began colonizing the southern Italian peninsula and Sicily, the area known as Magna Graecia (Greater Greece). By the sixth and fifth centuries BC, Greek civilization was at its peak in Italy. During this period, the great temples of the Doric order — the Greeks' greatest contribution to architecture — were built. The best surviving examples are at Paestum on the mainland and at Agrigento, Segesta, and Syracuse on Sicily. Here the principles of Doric architecture — harmoniously proportioned, fluted columns with a slight convexity (entasis) in the shaft, topped with a simple square capital — took shape before culminating in the Parthenon in Athens.

THE ETRUSCANS

Meanwhile, beginning in the eighth century BC, the mysterious Etruscans were gradually building up their empire in the central part of the peninsula. Very little of their architecture has survived, primarily because of the impermanence of the building materials they used — wood, rubble, and clay. What remains is made of stone or terra cotta: massive stone-block city gates in

Volterra, Perugia, and Todi (the Etruscans, not the Romans, deserve credit for being the first people since Babylonian times to use the arch in monumental architecture); bits of wall near Viterbo; and burial chambers outside Cerveteri and Tarquinia, hewn into the rock in sometimes ghostly simulations of real homes. The remains of temples consist mostly of stone foundations (the buildings were made of wood), although some fragments of terra cotta entablatures have also been unearthed. The temples were built along simple Greek lines; the Etruscans, however, originated the use of certain elements in their temples — the simple, unfluted columns of the Tuscan order, the high podium, the deep porch, and the wide cella — many of which the Romans later appropriated.

THE ROMANS

At the height of the Roman Empire in the first century AD, the state policy of bread and circuses generated a building boom of new theaters, amphitheaters, and stadia. Other civic needs called for factories, roads, bridges, aqueducts, triumphal arches, temples, basilicas, and even entire towns. Living conditions ranged from squalid to squanderous — blocks of tenements, urban houses with open atria, and luxurious villas.

In his *De architectura* (*Treatise on Architecture*), Vitruvius, the first-century BC Roman architect, suggests that many early Roman architects came from Greece. Even so, the Romans used Greek principles only to suit their own grandiose purposes; the Greek orders, especially the florid Corinthian (often combined with Ionic), provided mere decoration for massive Roman walls. The Romans even developed their own large-scale order — appropriately called *colossal* — to match the grandeur of their buildings.

The Romans introduced a variety of new building types. They turned the Greek temple inside out to invent the *basilica* for use as a meeting hall. The basilica is considered the most basic of all Roman buildings, a functional structure with solid walls on the outside and columns on the inside. The Romans also built the first standing amphitheaters (of which the *Colosseum* in Rome is the largest example), developed public baths (*thermae*), and introduced the triumphal arch. They also left many well-preserved examples of domestic architecture: At the ancient port of Ostia, for example, the *insulae*, concrete-and-brick tenements, survive, and the *domus*, the middle-class home, is in evidence at Herculaneum and Pompeii. Roman domestic architecture reached its height in the sprawling villa outside Tivoli that once belonged to the emperor Hadrian.

Besides their architectural achievements, the Romans were also highly skilled engineers. Although they did not invent the arch or the vault, they incorporated them throughout the empire in bridges, aqueducts, amphitheaters, and other structures. And while concrete and brick had previously been used as building materials, the Romans used them so extensively in their capital that the emperor Augustus boasted that he found a city of brick and turned it into a city of marble — only to have his successors leave it largely a city of concrete.

EARLY CHRISTIAN THROUGH GOTHIC ARCHITECTURE

Roman buildings set the style for early Christian churches. The long, narrow basilica and the centrally planned mausoleum became the churches and baptistries of a later era. Numerous examples of these fifth- and sixth-century buildings exist throughout Rome and, most prominently, in Ravenna, which also has the earliest *campanili,* or bell towers, added on to the churches in the ninth century.

During the Romanesque era, which in Italy began at the end of the ninth century, the use of baptistries and bell towers was common in Italian churches (the most famous bell tower is the Leaning Tower of Pisa). Italian Romanesque used brilliant white marble on church exteriors, as can be seen in Pisa, Lucca, and Pavia; brick was used extensively in Milan and Murano. During this period, the number of outside influences on Italian architecture was enormous: St. Mark's in Venice remained Byzantine; southern Italian architecture is Norman; and Sicilian structures of the period resemble Norman, Saracen, and even Arabic architecture.

Gothic cathedrals in Italy did not catch on the way they did north of the Alps for several reasons: the warmer climate called for thick walls with frescoes rather than the stained glass windows that predominated in the north, the traditional materials in Italy for churches were brick or colored marbles (not limestone), and Italy was already endowed with a centuries-old architectural tradition. Nevertheless, during the thirteenth and fourteenth centuries, Gothic cathedrals were built in Siena, Florence, Orvieto, and Milan (although Milan's Duomo — perhaps the most recognizably Gothic of all — wasn't completed until the nineteenth century). Among the magnificent examples of nonreligious Gothic architecture are the town halls of Perugia, Siena, and Florence and the Doge's Palace in Venice, which has been described as "the most successful nonecclesiastical building ever achieved in the Gothic style."

THE RENAISSANCE

The rebirth of classical principles, known as the Renaissance, that took place in Florence during the early fifteenth century was especially evident in architecture. Unlike the case of painting, there were tangible reminders everywhere of the classical past — buildings and ruins to be studied — and the architects of the time made a conscious effort to emulate the ancients: Leone Battista Alberti's (1404–1472) *De re aedificatoria* (*On the Art of Building;* 1452), the first architectural treatise of the Renaissance, was a deliberate nod to Vetruvius.

Like the artists of the era, Renaissance architects were major personalities with highly individual styles as well as multitalented "Renaissance men." For example, Filippo Brunelleschi (c. 1377–1446), who is considered the first Renaissance architect, was trained as a goldsmith and sculptor, and it was not until he lost the competition to design the bronze doors for Florence's baptistry that he took up architecture full time. After studying in Rome for many years, Brunelleschi returned to his native Florence to build what is regarded as the first Renaissance building, the *Spedale degli Innocenti* (Foundling Hospital). Soon afterward, he began the red tile dome of the Florence Cathedral. Rising, as Alberti described it, "above the skies, ample to cover with its shadow all the Tuscan people," the dome still dominates Florence. Brunelleschi's work, with its peaceful classical interiors of white plaster and contrasting gray stone known as *pietra serena,* set the style of Florentine architecture for centuries to come.

Alberti himself was one of the most fascinating personalities of the Renaissance, as noteworthy as Leonardo da Vinci for the variety of his talents. In addition to being a theoretician, playwright, musician, painter, mathematician, scientist, and athlete, he was also one of the most influential architects of the Renaissance. His extensive studies of the ancients strongly influenced his plans for many different types of buildings (although he never actually took part in building them). The façade of the Church of Santa Maria Novella in Florence has a central doorway based on the Pantheon and is the first Renaissance structure to use "harmonic proportions," a system of measurements based on ancient music theory, which later figured prominently in Renaissance architectural ideals. Alberti is also credited with spreading the Renaissance beyond Florence: The Tempio Malatestiano, a memorial based loosely on a Roman arch, was built in Rimini; the churches of San Sebastiano and Sant'Andrea, also classically derived, were erected in Mantua.

Milan also had its share of architectural activity during the Renaissance, introduced by the Florentine architect Michelozzo di Bartolomeo (1396–1492), with his Brunelleschi-derived Portinari Chapel in the Church of Sant'Eustorgio. Another Florentine architect, Antonio Averlino Filarete (c. 1400–c. 1470), worked at the court of the powerful Sforza family. Besides building the symmetrical Spedale Maggiore in Milan, Filarete was responsible for a curious architectural treatise that included plans for an ideal city called Sforzinda, the first entirely symmetrical town plan in Western history (as idealistic as it was, it included provisions for a brothel on the ground floor of a ten-story "Tower of Vice and Virtue").

The theme of symmetry was later taken up by the Sforza's most famous beneficiary, Leonardo da Vinci (1452–1519), who planned a number of symmetrical churches. Although the plans were never executed, they had a tremendous influence on Donato Bramante (1444–1514), who built many centrally planned structures in Milan before fleeing to Rome when the Sforzas lost power. The classical architecture in Rome greatly influenced Bramante's work: His small, circular Tempietto of San Pietro in Montorio (1502) is considered the first piece of High Renaissance architecture and the only one of the entire Renaissance that successfully captured the classical spirit.

The High Renaissance in Rome had a reverberating effect on northern Italian architects through its influence on Galeazzo Alessi (1512–1572), Michele Sanmicheli (1484–1559), and Jacopo Sansovino (1486–1570), who were active in the city in the early part of the century. Sanmicheli carried the style to his native Verona, where he resettled after the sack of Rome in 1527; Sansovino introduced it to Venice when he fled there the same year; Alessi applied it to a number of palaces in Genoa, where he settled in 1548.

Two other figures from the High Renaissance were also active in Rome: Bramante's pupil Raphael (1483–1520) and Michelangelo (1475–1564). Raphael's position as superintendent of Roman antiquities gave him the ideal opportunity to study classical architecture, as evidenced by his Villa Madama, which contains many elements derived from the Roman *thermae*. Michelangelo's most important architectural contribution in Rome was his work on the city's renowned religious landmark, St. Peter's, which was begun by Bramante and continued by Antonio da Sangallo (c. 1483–1546).

In Florence, Michelangelo touched off the movement known as Mannerism, so called because of its affected or "mannered" style. His Medici Chapel and Laurentian library staircase, with their deliberate distortion of classical elements, influenced a number of other Florentine architects, among them Bartolomeo Ammannati (1511–1592) (who supervised the building of the Laurentian library's vestibule staircase), Giorgio Vasari (1511–1574) (the Uffizi), and Bernardo Buontalenti (1536–1608) (the Galleria and Tribuna rooms in the Uffizi). Other Mannerist architects include Giulio Romano (1499–1546), who worked in Mantua; Pirro Ligorio (1510–1583), who designed the fanciful Villa d'Este in Tivoli; and Giacomo Barozzi da Vignola (1507–1573), who built the Church of the Gesù in Rome and continued Michelangelo's work on St. Peter's.

Another aspect of classical architecture, the villa, had its rebirth during the Renaissance. Giuliano da Sangallo (1445–1516) built a villa for the Medici family at Poggio a Caiano near Florence, actually designing a Roman temple portico as an entrance. Michelozzo (1396–1472) also built a number of villas for the Medicis in and around Florence, but the greatest villa architect of the era was Andrea Palladio (1518–1580), who worked in the region around Venice. Although his classically derived Teatro Olimpico in Vicenza and the Venetian churches of San Giorgio Maggiore and I1 Redentore are all masterpieces of Renaissance architecture, his villas had even greater influence outside Italy. The classical symmetry of places such as Villa Rotonda outside Vicenza and Villa Foscari at Malcontenta served as the inspiration for English and American estates centuries later. And, finally, as Alberti had done at the beginning of the Renaissance, in 1570 Palladio wrote a major treatise on architecture, *Quattro libri dell'architettura,* codifying the Renaissance architectural ideals of harmonic proportions and symmetry.

BAROQUE THROUGH NEOCLASSICAL ARCHITECTURE

The Baroque movement took its name from the Portuguese word *barocco,* used to describe pearls of odd shape. It began in Rome in the late sixteenth century to meet the needs of a rapidly expanding Catholic church for an architecture full of dramatic effect. Architects of the time delighted in creating new buildings, especially churches, on a grand scale, based on curved forms that conveyed a dizzying sense of movement.

After Carlo Maderno (1556–1629) finally completed the façade and nave of Michelangelo's St. Peter's Basilica, the architects who dominated the Baroque period were Pietro da Cortona (1596–1669), Gianlorenzo Bernini (1598–1680), and Francesco Borromini (1599–1667). Cortona, who was also a skilled painter, designed the Church of Saints Luke and Martina in Rome; with its rich decoration and giant columns, it is considered the first fully Baroque church. Bernini, equally well known as a sculptor, is credited for architectural work throughout Rome: At the Vatican he designed the oval, colonnaded piazza in front of St. Peter's, the giant baldacchino under Michelangelo's dome, and a grand staircase, the *Scala Regia,* in the Vatican Palace. In addition to his palaces and churches, Bernini built many of the fountains for which Rome is famous. Like Bernini, his rival Borromini made elaborate use of the oval, as in the churches of San Carlo and Sant'Ivo della Sapienza.

Though the Baroque style did not have the same explosive effect in other Italian cities that it had in Rome, it left remarkable traces throughout the peninsula. Baldassare Longhena's (1604–1682) octagonal Church of Santa Maria della Salute on the Grand Canal in Venice, although based on local Byzantine and Renaissance traditions, is Baroque in its sweeping theatricality. Bartolomeo Bianco (1590–1657) built the dramatic university in Genoa; Guarino Guarini (1624–1683) and Filippo Juvarra (c. 1676–1736) both erected Baroque buildings in Turin; and Giuseppe Zimbalo (1620–c. 1691) transformed the city of Lecce with his Baroque churches carved in the local golden sandstone. Finally, Luigi Vanvitelli (1700–1773) designed the magnificent 1,200-room Palazzo Reale at Caserta, outside Naples; begun in 1751, it is considered the last great Baroque building in Italy.

The Baroque was followed by a neoclassical movement, partly in reaction to the excesses of the Baroque and partly because of classical archaeological discoveries in Sicily and at Paestum. The neoclassical movement was especially strong in Venice, where Tommaso Temanza (1705–1789) built the Church of the Maddalena in 1760, Antonio Selva (1751–1819) put up the Teatro La Fenice from 1788 to 1792, and Giuseppe Jappelli (1783–1852) built the Caffè Pedrocchi in nearby Padua in 1816.

NINETEENTH CENTURY THROUGH THE PRESENT

The new techniques made possible by the Industrial Revolution had their effects on Italian architecture. In 1861, mass production of iron and glass enabled Giuseppe Mengoni (1829–1877) to design the prototypical shopping arcade, the Galleria Vittorio Emanuele in Milan. Two years later, Alessandro Antonelli (1798–1888) designed his Mole Antonelliana, the iron-supported tower in Turin.

Toward the end of the century, Art Nouveau had its exponent in Italy, Giuseppe Sommaruga (1867–1917), whose Palazzo Castiglioni (1901) in Milan is one of the best examples. The next major movement was the short-lived Futurism, whose major theorist was Antonio Sant'Elia (1888–1916), who believed that architecture could influence society for the better. Sant'Elia was killed during World War I, but his idealism was carried on by Giuseppe Terragni (1904–1943), who founded Gruppo 7, an avant-garde architects' cooperative, in 1926. Ironically, Terragni's best-known work, the Casa del Popolo (1936) in Como, was built in the service of the Fascists.

Other important modern architects are Pierluigi Nervi (1891–1979), who built sports stadiums in Florence (1930–32) and Rome (1957, 1959); Gio Ponti (1891–1979), whose Pirelli Building (1957) in Milan is one of the most influential skyscrapers in Europe; and Giovanni Michelucci (b. 1891), whose Le Corbusier–influenced San Giovanni Battista outside Florence, also known as the Church of the Autostrada del Sole (1961), is dedicated to those who lost their lives during the building of the superhighway.

Contemporary architects are very active in Italy; professionals from around the world watch biennial and triennial exhibitions in Venice and Milan with great interest. As it has been for centuries, Italy remains at the forefront of trends in architectural styles.

THE CITIES

BOLOGNA

Bologna, the principal city of the Emilia-Romagna region, is known to Italians by a variety of nicknames: *Bologna la Dotta* (the learned), *Bologna la Turrita* (the turreted), and *Bologna la Grassa* (the fat). The first sobriquet refers to the city's university, one of Europe's oldest, founded in the twelfth century and still thriving today. The second recalls the forest of medieval towers that once gave Bologna an astonishing skyline — sadly, few remain, but those that survive are indeed spectacular. Bologna la Grassa attests to the city's reputation as the gastronomic center of a country in which food occupies the same prominence as family, religion, and soccer.

Looking at Bologna's turbulent history, it is hard to imagine how the Bolognese have had time to do anything besides fight outsiders and each other. By rough count, the city has been battled over, stormed, occupied, conquered, and reconquered at least fifteen times — and that total doesn't include a minor odd revolt or two here and there.

Human settlement first appeared on the site of the present city sometime in the ninth century BC, an Iron Age civilization that was followed by the Etruscans. The Etruscans named their city Felsina, and the settlement grew rapidly until it became the Etruscan capital of the entire Po Valley. For about two hundred years (600–400 BC), the city enjoyed great prosperity as a result of the fertility of the surrounding plain. In fact, the extraordinarily productive farmland of Emilia-Romagna was to prove as much a curse as a blessing, since everybody wanted it.

The first marauders were the Gauls, who swooped down on ancient Etruria. They took Felsina and, some say, renamed the city Bononia, after the name of their Gaulish tribe, the Boia. Others say that the modern name of the city originated some two centuries later with the arrival of the Romans, who already had a flourishing seaport not far away at Rimini. In 190 BC, the Romans evicted the Gauls from Bologna and immediately set about building a new city, which was known as Bononia from this time on and gradually became Bologna. The Romans gave the city a single, extremely important reason to be: They built the consular road that joins Milan to Rimini, the Via Emilia, directly through the middle of it — and the road still slices through the heart of the city today.

Bologna's Roman period seems to have been tranquil except for a devastating fire in AD 53. In an odd twist of history, Nero, the Roman emperor at the time, insisted that Bologna be rebuilt; not long afterward he was to burn his hometown, Rome, to the ground.

With the decline of Roman influence, Bologna began to alternate between masters, a period that was to last, with few interruptions, until World War II. In 476, the city was taken by the Goths, who held it for less than a century. Then it came under the Byzantine rule of the Eastern Roman Empire. By the beginning of the eighth century, the Lombards had taken over the city; by the end of the eighth century, Charlemagne had taken it for the Franks — and promptly gave it to the pope.

A rebellion of the Bolognese in 1116 loosened the papal grip on the city, but it wasn't long before Frederick Barbarossa swept down from the north and conquered the entire area, Bologna included. Barbarossa wasn't to enjoy the fruits of his victories for too long, however. By 1176 he had been defeated at Legnano by the Lombard League, and the Bolognese immediately began a lengthy struggle to remain independent, this time resisting one of Frederick II's sons, Enzo, king of Sardinia. They succeeded, capturing Enzo and imprisoning him until the day he died. The palazzo in which the unfortunate king was kept still stands in the very center of the city and now bears his name.

During the next few centuries, the turmoil that afflicted the city was primarily home-grown: Three noble families battled for control — the Visconti, the Pepoli, and the Bentivoglio, with the last finally winning out. The Bentivoglios held Bologna until 1506, when the Warrior Pope, Julius II, wrested it from their control. Over the next several decades, the Bentivoglios tried many times to reconquer the city, but without success. Bologna was in papal hands until 1796, when it was lost again, this time to the French, who had invaded Italy under the command of Napoleon. Three times in twenty years (1796–1816) the city was passed back and forth between the French and their Austrian enemies.

By 1816, the Austrians had taken charge and, despite being evicted several times by the Bolognese themselves, they held effective sway until 1860, when the city passed, by plebiscite, to the Kingdom of Savoy and thus to the Kingdom of Italy. Bologna had little role in World War I, but in World War II, as the center of German resistance in the Po Valley (which the Germans used as a breadbasket for the fatherland), it was severely damaged. It took forty-three separate bombardments by the Allies to dislodge the German occupiers.

Despite all this martial to-and-fro, Bologna had time to build a city of great beauty and charm, remarkably intact, considering its warlike past. And as the great buildings and the arcaded streets that are Bologna's signature were going up, some magnificent meals were being served. Bolognese history — not to mention its civic pride — is inextricably bound up in its food. The fertility of the surrounding land made the city a target, and its culinary traditions marked it a worthy prize.

Ask any Italian where the best food in Italy is served and the answer is sure to be "my hometown." But that is just regional chauvinism — all Italians agree that the *second* best food in Italy comes from Bologna. Food — its preparation, presentation, and consumption — is serious business in Bologna. The city has given its name to the international classic *spaghetti alla bolognese* and, less notably, to "baloney." However, a visitor will soon learn that *spaghetti alla bolognese* is better here than anywhere else in the world and that baloney is unknown locally — in fact, a Bolognese would probably be hard pressed to find any connection between delicatessen baloney and its noble ancestor, mortadella, the highly spiced pork sausage that's been made hereabouts since Roman times. Once you've had the real thing, it will be very hard to settle for the pale imitation that carries Bologna's name.

In Italy, the dish for which *cucina bolognese* is most famous is a pasta called *tortellini,* tiny sachets stuffed with lean pork, grated cheese, eggs, and nutmeg. The best tortellini are made by hand — a good tortellini stuffer can make 6,000 an hour — and the Bolognese are quite prepared to pay more for handmade pasta than for the inferior machine-made variety. Bologna's ancient and more recent history is filled with references to the quality of tortellini — it has been featured in plays, songs, and poems. In fact, a Bolognese poet once wrote: "If the first father of the human race was lost for an apple, what would he not have done for tortellini?" Given this kind of ardor, it is not hard to believe that, in 1909, a Bolognese mailman was sentenced to six months in prison for assaulting a cocky Venetian who dared criticize the local tortellini.

For reasons that the Bolognese have never quite fathomed, Bologna has never really caught on as a stop for foreign visitors. This is both good and bad. Good because Bologna has not suffered tourist burnout. Hotel rooms are easy to find (except during one of the frequent major trade fairs), prices are moderate, and hotel workers and waiters haven't developed the surliness that afflicts a few of their counterparts in other parts of the country. Bad because Bologna deserves to be more widely appreciated. Despite the fact that Italians visit often — high-rollers from Rome and Milan have been known to zip up or down the *autostrada* just to have lunch in the city — foreigners are still relatively rare. However, much awaits the lucky few: beautiful buildings, fabulous shops, charming people, and, best of all, the food that made Bologna *la Grassa.*

BOLOGNA AT-A-GLANCE

SEEING THE CITY: Pisa is by no means the only city in Italy that boasts a leaning tower. In the heart of Bologna, in Piazza di Porta Ravegnana, are two leaning towers, side by side. The taller of the two, the Torre degli Asinelli, was built by the Asinelli family between 1109 and 1119. It soars 320 feet above the busy streets and leans 4 feet from the perpendicular. Steep stairs — 500 of them — lead to the top, and the vista from the viewing platform is nothing short of spectacular. On a clear day, all of Bologna is visible, and most of the surrounding province as well. It is open daily from 9 AM to 7 PM; admission is charged. The shorter of the twin towers is the Torre Garisenda, which dates from about the same time as its partner. It is a mere 160 feet high, and it is not open to visitors — just as well, perhaps, since it has an alarming 10-foot list. The Garisenda is thought to have once been as tall as its neighbor but was shortened for (understandable) reasons of safety in the 14th century. Taken together, the Torre Asinelli and the Torre Garisenda provide a good sense of the historic *Bologna la Turrita* — it is thought that there were once 180 such towers in the city.

SPECIAL PLACES: The heart of Bologna is made up of two adjoining squares, the huge Piazza Maggiore and the smaller Piazza del Nettuno, which takes its name from the robust statue of Neptune that decorates it. Clustered around these two majestic spaces are some of the major sights of the city.

CENTER

Basilica di San Petronio (Basilica of St. Petronius) – This huge church on one side of Piazza Maggiore is dedicated to St. Petronius, an early bishop of Bologna and the town's patron saint. It was begun in 1390, and although work went on for the next three centuries or so, it was never finished, as is immediately evident in the only partly decorated façade. The bottom third is faced in marble and graced with exceptional carvings over and around the three doorways. Particularly noteworthy is the center door, capped with a lovely Madonna and Child flanked by Saints Petronius and Ambrose, an early-15th-century work by the Sienese sculptor Jacopo della Quercia. The rest of the façade is unadorned, affording a good look at an Italian Gothic cathedral "under the skin," so to speak — this is considered a fine example of Gothic brickwork.

The first impression on entering the cathedral is one of vast, unadulterated space. The dimensions — 433 feet long, 190 feet wide, 144 feet high — while grand, shrink somewhat with the realization that the building was designed to be some *300 feet longer* and was meant to be surmounted by a dome soaring 500 feet from the floor. A depleted treasury and Bologna's unsettled history account for this more "modest" structure. (Outside, beyond the apse, is a row of columns erected as part of the unfinished plan.) The interior is notable not only for its size but for some highly original works of art in the 22 side chapels, the most peculiar of which is the *Inferno* of Giovanni da Modena in the Chapel of the Magi. This large painting is a particularly gruesome, but finely executed, fantasy vision of hell: A black beast single-mindedly devouring the damned through two mouths (one rather unconventionally placed) dominates a very busy group of devils as they fry, puncture, and flay hordes of sinners. The picture was meant to scare the living onto the straight and narrow — and probably succeeded. Set in the floor, and running the length of the nave at a slight angle to the main altar, is the meridian line of the astronomer Gian Domenico Cassini. Set down in 1655, the line in effect turned the entire church into a giant timepiece. A hole in the roof admits a ray of the sun that works its way along the line, showing local time. Although adjusted several times over the centuries, it is now seriously out of whack. Piazza Maggiore.

Palazzo del Podestà (Governor's Palace) – Directly across Piazza Maggiore from the basilica, this older building dates from the 13th century, although it was considerably remodeled about two hundred years later. The tower that surmounts it, called the Torre dell'Arengo, dates from the original structure and contains a massive bell that was rung in times of celebration or distress as a signal for the citizenry to gather in the piazza to hear the good or bad news proclaimed from the gallery. Nestled in the corners of the vaults of the archway are four sculpted figures representing the four patrons of the city: St. Petronius, St. Florian, St. Eligius, and St. Francis. The interior of the palazzo is open from time to time for exhibits on its upper floors. Piazza Maggiore.

Palazzo Comunale (Communal Palace) – Also facing Piazza Maggiore is this massive edifice, actually two buildings joined. The extreme difference in façade marks where one ends and the other begins. The Palazzo Comunale, also known as the Palazzo d'Accursio, has been the seat of the Bolognese city government since the 14th century. Over the entrance is a heavy bronze statue of Pope Gregory XIII, a native of Bologna who gave his name to the calendar still in use today. The 15th-century statue of the Virgin and Child, in terra cotta to the left of the pope, is by Nicolò dell'Arca, a Pugliese artist who worked extensively in Bologna. In the courtyard of the palace is a wide and gently sloping staircase said to be by Bramante; the width of the steps and their easy grade were designed specifically so they could be climbed by men on horseback — fully armed and mounted riders were always a feature of ceremonial occasions. On the first floor of the building is the Chamber of Hercules, taking its name from the giant statue of the mythical strong man that dominates the room. There is more sculpture on the second floor, in the Sala Farnese, the room in which Pope Leo X and King Francis I of France, the two most powerful men in the world at the time, met in secret in 1515. About 15 rooms are open to the public on this upper floor of the palazzo, all lavishly decorated and displaying paintings of the Bolognese school and other works that make up the Municipal Art Collections. The large windows afford excellent views of the piazza and the city. Closed Tuesdays. Piazza Maggiore (phone: 290526).

Fontana del Nettuno (Neptune Fountain) – Whether viewed from above, from the windows of the Palazzo Comunale, or face on at street level, the proportions and grace of this famous fountain are readily apparent. One of the best examples of a Renaissance fountain in this part of Italy, it was designed by Tomaso Laurenti but was actually constructed and sculpted (1566) by a French artist. His name, however, has been Italianized: no longer Jean de Boulogne, he is now known as Giambologna. The fountain was painstakingly restored in 1934. Piazza del Nettuno.

Palazzo di Re Enzo (King Enzo's Palace) – Built in 1200, this somber building has much within it to recall Bologna's violent past. From 1249 to 1272, it was the prison of the hapless King Enzo, who died here. One assumes that while Enzo was not exactly happy in it, he did live better than the other prisoners held in the bowels of the palazzo. In the courtyard of the building is a small church, Santa Maria dei Carcerati (St. Mary of the Prisoners), built to offer last rites to prisoners as they were taken from the palazzo to their execution in Piazza Maggiore just outside. The Carroccio, the medieval battle symbol of the warlike Bolognese, is usually kept inside the palace, although it has been removed for restoration. The Carroccio, consisting of an ox cart carrying an altar, a bell, and the sacred and secular banners of Bologna, was hauled into battle and defended to the death by an elite corps of soldiers drawn from the first families of the city. Closed Sundays and Monday mornings. Piazza del Nettuno.

Palazzo Archiginnasio – Now the town library, but originally the seat of the university, this palazzo was built in the 16th century. The courtyard, corridors, and staircases are covered with the coats of arms of early professors and students, and upstairs is a beautiful anatomical theater, which the custodian will open on request. Built in the 17th century and completely rebuilt following damage in World War II, it's paneled in wood and contains two interesting anatomical figures dating from 1735. Piazza Galvani 1.

Basilica di San Domenico (Basilica of St. Dominic) – Both this church and the site on which it stands are rich in associations with St. Dominic, who founded a convent on the spot in 1219 and died here in 1221. In the building itself, the sacristan will show, on request, the cell where he lived. An 18th-century renovation totally ruined the medieval character of the interior, but it still contains an exceptional work of art, the *Arca di San Domenico,* or tomb of the saint. Many artists contributed to this masterpiece, but the one who had the greatest hand in it was Nicolò da Bari, who became so famous for this work that he was ever after known as Nicolò dell'Arca. (Note that the term *arca* is an archaic one for a chest or tomb; it does not refer to an arch over the tomb.) The kneeling angel on the right of the tomb and the figures of St. Petronius (holding a model of Bologna in his arms) and St. Proculus are some of the earliest known works of Michelangelo. Be sure also to see the inlaid wooden choir stalls, made by a monk, Damiano of Bergamo, in the 15th century. Outside the church in the piazza are two curious aboveground tombs belonging to Rolandino de' Passeggeri and Egidio Foscherari, lawyers in Bologna in the 13th and 14th centuries. Piazza San Domenico.

Chiesa di Santa Maria della Vita (St. Mary of Life Church) – Stop in here to see the wonderful terra cotta *Pietà,* another masterpiece by Nicolò dell'Arca, done after 1485. Also known as the "Crying Marys," the group is full of movement, especially in the figure of Mary Magdalene, who is almost frantic in her grief. Via Clavature 10.

Chiesa di Santo Stefano (St. Stephen's Church) – The complex of churches that makes up the ancient church of Santo Stefano is one of the most interesting sights in Bologna. There is not one church here but four, and there once were seven. The four churches that remain — Santi Pietro e Paolo, San Sepolcro or Calvario, Crocifisso, and Santi Vitale e Agricola, the latter dating from the 5th century and said to be the oldest ecclesiastical building in Bologna — are united in a patchwork of adjoining cloisters and passages, making the complex an extremely quiet and restful place in a very busy city. The warren of rooms contains some odd and affecting devotional objects. San Sepolcro (Holy Sepulcher), for example, contains what the 12th-century Bolognese imagined a replica of the tomb of Christ would look like. It houses relics of St. Petronius. Beyond San Sepolcro is the Cortile di Pilato (Courtyard of Pilate). Legend has it that the deep basin in the center of this beautiful courtyard is the actual bowl in which Pontius Pilate washed his hands after the condemnation of Christ. The inscription on the rim, however, dates it only to the 9th century. Beyond the courtyard is an extremely old, rather rustic *presepio*, a nativity scene that becomes a shrine of particular importance for the children of Bologna at Christmas. The remaining courtyard is given over to a memorial to the Bergsalieri, the mountain troops of the Italian army, who achieved immortality in Italy by seizing Rome from the pope on behalf of the new Italian nation. Via Santo Stefano.

Pinacoteca Nazionale – This picture gallery near the university contains one of the most important collections of paintings in northern Italy. Here are first-rate examples by the immortals of Italian art as well as by distinguished foreigners: Giotto, Raphael, Titian, Tintoretto, El Greco. The huge exhibition space is beautifully restored, the paintings expertly placed and perfectly lighted. Closed Mondays. Admission fee. Via delle Belle Arti 56 (phone: 223774).

ENVIRONS

Santuario della Madonna di San Luca (Sanctuary of the Madonna of St. Luke) – On the way into Bologna is one of Bologna's most distinctive landmarks — a church perched on top of a hill and approached by what appears to be an attenuated version of the Great Wall of China. The church was built on Monte della Guardia in the 18th century, and its main point of interest is an heirloom inherited from a previous church built on the same spot, an image of the Madonna said to have been painted by St. Luke but more likely painted by a Byzantine artist in the 12th century. Visitors may not be moved to come all this way to see the Madonna (which is on view once a year in the Cattedrale di San Pietro, otherwise known as the Metropolitana, on Via dell'Indipendenza), but for those who like to climb to the tops of cupolas and bell towers, the seeming wall presents a challenge. Actually, it's a portico, the most remarkable of many such walkways in Bologna (see *Extra Special,* below). Built in the 17th and 18th centuries, it connects one of the old gates of the city, Porta Saragozza, and the church via a series of 666 covered and connected arches that climb uphill for a total distance of more than two miles. The view from the church is well worth the ascent, but most people take public transportation up and save the portico for a leisurely descent.

■**EXTRA SPECIAL:** Every city has a feature particularly its own — Big Ben, the Eiffel Tower, the Empire State Building — and Bologna is no exception. Here it is the arcade, or *portico.* Virtually all of Bologna's streets are lined with covered walkways, gracefully arched and vaulted passages that lead for miles through the city center, so that it is possible to walk from one end of town to the other in the rain without getting wet — except when crossing streets. All told, there are just under 30 miles of *portici,* and they have been around a long time. They were born sometime in the 11th or 12th century, when the old wooden city of the Dark Ages was being rebuilt in stone; porticoes went up in front of each building, and gradually they were joined to make the continuous complex seen today. By 1400 their existence had been codified — uniform heights and widths were established — and laws stated that new buildings had to join the arcades whether their owners wanted to or not. The *portici* have become as much a part of Bolognese life as tortellini and mortadella — they are always crowded with strollers, gossips, and students studying the manifestoes pasted on the inner walls. Not everybody has appreciated them, however. Goethe thought they were dark, ugly, and impractical. The local newspapers criticized him savagely for this heretical opinion and suggested that he might be happier elsewhere. Goethe left.

SOURCES AND RESOURCES

TOURIST INFORMATION: The *Ente Provinciale per il Turismo,* headquartered at Via Marconi 45 (phone: 237413), has two information offices in Bologna offering advice and assistance in English. One is in the center of the city, in Piazza del Nettuno (phone: 239660), and the other is at the main railway station, in Piazza delle Medaglie d'Oro (phone: 372220). Both are closed Saturday afternoons and Sundays.

Local Coverage – The newspaper that serves Bologna and the rest of the province is *Il Resto del Carlino,* one of Italy's oldest dailies. The *International Herald Tribune* can be purchased in the late afternoon on the day of publication at the larger newsstands around Piazza Maggiore and at the train station. A colorful local guidebook published in English, *Bologna: A City to Discover,* can be bought at newsstands, bookshops, and souvenir stands.

Telephone – The telephone prefix for Bologna is 051.

GETTING AROUND: Bologna is a city best seen on foot. Almost all the sights of note are near the city center, and the porticoes make pedestrian traffic easy in any weather.

Airport – *Aeroporto Civile Guglielmo Marconi,* Via Aeroporto 38, 4 miles northwest of the city center, serves domestic and international flights. Phone: 311570, 311578, 312259.

Bus – Service is excellent, comprehensive, fast, and inexpensive. Most lines run 24 hours a day, although frequency drops off considerably after midnight. A ticket costs 600 lire and must be purchased at tobacco shops or newsstands before boarding. Passengers cancel their tickets themselves once on board.

Car Rental – The major firms have rental offices both in the city itself and at the airport. *Hertz* (phone: 366918) is at Viale Mazzini 4/3; *Avis* (phone: 551528) is at Viale Pietramellara 35, very close to the train station.

Taxi – Hail taxis as they cruise, or reserve them in advance by phoning 534141. There are two major taxi stands, in Piazza Re Enzo and Piazza Galvani.

Train – The main train station, *Bologna Centrale,* is an important rail hub for central Italy. It's at Piazza delle Medaglie d'Oro, along Viale Pietro Pietramellara, at the head of Via dell'Indipendenza (phone: 372126).

MUSEUMS: Besides those mentioned in *Special Places,* a number of other museums in Bologna may be of interest.

Museo Carducci – The home of the poet, as he left it, with his library and manuscripts. Piazza Carducci 5.

Museo Civico Archeologico (Civic Archaeological Museum) – Egyptian and Greco-Roman antiquities, plus a notable collection of local Etruscan finds. Via dell'Archiginnasio 2.

Museo della Tappezzeria (Tapestry Museum) – Bolognese, Florentine, Venetian, and Oriental tapestries and fabrics, from the 16th through the 19th century. Via Barberia 13.

 SHOPPING: Bologna is one of the richest cities in Italy, and the quality and quantity of the merchandise for sale reflect its taste for the good life. The main shopping streets are Via Rizzoli, Via Ugo Bassi, Via dell'Indipendenza, Via D'Azeglio, and Via Farini. Virtually all the side streets running off these contain more shops stocking everything from puppets to high-fashion wear. Local handicrafts tend to be of the edible variety, and if there exists a more lavish foodshop in Italy than *Tamburini* (corner of Via Caprarie and Via Drapperie), it has yet to be found. Always busy, it stocks an unbelievable assortment of prepared meats, salads, vegetables, fish, soups, and sweets — everything fresh and delicious. Even if you are not hungry, it is a sight worth seeing. Some other shops of note:

Saia Bordoli – Fine, rare art objects; very expensive, but high quality. Piazza Galvani 6.

Cavazza – Men's and women's boots, made to order. Via Castiglione 48 and Piazza San Francesco 14.

Palazzo Lupari – An extensive complex of small boutiques selling jewelry, *objets d'art*, fur, luggage, perfume, and sportswear — all under one roof in a beautifully designed structure incorporating bits and pieces of the original 14th-century palazzo and blessed with a small luxurious tearoom for weary shoppers. Strada Maggiore 11.

Galleria Marescalchi – Bologna's finest art gallery, featuring important paintings by modern Italian masters such as De Chirico and Morandi. Via Mascarella 116.

Marisell – Clothes for women, including some of the best-known Italian designers. Via Farini 4. *Marisell* for men is just around the corner at Via D'Azeglio 13.

Monica Tornicelli – Bologna's outlet for products by Gucci and Salvatore Ferragamo. Via D'Azeglio 15.

1 & 2 – Less expensive, but still high-quality clothing for men and women. Via Rizzoli 7.

 SPECIAL EVENTS: At any given time of the year, Bologna is probably playing host to some industrial fair, convention, or congress. They range from the popular, such as the *International Fair of Contemporary Art* in April, to the esoteric, such as the *Packaging Machines and Materials Exhibition* in February. The *Children's Book Fair* (April) and the *Bologna Motor Show* (December) are perhaps the best known. More traditional events are definitely subordinate to such shows, but they do exist. For instance, every year, on the Sunday before Ascension Thursday in May, the 12th-century Madonna that's usually in the Santuario della Madonna di San Luca is carried down to the city amid great fanfare to be displayed in the Cattedrale di San Pietro (Metropolitana). She receives the homage of the faithful while there, attended by men in tuxedos, and then returns home the following Sunday at the head of a procession. The event is almost as old as the Madonna herself — it began in the early 15th century.

 SPORTS: Golf – There's an 18-hole course at *Chiesa Nuova di Monte San Pietro*, about 10 miles west of town (phone: 969100).

Horse Racing – Trotting races take place year-round at the *Ippodromo Arcoveggio*, Via di Corticella 102 (phone: 356015).

Soccer – The Bolognese are passionate supporters of their home team, *Bologna*, which plays from September to May at the *Stadio Comunale*, Via Andrea Costa 174 (phone: 411651, 411818).

Tennis – If you're serious, note that the late Harry Hopman established a training center about 4 miles out of Bologna. Week-long packages begin on Sundays and end on Saturdays. Contact the *Centro Internazionale Junior Academy,* Via Serrabella 1, Rastignano (phone: 743142). For more information, see *Tennis,* DIVERSIONS.

 THEATER: When Russian theater director Yuri Lyubimov was expelled from the Soviet Union, he found a home at Bologna's world famous *Teatro Arena del Sole,* Via dell'Indipendenza 44 (phone: 234815). Lyubimov has moved on, but the quality of the theater remains. The season runs from December to May. The other major theater in town, *Teatro Duse,* Via Cartoleria 42 (phone: 231836), stages an eclectic repertoire of modern and classical plays by both Italian and foreign playwrights.

 MUSIC: The magnificent 18th-century *Teatro Comunale,* Largo Respighi 1 (phone: 222999), is open once again after a long restoration. Bologna's opera season takes place here (usually from November or December through March), and both before and after that period, the orchestra presents a season of symphonic concerts. World-class singers, instrumentalists, conductors, and guest orchestras regularly appear, so tickets sell out quickly. More intimate musical events, such as chamber music concerts and recitals, take place at the *Teatro delle Celebrazioni,* Via Saragozza 236 (phone: 222999), an adjunct of the Teatro Comunale.

 NIGHTCLUBS AND NIGHTLIFE: Bologna is not blessed with a very active nighttime social scene. A typical night out consists of dinner at one of the city's fine restaurants followed by animated conversation over *grappa* and coffee. The best of the limited number of discos are *Charlie* (Vicolo Bianchetti 4), *Living* (Via di Corticella 218), and *Flamengo* (Via Toscana 50). No reservations are necessary, and they tend to be crowded with students from the university on weekends.

 SINS: Prostitutes of indeterminate age and sex cruise the dark streets around the train stations. The *Black Shadow Club* (Via Broglio 1) presents a tame, "sexy" floor show, and some of the nightclubs calling themselves "American Bars" feature some thirsty drinking companions. Oddly enough, there are two large pornographic movie theaters smack in the heart of historic Bologna, both a stone's throw from Piazza Maggiore, on Via Rizzoli and Via Caprarie.

BEST IN TOWN

 CHECKING IN: Hotels in Bologna fall into two distinct categories. The larger, commercial hotels are oriented to the needs of businesspeople and conventioneers, and the smaller, more intimate hostelries cater to the visitor at leisure. Most hotels in the first category are in the newer part of town, where streets are wider, traffic is heavier, and access to and from the train station, airport, and convention center is easy. The smaller hotels are mostly on quieter, narrower streets in the historic center, perfectly located for the tourist. The top hotels in town, listed as expensive, cost $75 and up for a double; moderate means $30 to $40; and inexpensive, $20 or less.

Royal Hotel Carlton – This modern 250-room establishment is generally considered Bologna's finest. Geared primarily to businesspeople, it offers huge, airy rooms, all with bath, mini-bar, color TV, and air conditioning. The staff is particularly attentive and eager to preserve the hotel's high standing in this very competitive city. The location, in the newer section of town near the busy Piazza dei Martiri, is good but not great. There is ample parking. Via Montebello 8 (phone: 554141). Expensive.

Albergo Al Cappello Rosso – Very near Piazza Maggiore, this is one of Bologna's best. The building itself is a 16th-century palazzo, but the ultramodern interiors seem closer to the 21st than to the 16th century. Each room has a TV, mini-bar, and radio, and the larger rooms have small kitchenettes. Most of the 35 rooms are grouped around an interior courtyard that has a tiny, vest-pocket garden. Service is very good. Via Fusari 9 (phone: 261891). Expensive.

Internazionale – First rate, with a convenient location, it has 140 fully appointed rooms with all the amenities the business traveler expects. The service is efficient, though a touch impersonal. Via dell'Indipendenza 60 (phone: 262685). Expensive.

Roma – One of the rarest birds around, a first-rate hotel at a moderate price, and it's on a pedestrian street only a block away from Piazza Maggiore. This best buy for the nonbusiness traveler has 80 comfortable rooms, a modest hotel dining room, a small indoor bar, and, in summer, a roof garden bar with fine views of the historic city center. There is excellent English-speaking service and ample — but not free — parking. Via D'Azeglio 9 (phone: 274400). Moderate.

Orologio – Small, unpretentious in decor and price, it offers basic, clean accommodation. It's perfectly located, facing the Palazzo Comunale, and some of the 32 rooms have excellent views of that beautiful building. Most have baths or showers. The Orologio is well run and could probably bump its rates up a bit and still sell out. Via IV Novembre 10 (phone: 231253). Inexpensive.

EATING OUT: Bologna's celebrity as the home of good food in Italy gives its restaurateurs something of a big reputation to justify. But on the whole, most live up to the challenge, though others fail outright and some surpass it. Tortellini, mortadella, and *spaghetti alla bolognese* are the items most closely associated with the city, but other culinary inventions are worth sampling as well. Lasagna, it is said, was born here, and most restaurants are sure to have *lasagne al forno* on their menus. Another pasta the Bolognese are credited with devising is *tagliatelle*, ribbons of golden noodles usually served with a sauce made of onions, carrots, chopped pork, and tomatoes — the traditional *ragù* served with any pasta ordered *alla bolognese*. Favorite second courses are *cotolette alla bolognese*, breaded veal cutlets baked with a dressing of ham, white wine, and white truffles; *maiale al latte alla bolognese*, pork roast simmered in milk with mushrooms; and *involtini alla bolognese*, little slices of veal wrapped around a stuffing of chopped pork and served in a sauce of onions, tomatoes, and butter. The best-known wine of the region is Lambrusco, a sparkling red that comes semisweet and dry. Lambrusco Reggiano is particularly good. Also consider trying Pagadebit, a dry white, and Trebbiano di Romagna, a characteristic white. In the list below, an expensive meal for two will cost $80 and up; a moderate one, $35 to $50; and an inexpensive one, $25 or less. Prices include service and a carafe of house wine.

Dante – In the past few years, it has established itself as one of Bologna's best restaurants. The menu frequently features some non-Italian entries, such as *cocktail di scampi* and *steak tartara*, and dishes from other parts of Italy, such as the *maccheroncini alla siciliana* among the pasta choices, but one of the specialties of the house is the quite regional *filetto di vitello all'aceto balsamico* (filet of veal in balsamic vinegar). There is a tasting menu for those who have difficulty deciding. In winter, closed Mondays, and Tuesdays at lunch; in summer, closed Saturdays and Sundays and part of August. Via Belvedere 2 bis (phone: 224464). Expensive.

Notai – This big, beautiful, turn-of-the-century restaurant stands apart from the crowd for two reasons: It has waitresses (very rare in Italy) and a circle of fans who say it is the best and most elegant restaurant in the city, if not the country. Decide for yourself by sampling traditional Bolognese dishes such as *tagliatelle Notai* and *scaloppine* of veal with porcini mushrooms. Trebbiano and Sangiovese are the best of an excellent collection of local wines. Closed Sundays. Reservations essential. Via de' Pignattari 1 (phone: 228694). Expensive.

Pappagallo – Once famed as the best eating place in Italy, it is still famous but no longer the best. The vaulted, dramatically decorated dining room is extremely elegant and boasts excellent service, with black-tied waiters hovering about to refill your glass the moment it is empty. Despite this close attention to detail, food pundits say that dining at Pappagallo just isn't what it used to be. That may be, but it certainly is possible to dine well here. Try the delicious tagliatelle with basil and mushrooms, the excellent breast of turkey, or the braised chicken in white wine sauce. Reservations necessary. Closed Mondays (and most Sundays in summer), a week in February, and most of August. Piazza della Mercanzia 3/C (phone: 232807). Expensive.

Cordon Bleu – This excellent hotel restaurant has a reputation for serving *piatti antichissimi,* very old traditional dishes, that still tantalize the palate — such as filet of beef flambéed with a sauce of puréed strawberries, a bit of ricotta, and cognac that comes from an old Estense recipe, and a thousand-year-old Pugliese dish, *purea di fave con la cicoria* (puréed beans with chicory). It also has an excellent wine list. Closed Sundays and from late July to late August. *Hotel Elite,* Via Aurelio Saffi 38 (phone: 437417). Expensive.

Bacco – A charming restaurant a little way out of town, in one of the quieter suburbs of the city. It serves not only Bolognese standbys such as lasagna and tagliatelle, but also rarer items such as vegetable mousse and a platter of fried vegetables and fruit. Since it is somewhat off the beaten track, it tends to draw local connoisseurs who appreciate the fine wine list and the relatively reasonable prices. Closed Sundays and the month of August. Via Lepido 193, Borgo Panigale (phone: 400218). Expensive to moderate.

Bitone – Also a bit out of the center, Bitone is one of Bologna's notable newer restaurants. Locals come here to dine on homemade pasta, delicious truffle and artichoke tarts, and perfectly grilled beef, lamb, and game in season. The home-made pastries are first rate, too, and the service is good. Closed Tuesdays and the month of August. Via Emilia Levante 111 (phone: 546110). Expensive to moderate.

La Torre – This fine restaurant, housed in a medieval tower in the corner of a tiny courtyard, caters to the elegant, upscale end of the market, but it's not quite as solemn a temple of food as *Pappagallo* or *Notai.* It serves many Bolognese delicacies, so it's an ideal spot for visitors who want a taste of the city's high life without the pomp and circumstance of its more famous establishments. Closed Sunday evenings and Mondays. Via Corte de' Galluzzi 5 (phone: 222448). Expensive to moderate.

Da Carlo – A wonderful place for a modestly priced dinner or lunch — particularly in summer when meals are served outdoors under a medieval *loggia.* The sausages, minestrone, braised pigeon — *piccione brasato* — or guinea hen with artichokes, and the desserts are all good, as is the service. Closed Tuesdays, 3 weeks in February, and a week in late August. Via Marchesana 6 (phone: 233227). Moderate.

Alla Grada – This large, noisy restaurant, in a modern building in the western quarter of the city, offers a menu including all the specialties that made Bologna famous: tortellini, tortelloni, and tortelli, as well as *lasagne alle spinaci* and *tagliatelle alla bolognese.* It bills itself as a *rosticceria,* meaning that a wide selection of spit-roasted meats is available for a hearty second course. Closed Wednesdays and 3 weeks in August. Via della Grada 6 (phone: 414803). Moderate.

Rosteria Luciano – This is a genuine anomaly — a restaurant that boasts a Michelin star but doesn't make diners pay an arm and a leg. As the name suggests, roast and baked meats are the specialty, the centerpiece being a very tender pork dish, *maialino di latte al forno.* Also try the "royal" salad of mushrooms and truffles, if it's on the menu (which is limited to a few items available on specific nights). Reservations necessary. Closed Tuesday evenings, Wednesdays, the month of August, and at Christmas. Via Nazario Sauro 19 (phone: 231249). Moderate.

Serghei – This unpretentious eatery provides simple country fare at a very reasonable price. The *tortellini alla Gorgonzola* is made the way it should be: heavy, creamy, and pungent with Italy's strongest cheese. This is a happy, family-run establishment, always crowded. Closed Sunday evenings, Wednesdays, and all of August. Via Piella 12 (phone: 232978). Moderate.

La Tavernetta – A quaint neighborhood eatery, La Tavernetta calls itself an *enoteca* (wine cellar). That also makes it a good place for a light lunch. It's in the heart of the old quarter and always attracts a good crowd of Bolognese looking for local specialties at a modest price. Closed Sundays and all of August. Piazza Malpighi 12 (phone: 236947). Moderate.

Da Bertino – One of the last of a dying breed — the neighborhood *trattoria.* It serves good, old-fashioned Italian cooking to regular customers who know exactly what to expect: nothing exotic, but good value for the money. Closed Sundays, Christmas through Epiphany, and two weeks in August. Via delle Lame 55 (phone: 522230). Inexpensive.

Birreria Lamma – A large, loud, noisy *birreria* (beer hall) that at first seems more Bavarian than Bolognese. The decor may be German, but the food is all Italian. There are good pasta dishes as well as chops, steaks, sausages, and roasts. Service tends to bustle along — you won't make friends with your waiter, but you won't wait long for your food either. This is just a few steps from the twin towers and a great place for lunch, though it's open continuously from 11:30 AM to 11:30 PM — almost unheard of in Italy. There is counter service. Closed Wednesdays. Via de' Giudei 4 (phone: 279422). Inexpensive.

FLORENCE

Florence, city of the arts, jewel of the Renaissance, symbol of Tuscan pride in grace and refinement, is for many an acquired taste. Rome has romance, Venice intrigue, and Naples a poignant gaiety — Florence may seem too austere, too serious, too severe. The elegance that is Florence does not seize a visitor immediately — not like the splashing fountains of Rome, the noisy laughter and song of Naples, the pastel chandeliers peeking out of patrician palaces along Venice's Grand Canal.

Next to the mellow tangerine hues of Rome, the pinks of Venice, and the orgy of color that is Naples, Florence is a study in neutral shades: blacks and whites, beiges and browns, a splattering of dark green. Its people seem less spontaneous and exuberant than Romans or Neapolitans, more hard-working and reserved, with an innate sense of dignity and pride.

Florentine *palazzi* are more like fortresses, at first glance rather forbidding and uninviting; the city's somber streets are lined with solid, direct architecture; its civic sculpture is noble and restrained. But this is only a superficial view. Step into the palaces and you will be awed by the beauty of fine details as well as by some of the world's greatest art treasures. Look at the fine Florentine crafts in gold, leather, and exquisite fabrics in the elegant but classically serious shops. It won't take long before you understand why the culture and art of Florence have attracted people from around the world through the centuries and why it is as much a favorite of artists, students, and expatriates today as it was during its apogee under the Medicis in the fifteenth century.

Florence was the home of Cimabue and Giotto, the fathers of Italian painting; of Brunelleschi, Donatello, and Masaccio, who paved the way for the Renaissance; of the Della Robbias, Botticelli, Leonardo da Vinci, and Michelangelo; of Dante Alighieri, Petrarch, and Boccaccio; of Machiavelli and Galileo. Art, science, and life found their finest, most powerful expression in Florence, and records of this splendid past fill the city's many galleries, museums, churches, and palaces, demanding attention.

Florence — *Firenze* in Italian — probably originated as an Etruscan center, but it was only under the Romans in the first century BC that it became a true city. Like so many other cities of its time, Roman Florence grew up along the fertile banks of a river, in this case the Arno, amid the rolling green hills of Tuscany. Its Latin name, *Florentia* ("flowering"), probably referred to the city's florid growth, although some historians believe it may have come from Florinus, the Roman general who besieged the nearby Etruscan hill town of Fiesole in 63 BC.

During the Roman rule, Florence became a thriving military and trading center, with its share of temples, baths, a town hall, and an amphitheater, but few architectural monuments of that epoch have survived. After the fall of the Roman Empire, it sank into the decadence of the Dark Ages, and despite a temporary reprieve during Charlemagne's eighth- and ninth-century European empire, it did not really flourish again until the late eleventh century. It was then that the great guilds were developed, the florin-based currency appeared, and Florence became a powerful, self-governing republic.

In the twelfth century, interfamily feuds were widespread, and more than 150 square stone towers — built for defense by influential families right next to their houses — dominated the city's skyline. Even so, during that and the next century, the Florentine population of about 60,000 (twice that of London at the time) was busily engaged in trade with the rest of the Mediterranean. The amazing building boom that was to follow, bringing about the demolition of fortified houses in favor of more gracious public and private *palazzi* and magnificent churches, reflected the great prosperity of the city's trading and banking families, its wool and silk industries, and the enormous strength of the florin.

As a free city-state or *comune,* Florence managed to maintain a balance between the authority of the Germanic emperors and that of the popes, overcoming the difficulties of internal struggles between the burgher Guelphs (who supported the pope) and the aristocratic Ghibellines (who were on the side of the Holy Roman Emperor). Eventually, by the late thirteenth century, the Guelphs won power and established a democratic government with the famous Ordinances of Justice. So began Florence's ascent, which would span three centuries and reach its height and greatest splendor under the Medici family.

Owing in large measure to the patronage of the Medicis, Florence became the liveliest and most creative city in Europe. Giovanni di Bicci de' Medici (1360–1429) founded this illustrious dynasty of merchants, bankers, and art patrons, and his son Cosimo the Elder (1389–1464) continued to gather artists around him. But it was Cosimo's grandson Lorenzo the Magnificent (1449–1492) who put Florence in the forefront of the Italian Renaissance. Today, the Medicis might be thought of as something of a political machine since they controlled — through their wealth and personal power alone — a city that was, in theory at least, still a democratic republic governed by members of the trade guilds. Their *de facto* rule was not uncontested, however. They suffered reversals, such as the Pazzi Conspiracy in 1478, and twice they were expelled — from 1494 to 1512, when a revolution brought the religious reformer Savonarola to power (and an attempt was made to reestablish democracy), and again from 1527 to 1530, when another republic was set up, only to fall to the troops of Emperor Charles V and lead to the Medici restoration.

Finally, in the late sixteenth century, their glory days behind them, the Medicis gained an official title. They became grand dukes (Cosimo I was the first), and Florence became the capital of the grand duchy of Tuscany. In the eighteenth century, the grand duchy of the Medicis was succeeded by that of the house of Lorraine, until Tuscany became part of the kingdom of Italy in 1860. From 1865 to 1871, Florence reigned as temporary capital of the kingdom, but with the capital's transfer to Rome, the history of Florence merges with that of the rest of Italy.

Two catastrophes in the twentieth century have caused inestimable damage to Florence's art treasures. In 1944, all the beloved bridges crossing the Arno — except for the Ponte Vecchio — were blown up by the Nazis. Reconstruction began as soon as the Germans retreated. Then, two decades later, in November 1966, the Arno overflowed its banks, covering the historic center with a muddy slime. Over 1,400 works of art, two million volumes of valuable books, and countless homes were damaged by flood waters that reached depths of 23 feet. The people of Florence, with help from all over the world, rose to the challenge. Before the flood waters had receded, they began the painstaking chore of rescuing their treasures from 600,000 tons of mud, oil, and debris.

Today, the city of Florence — with a population of more than half a million — is still a vital force in the arts, in culture, and in science, as well as an industrial, commercial, and university center and a leader in the fields of handicrafts and fashion. Note, indeed, how the Florentines dress — their fine attention to detail and the remarkable sense of style that turns an ordinary outfit into something personal and very special. And note the almost challenging local swagger. Then realize that these are people who wake up every morning to the marvels of Michelangelo, who literally live in a textbook of the fifteenth-century Renaissance. Their artistic and cultural heritage is unsurpassed, truly unique in the world. No doubt you'll agree, they have every reason to be proud.

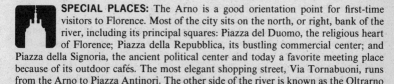

FLORENCE AT-A-GLANCE

SEEING THE CITY: The picture-postcard view of Florence is the one from Piazzale Michelangelo. From here, more than 300 feet above sea level, the eye embraces the entire city and neighboring hill towns as far as Pistoia, but it is the foreground that rivets the attention. The Arno with all its bridges, from Ponte San Niccolò to Ponte della Vittoria, the Palazzo Vecchio with its tower and crenellations, the Uffizi, the flank of Santa Croce, and numerous spires and domes are all in the picture. And looming over the whole, like a whale washed ashore in the land of Lilliput, is the massive Duomo, with its bell tower and giant red cupola. The *piazzale* is reached by a splendid tree-lined avenue called the Viale dei Colli, which begins at Ponte San Niccolò and winds up to the enormous square under the name of Viale Michelangelo. It then proceeds beyond the square as far as the Porta Romana under the names of Viale Galileo and Viale Machiavelli. From bridge to Roman Gate is a scenic 4-mile walk, but it's also possible to trace the same route aboard bus No. 13 from the station. Another extraordinary view, of Florence and the entire Arno Valley, can be enjoyed from the lookout terrace just before the Church of St. Francis, perched on a hill studded with cypress trees and sumptuous villas in neighboring Fiesole (see *Special Places*).

SPECIAL PLACES: The Arno is a good orientation point for first-time visitors to Florence. Most of the city sits on the north, or right, bank of the river, including its principal squares: Piazza del Duomo, the religious heart of Florence; Piazza della Repubblica, its bustling commercial center; and Piazza della Signoria, the ancient political center and today a favorite meeting place because of its outdoor cafés. The most elegant shopping street, Via Tornabuoni, runs from the Arno to Piazza Antinori. The other side of the river is known as the Oltrarno (literally "beyond the Arno"). Sights on this side include the Pitti Palace and Boboli Gardens, the churches of Santo Spirito and Santa Maria del Carmine, as well as Piazzale Michelangelo.

THE CATHEDRAL (DUOMO) COMPLEX

Il Duomo (The Cathedral) – The Cathedral of Santa Maria del Fiore was begun in 1296 by Sienese architect Arnolfo di Cambio and took 173 years to complete. Dominating a large double square, it is the fourth longest cathedral in the world (after St. Peter's in Rome, St. Paul's in London, and the cathedral of Milan) and is said to hold more than 20,000 people. The gigantic project was financed by the Florentine republic and the Clothmakers Guild in an age of faith when every city-state aspired to claim the biggest and most important cathedral as its own. Besides religious services, the Duomo has served as the site of major civic ceremonies and many noteworthy historical events, such as the Pazzi Conspiracy when Giuliano de' Medici was assassinated in 1478. The original façade, never completed, was destroyed in the 16th century and was replaced in the late 19th century. Whereas the exterior walls are encased in colorful marble (white from Carrara, green from Prato, and pink from Siena), the interior seems plain and cold, of a brownish-gray sandstone called *pietra forte* and soberly decorated in keeping with the Florentine character. Most of the original statuary that adorned the Duomo, including, most recently, Michelangelo's unfinished *Pietà*, has been moved to the Museo dell'Opera del Duomo (see below). The remains of the ancient church of Santa Reparata, the original cathedral of Florence, which came to light under the Duomo during the extensive excavation undertaken after the 1966 flood, are very interesting (take the staircase near the entrance on the right side of the nave). The crypt is particularly haunting.

The public competition for the design of the dome was won by a Florentine, Filippo Brunelleschi, who had marveled at the great engineering feat of ancient Rome, the dome of the Pantheon. The Renaissance architect's mighty cupola, built between 1420 and 1436, the first since antiquity, subsequently inspired Michelangelo as he faced the important task of designing the dome of St. Peter's in Rome. Brunelleschi's dome surpasses both the Pantheon and St. Peter's. It is over 371 feet high and 148 feet across and has double walls between which a 463-step staircase leads to a lantern at the top (also a Brunelleschi design). Because of restorations that have been under way for more than a decade, there is little available light for viewing the dome's immense fresco (begun by Vasari), reputedly the largest wall painting in the world. Still, the 40-minute climb up and down is well worth the effort for the breathtaking panoramic view from the top and for a true sense of the awesome size of this artistic and technical masterpiece. No, Virginia, there is no elevator.

Il Campanile (The Bell Tower) – The graceful freestanding belfry of the Duomo, one of the most unusual in Italy, was begun by Giotto in 1334 (when he was 67) and eventually completed by Francesco Talenti. The bas reliefs adorning the base are copies of the originals by Giotto and Luca della Robbia, which have been removed to the *Duomo Museum,* as have the statues of the Prophets (by various artists, including Donatello) that stood in the niches. The 414-stair climb to the top leads to a terrace with another bird's-eye view of Florence. No elevator.

Il Battistero (The Baptistry) – Dedicated to St. John the Baptist, the patron saint of Florence, the baptistry is a unique treasure, the origins of which are lost in time. The octagonal building may date from the 4th century, contemporary with the Church of Santa Reparata, while the facing of white and green marble dates from the 12th century and is typical of the Tuscan Romanesque style with an Oriental influence. To this day, the baptistry is still used for baptisms, and many a famous Florentine (such as Dante Alighieri) has been baptized here. On the feast of St. John the Baptist (June 24), the relics of the saint are displayed in the building and candles are lit in his honor (see

Special Events). The interior is covered with magnificent Byzantine-style mosaics by 13th- and 14th-century Florentine and Venetian masters, but the three gilded bronze doorways are the main tourist attraction. The *south doors,* by Andrea Pisano, are the oldest, dating from the early 14th century. In the Gothic style, they have 28 panels with reliefs depicting the life of St. John the Baptist and the cardinal and theological virtues. The *north doors* (1403–1424), in late Gothic style, were the result of a competition whose unanimous winner was Lorenzo Ghiberti (Brunelleschi was among the competitors). They, too, are divided into 28 panels, depicting scenes from the life of Christ, the Evangelists, and the Doctors of the Church. Ghiberti's *east doors,* however, facing the cathedral, are his masterpiece. In full Renaissance style, they were defined by Michelangelo as worthy of being the "gate of paradise." Begun in 1425 and completed in 1452, when Ghiberti was 74 years old, they are made up of ten panels illustrating Old Testament stories and medallions containing self-portraits of Ghiberti and his adopted son Vittorio (who designed the frame), as well as portraits of their principal contemporaries.

Admission is charged for the cathedral dome (closed Sundays), the crypt (closed Sunday afternoons), and the bell tower. Piazza del Duomo.

Museo dell'Opera del Duomo (Duomo Museum) – This museum contains masterpieces from the cathedral, the baptistry, and the bell tower, especially sculpture: Michelangelo's unfinished *Pietà* (the third of his four), Donatello's *Mary Magdalene,* the famous choir lofts (*cantorie*) by Luca della Robbia and Donatello, the precious silver altar frontal from the baptistry, fragments from the original cathedral façade, even the original wooden scale model of Brunelleschi's dome. Closed Sunday afternoons. Admission fee. Piazza del Duomo 9.

ELSEWHERE DOWNTOWN

Galleria degli Uffizi (Uffizi Museum and Gallery) – Italy's most important art museum is housed in a Renaissance palace built on the site of an 11th-century church (San Piero Scheraggio), the remains of which are incorporated in the *palazzo* and may still be seen. The splendor of this museum derives not only from the great works it contains but also from the 16th-century building itself, which was commissioned by Cosimo I and designed by Vasari (completed by Buontalenti) to house the Medicis' administrative offices, or *uffizi.* In 1581, Francesco I began converting the top floor into an art museum destined to become one of the world's greatest. The three corridors, light streaming through their great windows, are a spectacle in themselves, and the collection they contain is so vast — the most important Italian and European paintings of the 13th through the 18th century — that a good specialized guide or guidebook should be taken along (Luciano Berti's is excellent), and comfortable shoes are a must. Remember also to allow more time for a visit here than you ever thought you'd need in a museum. At the top of the monumental staircase (there is also an elevator) on the second floor is the Prints and Drawings Collection; the museum proper (painting and sculpture) is on the third floor. Fifteen rooms are devoted to Florentine and Tuscan masterpieces, including the work of Cimabue, Giotto, Fra Filippo Lippi, Paolo Uccello, Fra Angelico, Leonardo Da Vinci, and Michelangelo, not to mention other, non-Florentine painters such as Raphael, Titian, Tintoretto, Caravaggio, Rubens, Van Dyck, and Rembrandt. The Botticelli Room contains the master's *Birth of Venus* and his recently restored *Allegoria della Primavera* (*Allegory of Spring*) as well as other allegorical and mythological works, making this the most important Botticelli collection in the world.

For die-hards, an important collection of self-portraits lines the Vasari Corridor and may be visited by special arrangement. Among the portraits are those of Raphael, Rubens, Van Dyck, Velásquez, Bernini, Canova, Corot, Fattori, and Chagall. Even without the portraits, the half-mile walk would be fascinating. The corridor is actually a raised passageway built in the 1560s to allow members of the Medici court to move from their old palace and offices (Palazzo Vecchio and Uffizi) to their new palace (Palazzo Pitti) without having to resort to the streets. It crosses the river above the shops on the Ponte Vecchio and affords splendid views of the Arno, the Church of Santa Felicità, and the Boboli Gardens. Closed Mondays. Admission fee. To visit the Vasari Corridor, reserve directly at the Uffizi entrance or phone ahead (no extra fee for the visit). Loggiato degli Uffizi 6 (phone: 218341).

Palazzo della Signoria or Palazzo Vecchio (Old Palace) – This fortress-like palace, built by Arnolfo di Cambio between 1298 and 1314 as the seat of Florence's new democratic government of *priori,* or guild leaders, began as Florence's Town Hall and is still just that. From 1540 to 1550, it was temporarily the residence of the Medicis as they progressed from their ancestral home, the Palazzo Medici-Riccardi, to their new home in Palazzo Pitti. Although in a rather severe Gothic style, it is at once powerful and graceful, with a lofty tower 308 feet high. Beyond its rusticated façade is an elaborately ornate courtyard highlighted by Verrocchio's delightful fountain of a bronze cherub holding a dolphin (1476). The medieval austerity of the exterior also contrasts with the sumptuous apartments inside. The massive Salone dei Cinquecento (Salon of the Five Hundred) on the first floor, built in 1496 for Savonarola's short-lived republican Council of Five Hundred, is decorated with frescoes by Vasari. Don't miss also the Vasari-designed *studiolo,* Francesco de' Medici's gem of a study, with magnificent walls painted by Bronzino and Vasari. On the third floor is a new exhibition of 140 works of art removed from Italy by the Nazis and recovered by the late Rodolfo Siviero, the famed Italian art sleuth. Closed Saturdays. Admission fee. Piazza della Signoria.

Loggia dei Lanzi or Loggia della Signoria – Built between 1376 and 1382 for the election and proclamation of public officials and other ceremonies, it took its name in the 16th century from Cosimo I's Germano-Swiss mercenary soldiers (known in Italian as *lanzichenecchi*), who were stationed here. Today the *loggia* is a delightful open-air museum with masterpieces of sculpture from various periods under its arches. Particularly noteworthy are Cellini's *Perseus* and the Belgian sculptor Giambologna's *Rape of the Sabines.* Piazza della Signoria.

Ponte Vecchio – The "old bridge" is indeed Florence's oldest and the only one to survive Nazi destruction in 1944, although the houses at both ends were blown up by the Germans. Built on the site of an Etruscan crossing, the first stone version was swept away in a flood in 1333 and rebuilt in 1345, as it is now, with rows of shops lining both sides. The backs of the shops, supported on brackets, overhang the Arno. They were occupied by butchers until Cosimo I assigned them to gold- and silversmiths in the late 16th century.

Palazzo Pitti e Galleria Palatina (Pitti Palace and Palatine Gallery) – On the opposite side of the Arno from the Uffizi, and several blocks back from the riverbank, is a rugged, austere, 15th-century palace built to the plans of Brunelleschi, originally for the Pitti family. When it was bought by Cosimo I and his wife, Eleonora of Toledo, in the 16th century, it was enlarged and became the seat of the Medici grand dukes and later of the Savoy royal family until 1871. The enormous building now houses several museums: The Galleria Palatina, upstairs on the second floor and not to be missed, is devoted to 16th- and 17th-century art — works by Raphael (11 in all), Rubens, Murillo, Andrea del Sarto, Fra Filippo Lippi, Titian, Veronese, and Tintoretto, to name a few (there are over 650) — arranged in no apparent order. The gallery, in fact, still resembles a sumptuous palace apartment more than a museum. Priceless masterpieces hang seemingly at random in elaborately decorated rooms filled with tapestries, frescoes, and gilded stuccoes. The Appartamenti Monumentali (Royal Apartments), in another wing of the same floor and once inhabited by the Medici, Lorraine, and Savoy families in turn, are normally open to the public, but as we went to press they were closed for restoration. The Museo degli Argenti (Silver Museum), occupying 16 rooms on the ground floor and another must-see, is filled not only with silverware but also with gold, jewels, cameos, tapestries, furniture, crystal, and ivory of the Medicis. Still another museum, the Galleria d'Arte Moderna (Gallery of Modern Art), on the third floor, houses mainly 19th-century Tuscan works. There is also a Coach and Carriage Museum, temporarily closed. An entrance on the left side of the palace leads to the Boboli Gardens, which extend for acres and are open until dusk. A delightful example of a 16th-century Italian garden, they were laid out for Eleonora of Toledo and are studded with cypress trees, unusual statuary, grottoes, and fountains — plus the fairly new Galleria del Costume (Costume Gallery) in the Palazzina della Meridiana.

The Palatine Gallery and the Gallery of Modern Art are open daily except Mondays. The Silver Museum is currently open only on Sundays, Wednesdays, and Fridays, and the Costume Gallery on Tuesdays, Thursdays, and Saturdays. One admission fee covers the Palatine Gallery, the Silver Museum, and the Royal Apartments (when they are open). The Gallery of Modern Art is charged separately. The Boboli Gardens and Costume Gallery are free. Piazza dei Pitti (phone: 210323).

Palazzo del Bargello e Museo Nazionale (Bargello Palace and National Museum) – The Bargello is to sculpture what the Uffizi is to painting, yet for some reason it is visited far less frequently by tourists. The building, the Palazzo del Podestà, is one of the finest and best-preserved examples of Florence's 13th- and 14th-century medieval architecture. Inside, the entire school of Florentine and Tuscan sculpture is represented — Donatello, Verrocchio, Cellini, Michelangelo, the Della Robbias, and others. Closed Mondays. Admission fee. Via del Proconsolo 4 (phone: 210801).

Santa Croce (Church of the Holy Cross) – Italy's largest and best-known Franciscan church, Santa Croce was begun late in the 13th century and was enriched over the centuries with numerous works of art as well as tombs of many famous Italians, including Michelangelo, Machiavelli, Rossini, and Galileo (there is a funeral monument to Dante here, but he is buried in Ravenna). Under Santa Croce are the remains of an earlier chapel founded by St. Francis of Assisi in 1228. The church is particularly noteworthy for a wooden crucifix by Donatello, for chapels with frescoes by Taddeo and Agnolo Gaddi, and above all for the fresco cycles by Giotto in the Bardi and Peruzzi chapels. Go outside the church and turn left to visit the 14th-century cloister and the 15th-century Pazzi Chapel, a Renaissance gem by Brunelleschi, designed at the height of his career. During the 1966 flood, the waters reached the top of the cloister's arches and damage here was particularly severe. Piazza Santa Croce.

Galleria dell'Accademia (Academy of Fine Arts Gallery) – The original of Michelangelo's *David* was brought here from Piazza della Signoria (where one of many first-rate copies takes its place) in 1873. Since then, millions of visitors (about a million a year now) have come just to see this monumental sculpture carved from a single block of Carrara marble and, in the same room, the four unfinished *Slaves* that Michelangelo meant to adorn Pope Julius II's unrealized tomb for St. Peter's in Rome. During the summer, lines form down the street, and the doors often close when the gallery gets too crowded. Unfortunately, most tourists ignore the rich collection of Florentine paintings — from 13th-century primitives to 16th-century Mannerists — and the five new rooms opened in 1985 to display works that had never before been shown to the public. These include 14th- and 15th-century works and an extraordinary collection of Russian icons brought to Florence by the Lorraines when they succeeded the Medicis during the first half of the 18th century. Closed Mondays. Admission fee. Via Ricasoli 60 (phone: 214375).

Convento di San Marco (Museum of St. Mark) – Vasari described this monastery as a perfect example of monastic architecture. It was built in the 15th century by the Medici architect Michelozzo (who actually rebuilt a more ancient Dominican monastery) and its walls — as well as more than 40 monks' cells — were frescoed by Fra

Angelico (and his assistants), who lived here as a monk from 1435 to 1445. Now a Fra Angelico museum, it contains panel paintings brought from various churches and galleries in addition to the painter's wonderful *Crucifixion* (in the chapter house across the cloister) and his exquisite *Annunciation* (at the top of the stairs leading to the dormitory). In addition to the cells decorated by Fra Angelico, see the one used by the reforming martyr Savonarola. There are also paintings by Fra Bartolomeo (see his portrait of Savonarola), Ghirlandaio, Paolo Uccello, and others. Closed Mondays. Admission fee. Piazza San Marco 1.

Piazza della Santissima Annunziata – This square best preserves the essence of the Florentine Renaissance spirit. It has porticoes on three sides, a 16th-century palace (by Ammannati) on the fourth, plus an early-17th-century equestrian statue of Ferdinando I de' Medici by Giambologna in the middle. Most interesting is the portico on the east side, that of the Spedale degli Innocenti (Hospital of the Innocents), built in the early 15th century by Brunelleschi as a home for orphans and abandoned children, one of Florence's oldest charity institutions and the world's first foundling hospital. Except for the two imitations at either end, the ceramic tondi of swaddled babies are by Andrea della Robbia. Inside, the Galleria dello Spedale degli Innocenti contains works by Ghirlandaio and others. It is open daily, except Mondays, for an admission fee. The Chiesa della Santissima Annunziata (Church of the Most Holy Virgin Annunciate), on the north side of the square, is much loved by Florentine brides, who traditionally leave their bouquets at one of its altars after the wedding ceremony. The church was founded in the 13th century, but rebuilt in the 15th century by Michelozzo. The left door of the church portico leads into the Chiostro dei Morti (Cloister of the Dead), which contains the *Madonna del Sacco,* a famous fresco by Andrea del Sarto. The middle door leads into the church via the Chiostrino dei Voti (Little Cloister of the Vows), with frescoes by several famous artists of the 16th century including Del Sarto, Pontormo, and Rosso Fiorentino. Of the numerous artworks in the church itself, Andrea del Castagno's fresco of the Trinity, over the altar of the second chapel on the left, is one of the most prized.

Chiesa di San Lorenzo (Church of St. Lawrence) – This 15th-century Renaissance building was designed by Brunelleschi as the Medicis' parish church. A later façade, by Michelangelo, was never completed. The Sagrestia Vecchia (Old Sacristy), the earliest part of the church and one of Brunelleschi's most notable early creations, is remarkable for the purity and harmony of the overall conception. It contains, besides decorations by Donatello, the tombs of several Medicis including Giovanni di Bicci. Outside, a doorway to the left of the façade leads to the Chiostro di San Lorenzo and the Biblioteca Mediceo-Laurenziana (Laurentian Library), a Michelangelo masterpiece designed to hold the Medicis' collection of manuscripts — 10,000 precious volumes.

Cappelle Medicee (Medici Chapels) – Once part of San Lorenzo, these two famous Medici funerary chapels now have a separate entrance. The Cappella dei Principi (Chapel of the Princes), where Cosimo I and other grand dukes of Tuscany lie, is the later of the two, and it is a family burial vault supreme: The elaborately Baroque interior took all of the 17th and 18th centuries to complete. Note the fine examples of Florentine mosaic, fine inlay done with semiprecious stones. But the real attraction here is the other chapel, the Sagrestia Nuova (New Sacristy), a companion piece to the Sagrestia Vecchia (see Chiesa di San Lorenzo, above). This magnificent showpiece is by Michelangelo, who was commissioned by Cardinal Giulio de' Medici (later Pope Clement VII) and Pope Leo X (another Medici) to design both the interior — Michelangelo's first architecture job — and the statuary as a fitting resting place for members of the Medici family. Michelangelo worked on it from 1521 to 1533 and left two of the projected tombs undone, but those he finished — the tomb of Lorenzo II, duke of Urbino, with the figures of Dawn and Dusk, and the tomb of Giuliano, duke of Nemours, with the figures of Night and Day, are extraordinary. (Lorenzo il Magnifico and his brother Giuliano, the latter murdered in the Duomo, are buried in the tomb opposite the altar, which was not designed by Michelangelo.) Don't miss the feeling of this room as a whole — with its square plan and imposing dome (especially its unusual trapezoid windows), one almost has a sensation of soaring upward! Closed Mondays. Admission fee. Piazza Madonna degli Aldobrandini.

Palazzo Medici-Riccardi (Medici-Riccardi Palace) – Not far from San Lorenzo is the palace where the Medici family lived until 1540, when they moved to the Palazzo Vecchio. When Cosimo the Elder decided to build a mansion for the family, he first asked Brunelleschi to design it but rejected the architect's plans as too luxurious and likely to create excessive envy. So Michelozzo was the master responsible for what was to be not only the first Renaissance mansion but a barometer of the proper lifestyle for a Florentine banker as well. Be sure to visit the tiny chapel to see Benozzo Gozzoli's wonderful fresco of the Three Kings on their way to Bethlehem. Closed Wednesdays. Via Cavour 1.

Santa Maria Novella – Designed by two Dominican monks in the mid-13th century and largely completed by the mid-14th century (except for the façade, which was designed by Leon Battista Alberti and finished in the late 15th century), this church figures in Boccaccio's *Decameron* as the place where his protagonists discuss the plague of 1348, the Black Death. Michelangelo, at the age of 13, was sent here to study painting under Ghirlandaio, whose frescoes adorn the otherwise gloomy interior, as do others by Masaccio, Filippino Lippi, and followers of Giotto. See the Gondi and Strozzi chapels and the great Chiostro Verde (Green Cloister), so called for the predominance of green in the decoration by Paolo Uccello and his school. Piazza Santa Maria Novella.

Orsanmichele – This solid, square 14th-century structure once housed wheat for emergency use on its upper floors, while the ground floor was a church, and the whole was adopted by the city's artisans and guilds and used as an oratory — an unusual combination. Outside, the 14 statues in the niches representing patron saints of the guilds were sculpted by the best Florentine artists in the early 15th and 16th centuries. The interior is dominated by a huge 14th-century tabernacle of colored marble by Andrea Orcagna. On St. Anne's Day, July 26, the building is decorated with flags of the guilds to commemorate the expulsion of the tyrannical Duke of Athens from Florence on July 26, 1343. Via dei Calzaiuoli.

Mercato Nuovo (Straw Market) – This covered market near Piazza della Signoria dates back to the 16th century. It holds an amazing assortment of handbags, sun hats, and placemats in traditional Florentine straw and raffia; wonderful embroidery work; typical gilt-pattern wooden articles, and other souvenirs. The symbol of the market is the *Porcellino,* an imposing and slightly daunting bronze statue of a wild boar. Rub its shiny nose and toss a coin into the fountain to ensure a return visit. Piazza del Mercato Nuovo.

ENVIRONS

San Miniato al Monte – Near Piazzale Michelangelo, this small church, beloved by the Florentines, dominates the hill of the same name and looks out over a panorama of Florence and the surrounding hills — a romantic setting that makes it a particular favorite for weddings. One of the best examples of Florentine Romanesque architecture in the city, it was built from the 11th to the 13th century on a spot where St. Miniato, martyred in the 3rd century, is reputed to have placed his severed head after carrying it from Florence. The façade is in the typical green and white marble of the Florentine Romanesque style, as is the pulpit inside, and the geometric patterns on the inlaid floor are interestingly Oriental. Art treasures include Michelozzo's Crucifix Chapel, with terra cotta decorations by Luca della Robbia; Spinello Aretino's frescoes in the sacristy; and the Chapel of the Cardinal of Portugal, a Renaissance addition that contains works by Baldovinetti, Antonio and Piero del Pollaiolo, and Luca della Robbia. The cemetery adjoining the church contains a wonderful collection of Italian funerary art (the English painter Henry Savage Landor and Carlo Lorenzini, author of *Pinocchio,* are among those buried here). The fortifications surrounding the church were designed by Michelangelo as protection against the imperial troops of Charles V.

Fiesole – This beautiful village on a hill overlooking Florence and the Arno was an ancient Etruscan settlement and, later, a Roman city. The *Duomo,* begun in the 11th century and radically restored in the 19th century, is on the main square, Piazza Mino da Fiesole. Just off the square is the *Teatro Romano,* built about 80 BC, where classical plays are sometimes performed, especially during the summer festival (*L'Estate Fiesolana*), which is devoted primarily to music. Take the picturesque Via San Francesco leading out of the square and walk up to the Church of St. Francis, passing the public gardens along the way and stopping at the terrace to enjoy the splendid view of Florence. The church, built in the 14th and 15th centuries, contains some very charming cloisters, especially the tiny Chiostrino di San Bernardino. Fiesole is 5 miles north of Florence and can be reached by bus No. 7 from the city.

■**EXTRA SPECIAL:** Scattered about the Florentine countryside are a number of stately villas of the historic aristocracy of Florence, three of which are associated with the Medici family. On the road to Sesto Fiorentino, about 5 miles north of the city, are the 16th-century *Villa della Petraia* (originally a castle of the Brunelleschi family, rebuilt in 1575 for a Medici cardinal by Buontalenti) and, just down the hill, the 15th-century *Villa di Castello,* which was taken over by the Medicis in 1480. Both have lovely gardens and fountains by Tribolo. The *Villa Medici* at Poggio a Caiano, at the foot of Monte Albano, about 10 miles northwest of Florence, was rebuilt for Lorenzo il Magnifico by Giuliano da Sangallo from 1480 to 1485. The gardens of all three villas are usually open to the public daily, except Mondays. The interiors of the Petraia and Poggio a Caiano villas may also be visited, but hours and policies change; call 451208 for information regarding the former, 877012 for the latter. *Agriturist* runs organized excursions to the villas as well as to country estates in the neighboring wine-producing region. Contact *Agriturist,* Via del Proconsolo 10 (phone: 287838).

SOURCES AND RESOURCES

TOURIST INFORMATION: The tourist information office of the *Azienda Autonoma di Turismo,* Via Tornabuoni 15 (phone: 217459), will provide information, brochures, and maps of the city and the surrounding area, as will the *Ente Provinciale per il Turismo,* Via Alessandro Manzoni 16 (phone: 2478141). Also contact these offices for current information on museums and churches, as hours of opening change frequently and rooms or entire museums often close indefinitely for restoration or lack of custodians. For information on Tuscany, contact the *Regional Tourist Office,* Via di Novoli 26. Helpful for younger travelers is the *Student Travel Service* (*STS*), Via Zannetti 18r. The *US consulate* is at Lungarno Amerigo Vespucci 38 (phone: 298276). Numerous maps and pocket-size guidebooks to Florence, such as the *Storti Guides,* are published locally and are available at newsstands throughout the city. Two excellent locally published guides available in bookstores are by Luciano Berti and by Rolando and Piero Fusi. Background reading before your trip might include Mary McCarthy's classic *The Stones of Florence* (Harcourt; $4.95 paperback), a discussion of the history and character of the city as seen through its art, and Christopher Hibbert's *The House of Medici: Its Rise and Fall* (Morrow; $9.95), a study of the city's most influential family.

Local Coverage – The brochure *Florence Concierge Information* is usually available at hotels, and *Florence Today* can be found at the tourist information office. Florence's daily newspaper is *La Nazione.*

Telephone – The telephone prefix for Florence is 055.

GETTING AROUND: Most visitors find Florence one of the easiest European cities to navigate. Although it is fairly large, the scale is rather intimate, and it's easy to get just about anywhere on foot. Almost all the major sights are on the north side, or right bank, of the river, but even those on the Oltrarno ("beyond the Arno") side are within easy walking distance of the center in most cases. Visitors are sometimes confused by the numbering on Florentine buildings. Houses are numbered in either black or red. Black (*nero*) numbers indicate dwellings, while red (*rosso*) numbers — indicated by an "r" after the number in written street addresses — are commercial buildings (shops and such). The black and the red have little relationship to each other, so you may find a black number 68 next to a red 5!

Airports – The international airport nearest to Florence is Pisa's *Galileo Galilei Airport* (phone: 050-28088), a 1-hour train ride from Florence, but too often closed due to early morning fog. Florence's domestic airport, *Peretola Civil Airport,* Via del Termine 11 (phone: 370123), a 10-minute drive from downtown, has flights to Milan, among other cities.

Bicycle – Sources of bike and motorbike rentals are *Ciao & Basta,* Costa dei Magnoli 24 (phone: 293357 or 263985); *Garage Tavanti,* Via Tavanti 12r (phone: 486686); and *Program,* Borgo Ognissanti 96 (phone: 282916). Ride carefully!

Buses – *ATAF,* the city bus company, runs buses on about 40 city and suburban routes listed in the yellow pages of the telephone directory. Tickets, which should be purchased before boarding, are available at tobacco shops, in bars, and at some newsstands; they currently cost 400 lire. A 500-lire ticket can be used more than once, with a 1½-hour time limit. Children under 1 meter tall ride free. As there are no ticket collectors (only automatic stamping machines), many Italians do not buy tickets, but a passenger caught without one by the occasional controller is fined on the spot. The back door of the bus is for boarding, the middle for disembarking; the front door is only for season ticketholders. At rush hour, buses are impossibly crowded and it's sometimes difficult to get off at the desired stop. Walking is often faster and more enjoyable, but pedestrians are cautioned to watch out for buses and taxis that may travel the wrong way on many one-way streets.

Car Rental – *Avis,* Borgo Ognissanti 128r (phone: 213629); *Eurodrive,* Via della Scala 48r (phone: 298639); *Europcar,* Borgo Ognissanti 120r (phone: 294130); *Hertz,* Via Maso Finiguerra 33 (phone: 282260); and *Maggiore,* Via Maso Finiguerra 11 (phone: 294578).

Taxi – You can hail a cab that's cruising (it's available if the light on top is lit), pick up a cab at one of the numerous cabstands around the city, or call for one by dialing 4798 or 4390. Taxis are metered, but there are extra charges for night rides, luggage, station pickups, and the like.

Train – The main train station in Florence is *Stazione Centrale Santa Maria Novella,* near the church of the same name (phone: 278785).

MUSEUMS: Since museums are the city's top attraction, quite a few are listed under *Special Places.* A few more of the 70 or so museums in the city are listed here, along with additional churches and palaces whose artwork makes them, in effect, museums too. The tourist information office (phone: 217459) or the Superintendent of Museums and Galleries (phone: 218341) can provide information about hours.

Badia Fiorentina – The church of a former Benedictine abbey (*badia*), with a part-Romanesque, part-Gothic *campanile,* it was founded in the 10th century, enlarged in the 13th century, and rebuilt in the 17th century. Opposite the Bargello. Via del Proconsolo.

Casa Buonarroti – The small house Michelangelo bought for his next of kin, who decorated it with the master's early works. Via Ghibellina 70.

Casa di Dante – A small museum in what is believed to have been Dante's house, it documents his life, times, and work. Via Santa Margherita 1.

Cenacolo di Sant'Apollonia – The refectory of a former convent, containing Andrea del Castagno's remarkable fresco of the Last Supper (ca. 1450). Via XXVII Aprile 1.

Museo di Antropologia ed Etnologia (Museum of Anthropology and Ethnology) – First of its genre in Italy, continually enlarged, now with more than 30 rooms and a vast collection divided by race, continent, and culture. Via del Proconsolo 12.

Museo Bardini – Sculpture, tapestries, bronzes, furniture, and paintings. Piazza dei Mozzi 1.

Museo Firenze com'era (Florence "As It Was" Museum) – Collection of mainly 19th-century maps, paintings, documents, and photos illustrating aspects of the city over the centuries. There is also a permanent exhibition of works by the 20th-century artist Ottone Rosai. Via dell'Oriuolo 24.

Museo della Fondazione Horne (Horne Museum) – A jewel of a museum — paintings, drawings, sculptures, furniture, ceramics, coins, and unusual old household utensils, the collection of an Englishman, Herbert Percy Horne, bequeathed to the city in 1916 and set up in his 15th-century *palazzetto.* Via de' Benci 6.

Museo Stibbert – Vast collection (about 50,000 pieces) of art objects, antiques, arms from all over the world, and other curiosities left by the English collector Stibbert, with his villa and gardens. Via Federico Stibbert 26.

Museo di Storia della Scienza (Museum of the History of Science) – Scientific instruments, including Galileo's telescope, and odd curiosities documenting the development of modern science from the Renaissance to the 20th century. Piazza dei Giudici 1.

Museo degli Strumenti Musicali Antichi (Museum of Antique Musical Instruments) – Collection of musical instruments begun by Ferdinando de' Medici in the 17th century. Via degli Alfani 80.

Ognissanti (Church of All Saints) – Built in the 13th century and rebuilt in the 17th, it contains extraordinary frescoes by Ghirlandaio and Botticelli and is the burial place of the latter as well as of the family of Amerigo Vespucci. Piazza d'Ognissanti.

Palazzo Davanzati – A well-preserved 14th-century palace with 15th-century furniture, tapestries, and ceramics, also known as the Museo della Casa Fiorentina Antica or the Florentine House Museum. Via Porta Rossa 13.

Palazzo Strozzi – A masterpiece of Renaissance architecture, scene of the biennial international antique show in the fall. Piazza degli Strozzi.

Santi Apostoli (Church of the Holy Apostles) – Built in the 11th century, redecorated in the 15th and 16th centuries, and restored in the 1930s, it holds the flints said to have been brought back from Jerusalem during the Crusades and still used to light the Holy Fire in the Duomo for the Scoppio del Carro at Easter (see *Special Events*).

Santa Maria del Carmine – Dating from the second half of the 13th century, this Carmelite church was mostly destroyed in a fire in 1771, but the Corsini and Brancacci chapels were spared. The latter contains the Masaccio frescoes that inspired Renaissance painters from Fra Angelico to Raphael. Piazza del Carmine.

Santo Spirito (Church of the Holy Spirit) – One of Brunelleschi's last works, and a gem, notable as one of the finest examples of a Renaissance church as well as for some two dozen chapels with masterpieces by Donatello, Ghirlandaio, Filippino Lippi, Sansovino, and others. Piazza Santo Spirito.

Santa Trinità (Church of the Holy Trinity) – One of the oldest churches in Florence, built in the 11th century with a 16th-century façade. See the Ghirlandaio frescoes in the Sassetti Chapel — one shows the church with its original Romanesque façade. Piazza Santa Trinità.

SHOPPING: Shopping is absolutely wonderful in Florence, possibly Italy's most fashionable city. For clothing, the smartest streets are Via Tornabuoni, Via della Vigna Nuova, Via Calzaiuoli, and Via Roma. The shops lining the Ponte Vecchio sell beautiful gold and silver jewelry. Antiques, leather goods, and handmade lingerie are other specialties of Florentine shops. Stores are open 9 AM to 1 PM and 3:30 to 7:30 PM Tuesdays through Saturdays and 3:30 to 7:30 PM Mondays. Food stores close on Wednesday afternoons but are open Monday mornings. During the summer, afternoon opening and closing times are a half hour later.

Alex – The best in designer clothes for women — Gianni Versace, Yamamoto, Byblos, Claude Montana, Basile, Thierry Mugler. Via della Vigna Nuova 19r.

Antico Setificio Fiorentino – Fabulous fabrics, all handloomed. Via della Vigna Nuova 97r.

BM – English-language bookstore. Borgo Ognissanti 4r.

Beltrami – A chain of elegant, expensive leather shops: shoes, bags, jackets, pants, and the like. Via Calzaiuoli 31r, 44r, and 101r; Via dei Pecori 16r; Via Calimala 11r.

Benetton – Colorful sportswear for the young at heart. Via Por Santa Maria 66–68r, Via Calimala 2r.

Bijoux Cascio – Moderately priced jewelry, particularly in gold; the designs are the shop's own. Via Tornabuoni 32r.

Bottega Veneta – The local incarnation of the worldwide chain. Piazza Ognissanti 3–4r.

Mario Buccellati – Fine jewelry and table silver in traditional Florentine designs. Via Tornabuoni 71r.

Cirri – Lovely linens. Via Por Santa Maria 32–36r.

Corsellini – Handmade pipes and accessories. Via Panzani 49r.

Tanino Crisci – The most stylish shoe shop (for men and women) in the city. Via Tornabuoni 43–45r.

David – Leather bags, luggage, shoes, clothes. Via Roma 11–13r.

Feltrinelli – Art books. Via Cavour 12–20r.

Ferragamo – Italian headquarters for the well-known shoes, with the widest selection of styles and colors. Via Tornabuoni 16r.

Libreria Franco Maria Ricci – Fine books selected by the publishers of *FMR* magazine. Via delle Belle Donne 41r.

Gants – Gloves of the highest quality; Gants makes its own. Via Porta Rossa 78r.

Gerard – Way-out, punk, and exotic fashion for men and women. Via Vacchereccia 18–20r.

Gherardini – A century-old leather shop, also selling sunglasses and perfume, run by an old Florentine family (Mona Lisa was a Gherardini). Via della Vigna Nuova 57r.

Giannini – Stationers with class; the finest of Florentine paper products. Piazza Pitti 47r.

Gucci – The parent store of Italy's most chic leather and fashion purveyor. Less expensive than in the US, but expensive nonetheless. Via Tornabuoni 73r.

Happy Jack – Fine men's boutique; alterations done quickly. Via della Vigna Nuova 7–13r.

Inmarket – Benetton sweaters in the latest colors and styles. Via Calimala 6r.

Lily of Florence – American sizes in shoes. Borgo San Jacopo 20r.

Madova – Among Italy's most competent glovemakers. Via Guicciardini 1r.

Melli – Antique jewelry, ivory, silver, clocks. Ponte Vecchio.

Mercato Nuovo (Straw Market) – The covered market, with all sorts of items made of straw, wood, and leather. Piazza del Mercato Nuovo.

Mercato di San Lorenzo – An open-air market selling everything from used clothing to hot tripe sandwiches. Mohair sweaters are a good buy here. Piazza San Lorenzo.

Mujer – Original fashions for the adventurous woman. Via Vacchereccia 6r.

Neuber – British and Italian wools. Via degli Strozzi 32r.

Emilio Paoli – Straw market with class; locally produced gift articles and imports. Via della Vigna Nuova 24–28r.

Il Papiro – *Papier à cuve,* or marbled paper, a method of hand decoration invented in the 17th century; lovely stationery. Via Cavour 55r.

Parson – Trendy women's boutique. Via Tosinghi 16–18r.

La Pelle – Leather clothes made to order. Via Guicciardini 11–13r.

Pineider – Italy's most famous stationers. Piazza della Signoria 13r, Via Tornabuoni 76r, Via dei Cerretani 9r.

Pollini – Fashionable shoes and boots. Via Calimala 12r.

Pratesi – Elegant linens. Lungarno Amerigo Vespucci 8–10.

Primi Mesi – Embroidered crib and carriage sets; maternity, infants', and toddlers' wear. Via dei Cimatori 23r.

Principe – A small but elegant department store. Piazza degli Strozzi.

Libreria Salimbeni – Specializes in art books. Via Matteo Palmieri 14r.

Santa Croce Church – Top-quality leather boxes, wallets, and handbags from the school and retail shop operated by the church. Piazza Santa Croce.

Schwicker – Quality gifts by Florentine artisans. Piazza Pitti.

Seeber – English-language bookshop. Via Tornabuoni 70r.

Stefanel – Colorful sportswear. Piazza del Mercato Nuovo 34–36r.

Ugo Poggi – Florentine handicrafts in silver, china, and glass. Via degli Strozzi 26r.

Ungaro Parallèle – High fashion for women. Via della Vigna Nuova 30r.

UPIM – A large, moderately priced department store. Piazza della Repubblica.

Mario Valentino – Designer shoes and bags. Via Tornabuoni 67r.

Valmar – Specializes in decorative tassels and braids, perfect for everything from upholstery to belts. Via Porta Rossa 53r.

Zanobetti – Classic clothing for men and women. Via Calimala 22r.

 SPECIAL EVENTS: Florence is bathed in medieval splendor each year for festivities surrounding the *Festa di San Giovanni Battista* (St. John the Baptist's Day), June 24. Part of the tradition for the past several hundred years has been the *Calcio in Costume,* which consists of more than 500 men wearing colorful 16th-century costumes — with modern T-shirts — and playing a very rough game of soccer. Actually, because there are four teams, representing the old rival neighborhoods of San Giovanni, Santo Spirito, Santa Croce, and Santa Maria Novella (distinguishable by their green, white, blue, and red costumes, respectively), three games are played, two preliminaries and the finale. One is usually scheduled on June 24 and the other two within the week or two before or after that date. The game, which resembles wrestling, rugby, and soccer, with the round leather ball thrown more often than kicked, originated in the Roman *arpasto,* played on sandy ground by soldiers training for war. It evolved through the Middle Ages and the Renaissance (in 1530 there was a most famous match played by the Florentines in defiance of the imperial troops of Charles V who were besieging the city), lapsed for about a century and a half, and then was revived in 1930. Also revived was the preliminary parade of Florentine guild officials, followed by the four teams led by their resident noblemen on horseback (the best known of whom is the Marchese Emilio Pucci di Barsento, the fashion designer). Because the game and its 8,000 or so spectators constitute some danger to the fountains and statuary of Florence's historic *piazze,* it was moved at one point to the Boboli Gardens, but will probably be back soon on one of the squares.

Among other folkloric events is the centuries-old ceremony called the *Scoppio del Carro* (literally "bursting the cart"), which takes place traditionally on Easter Sunday in celebration of a Christian victory in one of the Crusades and culminates in a great fireworks display. A large cart filled with firecrackers and drawn by white oxen is brought to Piazza del Duomo and connected to the main altar of the cathedral by a metal wire. At the stroke of noon, when the bells announce the Resurrection of Christ, the Cardinal Archbishop of Florence sets off a dove-shaped rocket that runs along the wire to the cart. When the firecrackers in the cart explode, the Florentine spectators jump with joy, taking the event and the flight of the "dove" as a good omen for the future. Occasionally the dove doesn't make it, and sighs of something worse than disappointment fill the square, as this is considered a bad omen indeed. On Ascension Thursday each May, Florentines celebrate the *Festa del Grillo* by going to the Cascine, a park along the Arno at the edge of the center, and buying crickets in cages, only to set them free. The *Festa delle Rificolone,* September 7, is celebrated with a procession along the Arno and across the Ponte San Niccolò with colorful paper lanterns and torches.

SPORTS AND FITNESS: Check with your concierge about which sports facilities are open to the public. Most are private clubs.

Fitness Centers – *Sauna Finlandese,* Via Cavour 108 (phone: 587246); *Tropical,* Via Cavour 19 (phone: 210908).

Golf – There is a good 18-hole course at *Golf dell'Ugolino* in nearby Impruneta at Via Chiantigiana 3 (phone: 2051009). Closed Mondays.

Jogging – The best place to run is the Cascine, the long, narrow park along the Arno west of the center. To get there, follow the river to Ponte della Vittoria.

Soccer – See the *Fiorentina* in action from September to May at the *Stadio Comunale,* Viale Manfredo Fanti 4/6 (phone: 587858), a stadium designed by Pier Luigi Nervi.

Swimming – Swimmers will do best to stay at one of the following hotels (most other pools are private): *Crest, Croce di Malta, Jolly Carlton, Kraft, Minerva, Park Palace, Villa Belvedere,* or *Villa Medici* in the city, or *Villa La Massa* or *Grand Hotel Villa Cora* outside the city.

Tennis – *Circolo Tennis alle Cascine,* Viale Visarno 1 (phone: 490164, 356651); *Piazzale Michelangelo,* Viale Michelangelo 61 (phone: 6811880); *Il Poggetto,* Via Michele Mercati 24/B (phone: 460127).

THEATER: The principal theaters in Florence for Italian-language performances are the *Teatro Comunale,* Corso Italia 16 (phone: 2779236), which was temporarily closed for repairs at press time; the *Teatro della Pergola,* Via della Pergola 32 (phone: 2479651); the *Teatro Verdi,* Via Ghibellina 99 (phone: 296242); and the *Teatro Niccolini,* Via Ricasoli 5 (phone: 213282). Films in English are shown every night except Mondays at *Cinema Astro,* Piazza San Simone (near Santa Croce).

MUSIC: Opera begins earlier in Florence than in most Italian cities: The season at the *Teatro Comunale* (see *Theater*), the principal opera house and concert hall, normally runs from October to early January, with ballet in July. The annual *Maggio Musicale Fiorentino* festival, which attracts some of the world's finest musicians and singers, is held in May and June. The *Teatro della*

Pergola (see *Theater*) is the scene of Saturday afternoon concerts from autumn through spring. Open-air concerts are held in the cloisters of the *Badia Fiesolana* (in Fiesole) and of the *Spedale degli Innocenti* on summer evenings, as well as in other historic monuments such as the recently restored Church of Santo Stefano al Ponte Vecchio, now the home of the Regional Tuscan Orchestra.

NIGHTCLUBS AND NIGHTLIFE: A Florentine evening usually begins with an *aperitivo* at a *caffè* on Piazza della Signoria or Piazza della Repubblica, at *Harry's Bar,* Lungarno Amerigo Vespucci 22r (phone: 296700), or at the bar in the *Excelsior Hotel* (see *Checking In*). Among the popular discos are *Jackie O',* Via dell'Erta Canina 24 (phone: 216146); *Full-up,* Via della Vigna Vecchia 21r (phone: 293006); *Avenue,* Borgo degli Albizi 66r (phone: 214406); *Yab Yum,* Via Sassetti 5r (phone: 282018); and *Space Electronic,* Via Palazzuolo 37 (phone: 293082). *Tabasco,* Piazza Santa Cecilia 3 (phone: 213000), is gay. The *Salt Peanuts Club,* Piazza Santa Maria Novella 26r, has live jazz on weekends; *Club Chiodofisso,* Via Dante Alighieri 16r, has guitar music. The *Loggia Tornaquinci* is an elegant piano bar on the top floor of a 16th-century Medici building, Via Tornabuoni 6 (phone: 219148). Other piano bars include the *Caffè,* Piazza Pitti 9 (phone: 296241); the *Octopus,* Via del Parione 50 (phone: 294122); *Oberon,* Via dell'Erta Canina 12r (phone: 216516); and *Arcadia,* Via Pandolfini 26 (phone: 210013). The last two are also discos. There are piano bars at some hotels, such as *Anglo-American, Londra, Majestic,* and *Savoy.* Popular for drinks is the *Caffè Strozzi,* Piazza degli Strozzi 16–19r (phone: 212574), which has outdoor tables in good weather and an interesting crowd to watch.

SINS: The family that runs the Santa Maria Novella Pharmacy (Officina Profumo-Farmaceutica di Santa Maria Novella), Via della Scala 16, takes great *pride* in the frescoes by 17th-century artist Mariotti di Nardo that decorate their shop and in the fact that the business has operated continuously as a drugstore since it was founded by monks in 1612. The best place to satisfy *gluttonous* urges for some marvelous Italian ice cream is *Vivoli,* Via Isola delle Stinche 7. The flavors are as traditional as chocolate and strawberry and as exotic as grapefruit and tea. Other good *gelaterie* include *Pomposi* of the Bar Fiorenza, Via Calzaiuoli, and *Frilli,* Via di San Niccolò 51, on the other side of the river. More *lustful* urges are being satisfied these days in the shadows along Via del Porcellana.

BEST IN TOWN

CHECKING IN: Florence is well organized for visitors — it has more than 400 hotels to accommodate more than 20,000 transients. Still, somehow, it's hard to find a room in high season. The hotel count above and the list below include former *pensioni,* modest accommodations (something like boarding-houses) that are no longer officially designated as *pensioni,* although they still exist. A few still require that some meals be taken, and that is specified for those that do. At an expensive hotel, plan to spend from $120 to more than $300 a night for a double room. Moderately priced establishments cost between $80 and $120 a night; those listed as inexpensive will be $30 to $80.

Excelsior – Beside the Arno, just a short walk from the city center, traditional in both style and service. It is part of the reliable and efficient CIGA chain. The excellent terrace restaurant, *Il Cestello,* has a splendid view when the stained glass windows are open. The 207-room hotel is a favorite of Florentines and their guests. Piazza Ognissanti 3 (phone: 264201). Expensive.

Grand Hotel Villa Cora – A neoclassical villa built when Florence was the capital of Italy in the mid-1800s. The name comes from one of the many former owners, an ambassador. As a private villa, it hosted Napoleon III's widow, Eugénie, as well as Tchaikovsky's patron, the Baroness Von Meck. It offers 56 spacious rooms and some suites decorated in the original style, grand public rooms, and a magnificent garden with heated pool. About 2 miles from the chaotic city center, on the other side of the Boboli Gardens. Viale Machiavelli 18 (phone: 2298451). Expensive.

Regency Umbria – A small, 31-room patrician villa set in a quiet residential area and decorated with exquisite taste. Like its sister hotel in Rome, the *Lord Byron*, it offers calm and privacy, discreetly displaying its Relais et Châteaux crest at the entrance. There is a charming garden and an excellent restaurant. Piazza Massimo d'Azeglio 3 (phone: 245247). Expensive.

Savoy – A classic gem, conveniently situated in the heart of Florence, with most of its 100 rooms decorated in Venetian style. It has a popular piano bar. Piazza della Repubblica 7 (phone: 283313). Expensive.

Villa Medici – A reconstruction of the 19th-century Sonnino de Renzis Palace, situated halfway between the railroad station and the Arno. It has more than 100 charming, spacious rooms, a roof garden restaurant and a swimming pool. Via del Prato 42 (phone: 261331). Expensive.

Villa San Michele – This is dramatically set on the slopes below Fiesole, about 5 miles from Florence. Originally an ancient monastery built by the Davanzati family in the late 15th century and designed in part by Michelangelo, it became a private villa during Napoleon's day and was transformed into one of Tuscany's most romantic hotels in the 1950s. (Brigitte Bardot honeymooned here in the 1960s.) Restored to its former glory and recently under new management, it now has about 30 rooms with Jacuzzis, intimate dining indoors or out in the open-air *loggia*, fragrant gardens, a pool, and limousine service into the city. Open from March to mid-November. Via Doccia 4, Fiesole (phone: 59451). Expensive.

Grand Hotel Minerva – The 110 rooms are large and comfortably furnished, all with private modern baths. The staff is pleasant, and the hotel is near the train station, convenient to shopping and the major museums. Piazza Santa Maria Novella 16 (phone: 284555). Expensive to moderate.

Anglo-American – Located between the train station and the river, very near the Teatro Comunale. It has 118 recently refurbished rooms. Via Garibaldi 9 (phone: 282114). Moderate.

Grand Hotel Baglioni – A traditional hotel in refined Tuscan taste: parquet floors, solid furnishings, handsome carpets, sober — even somber — atmosphere and service. With nearly 200 rooms, it's near the railway station and only a short walk from the best shopping. The roof garden restaurant has an enviable view of the historic city. Piazza dell'Unità Italiana 6 (phone: 218441). Moderate.

Hotel de la Ville – Dark, quiet, and somber, the perfect hotel for light sleepers. Its double doors and storm windows provide an oasis in the center of Florence, just off the elegant Via Tornabuoni. About 70 rooms. Piazza Antinori 1 (phone: 261805). Moderate.

Jolly Carlton – This large, modern, 140-room hotel of the efficient Jolly chain has a pool and a wonderful view from the terrace. It's near the Cascine park. Piazza Vittorio Veneto 4/A (phone: 2770). Moderate.

Kraft – A modern, 66-room hotel in a nice area near the Teatro Comunale, with a panoramic roof garden restaurant sporting umbrella pines and a cypress tree, as well as a rooftop swimming pool. Via Solferino 2 (phone: 284273). Moderate.

Lungarno – Comfortable, functional, and cheerful. Set between the Ponte Vecchio and the Ponte Santa Trinità, it has about 70 modern rooms, the best of which have terraces and balconies overlooking the Arno. Borgo San Jacopo 14 (phone: 264211). Moderate.

Villa Villoresi – About 5 miles from the center of Florence and a noble home away from home. It dates from the 12th century, and for the last 200 years it has been the property of the Villoresi family, who turned it into a hotel in the 1960s and manage to impart a sense of family as well as history. Bedroom walls have frescoes, and meals are good. There is a pool in the garden among the olive trees. Via Ciampi 2, Località Colonnata, Sesto Fiorentino (phone: 4489032). Moderate to inexpensive.

Balestri – A clean, no-frills stopping-place overlooking the Arno. About 50 rooms, no restaurant. Piazza Mentana 7 (phone: 214743). Inexpensive.

Beacci Tornabuoni – This delightful former *pensione* occupies the top floors of a 14th-century palace on Florence's most elegant street. It's traditional yet cheerful and sunny, provides excellent service, and has a charming terrace. Half board is required during high season. Via Tornabuoni 3 (phone: 212645). Inexpensive.

Pensione Bencistà – This 15th-century villa, an inn among the olive trees near Fiesole, is a beautiful bargain for those whose shoestring does not stretch quite as far as the *Villa San Michele.* Half board is required. No phones in the rooms. Open mid-March to November. Via Benedetto da Maiano 4, between Fiesole and San Domenico (phone: 59163). Inexpensive.

Continental – An ideal, albeit noisy, location overlooking the Ponte Vecchio, this is as efficient as its sister hotel across the river, the *Lungarno,* which you can see from the terrace. No restaurant. Lungarno Acciaiuoli 2 (phone: 282392). Inexpensive.

Porta Rossa – One of Florence's oldest hotels (14th century, with a 13th-century tower), and perhaps in need of a little sprucing up. Balzac and Stendhal, they say, slept here. It has Renaissance public rooms (good for meetings in the commercial center of the city) and a terrace overlooking the Ponte Vecchio. Via Porta Rossa 19 (phone: 287551). Inexpensive.

Pendini – An old-style, family-run hotel for over a hundred years, in a building far older but recently renovated. Via degli Strozzi 2 (phone: 211170). Inexpensive.

Quisisana Ponte Vecchio – Between the Ponte Vecchio and the Uffizi, with a view of the former from a charming terrace. Lungarno Archibusieri 4 (phone: 216691). Inexpensive.

La Residenza – A small hotel, recently renovated, with a lovely terrace on Florence's best shopping street. Half board is required during high season. Via Tornabuoni 8 (phone: 284197). Inexpensive.

Silla – The large flowered terrace overlooks the river and a park on the Oltrarno side of town. A quiet, charming place with 3 large newer rooms on the third floor. No restaurant; usually closed in December. Via dei Renai 5 (phone: 284810). Inexpensive.

 EATING OUT: Back in the 16th century, Catherine de' Medici married King Henry II of France, and her cousin Maria de' Medici married Henry IV. The girls took to the French court — along with their trousseaus — their cooks and their recipes for creams, sauces, pastries, and ice creams. As an Elizabethan poet once said, "Tuscany provided creams and cakes and lively Florentine women to sweeten the taste and minds of the French."

Following their departure, the fanciness went out of Florentine food, and French cooking began to shine. But today, Florentine cooking, while simpler and more straightforward than during the Renaissance, is still at the top of the list of Italy's varied regional cuisines. No small contributing factor to this culinary art is the quality of the ingredients, as is the case with Florence's famed craftsmanship. Tuscany boasts excellent olive oil and wine, exquisite fruits and vegetables, good game in season, fresh fish and dried cod (*baccalà*) from its coast, as well as salami, sausages, and every kind of meat.

If you're a classic meat-and-potatoes person, nowhere will you rejoice more. Florence has the best beef in Italy, if not all of Europe. A *bistecca alla fiorentina,* thick and juicy on the bone and traditionally accompanied by new potatoes or white beans drenched in pure golden olive oil, is a meal fit for the fussiest royalty. You can roughly judge the price of a restaurant before entering by the cost per kilo (2.2 pounds) of its Florentine steak on the menu displayed outside. Fortunately, one steak is usually more than enough for two persons.

Meal hours in Florence are earlier than those in Rome, beginning by 12:30 or 1 PM for lunch and 7:30 or 8 PM for dinner. Many of the typical family-run restaurants are small, popular, and crowded. If you don't make a reservation, be prepared to wait and eventually share a table (single guests are often seated at a communal table — a respectable way of meeting the locals). Also unlike Rome, you won't be encouraged to linger over your dessert wine if there are people waiting for your table. Food, like almost everything else in Florentine life, is taken seriously — do your business and socializing elsewhere. A full meal for two including the house wine or the low-priced (but excellent) local Chianti at an expensive restaurant will cost between $50 and $130. Expect to pay between $25 and $50 at a moderate restaurant and between $15 and $25 at an inexpensive one.

Il Barrino – Originally opened by renowned singer Gino Paoli, this tiny, luxurious restaurant has changed hands often and has lost some of its glamour, but it continues to offer an interesting, although brief, menu and has the advantage of staying open later than most. Dinner only; closed Sundays and August. Reservations required. Via de' Biffi 2r (phone: 215180). Expensive.

Enoteca Pinchiorri – In the 15th-century Ciofi-Iacometti Palace, with a delightful courtyard for dining al fresco, this is possibly Italy's best restaurant and certainly the place for that grand dinner in Florence. The four chefs prepare exquisite nouvelle dishes such as mosaic of sweet and sour fish, sweetbread salad with shrimp sauce, and medallions of veal with capers and lime. The wine collection (60,000 bottles) is outstanding, understandably so, since the restaurant actually began as a wine showroom. Closed Sundays, Mondays at lunch, and August. Reservations required. Via Ghibellina 87 (phone: 242777). Expensive.

Harry's Bar – No relation to the famed eatery in Venice, but Americans flock here just the same. Italian specialties are best, though it's also the place to find a hamburger and french fries. Closed Sundays and mid-December to mid-January. Reservations recommended. Lungarno Amerigo Vespucci 22r (phone: 296700). Expensive.

Sabatini – Once Florence's top restaurant, but thoroughly outclassed in recent years. It's still quiet, dignified, and noted for its traditional cuisine, but quality has slipped. Some may find the standard menu far less interesting than those of less expensive *trattorie.* Closed Mondays. Reservations recommended. Via Panzani 9/A (phone: 211559). Expensive.

Cantinetta Antinori – Not quite a restaurant, but a typically rustic, yet fashionably chic, *cantina,* with food designed to accompany the Antinori wines. Perfect for a light lunch of salami or *finocchiona* with bread, *crostini* (chicken liver canapés), soup, or a modest hot dish such as tripe or *bollito* (mixed boiled meats). Closed Saturdays, Sundays, and August. Piazza Antinori 3 (phone: 292234). Expensive to moderate.

Coco Lezzone – Another Florentine favorite, serving authentic local food using the best ingredients with no pretenses. Try the *pappa al pomodoro,* a thick soup made of fresh tomatoes, herbs, and bread. This restaurant is crowded and hurried; don't expect to linger. Closed Sundays, Saturdays in summer, Tuesdays in winter, the last week of July, and all of August. Via del Parioncino 26r (phone: 287178). Expensive to moderate.

Otello – Busy and modern, with walls lined with paintings and a courtyard that's open in fine weather. Florentine specialties include grilled meats and *costola di vitello alla zingara* (veal in piquant sauce, gypsy style). Closed Tuesdays and part of August. Reservations required. Via degli Orti Oricellari 28r (phone: 215819). Expensive to moderate.

Da Noi – Currently *di moda* (in fashion), this small restaurant offers a menu that's extremely imaginative yet at the same time traditional. Try the *crespelle* (crêpes) stuffed with spinach and ricotta cheese in a sweet pepper sauce, or fresh fish prepared with sage and rosemary or with tarragon. Delicious desserts. Closed Sundays, Mondays, and August. Reservations recommended. Via Fiesolana 40r (phone: 242917). Expensive to moderate.

La Carabaccia – Named after an antique Florentine dish (none other than onion soup) favored by the Medicis. Its menu changes daily according to what's good at the market. Five starters and five main courses are generally offered, occasionally featuring parts of an animal you never thought you could eat (don't ask!). Very popular, informal, and unrushed. Reservations recommended. Closed Sundays, Mondays at lunch, and August. Via Palazzuolo 190r (phone: 214782). Moderate.

Le Cave di Maiano – A delightful stop in Fiesole, and sheer magic in early summer and fall for lunch under the linden trees with a view over a splendid valley. Indoors is warm, cozy, and rustic, as is the country-style cuisine, beginning with excellent prosciutto, *finocchiona* and other local salami, chicken and truffle croquettes, canapés of mozzarella and mushrooms, *crespelle* or ravioli, and the house specialty, *gallina al mattone,* spring chicken grilled on an open fire and seriously seasoned with black pepper and the purest virgin olive oil. Closed Thursdays, Sunday evenings, and August. Via delle Cave 16, Località Maiano, Fiesole (phone: 59033). Moderate.

Cibreo – Named after a historic Florentine dish, one so good it is said to have given Catherine de' Medici near fatal indigestion from overeating. The restaurant does not limit itself to the traditional Florentine fare it does so well, however. Genoese minestrone, eggplant Parmesan from the south, polenta from the Veneto, plus appetizing appetizers, soups, seafood, game, and desserts from some of the best bakeries in town are all on its menu, as are good wines. Al fresco dining in summer. Closed Sundays, Mondays, and from late July to mid-September. Reservations required. Via de' Macci 118r (phone: 677394). Moderate.

La Crêperie – As the name suggests, the specialty here is a vast assortment of crêpes, fillings, salads, and desserts. Closed Tuesdays. Reservations advised. Via Vecchietti 6–8–10r (phone: 294470). Moderate.

Garga – The unusual specialties include *zuppa di cavoli neri* (soup of a bitter, green local vegetable), *risotto* of leeks and bacon, and *gnocchetti verdi* (pasta of spinach and ricotta) — all exquisitely prepared. Only 5 tables; formerly a butcher shop. Closed Sundays. Reservations required. Via del Moro 40 (phone: 218094). Moderate.

Il Giardinetto – Fine Florentine and Bolognese cuisine, with a small courtyard for al fresco dining. Open later than most. Closed Mondays. Reservations required. Viale Giannotti 62r (phone: 680640). Moderate.

Hostaria Ganino (Ex-Mario) – A longtime Florentine favorite, this typically tiny Tuscan *trattoria* has recently changed hands and surpassed its former glory. Now run by a family of enthusiastic nonrestaurateurs, it provides few comforts (5 marble-topped tables covered with plain brown paper for tablecloths) but the best of Florentine cuisine, including fresh mushrooms and truffles in season and a justifiably famous cheesecake. Al fresco dining on the small square in good weather. Closed Sundays and August. Reservations advisable. Piazza dei Cimatori 4r (phone: 214125). Moderate.

Il Latini – This popular eatery, lodged in the former stables of the historic Palazzo Rucellai, serves solid and abundant fare such as hearty Tuscan soups, unpretentious meat platters, grilled fish, fresh vegetables, and traditional desserts. Very good value. Closed Mondays and at lunch on Tuesdays. Via Palchetti 6r (phone: 210916). Moderate.

La Loggia – On the most spectacular site in Florence, with a view over the entire city. It's run by some ex-*Sabatini* waiters who have transformed a once-mediocre restaurant into a Florentine favorite — especially pleasant during the summer for the panorama from the terrace. Closed Wednesdays. Reservations advised. Piazzale Michelangelo 1 (phone: 287032). Moderate.

Pierot – The specialty is seafood, especially on Tuesdays and Fridays. The menu is long and ever changing, depending on the availability of ingredients, but if you spot the traditional squid and beet dish called *inzimino di calamari e bietoline,* try it; also the chestnut ice cream for dessert. Closed Thursdays and the last 3 weeks of July. Reservations recommended. Piazza Taddeo Gaddi 25r (phone: 702100). Moderate.

La Sostanza – Popularly called *Troia,* literally a hog (also a woman of easy virtue), this is one of Florence's oldest and most famed *trattorie,* serving some of the best steaks in town. If you haven't had a *bistecca alla fiorentina* with Tuscan beans, get here early to beat the crowd. The place is picturesquely plain and tiny, the turnover as fast as the service (which can be rude if you try to linger). Closed Saturday evenings, Sundays, and August. Via del Porcellana 25r (phone: 212691). Moderate.

Tredici Gobbi – This was once known for Hungarian cooking, which still simmers on the back burner although Tuscan specialties have come to the fore. Closed Sunday evenings, Mondays, and August. Via del Porcellana 9r (phone: 298769). Moderate.

La Vecchia Cucina – New and out of the way, but with a *nuova cucina* worth trying when you've had your fill of wonderfully traditional Tuscan food. The innovative menu of a half dozen first and second courses is recited by the owner (tricky if you don't speak Italian), and it changes every week. Interesting wine list. Closed Sundays and August. Reservations recommended. Viale Edmondo De Amicis 1r (phone: 672143). Moderate.

Antico Fattore – In the shadow of the Uffizi, it's famous for its *ribollita* — a vegetable soup so thick with broccoli, bread, and white beans that a spoon stands up in it. The rest of the menu is equally hearty peasant fare. Closed Sundays, Mondays, and early July to early August. Via Lambertesca 1r (phone: 261215). Moderate to inexpensive.

Angiolino – Very good potluck and very economical, with a cozy ambience. On the Pitti side of the river. Closed Mondays. Via di Santo Spirito 36r (phone: 298976). Inexpensive.

Fagioli – A cheery, rustic ambience and a full bar. Enjoy the *passato di fagioli con pasta,* a thick soup of white beans and pasta. Closed Saturdays, Sundays, and August. Corso Tintori 47r (phone: 244285). Inexpensive.

Le Mossacce – Still largely frequented by habitués, it's filled with long paper-covered tables and serves good country cooking. The *ribollita* is the thing to try. Closed Saturday nights, Sundays, and August. Via del Proconsolo 55r (phone: 294361). Inexpensive.

Vecchia Bettola – A typical Tuscan *trattoria* with good home-style cooking and marble tabletops. Closed Sundays and Mondays. Viale Ariosto 32–34r (phone: 224158). Inexpensive.

GENOA

Two centuries ago, Genoa, along with Rome, Florence, and Venice, occupied a prime position on the itinerary of any Grand Tour of Europe. Today's visitors to Italy, however, often bypass the city entirely, little realizing that behind the sprawling port lies one of the country's most elegant, interesting, and sophisticated cities. The evidence of past wealth and power is still visible in its many monuments, great churches, countless palaces, lavish courtyards, and rich art treasures. The composer Richard Wagner even considered that "Paris and London, compared with this divine city, seem simply an agglomeration of houses and streets without any form."

Genoa — *La Superba* ("the proud") — was a flourishing port several hundred years before Christ. With a natural harbor on its southern flank and a semicircle of mountains as a landside frontier, its location has always been ripe for occupation and development. Since its steep terrain was obviously unsuitable for cultivation, the Genoese turned naturally to the sea — but not in the halfhearted style of a modest fishing community. For centuries the Genoese navy, along with the Venetian fleet on the far side of the peninsula, ruled the waves while its merchants traded with, and established outposts in, far-flung countries (the ruins of a Genoese fort have even been found in the Soviet Union, on the banks of the river Dniester).

The capital of Liguria and the fifth largest city in Italy, Genoa has a population of around 750,000. It stretches 25 miles along the coast and spreads up the hills that rise around the bay. Shipping is still the major industry, with related business — in communications, electronics, banking, insurance, and general commerce — also highly developed, making the city one of the most prosperous in Italy. But, remarkably, Genoa has managed to retain its historical legacy. The medieval city center is one of the largest in Europe (surpassed only by that of its archrival, Venice), and it is maintained not as a relic of the past or as a tourist attraction but as an active, thriving part of contemporary life. The vivid contrasts between, say, the *caruggi* — the winding ancient streets, some so narrow that you can touch opposite walls with outstretched arms — and the orderly planning of the modern town, with the elegant Piazza de Ferrari at its center, somehow seem entirely harmonious.

Although the etymological origin of the word *Genoa* is not certain, it probably derives from the Latin *janua,* meaning "door." This explanation is satisfactory at least in a figurative sense, since Genoa forms a natural inlet along the rocky and sometimes inaccessible Riviera coastline. Long before the Romans, the Greeks and the Etruscans used this place as a harbor; from here they traded goods and ideas, and penetrated inland. Pre-Roman Ligurians, the original Genoese inhabitants, had a settlement on the hill now called Santa Maria di Castello. By the fifth century BC the city was already an important port and trading center and an ally of Rome. Although Genoa was sacked and its inhabitants massacred in 205 BC by Magone, Hannibal's son, it soon reasserted itself, as it would each time it was plundered in the following centuries. With strong Byzantine and Christian connections, Genoa became a bishopric as early as AD 381. An invasion by barbarians in about AD 640, during which the original city walls were destroyed, roughly marked the end of the Roman era and the beginning of the Middle Ages. From the seventh century, when the Arabs conquered Spain, Genoese shipping — and indeed all Mediterranean trading — was continually under attack by Saracen pirates. Ironically, it was the city's constant struggle to maintain itself and survive Saracen attacks that led to the gradual rise of its powerful fleet. By the middle of the eleventh century, many Genoese were selling their landholdings and going over to shipping. By the twelfth century, the proud Genoese felt protected enough by their economy and their new city walls to refuse to pay tribute to Emperor Frederick Barbarossa.

Between the eleventh and thirteenth centuries, Genoa's rivals for sea power were Pisa and Venice. But with the defeat of Pisa in 1284, Genoa ensured its mastery over the Tyrrhenian Sea. The city had also begun a campaign to conquer the two Rivieras lying to its west and east. This was not fully achieved until the fourteenth century, and even thereafter some of the Ligurian cities periodically rebelled, especially Savona, which did not concede final surrender until 1541.

Genoa's prosperity was at its peak from the middle of the thirteenth to the fifteenth century, but politically it was continually threatened by external forces. After 1529, when the great leader Andrea Doria drew up a constitution that was to work effectively for the next 200 years, the city achieved relative peace under the protection of Spain. At its peak, it had settlements all over the Middle East — in Constantinople, Beirut, Syria, and Armenia, as well as in Egypt. Its merchants dealt in numerous profitable commodities, such as wheat, fish, fur, silk, wool, oil, wine, spices, and slaves. The Genoese were unusually tolerant to foreigners and foreign religions. In the sixteenth century they built a mosque in the port for galley slaves captured from the Barbary pirates. From as early as the fifth century, a large Jewish community existed in the city and was treated with comparative tolerance.

The ruins of the family house of Genoa's most famous citizen, Christopher Columbus — the gates of the original twelfth-century inner wall — still stand at the bottom of the Vico Diritto Di Ponticello, below the impressive Porta Soprana, but are hardly worth a visit. Columbus came from a family of humble weavers but earned a place for himself in world history when, in behalf of the Spanish queen, he discovered the New World in 1492. He also changed the fortunes of his native city, which up to that time had been a maritime power. Ironically, after the discovery of the Americas, Genoa was increasingly cut off from what came to be the most important trade routes; after its commercial loss, the city also lost much of its political power. Nevertheless, cordial relations with Spain, which had begun between Andrea Doria and Charles V, continued. For another two centuries Genoa provided Spain with outstanding military and naval leaders and handled vast amounts of trading between the mother country and the colonies. Genoese banks also financed many Spanish ventures in the New World. With their long-established, if highly secretive, strength, the banks ensured that the city would remain materially rich long after it had ceased to be a visible political power.

Although Genoa retained its own government until the beginning of the nineteenth century, in actuality it was overshadowed by other powers that controlled the politics and economics of Europe. When Napoleon defeated the Austrians and annexed the Genoese Republic to France, he effectively ended its independent history. But even after Napoleon's final defeat in 1815, when Genoa was united with the Kingdom of Sardinia, the nationalistic fervor within the city remained strong. Genoa, in fact, had been a center for the radical new politics of Jacobinism since 1796, and from then on it played a leading part in the Young Italy Movement. Founded in Genoa by Mazzini, the movement led to the Risorgimento and finally to the unity and independence of the whole of Italy. On September 20, 1870, Rome was finally liberated by Italian troops, thus completing the last stage of the unification. It is not surprising that this proud city, after contributing so much to Italy's unity, named its main thoroughfare — Via XX Settembre — to commemorate that date.

GENOA AT-A-GLANCE

SEEING THE CITY: Access by road or rail is via a series of tunnels carved through the rocks and under the houses; within the city, the hills that form a natural amphitheater entail plenty of slopes, steps, and underground passageways, as well as a number of elevators and funicular railways to get visitors to the city's best vantage points. A funicular runs every 15 minutes from Largo della Zecca up Monte Righi, where, at nearly 1,000 feet above sea level, the panorama spans several miles of the Riviera. This is also the best place from which to view the old city fortifications. From Via San Benedetto, another funicular climbs to Granarolo for an equally stunning view of the city, while a third funicular goes from Piazza Portello to Sant'Anna.

SPECIAL PLACES: Although Genoa proper is vast, the city center, which includes the historic section, is exceptionally concentrated, crisscrossed with steep, narrow, winding passages. It is, therefore, possible to see most of the interesting features of the town on foot, with occasional recourse to funicular. In fact, many of the sights cannot be seen or reached by car.

Cattedrale di San Lorenzo (Cathedral of Saint Lawrence) – Although it is not the oldest church in Genoa, San Lorenzo is the heart of the medieval city. For many centuries it was the scene of the principal acts of both church and state: ceremonies, celebrations, investitures, negotiations, judgments, and elections. Construction of the church began in 1099; consecration was in 1118. Saint Lawrence, to whom it was dedicated, is said to have passed through the city in the 3rd century on his way to Rome. An earthquake in 1222 damaged the building, and some years later a new Gothic façade was built to replace the Romanesque original. The alternating bands of black slate and white marble create an imposing and monumental effect. Entering the cathedral, a visitor is immediately impressed by the size of the interior and the richness of its design. The eye is led by the black and white pattern down the aisle and toward the nave and the spacious apse of the sanctuary. Renaissance frescoes depict moments in the life of

Saint Lawrence. Also of interest is the chapel of Saint John the Baptist, which houses sculptures by Sansovino and Guglielmo Della Porta, among others. It formerly held a silver casket containing the saint's ashes, brought from Jerusalem by Genoese crusaders; this is now in the treasury. Elsewhere in the cathedral is an unexploded bomb (now defused) that fell during World War II.

San Donato – This 11th-century church, a few minutes' walk from the cathedral, also exemplifies the transition from Romanesque to Gothic architecture. Its octagonal tower, rising above the conical roof, is formed by a central nave and flanking aisles. At the front of the church are heavy Roman columns; at the back, black and white medieval columns with imitation classical capitals. A splendid triptych hangs on the wall in the apse, making up for the lack of other ornamentation. Its panels, depicting the Adoration of the Magi, are attributed to the Flemish painter Joos van Cleve, who probably painted the work on a visit to Genoa in the early 16th century. The simplicity of this church inspires quiet reverence.

San Filippo Neri – Located in the northwest part of the old city in a piazza of the same name, this church and its adjoining oratory are exceptional examples of Genoese Baroque art. San Filippo founded the order known as the Oratorians in Rome in the mid-16th century. One of the founding fathers left a sum of money to the order to establish an oratory in his native Genoa. Construction of the church proper was completed in 1700. The chief features of the exterior are the *Virgin of the Immaculate Conception* marble group and a medallion with a portrait of San Filippo by Carlo Cacciatori of Carrara. The interior of the church is formed by a single nave with highly ornamental walls and vault. Next to the church is the oratory, built in 1750 by the architect Giovanni Battista Montaldo. This elaborate, impressive building is the home of a remarkable sculpture of the Virgin by Pierre Puget. With its swirling draperies and delicate execution, it is one of the artist's finest works. An outstanding mural by Giuseppe Davolio that continues from the wall onto the ceiling creates an impressive illusionistic vision.

Via Garibaldi – Originally known as Strada Nuova (New Street), this is the only street in Europe composed entirely of palaces. In the early 16th century, wealthy patrician families of Genoa expanded their living quarters beyond the severely cramped medieval city. The plan of the street, said to have been devised by the Perugian architect Alessi, eventually included 14 palaces. Many are still owned and inhabited by descendants of the original powerful families, several are now used for local government and commercial functions, and one or two are important museums. Of these, the following are the most interesting and accessible (see *Museums* for standard hours and admission fees).

Palazzo Tursi – Now the Town Hall, this is the largest and perhaps the most beautiful of all the palaces. Its façade is of the lovely roseate stone quarried in Finale Ligure. Among the many treasures housed within is a Paganini violin that is played every year on Columbus Day (October 12). Apply to the director of public relations inside the building to see the violin. Standard hours, except when council meetings are in progress. Via Garibaldi 9.

Palazzo Carrega-Cataldi – This building was commissioned by one of the greatest Genoese financiers, Tobia Pallavicino. Its exterior is severe, its interior very richly decorated. Among its most dazzling features is the Sala degli Specchi (Room of Mirrors), designed by Lorenzo de Ferrari. The glitter and sparkle of this wonderful room provide the setting, ironically, for the sober decisions of the Genoa Chamber of Commerce, which now owns the building. Standard hours; the Room of Mirrors is used for meetings and may not be open to visitors. Via Garibaldi 4.

Palazzo Bianco – This sumptuous palace contains a fine collection of paintings from the Genoese and Flemish schools, among them *Venus and Mars* by Rubens and *The Tribute Money* by Van Dyck. Open 9 AM to 1 PM and 3 to 6 PM Tuesdays through Saturdays, 9 AM to noon Sundays. Via Garibaldi 11 (phone: 291803).

Palazzo Rosso – Van Dyck lived in Genoa and was one of the city's most sought-after portrait painters. Many of his full-length portraits of Genoese citizens are housed in the Palazzo Rosso, along with some fine examples of Venetian works, including masterpieces by Titian and Veronese. Standard hours. Via Garibaldi 18 (phone: 282641).

Palazzo Spinola – Bequeathed to the state as a national gallery by the Spinola family in 1958, the building contains mainly 17th-century Genoese works but also some important ones by non-Italian artists. *Ecce Homo* by Antonello da Messina, one of the many hauntingly beautiful works at the palazzo, is also historically interesting as an example of painting techniques. It was Messina who introduced oil painting to Italy after his travels in the north. Standard hours. Piazza Pellicceria 1 (phone: 294661).

■ **EXTRA SPECIAL:** To the east of the medieval city are ancient fishing villages that seem virtually untouched by time. Boccadasse is noteworthy not only for its historical significance but also for its many fine *trattorie.* Nervi contains the lush Parco Nervi, where visitors can enjoy open-air theater in the summer. Other easily accessible coastal towns include San Remo, Camogli, Rapallo, Santa Margherita Ligure, Portofino, Chiavari, and Sestri Levante, all of which can be reached in less than an hour by train from Stazione Brignole, Piazza Verdi. Some destinations involve an easy bus connection from their inland stations to the coast.

SOURCES AND RESOURCES

TOURIST INFORMATION: There are two main tourist offices in Genoa. The one for the town is at Via Porta degli Archi 10 (phone: 541541); the other, serving the region, is at Via Roma 11 (phone: 581407). Office hours are 8 AM to 2 PM and 2:30 to 5:30 PM Mondays to Thursdays; 8 AM to 1 PM Fridays and Saturdays; closed Sundays. Other branches, with varying hours, are at the two train stations and the airport. *L'Agenda,* a calendar of events, and *Un Ospite in Liguria (A Guest in Liguria),* a multilingual booklet, are available free at the tourist offices, along with various pamphlets on museums, tours, and accommodations.

The *US consulate* is in the Banca d'America Building, Piazza Portello 6 (phone: 282741).

Local Coverage – *Il Secolo XIX (The Nineteenth Century)* is the most popular Genoese newspaper and also the most useful to visitors, as it has a good section on local events. Like many Italian newspapers, it is not published on Mondays; an alternative is *La Gazzetta del Lunedì.* Newsstands with English-language newspapers are all over the city. For general guidebooks or other reading material, try the English bookstore, *Bozzi,* on Via Cairoli 6, which is closed the first half of August.

Telephone – The telephone prefix for Genoa is 010.

GETTING AROUND: In the center of the city, walking is best, since many places of interest are in pedestrian zones or on very narrow streets. Street numbering can be confusing: According to the importance of an entrance, numbers may be black (for palaces, office blocks, banks) or red (for cafés, *trattorie,* hotels). Black and red numbers do not run consecutively; for example, the number 3 black may be followed by 14 red.

Airport – The *Aeroporto Internazionale di Genova Cristoforo Colombo* is at Sestri

Ponente, a 10-minute taxi ride from the city center. Bus service is available to the airport as well. The city terminal is at Via Petrarca (phone: 581316). The airport serves most of the main Italian cities, plus London, Frankfurt, Paris, and Zürich. For airport information, phone 600861 or 60071.

Boat – Various kinds of yachts can be hired by experienced sailors from the *Sailor's Center,* Via Lanfranco 1 (phone: 592089). Tickets for hour-long boat tours around the harbor, organized by the sailors' cooperative, are available at the landing stage to the right of the main marine station, called *Calata Zingari,* not far from Stazione Principe; for groups, call 265712 for bookings. There are roughly a half dozen trips a day, organized on an ad hoc basis and costing roughly 3,500 lire per person. Ferries run daily to Sardinia, and boats sail to Corsica, Sicily, and Tunisia. Services to Spain are currently not operating but may be reintroduced soon.

Bus and Tram – Services are frequent and reliable. Tickets (which also cover the funicular and lifts) can be bought at tobacconists and newsstands for 600 lire; they are valid for any number of journeys within a 1-hour period (misuse can result in an on-the-spot fine).

At main hotel desks, as well as at a kiosk beside the Stazione Principe, travelers can buy tickets for short coach tours of Genoa. The cost is 8,000 lire for roughly 3 hours, departing daily at 3:30 PM (2:30 PM in winter). The tours are a good way to get an overview of the city before starting out on an individual itinerary.

Car Rental – Cars are useful for day trips from Genoa but are more trouble than they're worth for touring within the city. All the major car rental firms have offices at the airport. In town, *Avis* is at Via Balbi 190 (phone: 255536); *Hertz* is at Via delle Casaccie (phone: 540906).

Taxi – For 24-hour service, call 2696. During the day, pay only the price registered on the meter; at night, there is a surcharge.

Train – There are two main stations in Genoa — *Stazione Principe,* Piazza Principe, and the newer *Stazione Brignole,* Piazza Verdi. Connecting bus and train services between them are fast and frequent, so this is a good way to hop from one side of town to the other. Both stations have frequent service to Milan (90 minutes on a fast train) and to towns along the Riviera. Phone: 284081 or 110.

 MUSEUMS: Genoa has many fine galleries, palaces, and museums. Nearly all have standard hours: 9 AM to 1:15 PM and 3 to 6 PM Tuesdays through Saturdays; 9:15 AM to 12:45 PM Sundays; closed Mondays. Admission is 1,000 lire; Sundays are free. The following are among the best.

Museo del Risorgimento – Visitors will have a better understanding of recent Italian history after visiting this museum, situated in the house where Mazzini was born. The building is 17th century, with original frescoes. Via Lomellini 11 (phone: 207553).

Lunardi Museum of American Studies – Displays on life in America illuminate the European view of contemporary American culture. The museum, housed in the 17th-century Villa Grüber, has a fine collection of pre-Columbian art. Corso Solferino 39 (phone: 814737).

Museo d'Arte Orientale (Museum of Oriental Art) – Here is one of Europe's largest collections of Oriental art. The original Japanese, Chinese, and Thai collection was donated by the painter Edoardo Chiossone. Villetta di Negro, Via Piaggio (phone: 542285).

 SHOPPING: There are two good department stores in Genoa: *La Rinascente,* Via Vernazza 5; and *Coin,* Via XII Ottobre 4. Many of the smaller, more exclusive stores are on the Via XX Settembre and the pedestrian-only Via Lucolli, while others are to be stumbled on while exploring the narrow streets of the medieval city. Food and clothing, as well as the crafts for which the region is famous — ceramics from Sestri Levante, fine laces, and silver and gold filigree — are all found here. Between Piazza Fontane Marose and Piazza della Zecca are a number of antiques shops that sell, among other things, curious objects relating to Genoa's seafaring past. In Piazza Lavagna a small, permanent flea market is worth a visit even if you are not looking for a bargain. The Genoese are great snackers, like most Italians, and it is not unusual to munch and shop at the same time. Look especially for shops bearing the sign *Torte e Farinate,* which feature local specialties. The majority of shops are closed on Sundays and on Monday mornings.

"Come tu mi vuoi" – Unique women's clothing. Vico Casana 8 (phone: 208920).

L'Enoteca – A small but rare selection of wines, particularly the better Ligurian wines not always available in restaurants. Via Porta degli Archi 31 (phone: 564071).

Gucci – A branch of the world-famous chain selling elegant leathers and other fine accessories, including luggage. Via XII Ottobre 18 (phone: 541447).

Klainguti – Homemade ice creams and cakes to rival the perfection of Romanengo's chocolates. Pleasant tearoom. Piazza Soziglia (phone: 296502).

Lucarda – Exceptional nautical clothing and accessories for both men and women. Via Sottoripa 61 (phone: 297963).

Pecchioli – Ceramics, crystal, other fine gift items. Via XX Settembre 126 (phone: 564914).

Pittahuga – Historic florist shop with attentive service. Piazza Portello 18 (phone: 298787).

Pietro Romanengo fu Stefano – For two centuries, the best handmade chocolates and other confections in Genoa. Via Soziglia 74 (phone: 297869).

 SPECIAL EVENTS: The Fiera Internazionale di Genova usually has an interesting fair or show. *Euroflora,* held there in the spring every five years (the next is scheduled for 1991), transforms the vast Fiera into an immense field of flowers. Piazzale Kennedy 1. Phone: 53911. The *International Festival of Ballet* is held in the beautiful Parco Nervi (see *Special Places* and *Music*) in July. The *International Boat Show,* the biggest of its kind in Europe, is held at the Fiera every October. The Nicolò Paganini violin contest, another annual international event, affords the winner the opportunity to play the famous instrument. Detailed information on all events can be obtained from the city tourist office.

 SPORTS: As you would expect, water sports are the most popular here. Genoa competes in an annual regatta against the three other ancient maritime republics — Pisa, Venice, and Amalfi. The contest alternates each year among the cities. Genoa will host it in 1990, during the first week of June.

Bocce – One of the most popular ball games in Italy, a bit like French *boules,* it is played in parks and squares all over the city. *Associazione Bocciofila Genovese,* Passa Zerbino 2 (phone: 810770).

Sailing – *Club Vela Pegli,* Via Lungomare di Pegli 40 (phone: 683213).

Soccer – Matches take place from September to May at the *Campo Sportivo Luigi Ferraris,* Via de Prà. The *genovesi* have two teams for which they root: *Genoa* (phone: 892431) and *Sampdoria* (phone: 813252).

Swimming – Pools are at *Stadio del Nuoto,* Via de Gaspari (phone: 368409), and *Sportiva Sturla,* Via 5 Maggio 2 (phone: 389325), both indoors; and *Gropallo,* Passeggiata Anita Garibaldi, Nervi (phone: 321311). The most popular (and crowded) beach for swimming is the Lido; take bus No. 31 from the city center. The nearby Ligurian resorts offer more attractive beaches.

Tennis – Courts at *Stadio del Tennis,* Via Albaro 74 (phone: 317604), and *Campo Tennis,* Via Campanella 4 (phone: 313056).

THEATER: The acclaimed Teatro di Genoa company has two theaters. The *Politeama Genovese* on Via Piaggio (phone: 893589) is the principal building, but productions also take place at the smaller *Sala Duse,* Via Bacicalupo 6 (phone: 873420). Various experimental works, as well as traditional Italian and international productions, can be seen in the small, well-established theaters *Alcione,* Via Canevari 47 (phone: 888686), and *Carignano,* Viale Villa Glori 8 (phone: 593533). The tiny *Teatro dell'Archivolto,* Salita Santa Brigida (phone: 281409), often presents works by traveling companies. During the summer, the *Comune di Genova* stages open-air programs under the title *Acquasola* in the public park near Piazza Corvetto. Detailed information about specific performances can be obtained from the theaters (box offices open from 3 PM) or from the main tourist offices.

 MUSIC: Most major musical performances are given in the century-old *Politeama Margherita,* Via XX Settembre (phone: 589329). This includes opera (the season is from mid-January to mid-June), classical concerts, and rock shows. In late June and July, concerts and international music and ballet festivals are held in the public gardens at Nervi.

 NIGHTCLUBS AND NIGHTLIFE: The best bet is to find a congenial restaurant, of which there are many, and settle in comfortably and enjoy a chat with your neighbors. There are two established nightclubs in Genoa: the *Orchidea,* Via Casaregis 28 (phone: 591559), and the *Astoria Club,* Via Quarnaro 7 (phone: 361195). Discos come and go, so it is best to ask at your hotel about popular places. *Anyway,* Via D'Annunzio 24 (phone: 543482), is currently the most popular. The *Louisiana Jazz Club,* Piazza Matteotti 20, swings on Thursday nights only. At the *Patio,* Via Oberdan 22, Nervi (phone: 321537), there is bluegrass on Mondays, jazz on Wednesdays, and bossa nova on Thursdays. For a late-night drink or just to hear some lullabies, try the piano bars: *American Bar La Marinetta,* Corso Italia 19 (phone: 310093), nightly except Tuesdays; or *Mix in Glass,* Piazza Leopardi 2 (phone: 363631), closed Sundays.

 SINS: Genoa, being a large port city, is as well versed in sins as in saints. The red-light district (once the city's Jewish ghetto) operates around Via Luccoli to Piazza Caricamento. Particularly under the elevated highway, this area can be unsavory. Naturally, the more deserted it becomes during the small hours of the night, the more careful you need to be. The *Bar Belgio* on Via di Sopraripa is a notable meeting place for skulky characters. All hotels, except those catering to the street trade, frown on improvised guests; usually a double room charge is levied. In the sleazier areas of town, be prepared for a document check by police. This is routine, and as long as you have valid identification, no trouble will ensue.

Another colorful, famous (or perhaps infamous) area is concentrated in Vico di Croce Bianca. Strictly speaking, this is a less dangerous zone and also great fun of an unsavory sort. Here, certain "Grandes Dames" of dubious age, sex, and pleasures have become celebrities. Many of these people have careers of more than 30 years.

BEST IN TOWN

 CHECKING IN: There are fewer hotels in Genoa than you might expect of a large, busy city. This is perhaps because most visitors stay nearby in the smaller resort towns, which are connected to the city by frequent train service and by two main roads. Nevertheless, Genoa has more than adequate facilities. The main tourist offices can help with arrangements. Hotels listed here as expensive charge around $80 or more for a double room with bath; moderate, $60 to $40; and inexpensive, $30 or less.

Colombia – Facing the Stazione Principe, just a 10-minute walk to the historic center, this CIGA hotel is the only luxury accommodation in Genoa. It has first-class service, a very good restaurant, and a "library-bar" (with phony books — just their spines) where snacks are also served. Television and babysitting services are available. Via Balbi 40 (phone: 261841). Expensive.

Savoia Majestic – Also facing the Stazione Principe and near the historic center. Not quite as luxurious as the *Colombia* but nonetheless very comfortable, with a good restaurant as well as a grill room and American bar. Via Arsenale di Terra 5 (phone: 261641). Expensive.

Bristol Palace – Although lacking the convenience of a restaurant, it is understandably one of the most popular hotels in Genoa because of its fashionable location and friendly, bustling atmosphere. The five floors are linked by a grand marble staircase. Via XX Settembre 35 (phone: 592541). Expensive.

Pagoda Residence – This ornate building, a real pagoda, built in the early 19th century by an eccentric sea captain returned from the Orient, has only 21 tastefully furnished, modern rooms. There is a large lounge, decorated with Baroque mirrors from Venice, as well as a restaurant and garden. Located in nearby Nervi, a 10-minute walk from Nervi station, which has frequent train service to Brignole, in the center of Genoa, and about 10 to 15 minutes by car from the city center. Via Capolungo 15, Nervi (phone: 328308). Expensive.

Astor – Previous to the opening of the *Pagoda Residence* in 1986, the *Astor* had no rival in Nervi. In a small park, this modern, comfortable hotel with restaurant and bar is only a brief stroll from the sea and the public gardens and open-air theater. Viale delle Palme 16, Nervi (phone: 328325). Expensive to moderate.

Metropoli – A homey, friendly establishment, with a sweet, pervasive fragrance of fresh polish and a central, though noisy, location (ask for a quiet room at the back). Vico Migliorini 8 (phone: 201538). Moderate.

Vittoria e Orlandini – Simple and comfortable, though not luxurious, with its own restaurant. Near Genoa's historic center and just minutes away from the magnificent Via Garibaldi. Via Balbi 33/45 (phone: 261923). Moderate.

Rio – For those who wish to sleep in the medieval section of town, the Rio is just off the port, very near the ancient church of San Siro. Comfortably simple, it does lack a restaurant. Closed for two weeks at Christmas. Via Ponte Calvi 5 (phone: 290551). Moderate to inexpensive.

Agnello D'Oro – The "Golden Lamb" is a bargain, one of the better hotels in this category. Rooms have air conditioning and telephones. Its restaurant is for guests only. Closed October to March. Vico delle Monachette 6 (phone: 262084). Inexpensive.

 EATING OUT: Ligurian culinary arts include many special dishes normally found only within the region; Genoese restaurants offer these either exclusively or combined with better-known national dishes. Some can be a little heavy — with lots of garlic and olive oil — but because they are so well prepared, they may not seem so. One such specialty, for example, is *pesto,* which is made from a variety of basil native only to Liguria, along with pine nuts, garlic, olive oil, and often Parmesan cheese, and is served on pasta, rice, *gnocchi,* or a locally made noodle called *trofie.* Other Ligurian treats are *focaccia,* a simpler version of pizza as we know it, served as a first course or appetizer; *polpettone,* a meat and vegetable loaf; and *torta Pasqualina,* a pie traditionally made with beets or artichokes. Veal is the most popular meat, though beef and other meats are plentiful. Naturally, the sea provides fresh fish and shellfish in abundance. The Genoese take great pride in their desserts, so most are homemade — *cucina casalinga.* Like other Italians, they eat out a lot, often with large family groups, ranging from infants to ancients. As a consequence, there are many restaurants in Genoa and nearby Boccadasse and Nervi, and prices are competitive. Prices given below are based on a meal for two, including wine but not liquor. Meals for two at restaurants categorized as expensive are about $50 or more; moderate, from $30 to $40; inexpensive, below $30. The price usually includes at least three courses with side dishes.

Da Giacomo – An unusually formal restaurant by Genoese standards. In a deluxe, modern environment, with spacious seating arrangements and first-class service, this establishment is popular with the *cognoscenti.* Dishes tend toward international favorites, though there are also many Ligurian specialties, especially seafood. An excellent wine selection is available, and the waiters are happy to offer advice. The menu changes daily but always includes both fish and meat. Closed Sundays. Reservations essential. Corso Italia 1 (phone: 369647). Expensive.

Gran Gotto – This small, elegantly appointed place has an exceptional kitchen specializing in regional dishes that are lighter and more easily digestible than usual. The *pesto* and the *ripieni* (stuffed) dishes are especially good. Try the fresh *pesce ripieno.* Homemade desserts such as lemonade sorbet and *antica torta di mele* (apple pie) are a fitting end to a sublime meal. Closed Sundays and for three weeks in August. Reservations advisable. Via Fiume 11 (phone: 564344). Expensive.

Harry's Bar – Informally chic decor and international food. Enjoy a cocktail at the lively bar before moving on to dinner. A first course worth noting is the *riso mantecato,* a light rice dish resembling a soufflé. Chicken alla Harry's is stuffed with prosciutto and cheese. Good French and Italian wines. Closed Wednesdays and part of July. Reservations essential. Via Donato Somma 13, Nervi (phone: 326074). Expensive.

Vittorio al Mare – Large, modern, and recently redecorated in very elegant style. Right on the sea, it has an open terrace for warm weather. Specialties include *scampi alla Vittoria,* made with champagne sauce, *branzino al sale* (seabass cooked under a salt crust), and *spaghetti all'aragosta,* with huge lumps of lobster. Closed Mondays and August. Belvedere Firpo 1, Boccadasse (phone: 312872). Expensive.

La Santa – This restaurant is in the 12th-century palace that once housed Saint Catherine of Genoa. Dining in its intimate, rather small environment, with soft lighting and traditional Ligurian furnishings, it's easy to feel transported to a bygone time. The food is outstanding: Oysters in season, ravioli stuffed with fish, and *tagliatelle* (noodle-like pasta) smothered in walnut sauce are fabulous possibilities. Don't miss *tiramisù* (pick me up), a chocolate confection with liberal splashings of Marsala. Closed Sundays. Via Indoratori 1/3 (phone: 293613). Expensive to moderate.

Saint Cyr – Comfortable but not spacious, this friendly, lively restaurant is particularly popular with the Genoese for lunch. Innovative selections include *timballo Arlecchino,* a casserole with spinach, fontina cheese, and tomato; *risotto ai funghi* (rice with mushrooms); and *filetto al Barolo* (steak smothered in a delicious red wine sauce). Light desserts include fresh fruit terrine and orange mousse. Closed Saturdays and Sundays, two weeks at Christmas, and the latter part of August. Piazza Marsala 4 (phone: 886897). Expensive to moderate.

Al Cucciolo – Spacious and modern, specializing in Tuscan dishes such as *pasta e fagioli* (with beans) and *fritto alla livornese* (fish fried with lots of garlic). Closed Mondays and August 1–25. Viale Sauli 33 (phone: 546470). Moderate.

Cardinali da Ermanno – Decorated with wooden figures and Tuscan terra cotta, this intimate, family-run bistro offers few Ligurian specialties, concentrating in-

stead on international dishes such as French crêpes and Swiss fondue, with a
particularly good truffle fondue in season. Closed Sundays and the latter part of
August. Via Assarotti 41 (phone: 870380). Moderate.

Del Mario – Housed in a 13th-century building, once the *loggia,* or assembly hall,
and now a national monument. Its menu is traditional and seasonal, with many
mushroom and truffle dishes. A very good *cima* (veal joint stuffed with vegetables
and eggs) and *stoccafisso* (stockfish soup), plus other Ligurian specialties, are
served in an extremely courteous and relaxed atmosphere. Closed Saturdays and
August 10–25. Reservations not usually necessary. Via Conservatori del Mare 35
(phone: 298467). Moderate.

Il 43 Rosso – Close to the theater district and one of the few places that remain
open for after-theater suppers, this boisterous, convivial restaurant is frequented
by actors as well as theatergoers. It serves typical Ligurian dishes and simple
wines. Closed Sundays and January. Via Palestro 43 (phone: 810225). Moderate.

Il Primopiano – In the center of the modern city, this well-established and pleasant restaurant serves Genoese specialties, particularly fish. The *risotto di
scampi* is very good, as are all the other rice dishes, and the *lasagne al pesto* is
excellent. Closed Sundays. Reservations essential. Via XX Settembre 36 (phone:
540284). Moderate.

Manvelina – For travelers along the coastal road to the east of the city, this is an
ideal place to stop for a meal. It is one of the region's best seafood restaurants,
specializing in dishes grilled on an open fire. Via Roma 278, Recco (phone:
0185-74128). Moderate.

Marinella – An inn as well as a restaurant, graced by sunlight, sea views, and
charming wooden fixtures. The menu is somewhat limited, but the seafood is
excellent. Try the seafood antipasto and the *fritto misto marinella,* a mixed fried
seafood dish. The Pigato wine is popular, as is the slightly bubbly Vermentino
Ligure. Closed Fridays. Passeggiata Anita Garibaldi 18, Nervi (phone: 321429).
Moderate.

Osvaldo – A very small and intimate restaurant, seating only 20 people. The fish
and pasta dishes are prepared in the simple Genoese manner, and there is a good
selection of Ligurian wines. Closed Mondays and for a month in July and August.
Via della Casa 2, Boccadasse (phone: 310004). Moderate.

Santa Chiara – Dine outdoors at this fish restaurant on the shore. The crêpes and
seafood risotto are especially good, the pasta homemade. Reservations necessary
on weekends. Capo di Santa Chiara 69, just beyond Boccadasse (phone: 308564).
Moderate.

Zeffirino – The five Belloni brothers run their restaurant in the tradition of their
father, Zeffirino. Their pasta is homemade in the *stirata,* or pulled, fashion —
by hand with long rollers. *Passutelli* is a ravioli stuffed with ricotta and fruit, a
recipe known only to the family. Other specialties are added daily to the ample
menu, which includes a good regional wine list. A large upstairs room is often used
for receptions and banquets; the smaller room downstairs is more intimate. Both
are decorated in a traditional style, all in wood, combining old Genoa with old
America. Closed Wednesdays. Reservations advisable. Via XX Settembre 20
(phone: 591990). Moderate.

Al Girone – Most of the food here is cooked on a grill over a log fire. Bolognese
specialties displace the usual Genoese. The *tortellini* are delicious, as is the exotic
risotto al curry. Closed Tuesdays and the last three weeks of September. Reservations essential. Via Boccadasse 19, Boccadasse (phone: 310391). Moderate to
inexpensive.

Gheise – The name of this quaint restaurant derives from the chants of the washer-
women at the nearby laundry, which has recently closed. Genoese specialties and

some excellent meat dishes, particularly Florentine steaks, are served. Closed Mondays and August. Via Boccadasse 29, Boccadasse (phone: 310097). Moderate to inexpensive.

7 Nasi – Enrico Nasi is one of seven children — hence the name of his restaurant, a friendly place on the beach offering its own pool and terrace. The fish is fresh daily, and the homemade desserts are very good. Closed Tuesdays. Via Quarto 16 (phone: 337357). Moderate to inexpensive.

Grattacielo – Situated below Porta Soprana, this smart *caffè* serves coffee, snacks, and ice cream (with photographs of various concoctions featured in an album-menu on each table) and occasionally features a pianist. Piazza Dante 26 (phone: 590402). Inexpensive.

Il Melograno – This small place is delightfully decorated in the Art Nouveau style and personally supervised by the charming, energetic couple who also do the cooking. The menu changes daily, with occasional Tuscan and other regional specialties as well as Ligurian. Ice creams and desserts are homemade. Closed Sundays and July. Via Maccaggi 62 (phone: 546407). Inexpensive.

Tonitto – This popular coffeehouse and *gelateria* sells a host of tempting flavors all made on the spot (and supplied to several other restaurants in town). Piazza Dante 31 (phone: 581077). Inexpensive.

MILAN

Milan is the financial and commercial hub of Italy and one of the most important business centers in the world. At first glance, it is a city of cold, uninspired skyscrapers, a city whose energizing force is money. Even the museum devoted to Leonardo da Vinci is a testament to his scientific and technical genius rather than to his artistic spirit. The people of Milan are industrious, sophisticated, chic, serious — not inclined to watch the world pass by from a sunny café table.

Although with nearly two million people Milan is second in size to Rome, many Milanese think of their city as Italy's real capital; it is arguably more powerful than Rome. There are over 400 banks in Milan. As a silk market, it rivals Lyon. Its International Trade Fair each spring draws tens of thousands of businesspeople from all over the world. Still, Milan's economic preoccupation is tempered by an appreciation of less mundane pursuits. It is La Scala, with its perfect acoustics and grand traditions, not the Milan Stock Exchange (*Borsa Valori*), that is the pride of the city. And the delicate Gothic spires of Milan's magnificent cathedral seem to soar in defiance of the stolid buildings around it.

Milan has survived a tumultuous history. Invading armies continually descended on it from the time it was a Celtic settlement called Mediolanum. The Romans subdued the city in 222 BC, and it eventually grew to rival Rome for primacy of the West. In AD 313, Constantine the Great officially recognized Christianity in the Edict of Milan, and with the coming of Christianity, Milan found a spiritual father in Bishop Ambrose (later proclaimed a saint), who accomplished the seemingly impossible task of conciliating church and state. This period was followed, however, by barbarian invasions by Attila, the Franks, and the Burgundians that shaped the fifth and sixth centuries.

Under the tyranny of civil rulers, the people of Milan turned even more to the religious authorities to protect them and represent their interests. By the mid-eleventh century, Milan had developed into one of the first Italian city-states and was ruled by bishops until Frederick Barbarossa invaded from Germany. When Barbarossa tried to extend his despotic rule to the surrounding Lombardian cities, however, the entire region united in the Lombard League to defeat him and win recognition of its independence.

In 1260, the Torriani became the first of the powerful families to rule Milan, but the Visconti seized power in 1277. Under the Visconti, particularly under Gian Galeazzo (1345–1402), Milan grew in wealth and splendor. When the Visconti family died out in 1447, Milan experienced three years of republican government before Francesco Sforza proclaimed himself duke. The most famous of the Sforzas was Ludovico il Moro (1451–1508), who brought Leonardo da Vinci, Donato Bramante, and other artists to Milan to enhance the city. After Ludovico's death, Milan fell to the invading French and, in

1713, to the Austrian Empire. At the beginning of the nineteenth century, Napoleon made Milan the capital of the Cisalpine Republic, but the tyrannic Austrian rulers returned when Napoleon fell.

In 1848, the Milanese staged a glorious five-day revolution, known in history as the Cinque Giornate. But it was nearly ten years before Milan was liberated and could throw its support to the Piedmontese king Victor Emmanuel of Savoy, who would become king of a unified Italy in 1860. During World War II, Milan was bombed fifteen times and many of its historic buildings were damaged extensively, but restoration and new construction began immediately. Contemporary Milan is surrounded by a massive industrial belt and a virtual maze of four-lane highways connecting it with the other northern industrial cities — Genoa, Turin, Venice, and Brescia — and, by the Autostrada del Sole, to Rome and southern Italy. Situated at the head of the Lombard plain, Milan is also the gateway to Italy's marvelous lake region along the Swiss border.

The city is prosperous and elegant; its people enjoy a high standard of living and a stimulating cultural and intellectual life. Whether you come on business, to attend the opera, to patronize the elegant Milanese fashion houses, or to admire the city's art treasures, you will find Milan's sophistication equal to that of London or Paris or New York, but always uncompromisingly Italian.

MILAN AT-A-GLANCE

SEEING THE CITY: For a grand view of Milan, the surrounding Lombard plain, the Alps, and the Apennines, climb the 158 steps, or take the elevator, to the roof of the Duomo (see *Special Places*). The stairway is entered from outside the north, or left, transept; the elevator is entered from the opposite transept. Both entrances are open daily and either way there is an admission fee. There is also a 350-foot viewing tower in Sempione Park (see *Special Places*).

SPECIAL PLACES: The huge *Piazza del Duomo* (*Cathedral Square*), with its perennial pigeons and ever-present pensioners, is one of the city's few pedestrian oases and is the heart of this bustling metropolis. Leading northward from Piazza del Duomo to Piazza della Scala is the elegant glass-domed arcade, the Galleria Vittorio Emanuele. Built in the last century under the direction of architect Giuseppe Mengoni, who later committed suicide, it has for decades been considered the *salotto,* or salon, of Milan for its exclusive shops, bookstores, cafés, and restaurants. Some of the city's tourist attractions are too far from the center to reach comfortably on foot, but ATM, the local bus and tram system, connects these sites efficiently, as does the relatively new subway system.

DOWNTOWN

Il Duomo (Cathedral) – The most magnificent Milanese monument is the white marble cathedral with 135 spires and more than 2,200 sculptures decorating its exterior. Take the time to go up to the roof, from which you can study the fine details of this forest of pinnacles, flying buttresses, and statues, and walk around to the *tiburio,* the base of the cathedral's central spire, which reaches a height of 354 feet and is topped by a golden Madonna. The interior of the cathedral, divided into five main aisles by an imposing stand of 58 columns, contains another 2,000 sculptures. The cathedral is considered the finest example of Gothic architecture in northern Italy, although its architectural peculiarities — it was begun in 1386 but not completed until 1813 — prevent it from being pure Gothic. Only St. Peter's in Rome is larger. Piazza del Duomo.

Teatro alla Scala (La Scala) – The most famous opera house in the world was built between 1776 and 1778 on the site of the church of Santa Maria della Scala. It was here that works by Donizetti, Rossini, Bellini, and Verdi were first acclaimed and where Arturo Toscanini conducted and was artistic director for many years. The Neoclassic building was damaged extensively during World War II but was rebuilt and reopened in 1946. Its acoustics are perfect. Traditionally, La Scala's season begins December 7, the feast of St. Ambrose, Milan's patron saint, and lasts until the end of May. The box office (phone: 80-70-41, 2, 3, or 4) is open daily, except Mondays, 10 AM to 1 PM and 3:30 to 5:30 PM (to 9:30 PM on performance days). The adjacent *Museo della Scala (Scala Museum)* has a rich collection of manuscripts, costumes, and other memorabilia documenting the theater's history. The museum is open daily for a small admission fee. Theater and museum are north of Piazza del Duomo, through the Galleria Vittorio Emanuele, on Piazza della Scala (phone: 80-53-418).

Museo Poldi Pezzoli (Poldi-Pezzoli Museum) – The Milanese nobleman Gian Giacomo Poldi-Pezzoli bequeathed his home and exquisite private art collection to the city in 1879. It includes some prime examples of Renaissance to 17th-century paintings and sculpture, Oriental porcelains, Persian carpets, and tapestries, including a Botticelli portrait of the Madonna, frescoes by Giovanni Battista Tiepolo, paintings by Pollaiolo and Fra Bartolomeo, and Giovanni Bellini's *Pietà.* Open daily, except Mondays. Small admission fee. A short walk from La Scala. Via Manzoni 12 (phone: 79-48-89).

Palazzo e Pinacoteca di Brera (Brera Palace and Art Gallery) – One of the most important state-owned galleries in Italy, and Milan's finest, is housed in the 17th-century Brera Palace. Its 38 rooms contain a broad representation of Italian painting, with particularly good examples from the Venetian and Lombard schools. The palace also has an important library (founded in 1770) of incunabula and manuscripts, plus a collection of books representing the printed output of the Milanese province since 1788. In the courtyard is a monumental statue of Napoleon I, depicted as a conquering Caesar. The art gallery is open daily, except Mondays. Small admission fee; free on Sundays. The library is open daily, except Sundays. A few blocks north of La Scala. Via Brera 28 (phone: 80-83-87).

Castello Sforzesco e Museo d'Arte (Sforza Castle and Art Gallery) – In the mid-15th century, Duke Francesco Sforza built this large, square brick castle on the site of a castle of the Visconti that had been destroyed. It became a fortress after the fall of the Sforzas and was damaged repeatedly in sieges before restoration began in the 19th century. Further damage from World War II has been repaired, and today the quadrilateral building contains the Museo d'Arte Antica (Museum of Antique Art). Among its treasures is the unfinished *Rondanini Pietà,* the last work of Michelangelo. The museum is entered from the courtyard of the residential part of the castle, the Corte Ducale. Closed Mondays and at lunchtime. West of the Brera. Piazza Castello (phone: 62-36, ext. 3940).

Beyond the castle is the beautiful 116-acre Parco Sempione (Sempione Park), with an aquarium, sports arena, and Neoclassic Arco della Pace (Arch of Peace), a triumphal arch with statues and bas-relief. The arch, on the model of Septimius Severus at Rome, marks the beginning of the historic Corso Sempione (Simplon Road) through the Alps to France, which was built by order of Napoleon.

Basilica e Museo di Sant'Ambrogio (St. Ambrose's Basilica and Museum) – The basilica was founded in the 4th century by Bishop Ambrose (later St. Ambrose), who baptized St. Augustine here. The bas-relief on the doorway dates from the time of St. Ambrose, and the two bronze doors are from the 9th century. The basilica was enlarged in the 11th century, and its superb atrium was added in the 12th century. Two other early Christian saints — Gervase and Protasius — are buried with St. Ambrose in the crypt. The ceiling of the apse is decorated with 10th-century mosaics. Above the portico is the Museo di Sant'Ambrogio (Museum of St. Ambrose), where you can see a 12th-century cross, a missal of Gian Galeazzo Visconti, and other religious treasures. The museum is open daily, except Tuesdays. Small admission fee. South of the Sforza Castle. Piazza Sant'Ambrogio 15 (phone: 87-20-59).

Santa Maria delle Grazie (The Church of St. Mary of Grace) – The interior of this recently restored brick and terra cotta church, representing a period of transition from the Gothic to the Renaissance, is decorated with some fine 15th-century frescoes. But the church, though beautiful in itself, is usually visited because Leonardo da Vinci's *The Last Supper* is on a wall of the refectory of the former Dominican convent next to it. *The Last Supper* was painted in tempera, which is not particularly durable, and though it has been restored several times, it has suffered considerable deterioration. Another attempt at restoration is under way. The convent is closed Mondays. Small admission fee. A few blocks northwest of Sant'Ambrogio. Piazza Santa Maria delle Grazie.

ENVIRONS

Certosa di Pavia (Carthusian Monastery) – Gian Galeazzo Visconti founded this monastery in 1396 as a family mausoleum. With its façade of multicolored marble sculpture and its interior heavily decorated with frescoes, Baroque grillwork, and other ornamentation, the monastery is one of the most remarkable buildings in Italy. It is conveniently reached from Milan by coach excursion or by road. Open daily, except Mondays. Sixteen miles from Milan, just off the Milan–Pavia Road.

Monza – The world-famous Monza *Autodromo* is the scene of the Italian Grand Prix Formula One race early in September each year. Visitors can drive around the course with its well-known seven corners for a small fee. The Autodromo is in a splendid park that was once part of the *Villa Reale* (Royal Villa) and now has golf courses, a racecourse, and a swimming pool as well as the auto track. The cathedral at Monza is also worth a visit. Built in the 13th and 14th centuries, it has a façade of white, green, and black marble, notable for its harmonious proportions and decorations. Monza is easily reached by bus or train; by road, it is 7 miles northeast of Milan on SS 36.

■**EXTRA SPECIAL:** Few people know it, but until the last century, Milan was crisscrossed by canals, or *navigli.* Today only two remain, and recently the city of Milan has reactivated some navigation on the Naviglio Grande. The *Elf-Milano* steamer departs regularly from the Milan dock (Via Gabriele D'Annunzio and Piazza Cantore) for trips through the Milanese countryside to places like Abbiategrasso and Vigevano. Fares range from $12 to $20. Information is available at the tourist board (EPT), Via Marconi 1 (phone: 80-96-62).

SOURCES AND RESOURCES

 TOURIST INFORMATION: General tourist information is available at the *Palazzo del Turismo of the Provincial Tourist Board* (Ente Provinciale per il Turismo, or EPT), Via Marconi 1 (phone: 80-96-62). The EPT will make hotel reservations within Milan and provide information on other regions of Italy. The *US consulate* is at Piazza Repubblica 32 (phone: 652-841).

Local Coverage – The tourist board can provide copies of *Tutta Milano,* a useful guide to activities, facts and phone numbers, and listings of restaurants and discos. The biweekly *Night & Day Milano* has bulletins on special events, and *Viva Milano,* a weekly entertainment newspaper, provides up-to-date information on shops, fairs, restaurants, and discos. Other publications, such as the monthly *Milano Mese* and *Un Ospite di Milano* (*A Guest in Milan*), which is produced by the Hotel Concierges Association, are often available in hotels.

The *Milan Trade Fair Center* is at Largo Domodossola 1 (phone: 49971).

Telephone – The telephone prefix for Milan is 02.

 GETTING AROUND: Much of the center of Milan has been closed to traffic, so it is far more convenient for visitors to use public transportation. Inexpensive day tickets that allow unlimited travel on the public transportation system can be purchased at the *ATM Ufficio Abbonamenti* at the Piazza del Duomo subway station, at the Stazione Centrale, and at the EPT on Via Marconi.

Airports – *Malpensa Airport* is about 28 miles (an hour's drive) from the center of Milan; a taxi ride into town can cost as much as 80,000 lire. Buses to Malpensa leave from Stazione Centrale (the main railway station), on the east side of the Galleria delle Carrozze, 2½ hours before every flight and cost 5,000 lire (phone: 27-29-74 or 66-90-836 for schedules). They also stop at the east entrance of Porta Garibaldi Station en route.

Linate Airport handles domestic traffic as well as some international — but not intercontinental — flights. Linate is 5 miles (15 minutes; longer if traffic is heavy) from downtown Milan; taxi fare into the city is about 12,000 lire. Buses to the airport leave from Porta Garibaldi Station every 20 minutes between 5:40 AM and 8:40 PM, stop at the Stazione Centrale, and cost 1,700 lire (phone: 7485-2200 or 7485-2207).

Although there is no regularly scheduled transport service between Malpensa and Linate airports, Alitalia occasionally provides group transfers if two Alitalia flights are involved.

Bus and Tram – The local bus and tram service, *ATM,* efficiently connects various points of the sprawling city. Tickets are sold at tobacconists and newsstands throughout the city and must be purchased in advance.

Car Rental – Most international and Italian firms are represented. *Avis, Europcar, Hertz,* and *Maggiore* all have counters at both Malpensa and Linate airports and at several locations in the city. Central reservations numbers are *Avis* (phone: 6981); *Europcar* (phone: 6071053); *Hertz* (phone: 20483); *Maggiore* (phone: 5243846). *Budget* is at Via Vittor Pisani 13 (phone: 6703151) and at Malpensa (phone: 868221) and Linate (phone: 7385639). *InterRent* is at Corso Como 4 (phone: 6570477, 6599417) and at Malpensa (phone: 868124) and Linate (phone: 733585). *Avis, Hertz,* and *Maggiore* also have locations at the train station.

Subway – The *Metropolitana Milanese* (MM) has two lines. The most useful for tourists is line 1, which runs south from near the main railway station, through Piazza del Duomo, and west beyond Piazza Santa Maria delle Grazie. Tickets are sold at coin-operated machines in each station.

Taxi – Taxis can be hailed while cruising, picked up at a cabstand, or called (phone: 83-88, 85-85, 67-67, 52-51). Meters begin at 4,000 lire plus arrival and waiting time if the cab is called by phone. Do not be surprised if the driver asks for a surcharge after 10 PM any evening or on Sundays or holidays. There is an additional small charge for baggage.

Train – Milan's main train station is *Stazione Centrale,* Piazzale Duca d'Aosta (phone: 67-500). Several smaller stations serve local commuter lines. The largest of these is Porta Garibaldi, from which trains depart for Turin, Pavia, Monza, Bergamo, and other points (phone: 66-20-78).

 MUSEUMS: In addition to those listed in *Special Places,* several other museums in Milan are worth a visit.

Museo della Scienza e della Tecnica Leonardo da Vinci (Leonardo da Vinci Museum of Science and Technology) – Via San Vittore 21 (phone: 46-27-09).

Museum of Milan – Via Sant'Andrea 6 (phone: 70-62-45).

Modern Art Gallery of the Villa Reale – Via Palestro 16 (phone: 70-28-19).

Museo del Risorgimento Nazionale (National Museum of the Risorgimento) – Via Borgonuovo 23 (phone: 80-53-598).

Biblioteca Ambrosiana (Ambrosiana Library) – Piazza Pio XI 2 (phone: 80-01-46).

Museo e Casa di Manzoni (Manzoni Museum and House) – Via Morone 1 (phone: 87-10-19).

Basilica di San Lorenzo Maggiore – Corso di Porta Ticinese 39.

Milan also has scores of art galleries with interesting shows. The following offer an excellent selection of contemporary and early-20th-century Italian art: *Ariete Grafica,* Via Sant'Andrea 5 (phone: 79-55-73); *Galleria Philippe Daverio,* Via Montenapoleone 6/A (phone: 79-86-95); *Centro Annunciata,* Via Manzoni 44 (phone: 79-60-26); *Arte Centro,* Via Brera 11 (phone: 86-58-88); *Cinque Fiori,* Via Fiori 5 (phone: 87-10-17); *Ars Italica,* Via Marconi 3/A (phone: 87-65-33).

 SHOPPING: With the proliferation of Italian design and fashion over the last ten years, Milan has become an international style center full of enticing, if expensive, shops, including the boutiques of most of Italy's major contemporary clothing designers. It is also a center for antiques and home furnishings. The main shopping area comprises the streets near Piazza del Duomo and La Scala, particularly the elegant Via Montenapoleone, Via della Spiga, and Via Sant'Andrea. The boutiques of top Italian designers, most of whom are based in Milan, are represented: *Giorgio Armani,* Via Sant'Andrea 9; *Gianni Versace,* Via della Spiga 4 and 25; *Enrico Coveri,* Via San Pietro all'Orto; *Missoni,* Via Montenapoleone 1; *Ferragamo,* Via Montenapoleone, and *Krizia,* Via della Spiga 23. In addition, many other elegant shops sell unusual, high-quality goods. Boutiques offering modern fashions and antique clothes are scattered throughout the old Brera quarter and around St. Ambrose's Basilica. Early in December, a flea market near the basilica features a wide selection of clothes, antiques, old books, and knickknacks. Shop hours generally are daily from 9 AM to 12:30 PM and 3:30 to 7:30 PM. Most shops are closed on Monday mornings.

Accademia – Fine menswear and accessories. Via Solferino 11.

Arflex – Armchairs and chaises that are produced by top designers and are among the best known in Italy. Via Durini 28.

Arte Antica – One of the city's best-known antique stores, with French porcelain, clocks, and furniture. Via Sant'Andrea 11.

L'Artisan Parfumeur – A new shop specializing in perfume and home scents. Via Francesco Sforza 3.

Guanti Berni – Beautiful leather gloves for men and women. Via Sant'Andrea.

Brigatti – Considered Milan's finest men's sportswear shop; also a ski boutique for the entire family. Corso Venezia 15.

Calderoni – Exquisite jewelry and silver. Via Montenapoleone 8.

Carrano – Stylish women's shoes. Via Sant'Andrea 21.

Centenari – Fine old prints and paintings. Galleria Vittorio Emanuele II, 92.

Cittone Oggi – One of Milan's most elegant and stylish furniture stores. Via Bigli 4.

Cose – Chic and trendy women's clothing. Via della Spiga 8.

Tanino Crisci – The best in finely crafted men's and women's footwear. Via Montenapoleone 3.

Decomania – Art deco objects and furniture. Via Fiori Chiari 5/9.

Erreuno – Elegant women's fashions. Via della Spiga 15.

Gobbi – One of the city's best-known jewelry stores. Galleria Vittorio Emanuele II (in the Octagon).

Franco and Aldo Lorenzi – Elegant travel and smoking accessories for men. Via Montenapoleone 9.

Orsi – A small, highly regarded antiques shop, with lovely 17th- and 18th-century furniture. Via Bagutta 14.

Peck – A specialty food shop, the main store of a gastronomic empire and a Milanese institution, not to be missed by those eager for the best in dried porcini mushrooms, truffles, pâtés, sausages, and cheese. Via Spadari 9. Other Peck stores are *Casa del Formaggio,* Via Speronari 3, and *Bottega del Maiale,* Via Hugo 3.

Provera – Top-quality wines (and free tasting). Corso Magenta 7.

Rubinacci – Top French designers and the store's own elegant line of women's fashions. Via Sant'Andrea 10.

Vittorio Siniscalchi – One of Milan's best custom shirtmakers for men. Via Gesù 8.

Stationery – The city's best-stocked stationery store, with interesting gadgets and office accessories. Via Solferino 3.

Alberto Subert – Fine Italian and imported antiques. Via della Spiga 22.

SPECIAL EVENTS: The annual *International Trade Fair* held in late April is one of the most important commercial fairs in the world. Although this is the city's biggest, various other trade fairs and exhibitions (including the showings of designer collections, the twice-yearly fashion fair, and the September furniture fair) occur almost every month except July and August, often making advance hotel reservations essential. Information and a year-round calendar of events can be obtained from the main Trade Fair office, Largo Domodossola 1 (phone: 49-971). In July and August, the city sponsors a variety of outdoor cultural events; sometimes restaurants join in by serving regional specialties in the parks. The opening of the opera season at *La Scala* each year on December 7 is the city's major cultural event.

SPORTS: For general information, contact the *Ripartizione Sport-Turismo* (Municipal Sports and Tourism Department), Via Marconi 2 (phone: 86-52-84). *Pronto Sport* (phone: 80-14-66) provides up-to-date information on sporting events.

Golf – There are several golf courses in the Milan area, the largest and most accessible of which is the 27-hole course at the *Golf Club Milano* in the park at nearby Monza (phone: 30-30-81).

Horseback Riding – There are two riding stables: *Centro Ippico Lombardo,* Via Fetonte 21 (phone: 40-84-270), and *Centro Ippico Milanese,* Via Macconago 20 (phone: 53-92-013). For more information, contact the Milan branch of *ANTE,* the national equestrian society, Via Piranesi 44/B (phone: 73-84-615).

Horse Racing – Thoroughbred and trotting races are run at the famous *Ippodromo San Siro* (phone: 45-21-854, 45-20-606) on the eastern outskirts of Milan.

Ice Skating – A rink is in operation from September through May at the Palazzo del Ghiaccio, Via Piranesi 14 (phone: 73-98). Skates can be rented at *Saini,* Via Corelli 136 (phone: 73-80-841).

Soccer – From September to May, both *Inter* and *Milan* play at *Stadio Comunale Giuseppe Meazza,* Via Piccolomini 5 (phone: 454123, 4084123).

Swimming – Public indoor pools include *Cozzi,* Viale Tunisia 35; *Mincio,* Via Mincio 13; and *Solari,* Via Montevideo 11. Open-air pools include *Lido,* Piazzale Lotto 15, near the San Siro Stadium; *Romano,* Via Ponzio 35; and *Piscina Olimpica* in the park at Monza.

Tennis – Public courts should be booked at least a week ahead of time. Some of the main courts are at *Bonacossa,* Via Mecenate 74 (phone: 506-1277); *Centro Polisportivo,* Via Valvassori Peroni 48 (phone: 236-6254); *Lido di Milano,* Piazzale Lotto 15 (phone: 39-16-67); and *Ripamonti,* Via Iseo 4 (phone: 645-9253).

 THEATER: You can take in classical Italian theater productions at the *Piccolo Teatro,* Via Rovello 2 (phone: 87-76-63); *Manzoni,* Via Manzoni 40 (phone: 79-05-43); *Salone Pier Lombardo,* Via Pierlombardo 14 (phone: 54-571-74); or the *Teatro Lirico,* Via Larga 14 (phone: 86-64-18). For avant-garde and experimental theater, try the *Teatro dell'Elfo,* Via Menotti 11 (phone: 71-67-91, 71-24-05); the *Centro Ricerca Teatro,* Via Ulisse Dini 7 (phone: 846-6592, 846-5693); or *Frigoriferia Suburbana,* Via Donatello 8.

 MUSIC: The renowned *La Scala* (see *Special Places*) is an obvious must for any opera fan, but ballets and concerts are also held here. Piazza della Scala (phone: 80-70-41). Concerts are held at *Auditorium Angelicum,* Piazza Sant'Angelo 2 (phone: 63-27-48), and *Conservatorio di Musica,* Via Conservatorio 12 (phone: 701-755). Tickets to the Angelicum are sold at Via Gustavo Favo 4 or at Ricordi Music Shop, Via Berchet 2.

 NIGHTCLUBS AND NIGHTLIFE: Milan has a variety of nightclubs offering both dinner and dancing. The most popular include *Charley Max,* Via Marconi 2 (phone: 87-14-16); *Caffè Roma,* Via Ancona 4 (phone: 87-69-60); and *Nepentha,* Piazza Diaz 1 (phone: 80-48-37). Top discos include *American Disaster,* Via Boscovich 48 (phone: 22-57-28); *Good Mood,* Via Turati 29 (phone: 655-93-49); *Plastic,* Via Umbria 120 (no phone); and *Odissea,* Via Besenzanica 3 (phone: 40-756-53). Jazz can be heard at several clubs, among them *Capolinea,* Via Ludovico il Moro 119 (phone: 47-05-24); *Ca'Bianca,* Via Ludovico il Moro 117; and *Le Scimmie,* Via Ascanio Sforza 49 (phone: 839-18-74). The latter also has rock or blues, as does *Magia,* Via Salutati 2 (phone: 48-45-53).

Milan has many cozy piano bars that are ideal for a late drink and snack. Try *Golden Memory,* Via Lazzaro Papi 22 (phone: 54-842-09); *Gershwin's,* Via Corrado il Salico 10 (phone: 84-977-22); or the elegant *Momus,* Via Fiori Chiari 8 (phone: 89-62-27).

 SINS: Striptease shows are featured at *Teatrino,* Corsia dei Servi 3 (phone: 79-37-16); *Maschere,* Via Borgogna 7 (phone: 70-55-84); *Venua,* Via Giardino 1 (phone: 80-503-30); and *Smeraldo,* Piazza 25 Aprile (phone: 66-27-68). Prostitutes solicit only at night on downtown streets. There are several soft-porn movie theaters, found under *Luci Rosse* in newspaper film listings.

BEST IN TOWN

CHECKING IN: As an international business center, Milan offers a wide range of accommodations for the visitor, from traditional, old-fashioned hotels to efficient, modern, commercial ones. Expensive hotels will cost from $180 to $270 a night for a double room; moderately priced hotels charge $80 to $175; and inexpensive hotels cost between $50 and $75. Unless otherwise noted, all Milan hotels accept major credit cards.

Excelsior Gallia – Built by the Gallia family in the early 1930s and recently restructured and redecorated in the grand style, this luxury hotel near the central train station is spacious, efficient, and friendly. Many consider its restaurant one of the city's finest (see *Eating Out*). 241 rooms and 12 suites. Piazza Duca d'Aosta 9 (phone: 6277). Expensive.

Grand Hotel Duomo – Much favored by the movers and shakers of Italian commerce. Bilevel rooms provide a businesslike sitting room, while touches of marble and Oriental carpets add swank to the contemporary decor. In the heart of town, just off Piazza del Duomo, but on a pedestrian street that ensures quiet. Via San Raffaele 1 (phone: 8833). Expensive.

Milano Hilton International – An attractive contemporary hotel in the new commercial center facing the main railway station about a mile north of the center and the cathedral. Tastefully decorated in a mixture of Italian provincial and modern styles. There is also a colorful, moderately priced Italian restaurant and a disco. The service is first rate. Via Galvani 12 (phone: 6983). Expensive.

Palace – Recently transformed by a $2.5-million renovation. Each floor has a different color scheme and the rooms have been decorated in ultramodern style. The smaller new wing is more conventional than the renovated old wing. Dining is on the roof garden or in the attractive *Casablanca* restaurant. Piazza della Repubblica 20 (phone: 6336). Expensive.

Principe di Savoia – A classic deluxe hotel with marble baths, antiques, thick rugs, air conditioning, and attractive dining and drinking facilities. Kitchenette apartments with balconies are in the new wing. The location is excellent: just north of the cathedral on a fashionable street away from the busy main road. Piazza della Repubblica 17 (phone: 6230). Expensive.

Executive – Next to the old airport bus terminal, about a mile from downtown Milan, this is an American-style hotel with a pleasant staff, deluxe rooms, and a good restaurant as well as saunas and a swimming pool that's covered in winter. Via Don Luigi Sturzo 45 (phone: 6294). Expensive to moderate.

Jolly President – This centrally located deluxe hotel has 235 comfortable rooms and a restaurant. Largo Augusto 10 (phone: 77-46). Expensive to moderate.

Europeo – Not far from the center of town, this fine hotel has its own peaceful garden, all the modern conveniences, and very good service. Via Canonica 38 (phone: 34-40-41). Moderate.

Lord Internazionale – A tiny budget hotel on a busy little shopping street near the cathedral. Rooms are quite small, but colorful and clean. It is most suitable for short stays. The lobby is cheerful and the management accommodating. There is no restaurant. Via Spadari 11 (phone: 86-24-20). Moderate.

Manin – This small, first-class hotel is about a half mile from *La Scala*. Some of the rooms have been renovated in a modern style; the older rooms are not impressive but are spacious and comfortable. There's also a very good restaurant and bar. Via Manin 7 (phone: 659-6511). Moderate.

Nasco – This new, American-style hotel is an excellent choice when downtown hotels are full. Via Spallanzani 40 (phone: 204-38-41). Moderate.

Manzoni – A small, pleasant hotel right in the city center. No restaurant, but there's a shopping mall nearby. Via Santo Spirito 20 (phone: 70-57-00, 70-56-97). Moderate to inexpensive.

Antica Locanda Solferino – A delightful tiny hotel with only 11 rooms, in the old Brera quarter a few blocks north of *La Scala*. This was once an old tavern and retains much of the *fin de siècle* charm in its furniture and decor. No credit cards. Must be booked far in advance. Via Castelfidardo 2 (phone: 659-9886). Inexpensive.

Centro – A small budget hotel in the heart of downtown Milan. Via Broletto 46 (phone: 87-52-32). Inexpensive.

EATING OUT: Milanese food, like much northern cuisine, differs from other Italian food in that butter is used more than olive oil. Look for special dishes made with the fabulous Italian white truffles, *tartufi bianchi,* from the neighboring Piedmont region, when they are in season between September and November. Rice replaces traditional pasta as the city classic, and *risotto alla milanese* is the favorite provender — best eaten with a steaming *ossobuco* (veal shank). Milan's expensive restaurants are the most expensive in Italy — expect to pay $75 or more for dinner for two; a moderately priced restaurant will cost $50 to $65; an inexpensive one will be $30 to $45. Prices don't include drinks, wine, or tips. It is a good idea to have reservations at any Milan restaurant and to check whether it accepts credit cards.

Gaultiero Marchesi – Italy's only three-star restaurant provides an elegant setting for a *nuova cucina* that the forces of Michelin consider the best in Italy. Closed Sundays, Mondays at lunchtime, and August. Reservations necessary. Via Bonvesin della Riva 9 (phone: 74-12-46). Very expensive.

Gallia's – Some of Milan's hotels provide fine dining, and one of the best hotel restaurants is at the *Excelsior Gallia,* where guests can savor traditional and nouvelle dishes in an elegant setting. Piazza Duca d'Aosta (phone: 6277). Expensive.

Giannino – Long known not only for its international cuisine but also for its sublime Tuscan cooking. The fish is excellent. As an appetizer, stop for a peek at the immaculate kitchen and the talented cooks at work — they're visible from the foyer. Closed Sundays and August. Via Amatore Sciesa 8 (phone: 5452948). Expensive.

Saint Andrews – This elegant downtown restaurant with dark-paneled walls and plush upholstery is a favorite of Milanese executives. Closed Sundays and August. Via Sant'Andrea 23 (phone: 79-31-32). Expensive.

Savini – Everything here, from the food to the decor, is classic and exquisite. Would that the food were more consistently topnotch. Ultraprofessional service in an atmosphere of 19th-century elegance: crystal chandeliers and red silk lampshades. The traditional northern Italian dishes are better choices than the Continental cuisine. Closed Sundays and August. Reservations recommended. Galleria Vittorio Emanuele II (phone: 805-8343). Expensive.

La Scaletta – The *nuova cucina* at this small, elegantly appointed two-room restaurant is so popular among Milanese diners that advance reservations are a must. Closed Sundays, Mondays, Christmas, New Year's, and August. Piazzale Stazione Porta Genova 3 (phone: 83-502-90). Expensive.

Aimo and Nadia – A husband and wife team from Tuscany run this small restaurant in an unprepossessing area of Milan, but the food is anything but anonymous. *Ovoli* (mushrooms) and Alba truffles are used in abundance, and the desserts are luscious. Closed Sundays and August. Via Montecuccoli 6 (phone: 41-68-86). Expensive to moderate.

Al Porto – The specialties at this family-run restaurant are fresh fish and friendly service. Closed Sundays and August. Piazza Cantore (phone: 832-1481). Expensive to moderate.

Alfio – It has a central location, an enclosed winter garden, and very good antipasti, *risotto,* and fish and meat dishes. Closed Saturdays and August. Via Senato 31 (phone: 70-06-33). Moderate.

Le Colline Pisane – This lively Tuscan *trattoria* serves fine food in pleasant surroundings. Closed Sundays and August. Reservations recommended. Largo La Foppa 5 (phone: 659-91-36). Moderate.

Gran San Bernardo da Alfredo – Some of the best regional cooking in town is served in this large, friendly restaurant. Try the classic Lombardy *cassoeula,* a stew of pork, sausages, carrots, and white wine, served with *polenta* (cornmeal mush). Closed Saturdays, Sundays, and August. Via Borgese 14 (phone: 38-90-00). Moderate.

Osteria del Vecchio Canneto – Definitely the place to try for wonderful fish. Sample the baked clams au gratin, the mixed fish grill, and the fine Abruzzi wine. Closed Sundays and August. Via Solferino 56 (phone: 659-84-98). Moderate.

Ristorante Peck – An offshoot of *Peck,* the elegant food emporium. There's a snack bar as well as the restaurant, which probably has the best wine list in town. Closed Sundays and August. Via Victor Hugo 4 (phone: 87-67-74). Moderate.

Rigolo – A large, friendly place that's a favorite of local journalists and businesspeople, this restaurant serves Tuscan specialties (such as thick, grilled steaks) and a superb selection of homemade desserts. Closed Mondays and August. Via Solferino 11 (phone: 805-97-68). Moderate.

Al Garibaldi – A new, unpretentious restaurant catering to Milan's young professional crowd. The kitchen dispatches topnotch food with professionalism and inventiveness. Closed Fridays, Christmas, and August. Via Montegrappa 7 (phone: 65-980-06). Moderate to inexpensive.

Giardino – Near the banks of the Naviglio River, this restaurant in a 19th-century courtyard spreads out under surrounding trees in summer and is enlivened by passing musicians. The food is simple but delicious, and the atmosphere is reminiscent of a 19th-century Milanese *osteria* (tavern). Closed Tuesdays. Alzaia Naviglio Grande 36 (phone: 839-9321). Moderate to inexpensive.

Quattro Mori – At this comfortable, family-run *trattoria* serving traditional Milanese food, try the fresh antipasto, veal cutlets, and grilled meats. Closed Sundays and August. Via San Giovanni sul Muro 2 (phone: 87-06-17). Moderate to inexpensive.

Along with its fine restaurants, Milan now boasts some of Italy's best *paninerie* (sandwich shops), which offer a variety of hot and cold sandwiches of sometimes unusual combinations. Try *Bar Magenta,* 13 Via Carducci (phone: 80-538-08), or *Paninomania,* Corso Porta Romana (phone: 57-68-27).

NAPLES

Naples, Gothic and Baroque under an azure sky, intellectual capital of the Mezzogiorno, and Italy's third most populated city, with nearly 1.5 million inhabitants, has often been described as one of the world's most beautiful seaports. Indeed, the magnificent Bay of Naples has long been lauded by its many illustrious visitors for its gently curving shoreline and palm-lined seaside avenues, its mild climate, sunny beaches, and romantic islands.

But Naples has always had a darker side. The brooding Mount Vesuvius, "its terror and its pride," ever hovering over the city, buried neighboring Pompeii and Herculaneum when it erupted in AD 79. And the eerie Campi Flegrei (Phlegrean Fields), a steaming volcanic area just north of the city whose violent beauty inspired both Homer and Virgil, was regarded by the ancients as the entrance to the underworld. More recently, the earthquake that devastated southern Italy in November 1980 took a tragic toll even in Naples, adding yet another major problem to the city's permanent ills of unemployment, crime, and disease.

For some visitors today, Naples is a disappointment. The old quarter, Spacca Napoli, is among the most densely populated areas in the world; infant mortality and unemployment rates are the highest in Italy — almost a third of the city's labor force is unemployed, and another estimated forty thousand persons derive their livelihood from smuggling. When a cholera outbreak in 1973 revealed that Naples had no sewers and was living on a beautiful but poisoned bay, "See Naples and die," once a popular saying beckoning visitors to the seductive charms of the city, suddenly acquired a morbid and foreboding significance. But the poor of Naples survive with a surprising stoicism, and the people themselves are one of the city's attractions, laughing off their many problems, helping each other with an extraordinary sense of warmth and humanity — they are a people incapable of hatred, of any kind of discrimination, yet strongly emotional, sensitive, full of fantasy. Just remember the best movies of the postwar school of Italian neorealism, directed by Roberto Rossellini, Vittorio De Sica, and Francesco Rosi, or the theatrical masterpieces of the famed Eduardo De Filippo, with the voluptuous figure of Sophia Loren representing the Neapolitan woman — madonna, mother, and *puttana* (whore) all in one.

Watch them live: Naples is like a theater of life. Stroll along Via Caracciolo and see the fishermen pulling in their nets, oblivious to the traffic behind them; buy lemons and oranges or sulfur water from men and women who transact their business across seventeenth-century marble tabletops; give in to the importuning of pizza vendors hawking their wares; or, when the jostling of the small, crowded streets becomes too much to bear, retire to a café table in the elegant Galleria Umberto I and watch well-dressed Neapolitans socialize over an afternoon coffee or aperitif.

Naples is famous for its music, its festivals, and its colorful arts. Neapolitan popular songs are, short of opera arias, the best-known tunes to have come out of Italy. In the seventeenth and eighteenth centuries, the works of a Neapolitan school of composers, whose forerunner and moving force was Alessandro Scarlatti, were just as well known; Vivaldi, Pergolesi, Paisiello, and Cimarosa drew capacity crowds. The city's opera house, Teatro San Carlo, built in 1737, remains one of the world's finest. A Neapolitan school of painting, characterized by realism and warm colors, flourished in the eighteenth and nineteenth centuries. In the eighteenth century, too, the famous Capodimonte porcelain factory was turning out highly elaborate pieces for members of the royal court, while less exalted folk artists were raising the making of nativity scenes, or Christmas cribs, into an art. The shepherds and angels of many an *ignoto napoletano* (unknown Neapolitan) live on in museums.

The city that was to spawn so much natural talent was founded as a Greek colony, probably in the seventh century BC, and was first called Parthenope, later Neapolis. Little remains of its earliest period. Then, along with the rest of the Italian peninsula, it became part of the great Roman Empire, and its intensely green countryside and sunny shores were soon studded with palatial villas of wealthy Romans who chose to spend the winters in Naples's milder climate.

But the tranquillity of the Roman period came to an end with the fall of the empire, and Naples sank into the abyss of the Dark Ages, as did all of Italy. The city came into its own again under the French rulers of the House of Anjou, who made it the capital of their Angevin kingdom of southern Italy in the thirteenth century, and continued its progress under the Catalonian rulers of the House of Aragon, who took control in 1442. Then, in 1503, Naples (with Sicily) became a part of Spain, ruled for more than two centuries by Spanish viceroys who exploited the Italian provinces for the benefit of the Spanish treasury; so heavily taxed were the commoners (nobles and clergy were exempt) that in 1647 they rose up, led by Masaniello, but the revolution was crushed. After a short period under Austrian rule, it was the turn of the Bourbons, who arrived in 1734 and established the Kingdom of the Two Sicilies with Naples as the capital. Its ancient dignity restored, Naples became one of Europe's major cities, attracting leaders in art, music, and literature until the unification of Italy in 1860. Economic and political problems gradually diminished Naples's prestige, however, and damage from World War II dealt a severe blow to an already sick economy.

Today, thanks to a busy port, Naples is an important industrial and commercial center. It is a city both wise and violent, religious and pagan, magical and dirty, old and new. It attracts thieves, tourists, artists, and lovers of beauty with a contagious gaiety and exuberant, if chaotic, vitality, a wealth of historical monuments, proximity to the Amalfi Coast, Capri, and the archaeological treasures of Pompeii and Herculaneum, and the magnificent — if somewhat tarnished — splendors of the romantic Bay of Naples.

NAPLES AT-A-GLANCE

SEEING THE CITY: Panoramic views of Naples and the bay are at every turn. Within the city, the outstanding view is from room 25 of the *Certosa di San Martino* (Carthusian Monastery of St. Martin), now a museum. Depending on the weather and the visibility, the most spectacular view is from Mount Vesuvius, 15 miles southeast of Naples. (See *Special Places*.)

SPECIAL PLACES: To make sightseeing easier, think of Naples as divided into the following sections: In the area roughly between Piazza Municipio and Piazza del Plebiscito, there are monumental buildings and relatively wide-open spaces. The Spacca Napoli quarter (the classic shots of streets strung with washing are taken here) and the historic center to the northeast have narrower, crowded streets. Farther inland is Naples on the hills, the Vomero being the principal hill and an elegant residential district. To the west of the Piazza del Plebiscito area is Naples by the bay. Where the workaday port ends, a lovely promenade begins along the shore before the port of Santa Lucia and extends as far as another port area, Mergellina. Most museums in Naples are open 9 AM to 2 PM weekdays, 9 AM to 1 PM holidays, and are closed Mondays.

DOWNTOWN

Castel Nuovo (New Castle) – This landmark on the Neapolitan waterfront, also called the *Castel Angioino* (Angevin Castle) or *Maschio Angioino,* was built in the late 13th century by Charles I of Anjou, who modeled it on the Castle at Angers. In the mid-15th century, Alphonse I of Aragon made substantial alterations. The triumphal arch sandwiched between two towers at the entry celebrates his entrance into Naples in 1443 and is an early example of Renaissance art in Naples. Inside the courtyard, the doorway to the Chapel of St. Barbara (or the Palatine Chapel), the only part of the castle remaining from Angevin times, is noteworthy, but the castle proper is not open to visitors. Piazza Municipio.

Palazzo Reale (Royal Palace) – Built in the early 17th century by Domenico Fontana for the Spanish viceroys, later enlarged and restored, this became the home of the Bourbon kings of Naples and was then inhabited from time to time by the kings of Italy. The niches on the façade contain statues of eight famous kings of the various dynasties that ruled Naples, including Charles I of Anjou, Alphonse I of Aragon, and Victor Emmanuel II of Italy. The palace is now a museum whose rooms contain original Bourbon furnishings, paintings, statues, and porcelain. Closed Mondays; admission fee. Piazza del Plebiscito (phone: 413888).

Piazza del Plebiscito – This vast semicircle cut off on one side by the *Palazzo Reale* is the center of public life in Naples. Directly opposite the palace is the *Church of San Francesco di Paola,* a copy of the Pantheon in Rome built by order of Ferdinand I of Bourbon in the early 18th century. Equestrian statues in the center of the square are of Ferdinand (by Canova) and Charles III of Bourbon.

Teatro San Carlo – Italy's second most famous opera house, 40 years older than La Scala, is just off Piazza del Plebiscito. Built under Charles of Bourbon in 1737 and inaugurated on the feast of its patron, St. Charles Borromeo, it was destroyed by fire in 1816 and thoroughly rebuilt in neoclassical style within six months, with Ionic columns, niches, and bas-reliefs on the outside and a fresco of Apollo and the Muses on the ceiling of the sumptuous auditorium — which seats 3,000 and has perfect acoustics. San Carlo audiences were the first ever to hear Bellini's *La Sonnambula,* Donizetti's *Lucia di Lammermoor,* and many other great works. Those not attending a performance can tour the theater in the morning by prior arrangement. Closed Mondays. Via San Carlo (phone: 417144).

Galleria Umberto I – Across the street from San Carlo, this is the perfect place to sit down for a *caffè* or an ice cream. The Victorian arcade of glass and steel, topped with a cupola, was built from 1887 to 1890 and is younger than the one in Milan.

Chiesa di Sant'Anna dei Lombardi (Church of St. Anne of the Lombards) – This church was built in the 15th century and rebuilt in the 17th century. It is best known for its Renaissance sculptures, particularly for the eight life-size terra cotta figures of the *Pietà* (1492) by Guido Mazzoni — extremely realistic and rather eerie when seen from the main part of the church (it's in a chapel to the right at the far end). Via Monteoliveto.

Chiesa di Santa Chiara (Church of St. Clare) – The church of the Poor Clares was built by order of Sancia of Majorca, wife of Robert I of Anjou, in the early 14th century. From the beginning, it was the church of the Neapolitan nobility. By the 18th century, it was covered with Baroque decoration, but following serious damage in World War II, it has been rebuilt in its original Provençal-Gothic style. Be sure to see the 14th-century tomb of Robert of Anjou behind the altar and then the adjoining Chiostro delle Clarisse (Cloister of the Poor Clares). This unique 18th-century cloister is a lovely bower of greenery and flowers studded with columns and lined with seats entirely covered with majolica tiles — a colorful, welcome surprise. Via Benedetto Croce.

Chiesa del Gesù Nuovo – Just across the square from Santa Chiara and quite a contrast: The interior of this late-16th-century church is full of Baroque marblework and painting. The unusual façade was originally built in the 15th century for a palace. Piazza del Gesù Nuovo.

Chiesa di San Lorenzo Maggiore (Church of St. Lawrence Major) – One of the most important medieval churches in Naples, it was begun in the late 13th century by French architects, who did the polygonal Gothic apse, and was finished in the next century by local architects. Boccaccio fell in love with Fiammetta in this church in 1334 and Petrarch, who was living in the adjoining monastery, came here to pray during a terrible storm in 1345. Piazza San Gaetano.

Duomo (Cathedral) – The cathedral of Naples is dedicated to the city's patron saint, San Gennaro. It was built by the Angevins in the late 13th and early 14th centuries on the site of a previous basilica dedicated to Santa Stefania, which had been built on the foundations of a Roman temple dedicated to Apollo. It also incorporates a smaller basilica dating from the 5th century and dedicated to Santa Restituta. Rebuilt several times, the Duomo's 19th-century façade still sports 15th-century doorways. It contains the famous Chapel of San Gennaro (third chapel on the right), a triumph of 17th-century Baroque art built in fulfillment of a vow made by Neapolitans for the passing of a plague. (The Latin inscription notes that the chapel is consecrated to the saint for his having saved the city not only from plague but also from hunger, war, and the fires of Vesuvius, by virtue of his miraculous blood.) Two vials of San Gennaro's dried blood are stored in a reliquary in the chapel, and twice a year, in May and September, all of Naples — or as many as the church and the street can hold — gathers to await the miracle of the liquefaction of the blood (see *Special Events*). If the miracle happens, all is well with the city. Via del Duomo.

Museo Archeologico Nazionale (National Archaeological Museum) – One of the most important museums in the world dedicated to Greco-Roman antiquity. Among its precious artworks are sculptures collected by Pope Paul III of the Farnese family during 16th-century excavations of the ruins of Rome, including two huge statues found at the Baths of Caracalla: the *Farnese Hercules,* a Greek copy of a bronze original by Lysippus, and the *Farnese Bull,* a Roman copy of a Hellenistic bronze, carved from a single block of marble. The museum is also the repository of art and artifacts removed from Pompeii and Herculaneum from the 18th century onward. Most impressive of these are the exquisite mosaics from Pompeii and the bronzes from the Villa dei Papiri at Herculaneum, especially the water carriers (or dancers) and the two athletes. Other items removed from Pompeii and Herculaneum include silverware and glassware, combs, mirrors, and other toiletry articles, some furniture, and foodstuffs, such as carbonized bread, olives, grapes, onions, figs, and dates. Two other important collections in this 16th-century palace — which was first a barracks and then the seat of the university until the Bourbon king of Naples turned it into a museum in 1777 — are the Santangelo collection of ancient coins and the Borgia collection of Egyptian and Etruscan art. Closed Mondays. Admission fee. Piazza del Museo (phone: 440166).

Catacombe di San Gennaro (Catacombs of St. Januarius) – The remains of San Gennaro lay in these catacombs from the 5th to the 9th century. On two levels, the catacombs date from the 2nd century and probably began as the tomb of a noble family that was later donated to the Christian community as a burial place. They are important for their early Christian wall paintings. Guided visits take place on Saturday and Sunday mornings. Admission fee. Off Via di Capodimonte, past the church of the Madre del Buon Consiglio.

Museo e Gallerie Nazionali di Capodimonte (Capodimonte Museum and Picture Gallery) – One of Italy's best collections of paintings from the 14th through the 16th century is displayed in the grandiose 18th-century palace of a former royal estate on the hills in the northeastern part of the city. A Simone Martini panel (1317) of Robert of Anjou being crowned king of Naples is one of the museum's treasures; other masters represented are Bellini, Masaccio, Botticelli, Correggio, and Titian, among whose portraits of the Farnese family is a well-known one of Pope Paul III. The royal apartments on the first floor include a marvelous parlor, the Salottino di Maria Amalia, completely built and decorated in Capodimonte ceramics (some of which were shattered in the 1980 earthquake). In the park surrounding the palace a wedding party is often having pictures taken — it's one of the Neapolitans' favorite backgrounds. Closed Mondays. Admission fee. Parco di Capodimonte (phone: 7410881).

Certosa di San Martino (Carthusian Monastery and National Museum of St. Martin) – Now a museum, this enormous monastery founded by the Angevin dynasty is beautifully situated on the Vomero Hill, next to an Angevin fortress, the *Castel Sant'Elmo.* The monastery was renovated in the 16th and 17th centuries (in the latter period by Cosimo Fanzago), so it is today a monument to the Baroque. The church immediately to the left as you enter is lavishly done in Baroque inlay of variously colored marbles and stones (see, too, the rooms behind the altar, including the one to the left with the intricate inlay of wood). In the museum the marvelous view from the belvedere of room 25 is said to have inspired the saying "See Naples and die." The museum contains a collection of 19th-century Neapolitan painting, a naval section, a collection of memorabilia from the Kingdom of Naples, and some striking 18th- and 19th-century *presepi,* or nativity scenes. The most famous is the *Presepe Cuciniello,* a room-size installation with countless figures and particularly graceful angels. Another *presepe* fits in an eggshell. Closed Mondays. Admission fee. Via Tito Angelini (phone: 377005).

Porto di Santa Lucia e il Lungomare (Santa Lucia Port and the Waterfront) – One of the best-known Neapolitan songs has immortalized this tiny port abob with picturesque fishing and pleasure boats. It is formed by a jetty that leads out from the mainland to a small island entirely occupied by the Borgo Marinaro, a so-called fishing village now populated largely with restaurants, and the Castel dell'Ovo (Egg Castle, not to be confused with the *Castel Nuovo,* described above). The fortress dates from the 12th century, but monks lived here even earlier, and in Roman times a patrician villa occupied the site. Santa Lucia is the focal point of seaside Naples: Via Nazario Sauro approaches it from the east; Via Partenope passes in front of it; and Via Caracciolo leads away from it to the west. The three together constitute Naples's *lungomare*, a broad promenade along the water that is *the* place in Naples to take the early evening *passeggiata* (stroll) and watch the sun go down. For at least half a mile of its length, Via Caracciolo is backed by the greenery of the *Villa Comunale*, or public park, which is stuffed with life — young lovers hugging, kids playing ball, grandparents taking the air with the grandchildren, fathers renting miniature cars for mere toddlers who are learning to become Neapolitan drivers. Ice cream is consumed by all.

ENVIRONS

Campi Flegrei (Phlegrean Fields) – Hot springs and sulfurous gases rise from this dark, violent volcanic area that extends west of Naples from Capo Posillipo to Capo Miseno, along the Gulf of Pozzuoli. Its name comes from the Greek, meaning "burning," and it is an area as rich in archaeological remains as in geophysical phenomena. The remains of the Greek colony of Cuma, founded in the 8th century BC, are about 12 miles west of Naples (closed Mondays; admission fee), as are remains of Roman baths at Baia (closed Mondays; admission fee). In Sophia Loren's hometown, Pozzuoli (8 miles west), the third largest amphitheater in Italy, built when the town was a major port in Roman times, can be visited (closed Mondays; admission fee). Also in Pozzuoli is a Roman temple, partially submerged in water, that reveals the effects of bradyseism, or "slow earthquake," to which the whole area is subject; less or more of the pillars is visible as the earth rises and falls. Lakes — such as Lago d'Averno and Lago Miseno — have formed in the craters of extinct volcanoes in the Campi Flegrei, but the Solfatara crater just north of Pozzuoli is merely dormant (its last eruption was in the 12th century). Full of steaming fumaroles and containing the remains of a Roman spa, it is open daily (admission fee). Pozzuoli is the last stop of the *metropolitana* from Piazza Garibaldi in Naples; Baia and Cuma are stops of the Ferrovia Cumana suburban train line leaving from Piazza Montesanto.

Vesuvio (Mount Vesuvius) – This active volcano about 15 miles southeast of Naples last erupted in 1944 and has averaged one eruption every 35 years over the past 300. Its most famous eruption was the one that buried Pompeii and Herculaneum in AD 79 (see *Campania and the Amalfi Coast* in DIRECTIONS). That explosion came from Monte Somma, 3,713 feet high, one of the volcano's two present-day summits; some 200 years later, another summit, Monte Nuovo, 4,189 feet high, formed, and this is the one that is now called Mount Vesuvius. A chair lift climbs to the top of Monte Nuovo, and an obligatory guide leads small groups of visitors along the path that follows the edge of the crater, allowing views down into the enormous cavity or out toward the sea and the surrounding towns. All that is visible of Vesuvius' cataclysmic power are the vapors rising from fumaroles, and the guide occasionally descends a bit into the crater for a better look at these vents. The chair lift runs daily, except in November, from 10 AM until late afternoon. Fees are charged for parking and for the ascent. To reach Vesuvius by public transportation, take the Circumvesuviana railway (Napoli–Barra–Torre del Greco–Torre Annunziata line) from Stazione Circumvesuviana, near the main train station in Naples. Get off at Herculaneum (Ercolano) and take a bus to the chair lift. Don't go on an overcast day.

■**EXTRA SPECIAL:** No stay in Naples is complete without a sunny drive up the famed promontory of Posillipo, a few miles southwest of the center, perhaps culminating in an al fresco lunch at Marechiaro overlooking the southern end of the Bay of Naples. The road from Mergellina climbs past villas and fragrant gardens, becoming Via Nuova di Posillipo, which was begun by order of Murat, king of Naples, and completed in 1830. Don't miss the view of Cape Posillipo (from Via Ferdinando Russo just past Piazza Salvatore di Giacomo) before continuing up Via Nuova di Posillipo to the winding Via Salvatore di Giacomo, which ends at Marechiaro, a most picturesque fishing village built high above the sea. It was made famous by a song of the same name written by Salvatore di Giacomo, the first line of which is inscribed in the wall of an old house overlooking the water, marking the window celebrated in the song. On the way down, stop at the Parco della Rimembranza for spectacular views of the Bay of Naples on one side and the Bay of Pozzuoli on the other.

SOURCES AND RESOURCES

TOURIST INFORMATION: For general information, brochures, and maps of Naples and its environs, contact the *Ente Provinciale per il Turismo,* Via Partenope 10/A (phone: 406289). Branches or booths are at the Stazione Centrale, the Stazione di Mergellina, and the Aeroporto di Capodichino. The *Azienda Autonoma di Soggiorno e Turismo* (AAST, or local tourist office) is headquartered in the Palazzo Reale at Piazza del Plebiscito (phone: 418744), and it also has branches including those at Piazza del Gesù Nuovo and at Castel dell'Ovo. The *Associazione Alberghi per la Gioventù* (*Association of Youth Hostels*) is at Via del Chiostro 9 (phone: 320084). The *US consulate* is at Piazza della Repubblica (phone: 660966).

Local Coverage – Among its other brochures, the AAST puts out an interesting one entitled "Naples — The Old City: A Stratified Multiple Itinerary Map" that traces four itineraries through the historic center (roughly the area between Piazza del Gesù Nuovo and the Duomo), each route corresponding to a period in Neapolitan art: Medieval, Renaissance, Baroque, and Rococo. The office also publishes a useful booklet, *Qui Napoli,* which is distributed monthly to the better hotels. Listings are in Italian and English. The Neapolitans' daily newspaper is *Il Mattino.*

Telephone – The telephone prefix for Naples is 081.

GETTING AROUND: Many of the sights are easily accessible by foot. For others, such as the Parco di Capodimonte and sights on the Vomero, alternate means of transportation are desirable. Do everything you can to avoid driving in the city: Neapolitan traffic jams belong in the *Guinness Book of World Records.*

Airport – *Capodichino Airport* serves mostly domestic and some international flights. A taxi ride from downtown takes from 15 to 45 minutes, depending on traffic, and costs from 5,000 lire to 15,000 lire; from the airport to downtown, the fare is double that shown on the meter. Night and holiday rides cost extra, as does baggage; ask to see the *tabella* (fare table). There is no airport bus, but bus No. 14 from the main train station, *Stazione Centrale,* stops at the airport. The trip takes 30 minutes to an hour depending on traffic.

Boats – Ferries and hydrofoils for Capri, Ischia, and Procida leave from the *Molo Beverello,* in front of Piazza Municipio and the Castel Nuovo, or from Mergellina's *Porto Sannazzaro.*

Bus and Tram – Main routes and schedules are listed in the supplement to the telephone directory, *TuttoCittà.* Tickets must be bought in advance at a tobacco shop or newsstand.

Car Rental – Major international firms are on Via Partenope: *Avis,* Via Partenope 32 (phone: 407333); *Europcar,* Via Partenope 38 (phone: 401454); *Hertz,* Via Partenope 29 (phone: 400400). Only a few gas stations are open at night. Check with your hotel or see the listings in *Qui Napoli.*

Funicular – Four funicular lines connect lower-lying parts of Naples to neighborhoods on the hills. Of the three that go to the Vomero, the *Funicolare Centrale,* from Via Toledo to Piazza Fuga, and the *Funicolare di Montesanto,* from Piazza Montesanto to Via Morghen, are useful for visiting the Certosa di San Martino. The fourth funicular connects the Mergellina area to the Posillipo area.

Subway – The *metropolitana* runs from Napoli Gianturco to Pozzuoli Solfatara, making useful stops at the Stazione Centrale, Piazza Cavour (near the National Archaeological Museum), Piazza Montesanto and Piazza Amedeo (near funiculars), Mergellina, Campi Flegrei, and elsewhere.

Taxi – Taxis can be hailed while they cruise or may be picked up at any cabstand. For a radio-dispatched taxi, call 364444 or 364340. Do not use unmetered taxis and do not expect the driver to make change.

Train – Naples's main train station is *Stazione Centrale,* Piazza Garibaldi (phone: 264644). Trains to Herculaneum, Pompeii, and Sorrento, operated by the suburban railway *Ferrovia Circumvesuviana,* leave from the nearby *Stazione Circumvesuviana,* Corso Garibaldi (phone: 269601), reached by the down escalator from Stazione Centrale. Trains to Campi Flegrei points, operated by another suburban railway, *Ferrovia Cumana,* leave from Piazza Montesanto (phone: 313328).

MUSEUMS: In addition to those mentioned in *Special Places,* a number of other museums and churches are impressive.

Aquarium – One of the oldest, if not *the* oldest in Europe (1872), housing some 200 species of Mediterranean marine life. Villa Comunale.

Museo Civico Filangieri (Filangieri Civic Museum) – Arms, furniture, porcelaih, costumes, and paintings, housed in the 15th-century Palazzo Cuomo. Via Duomo 288.

Museo Duca di Martina (Duke of Martina Museum) – Ivories, enamels, china, and majolica, European and Oriental, displayed in the Villa Floridiana, a small neoclassical palace in the Vomero section, with splendid gardens and a panoramic view of the bay. Via Cimarosa.

Museo Principe Aragona Pignatelli Cortes (Prince of Aragon Pignatelli Cortes Museum) – A collection of 19th-century furniture and china, plus a coach museum with French and English carriages in the surrounding garden. Riviera di Chiaia.

Cappella Sansevero (Sansevero Chapel) – The funerary chapel of the Sangro family, containing the *Veiled Christ* by Giuseppe Sammartino and many other 18th-century sculptures. Via Francesco De Sanctis 19.

Chiesa di San Domenico Maggiore (Church of St. Dominic Major) – A 14th-century church, frequently restored, containing the famous crucifix of St. Thomas Aquinas and paintings by Titian, Luca Giordano, Solimena, Simone Martini, and others. Piazza San Domenico.

Chiesa di San Gregorio Armeno (Church of St. Gregory of Armenia) – A Baroque church worth a visit for its famous nativity scene. Via San Gregorio Armeno.

Chiesa di San Paolo Maggiore (Church of St. Paul Major) – A church of the late 16th century, wonderfully Neapolitan Baroque in style, with paintings by Stanzione, Solimena, and Paolo de Matteis. Piazza San Gaetano.

Chiesa di Santa Maria del Carmine – A 13th-century church with a venerated image of the Madonna and an adjacent tower that is the scene of a mock burning each July 16 (see *Special Events*). Piazza del Carmine.

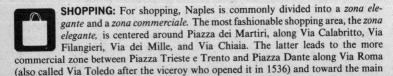

SHOPPING: For shopping, Naples is commonly divided into a *zona elegante* and a *zona commerciale.* The most fashionable shopping area, the *zona elegante,* is centered around Piazza dei Martiri, along Via Calabritto, Via Filangieri, Via dei Mille, and Via Chiaia. The latter leads to the more commercial zone between Piazza Trieste e Trento and Piazza Dante along Via Roma (also called Via Toledo after the viceroy who opened it in 1536) and toward the main railroad station along Corso Umberto I. Ceramics and porcelains have been sold here since the Bourbon kings founded the Capodimonte school and factory in the 18th century. Although original Capodimonte pieces are collectors' items and Capodimonte-style figurines are produced by companies all over Italy, the production of more traditional ceramics, in popular folk styles, continues to thrive in Naples and the vicinity. Another important product of the area is coral, much of which, it is said, is now imported from Southeast Asia but handcrafted nevertheless in nearby Torre del Greco, where there are several large factories and showrooms (*Giovanni Apa,* in Torre del Greco, just off the Naples-Pompeii Highway, is one source of coral and cameos). Neapolitan street markets are very colorful (always beware of pickpockets and *scippatori,* who speed by on motorbikes, grabbing bags and gold chains from shoulders and necks as they go). Among the markets are *Resina,* for new or used clothing and fabrics; *Spacca Napoli,* for books and silver objects; *Antignano,* for fabrics, household goods, and food; *Corso Malta,* for shoes and bags; and, at Christmas, San Liborio, for traditional Neapolitan nativity figures. Antiques shops are found mostly in the area around Piazza dei Martiri and Via Santa Maria di Costantinopoli.

Baracca e Burattini – Opposite the entrance to the archaeological museum, an artisan shop selling masks, marionettes, and lovely dolls. Piazza del Museo 2.

Chiurazzi – Bronze reproductions of sculptures in the archaeological museum, in all sizes. Via ai Ponti Rossi 271.

Coin – A good department store. Via Scarlatti 10.

La Rinascente – Another good department store. Via Roma 343.

Il Sagittario – Curious leather goods (masks, sculptures). Via Santa Chiara 10/A.

La Soffitta – Hand-painted ceramics. Via Benedetto Croce 12.

 SPECIAL EVENTS: Twice a year (on the Saturday preceding the first Sunday in May and on September 19), Neapolitans crowd into the Duomo of San Gennaro and pray for the miracle, the liquefying of the dried blood of their patron saint that is kept in two vials in a chapel of the church. The miracle is supposed to have first occurred on the hands of a bishop transporting the body after San Gennaro's martyrdom in Pozzuoli on September 19, 305, and it has been happening regularly since the first recorded recurrence in 1389 — regularly, but not *always.* The event is something of a mass fortunetelling, because when it fails, some disaster is expected to befall the city — in the past it might have been plague; in the future it could be Vesuvius. The miracle lets Naples know that the saint is still with them, and nowhere is the atmosphere more alive with anticipation than in the chapel downstairs where San Gennaro's bones are kept and the people plead for a sign. Other important festivals celebrate the feast of Santa Maria del Carmine on July 16 and the Madonna di Piedigrotta, which lasts several days in early September.

SPORTS AND FITNESS: Most sports facilities belong to private clubs, so check with the concierge of your hotel about which may be open to the public.

Fitness Centers – *Athletic Club* (men) and *Silhouette* (women), Via Fiorentini 21 (phone: 313160, 313342).

Jogging – One good place to run is the *lungomare* (seafront promenade) along Via Partenope and Via Caracciolo from the port of Santa Lucia to the Mergellina. The *Villa Comunale,* the park behind Via Caracciolo, is another good spot.

Soccer – From September to May, *Napoli* plays at the *Stadio San Paolo,* Piazzale Vincenzo Tecchio, Fuorigrotta (phone: 615623, 619205). Its capacity is 100,000 fierce fans.

Swimming – The polluted Bay of Naples is not the best spot for water sports, but there are fine seaside resorts on the islands and along the Amalfi Coast.

Tennis – Several tennis clubs have public courts, including *Tennis Club*

Vomero, Via Rossini 8 (phone: 658912), and *Tennis Club Napoli,* Villa Comunale (phone: 384801).

 THEATER: Even if you don't understand the Neapolitan dialect, you may enjoy a performance by the renowned Repertory Group of Eduardo De Filippo at the *Teatro San Ferdinando,* Piazza Teatro San Ferdinando (phone: 444500). Other theatrical groups perform at the *Politeama,* Via Monte di Dio (phone: 401643); *Cilea,* Via San Domenico, at Corso Europa (phone: 656265); *Sannazaro,* Via Chiaia 157 (phone: 411723); and *Bracco,* Via Tarsia 40 (phone: 347005).

 MUSIC: The season at the *Teatro San Carlo,* Via San Carlo, one of the finest opera houses in the world, generally runs from December through most of June. Then, from mid-September through mid-November, the theater hosts a series of symphonic concerts, the Concerti d'Autunno (Autumn Concerts). Box office open daily, except Mondays (phone: 418490, 418266). Other symphony and chamber concerts, by groups such as the Associazione Alessandro Scarlatti, the Accademia Musicale Napoletana, and others, are scheduled frequently at *Auditorium RAI-TV,* Via Guglielmo Marconi (phone: 610122), at *Conservatorio di Musica San Pietro a Maiella,* Via San Pietro a Maiella (phone: 459255), in the church or cloisters of *Santa Chiara,* Via Benedetto Croce (phone: 207697, 320582), and in numerous other churches about town. In the summer, concerts are also held in the gardens at *Capodimonte.*

 NIGHTCLUBS AND NIGHTLIFE: Like most port towns, Naples has a number of seedy bars and rip-off joints to be avoided. Currently acceptable discotheques are *Shaker,* Via Nazario Sauro 24, and *Damiani,* Via Domiziana. Some good places on Via Manzoni are *Papillon* and the *Accademia. Harry's Bar,* behind the *Excelsior* at Via Lucilio 11 (phone: 407810), is the spot for a quiet drink or a late dinner in an elegant setting. *Il Gabbiano,* also near the principal hotels at Via Partenope 26, is a piano bar that serves late snacks (phone: 411666). The newest and most elegant restaurant and nightclub is *Rosolino,* Via Nazario Sauro 5–7 (phone: 415873).

 SINS: You'll find people hawking many black market goods; buy them at your own risk: Some "Marlboros" are Neapolitan-made and quite rough, and the whiskey bottles may contain tea or colored water. Stolen goods are also widely offered for sale — and they could be yours. Watch your wallet and don't ever leave possessions in a parked car.

BEST IN TOWN

CHECKING IN: An expensive hotel in Naples will charge from $100 to $220 a night for a double room; moderately priced hotels range from $60 to $100; and inexpensive ones cost $30 to $60.

Excelsior – Naples's only truly deluxe hotel, part of the reliable CIGA chain, it dominates the port of Santa Lucia, with terraced seaside rooms overlooking the 12th-century Castel dell'Ovo, the old fishing village of Borgo Marinaro, and the whole bay. The *Casanova Grill* takes some prizes, too (see *Eating Out*). There are 140 air conditioned rooms and a garage nearby. Via Partenope 48 (phone: 417111). Expensive.

Vesuvio – Close to the *Excelsior,* it faces the picturesque port of Santa Lucia. It has 179 medium-sized rooms, good baths, a decor ranging from period style to modern, a garage, and air conditioning. Via Partenope 45 (phone: 417044). Expensive to moderate.

Britannique – It offers Swiss management and efficiency and is hospitable and very clean. Most of the 76 rooms in this old converted villa are large, and since it's set on a panoramic hillside up and back from the waterfront, most have attractive views. Corso Vittorio Emanuele 133 (phone: 660933). Moderate.

Royal – A third hotel on the Santa Lucia waterfront, this one is Naples's biggest, with 300 rooms. It's modern and busy, and it has a rooftop pool, a garage, and air conditioning. Via Partenope 38 (phone: 400244). Moderate.

Mediterraneo – This has a convenient location in the commercial center of town, behind Piazza Municipio, but it's not very romantic. Garage and air conditioning; more than 250 rooms. Via Nuova Ponte di Tappia (phone: 312240). Inexpensive.

Miramare – Also conveniently located, but with the added attraction of the waterfront. Reputable, comfortable, and small (26 rooms), it offers good service and a pleasant atmosphere. No restaurant, but very near *La Cantinella* (see *Eating Out*). Via Nazario Sauro 24 (phone: 416775). Inexpensive.

Rex – A reliable family hotel in the Santa Lucia quarter, with 40 rooms and no restaurant. Via Palepoli 12 (phone: 416388). Inexpensive.

San Germano – A few miles' drive from the center of Naples in rather nondescript surroundings at the crossroads for the *Ippodromo di Agnano* racecourse. It has some 100 pleasant rooms, a lovely garden, a swimming pool and nearby tennis courts, a garage, and air conditioning. Via Beccadelli 41 (phone: 7605422). Inexpensive.

EATING OUT: While Italian food is not all pasta and pizza, both originated in Naples and are staples of southern Italy. Here pasta is almost always eaten as a first course at lunch, while it is usually replaced at the evening meal by a light broth or soup (if the evening meal itself hasn't been replaced altogether by pizza, which is generally served only in the evenings). Naples is the home of *spaghetti c'a pummarola* (*spaghetti al pomodoro* in proper Italian), born of the mating of pasta with the tomato not too long after the latter arrived in Italy from South America in the 16th century. It is still the most popular pasta dish, easily prepared, vividly colorful, fragrant with additions of basil or parsley, oregano, and garlic, and topped with tangy Parmesan cheese. Other Neapolitan favorites are *vermicelli con le vongole* (pasta with clams, with or without tomatoes, in a garlic and olive oil sauce) or *con zucchine* (with zucchini, garlic, and oil) and *pasta e fagioli* (a very thick white bean soup with short pasta).

Naples is seafood country, and the best main course here is simple fresh fish grilled and seasoned with olive oil and lemon. But if you're watching your budget, be careful. Most good fish is sold by weight at restaurants, and you'd do well to avoid those whose prices are listed on the menu *al kilo* (per kilogram), which can turn an otherwise modest bill into a major monetary setback. Exceptions to this rule are lesser fish such as *alici* (anchovies), which, when fresh, can be tastefully prepared in oil, garlic, and parsley, and *fritto misto,* a mixture of fried shrimp, squid, and small local fish. One piece of advice: Don't ever eat raw seafood that may have come from the polluted Bay of Naples. Local meat, not of very good quality, is usually served drowned in a tomato (*pizzaiola*) or other sauce. Dinner for two with a house wine will run from $60 to $100 at a restaurant listed as expensive, from $30 to $60 at a moderate one, and from $15 to $30 at an inexpensive one.

Casanova Grill – A delightfully intimate restaurant for such a grand hotel as the *Excelsior,* it offers a wide selection of enticing antipasti, plenty of fresh fish,

Neapolitan specialties such as pasta with seafood, a remarkable fish soup, and roast baby lamb with rosemary and garlic — all prepared and served with care and refinement. Hotel Excelsior, Via Partenope 48 (phone: 417111). Expensive.

Giuseppone a Mare – Traditionally one of Naples's best fish restaurants, with incomparable views from Cape Posillipo. But lately it seems that the prices keep going up while the quality goes slowly down. Still, it's worth knowing about if you're in the Posillipo area. Closed Sundays and from Christmas through New Year's. Via Ferdinando Russo 13, Capo Posillipo (phone: 7696002). Expensive.

Rosolino – An elegant supper club, piano bar, and nightclub in the Santa Lucia quarter, just a skip and a jump from the *Excelsior* and *Vesuvio* hotels. The restaurant is open at lunch, too. Closed Sundays. Reservations required at dinner. Via Nazario Sauro 5–7 (phone: 415873). Expensive.

La Cantinella – A favorite of Neapolitans, visiting dignitaries, and tourists staying nearby along the picturesque port of Santa Lucia. Fresh fish, as everywhere, is at a premium, but local clams and mussels mated with a hint of garlic, parsley, and *pummarola* or tomato, and lavished on a steaming plate of linguine constitute one of the great pleasures of southern Italian life, within reach of everyone's pocket. The service is friendly and efficient. Closed Sundays. Via Cuma 42 (phone: 404884, 405375). Expensive to moderate.

La Fazenda – Very Neapolitan, serving homemade garlic bread, wonderful pasta dishes, fresh fish, home-raised chickens, and exquisite desserts. In the Posillipo area, the surroundings are rustic, with spectacular views of the bay and flowers everywhere. Closed Sundays and 2 weeks in August. Calata Marechiaro 58 (phone: 7697420). Expensive to moderate.

La Sacrestia – Dine al fresco on delicious Neapolitan dishes such as *scazzette di Fra' Leopoldo* (homemade pasta stuffed with ricotta) or one of the several fish dishes. On a hillside beyond Mergellina. Closed Wednesdays (but Sundays in July and August). Via Orazio 116 (phone: 664186). Expensive to moderate.

San Carlo – A favorite of politicians at lunch and of theatergoers at dinner, given its location near San Carlo and the Royal Palace, municipal and regional administrative offices. It's small, quiet, very good, and open late. Closed Sundays and from late July through August. Reservations advisable. Via Cesario Console 18 (phone: 417206). Expensive to moderate.

Amici Miei – Traditional Neapolitan cuisine is served in a traditionally elegant ambience in one of the elegant residential zones of Naples, near the Politeama Theater. Closed Mondays and August. Via Monte di Dio 78 (phone: 405727). Moderate.

Ciro a Santa Brigida – In the center of town, this has been one of the best and busiest of Naples's *trattorie-pizzerie* since the 1920s. Sample the great variety of fresh fish or pastas such as *lasagne imbottite* and *maccheroni alla siciliana*. This is also a good place for *pastiera,* a typical Neapolitan dessert made of ricotta and wheat. Closed Sundays. Via Santa Brigida 71 (phone: 324072). Moderate.

Don Salvatore – It has been said that "Mergellina without Don Salvatore would be like Naples without Vesuvius." It's a longtime Neapolitan favorite where everything is good, from antipasto to pasta, fish, meat, and pizza (served evenings only). Closed Wednesdays. Via Mergellina 5 (phone: 684402). Moderate.

Dora – The ambience here is that of a small fishing boat, and the fish served is first class. Try the *linguine all'aragosta* (pasta with crayfish). Closed Sundays and August. Via Ferdinando Palasciano 30 (phone: 684149). Moderate.

Il Gallo Nero – Elegant dining in an antique-filled 19th-century villa or on a terrace with a splendid view of Mergellina. Classic favorites as well as sensible innovations are on the menu, plus fresh fish and imaginative meat dishes. Open evenings only, except Sundays, when it's open for lunch only; closed Mondays and August. Via Tasso 466 (phone: 643012). Moderate.

La Bersagliera – In good weather, the Borgo Marinaro facing the Castel dell'Ovo can't be beat for local color. And this is the only one of the "made for tourists" portside restaurants that makes the grade: Sometimes a dose of sun in a spectacular setting is worth more than a flawless meal. A surprisingly inexpensive mixed grill of seafood includes a surprisingly tender, tasty fresh squid — a dish certainly worth a repeat visit. Naples's famous *scugnizzi* (streetwise waifs) ask for pieces of bread as they pass by between swims in the polluted bay. Closed Tuesdays. Borgo Marinaro, Santa Lucia (phone: 415692). Moderate to inexpensive.

Il Pulcinella – This is a genuine family restaurant, cozy, friendly, and delicious. Closed Mondays and from July to September — but it's really a winter ambience anyway. Vico Ischitella 4 (phone: 422494). Moderate to inexpensive.

Pizzeria Bellini – This is one of the city's oldest *pizzerie*. Besides a vast assortment of pizza (the most famous with fresh basil and tomato), there are pasta, fish, and meat dishes. Closed Wednesdays. Via Santa Maria di Costantinopoli 80 (phone: 459774). Inexpensive.

Vini e Cucina – The food is delicious — real home cooking, Neapolitan style — and so this little Mergellina restaurant is increasingly popular and often impossibly crowded. Closed Sundays. Corso Vittorio Emanuele 762 (no phone). Inexpensive.

PALERMO

Capital of Sicily as well as its chief seaport, Palermo (from the Greek *panoramus,* meaning "broad harbor") is bordered on one side by the blue Tyrrhenian Sea and on the other by the dusty-brown Apennines. It nestles on the edge of a fertile plain known as the Conca D'Oro, or Golden Valley (sometimes translated as the "Golden Conch Shell"), named for the gleaming orange groves that used to encircle the city.

Despite its name, the city was never Greek. It was founded between the sixth and eighth centuries BC by the seafaring Phoenicians, later becoming a colony of Carthage. In AD 254, it was conquered by the Romans. Over succeeding centuries, it was invaded by Saracens, Normans, Swabians, Angevins, and Spaniards, each of whom influenced the city's monuments and customs. Under the Arabs, who conquered the city in AD 831 and ruled it until their defeat in 1072 by the Norman king Roger the First, Palermo became a major Mediterranean center (in the tenth century the city reportedly had 300,000 inhabitants). Subsequent wars between various European monarchs led to alternating periods of prosperity and decline until the city was annexed by Italy in 1860.

In more recent history Palermo — like much of Sicily — has been under the influence of the criminal organization well known as the Mafia, which has exerted significant economic as well as political influence and subjected the city to a succession of bloody gang wars. In this decade, however, the people of Palermo, led by honest politicians and a group of committed Roman Catholic priests, have begun to fight back. The Sicilian government has been diligent in investigating Mafia activities and bringing hundreds of gangland suspects, as well as the organization itself, to trial.

Today, the historic center of Sicily's major port city is a hodgepodge of narrow streets, broad squares, bustling outdoor markets, luxuriant subtropical gardens, Byzantine domes, Gothic churches and cathedrals, Spanish Baroque chapels, and decaying seventeenth-century palaces. Although the twentieth century has certainly made itself felt here, life in Palermo today is still a study in contrasts: In some areas, such as the Vucciria market, which resembles an Arab bazaar, the cacophony of automobile horns from snarled traffic is drowned out by the cries of fishmongers and greengrocers. In this and other markets, like the Capo or Ballaro, ripe red tomatoes, deep purple eggplants, bell peppers, artichokes, zucchini, onions, oranges and lemons, pumpkins, persimmons, and prickly pears are piled high alongside tables of fresh-killed kid or lamb and the seafood catch of the day.

Downtown, where businesspeople manage their shipping, construction, and commercial affairs in modern offices, courtly gentlemen with appreciative roving eyes still stroll unhurriedly, sometimes lingering over their cappuccinos and brioches, the better to admire the ladies. The Sicilian regional government sits in a twelfth-century Arab-Norman palace (Palazzo dei Normanni). And the best sweets in town — such as the Arab-derived "joy of the throat," a mound of pistachio-flavored almond paste — are still made by a small group of Benedictine nuns cloistered in the central downtown area.

Palermo has many points of international artistic interest. The imposing Norman cathedral, from which Cardinal Salvatore Pappalardo now frequently rails against the city's criminals, dates back to the twelfth century. The center of town is the four-cornered Quattro Canti intersection, with its Spanish Baroque design. And the majestic Renaissance fountain in the Piazza del Municipio casts a spell of the past in the fading evening light. The small Martorana church in central Piazza Bellini has beautiful Byzantine mosaics, as does the incomparable cathedral in the nearby town of Monreale. The 8,000 mummies that line the walls of the Capuchin Convent's catacombs are an eerie reminder of those who came before.

But if the waves of invaders left their mark on the city's art and architecture (as well as on the physical traits of its populace — witness the blond, blue-eyed Sicilians who are probably descended from Normans), they have left an even more obvious imprint on the island's distinctive cuisine. Because of its hot, sunny climate and variable topography, which includes some extremely fertile areas, Sicily has always been blessed with a surfeit of high-quality culinary resources. Its vegetables and fruits are said to be the tastiest in Italy, perhaps in Europe. The fish is fresh and abundant. (The local meats, primarily kid and lamb, are a little less plentiful but excellent.) Four centuries of Arab domination, along with the influence of other "visitors," left an exotic gustatory heritage. Many Sicilian recipes include pine nuts, raisins, and sweet-and-sour condiments. Sweet desserts of almond paste, ricotta cheese, and candied fruits also seem to be of Arab origin. The best known of these are the *cassata siciliana* (sponge cake with ricotta and candied fruits), *cannoli* (pastry cones filled with sweet ricotta paste), and *frutta della Martorana* (marzipan), in the shapes of fruits, vegetables, and even pasta.

Sicily's best-known dishes are probably its pastas — with sardines, tomatoes and eggplant, or yellow broccoli. Swordfish, sliced in steaks or formed into meatballs or cold stuffed rolls, is also among the island's favorites, as is the famous *falsomagro* ("falsely thin"), a veal roll stuffed with eggs, cheese, tomatoes, and fresh herbs.

PALERMO AT-A-GLANCE

 SEEING THE CITY: Palermo is bordered on the north by 1,800-foot Monte Pellegrino (Pilgrim's Mountain), which Goethe described as "the most beautiful promontory in the world." The headland, defended by Carthage against Rome for three years during the First Punic War, is 9 miles from Palermo by car and can be reached by the winding Via P. Bonanno. There are impressive views of the city below and of the fertile Conca d'Oro plain beyond at almost every turning. The best view is from the terrace of the abandoned *Castello Utveggio Hotel.* The road continues to the *Sanctuary of Santa Rosalia,* the patron saint of Palermo, and then down to the beach of the *Mondello* resort.

SPECIAL PLACES: Palermo begins at the mouth of a wide bay and stretches back toward the interior. The old city center, near the bay, can be covered fairly easily on foot, but some of the sites worth seeing require transportation. When touring, remember that some churches close at noon or 12:30 PM and do not reopen until 4 or 5 PM. Carry a handful of 100-lire pieces to operate the machines that provide extra lighting or recorded explanations.

Quattro Canti (Four Corners) – This four-cornered crossroads (sometimes called *Piazza Vigliena*) is the heart of the old city. It is the intersection of Via Maqueda and Corso Vittorio Emanuele; from here it is a short walk to many of Palermo's principal monuments. The four façades at Quattro Canti, built in the early 17th century, are fine examples of Spanish Baroque architecture. The fountains are decorated at ground level with statues representing the four seasons; at the next level, with four of Sicily's Spanish kings; and yet higher, with four of the city's women saints.

San Giuseppe dei Teatini (Saint Joseph of the Theatine Fathers) – St. Joseph's Church stands on the southwest corner of the Quattro Canti; its entrance is on Corso Vittorio Emanuele. The façade is simple, but the Spanish Baroque interior is notable for its rich detail. The frescoes on the roof of the vault are copies of the originals that were destroyed when the church was bombed in 1943.

Piazza Pretoria, or Piazza del Municipio (City Hall Square) – From the Quattro Canti, just a few steps along Via Maqueda, is Piazza Pretoria. In its center is a huge, slightly elevated fountain designed by 16th-century Florentine sculptors. Beautifully illuminated at night, the fountain is known by local residents as the Fountain of Shame because the statues are very explicitly naked. The city hall palace, originally called Palazzo delle Aquile (Palace of the Eagles), dates from 1463 and has been restored several times. A small street on the left of the palace leads to *Piazza Bellini,* the third part of this central monumental complex.

Chiesa di Santa Caterina (Church of Saint Catherine) – If you enter Piazza Bellini from Piazza Pretoria, Santa Caterina, built between 1566 and 1596, is to the left. Its late Renaissance façade (the cupola is especially lovely) suggests little of the polychrome marble decoration within, a splendid example of Spanish Baroque style. Except for Sunday mornings from 8 AM to noon, the church is rarely used for services.

La Martorana, or Chiesa di Santa Maria dell'Ammiraglio (Church of Saint Mary of the Admiral) – Facing Santa Caterina in Piazza Bellini is Palermo's single most famous church and one of the few Greek Orthodox churches in Italy today. The first visible feature is the strikingly beautiful Norman campanile, which dates from the 12th century. The interior, where the original central Greek cross plan can still be detected, is decorated with intricate Byzantine mosaics. Originally named for its founder, George of Antioch, admiral to the fleet of King Roger I, the church was later ceded to the nearby monastery founded in 1193 by Eloisa Martorana. Open daily, 8:30 AM to 1 PM and 4 to 7:30 PM (it closes earlier in winter).

Chiesa di San Cataldo (Church of Saint Cataldo) – Opposite La Martorana is this tiny church, which dates from the Norman period but has clear evidence of the city's Arab heritage in its three small red domes. Because of the untimely death of its founder, Admiral Maio of Bari, it was never fully decorated. It does have its original mosaic floor and rows of original columns, and the altar still bears the ancient symbols of the lamb and the cross. This church has no electricity, so it must be seen during daylight. Ask the caretaker for the key (which you must remember to return when you leave).

Chiesa del Gesù (Church of Jesus) and Casa Professa – Across Via Maqueda, the narrow Via Ponticello leads to the first church built by the Jesuits in Sicily (1564) and now their local headquarters. The church has a sober façade and a richly decorated interior. Located in the heart of the Alberghiera quarter of Palermo, one of the city's poorest and liveliest neighborhoods, it is only a few steps from Piazza Ballaro, where a colorful morning market flourishes. Also nearby is the Chiesa del Carmine.

Duomo (Cathedral) – From Quattro Canti, Corso Vittorio Emanuele leads to Piazza della Cattedrale. There, a small park with palm and other trees stands before the imposing Cattedrale di Santa Maria Assunta (Cathedral of Saint Mary of the Assumption). Begun in 1185 by an English archbishop, the final building has assumed a Gothic-Catalan style with pronounced Moslem influences, typical of much of Sicily. The main entrance, from the park, is through the great south porch with its carved wooden doors; the column on the left is inscribed with a verse from the Koran. The spacious interior houses the tombs of six former Sicilian monarchs and their relatives. The *Duomo* is interesting, too, for its campanile, choir, and treasury. Usually open daily, 7 AM to noon and 4 to 7 PM (phone: 334373).

Palazzo dei Normanni, or Palazzo Reale (Palace of the Normans, or Royal Palace) – From the exit at the back of the *Duomo,* the *Palazzo Arcivescovile,* or archbishopric (connected by a bridge to the *Duomo*), is on the right, with Piazza della Vittoria, a square traditionally used for public celebrations, on the left. Also on the left is the *Palazzo dei Normanni.* Originally built by the city's Arab occupiers and subsequently modified by both the Normans and the Spaniards, this building has always been the residence of Sicilian rulers. Today it houses the Sicilian regional government. The royal apartments on the top floor have beautiful mosaics. The Cappella Palatina (Palace Chapel), with its Saracen carved ceilings and columns and Greek Byzantine mosaics, is considered one of the finest examples of Arab-Norman art in Sicily. To some extent, visiting hours depend on political necessity. The royal apartments are generally open 9 AM to noon Mondays, Fridays, and Saturdays. The chapel is open daily, 9 AM to 1 PM and 3 to 5 PM, and closed Wednesday and Sunday afternoons and holidays. Piazza del Parlamento (phone: 485694).

Chiesa di San Giovanni degli Eremiti (Church of Saint John of the Hermits) – Not far from the Palazzo dei Normanni is a lovely Arab-Norman church built in 1132 at the request of King Roger II. It has picturesque pink domes and a cloister with a luxuriant tropical garden. Via dei Benedettini 18 (phone: 212633).

Chiesa di San Domenico – Taking Corso Vittorio Emanuele from the Quattro Canti toward the port (and away from the Duomo), turn left onto Via Roma. Past the entrance to the Vucciria market are the Piazza and the Church of San Domenico. Many well-known Sicilians are buried inside this large church. The Oratorio del Rosario di San Domenico behind it boasts a masterpiece, the *Madonna del Rosario,* painted by Van Dyck after he fled the plague in Palermo in 1628.

Museo Nazionale Archeologico (National Archaeological Museum) – Next to the post office on Via Roma is one of the most important historical museums in Italy. It is not large (only two floors) but has an excellent collection of Phoenician, Egyptian, Punic, Greek, and Roman artifacts, including the famed metopes of the Selinunte Greek temples. Open 9 AM to 2 PM Tuesdays through Saturdays; to 1 PM Sundays; closed Mondays. Admission fee. Via Olivella (phone: 587825).

Oratorio di San Lorenzo (Oratory of Saint Lawrence) – Walking east on Corso Vittorio Emanuele, beyond Via Roma, the narrow Via Immacolatella is on the left. The oratory, at No. 5, contains a sculpture by Serpotta and a painting by Caravaggio. The custodian will let visitors in.

Galleria Nazionale della Sicilia (National Gallery of Sicily) – The Palazzo Patella, or Abatellis — a late Gothic–Catalan structure on the edge of the Kalsa neighborhood near the port — houses the National Gallery. Tastefully arranged, its exhibits well documented, the gallery contains interesting paintings and sculptures from many Sicilian periods. Open 9 AM to 2 PM Saturdays through Thursdays; to 1 PM Sundays; closed Fridays. Via Alloro 4 (phone: 233317).

Convento dei Cappuccini (Convent of the Capuchin Friars) – For even the most unimpressionable, the catacombs of this ancient convent are an amazing sight, containing the desiccated bodies, some naturally mummified, of more than 8,000 priests, other professionals, workmen, women, and children of old Palermo. Donations requested. Open 9:30 AM to noon and 3:30 to 5:30 PM Mondays through Saturdays; 9:30 AM to noon Sundays and holidays. Via Pindemonte (phone: 212633).

Orto Botanico (Botanical Gardens) – The gardens are situated alongside Villa Giulia, off Via Lincoln on the eastern edge of Palermo. The 17th-century design and lush subtropical vegetation make interesting visuals. Open 9 AM to noon and 2 to 4 PM Mondays through Saturdays, October through May; 9 AM to 2 PM June through September.

Palazzo della Zisa (Palace of Zisa) – La Zisa, from the Arabic *El Aziz* (The Magnificent), is one of several pleasure palaces built by the Norman kings outside the city proper. The former residence of King William, who reigned from 1156 to 1166, it is a splendid example of Arab-Fatimid architecture, one of the most important of the surviving Arab-Norman secular monuments in Sicily. Closed for restoration at press time. Vicolo Zisa (Bus No. 24).

■ **EXTRA SPECIAL:** Palermo has several bustling outdoor markets with long-standing traditions that provide a colorful and interesting view of everyday life in the Sicilian capital as well as a hint of the city's Arabic background. The biggest of these, and the most famous — having been immortalized in a painting of one of Sicily's major contemporary artists, Renato Guttuso — is the *Vucciria* (originally Bucceria, from the French, *boucherie,* or slaughterhouse). First a meat market, the Vucciria later became a vegetable market but is now an outlet for foods of all kinds: fish of varied stripes and sizes, local meats, cheeses, fresh fruits and vegetables, spices, dried fruits and nuts, and even some nonfood products, such as transistor radios and cassettes. Not far from the port, the Vucciria stretches from Via Roma to the sea and from the Church of San Domenico to Corso Vittorio Emanuele. It is noisy and crowded (watch out for your wallet or purse) but wonderfully vivid and alive.

Added attractions in the Vucciria are a small restaurant called the *Maestro del Brodo* (The Broth Master), Via Panieri 7, where various broth dishes can provide an inexpensive meal for about $6; the *Shangai,* Viccolo Mezzani 34, where in warm weather diners sit on a terrace overlooking Piazza Caracciolo while sampling pasta *con le sarde* (sardines), *con broccoli,* or *alla norma* ("as usual," with eggplant); and the tiny *Taverna Azzurra,* Discesa dei Maccheronai (Sloping Street of the Macaroni Makers), where locals gather for a glass of *zibibbo* (sweet wine), Sangue Siciliano (Sicilian Blood, another sweet wine), or Marsala.

ENVIRONS

There are several interesting day trips from Palermo. Most can be done by bus, but for speed and convenience we suggest a taxi or private car.

La Favorita – About 2½ miles from the city center is a wonderful park at the foot of Monte Pellegrino. La Favorita has many sports facilities; its landscaping, commissioned by 19th-century Bourbon kings, is special. On the same excursion, visit the mountain and the Santa Rosalia sanctuary, enjoying fine views of Palermo, the coastline, and the attractive seaside resort of Mondello, about 7 miles from the city.

Piana degli Albanesi – This Albanian settlement, one of the island's most interesting, was founded in 1488. Its inhabitants retain their ancient dialect and observe Greek Orthodox traditions. Easter and Epiphany are especially colorful celebrations. About 14½ miles from Palermo; buses leave several times a day from Stazione Centrale on Piazza G. Cesare.

Monreale – Five miles southwest of Palermo is the hilltop town of Monreale, site of the famous cathedral of Santa Maria la Nuova, built by King William II between 1172 and 1176. This is indisputably the most important Norman church in Sicily and contains some of the most impressive medieval artwork. The façade is grand, but nothing to compare with the vast interior, the walls of which are almost entirely covered with mosaic scenes from the Old and New Testaments. One of the most stunning depictions, the full-length figure of Christ kneeling in benediction, is in the apse. The wooden choir is beautiful, as are the sarcophagi of several Sicilian kings and queens. (This is one of the many churches in Sicily where visitors need 100-lire pieces to operate temporary lights in order to see the art.) A small admission fee is charged for access to the roof, from which it's possible to view the cloister next door and the fertile Conca D'Oro plain below the town. Open daily, 7:30 AM to 12:30 PM and 3 to 7 PM. (A taxi from Palermo — round trip, including an hour's wait — costs about $15.)

On the south side of the cathedral is the 12th-century *chiostro* — Cloister of the Benedictines — which is enclosed by double rows of individually designed columns, many of which are decorated with reliefs or mosaics. Open 9 AM to 2 PM in winter, 9 AM to 1 PM and 4 PM to sunset the rest of the year; closed Tuesdays. Buses from Piazza Verdi in Palermo.

During a visit to Monreale, travelers may want to have a meal here. Try *La Botte,* with its vast selection of antipasti, plus old-time Sicilian dishes such as artichokes with tuna and shrimp; spaghetti with ricotta cheese or with tuna, capers, and olives; and *falsomagro,* the classic Sicilian meat loaf. Closed Mondays and in August and September. Contrada Lanzitti, SS186 (phone: 414051). Inexpensive.

FULL-DAY EXCURSIONS

Erice and Segesta – Erice is a lovely medieval village about 62 miles west of Palermo along the coast road toward Trapani. It was known in antiquity throughout the Mediterranean for its temple to the goddess of fertility, Venus Erycina. It also has two interesting castles and the lovely Chiesa Matrice. Its mountain perch above the sea provides a number of impressive views, but the little town is often shrouded in fog, particularly in winter, so try to visit in good weather and early in the day. On the way back to Palermo, stop at Segesta, where there are well-preserved ruins of a Doric temple dating from the 5th century BC.

Cefalù – A pleasant drive about 47 miles along the coast road east of Palermo includes the picturesque town of Cefalù, an ancient Greek cliffside seaport. Its 12th-century cathedral has mosaics to rival those of Monreale. The old town, dating from 1130, consists of nine parallel streets.

SOURCES AND RESOURCES

TOURIST INFORMATION: General tourist information regarding Palermo and its environs is available at the *Ente Provinciale per il Turismo* (*EPT*) office at Piazza Castelnuovo 35 in downtown Palermo (phone: 583847). The EPT also has lists of hotels. Other EPT branches are at the domestic terminal (phone: 230032) and the international terminal (phone: 281986) of the airport, as well as at the train station (phone: 233808). The *US consulate* is at Via Vaccarini 1 (phone: 291-532-35).

Local Coverage – Two daily papers are published in Palermo: *Giornale di Sicilia* and *L'Ora.*

Telephone – The telephone prefix for Palermo is 091.

GETTING AROUND: Downtown thoroughfares are few, so traffic in Palermo is, to say the least, chaotic. Rush hour often lasts for most of the day. Allow plenty of time to get where you're going.

Airport – Domestic and international flights operate from the *Punta Raisi Airport,* 20 miles outside the city. Buses to the airport run from the terminal at Via Mazzini 59. Taxis are available but are very expensive.

Boat – Maritime departures for the Italian mainland, Tunisia, and some of the Sicilian islands are from the maritime station at the Vittorio Veneto dock.

Bus – Because of the traffic jams, travel by public bus is not always a good idea. Assess the traffic situation and the amount of time at your disposal before committing yourself to a bus ride. Tickets are 400 lire per ride and can be bought at shops with a sign reading "Biglietti A.M.A.T." The Sicilian intercity bus company, S.A.I.S., Via Balsamo 16, also provides daily bus service between Palermo and most Sicilian cities.

Carrozze – Sometimes called *carrozzelle,* these horse-drawn cabs are a pleasant way to get around in the evening when there is little traffic. It is best to work out the price with the driver beforehand; otherwise you may find the hansom's meter conveniently broken when your drive is over.

Car Rental – Possible through most international and Italian firms, but driving a private car through the city is not recommended for anyone who isn't a longtime resident of Italy.

Taxi – Cabs are relatively inexpensive and can be picked up at a downtown stand or called by your hotel (radio taxi phone: 513311). Taxi meters start at 1,500 lire; the minimum price for any ride is 3,000 lire, with an additional charge of 1,000 on Sundays and holidays and evenings after 10 PM. Luggage costs 200 lire per bag. Since it is often hard to find taxis outside the immediate central city, it is a good idea to ask a cab to wait while you visit a site.

Train – The main train station is the *Stazione Centrale* at Piazza G. Cesare (phone: 230806, 233808).

MUSEUMS: Besides those mentioned in *Special Places,* Palermo has a number of museums of special interest.

Museo Internazionale delle Marionette (International Museum of Marionettes) – Collection of puppets from various parts of Sicily. (See also *Italy's Museums and Monuments,* DIVERSIONS.) Open 10 AM to 12:30 PM and 5 to 7 PM Mondays, Wednesdays, and Fridays. Piazza Marina 19 (phone: 328060).

Galleria d'Arte Moderna (Gallery of Modern Art) – Collection of works by painters from Sicily and elsewhere in southern Italy. Open 9 AM to 1 PM Tuesdays through Saturdays; also 4:30 to 7:30 PM Tuesdays and Thursdays. Via F. Turati 10 (phone: 588951).

Museo Etnografico Pitrè (Pitrè Ethnological Museum) – Art and folklore collection illustrating all aspects of Sicilian life. Near the Palazzina Cinese (Chinese Palace) in the Parco della Favorita estate, which can be reached by taxi or public bus No. 14 or 15. Open daily, 8:30 AM to 1:30 PM and 3 to 5 PM; closed Friday mornings. Via Duca degli Abruzzi (phone: 461060).

Museo Archeologico della Fondazione Mormino (The Mormino Foundation Archaeological Museum) – In the Banco di Sicilia building. Includes a variety of prehistoric and ancient pottery. Open 9 AM to 1 PM and 3 to 5 PM except Saturday afternoons, Sundays, and holidays. Via Roma 185 (phone: 585144).

SHOPPING: Like many smaller Italian cities, Palermo has a compact, central shopping district with several stores as elegant as those in Rome, Florence, and Milan. All the famous Italian designers have shops or outlets here; leather and fine linen products may be less expensive than elsewhere in Italy.

Hand-crafted items include ceramics, willow baskets, embroidered fabrics, clay crèche figures, and replicas of the famed Sicilian puppets and horse carts. Marsala wine and marzipan candy are two of the prime gastronomic products available.

Most Palermo stores are open daily, 9 AM to 1 PM and 4 to 7:30 PM. Most stores are closed on Monday mornings; food stores on Wednesday afternoons. All shops are closed on Sundays and holidays, including January 1, April 25, May 1, August 15, November 1 and 4, and December 8, 25, and 26.

Some of the better shops include:

Giovanni Alongi – Menswear, from shoes to evening wear. Via Ruggero Settimo 46/A.

Battaglia – Top-label women's clothing, Via Ruggero Settimo 76; menswear, Via Ruggero Settimo 97.

La Botteguccia – Women's sportswear; imaginative and innovative daytime and evening wear. No credit cards. Piazza Ungheria 11. Branch store for older women right across the street.

Convent of St. Benedict – Traditional Palermo cakes and cookies prepared and sold by the Benedictine nuns. Open daily, 9:30 AM to 6:30 PM; closed Wednesday afternoons. Piazza Venezia 38/A.

Emporio Roma – Gifts, hardware, houseware, appliances. Via Roma 230–238.

Fecarotta – Fine Sicilian, Italian, and other European antiques. Via Belmonte 108/B.

Libreria Flaccovio – The best bookstore in town; wide selection of art books, guidebooks, and books in English. Via Ruggero Settimo 37.

Harabel's – Elegant women's wear. Via M. Stabile 189.

Harper – Small, well-organized department store carrying men's, women's, and children's clothing as well as housewares and gift items. Via Ruggero Settimo 31.

Lorizzo – Attractive men's clothing. Via Belmonte 114.

Ma Gi – Fine jewelry and silver. No credit cards. Via Ruggero Settimo 45.

Fratelli Magri – One of the city's oldest and best-known bakeries. Via Carini 42.

Mangia, R – Fine regional food products, well packaged and fresh. Via Belmonte 116.

MaxMara – Stylish, moderately priced women's sportswear. Via della Libertà 24/B.

Prezioso – Fine women's clothing and leather goods. Via della Libertà 14/A.

De Simone – Artistic ceramics. Via M. Stabile 133.

Spatafora Calzature – Branch of a well-known chain offering moderately priced Italian shoes. Via Magueda 111–113.

Tullio – Beautiful leather goods. Via Belmonte 104B.

SPECIAL EVENTS: Every November there is a two-week *Marionette Festival* at the *Museo Internazionale delle Marionette*, Piazza Marina 19 (phone: 328060), and other theaters. *Festino di Santa Rosalia,* the feast days of Santa Rosalia, the patron saint of Palermo, falls in July, culminating on July 15 with a street procession in which a statue of the saint is carried joyfully through the city. In early September there is a procession to the sanctuary on nearby Monte Pellegrino.

SPORTS: The Palermo area is blessed with many pleasant beaches. Thus (except for tennis and horseback riding) sports enthusiasts take to the water.
Horseback Riding – *SECEP,* Viale Diana, Parco della Favorita (phone: 528395); *Società Palermitana Equitazione,* Viale Diana, Parco della Favorita (phone: 513935).

Soccer – From September to May, *Palermo* — in the pink shirts and black shorts — plays at the *Stadio Comunale,* Viale del Fante 11 (phone: 513643, 523869).

Swimming – The city's main beach resort is *Mondello,* 7 miles north. Most of the long, sandy beach is taken up by *stabilimenti balneari* (bathing establishments), which charge an entrance fee for those who wish to use the facilities (showers, cabins, and so on). According to Italian law, anyone is free to use the beach without paying, as long as bathers stay within the first 5 meters of the shoreline. Those who pay the admission fee, however, may also rent chairs, take showers, and use the pool if there is one. Another beach, in the small fishing village of *Sferracavallo,* lies beyond the rocky spur of Monte Gallo, a few miles farther west. It is somewhat less commercial, and the water is delightfully clear. *Solunto* and *Porticello,* east of Palermo, also have good beaches.

One swimming pool can be recommended: *Piscina Comunale* (City Swimming Pool), Viale del Fante 11 (phone: 510558).

Tennis – *Castelforte Tennis Club,* Viale Olimpico 12 (phone: 454886); *Circolo del Tennis,* Viale del Fante 3 (phone: 362552). The *Palermo Grand Prix* tournament is held in October.

Water Sports – For information on sailing, try *Circolo della Vela Sicilia,* Viale Regina Elena 1 (phone: 450182, 450333). *Club Sci Nautico Mondello,* Via Piano Gallo, Mondello (phone: 455500), will get you onto water skis. For windsurfing, there's *Albaria Windsurfing Club,* Viale Regina Elena 95 (phone: 454034).

THEATER AND MUSIC: Since the closing of the 19th-century *Teatro Massimo* for restoration, the major theater in Palermo is the *Politeama Garibaldi,* Piazza Ruggero Settimo (phone: 212334), which generally produces classical theater or concerts. In summer, a program of ballet, jazz, and classical music is offered at the *Teatro del Parco di Villa Castelnuovo,* an open-air theater by the sea. Tickets are available through the *Politeama.* Concerts are also held at the *Sala Scarlatti* of the Music Conservatory, Via Squarcialupo 45, or at *SS Salvatore Auditorium,* Corso Vittorio Emanuele 396.

Palermo has a long history and tradition of puppet theaters. Performances are held at the *Museo Internazionale delle Marionette,* Piazza Marina 19 (phone: 328060), Fridays at 6 PM. Other theaters sometimes used for puppet shows are *Figli d'Arte Cuticchio* (the name is from a family of puppet makers), Via Bara 95 (phone: 329194, 323400); the *Teatro Ippogrifo,* Vicolo Ragusi 6 (phone: 329194); *Compagnia A. Mancuso,* Piazza Sturzo (phone: 247508); and *Voci dalla Sicilia,* Via Lombardia 25 (phone: 296929).

NIGHTCLUBS AND NIGHTLIFE: There are several small piano bars, where conversation and liquid refreshment can be enjoyed against a musical background. The best are at *Grande Albergo e delle Palme* and *Villa Igiea* (see *Checking In*) and at *Mazzara,* Via Generale Magliocco 15 (phone: 321366), and the *Collica,* Via Notarbartolo 6 (phone: 6252040). For those with a yearning to dance, there are several nightclubs and discotheques, especially along Viale Strasburgo: *Anyway,* Via Maggiore Toselli; *Cerchio,* Viale Strasburgo; *Speak Easy,* Viale Strasburgo 34 (phone: 518486); and *Pare Choc,* Via dei Nebrodi 55. But you will find that most Sicilian nightlife is at home. There is much socializing among families and friends, either at each other's homes or in the many fine neighborhood restaurants.

BEST IN TOWN

CHECKING IN: In Palermo, as throughout Sicily, hotels are considerably less expensive than elsewhere in Italy. Those rated as expensive charge from $100 to $150 for a double room; moderate, from $50 to $100; and inexpensive, less than $50.

Villa Igiea Grand – This sprawling, elegant villa in a seaside park 2 miles out of the city center is Palermo's only luxury hotel, complete with tennis courts, swimming pool, and beach. Rooms are beautifully decorated; service is excellent. The only disadvantage is the need for transportation into town. Via Belmonte 43 (phone: 543744). Expensive.

Excelsior Palace – Recently refurbished and refurnished, this 86-room downtown establishment has been turned into a jewel of comfort. A short walk from the main shopping center. Some rooms overlook the fasionable Via della Libertà, one of Palermo's busiest (and noisiest) streets. Via Marchese Ugo 3 (phone 266155). Moderate.

Grande Albergo e delle Palme – Richard Wagner stayed in this hotel, formerly the Palazzo Ingham, in 1882, just after he completed *Parsifal,* and the word is that Mafia bigwigs held summit meetings here in the 1950s. Today this large, centrally located hotel is a home away from home for Italian businesspeople, politicians, and traveling journalists (not to mention tourists). Good service, good food, good bar. Via Roma 396 (phone: 583933). Moderate.

Mondello Palace – A pleasant, 83-room resort hotel with a pool, garden, and private beach. Viale Principe di Scalea, Mondello (phone: 450001). Moderate.

Politeama Palace – Across the street from the *Politeama Theater* and fine for short stays. Piazza Ruggero Settimo 15 (phone: 322777). Moderate.

President – Closer to the port and less central than several of the others mentioned, but still conveniently downtown. Via Francesco Crispi 230 (phone: 580733). Moderate.

Splendid Hotel La Torre – On the far end of the Mondello beach, this modern hotel has all private outdoor facilities, including pool, park, and beach. Via Piano Gallo 11, Mondello (phone: 450222). Moderate.

Europa – Small and comfortable, with a convenient downtown location. Via Agrigento 3 (phone: 266673). Inexpensive.

Mediterraneo – Comfortable, with adequate services and facilities. Via Rosolino Pilo 43 (phone: 581133). Inexpensive.

 EATING OUT: Food in Palermo is distinctive for its combination of Arab, Norman, and Spanish influences and for the quality of its super-fresh ingredients (provided by the markets described in *Extra Special*). Expect to pay over $60 for a meal for two, including wine, at the city's few luxury eating places, listed as expensive; from $40 to $60 in the moderate category; and less than $40 for an inexpensive meal.

Charleston – This elegant downtown restaurant is one of Sicily's most famous. It has beautiful Art Nouveau decor and excellent food. Specialties include eggplant Charleston (stuffed with pasta) and grilled stuffed swordfish rolls. Closed Sundays and from mid-June to mid-September. Reservations advised. Piazza Ungheria 30 (phone: 321366). Expensive. (In summer, *Charleston* has a branch at *Mondello,* Viale Regina Elena; phone: 450171.)

Gourmand's – Palermo businesspeople and politicians favor its quietly modern decor, discreet service, and good Sicilian cooking. Try the *risotto* with lobster and the vegetable antipasti. Closed Sundays and August 10–20. Reservations advised. Via della Libertà 37 (phone: 323431). Expensive.

Renato–L'Approdo – One feature of this attractive restaurant is its excellent wine cellar, with some 70,000 bottles from which to choose. Another is its varied menu. Closed Wednesdays. Via Messina Marina 28 (phone: 470103). Expensive.

Sympathy Trattoria – Some people say that at *Sympathy* as much Brooklynese is spoken as Sicilian. The fish is excellent in this colorful place, and you can never be sure just what the person at the next table does for a living. Via Piano Gallo 18, Mondello (phone: 454470). Moderate.

Terrazza Fiorita – For dining *en ville* on a summer evening, try this rooftop garden restaurant where the choice of both antipasti and main dishes is enticing. In the *Grande Albergo e delle Palme.* Open evenings only, July to September. Via Roma 389 (phone: 583933). Moderate.

Gambero Rosso – The imaginative menu includes such interesting selections as pasta with oysters, *risotto* with seafood sausage, and delectable imperial shrimp. Closed Mondays and November. Via Piano Gallo 30–32, Mondello (phone: 454685). Moderate to inexpensive.

A'Cuccagna – A relaxing *trattoria* right in the center of town, featuring an impressive self-serve antipasto display and many typical Palermo dishes. Closed Mondays. Via Principe di Granatelli 21/A (phone: 587267). Inexpensive.

N'grasciata, Osteria del Pesce Fresco – Fish is the thing at this characteristically simple harbor restaurant. You could start with a plate of tiny fried baby fish (*u'sciabbacheddu,* in Sicilian dialect) or slices of *bottarga* (pressed tuna roe). Pasta with *bottarga* is a specialty. Closed Sundays. Via Tiro a Segno 12, in the Sant-'Erasmo neighborhood (phone: 230974). Inexpensive.

Primavera – For sampling basic Sicilian dishes such as pasta with sardines, broccoli, or eggplant, this small, family-run *trattoria* is ideal. Go early. Closed Fridays. Piazza Bologni 4 (phone: 329408). Very inexpensive.

Shangai – This small *trattoria* overlooking the heart of the Vucciria market has become a landmark (see *Extra Special*). Classic Sicilian antipasti and pasta dishes, at times accompanied by owner Benedetto Basile's verses. Closed Wednesdays. Vicolo Mezzani 34 (phone: 589773). Very inexpensive.

ROME

If you're traveling from the north, you'll quickly understand why *Italia meridionale,* or southern Italy, begins in Rome: ancient stone ruins basking in the southern sun, Baroque swirls teasing the senses at every turn, religious art exploding with color and Catholic sensuality — celebrating life with the conspicuous *joie de vivre* (here known as *gioia di vivere*) of southern Europe. Rome reaches out to your senses, blinding you with colors, beckoning you to stay. Its appeal is gripping and obviously romantic, inspiring throughout history many an illustrious northern visitor — among them Goethe, Keats, Byron, and Shelley — though today these romantic souls might be repelled by the insufferable noise, the screaming traffic, the exasperating strikes, political demonstrations, and general chaos of modern Rome. Yet despite the familiar symptoms of contemporary blight, Rome remains the Eternal City, ancient capital of the Western world, and center of Christianity for nearly 2,000 years.

Rome lies roughly in the center of the region of Lazio (Latium), just below the knee of boot-shaped Italy, between the Tyrrhenian Sea to the west and the Apennine Mountains to the east. The Tiber River gently curves through the city, with ancient Rome on its left bank, Vatican City and Trastevere (*tras* means across; *tevere,* Tiber) on its right. The original seven hills of Rome are all on the left bank, as is its modern center — the shopping areas that surround Piazza di Spagna (the so-called Spanish Steps), Piazza del Popolo, Via del Corso, Via del Tritone, and the legendary Via Veneto, celebrated in Fellini's film *La Dolce Vita.*

The third-century Aurelian Walls still surround ancient Rome as well as most of papal and modern Rome. The city is unique because its fine buildings span so many centuries of history. There are ancient Roman remains, the most famous of which are the Colosseum and the Forum; buildings from the early Christian period such as the Castel Sant'Angelo; and a wealth of dazzling Renaissance and Baroque architecture — from St. Peter's itself to Piazza del Campidoglio, the square designed by Michelangelo. The city abounds in churches, palaces, parks, *piazzas,* statues, and fountains — all of which sparkle in the golden light and clear blue sky of the region.

Even Rome's beginnings are shrouded in a romantic legend that attributes the city's birth to Romulus and Remus, twin sons of the war god Mars and Rhea, a vestal virgin who encountered Mars in a forest one day. The babies, left to die on the shore of the Tiber River at the foot of the Palatine Hill, were rescued and suckled through infancy by an old she-wolf and grew up to lead a band of adventurers and outlaws. Romulus, the stronger leader of the two, is said to have founded Rome in 753 BC, killing his brother to become its first king.

But traces of habitation earlier than that have been found on the Palatine Hill, one of the original seven hills — which today are indistinguishable — and site of Roma Quadrata, a primitive Rome squared off by a surrounding rectangular wall. More likely, the traditional founding date refers to a time when the first settlements of shepherds and farmers on the Palatine took on the shape of a city and the Latins, Sabines, and Etruscans who peopled the area had fused under one system of laws. The name *Roma* was probably a derivation of *Ruma,* an Etruscan noble name.

Following a succession of seven legendary kings, a republic was declared in 509 BC, and a period of expansion began. By 270 BC or so, the entire Italian peninsula was under the protection of Rome, and the resulting political unification brought about a cultural unity as well, a new Roman style in art and literature. Hannibal's defeat at Zama in 201 BC, an event that brought the Second Punic War to an end, prepared the way for further expansion: Rome's dominion over the Mediterranean and its eventual supremacy over Alexander the Great's empire in the East and over Spain and Gaul in the West.

A long period of civil war ended with Julius Caesar's defeat of Pompey in 48 BC, but the brilliant conqueror of Gaul was assassinated in the Senate four years later. His great-nephew and heir, Octavian, continued in the victorious vein, becoming, with the honorific name of Augustus, Rome's first emperor and one of its best administrators. Augustus is said to have found Rome a city of brick and to have left it a city of marble; the Theater of Marcellus and the Mausoleum of Augustus are among his many fine constructions that survive today.

The reign of Augustus (27 BC–AD 14) saw Roman civilization at its peak, and it ushered in two centuries of peace throughout the empire known as the Pax Romana. Wherever they went, the Romans introduced brilliant feats of engineering and architecture, as well as their own culture, government, and law. Persecution of the Christians, which had begun as early as Nero's reign — he blamed the burning of Rome on the new sect and executed large numbers of them in AD 64 — came to an end in the early fourth century, when Constantine the Great issued the Edict of Milan, guaranteeing freedom of worship for all religions. But Rome by now had become top-heavy with its own administration; the empire was divided in 395, with an eastern section in Byzantium (Constantinople, now Istanbul). This was the beginning of the end.

Rome's grandeur had long passed by the fifth century, when a series of economic crises, internal decadence and corruption, and repeated barbarian invasions led to the fall of the empire with the deposition of its last emperor, Romulus Augustulus, in 476.

Thus began the Dark Ages, punctuated by struggles between the empire and the Church, which was centered in the papacy at Rome. The Holy See, under Pope Clement V, actually fled Rome in the fourteenth century, taking up residence in Avignon, France, for seventy years. During that period, the city of Rome declined, and its population, which had been as many as a million at the time of Augustus, shrank to less than 50,000. The Capitoline

Hill and once-bustling Roman Forum became pastures for goats and cows. Sheep grazed in St. Peter's.

The popes returned in 1377, and Rome again became the capital of the Catholic world. Under papal patronage it was soon reborn artistically and culturally. During the fifteenth century, restoration of St. Peter's began, prior to its complete reconstruction; the Vatican complex was built; and new palaces, churches, and well-planned streets changed the face of the city. Powerful popes commissioned artists and architects to beautify Rome, and their genius created sumptuous palaces, splendid villas, and squares adorned with fountains and obelisks, until a second city grew out of the ruins of ancient Rome to match its former splendor. The seventeenth century brought the birth of Baroque Rome, with its dominating figure, architect, sculptor, and painter Gian Lorenzo Bernini, whose masterpieces perhaps best symbolize the spirit of this magnificent and undeniably theatrical city.

The comfortable security of the popes was shaken by the arrival of Napoleon Bonaparte in 1798. He soon set up a republic of Rome, deporting Pope Pius VI briefly to France, and in 1805 he was crowned king of Italy, proclaiming Rome a sort of second capital of the French Empire. In 1809, Napoleon declared the papal territories a part of France and in return was excommunicated by Pope Pius VII, who was deported to Fontainebleau. By 1815, the Napoleonic regime had collapsed, the papal kingdom was reconciled with France, and the pope was back in Rome, but the sparks of nationalistic passion had already been ignited in Italian hearts.

Friction between papal neutralism and patriotic fervor drove Pope Pius IX out of Rome to Gaeta in 1848. In 1849, Rome was again proclaimed a republic under the leadership of patriot Giuseppe Mazzini. Twice the French tried to restore the temporal power of the pope in Rome, meeting strong resistance from republican forces led by Garibaldi. Finally, in 1870, the Italians entered Rome through a breach in the Aurelian Walls at Porta Pia and incorporated the city into the kingdom of Italy. That act dissolved the pontifical state and made Italian unity complete. A year later, Rome became the capital of the kingdom.

Mussolini's march on Rome in 1922 began the infamous Fascist regime that lasted until his downfall some twenty years later. The city was then occupied by the Germans until its liberation in 1944 by the Allies. In 1946, a referendum was held, and Italy was declared a republic again — just as it had been nearly 2½ millennia earlier!

Today Rome is still the capital of Italy and of the Catholic church, as well as home to about four million people (increased from 260,000 inhabitants in 1870). Many Romans are employed in tourism and in government offices — in a city often strangled by bureaucratic problems. Aside from filmmaking (in its cinematographic heyday, the filmmaking activity at Cinecittà gained Rome the nickname "Hollywood on the Tiber") and a certain amount of printing, as well as small-scale production of foodstuffs, pharmaceutical products, building materials, plastics, glass, some clothing, and handmade goods, there is not much industry in Rome.

Yet for a society with significant problems — double-digit inflation, insufficient housing, impossible traffic — Romans today still enjoy a relaxed way of life, as they have done for centuries. Perhaps nowhere north of Naples is the *arte di arrangiarsi* — the art of making do or surviving with style — learned with such skill and practiced with such a timeless sense of resignation.

The *dolce vita* nightlife, more a figment of Fellini's imagination than a reality for any more than a handful of rich or famous Romans, has become somewhat subdued, but Romans today enjoy the same sweet life they always have. Despite the country's pressing problems, an air of conviviality pervades.

Three-hour lunches are still an essential part of life, and a sunny day at any time of the year fills the cobblestoned squares with diners at open-air *trattorie.* You'll see them involved in animated conversation over their robust Roman food and inexpensive carafe wine from the Castelli (the surrounding hill towns such as Frascati). Most visitors are pleased to "do as the Romans do." No sense worrying about the city's crushing debts if the inhabitants don't. And even with many of its museums and ruins half shut because of lack of custodians, there are still more than enough to satisfy the most enthusiastic tourist.

Roma, Non Basta Una Vita (*Rome, a Lifetime Is Not Enough*) by the late Italian author and journalist Silvio Negro hints, with justification, at the impossibility of ever knowing everything about this city. For visitors who harbor the illusion of having seen all the ruins, churches, and monuments of Rome's glorious past, it may be time to begin discovering the countless hidden treasures, best done by walking the back streets and alleyways of the historic center (which is now, for the most part, a pedestrian zone).

If you feel suffocated by city life, try a day or two in the neighboring countryside. The surrounding Lazio region, sandwiched between the Tyrrhenian Sea and the Apennine Mountains, offers seaside resorts, rolling hills topped by medieval towns, picturesque lakes, rivers and green meadows studded with umbrella pines, cypress trees, and wildflowers. Take an organized excursion to the Villa d'Este and Hadrian's Villa in Tivoli; to the Castelli Romani, or Roman hill towns, where the pope has his summer home; or to the excavations of Ostia Antica, the ancient port of Rome.

But take time to sit back and enjoy Rome. Visit the Forum and the Colosseum by day, and return at night when the ruins are bathed in gentler light to meditate over the rise and fall of ancient Rome. Watch the play of water in the Trevi Fountain or any of Rome's nearly 1,000 other fountains of every size and shape. See the ancient Roman Theater of Marcellus, which has been a Roman amphitheater, a medieval fort, and a Renaissance palace and which now contains apartments. Enjoy the superb cooking of the Lazio region. Ride a bicycle or jog in the Villa Borghese. Sip an *aperitivo* on the famed Via Veneto.

Locally it is believed that on the last day of the world, while all humans brood and repent, the Romans will throw a great farewell party, a gastronomic feast to end all, with wine flowing from the city's many fountains. With the apocalypse not yet at hand, and despite the agonies besetting the country at large, the Eternal City remains eternally inviting.

ROME AT-A-GLANCE

SEEING THE CITY: You can enjoy a magnificent view of all of Rome and the surrounding hill towns from *Piazzale Garibaldi* at the top of the Gianicolo (Janiculum Hill). It's best at sunset. Another panoramic view of the city comes into focus after you've climbed to the top of *St. Peter's* dome. For a view of Rome dominated by St. Peter's, go to the terrace of the *Pincio*, a small public park next to the Villa Borghese, above Piazza del Popolo. And the most unusual view is of the dome of St. Peter's as seen in miniature through the keyhole of the gate to the priory of the Knights of Malta on Piazza dei Cavalieri di Malta at the end of Via di Santa Sabina, on the Aventine Hill. The picturesque piazza was designed by engraver Piranesi, a surrealist in spirit though he lived in the 18th century.

SPECIAL PLACES: Rome cannot be seen in a day, three days, a week, or even a year. If your time is limited to a few days, you'd best get a general idea of the city by taking an organized bus tour or two. Then, when you've seen where your interests lie, grab your most comfortable walking shoes and a map. Most of historic Rome, which is also the city's center today, is within the 3rd-century Aurelian Walls and is delightfully walkable.

For practical purposes, the must-sees below are divided into ancient, papal, and modern Rome, but elements of two or all three categories are often found in one site — such as a sleek, modern furniture shop in a Renaissance palace built with stones from the Colosseum. A further heading is dedicated to the palaces, fountains, splendid piazzas, and streets of Rome. The ancient center of the city is very close to *Piazza Venezia*, the heart of the modern city, and most of the sights of ancient Rome are around the Capitoline, Palatine, and Aventine hills. They can be seen on foot — though of course they were not built — in one day. Much of papal Rome is centered in the Vatican, but since all of Rome is a religious center, some of its many fascinating and beautiful churches are included under this heading. (For other churches, and for museums not mentioned below, see "Museums" in *Sources and Resources.*)

Many of the museums, monuments, and archaeological sites run by the state or city are closed on Mondays. Opening and closing hours change often (some close indefinitely because of strikes, personnel shortages, or restorations — it is estimated that only a third of Italy's artworks are exhibited), so check with your hotel or the tourist office before starting out. Where possible, we have listed hours that seem relatively reliable.

Warning: Although the terrible crime wave of a few years ago has subsided, one must still be aware of pickpockets all around the city. They are especially numerous at the most popular tourist spots, even though plainclothes police scour these areas. Watch out particularly for gypsy children who will beg or ask for a light while accomplices make straight for your wallet.

ANCIENT ROME

Colosseo (Colosseum) – It's said that when the Colosseum falls, Rome will fall — and the world will follow. This symbol of the eternity of Rome, the grandest and most celebrated of all its monuments, was completed in AD 80, and it is a logical starting point for a visitor to ancient Rome. See it in daylight, and return to see it by moonlight. The enormous arena, ⅓ mile in circumference and 137 feet high, once accommodated 50,000 spectators. To provide shade in the summer, a special detachment of sailors stretched a great awning over the top. There were 80 entrances (progressively numbered, except for the four main ones), allowing the crowds to quickly claim their marble seats, and underneath were subterranean passages where animals and other apparatus were hidden from view. In the arena itself, Christians were thrown to lions, wild beasts destroyed one another, and gladiators fought to the death. Gladiatorial combats lasted until 404, when Onorius put an end to them (possibly after a monk had thrown himself into the arena in protest and was killed by the angry crowd); animal combats were stopped toward the middle of the 6th century.

The Colosseum was abused by later generations. It was a fort in the Middle Ages; something of a quarry during the Renaissance, when its marble and travertine were used in the construction of St. Peter's and other buildings; and in the 18th century it even became a manure depot for the production of saltpeter. Yet it remains a symbol of the grandeur of Rome. Open daily. Admission fee for the upper level. Piazzale del Colosseo.

Palatino (Palatine Hill) – Adjacent to the Colosseum and the Roman Forum, the Palatine is where Rome began. Its Latin name is the source of the word *palace.* In fact, great men — Cicero, Crassus, Mark Antony — lived on this regal hill, and the emperors of Rome — Augustus, Tiberius, Caligula, Nero, Domitian, Septimius Severus — built their palaces here, turning the hill into an imperial preserve. A 12th-century author called the spot the "palace of the Monarchy of the Earth, wherein is the capital seat of the whole world." In ruins by the Middle Ages, the ancient structures were incorporated into the sumptuous Villa Farnese in the 16th century, and the Farnese Gardens were laid out, the first botanical gardens in the world.

The Palatine is a lovely spot for a walk or a picnic. See especially the so-called House of Livia (actually of her husband, Augustus), with its remarkable frescoes; Domitian's Palace of the Flavians, built by his favorite architect, Rabirius; the impressive stadium; the view from the terrace of the Palace of Septimius Severus; and the remains of the Farnese Gardens at the top with another superb panorama of the nearby Forums. Closed Tuesdays. Admission fee includes the Roman Forum. Enter at Via di San Gregorio or by way of the Roman Forum on Via dei Fori Imperiali.

Foro Romano (Roman Forum) – Adjoining the Palatine Hill is the Roman Forum, a mass of ruins overgrown with weeds and trees that was the commercial, civic, and religious center of ancient Rome. Here stood several large ceremonial buildings, including three triumphal arches, two public halls, half a dozen temples, and numerous monuments and statues. Set in what was once a marshy valley at the foot of the Capitoline Hill, the Forum was abandoned after the barbarian invasions and had become a cattle pasture by the Renaissance. When excavations began during the last century, it was under 20 feet of dirt.

Highlights of the Forum include the triumphal Arch of Septimius Severus, built by that emperor in AD 203; the Arch of Titus (AD 81), adorned with scenes depicting the victories of Titus, especially his conquest of Jerusalem and the spoils of Solomon's Temple; the ten magnificent marble columns — with a 16th-century Baroque façade — of the Temple of Antoninus and Faustina; the eight columns of the Temple of Saturn (497 BC), site of the Saturnalia, the precursor of the Mardi Gras; three splendid Corinthian columns of the Temple of Castor and Pollux (484 BC); the Temple of Vesta and the nearby House of the Vestal Virgins, where highly esteemed virgins guarded the sacred flame of Vesta and their virginity — under the threat of being buried alive if they lost the latter. The once imposing Basilica of Maxentius (Basilica di Massenzio), otherwise known as the Basilica of Constantine, because it was begun by one and finished by the other, still has imposing proportions: 328 feet by 249 feet. Only the north aisle and three huge arches remain of this former law court and exchange.

As this is one of the most bewildering archaeological sites, a guide is extremely useful, especially for short-term visitors. A detailed plan and portable sound guide are available at the entrance. Closed Tuesdays. Admission fee includes the Palatine Hill. Entrance on Via dei Fori Imperiali, opposite Via Cavour.

Fori Imperiali (Imperial Forums) – Next to the Roman Forum and now divided in two by Via dei Fori Imperiali is the civic center begun by Caesar to meet the demands of the expanding city when the Roman Forum became too congested. It was completed by Augustus, with further additions by later emperors. Abandoned in the Middle Ages, the Imperial Forums were revived by Mussolini, who constructed Via dei Fori Imperiali in 1932.

Two of the major sights are Trajan's Forum and Trajan's Market. Trajan's Forum, although not open to visitors, can be seen from the sidewalk surrounding it. It is memorable for the formidable 138-foot-high Trajan's Column, composed of 19 blocks of marble and unfortunately temporarily covered with scaffolding. The column is decorated with a spiral frieze depicting the Roman army under Trajan during the campaign against the Dacians — some 2,500 figures climbing toward the top where, since 1588, a statue of St. Peter has stood instead of the original one of Trajan. The Market (entered at Via IV Novembre 94) is a three-story construction with about 150 shops and commercial exchanges. Admission fee for Trajan's Market, which is closed Mondays. Via dei Fori Imperiali.

Carcere Mamertino (Mamertine Prison) – Just off Via dei Fori Imperiali between the Roman Forum and the Campidoglio is the prison where Vercingetorix died and where, according to legend, St. Peter was imprisoned by Nero and used a miraculous spring to baptize his fellow inmates. From 509 to 27 BC, it was a state prison where many were tortured and slaughtered. Much later, the prison became a chapel consecrated to St. Peter (called *San Pietro in Carcere*). To Charles Dickens it was a "ponderous, obdurate old prison . . . hideous and fearsome to behold." The gloomy dungeons below, made of enormous blocks of stone, may be the oldest structures in Rome. Via San Pietro in Carcere off Via dei Fori Imperiali.

Pantheon – This, the best preserved of Roman buildings, was built in 27 BC by Agrippa, who probably dedicated it to the seven planetary divinities, and rebuilt by Hadrian in AD 125. It became a Christian church in 606 and contains the tombs of Raphael and the first two kings of Italy. The building is remarkable for its round plan combined with a Greek-style rectangular porch of 16 Corinthian columns (3 were replaced in the Renaissance), for the ingenuity evident in the construction of the dome, and for its balanced proportions (the diameter of the interior and the height of the dome are the same). Piazza della Rotonda.

Terme di Caracalla (Baths of Caracalla) – These are in the southern part of the city, near the beginning of the *Appia Antica*. Built in the 3rd century, they accommodated 1,600 bathers, but all that's left are sun-baked walls and some wall paintings. The vast scale makes a picturesque ruin, however, and Shelley composed his famous *Prometheus Unbound* here. In summer, a stage and bleachers go up and the baths become the site of the Rome Opera's outdoor opera season. Closed Mondays. Enter on Viale delle Terme di Caracalla, just short of Piazzale Numa Pompilio.

Porta San Sebastiano (St. Sebastian Gate) – This majestic opening in the 3rd-century Aurelian Walls (which encircle the city of Rome for 12 miles, with 383 defense towers) marks the beginning of the Appia Antica. Every Sunday morning, guided tours walk along the walls from Porta San Sebastiano to Porta Latina, affording good views of the Baths of Caracalla, the Appia Antica, and the Alban hills in the distance. The *Museo delle Mura* (*Museum of the Walls*), incorporated into the two towers of the gate, contains local archaeological finds.

Via Appia Antica (Appian Way) – Portions of this famous 2,300-year-old road are still paved with the well-laid stones of the Romans. By 190 BC the Appian Way extended all the way from Rome to Capua, Benevento, and Brindisi on Italy's southeastern coast. Although its most famous sights are the Catacombs (see below), many other interesting ruins are scattered along the first 10 miles of the route, which were used as a graveyard by patrician families because Roman law forbade burial (but not cremation) within the walls. Among the sights worth seeing is the *Domine Quo Vadis chapel,* about ½ mile beyond Porta San Sebastiano. This was built in the mid-9th century on the site where St. Peter, fleeing from Nero, had a vision of Christ. St. Peter said "Domine quo vadis?" (Lord, whither goest thou?). Christ replied that he was going back to Rome to be crucified again because Peter had abandoned the Christians in a moment of danger. Peter then returned to Rome to face his own martyrdom. Also see the *Tomb of Cecilia Metella,* daughter of a Roman general, a very picturesque ruin not quite 2 miles from Porta San Sebastiano.

Catacombe di San Callisto (Catacombs of St. Calixtus) – Of all the catacombs in Rome, these are the most famous. Catacombs are burial places in the form of galleries, or tunnels — miles of them, arranged in as many as five tiers — carved underground. Marble or terra cotta slabs mark the openings where the bodies were laid to rest. Early Christians hid, prayed, and were buried in them from the 1st through the 4th century. After Christianity became the official religion of Rome, they were no longer necessary, but they remained places of pilgrimage because they contain the remains of so many early martyrs. St. Cecilia, St. Eusebius, and many martyred popes are buried here. Take a guided bus tour or a public bus. At the catacombs, guides, who are often priests, conduct regular tours in several languages. Closed Wednesdays; admission fee. Via Appia Antica 110.

Terme di Diocleziano (Baths of Diocletian) – West of the center of Rome, not far from the train station, are the largest baths in the empire, built in AD 305 to hold 3,000 people. The site now houses both the *Church of Santa Maria degli Angeli,* adapted by Michelangelo from the hall of the tepidarium of the baths, and the *Museo Nazionale Romano* (*National Museum of Rome*). The museum, one of the great archaeological museums of the world, contains numerous objects from ancient Rome — paintings, statuary, stuccowork, bronzes, art objects, and even a mummy of a young girl. Admission fee to the museum, which is closed Mondays. The church is on Piazza della Repubblica; the museum entrance is on Piazza dei Cinquecento.

Castel Sant'Angelo – Dramatically facing the 2nd-century Ponte Sant'Angelo (St. Angelo Bridge — lined with statues of angels by Bernini), this imposing monument was built by Hadrian in AD 139 as a burial place for himself and his family, but it subsequently underwent many alterations, including the addition of the square wall with bastions at each corner named after the four Evangelists. In its later role as a fortress and prison, it has seen a lot of history, especially in the 16th century: Some of the victims of the Borgias met their end here, popes took refuge from antipapal forces here (an underground passage connects it to the Vatican), and Benvenuto Cellini spent time as a prisoner on the premises. Opera fans also know that the last act of Puccini's *Tosca* takes place here. It is now a museum containing relics, works of art, ancient weapons, and prison cells. Closed Mondays. Admission fee. Lungotevere Castello.

Teatro di Marcello (Theater of Marcellus) – Begun by Caesar, completed by Augustus, and named after the latter's nephew, this was the first stone theater in Rome and was said to have been the model for the Colosseum. It seated from 10,000 to 14,000 spectators and was in use for over 300 years. During the Middle Ages, what remained of the edifice became a fortress, and during the 16th century the Savelli family transformed it into a palace, which later passed to the powerful Orsini family. The sumptuous apartments at the top are still inhabited by the Orsinis, whose device of a bear (*orso*) appears on the gateway in Via di Monte Savello, where the theater's stage formerly stood. Via del Teatro di Marcello. The palace can be visited only with a permit from City Hall: *Comune di Roma,* Ripartizione X, Via del Portico d'Ottavia 29.

Largo Argentina – Just west of Piazza Venezia are the remains of four Roman temples, which, still unidentified, may be the oldest relics in Rome. The area is also home to Rome's largest stray cat colony. Corso Vittorio Emanuele II.

Piramide di Caio Cestio (Pyramid of Caius Cestius) – In the southern part of the city, near the Protestant Cemetery, is Rome's only pyramid. Completely covered with white marble, 121 feet high, it has a burial chamber inside decorated with frescoes and inscriptions. Piazzale Ostiense. The interior can be visited only with special permission from the *Sovrintendenza Comunale ai Musei, Monumenti,* Piazza Caffarelli 3.

PAPAL ROME

Città del Vaticano (Vatican City) – The Vatican City State, the world's second smallest country (the smallest is also in Rome, on Via Condotti), fits into a land area of less than one square mile within the city of Rome. Headquarters of the Roman Catholic Church, the Vatican has been an independent state under the sovereignty of the pope since the Lateran Treaties were concluded in 1929. The Vatican has its own post office and postage stamps (thriving right now with the surrounding Italian post offices functioning so badly — do all your mailing from here!), its own printing press and newspaper (*Osservatore Romano*), its own currency, railway, and radio station. Its extraterritorial rights cover the other major basilicas (Santa Maria Maggiore, San Giovanni in Laterano, and San Paolo fuori le Mura), the pope's summer home at Castel Gandolfo, and a few other buildings. The Vatican is governed politically by the pope and protected by an army of Swiss Guards whose uniforms were designed by Michelangelo.

General audiences are held by the pope every Wednesday at 11 AM year-round on St. Peter's Square; special audiences can be arranged for groups of 25 to 50 persons. Recently, behind-the-scenes tours that take visitors to places in the Vatican ordinarily closed to the public (such as the mosaic school, the radio station, railway terminal, and so on) have been offered. Buy the tickets at the *Vatican Tourist Information Office,* St. Peter's Square.

Piazza San Pietro (St. Peter's Square) – This 17th-century architectural masterpiece was created by Gian Lorenzo Bernini, the originator of the Baroque style in Rome. The vast, open area is elliptical, with two semicircular colonnades, each four deep in Doric columns, framing the façade of St. Peter's Basilica. The colonnades are surmounted with statues of saints. An 83½-foot obelisk, brought from Heliopolis to Rome by Caligula, marks the center of the square and is flanked by two fountains that are still fed by the nearly 4-century-old Acqua Paola aqueduct. Find the circular paving stone between the obelisk and one of the fountains and turn toward a colonnade: From that vantage point it will appear to be made up of only a single row of columns.

Basilica di San Pietro (St. Peter's Basilica) – The first church here was built by Constantine on the site where St. Peter was martyred and subsequently buried. Some 11 centuries later, it was the worse for wear, so renovation and then total reconstruction were undertaken. Michelangelo deserves a great deal of the credit for the existing church, but not all of it: Bramante began the plans in the early 16th century, with the dome of the Pantheon in mind; Michelangelo finished them in mid-century, thinking of Brunelleschi's dome in Florence. Giacomo della Porta took over the project at Michelangelo's death, actually raising the dome by the end of the century. In the early 17th century, Carlo Maderno made some modifications to the structure and completed the façade, and by the middle of the century, Bernini was working on his colonnades. The vast dome of St. Peter's is visible from nearly everywhere in the city, just as the entire city is visible from the summit of the dome. You can go up into the dome by elevator for a fee — then take a staircase to the top for a panoramic view of Rome or a bird's-eye view of the pope's backyard.

The door farthest to the right of the portico is the Holy Door, opened and closed by the pope at the beginning and end of each Jubilee Year, usually only four times a century. The door farthest to the left was done in the 1960s by the contemporary Italian sculptor Giacomo Manzù. Among the treasures and masterpieces inside the basilica are the famous *Pietà* by Michelangelo (now encased in bulletproof glass since its mutilation and restoration several years ago) and the *Baldacchino* by Bernini, a colossal Baroque amalgam of architecture and decorative sculpture weighing 46 tons, as well as the 13th-century statue of St. Peter by Arnolfo Di Cambio, his toes kissed smooth by the faithful. The interior of St. Peter's is gigantic and so overloaded with decoration that it takes some time to get a sense of the whole. Piazza San Pietro.

Musei Vaticani (Vatican Museums) – The Vatican's museum complex houses one of the most impressive collections in the world, embracing works of art of every epoch. It also contains some masterpieces created on the spot, foremost among which is the extraordinary Sistine Chapel, with Michelangelo's frescoes of the Creation on the ceiling (painted from 1508 to 1512) and his Last Judgment on the altar wall (1534–1541). These are currently undergoing extensive restoration, begun in 1980 and expected to last 12 years, but the removal of centuries of soot from some parts has already revealed such a vibrancy in Michelangelo's use of color that a new lighting system is being prepared for the chapel and footnotes are being added to art histories. While Michelangelo was painting the Sistine Chapel ceiling for Pope Julius II, a 25-year-old Raphael was working on the Stanza della Segnatura, one of the magnificent Raphael Rooms commissioned by the same pope, which would occupy the painter until his death. Also part of the Vatican museum complex are the Pio-Clementino Museum of Greco-Roman antiquities, which houses such marvelous statues as *Laocöon and His Sons* and the *Apollo Belvedere;* the Gregorian Etruscan Museum; the Pinacoteca or Picture Gallery; the Library; and the new Gregorian Profane, Pio-Cristiano, and Missionary-Ethnological sectors. Admission fee. Open 9 AM to 2 PM (longer in summer); closed Sundays, except the last Sunday of the month. Admission fee; free the last Sunday of the month. Entrance on Viale Vaticano.

San Giovanni in Laterano (Church of St. John Lateran) – Founded by Pope Melchiades in the 4th century, this is the cathedral of Rome, the pope's parish church, in effect. It suffered barbarian vandalism, an earthquake, and several fires across the centuries, so that its interior was largely rebuilt in the 17th century by Borromini, who maintained the 16th-century wooden ceiling (the principal façade belongs to the 18th century). Older sections are the lovely cloisters, dating from the 13th century, and the baptistry, from the time of Constantine. The adjoining Lateran Palace was built in the 15th century on the site of an earlier one that had been the home of the popes from Constantine's day to the Avignon Captivity and that had been destroyed by fire. In front of the palace and church is the Scala Santa (Holy Stairs), traditionally believed to have come from the palace of Pontius Pilate in Jerusalem and to have been climbed by Christ at the time of the Passion. The 28 marble steps, climbed by worshipers on their knees, lead to the Sancta Sanctorum, once the popes' private chapel (not open to the public, but visible through the grating). Both the chapel and the stairs were part of the earlier Lateran Palace but survived the fire. Also in the piazza is the oldest obelisk in Rome. Piazza di San Giovanni in Laterano.

Santa Maria Maggiore (Church of St. Mary Major) – A 5th-century church, rebuilt in the 13th century, with an 18th-century façade and the tallest campanile in Rome. It has particularly interesting 5th-century mosaics and a ceiling that was, according to tradition, gilded with the first gold to arrive from the New World. Piazza di Santa Maria Maggiore.

PIAZZAS, PALACES, AND OTHER SIGHTS

Piazza del Campidoglio – The Capitoline was the smallest of the original seven hills, but since it was the political and religious center of ancient Rome, it was also the most important. When the need arose in the 16th century for some modern city planning, the task was given to someone worthy of the setting. Thus, the harmonious square seen today, with its delicate, elliptical, star-patterned pavement centered around a magnificent 2nd-century bronze equestrian statue of Marcus Aurelius (removed for restoration), is the design of none other than Michelangelo. The piazza is flanked by palaces on three sides: Palazzo Nuovo and Palazzo dei Conservatori, facing each other and together making up the *Musei Capitolini* (*Capitoline Museums*), and the Palazzo Senatorio, between the two, which houses officials of the municipal government. The Musei Capitolini are famous for an especially valuable collection of antique sculptures, including the *Capitoline Venus,* the *Dying Gaul,* a bronze statue (known as the *Spinario*) of a boy removing a thorn from his foot, and the *Capitoline Wolf,* an Etruscan bronze to which Romulus and Remus were added during the Renaissance. Admission fee for the museums, which are closed Mondays.

Piazza di Spagna – One of the most picturesque settings of 18th-century Rome was named after a palace that housed the Spanish Embassy to the Holy See. The famous Spanish Steps were actually built by the French to connect the French quarter above with the Spanish area below. One of Rome's fine French churches, Trinità dei Monti, hovers over the 138 steps at the top. At the bottom of the steps — which in the spring are covered with hundreds of azaleas — is the Barcaccia fountain, depicting a sinking barge inspired by the Tiber's flooding in 1589. Modern art historians disagree on whether this fountain, the oldest architectural feature of the square, was designed by Pietro Bernini or his son, the famous Gian Lorenzo Bernini. The house where John Keats spent the last three months of his life and died in February 1821 is next to the Spanish Steps at No. 26. It is now the *Keats-Shelley Memorial House,* a museum dedicated to the English Romantic poets, especially Keats, Shelley, Byron, and Leigh Hunt, with a library of more than 9,000 volumes of their works. Admission fee for the museum, which is closed weekends.

Via Condotti – A sort of Fifth Avenue of Rome, lined with the city's most exclusive shops, including *Gucci, Bulgari,* and *Ferragamo.* Only a few blocks long, it begins at the foot of the Spanish Steps, ends at Via del Corso, and is a favorite street for window-shopping and the ritual evening *passeggiata,* or promenade, since it is — like much of the area — closed to traffic. Via Condotti's name derives from the water conduits built under it by Gregory XIII in the 16th century.

One of Via Condotti's landmarks is the famous *Caffè Greco* at No. 86, long a hangout for Romans and foreigners. Among its habitués were Goethe, Byron, Liszt, Buffalo Bill, Mark Twain, Oscar Wilde, and the late Italian painter Giorgio de Chirico. The place is full of busts, statues, and varied mementos of its clientele, and the somber waiters still dress in tails. Another landmark, at No. 68, is the smallest sovereign state in the world, consisting of one historic palazzo. If you peek into its charming courtyard, you'll see cars parked there with number plates bearing the letters SMOM, the initials of the Sovereign Military Order of Malta. Besides its own licenses, the order also issues just a few passports and has its own diplomatic service and small merchant fleet.

Piazza del Popolo – This semicircular square at the foot of the Pincio was designed in neoclassical style by Valadier between 1816 and 1820. At its center is the second oldest obelisk in Rome — dating from the 13th century BC. Twin-domed churches (Santa Maria di Montesanto and Santa Maria dei Miracoli) face a ceremonial gate where the Via Flaminia enters Rome. The piazza's two open-air cafés, *Rosati* and *Canova,* are favorite meeting places.

Piazza Navona – This harmonious ensemble of Roman Baroque is today a favorite haunt of Romans and tourists. It is also one of Rome's most historic squares, built on the site of Domitian's stadium. In the center is Bernini's fine *Fontana dei Fiumi* (*Fountain of the Rivers*), the huge figures representing the Nile, Ganges, Danube, and Plata. On the west side of the square is the church of Sant'Agnese in Agone, much of it the work of a one-time Bernini assistant, Borromini. There was little love lost between the two men, and according to the Romans, the hand of the Plata figure is raised in self-defense, just in case the façade of the church falls down, while the Nile figure hides under a veil to avoid seeing Borromini's mistakes. From the 17th to the mid-19th century, the square was flooded on August weekends, and the aristocrats of the city cooled off by splashing through the water in their carriages. Now, during the Christmas season and until Epiphany, it is lined with booths selling sweets, toys, and Christmas crib figures.

Piazza Farnese – This square is dominated by Palazzo Farnese, the most beautiful 16th-century palace in Rome. Commissioned by Cardinal Alessandro Farnese (later Pope Paul III), it was begun in 1514 by Sangallo the Younger, continued by Michelangelo, and completed by Della Porta in 1589. Opera fans know it as the location of Scarpia's apartment in the second act of Puccini's *Tosca.* Today it is occupied by the French Embassy and can be visited only by special permission. The two fountains on the square incorporate bathtubs of Egyptian granite brought from the Baths of Caracalla.

Piazza Campo dei Fiori – Very near Piazza Farnese, one of Rome's most colorful squares is the scene of a general market every morning. In the center, surrounded by delicious cheeses, salamis, ripe fruit and vegetables, and *fiori* (flowers) of every kind, is a statue of philosopher Giordano Bruno, who was burned at the stake here for heresy in 1600. Watch your wallet — this is a hangout for thieves.

Piazza Mattei – A delightful clearing on the edge of the ancient Jewish ghetto, this small square's famous *Fontana delle Tartarughe* (*Fountain of the Tortoises*), sculpted in 1585 by Taddeo Landini, is one of Rome's most delightful: Four naked boys lean against the base and toss life-size bronze tortoises into a marble bowl above. The water moves in several directions, creating a magical effect in the tiny square.

Piazza del Quirinale – The Quirinal Palace was built by the popes in the late 16th to early 17th century as a summer residence, became the royal palace after the unification of Italy, and is now the official residence of the president of Italy. The so-called *Monte Cavallo* (*Horse Tamers'*) *Fountain* is composed of two groups of statues depicting Castor and Pollux with their horses and a granite basin from the Forum once used as a cattle trough. The obelisk in the center is from the Mausoleum of Augustus. The square affords a marvelous view of Rome and St. Peter's.

Fontana di Trevi (Trevi Fountain) – Designed by Nicola Salvi and completed in 1762, the Trevi Fountain took 30 years to build and is the last important monumental work in the Baroque style in Rome. It is incongruously situated in a tiny square surrounded by narrow, cobblestoned streets, so that one comes upon it, in all its magnificence, all of a sudden, at the turn of a corner. A colossal Oceanus in stone rides a chariot drawn by seahorses and surrounded by a fantasy of gods, tritons, and horses. According to legend, you will return to Rome if you throw a coin over your left shoulder into the fountain. Young Roman men like to congregate in the small square on summer evenings, trying to pick up foreign girls. Some prefer to pick your pocket — so be careful. Piazza di Trevi.

Piazza Barberini – At the foot of Via Veneto, this square in northern Rome has two of Bernini's famous fountains: the *Triton Fountain* in travertine, representing a triton sitting on a scallop shell supported by four dolphins and blowing a conch; and the *Fountain of the Bees* on the corner of the Veneto, with three Barberini bees (of that family's crest) on the edge of a pool spurting thin jets of water into the basin below.

Villa Borghese (Borghese Gardens) – In the northern section of the city, this is the most magnificent park in Rome, with hills, lakes, villas, and vistas. It is the former estate of Cardinal Scipione Borghese, designed for him in the 17th century and enlarged in the 18th century. Rome's zoo is here, as well as two museums: the *Galleria Borghese,* housed in the cardinal's small palace and noted for its Caravaggios, its Bernini sculptures, and Antonio Canova's statue of the reclining *Pauline Borghese;* and the *Galleria Nazionale d'Arte Moderna,* with its Italian modern works. The Villa Borghese is a wonderful place to sit in the shade of an umbrella pine on a hot summer day: Enter through the Porta Pinciana, at the top of Via Veneto, or through the Pincio, which it adjoins. The main entrance is at Piazzale Flaminio, just outside the Porta del Popolo.

Cimitero Protestante (Protestant Cemetery) – In the southern part of the city, behind the pyramid of Caius Cestius, the Protestant Cemetery is principally a foreign enclave that harbors the remains of many adopted non-Catholics who chose to live and die in Rome: Keats, Shelley, Trelawny, Goethe's bastard son, and the Italian Communist leader Gramsci. There is nothing sad here — no pathos, no morbid sense of death — and few gardens are so delightful on a spring morning. Via Caio Cestio 6.

MODERN ROME

Monumento a Vittorio Emanuele II (Monument to Victor Emmanuel II) – Sometimes called the Vittoriano, this most conspicuous landmark of questionable taste was completed in 1911 to celebrate the unification of Italy. Built of white Brescian marble and overshadowing the surrounding mellow tones of old Rome in size, it is often derided by Romans as the "wedding cake" or the "typewriter." It contains Italy's Tomb of the Unknown Soldier from World War I, and the top affords a view of the network of modern boulevards built by Mussolini to open out the site of ancient Rome: Via dei Fori Imperiali, Via di San Gregorio, Via del Teatro di Marcello, and Via Nazionale — a busy and somewhat chaotic shopping street leading to the railroad station. Turn your back to the monument, and note the 15th-century Palazzo Venezia to your left. It was from the small balcony of this building, his official residence, that Mussolini made his speeches. Piazza Venezia.

Via Vittorio Veneto – Popularly known as Via Veneto, this wide, tree-lined street winds from Porta Pinciana down past the American Embassy to Piazza Barberini. The portion around Via Boncompagni is lined with outdoor cafés; however, the once elegant street now attracts a mixed bunch — from down-and-out actors and decadent Roman nobility to seedy gigolos and well-to-do American tourists and businesspeople staying in the fine hotels nearby. The entire area, including adjacent Via Bissolati, is heavily guarded by police after several recent terrorist attacks.

Porta Portese – Rome's flea market takes place on the edge of Trastevere on Sunday mornings from dawn to about 1 PM. It's a colorful, chaotic happening. Genuine antiques are few and far between, quickly scooped up before most people are out of bed. Still, you'll find some interesting junk, secondhand clothes, pop records, used tires and car parts, black market cigarettes — everything from Sicilian puppets to old postcards, sheet music, and broken bidets. Some say that if your wallet is stolen at the entrance, you'll find it for sale near the exit. Via Portuense.

OUT OF TOWN

Esposizione Universale di Roma (EUR) – Mussolini's ultramodern quarter was designed southwest of the center for an international exhibition that was supposed to have taken place in 1942 but never did. It's now a fashionable garden suburb and the site of international congresses and trade shows as well as of some remarkable sports installations built for the Olympic games of 1960, including the Palazzo dello Sport, with a dome by Pier Luigi Nervi. EUR also has some interesting museums, such as the *Museo della Civiltà Romana* (*Museum of Roman Civilization*), worth seeing for its thorough reconstruction of ancient Rome at the time of Constantine. Admission fee for the museum, which is closed Mondays. Piazza Giovanni Agnelli 10.

Ostia Antica – This immense excavation site about 15 miles southwest of Rome was once the great trading port of ancient Rome, much closer to the mouth of the Tiber than it is today. Fairly recently uncovered, the ruins are picturesquely surrounded with pines and cypresses. They have not had much chance to crumble and they reveal a great deal about the building methods of the Romans.

A visit takes about half a day. Among the chief sites are the Piazzale delle Corporazioni (Corporations' Square), once 70 commercial offices, with mottoes and emblems in mosaics revealing that the merchants here were caulkers, ropemakers, furriers, and shipowners from all over the ancient world; the capitolium and forum, baths, apartment blocks, and several private houses, especially the House of Cupid and Psyche; and the restored theater, used in the summer for classical plays in Italian translation. Recent excavations have uncovered evidence of the town's Jewish community. Take the Decumanus Maximus to the end, turn left, and a few hundred yards away, on what was once the seashore, a synagogue stands, a moving testimonial to the Jewish presence in Rome in earliest times. A local museum traces the development of Ostia Antica and exhibits some outstanding statues, busts, and frescoes. Closed Mondays. Admission fee. To reach Ostia Antica, take the *metropolitana* (not all trains, however) from Stazione Termini, a train from Stazione Ostiense, an ACOTRAL bus from Via Giolitti, a car, or even a boat (see "Getting Around," *Sources and Resources*).

The *Lido di Ostia* or *Lido di Roma* is 2½ miles southwest of Ostia. It's the most popular, most polluted, and most crowded seaside resort in the vicinity of the city. There are more pleasant beaches both north and south of Rome.

Castelli Romani – Rome's "castles" are actually 13 hill towns set in the lovely Alban Hills region southeast of Rome, an area where popes and powerful families of the past built fortresses, palaces, and other retreats. The mountains, the volcanic lakes of Nemi and Albano, chestnut groves, olive trees, and vines producing the famous Castelli wine continue to make the area a favorite destination of Romans who want to get away from the city on a summer day. Particularly charming are *Frascati,* known for its villas and its wines; *Grottaferrata,* famous for its fortified monastery; beautiful *Lake Nemi,* with its vivid blue waters and wooded surroundings, where Diana was worshiped; and *Monte Cavo,* a mountain whose summit can be reached by a toll road and which offers a panorama of the Castelli from a height of 3,124 feet. The Castelli Romani are best seen on an organized tour or by car. (For more information and a suggested itinerary, see *Lazio* in DIRECTIONS.)

■ **EXTRA SPECIAL:** Fountain fans should not miss *Tivoli,* a charming town perched on a hill and on a tributary of the Tiber (the Aniene) about 20 miles east of Rome. It's famous for its villas, gardens, and, above all, cascading waters — all immortalized by Fragonard's 18th-century landscapes. Called *Tibur* by the ancient Romans, it was even then a resort for wealthy citizens, who bathed in its thermal waters, which remain therapeutic to this day.

The *Villa d'Este,* built for a cardinal in the 16th century, is the prime attraction — or rather, its terraced gardens are. They contain some 500 fountains, large and small, including the jets of water lining the famous Avenue of the Hundred Fountains and the huge Organ Fountain, so named because it once worked a hydraulic organ. The villa and gardens are open daily for a fee; on summer nights the fountains are beautifully illuminated, and there's a a sound-and-light show. Nearby, the *Villa Gregoriana,* built by Pope Gregory XVI in the 19th century, has sloping gardens and lovely cascades (which are best on Sundays, since most of the water is used for industrial purposes on other days), but it is definitely to be seen only after you have seen the Villa d'Este. It, too, is open daily for a fee.

Only 4 miles southwest of Tivoli is the *Villa Adriana* (*Hadrian's Villa*), the most sumptuous of the villas left from ancient Roman times. It was built during AD 125–134 by the emperor Hadrian, whose pleasure was to strew the grounds with replicas of famous buildings he had seen elsewhere in his empire. Extensively excavated and surrounded by greenery, the ruins of the villa include the Maritime Theater, built on an island and surrounded by a canal; the Golden Square in front of the remains of the palace; and the Terrace of Tempe, with a view of the valley of the same name. There are statues, fountains, cypress-lined avenues, pools, lakes, and canals. Closed Mondays. Admission fee. You can see Tivoli with a guided tour or take an ACOTRAL bus from Via Gaeta or a train from Stazione Termini. Villa Adriana is also reachable by bus from Via Gaeta, but note that while one bus, leaving every hour, stops first at Villa Adriana and then at Tivoli, the other, leaving every half hour, goes directly to Tivoli and entails getting off at a crossroads and walking about a half mile to Villa Adriana.

SOURCES AND RESOURCES

 TOURIST INFORMATION: The *Ente Provinciale per il Turismo* for Rome and Lazio, headquartered at Via Parigi 11 (phone: 461851), has its main information office at Via Parigi 5 (phone: 463748), with branches at Stazione Termini and at Leonardo da Vinci Airport at Fiumicino. There are also branches at the Salaria Ovest and Frascati Est service areas of the A1 and A2 highways for those arriving by car. The *US Embassy and consulate* are at Via Vittorio Veneto 119/A and 121, respectively (phone: 46741).

For some good background material about Rome, see Georgina Masson's *Companion Guide to Rome* and Eleanor Clark's *Rome and a Villa,* both delightfully amusing. A locally published book on the city's hidden treasures, *In Rome They Say,* by Margherita Naval, is also good reading. There are several English-language bookstores in the Spanish Steps area: the *Lion Bookshop,* Via del Babuino 181, *Anglo-American Book Company,* Via della Vite 57, the *Economy Book Center,* Piazza di Spagna 29, and the *Bookshelf,* Via Due Macelli 23 (in the Tritone Gallery).

Local Coverage – The *International Courier* is an English-language daily newspaper published in Rome and available at most newsstands. Consult *This Week in Rome* or *A Guest in Rome* for varied information on theaters, galleries, and special exhibitions; *Wanted in Rome* contains classified ads, some coverage of local events, and advice.

Telephone – The telephone prefix for Rome is 06.

GETTING AROUND: Airports – *Leonardo da Vinci Airport at Fiumicino,* about 21 miles from downtown Rome, handles both international and domestic traffic (phone: 60121). The trip by taxi takes about 45 minutes and costs roughly 40,000 lire (from Fiumicino to Rome, double the charge shown on the meter; from Rome to Fiumicino, a supplement of 12,500 lire is added to the meter charge; additional costs for baggage and night or holiday trips). ACOTRAL buses run between the airport and the city air terminal on the Via Giolitti side of Stazione Termini, the central railway station. Buses leave every 15 minutes and cost approximately 4,500 lire. *Ciampino Airport* handles mostly charter traffic (phone: 4694). A taxi ride into Rome takes 30 minutes and costs about 25,000 lire. ACOTRAL buses leave the airport every 30 minutes for Cinecittà, where you pick up the subway to Rome. *Urbe Airport* is for private planes; it's a 15-minute taxi ride from the center, and public transport (by bus) is also available. Via Salaria 825 (phone: 8120524).

Bicycle and Moped – Rent a bike at *I Bike Rome,* Lungotevere Marzio 3 (phone: 6543394). To rent a moped or scooter, try *Scoot-a-long,* Via Cavour 302 (phone: 6780206), or *Motonoleggio,* Via della Purificazione 66, near Piazza Barberini (phone: 465485).

Boat – From April through October, weather permitting, the *Tiber I* carries 150 passengers on a cruise along the river from Ponte Marconi in Rome to Ostia Antica, the ancient port of Rome. The return is by bus. For reservations, phone *Tourvisa* at

493483 or 4950284 or the *Associazione Amici del Tevere* (*Friends of the Tiber Society*) at 6370268.

Bus – *ATAC* (*Azienda Tramvie e Autobus Comune di Roma*), the city bus company, is the backbone of Rome's public transportation system (phone: 4695). Buses — and a few tram lines — run frequently throughout the city, particularly through the center, and fares are still among the cheapest in Europe. But beware — most central routes are extremely crowded, getting off where you'd like is sometimes impossible, pickpockets are rampant, and service after midnight or 1 AM is not nearly as frequent or ubiquitous as day service. Tickets, which currently cost 700 lire, must be purchased before boarding and are available at certain newsstands, tobacco shops, and bars. Remember to get on the bus via the back doors, stamp your ticket in the machine, and exit via the middle doors (the front doors are used only by *abbonati* — season ticketholders). Visitors can save money by buying books of 10 tickets, half-day tickets, or full-day tickets. Weekly tourist tickets and route maps are sold at the ATAC information booth in Piazza dei Cinquecento. Bus service to points out of town is run by ACOTRAL, including buses to Leonardo da Vinci Airport at Fiumicino (phone: 57531). The Rome telephone directory's *TuttoCittà* supplement lists every street in the city and contains detailed maps of each zone as well as postal codes, bus routes, and local taxi stands.

Car Rental – Major car rental firms such as *Avis,* Via Sardegna 38/A (phone: 4701228), *Europcar,* Via Lombardia 7 (phone: 547811), and *Hertz,* Via Sallustiana 28 (phone: 549921), as well as several reliable Italian companies such as *Maggiore,* Via Po 8/A (phone: 851620), have offices in the city and at the airport and railway stations. Note that gas stations close at lunchtime and at 7 PM in winter, 7:30 PM in summer. Most are closed Sundays. Self-service stations operate with 10,000-lire notes.

Subway – The *metropolitana,* Rome's subway, consists of two lines. The new line, Linea A, opened in 1980, runs roughly east–west, from an area close to the Vatican, across the Tiber, through the historic center (Piazza di Spagna, Piazza Barberini, Stazione Termini), and to the eastern edge of the city just past Cinecittà. Linea B, which is partly an underground and partly a surface railroad and has been in operation since the 1950s, runs north–south, from Stazione Termini, to the Colosseum, and down to the southern suburb of EUR. The fare is 700 lire; subway entrances are marked by a large red *M.*

Taxi – Cabs can be hailed or found at numerous stands, the locations of which are listed in the yellow pages with their phone numbers. The *Radio Taxi* telephone numbers are 3570, 3875, 4994, and 8433. Taxi rates are increasing regularly, and drivers are obliged to show you, if asked, the current list of added charges. After 10 PM, a night charge is added, and there are surcharges on holidays and for suitcases. By taxi, the trip between Rome and Leonardo da Vinci Airport at Fiumicino (about 21 miles) takes about 45 minutes. From Fiumicino to Rome, the charge is double the meter; from Rome to Fiumicino, pay the meter plus 12,500 lire.

Train – Rome's main train station is *Stazione Termini* (phone: 4775 for information; 110 for reservations). There are several suburban stations, but the visitor is unlikely to use them, except *Stazione Ostiense,* from which trains depart for Ostia Antica and the Lido di Ostia.

MUSEUMS: Many museums are described in *Special Places.* The following is a list of additional museums of interest, including some churches not to be overlooked because of their artistic value.

Villa Giulia – A remarkable Etruscan collection housed in a 16th-century villa by Vignola. Piazzale di Villa Giulia 9.

Galleria Nazionale d'Arte Antica (National Gallery of Ancient Art) – Paintings by Italian artists from the 13th to the 18th century, plus some Dutch and Flemish works. Palazzo Barberini, Via delle Quattro Fontane 13.

Galleria Spada – Renaissance art and Roman marble work from the 2nd and 3rd centuries. Palazzo Spada, Piazza Capo di Ferro 13.

Galleria Doria Pamphili – The private collection of the Doria family, Italian and foreign paintings from the 15th to the 17th century. Palazzo Doria, Piazza del Collegio Romano 1/A.

Museo Nazionale d'Arte Orientale (National Museum of Oriental Art) – Pottery, bronzes, stone, and wooden sculpture from the Middle and Far East. Via Merulana 248.

Museo di Roma (Museum of Rome) – Paintings, sculptures, and other objects illustrating the history of Rome from the Middle Ages to the present. Piazza San Pantaleo 10.

Museo di Palazzo Venezia – Tapestries, paintings, sculpture, and varied objects. Via del Plebiscito.

Galleria Colonna – The Colonna family collection of mainly 17th-century Italian paintings. Palazzo Colonna, Via della Pilotta 17.

Sant'Agostino (Church of St. Augustine) – A 15th-century church containing the *Madonna of the Pilgrims* by Caravaggio and the *Prophet Isaiah* by Raphael. Piazza di Sant'Agostino.

Sant'Andrea al Quirinale (St. Andrew at the Quirinale) – A Baroque church by Bernini, to be compared with Borromini's church on the same street. Via del Quirinale.

San Carlo alle Quattro Fontane (St. Charles at the Four Fountains) – A small Baroque church by Borromini, it was designed to fit into one of the pilasters of St. Peter's. Via del Quirinale, corner Via delle Quattro Fontane.

San Clemente – An early Christian basilica with frescoes and a remarkable mosaic. Piazza di San Clemente.

San Luigi dei Francesi (St. Louis of the French) – The French national church, built in the 16th century and containing three Caravaggios. Piazza San Luigi dei Francesi.

Santa Maria d'Aracoeli (St. Mary of the Altar of Heaven) – A Romanesque-Gothic church with frescoes by Pinturicchio and a 14th-century staircase built in thanksgiving for the lifting of a plague. Piazza d'Aracoeli.

Santa Maria in Cosmedin – A Romanesque church known for the *Bocca della Verità* (*Mouth of Truth*) in its portico — a Roman drain cover in the shape of a face that, according to legend, will bite off the hand of anyone telling a lie. Piazza della Bocca della Verità.

Santa Maria sopra Minerva (St. Mary over Minerva) – Built over a Roman temple, with (unusual for Rome) a Gothic interior and frescoes by Filippino Lippi. Piazza della Minerva.

Santa Maria del Popolo (St. Mary of the People) – Early Renaissance architecture, a Baroque interior, and two masterpieces by Caravaggio. Piazza del Popolo 12.

Santa Maria in Trastevere – An ancient church, the first in Rome dedicated to the Virgin, with 12th- and 13th-century mosaics. Piazza Santa Maria in Trastevere.

Santa Maria della Vittoria (St. Mary of the Victory) – Baroque to the core, especially in Bernini's Cornaro Chapel. Via XX Settembre.

San Pietro in Vincoli (St. Peter in Chains) – Erected in the 5th century to preserve St. Peter's chains, this church contains Michelangelo's magnificent statue of Moses. Piazza di San Pietro in Vincoli.

Santa Sabina – A simple 5th-century basilica, with its original cypress doors and a 13th-century cloister and bell tower. Piazza Pietro d'Illiria.

 SHOPPING: Like Florence and Milan, Rome is a wonderful place to shop. You'll find the great couturiers here, many of whom have boutiques, and most important Italian firms have branches here. The best buys are in leather goods, jewelry, fabrics, shoes, and sweaters.

The chic-est shopping area is around the bottom of the Spanish Steps, beginning with the elegant Via Condotti, which runs east to west and is lined with Rome's most exclusive shops, such as *Gucci, Bulgari,* and *Ferragamo.* Running parallel to Via Condotti are several more streets with fashionable boutiques, such as Via Borgognona (*Fendi,* more *Gucci, Versace, Missoni,* and *Testa*), Via delle Carrozze, Via Frattina (for costume jewelry, lingerie, and some ceramics), Via Vittoria, and Via della Croce (known particularly for its delicious delicatessens) — most closed to traffic. All of these streets end at Via del Corso, the main street of Rome, which runs north to south and is lined with shops carrying the latest fashions in shoes, handbags, and sportswear, particularly along the stretch between Piazza del Popolo and Largo Chigi, where Via del Tritone begins. There are some fine shops along Via del Tritone, Via Sistina, and in the Via Veneto area.

On the other side of the river toward the Vatican are two popular shopping streets that are slightly less expensive, Via Cola di Rienzo and Via Ottaviano. Also less expensive and more central is Via Nazionale, near the railroad station. For inexpensive new and secondhand clothes, visit the daily market on Via Sannio, near San Giovanni, and the flea market on Sunday mornings at Porta Portese. For old prints and odds and ends, try the market at Piazza della Fontanella Borghese, every morning except Sundays; antiques can be found along Via del Babuino, Via dei Coronari, Via Margutta, and Via Giulia.

The following are but a few recommended shops in Rome:

Alexander – An outstanding boutique for women. Piazza di Spagna 49–50.

Annette – Knitwear in American sizes. Piazza di Spagna 35.

Anticoli – A good place for sweaters. Via del Corso 333 and Via del Tritone 133.

Giorgio Armani – High fashion for men and women. Via del Babuino 102.

Bertè – Old and new toys. Piazza Navona 107–111.

Laura Biagiotti – Elegant women's wear. Via Vittoria 30.

Bises – A place for fine fabrics. Via del Gesù 93. Bises' *Boutique Uomo,* for men, is at Via del Gesù 54.

Bomba e De Clercq – Exclusive sweaters and blouses with handcrafted details. Via dell'Oca 39, behind Piazza del Popolo.

Borsalino – World-renowned hats. Via IV Novembre 157/B.

Buccellati – An expensive jeweler specializing in Florentine silver, gold jewelry, and antiques. Via Condotti 31.

Bulgari – One of the world's most famous high-style jewelers, offering fabulous creations in gold, silver, platinum, and stones. Via Condotti 10.

Roberta di Camerino – Women's wear, handbags, umbrellas, and other items. Piazza di Spagna 30.

Capodarte – The latest styles in shoes and boots, many with matching bags. Via Sistina 14/A.

Coin – Newest and most fashionable of Rome's comparatively small department stores. Good boutique wear, leather goods, knits, gifts. Piazzale Appio, near the San Giovanni metro station. *Coin Lei,* Viale Libia, is for women only.

Di Cori – A good place for gloves. Piazza di Spagna 53 and Via del Tritone 52.

Croff Centro Casa – Household supplies and gifts, some of Italian design and some imports. Via Cola di Rienzo 197, Via Tomacelli 137, and Via XX Settembre 52.

Fendi – Canvas and leather bags, baggage, and clothing. Via Borgognona 39; shoes at Via Borgognona 4/E.

Ferragamo – For high-style women's shoes. Via Condotti 66.

Gianfranco Ferre – High fashion for women. Via Borgognona 42/B.

Filippo – An avant-garde boutique with fairly reasonable prices. Via Borgognona 7 bis and Via Condotti 6.

Fiorucci – Famed, funky sportswear and shoes. Via Genova 12, Via della Farnesina 19, Via Nazionale 236, and Via della Maddalena 27.

Forlani – A friendly, small boutique for women, with reasonable prices. Via del Lavatore 92, near Trevi Fountain.

Fornari – Fine silver and other gifts. Via Frattina 71–72.

Maud Frizon – Very original shoes for women, with corresponding prices. Via Borgognona 38.

Nazareno Gabrielli – Leather goods. Via Sant'Andrea delle Fratte 3–5 and Via Borgognona 29.

Galtrucco – All kinds of fabrics, especially silks. Via del Tritone 23.

Gucci – Famous for men's and women's shoes, luggage, handbags, and other leather goods. Via Condotti 8 and Via Borgognona 25 (the latter belongs to a Gucci son and is younger in style).

Krizia – Elegant women's boutique. Piazza di Spagna 11/B.

Laurent – Good buys in leatherwear. Via Frattina 3.

Lio Bazaar – Amusing women's shoes. Via Borgognona 35.

Maccalè – Yet another fine boutique for women. Via della Croce 69.

Bruno Magli – Top-quality shoes and boots of classical elegance. Via Veneto 70, Via del Gambero 1, and Via Cola di Rienzo 237.

Miranda – Colorful women's woven shawls and jackets. Via delle Carrozze 220.

Missoni – High-fashion knitwear. Via Borgognona 38/B. *Missoni Uomo,* for men, is at Piazza di Spagna 78.

Ottica Scientifica – Eyeglasses and contact lenses fitted by one of Rome's best and most scrupulous optometrists; camera supplies also. Via delle Convertite 19, near Piazza San Silvestro.

Carlo Palazzi – Creative, high-quality fashions for men. Via Borgognona 7/C.

Pineider – Italy's famed stationer. Via Due Macelli 68–69 and Piazza Cardelli.

Polidori – Exclusive menswear and tailoring. Via Condotti 84 and Via Borgognona 4/C; fabrics at Via Borgognona 4/A.

Ramirez – Latest shoe fashions at reasonable prices. Via del Corso 73 and Via Frattina 85/A.

Rinascente – One of Rome's few department stores, sometimes offering good buys. Piazza Colonna and Piazza Fiume.

Sabatini – Best buys on film and camera equipment, catering to the professional photographer. Via Germanico 166/A (downstairs).

Salato – For famous-make Italian men's and women's shoes at reasonable prices. Via Veneto 104 and 149 and Piazza di Spagna 34.

Sansone – Italy's largest selection of Italian and imported luggage, trunks, and travel bags. Repairs and custom designs. Via XX Settembre 4.

Al Sogno Giocattoli – Toys, including huge stuffed animals. Piazza Navona 53.

Spazio Sette – Elegant design products from Italy, Scandinavia, and other places; gifts for those who have everything. Via Santa Maria dell'Anima 55, behind Piazza Navona.

Testa – Offbeat, resort, and casual clothes for men. Via Borgognona 13 and Via Frattina 104–106.

Trimani – Rome's oldest wine shop. Via Goito 20.

Trussardi – Fine handbags, luggage, and leather clothing. Via Bocca di Leone 27.

Valentino – Bold, high-fashion clothes for men and women. Via Condotti 13 for men, Via Bocca di Leone 15–18 for women; haute couture salon at Via Gregoriana 24.

Mario Valentino – Fine shoes and leather goods. Via Frattina 58 and 84.

I Vergottini – Beauty products by Milan's famed hair stylist. Via del Lavatore 44 (phone: 6780784 for hair appointment).

Gianni Versace – Another name in high fashion. Via Borgognona 41 and Via Bocca di Leone 29.

SPECIAL EVENTS: The events of the church calendar — too numerous to mention here — are extra special in Rome. For *Natale* (Christmas), decorations go up around the city, churches display their *presepi* (nativity scenes), and a colorful toy and candy fair begins in Piazza Navona. The season, including the fair, lasts until *Epiphany,* January 6, when children receive gifts from a witch known as the Befana to add to those that Babbo Natale (Father Christmas) or the Bambino Gesù (Baby Jesus) brought them at Christmas. The intervening *Capodanno* (New Year's) is celebrated with a bang here, as in much of the rest of Italy — firecrackers snap, crackle, and pop from early evening, and at midnight, all manner of old, discarded objects come flying out of open windows. (Don't be on the street!) During the *Settimana Santa* (Holy Week), the city swarms with visitors. Religious ceremonies abound, particularly on Good Friday, when pilgrims, on their knees, climb the Scala Santa at St. John Lateran, and the pope conducts the famous *Via Crucis* (*Way of the Cross*) procession between the Colosseum and the Palatine Hill. At noon on Easter Sunday, the pope pronounces the *Urbi et Orbi* blessing in St. Peter's Square. The day after Easter is *Pasquetta* (Little Easter), when Romans usually go out to the country for a picnic. The arrival of spring is celebrated in April with a colorful display of potted azaleas covering the Spanish Steps; in May, a picturesque street near the Spanish Steps, Via Margutta, is filled with an exhibition of paintings by artists of varied talents. (The Via Margutta art fair is repeated in the fall.) In May, too, Villa Borghese's lush Piazza di Siena becomes the site of the *International Horse Show,* and soon after that is the *International Tennis Championship* at Foro Italico. An antique show also takes place along the charming Via dei Coronari (near Piazza Navona), and there's an *International Rose Show* at the delightful Roseto di Valle Murcia on the Aventine Hill. In late May or June, the vast *Fiera di Roma,* a national industrial exhibition, takes place at the fairgrounds along Via Cristoforo Colombo. In mid-July the *Festa di Noiantri* is celebrated in one of Rome's oldest quarters, Trastevere. This is a great pagan feast, involving plenty of eating, music, and fireworks — as filmed by Fellini in his surrealistic/realistic *Roma.*

There are also innumerable characteristic *feste* or *sagre* (the latter meaning "consecrations," usually of some local food or beverage at the height of its season) in the many hill towns surrounding Rome. One especially worth a visit is the *Sagra dell'Uva* (consecration of the grape), the first Sunday in October at Marino, where residents celebrate the new vintage by selling grapes from stalls set up in the quaint old streets and by running wine instead of water in the fountain in the main square! Another happening worth seeing is the *Infiorata* at Genzano di Roma. On a Sunday in mid-June, a brightly colored carpet of beautifully arranged flowers is laid along the entire Via Livia. Both towns are about 15 miles south of Rome in the *Castelli Romani* (see "Out of Town" in *Special Places*).

SPORTS AND FITNESS: Auto Racing – The *Autodromo di Roma* (Valle Lunga racetrack), Campagnano di Roma, Via Cassia, km 34 (phone: 9041027). Take a bus from Castro Pretorio.

Fitness Centers – Try the *Aldrovandi Health Center* at the *Aldrovandi Hotel,* Via Ulisse Aldrovandi 15 (phone: 841091), or the *American Aerobic Association,* Via Giovanni Amendola 5 (phone: 4754496), run by a former Jane Fonda Workshop instructor.

Golf – Both the *Circolo del Golf Roma,* Via dell'Acqua Santa 3 (phone: 783407), about 8 miles from the center, and the *Olgiata Golf Club,* Largo Olgiata 15 (phone: 3788004), about 12 miles, have 18-hole courses and extend guest privileges to members of foreign clubs. Both closed Mondays.

Horseback Riding – For lessons at various levels of proficiency, rentals by the hour (sometimes a subscription for several hours is required), or guided rides in the country, contact the *Circolo Ippico Appia Antica,* Via Appia Nuova, km 16.5 (phone: 600197), *Società Ippica Romana,* Via dei Monti della Farnesina 30 (phone: 3966214), *Circolo Ippico del Tebro,* Via Tiberina 198 (phone: 6912974), or *Circolo Buttero Fontana Nuova,* near Sacrofano, outside Rome (phone: 9036040).

Horse Racing – Trotting races take place at the *Ippodromo Tor di Valle,* Via del Mare, km 9 (phone: 6564129). Flat races take place at the *Ippodromo delle Capanelle,* Via Appia Nuova, km 12 (phone: 7993143), in the spring and fall.

Jogging – The best place for running is the *Villa Borghese;* enter at the top of Via Veneto or from Piazza del Popolo.

Soccer – Rome boasts two highly competitive teams, *Roma* and *Lazio,* which play regularly on Sundays from September to May at the *Stadio Olimpico,* Foro Italico (phone: 36851).

Swimming – The pools at the *Cavalieri Hilton,* Via Cadlolo 101 (phone: 3151), and the *Aldrovandi,* Via Ulisse Aldrovandi 15 (phone: 841091), are open to nonguests for a fee. Public pools include the *Piscina Olimpica* at Foro Italico (phone: 3608591, 3601498) and the *Piscina delle Rose* at EUR (phone: 5926717). The beach nearest Rome is at Ostia, and it's polluted, very crowded, and strung from end to end with bathing establishments charging a fee for entry and use of changing rooms. There are stretches of free beach at *Castel Fusano* and *Castel Porziano,* southeast of Ostia; the first is reachable by subway from Stazione Termini (not all trains). *Fregene,* farther north along the coast, is very popular with fashionable (and mostly topless) Romans. There's also swimming at *Lake Bracciano,* about 20 miles north of Rome.

Tennis – Most courts belong to private clubs. Those at the *Cavalieri Hilton,* Via Cadlolo 101 (phone: 3151), and at the *Sheraton Roma,* Viale del Pattinaggio (phone: 5453), are open to nonguests for a fee. There are public courts at the *Foro Italico* (phone: 3619021).

Windsurfing – Windsurf boards and lessons are available at *Castel Porziano* (*primo cancello,* or first gate); at the *Stabilimento La Baia* (phone: 6461647) and the *Miraggio Sporting Club* (phone: 6461802) in Fregene; and at the *Centro Surf Bracciano* (phone: 9024568) at Lake Bracciano.

THEATER: During the theater season, approximately October through May, check *This Week in Rome* for listings. Most theater in Italian consists of revivals of the classics (including English and French classics in translation) and some avant-garde works. The principal theaters are the *Teatro Eliseo,* Via Nazionale 183 (phone: 462114), the *Teatro Argentina,* Largo Argentina 52 (phone: 6544601), and the *Teatro Quirino,* Via Minghetti 1 (phone: 6794585). To see something in English, check the *Workshop Theater* at St. Paul's American Church (Anglican-Episcopal), Via Napoli 58, and *Alla Ringhiera,* Via dei Riari 81 (phone: 6568711). A season of classical drama (in Italian and sometimes in Greek) is held in July each year in the open-air *Teatro Romano di Ostia Antica* (phone: 5651913). *Teatro Sistina,* Via Sistina 129 (phone: 4756841), is Rome's best music hall, offering top-class, often imported musical entertainment Monday nights, when the regular rep is resting (in the fall, they usually run top-name Brazilian entertainment Monday nights). For films in English, check the newspapers for *Cinema Pasquino,* Vicolo del Piede in Trastevere (phone: 5803622).

MUSIC: For current schedules, check *This Week in Rome.* The regular opera season at the *Teatro dell'Opera,* Piazza Beniamino Gigli 1, corner Via Firenze (phone: 461755, 463641), runs from December through May, and during July and August there is a summer opera season at the *Baths of Caracalla.* (Tickets for the latter are on sale at the Teatro dell'Opera box office or, on the day of performance, at Caracalla.) The *Rome Ballet Company* also performs at the

Teatro dell'Opera. Rome's RAI symphony orchestra, one of four orchestras run by Radiotelevisione Italiana, the state television network, holds its concert season at the *Auditorio del Foro Italico,* Piazza Lauro de Bosis 28 (phone: 390713), from October to June. In roughly the same months, the venerable *Accademia Nazionale di Santa Cecilia* gives first-class concerts with international guest artists, either at the *Auditorio Santa Cecilia,* Via della Conciliazione 4 (phone: 6541044), or at the smaller *Sala Concerti* (Concert Hall), Via dei Greci 18 (box office at Via Vittoria 6; phone: 6790389). In July and August, there's an outdoor season at the Campidoglio. Also between October and May, the *Accademia Filarmonica Romana* sponsors a series of concerts at the *Teatro Olimpico,* Piazza Gentile da Fabriano 17 (phone: 3962635) — its summer season is held in the garden at its headquarters, Via Flaminia 118 (phone: 3601752) — and the *Istituzione Universitaria dei Concerti* holds concerts at the *Auditorium San Leone Magno,* Via Bolzano 38 (phone: 3964777), and at the university's *Aula Magna.* From November to April, there are concerts at *Auditorio del Gonfalone,* Via del Gonfalone 32 (phone: 655952), and around Rome by *Coro Polifonico Romano.* Still other musical groups use the *Teatro Ghione,* Via delle Fornaci 37 (phone: 6372294). Finally, there are concerts in many, many churches throughout the year, and music festivals — classical, jazz, pop, and folk — outdoors in the parks and piazzas during the summer. For jazz and other modern music in clubs, see *Nightclubs and Nightlife* below.

NIGHTCLUBS AND NIGHTLIFE: Night spots are born and die so quickly, slip into and out of fashion so easily, it is best to inquire at your hotel about what is currently popular. At the moment, the most fashionable are the *Open Gate,* Via San Nicola da Tolentino 4 (phone: 4750464); *Isteria,* Via Giovannelli 12 (phone: 864587); and *Jackie O',* Via Boncompagni 11 (phone: 461401). Both Jackie O' and Open Gate are also restaurants, but be prepared to spend. *Bella Blu,* Via Luciani 21 (phone: 3608840), is also elegant, somewhat calmer, with a small, pricey restaurant. The *Acropolis* (formerly *Much More*), at Via Luciani 52 (phone: 870504), *Piper '80,* at Via Tagliamento 9 (phone: 854459), *Executive Club,* at Via San Saba 11/A (phone: 5782022), and *Super Sonic,* at Via Ovido 17 (phone: 6548435), are preferred by the younger set, punks and teenagers generally. The Acropolis has an all-night restaurant; the Piper features a different event (video, breakdance, fashion shows, etc.) every evening; the Executive admits women for free on Wednesdays and Sundays; and the Super Sonic is especially new wave (it even has wavy floors!), with super-popular Thursday night parties. *La Makumba,* Via degli Olimpionici 19 (phone: 3964392), jumps with African, Caribbean, and Latin rhythms, as does *Dorian Gray,* Piazza Trilussa 41 (phone: 5818685). *Gil's,* Via Romagnosi 11/A (phone: 3611348), is also rather exotic, but only in decor. A special summer treat is the *Apollonia,* near the Via Appia Antica at Via Tor Carbone 41 (phone: 7990680), where you can dine, dance, and swim in the pool. *Easy Going,* Via della Purificazione 9 (phone: 4745578), is for gays, as are the *St. James,* Via Campania 37/A (phone: 493706), *Angelo Azzurro,* Via Cardinale Merry del Val (phone: 5800472), *L'Alibi,* Via di Monte Testaccio 44 (phone: 5782343), and the new *Oscar Club,* near Piazza del Popolo at Via Principessa Clotilde 11 (phone: 3610284), a rather New York–style combination of art gallery, bar, and restaurant that opens at 5 PM daily and for Sunday brunch (noon to midnight). Of these, the St. James, the first gay place in Rome, is the most traditional, with a jacket-and-tie atmosphere. You may be asked to pay a "membership fee" in some Rome clubs or may be refused entry altogether if the doorman doesn't like your looks.

Other clubs include *Il Veleno,* Via Sardegna 27 (phone: 493583), decorated in mock-ancient-Roman style with marblelike columns; *Fonclea,* Via Crescenzio 82/A (phone: 353066), which is also a beer hall with board games and a restaurant; *La Cage aux*

Folles, Via Gregoriana 9 (phone: 6790490); *Club 84,* Via Emilia 84 (phone: 4742205); *L'Incontro,* a disco and piano bar at Via della Penna 25 (phone: 3610934); the *Cavalieri Hilton*'s *La Pergola* roof garden, Via Cadlolo 101 (phone: 3151); and *New Life,* Via XX Settembre 90–92 (phone: 4740997). The *Hostaria dell'Orso* has a disco upstairs (*La Cabala*) and a quiet comfy piano bar (*Blue Bar*) with guitarists on the main floor. At *L'Arciliuto,* an intimate musical salon and bar in what is reputed to be Raphael's old studio on Piazza Montevecchio, a pianist accompanies the owner–guitarist–lutist–music historian, whose repertoire includes ancient madrigals, classic Neapolitan love songs, and current Broadway hits. There are several other bars with music but no dancing, such as the very yuppy *Hemingway,* Piazza delle Coppelle 10, near the Pantheon (phone: 6544135), which has tables outdoors in good weather; *Privilege,* Via San Nicola da Tolentino 22 (phone: 4746888); *Le Nane,* Via Paolo Mercuri 21 (phone: 6545132); *Birdland,* Passeggiata di Ripetta 33 (phone: 6786312); *Reginé,* Via del Moro 21; *Aldebaran,* Via Galvani 54; *La Privé,* Via della Penna, behind Piazza del Popolo; the *Tartarughino,* Via della Scrofa, which is also a very chic restaurant; *Cappello a Cilindro,* Via del Vantaggio 47; and several hotels and cafés in the Via Veneto area, such as the *Eden Hotel*'s *Roof Garden Bar,* the *White Elephant, George's,* and the *Hotel Aldrovandi* across the park. *Manuia,* Vicolo del Cinque 54–56 in Trastevere (phone: 5817016), is a restaurant as well as a piano bar that traditionally has live Brazilian music.

The most fashionable spots for the predinner *aperitivo* are the *Caffè Greco* or the *Baretto* on Via Condotti, *Rosati* or *Canova* on Piazza del Popolo, and *Harry's Bar, Carpano,* the *Café de Paris, Doney's,* or others on Via Veneto. Currently *alla moda* also is the little *Bar della Pace* on Piazza della Pace behind Piazza Navona, which is frequented by vendors from the nearby market in the morning and prelunch period, and then later in the day (until 3 AM) by all types from artists and filmmakers to punks and politicians who, when the little marble tables fill up, rest their drinks and their bottoms on cars parked in the square.

After dinner, a lot of Italians converge at the tiny, busy Piazza Sant'Eustachio, where the *Bar Eustachio* serves what is reputed to be the best coffee in town (but this is more an Italian-style espresso bar where a quick coffee is downed while standing, more a shot of caffeine than cause for lingering). Then, on summer evenings, the after-dinner crowd often moves toward one of the many *gelaterie* in Rome, some of which are much more than ice cream parlors, since they serve exotic long drinks and *semifreddi* (like the famous *tartufo* at Piazza Navona's *Tre Scalini*), and a few have lovely gardens and even live music. *Selarum,* Via dei Fienaroli 12, and *Fassi,* Corso d'Italia 45, have both gardens and music. Perhaps the best-known *gelateria,* however, is *Giolitti,* Via degli Uffici del Vicario, not far from Piazza Colonna (closed Mondays). Others are the *Gelateria della Palma,* at the corner of Via della Maddalena and Via delle Coppelle, and *Fiocco di Neve,* Via del Pantheon 51 (both near the Pantheon); *Gelateria Sahara,* Piazza San Pancrazio 17–18, in Trastevere; and *Biancaneve,* Piazza Pasquale Paoli 1, where Corso Vittorio Emanuele II meets the Lungotevere dei Fiorentini. Favorites in the Parioli residential district are *Gelateria Duse* (also called *Giovanni*), Via Eleonora Duse 1/D; *Bar Gelateria Cile,* Piazza Santiago del Cile 1–2; and the nearby *Giardino Ferranti,* Via Giovanni Pacini 29.

For an open-air nightcap, the Piazza Navona bars are popular; a rather seedier late-night bunch hangs out at Piazza del Pantheon; while tourists, tarts, and gigolos stake their claims to various vantage points along Via Veneto. For a late-night snack, there are plenty of places, some with music, poetry readings, video, or other attractions. Most popular are *Le Cornacchie,* Piazza Rondanini 53, *La Poeteca,* Vicolo dei Soldati 47, *Chef du Village,* Via del Governo Vecchio, and *Amarcord,* Via del Boschetto 73. Open to about midnight are *Il Calice,* Via dei Delfini 20, and *Il Calisé,* Via Col di Lana 14–16. Others are *Gamela Vini,* Via Frangipani 35, *Cul de Sac,* Piazza Pasquino,

Spaghetti House, Via Cremona 5/A, and *Coffee Shop No Stop,* Piazza Euclide 43 in Parioli.

Folk music can be heard at the *Folkstudio,* Via Gaetano Sacchi 3 in Trastevere (phone: 5892374), *El Trauco,* Via Fonte dell'Olio 5 (phone: 5895928), and *Le Cabanon* (see *Eating Out*). Jazz is the thing at *Music Inn,* Largo dei Fiorentini 3 (phone: 6564934), *Mississippi Jazz Club,* Borgo Angelico 16 (phone: 6540348), *Saint Louis Music City,* Via del Cardello 13/A (phone: 4745076), *Tusitala,* Via dei Neofiti (phone: 6783237), *Alexanderplatz,* Via Ostia 9 (phone: 3599398), *Big Mama,* Vicolo San Francesco a Ripa 18 (phone: 582551), and the *Billie Holiday Jazz Club,* Via degli Orti di Trastevere 43 (phone: 5816121). Roman music can be heard at the supper clubs *Fantasie di Trastevere,* Via di Santa Dorotea 6 (phone: 5892986), *Da Meo Patacca,* Piazza dei Mercanti 30 (phone: 5816198), and *Da Ciceruacchio,* Via del Porto 1 (phone: 580-6046), all in the heart of Trastevere. If you're curious about cabaret in Italian, go to *Il Bagaglino* (*Salone Margherita*), Via Due Macelli 75 (phone: 6791439), or *Il Puff,* Via Gigi Zanazzo 4 (phone: 5810721). The city's English-speaking community frequents the *Fiddler's Elbow,* near Santa Maria Maggiore, the *Falcon,* near Piazza Barberini, and the *Little Bar,* Via Gregoriana 54/A.

 SINS: Although prostitution was declared illegal in 1958, that law, like most laws in Italy, has been blatantly ignored. The *bordelli* closed down, sending most *prostitutes* (more vulgarly called *puttane*) out on the streets with less medical control — so be careful. Call girls, or *ragazze squillo,* can often be procured with the help of your friendly hotel *portiere* or those freelance, multilingual tour guides who hang around the better hotels soliciting customers. Some can be found sitting alone at the tables of the more popular cafés near the top of Via Veneto. (An Italian lady would never sit alone, so don't worry about making a great gaffe.) Sit next to her, or tactfully solicit assistance from a smiling waiter. The best streetwalkers' beat is the lower part of Via Veneto; Via Sistina and Via Francesco Crispi are less expensive. Pretty prohibitive (though not in price) are the girls (some as ancient as their surroundings) along the streets circling the Baths of Caracalla, along the Via Appia Antica, and on the truck routes leading into the city. They often keep warm and attract potential customers by building bonfires along the road.

Unlike prostitution, *gluttony* is not illegal; it can be enjoyed indoors or outdoors, and it is probably Rome's most popular sin. So by all means, do as the Romans do, and gorge yourself on the Italian ice cream in Piazza Navona, comparing the famous *tartufo* at *Tre Scalini* with the *gelati* of *Giolitti* near Piazza Colonna. And whatever you do, don't miss out on *fettuccine all'Alfredo,* which is hard to beat for calories — pasta plus cream plus butter plus cheese. Enjoy it now; you can diet later.

BEST IN TOWN

 CHECKING IN: Of the more than 500 hotels in Rome, the following are recommended either for some special charm, location, or bargain price in their category. Those without restaurants are noted, although all serve an optional breakfast, and all have heating and telephones in the rooms unless otherwise stated. You'll pay from $140 to more than $300 for a double room with bath in the hotels listed as expensive, from $75 to $140 in the moderate category, and under $75 (as low as $30) in the inexpensive category.

Cavalieri Hilton International – Far from the historic center of Rome, at the top of a lovely hill (Monte Mario) overlooking much of the city, with shuttle buses to Via Veneto and Piazza di Spagna running hourly during shopping hours. But the swimming pool is especially desirable in summer, and the rooftop restaurant,

La Pergola, has been gathering high praise from food critics. A resort hotel with year-round swimming, tennis, sauna, and other diversions, it has 400 rooms. Via Cadlolo 101 (phone: 3151). Expensive.

Eden – Among the most elegant in Rome, this hotel has excellent service, an intimate roof garden restaurant, and a panoramic bar. There are 116 air conditioned rooms with TV. Via Ludovisi 49 (phone: 4743551). Expensive.

Excelsior – Big, bustling, but efficient, it dominates Via Veneto, next to the US Embassy. It's a favorite with Americans, and the bar is a popular meeting place. There are 394 rooms in this member of the CIGA chain. Via Vittorio Veneto 125 (phone: 4708). Expensive.

Le Grand Hotel et de Rome – The pride of the CIGA chain in Rome and tradition-ally the capital's most dignified hotel, the Grand is truly grand — formal, well run, and elegant in style and service. It has 175 rooms and a central location, although not exactly the "right address," between the railroad station and the Via Veneto area. Via Vittorio Emanuele Orlando 3 (phone: 4709). Expensive.

Hassler–Villa Medici – Perched at the top of the Spanish Steps and within easy striking distance of the best shopping in Rome, favored by a loyal clientele. Although it's not quite as deluxe as a decade ago, each of the 101 rooms has a certain charm. The roof garden restaurant has one of the city's most splendid views. Piazza Trinità dei Monti 6 (phone: 6792651). Expensive.

Lord Byron – A small (47 rooms) first-rate hotel in the fashionable Parioli residential district, this was once a private villa, and it maintains the atmosphere of a private club. It has a good restaurant, *Le Jardin* (see *Eating Out*). Via Giuseppe de Notaris 5 (phone: 3609541). Expensive.

Sheraton Roma – Rome's largest hotel (622 rooms) opened in the early 1980s and sprawls over the modern suburb of EUR, an area that was originally developed by Mussolini for a world's fair and is connected to the center of town by bus and subway. The hotel has full 24-hour room service (rare in Italy), a piano bar, swimming pool, tennis courts, and sauna. Viale del Pattinaggio (phone: 5453). Expensive.

Aldrovandi – This quiet hotel in a fashionable residential area next to the Villa Borghese and not far from Via Veneto has a delightful park with a swimming pool and a full-facility health club. No restaurant; 139 rooms. Via Ulisse Aldrovandi 15 (phone: 841091). Moderate.

Anglo-Americano – Just off Piazza Barberini, it has 115 rooms, and the back ones look out on the garden of Palazzo Barberini. Via delle Quattro Fontane 12 (phone: 472941). Moderate.

Atlas – On a street made famous by World War II, with 40 recently renovated rooms and a flowered roof garden. It has no restaurant but enjoys a central location. Via Rasella 3 (phone: 462140, 4757739). Moderate.

Cardinal – On Renaissance Rome's most stately street, this restored palace (at-tributed to Bramante) is convenient for exploring some of the city's hidden treas-ures but not for shopping in the city center. No restaurant; 66 rooms. Via Giulia 62 (phone: 6542719). Moderate.

Cicerone – This is in the residential and commercial area of Prati on the Vatican side of the river, but convenient nevertheless because it's just across from Piazza del Popolo and the Spanish Steps. It has modern and spacious public areas, 237 well-appointed guestrooms, friendly, attentive service, and a large garage. Via Cicerone 55/C (phone: 3576). Moderate.

Eliseo – Just off Via Veneto, this has traditional furnishings (with a slightly French air) in the public rooms and in some of the 50 guestrooms; others are super-modern. A panoramic roof restaurant looks out over the tops of the umbrella pines in the Villa Borghese. Via di Porta Pinciana 30 (phone: 460556). Moderate.

Flora – At the top of Via Veneto right next to the Villa Borghese, the *Flora* is traditional, reliable, and not without charm. It has 177 rooms. Via Vittorio Veneto 191 (phone: 497821). Moderate.

Forum – Built around a medieval tower in the middle of the Imperial Forums, this charming 82-room hotel is a bit out of the way but worth any inconvenience for the spectacular view of ancient Rome from its roof garden. Via Tor de' Conti 25 (phone: 6792446). Moderate.

D'Inghilterra – Extremely popular with knowledgeable travelers, it has numbered Anatole France and Ernest Hemingway among its many illustrious guests. It's very near the Spanish Steps and the central shopping area. No restaurant; 105 rooms. Via Bocca di Leone 14 (phone: 672161). Moderate.

Nazionale – Another old favorite (of Sartre and de Beauvoir, among others), its 78 rooms are very central, next to the Chamber of Deputies, between Via del Corso and the Pantheon. Piazza Montecitorio 131 (phone: 6789251). Moderate.

Parco dei Principi – This modern hotel is on the edge of Villa Borghese in the Parioli residential district, not far from Via Veneto. It has 203 rooms and a small swimming pool in a lovely garden. Via Gerolamo Frescobaldi 5 (phone: 841071). Moderate.

Raphael – Behind Piazza Navona, it's a favorite of Italian politicians (it's near the Senate and the Chamber of Deputies), but it has been slipping lately. It has 85 rooms. Largo Febo 2 (phone: 6569051). Moderate.

La Residenza – An exceptional bargain on a quiet street just behind Via Veneto. With only 27 recently renovated and luxurious rooms, it feels much more like a private villa than a hotel. Book well in advance. No restaurant. Via Emilia 22 (phone: 6799592). Moderate.

Sitea – Gianni de Luca and his Scottish wife, Shirley, have bestowed the coziness of a private home on their 40-room, 5-floor hotel opposite the *Grand*. Rooms have high ceilings, crystal chandeliers, and hand-painted Florentine dressers. Other amenities: sitting rooms, a sun-drenched penthouse bar, and a rustic dining room with a rooftop view. Via Vittorio Emanuele Orlando 90 (phone: 4751560). Moderate.

Gregoriana – On the street of the same name — high fashion's headquarters in Rome — this tiny gem attracts the fashionable. Its decor is reminiscent of art deco, with room letters (rather than numbers) by 1930s fashion illustrator Erté. No restaurant; 19 rooms. Via Gregoriana 18 (phone: 6794269 or 6797988). Moderate to inexpensive.

Degli Aranci – This small, quiet hotel in the Parioli residential district has 42 rooms. No restaurant. Via Barnaba Oriani 11 (phone: 805250). Inexpensive.

Carriage – Another small inn (24 rooms) without a restaurant, this is on the picturesque street where the grand touring carriages (*carrozze*) of the 18th century were cleaned and repaired. It's a mere hop from the Spanish Steps, but it's beginning to get a little tacky. Via delle Carrozze 36 (phone: 6795166). Inexpensive.

Columbus – This 107-room hotel in a restored 15th-century palace is right in front of St. Peter's. Antique furniture, paintings, and a garden add a lot of atmosphere for the price. Via della Conciliazione 33 (phone: 6565435). Inexpensive.

Dinesen – Off Via Veneto and next to the Villa Borghese, the 24 rooms in this charming hotel are a real bargain. No restaurant. Via di Porta Pinciana 18 (phone: 4754501, 460932). Inexpensive.

Fontana – A recently restored 13th-century monastery next to the Trevi Fountain, with 28 cell-like rooms — some facing the fabulous fountain — and a lovely rooftop bar. Piazza di Trevi 96 (phone: 6786113). Inexpensive.

King – The 75 rooms in this well-positioned hotel are reasonably priced. No restaurant. Via Sistina 131 (phone: 4741515). Inexpensive.

Margutta – Try for the two rooms on the roof, complete with fireplaces and surrounded by a terrace. This 21-room hotel is near Piazza del Popolo. No restaurant. Via Laurina 34 (phone: 6798440). Inexpensive.

Sant'Anselmo – This is a beflowered bargain in a small villa on the Aventine Hill. It has about two dozen rooms and a family atmosphere, but no restaurant. Piazza di Sant'Anselmo 2 (phone: 573547). Inexpensive.

Scalinata di Spagna – Spectacularly placed overlooking the Spanish Steps, it's opposite the deluxe *Hassler.* No restaurant and no phones in the 14 rooms. Piazza Trinità dei Monti 17 (phone: 679-3006). Inexpensive.

 EATING OUT: The ancient Romans, not exactly known for their culinary conservatism, were the originators of the first fully developed cuisine of the Western world. Drawing on an abundance of fine natural ingredients from their Mediterranean backyard, and inspired by influences from Greece and Asia Minor, they evolved a gastronomic tradition still felt in the kitchens of Europe today.

While the lavish and exotic banquets of exaggerated proportions described in detail by Roman writers such as Petronius and Pliny no doubt existed, they were relatively infrequent and probably more a vulgar show of *nouveaux riches* than typical examples of local custom. The old nobility, then as now, must have found such conspicuous consumption in poor taste, and, in fact, the beginnings of genuine Roman gastronomic traditions were more likely among the humble masses.

Today nothing resembles Roman cooking more than real Roman people — robust and hearty, imbued with a total disregard for tomorrow. There's no room in the popular Roman philosophy of *carpe diem* ("seize each day as it comes") for concern about cholesterol or calorie counting or preoccupations with heartburn, hangovers, or garlic-laden breath. These considerations disappear before a steaming dish of fragrant *fettuccine,* deep-fried *filetti di baccalà* (strips of salt cod), or *fagioli con le cotiche* (white haricot beans slowly stewed with thick slices of pork rind) — all accompanied by the abundant wines of the surrounding hill towns, the Castelli Romani (which cannot possibly produce the quantity available in Roman *trattorie* — so if a first sip of the house wine isn't quite right, buy a bottled wine). Other Roman specialties to sample are *saltimbocca alla romana* (which means literally "jump in the mouth," because it's so tasty), *scaloppine* of veal covered with sage and ham and simmered in Marsala wine; and *abbacchio al forno,* milk-fed baby lamb roasted whole with garlic and rosemary, or *abbacchio brodettato,* lamb cooked in a sauce of egg yolks and lemon juice, or *scottadito,* "finger-burning" tiny grilled lamb chops. On festive occasions, tender suckling pig (*porchetta*) is stuffed with herbs, roasted, thickly sliced, and sold at stands on the streets with rough-textured crusty bread. Otherwise, pork usually takes the form of ham (*prosciutto*) or sausages (*salami, salsicce*). Then there is rabbit (*coniglio*), kid (*capretto*), fowl and game of all sorts, and all the entrails of animals — such as lamb's heart (*coratella*), sweetbreads (*animelle*), tripe (*trippa*), and kidneys (*rognoni*) — with which the Romans do wonders.

Pasta dishes include the incredibly simple *spaghetti alla carbonara* (with salt pork, eggs, plenty of black pepper, and Rome's pungent *pecorino* cheese), *bucatini all'-amatriciana* (a form of thick spaghetti in a tomato sauce with onions, bacon, and more *pecorino*), *penne all'arrabbiata* (short pasta in a tomato and garlic sauce "rabid" with hot peppers), and the familiar *fettuccine all'Alfredo* (handmade strips of egg pasta in a butter, cream, and Parmesan cheese sauce).

Fresh seasonal vegetables, which are often treated as a separate course, provide the base for many a savory antipasto, accompany the main dish, and are even munched raw — for instance, *finocchio al pinzimonio* (fennel dipped into the purest olive oil seasoned with salt and pepper) — after a particularly heavy meal to clean the palate.

Several local greens are unknown to visitors, such as *agretti, bieta, cicoria,* and *broccolo romano* — the last two often boiled briefly and then sautéed with olive oil, garlic, and hot red peppers. Salad ingredients include the red *radicchio,* crunchy *puntarelle* (served with an anchovy and garlic dressing), bitter arugula, or rocket (called *rughetta* in Rome), and the juicy tomatoes so cherished during the sultry summer months when they are served with ultra-aromatic basil — the sun's special gift to Mediterranean terraces and gardens. Tomatoes are also stuffed with rice and roasted; yellow, red, and green sweet peppers, eggplant, mushrooms, green and broad beans, and zucchini are favorite vegetables for antipasto; while asparagus and artichokes are especially prized in season. The latter are stuffed with herbs and garlic, boiled, and served with olive oil seasoning *alla romana,* or opened out like flowers and deep-fried *alla giudia* (Jewish style). Then there are beans (*fagioli*), lentils (*lenticchie*), and chickpeas (*ceci*), which often accompany pork dishes or are combined with pasta for a hearty soup.

After such a meal, Romans normally have fresh fruit for dessert, although there is no shortage of sweet desserts (such as *montebianco, zuppa inglese,* and, of course, ice cream). For a final *digestivo,* several bottles are often brought to the table. They may include *sambuca romana* (it has an aniseed base), *grappa* (made from the third and fourth grape pressing and normally over 60 proof!), and some sort of *amaro* (which means "bitter," but is more often quite sweet). Fancier restaurants suggest whiskey or chilled Russian or Polish vodka. Whew!

A visit to Rome can be gastronomically limited to tasting Roman fare. But as the capital of Italy, the Eternal City has long collected cultural tribute from the rest of the peninsula, and almost all gastronomic roads of Italy lead to Rome. The country's many regional cuisines may all be sampled within the confines of the 3rd-century Aurelian Walls that enclose the old city — from the tomato-laced specialties of Naples and the garlic-filled dishes of Sicily to the creamy fare of Bologna and the light rice dishes of Venice and the Friuli region.

It is possible to have a full meal, including house wine, for as little as $6 in a modest restaurant, while the same fare may cost twice that amount if the restaurant is even marginally fashionable. Most dining is à la carte, although a *menu turistico* (a selection of a few fixed-price meals) is offered at some unpretentious *trattorie* for very reasonable prices. Less expensive still are the quick-service, often cafeteria-style, *rosticcerie* and *tavole calde* (literally "hot tables"). Most café-bars serve sandwiches as well as that delicious and filling health snack *frullato di frutta* (a mixture of frothy liquidized fruit and milk), which is as inviting as a swim on a hot summer day. Be careful when ordering fresh fish or Florentine steaks *al kilo* — by weight — as this may swell a bill way out of proportion, even at average-priced restaurants. Dinner for two (with wine) costs from $50 to more than $100 in restaurants classed as expensive; $25 to $45 in moderate restaurants; and $15 to $25 in those listed as inexpensive.

Il Bacaro – A tiny, exclusive gastronomic refuge with a total seating capacity of 20. Innovative cuisine is accompanied by an intelligent selection of wines (let the staff choose the wines for each course). The unwritten menu changes daily but usually includes *originalissimi* homemade pasta dishes such as *tortelli di magro ai peperoni* (pasta stuffed with greens and ricotta cheese and served in an amazingly delicate sauce of sweet peppers). Open evenings only; closed Sundays. Reservations a must. Via degli Spagnoli 27 (phone: 6564110). Expensive.

Le Cabanon – French and Tunisian food are served in an intimate ambience accompanied by Mediterranean melodies sung by the well-traveled owner, Enzo Rallo. South American or Francophile singers ably fill in the gaps. The usual onion soup and *escargots,* as well as a delicious Tunisian *brik à l'oeuf* (a pastry concealing a challengingly dripping egg within), couscous, and *merguez* sausages are among the choices. Open evenings only, late; closed Sundays and August. Reservations advisable. Vicolo della Luce 4 (phone: 5818106). Expensive.

Il Cardinale – In a restored bicycle shop off the stately Via Giulia, decorated in a cozy turn-of-the-century style, this eatery produces such fine dishes as *timballo di maccheroni in crosta dolce* (baked pasta in a pastry shell) and *aliciotti con l'indivia* (an anchovy and endive dish), as well as good *soufflé alla francese.* Closed Sundays and August. Reservations necessary. Via delle Carceri 6 (phone: 6569336). Expensive.

Carmelo alla Rosetta – Carmelo is as Sicilian as the fish he flies in daily from Mazara del Vallo, Sicily, and his small *trattoria,* disguised as a fishing boat, smells of salt water and sun, with just a hint of garlic. Not only does he manage to find some of the best oysters in Italy, but his chef grills, fries, boils, or bakes to perfection any — or a mixture of all — of the fish and seafood available. He also whips up a mean *pappardelle al pescatore* (wide noodles in a garlicky, piquant tomato sauce with mussels, clams, and parsley). Closed Sundays, Mondays at lunchtime, and August. Reservations advisable. Via della Rosetta 9 (phone: 6561002). Expensive.

Alberto Ciarla – Alberto, long an impassioned diver and spearfisherman, is another restaurateur who knows where to find the fresh fish that's at such a premium in Rome. Following a recent visit to the Far East, he now also offers several raw fish dishes (the polluted Mediterranean all around does not inspire confidence) and is constantly trying new recipes to adorn his top-quality ingredients. Some work, and some do not. The *pasta e fagioli,* a bean soup, does not mate well with seafood, for instance, but some of his herb sauces are a welcome change from the more usual ways of preparing Italy's favorite food. In good weather, there's al fresco dining on a little piece of a Trastevere street. Open for dinner only. Closed Sundays. Reservations advisable. Piazza San Cosimato 40 (phone: 5818668). Expensive.

Cucurucu – Delightful gardens overlooking the Tiber provide one of Rome's most pleasant summer settings for dining al fresco, while inside it's cozy and rustic. The *antipasti* are good, and so are the meats grilled on an open fire. Ask for *bruschetta con pomodori* (toasted country bread smothered in fresh tomatoes and oregano) and *insalata di rughetta* (a salad of Rome's deliciously bitter arugula, in summer only). Closed Mondays. Via Capoprati 10 (phone: 354434, 382592). Expensive.

Girarrosto Toscano – Brightly lit and bustling, a perfect place for indecisive but hungry nonlinguists. There's little opportunity here to choose from the Tuscan menu, or to speak at all. If you don't say no, you'll be brought various salamis, prosciutto, and fresh ricotta cheese, followed by some *fettuccine al prosciutto,* at which point you'll be asked about a main course. Simply nod positively and you'll probably be served a sizzling Florentine steak grilled to perfection. The rest is perfect, too, but this is not a restful place. Closed Wednesdays and 2 weeks between late July and early August. Reservations necessary. Via Campania 29 (phone: 493759). Expensive.

Le Jardin – This is a rare oasis of quiet and refinement in an increasingly chaotic city. The ambience is sheer elegance, the result of a combination of antiques and top modern Italian design — not to mention the white-gloved gentlemen who serve with perfect professionalism. The menu — light nouvelle cuisine, Italian style — includes such dishes as flan of watercress with scallops, pasta with quail and wild porcini mushrooms, and fresh sturgeon with white wine and mussels, and the fanciful wine list offers poetic descriptions along with an invitation to re-create the true art of living. Since this is one of Rome's most expensive restaurants, one comes expecting perfection, and although there has been some quibble lately about the food (a question of faint praise), one is not gravely disappointed. Closed Sundays. Reservations necessary. *Hotel Lord Byron,* Via Giuseppe de Notaris 5 (phone: 3609541). Expensive.

Papà Giovanni – Giovanni's son Renato now runs the show with great aplomb, though the service often leaves much to be desired. It's small and intimate, with paintings and wine bottles lining the walls, and the bar is very well stocked — sip a kir as an *aperitivo* while choosing from over 700 wines. The cuisine is basically refined Roman, with truffles a seasonal specialty. Try *panzerotti al tartufo* (small ravioli with truffles) and *stufatino alla romana* (colorful Roman beef stew served on a hot king-size plate). Closed Sundays and August. Reservations necessary. Via dei Sediari 4 (phone: 6565308). Expensive.

Il Pianeta Terra – A new entry on the Roman gastronomic scene, this Planet Earth comes close to paradise. A young couple, a Tuscan and a Sicilian, has created an elegant and rustic, traditional yet adventurous dining place in the heart of Rome. Starters such as ravioli stuffed with sea bass in a pistachio sauce or pasta with clams and broccoli lead to exciting main courses such as the pigeon stuffed with artichokes or with oysters and clams, and to delicate desserts such as carrot cake with chocolate and almonds. The wine list is intelligent. Open evenings only; closed Mondays and from mid-July through August. Reservations necessary. Via Arco del Monte 94–95 (phone: 6569893). Expensive.

Pino e Dino – A southerner and a northerner have created a menu of exciting regional dishes, from the robust *pasta e broccoli alla calabrese* (for women diners it's served with a delicate rose) to *capretto abruzzese arrosto* (roast Abruzzi kid). The restaurant is on one of Rome's more picturesque squares, but a summer meal *all'aperto* is only slightly more enticing here than a cozy winter meal indoors surrounded by wine bottles and artisan products from all over Italy. The two boys can be terribly touchy, so don't arrive late for your reservation. Closed Mondays and most of August. Piazza di Montevecchio 22 (phone: 6561319). Expensive.

San Luigi – Another new addition to the Roman scene, off the beaten track on the Vatican side of the river. Softly lit and cozy, refined yet homey, this is a family affair: Giuliana, *la mamma,* brought from her Neapolitan home some patrician and peasant recipes, a creative gastronomic streak, and a few sons and others to keep it *in famiglia.* The cuisine is not, however, strictly southern, nor even strictly Italian, and the innovative menu changes constantly. Open for dinner only; closed Sundays, August, and Christmas holidays. Reservations. Via Mocenigo 10 (phone: 350912). Expensive.

Taverna Giulia – Authentic Genoese cuisine, with the addition of a few French dishes, is featured here, in the heart of Renaissance Rome (at the end of Via Giulia). *Crostini al salmone* (smoked salmon canapés) make a good starter, followed by *trenette al pesto* (thin noodles in a sauce of fresh basil, garlic, pine nuts, and olive oil) and *stinco al forno* (roast shoulder of veal in a flaky pastry shell). There are a few outdoor tables during the summer. Closed Sundays and August. Reservations advisable. Vicolo dell'Oro 23 (phone: 6569768, 6564089). Expensive.

El Toulà – One of Rome's best for more than two decades. The decor is elegant: softly lit warm browns and beiges, antique paintings, fresh flowers, and deep chairs. The cuisine is international, but the regional (Venetian) dishes outshine all others — and the simpler the better. Try the *risotto nero di seppie* (a rice dish black with cuttlefish ink), *radicchio di Treviso ai ferri* (grilled red lettuce), and *gigot alla menta* (roast lamb with mint sauce). There's an impressive wine list. Closed Saturdays at lunch, Sundays, and August. Reservations necessary. Via della Lupa 29/B (phone: 6781196). Expensive.

Alvaro al Circo Massimo – Let Alvaro suggest what's best that day and you'll not go wrong, whether it's fresh fish, game such as *fagiano* (pheasant) or *faraona* (guinea hen), or mushrooms (try grilled porcini). The ambience is rustic indoors, and there are tables outdoors during the summer. Reservations are generally not necessary. Closed Mondays. Via dei Cerchi 53 (phone: 6786112). Expensive to moderate.

La Majella – On a delightful square colorfully illuminated in the summer for outdoor dining, this efficient organization with delicious food owes its fame and popularity to owner-manager Signor Antonio. The pope, while still a cardinal, was among his clientele, and the menu is nearly as long as the Bible. Fresh seafood is the major attraction. Closed Sundays and a week in August. Reservations advisable. Piazza Sant'Apollinare 45 (phone: 6564174). Expensive to moderate.

Osteria dell'Antiquario – This small hostelry on a picturesque little square along the antique shop–lined Via dei Coronari prides itself on genuine Roman fare, well prepared with the finest seasonal ingredients. Closed Sundays. Reservations advisable. Piazza San Simeone 27 (phone: 659694). Expensive to moderate.

Piccolo Mondo – Not exactly a "find," this cheerful and busy restaurant behind Via Veneto has been popular with Italians and foreigners for years. Among the many varied *antipasti* displayed at the entrance are exquisite *mozzarellini alla panna* (small balls of fresh buffalo's milk cheese swimming in cream) as well as eggplant and peppers prepared in several tempting ways. The good-natured waiters ply you with far too many tastes of different pasta dishes, leaving little hope of arriving at a main course. There are tables on the sidewalk in good weather. Closed Sundays and most of August. Reservations recommended. Via Aurora 39 (phone: 4754595). Expensive to moderate.

Piperno – A summer dinner outdoors on this quiet Renaissance *piazzetta* next to the Palazzo Cenci — which still reeks "of ancient evil and nameless crimes" — is sheer magic. Indoors it is modern and less magical, and the classic Roman-Jewish cooking can be a bit heavy. *Pasta e ceci* (pasta and chickpea soup) is always good, and the great specialty is *fritto vegetariano* (zucchini flowers, mozzarella cheese, salt cod, rice and potato balls, and artichokes — the latter *alla giudia,* Jewish style — all individually deep fried, the artichokes golden brown, crisp, and crackling). Closed Mondays and August. Reservations necessary. Monte de' Cenci 9 (phone: 6540629). Expensive to moderate.

Taverna Flavia – It's been fashionable with the film world, journalists, and politicians for over 30 years. Owner Mimmo keeps their autographed pictures hanging on the walls, and the *Sardi's* style survives, despite the crash of "Hollywood-on-the-Tiber" more than a decade ago. This is fun for the would-be trendy, and it's open until quite late. Closed Sundays and August. Reservations necessary. Via Flavia 9–11 (phone: 4745214). Expensive to moderate.

Da Zorzetto – Distinguished northern (Veneto) cuisine with a few international additions, a quiet ambience, and friendly service. Start with an antipasto of *bresaola* or *soppressa veneta* or with the exceptional rice dish *risotto alla Zorzetto.* Fish or frogs' legs if available, game in season, and pepper steak or thinly sliced *carpaccio* (raw beef) are other good bets. Try a house wine from Venice's low-lying region, Tocai white or Cabernet red. Closed Sundays. Reservations recommended. Via Flavia 63–65 (phone: 486487). Expensive to moderate.

Dal Bolognese – Strategically set next to the popular *Caffè Rosati* on Piazza del Popolo and with a menu nearly as long as the list of celebrities who frequent this fashionable eatery. It's run by two brothers from Bologna. Although the food quality has been slipping lately, star-gazers will still enjoy such specialties as homemade *tortelloni* (pasta twists stuffed with ricotta cheese) and the *bollito misto* (boiled beef, tongue, chicken, pig's trotter). There are tables outdoors in good weather. Closed Mondays and most of August. Reservations necessary. Piazza del Popolo 1 (phone: 3611426). Moderate.

La Campana – This unprepossessing place is favored by everyone from neighborhood folk to the stars and staff of RAI, Italian radio-television. Waiters help decipher the menu, which tempts most diners with perfect *carciofi alla romana* (fresh artichokes in garlic and oil), *tonnarelli alla chitarra* (homemade pasta in an egg and cheese sauce), and ricotta-filled ravioli with butter and fresh sage. Closed Mondays and August. Vicolo della Campana 18 (phone: 655273, 6567820). Moderate.

Casina Valadier – In one of the world's most enchanting locations, this is worth an al fresco lunch if only for the peace and beauty of its setting in the Borghese Gardens. Light is best: Try the *bresaola* or prosciutto, *insalata caprese* (mozzarella and tomato salad), or *salade niçoise*. There's good people-watching, especially in the spring and fall. Closed Tuesdays. Pincio, Villa Borghese (phone: 6792083). Moderate.

Il Drappo – Drapes softly frame the two small rooms of this *ristorantino* run by the brother-sister team of Paolo and Valentina Tolu from Sardinia. The Tolus offer a delicate cuisine based on robust island fare but add fragrance with wild fennel, myrtle, and herbs. The short (but innovative) menu, recited by Paolo and artfully prepared by Valentina, always begins with mixed *antipasti* including *carta di musica* (hors d'oeuvres on crisp Sardinian wafers). Closed Sundays and 2 weeks in August. Reservations required. Vicolo del Malpasso 9 (phone: 657365). Moderate.

Da Luciano – A restaurant in Rome's Jewish ghetto (one of the oldest in the world), with outdoor tables on one of the city's most colorful streets. *Luciano's* serves authentic old Roman-Jewish (kosher) dishes such as pasta with broccoli, red mullet with grapes and pine nuts, and an amazingly light, breaded, deep-fried mixture of vegetables (onions, potatoes, zucchini flowers, and so forth). Plans are under way to provide after-dinner music — live, classical, or jazz — at the end of the long, narrow dining room. Closed Tuesdays (but not always — call ahead). Via Portico d'Ottavia (phone: 6561613). Moderate.

Nino's – A reliable place, frequented by artists, actors, and aristocrats, and near the Spanish Steps, *Nino's* is truly Tuscan. The cuisine is composed of best-quality ingredients, ably yet simply prepared, and the service is serious, if not exactly heart-warming. Specialties: *zuppa di fagioli alla Francovich* (thick Tuscan white bean soup with garlic), *bistecca alla fiorentina* (thick succulent T-bone steak), and for dessert, *castagnaccio* (semisweet chestnut cake). Closed Sundays. Reservations advised. Via Borgognona 11 (phone: 6795676). Moderate.

Trattoria del Pantheon (Da Fortunato) – A favorite of politicians, businesspeople, and the conservative *borghesia*. It's a serious restaurant, entirely reliable, serving nothing but the most traditional Roman dishes, cooked to perfection, using the very best ingredients. Service is extremely professional, the house wine genuine and good. What more could one ask? From its outdoor tables in good weather, a view of the Pantheon at the end of the little street. Via del Pantheon 55 (phone: 6792788). Moderate.

Vecchia Roma – The setting is truly out of a midsummer night's dream on magical Piazza Campitelli on the fringe of Rome's Jewish quarter. The menu is varied, the ingredients fresh, the salads many and unusual. Closed Wednesdays and two weeks in August. Reservations recommended. Piazza Campitelli 18 (phone: 6564604). Moderate.

Arnaldo – A charming grotto of sorts, decorated with curiosities that reveal Arnaldo's passion for the ballet. Not surprisingly, dancers are among his clientele. The cuisine features unusual combinations of pasta and vegetables and pork with various fruit sauces as well as traditional fondue Bourguignon or steak tartare with caviar. Closed Tuesdays and a week in August. Via di Grotta Pinta 8 (phone: 6561915). Moderate to inexpensive.

Il Falchetto – Conveniently set off Via del Corso, with a few outdoor tables in fine weather, this might seem a tourist's haven. But knowledgeable Romans fill the small rooms even in the gray days of winter. One of the pasta specialties to try is *paglia e fieno al salmone* (green and yellow noodles with a creamy smoked salmon sauce). The imaginative game, veal, and fish dishes are also delicious. Closed Fridays. Via Montecatini 12–14 (phone: 6791160). Moderate to inexpensive.

Mario – A Tuscan favorite, with the usual Tuscan specialties such as Francovich soup, Florentine steaks, and delicious game in season, all prepared with admirable care and dedication by Mario himself, but served by only three overworked waiters. Closed Sundays and August. Via della Vite 55 (phone: 6783818). Moderate to inexpensive.

Ar Galletto – A beautiful warm-weather spot, it's set on Piazza Farnese opposite the finest Renaissance palace in Rome. By all means dine outside (inside is dreary). Try Rome's favorite *bucatini all'amatriciana* (thick spaghetti with tomato, bacon, and onion sauce) or *galletto alla diavola* (spring chicken heavily peppered and grilled to a crunch). Closed Sundays. Piazza Farnese 102 (phone: 6561714). Inexpensive.

Carmelo – It's a *trattoria,* Sicilian style, with strolling minstrels and such typical specialties as *maccheroni con melanzane, pasta con i broccoli,* and *pescespada alla messinese* (fresh swordfish in season, Messina style). Closed Mondays. Via Roma Libera 5–7 (phone: 5818088). Inexpensive.

Da Ciccio – Similar to *Carmelo,* but Calabrian, serving *antipasti alla calabrese,* pasta with broccoli or eggplant, and other southern specialties. In Trastevere, this is busy, noisy, musical, and good fun — depending on the crowd, you're likely to hear a singalong, Italian style, with an American tune thrown in. Closed Sundays. Reservations recommended. Via dei Genovesi 37 (phone: 5816017). Inexpensive.

Ettore Lo Sgobbone – A *trattoria* set on a rather dreary, but typically working-class street that is popular with newspaper and TV journalists and noted for its unpretentious northern home-style cooking. Pasta and rice (*risotto*) courses are excellent: Try the simple *tonnarelli al pomodoro e basilico* (pasta with fresh tomato and basil sauce) or *risotto nero di seppie* (rice cooked with cuttlefish and its ink). Closed Tuesdays. Reservations recommended for the few tables outdoors. Via dei Podesti 8–10 (phone: 390798). Inexpensive.

La Fiorentina – This favorite Roman pizzeria, with wood-burning oven and grill, is in residential Prati on the Vatican side of the river. It serves pizza even at lunchtime, a rarity in Italy. Tables on the street in good weather. Closed Wednesdays. Via Andrea Doria 22 (phone: 312310). Inexpensive.

La Fraschetta – A crowded restaurant/pizzeria in Trastevere with good Roman pasta dishes (*alla carbonara, all'amatriciana*) and pizzas. Closed Mondays. Via San Francesco a Ripa 134 (phone: 5816012). Inexpensive.

Da Giulio – Another bargain for budget-minded travelers, on a tiny street off Via Giulia in a historic building. A few tables line the sunless street in the summer, and inside is most pleasant — if a bit noisy — with an original vaulted ceiling and paintings by local artists. Roman family-style cooking. Closed Sundays. No reservations. Via della Barchetta 19. Inexpensive.

Isole del Sole – A converted houseboat on the Tiber offers a variation on the theme of al fresco dining and a pleasantly light cuisine. Try *pasta alla checca con rughetta* (pasta with a marinated fresh tomato and arugula salad) and *carpaccio* (thin slices of raw beef seasoned with olive oil, lemon, and flaked Parmesan cheese). Closed Mondays. Under Ponte Matteotti; walk down to the river from Lungotevere Arnaldo da Brescia (phone: 3601400). Inexpensive.

Le Maschere – For a taste of Calabria's Costa Viola, fragrant with garlic and devilish with red peppers, try this rustic and charming 17th-century cellar near Largo Argentina. The fare is not for fragile stomachs: *antipasti* of tangy salamis and tomatoes dried in the southern sun with garlic and herbs; pasta with broccoli or eggplant, or the traditional *struncatura* (handmade whole wheat pasta with anchovies, garlic, and bread crumbs); *stoccafisso* (salt cod stew with potatoes) or meats grilled on an open fire; pizzas and Calabrian sheep's milk cheese. Open for dinner only. Closed Tuesdays and part of August. Via Monte della Farina 29 (phone: 659444). Inexpensive.

Otello alla Concordia – A delightful *trattoria* in the middle of the Piazza di Spagna shopping area, with certain tables reserved for habitués and a colorful courtyard for fine-weather dining. The menu is Roman, and it changes daily, depending a great deal on the season. A regular reliable is *cannelloni alla concordia.* Closed Sundays, Christmas week, and the first week in January. Reservations not accepted. Via della Croce 81 (phone: 6791178). Inexpensive.

Palmerie – A trendy restaurant with 1950s fashions and ambience, and marble-topped tables with paper mats. The fixed-price menus appeal to the young. Dinner only; closed Mondays. Reservations recommended on Fridays and Saturdays. Via Cimarra 4–5 (phone: 4744110). Inexpensive.

Polese – This is a bargain any time of the year, either outside under the trees of the spacious square or inside the intimate rooms of the Borgia palazzo. A great summer starter is *bresaola con rughetta* (cured beef with arugula, seasoned with olive oil, lemon, and freshly grated black pepper), and the *pasta al pesto* is fine year-round. Closed Tuesdays. Reservations taken reluctantly (come and wait your turn). Piazza Sforza Cesarini 40 (phone: 6561709). Inexpensive.

SIENA

True to the traditional pattern of settlement in Tuscany, Siena sits on top of a hill or, rather, on top of three hills, enclosed in high walls — an age-old vision, the exact color of which every one of us has known since opening our first box of crayons. With a little bit of imagination, enough to ignore the twentieth-century traffic, it is easy to feel like a medieval traveler approaching the walls looking for access through a gateway or portico carved with the Sienese coat of arms. Inside, drawn into the labyrinth of narrow steets that snake through the medieval fabric of the city, the feeling does not dissipate. Few modern buildings disturb the illusion; it's as though medieval Siena were merely playing host to modern life. Much the same can be said about many other Italian or European cities, but here it's particularly apt.

After Florence, Siena has probably the richest artistic heritage in Tuscany, but unlike Florence, it remains more of a medieval than a Renaissance city, its overall thirteenth- and fourteenth-century Italian Gothic look a result of certain vicissitudes of its history. But there are other differences between the two cities. Siena is a lot smaller. It has the friendly spirit of a well-to-do provincial town in the midst of an agricultural region, not the refinements and sophistication of the region's cultural capital. Also, while the elegance and pride of the Florentines is sometimes seen as verging on hauteur, the quality most frequently attributed to the Sienese is a kind of sincere politeness, a soft-spoken charm — *gentilezza*.

The late Italian writer Curzio Malaparte points out in his wonderfully satirical evaluation of his fellow Tuscans that if you ask a Florentine saint some news about heaven, you will get an answer, but in a tone of voice that casts doubt on your worthiness to go there. Ask San Bernardino of Siena, however, and you will be told not only what heaven is, where it is, and the shortest road to take, but also how many rooms it has, how many kitchens, and what's cooking in the pot. Something of the same air of affectionate intimacy pervades Sienese speech, peppered with diminutives (it is said the Sienese speak Italy's purest Italian), and Sienese painting, which continued to delight in pretty Madonnas while the Florentines wrestled with problems of depth and perspective. (Look closely at the backgrounds of those lovingly rendered Sienese panels, and you sometimes *can* see what's on the back burner.)

Florence was a menacing presence throughout much of Siena's history, and in a certain sense it was Florence that arrested Siena's development and caused it to remain the medieval gem it is today. One legend has it that Siena was founded by the Senes Gauls; another recounts that it was founded by Senio, son of Remus, one of the founding brothers of Rome, and hence the Roman she-wolf on the Sienese emblem. Regardless of its origin, Siena was certainly an Etruscan city and then a military stronghold under the Romans until it finally began to flourish as a center of commerce, finance, and culture in the Middle Ages. At the same time, Siena's wealth and trade became the envy of her Tuscan neighbors, prompting continual warfare with the Florentine city-state in particular. By 1235, the mightier military strength of Florence forced Siena to accept harsh peace terms.

But that was merely round one. On September 4, 1260, the Sienese dealt the Florentines such a resounding defeat at Montaperti, a hill east of the city, that it is remembered to this day. Having exorcized Florentine dominance, good sense prevailed, and under a nine-member government of merchant families (Governo dei Nove), peace was made and Siena embarked on one of its most enlightened and prosperous periods. Some of the city's most noteworthy buildings, such as the Palazzo Pubblico, the Palazzo Chigi-Saracini, and the Palazzo Sansedoni, as well as plans to enlarge the cathedral, date from this time. It was a golden age for painting, too — Duccio di Buoninsegna and Simone Martini were making names for themselves beautifying palaces and churches.

The good times lasted until 1355, when, following a severe drought and then a terrible outbreak of plague in 1348, civil discontent brought about a rebellion of leading noble families and a series of short-lived governments. Would-be conquerors came from farther afield until, in 1554, a 24,000-man army of Spanish, German, and Italian troops under the command of the Florentine Medici family laid siege to the city. A year later, Siena fell. Cosimo I de' Medici became its ruler and Siena was taken as a part of the grand duchy of Tuscany, first under the Medicis and then under the French house of Lorraine, until it passed, with Tuscany, to the Kingdom of Italy in 1860.

It was probably due to Siena's absorption by Florence that the city stayed as small and as resolutely medieval-looking as it is. What's more, it was probably due to their loss of independence that the Sienese invested their annual Palio — the reckless bareback horse race around the treacherous Piazza del Campo — with so much civic passion. There are two runnings of this madcap race, one on July 2 and one on August 16. Both originated long ago as the popular part of religious festivities, the former in honor of the Madonna di Provenzano, the latter in honor of Our Lady of the Assumption. The August 16 Palio, the more important of the two, has been documented as far back as 1310; the July 2 Palio was instituted in 1656.

Then, as now, the city was divided into *contrade,* or districts, which compete against each other with one horse and rider each. The city once had fifty-nine contrade; now it has seventeen, with quaint names such as Bruco (caterpillar), Tartuca (tortoise), Chiocciola (snail), Drago (dragon), and Leocorno (Unicorn). Keep an eye on the corners of buildings as you walk around town, and you'll see the *contrade* marked off with their symbols just as streets are with their names. Each *contrada* has its own patron saint, a church where the saint is worshiped, and a feast day in the saint's honor, and each *contrada* has its own fountain, not in the church, where its babies are baptized a second time.

A Sienese is born into his *contrada* and roots for it all his life, so when the day of the Palio rolls around, after months of preparation, spirits are as high as they are in a neighborhood bar in Brooklyn during the World Series. The day begins, now as then, with a mass in the Cappella di Piazza and the hanging of the *contrada* banners in either the church of Santa Maria di Provenzano or in the Duomo. Among the banners is the *palio* itself, the banner that goes to the victor. (A *palio* is a banner, but since it is one that is the prize of a competition, the word now also refers to the competition itself and has a double meaning, something like "stakes.") In the early afternoon, each horse is taken to its local *contrada* church to be blessed (it's considered a good omen if the horse leaves something behind). Then, later in the afternoon, comes the most magnificent historical procession in Italy — a parade of dignitaries such as might have taken place in the days of the Sienese Republic, delegations from all the *contrade* in full fifteenth-century regalia, trumpeters, and *sbandieratori* (flag bearers) who wave, toss, and manipulate their flags in intricate synchronized routines.

The race takes at most three minutes, but it's hardly an anticlimax. While thousands of the spectators are tourists, the enthusiasm and joy shown by the winning *contrada* indicate that this is not merely an attraction staged for tourists but a deeply felt tradition. The victorious jockey is carried around town in triumph, and at the subsequent outdoor banquet in the winning *contrada,* the winning horse is treated as an honored guest. Palio time is definitely the time to visit Siena *if* you don't mind massive crowds and *if* you make all arrangements well in advance. If you miss it, well, you still might catch sight of a clutch of little boys, perhaps standing in a slice of late afternoon shade by the Duomo, wielding, waving, throwing the flag, practicing. The image will stay with you. All the Palio pageantry may be only one expression of Siena's past, but it's the one that most vividly captures the imagination.

SIENA AT-A-GLANCE

SEEING THE CITY: The best spot for a bird's-eye view of Siena is the top of the *Torre del Mangia,* next to the Palazzo Pubblico in Piazza del Campo, from which one can see not only all of the Campo below and across a sweep of red tile roofs to Siena's other major monumental complex, the Duomo, but also out to the surrounding hills. Another vantage point for bringing it all into focus is from the top of what the Sienese call the *Facciatone,* or big façade, actually the façade of the never-finished *Duomo Nuovo* (New Cathedral), which now houses the Museo dell'Opera del Duomo. Among other things, there's a good view of Piazza del Campo and the Torre del Mangia from here. Still another view is that from the *Fortezza Medicea* (see *Extra Special*), which should be saved for the end of a visit.

SPECIAL PLACES: A glance at the map shows that all of Siena seems to gravitate toward the fan-shaped Piazza del Campo. In fact, since Siena is no bigger than a large provincial town, almost all of its sights are within walking distance of this center of gravity. Be aware, however, that the town's narrow streets wind uphill and downhill, and sometimes turn into steps, so comfortable walking shoes are necessary.

Piazza del Campo – Siena's main square is certainly one of the beautiful old squares of Europe. It's on a slant, and its brick paving is divided into nine sectors, a number that harks back to the 13th and 14th centuries, when the city was ruled by a government of nine men who did much to create the cityscape that remains today. The nine sectors converge on the piazza's lower side, in front of the *Palazzo Pubblico* and the adjacent *Torre del Mangia.* Facing them on the higher side is the Fonte Gaia, a monumental fountain that was decorated with reliefs by Jacopo della Quercia (reproductions take the place of the 15th-century originals, which are now in the Museo Civico in the Palazzo Pubblico). Its name — the "gay" fountain — alludes to the fact that the arrival of water in the piazza sparked no end of festivity in the 14th century. All around the semicircular edge of the piazza are medieval and Renaissance palaces, one of the most noteworthy of which is the *Palazzo Sansedoni,* with a curved façade. It dates from the 13th and 14th centuries but became a single residence in the 18th century. At Palio time, the windows of the palaces are hung with ancient banners, the center of the piazza is stuffed with spectators, and the roadway all around turns into the route of the historical procession — and then the Palio racetrack.

Palazzo Pubblico – The elegant façade of this Gothic building is slightly curved, in keeping with the unusual outline of the Campo. It is Siena's city hall, as it has been since it was built between 1297 and 1310, but because part of it has become a museum, it is accessible to visitors. The adjacent bell tower, the *Torre del Mangia,* was added in the mid-13th century. It takes its name from a one-time bell ringer, Giovanni di Duccio, who was evidently a man of prodigal habits and better known to the Sienese as *Mangiaguadagni* (Spendthrift). The pillared and roofed structure at the base of the tower is the Cappella di Piazza, built from 1352 to 1376 to fulfill a vow made during the plague of 1348.

Inside the Palazzo Pubblico are beautifully proportioned rooms that give a sense of tangible authority rather than grandeur, and the frescoes with which they were decorated remain, although not in their pristine state. The world map that gave the Sala del Mappamondo its name is gone, but in the same room it's still possible to see the *Maestà* (1315) of Simone Martini, the great Sienese painter's first masterpiece. (It is much deteriorated and was already restored by the painter himself in 1321.) The fresco of *Guidoriccio da Fogliano* (1328) in the same room has long been attributed to Martini, although its authenticity has recently become a point of controversy. Below that is a Madonna and Child by the earlier Sienese painter Guido da Siena, dated 1221 but commonly held to have been done in the latter half of that century and to have been repainted in part by another great master of the Sienese school, Duccio di Buoninsegna. The next room, the Sala della Pace, is decorated with a series of allegorical frescoes on the subject of good and bad government. Painted between 1338 and 1340, they are the most extensive fresco cycle of the Italian medieval period with a secular subject and the most important works of their creator, Ambrogio Lorenzetti, a painter who was much influenced by Giotto and who probably died in the plague not too many years after completing them. One of the frescoes is particularly noteworthy for its early rendering of the Sienese urban scene and for its early use of landscape as a subject rather than a background. The museum also contains the originals of Jacopo della Quercia's reliefs for the Fonte Gaia. Open daily. Admission fee. Piazza del Campo (phone: 292111).

Duomo – This landmark, dedicated to Santa Maria dell'Assunta (Our Lady of the Assumption), is one of the most beautiful medieval churches in Italy. In many ways, it is a chronicle of the artistic and political history of Siena. It was begun in 1196, during the early stages of Siena's development as a city-state, and much of what is seen today was completed in the 13th century. But in the 14th century, with a growing population and the example of Florence's huge Duomo, the city's plans for the cathedral also grew. It was decided that the existing church should form the transept of a newer, much larger church, so construction began again, in 1339. By 1355, money problems and the plague had put an end to the super-church dream but not before the façade of the new church had been built. (It is this piece of unfinished architecture, off to the right of the Duomo, that the Sienese call the *Facciatone,* or big façade.) Attention returned in the late 14th century to finishing the old Duomo, and the result is an imposing, if somewhat irregular, white marble basilica with characteristic black stripes. The lower level of the façade, largely Romanesque, is dominated by the stone carving of Giovanni Pisano, whose work decorates many Tuscan churches. The upper level, Siena's response to the magnificent façade of the Duomo in Orvieto, is full 14th-century Gothic. The mosaics at the top, whose gold backgrounds catch the sun like mirrors playing with a beam of light, are from the 19th century.

The interior of the church is rich in art treasures, not the least of which is the floor, done from the mid-14th century to the mid-16th century and divided into 56 squares, each recounting a different biblical story in inlaid marblework. The scenes are the work of more than 40 different, mostly Sienese, artists (there are several by Beccafumi), and although many are visible all year, the most precious are kept covered in the interests of conservation and can be seen only from August 15 to September 15. Another treasure is the magnificent marble and porphyry pulpit by Nicola Pisano, Giovanni's father, sculpted with the help of his son and Arnolfo di Cambio. (Giovanni's own great pulpit sits in the Duomo at Pisa.) Lovers of the Renaissance should look at the chapel of San Giovanni Battista, which has frescoes by Pinturicchio (note the two portraits of Alberto Aringhieri). Pinturicchio also painted the lively, vivid frescoes recounting the life of Pope Pius II (Enea Silvio Piccolomini) in the Libreria Piccolomini, off the left side of the nave. The library, built in 1495 by the pope's nephew (who later became Pope Pius III) to house the uncle's precious collection of books, also contains a famous Roman statue of the Three Graces. Admission fee for the library. Piazza del Duomo.

Battistero – Siena's baptistry is down a flight of stairs to the right of the cathedral, behind the apse. A 14th-century building, it is best known for its baptismal font, designed by Jacopo della Quercia and considered a work of transition from the Gothic to the Renaissance. A collaborative effort, it has two bronze angels by Donatello, as well as bas-reliefs around the basin by Donatello, Lorenzo Ghiberti, and others. Piazza San Giovanni.

Museo dell'Opera del Duomo (Cathedral Museum) – Also known as the *Museo dell'Opera Metropolitana,* this contains mainly works that have been taken from the cathedral. Almost as interesting as the works themselves is their setting: the Duomo Nuovo, the unfinished extension of the cathedral that was planned and then abandoned in the mid-14th century. A visitor can only imagine its potential magnificence from the five huge Gothic arches that still stand and would have been the nave. Three of these have been closed off to form the museum. On the ground floor are ten statues of Old Testament figures carved by Giovanni Pisano for the Duomo façade (the statues on the façade now are reproductions) and a stone relief panel of the Madonna and Child carved by Jacopo della Quercia for one of the side altars. Upstairs is the masterpiece that made Duccio di Buoninsegna's career, the *Maestà* (1308–1311), which was carried from his workshop to the high altar of the cathedral in solemn procession. Originally it showed the Madonna and Child on the front and the 26 scenes of the Passion on the back (it was sawed in two in the 18th century), with smaller scenes of the life of Christ and the Virgin above and below. (Nineteen of these smaller panels remain; others are in museums in the US and Great Britain.) Still another masterpiece is Simone Martini's *Blessed Agostino Novello and Four of His Miracles* (1330). From the museum it's possible to climb to the top of the Duomo Nuovo façade — the Facciatone — for a splendid view of the town. Open daily. Admission fee. Piazza Jacopo della Quercia.

Pinacoteca Nazionale – The National Picture Gallery is a must for a clear understanding of Sienese art from the 12th to the 17th century. Housed in the beautiful 15th-century Palazzo Buonsignori, here are 40 rooms filled with Sienese masterpieces — from Guido da Siena, Duccio, Simone Martini, Pietro and Ambrogio Lorenzetti,

Beccafumi, and more. Closed Mondays. Admission fee. Via San Pietro 29 (phone: 281161).

Chiesa di Sant'Agostino – Stop here to see Perugino's *Crucifix and Saints* (1506) and, in one of the chapels, the *Slaughter of the Innocents* (1482) by Matteo di Giovanni, *Madonna with Child and Saints* by Ambrogio Lorenzetti, and the *Epiphany* by Sodoma over the altar. The church was built in the 13th and 14th centuries and underwent Baroque modifications in the 18th century. Prato di Sant'Agostino.

Palazzo Chigi-Saracini – Like many Sienese palaces and churches, this was begun in the 12th century, finished in the Gothic style in the 14th century, and later altered and restored. Originally built for one of the leading families of Siena, it is now the seat of the *Accademia Musicale Chigiana* and a music school whose international summer students congregate around the carved stone well in the delightful courtyard. The interior can be visited on request: Its lofty ornate rooms are decorated with some of the gems of Sienese art of the 13th to 17th centuries. Concerts are held in the palace's music room, which is adapted from the noble apartments and is Siena's main concert hall. To visit the interior, apply to the *Accademia,* Via di Città 89 (phone: 46152).

Palazzo Piccolomini – A mid-15th-century Renaissance palace in the midst of medieval Siena, this was once the home of the family of Pope Pius II and now houses the state archives, with a wealth of documents and statutes pertaining to Siena's turbulent history. (Archives closed Sundays.) Farther down the street are the *Logge del Papa,* three graceful Renaissance arches that Pius II had built in his family's honor. Via Banchi di Sotto.

Museo Archeologico Nazionale (National Archaeological Museum) – The collection here provides a sense of Siena in its very earliest days. Exhibits range from prehistory to the Roman period and include Etruscan funeral urns from the 3rd century BC and Greek and Roman statues and statuettes dating from the 6th century BC. Closed Wednesdays. Admission fee. Via della Sapienza 3 (phone: 44293).

Basilica di San Domenico – Approach from Via della Sapienza for a breathtaking glimpse of the *Duomo* and its bell tower as well as of the *Torre del Mangia* next to the Palazzo Pubblico. San Domenico is a massive, severe-looking monastic Gothic building begun in 1226 and completed in the 15th century, while the graceful bell tower next to it was built in 1340. Inside, the spacious, simple majesty of this austere church — in the unusual T-shape of an Egyptian cross — is interrupted with shafts of light from modern stained glass windows. See the Chapel of St. Catherine, which is adorned with Sodoma's early 16th-century frescoes of the mystic Sienese saint who was a member of the Dominican order and who eventually became one of the two patron saints of Italy (with St. Francis of Assisi). A reliquary in the same chapel contains the head of St. Catherine, while another chapel, the Cappella delle Volte, contains a fresco of her that was done by a contemporary, Andrea Vanni, and is held to be the only authentic portrait of the saint in existence. Piazza San Domenico.

Santuario Cateriniano (House of St. Catherine) – St. Catherine lived from 1347 to 1380, and by 1464, only a few years after her canonization, her house was turned into a sanctuary. Despite the sacred transformation, the addition of chapels, and the 15th- and 16th-century paintings showing scenes from her life, there is still a homey atmosphere about what was once an ordinary household. The adjoining church of Santa Caterina in Fontebranda, facing Via Santa Caterina, is part of the sanctuary; once the dyer's shop of her father, it too contains frescoes and statues of the saint. Open daily. If it is not open, the custodian is at Via Camporegio 31 (phone: 44177). Costa di Sant' Antonio.

Fonte Branda – One of Siena's oldest and best-loved fountains stands at the end of Via Santa Caterina, not far from the sanctuary. There are references to it as far back as 1081, but it was rebuilt in the mid-13th century, when it was given its present triple-arched mini-fortress form with the emblem of Siena in the middle.

Basilica di San Francesco – Begun in the 14th century and originally Gothic in style, this was much changed externally by later building, Baroque additions following a 17th-century fire, and a modern façade. Still, the interior, in the shape of an Egyptian cross, retains the characteristic alternating layers of black and white marble. Detached frescoes by Pietro Lorenzetti (the *Crucifixion*) and Ambrogio Lorenzetti (the other two) are in the side chapels. The church gives onto the ex-convent of St. Francis and a wonderful Renaissance cloister. Piazza San Francesco.

Oratorio di San Bernardino – This two-tiered oratory was built in the 15th century on the spot where Siena's beloved second saint, the Franciscan San Bernardino (1380–1444), preached his sermons (quite lively ones, evidently — his gift for persuasion caused him to be made the patron saint of advertising and public relations by Pope John XXIII). The upper floor of the oratory is gracefully decorated with stuccoes and is frescoed with images of the Madonna and saints (including San Bernardino himself) by some notable 16th-century artists: Sodoma, Girolamo del Pacchia, and Beccafumi. To visit, contact the custodian (phone: 289081). Piazza San Francesco 6.

Basilica di Santa Maria dei Servi – Set away from the center, on a rise that offers a splendid view of the Duomo, it has a simple 13th-century façade and bell tower, and an interior that mixes Gothic with Renaissance splendor. Among the works of art are a *Madonna* (1261) by Coppo di Marcovaldo and one by Lippo Memmi. Piazza Alessandro Manzoni.

■**EXTRA SPECIAL:** Besides the Torre del Mangia and the Facciatone, one other special spot in Siena offers a panoramic view of all the palaces and churches, the red-roofed expanse cut through by winding streets. This is the *Fortezza Medicea,* also known as the *Forte di Santa Barbara,* a defensive fortress built in 1560 by Cosimo I of the Florentine Medici family shortly after his arrival in Siena as the city's conquerer. Now it's a city park, and although anyone standing on its battlements is no longer master of all he or she surveys, he or she does still survey quite a lot, both of the city and of the surrounding countryside, in all directions. But the view is not the only reason to visit this well-preserved fort at the end of a long day's sightseeing. Inside, part of the space is given over to the *Enoteca Italica Permanente,* a showroom and outlet for all the best Italian wines, including the excellent Chianti bottlings for which the province is famous. The most demanding restaurateurs do their shopping here, but so can the enthusiastic individual, and some of the local wines can be tasted before purchase. The cellars are open daily, 3 PM to midnight. Fortezza Medicea (phone: 288497).

SOURCES AND RESOURCES

TOURIST INFORMATION: Siena's *Azienda Autonoma di Turismo* is at Via di Città 43 (phone: 42209), and there is a branch information office right in Piazza del Campo (phone: 280551). It's open daily in summer but closed Sundays off-season.

Local Coverage – The Sienese read Florence's daily newspaper, *La Nazione.* Many shops in the heart of town carry guidebooks in English.

Telephone – The telephone prefix for Siena is 0577.

GETTING AROUND: Since so many of the narrow streets in the center of this city are closed to traffic, the only way to get around is on foot. Several car parks situated around the walls make any walk to the center easy enough for even the most reluctant pedestrian.

Bus – Siena has local bus service; one of the main stops for most of the buses is Piazza Matteotti. Buses for destinations in and around Tuscany usually leave from Piazza San Domenico. Call SITA (phone: 289069) for information on the latter.

Car Rental – The big international chains are not represented, but there are many smaller firms. Try *Auto Noleggi ACI,* Viale Vittorio Veneto 47 (phone: 49118), run by Italy's main automobile club, or *Auto Noleggio Intercar Eurodrive,* Via San Marco 96 (phone: 41148), which also rents motor scooters and will arrange chauffeured trips in the area.

Taxi – *Consorzio Taxisti Senesi* (phone: 49222). There are cabstands at the train station and at Piazza Matteotti.

Train – The main train station is at the foot of the hills, at Piazzale Fratelli Rosselli, a short taxi ride from the city center (phone: 280115).

MUSEUMS: The most important museums of Siena are listed under *Special Places.* In addition, the following may be of interest.

Biblioteca Comunale degli Intronati – Ancient religious and civic manuscripts and beautifully illuminated sacred books. Via della Sapienza 5.

Musei dell'Accademia dei Fisiocritici – A geomineralogical museum and a zoological museum with prehistoric fossils, shells, and skeletons found in the surrounding area. Piazza Sant'Agostino 4.

Orto Botanico – Botanical gardens. Via Pier Andrea Mattioli 4.

SHOPPING: Sienese shops are a mixture of extreme sophistication and rustic simplicity. While leading names in Italian fashion are in evidence in clothing and shoe stores, local craftsmanship can be found in the numerous ceramic and pottery shops selling original designs, as well as excellent copies of medieval and Renaissance Sienese items. The shops lining the main streets — Banchi di Sopra, Banchi di Sotto, and Via di Città — in the vicinity of Piazza del Campo are fertile ground for all of Siena's specialties, including the numerous culinary delicacies to be found in this area. Siena is particularly famous for *panforte,* a rich, spiced fruit and nut cake; *ricciarelli* (almond pastries); and salami. Wines can be bought at the *Enoteca Italica Permanente* in the Fortezza Medicea (see *Extra Special*) or at any local grocer. Siena also has branches of the all-purpose *Upim* and *Standa* department stores that are found in every major Italian city. One favorite souvenir quest is the attempt to collect a set of flags, mugs, or plates that carry each of the crests of Siena's 17 surviving *contrade.*

Antichità Saena Vetus – High-quality antiques and some small pieces for the bargain hunter. Via di Città 53.

Art Shop – Exquisitely made paper products — notebook covers, picture frames, large folders, tiny boxes — made with seventeenth-century methods. Via di Città 17.

La Balzana – An antiques shop, selling Tuscan and other Italian antiques and bric-a-brac. Via della Sapienza 26.

Le Botteghe Piccole – Custom-made jewelry. Via dei Rossi 83.

Cabibbe – A good place for women's wear. Banchi di Sopra 9.

Castelnuovo – Original, wearable men's clothes. Banchi di Sopra 55–57.

Ceccuzzi – Beautiful Italian fabrics as well as made-to-measure and ready-made clothes. Banchi di Sopra 1 and Via dei Montanini 32–36.

Ceramiche Santa Caterina – A wide-ranging display of local pottery. Via Pier Andrea Mattioli 12 and Via Camporegio 9.

Fendi – Leather goods by the world-famous designers. Via dei Rossi 30.

Mercatissimo della Calzatura e Pelletteria – Fine, reasonably priced leatherwork. Viale Curtatone 1.

Mori – An extensive selection of shoes, bags, and belts. Banchi di Sopra 32 and 68.

Provvedi – One of the best stocked of the many ceramics shops in this area. Via di Città 96.

Quasar – A delightful collection of hand-painted ceramics. Via Aretina 1.

Quercioli – Jewelry, some of it from the nearby workshops of Arezzo, a leading jewelmaking town. Banchi di Sopra 5.

Luisa Spagnoli – A good place for women's clothing. Banchi di Sopra 65–67.

 SPECIAL EVENTS: The *Palio,* Siena's famous bareback horse race around the outer edge of the Piazza del Campo, has been going on since the 14th century. One of Italy's major traditional events, it is run twice, once on July 2 for the feast of Santa Maria di Provenzano and once on August 16 in honor of Maria Santissima Assunta in Cielo (Our Lady of the Assumption), to whom the cathedral is dedicated. The races involve months of preparation on the part of each *contrada,* but the actual Palio activities begin three days or so before each race, with the selection of horses, a lottery to choose which of the 17 *contrade* will run (the Campo track can accommodate only 10 horses), and several rehearsals. The night before the race a banquet is held in each *contrada* (visitors may attend). The next day, various religious activities fill up the morning; then, in the afternoon, horses are blessed in the local churches. In late afternoon, the Torre del Mangia bell sounds, and one of the most spectacular parades imaginable files into Piazza del Campo — representatives of the city and of all the *contrade,* every marcher in historic costume. This is followed by the race itself. There are no rules, so drugging of horses and bribing of jockeys goes on right up to post time. The Sienese are by now worked up to a fever pitch, and even though the race is over in a few minutes, celebration in the winning *contrada* goes on all night and the next day. Finally, in September, the two winning *contrade* hold a huge outdoor banquet, with the winning horses at the head of the table — understandably, since more horses than riders finish the race, and it can be won by a riderless horse.

Tickets for the Palio are not easy to come by. Most of the grandstand seats on the perimeter of the course belong to the Sienese, almost by birthright. Remaining seats sell out well in advance and are expensive. It's possible to order them before arrival from *Agenzia Viaggi SETI,* Piazza del Campo 56, 53100 Siena, but only if you write far in advance (they cost 90,000 lire each in 1986). Locally, they are sold by shops in and around Piazza del Campo, and the demand for them is so great that spaces at the windows of homes around the Campo are sold, too, and scalping is rampant. Nonticketholders can stand in the mass of humanity in the middle of the piazza without charge, but early arrival is imperative to ensure a view (pick a high spot near the Fonte Gaia). Another alternative is to buy a ticket (10,000 lire in 1986) for one of the *prove,* or rehearsals, that take place on the three days preceding each Palio. The regal pageantry is missing at these trial heats, but it's still possible to feel a bit of the spirit. Occasionally, too, a third Palio is declared for some special reason (as in 1986, in honor of a local government anniversary).

For those not planning to visit Siena at Palio time, but still looking for a taste of it, note that each *contrada* has its own feast day when its church and the museum in which it keeps the silk Palio banners are open to the public. The tourist information office can provide a list of these days, all of which occur between April and October.

SPORTS: Horseback Riding – The *Club Ippico Senese,* Località Pian del Lago (phone: 53277), offers riding lessons and countryside treks.

Soccer – From September to May, *Siena* plays at *Stadio Comunale Il Rastrello,* Viale dei Mille 3 (phone: 280937), near the Fortezza Medicea.

Swimming – The outdoor municipal swimming pool in *Piazza Amendola* (phone: 47496), on the northwest edge of the city, is open in the summer months.

Tennis – There are clay courts at *Circolo Tennis Siena,* Località Vico Alto (phone: 44925 or 283397), just outside the walls on the northwest side of the city.

MUSIC: Siena has no opera company, but the highly active *Accademia Musicale Chigiana* more than makes up for this deficit in July and August, when its summer school for professional and advanced musicians is in session. For the duration of the program, students make regular concert appearances, as soloists or in ensembles, and at the same time the Academy sponsors an approximately month-long series of concerts, the *Settimane Musicali Senesi* (Sienese Musical Weeks), featuring well-known guest artists. The events take place in the Palazzo Chigi-Saracini music room — Siena's main concert hall for performances at other times of the year as well — or in any of the city's innumerable palaces and churches. For information, contact the *Fondazione Accademia Musicale Chigiana* (phone: 46152).

NIGHTCLUBS AND NIGHTLIFE: As in most Italian cities, at least in the summer, nightlife to the average Sienese simply means wandering through the city and stopping at the occasional café that's open late in the Campo. There are always groups of people congregated around the fountain here or elsewhere in some small piazza, in animated discussion. Greater stimulation is possible at two discotheques, *Club Enoteca,* adjacent to the wine cellars of the Fortezza Medicea (phone: 285466), open Thursdays through Sundays, and the more centrally located *Bijoux Noir,* Via Pantaneto 13 (phone: 288379), closed Wednesdays. The *Pub,* Via Pantaneto 48 (phone: 43183), is a gathering place for drinking, music, and conversation, while *Tinapica,* Via Roma 6 (phone: 220707), is a cozy piano bar. Both of the latter are closed Tuesdays.

SINS: In the absence of any formal red-light district, hotel bellhops are the best source of information. In general, the sins most commonly indulged in here could be classified under *gluttony* and *excessive drinking,* given the hearty country food and the wealth of good wines available. Fortunately, this part of Tuscany has developed a way to deal with the aftereffects of such overindulgence. There are numerous small spa towns in the area where naturally hot water bubbles up into swimming pools and where massages and other types of therapy can be had. The hotels are cheerful, reasonably priced, and they (oops!) serve good food. Just ask the tourist information office.

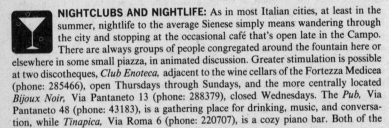

BEST IN TOWN

CHECKING IN: It is unwise to arrive in Siena without a hotel reservation between May and October. Because of the size and popularity of the town, its 30 or so hotels, both inside and outside the walls, are usually booked solid for most of the tourist season. It is definitely a mistake to arrive in town unexpectedly on Palio days and the days immediately preceding them. Prices in the larger out-of-town hotels, some of which are converted Renaissance villas, are expensive, from $100 and up for a double room with bath. Moderate means prices ranging from $50 to $90 for a double, and inexpensive means less than $50.

Certosa di Maggiano – Among the cypress trees and vineyards, this hotel has a unique atmosphere of seclusion and meditation, which is not surprising because it began in the 14th century as a monastery. A short taxi or bus ride outside the city walls, it has several spacious sitting rooms, Renaissance furniture, and a permanent show of ancient manuscripts and documents. A large, well-kept garden contains a heated swimming pool and tennis courts, and there is a highly recommended restaurant (see *Eating Out*). The rooms are few (only 14), however, so book well in advance. Closed December through February. Via di Certosa 82 (phone: 288180). Very expensive.

Park – The building originally held a castle-cum-villa, built in 1530, of the local well-to-do Gori family. They chose the spot for its dominating position (and, therefore, its easy defendability) as well as for the healthy air and attractive countryside views of olive trees and rolling hills. Today's traveler can enjoy the same, with the addition of a swimming pool and tennis courts unobtrusively integrated into a romantic, slightly decadent-looking Italian garden surrounded by a small wood of oak and beech trees. There are 69 rooms in this link in the CIGA chain, all with air conditioning (color TV on request), and the restaurant is good (see *Eating Out*). A short taxi or bus ride from the city center. Via di Marciano 16 (phone: 44803). Expensive.

Villa Scacciapensieri – A bit over a mile from the city center, this family villa, built a little over a hundred years ago, is another romantic spot in the Sienese countryside. With its large garden and outlook onto both the city and the surrounding vine-clad hills, tennis court, swimming pool, and excellent cuisine, plus regular bus service into town, this is an ideal stopping-place from which to enjoy sightseeing trips in Siena or forays into the Chianti hills. Closed October to mid-March. Via di Scacciapensieri 24 (phone: 41442). Expensive.

Castagneto – Set below the city walls at the foot of the western side of Siena, this small but comfortable hotel offers splendid panoramas from its own garden. There are 11 rooms with private showers; no restaurant. Closed December through February. Via dei Cappuccini 55 (phone: 45103). Moderate.

Garden – In a new section of the city a short taxi or bus ride from the center. Some of the rooms are in a 16th-century villa that has public rooms with Pompeii-style frescoes on the ceilings; other rooms are in an adjoining new building erected in the old Tuscan style. A reasonably priced hotel with a swimming pool, a restaurant, a lovely garden setting, and good views of the city from its grounds. Only 2 of the 67 rooms have bathtubs; the rest, showers only. Via Custoza 2 (phone: 47056). Moderate.

Palazzo Ravizza – This 17th-century villa is a well-appointed hotel within easy walking distance of the main sights of Siena. It is surrounded by its own garden and provides a peaceful, yet central, vantage point from which to enjoy the city. There are 28 rooms and a restaurant for guests only, open evenings (in high season, you must take breakfast and dinner daily). Closed November to March. Pian dei Mantellini 34 (phone: 280462). Moderate.

Chiusarelli – Set just below the imposing walls of the Basilica di San Domenico and the Fonte Branda on the western outskirts of the city, yet within easy reach of the center. There are 50 rooms, a restaurant, and a small garden. Viale Curtatone 9 (phone: 280562). Inexpensive.

Duomo – A good hotel for a comfortable, reasonably priced stay in town, this is in the heart of medieval Siena, a 5-minute walk from the Duomo and within easy reach of Via di Città, one of the main shopping streets. There are 14 rooms; no restaurant. Via Stalloreggi 38 (phone: 289088). Inexpensive.

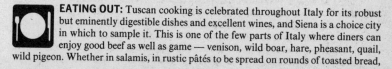 **EATING OUT:** Tuscan cooking is celebrated throughout Italy for its robust but eminently digestible dishes and excellent wines, and Siena is a choice city in which to sample it. This is one of the few parts of Italy where diners can enjoy good beef as well as game — venison, wild boar, hare, pheasant, quail, wild pigeon. Whether in salamis, in rustic pâtés to be spread on rounds of toasted bread,

or served with lentils or beans, these seasonal delights are a staple of the area's hearty country cuisine. Sienese cooks are also handy with vegetable dishes and are well versed in the making of soups, such as the rich vegetable broth with bread and poached egg known as *acqua cotta* (literally, "cooked water") and the equally straightforward *ribollita* ("reboiled"), which originated as household leftovers cooked in broth but which in restaurants has become a delicious meat-based broth and vegetable soup. Mushrooms are found in abundance. Gathered fresh from the surrounding wooded areas and served in a variety of ways, they can be a main course or a side dish. Cheeses are traditionally made from sheep's and cow's milk, the most prevalent being *caciotta,* which can be mild and soft or seasoned to become salty and hard. Wines range from the local Chianti to the finer-quality wine — arguably the best red wine in Italy — from the Brunello grapes of nearby Montalcino to the dry but robust Tuscan whites, such as Vernaccia from San Gimignano or Bianco Vergine della Valdichiana. And then there is the traditional sweet dessert wine, Vin Santo.

Siena is essentially an informal city, and while the more expensive hotels offer an elegant ambience befitting their ratings, the average restaurant tends to be more homey — though the food is no less delectable for being served in relaxed surroundings. Service is friendly, and waiters are happy to help bewildered foreigners through the menu. In the listings below, a meal for two in an expensive restaurant will cost $90 and up, including house wine, while the moderate restaurants charge from $40 to $80. Inexpensive is under $40.

Certosa di Maggiano – The cuisine in this delightful country hotel, transformed from a 14th-century monastery, goes beyond the Tuscan border to include such dishes as tortellini soufflé, shrimp fricassee, and sole with asparagus. Most of the dishes on the menu are made from locally grown ingredients, the choice of dessert changes daily, and there is an excellent choice of wines. Reservations are required because of limited seating. Via di Certosa 82 (phone: 288180). Expensive.

Park Hotel – For Tuscan cooking par excellence, try the restaurant of this 16th-century villa hotel. Original salads of mushrooms and white beans are bathed in the purest olive oil, soups are made from freshly gathered mushrooms, and fresh fish is brought in from the Tuscan coast. Homemade cheeses and cakes, and a vast selection of wines, complete a memorable meal. Via di Marciano 16 (phone: 44803). Expensive.

Grotta di Santa Caterina–Da Bagoga – This lively restaurant named after a Palio jockey gets overcrowded during Palio time and often during the rest of the season as well, so it's best to eat here off-season. Palio mementoes decorate the walls, and the menu is classic Tuscan fare — roast meats and game. Closed Mondays. Via della Galluzza 26 (phone: 282208). Moderate.

Da Guido – In the heart of the old city, and one of the most characteristic of the inner city's wood-beamed restaurants, with an equally characteristic cuisine. This is one of Siena's favorite haunts, and it should be avoided at the height of the tourist season. Closed Mondays and most of July. Vicolo Pier Pettinaio 7 (phone: 200042). Moderate.

Al Mangia – Since it's right in Piazza del Campo, this well-known Sienese restaurant is inundated in summer by Palio fans and other visitors. At other times, however, it makes a pleasant eating place, with tables outside looking toward the handsome Palazzo Pubblico. The menu is particularly good for game and mushroom dishes. Closed Mondays. Piazza del Campo 43 (phone: 281121). Moderate.

Al Marsili – A handsome vaulted restaurant near the Duomo, this is another prime Sienese eating place rooted in Tuscan tradition, but it has its own original dishes as well. Fresh vegetables form the basis of some of the regulars' favorites: zucchini in casserole, chickpeas with garlic and rosemary, and vegetable *sformati* (mousses). Mushroom pâté is spread on toasted country bread for an hors d'oeuvre, and game — guinea fowl, wild duck, or pigeon, roasted or served with one of the inimitable house sauces — is prominent among the meat dishes. Closed Mondays. Via del Castoro 3 (phone: 47154). Moderate.

Tullio ai Tre Cristi – Expect unpretentious but high-quality cuisine. The suckling pig with porcini mushrooms is particularly good — or the porcini can be served whole as a main dish. Mushrooms prepared in a variety of ways are among the specialties here, along with vegetable mousses. Closed Mondays. Vicolo Provenzano 1 (phone: 280608). Moderate.

Il Biondo – This large, modern restaurant at the edge of the old city center adds fresh fish dishes, such as spaghetti with anchovies, to an otherwise Tuscan menu, which often features fried lamb and artichokes, grilled pork liver, and pork and sausage on skewers. Closed Mondays. Vicolo del Rustichetto 10 (phone: 280739). Moderate to inexpensive.

Le Campane – Between the Duomo and Piazza del Campo, it's one of the few restaurants in Siena where a staple on the menu is fish, served in cannelloni or with pasta. Also on the menu are house variations on classic Tuscan soups such as *ribollita* and a vegetable main dish of artichokes in a sort of quiche. Charcoal-grilled meats and veal *scaloppine* with fresh tarragon are other entrées, and desserts include homemade pine nut tarts accompanied by sweet, locally produced Vin Santo. Closed Mondays. Via delle Campane 4 (phone: 284035). Moderate to inexpensive.

Nello La Taverna – The informal, friendly atmosphere makes this a popular place with the Sienese as well as with visitors. A good place to try traditional Tuscan *acqua cotta,* or pasta served with a sauce or, as in the tagliatelle with tarragon, simply with fresh herbs. The veal fricassee with mushroom cream sauce is good, too. Closed Mondays and February. Via del Porrione 28 (phone: 299043). Moderate to inexpensive.

Osteria Le Logge – Farther down the street, with slightly more upscale flights of fancy, this is a meeting place for the intelligentsia where good wine, food, and conversation are the rule. Taste a rustic Sienese bean soup, *crostini* (toasted rounds of bread) with game and mushroom pâté, or classic meat and game dishes with a sprinkling of truffles, in season. A home-produced *caciotta* dominates the cheese selection, and the house wine is an excellent local Chianti. Closed Sundays and June. Via del Porrione 33 (phone: 48013). Inexpensive.

TAORMINA

Set on the slopes of Monte Tauro (Mountain of the Bull), looking out at snow-capped Mount Etna and the blue Ionian Sea, this little town is easily one of the world's loveliest resorts. For twenty centuries, Taormina has offered visitors the amenities of a restful vacation against the backdrop of exquisite natural beauty. Its purpose is reflected in its current composition: a year-round population of only 10,220 people with more than seventy hotels and *pensioni* in the town itself and another twenty-five in the seaside suburb of Mazzarò.

A peacefully beautiful place — ancient and medieval stone buildings are framed by green palm trees and fuchsia bougainvillea vines — in recent times Taormina has been known primarily as a refuge for rich and cultured Europeans. The first modern hotel was built in 1874; others followed, many built with British capital. After a stay by Emperor Wilhelm II of Prussia, it became a well-known aristocratic watering spot. By the turn of the century, it was popular not just with crowned heads but with the families of European financiers. It was not unusual for the Rothschilds, the Krupps, and the Vanderbilts to take vacations here, while still later it became a favorite spot for artistic personalities such as British writer D. H. Lawrence and German photographer Wilhelm von Gloeden. (Von Gloeden shocked the locals when he took to photographing local lads, often in the nude, posed as small Greek gods.)

Taormina has historical roots that go far back in time. Tombs built by the Siculi (Italian tribes that migrated to Sicily 1,300 years before Christ) have been discovered nearby, proving that the area has long been settled. In 735 BC, Greek sailors founded the nearby city of Naxos. For several centuries, there was bitter rivalry among Greek colonies in Sicily. When Naxos was destroyed by Dionysius of Syracuse in 403 BC, the Siculi survivors founded Tauromenium. This town, too, was wiped out by Dionysius but was soon refounded. In 358 BC, with the support of the Naxian survivors, a new state was established by Andromachus. His son, Timaeus of Taormina, became the city's chief historian.

The Romans gave Taormina considerable autonomy. Despite the vicissitudes of the empire (and the emperors' internal rivalries), it seems to have enjoyed centuries of peace and prosperity, attracting patrician vacationers. The area was known for its fruits, vegetables, olives, and grapes, as well as for its marble, but its primary importance was military — the natural harbors below and the rocky lookout points above were a strategic advantage.

After the fall of Rome and the brief period of domination by barbarian tribes, Taormina — like the rest of Sicily — fell under the influence of the Byzantine Empire. It became an archbishopric and, for a while, was the most important city in eastern Sicily. It fell to the Arabs in 902, and for the next several centuries it was variously dominated by the Swabians, the Normans, the Angevins, and the Aragonese. When King Martin died without heirs in 1411, King Ferdinand sent his son John to the island, and for the next three centuries all of Sicily was ruled by Spanish viceroys. During the latter part of this period, Taormina suffered a major fire and a severe earthquake; it lost population and sank into obscurity. Little changed during the eighteenth and nineteenth centuries under the Bourbons, the Savoys of Piedmont, and the Hapsburgs of Austria.

The town's fortunes began to change after Italian unification in 1860. With the stabilization of government and development of transportation, it was soon discovered by wealthy German and British travelers. In a short time, its hotel industry burgeoned. Taormina today is known for the cultivation of citrus fruits, olives, and the wine commonly known as the "red wine of Etna," but there is no doubt that mass tourism is the city's principal source of revenue. Fortunately, its governors have succeeded in protecting Taormina from the defacement that can result from invasions of vacationers. It has taken on a role in Italian cultural life as well — theatrical, film, and literary festivals are held here annually — so this enchanting city of gardens and medieval monuments continues to offer its visitors, in the words of Guy de Maupassant, "all that seems made on the earth to entice eyes, spirit, and imagination."

TAORMINA-AT-A-GLANCE

SEEING THE CITY: Taormina, with its stone buildings, flowered balconies, and lush subtropical vegetation, appears to be a physical outgrowth of the surrounding mountainous landscape. A good view of the town can be had from the ruins of the Castello (castle) on the summit of Monte Tauro; the sea is accessible from here by foot or by car along the road to the village of Castel Mola. There's an even better view from Castel Mola itself, about three miles away. Taormina, however, is best known for the stunning view of the town, the sea, and — in the distance — volcanic Mount Etna, visible from the well-preserved Greek (later Roman) theater. In town, from Piazza IX Aprile, off the central Corso Umberto, there is a lovely view of the sea and coastline below.

SPECIAL PLACES: The town itself is tiny, with most shops, restaurants, and other attractions on or just off the main street, Corso Umberto. The smaller crossroads are often merely pedestrian staircases hewn into the rock.

Corso Umberto (Umberto Avenue) – The central street of Taormina, now closed to automobile traffic, runs horizontally through the town from Porta Messina to Porta Catania. The street runs over the outskirts of what was the ancient Greek city of Tauromenium and through what is still known as the *Borgo Medioevale* (Medieval Township). With its many cafés and benches, this street is where the locals take their evening and Sunday strolls. It is undoubtedly the best place in Taormina for watching neighbors and strangers alike, a favorite Sicilian pastime.

Teatro Greco (Greek Theater) – A short walk along the *corso* from Porta Messina is Piazza Vittorio Emanuele. From this square, turn left and walk along Via del Teatro Greco directly to one of Sicily's most impressive and well-preserved archaeological ruins. The original structure, probably built in the 3rd century BC, is the second largest ancient theater in Sicily after the one in Syracuse. The *cavea,* the graduated rows of seats, was carved out of the hillside and surmounted by a portico of marble columns. Under the Romans, the theater was significantly rebuilt for use as a gladiatorial arena. The view from the theater is fine, and the acoustics are so good that it is still used during summer arts and film festivals. Next door is a small antiquarium with relics of the ancient city. The theater is open daily, 9 AM to shortly before sunset. Admission is 2,000 lire; free on Sundays.

Palazzo Corvaia (Corvaia Palace) – In Piazza Vittorio Emanuele stands Palazzo Corvaia, an impressive late-14th-century building with a crenelated façade. Built on the site of the ancient Roman forum, the palazzo originally housed the Sicilian parliament. It is also thought to have been the residence of Queen Bianca of Navarre. In the 16th century it was passed on to the Corvaia family. Windows and other decorations, such as the black and white lava inlay ornamentation, are typically Catalan-Gothic in style. There is a picturesque inner courtyard with a 13th-century stone staircase. Palazzo Corvaia today houses the *Azienda Autonoma* travel information office.

Chiesa di Santa Caterina (Church of Saint Catherine) – This small church next to Palazzo Corvaia has a fine statue of Saint Catherine, three handsome Baroque altars, and a gloomy downstairs funeral chamber. Behind the church are the remains of a small Roman theater, or *odeon,* where musical performances were held in ancient times.

Naumachia – Farther west along Corso Umberto is the Via Naumachia, which leads to the remains of an ancient cistern and its arcaded retaining wall. The Romans used naumachiae to stage mock sea battles. Some archaeologists believe this one may have been part of a gymnasium.

Piazza IX Aprile (Ninth of April Square) – Corso Umberto continues west to a charming square, complete with jacaranda trees and a lovely 19th-century iron lamp-post. Passersby stop here for an *aperitivo* at one of the several outdoor cafés or to enjoy the panoramic view of the Greek theater, Mount Etna, and the sea below. To the left as one enters the square (which is simply a broadening of the *corso*) is the tiny 15th-century *Chiesa di Sant'Agostino,* now the public library. On the right, up a double staircase, is the *Chiesa di San Giuseppe,* with its charming Baroque façade. And at the end of the square stands the *Torre dell'Orologio* (Clock Tower), which is the entrance-way to the *Borgo Medioevale.* The present tower dates from the 12th century, but its foundations are believed to be much older.

Borgo Medioevale (Medieval Township) – This district preserves many architectural details from the Middle Ages. Note especially the Gothic windows and doors at Nos. 122, 176, 190, 228, and 241. Up a staircase on the right is *Palazzo Ciampoli,* which dates back to 1412 and is now a hotel.

Duomo (Cathedral) – San Nicola di Bari (Saint Nicola of Bari), the duomo of Taormina, is a severe 13th-century church of rough-hewn stone. Its crenelated walls have a decidedly Norman appearance. Its interior is in the form of a Latin cross — the nave and two aisles are separated by columns of Taormina rose marble. Note the 15th-century triptych *Visitation of Mary to Elizabeth, Saint Joseph, and Saint Zachariah,* by Antonio Giuffrè, and other medieval religious paintings.

Piazza del Municipio and Porta Catania (Municipal Square and Catania Gate) – The duomo's main portal opens out onto Palazzo Municipio, where there is a Baroque fountain. Across the *corso* is what is left of the *Chiesa del Carmine,* including its campanile. The *corso* comes to an end at the arch of Porta Catania, which is also called *Porta del Tocco* (Tolling Gate) because in Norman times the people of Taormina gathered here when the bells were rung. It is inscribed with the date 1440 as well as the Taormina and Aragon coats of arms. To the left is the *Palazzo del Duca di Santo Stefano,* a massive Gothic residence.

Convento di San Domenico (Convent of Saint Domenic) – Just downhill from Piazza del Municipio is the Chiesa di San Domenico, whose campanile commands a lovely view. The nearby convent has been a hotel — the *San Domenico Palace* — since 1896 and is today probably one of the most luxurious and tastefully beautiful resorts in all of Italy (see *Checking In*). The hotel has preserved the original monastic furnishings and art objects. The 15th-century cloister with its fine marble well has been glass enclosed. The gardens are lush; the views of the sea and Mount Etna are spectacular. (The management does not encourage uninvited guests.)

■**EXTRA SPECIAL:** *Via Roma* winds down from San Domenico, providing the viewer with exceptional panoramas, to the *Giardino Pubblico* (Public Gardens). Once part of the nearby Villa Cacciola, the park was taken over by the city in 1922 and has been open to the public ever since. Not only are the views from the park splendid, but the colorful Mediterranean subtropical vegetation is enhanced by odd Babylonian-style structures erected in the last century for the villa's mistress, Lady Trevelyn. A stroll in these well-tended formal gardens is truly a sensual experience.

ENVIRONS

Lido di Mazzarò (Mazzarò Beach) – A summer vacation in Taormina also means sun and sea, with the accompanying gastronomic delights. Most people staying in Taormina swim at the Lido di Mazzarò, a long, well-equipped beach lined with numerous hotels, cafés, and restaurants. There are footpaths to the beach, and a *funivia* (cable car) operates regularly between Mazzarò and a point just outside Porta Messina. A one-way ticket for the 3-minute ride costs 800 lire. Other pleasant beaches in the area are *Spisone* and *Giardini-Naxos*, for which there is regular bus service, and *Capo (Cape) Schiso.*

Castel Mola – Three miles away and 1,800 feet above sea level is a tiny village that overlooks Taormina and the ruins of its medieval castle. Historians believe Castel Mola may have been the ancient city of Mylai, which was used as a place of hiding by refugees of various wars in the area. It was destroyed by the Arabs in AD 902.

Giardini-Naxos – Naxos was the oldest Greek colony in Sicily. There are few traces of the ancient city, but excavations begun in 1967 have unearthed some of the basalt blocks from the town's defensive walls. Its location on Capo Schiso, a peninsula of lava rock, is striking. *Giardini,* the new sea resort, is less than 3 miles south of Taormina. It was from this spot that the Italian patriot Giuseppe Garibaldi sailed with about 5,000 troops to fight for Italian unification in 1860.

Forza D'Agrò and Capo Sant'Alessio – The tiny medieval town of Forza D'Agrò is only a short drive north of Taormina. Both the *Chiesa della Trinità* (Church of the Trinity) and the *Chiesa di San Francesco* (Church of Saint Francis) contain interesting paintings and artifacts. Nearby is *Capo Sant'Alessio,* a twin-peaked rock cliff separating two beaches and topped by a medieval castle.

Alcantara Gorge – A winding road toward the interior from Giardini leads to the scenic Alcantara Valley. After the viaduct in Contrada Larderia, one comes to the gorge, a narrow split in the lava rock, plunging precipitously down to the river.

Monte Etna – The biggest volcano in Europe — and still very active — Etna was believed by the ancients to be the forge of Hephaestus, the Greek god of fire. It was also associated with the legend of the Cyclops Polyphemus, who waylaid Ulysses on his way through the Straits of Messina. (*Etna* comes from the Greek *aitho,* or "eye burn.") The mountain's earliest known eruption, in 475 BC, was recorded by Pindar and Aeschylus. We know of 135 eruptions since. Several times — notably in 1669 when it destroyed Catania — its lava has reached the sea. It still smokes and rumbles frequently, indicating that a major eruption is possible at any time. Its several craters, especially the main caldera, are fascinating geologically, and the view from the summit, including most of Sicily, the Lipari Islands, and Calabria, is awesome. A consideration of weather conditions and the volcano's current activity is advisable before going up the mountain, however. There are several approaches to Etna from Taormina. The nearest is by way of Fiumefreddo. Drive south on SS114, then take SS120 northwest to Linguaglossa; bear left to the village of Mareneve. A minibus carries visitors from there to within a short walk of the caldera. Farther south there are easy approaches from either Nicolosi or Zafferana. At Nicolosi-Nord a cable car climbs to within about 7,500 feet; 4-wheel-drive vehicles to the top are available from there. Plan to spend at least half a day on the volcano; wear warm clothing and sturdy shoes. It's also fun to make the trip at night, when lava glows eerily red in the caldera, and then stay to see the sunrise — a poetic experience. (For further information on Mount Etna, see *Sicily and the Lipari Islands,* DIRECTIONS.)

SOURCES AND RESOURCES

TOURIST INFORMATION: The Taormina *Azienda Autonoma di Soggiorno e Turismo,* in the back of Palazzo Corvaia, is open daily, except Sundays, 8 AM to 2 PM and 4 to 6 PM (phone: 23243). The office provides several brochures and pamphlets on Taormina, its services, and surroundings, as well as information about hotels, although it does not make reservations. Do this directly or through the *Compagnia Italiana Turismo* (*CIT*), Corso Umberto 101 (phone: 23301, 23302, or 23303), or any private agency.

Telephone – The telephone prefix for Taormina is 0942.

GETTING AROUND: Walking is the easiest and most enjoyable way around town. A car is useful for excursions.

Buses – There is regular bus service from the terminal, in front of the *Miramare Hotel,* to most nearby towns, including Mazzarò, Castel Mola, Forza d'Agrò, and Giardini-Naxos. The bus company, *SAIS,* also offers tours to Agrigento, Alcantara, and Siracusa (phone: 23494).

Car Rental – The major car rental companies all have offices in Taormina.

Taxi – Taxis can be hired for special excursions. Stands are at Piazza Badia (phone: 23000), Piazza Duomo (phone: 23800), the Giardini-Naxos train station (phone: 51150), and Mazzarò (phone: 21266). A taxi ride to the Catania airport takes about 40 minutes. Prices are by meter or negotiable beforehand.

Trains – Trains to and from Messina and Catania and other points arrive regularly at nearby Giardini-Naxos, where taxi and bus services to Taormina are available.

SHOPPING: Taormina has perhaps the best selection of antiques, ceramics, jewelry, and lace handiwork in all of Sicily. Conveniently, most of the shops are concentrated on the main street, Corso Umberto, which winds from one end of the old town to the other. The *corso* is off limits to cars, making it ideal for leisurely strolls and window-shopping. It is also an unusually beautiful street, with bougainvillea-filled balconies, shady piazzas, outdoor cafés, and irresistible pastry shops.

The *Bar Mocambo,* in Piazza IX Aprile, is a favorite spot for a cappuccino or an *aperitivo.* Its outdoor tables are perfect for people-watching. Inside, the café's walls are decorated with enlargements of Wilhelm von Gloeden's famous turn-of-the-century photographs of Sicilian boys — some dressed as ancient Greeks or as girls, some seminude.

The ubiquitous *Benetton* has an outlet on the *corso,* but far more interesting are the scores of small stores selling antiques and ceramics. Shops are open daily, including Sundays, 9 AM to 1 PM and 4 to 9:30 PM in summer, or 3:30 to 7:30 PM in winter. Most accept major credit cards.

Casa d'Arte Ita – Fine silver, porcelain, antique furniture, and other art objects. Corso Umberto 148 (phone: 3060).

Galeano (Concetta) – Beautiful hand-embroidered lace tablecloths and bedspreads in linen and cotton. Piazza Duomo, facing the cathedral.

Gioielleria Giuseppe Stroscio – Finely crafted modern and antique jewelry. Corso Umberto 169 (phone: 24865).

Il Gaucho – Casual and dressy shoes for men and women. Corso Umberto 118.

Maru – Fendi furs and leathers. Corso Umberto 83 (phone: 24218).

Mazzullo – Elegant clothing and accessories for men and women. Corso Umberto 35 (phone: 23152).

Carlo Panarello – Tasteful selection of Sicilian ceramics and antiques. Corso Umberto 122 (phone: 23910).

Parrucchiere Elle – Taormina's best beauty salon. Corso Umberto 99 (phone: 23997).

Ritrovo Tamako – Café and pastry shop, homemade marzipan in the form of fruits and vegetables, delicious *cannoli,* praline almonds, and other Sicilian pastries. Corso Umberto 141 (phone: 24782).

Scrupoli – Trendy fashions for women. Via Bagnoli Croce 10 (phone: 23735).

Stefanel – Moderately priced sportswear for men and women. Corso Umberto 117 (phone: 24886).

Vadala – Designer clothes for men and women. Corso Umberto 191 (phone: 25163).

R. Valentino – Vast, cheerful selection of Sicilian pottery, local handicrafts, and gift objects. Corso Umberto 98 (phone: 23960).

 SPECIAL EVENTS: Every summer, beginning on July 18, Taormina hosts a 2-month arts festival that consists of about 10 days of films and a month or more of theatrical and dance productions, many of which are held in the *Teatro Greco* (see *Special Places*). The program for the festival is available in June from the *Azienda Autonoma di Soggiorno e Turismo,* Palazzo Corvaia (phone: 23243).

 SPORTS: Sports here are limited to water sports and tennis. Most major hotels have arrangements with bathing establishments at Mazzaro, Spisone, Isolabella, and Mazzeo; a list is available at the tourist information office.

Tennis – Book a court through the *Tennis Club of Taormina,* Via Bagnoli Croce (phone: 23282).

Water Skiing – Arrangements can be made with the *Water Ski Club,* Villagonia, Via Nazionale (phone: 52283).

 THEATER AND MUSIC: In August a concert and ballet series is offered at the *Teatro Greco* (see *Special Places*). A schedule of performances is usually available from the tourist information office at the beginning of the summer.

 NIGHTCLUBS AND NIGHTLIFE: Taormina's classiest nightclub is *Tout Va-Aurelio,* a former gambling casino set in a huge park. It has an excellent restaurant, piano bar, and discotheque. Open daily to 4 AM, June through September and on weekends year-round. Via Pirandello 70 (phone: 24460) (see also *Best in Town*). Other nightclubs with live music and dancing are *La*

Giara, Via La Floresta 1 (phone: 23360), and *L'Ombrello,* Piazza Duomo (phone: 23733). For traditional Sicilian music, visit *Grotta Di Ulisse,* Salita Dente 3 (phone: 23394). The most popular late-night discotheques (in high season) are *Septimo,* Via S. Pancrazio 50 (phone: 25297), and *Le Perroquet,* Piazza San Domenico (phone: 24808).

BEST IN TOWN

 CHECKING IN: Hotels are Taormina's major commercial resource. Usually modern, comfortable, attractive, and well equipped, they are occasionally elegant as well. Service is generally good to excellent. Expect to pay around $100 for a double room at hotels rated as expensive; from $75 to $90 at those rated as moderate; and under $55 at those rated as inexpensive.

San Domenico Palace – A superlative hotel, one of Italy's best, this former 15th-century Dominican monastery has luxurious rooms furnished with antiques, an elegant restaurant and bar, beautiful gardens, a swimming pool, and private beach facilities. (See also *Special Places.*) Service is impeccable. Piazza San Domenico 5 (phone: 23701). Very expensive.

Grand Albergo Capo Taormina – Large and modern, it has a swimming pool and excellent beach facilities. Closed December through February. Mazzarò (phone: 24000). Expensive.

Mazzarò Sea Palace – Luxurious and right on the beach, with a good restaurant and swimming pool. Closed November through March. Mazzarò (phone: 24004). Expensive.

Bristol Park – Elegant and medium-sized, with a good restaurant, swimming pool, and splendid views of the sea and Mount Etna. Closed November through February. Via Bagnoli Croce 92 (phone: 23006). Moderate.

Timeo – An old villa, tastefully renovated, with turn-of-the-century charm in a beautiful setting, right next to the ancient Greek theater. There is a lovely garden and terrace, both with a view of the sea. Via Teatro Greco 59 (phone: 23801). Moderate.

Villa Sant'Andrea – Once the summer home of a British family, this small hotel overlooking the bay has charming rooms, most with sea views, a beautiful terrace restaurant, and a lush private garden. Closed January and February. Mazzarò (phone: 23125). Moderate.

Villa Belvedere – True to its name, this lovely hotel offers great views of Mount Etna and the sea. Its 40 rooms are pleasantly decorated and comfortable; its swimming pool is set in a tranquil garden. Closed November through mid-March. Via Bagnoli Croce 79 (phone: 23791). Inexpensive.

Villa Paradiso – Small and centrally located, overlooking the sea, with an excellent restaurant and the best view of Mount Etna. Closed November to mid-December. Via Roma 2 (phone: 23922). Inexpensive.

 EATING OUT: Most of the hotels in Taormina have their own dining rooms, but don't hesitate to sample the local restaurants as well. These, for the most part, are pleasant, often have lovely views, and in general are less expensive than comparable restaurants in northern Italy. Whenever possible, try the local specialties, particularly the fish and succulent fresh vegetables such as eggplant, artichokes, and squash. The pasta is delicious. Expect to pay $50 or more for a meal for two at restaurants categorized as expensive; between $30 and $40 at those listed as moderate; and under $25 at inexpensive restaurants. Prices do not include wine or tip.

L'Oliviero – Housed in the *Hotel Villa Sant'Andrea,* by the sea, with a lush outdoor terrace. Specialties include crabmeat *risotto*, mixed fish fry, and tournedos of beef. Excellent Sicilian wines. Closed January and February. Via Nazionale 137 (phone: 23125). Expensive.

Villa Le Terrazze – Dine outdoors and enjoy a beautiful coastal view. Specialties include an antipasto of marinated raw swordfish, *tagliolini* with salmon, and grilled lobster; for dessert, try an almond parfait with chocolate sauce. Closed Mondays and November through March. Corso Umberto 172 (phone: 23913). Expensive.

Giova Rosy Senior – Overlooking the ancient Greek theater, this delightful *trattoria* with a flower-filled terrace serves excellent pastas and fish dishes, including large shrimp in vodka sauce and swordfish sausage *en papillote*. Closed Mondays and from January 28 through February. Corso Umberto 38 (phone: 24411). Expensive to moderate.

Da Lorenzo – Located in the center of town, with a pleasant garden for outdoor dining, it serves traditional Sicilian cuisine, including an excellent *spaghetti alla Norma* (with eggplant). Closed Tuesdays. Via M. Amari 4 (phone: 23480). Expensive to moderate.

La Botte – This favorite late-night spot serves good pizza, grilled meats, and Sicilian dishes. Closed Mondays. Piazza San Domenico 4 (phone: 24198). Moderate.

Ciclope – Typical Sicilian cooking, with a particularly good selection of antipasto dishes. Closed Wednesdays and January. Corso Umberto (phone: 23263). Moderate.

Da Giovanni – This bright, family-run restaurant, with a spectacular view of the sea, offers good fish dishes. The enormous fish soup, made with the catch of the day, is a meal in itself. Closed Mondays. Via Nazionale, Isolabella (phone: 23531). Moderate.

Il Pescatore – Perched above the bay and considered by many to be Taormina's best restaurant. The menu features mainly fish, with very good *cannelloni* and rice *alla pescatora* (with seafood). Closed Mondays and November through February. Mazzarò (phone: 23460). Moderate.

Tout Va–Aurelio – A fashionable establishment in a private park, with a piano bar and discotheque, this restaurant serves Continental and Italian cuisine, both prepared with originality. Closed mid-September through May. Via Pirandello 70 (phone: 23824). Moderate.

La Buca – Pleasant outdoor dining on typical Sicilian cuisine — grilled meats and fish, good homemade pasta. Closed Mondays and December. Corso Umberto 140 (phone: 24314). Moderate to inexpensive.

Il Delfino – Good fish is served at this bayside restaurant, with its own private swimming facilities. Closed November through mid-March. Via Nazionale in Mazzaro (phone: 23004). Moderate to inexpensive.

Ficodindia – A beachside restaurant featuring pasta with sardines and an excellent entrée of fish simmered in a sauce of capers, tomatoes, and olives. Closed Mondays, January, and February. Via Appiano (phone: 36301). Moderate to inexpensive.

TRIESTE

Once the major port of the Hapsburg Empire, a glamorous commercial and cultural center on the Adriatic that suffered a steady decline after World War I, Trieste is a city far overshadowed by its past. Today it is all but forgotten by the rest of Italy, tucked away in the northeasternmost corner of the peninsula, ninety miles northeast of Venice and right on the border with Yugoslavia. But if present-day Trieste seems faded compared with the bustling seaport of a century ago, much of its old fascination still lingers.

Tourists will find very little of the great monuments, antiquity, and art treasures that are so plentiful in other Italian cities. Trieste's special appeal is its ambience and people, Old World elegance, and interesting mixture of cultures. Triestines will tell you that their city has two souls, one worldly and the other provincial, and the pleasure of a visit lies in experiencing these contrasts. Traces of Trieste's cosmopolitan past are evident in its religious and ethnic diversity, its grand old hotels, the strong Slavic flavor, a richly varied local cuisine, and its Viennese-style cafés. Yet it is essentially a quiet little town, which the Italian Census Búreau recently ranked as the most livable in Italy. This distinction hardly qualifies as a major tourist attraction, but it does suggest the easy pace and tranquillity that can make a visitor's stay here so pleasant.

Trieste also boasts a wonderful natural setting, from the beautiful harbor and coastline to the rich countryside of its surrounding mountains in the Carso, Trieste's highland. Of architectural interest are its handsome examples of eighteenth- and nineteenth-century neoclassicism, including the Teatro Verdi (the opera house), the old Stock Exchange, the Offices of the Captain of the Port, and the splendid Church of Sant'Antonio. Its magnificent Piazza dell'Unità d'Italia, with one side open to the sea, is unique in Italy, and the lively Piazza Ponte Rosso (see *Extra Special*) has to be one of the most picturesque squares in the world. And no visitor should leave the city without taking a long and leisurely stroll along the seafront.

To understand Trieste is to grasp the sense of loss that permeates the air, creating a nostalgic, somewhat romantic mood. The city still laments the transferral of its environs to Yugoslavia after World War II, and there is a growing sense of isolation from the rest of Italy. Much like the local weather, which can be gloriously sunny in summer but suffers from a cold, sometimes fierce, wind from the north called the *bora* in winter, the Triestine character is a curious blend of Mediterranean and more northern elements. In casual contact this comes across as exuberance tempered by melancholy.

Trieste's origins go back to Roman times, when it was a small port known as Tergestum. By the Middle Ages it had become an independent municipality that periodically fell under domination by Venice, then the major power in the Adriatic. In 1382, Trieste placed itself under the protection of the

Austro-Hungarian Empire, where it remained for more than five hundred years (interrupted briefly when Napoleon's armies occupied the town in the early 1800s). Only after the Hapsburg emperor Charles VI declared the city a free port in 1719 did Trieste attain real importance. The decree launched the city's fortunes as the empire's major gateway to the world. But it was Charles's daughter, Empress Maria Theresa, who is generally credited with creating modern Trieste. In the mid-eighteenth century the empress enlarged the seaport and revamped the city, laying out a neat grid of streets in the quarter named after her, the Borgo Teresiano, which is still considered the "new" part of town. She improved public education, encouraged local industry, and lifted the constraints that confined Trieste's Jewish community to a ghetto.

The lure of commerce attracted foreign merchants and entrepreneurs from all over the Mediterranean and central Europe. By the mid-1800s, Trieste's population had soared to over 150,000, nearly ten times that of the previous century. The newcomers blended into the city's fabric without losing their distinct identities. This mutual tolerance is evident in the variety of churches in Trieste: Catholic, Protestant, Serbian Orthodox, Waldensian, Anglican, and Methodist. A magnificent synagogue built in 1912 is still active, although the once sizable Jewish community, whose roots in Trieste go back at least seven centuries, has shrunk to only a few hundred.

By the end of the nineteenth century, Trieste had become a center of trade, finance, and banking, the birthplace of the modern insurance company, and Austria-Hungary's great emporium for central Europe. A prosperous bourgeoisie built stately homes in the Teresiano quarter, several of which can be visited as museums today. The city also nurtured some great writers, including James Joyce, who lived here with his family from 1904 to 1915, supporting himself by teaching English. Much of his autobiographical novel *A Portrait of the Artist as a Young Man* was written here, as well as parts of his masterpiece *Ulysses.* The local tourist board distributes a small booklet in English that provides a "Joycean" walking tour of the city, pointing out his haunts and homes. One of Joyce's most devoted pupils, the businessman Ettore Schmitz, launched a writing career of his own under the name Italo Svevo and together with fellow Triestine writer Umberto Saba helped launch a new Italian literature. In a letter that looks back at his time in Trieste, Joyce says: "I cannot begin to give you the flavor of the old Austrian Empire. It was a ramshackle affair, but it was charming, gay, and I experienced more kindness in Trieste than ever before or since in my life."

Although Trieste had strong Austrian and Slavic overtones, it remained essentially Italian. In the late 1800s the struggle for union with Italy gained force. The Italian composer Giuseppe Verdi (who created two works for Trieste's opera house) became a symbol of this cause, and disorders usually erupted wherever his music was played. Trieste also had a local martyr, Guglielmo Oberdan, a deserter from the Austrian army who returned to the city with the goal of assassinating Emperor Franz Joseph but was arrested and executed before he could carry out his plan.

Sadly, unification with Italy in 1918 signaled the city's demise. The new frontier severed Trieste from its German and Slav hinterland, leaving it, in the words of historian Denis Mack Smith, "a head without a body." World War I seriously damaged the port and local industry, and Trieste never regained the prosperity of its prewar days. The Nazis occupied it in 1943 and established a concentration camp at an old rice-processing plant outside town (the Risiera di San Sabba has become a memorial to the Resistance and is open to visitors). After the war, the territory bordering Trieste — most of the Istrian peninsula and the Karst (Carso), predominantly Slovenian — was transferred to Yugoslavia, and in 1947 the city itself, also in dispute, was proclaimed a free territory under United Nations administration. Trieste remained a city without a country for seven years until it was finally returned to Italy in 1954, along with a sliver of Istrian coast. Ten years later it became the capital of the region known as Friuli–Venezia Giulia.

Today more than half of the city's 250,000 residents are retired. Most of the others are involved in Trieste's traditional occupations: banking, trade, and import-export. A large Slovenian minority continues to run its own cultural and educational facilities, while the location here of the prestigious International Center for Nuclear Physics has given Trieste a certain stature in the scientific community, too.

As the dividing point between East and West, Trieste is vulnerable to policies on both sides of its frontier. Its port has suffered from the crisis in Italy's steel and shipbuilding industries, and a 1982 travel tax imposed by the Belgrade government all but eliminated the regular influx of Yugoslav shoppers, bringing many Trieste stores to the verge of bankruptcy. After lengthy negotiations Belgrade recently lifted the tax, and more Yugoslavs are crossing the border to buy blue jeans, coffee, appliances, and machine replacement parts. But inflation at home has reduced their purchasing power.

Visitors, however, have a hard time perceiving these economic hardships. The city is full of elegant shops and fine restaurants, and Triestines enjoy a comparatively high standard of living. Most important, Trieste's appealing ambience and the echoes of its glorious past are still here for all to savor.

TRIESTE AT-A-GLANCE

SEEING THE CITY: For a spectacular panorama of Trieste, its harbor, coast, and the mountains of Istria, take the No. 2 tram or the No. 4 bus from Piazza Oberdan to the village of Opicina, 1,000 feet above sea level. Get off two stops before the end, at the *Obelisco di Opicina.* Both the tram and the bus run every 20 minutes. Another good vantage point is the hilltop *Castello di San Giusto* (see *Special Places*), which can be reached by foot, taxi, or the No. 24 bus. The *Molo Audace,* a pier that juts out into the harbor near Piazza dell'Unità d'Italia, is a favorite promenade and offers a beautiful view of the city, sea, and hills.

SPECIAL PLACES: Piazza dell'Unità d'Italia is the heart of Trieste and the natural starting point for a walking tour of the city, as most of the major attractions are nearby. To the north of it is the area called Borgo Teresiano, the business, cultural, and commercial center, encompassing Trieste's opera house in Piazza Verdi, the neoclassical palace of the Borsa Vecchia (the former Stock Exchange) in Piazza della Borsa, and avenues and side streets lined with elegant boutiques, old cafés, and colorful food shops. The district is bisected by the Canal Grande, which once allowed ships to sail right into Piazza Ponte Rosso. To the south of Piazza Unità, the winding streets of the old medieval city lead past the Roman amphitheater and a Roman gateway, the so-called Arco di Riccardo, to the Colle di San Giusto, a hill named after Trieste's patron saint. Perched on top of the hill are the old fortress and the 14th-century church that dominate the town. It's a good walk to the hill (or, better, take bus No. 24 up and walk down), but vehicular transportation is needed to get to Miramare Castle, the most unusual and spectacular of Trieste's sights, as well as to the Grotta Gigante.

CENTER

Piazza dell'Unità d'Italia – A spacious, truly breathtaking square. Enclosed on three sides by stately 19th-century *palazzi* — the Palazzo Comunale (Town Hall), the Palazzo del Governo (Prefecture), and the building housing the once powerful Lloyd Triestino shipping line — the piazza is open to the sea on its west side, which sweeps right up to the Adriatic. By all means, take an outside table at *Caffè degli Specchi* and take it all in.

Castello di San Giusto – This 15th-century castle was built by the Venetians on the site of a Roman fort. Its bastions command a wonderful view of Trieste. In recent decades, the castle has been tastefully restored, and today it houses the city's tourist information office as well as an extensive collection of old arms and armor. The museum is open mornings only and closed Mondays. Admission fee. Colle di San Giusto.

Cattedrale di San Giusto – Dedicated to the city's patron saint, the 14th-century cathedral is a curious amalgam of two earlier churches, from the 5th and 11th centuries, which in turn were built on the site of an ancient Roman temple. The decision to incorporate the previous structures into the new, grander cathedral reflects the characteristic practicality of the Triestines, and the result is a unique but appealing blend of styles. The simple, Romanesque façade is embellished by a Venetian Gothic rose window. The five-nave interior contains some handsome Byzantine mosaics, a 9th-century baptismal font, a 16th-century wooden Pietà, and a small collection of holy relics and artworks. Piazza della Cattedrale, Colle di San Giusto.

Orto Lapidario (Lapidary Garden) – Just downhill from San Giusto, this is one of the most romantic spots in Trieste, with a Byronesque feel to it. Formerly the church's graveyard, it was transformed in the middle of the last century into a stone garden of archaeological finds. Strolling among the ruins one comes across Roman tombstones, fragments of altars, memorial tablets, urns, and other statuary. Off to one side, a neoclassical temple, built in the last century, houses a sculptured monument to the famous German archaeologist Johann Winckelmann, who was murdered in Trieste in 1768. The garden also contains the *Museo Civico di Storia e d'Arte,* which has a small, eclectic collection of ancient art and artifacts. Of particular interest are Egyptian burial objects and several mummies; Roman jewelry, busts, and urns; pre-Roman bronzes; and an extensive coin and medal exhibit. Open mornings only, closed Mondays. Admission fee. Via della Cattedrale 15.

Civico Museo Revoltella – The Baron Pasquale Revoltella, a Venetian financial tycoon of the mid-19th century, bequeathed his palazzo and private art collection to the city. The gallery (closed for renovation, with reopening expected in 1987) contains several works by major 19th-century Italian artists. Revoltella specified, however, that his home should also be used as a showcase for contemporary art, and there are frequent exhibits of new artists. Of particular interest are the museum's upper floors, which have been maintained as they were in the baron's day. The ornate furnishings and luxurious quarters give a good idea of how affluent families lived in the last century. Open mornings only, closed Mondays. Via Diaz 26 (phone: 300938).

Museo del Mare (Maritime Museum) – This delightful museum, tastefully modernized, contains all kinds of objects that illustrate the history of navigation and fishing. In addition to nautical instruments and maps, there are wonderful scale models of a wide variety of vessels. One room is devoted to Guglielmo Marconi, and upstairs there are superbly crafted three-dimensional scenes depicting various kinds of fishing. Open mornings only, closed Mondays. Admission fee. Via Campo Marzio 1 (phone: 304885).

Museo Morpurgo – This home of a wealthy family has been turned into a museum, complete with original furniture, gilded mirrors, Venetian chandeliers, paintings, and sculpture. Although officially open every morning except Mondays, museum hours are extremely erratic, depending on the availability of its small staff. Visitors have to ring a downstairs doorbell to be admitted. Admission fee. Via Imbriani 5 (phone: 794054).

ENVIRONS

Castello di Miramare (Miramare Castle) – At the tip of a wooded promontory overlooking the Bay of Grignano and surrounded by a magnificent park, this white turreted castle has a past as romantic as its setting. It was built in 1860 for Archduke Maximilian and his wife, Princess Carlotta of Belgium, who spent three happy years here before Maximilian was persuaded to take over as emperor of Mexico. The ill-fated Hapsburg prince was soon executed by the Mexican republican army of Benito Juárez, and his wife went insane. The sumptuous rooms of the castle are maintained exactly as they were when the royal couple was in residence. The throne room, chapel, several parlors, the royal bedrooms, and Maximilian's fine library — all filled with precious furniture, paintings, antique vases, and art objects — are open to the public. Visitors are also free to stroll through the beautiful 55-acre park, which contains a small café. The castle is open mornings year-round, and there is a small admission charge, except on Sundays. The guided tours in English are a must. On summer evenings, the royal couple's sad tale is told in a dramatic hour-long sound-and-light show. Miramare is about 5 miles north of Trieste, a 10-minute taxi ride that costs up to $5. An alternative is to take the No. 6 bus from the train station to Barcola, and then change to the No. 36 bus. In summer, transportation to the castle from Trieste is available by boat.

Grotta Gigante (Giant Grotto) – About 10 miles north of Trieste, this enormous cave is the largest natural cavern known today, and it is considered a speleological wonder. The cave has been equipped with stairways and lighting, and there are 45-minute guided tours every half hour. There is also a small museum of local archaeological finds. Open daily, except Mondays. Admission fee (phone: 227312). The cave can be reached by the bus or tram to Opicina.

■**EXTRA SPECIAL:** To fully grasp the special nature of Trieste, every visitor must stroll along the *riva,* its waterfront promenade, and take in the harbor, the ships, the surrounding hills, the fishermen's shops, and the restaurants. This was one of James Joyce's favorite walks, and it has been an inspiration to generations of Trieste writers. The stroll should include a stop at the huge enclosed fish market — the *Grande Pescheria* — on the waterfront just south of Piazza dell'Unità d'Italia. Another must is a visit to *Piazza Ponte Rosso.* The Grand Canal that bisects this unusual square was dug in the 18th century to allow trading ships to sail into the business district. Today it serves as a dock for pleasure craft. But the piazza is still a lively center of commerce, with outdoor food and flower markets, and numerous clothing stalls frequented primarily by Yugoslav shoppers. Rising like an ancient Greek temple at its far end is the *Church of Sant'Antonio,* one of Trieste's most striking neoclassical monuments.

Some 7 miles southwest of the city (about a 20-minute ride by car or the No. 20 bus), the tiny fishing village of *Muggia* is well worth a visit. This jewel of a harbor, once part of the Republic of Venice, is virtually unknown to tourists and, indeed, to most Italians outside Trieste. It has a miniature main square with an exquisite 13th-century cathedral. There are several excellent seafood restaurants, which make this a perfect lunchtime excursion.

SOURCES AND RESOURCES

TOURIST INFORMATION: General tourist information is available at Trieste's *Azienda Autonoma di Soggiorno e Turismo,* which has its main office inside the Castello di San Giusto (phone: 750002). Travelers can cross into Yugoslavia by bus, train, boat, or car. Tourist visas are issued at the border for a nominal fee. For fares and schedules, inquire at the tourist information office, at the Trieste bus terminal near the central railroad station, or at the Opicina train station (phone: 211682). The *US consulate* is at Via Roma 9, 4th floor (phone: 68728, 68729).

Local Coverage – The tourist office plans to begin printing weekly guides soon, but meanwhile it provides pamphlets with listings of museums, special events, theater and concert halls, and day excursions. Hotels have information about evening activities. The local Italian-language daily newpaper is *Il Piccolo.*

Telephone – The telephone prefix for Trieste is 040.

GETTING AROUND: The city is small, and most of the main points of interest are easily accessible on foot.

Airports – Trieste's airport, *Ronchi dei Legionari,* is 20 miles northwest of the city and served by domestic flights only. An airport bus operates between the airport and the central railroad station on Viale Miramare. The nearest international airport is Venice's *Marco Polo Airport.*

Bus – Service is good within the city and to nearby points of interest. Tickets are sold at newsstands and tobacconists and must be purchased before boarding.

Car Rental – *Hertz* and *Avis* have local offices.

Taxi – Taxis are expensive, but given the city's small size, rides to the most likely tourist spots should be less than $5. There are numerous cabstands, and a 24-hour *Taxi Radio Trieste* service (phone: 775665).

Train – *Stazione Trieste Centrale* is on Viale Miramare (phone: 418207).

MUSEUMS: The museums of most interest to visitors are discussed in *Special Places.* But time permitting, several others are worth a visit. Unless otherwise indicated, they are open mornings only and closed Mondays.

Museo Teatrale (Theater Museum) – Housed in the Teatro Verdi, this small museum contains several thousand old librettos, manuscripts, books, and photographs related to opera, and a fine collection of musical instruments. Open during intermissions and Tuesday and Thursday mornings. Piazza Verdi 1 (phone: 61980).

Acquario Marino – A public aquarium on the waterfront with a wide variety of Adriatic marine life. Riva Nazario Sauro 1 (phone: 306201).

Museo del Risorgimento (Museum of the Risorgimento) – A small collection of artifacts and paintings illustrating Trieste's struggle to become part of Italy. Via XXIV Maggio 4 (phone: 60236).

SHOPPING: Trieste is less a shopper's paradise than Milan or Rome is, but it has a fine selection of the designer clothes, sportswear, shoes, and leather goods for which Italy is famous. It is also an easy and extremely pleasant place to shop. Most of the best boutiques are concentrated in the area from Piazza della Borsa to Piazza Goldoni, including the main avenue Corso Italia, the elegant 19th-century Galleria Tergesteo shopping arcade, and numerous side streets. An added attraction are the nautical shops that line the waterfront, selling boating accessories and clothing. Two hidden alleyways (Via del Ponte and Via delle Beccherie) behind Piazza dell'Unità d'Italia are lined with antiques shops and old curio shops — a kind of mini–flea market — that are great for browsing and for some good buys. If you want to check out the blue jeans that bring Yugoslav shoppers to Trieste, stop by Piazza Ponte Rosso any morning. It's also the best place to buy fresh fruit and vegetables. Although Trieste is not particularly known for handicrafts, a few bottles of the excellent wines made in the region make a worthwhile purchase. In addition to the shops listed below, *Gucci*, Corso Italia 21, and *Fendi*, Capo di Piazza 1, are represented in Trieste. Shop hours are 8:30 AM to 12:30 PM and 3:30 to 7:30 PM. Most are closed Monday mornings.

Ambassador – A wide selection of designer clothes (including Armani, Missoni, and Valentino) for men. Piazza della Borsa 3 (phone: 68118).

Beltrame – A large store for the whole family, selling casual and designer clothes, coats, and furs. Corso Italia 25 (phone: 65366).

La Bomboniera – A tiny jewel of a shop, 120 years old, with etched-glass doors, carved walnut shelves, and an original Bohemian glass chandelier. It sells pastries and beautifully wrapped chocolates. Via XXX Ottobre 3 (phone: 62752).

Coin – A good, general-purpose department store. Corso Italia 16 (phone: 614312).

Max Mara – Fine sportswear for women at significantly less than what this fashionable label costs in the US. Via Carducci 23 (phone: 631334).

Le Monde – Trendy fashions for men and women. Passo San Giovanni 1 (phone: 62237).

Christine Pelletterie – Fine leather clothes, shoes, and accessories for men and women. Piazza della Borsa 15 (phone: 64110).

Spangher – A large, slickly modern waterfront shop with the latest in nautical equipment and elegant sailing clothes, shoes (including designer rubber boots), and accessories. Riva Gulli 8 (phone: 305158)

Stefanel – A *Benetton*-type chain with a lively selection of moderately priced sweaters and slacks for both sexes. Corso Italia (phone: 61659).

Trussardi – Elegant sportswear and accessories for men and women by the well-known Milanese designer. Via San Nicolò 27 (phone: 68087).

Vecchia Europa – A tasteful selection of antique objects, art, furniture, and jewelry. Via Armando Diaz 1/C (phone: 690564).

V. Zandegiacomo – Elegant smoking and grooming articles for men, and quality silver, china, and glassware. Corso Italia 1 (phone: 37591).

SPECIAL EVENTS: Each spring on Pentecost Sunday, the nearby fishing port of Muggia (about a 20-minute car ride from Trieste) holds a colorful *Carnevale*, with huge floats and costumed parades through the town. Trieste's annual *International Trade Fair* is held the last two weeks in June. From July through mid-August, a popular *Festival dell'Operetta* takes place at the Teatro Stabile–Politeama Rossetti. Other summer events include outdoor concerts, ballets, and plays at the *Castello di San Giusto;* classical drama performances amid the ruins of the *Teatro Romano;* and evening sound-and-light shows at *Miramare Castle.* Every September, the *Settembre Musicale* festival features classical concerts by first-rate guest musicians and ensembles in the city's churches.

SPORTS: Besides the tourist office, the *Municipal Youth, Sports, and Leisure Department* (*Ripartizione Comunale Gioventù, Sport, e Tempo Libero*) has information on sports facilities in the city.

Golf – The *Golf Club Trieste* has an 18-hole course roughly 4 miles (20 minutes) from the center. Closed Tuesdays. 80 Padriciano (phone: 226159).

Horse Racing – Trotting races are run twice a week at the *Ippodromo di Montebello,* Piazzale de Gasperi 4 (phone: 732094).

Sailing – In the summer, sailboats can be rented at *Società Triestina della Vela,* Pontile Istria 8 (phone: 305999) and at *Società Triestina Sport del Mare,* 1/D Molo Venezia (phone: 303580).

Soccer – From September to May, *Triestina* plays at *Stadio Comunale Grezar,* Piazzale Valmaura (phone: 812210).

Swimming – There's an indoor municipal pool at Riva Gulli 3 (phone: 306024). The Trieste coastline is dotted with rocky beaches (the ones in Muggia and the resort town of Barcola are particularly nice), several of which have water sport facilities in the summer.

Tennis – Courts can be booked by the hour at *Tennis Club Park Hotel Obelisco,* Via Nazionale 1, Opicina (phone: 212756).

 THEATER: The *Teatro Stabile–Politeama Rossetti,* Viale XX Settembre 45 (phone: 69406 or 567507), is Trieste's major theater for top national productions. *Teatro Cristallo,* Via Ghirlandaio 12 (phone: 65700 or 741475), offers a mixture of avant-garde and traditional theater by repertory groups from all over Italy. Plays for the local Slovene community are staged at the *Teatro Sloveno,* Via Petronio 4 (phone: 734265).

 MUSIC: Trieste is a music-loving city, with classical concerts year-round. But its major attraction is the beautiful 19th-century opera house *Teatro Comunale Giuseppe Verdi,* Piazza Verdi 1 (phone: 631948), similar to Milan's La Scala and one of the best run in Italy. The opera season lasts from mid-October through April. Concerts and other musical events are held at the *Conservatorio Tartini,* Via Ghega 12 (phone: 630087), and at the *Teatro Cristallo,* Via Ghirlandaio 12 (phone: 741475).

 NIGHTCLUBS AND NIGHTLIFE: Despite its cosmopolitan aspects, Trieste is still a town that closes down rather early in the evening. But it does have its pockets of after-hours vitality. The hot discotheque is *Il Mandracchio,* Passo di Piazza 1 (phone: 64464). Other good discos are *Big Ben,* Viale Miramare 285, about 5 miles outside the city in Barcola (phone: 421452), and *Nepenthes,* 67 Duino, near the airport (phone: 208607). The *Bottega del Vino* (phone: 705959), an elegant piano bar and restaurant occupying the former stables of the Castello di San Giusto, offers romantic dining and dancing until 1 AM, except Tuesdays. Another popular late-night restaurant is the stylish *Elefante Bianco,* on the waterfront near Piazza dell'Unità d'Italia, at Riva Tre Novembre 3 (phone: 60889).

 SINS: The best local striptease show is at *Il Carillon,* a cabaret-restaurant at Via San Francesco 2 (phone: 732427). Soft-porn films are shown at the *Cinema Nazionale,* Viale XX Settembre 30 (phone: 723351), and at the art nouveau *Eden Cinema,* Viale XX Settembre 35 (phone: 794741).

BEST IN TOWN

 CHECKING IN: For a small city, Trieste has a surprisingly varied selection of hotels, some of which recall its glamorous past. As it is still relatively undiscovered by foreign tourists, local prices are quite reasonable. The best hotels in town, listed as expensive, cost up to about $100 for a double room. Hotels in the moderate category charge $50 to $75 for a double; inexpensive ones, $45 or less. The hotels listed below as moderate and inexpensive do not have air conditioning, but keep in mind that summers are rarely very hot here.

Adriatico Palace – A large luxury hotel overlooking the sea in Grignano, about 4 miles from Trieste, near Miramare Castle. It tends to host conventions of the nearby International Center of Nuclear Physics but has plenty to offer the independent visitor, including private beach facilities and swimming pool, a restaurant, and a magnificent terrace. Closed November through March. Via Grignano 9 (phone: 224241). Expensive.

Duchi d'Aosta – Small and truly elegant, with an ideal location right on Piazza dell'Unità d'Italia. Built in the late 19th century, the rooms have been tastefully modernized and equipped with air conditioning, television, and a small refrigerator bar. Exquisite decor and friendly service (the hotel is part of the prestigious CIGA chain) make it a jewel of a place to stay. Ask for a corner room looking out at the square and the waterfront. The ground-floor *Harry's Bar* offers an intimate setting for cocktails, and the adjoining *Grill Room* (see *Eating Out*) is one of the city's finest restaurants. Piazza dell'Unità d'Italia 2 (phone: 62081). Expensive.

Savoia Excelsior Palace – Some critics claim the modernization of this grand old hotel overlooking the waterfront has destroyed its Old World elegance, but guests will find the rooms more comfortable and equipped with all the amenities. Nostalgic patrons can still find some of the former ambience in the spacious lobby. Many of the 150 rooms (including several suites and apartments) have wonderful views. There is also a restaurant and piano bar. Riva del Mandracchio 4 (phone: 7690). Expensive.

Jolly – Near the station, this is a modern, efficient hotel, part of a national chain that caters mainly to businesspeople. It lacks the special character and decor of the other good hotels, and service tends to be impersonal. Corso Cavour 7 (phone: 7694). Expensive to moderate.

Colombia – The pick of hotels in the moderate-priced category. A real value, with modern, carpeted rooms and tiled baths, an attractive lobby and bar, and a particularly nice concierge. It's near the train station. Via della Geppa 18 (phone: 69434). Moderate.

Continentale – Pleasant and small, opposite a house where James Joyce once lived, on a quiet side street in the center of town. Rooms are spacious and very clean, and about 20 of the 53 have tiled baths. There's a bar and small breakfast room. Via San Nicolò 25 (phone: 65444). Moderate.

Corso – Modest but conveniently set in the best shopping area. The decor is unremarkable, but all the rooms are clean and functional, and about half have private baths. The 19th-century writer Stendhal is said to have spent several months here. Via San Spiridione 2 (phone: 630131). Moderate to inexpensive.

Abbazia – This recently renovated small hotel near the train station is nicely decorated for its genre. Most of the 21 rooms have private baths. It seems to be a favorite of Italian businesspeople. Via della Geppa 20 (phone: 61330). Inexpensive.

Al Teatro – An old-fashioned hotel near the opera and thus popular with musicians. The rooms are simple but comfortable, some with wood parquet floors. Only 12 of the doubles have private baths. Capo di Piazza 1 (phone: 64123). Inexpensive.

EATING OUT: Trieste's cuisine is a hearty blend of northern Italian and middle-European cooking, and it offers a wide variety of characteristic dishes. As might be expected in a port city, the fish is superb, and there are plenty of fine seafood restaurants. But pork, beef, veal, and venison are also local specialties. One pleasant Triestine tradition that's especially convenient for visitors is the informal "buffet," which offers home-cooked meals that are consumed with beer or wine at standup counters (some have stools) or at small tables. Buffets offer the best sausages, ham, and salami, in addition to such typical dishes as goulash, *tafelspitz* (tender cuts of boiled beef), and *jota,* a thick bean soup with sauerkraut, served at room temperature. Trieste has the added advantage of being in good wine-producing country. Excellent regional wines include Pinot Grigio, Tocai, and Merlot. Beer is also extremely popular; in addition to the full range of Italian brands, there are plenty of imports from Germany and Austria. Desserts are decidedly Austro-Hungarian in origin: rich cakes and strudels, coffee rings, and Sacher tortes. Among the restaurants listed, expect to pay $45 to $60 for a three-course meal for two without wine at restaurants categorized as expensive; $30 to $40 at moderately priced restaurants; and under $25 at inexpensive ones.

Harry's Grill – This elegant hotel restaurant once belonged to the Cipriani family that runs the famous *Harry's Bar* in Venice. The current owners have maintained its Old World charm and offer a refined cuisine of regional and international inspiration. The filet mignon is excellent, and there is a good selection of pasta and fish dishes. More indulgent diners might want to try some beluga caviar at about $100 per portion, but there are other appealing appetizers that cost considerably less. *Hotel Duchi d'Aosta,* Piazza dell'Unità d'Italia 2 (phone: 62081). Very expensive.

Antica Trattoria Suban – A well-known restaurant in a country house a few miles from the center of town, it has been in the same family for over 100 years. It has a lively, elegantly rustic atmosphere and an excellent menu and wine list. Try the *crespelle al radicchio rosso* (crêpes with grilled *radicchio,* a lettuce-like red salad leaf) or the crêpes with basil and cream sauce as an appetizer, followed by one of the superb steak or veal dishes. This is regional cooking at its best. Closed Tuesdays and August. Reservations advised. Via Comici 2 (phone: 54368). Expensive.

Ristorante alla Marinella – A pleasant, 10-minute walk from the Miramare Castle, this huge restaurant on the sea has a beautiful view of the coast and excellent seafood. The *risotto* with scampi is particularly good. Closed Sunday evenings and Mondays. Viale Miramare 323, Barcola (phone: 410986). Expensive.

All'Adriatico da Camillo – A small, friendly place that serves simple but excellent regional dishes, including a hearty goulash, *brasato* (pot roast), and homemade Austrian-style desserts. Vegetables and fish are always the best of the season. Closed Mondays and August. Via San Lazzaro 7 (phone: 65680). Moderate.

Al Bragozzo – Fish is the specialty of this cheerful, wood-paneled restaurant along the waterfront. Customers can help themselves to a wide variety of fish *antipasti* and choose their main dish from the fresh catch of the day. The homemade *ravioli Miramare,* stuffed with shrimp, salmon, and heavy cream, is not to be missed. Closed Sundays and Mondays. Riva Nazario Sauro 22 (phone: 303001). Moderate.

Ai Fiori – Traditional food with a touch of fantasy is served in a charming and intimate setting. The menu changes daily, but the focus remains finely prepared fish and pasta dishes. Try the artichoke soup or the exquisite *risotto* made with oysters and champagne. Closed Tuesdays and Wednesdays, Christmas through New Year's Day, and mid-June to mid-July. Piazza Hortis 7 (phone: 300633). Moderate.

Al Granzo – A favorite seafood restaurant, with a waterfront terrace overlooking the huge, enclosed fish market. Specialties include spaghetti with crabmeat, fish soup, and a delicate seafood *risotto,* as well as delicious homemade desserts — particularly the chocolate cream pastry called *rigojanci,* a local specialty of Hungarian origin. Owners Dario and Tullio, who both speak English, are exuberant hosts. Closed Wednesdays. Piazza Venezia 7 (phone: 762322). Moderate.

Buffet Benedetto – One of the best buffets in town, it also has ample room for sit-down dining, and its homey, wood-paneled decor, much like an Alpine tavern, is nicely complemented by the friendly service. This is a place for hearty meat and potato dishes such as goulash and *stinco di maiale* (roast shank of pork), and it also serves excellent *gnocchi,* with a meat or cheese sauce. For quicker, standup meals, the buffet offers a variety of salamis, cold meats, and salads. Try the exquisite *marrons glacés* (candied chestnuts) made fresh every day, for dessert. Closed Mondays and August. Via XXX Ottobre 19 (phone: 36409). Moderate.

Nastro Azzurro – A popular lunch spot for businesspeople, and considered one of the best seafood restaurants in town. It consists of one large room with brass chandeliers and a sumptuous display of shellfish appetizers, the catches of the day, and rich desserts. Fish is prepared in every way possible and also appears in delicious pasta and *risotto* dishes. Closed Saturday evenings and Sundays. Riva Nazario Sauro 10 (phone: 305789). Moderate.

Sacra Ostaria – Housed in a former inn where a Hapsburg prince once slept, this landmark restaurant, one block from the sea, has the feel of an old tavern that has been tastefully modernized. Open all day for drinks and cold-cut snacks, the restaurant has a fine menu of fish and meat dishes, a legendary homemade Sacher torte, and an exceptional wine list. Meals are served until midnight, and there is a pleasant outdoor garden for summer dining. Closed Mondays. Via Campo Marzio 13 (phone: 304791). Moderate.

Buffet Borsa – A popular lunchtime spot for downtown shoppers and office workers eating on the run. The fare consists of good goulash, sandwiches, and grilled meats. It's friendly but tiny — just a few tables and some counters with stools. Closed Sundays. Via Cassa di Risparmio 2 (phone: 630165). Inexpensive.

Siora Rosa – This small, lively neighborhood buffet has a cozy atmosphere and an irresistible aroma wafting from its kitchen. The food is genuine Triestine fare: roast pork, *cotechino* (a kind of cooked salami), hot boiled ham with horseradish, and liver with onions. This is a good place to try *jota* soup, and for a light lunch there are sandwiches and salads. Closed Saturday evenings and Sundays. Piazza Hortis 6 (phone: 301460). Inexpensive.

 CAFFÈS AND BARS: The coffeehouse tradition is an important part of Trieste life, and there are several historic *caffès* in which to enjoy a leisurely coffee or light snack. When ordering, keep in mind that, here, *cappuccino* means an espresso in a small cup with a bit of steamed milk. For the standard large cup of *cappuccino* served in the rest of Italy, ask for a *caffè latte.* The 150-year old *Caffè degli Specchi,* in Piazza dell'Unità d'Italia, was modernized in the 1960s and remains the fashionable meeting place. Its splendid outdoor setting makes it the best place to see and be seen while sipping an *aperitivo* or savoring a *gelato.* It's open until 11:30 PM daily, except Mondays. For true Old World atmosphere, nothing beats the *Caffè San Marco,* Via Cesare Battisti 18, two cavernous rooms with high ceilings, black wrought-iron lamps, golden wall friezes, and red marble tables where regulars play cards or read newspapers all day. Linger for hours over a cup of coffee or toasted sandwich any day except Wednesdays, from 7:30 AM until midnight. Unfortunately, there are no pastries other than a large jam-filled cookie. The elegant *Bar Tergesteo,* in the Galleria Tergesteo shopping arcade, Piazza della Borsa 15, has antique wooden tables and glittering Venetian crystal chandeliers. It's a good spot for a light snack or pastry, or a late drink after the opera. Open 7:30 AM to 11:30 PM, except Mondays.

TURIN

Turin (Torino) is the richest city in Italy — and any Italian will tell you why: The Turinese simply work harder than the rest of their compatriots. This should not give the visitor the idea that Turin is an all work and no play industrial city. Far from it. A stroll down Turin's main shopping street, Via Roma, proves that the inhabitants are blessed with excellent taste and the means to indulge it. Block after block on Via Roma — and elsewhere in the city — features luxury shops selling everything from the latest fashions to antique treasures.

It is obvious that the Turinese work hard to enjoy the fruits of their labors. But to be entirely honest, the people of Turin do tend to go to bed a little earlier than in the rest of Italy — the dinner hour begins closer to seven o'clock than to eight; many restaurants close by ten — but the locals seem to feel that this is a small price to pay for the rewards their labors afford them.

The image the Turinese present to the rest of the country is one of hard-working sobriety, but this is not quite accurate. In fact, there seems to be a curious dichotomy at work in this city — a second face carefully concealed from outsiders. For example: the vast wealth of Turin derives from the massive heavy industrial projects that ring the city, notably the enormous plants producing Italy's low-priced Fiat automobiles; yet Turin is also home to the finest names in automotive haute couture, car designers like Bertone, Pininfarina, and Giugiaro — names that quicken the pulse of car buffs the world over. The Turinese are not famous for being big drinkers, yet they have invented some of the best-known drinks in the world: Martini, Cinzano, and Carpano vermouths were invented and are still made in Turin. Turinese cuisine is elaborate and delicious; fanciful pastries and sweet, sweet chocolate concoctions are prized, yet Turin is the proud birthplace of the simple *grissino* — the breadstick.

Perhaps the oddest example of Turin's split personality is that the city is the undisputed capital of black magic in Italy. These same no-nonsense Turinese who seem so down-to-earth and efficient by day are dedicated followers of their horoscopes. The more superstitious regularly seek out the wisdom of fortunetellers and soothsayers, known as *maghi* and *chiromanti*. If they are in need of some serious black magic, they might go in search of a *stregone* who will cast a spell — for a healthy fee. Practitioners of the black arts are not hard to find. They advertise in newspapers, and there are several pages of them in the Turin yellow pages. The various first-class exorcists who are said to make Turin their base are harder to find — presumably they will contact you. Native-born Turinese claim that none of this necromancy is home grown but rather that it was imported by the suspicious southerners who came north in droves after the war to work in the newly rebuilt car factories. Nevertheless, a certain portion of the native Turinese have also taken to the occult in a big way.

Turin's roots lie deep in history. Conveniently placed on the banks of the Po River, the original city was laid out as a garrison town for the Romans who were working their way north in their ultimate conquest of Gaul. These ancient founders have left a notable legacy. The grid street pattern still visible today was laid out by the Romans. Successive rulers of the city saw no need to alter it — in fact, they added to it.

The Roman heritage of the city notwithstanding, it is impossible to divorce the history of Turin from a great noble family, the House of Savoy. This aristocratic family, possessed of a lineage longer, it is said, than that of any other nobility in Europe, made Turin the capital of its vast duchy in the eleventh century. Over a span of nine centuries, the citizens of Turin saw their fortunes soar under such enlightened rulers as Charles Emmanuel III and at times sink to sickening depths as their city was threatened by many enemies. For every enlightened Savoyard ruler, however, there seemed to be a dozen soldier-dukes. The history of Turin is, therefore, a martial rather than a cultural one.

Twice in its history Turin experienced lengthy and severe sieges at the hands of the French. Both sieges lasted months, yet at neither time was the city taken (once the French were turned back by the heroism of a single man; see "Pietro Micca Museum" in *Museums*). From their strong capital, the House of Savoy spent much of their tenure conquering additional territory (they acquired the Kingdom of Sardinia in the eighteenth century) or repulsing invaders. Charles Albert of Savoy expelled the Austrians from his lands in the early nineteenth century, although Turin did fall (like the rest of northern Italy) to the armies of Napoleon in 1798.

But Turin and the House of Savoy had a greater role to play in the destiny of nations. It was here that the first murmurs of the new Italian state — a unified Italy — were heard. The able and intelligent Victor Emmanuel II and his wise, if rather cold, prime minister, Count Camillo Cavour, became the chief movers and shakers of Italian unity. If Garibaldi can be considered the George Washington of Italian independence, then Cavour was its Thomas Jefferson. Cavour enlisted the aid of the French in a war against Austria (which was the major impediment to Italian unity) and, following two stunning victories at Magenta and Solferino (battles said to have been so bloody that the blood-soaked earth gave their names to dark red pigments on a painter's palette), broke the power of foreign interventionists in Italy. By 1861 the Kingdom of Italy had been proclaimed, with Turin its capital. In 1870 Rome was given that honor, but the king who ruled in Rome was Turinese, Vittorio Emanuele II of the House of Savoy.

The dynamic struggles for independence did not leave Turin spent, doomed to look back on the good old days forever. The Piedmontese faction was a power with which to reckon in Rome — a Turin-born son of the new kingdom would always have a voice in the running of the country. But more important, Turin rapidly caught up with its European economic rivals, whose industrial revolutions had a two-decade start on Italy's. Fiat and, later, Lancia were the leaders of this industrialization. It was the influx of workers to a traditionally independent-minded town that made Turin sit rather uneasily with fascism. Through the Fascist period anti-Fascist cells were at work in the city; when, in 1943, the Germans assumed control of northern Italy, open warfare broke out between partisan bands and the Nazis in and around the city. In addition, there were almost daily air attacks by the Allied air forces.

Yet the city survived and ultimately prospered. It was the cornerstone of the Italian Economic Miracle that followed World War II, and it became the center of modern Italian writing. First published out of Turin were such important authors as Italo Calvino (*If on a Winter's Night a Traveller*), Primo Levi (*The Truce, If There Is a Man, The Periodic Table*), and Cesare Pavese (*The Good Summer*).

It's an old joke in Italy: "If the government needs more money, we'll just make them work harder in Turin." It might be true, but the rest of the country can be sure that the "somber," high-living, superstitious, well-fed Turinese will do their part — and keep the lion's share for themselves.

TURIN AT-A-GLANCE

SEEING THE CITY: In the heart of the city is the dramatic and rather oddly designed tower of the *Mole Antonelliana.* It is some 300 feet high, and the viewing platform at the 275-foot mark provides a commanding view of the city and the Alps beyond. Begun in 1863 as part of Turin's synagogue, the congregation that commissioned it objected to its unorthodox design (it looks like a cross between a very large greenhouse and a very thin pagoda), leaving it to the city to either demolish or finish it. It was completed in 1890. An elevator takes visitors to the base of the spire. Open daily, except Mondays, 9 AM to 7 PM. Admission 500 lire. Via Montebello 20 (phone: 8398314).

A magical nocturnal view of the city is available from the terrace of the *Convento dei Cappuccini,* situated on the far bank of the Po. (Cross the river at Ponte Vittorio Emanuele 1 and follow signs for Via M. Giardino.)

SPECIAL PLACES: *Piazza San Carlo* is the heart of this busy town, and the square itself is an impressive architectural unity, incorporating the twin churches of *Santa Cristina* and *San Carlo,* which frame Via Roma. The equestrian statue dominating the square is of Emanuele Filiberto, the first of the House of Savoy to make Turin a capital. Elegant shops front the square, particularly some fine antiques shops and antiquarian bookshops. Weather permitting, the cafés that ring the square put out tables and chairs for their customers. Piazza San Carlo is *the* place to sip one of Turin's famous *aperitivi* and feel the vibrant city bustling all around. Not far away is the smaller, quieter *Piazza Carignano.* Packed into this tranquil square are some of Turin's best-known sights: the massive Baroque *Palazzo Carignano,* home of the first Italian parliament, and the *Academy of Sciences,* which houses the world-famous Egyptian collection. There is also the ancient and venerable *Ristorante del Cambio,* a favorite haunt of Cavour. (Most of the places recommended here are in the city center, an area flanked on the south by Corso Vittorio Emanuele, on the east by Corso Inghilterra, on the north by Corso Regina Margherita, and on the west by the Po River. Many sites are within walking distance of each other.)

Cappella della Santa Sindone (Chapel of the Holy Shroud) – Within the 15th-century Duomo di San Giovanni (Saint John's Cathedral) is the chapel containing

Turin's most famous possession, the Holy Shroud. Behind the apse stands the awesome black marble chapel of the *santissima sindone*. On the altar is a black marble urn containing the Holy Shroud, in which it is said the body of Christ was wrapped following his crucifixion. The shroud has not always been in Turin. Although specifically mentioned in the Gospel of Matthew, no trace of cloth was known until it turned up in Cyprus centuries after Christ's death. From Cyprus it traveled to France, where it is thought to have been acquired by the Savoys in 1578. The sheet, rarely exhibited, does demonstrably show the features of a man who suffered crucifixion — specifically in the manner described in the Gospels. While millions believe the features to be those of Christ, the Vatican has been reluctant to acknowledge them as such. The Church, however, treats the shroud as a holy relic, and belief in its validity has been enhanced since the present pope agreed to accept the shroud as a gift from the archbishop of Turin to the Holy See. Some testing has been done on the cloth, and some say there is evidence to suggest that the cloth is of the correct date (early 1st century) and that its origins are in the Middle East. As for the imprint of the man on the cloth itself, how and when it appeared, dozens of theories exist (none is irrefutably supported by scientific data). Although technically belonging to the Vatican, the shroud will always remain in Turin. It is kept in a silver casket, within an iron box enclosed in the marble urn on display. The only two keys are held by the Archbishop of Turin and the Palatine Cardinals, the group of senior churchmen based permanently at the Vatican. A large reproduction of the shroud, itself shown to the public on very rare occasions, stands in the chapel. Open daily, except Monday afternoons, 7 AM to noon and 3 to 7 PM. Piazza San Giovanni.

Palazzo dell'Accademia delle Scienze (Academy of Sciences) – A 17th-century palace designed by Guarino Guarini houses three notable art and antiquity collections. All are open 9 AM to 2 PM Tuesdays through Saturdays, to 1 PM Sundays; closed Mondays. Admission 3,000 lire. Piazza Carignano.

   Museo Egizio (Egyptian Museum) – It is said that Turin's collection of Egyptian artifacts is second only to that of the National Museum in Cairo. By far the most exciting exhibit in the museum is the entire Temple of Ellessya (dating from 15 BC). The presentation of this stone temple to the museum was a reward for the museum's work in saving ancient sites lost forever by the building of the Aswan High Dam (which created Lake Nasser, submerging hundreds of square miles in Upper Egypt). Overall, the museum includes precious and rare objects dating from the earliest civilization in Egypt to the full flowering of its culture in the 17th and 18th Dynasties.

   Galleria Sabauda (Savoy Gallery) – The gallery houses a fine collection of Flemish and Dutch paintings, including notable examples by Van Eyck, Memling, and Rembrandt. Italy is well represented by various Piedmontese, Tuscan, and Venetian masters, among them Mantegna, Guardi, Fra Angelico, and Veronese. Of particular interest are Palladio's *Tobias and the Angel* and Bronzino's *Eleanora of Toledo*.

   Museo dell'Antichità (Museum of Antiquity) – This is an archaeological museum housing artifacts from prehistory to late Roman times, including weapons, tools, coins, pottery, and sculpture.

Palazzo Madama (Madama Palace) – It is possible to see every phase of Turin's history in the architecture of this, one of the town's most imposing buildings. It incorporates the remains of a gate dating from the time of the Roman founders. In the Middle Ages, the palazzo became a Savoy stronghold, and over the years it was enlarged until, in the 17th century, its military value diminished and it became the household of the "Madama Reale" (loosely, dowager duchess) Maria Cristina, widow of Vittorio Amedeo II of Savoy. In 1721 the Baroque façade was added by the brilliant Sicilian architect Filippo Juvara. The palazzo now houses the Museo d'Arte Antica

(Museum of Ancient Art), something of a misnomer, as the bulk of the collection — certainly the masterpieces — dates from the late Middle Ages, the Renaissance, and the 17th and 18th centuries. One large gallery contains a Venetian state barge once belonging to the king of Sardinia. Open 9 AM to 7 PM weekdays, 10 AM to 1 PM and 2 to 7 PM Sundays; closed Mondays and public holidays. Admission 1,500 lire; free on Sundays. Piazza Castello.

Palazzo Reale (Royal Palace) – This rather plain 17th-century building was the home of Savoy rulers until 1865. The first floor has excellent examples of furniture and decoration from the 17th and 18th centuries. There is a fanciful Chinese room with some excellent porcelains. In the gallery attached to the library is a Leonardo da Vinci self-portrait. Open 9 AM to noon and 2 to 4 PM weekdays in winter; 9 AM to 12:30 PM and 3 to 5 PM weekdays in summer; 9 AM to 1 PM weekends and holidays; closed Mondays. Admission 1,500 lire. Piazza Castello.

Chiesa di San Lorenzo (Church of Saint Lawrence) – Near the Palazzo Reale is a 17th-century church that served as chapel for the ruling family. Designed by Guarini, its somber façade belies its sumptuous Baroque interior. Piazza Castello.

Armeria Reale (Royal Armory) – Nowhere is the martial past of the House of Savoy more clearly documented than in the Royal Armory, which houses a rich collection of arms and armor dating from Roman times to the Napoleonic era. (At press time the collection was closed for restoration.) Open daily, except Mondays, 9 AM to 2 PM. Piazza Castello.

Parco del Valentino (Valentino Park) – In the southern part of the city, set along the banks of the Po River, is a broad swatch of park containing an imitation castle constructed in the mid-1600s by the Francophile Maria Cristina. The castle is an almost perfect reproduction of a French château. Nearby is a newer (1884) reproduction, the *Borgo Medioevale* (Medieval Village). The houses of the village are patterned after those in the Piedmont region, the castle after Valle d'Aosta. Open daily, except Mondays and holidays, 10 AM to noon and 3 to 7 PM.

Museo Nazionale d'Artiglieria (National Artillery Museum) – Housed in the *Mastio della Cittadella*, the only remaining tower of the 16th-century citadel, this collection contains firearms from the history of Turin. Open 9 to 11 AM Tuesdays and Sundays, 9:30 to 11:50 AM and 3 to 5:20 PM Thursdays and Saturdays; closed Mondays, Wednesdays, and Fridays. Corso Galileo Ferraris.

Palazzo Carignano (Carignano Palace) – Originally built for the Carignano princes in the 17th century, this palace has two noteworthy façades: The one toward Piazza Carignano was designed in the Baroque style by Guarini; the other, toward Piazza Carlo Alberto, was added nearly two centuries later by Ferri and Bollati. The palazzo was the seat of the first Italian parliament and the birthplace of Victor Emmanuel II. It houses the *Museo Nazionale del Risorgimento* (*National Museum of the Risorgimento*), which displays documents and relics of the Italian unification movement. Open daily, 9 AM to 6 PM, 9 AM to noon Sundays; closed Mondays. Admission fee.

Museo dell'Automobile (Automobile Museum) – A huge collection of auto memorabilia, including 160 cars, documenting the entire history of the internal combustion engine. There is a vast research library as well. Open daily, except Mondays, 9:30 AM to 12:30 PM and 3 to 7 PM April to October, 10 AM to 12:30 PM and 3 to 5:30PM November to March. Corso Unità d'Italia 40 (south of the city center).

Museo Nazionale della Montagna (National Alpine Museum) – Located on the Monte dei Cappuccini, overlooking the river and the city, is a small museum devoted to Piedmontese mountain life, culture, and alpinism. Open daily, 8:45 AM to 12:15 PM and 2:45 to 7:15 PM. Admission 2,000 lire. Via G. Giardino 39.

ENVIRONS

Sacra di San Michele – Perched on the edge of the San Michele ravine, this ancient Benedictine monastery was built by a group of French monks in 998. It takes its name from the miraculous appearance of Saint Michael, who is said to have appeared in midair to catch a falling child. The abbey, now overseen by Rosminian priests, commands an astonishingly beautiful position high above the Dora Riparia Valley. The "staircase of the dead" leads to the marble portal, which has strong Romanesque bas-reliefs — some decidedly more profane than sacred (zodiacal symbols, women offering their breasts to serpents, etc.) — as well as the stories of Cain and Abel and of Samson and Delilah. From the esplanade surrounding the Romanesque Gothic church at the summit are beautiful views of the Dora Valley, the Po Plain, and the Turin Plain. Open daily, 9 AM to noon and 2 to 7 PM. On route SS25, 23 miles (about a half-hour drive) west of the city.

Palazzo Stupinigi (Stupinigi Palace) – Built in the 18th century as a hunting lodge for the Savoy family, the design of this beautiful palace (sometimes called the Villa Reale or *la palazzina di caccia*) has all the clarity and authority of a great work of art. Filippo Juvara, whose signature is indelibly stamped on Turin, was the architect. Although "merely" a hunting lodge, it was Napoleon's home before he assumed the crown of Italy. It is now a museum of 18th-century furniture — some of it lovely — but it is the building, with its noble sculpture of a stag stamped against the Alpine sky, that one comes to see. Guided tours only. Open daily, except Mondays, 10 AM to noon and 3 to 6 PM in summer; 10 AM to 12:30 PM and 2 to 5 PM in winter. Admission 1,000 lire. On the Pinerolo road (SS23), less than 7 miles south of Turin.

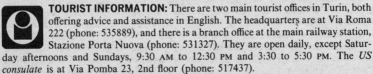

SOURCES AND RESOURCES

TOURIST INFORMATION: There are two main tourist offices in Turin, both offering advice and assistance in English. The headquarters are at Via Roma 222 (phone: 535889), and there is a branch office at the main railway station, Stazione Porta Nuova (phone: 531327). They are open daily, except Saturday afternoons and Sundays, 9:30 AM to 12:30 PM and 3:30 to 5:30 PM. The *US consulate* is at Via Pomba 23, 2nd floor (phone: 517437).

Local Coverage – The Turin daily newspaper is *La Stampa,* considered one of the finest papers in Italy. Its readership and influence extend well beyond the city. The *International Herald Tribune* and the Rome-based *International Courier* represent the English press in Turin. Both can be purchased late on the day of publication at the larger newsstands or at the train station. A useful booklet, *This Week in Turin,* is available free at hotels, tourist offices, the train station, and the airport.

Telephone – The telephone prefix for Turin is 011.

GETTING AROUND: Airport – There are daily connecting flights to all major European cities from the Turin international airport, *Città di Torino,* in Caselle (phone: 5778361, -2, -3, or -4). Bus service and taxis to Turin are available.

Bus and Tram – Turin has an extensive bus and tram service. There is even a country trolley line serving the outskirts of the city. Very few of the buses, trams, or trolleys run all night. Tickets must be purchased before boarding at cigarette shops or some newsstands and are validated on board. For information about schedules, call *Autostazione Terminal* (phone: 442525).

Car Rental – The major firms have offices in Turin: *Avis,* Via Corso Turati 15/G (phone: 500852, 501107, 503263, and 505568), at the airport (phone: 4701528), and at the railway station (phone: 6699800); *Hertz,* Corso Marconi 19 (phone: 6504504), and at the railway station.

Taxi – Taxis can be hailed as they cruise or at one of the taxi stands on the major streets — Via Po, Via Roma, and so on.

Trains – Turin is an important railway center for northern Italy. The *Stazione Porta Nuova* is on the Corso Vittorio Emanuele II, one of the city's most important streets (phone: 544471).

 MUSEUMS: Besides those mentioned in *Special Places,* Turin has a number of galleries and museums of special interest:

Anthropology and Ethnology Museum – Via Accademia Albertina 17.
Gallery of the Albertine Academy of Fine Arts – Via Accademia Albertina 6.
Gallery of Modern Art – Via Magenta 31.
National Cinema Museum – Piazza San Giovanni 2.
Natural History Museum Don Bosco – Viale Thovez 37.
Pietro Micca Museum – Via Guicciardini 7.

 SHOPPING: The most elegant shopping street is Via Roma, which runs from the Porta Nuova railway station to Piazza Castello. Along this busy thoroughfare, or just off it, are a number of the shops that allow the hard-working Turinese to enjoy the fruits of their labors. Via Garibaldi is also a mother lode of fine shops, some less expensive than those on Via Roma. As Via Garibaldi is closed to motor traffic, shopping here can be a bit less frantic than elsewhere.

The Turinese are artists when it comes to producing and consuming chocolate. *Peyrano,* Corso Moncalieri 47, has been making chocolate for a number of royal houses for centuries. The firm specializes in bitter and liqueur chocolates; the prices, unfortunately, are rather high. Other top-quality makers of Turin's favorite sweet are *Stratta,* Piazza San Carlo 191, and *Caffarel* (distributors to the city's best *caffès* and *pasticcerias*).

Other fine shops are:

De Candia – For the well-dressed Torinese male. Piazza San Carlo 175.

Durando – Large selection of the finest furs — capes, jackets, stoles, and full-length coats — well suited to the Alpine air or a first night at the theater. Via Roma 77.

Lenci – World-famous for antique porcelain and hand-carved dolls. Via San Marco 56/b.

Olimpic – Extremely elegant shop known for its classic women's and men's clothing. Piazza San Carlo 82.

Visetti – A breathtaking selection of lingerie in silks, satins, crêpes des Chine, and good old-fashioned cotton to keep out the Alpine chill. Via Roma 247.

 SPECIAL EVENTS: As might be expected in a city that makes much of its living from automobiles, the biggest event is the *International Car Show,* held in even years at the fairgrounds on Corso Massimo D'Azeglio. The show takes place in the spring, usually in late April or early May. Since the city is overrun with conventioneers who crowd every hotel, restaurant, and shop, it is suggested that only devoted autophiles visit Turin during this period. Other events at the fairgrounds include the *International Vacations Salon* (February); the *International Salon of Domestic Arts* (March); the *Oscar Award* competition for the best shoes (June); the *International Shows of Technology and*

Mountain Sports (October); and the *International Industrial Vehicle Expositions* (November).

SPORTS: Horse Racing – There are flat races most of the year, except during August and the height of the winter, at *Vinovo,* near Stupinigi.

Golf – The *Torino Golf Club* maintains a championship course at Mandria Park (see *Great Italian Golf,* DIVERSIONS). In addition, there is a 9-hole course at *Parco della Madonna,* 10 miles from the city center. Other courses are at *I Roveri* and *Stupinigi,* slightly more distant from the city.

Soccer – From September to May, both *Torino* (phone: 393496, 327474) and *Juventus* (phone: 390292) — "la Juve" in headlines and graffiti — play at *Stadio Comunale,* Corso Sebastopoli 123.

Swimming – The municipal swimming center has both covered and uncovered pools. Admission 1,500 lire. Corso Sebastopoli 123.

THEATER AND MUSIC: Operas, symphonies, ballets, and any number of plays may be running concurrently. There is no "season" as such — productions go on year-round. The best way to find out what Turin is offering on a daily basis is to consult *La Stampa* or *This Week in Turin.* Activities are usually centered on the *Teatro Regio* (Royal Theater) and the *Opera House* in Piazza Castello. Both publish extensive calendars of events. Other theaters of note are *Stabile di Torino,* Via Rossini 8; *Teatro Carignano,* Piazza Carignano; and *Teatro Alfieri,* Piazza Solferino. Symphony concerts and chamber music can be heard at the *Auditorium della RAI,* Via Rossini 15.

NIGHTCLUBS AND NIGHTLIFE: The Turinese do not dance the night away. Such nightclubs as the city possesses are located mostly in the area around the Porta Nuova railway station. Some clubs come and go so fast that they are known by word of mouth only. Hotel porters are the best sources of information on the discotheques, pubs, and piano bars that have brilliant, but brief, life spans.

SINS: The Turinese are afflicted with two great sins. The first is enormous *pride* in their history and economic accomplishments. They feel that they more or less gave Italy to the Italians. Now, having given it, they sometimes feel they are picking up the entire tab for it. (The rest of the country suffers from envy of Turin. Any number of Italian cities are more beautiful, older, more cultured — but none are as well run, efficient, or rich.) You can only admire Turin (or you can envy its people), but you can actively indulge in the city's other great sin — the passion for sweets (see *Shopping* for chocolates and "Coffeehouses" in *Eating Out*).

BEST IN TOWN

CHECKING IN: Turin has a parking problem, so visitors who are driving should ask the management of any hotel (or a travel agent) whether garage space is available. Hotels that charge more than $80 a night for a double room are classified here as expensive; those that charge between $60 and $80 are moderate; $50 or less, inexpensive.

Jolly Hotel Principi di Piemonte – Turin's finest hotel is in the heart of town, not far from the train station. Rooms are large, some grand, and the service is superlative. Via P. Gobetti 15 (phone: 519693). Expensive.

Grand Hotel Sitea – After recent reconstruction, plans now call for a new roof garden. Each of the spacious rooms has air conditioning, color television, a minibar, and a direct-dial phone. Central location and excellent service. Via Carlo Alberto 35 (phone: 55701719). Expensive.

Ligure – Another of the *Jolly* hotel chain, this one opened in 1984. It is directly opposite the Porta Nuova station. Piazza Carlo Felice 85 (phone: 55641). Expensive.

Turin Palace – A large hotel next to the railway station, with an excellent restaurant and conference facilities. Via Sacchi 8 (phone: 515511). Expensive.

Villa Sassi – A good choice for those who want to escape the noise and bustle of the city center. Three miles from downtown (follow signs for Pino Torinese and Chieri), this 17th-century country house is set in a beautifully landscaped park. There are 12 elegant rooms, and its restaurant is the best in Turin (see *Eating Out*). Via Traforo del Pino 47 (phone: 890556). Expensive.

City – Small and modern, with an attractive little garden and a late-night grill that serves hot snacks (no restaurant). Via F. Juvara 25 (phone: 540548). Expensive to moderate.

President – Each room has a terrace overlooking an enclosed garden. The hotel boasts a cheerful, modern environment and a helpful staff. Only breakfast is served, and there is a small bar. Via A. Cecchi 67 (phone: 859555). Moderate.

Europa – Once the haunt of local nobility, it fell on hard times for a while. It has recently been renovated, however, and has again become a pleasant place to stay. Ask for a quiet room with a bath. Piazza Castello 99 (phone: 543765, 5434238). Moderate to inexpensive.

EATING OUT: The cuisine of Turin, like northern Italian cooking in general, is similar to that of the French in method — but very different in ingredients. Piedmont is especially rich in special delicacies, some as simple as the breadstick. Others are more exotic: fabulous white truffles, for instance, are hunted at night, not by pigs, as in France, but by dogs — in fact, there is a special school at Rodi that does nothing but turn ordinary hounds into truffle hunters. This range of culinary delights and a plethora of cheeses and hot appetizers make dining in Turin a distinctly different experience. Meals for two that cost more than $70 are categorized here as expensive; those between $40 and $70, moderate; and $40 or less, inexpensive.

Villa Sassi – The best restaurant in Turin, in the hotel by the same name. It's 3 miles from the city center but well worth the drive. Specialties include salmon marinated in raspberry vinegar, and breast of duck with local herbs. Any pork dish is sure to be outstanding. The service is excellent. Closed August. Reservations essential. Strada al Traforo del Pino 47 (phone: 890556). Expensive.

Del Cambio – A little piece of Turin history. A scarf in the Italian colors still marks the table that Cavour frequented, and some of the waiters, who wear black tails, white gloves, and aprons, look as if they could have waited on him. Although the braised beef in Barolo wine is exceptional, one comes here most for the history and the atmosphere. Closed Sundays and August. Reservations essential. Piazza Carignano 2 (phone: 546690). Expensive.

Vecchia Lanterna – A quiet, hospitable place that makes the most of the local duck and pork dishes. Any meal begun with a terrine of duck foie gras is bound to be a success. Closed Saturdays at lunchtime, Sundays, and August. Reservations necessary. Corso Re Umberto 21 (phone: 537047). Expensive.

I Due Lamponi – The atmosphere is like that of a 19th-century drawing room, with a high, barrel-vaulted ceiling and a rather somber decor. A wide range of Piedmontese hot appetizers is served, as well as excellent *agnolotti* (large ravioli) stuffed with pheasant. Closed Sundays. Reservations suggested. Via C. Alberto 45 (phone: 546721, 555292). Expensive to moderate.

Gatto Nero – Turin's best fish restaurant is an inconspicuous place. It has no street sign, but behind its large windows there are usually some 80 diners enjoying excellent fish, shellfish, and steaks. Closed Sundays and August. Corso Filippo Turati 14 (phone: 590414). Expensive to moderate.

San Giorgio – Enjoy an evening of dining and dancing at this lakeside restaurant with a lovely view. Closed Tuesdays. Borgo Medioevale Valentino (phone: 682131). Expensive to moderate.

Il Blu – A large, lively restaurant serving a good selection of salads and charcoaled entrées, including local sausages and meats. Service is rapid without being rushed; the decor, bright without being gaudy. Closed Sundays. Corso Sicardi 75 (phone: 545640). Moderate to inexpensive.

Tre Galline – Experience the full range of Piedmontese hot appetizers: breadsticks, boiled meats, *fondutas*, so many first courses that the second course is almost irrelevant. Closed Mondays and August. Via Bellezia 37 (phone: 546833). Inexpensive.

COFFEEHOUSES: Turin is home to some of Italy's most celebrated coffeehouses — many of which are 19th-century palaces — where customers can overdose on pastries and chocolates. Among the best known, and certainly the oldest, are *Baratti* and *Milano,* in Piazza Castello. These two grand old establishments are dark and intimate. Dating from the same era, yet ages away in decor, are the *San Carlo* and the *Torino,* in Piazza San Carlo. The interiors of these two are a riot of mirrored gilt and stucco. Another not to be missed is *Zucca,* at Via Roma 296.

VENICE

Venice is one of the world's most photic — and photographic — cities. As the sun sets, it burnishes the old buildings with a splendid, rosy glow that is reflected, then refracted, in the waters of the canals. The city is luminously beautiful, both in radiant, peak-season August and in bleak, wet November. And it is painfully beautiful when suddenly, on some late-winter morning, the rain trickles to a halt, the cloud curtains part, and trapezoids of sunlight reheat the ancient stones. Then there is an ineffable sense of renewal as the café tables are set up again in St. Mark's Square, and pigeons and waiters alike swoop out from the dark arcades while an orchestra begins another airy melody. Little wonder that, long before photography, Romantic painting flourished here.

Venice is 117 islets separated by 150 canals and joined by 400 bridges on Italy's northeastern Adriatic coast. A three-mile bridge reaches across the Laguna Veneta (Venetian Lagoon), connecting it to the mainland near the small town of Mestre. The city is protected from the force of the Adriatic Sea by the natural breakwater of the Lido, a long, narrow sandbar that is one of the most fashionable resorts on the Adriatic.

The lagoon city began as a place of refuge from the violent barbarian invasions of the fifth century; mainland inhabitants fled to the isolated islands. As communities grew up, the islands became connected to one another, and Venice developed into a powerful, flourishing city-state. During the Crusades, this little maritime republic came to dominate the entire Mediterranean, and the winged Venetian lion, symbol of St. Mark, the city's protector, stood guard over a network of palaces from the Strait of Gibraltar to the Bosporus. This was the city of Marco Polo.

Renaissance Venice was the focal point for the great trade routes from the Middle East, and the markets beside the city's Ponte di Rialto (Rialto Bridge) were a pulse of European commerce. The doges — the city's rulers — celebrated their mastery of the Mediterranean with an annual ceremony of marriage to the sea, and the golden ducats that overflowed the city's coffers financed some of the world's most spectacular art and architecture. The Venetian school of painting, which produced magnificent colorists, began with Giorgione and achieved its apogee in the sixteenth century with Titian Vecellio, Paolo Veronese, and Jacopo Tintoretto. The proud, thousand-year Venetian independence ended with the Treaty of Campoformio in 1797, when Napoleon traded the territory to Austria. In 1866, after nearly seventy years of Bonaparte and Hapsburg domination, the city was joined to newly unified Italy.

The city today has a population of nearly 400,000, including some who live in the industrialized areas on the mainland side of the lagoon. The millions of tourists who swarm through its narrow streets and tiny squares make up

Venice's chief industry — and they leave behind well over $100 million a year. A gaudy party atmosphere reigns from Easter to October, with a midsummer explosion sometimes as crass as it is colorful: the landing stages jammed and listing with tour groups, long lines waiting for frozen custard by the Doge's Palace, and the big Lido ferries packed with sun-scorched day-trippers. Hawkers and hustlers populate every corner. In its way the scene is as vibrant, insistent, chaotic, and vulgar as anything from the days of the international market on the Ponte di Rialto.

And yet, even on *Ferragosto* weekend, Italy's state holiday in August, it's still possible to turn deliberately from the main thoroughfare and string together a few random rights and lefts to find yourself in a haven of quiet back alleys, on a tiny bridge across a deserted canal, in the middle of a silent, sun-baked *piazzetta,* with a fruit stall, a splashing fountain — and not a tourist in sight.

Venice in winter is a totally different experience: placid, gray, and star-tlingly visual. Suddenly, there is no one between you and the noble palaces, the soaring churches, the dark canals. Only the mysterious masked merriment of *Carnevale,* in mid-February, interrupts the chilly repose of the time when Venice is most emphatically a community of Venetians.

Not everyone loves Venice. D. H. Lawrence called it "an abhorrent, green, slippery city," and it does have a dark, decadent quality, sometimes a damp depressiveness. (An inscription on a sundial says, "I count only the happy hours.") But few cities have attracted so many illustrious admirers. Shake-speare set one of his best-known plays, *The Merchant of Venice,* here. Galileo Galilei used the bell tower in St. Mark's Square to test his telescope. Richard Wagner composed here. Lord George Byron and Henry James wrote here. It's not hard to feel the ghosts of these and others who, as James said, "have seemed to find [here] something that no other place could give."

VENICE AT-A-GLANCE

SEEING THE CITY: The traditional vantage point from which to admire Venice is the summit of the 324-foot red *campanile* (bell tower) in St. Mark's Square. The view on all sides is breathtaking — from the red-shingled roof-tops and countless domes of the city to the distant islands that dot the wide lagoon. There's an elevator to the top or, for the heartier, a ramp. Open daily. Admission fee.

For a bird's-eye view of St. Mark's Square itself (and the rest of the lagoon city), take a short boat ride to the *Isola San Giorgio* (No. 5 ferryboat from the Riva degli Schiavoni — one stop) and ride the elevator to the top of the church tower. The church itself, a masterpiece by Andrea Palladio, contains two major works by Tin-toretto. It also has beautiful carved wooden choir stalls depicting the life of St. Bene-dict. Admission fee.

SPECIAL PLACES: *St. Mark's Square* is the center of life in Venice; from here sightseers can board steamers to the Lido and other islands as well as to the various quarters of the city. The *Corso della Gente* is not a street, but a phrase Venetians use to describe the "flow of people" that roughly parallels the Grand Canal, snaking through the heart of the city from the bridge (Ponte degli Scalzi) near the Santa Lucia Railway Station to St. Mark's Square. You can follow it instinctively without once asking for directions.

DOWNTOWN

Piazza San Marco (St. Mark's Square) – Napoleon called this huge marble square the finest drawing room in Europe. Bells chime, flocks of pigeons crisscross the sky, violins play, couples embrace in the sunset — while the visitor takes it all in from a congenial café. A mere turn of the head allows you to admire St. Mark's Basilica, the Doge's Palace, the 9th-century bell tower, the clock tower where giant bronze Moors have struck the hours for five centuries, the old law courts, and the old library, which now houses the archaeological museum. In the *piazzetta,* through which the square opens onto the Grand Canal, there are two granite columns — one topped by the Lion of St. Mark, the other by a statue of St. Theodore.

Basilica di San Marco (St. Mark's Basilica) – This masterpiece of Venetian-Byzantine architecture was built in 830 to shelter the tomb of St. Mark, whose bones had been smuggled out of Alexandria. When first built, it was not a cathedral but a chapel for the doges. The present basilica was constructed during the 11th century, but the phenomenal decoration of the interior and exterior continued well into the 16th century. The basilica has a large dome and four smaller ones; its imposing façade of variegated marble and sculpture has five large doorways. The four famous bronze horses that have adorned the central doorway since 1207, when they were brought here after the sack of Constantinople, were removed in 1980 for restoration. Plaster replicas have taken their place in the doorway, and the originals are now on permanent display in the basilica's museum. Inside, the walls are encrusted with precious art, rare marbles, and magnificent mosaics. Behind the high altar in the chancel is the famous gold altarpiece, the *Pala d'Oro,* and the basilica's treasury includes rare relics as well as Byzantine goldwork and enamels. Open daily. Small admission fee for the chancel and treasury. Piazza San Marco.

Palazzo Ducale (Doge's Palace) – Next to the basilica is the pink and white palace with an unusual double *loggia* that served as the residence of the doges and the seat of government. The finest room in the palace is the Grand Council Chamber, containing paintings by Tintoretto and Veronese. You may also visit the doge's apartments and the armory. The palace is connected to the old prisons by the famous *Ponte dei Sospiri* (Bridge of Sighs), whose name comes from the lamentations of prisoners supposedly taken across the bridge to be executed. Open daily. Admission fee. Piazza San Marco (phone: 5236830).

Grand Canal – Lined with some 200 marble palaces built between the 12th and the 18th century, the Grand Canal has been called the finest street with the finest houses in the world. On the right (east bank) are the *Palazzo Vendramin-Calergi,* where Wagner died, now the winter home of the *Municipal Casino* (see *Sins*); the *Ca' d'Oro* (Golden House), so called because its ornate façade once was entirely gilded; the *Palazzo Mocenigo,* where Lord Byron lived; and *Palazzo Grassi,* now also called *Palazzo Fiat,* an art museum recently bought and refurbished by the Agnelli family. On the left (west bank) are the *Palazzo Pesaro,* which houses the modern art gallery, and the *Palazzo Rezzonico,* an architectural jewel that contains the civic museum of 18th-century art. A good way to see all of these beautiful *palazzi* is to take a slow boat ride over the entire 2-mile length of the Grand Canal.

Chiesa di Santa Maria della Salute – Dedicated to the Madonna for delivering Venice from a plague, this 17th-century Baroque church is just across the Grand Canal from St. Mark's Square. Its octagonal shape and white Istrian limestone façade are easily recognizable in innumerable paintings of Venetian scenes and panoramas. Inside are paintings of the New Testament by Titian and Tintoretto.

Chiesa del Redentore (Church of the Redeemer) – A must for architectural enthusiasts, this 16th-century church is known for its perfect proportions and remarkable harmony both inside and out. It was built by Andrea Palladio on a point of the Giudecca Island, a short ferry ride (take a No. 5) from St. Mark's by way of Isola San Giorgio. The yearly Feast of the Redeemer (the third Sunday in July; see *Special Events*) used to be attended by the doge, who reached the church across a bridge of boats. Campo Redentore.

Galleria dell'Accademia (Gallery of Fine Arts) – Brief but frequent visits are the best way to savor the rich contents of this great art gallery. Of particular interest are Veronese's *Supper in the House of Levi,* Titian's *Presentation of the Virgin,* Tintoretto's *Transport of the Body of St. Mark,* and Giorgione's *Tempesta.* The paintings of Venice by Antonio Canaletto, Francesco Guardi, and Gentile Bellini are the academy's most Venetian selections, both by subject and artist, and meld all impressions of the city. Closed Mondays. Admission fee; free on Sundays. Campo della Carità.

Museo del Settecento Veneziano (Museum of Eighteenth-Century Venice) – Built in the 17th century, *Ca' Rezzonico* — the palace that has housed the museum since 1936 — has a magnificent exterior that is best observed from the Grand Canal (in turn, its windows afford superb views of the canal). In addition to holding the most sumptuous treasures of 18th-century Venetian art, the palace itself is worth visiting for its grandiose decor and its frescoes by Giandomenico Tiepolo and his son Giambattista. Closed Fridays. Admission fee. Dorsoduro Ca' Rezzonico (phone: 5224543).

Scuola di San Rocco (Great School of San Rocco) – The Venetian *scuola* was not a school, but something of a cross between a trade guild and a religious brotherhood that supplied wealthy patronage for the arts. San Rocco contains a rich collection of Tintorettos — some 56 canvases depicting stories from the Old and New Testaments. Open daily. Admission fee. Campo San Rocco.

Chiesa di Santa Maria Gloriosa dei Frari (St. Mary's Church) – Known simply as *Frari,* this church is considered by many to be the most splendid in Venice after St. Mark's. It contains three unquestioned masterpieces: the *Assumption* and the *Madonna of Ca' Pesaro,* both by Titian, and Giovanni Bellini's triptych on the sacristy altar. An excellent way to appreciate its beauty is to attend an early morning mass before the tourists come. Next to the *Scuola di San Rocco.* Campo dei Frari.

Chiesa di Santa Maria del Carmelo (Church of Our Lady of Mount Carmel) – Also known as the *Chiesa dei Carmini* (*Church of the Carmelites*), this 14th-century Gothic church with a 17th-century campanile — crowned by a statue of the Virgin — still has original gilded wooden ornamentation in its nave. Its walls are lined with many 17th- and 18th-century paintings. The cloister adjacent to the church (see the next entry) now belongs to the State Institute of Art. Campo Santa Margherita.

Scuola Grande dei Carmini (Great School of the Carmelites) – Next to the Carmelite Church, this gracious 17th-century palace contains the most extensive collection of works by Giambattista Tiepolo anywhere in Venice. Paintings and frescoes adorn the interior. Campo Santa Margherita.

Scuola San Giorgio degli Schiavoni (School of St. George of the Slavonians) – This small building, beyond St. Mark's Square in a part of the city most visitors do not tour, contains one of the city's most overlooked treasures: the frieze of paintings by Vittore Carpaccio depicting stories of St. George, St. Jerome, and St. Tryphon. Closed Mondays. Admission fee. Castello, Calle dei Furlani.

ENVIRONS

The Lido – For most of the 20th century, this shoestring island — across the lagoon from Venice proper — has been one of the world's most extravagant resorts. Indeed, the word *lido* has come to mean, in much of the world's lexicon, any fashionable, luxuriously equipped beach resort. There has always been a touch of decadence to the

Venetian Lido with its elegant rambling hotels, sumptuous villas, swank casino, and world-weary, wealthy clientele. Thomas Mann used the Lido's posh *Grand Hotel des Bains* (see *Checking In*) as a background for his haunting novella *Death in Venice*. Today, thousands of cabins and cabanas line the Lido's fine sandy beaches, and purists assert that the old resort has gone to seed. But the tourists still come by the thousands — some drawn by the tinsel of an international cinema festival, others by the trendiness of a pop music celebration, but most lured by the legendary Lido ambience. There are buses on the island, which can be reached by frequent boat service from Riva degli Schiavoni. There is also a car ferry from Piazzale Roma.

Murano – This island has been the home of Venetian glassmaking since the 13th century. Visitors can watch the glass blowing and molding processes at one of the island factories but should be aware of the high-pressure tactics used to sell the glass. The island's *Museo Vetrario* (*Glassworks Museum*), Fondamenta Giustinian 8, has one of the world's best collections of Venetian glass. Closed Tuesdays. Admission fee; free Sundays. Murano is 15 minutes by steamer from Fondamenta Nuove.

Burano – The colorful homes, small boats, and nets and tackle of the fishermen who live here add charm to this little island, best known as a center of lacemaking, still practiced by some island women. Burano is 30 minutes by steamer from Fondamenta Nuove.

Torcello – This was one of the most prosperous colonies on the lagoon in the 5th and 6th centuries, but as Venice grew, Torcello declined. The main square is now overgrown with grass. Most of the cathedral, as it appears today, dates from the early 11th century. It has several fine Byzantine mosaics and an interesting iconostasis. The island is 45 minutes by steamer from Fondamenta Nuove.

■**EXTRA SPECIAL:** The so-called *Brenta Riviera* was where all Venetians who could afford them built summer residences in the 16th century. So many Venetian villas were built along the Brenta Canal that it seemed to be an extension of the Grand Canal. During the 17th and 18th centuries a luxurious barge, *Il Burchiello*, made a daily trip along the Brenta, which links Venice and Padua. Today's tourist can enjoy the same cruise in the summer by motorized boat from Pontile Giardinetto near St. Mark's Square. The excursion, which includes lunch in Oriago and a bus return from Padua, takes a full day. Apply to *Compagnia Italiana Turismo* (*CIT*), St. Mark's Square (phone: 85480), for information. (It is also possible to tour the area by car on a road that roughly parallels the canal. See *The Veneto* in DIRECTIONS.)

South of Venice is the island of *Chioggia*, once a major stronghold of the Venetian Republic. Now little more than a fishing port, it retains tantalizing traces of its past glory. The 13th-century *Church of San Domenico* displays works by Carpaccio and Tintoretto; the highly decorated Baroque altar contrasts with its simpler surroundings. There are numerous other small churches in Chioggia, some in a poor state of repair, but all with significant works of Venetian art. The *duomo*, or cathedral and bishopric, which stands at the end of Corso del Popolo, is a grandiose 17th-century building reconstructed on the ruins of the original 12th-century church. Inside are paintings that recount some of the history and sacred legends of Chioggia. Around the corner is the celebrated *Piazza Vescovile*. Bordered by plane trees and an ornamented balustrade, it has been a favorite subject for painters through the ages. Chioggia can be reached by boat, passing several other lagoon islands on the way, or by bus from the train station of Piazzale Roma. On the waterfront is an excellent, inexpensive restaurant, *El Gato*, which specializes in lagoon fish, served with fresh salads and local wines.

SOURCES AND RESOURCES

TOURIST INFORMATION: A free pocket-sized map of Venice, listing the various boat routes around the city, is available from the *Azienda Autonoma di Soggiorno e Turismo,* 4089 Rialto, Palazzo Martinengo (phone: 30313, 30399) or from the *Ente Provinciale per il Turismo* in the Santa Lucia railroad station (phone: 715016, 715288). Both organizations provide tour guides for small groups. The *Associazione Guide Turistiche Calle delle Bande,* Castello 5267 (phone: 709038), has a list of multilingual tour guides whose fixed rates are approved by the local tourist board. The nearest *US consulate* is in Trieste, Via Roma 9 (phone: 040-68728).

Local Coverage – *Venezia Per Conoscere La Città* is a useful multilingual booklet published weekly and available at newsstands; it lists up-to-date museum schedules, special events, entertainment programs, and other activities. *The Companion Guide to Venice* by Hugh Honour (London: Collins; $6.95) is a sensitive, well-written guide to the city; it is available in many bookstores.

Telephone – The telephone prefix for Venice is 041.

GETTING AROUND: There are no cars in Venice. After crossing the Ponte della Libertà, visitors leave their cars in the lots and garages at Piazzale Roma. People walk, and traffic moves on water.

Airport – *Aeroporto Marco Polo* (phone: 661262) serves both domestic and international flights. It is 8 miles from the city and is reachable by *motoscafo* (motorboat) service, which leaves from St. Mark's Square and costs 10,000 lire per person. A private motorboat taxi for up to four people is 80,000 lire, including bags. *ATVO* bus service from the parking area of Piazzale Roma (across the Grand Canal from the Santa Lucia train station) costs 3,500 lire per person. Ask for time schedules at *Compagnia Italiana Turismo,* St. Mark's Square, or at the tourist office in Piazzale Roma. Also consult the weekly booklet *Un Ospite a Venezia (A Guest in Venice),* available at newsstands.

Bus and Train – The bus station (phone: 27402) is at Piazzale Roma; the train station, Stazione Santa Lucia (phone: 715555), is across the Grand Canal from the bus station.

Gondola – An hour's tour of the city in one of these sleek, black boats can cost you as much as $50, but for 15¢ you can get a short sample by taking a canal ferry, called a *traghetto,* across the Grand Canal at various points some distance from the bridges. If it's the gondoliers' barcaroles you've been waiting to hear, you can enjoy them for free by leaning over one of the bridges as they pass by in the evening.

***Motoscafi* and *Vaporetti* –** The little steamers that make up the municipal transit system are cheap and fun. The *motoscafi* are express boats, making only a few important stops. The *vaporetti* are much slower. No. 1 chugs leisurely along the whole length of the Grand Canal, and No. 5 meanders for more than an hour through interesting parts of the city. Tickets cost between $1.50 and $2.50.

MUSEUMS: Besides those mentioned in *Special Places,* Venice has a number of museums of special interest:

Civico Museo Correr (Correr Civic Museum) – Piazza San Marco.

Galleria Giorgio Franchetti (Franchetti Gallery) – Ca' D'Oro, Cannareggio 3932 (phone: 38790).

Museo Archeologico (Archaeological Museum) – Piazza San Marco.

Museo d'Arte Moderna (International Gallery of Modern Art) – Ca' Pesaro, Santa Croce (phone: 5224127).

Museo Guggenheim (Guggenheim Museum) – Palazzo Venier dei Leoni, San Giorgio 701 (phone: 706288). Closed November through April.

Palazzo Grassi (also called Palazzo Fiat) – Canal Grande.

 SHOPPING: Venetian glass is a seductive item, but not all of it is of high quality. Do a bit of comparison shopping first, and if you can, visit the museum and factories on *Murano* (see *Special Places*). Also consider the inexpensive necklaces of colorful Venetian glass beads. Other items worth purchasing are the traditional handmade paper *Carnevale* masks, which are currently enjoying a renaissance. Two of the best mask workshops are at Piazza San Paolo 2008/A and at 1077/A Calle de l'Ogio o de la Rughetta (midway between the Rialto and St. Mark's Square). In addition, there are many fine jewelry stores on the Ponte di Rialto.

The *Mercato di Rialto*, near the Rialto Bridge, is one of the city's most colorful outdoor food markets. It is fascinating to wander here, even if you aren't shopping. During the Middle Ages, this area was the Wall Street of Europe, since Venice was queen of the seas and, therefore, queen of trade. In those days, spices, silver, and silks from the overland Eastern trade route were all sold here, and banks surrounded the area. Now it is more the staples of life that are sold from the small stalls — fruits and vegetables, coffee and cheeses, fresh game and seafood. The sounds and smells are pure Venice.

Venice's main shopping district is the area directly surrounding St. Mark's Square or in the adjacent Merceria. While most shops are open in the mornings from 9 AM to 1 PM, they close for a long lunch, reopen around 3:30 PM, and remain open until 7 or 7:30. Most Venetian merchants accept major American credit cards.

Barozzi – Antique furniture, mainly Venetian. Via XXII Marzo 2052.

Domini – Fine silverware and china. Calle Larga San Marco 659–664.

Duca d'Aosta – Sports clothes, accessories, formerly for men only, but women's wear is now available across the street. Merceria del Capitello 4945.

Elysée – Elegant footwear. San Luca 4485.

Fendi – Chic clothing and leather. Salizzada San Moisè, Piazza San Marco.

Fortuny – Fine fabrics. Piazza San Marco 2251 and Calle Larga XXII Marzo.

Jesurum & Co. – Lace and other needlework. Ponte Canonica and Piazza San Marco.

Libreria Antiquaria La Fenice – Old books and prints. Campo San Fantin and Piazza San Marco 1850.

Mondo Novo – Papier-mâché masks — alligators, camels, and mummies — for *Carnevale*. Campo Santa Margherita.

Nardi – Beautiful jewelry in the Venetian tradition. Piazza San Marco 69.

Piazzesi – Notebooks, boxes, albums, and other gift articles crafted from handmade marbleized papers in classic Italian style. San Marco 2511.

Salviati – A 100-year-old firm with the highest traditions of craftsmanship in Venetian glass. Shops at San Gregorio 195, Piazza San Marco 78, and the glassworks museum in Murano.

 SPECIAL EVENTS: In late February, Venetians celebrate *Carnevale*, a 10-day pre-Lenten fete that includes outdoor masked balls, 24-hour street theater, and pop music. On the night between the third Saturday and Sunday in July, illuminated gondolas glide along the canals while musicians play from barges on the lagoon and fireworks paint the sky. This is the *Festa del Redentore* (Feast of the Redeemer; see also *Italy's Most Colorful Festas*, DIVERSIONS), one of the most special celebrations of the year in Venice. No one goes to bed before dawn. On the first Sunday in September, gondola races and a procession of decorated barges filled with Venetians in Renaissance dress highlight the *Regata Storica* (Historic Regatta) on the Grand Canal. An *International Film Festival* is held on the Lido in late August and early September, and in even-numbered years the important *Esposizione Internazionale d'Arte Moderna* (International Exposition of Modern Art) takes place in a small park beyond the Riva dei Sette Martiri from June through October.

 SPORTS AND FITNESS: The visitor to Venice gets plenty of exercise climbing up and down its hundreds of bridges. For more organized sports, one must move to the open spaces of the Lido.

Fitness Center – *La Palestra,* Campo della Guerra 510 (phone: 25957), is the only fitness center in Venice open to nonmembers.

Golf – The *Golf Club Lido di Venezia* is a championship course at the far western end of the Lido (phone: 731015). (See also *Great Italian Golf* in DIVERSIONS.) It's reached by the No. 11 boat from Riva degli Schiavoni or by the C bus from Santa Maria Elisabetta, the main Lido dock.

Jogging – Just east of St. Mark's Square, the Riva degli Schiavoni runs southeast along the water toward the Riva dei Sette Martiri and the Giardini Pubblici (public gardens) — a good 20-minute jog. Runners may also jog on the Lido beach.

Soccer – From September to May, *Venezia* plays at *Stadio Comunale P. L. Penzo,* S. Elena (phone: 87418).

Swimming – The northern end of the Lido has municipal beaches, all of which charge admission. Other beaches are the domain of the great luxury hotels of the Lido, but cabanas are available for an entrance fee.

Tennis – The *Tennis Club,* Lungomare Marconi 41/D (phone: 60385), has seven courts (two covered; two lighted). Nonmembers can also play at the *Henkell Club,* Via Malamocco (phone: 760122), or the *Tennis Club Lido,* Via Sandro Gallo 163 (phone: 760594).

Yachting – The *Ciga Yacht Club* hires out sailing boats or gives lessons to enthusiasts through the *Hotel Excelsior Palace* (see *Checking In*) on the Lido (phone: 760201).

 THEATER: Music, rather than drama, is the performing art of Venice. However, the *Teatro Verde,* on the little island of San Giorgio Maggiore just across from Piazza San Marco, is a lovely outdoor amphitheater that looks out over the lagoon. It's a marvelous place to spend a summer evening, even if you're watching a classic theater piece done in an incomprehensible Venetian dialect. Another pleasant theater for traditional and contemporary productions is *Teatro Goldoni,* Calle Goldoni 4650/B, San Marco (phone: 707583).

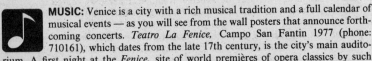 **MUSIC:** Venice is a city with a rich musical tradition and a full calendar of musical events — as you will see from the wall posters that announce forthcoming concerts. *Teatro La Fenice,* Campo San Fantin 1977 (phone: 710161), which dates from the late 17th century, is the city's main auditorium. A first night at the *Fenice,* site of world premières of opera classics by such composers as Verdi and Rossini, is a highlight of the social season. Its gold and pink plush interior is pure Venetian; tours are permitted when rehearsals are not in progress. In summer, open-air concerts are held in the courtyard of the Doge's Palace, and there are concerts in various churches (where the acoustics are fabulous). If possible, attend a performance by either of the city's stellar chamber music groups: the *Solisti Veneti* or the *Sestetto a Fiati di Venezia* (Venice Wind Sextet). In winter, too, you can attend concerts in churches and in the ornate salons of palaces such as the 17th-century *Palazzo Labia* (now the Venice office of Italian state radio and television).

NIGHTCLUBS AND NIGHTLIFE: *Antico Martini,* San Marco 1983 (phone: 37027), is Venice's chic-est night spot. Next to the *Teatro La Fenice,* which supplies it with a glossy, after-theater crowd, it has a floor show, dancing, a pleasant outdoor terrace, and good food (see *Eating Out*). As long as the weather holds, the city's best nightlife is the nonstop show in *Piazza San Marco.* Take up residence in one of the cafés, listen to the schmaltzy orchestra, and watch the world go by. Popular places for rock and disco are the *Piper Club,* on the Lido at 125 Lista di Spagna (phone: 716643), and *El Souk Disco,* Accademia 1056/A (phone: 700371).

 SINS: Venice encourages *dolce far niente* ("sweet idleness"), so enjoy *sloth* turned into fine art. The *Municipal Casino* is at the Lido (phone: 760626) from April through September and at the elegant Palazzo Vendram-in-Calergi (phone: 710211) on the Grand Canal from October through March. Just past the narrow end of Piazza San Marco is the *Frezzeria,* where there is *lustfully* lively late-night traffic.

BEST IN TOWN

 CHECKING IN: Your first decision is whether to stay out at the Lido or right in the center of town. But even if you stay in the center, it's easy to use the frequent ferry service (from Riva degli Schiavoni) any time you feel the urge to swim or play a game of tennis. Expensive hotels here will charge from $250 to $500 per night for a double; moderately priced hotels, $100 to $250; and inexpensive ones, $50 to $100.

Gritti Palace – There are those — Ernest Hemingway was one — who would rather stay in this small crown jewel than anywhere else in Europe. Once the Renaissance residence of Venetian nobility, this hotel is famous for its excellent service, classic dining room, and beautiful dining terrace on the canal. Campo Santa Maria del Giglio 2467 (phone: 794611). Expensive.

Cipriani – On the serene Isola Giudecca, this charming hotel has a peaceful, luxuriant garden, a swimming pool, and stunning views of the lagoon. Very formal, very capable service that's a throwback to a more elegant, opulent age. Frequent shuttle service transports guests to and from St. Mark's Square in 5 minutes. Fine restaurant. Open April through November. Giudecca 10 (phone: 707744). Expensive.

Bauer Grünwald – Visiting royalty often stays in the poshest suites in this Grand Canal hotel near St. Mark's Square. Its roof garden offers one of the loveliest vantage points from which to admire the city. Campo San Moisè 1459 (phone: 5231520). Expensive.

Danieli – One of Venice's oldest and most romantic hotels (and one of the biggest) was once the residence of a 14th-century doge. It has a modern annex that is less evocative but is still a favorite for wealthy honeymooners. Riva degli Schiavoni 4196 (phone: 26480). Expensive.

Londra Palace – This charming hotel on a popular promenade offers wonderful views of the Bacino di San Marco and the Byzantine Chiesa di San Zaccaria. All 69 rooms have modern bathrooms, and many have private balconies. Other amenities include an elegant bar and a very good restaurant. Riva degli Schiavoni 4171 (phone: 700533). Expensive.

Grand Hotel des Bains – On the Lido, this luxurious and gracefully old-fashioned hotel is where Visconti filmed much of *Death in Venice.* It has spacious rooms and renovated bathrooms. The stately porticoed hotel is across the road from the private beach. Open April through October. Lungomare Marconi 17, Lido (phone: 765921). Expensive.

Excelsior Palace – This luxurious modern hotel on the Lido has its own fine restaurant, beach, tennis courts, and golf course. Open April to October. Lungomare Marconi 40, Lido (phone: 5260201). Expensive.

La Fenice et des Artistes – Just alongside the *Teatro La Fenice* (see *Theater*), this hotel is popular with performers and musicians. It consists of four buildings around a pretty garden and has comfortable, well-appointed rooms. One of the city's fine restaurants, *Taverna La Fenice* (see *Eating Out*), is downstairs. Campo San Fantin 1937/A (phone: 5232333). Expensive.

Europe and Regina – With a terrace overlooking the Grand Canal, this gracious hotel offers a fine view of the Chiesa di Santa Maria della Salute. Calle Larga XXII Marzo 2159 (phone: 700477). Expensive to moderate.

Monaco and Grand Canal – The intimate seclusion of this homelike hotel is just one minute's walk from St. Mark's Square. Constructed from three 18th-century family houses, it has its own flowered terrace on the Grand Canal. San Marco 1325 (phone: 70021). Expensive to moderate.

Ala – Across a small square from the *Gritti,* this hotel has many of the more expensive hotel's advantages at about one-third the cost. The atmosphere is gracious and intimate. It's about equidistant from Piazza San Marco and the Galleria dell'Accademia (see *Special Places*). Campo Santa Maria del Giglio 2494 (phone: 708333). Moderate.

Do Pozzi – A small, attractive hotel just a block away from Piazza San Marco, it has a pleasant atmosphere and a lively canalside restaurant, *Da Raffaele.* Calle Larga XXII Marzo 2373 (phone: 707855). Moderate.

Etap-Park – This modern, luxurious hotel is a short walk from Piazzale Roma, the first stop for everyone en route from the airport by bus or car. It has easy access to the main *vaporetto* lines to all parts of Venice. Santa Croce 245–246 (phone: 5285394). Moderate.

Flora – This small jewel of a hotel has a lovely patio and garden. The atmosphere is tranquil and gracious. Just around the corner from Piazza San Marco. Closed November through January. Calle Larga XXII Marzo 2283/A (phone: 705844). Moderate.

Bonvecchiati – This comfortable, 86-room hotel near St. Mark's Square is tastefully decorated and boasts an impressive collection of contemporary art. 4488 Calle Goldoni (phone: 5285017). Moderate.

Quattro Fontane – Transformed from a villa built last century, this quiet hotel with excellent service offers the peace of an English country garden. It still has the air of a family dwelling, with antique furniture of various origins. Via Quattro Fontane, Lido (phone: 5260227). Moderate.

Santa Chiara – This small hotel on the Grand Canal — with beamed ceilings and antique furniture — is particularly convenient for guests arriving by car (Piazzale Roma is around the corner). Private garage space. Easy access to the main *vaporetto* stops. Santa Croce 548 (phone: 706955). Moderate.

Torino – Tucked in a corner near fancier hotels, this comfortable place is within easy reach of *La Fenice.* Calle delle Ostreghe 2356 (phone: 705222). Moderate to inexpensive.

Kette – Tucked in a quiet spot between *La Fenice* and St. Mark's Square, this charming and efficient hotel is within strolling distance of several Grand Canal palazzi. Piscina San Moisè–San Marco 2053 (phone: 707766). Inexpensive.

La Residenza – This delightful 14th-century building is little more than a stone's throw from the busy Riva degli Schiavoni. Closed mid-January to mid-February and mid-November to mid-December. Campo Bandiera e Moro (phone: 5285315). Inexpensive.

Pensione Accademia – Also known as *Villa Maravegie,* this tranquil, rather stately establishment is near the Galleria dell'Accademia. It has a lovely garden with a view down a small canal to the Grand Canal. With wide vestibules, high ceilings, and the ambience of a private home from another era. Dorsoduro 1058–60 (phone: 710188). Inexpensive.

 EATING OUT: One of life's great pleasures is dining out in Venice in good weather — alongside a canal, on one of the wide, sunny squares, or in a little garden shaded by vine leaves. But in winter the crowded tables and warm interiors offer refuge from the misty, melancholy streets. Prices for dinner for two, with wine, range from $70 to $100 at an expensive restaurant; $50 to $70 at a moderate one; and $30 to $45 at an inexpensive one. Don't plan to linger too late; most restaurants take their last orders at about 10:30 PM.

Club del Doge – Part of the *Gritti Palace* hotel on the Grand Canal, this is the place for fine food in deluxe surroundings. In good weather, diners are served on a canalside terrace. Reservations advised. Campo Santa Maria del Giglio 2467 (phone: 794611). Very expensive.

Antico Martini – Venice's classiest restaurant, across the square from *La Fenice* (see *Theater*), is open daily, although dinner only is served on Tuesdays and Wednesdays. The *cocktail di crostacei* (seafood cocktail) and the *filetto di sogliola* (filet of sole) are dishes of national repute. Open March 15 through November 30. Reservations required. Campo San Fantin 1938 (phone: 5224121). Expensive.

Harry's Bar – Long a Venetian landmark, and the city's only restaurant with two Michelin stars, this popular spot is crowded with tourists in summer, but it makes an elegant, international rendezvous in the off-season. The food is splendid 12 months a year, though it may be a bit overpriced. The *Bellini* cocktail was born here. Closed Mondays and January. Reservations advised. Near the San Marco motorboat station. Calle Vallaresso 1323 (phone: 5236797). Expensive.

Locanda Cipriani – The almost pastoral tranquillity of the garden makes this a perfect place for a leisurely lunch. The restaurant, under the same management as *Harry's Bar,* sits on an ancient piazza on the sleepy island of Torcello (see *Special Places*). You can get lunch and transportation in one fare by taking the motor launch that leaves from the dock adjacent to *Harry's Bar* at noon and brings diners back after lunch. Open daily, except Tuesdays, March 15 through October. Reservations advised in summer. Piazza Torcello, Torcello (phone: 730757). Expensive.

La Colomba – Sooner or later, everyone drops in at this favorite Venetian hangout. Large and crowded, the restaurant has a lovely outside terrace, a creative array of seafood specialties, and modern art on the walls. Try *cartoccio Colomba,* Adriatic fish baked in a paper bag. Closed Wednesdays from November through May. Piscina di Frezzeria 1665 (phone: 5221175). Expensive.

La Caravella – It has a typically Venetian atmosphere, and the chef's specialties include scampi in champagne and filet mignon. Closed Wednesdays. Reservations advised. Largo XXII Marzo 2397 (phone: 708901). Expensive.

Al Giglio – Set in a charming piazza, this intimate restaurant offers very good fish and meat dishes in an atmosphere of calm and elegance. Closed Wednesdays and December and January. Reservations advised. Near Piazza San Marco, Campo Santa Maria del Giglio (phone: 89456). Expensive to moderate.

Malamocco – A favorite of after-theater crowds, with its 18th-century decor and pretty garden for outdoor eating. Specialties include *carpaccio* (slices of fine raw beef dressed with oil and lemon) and *pesce al cartoccio* (fish roasted in paper). Campiello del Vin 4650 (phone: 27438). Expensive to moderate.

Al Graspo de Uva – This colorful, popular restaurant in an old blacksmith's shop offers great Venetian food and a good selection of wines. Closed Mondays and Tuesdays. Calle Bombaseri 5094 (phone: 5223647). Expensive to moderate.

Noemi – Salmon mousse and shrimp pâté are the specialties at this lesser-known (but still one-star), cozy, family-run restaurant. Closed Sunday evenings and Mondays and January 5 to February 15. Calle dei Fabbri 909–912 (phone: 25238). Expensive to moderate.

Alla Madonna – This is a brightly lit, lively restaurant on a little side street near the Ponte di Rialto. It has a fixed menu daily featuring Venetian specialties. Closed Wednesdays, the first week in August, and December 24 to January 31. Calle della Madonna 594 (phone: 5223824). Moderate.

Da Valentino – On the Lido, this small restaurant with garden and terrace serves Venetian fish and meat specialties, including game in season. Homemade desserts and good local wines are an integral part of any meal here. Seating is limited, so book in advance. Closed Mondays and October through mid-November. San Gallo 81 (phone: 5260128). Moderate.

Caffè Orientale – In a particularly delightful spot near the Ponte dell'Accademia, this relatively new restaurant is adapted both for working Venetians' and foot-weary tourists' lunches. The menu (be prepared for Venetian dialect) includes Adriatic fish specialties as well as meat and vegetables. A bargain. San Polo 2426 (phone: 719804). Moderate.

Osteria da Fiore – Fish only — accompanied by Venetian vegetable specialties such as mushrooms, artichokes, and *radicchio* — is served in this former hostelry. Closed Sundays, Mondays, and the last three weeks of August. Calle dello Scaletèr, San Polo 2202 (phone: 37208). Moderate.

Taverna La Fenice – This elegant restaurant, popular with performers, musicians, and theatergoers, is part of the hotel *La Fenice et des Artistes* (see *Checking In*). Its food and decor are characteristically Venetian. Closed Sundays and January. Reservations suggested. Campiello Marinonio 1938 (phone: 5223856). Moderate.

Trattoria Do Forni – Open all year in the *Montecarlo Hotel.* Fish of various sorts are a specialty here, on a menu that's extensive and varied. A favorite dining spot for Venetians. Closed Thursdays. Calle Specchieri 468 (phone: 5237729). Moderate.

Al Teatro – An after-show meeting place for performers, musicians, and hungry roulette players, this popular *rosticceria* serves everything from a late-night pizza to a five-course meal. Next to *La Fenice.* Closed Mondays. Campo San Fantin (phone: 21052 or 37214). Inexpensive.

Antica Bessetta – Venetian home cooking is hard to beat, and here it is at its best in the vegetable and pasta dishes as well as in the more sophisticated fish special-ties. Closed Tuesdays, Wednesdays, and mid-July to mid-August. Calle Salvio 1395 (phone: 37687). Inexpensive.

Antica Locanda Montin – Simple decor, simple food, and some of the city's most interesting people are found in this out-of-the-way restaurant, usually referred to simply by its last name. It's popular with artists and journalists and has a cool, attractive arbor. Closed Tuesdays and Wednesdays. Near Campo San Barnaba. Fondamenta Eremite 1147 (phone: 27151). Inexpensive.

Caffè Florian – This beautiful, slightly frayed *caffè* looks out on the entire St. Mark's scene. It's the perfect site from which to watch the world go by while sipping coffee and nibbling a sweet confection. San Marco 57. Inexpensive.

Da Ivo – Good, solid food is found at this *trattoria* frequented by more locals than tourists. Try the *pappardelle alla marinara* for the pasta course. Closed Sundays and January. San Marco, Calle dei Fuseri 1809 (phone: 5285004). Inexpensive.

Lavena – The most intrepid of the St. Mark's cafés. Waiters serving drinks and coffee to patrons (occasionally in hip boots) while the rain pelts down and the whole square floods demonstrate the determination of servers and guests alike. San Marco 133. Inexpensive.

Osteria Ca' d'Oro alla Vedova – This attractive restaurant has a particularly well stocked wine cellar to accompany its Venetian fish and vegetable dishes and Veneto cheeses. Cannaregio, Strada Nova 3912 (phone: 85324). Inexpensive.

VERONA

While the Venetians are all *gran signori* (fine gentlemen) and the people of Padua are *gran dottori* (very learned), the Veronese — as the old saying goes — are all *tutti matti* (quite mad). We don't mean insane, but mad as in March hares, enjoying a rollicking good time. Even the statues, somber in some cities, smile here, evidently enjoying some local joke.

The Veronese love to drink their excellent wines, the Soaves and Valpolicellas of the region, and when they have had a little to drink, they love to sing. A favorite meeting place for drinking and singing is the *osteria* (inn), and there seems to be one on almost every street in old Verona. Here a glass of wine costs about twenty-five cents, and the conversation is very loud, usually because the Veronese are discussing the exploits of their soccer team, of which — like all Italian cities — they are inordinately proud.

Or, if it is January or February, the uproar could be about the election of the Gnocchi King of *Carnevale.* This is a tradition that goes back to the sixteenth century, when a rich lord of Verona distributed flour among the poor of the city to make *gnocchi,* a local pasta dish. To this day, Gnocchi Friday is the height of *Carnevale,* when the fun-loving Veronese are even madder than usual!

Although Verona was known as *piccola Roma* (little Rome) during Roman times — as the massive Arena, the arched stone doors such as the Porta Borsari, and the fragments of ancient pillars and walls amply attest — the overwhelming impression today is medieval. There are battlements, turrets, slits in the walls from which archers fired their arrows, and cobbled streets that seem left over from the times of the Montagues and Capulets, whom visitors can easily imagine clattering across the Ponte di Castelvecchio.

As a border town, Verona played a key role in Italy's past. After the Romans, the city was ruled by the Goths and King Theodoric, followed by two centuries of Lombards, until it was conquered by the Franks and Charlemagne in 774. The grand masters left their imprints on the city, especially under the doges and their Venetian Republic, a time known as the Serenissima, during which Verona contributed to the Italian Renaissance with painters such as Paolo Veronese and architects like Michele Sanmicheli. The Venetians were ousted in 1797 by Napoleon, whose government was in turn ousted in 1814 by the European coalition. Verona was then ruled by the Hapsburgs until the Italian unification in 1860.

The rule of the Della Scala family had the most lingering effect on Verona. Known as the Scaligeri, the family reigned from 1262 to 1387, during which time Romeo is supposed to have courted Juliet and "with love's light wings did o'erperch these walls" into the Capulet garden. It was the Scaligeri who gave Verona so many of the city's monuments, such as the *Arche Scaligere,* where the family is buried; the *Castelvecchio,* now the city's main museum; the old *Town Hall;* and *Piazza dei Signori* (Lords' Square). Many of the churches grew in splendor during the rule of the Scaligeri, and it was a time of great cultural awareness. The poet Dante Alighieri stayed in the Palazzo Scaligero during his Florentine exile as a guest of Cangrande I della Scala, whom he immortalized in the 17th canto of his *Paradiso.*

Long before Romeo and Juliet, Verona claimed to be Italy's city of love. A legend tells how the Adige River, cascading down from the glacier in the mountains above the city, fell in love with Verona. The love was fiercely contested by the goddess Diana — to whom Verona had pledged a vow of chastity. Diana condemned the city to die in the watery embrace of its suitor, which wound lovingly around the city in the shape of an *S,* for *sposa* (bride). But love prevailed. Verona did not die, and to this day it remains enclosed within the wide curves of the river and within the series of city walls built by succeeding overlords.

During the thirteenth century, the poor people actually lived under the arches of the Roman Arena and had to pay rent for their humble dwellings, until they were turned out to make way for the city's red-light ladies, who in those days had to wear a cap with a rattle on the peak to differentiate them from honest women. In fact, Verona has always been "lived in" by the Veronese, and the city's monuments, however ancient and revered, are still just as much a part of day-to-day life as they always were. The Arena, which once featured gladiators and lions and, later, medieval jousters, still dominates the city; during its world-famous opera season, it is an important part of civic life. The Scaligeri palaces have become government offices. The daily market is held in *Piazza delle Erbe* on the site of the old Roman forum. Lawyers and judges still ascend the *Scala della Ragione* (Stair of Reason) as they did in the fifteenth century.

Verona is a small, compact city, only a quarter of an hour's walk end to end. But it has much to see. The visitor should come equipped with comfortable shoes and be prepared to walk, walk, walk the cobbled streets, taking time to look up at the façades of the buildings (some of them, like No. 4 on Via San Cosimo, are almost grotesque). The diligent roamer will soon discover that not only Romeo and Juliet but everyone in Verona had a balcony. It will also quickly become apparent that Romeo and Juliet are only one reason to come to Verona and the least haunting of the impressions visitors will carry home.

VERONA AT-A-GLANCE

SEEING THE CITY: The *Torre Lamberti* (Lamberti Tower) rises to 272 feet in Piazza delle Erbe in the heart of old Verona. Fortunately, there is an elevator as well as stairs to the top, from which there is a fine view of the city. Open daily, except Mondays, 8:30 AM to 1:30 PM in winter, 8:30 AM to 7 PM in summer.

On the other side of the *Ponte di Pietra* (Stone Bridge) from the *Torre Lamberti* are the *Teatro Romano* (Roman Theater), founded by Augustus, and the *Castel San Pietro* (St. Peter's Castle), built by the Austrians in the 19th century. Both places afford good views of Verona. The *Scalone di San Pietro* (St. Peter's Stairway) is steeped in legend. The higher one climbs, the more of the city is visible on the horizon. Here King Albion, king of the Lombards, was killed at the instigation of his wife, Rosamund. On the same side of the river is the *Giusti Garden,* a 16th-century formal Italian garden with terraces overlooking the city (see *Special Places*).

 SPECIAL PLACES: Other cities have their museums and picture galleries. Verona has churches, although many are so dimly lit that one can only guess at the artistic and architectural wonders lurking in the transepts and side chapels. There are so many churches, so large, so awe-inspiring, that it is hard to believe there were ever enough Veronese to fill them. They all close for a long lunch from 1 to 4 PM.

Duomo (Cathedral) – The most important church in Verona is this 12th-century Romanesque basilica with a 15th-century Gothic nave. It is located in the old section of the city near the *Ponte di Pietra.* The choir screen separating the altar from the rest of the church is attributed to Sanmicheli. At the end of the nave, in the Nichesola chapel, is Titian's *Assumption of the Virgin Mary.* Behind the cathedral is the little 12th-century church of San Giovanni in Fonte, one of the most important examples of Romanesque architecture in Verona. It is named for the huge octagonal baptismal font in red stone, its eight sides showing scenes from the life of Christ. Piazza Duomo.

Chiesa di Sant'Anastasia (Church of Saint Anastasia) – This basilica was built on the site of a much older church. Although the foundations were laid in 1290 by the Dominicans, the basilica was not finished until 1481. The vaulted ceiling is supported by massive red Veronese marble columns. Two *gobbi,* or hunchbacks, support the holy water fonts at the foot of the first column on either side of the nave. There is something uncannily realistic in the resigned expressions and torn trousers of the *gobbi,* as if they were carrying the weight of the Catholic church on their shoulders. In the sacristy to the left is *St. George and the Princess,* the famous fresco by Pisanello. Illuminate the picture by putting a 100-lire coin into the machine. It is like a fairy-tale painting with a knight in armor, a damsel in distress, a castle in the clouds, and, in the foreground, the unexpectedly large rump of a white charger. Corso Sant'Anastasia.

Chiesa di San Zeno Maggiore (Church of Saint Zeno Major) – This is the only site around town that requires a bus or a taxi to reach. Zeno is the patron saint of Verona. His black-faced, laughing statue is seated on its bishop's throne in a small apse to the left of the altar. The 48 panels of the magnificent bronze doors show scenes of the Old and New Testaments, and the triptych above the main altar is a depiction of the Madonna with angel musicians and saints by Andrea Mantegna. The ceiling of the nave looks like an upturned wooden ship's keel. Piazza San Zeno 2.

This basilica is not to be confused with the tiny church called *San Zeno in Oratorio* on Via A. Provolo, near the Castelvecchio Museum. The smaller church contains an enormous boulder that is supposedly the stone on which the laughing Saint Zeno used to sit fishing by the Adige River.

Chiesa di San Fermo Maggiore (Church of Saint Firmanus Major) – This is, in fact, two churches in one. The lower church, which parishioners use in winter, is pure Romanesque; the upper and larger church, altered by the Franciscans in the 13th century, has a more Gothic aspect. The interior is decorated with frescoes by Veronese painters from Turone (see his *Crucifixion*) to Pisanello (the *Annunciation*). The ceiling here, as at San Zeno, looks like a ship's keel. Via Dogana 2.

Chiesa di San Lorenzo (Church of Saint Lawrence) – Still remaining here are the *matronei,* or women's galleries, running above the two lateral naves. (Men and women used to worship separately.) Two cylindrical towers of striped stone and brick were the entrances to the galleries. Via Cavour 28.

Chiesa di Santo Stefano (Church of Saint Stephen) – Time permitting, walk over the *Ponte di Pietra* and visit this church, believed to have been built in the time of Theodoric the Goth. Tradition dates its foundations to around AD 415. It is thought to have been the cathedral of Verona for more than three centuries. More than 20 Veronese bishops are buried here, and the façade is inscribed with records of important events, as they are in a family Bible. Via Vicino Ponte di Pietra.

Chiesa di Santa Maria in Organo (Church of Saint Mary in Organo) – Known for the remarkable marquetry (inlaid pictures in wood) on the backs of the wooden choir stalls and in the sacristy. Executed around 1499 by Fra Giovanni da Verona, they contain 32 types of wood, endowing them with extraordinary nuances of light and color. Piazza Santa Maria.

Chiesa di San Giorgio in Braida (Church of Saint George in Braida) – This later building, constructed from 1536 to 1543, lacks the powerful atmosphere of some of the earlier Romanesque churches, but it is rich in artwork. Paintings include a large Tintoretto, *The Baptism of Christ,* over the entrance and a Veronese, *The Martyrdom of St. George,* on the end wall of the apse. The design of the cupola and the unfinished campanile are attributed to Sanmicheli. Lungadige San Giorgio.

Giardino Giusti (Giusti Garden) – Across the Adige from the old city is a formal garden that was designed by its 16th-century owner, Count Agostino Giusti. Laid out behind a palazzo of the same name, the garden is composed of formal walks with box-hedge mazes geometrically arranged around statues and fountains. The place is a child's delight, a series of terraces and stairs leading to what in gardening terms are called follies and hahas. Open daily until sunset. Via Giardino Giusti (phone: 38029).

Piazza delle Erbe (Square of the Herbs) – Every day octagonal white umbrellas shade the stalls of this market square, where you can buy food, especially fruits and vegetables, flowers, and clothing. There is even an *arrotino* (knife grinder). On the fountain is a Roman statue known as Madonna Verona (Lady Verona), who holds a scroll declaiming, *Est iusti latrix urbs haec et laudis amatrix* ("the city is proud of her justice and fond of praise"). The statue is the only visible remains of the Roman forum that was at this site. Evidence of the forum was discovered about 10 feet below ground when a hole was being dug for the flagpole. At the northwest end of the square is the Baroque façade of *Palazzo Maffei,* with statues of Greek gods along the roof. At the same corner is the beautifully frescoed 14th-century *Casa Mazzanti.* Next to the Casa Mazzanti, leading into the Mercato Vecchio square, is the *Arco della Costa,* an arch from which hangs a prehistoric whale bone, also discovered under the square during excavations, evidence that millennia ago this entire area was under the sea.

Romeo e Giulietta (Romeo and Juliet Homes and Tomb) – Juliet's house, with its famous balcony, is beautiful, but it is empty of anything except its graffiti-covered walls. Romeo's house is but a façade, albeit with battlements. It is easier to be caught up in the immortal love story at Juliet's tomb, which, although also empty, is in the evocative crypt of the cloisters of San Francesco al Corso. Lord Byron found it so romantic that he purloined little pieces of marble from the tomb to make into jewelry for his current *innamorata.* Juliet's house is at Via Cappello 23, in the middle of the shopping center (phone: 38303). Open daily, except Mondays, 9 AM to 7 PM. Romeo's house, on Via Arche Scaligere near Piazza Indipendenza, can be viewed from the street only. The tomb is on Via del Pontiere (phone: 25361). Open daily, except Mondays, 8 AM to 6 PM in winter, to 7 PM in summer.

Castelvecchio Museum – Verona does not have many museums, but the Castelvecchio Museum is very special. Also called the *Museum of Art,* it is in the Scaligeri castle, which looks like a set for *The Prisoner of Zenda.* Like the Castello Sforzesco in Milan, this 14th-century building is as interesting as its exhibits. The galleries span its battlements and its buttresses and lead over a little bridge where the famous statue of Cangrande della Scala, Lord of Verona from 1311 until 1329, sits smiling on its horse. The museum houses a large collection of Romanesque, Gothic, and Renaissance sculpture, as well as an impressive array of Madonnas — of the Fan, of the Rose Tree, of the Quail, of the Goldfinch, and of the Passion. Famous Italian painters are well represented here — Crivelli, Tintoretto, Guardi, Tiepolo, and the great Veronese painter Paolo Caliari, known as Il Veronese. Open daily, except Mondays, 8:30 AM to 7 PM. Via Castelvecchio (phone: 594734).

Caffè Dante – This old-fashioned coffeehouse is in the heart of old Verona, in Piazza dei Signori, with Scaligeri monuments all around and a statue of the family's most famous guest, Dante Alighieri, in the middle of the square. The restaurant has marble tables and plush armchairs, a little worse for wear. In the afternoons the tables in the back room are taken by chess players. In 1866, to mark the annexing of Verona to a unified Italy, the ceiling was painted with oval portraits of Italy's great patriots — Garibaldi, Mazzini, Cavour, etc. Light refreshment, as well as history, is to be had here. Closed Thursdays. Piazza dei Signori (phone: 30546).

Arena – Nowadays the enormous Roman Arena is the opera house and still an important component of Veronese life. It is in the middle of Piazza Brà, the largest square in Verona. (*Brà* perhaps comes from the German word *breit,* "wide.") From a balcony in this square Garibaldi declared *Roma o Morte* — Rome or die. Today the square is filled with sidewalk cafés. During the 1985 Christmas holiday season, a giant comet made of 70 tons of white iron and steel and welded together with 2,763 nuts and bolts seemed to land in the middle of the square, the tip of its tail resting on the lip of the Arena. The Arena is closed to visitors on Mondays. In opera season (July and August), it is open 8 AM to 1:30 PM; otherwise, 8:30 AM to 5:30 PM in winter, to 6:30 PM in summer (phone: 590966). See also *Music.*

ENVIRONS

Lago di Garda (Lake Garda) – Less than 25 miles from Verona is one of the most beautiful Italian lakes. The climate in this area is mild, and in the warmer months there are facilities for bathing and sailing. In high summer it gets crowded. The lake is surrounded by picturesque villages and vineyards, and there are plenty of good restaurants.

SOURCES AND RESOURCES

TOURIST INFORMATION: General tourist information is available at the *Azienda di Soggiorno di Verona,* Via Anfiteatro 6/B (phone: 592828). Ask for free publications: the four-language guide, *Passport Verona;* the restaurant guide, *Verona Anni 80;* and the city map that locates principal monuments, *Verona Anni 80.* The *Verona Trade Fair Center* is at the gates of the city on the Bologna side (phone: 588111).

Local Coverage – The daily paper of Verona and the province is *L'Arena di Verona.*

Telephone – The telephone prefix for Verona is 045.

GETTING AROUND: This is a town for walking. Park outside the gates and walk from there. (It is unlikely that a car would be stolen, but it would be unwise to leave anything of value visible in it.)

Airport – Verona is served for domestic flights only by *Verona-Villafranca Airport,* about 7 miles out of town (phone: 513039). Bus and taxi service into Verona is available.

Bus – Verona has an extensive municipal bus service. Tickets are inexpensive; buy them beforehand at tobacconists. Buses that serve the province and Lake Garda depart from Piazza Brà, Piazza Cittadella, and Piazza Isolo (phone: 34125).

Car Rental – Representatives of the major car rental firms are at Porta Nuova, the main train station.

Taxi – Feet do wear out sometimes; fortunately, a taxi rarely costs more than $3. There is a cabstand at Piazza Brà; or call *Radio Taxi* (phone: 532666).

Train – Insist on *rapido,* or at least direct, trains. The main station, *Porta Nuova,* is at the south end of the Corso Porta Nuova (phone: 28312, 28313).

MUSEUMS: Apart from the Castelvecchio Museum, mentioned in *Special Places,* Verona has a few smaller museums.

Teatro Romano e Museo Archeologico (Roman Theater and Archaeological Museum) – Ancient theater near fortress and castle complex; antiquity museum. Open daily, except Mondays, 8 AM to 2 PM. Via Regaste Redentore (phone: 8000360).

Museo Lapidario Maffeiano (Maffeiano Lapidary Museum) – The oldest in Europe, with stone plaques, statues, urns, and reliefs. Open daily, except Mondays, 7:30 AM to 7:30 PM. Portoni della Brà (phone: 590087).

Museo Civico di Storia Naturale (Natural History Museum) – In Sanmicheli's Palazzo Pompei. Open daily, except Fridays, 9 AM to 12:30 PM and 3 to 6 PM. Lungadige Porta Vittoria 9 (phone: 21987).

Biblioteca Capitolare (Capital Library) – The oldest functioning library in Europe, with manuscripts, parchments, codices, and so on. Open 9:30 AM to 12:30 PM and 4 to 6 PM Mondays, Wednesdays, and Saturdays. Piazza Duomo 13 (phone: 596516).

SHOPPING: The province of Verona produces shoes for all of Italy and abroad — one-tenth of the country's entire production. Drive along the main road toward Lake Garda, through Bussolengo, and buy directly from the factories at very low prices. Verona is also known for its reproductions of antique furniture. Drive the *strada dei mobli* (furniture road) toward Legnago and visit the artisans' workshops.

In the center of town are two streets devoted almost exclusively to authentic antiques, Via Sant'Anastasia and Via Sottoriva, especially the latter. Stores here are tucked away under medieval arches. Their façades date from the 3rd and 4th centuries.

The main shopping street is Via Mazzini, which branches right into Via Cappello, the site of Juliet's home. Like most of the historic center, this is a pedestrian zone. All the big names in Italian fashion are here: *Richard Ginori, Pollini, Gianni Versace,* and *Ritzino,* for example, as well as the big department stores *Coin* and *Upim.* Many of the shops have outlets in other towns, but the stores listed below are found only in Verona. Most are closed on Monday mornings and during lunch, from 1 to 3:30 or 4 PM.

Alloni – Spectacular flower shop specializing in dried herbal and floral arrangements. Corso Porta Nuova 11 (phone: 596077).

Bon Bon – Children's clothes. Via Cappello 25 (phone: 594727).

Calima – Embroidered linens and lace. Via E. Noris 6/B (phone: 22427).

Canestrari – The oldest jeweler in Verona. The shop looks a bit like Aladdin's cave. Via Cappello 35 (phone: 594763).

Il Cassettone – Embroidered linens and lace. Vicolo Crocioni 3 (phone: 590077).

Cose di E. Passeroni & S. Tapparini – New and antique silver. Via Mazzini 63 (phone: 596596).

Faraoni – Fashion boutique specializing in Kenzo clothes. Via Ponte Nuovo 7/D (phone: 590989).

Fulmine del Guanto – Gloves. Via Mazzini 44 (phone: 595512).

Libreria Ghelfi Barbato – Old-fashioned bookstore; many books in English. Via Mazzini 21 (phone: 22306).

Mantellero – High-class men's hats and women's hosiery in a hallowed atmosphere. Via Mazzini 59 (phone: 31607).

New Galles – Fashion, including Emporio Armani styles. Via A. Cantore 4 (phone: 31555) or Galleria Catullo 1/B (phone: 590502).

Pasticceria Cordioli – Traditional coffee bar and pastry shop. Via Cappello 39 (phone: 23055).

Principe – Verona's local shoe store. At the very beginning of Via Mazzini (phone: 21165). Also *Principino,* for children. Via Cappello 35 (phone: 22443).

Venus – *Profumeria* — perfume, makeup, and toiletries. A local branch of Elizabeth Arden. Via Mazzini 29 (phone: 22955).

 SPECIAL EVENTS: Verona has a large trade fair center with an international following. Although some of the exhibitions are of limited interest to the layperson (such as the fair for agricultural machinery), many others are well worth browsing. In April, the *VinItaly* wine fair offers a complete panorama of Italy's wines — and a taste of them as well. *Herbora,* in May, specializes in herb-based products. In September, *Marmomacc* shows all the marble, granite, and other stone produced in Italy today, much of which comes from the Verona area. In November, *Fiera dei Cavalli* is very popular with horse buffs from all over the country.

Every two years an *Antiques Fair* is held in the Palazzo della Gran Guardia. Another very special event is the *Rassegna del Presepe* (Christmas Crèche Exhibition), which is held in the Arena from December 1 to February 9. There's no need to celebrate Christmas to be fascinated by this international collection of historic crèches.

 SPORTS: Sports do not seem to be very high on the agenda for visitors to the city, perhaps because they get quite enough exercise just walking around. The Veronese ski in the mountains above the city, about an hour away by car (see *Italy's Unparalleled Skiing,* DIVERSIONS), and in summer they go sailing on Lake Garda (see *Special Places*).

Soccer – Every other Sunday, from September to May, *Verona* plays at *Stadio Comunale, Marc'Antonio Bentegodi,* Piazzale Olimpia (phone: 574992).

 THEATER AND MUSIC: The *Arena di Verona* opera season, spanning July and August, is a major musical phenomenon in Italy. World-famous stars perform in the *Arena*'s vast oval auditorium. Although the soprano can look very small if you're sitting near the lip of the *Arena,* she's still visible and, more important, audible from anywhere. Prices for the best seats are expensive; higher up and to the sides, they are more reasonable. The rest of the year there is excellent music, including opera, at the *Teatro Filarmonico,* where the tickets are less expensive. In summer ballet performances are given in the *Roman Theater* on the other side of the river. All bookings are made through the *Ente Lirico Arena di Verona,* Piazza Brà 28, 37100 Verona (phone: 596517, 28151). You can book in advance by mail or phone.

 NIGHTCLUBS AND NIGHTLIFE: Popular nightclubs in the city center are *Arabel's Dinner Club,* Via Tezone 7 (phone: 595545), which doubles as a piano bar (closed Wednesdays); *Excalibur Club,* Stradone A. Provolo 24 (phone: 594614) welcomes nonmembers (closed Mondays); *Campidoglio,* Piazzetta Tirabosco 4 (phone: 594448), a piano bar specializing in 1960s music, with live music after midnight (closed Mondays); and *Café Jazz Beer Jose,* Via Sant'Egidio 8 (phone: 592958), offering jazz in a 14th-century palazzo (closed Tuesdays).

 SINS: The Veronese confess to *overindulgence* in food and wine. *Salumerie,* or fine food stores, always have a counter for freshly prepared delicacies that can be packed for picnics along the Adige River. The two most famous stores are *Spega,* Via Stella 11 (phone: 34998), and *Sinico,* Via Leoni 5 (phone: 22581 or 31193). For wine sampling, there are no fewer than 26 *osterie* between the bends of the Adige River.

BEST IN TOWN

 CHECKING IN: Verona has one very expensive hotel, where the rate is $160 a night for a double room; all others are very reasonably priced. Hotels rated as moderate are between $40 and $60; inexpensive, $30 and less.

Due Torri – The entrance hall is like the throne room of a doge's palace, and, indeed, the whole hotel is furnished with antiques. This luxury hotel is one of Italy's finest. Piazza Sant'Anastasia 4 (phone: 595044). Very expensive.

Accademia – An old-fashioned hotel just off Via Mazzini, the main shopping street, this is traditionally *the* hotel for tourists in Verona. Via Scala 10–12 (phone: 596222). Moderate.

Antica Porta Leona – Just around the corner from Juliet's house and Via degli Amanti (Lovers Street), this charmingly redecorated hotel is on one of the quaintest corners in Verona. Corticella Leoni 3 (phone: 595499). Moderate.

Touring – A turn-of-the-century hotel in the heart of old Verona. Via Q. Sella 5 (phone: 590944). Moderate.

Bologna – Just off Piazza Brà, this unpretentious modern hotel has a newly renovated restaurant with a sidewalk terrace looking out toward the Arena. Piazzetta Scalette Rubiani 3 (phone: 26830, 26990). Moderate.

Aurora – Economical accommodations for those who appreciate a hotel's view more than its comforts. Ask for a room overlooking the white umbrellas of the market square. Piazza delle Erbe (phone: 594717, 597834). Inexpensive.

Ciopetta – Centrally located, behind the Arena and Piazza Brà, a family restaurant that also has rooms above, none with private bath. It has lots of atmosphere, though. Vicolo Teatro Filarmonico (phone: 26843). Inexpensive.

EATING OUT: Veronese menus differ only slightly from those elsewhere in northern Italy, and the overall standard is high. Local specialties include *gnocchi*, little dumplings made of flour and potatoes (best when handmade — *fatti a mano*), that come with a variety of sauces, from the classic meat or tomato to butter and sage. An interesting local pasta dressing is made with *ortiche* (nettles), which taste a little like broccoli. For the main course, Verona is famous for its boiled meats, not just the usual cuts, but less expected parts of different animals — such as *testina* (head), which is always served with *pearà*, a bread sauce spiced with pepper. If you are not squeamish, you might try another typical dish, *pastissada*, a horse meat stew, served with *polenta*, yellow cornmeal pudding, a staple served all over the Veneto region. In the Veronese version, it is served in solid strips, usually toasted. On the whole, eating out in Verona is very inexpensive, especially in the simple *trattorie* and small restaurants. Restaurants rated as expensive cost about $60 for two, including wine; moderate cost about $40. It is possible for two people to have a full meal with wine for as little as $20.

12 Apostoli – One of Italy's most celebrated restaurants, dating back 200 years. We think it is not quite as good as it used to be, but it's still an experience — original recipes, excellent wines, Renaissance-style decor. Closed Sunday evenings and Mondays. Vicolo Corticella San Marco 3 (phone: 596999). Expensive.

Groto de Corgnan – It's worth driving the 12½ miles to Sant'Ambrogio to experience this eatery. A lengthy, variable menu. Closed Sundays. Via Corgnano 41, Sant'Ambrogio di Valpolicella (phone: 7731372). Expensive.

Ristorante Le Arche – Excellent fish in an aristocratic atmosphere. Closed Sundays and Mondays at lunchtime. Via Arche Scaligere 6 (phone: 21415). Expensive.

Ristorante Il Desco – Save this elegant restaurant for a romantic evening. Begin with the fondue specialty, *budino di formaggio con fonduta.* Closed Sundays. Via Dietro San Sebastiano 7 (phone: 595358). Expensive.

Ristorante Nuovo Marconi – Elegant Belle Époque decor is the backdrop for painstakingly prepared Veronese specialties. Closed Sundays and Tuesday evenings. Via Fogge 4 (phone: 591910). Expensive to moderate.

Ristorante Torcoloti – Old-fashioned elegance, perfect for a quiet dinner. Appetizers are excellent, especially the combination *tris della casa,* three kinds of stuffed pasta. Closed Sundays and Monday evenings. Via Zambelli 24 (phone: 26777, 30945). Moderate.

Il Cenacolo – Choose from a wide selection of entrées; the fixed-price menu seems endless. Closed Saturdays at lunchtime and Tuesdays. Via Teatro Filarmonico 10 (phone: 33932). Moderate.

Armando – Unassuming (but excellent) fish restaurant next to an *osteria* of the same name. Closed Mondays. Via Macello 8 (phone: 25892). Inexpensive.

Ristorante La Greppia – Imaginatively renovated, ideal for lunch; try the boiled meats. Closed Mondays. Vicolo Samaritana 3 (phone: 34577). Inexpensive.

Trattoria Fontanina – A friendly, family-run establishment. Closed Monday afternoons and Tuesdays. Piazzetta Chiavica (phone: 31133). Inexpensive.

Pizzeria Marechiaro – We give this place a zero for atmosphere and a ten for pizza. Closed Wednesdays. Via Sant'Antonio 15 (phone: 34506). Very inexpensive.

 CAFFÈS AND WINE BARS: To better enjoy the local wines, join the Veronese in one of their *osterie,* of which there are no fewer than 26 between the bends of the Adige River. Many have a history almost as old as Verona itself, and some have given their names to the streets on which they stand, such as *Osteria La Pigna,* Via Pigna 4/B (closed Sundays). *Osterie* usually serve food — such as little open sandwiches with anchovies, cheese, or ham — to ballast the wine. Some offer a full, medium-priced meal, although they have lost the traditional atmosphere of hubbub and camaraderie in the process. Try *Bottega del Vino,* Via Scudo di Francia 3 (closed Sundays; phone: 34535). More typical is *Osteria Le Vecete,* Via Pellicciai 32 (closed Saturday afternoons and Sundays), where the emphasis is on drinking. The quality of the local house wines is surprising, even in the humblest *osteria.* This is one of the few regions of Italy where red and white wines are equally good.

DIVERSIONS

For the Body

Italy's Unparalleled Skiing

 Not so long ago a pastime of privilege solely for sporty Milanese industrialists and *Alpini* mountain troops on furlough, skiing has exploded into high fashion in Italy. Nowhere else in Europe are the moon boots as furry, the faces as bronzed, and the styles as avant-garde. Some large international resorts like Cervinia, Cortina, and Sestriere have it all — a vast array of runs and lifts, troops of multilingual instructors, a selection of winter sporting opportunities such as ice skating and tobogganing, cornucopias of shops, shimmering hotels, high-speed nightlife, and the glossy aura of Europe's leisured classes. But there are also lots of cozier, *famiglia*-oriented villages, many of them linked to a constellation of neighbors by far-reaching networks of chair lifts and cable cars.

Increasingly available is the all-region *tessera,* a pass that permits a skier to schuss hundreds of kilometers of trails with a single document. One of the best, the *Superski Dolomiti* pass, offers access to more than 450 lifts serving more than 675 miles of ski trails, an authentic orgy of Alpine ski touring from village to mountain pass and mountain pass to village. District passes that permit use of some portion of these 450 lifts — as much territory as most intermediates would be able to cover in a couple of weeks of skiing — are also available and are somewhat less expensive.

The best of Italy's ski towns are strung through the Alps across the northern tier of the country. Resorts in the French-flavored Valle d'Aosta are situated on natural balconies with stunning views of Mont Blanc (Monte Bianco here), the Matterhorn (which Italians know as Monte Cervino), Italy's own Monte Rosa, and other celebrated Alpine peaks; the opening of the Mont Blanc and Great St. Bernard tunnels and the construction of the Aosta–Po Valley *autostrade* have made the area easily accessible. There's also the German-speaking Alto Adige and the craggy pink peaks of the Dolomites — named for the 18th-century French geologist Déodat de Dolomieu — which rise fantastically out of valleys. With their spires and towers, deeply grooved boulders and huge terraces, and sheer vertical faces on all sides, the Dolomites do not look particularly skiable. But wide-open ledges and snowfields above, and tree-covered lower slopes below, provide sport enough to last a lifetime. That this area is also known as the South Tyrol gives a clue to the culture here — equal parts Teutonic and Mediterranean.

Surprisingly, there is also some very serviceable skiing within striking distance of southerly cities better known for their sunny summer languor — Abetone near Florence; Terminillo, Campo Imperatore, and Ovindoli near Rome; and Roccaraso, equidistant from Rome and Naples. It's even possible to ski on Mount Etna — volcanic activity permitting — and cool off afterward in the Sicilian sea.

Throughout most of these regions, those who like their luxury rugged can hire a helicopter for a quick trip up to their choice of high-altitude moonscape and the subsequent opportunity to carve their way back through miles of glittery virgin powder. If your pleasure is the trudgery known as *sci di fondi* — cross-country skiing —

you'll be glad to know that the sport is booming here; a wide choice of trails and excursions (and a good supply of the necessary equipment) are readily available. And no matter where you go, there's a very high standard of cooking in the dining rooms adjacent to the slopes. Italians demand that of their resorts (or why go?).

Words of caution: If you need an English-speaking instructor from the area's ski school, say so when signing up or risk learning to recognize "Bend your knees" spoken in all too faultless Italian. Know the local trail markings — green for novice, blue for intermediate, and red for expert. Be prepared for sometimes hair-raising traffic — both on the mountain roads and on the slopes. Since skiing as a mass activity is a Giovanni-come-lately in Italy, the average level of expertise is lower than in Switzerland or Austria, and traditions of slope safety and etiquette are not at all hallowed. Avoid crowded Christmastime if you can, and remember that the Italian school vacation extends through Epiphany on January 6. Take advantage of lunchtime — the quiet time in all seasons as skiers *all'italiana* down their regulation peaks of pasta. And remember that the same ebullience that makes an Italian so vocal in a lift line also leads to easily made friendships elsewhere in the resort.

BORMIO, Lombardy: In ancient times, Romans traveled to Bormio to cure gout, diabetes, and allergies in the natural hot water bubbling from its nine springs. Now Italians from every corner take to the heights in a two-stage cable lift that carries them above the lower mountain and its soft snow and forest-edged runs to 6,500 feet (2,000 meters) and on to the wide-open snowfields at about 9,800 feet (3,000 meters). Then, at the end of each bracing day's runs, they return to agreeably relaxed Bormio and a warm reception, Bormio style. That means enjoying the tumble of buildings and cobbled streets that infuses the town with charm throughout the year, with or without the snow, and doing as those ancient Romans did — in the thermal center in town or, a 15-minute taxi ride into the mountains, at the original Roman baths. (The original sauna is in a cave, and the pools are naturally heated — hot, hotter, hottest.) At nearby Passo dello Stelvio, summer skiing is a serious business, and no fewer than 16 schools help keep the high-altitude glaciers populated even at high noon in July — which, incidentally, is the time of year for a would-be sybarite to learn to ski. Details: *Azienda Autonoma di Soggiorno,* Cura e Turismo, Via allo Stelvio 10, 23032 Bormio (Sondrio); phone: 0342-903300.

CANAZEI, Trentino–Alto Adige: Busy, friendly, and not overly chic, surrounded by the most decorative mountains in Italy — the Sella, Marmolada, and Sassolungo sections of the distinctively dramatic Dolomite range. The more than 60 miles (100 km) of trails here are linked with the extensive networks of neighboring Val Gardena and Val Badia, so there's no shortage of skiable terrain, and the valley ski schools are known for their professionalism and highly developed teaching methods. The covered swimming pool and the brand-new skating rink will burn off any unused energy. Details: *Azienda Autonoma di Soggiorno e Turismo,* Via Roma 24, Canazei (Trento); phone: 0462-61113.

CERVINIA, Valle d'Aosta: In the Italian shadow of the Matterhorn, this is one of the most popular Italian mountain resorts — partly because of its open, sun-bathed position; partly because of its majestic mountain-rimmed setting on the Monte Rosa plateau; partly because of its altitude, which begins at over 6,500 feet (2,000 meters) and guarantees an abundant harvest of snow in an average year; and, last, because the spring skiing is superb. The trails are mostly smooth and forgiving — it's possible to stay on the slopes all day without ever bending your knees. The lift system is also one of Italy's most sophisticated, and the town is linked to neighboring Val Touranche; on a clear day you can also ski to Switzerland, passport in your parka, over the saddle to Zermatt. Every type of winter sport is on tap, from cross-country skiing to ice hockey and bobsledding, and if the looks of the place are unexceptional, the atmosphere is agreeably frenetic; chic shops, discos, skiers dressed at least to maim (both on and off the slopes), and Maseratis with roof racks full of Rossignols. Quaint it ain't. Details: *Azienda Autonoma di Soggiorno e Turismo di Breuil-Cervinia,* Via J. A. Carrel 29, 11021 Cervinia (Aosta); phone: 0166-94136.

CHAMPOLUC, Valle d'Aosta: Tucked into the end of the sunny Val d'Ayas under Monte Rosa, Champoluc has been mercifully ignored by the great mass of European skiers; the fur-coated folks with year-round suntans gravitate to nearby Cervinia and Courmayeur, also in the Aosta Valley, so Champoluc has kept its countrified air. But the facilities are as complete as the town life is simple. Including the facilities of the neighboring areas of Frachey, Staval, Orsia, and Gressoney, a total of about 27 lifts serves over 120 miles (200 km) of trails, offering skiing for every level. There's even an 18-mile (30-km) cross-country trail. Glamorous hotels are not part of Champoluc life, and quiet is the order of the evening. High school French aids communication with the hospitable natives, whose dialect is heavily Gallicized. Details: *Azienda Autonoma di Soggiorno,* Piazza Centrale, 11020 Champoluc (Aosta); phone: 0125-307113.

CORTINA D'AMPEZZO, Venetia: The country's number-one ski resort attracted its first tourists — English, German, and Austrian mountain climbers — in the mid-19th century; skiing began here early in the 20th century. But the ski trade didn't really boom until the town hosted Italy's first Winter Olympics in 1956. Now among the Alps' best-equipped and most cosmopolitan ski resorts, it counts a huge, open, blond-wood Olympic Ice Stadium among its special offerings, along with a location amidst the toothy spikes of the Dolomites at the heart of the *Superski Dolomiti* region. Add the resort's own network of four ski areas, and the resulting package draws a stylish international set that nourishes the department stores, big hotels, and scores of smart boutiques and eateries that crowd the long, narrow main street, Corso d'Italia. As a reminder that Venice and the Mediterranean are only a few hours away, a powerful sun is always present, even in February and March. Details: *Azienda Autonoma di Soggiorno e Turismo,* Piazzetta San Francesco 8, 32043 Cortina d'Ampezzo (Belluno); phone: 0436-2711.

CORVARA, Trentino–Alto Adige: Corvara is the principal departure point for the *Carosello,* the Dolomite circuit that connects five downhill areas and countless skiing experiences and that, together with a mega ski pass, provides access to about 250 miles (400 km) of linked trails. Located in one of the few valleys where residents still speak Ladin (a language said to have come down from the Latin of Romans who came here in the 4th century, similar to Switzerland's Romansh), Corvara itself has a bucolic flavor, despite the modish tone of its shops, cafés, and discothèques. If you long for the Great Indoors, there's heated swimming, covered tennis, and high-Alpine bowling. Details: *Azienda Autonoma di Soggiorno e Turismo,* Palazzo Comunale, 39033 Corvara in Badia (Bolzano); phone: 0471-83176.

COURMAYEUR, Valle d'Aosta: Among the most glamorous of Italian ski resorts, and one that some call the friendliest in the Alps, it is stunningly situated in the middle of 12 peaks above 13,000 feet (4,000 meters), the magical tag of mountain supremacy in Europe. The dramatic south-facing side of the Mont Blanc massif looms above, and over two dozen lifts make more than 60 miles (100 km) of ski runs accessible to both beginners and experts; the area is heaven for intermediates, with enough *auto-strade*-on-snow trails to boost any ego and enough moguls to remind you that there's always more to learn. Meanwhile, snow pioneers accompanied by guides can ski across Monte Bianco and over the French border to Chamonix. Such facilities and terrain attract important skiing competitions all winter and, with them, the sleek international set and modern Milan-Turin managerial money. The even more upwardly mobile use helicopters as transport to powdery plateaus. The beauties of the old-fashioned town itself will satisfy valley types: four cross-country circuits ranging in length from 3½ to 12 miles (6 to 20 km), the new snow-golf course, an arpeggio of high-decibel discotheques, and a place called the *American Bar,* presided over by the affable Giorgio. Summer skiing keeps the Gigante glacier from getting lonely during the off-season. Details: *Azienda Autonoma di Soggiorno e Turismo,* Piazzale Monte Bianco, 11013 Courmayeur (Aosta); phone: 0165-82060.

LAVEROGNE, Valle d'Aosta: A tiny one-tow town in the Valgrisenche, a bit off the highway that speeds the world to chic Courmayeur, Laverogne has only a single ski lift, no nightlife, and no grand hotels. It simply offers the opportunity to travel back in time, to see the Italian mountains as they were 40 years ago before Italy high-styled skiing for the new leisure class. Go before it's too late, and be prepared for off-trail exploring, strapping on sealskins for steep ascents, and quaffing thermosfuls of *vino brulé* (but bring your own). If all this is too serene and relaxing, rest assured that high society is only a sleigh ride away. Details: *Ente Provinciale per il Turismo,* Piazza E. Chanoux, 110 Aosta; phone: 0165-35655.

LIVIGNO, Lombardy: Not so long ago, this curious, little-known village of distinctive wooden houses strung out along a valley on the Swiss-Italian border was exclusively the domain of cross-country ski wanderers; its only road was regularly blocked by heavy snowfalls. Now, thanks to enthusiastic, but not excessive, development and the construction of a tunnel into Switzerland as an alternative means of egress, it offers a good deal of attractive skiing and accommodation, plus ice skating, tobogganing, a pretty lake, gentle landscape, and a pleasantly lost horizon. Yet it still caters to a reasonably limited clientele, particularly compared with some of the great ski mills across the border. Diehards can shop for duty-free items in the chalets-turned-shops along the main street, thanks to Livigno's special border-town dispensation. Details: *Azienda Autonoma di Soggiorno e Turismo,* Plaza dal Comun, 23030 Livigno (Sondrio); phone: 0342-996379.

MADONNA DI CAMPIGLIO, Trentino–Alto Adige: The least cosmopolitan of Italy's Big Five — a group that also includes Cervinia, Cortina, Courmayeur, and Sestriere — this resort is not widely known outside the country. So instead of the high-powered international set, the slopes are full of sleek and stylish northern Italians who are serious about their snow. The facilities for which they come are world-class: helicopters to ascend to the farthest peaks for guided all-day descents and three dozen lifts fanning out from the town to serve four separate areas with 60 miles (100 km) of slopes and trails. The possibilities run the gamut from ballroom slopes for novice snowplowers to the steep and bumpy terrain favored by high-tech slalomers. The town itself is Tyrolean in style, though there are modern structures in the Campo Carlo Magno section, and it is surrounded by beautiful pine forests and lakes — all dominated by the awesome sawtooth skyline of the Brenta Dolomites. Snowcats can haul hardy skiers up to one of the slopeside refuges for dinner and then back down in time for action in one of the town's discos, if that's your pleasure. Details: *Azienda Autonoma di Soggiorno,* 38084 Madonna di Campiglio (Trento); phone: 0465-41026.

MOENA, Trentino–Alto Adige: This Italian capital of cross-country skiing, in a sunny valley at the bull's-eye of the Dolomites, is the starting point for the annual competition known as the Marcialonga, a circuit of 43 miles (70 km) that attracts cross-country fans from all over Europe. During the rest of the season, trails are exceptionally well maintained, and the town is cheerful, bustling, and unpretentious. A favorite of vacationing families, it offers an order of luxury lower than that of some of its glossy neighbors, and prices are the opposite of exorbitant. Details: *Azienda Autonoma di Soggiorno,* Piazza Cesare Battisti 33, 38035 Moena (Trento); phone: 0462-53122.

ORTISEI/VAL GARDENA, Trentino–Alto Adige: Tucked below the broad open plateau of the Alpe di Siusi in the lushly wooded Val Gardena, sunny Ortisei is lively and pretty, with ornately decorated houses and shops overflowing with wood carvings. The atmosphere is decidedly South Tyrolean — you'll hear German as well as the local

Ladin language — and the food more Teutonic than Mediterranean. From the main square, buses fan out to all adjacent valleys, and a five-minute cable car ride hoists skiers 2,625 feet (800 meters) to a bounty of ski trails linked to the 600 miles (1,000 km) of the *Superski Dolomiti* facilities. One of the most attractive sections is the Sella Ronda, over 16 miles (26 km) of lift-connected runs around the Sella mountain massif; easy enough even for beginners, it's best done on Tuesdays or Wednesdays, when less-trafficked lifts make it possible to cover the maximum territory. If you care more about serious skiing than village life, stay at Alpe di Siusi itself at 5,900 feet (1,800 meters), where you'll have nine hours of sunlight in January and guaranteed snow. Details: *Azienda Autonoma di Soggiorno e Turismo,* Piazza Stetteneck, 39046 Ortisei (Bolzano); phone: 0471-76328.

SAN MARTINO DI CASTROZZA, Trentino–Alto Adige: Under the rose-colored peaks of the Dolomites' theatrical Pale di San Martino, this long-established center in the Valle del Cismon enjoys the twin Italian advantages of a southern exposure and protection from icy northern winds. Yet at 4,760 feet (about 1,450 meters), there is reliable snow on the piney trails that skirt the village, and the local master ski pass admits skiers to the multiple joys of the *Superski Dolomiti* system. The *Drei Tannen* has the best food in town; don't depart without the traditional *polenta e salsiccie* — a tomato-sauced cornmeal and sausage parlay served on homemade wooden trenchers. It is also almost obligatory to swig a little of the incendiary local *grappa,* especially on gelid early-morning runs from the high Rosetta. Details: *Azienda Autonoma di Soggiorno e Turismo,* Via Passo Rolle 15, 38058 San Martino di Castrozza (Trento); phone: 0439-68101.

SAN SICARIO, Piedmont: Designed and built from scratch in the late 1960s with the hard-core skier in mind, this high-powered, very Italian ski center offers not one whit of the quaint, and its complex of hotels and mini-apartment residences, accessible by silent monorail from the covered parking lot, is the ultimate in contemporaneity. The no-traffic regime guarantees stressless days and sleepful nights, and the location in the middle of an extensive trail network known as the *Via Lattea* (Milky Way) — a consortium of nine ski towns and their collective lift systems — takes care of the skiing. The comfort, convenience, and quality of the facilities more than make up for the lack of local color — especially for 9-to-5 trailaholics. Details: *Azienda Autonoma di Soggiorno,* Piazza Vittorio Amedeo 3, 10054 Cesana (Torino); phone: 0122-89202.

SAPPADA, Venetia: The language is German and the food Austrian. But the currency is still Italian in this town off the beaten trails just south of the border. Ideal for seekers of the small but *bello,* Sappada has 30 miles (50 km) of varied and well-groomed skiing as well as opportunities for cross-country trekking. The friendly hotels are mostly pocket-sized and family-run, and there is a broad selection of short-term apartment rentals in balconied chalets. Evening entertainment centers on hot *vino brulé* (mulled wine) or cold beer, not brassy disco dancing. The costumed carnival merriment of February is an added dividend. Details: *Azienda Autonoma di Soggiorno e Turismo,* Via Bach 12, 32047 Sappada (Belluno); phone: 0435-69131.

SAUZE D'OULX, Piedmont: Lift-linked to the bigger, brassier centers of Sestriere and San Sicario, and thereby to the 240 trail miles (400 km) of the Via Lattea, Sauze d'Oulx itself is a smaller, more easygoing, and less sophisticated snow haven — an excellent choice for those preferring ski-borne access to the widest possible range of trails with less conspicuous merriment off-trail. Close to the border, Sauze d'Oulx has been a favorite with the French since the early part of the century. It is also very popular with the British, and English — of a sort — is widely spoken. The mountain terrace of the Val di Susa, at 4,900 feet (1,500 meters), is a wind-free suntrap — ideal for mid-winter tanning, and rows of maidens in deck chairs can usually be seen cupping aluminum reflectors under their chins while turning their tawny faces phototropically. Wide north-facing slopes and open larch woods mean a long season of powder and fine trails of the calendar art variety. The town itself is a charmer — buildings leaning this way and that over the twisting streets, a 15th-century fountain in the plaza. Dedicate evenings to the *fonduta* — the Italian answer to Swiss fondue, chased with a local Arneis or Erbaluce di Caluso wine. Details: *Azienda Autonoma di Soggiorno e Turismo,* Piazza Assietta, 10050 Sauze d'Oulx (Torino); phone: 0122-85009.

SESTRIERE, Piedmont: Like Courcheval in France, Sestriere was carved out of snowy emptiness expressly to create a fabulous location for skiing, "a kind of skiing university in which the ordinary ski runner who usually knows nothing at all about mountains can graduate to an expert winter mountaineer" by working through its runs, according to a 1934 guidebook to the area. "Here," the guidebook goes on, "all is for the ski, for the slope . . . the most satisfying creation of the industrial revolution on the snows of the Alps." The main square is named for Fiat founding father Giovanni Agnelli, whose vision spawned the whole thing. His ideas have held up remarkably well. In season, excellent high-altitude runs rise from a base of about 9,200 feet (2,803 meters) for all levels of skier, and it's possible to ski here for a week without ever repeating a run — especially when you take advantage of the facilities of other Via Lattea resorts. The ski instruction is excellent, the mood chic and modern, and the condos comfortable. The sun shines abundantly, and there are large terraces with plenty of deck chairs and umbrella tables from which to enjoy it. And although there's no sense of village life, Sestriere is eminently lively in season. It's an especially marvelous place to ski on weekdays. High-season weekends, when big tour buses arrive from Turin, 55 miles (90 km) distant, are another matter. Details: *Azienda Autonoma di Soggiorno e Turismo,* Piazza Giovanni Agnelli 11, 10058 Sestriere (Torino); phone: 0122-76045.

Tennis

It wasn't too long ago that only a select group of Italians donned tennis whites for an afternoon of tennis, 5 o'clock tea, and 7 o'clock cocktails. Tennis was a game of the elite.

Then, after Italy produced a few champions in the 1950s, Italians began viewing tennis through new eyes. Hundreds of clubs were established all over the country and everyone rushed to join. Networks broadcast major international tournaments, and now it's often very hard to find a free court.

The traveling tennis player will find most of the activity at private tennis clubs, admission to which can usually be arranged by the better hotels for their guests. In addition, many hotels, particularly those in prime resort areas, have at least a court or two. Everywhere, clay is the preferred surface, and regulation tennis shoes, as well as accepted tennis attire, are usually required.

At a number of tennis instruction camps, both adults and children can work on their strokes in gorgeous surroundings — by the sea, in the mountains, or in the countryside. Fitness centers, swimming pools, saunas, and solaria are the usual companions to serious instruction by *Federazione Italiana Tennis* (Italian Tennis Federation) coaches. And the atmosphere is always friendly and relaxed.

For a complete listing of Italian tennis clubs and for general information about the game in Italy, contact the Federation at Viale Tiziano 70, 00100 Roma (phone: 06-36851). Here are some of the best net bets.

CENTRO INTERNAZIONALE JUNIOR ACADEMY, Bologna, Emilia-Romagna:
One of the most successful Davis Cup coaches in history, the late Harry Hopman,

established this training camp and another in Florida. The likes of Mal Anderson, Ashley Cooper, Roy Emerson, Neal Fraser, Lew Hoad, Rod Laver, John Newcombe, Ken Rosewall, Frank Sedgman, and Fred Stolle all worked with Hopman; Vitas Gerulaitis, Andrès Gomez, and others have trained at his center in the US. So it should come as no surprise that this place in the hills of Rastignano, near Bologna, is Italy's most intensive tennis training center. From beginners through champions, everyone follows the regimen the founder designed to "take the best in your game and make it better." Coaches analyze students' physique, personality, adaptability, natural aptitude, and current tennis ability and prescribe a program of standardized drills. The tennis facilities are abundant — 19 indoor courts (5 in geodesic domes) and 6 outdoor clay courts, all lighted — and so are the possibilities for taking the kinks out of your other games. There's an Olympic-size pool, a well-equipped health club and gym, and a small soccer field for *calcetto.* Complete week-long tennis packages for all ages are available year-round. The week includes 5 hours of tennis daily, with one instructor for every 4 students. Prices range from 950,000 lire to 1,100,000 lire weekly, depending on the season. Details: *Centro Internazionale Junior Academy,* Via Serrabella 1, 40065 Rastignagno (Bologna); phone: 051-743142.

SPORTING CLUB GAVARNO, Bergamo, Lombardy: Located in gentle hill country, the Sporting Club Gavarno sponsors tennis clinics from June through August under the supervision of former national team member and Tennis Federation trainer Pier Franc Bonaiti. Groups of four are organized according to ability and train for 3 hours each day. Lodging is in four- or eight-bed dorm rooms or, by special arrangement, at nearby hotels (though a car is required). Swimming, squash, badminton, Ping-Pong, and a health club are also available. Details: *Sporting Club Castello di Gavarno,* Via Gavarno 18, 24020 Scanzorosciate (Bergamo); phone 035-659202.

BRUCOLI, Sicily: Tennis is the focus at this Valtur vacation village, where former Italian Davis Cup team member Orlando Sira heads a program of clinics offered weekly from May through August. There are 3 hours of lessons daily or a more intensive 5- or 6-hour program. Ball machines, videotape units, and other high-tech instructional items are available on the court. Sailing, windsurfing, horseback riding, canoeing, and aerobics are also offered; underwater photography and bridge are a welcome change of pace for those whose muscles have given out. Clinics range in cost from 350,000 to 650,000 lire per week. Details: *Valtur Office,* Via Milano 42, 00184 Roma; phone: 06-4706238 or 06-4706239.

BAIA DI CONTE, Alghero, Sardinia: The clearly Catalanian Spanish port-and-resort of Alghero, set amid olive and eucalyptus trees, and the attractive seaside Baia di Conte Hotel are ideal for spicing stroke drills with Sardinian scenery. At hotel tennis camps, available for adults and children from June through September, certified instructors and coaches divide participants into groups of eight according to ability and work on their games using videotape analyses and ball machines as necessary. A fitness room, sauna and whirlpool, windsurfing boards, and horseback riding are available; guests can unwind in the evening in the hotel's disco. Rates range from 500,000 to 700,000 lire per week, depending on the season. Details: *Baia di Conte,* Alghero (Sardegna); phone: 079-952003 or 079-951109.

IL CIOCCO, Lucca, Tuscany: The summer tennis camps of this international vacation center in a vast natural reserve in the Garfagnana hills are organized primarily for 8- to 15-year-olds. However, adults can use the courts and arrange coaching sessions with the instructor, and, off the courts, enjoy the solarium, sauna, health club, pool, horseback riding, and hiking. Lodging is in the hotel or in cozy little chalets in the surrounding woods. Details: *Il Ciocco,* Centro Turistico Internazionale, 55020 Castelvecchio Pascoli (Lucca); phone: 0583-710021.

INTERNATIONAL TOURNAMENTS

If you're accustomed to the respectful hush of Wimbledon, the noisy Italian crowds can strike a jarring note. But if you just think of the noise as heartfelt enthusiasm, attending a tournament in Italy can be a cultural as well as a sporting experience. The top tournaments at which this very Mediterranean show of excitement is most evident include most of the following:

> *International Italian Indoor Grand Prix,* Milan, March.
> *Bari Grand Prix,* April.
> *Italian International Grand Prix,* Foro Italico, Rome, May.
> *Florence Grand Prix,* May.
> *International Virginia Slims Tournament,* Taranto, May.
> *Bologna Grand Prix,* June.
> *Women's Virginia Slims,* Perugia, July.
> *Palermo Grand Prix,* October.

For exact dates and information on purchasing tickets, contact the *Federazione Italiana Tennis,* Viale Tiziano 70, 00100 Roma (phone: 06-36851). For news about the sport in Italy, consult the country's major tennis publications: *Matchball, Il Tennista,* and *Tennis Italiano.*

Great Italian Golf

The British brought golf to Italy around the turn of the century, but it was another 50 years before the game acquired any degree of popularity — and then it remained an activity of the very social or the very rich. Now an increasing number of foreign golfers have discovered that Italy's 80 or so courses offer the perfect formula for a golfing vacation: a beautiful natural setting, an ideal climate nearly year-round, and some rather challenging sport. The result is that 20 new courses are currently being built, and the Italian golf devotees' explanation of the nation's relatively small number of courses — that they're looking for quality rather than quantity — is beginning to gain some credibility. It is also increasingly possible to find layouts that begin to measure up to the criteria for a great course articulated over 40 years ago by Bobby Jones: It should "give pleasure, and . . . to the greatest number of players . . . because it will offer problems many may attempt according to his ability. It will never become hopeless for the duffer nor fail to concern and interest the expert; and it will be found, like Old St. Andrews, to become more delightful the more it is studied and played."

As Italy becomes more involved with golf, it has become more apparent that the country is full of spots that seem to have been created just to hold a golf course: layouts by the sea, courses in the mountains, and more.

Some of the best are listed below. Greens fees range from 10,000 to 40,000 lire on weekdays, slightly more on weekends; some courses accept credit cards, and some do not. The courses are very crowded on weekends, so if that's when you want to play, reserve a tee time well ahead, either through your hotel or by contacting the club directly. All Italian golf clubs extend reciprocal privileges to foreigners with a membership card or other evidence of club membership at home.

For complete information about golf in Italy and Italian golf clubs, contact the *Italian Golf Federation,* Via Flaminia 388, Roma; phone: 06-394641.

BY THE SEA

GARLENDA GOLF CLUB, Garlenda, Liguria: Winters are mild, springs gentle, and summers temperate on the Italian Riviera, so there's no season to the pleasures and challenges of this course. Just as the first holes have lulled you into relaxation, the 12th hole comes along, a long and very treacherous par 4. It's followed by a long par 3 that crosses a stream, and, three holes later, a par 4 with a left-hand dogleg. Even then, the average duffer has a good chance of making a few pars here. The most convenient lodging is next door at the *Golf Hotel La Meridiana.* Details: *Garlenda Golf Club,* Via del Golf 7, 17030 Garlenda (Savona); phone: 0182-580012, 0182-580013.

PEVERO GOLF CLUB, Porto Cervo, Sardinia: When Robert Trent Jones created this "emerald jewel in the Costa Smeralda crown," one of the world's great seaside courses, he gave free reign to his sense of the dramatic, and the resulting layout is a direct reflection of his raw materials — a narrow, rising and plunging, sea-edged neck of land patched with granite outcrops, pine, broom, gorse, lavender, poppy, lupin, and juniper that blazes with color in the spring. This is a tiger of a course, and perhaps the greatest difficulty is making a good recovery shot out of the rough. Major traps are found at the 3rd, 11th, and 15th holes. Rated fifth on *Golf Digest*'s top 15 European courses. Closed Tuesdays. Details: *Pevero Golf Club,* 07020 Porto Cervo (Sassari); phone: 0789-96072, 0789-96210.

GOLF CLUB PUNTA ALA, Punta Ala, Tuscany: Set in southern Tuscany's Maremma, near the meeting place of the Tyrrhenian and the Ligurian seas opposite the isle of Elba, this 6,720-yard course has been a standout among Italian layouts since 1964, when it was carved out of a pine woods on rolling terrain that stretches down to the sea. Long and tough from start to finish, it has been seeded with a special Korean grass known for its even growth, so players are almost able to hit a driver off the fairways. Caution is required on the 5th and 12th holes; the 8th confronts players with a long par 4 on a steep uphill slope. High summer temperatures (albeit tempered by sea breezes) add to the challenge. Open daily. Punta Ala itself is a prime destination for sports of all types, particularly swimming, sailing, and riding. Details: *Punta Ala Golf Club,* Via del Golf 1, 68040 Punta Ala (Grosseto); phone: 0564-922121.

GOLF CLUB DEGLI ULIVI, San Remo, Liguria: Named for the olive groves through which the course unfolds, this 6,020-yard layout, rebuilt in 1972, offers panoramic sea views, narrow fairways, undulating greens, and a valley location that protects players from the sea winds. Tee shots must be precise, but otherwise this is a course for relaxation. Closed Tuesdays. Details: *Golf Club degli Ulivi,* Strada Campo Golf 59, 18038 San Remo (Imperia); phone: 0184-63093.

ALBERONI GOLF COURSE, Venice: At 6,356 yards, this spectacular seaside layout at the far western end of Venice's famed Lido is long for a Continental course. And with tees and greens surrounded by groves of pines, olives, and poplars, it can also be demanding. However, it is extraordinarily well balanced. There are par 5 holes that call for long hitting, as well as other holes that require all the other golfing skills. Concentration is paramount, especially at the 7th hole, the longest par 4, where two bunkers guard the green; the 8th hole, which has a blind approach; and the 14th, which forces a player to avoid a gaggle of scattered traps. Details: *Golf Club Lido di Venezia,* Via del Forte, 30011 Alberoni (Venezia); phone: 041-731015.

NEAR MAJOR CITIES

MILANO GOLF CLUB, Milan: These 27 holes are in the heart of Monza Park, a few miles north of Milan, on the former estate of Umberto I (who was assassinated here in 1900). The site of several major tournaments, it also has pros that rank among Italy's best, and the physical facilities are first rate. Closed Mondays. Details: *Golf Club Milano*, 20052 Parco di Monza (Milano); phone: 039-303081, 039-30382.

OLGIATA, Rome: The preferred Italian venue for most major international tournaments, the west course is tough and demanding — particularly for the power golfer who may be short on precision. British course architect C. K. Cotton started with plenty of space, so there's never a feeling of congestion. At the same time, he gave every hole a character all its own, balancing the course as a whole to challenge every facet of a player's skill and strategic abilities. The large greens have narrow bunkered entrances, the levels change (though never too drastically), and there's scarcely a straight hole on the course. There's also a 3,092-yard, 9-hole east course. Closed Mondays. Details: *Olgiata Golf Club*, Largo Olgiata 15, 00123 Roma; phone: 06-3789141.

GOLF CLUB ROMA, Rome: Rome's golf devotees love this undulating 6,344-yard layout near the Acquasanta Springs nine miles north of Rome. It is probably the most prestigious course in all of Italy. The most strenuous test of shot-making is posed by the strong winds that normally sweep across its pines, cypresses, and oaks. Accuracy is a must. Details: *Golf Club Roma*, Via Appia Nuova 716/a, Località Acquasanta, 00178 Roma; phone: 06-783407, 06-786129.

TORINO GOLF CLUB, Turin, Piedmont: On a classic championship layout with wide fairways, these 27 holes in Mandria Park unwind along flat terrain scattered with trees and water hazards. Even Sunday players have a fighting chance here; the course is fairly forgiving and allows for errors and recovery. Site of many Italian championships, the club is considered very exclusive. The clubhouse is quite charming. Closed Mondays. Details: *Golf Club Torino*, 10070 Fiano Torinese (Torino); phone 011-9235670, 011-9235440.

IN THE HILLS

CIRCOLO GOLF VILLA D'ESTE, Como, Lombardy: This interesting hillside course on the banks of Lake Montorfano, an arduous test of shot-making that some consider the toughest par 69 in Europe, has hosted major international tournaments since it was constructed in 1926. Unwinding through chestnut, birch, and pine groves, its 6,066 yards offer not a single opportunity for relaxation. The fairways, while not cramped, are bordered by trees and roll and dip inexorably toward the lake, so that both accuracy and power are essential every step of the way. The layout was built by the lush *Villa d'Este Hotel*, though it is no longer involved in the club's operation. It does, however, still provide the perfect pampering headquarters at which to find succor from soaring scores. Open daily, March to December. Details: *Circolo Golf Villa d'Este*, Via Cantù 13, 22030 Montorfano (Como); phone: 031-200200. (See also *Italy's Most Memorable Hostelries.*)

CIRCOLO GOLF FIRENZE, Florence: Nestled in the Chianti hills, this layout is not very long, but its numerous trees and bushes, bunkers, and out-of-bounds require concentration and accuracy. The 4th hole is a long, downhill par 3, the 5th a long par 4 through an olive grove. Wine tasting before a round is not advised. Closed Mondays. Details: *Circolo Golf Firenze*, Via Chiantigiana 3, 50015 Grassina (Firenze); phone: 055-2051009.

GOLF CLUB SESTRIERE, Sestriere, Piedmont: Known as the highest 18-hole course in Europe, this one in the western Alps is open only in July and August. After then, it's snow, snow, snow. Major challenges are the strong winds that often start up when players least expect them; be prepared. Watch out for the 9th hole, a long, uphill par 4 that plays to a very small green, and the 18th hole, where it's all uphill — and steep. Details: *Golf Club Sestriere*, Piazza Agnelli 4, 10058 Sestriere (Torino); phone: 0122-76276, 0122-76243.

GOLF CLUB CANSIGLIO, Vittorio Veneto, Venetia: Robert Trent Jones designed this 9-hole course on a limestone plateau with a good deal of wide-open space peppered by natural obstacles and double tees. Careful shots are in order. Open daily, April to November. Details: *Golf Club Cansiglio,* c/o A.A.S.T., 31029 Vittorio Veneto (Treviso); phone: 0438-585398.

Beaches

 Italy's 5,000 miles of coastline are continually washed by the historic dark waves of the Ligurian, the Tyrrhenian, the Ionian, the Adriatic, and the Mediterranean. From Portofino to Trapani, the choice of beaches is as dazzling as the midsummer sun. Sun worshipers can sprawl on wide swaths of downy sand at Viareggio, hike down a cliff-hanging path to a craggy Calabrian cove, share a dry martini with a titled fellow beachcomber, plunge off a pedal boat on the far side of Sardinia, or overdo it on fish and Frascati at suburban Rome's Fregene. To get away from everybody else who's getting away from it all, it's a simple matter to head for the northern coast of the Gargano, near the obscure fishing village of Vieste, where a 40-mile-long strand is punctuated at either end by two huge dunes, or travel to the garland of islands that rings Italy's coast — Elba, Giglio, Ponza, Ischia & Co. — for the country's freshest fish and crystal-clearest waters.

Most of Italy's best beachfronts are listed below. But wherever you decide to establish your beachhead, do it in June, July, September, or October. In August, all of Italy seems to slide down to the sea, and on even the tiniest postage stamps of sandy coastline, coconut-scented sun-seekers jockey aggressively for meager patches of sand and salt water. But on a balmy Columbus Day, a beach-loving visitor can savor a semiprivate Capri and be positively lonely on the Lido.

LIPARI, or AEOLIAN, ISLANDS, Sicily: Movie buffs know this chain of ancient volcanoes north of Milazzo, off the Sicilian coast, as the setting for Roberto Rossellini's *Stromboli,* starring Ingrid Bergman; classics majors may remember it as the home of Aeolus, the god of the winds, and a notable stop on Odysseus' grand tour. Each of the landfalls has its own magic. Lipari, the busiest and easiest to reach, is a subtle mosaic of pastel houses, buff-colored beaches, and turquoise waters. At Vulcano, the more adventurous can climb to the summit of the broad crater for fine views over the archipelago and splash in the thermal springs near the shore of Porto di Levante. On Stromboli, stroll up the cone-shaped crater on a moonlit night to see the fiery bubbles of lava and showers of stone explode against the sky and then fall tamely back into the crater. Scuba divers choose the clear waters of Panarea or Salina, and those seeking solitude visit wild and secluded Alicudi or Filicudi. The archipelago can be reached by boat from six mainland cities, including Naples. Go early in the season; the water is warm enough for swimming by late May. Details: *Azienda Autonoma di Soggiorno e Turismo dell Isole Eolie,* Corso Vittorio Emanuele 253, 98055 Lipari (Messina); phone: 090-9811410.

AMALFI COAST, Salerno, Campania: The Sorrento Peninsula — the finger of land curling around the Bay of Naples and pointing to the island of Capri — is mountainous and brilliant with flowers. Its southern exposure is edged by a narrow road that has been famous for breathtaking views and heart-stopping curves since it was carved out of the rock in the mid-19th century. Break up the dizzying drive through its tunnels, over its bridges, and atop its cliffs with a stay in Positano, where chalk-white houses cling to the hillside that dives down to the busy seafront, and minuscule boutiques display rainbows of trendy summer styles. For the best swimming, rent a boat with enough motor to take you a few kilometers away from the gladding crowd. Yachts anchor off the coast at the privately owned islands of I Galli. One of the sleekest hotels in Italy, the *San Pietro* (described in *Italy's Most Memorable Hostelries*), perched south of town, has its own private beach.

Once an independent republic with a population of over 100,000, Amalfi rivaled cities such as Genoa and Pisa during the medieval struggle for power in the Mediterranean. It remains small and charming despite its grandiose history and today's continued assaults by Nordic tour buses, whose merry regiments briefly besiege the shops and cafés but blissfully decamp (usually) by nightfall. The best beaching is to be enjoyed in early morning before the carnival comes to town. Details: *Azienda Autonoma di Soggiorno e Turismo,* Via del Saracino 2, 84017 Positano (Salerno); phone: 089-875067; *Azienda Autonoma di Soggiorno e Turismo,* Corso Roma 19, 84011 Amalfi (Salerno); phone: 089-872619.

CAPRI, near Naples, Campania: The most famous, most expensive, and most crowded of all Italian islands, Capri (*ca*-pri, not ca-*pree*) is also one of the most beautiful places in the world. To be sure, it's necessary to keep your distance in July and August, when the little main square and the Marina Piccola beach become twin cans of Mediterranean sardines. But during the off-season, on a sunny November Wednesday, say, it's absolutely incomparable, with sapphire sky and sea, heady aromas from hillside lemon groves perfuming the air, lush purple explosions of wisteria at every turn. The principal pleasures: funicular rides from the boat dock, lazy morning orange juice in one of the piazzetta cafés, afternoon jaunts to the marina, rowboat rides out around the grottoes, the hair-raising minibus ride back up the hairpin road to town, and spooky moon-shadowed rambles to the pagan shrine of the Matromania cave. The Roman emperor Tiberius built 12 villas here to honor the 12 Olympian deities, and his Villa Jovis — from which he ruled the empire for a decade — is a wonderful walk with a view. From the peak of the island it's possible to see all the way to Calabria. Details: *Azienda Autonoma di Soggiorno,* Piazzetta Ignazio Cerio 11, 80073 Capri (Napoli); phone: 081-8370424.

COSTA SMERALDA, Sardinia: It's remarkable what the Aga Khan and $200 million can do for a primitive island coastline. Centuries of invasions by Libyans, Phoenicians, Saracens, Romans, and Spaniards had driven Sardinians into the mountains, leaving the island's rugged, rocky coastline largely uninhabited. Then, in the space of just a few years, the stretch between the port of Olbia and the island's tip at La Maddalena went from wasteland to Emerald Coast — now the country's most glamorous beach complex. The boulders are still there and the water is still an incredibly cloudless cobalt, but scattered from cove to cove are four elegant hotels tastefully designed so that they seem to grow gracefully out of the landscape — the Moorish-style, chalk-white *Romazzino* (90 rooms); the *Cervo* (family-oriented and Spanish-inspired); the 25-bungalow, ultra-private *Pitrizza;* and the biggest of all, the *Cala di Volpe* (described in *Italy's Most Memorable Hostelries*). Each has its own beaches, which are separated from the main hotel grounds so that guests can enjoy total seclusion. And when one crescent of sand gets crowded, it's only a short hike around the bend to find another, equally pretty — one statistics maven counted 83 strands on the Costa Smeralda's 35 miles of coast. When there is a crowd, it can get very fancy, particularly when the yacht fleet's in at Porto Cervo (you might see Princess Caroline, Lord Snowdon, King Hussein, or any number of other sheiks or bluebloods). But everyone on the Costa Smeralda comes here for the laid-back sun-and-sea life, so it all stays superbly simple. Facilities off the beach include golf on one of Italy's best courses, tennis, boating, and water skiing, all shared by the four hotels. Boat and air connections with several mainland cities are available — but remember to make midsummer reservations well in advance or you may vacation in a sleeping bag on the dock at Civita-vecchia. Details: *Azienda Autonoma di Soggiorno e Turismo,* Viale Costa Smeralda, 07021 Arzachena (Sassari); phone: 0789-82624.

FORTE DEI MARMI, Lucca, Tuscany: The Italian Riviera is really like a gigantic seaside café, and the chief amusement is watching the passing — or sprawling — parade: the phalanxes of candy cane–striped umbrellas, deck chairs, and beach cabins, the fleets of pedal boats, the sippers of Campari, the builders of sand castles, the narcissistic waders, the ostentatious players of volleyball. And the whole expanse of coast between the Lido di Camaiore and the bustling resort town of Viareggio is really one long marina. Patrician families from Rome, Florence, and Turin have been coming here every summer since the last century, though many of their pined and palmed seafront villas have been transformed into small hotels (the *Augustus* once belonged to the Agnelli clan). Though the air is perfumed with mimosa and eucalyptus, never expect romantic solitude (though by comparison with other parts of the coast, Forte Dei Marmi is almost sedate). Details: *Azienda Autonoma di Soggiorno,* Piazza Marconi, 55042 Forte dei Marmi (Lucca); phone: 0584-80091.

MARATEA, Potenza, Basilicata: Fishermen have plied the transparent waters of this enchanted coastline since Greek times, but the pleasantly unpretentious town of Maratea, at the ankle of Italy's boot, was virtually unknown 20 years ago; even today few foreigners make their way this far down the coast. Those who do find beaches ranging from blanket-sized to roomy and a shoreline jagged with cliffs, crags, coves, and caves. The Apennines reach almost to the sea here, leaving just enough space for a huddle of russet roofs and a riot of low-growing rosemary, myrtle, and broom between the pines and olive trees. Maratea harbors the sumptuous *Santavenere Hotel,* whose affluent northern clientele sometimes seems an anomaly surrounded by the simplicity of the town; there are also more modest accommodations, plus pensions and private rooms, for beachcombers of other classes. Details: *Azienda Autonoma di Soggiorno e Turismo,* Piazza del Gesù, 85040 Maratea (Potenza); phone: 0973-876129.

MONTE ARGENTARIO, Grosseto, Tuscany: Halfway between Rome and Pisa on the Tyrrhenian coast, Monte Argentario has all the advantages of an island, but none of the drawbacks. The air is clear and tangy, the vegetation lush and fragrant, the sea spreads out on all sides, and, with a narrow causeway linking the promontory to Orbetello and the mainland coast road, there's no fuss over ferries. The Porto Ercole side of the mountain is frequented by nouveau-*ricco* Roman and landed aristocracy; Holland's Queen Beatrice has her vacation home here, the "White Elephant." Summer at the secluded, exclusive *Pellicano Hotel,* and you won't have to worry over your un-crowned head about villa upkeep. Rent a boat at recently developed *Cala Galera* nearby, one of the largest marinas on the coast with space for 750 boats. Try to lunch at Porto Santo Stefano when the swordfish catch comes in. And should the water seem bluer on the other side of the strait, catch a ferry to the unblemished isles of Giglio and Giannutri. Details: *Azienda Autonoma di Soggiorno e Turismo della Costa d'Argento,* Corso Umberto 55a, 58019 Porto Santo Stefano (Grosseto); phone: 0564-814208; *Ufficio Informazioni,* Isola del Giglio, Giglio Porto, Via Umberto 148, 58013 Isola del Giglio (Grosseto); phone: 0564-809265.

PORTOFINO, Genoa, Liguria: Genoa divides the 180-mile-long marina known as the Italian Riviera midway along its gentle curve; Portofino is the jewel in the crown of the glittering Riviera di Levante (Riviera of the Rising Sun), which stretches east and south of the sprawling port city. A motley tumble of little houses clustered around a miniature natural harbor where yachts purr in at sunset in time for Campari-and-soda hour, Portofino mixes the scenically savage and the luxuriously manicured. Set like a chunk of coral on its hilly perch above the town, the *Hotel Splendido,* a three-tiered pink and white manse that once belonged to one of Liguria's noblest families, is a case in point. Don't miss the two-hour walk to the Benedictine Abbey at San Fruttuoso and the grilled shrimp at the little restaurant on the beach. Details: *Azienda Autonoma di Soggiorno,* Via Roma 35, 16034 Portofino (Genova); phone: 0185-69024.

SENIGALLIA, Ancona, Marches: With miles of pale, velvety sand sloping gently into a warm and shallow sea, the Adriatic coast offers Italy's most immaculate strands. Less frantic in high season than more northerly parts, Senigallia is a prime destination for the sand castle set. Hundreds of family-run pensions and hotels, in all price ranges, are scattered along a tidily modern beachfront; the historic old center represents the Renaissance and the Baroque in pleasing harmony with a fortress, a palace, a church, a cathedral, and a papal wall that can be visited each day after a swim and lunch. An aged synagogue is a poignant reminder of a once-flourishing Jewish community. Details: *Azienda Autonoma di Soggiorno,* Piazzale Morandi, 60019 Senigallia (Ancona); phone: 071-64844.

SPERLONGA, Latina, Latium: Attracting an intensely casual young crowd in June and July, and families with station wagons during the national holiday month of August, this town is a Moorish labyrinth of white buildings, staircases, and alleyways stacked compactly on a seaside ledge, with the beach stretching below in a silken crescent. A few kilometers away is the Grotto of Tiberius, where that jovial imperial degenerate maintained a huge marine theater and his own personal pleasure dome. A little-known museum there houses several ancient monumental sculptures pieced together from thousands of fragments found buried in the grotto's pools and sands. Sperlonga itself, easily reached from both Rome and Naples, has only a handful of modest hotels; the lively *Corallo,* right in town, has a staircase that plummets to the beach. After you climb back up at day's end, you'll be ready for a swim. Details: *Pro Loco,* Corso San Leone 22, Sperlonga (Latina); phone: 0711-54796.

TAORMINA, Messina, Sicily: In Taormina, a medieval city carved into the side of Monte Tauro, visitors look up to the puffing, snow-covered Mount Etna and down into the warm, transparent seas of Sicily. It's also a place for exploring Greek and Roman ruins; trekking to the tower of Castelmola for the last word in panoramic views; glancing at the lace and embroidery shops; then settling in for some serious *aperitivo*-sipping and *passeggiata*-ogling at a café on the Corso Umberto, where pomaded, cream-suited Latin lover-boys still try to rub elbows with fetching blond maidens from the north. Evenings are for concerts or dance recitals at the outdoor Greek theater, as flowers perfume the soft air and reflections of the lights of fishing boats dance in the midnight sea. In August, the town tinsels with film festival followers, and the movie-set terrace of the glamorous *Hotel San Domenico* (described in *Italy's Most Memorable Hostelries*) blossoms with semi-famous faces. Details: *Azienda Autonoma di Soggiorno,* Palazzo Corvaia, 98039 Taormina; phone: 0942-23243.

LIDO OF VENICE, Venetia: Just a reminder that while travelers are closely examining the most beautiful city in the world, it's also possible to swim, sunbathe, and eat fresh shrimp on the Lido, a long, skinny island bordered on one side by the sea and on the other by the lagoon, just a short boat ride from downtown Venice. Besides golf, tennis, riding, and boating, there are acres and acres of fine, soft sand — some handsome and public, some the combed-and-groomed-and-cabana-lined private reserves of the great rambling seafront hotels that give the resort its air of slight decadence (the *Grand Hotel des Bains* was the setting for Thomas Mann's novella *Death in Venice*). Whichever patch of beach you choose for morning sun worship, it's still a snap to be strolling along the Venetian canals or sitting at a café in Piazza San Marco by late afternoon — and that sure beats the usual range of après-swim choices. (If you're willing to travel just a little farther afield, try the Lido di Jesolo. It lacks the Lido's tradition, but it's more charming in other ways. And the waters are bluer.) Details: *Azienda Autonoma di Soggiorno,* Rialto 4089, 30124 Venezia; phone: 041-26110.

Sailing the Seas of Italy

 Some of the greatest sailors who ever lived were Italians: Christopher Columbus, Amerigo Vespucci, Giovanni da Verrazano, and Giovanni Caboto, whom the world knew better as John Cabot. When these daring men set sail, the sea was a way of life. And since three-fourths of their country is surrounded by water, it should come as no surprise that Italians still take to the sea with great gusto. The country's four seas — the Tyrrhenian, the Ligurian, the Adriatic, and the Ionian — are each adventures that include charming ports, picturesque villages, crumbling ruins, historical monuments, elegant resorts, secluded coves, and incomparable beaches. Dock at any harbor and sample some of the country's finest cuisine or relax in a waterfront *caffè*. Or leave the crowds behind entirely and set sail for remote beaches on nearby islands.

Here are some of the best waters for sailing around Italy, as well as our selection of the prime ports of call.

THE TYRRHENIAN SEA: The most difficult sailing in the Mediterranean, the Tyrrhenian can be dangerous to small craft because of strong breezes, strong waves, and the *libeccio* — a treacherous southwest wind that strikes terror in the hearts of even the most competent experts. But as any sea enthusiast will tell you, the coastline here has what it takes to make those fears conquerable: sandy beaches, high peaks and promontories, quaint fishing villages, fine resorts, and the world's most beautiful islands. Capri, Ischia, and Sardinia alone can transform a simple cruise into a romantic and spectacular escapade.

Indeed, approaching Capri from the sea is one of the most breathtaking sailing experiences in Italy. As you sail on and through the sapphire sea that surrounds this fabulous island, the scene framed by a cloudless sky, you have no doubt why even the most jaded travelers call this one of the most gorgeous places on earth. It's a special treat to explore hidden coves, visit the famed Blue Grotto, call at the less known (but equally dramatic) Green Grotto, and stop at the Tiberian Baths.

The coast near Naples is all cliffs, fantastically sea-carved promontories, Saracen towers, and peaceful seaside towns — legendary Sorrento, villa-studded Posillipo, Moorish-looking Amalfi, and Positano ("a dream place that isn't quite real," according to John Steinbeck).

In Tuscany, farther north, visit Monte Argentario and Porto Ercole, walk along centuries-old cobblestone streets, or climb to high lookout points for bird's-eye views of the littoral.

And don't forget the Tuscan Archipelago. You can sail around the island of Monte Cristo — "Treasure Island" to Alexandre Dumas — now a nature reserve. On the island of Giannutri, there are Roman remains to prowl and, on Giglio Island, an ancient castle and its fortifications to tour.

The knobby island of Elba, a gigantic, half-submerged mountain that is the largest landfall in this island group, is a splendid combination of rocky shores, sandy beaches, impressive mountains that descend straight to the sea, and clean waters whose depths hide ancient wrecks, rusted anchors, broken amphoras, and other relics of eras long past. The area around Sant'Andrea is particularly favored among boaters equipped with scuba gear.

The ultimate Tyrrhenian sailor's destination may be sun-washed Sardinia. The island's Costa Smeralda (Emerald Coast) radiates wealth and sophistication. Don't miss Porto Cervo, Porto Rotondo, and Golfo Aranci.

For charters in the Tuscan Archipelago: *Centro Nautico Italiano,* Piazza Signoria 31r, 50122 Firenze; phone: 055-287045.

For sailing along the Tuscan coast and Sardinia: *Mario Lorenzoni,* Via degli Alfani 105r, 50100 Firenze; phone: 055-284790.

For sailing around Sardinia: *Sarda Sailing Club,* Via De' Pignattari 1, 40124 Bologna; phone: 051-272610.

For sailing in the Tuscan Archipelago and around Sardinia: *Renato Lessi,* Località Porto, 58040 Punta Ala, Grosseto; phone: 0564-922793 and 920710.

For sailing around Sicily: *Salpaancore,* Via Mariano Stabile, Palermo, Sicilia; phone: 091-331055.

THE LIGURIAN SEA: The going is a bit smoother in this body of water that laps at the strands of the Italian Riviera in central and northern Italy. Along the Tuscan and Ligurian coasts, beautiful old villas stand proudly on seaside cliffs, as if craning their necks to get a better glimpse of the view. Portovenere, an important harbor in Roman times and now a reference point for all sailors, is dreamy and picturesque — worth a special trip. The sight of the Genoese Gothic Church of San Pietro, rising dramatically out of sheer rock, overwhelms most visitors when first seen from the water. Ancient houses dating back 600 years (and more) line the port and its main street.

The other must is Portofino, the celebrated port and resort near Genoa, extravagantly praised among globetrotters as "the world's pearl." The rich and famous come here for luxurious hotels, superb restaurants, and stylish boutiques; everyone enjoys the scenery — the tumble of brightly colored houses, crystal-clear blue sea, olive trees, sea pines, and a lighthouse.

THE ADRIATIC AND IONIAN SEAS: The coastline here is linear and sandy rather than rocky and craggy, except in the south, so avid sailors usually prefer the Ligurian and Tyrrhenian alternatives. However, several ports can make a cruise here eminently enjoyable.

Muggia, an ancient Venetian village near Trieste is justly famous for its summer music festivals and folklore exhibits. The ancient seaside fishing town of Chioggia, in the Veneto region, has one of the largest and most picturesque fish markets in Italy and two canals photogenically packed with fishing boats.

In Apulia, to the south, fishing villages, historical sites, and archaeological remains abound. The mountain promontory of Gargano, the spur of Italy's boot, is edged with long, luxuriant strands, exotic rock formations, fantastic caves, and tiny coves perfect for picnicking. Vieste, an ancient fishing village with a medieval castle, is coming into its own as a resort. Manfredonia, Rodi Garganico, and whitewashed, cliff-top Peschici are other worthy ports of call. Just off shore are the jewel-like Tremiti Islands, virtually beachless fragments of rock that attract snorkelers and divers.

As the Adriatic flows into the Ionian, it becomes the Mediterranean's deepest sea, extending from Apulia to Basilicata and Calabria over to Sicily. Be sure to visit Gallipoli (in Apulia). This "Venus of the Ionian" shows off a wealth of historical, artistic, and archaeological treasures, not the least of which is the *Marechiaro,* the city's best restaurant, perched on a large rock surrounded by water and connected to the mainland only by wooden planks. Details: *Skimar,* Piazzetta Pattari 4, 20122 Milano; phone: 02-809166. There is also an office in Chioggia.

MORE SAILING INFORMATION

Local yacht clubs can be very helpful. In addition, there are several other reliable sources of information, among them:

Federazione Italiana Vela, Viale Brigate Bisano 22, 16129 Genova; phone: 010-565723, 010-575723.

Charter & Charter, Piazza Municipio 84, 80133 Napoli; phone: 081-310101.

Renato Lessi, Località Porto, 58040 Punta Ala, Grosseto; phone: 0564-922793, 0564-920710. For sailing in many parts of Italy.

Centro Nautico Glenans, Isola di San Clemente, Venice; phone: 041-700320. For sailing courses and cruises.

Vela/Marclub, Via Crocifisso 4, Milano; phone: 02-8691087. For sailing courses on Maddalena Island, Sardinia.

CANOEING

Canoeing is rapidly becoming a popular sport in Italy, and 250 clubs are currently affiliated with the Italian Canoe Federation. Each year from March to September, these organizations host a number of regional, national, and international competitions. In addition, they sponsor instructional programs for canoeists of all abilities on the best canoeing waters of the country — those in northern Italy, particularly in the Alpine regions. Among the better schools are the following:

Canoe School of Valesia, Via Lomellina 46, 20133 Milano; phone: 06-7388685 or, in summer, 0163-53653. Rafting tours of the Alpine rivers are also available.

Capeggio Dolomiti di Brenta, c/o Renzo Mariani, Dimaro, Trento; phone: 045-59818.

Canoe Club Milano, c/o Valerio Zacchi, Via San Martini 5, Milano; phone: 02-6892086.

LAKE AND CANAL CRUISING

With the exception of the Po River, Italy's largest, Italian rivers are so shallow and rocky that river cruising is virtually nonexistent. The lakes are another matter, though, and the country's several organized boat excursions may well prove a highlight of your Italian sojourn.

LAKE MAGGIORE, Piedmont: The shores of this 40-mile-long, island-studded expanse of blue, nestled at the foot of the northern Italian mountains, are sometimes rugged, sometimes lush with tropical vegetation — magnolias, azaleas, palms, and orange and lemon trees. Lake cruises here provide a view of the 14th-century castle of Rocca di Angera, the lovely town of Ispra, and the sanctuary of Santa Caterina del Sasso. In the center of the lake are the sweetly scented Borromean Islands. The baroque fantasy known as Isola Bella (Beautiful Island), the busiest and most famous, is capped by viewful gardens and inhabited by lacy albino peacocks; if you can somehow overlook the covey of ticky-tacky souvenir stands, it is a splendid sight. Isola Madre (Mother Island) has even more splendid gardens, luxuriant with 140-year-old cypress, massive palms, and 80-yard-long wisterias. Isola dei Pescatori (Fishermen's Island) is a simple folk legend of a place, with narrow alleyways and a pretty port full of little red and yellow houses. On the mainland is Stresa, a slightly stuffy, stately resort that livens up in September, when the annual festival of lyrical music comes to town. Details: *Skimar,* Piazzetta Pattari 4, 20122 Milano; phone: 02-809166.

THE CANALS OF VENICE: It may be hard to swallow the instinctive reluctance to do anything so expressly aimed at gawking tourists as hiring one of the gondolas that, elegant as black swans, ply the Venetian canals. But once you overcome your misgivings, you're in for an experience that is poetic, mysterious — and worth every one of the vast number of lire that it will doubtless cost. It's a unique experience, particularly at night, when the pale moonlight drapes the city's medieval palaces in silver, and the

Lido, the island of San Giorgio Maggiore, and the Giudecca all become a heart-stopping stage that calls to mind Robert Browning's *In a Gondola* and Thomas Mann's *Death in Venice*. Rates — 30% higher after dark — vary little from one gondolier to another; choose one who is pleasant (and perhaps not too talkative, since twisting around to keep up your end of the conversation can get uncomfortable). And if you choose against the gondola because of price or principle, remember that Venice boasts the only public transportation system that actually adds to the joy of the city. Take your pick of *traghetti, motoscafi,* and *vaporetti,* depending on where you want to go and how fast. With a good map, it's possible to master the transportation system in about 10 minutes. To get started, see "Getting Around" in *Venice,* THE CITIES.

VENETO WATERWAYS, Venetia: During the 16th century, every Venetian who could afford it built a summer residence along the Brenta Canal, and the so-called Brenta Riviera was born. A cruise from Venice along its peaceful green waters conjures up images of the trip as it doubtless was made regularly by the nobility during the 17th and 18th centuries. The vessel is the luxurious barge *Il Burchiello,* and the scenery is a string of classical villas designed by Andrea Palladio and his contemporaries. The excursion, which includes lunch at Oriago and a bus return from Padua, begins just after 9 AM at the Pontile Giardinetto near St. Mark's Square and takes a full day. Details: *Compagnia Italiana Turismo (CIT),* St. Mark's Square; phone: 041-85480; *Siamic Express,* Via Trieste 42, 35100 Padova; phone: 049-660944. See also *Villa Foscari* in *Italy's Museums and Monuments.*

Fishing

The truth is that catching a fish in Italian waters is tougher than elsewhere in the world. The indiscriminate angling of the past and the pollution of the present have taken their toll, not only on countless Italian rivers, streams, and lakes but also on its seas — the Tyrrhenian, the Adriatic, the Ligurian, and the Ionian. So the mere act of reeling in a live one in Italy brands the sportsman as a force to be reckoned with.

Nonetheless, fishing can provide some real adventure during an Italian tour. The Alps and the Apennines give life to diverse water systems, and with a bit of patience and some luck, there's a fish waiting to be caught somewhere. If not, there's always peace and quiet — and the delightful Italian scenery.

SEA ANGLING

Three-fourths of Italian territory is coastal, and on many islands the fishing is actually quite good — most notably around Sicily and Sardinia.

No license is needed to fish in these waters. However, there are regulations on size, species, seasons, and the like. For the particulars, check with the *Italian Fishing Federation (Federazione Italiana Pesca Sportiva e Attività Subacquea,* or *FIPS*), Viale Tiziano 70, Roma (phone: 06-36851). For local direction, get the address and phone number of the FIPS office nearest the area where you plan to fish. Information about charter and party boats is readily available from yacht clubs, and it's easy to rendezvous with local fishermen (and hear a few good yarns) at local bait-and-tackle shops. Don't worry about the language barrier. The Italian who speaks no English will probably rush off to grab a countryman who does.

Another good information source is the magazine *Pesca Mare,* available on newsstands or through its offices at Viale Volta 173, 501131 Firenze (phone: 055-574774, 055-570144). The staff can be quite helpful.

ADRIATIC SEA: Most Italian anglers know this body of water as Old Faithful — especially for blue shark (May through September) and giant tuna (late July through late October). Porto Barricata and Albarella are the chief angling centers, and the *Porto Barricata Fishing Club* (phone: 0426-89125) organizes numerous annual tournaments.

For information about charters and fishing schools, contact *Gianni Bison,* GIBI, PO Box 67, Piazza San Cuore 27, Abano Terme (Padova) (phone: 049-668353). The *Pesaro Yacht Club* (phone: 0721-33074) can also be helpful.

LIGURIAN SEA: Here, along the Italian Riviera, the resorts of Alassio, Rapallo, and busy, sometimes chaotic San Remo are the best centers for big-game fishing. For details, contact the local yacht clubs and the Azienda Autonoma di Soggiorno e Turismo (Tourist Board) of each town.

TYRRHENIAN SEA: Punta Ala, in southern Tuscany, is an angling hot spot, especially in September and October, when hundreds of giant tuna pass offshore. For details on fishing trips and charters, contact *Renato Lessi,* Località Porto, 58040 Punta Ala, Grosseto (phone: 0564-922793, 0564-920710). Mr. Lessi can introduce traveling anglers to local fishermen equipped to take them out fishing — and share their secrets.

Near the islands, where the waters are generally cleaner, fishing is even better. Sardinian action centers on Cagliari in Carlo Forte and the Asinara Gulf. For details, contact the *Ente Provinciale per il Turismo–Cagliari.* In Sicily, the best fishing, especially for tuna, is near the port of Milazzo. Your best contact is the *Azienda Autonoma di Soggiorno e Turismo–Milazzo.* Waters off the island of Ischia, near Naples, can also yield full creels. For information, contact the *Ente Provinciale per il Turismo–Naples;* the *Azienda Autonoma di Soggiorno e Turismo–Ischia;* and *Ischianautica,* Via Jesolino 92, Ischia.

The Tyrrhenian Sea is also the best place for surf casting — shore fishing from rocks, beaches, and piers — or rod fishing from small boats. Quarry include bass, bogue, conger, cuttlefish, grouper, moray eel, mullet, saddled bream, and scad.

FRESHWATER ANGLING

Italy's prime freshwater sport is in northern Italy, especially in the Alps, Piedmont, Lombardy, Venetia, and Emilia-Romagna.

The northern Italian lakes — Como, Maggiore, Garda, and Iseo — are good for perch, pike, trout, and carp, shiners, and other fish of the cyprinid family. Mountain streams and rivers can produce good catches of brown and tiger trout. The fish population of valley rivers is varied. Sturgeon can be found in abundance in the Ticino and Po; in the former, you'll also find tiger trout. Canals, ponds, coves, and creeks of flatter areas are full of perch and pike.

Italy's main lakes are populated by those species and others — fallax lacustris, twaite shad, and brown trout. The latter can be caught from shore with minnows during the hotter months. Lake Garda is the place to cast for carp. The Magra River, between the regions of Liguria, Tuscany, and Emilia-Romagna, is home to a variety of trout, as are the Abruzzo and Molise regions, where numerous slow-current rivers are found.

Latium is fine for pike and perch, whereas the rest of central Italy offers an abundance of salmonoid *Coregonus italicus* — a member of the family that also includes trout and whitefish.

Licenses are required for freshwater fishing. They cost approximately $5 and can be obtained in any town hall or municipality, in the section called *Ufficio Caccia e Pesca* (*Office of Hunting and Fishing*). A temporary fishing license can also be obtained through the *Italian Fishing Federation* (*FIPS*), Viale Tiziano 70, Roma (phone: 06-36851), or at its provincial offices, which can be found in every city and large town.

FIPS can also give advice on all the open and closed seasons, creel limits, and permitted bait and tackle — which vary from one species (and region) to another. In addition, the organization owns fishing rights to many streams and small lakes. To fish them, simply apply to one of its offices. Be sure not to attempt to fish its waterways without membership as they are well patrolled and the fines are steep — even for foreigners who have made an honest mistake.

For further information, consult the publication *Pescare,* available on newsstands or from the publishers (Viale Milton 7, 50129 Firenze; phone 055-490750, 055-489331, 055-473915). Staff members will gladly answer any question you might have on Italian freshwater fishing. Once you've decided on a location for your angling expedition, get additional details from the nearest Azienda Autonoma di Soggiorno e Turismo (Tourist Board), fishing club (get addresses from FIPS), or bait-and-tackle shop.

Horsing Around, Italian Style

 When you begin to believe that Italians are irretrievably wedded body and soul to their automobiles, remember that Italy's equestrian tradition goes back to the *condottieri* — the great mounted warrior-princes of the Renaissance. Notice, too, sometime just how many Olympic medals the Italians gallop off with in the four-footed competition. And then consider how many fine places there are for the horse-loving tourist to pursue his or her avocation, from the Alpine top of the boot to the Sicilian stirrup. You may change your mind about Italians and autos.

There are manicured manors where counts cantored, completely informal farmhouses converted to equitation to supplement faltering agricultural income, and all manner of establishments in between. For extensive information about simple, rustic accommodations throughout Italy, contact *Agriturist,* Corso Vittorio Emanuele 101, 00186 Roma, and the *National Association for Equestrian Tourism* (*ANTE*), Largo Messico 13, 00198 Roma (phone: 06-864053). A representative selection of Italy's equitation establishments follows.

ALABIRDI, Arborea, Sardinia: Surrounded by pine woods near the beach on Sardinia's west coast, this complex of hotel, bungalows, and mini-apartments — one of Italy's best-equipped equitation centers — offers dedicated riders a choice of 40 horses and six first-rate instructors. The training is high-powered, with an emphasis on acquiring close-to-professional expertise. But there are also rambling excursions both along the shore and into the neighboring countryside. That the sea is always at your stirrup tips is especially welcome in summer at the end of a tough day in the saddle. In spring and fall, there are vast flocks of migrating birds to observe, and the exotic flamingo and heron are regular winter visitors. Details: *Alabirdi,* Strada a Mare 24, 09021 Arborea (Oristano); phone: 0783-48268.

LA MANDRIA, Candelo, Piedmont: There really was gold in them thar hills, and in a day's ride from La Mandria you'll still see hopefuls panning for it in shallow riverbeds that cross the wild Baraggia plateau, where this equestrian holiday center is situated. The skilled and exacting management offers holidays in all-sized portions, from the equivalent of an afternoon's snack to a fortnight-long banquet that has riders traveling past ancient Roman gold mines or recently reclaimed trails between abandoned medieval castles. The plateau is on tens of thousands of acres of state property, all forest-covered and uninhabited, and riding out from this once-fortified medieval village seems almost like time travel, though Candelo is only about an hour's drive from either Turin or Milan. Some 20 horses and a half dozen ponies are available to the 16 guests who can be accommodated in the restored farmhouse and the 10 who lodge in the annex; overnight trips include accommodations in modest inns en route. Expert riders can go wherever they wish and leave their youngsters in experienced hands. The food here features local country dishes, complemented by some very urbane wines. Details: *Tenuta La Mandria,* 13062 Candelo (Vercelli); phone: 015-53078.

LA SUBIDA, Cormons, Friuli–Venezia Giulia: The countryside in this rural northeast corner of Italy, bordering Yugoslavia, is a patchwork of meadows and pastures, orchards and vineyards, chestnut forests and rustic churches, farms and mountain views; and this center is in perfect keeping with its surroundings. A handful of little wooden houses, set on a verdant hillside, provide apartment lodgings, and the handsome family-run *trattoria* provides grilled specialties typical of the nearby Julian Alps, as well as the local polenta, lightly smoked hams, potato-and-fruit dumplings (*knödel*), and all manner of game. The main business of every day is riding, and a saunter up to the ruins of the castle at Monte Quarin opens a view that stretches from the Alps to the Adriatic. However, La Subida also has a pool, a children's playground, a stable of bicycles, and a lighted tennis court. Guests normally require long hours in the saddle to work off the richness of the cuisine. The wine of the local Collio area is superb, and in short supply elsewhere, and it makes a very festive end to a day on the trail. Details: *La Subida,* Località Monte Subida 22, 34071 Cormons (Gorizia); phone: 0481-60531.

BADIA MONTESCALARI, Figline Valdarno, Tuscany: Set on 500 acres of hillside farmland a few miles from Florence, this handsomely furnished converted abbey dates from the 11th century. Now, nearly a thousand years later, guests canter the Badia's horses along country roads and up steep mule paths to viewing points that embrace the whole Tuscan tableau. Accommodations are in nine beautiful rooms adorned with antique furniture, brick floors, and beamed ceilings. In the dining room, a vaulted stone hall with a princely fireplace, meals are based on the farm's own fresh output — wine and olive oil, eggs and chicken, cheese, lamb, and vegetables. Details: *Badia Montescalari,* Via di Montescalari 129, 50063 Figline Valdarno (Firenze); phone: 055-959596.

RENDOLA RIDING, Montevarchi, Tuscany: The proprietor of this pastoral riding center goes by the very Anglo-Saxon name of Jenny Bawtree. But the setting, the food, and the gracious simplicity of the farmhouse accommodations are pure Tuscan, and the bridle paths rise and fall over the vineyard-clad hills of Chianti itself. This is art and wine country, and Arezzo, Florence, and Siena are comfortable day trips away — by motorized horsepower for the saddle-weary. In the sun-baked summer months, the party moves to a mountain lodge in the cool woods of Vallombrosa, and the excursions wind through forests and greener pastures. Beginners start with a few lessons in the training ring (*maneggio*) before going out for brief outings; experts join 2- to 5-day trips around the area. Rendola Riding has 15 horses and can house an equal number of bipeds year-round. Details: *Rendola Riding,* 52020 Rendola Valdarno (Arezzo); phone: 055-0987045; in summer, *Centro Equitazione Vallombrosa,* 50060 Saltino (Firenze); phone: 055-862018.

RIFUGIO PRATEGIANO, Montieri, Tuscany: At this stone-faced, wooden-shuttered hotel high in the hills between Siena and the Tyrrhenian coast, beginners can alternate riding lessons with lounging sessions around the swimming pool and garden, while more experienced equestrians can range over the establishment's woods and meadows, along Etruscan roads, across burbling streams, and to hidden ruins. Tiny lakes, miniature churches, stark castles, and winding pathways to the sea, discovered during the day's ride, are the topics of dinnertime conversation. Choose from a dozen guided itineraries, with the mountaintop village of Gerfalco, the glorious abandoned abbey of San Galbano, and the ancient baths of Galleraie as prime points of interest. Montieri itself is attractive and unspoiled, and Siena, Volterra, and San Gimignano are all within easy reach by car. Details: *Rifugio Prategiano,* 58026 Montieri (Grosseto); phone: 0566-997703.

FATTORIA CERRETO, Mosciano Sant'Angelo, Abruzzo: For those who want sea and saddle as a daily double, here is the best bet. Whether guests headquarter in one of the four rooms at the farm itself or at the *Hotel Smeraldo,* in a grove of pine and eucalyptus at Giulianova on the Adriatic a few miles away, it's a delight to ride all morning and then while away entire afternoons stretched out in the sun. The atmosphere is cheerful and countrified; the town of Giulianova (pop. 15,000), which has several good restaurants, is the destination of choice for those seeking something a bit more worldly. The farm's 20 horses are well trained, with good mounts for riders of any level of skill. The horses are also excellent for mounted exploration of the area, and week-long trips that cover 100 miles or more in the Abruzzo foothills can be arranged. Details: *Fattoria Cerreto,* Colle Cerreto, 64023 Mosciano Sant'Angelo (Teramo); phone: 085-863806.

LE CANNELLE, Parco dell'Uccellina, Tuscany: The atmosphere at this parkland establishment is rough and ready, and the devotion to riding is single-minded. Paths wander through wild Mediterranean brush or along vast deserted expanses of parkland beach. Wild boar, fox, and horned white cattle are the only intruders. Housing is in eight unadorned bungalows, and guests bring and prepare their own provisions. Since only one Land Rover is permitted on the single bumpy road connecting Le Cannelle to civilization, visitors must call ahead to request pickup at the entrance to the protected area. Details: *Le Cannelle,* Parco dell'Uccellina, 58010 Talamone (Grosseto); phone: 0564-887020.

FONTANA PILA, Pontelatone, Campania: Set on four thousand acres of vineyard, orchard, and pastureland, this establishment just north of Naples, near the medieval town of Caserta, has some 20 horses for visiting riders and another score that local owners board permanently in the well-groomed stables. Opportunities for manège, jumping, instruction, and mounted excursions are varied and ample. Forty guests can be housed in the center's comfortable double rooms, and there are facilities for campers as well. For un-reiny days, there's boating and fishing on the nearby Volturno River; hunting for boar, pheasant, and fox in the area; and sightseeing aplenty (the Norman cathedral at Capua, the royal palace at Caserta). When in Caserta, try the spaghetti with eggplant and mozzarella at the *Antica Locanda Massa* and the assortment of game at *La Castellana.* Details: *Fontana Pila,* Via Ponte Pellegrino 69, 81050 Pontelatone (Caserta); phone: 0823-878107.

ROME, Latium: There are several riding schools and clubs inside the capital, and dozens more in the countryside surrounding the city. A regional branch of the *National Association for Equestrian Tourism* (*ANTE*) arranges special events for riders and can provide a complete list of local facilities. Better than almost any other Italian experience anywhere, a day trip through woods and vineyards to a tiny Roman amphitheater will help a visitor envision what Italy was like before the Fiat Age. Details: *ANTE,* Via Montesanto 68, Roma; phone: 06-353428.

Elsewhere in and around Rome, a number of establishments can provide information on sporting opportunities:

Società Ippica Romana, Via Monti della Farnesina 1, Roma; phone: 06-3966386.
Associazione Sportiva Villa Borghese, Via del Galoppatoio 23, Roma; phone: 06-3606797.
Circolo Ippico Appia Antica, Via Appia Nuova/km 16,500, Roma; phone: 06-600197.
Centro Ippico Monte del Pavone, Via Valle di Baccano, Campagnano (Roma); phone: 06-9041378.

OTHER EXPERIENCES OF EQUINE ITALY

In addition to equestrian vacations such as those detailed above, another handful of Italian experiences should be on every horse lover's Italian must-see list:

The Lipizzaner Stud – Italy's prime reserve of the princely white prancers that staff Vienna's renowned Spanish Riding School is at Monterotondo, a half hour's drive from Rome.

Palio – A no-holds-barred race around the packed Piazza del Campo in Siena, with every rider garbed in Renaissance costume. Twice yearly, July 2 and August 16. See *Siena* in THE CITIES.

Fiera dei Cavalli – A gigantic November fair and market that turns Verona into a thousand-horse town, with colorful sales and auctions, races, exhibitions, and a show of everything that's new and stylish in riding equipment.

Annual Horse Show, Rome – Held in the Piazza di Siena in the Villa Borghese park every May, it offers some of Europe's best jumping competition and ends with a breathtaking *carabinieri* cavalry charge.

Le Capannelle Racetrack – If you have a free sunny Sunday afternoon in Rome and a couple of dollars burning a hole in your pocket, blow the whole packet here, just beyond Ciampino Airport. The atmosphere is Italy's turfiest.

Biking

 With the Alps across the top and the Apennines down the middle, there's not a great deal of flat terrain left for leisurely pedaling. But this is a nation of great bicycling traditions, and every Sunday on country roads all over the boot legions of capped and uniformed bicyclists hunch over their handlebars, pretending to be Saronni or Fausto Coppi.

The bicycle is also the nimblest transportation through the traffic-strangled cities, and most foreign pedalers can easily manage the Seven Hills of Rome in low gear. But a word to the two-wheeled: Italian automobile drivers consider cyclists more a nuisance than folks entitled to a share of the roadway. Ride with extreme caution — and a solid helmet. (For more details, see "Biking" in *Camping and Caravanning, Biking, and Hiking,* GETTING READY TO GO.)

THE ITALIAN LAKES: The Italian lake region provides some of Italy's best cycling. The roadways are fairly flat, particularly around the lakes themselves, the summer temperatures moderate, the towns attractive and well spaced, and the landscape a lyrical mix of lemon groves, palm trees, and other subtropical vegetation against an Alpine backdrop. Visitors can stop at each of the five lakes, one by one, or cyclists with 2 weeks' vacation and the stamina to go 500 miles (300 km) can take a once-in-a-lifetime two-wheel ride around them all.

This circuit begins on Lake Como at Menaggio, an inviting resort town of considerable charm, then travels north to Gravedona, follows the lake shore around its northern tip, and heads southward, skirting Lago di Lecco's eastern shore.

To visit Lake d'Iseo and Lake Garda, the next lakeland destinations, the route passes through the busy center of Bergamo. Make a stop in the charming medieval part of the town, set high above the Lombardy plain, before continuing on to Lake d'Iseo, where George Sand's heroine Lucrezia came to live with her Prince Karol, and the dominant scenic elements are wild mountainsides and lots of shimmering gray-green olive trees. Circle this scenic, less-developed lake, passing through Sarnico, Lovere, and Iseo, and then head for Garda.

The largest and arguably the most spectacular of the Italian lakes (the poet Virgil called it a sea), Garda is wild and alpine in the north, softer and greener to the south. The stretch between Salò, Mussolini's last headquarters, and Riva del Garda is lush, verdant, and entirely spectacular, particularly when the late afternoon sunlight gilds the eastern shore; in 27 miles (44 km), this road follows the *corniche* over 56 bridges and burrows through 70 tunnels.

Having pedaled through the olive groves, vineyards, and cypress stands of the eastern shore, head back to Como and admire its shores crowded with fig and mulberry trees. Pedal alongside wilder and more exotic Lake Lugano and finally to Lake Maggiore, where Hemingway set *Farewell to Arms,* and the little town of Luino. From there, circle broad Maggiore, weaving in and out of Switzerland. Hostels, campgrounds, and hotels dot the way. Just stay out of the area in August, Italy's vacation rush hour. Details: *Ente Provinciale per il Turismo,* Piazza Cavour 16, 22100 Como; phone: 031-262091.

ROME: Few tourists (and fewer Romans) ever see the verdant Rome it's possible to enjoy on the Villa Circuit, which travels 18 miles (30 km) from one major public park to another, all former private estates. Start on the silent residential Aventine Hill, cross the Tiber, and climb up the Gianicolo to the vast Villa Doria Pamphili. Dozens of otters, descendants of a single pair brought here as part of an experiment, waddle and paddle around the lake in the parks' center. Pass by St. Peter's, cross the river again, and pedal through the Villa Borghese gardens. The Pincio terrace, overlooking Piazza del Popolo, offers the classic view of Rome captured by northern painters in love with the city's unique light. Then slake your thirst in grand style at the *Casina Valadier,* a regal 19th-century refreshment stand where all Rome seems to pleasure itself on sunny Sundays. From there, it's a short ride to the Villa Ada, wooded and aristocratic — our final suggested stop. Nino Collalti, Via del Pellegrino 82, Roma (phone: 06-6541084), has rental bikes, including tandems with two, three, and even four places.

IL GIRO D'ITALIA: If you happen to have a spare semester to train, a 10-speed Bianchi bike, and the stamina of Stallone, you might attempt to follow in the tire treads of the speed demons who participate in this 3-week-long May (or early June) bike race — one of the great sports events of Italy's year. The competition has been going on for 70 years, covering 2,400 miles (about 4,000 km) and climbing a grueling assortment of Alpine passes. Followed passionately both on television and by cheering crowds along the nation's roads, this galvanizing marathon is the Wimbledon and Kentucky Derby of biking champions. The route changes each year and is announced in February by its newspaper sponsor, *La Gazzetta Sportiva.* Details: *Federazione Ciclistica Italiana,* Via L. Franchetti 2, 00196 Roma; phone: 06-36857255.

Walking

Despite the more familiar images of thronged *piazze* and medieval quarters as compact as a box of stone dominoes, a striking 21% of all Italy is still wooded, and wild mountains loom over a good deal more. The Aosta Valley alone offers a dozen peaks over 13,000 feet (4,000 meters) and a hundred-odd glaciers. The available wilderness ranges from northern tundras to subtropical woods and is home to wolf, brown bear, moufflon, ibex, and other fauna largely extinct in the rest of Europe. Despite the web of *autostrade* that now laces this passionately automotive country, hikeable, bikeable dirt roads still veer off the most beaten tourist tracks. In the Alps, many of these are dotted with mountain huts (*rifugi*) that provide bed, blankets, and board tasty enough that you don't forget where you are.

So hurry and see the countryside while the supply lasts — let your feet rush in where your Fiat cannot tread. Tromp from Tuscan hill town to Tuscan hill town, with a loaf of bread under your arm and a wineskin of Brunello di Montalcino over your shoulder. Trek from *rifugio* to *rifugio* along the spiky, soaring ridges of the Dolomites. Wander from cliffside pasta to seaside *gelato* along the old Roman mule paths of Capri.

For simple, rustic accommodations in some of Italy's most walkable areas, consult the directory of farms and chalets published by *Agriturist,* Corso Vittorio Emanuele 101, 00186 Roma (phone: 06-6512342). (For more details on accommodations, see *Camping and Caravanning, Biking, and Hiking,* GETTING READY TO GO.)

PARCO NAZIONALE DEL GRAN PARADISO, Aosta, Valle d'Aosta: Some of Europe's highest mountains — Monte Bianco (a.k.a. Mont Blanc), Monte Cervino (known outside Italy as the Matterhorn), and Monte Rosa — stand on the border between Italy, France, and Switzerland and protect this green ribbon of valley from the colder, wetter weather of the north. But the relatively mild climate is only one reason that the spacious Gran Paradiso National Park, tucked in a large corner of the Valle d'Aosta, lives up to its name for dedicated walkers.

When Italy was a kingdom, the royal hunting parties rode in these hills along 43 miles (70 km) of high-altitude bridle paths — and all of these can be hiked today. There are also a number of well-appointed mountain huts (open all summer) and wildlife galore, which is most often visible at day's end by those who lodge in one of the *rifugi:* when the day-trippers have gone, the ibex and chamois that populate the park come loping down the mountainsides, and it's very pleasant to spend the evening hours watching them leap and wrestle in the fading light. Otherwise, the best base for walking is either small, quiet Degioz in the neighboring Valsavaranche, or busy, cheerful Cogne, which organizes guided mountain excursions for visitors. Details: *Ufficio Informazioni Turistiche Regionale,* Piazza E. Chanoux 8, 11100 Aosta; phone: 0165-35655.

PARCO NAZIONALE DELLO STELVIO, Bormio, Lombardy: The largest protected area in Italy, this park just south of Switzerland offers some of the most attractive hiking in the Alps. Deer, chamois, ibex, marmots, and wild goats populate the park, and hikers have occasion to encounter many of them on most local rambles. One particularly interesting tour is the 5-day trip to the massif of the Gran Zebrù, which represents about 25 hours of solid trekking from Sant'Antonio near Bormio, up the Gran Zebrù, and back to Santa Caterina Valfurva. En route, there are several refuges and marvelously varied scenery — glaciers, Alpine tundra, evergreen forests. However, since the paths can be steep, this is definitely for experienced walkers only. For other treks for lesser levels of expertise, and for information about expert guides, contact the park management: *Direzione Parco Nazionale dello Stelvio,* Via Monte Braulio, 23032 Bormio (Sondrio); phone: 0342-901582.

ISOLA DI CAPRAIA, Tuscany: When you make the 2-hour ferry ride here from Livorno and the teeming Italian Riviera, expect a tiny port village, a castle, no boutiques, no nightlife, very few tourists, and some wonderful walking through an untouched Mediterranean landscape. One path leads to the Punta della Bella Vista, a perfect wide-angle view of coast and shimmering Ligurian Sea. Other walking routes wind along hillsides perfumed with wild lilies and jasmine, brilliant with heather, rosemary, and cyclamen. Bird watchers will find kindred souls and expert guides. The rare Corsican gull nests on these shores; it can live only where the sea is pure and limpid. For swimming, rent a boat to sail to the tiny secluded coves a few minutes from the port. The prettiest among the handful of hotels and *pensioni* is *Al Saracino.* Private rooms are available, especially after August 20 or in the early summer. Details: *Pro Loco,* 57032 Isola di Capraia (Livorno); *Al Saracino,* 57032 Isola di Capraia (Livorno); phone: 0586-905018.

LAGO DEL MIAGE, Courmayeur, Valle d'Aosta: A 3-hour ramble from the mountain town of Courmayeur leads to this sky-blue glacier lake surrounded by beautiful woods. The vista of the neighboring Monte Bianco group is stupendous. The area offers many other mountain hikes, including a demanding 10-day circuit of Monte Bianco itself. Details: *Azienda Autonoma di Soggiorno e Turismo,* Piazzale Monte Bianco, 11013 Courmayeur (Aosta); phone: 0165-842060.

CINQUE TERRE, La Spezia, Liguria: Perched on the rocky coast north of La Spezia, these five villages, world-famous for their wine, are accessible only on foot or by train. Once there, paths and trails along the beach, or through the vineyards and olive groves, will lead you from one to the other in the course of a day or two. There's fine swimming — and a chance to ogle the craggy coast views — all along the way. Details: *Ente Provinciale per il Turismo,* Viale Mazzini 47, 19100 La Spezia; phone: 0187-36000.

THE BRENTA DOLOMITES, Madonna di Campiglio, Trentino–Alto Adige: Only the most fearless walkers will want to tackle the hiking trails of this region. Along these *vie ferrate* (iron trails), bracelets and necklaces of iron cable have been anchored to the mountain at just the point that most sensible mortals would elect to turn back. (A prime example is the Via delle Bocchette — the "route of tiny passageways" — where the path clings precariously to the sides of sheer rock wall hundreds of feet above the gashes between the mountains.) Elsewhere, ladders are embedded in scrambles too steep for hands and knees. If the illusion, generally of grave danger, becomes too real, retreat to the delights of the *Madonna di Campiglio* resort, where golf and swimming keep guests risklessly active at close to the same altitude. Details: *Azienda Autonoma di Soggiorno,* 38084 Madonna di Campiglio (Trento); phone: 0465-41026. See also *Italy's Unparalleled Skiing.*

MONTE BALDO, Malcesine, Venetia: The little chain of mountains that separates Lake Garda from the Adige River is a garland for walkers interested in plants and flowers. The unusual varieties found here attract professional as well as amateur botanists. Dramatic views over the lake are an added delight. Details: *Comunità Montana del Baldo,* Via A. De Gasperi 45, Caprino Veronese (Verona); phone: 045-621600.

THE CATINACCIO DOLOMITES, Nova Levante, Trentino–Alto Adige: Located about 12 miles (20 km) north of Bolzano, this sturdy, simple mountain town, known as Welschnofen by its German-speaking population, makes a fine base for walkers of every degree of expertise. Gentle, shady forest paths strike out in all directions. To the west is hill country and a descent to the Adige Valley and civilization. The rugged Latemar massif is to the south. Eastward are the long, rose-colored ridges of the Dolomites' Catinaccio range. Cable cars and chair lifts have made approaches to their dramatic footpaths much easier, and strenuous climbs are no longer a necessary ingredient of a trek here. But the ambitious and experienced will find challenging *vie ferrate* (iron trails), with cables and ladders at crucial points; real experts can try the towering spirits of the Vaiolet. Refuges at frequent intervals provide both lunches and overnight lodging. Plan on half a day in engaging Bolzano, which is more Austrian than Italian — like most of the Alto Adige region. Details: *Azienda Autonoma di Soggiorno e Turismo,* Via Carezza 5, 39056 Nova Levante (Bolzano); phone: 0471-613126.

SAN FRUTTUOSO, Portofino, Liguria: Instead of the ordinary half-hour boat ride from the resort town of Camogli to this fascinating medieval abbey, walk an extraordinary hour and a half from Portofino with the sea and shoreline at your feet around every bend. The final reward is a picture-book inn on the beach accessible only by water or on foot. Details: *Azienda Autonoma di Soggiorno,* Via Roma 35, 16034 Portofino (Genova); phone: 0185-69024.

PARCO NAZIONALE DEL CIRCEO, Sabaudia, Latium: A dangerous land of sorcery and spells when Odysseus passed through 3,000 years ago, the scene of Circe's mythical magic is now an enchanting national park on the edge of the Tyrrhenian Sea. In the landscape where Odysseus brought down a deer, the modern visitor can still catch glimpses of wild boar, fox, and hare. An experienced hiker should make the deceptively hard scramble over the promontory of Monte Circeo, which seems, when seen from the north, to rise from the sea like the figure of a reclining woman. From there, trekkers get to enjoy the fine view of the Pontine Islands, one of which, Zannone, is under park jurisdiction and can be visited by hiring a private boat from the popular resort island of Ponza. The park itself has a dozen or more easy walks through oak forests and low Mediterranean brush, often on trails used long ago by woodcutters and the *carbonai,* who once made charcoal here. The four coastal lakes, part of the park complex, teem with birdlife in spring and fall. Only about 49 miles (80 km) south of Rome, Circeo makes a fine overnight excursion from the capital, especially for those traveling with children and those needing a break from a rich diet of ruins. Details: Parco Nazionale del Circeo, Via C. Alberto 107, 04016 Sabaudia (Latina); phone: 0773-57251.

FORESTA MONTARBLU, Seni, Sardinia: It takes an experienced Alpine climber to make his or her way through the gorges and up and down the cliffs of this wild Sardinian forest. But in return for the effort, the intrepid get to glimpse types of eagles, vultures, buzzards, and other species seldom viewed elsewhere. Maps are available for three equally savage itineraries. Details: *Foreste Demaniali,* Ufficio Amministrazione, Via Trieste, 08100 Nuoro; phone: 0784-35730.

FORESTA UMBRA, near Vieste, Apulia: The Gargano promontory in the southern region of little-visited Apulia, on the spur of the boot, is best known for its beaches and animated resorts. But high above the coastal commotion is a shady, miraculously surviving 30,000-acre Eden of firs, oaks, maples, beeches, and giant ferns, such as Aeneas must have seen in his antique wanderings; even wild boar still roam free. Stay in the simple refuge-hotel and spend a piney and pensive day walking along the silent forest paths. Details: *Azienda Autonoma di Soggiorno e Turismo,* Piazza Santa Maria Delle Grazie 8–9, 71019 Vieste (Foggia); phone: 0084-78755.

LONG-DISTANCE HIKING

THE E-5 LONG-DISTANCE EUROPEAN FOOTPATH: The international long-distance footpaths that have been marked by modern pilgrims and crusaders since 1969 and are maintained by walking clubs and associations in 15 countries are a fantasy come true for dedicated walkers through Europe. Two of the six that criss-cross Europe from Denmark to Spain, Holland to Yugoslavia, pass through Italy. The E-1 is unmarked for most of its length in Italy, though about 24 miles (40 km) near Genoa are kept up with care. The E-5, a better choice, is 370 miles (600 km) and 26 days long. It begins in Konstanz, West Germany, enters Austria at Bregenz, and reaches Italy at the Timmelsjoch, north of Merano. It then winds down the Passeier Valley, rich in fruit trees and vineyards; climbs into the Sarntal Alps; rolls and dips along a series of ridges and high valleys to Bolzano; heads south above the Adige River valley to just north of Trento, Lake Santo; and then swings through the southern Dolomites and heads southeast to Venice. Two compact German publications describe the complete route in detail, with maps, addresses, photos, and other information needed to walk each section: *Europäischer Fernwanderweg E-5,* published by Fink-Kümmerly & Frey (Gebelsbergstrasse 41, D-7000 Stuttgart, Germany), and *Deutscher Wanderverlag,* c/o Dr. Mair & Schnabel & Co. (Haussmannstrasse 66, D-7000 Stuttgart, Germany). Other details: *Provincia Autonoma di Trento,* Assessorato al Turismo, Corso 3 Novembre 132, 38100 Trento; phone: 0461-901111.

GRANDE ESCURSIONE APPENNINICA: Inaugurated in 1983 by the celebrated Italian climber Reinhold Messner, this "green autostrada" through the central Apennines is evidence of a newly aroused Italian interest in hiking and the environment. Its approximately 250 miles (400 km) extend from the tricornered border of Umbria, the Marches, and Tuscany to the point where Tuscany joins Liguria and Emilia-Romagna, near the Tyrrhenian coast. It presents no particular technical difficulties and offers superb walking through the heartland of the most poetic areas of Italy. Details: *Gruppo Trekking Firenze,* Piazza San Gervasio 12, 50100 Firenze; phone: 055-585320.

GRANDE TRAVERSATA DELLE ALPI: This challenging, newly developed itinerary — the "Great Crossing of the Alps" — stretches east and north of Turin, from the Maritime Alps near the French border nearly to Switzerland, above Lake Maggiore. Its more than 400 marked miles (650 km) cross the region's most beautiful valley and take in 84 refuges (open July to September). One of the most interesting sections begins in Susa, a town easily reached from Turin, and leads north to Il Truc, Usseglio, Balme, and Ceresole. It's also possible to continue into the Valsavaranche in the Gran Paradiso National Park. All hiking is at fairly high altitudes, from 4,900 to 8,200 feet (1,500 to 2,500 meters), and often follows old mule paths between abandoned mountain villages. The Grande Traversata does require a good level of physical fitness but is not a particularly difficult route. There are, however, a few strenuous ascents and descents that may inspire wistful memories of the mules. Details: *Comitato Promotore GTA,* Ente Provinciale per il Turismo, Piazza CLN 226, 10100 Torino; phone: 011-5355181; *Comitato Promotore GTA,* Via Barbaroux 1, 10100 Torino; phone: 011-514477.

Hunting

 Whether out of love of sport or from necessity dictated by legendary appetites, the ancient Romans took their hunting very seriously. Special animal breaking parks were created to make sure that everyone got his share, and there were no controls or restrictions at all on hunting (an anomaly in a nation that had laws for just about everything else).

Today, things are drastically different. To put the brakes on a situation in which hunting is increasingly popular and game increasingly scarce, all kinds of regulations — both regional and national — are imposed on what can be hunted, how, when, and where (far too many regulations in the opinion of many). Whether you want to go for wildfowl, starling, partridge, pigeon, thrush, finch, skylark, hare, or wild boar — the most common quarry — or for other protected species of deer, fox, wolf, or bear, you will be confronted by a discouraging snarl of red tape.

However, hunting takes its enthusiasts into some of the country's wildest, most remote, and least-known areas — an experience rewarding enough in itself to justify the trouble. And a wild boar hunt is one of the ultimate hunting adventures.

While it is possible to hunt in almost every part of Italy except the Alpine regions, where hunting is for residents only, there are a handful that Italian hunters consider the best choices for visitors.

LOMBARDY: The low, marshy lands of this part of northern Italy are excellent for duck, pheasant, and gray partridge. Details: *Federazione Italiana della Caccia, Sezione Provinciale, Via San Tecla 5, 20122 Milano;* phone: 02-807996; *Ente Produttori Selvaggina, Via San Tecla 5, 20122 Milano;* phone: 02-873369.

TUSCANY: Italian hunters are unanimous in acclaiming the Maremma, near the Tyrrhenian Sea in southern Tuscany, for its wild boar hunting — undoubtedly the most exciting quarry in Italy. The area is also one of the most beautiful and secluded spots in the country, and the hunting is in typical Mediterranean maquis and thick pine forests. Details: *Federazione Italiana della Caccia, Sezione Provinciale, Via Massimo d'Azeglio 3, 58100 Grosseto;* phone: 0564-22003.

Two game reserves can also supply information: *Riserva Turistica di Caccia della Maremma Toscana, Capalbio* (Grosseto); phone: 0564-896022; *Azienda Turistico-Venatoria "Il Bargello,"* Capalbio (Grosseto); phone: 0564-896115.

Tuscany is also a good choice for pheasant, wild rabbit, and partridge. Details: *Federazione Italiana della Caccia, Sezione Provinciale, Via de' Banchi 6, 50122 Firenze;* phone: 055-216875; *Ente Produttori Selvaggina, Piazza San Firenze 3, Firenze;* phone: 055-212056.

Two game reserves can be contacted directly: *Diana Turistico Venatorio, Via Enrico Dandolo 15, Lido di Venezia;* phone: 041-765765; *Azienda Faunistico Venatorio, Badia di Susinana, Palazzuolo sul Senio (Firenze);* phone: 055-8049043.

LATIUM: This part of central Italy is considered very good for pheasant shooting. There is also some wild boar (though the best bet is still the Maremma). Details: *Federazione Italiana della Caccia, Sezione Provinciale, Via Sommacampagna 9, 00185 Roma;* phone: 06-4759945; *Ente Produttori Selvaggina, Via Lucrezio Caro 51, Roma;* phone: 06-383893.

APULIA: Still a vast wilderness, Apulia probably has more game animals than any other region in Italy, so it's not surprising it's such a favorite with Italian hunters who go after wild boar, pheasant, gray partridge, hare, and deer. Details: *Federazione Italiana della Caccia, Sezione Provinciale, Via dei Peroni 25, 73100 Lecce;* phone: 0832-41847; *Federazione Italiana della Caccia, Sezione Provinciale, Via Imbriani 111, 70121 Bari;* phone 080-540095; *Ente Produttori Selvaggina, Via Quintino Sella 12, Barletta (Bari);* phone: 0883-36100. Also, contact the game reserve *Riserva di Pugno Chiuso, Albergo del Faro, Vieste (Foggia);* phone: 0884-79011.

SARDINIA: One of the most beautiful spots in all of Italy, Sardinia is more than a millionaire's playground and a sea lover's paradise. Its many secluded highland areas are also an ideal setting for the hunt. Game animals still abound, particularly pheasant and wild boars — here smaller than in Maremma but just as wild and wary. Details: *Federazione Italiana della Caccia, Sezione Provinciale, Via Bruscu Omnis 16, 09100 Cagliari;* phone: 070-668933.

PROCEDURES AND INFORMATION

A hunting vacation must start out with an adventure into Italy's complex bureaucracy because organizations that can arrange hunting vacations or get together hunting parties are almost nonexistent. If you're still game for a hunting adventure, then this is what you must do.

First, decide when to go; Italian hunting season runs from August 18 through May 10, with some interruptions depending on the quarry and the region.

Next, contact the *Italian Hunting Federation* (*Federazione Italiana della Caccia;* also called *Federcaccia*), Viale Tiziano 70, 00100 Roma (phone 06-36851, 06-394871, 06-394872). Find out what kinds of rifles are allowed if you want to bring your own. (Write or call well in advance of your trip.)

For information about where to go, where to rent rifles, obtain permits, and find lodging, contact the *Ente Produttori Selvaggina,* which can be found in all Italian cities.

Then, equipped with a hunting license and gun permit from your country of origin and an export permit for your rifle, go to the *Ufficio Caccia e Pesca* (*Office of Hunting and Fishing*) in the provincial administration office or the town hall in the area or town where you plan to hunt. You will be asked to establish a temporary domicile, which will be your hotel. Pay the state and regional tax ($30 to $50, depending on where you'll be hunting and what gun you use). Then, if your own insurance coverage for hunting accidents does not cover you for Italy, get a temporary policy through the Italian Hunting Federation.

Also take a few minutes to stop in a shop that sells firearms and hunting equipment. You'll pick up precious bits and pieces of information and also learn something about Italian hunting customs and traditions. Language isn't a barrier — you're bound to find someone who speaks English.

Italian magazines are always a good source of information, and the staff of the hunting magazine *Diana,* available on newsstands, is more than willing to help visiting hunters. Offices are at Viale Milton 7, 50129 Firenze (phone: 055-490750, 055-489331, 055-473915).

For the Mind

Twenty-Five Centuries of History: Italy's Museums and Monuments

 Napoleon determinedly exported a significant portion of Italy's art treasures to France, but even so, what remains could easily fill a planet or two. Parochial museums house ancient booty from local excavations. Villas from the 17th century overflow with 16th-century paintings, 1st-century sculptures, and quite a bit from all the centuries in between. The massive state museums have basements stuffed with the national artwork of 2,500 years ago.

Faced with all this, a visitor to Italy will be well advised to master the fine art of museumgoing. There is something essentially numbing about the means by which we normally view the world's greatest art, so when visiting the giant Italian warehouses of beauty, stop first to thumb through the catalogue and finger the postcards to get an idea of what the collection includes — and where you'll find it. Determine in advance what you most want to see, and don't try to cover everything. If you attempt a single heroic sweep of the thousand rooms of the Vatican Museum, you may develop a dread case of Titian-fission, where all the Madonnas blend into one polychromatic blur. And when you look at paintings at random, study a picture before you inspect the nameplate — that's the best way to quickly determine what you really like, as opposed to what you're supposed to like. And try to give luncheons and Leonardos equal attention.

Break away from the gargantuan museums in any way you can. Don't forget that single altarpiece in the empty village church, the grouping of portraits adorning the fireplace of the ancient mansion — art in the environment for which it was created. Try building an excursion around a manageable number of goals. For instance, cruise the gentle Tuscan countryside painted by Piero della Francesca, stopping to see his masterpieces in the church of San Francesco in Arezzo and the Palazzo Comunale of Sansepolcro, his birthplace. Long after you're hazy on roomfuls of Raphaels, you'll remember della Francesca's solitary *Madonna del Parto* in the tiny pastoral chapel of Monterchi, 72 miles south of Florence.

And visit a gallery or an auction house occasionally, just to remind yourself that once it was *all* for sale.

Note: Most of the opening and closing times listed below should be right most of the time. But museum hours in Italy are often rearranged owing to personnel shortages, labor disputes, surprise restorations, and as many other causes as there are paintings in the Uffizi. Caveat visitor.

PARCO DEI MOSTRI, Bomarzo, Latium: Cloistered by a protective forest and a placid countryside that's a day trip north of Rome, this sculpture park on the grounds of the Duke Paolo Giordano Orsini's 16th-century villa is like a 400-year-old spookhouse in the woods or an odd precursor to Disneyland. Gargoyle doorways invite visitors to enter through gaping mouths. A lopsided miniature villa suggests an outdoor wax museum visited on a warm day. A cute baby elephant with hollowed-out eyes carries an eroded, androgynous figure on its back and a dead Roman soldier in its trunk. Open daily, 9 AM to dusk. Details: Parco dei Mostri, 01020 Bomarzo (Viterbo); phone: 0761-424029.

BARGELLO PALACE AND NATIONAL MUSEUM, Florence: The impressively fortified exterior is an apt reminder of its earlier functions — first as a prison, then as the heavily guarded residence of the city's *podestà*, or chief magistrate. But within the severe 13th- and 14th-century ramparts is a gracious courtyard and a cornucopia of Florentine and Tuscan Renaissance sculpture. The collection's centerpiece is Donatello's effeminate *David*, sporting a helmet that looks like a flowered Easter hat and balancing with ballerina-like grace on Goliath's severed head. You'll also see several early Michelangelos and the Giambologna *Mercury*, who, poised precariously on one foot, looks as if he is about to launch himself into 16th-century space. Open 9 AM to 2 PM Tuesdays through Saturdays, 9 AM to 1 PM Sundays and holidays; closed Mondays. Details: *Bargello*, Via del Proconsolo 4, 50100 Firenze; phone: 055-210801.

GALLERIA DELL'ACCADEMIA, Florence: Unlike the great, and often bewildering, warehouses that hold more than 700 years of art, this compact museum provides a single, unified experience — of perfection. Its core is the 19th-century hall built especially to fit around Michelangelo's majestic *David*. No matter how many postcards and reproductions you may have seen of this gigantic boy, relaxed and self-confident in the moment before dispatching Goliath, the first in-person vision of him is always intensely dramatic. Don't ignore the rest of the rich collection. Retrace your steps through the hall to enter the tortured world of *The Prisoners*. Originally intended for the tomb of Pope Julius II, these figures try desperately to wrench themselves out of the rough stone blocks that Michelangelo never finished sculpting. In the next room is the splendid *Cassone Adimari*, a 15th-century Tuscan wedding chest, across whose delicately painted panels moves a procession of lavishly robed and coiffed gentlewomen and graceful, multicolored courtiers. Together, these three masterpieces seem to embody the spirit of the Renaissance — its boundless optimism and faith in humanity, its struggle toward freedom from the oppressive past, its festive joy in sheer physical beauty. Open 9 AM to 2 PM Tuesdays through Saturdays, to 1 PM on Sundays and holidays; closed Mondays. Details: *Galleria dell'Accademia*, Via Ricasoli 60, 50100 Firenze; phone: 055-214375.

GALLERIA DEGLI UFFIZI, Florence: One of the world's great museums. While hiking through its glowing rooms, awash in the golden tides of the Italian Renaissance, reflect on the fact that over 90% of Italy's artistic patrimony is stacked in dingy storerooms, hanging in museum wings permanently closed for lack of personnel, and adorning the offices of petty bureaucrats in obscure ministries and consulates out of public view. Consequently, what is hung here is the *crema della crema della crema* by Botticelli, Caravaggio, Piero della Francesca, Giotto, Leonardo, Raphael, and virtually every other major Italian artist. Particularly beautiful, and often overlooked, are the 13th- and 14th-century religious paintings on wood panels. The Renaissance palace that houses these marvels was designed by Vasari in 1560 as the offices (*uffizi*) for Medici administrators. Open 9 AM to 2 PM Tuesdays through Saturdays, to 1 PM on Sundays; closed Mondays. Details: *Galleria degli Uffizi*, Loggiato degli Uffizi 6, 50100 Firenze; phone: 055-218341. See also *Florence*, THE CITIES.

MONASTERY OF SAN MARCO, Florence: Even this placid cedar-shaded cloister knew its share of the daily violence of 15th-century Florentine life. Until 1498, when he was burned at the stake, it was the home of the Dominican monk Savonarola, who declaimed against the arts and the pleasures of the senses and even organized a bonfire for deviltry such as books, paintings, and musical instruments while the sensual and artistic Florentines quaked in their boots. Now the ideal museum, the monastery has remained just as it was at that time. Painted into the white wall of each plain cell is a single masterpiece intended by the artist Fra Angelico, another longtime Dominican, to encourage meditation. Stand in solitary silence, with a fresco of St. Francis preaching to the birds as your only companion, and it is not hard to imagine the monastic life. Better-known works by this pure and delicate artist — the *Annunciation*, for example — are more publicly displayed. Don't miss the airy, light-filled library, where Savonarola was arrested and which has a stunning collection of illuminated manuscripts. Open 9 AM to 2 PM Tuesdays through Saturdays, to 1 PM on Sundays and holidays; closed Mondays. Details: *Museo di San Marco*, Piazza San Marco 1, 50100 Firenze; phone: 055-210741.

PALAZZO PITTI AND GIARDINO DI BOBOLI, Florence: With an appetite for exploring Italian Renaissance glories whetted at the Uffizi, a museumgoer is ready for the enormous banquet at this once-private estate, luxuriously sprawled across the Arno on an entire Florentine hillside. Five separate museums, including collections of Tuscan impressionists and other modern art, plus a carriage display, are housed in the 104,000-square-foot Palazzo Pitti — a magnificent Renaissance villa designed by Brunelleschi under commission from banker Luca Pitti, with wings by other architects commissioned by its later owners the Medicis. Just the carefully selected collection of 16th- and 17th-century works in the Palatine Gallery includes 22 Raphaels and masterpieces by Rubens, Titian, Tintoretto, Van Dyck, Velásquez, and Fra Filippo Lippi. Behind the tri-level façades of rough-hewn rock are scores of resplendent drawing rooms, bedrooms, waiting rooms, reception rooms, and dining rooms. As the Medicis intended, the effect is nothing short of overwhelming. Walk off the rich diet of masterpieces with a stroll through the pleasantly asymmetrical *Giardino di Boboli* (*Boboli Gardens*), where the Medicis entertained their friends and Florentine matrons now pasture their children. This monument of sculpted and terraced nature, studded with cypress, unusual statuary, fountains, and grottoes, took half a century to complete. Be sure to take the 15-minute hike directly up the hill to the Porcelain Museum. Open 9 AM to 2 PM Tuesdays through Saturdays, to 1 PM on Sundays and holidays; closed Mondays. Details: *Palazzo Pitti*, Piazza Pitti, 50100 Firenze; phone: 055-213440.

VILLA FOSCARI, "LA MALCONTENTA," Malcontenta, Venetia: Sitting placidly on the shores of the Brenta Canal, this superbly simple villa, to which a Foscari family member banished his wife, is one of the stops in the full-day boat cruise between Venice and Padua. Boxy, with the façade of a Greek temple on each side, it is one of many aristocratic homes in this area by the 16th-century architect Palladio, whose classicism influenced notable 18th- and 19th-century English and American buildings from Knole to the White House. Open Tuesdays, Saturdays, and the first Sunday of the month from May to October. (*The Veneto* in DIRECTIONS describes the road that roughly parallels this canal.)

The tourist vessel *Il Burchiello* follows the same route as its namesake, a luxurious 17th-century craft that shuttled back and forth between the two towns. Also along the canal are the Villa Pisani and its fine gardens and maze at Stra, where Hitler and Mussolini first met in 1934, and the Villa Foscarini at Mira, where Lord Byron wrote part of *Childe Harolde* in 1817. Relax and enjoy gliding along at the speed of the Renaissance. *Il Burchiello* operates daily, except Mondays, April through October.

Details: *Villa Foscari*, 30030 Malcontenta (Venezia); phone: 041-969012; *Compagnia Italiana Turismo* (*CIT*), St. Mark's Square, Venezia; phone: 041-85480; or *Siamic Express*, Via Trieste 42, 35100 Padova; phone: 049-660944.

MUSEO ARCHEOLOGICO NAZIONALE, Naples: Originally built as a 16th-century palace and later expanded for use as a university, Naples' prime museum now houses one of the most important archaeological collections in the world — one that's the size of a neighborhood. On a first visit, head past the hordes of ancient pots and pendants, baubles and busts, and concentrate on the finest part of its collection — the sculptures, paintings, and mosaics from Pompeii and Herculaneum. Except for the little that remains on these sites, this collection represents virtually everything that was buried under the tons of ash and pumice and the avalanche of hot gases and rocks that covered the two cities when Vesuvius erupted in the 1st century AD. Preserved in a blanket of volcanic debris for 1,800 years, everything was carefully excavated, allowing visitors to view wooden furniture, delicate surgical instruments, weighing scales, and even entire heating and lighting systems from the dead cities.

Among the marble sculptures that populate the museum's entire ground floor is a muscle-bound Hercules who once held up a hefty section of wall in Rome's Baths of Caracalla (described in *Remarkable Ruins*). Open daily, 9 AM to 2 PM. Details: *Museo Archeologico Nazionale,* Piazza Museo, 80100 Napoli; phone: 081-440166.

CARAVAGGIO COUNTRY, Rome: If you wake to a Roman morning too sun-bathed and gleaming to spend the day as a museum shut-in, combine some shopping, strolling, and snacking with a treasure hunt for the half dozen major works by the talented 17th-century painter and street-brawler Caravaggio, a notorious libertine who nonetheless revolutionized religious painting by setting his scenarios in lifelike locales and populating them with realistic, rather than idealized, characters. These are distributed throughout what art historian Howard Hibbard called "Caravaggio Country" — the alleys, markets, and sun-shot piazzas that provided his models during his brief, tempestuous Roman career.

Begin at the church of *Santa Maria del Popolo,* just inside the Roman walls. On the sides of a dimly lit chapel are his *Conversion of St. Paul* and *Crucifixion of St. Peter.* After stopping for a cappuccino and a nut croissant at *Rosati's,* across the street, head for the once-suburban estate of the Borghese family. Wander through its huge park, then visit the Galleria Borghese, a fine, manageable museum whose roster of Caravaggios includes the dramatic *Madonna dei Palafrenieri* and a roomful of others. Then on to the virtual geometric center of Rome, Piazza Navona, where the hordes seem oblivious to the proximity of great art just a couple of blocks to the east at the mid-16th-century church of San Luigi dei Francesi, on Via della Dogana Vecchia. Three paintings there portray the life of St. Matthew, among them the *Calling of St. Matthew,* arguably the single most famous of Caravaggio's images, and the *Martyrdom of St. Matthew.* Ten minutes away is the church of Sant'Agostino, with its *Madonna of the Pilgrims,* a tender painting of a Madonna modeled on Caravaggio's mistress, cradling a round and energetic *bambino;* note the dirty feet of the pilgrims, a controversial note of realism at the time it was painted in 1604, six years before Caravaggio contracted malaria and died. Finish your tour with a pistachio ice cream cone at nearby *Giolitti's.* Churches are usually open daily from 7 AM to noon and from 4 to 6 PM.

For other Caravaggio explorations, visit the *Doria Pamphili Gallery* in the Palazzo Doria Pamphili near Piazza Venezia, and the Palatine Gallery in the Vatican Museums, which houses the famous *Entombment of Christ.*

PANTHEON, Rome: Come to this most perfectly preserved of ancient Roman buildings in the morning to witness the column of rain or sunshine that plunges through the giant round oculus in the middle of the roof. Visit again at twilight to sit on the steps of the fountain facing it, and watch the procession of clinging couples, soldiers on leave, families on tour, and the soccer players whose game in the portico has probably been going on since the fall of Rome. The Pantheon's proportions — its height equals the diameter of the dome — give it an aura of classical calm no matter who is coming or going. The structure was also a remarkable feat of engineering, the magnitude of which is suggested by the fact that the diameter of its dome was unsurpassed until the construction (with prefab concrete) of the Palazzo dello Sport for Rome's 1960 Olympic Games. The bronze doors are originals; the street level has risen since its construction by Hadrian in approximately AD 120, and the original staircase that led up to its colonnaded entrance has been replaced by a traffic-free *piazza* that slopes down to it. Initially a pagan temple to all the gods, the spacious, cylindrical Pantheon became a Christian church in 606; it now holds the tombs of the the the first two kings of Italy and of the painter Raphael (whose epitaph reads "Here lies Raphael: While he lived the great mother of all things feared to be outdone; and when he died she feared too to die"). Open 9 AM to 2 PM Tuesdays through Saturdays, to 1 PM on Sundays and holidays; closed Mondays. Details: *Pantheon,* Piazza della Rotonda, 00100 Roma.

THE VATICAN MUSEUMS, Rome: Occupying palaces constructed by popes from the 13th century onward, the Vatican collections are among the most impressive in the world, comprising works of every epoch. But seeing even a part of them poses a challenge. The pleasures are interspersed with a fair assortment of priceless objects in glass cases with which most people really don't want to bother. And there are not only the usual population of other museum visitors but also sizable bands of Vatican visitors and other pilgrims vying for space in front of the objects that one does want to see. The Sistine Chapel, in particular, sometimes seems more like a very tastefully decorated subway during rush hour. The solution: Visit at 9 AM sharp. Grab a ticket and scurry past what seems like kilometers of papal robes, old maps, and tomb inscriptions until you've left the school groups and Ecuadorian nuns far behind. Your destinations are the *Raphael Rooms;* the Apollo Belvedere, the Laocöon Group, and other classical statuary in the *Pio-Clementino Museum;* and the works of Fra Angelico, Giotto, and Filippo Lippi in the *Pinacoteca* (Picture Gallery). Open 9 AM to 2 PM Mondays through Saturdays, to 5 PM around Easter and from July through September, and 9 AM to 1 PM on the last Sunday of every month (with free admission); closed on other Sundays. Details: *Musei Vaticani,* Viale Vaticano, 00100 Roma; phone: 06-6983333.

VILLA D'ESTE, Tivoli, Latium: The seven terraced acres of gardens at this 16th-century villa are a tour de force of hydraulics, and the best time to visit is a warm summer afternoon when the more than 500 fountains, pools, and water jets seem a marvel of outdoor air conditioning. The gardens' centerpiece is a two-story fountain that creates a sheet of water behind which visitors can walk and still stay relatively dry. In spring and summer, there is something almost tropical about the lush vegetation that climbs up walls and around statues but stays primly off the gravel paths. It makes an ideal excursion for kids with its endless possibilities for florid fantasy and damp mischief. Start earlier in the day from Rome and enjoy a double feature, with morning at the emperor Hadrian's spectacular Villa Adriana (described in *Remarkable Ruins*) and a lunchtime intermission in the engaging town of Tivoli. Open from 9 AM to an hour before sunset. Details: *Villa d'Este,* 00019 Tivoli (Roma); phone: 0774-22070.

CARLO BISCARETTI DI RUFFIA AUTOMOBILE MUSEUM, Turin, Piedmont: Since Turin is in the heart of Italian car country, it is entirely appropriate that one of its major museums is devoted to the history of the automobile and its ancestors from 15th-century wind-powered contraptions to the development of the city's sprawling Fiat industrial complex. Started by an aficionado of things automotive in the mid-1950s, the museum now houses 150 vehicles, including a steam-powered tricycle from 1891 and the car that won the 1907 Paris-to-Peking motor race by covering the distance in 44 days. The first tentative efforts of such distinguished makers as Lancia, Ferrari, and Alfa Romeo are on display, along with some perfectly preserved legends — a 1916 Rolls Royce Silver Ghost, a 1933 Bentley, a 1916 Model T Ford. Open 9:30 AM to 12:30 PM and 3 to 7 PM Tuesdays through Saturdays; closed Sundays and Mondays. Details: *Carlo Biscaretti di Ruffia Automobile Museum,* Corso Unità d'Italia 40, 10100 Torino; phone: 011-677666.

Theater, Music, and Opera

Italy has been a land of patrons and performers since the flush days of the Medici. Noble courts throughout the peninsula maintained private orchestras. Comedians *dell'arte* found the palace gates flung wide open with welcome. Now, where the aristocracy is too impoverished to treat, the government has rushed in, and virtually every fair-sized city has its publicly funded concert hall and *teatro stabile* (repertory theater), and some 40,000 subsidized musical events a year crowd the Italian calendar. As a result, ticket prices are far more reasonable than in the US — as long as they are purchased before the familiar *esaurito* ("all sold out") strip is pasted across the poster outside the theater.

Even outside Milan (the seat of music publishing and the home of a sophisticated and varied concert season) and Rome (the first city of Italian music), concerts are definitely a growth stock. Far from keeping audiences away, the widespread ownership of compact disc players and Walkman cassette players has actually brought down the average audience age. Increasingly, venues include not only staid and sterile local auditoriums but also Renaissance *palazzi* and medieval churches, *piazzas,* and flower-edged cloisters and courtyards. A recent Roman summer festival offered a strong quartet concert on a barge moored off the tiny Tiber Island. And you've never really heard Bach until you've heard his music reverberating through a Baroque basilica.

Long more popular than classical music in Italy, opera continues to boom. Bricklayers really do whistle *Traviata* as they trowel; your loge-mates may hum along with *Butterfly.* Though the days have passed when fiascos automatically ended with a shower of rotten vegetables, there are still lots of lusty boos when the diva turns out to be a dog — and bravos when the tenor hits a string of flawless high C's. Lately, too, some of the country's dowager opera houses have been refitted with modish new finery.

In the theater, Goldoni and Pirandello are perennial favorites — with Guglielmo Shakespeare a close second. Theatrical activity is more national than metropolitan; companies usually do a limited run in major cities and then go out on tour — so travelers may well catch something in the provinces that they just missed in the capital. The stutter-and-mutter traditions that have reigned in much of the US since the rise of the Actor's Studio have no place here. The Italian stage style is definitely declamatory. Just think of it as reflecting the greater melodrama of daily Italian life.

SOCIETÀ AQUILANA DEI CONCERTI BARATTELLI, L'Aquila, Abruzzo: The nation's most impressive example of low-budget, high-quality music can be found in this Apennine city, the jumping-off point for visits to the Abruzzo National Park. That it has a musical reputation of a city many times its size is all the more impressive because this is the capital of one of Italy's poorer regions. Behind the reputation is an enterprising native lawyer, who not only founded the distinguished Abruzzo Symphony Orchestra but also has been able to recruit some of Europe's most prestigious artists for his Barattelli Society's chamber concert series, held in a tiny auditorium with state-of-the-art acoustics that is nestled picturesquely inside the city's 15th-century castle. An evening here is a perfect finale to a day's ramble in the neighboring wilderness. Details: *Società Aquilana dei Concerti Barattelli,* Il Castello Cinquecentesco, 67100 L'Aquila; phone: 0862-24262.

PICCOLO TEATRO, Milan: Since its creation just after World War II, the so-called Little Theater has been the most vital force of the Italian stage. The mission of its ever-active founder and godfather, Giorgio Strehler, was to make the theater a medium of popular culture; toward that end, the repertory is eclectic and international, the staging vigorous and imaginative, and its public the same patrician group glimpsed the evening before at *La Scala*. After a decade of debate, the Piccolo has finally moved to new, less *piccolo* quarters. Details: *Piccolo Teatro,* Teatro Studio, Via Rivoli 6, 20100 Milano; phone: 02-8050190.

TEATRO ALLA SCALA, Milan: Built between 1776 and 1778 on the site of the church of Santa Maria della Scala and then restored to rococo glory in 1948 after Allied bombing damaged it during World War II, La Scala has always been a prince among opera houses. Works by Donizetti, Rossini, Bellini, and Verdi were first acclaimed here, and Arturo Toscanini, conductor and artistic director for years, reintroduced the works of Verdi during his tenure. The house has never lost its aristocratic aura, and its opening night on Saint Ambrose Day (December 7) is a glittering, celebrity-studded gala. Though the repertory tends toward the conservative, the glamorous tradition of world premières continues: *L'Altra Storia,* co-produced by composer Luciano Berio and the eminent author Italo Calvino, opened in 1985 with all the hoopla bestowed on the debuts of *Otello* and *Pagliacci* a century ago. With legendary perfect acoustics, a performance here is truly exhilarating — and also expensive. Tickets for each season's performances, presented December through May, are passionately pursued and hard to come by — especially those to old favorites. Tickets can be purchased from the box office in advance; at the last minute, concierges at the city's deluxe hotels often can get positive results for a consideration. There are also vocal recitals during the summer as well as performances of the *Filarmonica della Scala,* perhaps Italy's finest orchestra, which has begun concertizing without vocals lately. Details: *Teatro alla Scala,* 2 Via Filodrammatici, 20100 Milano; phone: 02-88791 or, for tickets, 02-807041.

RAI ORCHESTRAS, Milan, Naples, Rome, Turin: A household word from the Alps to the Ionian, RAI — which stands for *Radio Televisione Italiana,* the state network — is among the most influential organizations on the national music scene because it sponsors a symphony orchestra and chorus in each of Italy's four largest cities, each with its own full-length season and its own auditorium. Although the *Alessandro Scarlatti Orchestra* in Naples is probably best known, those in Milan and Turin are first rate and produce some of Italy's finest recordings. The Rome orchestra produces a regular season at the Foro Italico; gives a special concert for the Pope once a year, either in St. Peter's or in the Vatican's giant Sala Nervi; and premières many contemporary works at the Villa Medici in an annual festival in September. Occasionally, all the RAI artists combine forces, as with the legendary triple-chorus-and-orchestra spectacular of Mahler's Eighth Symphony at St. Mark's Basilica in Venice. On the other hand, the parent organizations also break down into pocket-sized chamber and choral groups. A chief mission of the RAI is to keep alive many little-performed works from past centuries. But it also has a virtual monopoly on symphonic pieces by contemporary composers. Tickets are kept at popular prices, and many concerts are televised. Details: *Auditorio del Foro Italico,* Piazza de Bosis 28, 00100 Roma; phone: 06-390713.

TEATRO SAN CARLO, Naples: Built under Charles III of Bourbon in 1737, destroyed by fire in 1816, and thoroughly rebuilt in neoclassical style within six months, Italy's second most famous opera house would be worth a visit if only for a view of the flamboyant rococo reception hall. Talented and progressive new direction of the theater where Bellini's *La Sonnambula,* Donizetti's *Lucia di Lammermoor,* and many other operatic classics had their premières has sparked a full-blown renaissance, with the consequence that an evening here is one of Italy's lushest musical experiences. Although San Carlo can seat twice as many as La Scala, it is perpetually packed. The spectators — as passionate about Pergolesi, Paisiello, and Puccini as they are about politics and soccer — tend to be vociferous. Join them: It's part of the fun, and the performers expect it (sometimes they've even paid for it). A bonus is the relatively low ticket prices compared to those found at other temples of European opera. Travelers not attending a performance can tour the theater in the morning, by prior arrangement. Details: *Teatro di San Carlo,* Via Vittorio Emanuele III, 80100 Napoli; phone: 081-417144 or, for tickets, 081-418266.

TEATRO DI OSTIA ANTICA, Ostia Antica, Latium: Beautifully restored in 1927, this Roman amphitheater is at center stage of the ancient, once-flourishing port town of Ostia, a half hour's drive or subway ride from downtown Rome. The summer season offers a mix of Roman and Greek classics in their natural habitat as well as more modern pieces performed in the grand manner. This is the perfect last act to a day that includes a visit to the vast excavations, a picnic lunch among the ruins, swimming on the beaches at modern Ostia (or prettier Fregene), and a fish dinner by the sea. Details: *Ente Provinciale per il Turismo,* Via Parigi 11, 00185 Roma; phone: 06-461851.

MUSEO INTERNAZIONALE DELLE MARIONETTE, Palermo, Sicily: Marionette theater, which made its way to Sicily through Spain and Naples in the mid-19th century, has been a fundamental part of the island's peasant culture. But only recently has it begun to be acknowledged as a real art form. This entrancing museum, housed in an 18th-century baronial palace, contains specimens from China, Java, Burma, and points west, and a theater where puppet shows regularly take place on Fridays. During November and December, the annual Sicilian Marionette Festival held here and at the nearby *Teatro Dante* brings puppet troupes from as far as Sweden and Malaysia, France and India. And in mid-November, the associated *Teatro Biondo* stages the unique *Torneo dei Pupi* — a theatrical tournament among all the Sicilian puppet companies. Museum hours are 10 AM to 12:30 PM and 5 to 7 PM on Mondays, Wednesdays, and Fridays. Details: *Museo Internazionale delle Marionette,* Piazza Marina 19, 90100 Palermo; phone: 091-328060.

AMICI DELLA MUSICA, Perugia, Umbria: Held at the 13th-century Palazzo dei Priori, the chamber concert series of the *Amici della Musica* (friends of music) is both a rare musical experience and the highlight of the social season in this storybook 15th-century town surrounded by a soft gold and green patchwork of cornfields and olive groves. Despite its small size, the town is the capital of the flourishing Umbria region and, as such, attracts artists of the caliber of a Backhaus, Pollini, or Accardo; Claudio Abbado has conducted the European Youth Orchestra here. During August, the harmonies switch from Bach to bop for the *Umbria Jazz Festival,* and the cobbled streets swing to the likes of Miles Davis and Annette Colman as well as a number of younger jazz musicians and blues singers from all over Europe. The *amici della musica* are by this time at the Riviera listening to Stravinsky in stereo. Details: *Associazione Amici della Musica,* Via San Prospero 23, 06100 Perugia; phone: 075-72392.

ACCADEMIA NAZIONALE DI SANTA CECILIA, Rome: Named in dignified Latin style for the patron saint of music and established in 1566 by Pierluigi da Palestrina, this organization serves a host of functions: managing Rome's symphony orchestra in residence, staging its concerts in the Vatican's stark Pio Auditorium on Sunday afternoons (with reprises on Monday and Tuesday evenings) from October to June, and orchestrating Bach-to-Berg chamber performances in the academy's own delightful hall on Friday evenings. Honorary director Leonard Bernstein appears at least once a year, and a guest conductor system brings visiting conductors such as Maazel, Abbado, Giulini, and Sawallisch. Yuppies and university students are swelling the once rather elderly ranks of the city's concert goers, and large chunks of tickets are sold by subscription, so be prepared to queue to snare a seat. In summer, Santa Cecilia moves out into the open and presents evening concerts in the hilltop *Piazza del Campidoglio.* Since seats here are not numbered, it is wise to find your place an hour or more before the music begins, settle down with a picnic supper, and enjoy the summer sunset in the company of Michelangelo's majestic architecture. During the interval, stroll behind the square for Rome's best overview of the Forum by night. Details: *Accademia Nazionale di Santa Cecilia,* Via della Conciliazione 4, 00100 Roma; phone: 06-6541044.

IL BAGAGLINO, Rome: Italy's prime example of authentic cabaret theater and one of the most *au courant* ways to spend an evening in Rome, this lively, funny, and insolent tradition of over two decades throws irreverent tomatoes at every one of the country's current concerns. The show changes every three months, but the mercurial comic Oreste Lionello, who also dubs the voice of Woody Allen in Italian versions of Allen's films, is usually the star. The setting is a refurbished cabaret with the audience sipping at tiny tables and nibbling pasta during intermission. To keep up with the puns and one-liners, you'll need to be nimble with Italian — or just laugh every time you catch the name of the current prime minister. Details: *Il Bagaglino,* Salone Margherita, Via Due Macelli 75, 00100 Roma; phone: 06-6798269.

TEATRO REGIO, Turin: Opera in Turin reflects the progressive spirit of the city, the first capital of modern Italy and currently its center of political liberalism. The Teatro Regio, a new 1,800-seat hall that opened in 1973 with Maria Callas singing Verdi's *I Vespri Siciliani,* is the national testing ground for budding young vocal talent, and a significant portion of the works staged here are contemporary. When electronic opera arrives, this is where it will beep. Details: *Teatro Regio,* Piazza del Castello 215, 10100 Torino; phone: 011-549126 or, for tickets, 011-548000.

TEATRO LA FENICE, Venice: An *istituzione nazionale* since 1792, this structure is unprepossessing in appearance, a titan on the local arts scene, and an architectural marvel within, from its wonderfully symmetrical grand staircase and mirrored corridors to the magnificent chandeliers, the scallop-topped velvet curtain, and the ceiling resplendent with rosy cherubs. Culturally there are performances for every taste and every season. La Scala's greatest rival for national pre-eminence, the Venice Opera, which has premièred Verdi's *Attila, Ernani, Rigoletto, La Traviata,* and *Simone Boccanegra* as well as Stravinsky's *Rake's Progress* and Britten's *Turn of the Screw,* raises its curtain annually in November, with all of the city's private gondola set in attendance. Also based here is the Agon Ballet, the country's most gifted dance troupe, which alternates with the opera in staging productions. Chamber concerts are presented in the *Sale Apolline* throughout the year; the plums are the performances by the distinguished *I Solisti Veneti.* During the summer, music fills the languid Venetian evening in enthralling open-air venues such as the courtyard of the Doge's Palace, and in midautumn the city hosts the International Contemporary Music Festival, which has premièred works by the most renowned modern composers on either side of the Atlantic — Boulez and Berio, Cage and Carter, Stockhausen and Feldman and Maderna among their number. After concerts, the Fenice-side *trattoria Al Teatro* becomes the center of Europe's musical universe. Details: *Teatro La Fenice,* Campo San Fantin, 30100 Venezia; box office phone: 041-710161.

ARENA DI VERONA, Verona, Venetia: The most spectacular outdoor opera performances in Italy are dramatically set in a 1st-century amphitheater in a stadium a stone's throw from the houses of Romeo and Juliet, on a site that has seen gladiators and lions and has served as fortress, marketplace, jousting field, and repertory theater before its bleachers first echoed with *Aïda* during the Verdi centenary celebrations of 1913. That prolific composer has remained the centerpiece of the Verona opera season, and every summer during July and August, Radames and Rigoletto, Alfredo and Otello belt out their passions on a stage twice the size of La Scala's, in front of audiences of half a million who have made pilgrimages here from every corner of Europe. Three operas are grandiosely staged every season (Bizet, Donizetti, Gluck, Puccini, and Wagner are other mainstays), along with a densely populated ballet, and a few select concerts. The acoustics are perfect, directors and performances top rank, tickets expensive by Italian standards, and lodgings hard to come by for the duration — so book well in advance. Afterward, stop for *gelato* on the *piazza* and study the contrast among the classical, medieval, and contemporary notes all around you. Details: *Arena di Verona,* Piazza Brà 28, 37100 Verona (phone: for information, 045-590966; for tickets, 045-596517, -28151).

MUSEO PUCCINI, near Viareggio, Tuscany: A shrine for music devotees, this remarkable lakeside villa 15 minutes' drive from Viareggio was Puccini's home from 1891 until 1921 and is well worth a detour. Now a scrupulously maintained museum, the house and grounds where *La Bohème* was first hummed are exactly as they were when he died, and so is the Förster upright piano from which he conjured up a lifelong explosion of *bel canto.* You may visit the chapel where he and his family are buried, admire the rooms with their gloomy *fin de siècle* furniture, amble through the gardens, and, in the armory, admire the assortment of rifles that the maestro kept for hunting moor hens. Come on a sunny day and lunch on the wharf; better still, if you are in the area in late July or early August, combine an afternoon visit with dinner and an evening of the Puccini Opera Festival, glamorously staged at the edge of the lake. Details: *Torre del Lago, Puccini Museum,* Villa Puccini, Belvedere Puccini, 55048 Torre del Lago (Lucca); phone: 0584-341093.

TEATRO OLIMPICO, Vicenza, Venetia: Designed by the late-Renaissance architect Palladio, this superb classical edifice, with its playful perspectives and orgy of ornament, was conceived to amuse the leisure class of 16th-century Vicenza and remains among the most stylish stages in Europe. Local repertory theater alternates with productions by touring companies during the April-to-October season; if you can't make it, visit the building anyway. Details: *Teatro Olimpico,* Piazza Matteotti, 36100 Vicenza; phone: 0444-34-381.

TEATRI STABILI: The heart of Italian theater is its group of 15 *teatri stabili* — regionally or municipally sponsored repertory companies that perform in their own theaters in most of the country's major cities as well as tour up and down the peninsula. In addition to premièring most contemporary Italian plays, they offer at least their share of foreign works — and thereby vary the diet that more traditional Italian companies serve the Sunday matinee crowd. Be on the lookout for the *Teatro di Genoa,* the *Centro Teatrale Bresciano,* the *Teatro di Roma* at the Argentina Theater, and *ATER Emilia-Romagna* at the Arena del Sole in Bologna. Contact local or regional tourist offices for details.

Italy's Most Colorful Festas

 The national delight in gregarious ritual means that hardly a day passes in Italy without some community of even a few hundred souls celebrating some village-shaking historical event, some traditional food, or some local saint. There are harvest festivals, banquets of music, masked carnival balls in candlelit palaces. Florence stages a medieval soccer match in its Piazza della Signoria, pungent Alba a Festival of the Truffle, Cavesana a feast consecrated to San Giorgio, the patron of oxen. Whether at the Tournament of Noses in Soragna, the live chess game at Marostica, the goose race of Lacchiarella, the Mongrel Fair in Mango, or the feast of Celibates at Casto (which means "chaste"), banners are draped from every windowsill, lights are strung up, processions shuffle to the rejoicing of the town band, celebrants dance in the *piazza* — and everyone commemorates whatever it was with a *porchetta* sandwich.

Here are some of the most festive of Italian festas.

SAGRA DEL TARTUFO, Alba, Piedmont: This knobby cratered nugget, worth ten times its weight in silver, is the main pleasure of any food lover's autumn and the chief honoree in Alba, the truffle capital of Italy, at a series of October goings-on. The culmination of the festivities occurs during the first weekend in November with an orgy of truffle madness: contests, auctions, truffle hound competitions, cooking demonstrations, and innumerable tastings and sniffings of the gloriously ugly fungus. Details: *Pro Loco,* Alba (Cuneo); phone: 0173-497118.

FOIRE DE SAINT OURS, Aosta, Valle d'Aosta: At the end of every January, following a tradition that goes back a thousand years, artisans from 12 mountain valleys around Aosta gather to show off the goods they've made by hand during the long winter months. Hundreds of stands exhibit items in wood, wrought iron, lace, wool, and straw — all for sale. Visitors can fight the cold with the region's famous cheese *fonduta* and its wicked *caffè valdostano,* a spiked-and-spiced coffee served in strange, many-spouted wooden receptacles. The bright parkas and brown faces adorning fellow shoppers confirm that you're not far from Italy's finest skiing. Details: *Azienda Autonoma di Soggiorno e Turismo,* Piazza Emilio Chanoux 3, 11100 Aosta; phone: 0165-33352.

VENDEMMIA DEL NONNO, Castagnole Monferrato, Piedmont: The second Sunday of October, while the tangy odor of pressed grapes suffuses the streets of small towns all over Italy, this village enacts an authentic old-fashioned grape harvest, a *Vendemmia del Nonno,* the way grandfather used to do it. Family groups work together in the vineyards, heap carts high with the richly colored fruit, trample it with bare feet, and feast raucously at day's end at a community supper that features the traditional *bagna cauda,* a savory anchovy and garlic vegetable dip. Don't miss the local wines — Barbera, Grignolino, Dolcetto, and the precious Ruché, a robust red produced only in small quantities and only in this area. Details: *Pro Loco,* 14030 Castagnole Monferrato (Asti); phone: 0141-292123.

RASSEGNA MEDITERRANEA DEGLI STRUMENTI POPOLARI, Erice, Sicily: Folk musicians from all over the Mediterranean — and as far abroad as Scotland and Scandinavia — descend on this pretty Sicilian hill town every year in early December to play and display bagpipes, flutes, lutes, tambourines, Jew's harps, and other folk instruments. Only a decade old, the festival is a fine time to visit ancient and mysterious Erice, where ivy-covered buildings of Arab, Gothic, and Baroque design line the cobbled streets. The haunting music makes a perfect soundtrack for wide-screen views from the town's Norman castle overlooking Trapani and the Sicilian coast. Details: *Azienda Autonoma di Soggiorno e Turismo,* Viale Conte Pepoli 56, 91016 Erice (Trapani); phone: 0923-869173.

MAGGIO MUSICALE FIORENTINO, Florence: Programs at this event, Italy's answer to the king of European music festivals at Salzburg, are so diverse that they seem a conscious attempt to avoid musical chauvinism; you're as likely to hear Berg and Stravinsky as Italian composers like Rossini and Puccini. Some of the concerts are held in the magical Boboli Gardens — lovely and quintessentially Italian, especially on a June evening. Despite a name that translates "Florentine Musical May," the goings-on continue right through June. Details: *Maggio Musicale Fiorentino,* Teatro Comunale, Via Solferino 15, 50123 Firenze; phone: 055-272841.

L'INFIORATA, Genzano, Latium: On the Sunday after Corpus Domini in early June, the long street that slopes up to the church of Santa Maria della Cima in this hill town just outside Rome is completely, fragrantly carpeted with flowers worked into elaborate abstract designs, copies of famous artworks, or biblical scenes. Everyone in town, and visiting Romans by the score, turn out to see the gaudy show and then pile into nearby country restaurants to fork down foothills of fettuccine with lemon-hued liters of the local Castelli wine. Follow their example. And don't leave Genzano without a wheel of the bread that bears the town's name — a dusky, rustic, crusty delight. Details: *Azienda Autonoma di Soggiorno e Turismo dei Laghi e Castelli Romani,* Via Olivella 2, 0041 Albano Laziale (Roma); phone: 06-9321323.

LA CORSA DEI CERI, Gubbio, Umbria: This most beautiful and perfectly preserved of Italian towns honors its patron saint, Ubaldo, on May 15 with an unusual and spectacular event that brings native Gubbini back home from all over the world. Three *ceri* — gigantic wooden structures resembling Brobdingnagian candles that are topped with tiny, but resplendently attired, statues of St. George, St. Anthony, and St. Ubaldo — are fixed to mammoth litters. Then troupes of bearers tote them at top speed up and down through the town's steep, narrow medieval alleys to the summit of Monte Ingino, where St. Ubaldo's glass coffin occupies a crumbling basilica; St. Ubaldo's candle always arrives first. Townspeople and tourists pack the streets to watch the colorful event, and flags, food, and religious fêtes are the order of the day. If you're in town on the last Sunday of May, stop in Piazza della Signoria to see the showy annual crossbow contest, which carries on the tradition of rivalry between the men of Gubbio and those of nearby Sansepolcro. Details: *Azienda Autonoma di Soggiorno e Turismo,* Piazza Oderisi 6, 06024 Gubbio (Perugia); phone: 075-922493.

SAGRA DELL'UVA, Marino, Latium: When this town on the slopes just southeast of Rome celebrates its grape harvest on the first Sunday of October, wine actually flows from its Fountain of the Moors. After the sacred thanksgiving rites of the morning (procession, grape offering to the Madonna, and ritual restaurant feasts), the day turns pleasantly pagan, with allegorical floats, roast suckling pigs, garish street stands, and gushing wine (gratis) — the straw-golden dry white of the Alban hills. Meanwhile, the mood builds from merry to mildly wild, and celebrants routinely stagger on until late at night. Details: *Ente Provinciale per il Turismo,* Via Parigi 11, 00185 Roma; phone: 06-461851.

EASTER WEEK: The collective passion for ritual has all Italy in its grip during the four days preceding Easter Sunday, as nearly every village and town throughout the nation stages some special procession or ceremony. Some of these are derived from ancient pagan practices and some from medieval customs. The pageantry in Sicily is particularly colorful. On Good Friday night in Palermo, the air throbs with haunting Sicilian funeral music, and barefoot penitents labor down the main streets under the weight of massive crosses in an extraordinary display.

In Nocera Tirinese, near Catanzaro, Sicily, penitents wound their legs with shards of glass fixed into corks and dry the blood with wine and vinegar as they follow rough-hewn statues of the Madonna and Christ in procession.

In Cascia, near Perugia, hooded figures keep a 700-year-old tradition alive by carrying heavy crosses and wearing chains on their legs while trudging through the Stations of the Cross.

In Chieti, in Abruzzo, the whole town center is illuminated by candlelight, and 150 musicians chant the *Miserere* as a solemn procession slowly winds down the streets.

Details: *Italian Government Travel Office.* For Palermo, *Ente Provinciale per il Turismo,* Piazza Castelnuovo 35, 90141 Palermo; phone: 091-583847.

SAN RANIERI E GIOCO DEL PONTE, Pisa, Tuscany: Every town in Italy has its own saint with his or her own special day and mode of celebration. In Pisa, the saint is Ranieri, and the celebrating begins on the night of June 16, as candles flicker enchantingly around the buildings along the Arno. The next day, eight-rower teams in 16th-century costume compete in a hotly contested race on the river and then scale a high post to claim the victory flag.

On the first Sunday in July, the strongest men from each side of the river don medieval finery and join a gigantic tug of war on the Ponte di Mezzo — according to a tradition rooted in far more lethal local skirmishes. If you're inclined to visit the Leaning Tower, try to time your arrival to coincide with one of these two raucous happenings.

Details: *Ente per il Turismo di Pisa,* Lungarno Mediceo 42, 56100 Pisa; phone: 050-20351.

LA FESTA DI NOIANTRI, Rome: For a boisterous week in mid-July, when the richest Romans have fled to the sea or the mountains, the teeming Trastevere quarter becomes one sprawling outdoor *trattoria*. As night falls and the air cools, streetlights illuminate rows of tables stretching for blocks, restaurant blending with pizzeria melting into café. Merrymakers pack the streets, musicians stroll, garish stands jam the main avenue, piazzas become dance floors and open-air cinemas, and — because there is a religious foundation to all this — the Madonna del Carmine Church stays open as late as the watermelon stands. The *noiantri* of the celebration are "we others" — the people of Trastevere who consider themselves the only true Romans and choose to honor their neighborhood when *those* others have fled the heat. Details: *Ente Provinciale per il Turismo,* Via Parigi 11, 00185 Roma; phone: 06-461851.

IL PALIO, Siena, Tuscany: On July 2 and August 16 every year, the whole city comes alive with Palio fever for this wild and exciting medieval horse race around the central Piazza del Campo. The pageantry is incomparable, from the monumental costumed procession that kicks off the celebration the night before to the post-race all-night celebration of the victorious *contrada,* where the beast dines at a jubilant open-air banquet. The jockeys are notorious for their treachery, and there are absolutely no rules — even a riderless horse can finish in the money. Details: *Azienda Autonoma di Soggiorno e Turismo,* Via di Città 43, 53100 Siena; phone: 0577-42209. For further details, see *Siena,* THE CITIES.

FESTIVAL DEI DUE MONDI, Spoleto, Umbria: Founded in 1957 by Maestro Gian Carlo Menotti, this celebrated mid-June event brings together performers from both sides of the Atlantic for three weeks of dance, poetry readings, concerts, drama, opera, and art exhibits notable for their diversity, quality, and sizable number of new works. Equally noteworthy is the setting. The capital of the dukes of Lombard from the 6th to the 8th century, it is picturesque and full of narrow vaulted passages and interesting nooks and crannies, quaint old shops, and colorful markets. The final concert is traditionally held in front of the 12th-century cathedral, with the audience sitting on the majestic stairway that overlooks it in the shadow of handsome palaces and hanging gardens. Menotti himself is still actively involved. Details: *Festival dei Due Mondi,* Via Margutta 17, Roma; phone: 06-6783262.

FESTIVAL INTERNAZIONALE DI MUSICA ANTICA, Urbino, Marches: For 10 days every year in late July, instrumentalists, dancers, singers, and theoreticians — both amateur and professional — from the four corners of Europe and the United States converge on this ancient hill town in the Marches, Raphael's birthplace, for the most important Renaissance and Baroque music festival in Italy. The streets vibrate with the tottling of recorders, the strumming of lyres, the melodies of the viols, and the high C's of sopranos. Courses are offered at all levels and for all ages in the principal ancient instruments, voice, music history, and dance (both folk and courtly), and ambitious artisans can learn to construct their own harpsichords and lutes. There are ample opportunities to perform with other musicians, and the chorus, open to all, serenades in the main piazza on the last day. An evening concert series focusing on music composed before 1750 runs through the summer. Details: *Società Italiana del Flauto Dolce,* Viale Angelico 67, 00195 Roma; phone: 06-354441.

LA FESTA DEL REDENTORE, Venice: A deadly plague ravaged the city in the late 16th century, and this Feast of the Redeemer is how Venice has been commemorating its end every year for centuries, the night between the third Saturday and Sunday in July. It begins quietly enough with pilgrimages to Palladio's Church of the Redeemer on the Giudecca and with the mounting of two bridges of boats across the Grand Canal, and ends with a bang — the sound and light of Italy's most electrifying fireworks exhibition. Dazzling cascades, spinning wheels of sparks, and explosions of color surprise the night sky until dawn. The lagoon is almost solid with boats, and the water's edge jammed with everyone who isn't afloat. At midnight, a grand and impressive barge full of flowers makes its stately way down the Grand Canal, and before dawn the hardy head for the Lido to greet the sunrise with a ritual swim. Details: *Azienda Autonoma di Soggiorno e Turismo,* Rialto 4089, 30124 Venezia; phone: 041-5230313.

LA FIERACAVALLI, Verona, Venetia: Whether you ride, raise, or simply relish horses, there's something for you at this November fair, a four-day medley of exhibitions, competitions, racing, jumping, dressage, and merchandising. Thousands of animals of all breeds compete for prizes and are sold at auction. The newest and best gear for the intelligent care and feeding of the horse is on display, and hundreds of dealers and shoppers from all over Europe are on hand to snap it up. Italy's best horsemen, the mounted Carabinieri, are resplendent in their Napoleonic uniforms. Details: *Ente Provinciale per il Turismo,* Via Carlo Montanari 14, 37122 Verona; phone: 045-25065.

CARNIVAL, Viareggio, Tuscany: During the three weekends before Lent, this summer seaside resort is a whirl of Carnival costumes, confetti, and floats that climaxes during a grand Sunday afternoon parade of leering dummies, pert majorettes, and immense floats that unequivocally demonstrate coastal Viareggio's shipbuilding expertise.

Such goings-on, plus theater, music, masked balls, sporting events, and fireworks displays, have always been Carnival staples all over Italy. But in the last few years, a Carnival mania seems to have swept Europe, and while the kindergarten crowd is dressing up as Superman and Cinderella, butchers and bankers don Rambo and Robespierre masks to dance down the roads, their spirits dampened not one whit by the unpredictable weather. Bassano del Grappa, Venice, and Verres (Valle d'Aosta) are other venues for Carnival bacchanalia.

Details: *Azienda Autonoma di Soggiorno e Turismo,* Viale Carducci 10, 55049 Viareggio (Lucca); phone: 0584-48881.

LA SAGRA DEI CUOCHI DEL SANGRO, Villa Santa Maria, Abruzzo: For three days every year in early October, gifted master chefs who hail from this small town in the Sangro River Valley return to their hometown to demonstrate their art in an appetizing festival that honors culinary talents stretching back to the Renaissance. Details: *Pro Loco,* 66047 Villa Santa Maria (Chieti); phone: 0872-94316.

The Antiques Lover's Guide to Italy

Though Italian cities preserve some of the finest collections of antiquities in the world, buying genuine antiques is not an easy matter. Plenty of dealers are willing to sell small relics of ancient Rome or Etruscan civilization, but even if these items were genuine, the strict control on exporting antiquities would make it impossible for foreign purchasers to take them home. At the same time, the kinds of handsome household items of later periods that predominate in the antiques trade of countries like England and Scotland are uncommon in Italy; poorer than other European nations, it never had a large middle class to demand luxury goods in quantity. The objects of value that do exist were almost always made for large noble families who have passed them down — or sold them at prices far beyond the means of the average buyer.

There is, however, a thriving antiques trade in Italy, particularly in Florence, Rome, and Milan. Many dealers trade in non-Italian goods. Many of the moderately priced antiques found here are English; silver is an especially common stock item. And since the antiques market in Italy is generally softer than that in London or New York, such items could well cost less than at home.

WHAT TO BUY

Italian antiques do exist in several categories. Candlestick holders and marionettes, Sicilian puppets, and lamps made from opaline are good finds, as are figurines from the traditional Christmas *presepe* (nativity scene). Also look for the following:

CHINA AND GLASS: There is a lot of Venetian glass about, but it is very hard to tell its age without expert advice. The original Venetian crystal tended to be of a darker, smoky hue.

COPPER AND BRASS: You don't have to be an expert to find good pieces of domestic copper and brass. These metals were used for domestic utensils and, therefore, no imprints were used. The oldest pieces were shaped with a hammer and are of irregular thickness. Northern Italy is the most reliable source.

FURNITURE: Most genuinely old Italian furniture is very heavily restored or extremely expensive. What is available is often not nearly as beautifully finished as pieces made in England or France; design was generally considered more important. Renaissance furniture is particularly sought after and difficult to find at reasonable prices. Popular versions of *barocchetto* (baroque) furniture, however, as well as *rustico* (rustic furniture), are still available, usually in the provincial cities of central and northern Italy.

JEWELRY: Though Italy is one of the world's major centers of modern goldsmithing, much antique jewelry sold here is imported. However, the market offers some very beautiful and ornamental earrings — mostly produced in Gaeta in Latium and largely found now in the south. Serving as a constant reminder of the beloved, these were traditionally used instead of engagement rings by peasant girls who worked in the fields, where a ring would have been a nuisance.

PAINTINGS: Since Italians are the world's experts at restoration, there are plenty of appealing pictures on the market. But don't automatically assume they'll be as authentic (or as valuable) as they are handsome. Italian regional loyalties, which in past centuries gave rise to distinctive local schools of painting, are expressed today by the high demand among each region's collectors for the works created there. Consequently, dealers in Venice try to stock examples of the Venetian school, Genoese dealers works of the Genoese school. Works by non-Italian artists painted during Grand Tour days may be underpriced.

PICTURE FRAMES: Gilded-and-carved wood-and-glass frames can still be found fairly easily — though you need a very large wall to hang them and a large bank account to pay for those made during the Renaissance. More practical are the little dressing table frames made in mahogany. They are not outrageously expensive and are widely sold.

POTTERY: Production of majolica — the tin-glazed and richly colored and ornamented earthenware pieces Italians know as *maiolica* or *faïence* — reached its zenith in the northern Italian towns of Deruta, Faenza, Gubbio, and Urbino during the Renaissance. In the middle of the 16th century, potters in Faenza introduced a lacy, Baroque style of "white" pottery, called *bianchi di Faenza,* which remained popular well past the middle of the 17th century. Both types of pottery are much sought after. There are many clever copies, and antiques dealers tell of colleagues who commission pieces and then have them joined together with copper wire so that the finished vessel looks authentically old.

PRINTS: The mapmaker of the medieval world, Italy created maps by the score beginning in the 14th century. Prints were also widely issued. Many of those available today have been reproduced on old paper or pulled out of old books. However, the stallholders in Rome's Piazza Borghese sell the real thing and are very helpful and knowledgeable. Venice, a center for engraving in the 15th century, is also a good source.

WHERE TO SHOP

For a comprehensive listing of antiques dealers by region and specialization and of major fairs, consult the *Guida OPI dell'Antiquariato Italiano,* published by Tony Metz, and the *Catalogo dell'Antiquariato Italiano,* published by Giorgio Mondadori. Both are in Italian.

FLORENCE: There are dozens of antiques shops in Florence, and the concentrations are highest along Via dei Fossi, Via Maggio, the Ponte Vecchio, and Borgognissanti. On the latter, the following establishments are good: *Bruzzichelli, Daninos, Fioretto, Fratelli Romano, Palloni, Pierini, Romano, Ventura.*

Other good dealers include the following.

Bartolozzi – Via Maggio 18. Furniture and works of art.

Giuseppe Bellini – Lungarno Soderini 5. The doyen of local dealers, a generalist.

Berti Berto – Via dei Fossi 29r. Majolica.

Carlo Carnevali – Borgo San Jacopo 64. Majolica.

Del Bravo – Lungarno Vespucci 6r. Old dolls.

Kolligian-Francheschi – Piazza dei Frescobaldi 2/r. Picture frames.

There are junk markets in Piazza dei Ciompi (daily) and Piazza Tasso (Saturdays). Bargains are there for the finding, and haggling is the rule. Curiosities are also commonly found in the early morning under the loggias of the Mercato Nuovo (Straw Market), near Piazza della Signoria.

The premier Italian antiques fair is Florence's *Mostra d'Antiquariato,* held in mid-September of odd-numbered years in the Palazzo Strozzi.

MILAN: Shops are more spread out here than in other cities. However, there are some groupings concentrated on Via Bagutta, Via Bigli, Via Montenapoleone, Via Sant'Andrea, Via Santo Spirito, and Via della Spiga, a narrow pedestrian cul-de-sac lined with marble benches and trees. Try the following dealers.

Marco Brunelli – Via Montenapoleone 18.

Aldo Pavesi, – Via Vincenzo Monti. Majolica.

Aldo Rossini – Corso Venezia. Majolica.

Franco Sabatelli – Via Fiori Chiavi 5. Picture frames.

A. Subert – Via della Spiga 22. Silver, faïence, scientific items.

The local auction houses are *Christie's,* Via Borgogna 9 (phone: 02-794712), and *Finarte,* Piazzetta Bossi 4 (phone: 02-877041).

The city's most important antiques fair, the annual *Feria di Sant'Ambrogio,* takes place in Piazza Sant'Ambrogio and adjoining streets for 15 days beginning December 7.

ROME: Italy's major center for antiques hunting is Rome, and most of the largest and most reliable dealers are on Via del Babuino, which runs from Piazza di Spagna to Piazza del Popolo. Among them are:

Apolloni – Via del Babuino 133.

Di Castro – Piazza di Spagna 5.

Di Giorgio – Via del Babuino 182.

Fallani – Via del Babuino 58–A. Sculpture.

Arturo Ferrante – Via del Babuino 42/43.

Olivi – Via del Babuino 136.

Marcello and Carlo Sestieri – Piazza di Spagna 81. Small objects.

Other good shopping streets are Via Margutta, behind Via del Babuino, Via del Governo Vecchio, Via di Panico, Via dei Coronari, Via Monserrato, and the Campo

Marzio area. (Via dei Coronari is especially delightful for strolling during the annual autumn antiques fair, when all the shops are open at night.) In the ancient Roman suburb known as the Suburra, near the Roman Forum between Via Cavour and Via Nazionale, there are a number of small, interesting shops — many of them selling art nouveau. The restorers in Via Boschetto are a good source of reasonably priced 19th-century furniture. The following dealers in these areas and elsewhere are worth a visit.

Art Import – Via del Babuino and Piazza Borghese 2. Silver.

L'Art Nouveau – Via dei Coronari 221. Old dolls.

Carboni – Piazza Augusto Imperatore 7. Small objects.

Giacomo Cohen – Via Margutta 83. Carpets.

Luciano Cohen – Via Margutta 65. Carpets.

Guiseppe Costantini – Piazza Navona 104. Majolica.

Enrico Fiorentini – Via Margutta 53b. Marble.

Luigi Funghini – Via di Ripetta 149. Majolica.

Galleria Spada – Via Giulia 145. Small objects.

Gasparrini – Via di Fontanella Borghese 46. Oil paintings.

Gussio – Via Laurina 27a. Majolica.

Cesare Lampronti – Via del Babuino 67. Oil paintings.

Lo Turco Saro – Via dei Pianellari 17. Puppets.

Lukacs-Donath – Via Veneto 183. Porcelain.

Piero di Nepi – Via del Babuino 87. Carpets.

Pacifici – Via Giulia 174. Bronzes and arms.

Passato Prossimo – Via del Boschetto 1/b. Old dolls.

Tanca – Salita dei Crescenzi 12. Antique jewelry and silver.

Tuena – Via Margutta 57. Antique marble.

Giorgio Ungarelli – Via Bando di Santo Spirito 46. Majolica.

Raoul Vangelli – Via Margutta 52. Small objects.

In addition, look for good prints as well as other items at the stalls in Piazza Borghese, and visit the auction houses:

L'Antonina – Piazza di Spagna 93; phone: 6794009.

Christie's – Piazza Navona 114; phone: 6541217.

Finarte – Via Margutta 54; phone: 6786557.

Sotheby's – Piazza di Spagna 90; phone: 6781798.

Finally, the Sunday morning flea market at Porta Portese can be fun. However, it's said that anything you see there of real value has probably been stolen. Never pay the first price quoted.

RULES OF THE ROAD FOR YOUR ODYSSEY OF THE OLD

Buy for sheer pleasure, not for investment. Forget about the carrot of supposed retail values that dealers habitually dangle in front of amateur clients. If you love something, it will probably ornament your home until the Colosseum falls.

Buy the finest example you can afford of any item, in as close to mint condition as possible. Chipped or broken "bargains" will haunt you later with their shabbiness.

Train your eye in museums. These are the best schools for the acquisitive senses, particularly as you begin to develop special passions.

Get advice from specialists when contemplating major acquisitions. Much antique furniture and many paintings have been restored several times over, and Italian antiques salespeople, particularly in Rome, are more entertaining than knowledgeable. If you want to be absolutely certain that what you're buying is what you've been told it is, stick with the larger dealers. Most auction houses have an evaluation office whose experts will make appraisals for a fee. Even museums in some cities can be approached. In Rome, two useful contacts are Sally Improta at the *Bottega di Montevecchio* (an appraisers' association of American members who will advise, for a commission) and *Art Import* on Via del Babuino (a British firm specializing in British antiques but knowledgeable about the trade in general).

Don't be afraid to haggle. Only a few of the large dealers have *prezzi fissi* (fixed prices). The others will decide for themselves how much you can afford and charge accordingly. So the rule of thumb is to bargain wherever you don't see the *prezzi fissi* sign. A word of warning: While most larger dealers take credit cards, smaller shops do not.

When pricing an object, don't forget to figure the cost of shipping. Around 30% of the cost of the item is about right for large items. Italian firms are expensive, so the best idea is to stick to the bigger international shipping firms, which offer a door-to-door service to New York as well as advice about required export licenses. The following Rome firms could be helpful.

Bolliger – Via dei Buonvisi 61; phone: 06-6857161. Also at Piazza Mignanelli 22; phone: 06-6786864.

Emery Air Freight – Fiumicino Airport; phone: 06-6011444.

Speedy International Transport – Via G. B. Molinella; phone: 06-6471050.

Note that the Italian government requires that any object of possible historical interest to the Italian state be declared and has levied an export tax on goods exported to the United States.

Churches and Piazzas

Whether it's a sleek designer space ringed with chic *caffès* or a rustic square sprouting vegetable stalls, Italy's piazzas are the acknowledged centers of local activity. Revolutions are preached there, crowds harangued, heretics burned, confetti sprinkled. Every day marks a new period in the perennial urchin-league soccer match. Every evening, tables and chairs are hauled onto the sidewalk, and a new hand is dealt in some card game that seems to have been in progress since the sack of Rome. And every Sunday, at the end of mass in the late morning, a churchful of the faithful pours out onto the square for a round of village gossip before lunch. The church, drawing its patrons from the teeming society just outside its portals and representing a supremely Italian mix of diversion and devotion, is the *raison d'être* of almost every piazza in Italy. Their styles range from plain to grandiose, from peasant church tacked as afterthought onto the dusty piazza of a one-priest town to St. Peter's, with its oval square designed to allow optimum admiration of the basilica's façade.

So when making a list of touristy tasks, put "sloth" and "idleness" very near the top and spend a large, lazy slice of as many days as possible doing as the Romans do — sitting and sipping and stretching and strolling on a glorious Italian piazza in front of a lush Italian church like those listed below. Here, indeed, the *far niente* (doing nothing) for which Italy is well known is truly *dolce* (sweet).

BASILICA DI SAN FRANCESCO, Assisi, Umbria: This handsome, elaborate double church was erected for the greater glory of the homely St. Francis in 1228, two years after his death, amid protests from Franciscans who thought such a structure inconsistent with their sect's consecration to a life of poverty. The colossal complex, which includes a Franciscan monastery and two churches (one on top of the other), towers over the roofs and alleys clustered on the Umbrian hillside town. The façade is a curious mixture of stolid squareness and Gothic fancy embroidered in light pink stone, and the windowless tower dissolves into a row of slender arches at the top. The rich artwork includes the portrait by Cimabue of a melancholy, slightly cross-eyed St. Francis and a famous series of 28 frescoes by Giotto depicting the saint's hyper-saintly life.

SANTA MARIA DEL FIORE AND PIAZZA DEL DUOMO, Florence: Henry James rhapsodized that this stupendous 13th-century structure — the fourth largest cathedral in the world — was "the image of some mighty hillside enameled with blooming flowers." No less overwhelming today, a visit here is a series of vivid vignettes as unforgettable as Florence itself. Stand at the top of the cupola, and you're afloat in a realm of pink, green, and white marble, with a bird's-eye view of toy pigeons and toy people in the double-sized piazza below. Or climb the endless steps to the top of the bell tower designed by Giotto, and look out over a sea of shingles — those of the cathedral's own lordly Brunelleschi dome blending with those of the rusty rest of the roofs of Florence. Come to earth through the poised and soberly decorated gray and white *pietra forte* interior — stopping, perhaps, for a haunting few minutes at the crypt — and, before you know it, the piazza's rousing rabble is all around you. In front of the church is the octagonal baptistry of St. John the Baptist (San Giovanni), which was Florence's cathedral from the time it was built (in perhaps the 4th century) until the construction of Santa Maria del Fiore. It was clothed in its present marble stripes in the 12th century and is still used for baptisms — Dante Alighieri was baptized here. The royal gilded bronze-relief doors on the east, which Ghiberti spent 27 years of his life creating, rang in the Renaissance and were dubbed by Michelangelo as worthy of being "the gates of paradise." Just to the rear of the Duomo, at Piazza del Duomo 9, is the *Museo dell'Opera del Duomo (Duomo Museum)*, which houses two masterworks of Renaissance sculpture — Donatello's gaunt and tormented (but still elegant) statue of Mary Magdalene and an oddly powerful but unfinished Michelangelo *Pietà*, which the artist finally broke up in frustration. For further details, peruse the Duomo section in *Florence,* THE CITIES.

PIAZZA DELLA SIGNORIA, Florence: With the giant, needlelike tower of the Palazzo Vecchio shooting straight up from its base in Piazza della Signoria, this is a noteworthy spot, not the least because of the towering, weathered copy of Michelangelo's *David,* the emblem of the city, that stands at its portal. It has also been the heart of Florence for a millennium. Over the troubled centuries of the Renaissance, the square was gradually expanded as powerful families razed the houses of the rivals they expelled. It was here, in the heart of what modern Italy knows as its prime magnet for consumer vanities, that the puritanical priest Savonarola organized his 1497 "Burning of the Vanities," a bonfire fed with purported lewd drawings, books, and other trinkets of worldly corruption. And it was also here that Savonarola himself was hanged and burned, on a spot now marked by an etched inscription. Now that the violence has given way to the peaceful ringing of the bells every quarter of an hour, which along with the throaty clucking of the pigeons are the dominant sounds, the piazza is shiningly beautiful, all the more so because of the adjacent Loggia dei Lanzi — so called because Cosimo the Younger stationed mercenary guards known as *lanzichenecchi* under its overhanging roof, where a small collection of statues now stands.

IL DUOMO, Milan: This frilly, glistening monument at the heart of Milan — Italy's largest cathedral next to St. Peter's — is something of an anomaly in modern, fast-paced Milan. With its arched flying buttresses, its gargoyles, and its statues perching perilously on narrow spires, it is the fullest-fledged example of Italian Gothic. Though nearly 50 yards high and big enough inside to seat 40,000, it manages to be less forbidding than its French counterparts because of the lightness of its white marble exterior. The cornerstone was laid in the late 14th century, and construction continued for more than 450 years, drawing on the talents of generations of architects, both Italian and imported, until it was completed in the early 19th century; statuary was added well into the 20th. Seen from the inside, the stained glass windows depicting Old and New Testament scenes are so huge that the roof seems supported by shafts of colored light.

For an account of the cathedral's history and a look at some fine sculpture and reliefs, visit the *Museo del Duomo* (*Cathedral Museum*) across the piazza.

CERTOSA DI PAVIA (CHARTERHOUSE OF PAVIA), near Pavia, Lombardy: This monumental monastery of glowing brick is wonderfully out of place in the quiet Lombard countryside just outside Pavia, on the banks of the Ticino, just an hour from Milan. When the dozens of architects, painters, sculptors, and builders who pieced it together during most of the 15th century were finished, it was an exuberantly decorated mini-city with its own unique urban sprawl. It has its own train station (station stop Certosa) and even a skyscraper of sorts (the octagonal cupola of its church, which towers five stories above everything else in the area). The arcades of its two cloisters are decorated with terra cotta reliefs, and the roofs are spiky with the chimneys of the Cistercian priests' cottages — tiny villas, each with two floors and a garden, which the religious occupants leave seven times daily to visit the church for prayers. They have taken a vow of silence; monks, who have not, are available to lead tours of the complex. The monastery is now open to the public, and several of the cells can be visited.

CAMPO DEI MIRACOLI (FIELD OF MIRACLES), Pisa, Tuscany: The rakishly tilted bell tower that attracts flocks of tourists in search of a new angle for their photography is only the most famous feature of this "Field of Miracles" at the edge of the city, where the cathedral, baptistry, and cemetery sit pensively on the emerald grass. Try to find a moment, perhaps at dusk, to peregrinate in solitude among the gleaming and magically simple buildings. They were built during the period that began in 1063 with the commencement of construction on the cathedral and ended in the mid-14th century with the completion of the cloistered cemetery. In the cathedral, be sure to see the ivory Madonna with Child leaning backward along the curve of the elephant's tusk out of which it is carved, and the intricately sculpted pulpit — both by the 14th-century artist Giovanni Pisano. And stroll through the Camposanto, the cemetery whose earth was brought by the Crusaders from Mount Calvary; the frescoes on the walls that surround it depict heaven, hell, life, death, and the cosmos, all in powerful style. Try to arrange to be here on June 17 for the *festa* of the city's patron, San Ranieri, when the piazza, Tower, and the Arno are dramatically aflicker with the light of dozens upon dozens of slow-burning torches known as *fiaccole*. For more details, see *Italy's Most Colorful Festas*.

BASILICA DI SAN VITALE, Ravenna, Emilia-Romagna: The naked brick exterior of this knobby, octagonal church, built between 526 and 547 — probably based on a much older church in Constantinople — conceals an Oriental treasure of an interior, brilliant with mosaics populated by royalty and gaudy birds and heavily embellished with columns whose capitals are encrusted with gingerbread curlicues. The imperial decoration climaxes in the apse. Depicted in a majestic fablescape of tiny colored stones at either side of the altar, Emperor Justinian and Empress Theodora, dressed in ornate Eastern robes and bearing the chalice containing the wine of the sacrifice of Christ in her hands, lead a stately procession toward Jesus. The infinitesimal stones are angled this way and that, and the effect as their blues, greens, golds, and whites catch the light is dazzling.

Installed during the 6th century, when the port of Ravenna was the capital of the western provinces of Justinian's Byzantine Empire — and at the height of its prosperity — this fabulous mosaic is one of the chief glories of Ravenna, a city whose early Christian churches are full of such wonders. To see more, don't fail to visit the adjacent 5th-century Tomb of Galla Placidia, Emperor Honorius' sister; the Orthodox baptistry; the 6th-century Church of Sant'Apollinare Nuovo; the small Museo Arcivescovile, near Piazza Duomo, whose collection is small but exquisite; and the 6th-century Sant'Apollinare in Classe. For further details, consult the Ravenna section in *Emilia-Romagna*, DIRECTIONS.

PIAZZA NAVONA, Rome: This pedestrian island in the middle of traffic-snarled Rome retains the elliptical shape, and much of the function, of the ancient Roman racetrack whose site it now occupies. But the chariots have been replaced by children on bicycles who cut nimble paths between unsuspecting photographers and rolling soccer balls. In summertime, people cluster to watch the progress of while-you-wait caricature artists or drop coins in the regiments of open guitar cases. Jugglers, fire-eaters, and long-haired bongo players vie for the attention of passersby. Hack artists peddle their watercolor cityscapes. In winter, from Christmastime through Epiphany, the piazza is crowded with booths full of sweets, toys, crèche figures, and goodies-stuffed stockings. In the middle of it all is the famous Pietro Bernini fountain, *Fontana dei Fiumi* (*Fountain of the Rivers*), which represents as powerful, writhing human figures what the 17th century considered the world's four great rivers — the Nile, Ganges, Danube, and Plata. There was no love lost between Bernini and his former pupil Borromini, who designed the church of Sant'Agnese on the west side of the square. So the Rio della Plata is shrinking in horror from it, and the Nile has its head covered — some say to avoid seeing the church.

PIAZZA SAN PIETRO, Vatican City, Rome: Since the first basilica of St. Peter's was built in the 3rd century by order of the emperor Constantine on the site where St. Peter was martyred and subsequently buried, millions of pilgrims have crossed continents by plane, train, car, carriage, and on foot to get to this vast elliptical space, the main square of Christendom. Every Wednesday morning, thousands pack between the welcoming arms of Bernini's two semicircular statue-topped Doric colonnades to hear and see the Pope on his Vatican Palace balcony. (The best comment on the efficiency of the Vatican is that, despite the hordes, the place is spotless.)

The present basilica, ordered after 11 centuries had left its predecessor somewhat the worse for wear, took a good chunk of the Renaissance to build and drew on the talents of Bramante, Michelangelo, and others. Among its myriad wonders are Michelangelo's *Pietà* (encased in bullet-proof glass since its mutilation and restoration several years ago); Bernini's *Baldacchino,* a 46-ton bronze altar canopy so elaborate it is really more architecture than sculpture; and the climb through the innards of Michelangelo's cupola for a glorious view into the well-shielded Vatican gardens and out over the entire city.

The whole place is overwhelming; save your first impression for a moment when you're fresh and firm-legged, and don't try to see it in tandem with the vast Vatican museums. For further details, consult "Special Places" in *Rome,* THE CITIES.

PIAZZA DI SPAGNA, Rome: The thing to do at this picturesque relic of 18th-century Rome can be summed up in a single word: nothing. Refresh yourself at Bernini's gushing, boat-shaped fountain, the *Barcaccia.* Recline on the voluptuous curving staircase. Almost magically, you'll find yourself impelled to stay right where you are. It has been this way for years. The stagelike set of 138 travertine stairs, known to everyone but locals as the Spanish Steps (after a palace that housed the Spanish Embassy to the Holy See), climbs to the twin-turreted church of Trinità dei Monti and the green sprawl of the Villa Borghese park beyond. In the wings at No. 26, with a window onto the staircase, is the house where John Keats died in 1821, now a museum devoted to him and his fellow Romantics. In May, the stairs are covered with red, pink, and white azaleas; at Christmastime, the platform midway up is the site of an il-luminated, near-life-sized crèche. Rome's answer to New York's Fifth Avenue, Via Condotti runs from the foot of the Spanish Steps to Via del Corso and is a favorite spot for window-shopping and the ritual evening *passeggiata* (promenade). (Also see "Special Places" in *Rome,* THE CITIES.)

PIAZZA DEL CAMPO, Siena, Tuscany: From the hazy horizon of Tuscan hills beyond the city walls, all Siena seems to slide down into the seashell-shaped Piazza del

Campo, one of Europe's most beautiful old squares. Begin your visit on one of the streets that circle it slightly above. Walk down a flight of stairs, through a dark archway, and then into the splash of sunlight that washes the piazza. Look around you. Your dazzled gaze dips toward the Palazzo Pubblico, halts momentarily against its stern, elegant battlements, and then soars up through the brown brick tower and its marble cap straight into the sky. All around the piazza's edge are medieval and Renaissance palaces — most notably the curved-fronted Palazzo Sansedoni, which dates from the 13th and 14th centuries. Twice each summer, in July and August, ancient banners hang from the windows of the palaces, the late-breakfast-takers give way to crowds of spectators, the piazza's usual languid atmosphere gives way to chaos, and the roadway all around turns into the route of a costumed procession and then becomes a racetrack for the Palio — hours of medieval pomp climaxed by a fierce horse race that follows traditions going back centuries. For further details, see "Special Places" in *Siena*, THE CITIES, and *Italy's Most Colorful Festas*.

IL DUOMO, Siena: Siena's cathedral, dedicated to Santa Maria dell'Assunta, rose mysteriously out of the 12th century and seems to be knotted into the thick skein of houses around it. Coated inside and out with the black and white marble stripes typical of Italian Gothic, it is both meticulously crafted down to the smallest detail and perfectly balanced — despite the shaggy remains of an abortive 14th-century attempt to double its size. Once inside, weave through the exquisitely carved patches of floor bathed in the amber light of the stained glass windows; each of the 56 squares tells a different biblical story in inlaid marble. (Some are so precious they are kept covered except from August 15 to September 15.) Next door is the *Museo dell'Opera del Duomo* (*Cathedral Museum*), which occupies what's left of the 14th-century enlargement. Its breathtaking collection of Sienese medieval paintings includes the *Maestà* of Duccio di Buoninsegna. For further details, see "Special Places" in *Siena*, THE CITIES.

PIAZZA SAN MARCO, Venice: Italy's square of squares, proudly placed at the entrance to the city on the Grand Canal and the center of Venetian life, is a glittering testimony to the opulence of the Venetian Empire in the East. The shimmering pattern of inset marble on the façade of the Doge's Palace, the polychrome Basilica, the pair of giant bronze Moors that have struck the hours at the clock tower for 500 years, the granite columns topped by the lion of St. Mark and the statue of St. Theodore, the pigeons and the violins, and even the brightly tinted T-shirts and café chairs, all give the piazza the gleam of some fairy-tale Oriental pavilion. It's not hard to understand why Napoleon called it Europe's finest drawing room and why, among all the squares of Venice, this is the only one that Venetians call a *piazza* (the other public spaces are known as *campi* — fields — because they were once unpaved). Galileo Galilei tested his telescope from the summit of the 324-foot-high, 9th-century red campanile, the traditional viewpoint over the city's red-shingled rooftops and domes to the lagoon and its distant islands; don't miss it. Also visit the 9th-century Venetian-Byzantine *Basilica of San Marco*, a masterpiece of sinuous curves, massive domes, and a profusion of supportive pillars built as a chapel for the doges and a shelter for the tomb of St. Mark. When the Venetians sacked Constantinople in 1203, they carted back a whole city full of gold, jewels, and mosaic tiles with which to lavishly decorate this church — a process that continued through the 16th century. The 10th-century painting known as the bejeweled *Madonna Nicopeia*, a part of this booty, is now exhibited in a chapel of its own.

Remarkable Ruins

 The only museums in the world where picnics and dogs are allowed, and where sightseeing is ideally combined with a sunbath, a game of touch football, or a bottle of wine, historic ruins have always been part of Italian life. In the last century, cows grazed along protruding bits of now-priceless antique wall. The disfigured Roman street-corner torso called Pasquino served under Rome's more repressive popes as one of the "talking statues" on which sometimes witty protesters hung anonymous slogans and insults. And every government since Mussolini's has tried to dig up, fence off, and charge admission to the thousands of ruins peppering the peninsula.

But there are simply more of them than anyone can catalogue. In Rome alone, there are so many buried theaters and villas that building the city's skimpy subway system took 20 years — in good part because of the labyrinth of subterranean treasures that had to be dodged.

Each ruin is in its own distinctive state of decay, and the most romantic may not necessarily be the most historically significant. And each complex of ruins has its own particular mood and its own prime viewing time during the year. The spectacular hilltop temples, with views that plummet over rocks submerged 40 feet below the sea, belong to clear, hot summer days. For urban experiences like Pompeii or the Roman Forum, try a rainy day in February, when you'll have the place all to yourself. Whatever you do, by all means make the pilgrimage through the ice cream and soda peddlers at some time during your Italian sojourn to pay homage to these ancient places. Be sure to check schedules in advance; many of the most important sites are closed on Mondays or Tuesdays and on holidays. And always keep an eye peeled for the unobtrusive yellow signs that point down dusty roads. Together with the handful of superbly interesting destinations sketched below, the moss-covered stumps of column in the middle of the woods that are found in this fashion may turn out to be the best part of the journey.

TARQUINIA AND CERVETERI, Latium: Virtually all that is known of the remote, but hauntingly familiar, Etruscan civilization comes not from excavation of their cities but from excavation of their burial grounds (*necropoli*), virtual cities themselves of underground chambers and dome-shaped tombs. Though their inscriptions are written in a language that still baffles experts, the scenes of elaborate lovemaking and jovial banqueting inside tell a story equivalent to thousands of words. The Vatican Museum and the Villa Giulia in Rome both have extensive collections of the angular, modern-looking household objects the Etruscans buried with their dead. Equally worthwhile are the more intimate displays in the medieval towns of Tarquinia and Cerveteri, which superseded Tarquinii and Caere, two of the most important cities of ancient Etruria. The cozy museum buildings are so old it's easy to forget that they are 1,500 years younger than the tools, weapons, and pots they contain. Closed Mondays. Details: *Ente Provinciale per il Turismo,* Via Parigi 11, 00185 Roma; phone: 06-461851.

HERCULANEUM AND POMPEII, Campania: Shortly after noon on August 24, in the year AD 79, Mount Vesuvius erupted, and the busy port city of Pompeii and the smaller, quieter town of Herculaneum were buried under tons of ashes, pumice, and other volcanic debris. Pompeii, which was then, and is now, a thrumming business center of about 30,000, was effectively embalmed. Excavations that began in the 18th century have unearthed almost two-thirds of the place. Hundreds of buildings are still standing — cramped houses from poor neighborhoods as well as sumptuous villas complete with interior gardens, central heating, and libraries. It's like a set for a 1st-century period movie or a huge, three-dimensional still life. Much of the artwork is kept in nearby Naples' *Museo Archeologico Nazionale* (*National Archaeological Museum*), but there's enough here to leave a visitor thoroughly exhausted — and still feeling that there are a few blocks of marble unturned. Some high points: The Antiquarium building, which contains, among other things, the plaster casts of victims buried in the molten rock; the cross on the wall of Herculaneum's Casa del Bicentenario, possibly the oldest known example of Christian worship; the finely detailed frescoes at Pompeii's Villa dei Misteri, depicting the rites of initiation into the mysteries of the cult of Bacchus; and the obscene drawings and graffiti on the walls of the Lupanara, the town brothel. To get away from the tourist jam that snarls the city from May to September, hike up to the still-steaming crater of Vesuvius, where it's possible to fry an egg on a rock for lunch. Closed Mondays. Details: *Azienda Autonoma di Soggiorno,* Via Sacra 1, 80045 Pompeii (Napoli); phone: 081-8631041.

NORA, Gonnesa, Sardinia: Jutting out into the sensuously limpid water for which Sardinia is famous, this area on the island's southern tip bears traces of 4,000 years of population. Primitive stone huts, called *nuraghi,* that date from 1500–2000 BC dot the countryside and make up the Bronze Age village of Seruci (not far from the modern town of Gonnesa). Remains of the ancient city of Nora, founded by the Phoenicians in the 9th century BC, are here as well, and above them are later, Roman ruins. At the center of the city is the temple to the Phoenician goddess Tamit, made of large, irregular blocks of stone. In addition, much of the Roman city remains, including a theater and some intricate decorative mosaics. A special bonus of a visit here: Nora is well off the path beaten by most tourists. Details: *Ente Provinciale per il Turismo,* Piazza Matteotti 1, 09100 Cagliari (Sardegna); phone: 070-651604.

OSTIA ANTICA, Latium: This much underrated and undervisited ruined sprawl at the mouth of the Tiber — in remarkably good condition because the excavations are relatively recent — was once among the most important trading centers of the empire. It had a population of 100,000, was a meeting place for sailors and merchants from all over Europe and northern Africa, and boasted remarkable cultural and religious diversity — obvious today from the remains of its synagogue, several Christian chapels, and the dozen or so temples to the Persian sun god, Mitra. A pile of columns marked with the name of their owner, Volusianus, and lying on what used to be a wharf, is a poignant symbol of its fall from prosperity, brought on by a malaria epidemic and the silting up of the harbor. In summer, boats from downtown Rome transport visitors to view classical plays in Ostia's antique theater. Closed Mondays. Details: *Ente Provinciale per il Turismo,* Via Parigi 11, 00185 Roma; phone: 06-461851.

PAESTUM, Campania: The massive temples of Paestum, gleaming bone-white against the dark greens and browns of the brush-covered mountains south of Salerno, provide an almost unique opportunity to see a Greek town that has not been surrounded by modern structures. Founded by the Greeks in the late 7th century BC as Poseidonia, it was inhabited successively by the early Italic tribes, the Romans, and the early Christians. Consequently, the ruins are a catalogue of the changing styles of 700 years of art. The weathered, but ruggedly eternal, remains of three major temples — their parades of columns remarkably intact among the cypress trees, oleander, and fragrant herbs — show how quickly the Greeks solved aesthetic problems. They were built within a century of each other, and one of them is considered the most beautiful Doric temple in the world. Rediscovered only in the 18th century, after centuries of hiding among malarial swamps and giant trees, Paestum is also home to the only known examples of classical Greek painting. One fresco from the Tomba del Tuffatore (Tomb of the Diver), a 1968 discovery now housed in Paestum's museum, shows an athlete plunging into the water, a look of Olympic concentration on his face. Details: *Azienda Autonoma di Soggiorno,* Piazza Basilica Paleocristiana, 84063 Paestum (Salerno); phone: 0828-811016.

VILLA ROMANA DEL CASALE, Piazza Armerina, Sicily: This 4th-century Roman villa of a late Roman emperor named Maximian, located in the almost exact center of Sicily, is full of beautifully preserved mosaics depicting mythical acts of heroism, hunting scenes, races, and cupids harvesting grapes. The busy hunters, struggling heroes, and frightened running bulls and deer are powerfully realistic; tiny colored mosaic stones outline each tensed muscle. One scene of women bathing, remarkable for its subtle shadings of flesh color, shows that bikinis were already in style during the Roman Empire. No textbook of ancient history could ever tell the story of Roman life as vividly as this. Elsewhere in Sicily, there are almost more ruins than can be counted — to start, at Agrigente, Palermo, Segesta, Selinunte, and Syracuse. Details: *Azienda Autonoma di Soggiorno,* Piazza Garibaldi, 94015 Piazza Armerina (Enna); phone: 0935-81201.

COLOSSEUM, Rome: Every week beginning in AD 80, at a time when Romans supplied free entertainment to their populace on a scale unique in the history of the planet, 50,000 spectators packed this stadium for an afternoon of gory Roman fun. Hundreds of gladiators did battle to the death and unarmed Christians wrestled hungry lions; on state occasions, the Colosseum was flooded and naval battles staged. Since then, a large chunk of outer wall is gone — Renaissance construction workers regularly chopped away at the structure when they needed marble for St. Peter's and assorted *palazzi.* Buttresses were erected by Pius VIII (1800–1823) to keep the structure from caving in on itself. Henry James's Daisy Miller went there against her elders' advice, caught Roman fever (as malaria was called then), and died of it. The luxuriant vegetation she went to see by moonlight (the 420 exotic species prompted two books on Colosseum flora and countless rhapsodies by Dickens, Byron, and other Victorians) has been entirely weeded out, a situation "much regretted by lovers of the picturesque," according to the 19th-century writer Augustus Hare. The floor was then excavated to reveal the locker rooms underneath — with separate but equal facilities for lions and Christians. The lions have long been replaced by stray cats, but the allure of the structure is as strong as ever, and visitors instinctively appreciate the genius of the engineers who found a way to erect such a gigantic structure on marshy ground (a challenge even today) and who designed it so that immense and often rowdy crowds could enter, claim seats, and exit with ease through its 80 *vomitoria.* Experiencing its immensity, it's easy to understand how Romans could think that were the Colosseum to fall, so would Rome — and the world itself. Until recently, contemporary visitors have always had to cross a fatal torrent of traffic that promised to be no less lethal than Roman fever to get there, but when the piazza in front was finally closed to cars, this dangerous obstacle was eliminated. Details: *Ente Provinciale per il Turismo,* Via Parigi 11, 00185 Roma; phone: 06-461851. See also "Special Places" in *Rome,* THE CITIES.

FORUM AND THE PALATINE, Rome: Begin your visit to ancient Rome on top of the first of Rome's seven hills, where Romulus and Remus were supposedly suckled by a she-wolf and where Rome began, because you'll be too tired to get up there *after* seeing the Forum. Bring picnic, kids, dogs, sketch pads, and cameras. The Palatine offers fine views through the framework of pine trees over ancient and modern Rome. Marble columns tower romantically over fields of flowers scattered with carved chunks of marble. Ruins of the luxurious imperial villas that once covered most of the hill — the reason that the Palatine is the namesake of all the world's palaces — stand next to the remains of the mud huts where Rome's founders settled in the 8th century BC. Painters such as Claude Lorrain and Jean Baptiste Camille Corot created canvas after canvas depicting this ruin-scattered landscape; to judge from their work and that of their contemporaries, all Rome must have once looked like this. Seeing it inspired the English to pioneer a whole new style in landscape gardening.

Following in the footsteps of early Romans, climb down from the Palatine to the low area that grew from a neutral meeting ground of hilltop tribes into the center of downtown ancient Rome to become the Forum. Actually made up of many different fora, it was once an agglomeration of open-air markets, shopping malls, government buildings, temples, and public meeting spots, and their ruins can all be seen. Along its Via Sacra, Julius Caesar returned from the wars in triumphal processions, and at its Basilica Julia, Mark Antony harangued the crowd after Caesar was killed. It was the business center of the empire as well as its religious and political center, and still embedded in the floor of the Basilica Emilia are the coins that melted in fires during the sack of Rome in the 5th century. During the Middle Ages, the Forum was covered with dirt and garbage and called *Campo Vaccino* (Cow Field); when excavations began in the 19th century, a good deal of it was 20 feet under. Today, much of the Forum lies beneath the roaring traffic of Via dei Fori Imperiali. What is left is a white, open jungle of fallen columns and headless statues; the detailed plan available at the entrance is a must. Don't miss the Forum of Trajan, which is separate from the rest and the best preserved of all. Keep in mind that this neighborhood becomes dangerously hot at midday in summer. Closed Tuesdays. Details: *Ente Provinciale per il Turismo,* Via Parigi 11, 00185 Roma; phone: 06-461851. See also "Special Places" in *Rome,* THE CITIES.

BATHS OF CARACALLA, Rome: This grandiose tribute to the human body was built on 27 acres by the emperor Caracalla in the 3rd century AD. Each of the sunken, mosaic-covered floors visible today was the bottom of a single pool. To get an idea of size, follow the curve of an imaginary arch up from one still-standing base; the other side is hundreds of feet away. Each one of these huge pools was heated to a different temperature by an elaborate underground central heating system, and the whole complex was open to the public. For a nominal fee, the citizens of Rome could pass from tub to tub, soaking in the steaming water of the circular *caldarium,* rubbing elbows with friends in the *tepidarium,* and talking brisk business in the *frigidarium.* Changing rooms, dry steam rooms, and gymnasia flanked the pool rooms. Everything about this glorified bathtub of ancient times is big — so it's entirely appropriate that the outdoor opera and ballet performances staged in the *caldarium* in July and August are blockbusters. (A recent *Aïda,* for instance, was complete with prancing horses and a ponderous pachyderm.) It seems entirely fitting that Percy Bysshe Shelley composed his *Prometheus Unbound* here. Closed Mondays. Details: *Ente Provinciale per il Turismo,* Via Parigi 11, 00185 Roma; phone: 06-461851.

VIA APPIA ANTICA AND THE CATACOMBS, Rome: Somber but refreshingly cool, the 2nd-century Catacombs are the miles of underground tunnels where the early Christians practiced their outlawed cult in secrecy, hid when necessary, and, behind slabs of marble or terra cotta, buried their dead — among them St. Cecilia, St. Eusebius, martyred popes, and others. The Catacombs of St. Calixtus and St. Sebastian, two of the most striking, are both notable for their examples of early Christian painting. Both are on the Via Appia Antica (Appian Way), the former closed Wednesdays, the latter Thursdays.

Back with the sun and the pagans aboveground, explore the rest of the Appia Antica, one of the most important of all the roads that led to Rome. From the time of its construction between Brindisi and the capital, beginning in 312 BC, it was the primary link to distant outposts. Now lined with broken columns, headless statues, umbrella pines, and secluded villas, this sleepy haven for lovers and families is still partly paved by the same large, jagged slabs of stone that surfaced Roman roads from Egypt to Gaul during the empire. Off the road stand some of the arches whose sloping tops carried water, gravity-fed, from miles-distant springs to Rome's public fountains and houses of the wealthy. Have dinner at one of the many family-run *trattorie* that line the Appia as you approach the city walls. Details: *Ente Provinciale per il Turismo,* Via Parigi 11, 00185 Roma; phone: 06-461851. See also "Special Places" in *Rome,* THE CITIES.

SEGESTA, Sicily: On the side of a barren, savage hill appropriately called the Monte Barbaro, the massive temple of Segesta sits eerie and solitary and silent, except for the clanging of boats' bells, and it dwarfs any mortal who braves the long staircase up from the road to see it. Destroyed by the Saracens in about AD 1000, it has no roof today and probably had none when it was built in the 5th century BC as a place of open-air sacrifices within a ring of 36 giant columns. The stark Greek amphitheater spread out in the sun-scorched wilderness above the temple would make an ideal spot for a UFO landing or a divine revelation. Details: *Ente Provinciale per il Turismo,* Corso Italia 20, 91100 Trapani (Sicilia); phone: 0923-27273.

TAORMINA, Sicily: Go to the Greek theater to watch the sunset during July. Peer through the breach in the scene where the wall has politely disintegrated, and look over the roofs of the steeply tiered town toward the sea and the natural fireworks coming from still-active Mount Etna. Though built by Hellenic colonizers in the 3rd century BC, the semicircular amphitheater seems an organic part of the landscape. In summer, however, there is also some manmade entertainment, and the outdoor concerts are superb. But then, even an organ-grinder would sound like Horowitz in this setting. Closed Mondays. Details: *Azienda Autonoma di Soggiorno,* Piazza Santa Caterina, 98039 Taormina (Messina); phone: 0942-23243.

VILLA ADRIANA, Tivoli, Latium: The sophisticated emperor and amateur architect Hadrian enjoyed this stately pleasure dome just outside Rome for only four years before his death in AD 138. But it was a one-man city, and every detail of its two swimming pools, two libraries, gymnasium, theater, thermal baths, courtyards, tree-lined avenues, and dozens of buildings was perfect. Each window in each of the hundreds of rooms was placed for the best possible view of the gentlest of the estate's rolling hills. Jets of water spouted strategically in every corner, statues from all over the empire surrounded the pools, and romantic nooks for secluded contemplation were sculpted out of nature so as to appear that they'd always been there. Still standing is a marine theater — a delightful little island construction accessible by bridges. The villa's sculpture is now in museums all over Europe, and many of the buildings have been replaced by beautiful olive groves, but copies of the statues are set between the Corinthian columns along one of the swimming pools, the Canopo, to suggest the magnitude of Hadrian's vision of home, sweet home; a scale model at the entrance gate reproduces the entire layout. Closed Mondays. Details: *Azienda Autonoma di Soggiorno,* Vicolo Missione 3, 0019 Tivoli (Roma); phone: 0774-21249.

L'ARENA DI VERONA, Verona, Venetia: Rising majestically out of the sunny, noisy, populous Piazza Brà, a short walk through the quiet streets from the houses of Romeo and Juliet, this splendor of 1st-century classical Roman architecture is one of the few Roman amphitheaters still in use. During Verona's summer opera season, it is a showcase of splendid classical music. The audience sits on marble benches 2,000 years old; the inner wall, scenery, and staircase are intact; and the acoustics are perfect. In fact, the structure qualifies as a ruin only because of the crumbled state of the outer ring, of which only a small section remains. Sample some ice cream in one of the numerous cafés on the piazza and contemplate how the structure's giant pink and white marble arches contrast with the lights and darks of Verona's many medieval buildings. Closed Mondays. Details: *Ente Provinciale per il Turismo,* Piazza Brà 10, 37122 Verona; phone: 045-30086.

For the Experience

Italy's Most Memorable Hostelries

 Sooner or later, whenever the world was too much with them, the Greta Garbos and Winston Churchills, Richard Wagners and Liz Taylors of every era slept here. Even the pleasure-loathing Lenin couldn't resist a season on Capri.

None of this should come as a surprise to anyone who has ever experienced the pleasures of Italian hostelries. Like one big room with a view, Italy is full of princely villas, magnificent monasteries, and other handsome accommodations lovingly and lavishly ransomed from the past. These historic hostelries supply the perfect excuse to avoid the anonymous glass-and-concrete business domes of postwar Italy.

ALBERGO DEI TRULLI, Alberobello, Apulia: One of the main attractions of little-visited Apulia, the narrow streets of Alberobello are lined with clusters of more than 1,000 *trulli* — tiny whitewashed, beehive-shaped houses. Found only in this part of southern Italy, the design is prehistoric and pagan and conjures up images of gnomes' houses or sorcerers' lairs. This hostelry provides the opportunity to actually lodge in one of them. Each cozy room is an authentic individual *trullo,* complete with patio, bathroom, bedroom, and miniature living room with fireplace. When you emerge from your room, the Castellana Grottoes and the antique town of Martina Franca nearby are worthy destinations for Apulian jaunts; the Gargano promontory to the north and the Gulf of Taranto to the south, both within day-tripping distance, offer some of Italy's least footprinted beaches. Details: *Albergo dei Trulli,* Via Cadore, 70011 Alberobello (Bari); phone: 080-721130.

GRAND HOTEL QUISISANA, Capri, Campania: When Doctor Clark, a British physician, founded his little sanatorium in the middle of the last century, he chose the sunniest and least windy corner of Capri — and named the spot *qui si sana,* meaning "Here you get well." The hotel grew and prospered, and today enjoys perfect health in the heart of Capri as one of Italy's best-known and most glamorous holiday spots. The notion of a vacation curing anything seems quaint now, so it's to the well-off — not the ill — that this hotel currently caters, a crowd that wouldn't shop anywhere but at Fendi or Armani, except maybe Valentino. Only the service is still superbly old-fashioned, and its three-star oval swimming pool, celebrated terrace bar, and international parade of guests are great for what ails you. Capri itself makes the rest of the world and its problems seem sweetly irrelevant; the vital issues here are the flawless sea, the endless bouquet of flowers, the wish-you-were-here sunny-Italy sunshine. Closed November through March. Details: *Grand Hotel Quisisana,* Via Camerelle 2, 80073 Capri (Napoli); phone: 081-8370788.

GRAND HOTEL VILLA D'ESTE, Cernobbio, Lombardy: Between its construction by a luxury-loving Cardinal Tolomeo Gallio in 1568 and its conversion to a hotel in 1873, this sumptuous tandem of villas on mountain-framed Lake Como passed through the hands of those noble families Torlonia and Orsini who seem to have owned every worthwhile piece of Renaissance real estate under the Italian sun. Its residents have numbered bluebloods by the score — among them George IV's wife, Princess Caroline, whose behavior inspired this ditty: "Most gracious Queen, we thee implore/To go away and sin no more/Or if that effort be too great/To go away at any rate." Now nudged into the 20th century with grace and style, the place must rank with the top half-dozen resort hotels on the planet. And you don't have to be a prince of the church, or even a princess, to stroll through the 20-acre park on pathways across velvet lawns or through groves of pine and cypress, promenade under the lindens alongside the lake, mount the monumental staircase, wander through the columned-and-chandeliered corridors, and hold court in the sauna. Days begin here as all days should in the best of all possible worlds, with a lakeside chalice of orange juice and champagne. There's a squash court, two swimming pools (one of which miraculously floats raft-like in the waters of the lake), eight tennis courts, and a nightclub to offer dizzying possibilities for distraction during the remaining hours. Every inch of the place is absolutely gorgeous and superbly maintained, and the level of service is never less than impeccable. The nearby mountains and lake guarantee cool weather even in the hottest of Italian summers. The food in the less formal grill room (called the "Sporting Club" by some) is far better at dinner than the dining room fare. And if you feel like changing lakes in mid-visit, lovely, lively Lugano is just up the block, across the Swiss border. Closed November through March. Details: *Grand Hotel Villa d'Este,* Via Regina 40, 22010 Cernobbio (Como); phone: 031-511471.

MIRAMONTI MAJESTIC GRAND HOTEL, Cortina d'Ampezzo, Venetia: In the craggy heart of the Dolomites, a few kilometers above the glitter of Italy's most sophisticated mountain resort, surrounded by a parkful of pines, this venerable hotel still has one courtly toe in the 19th century. But the sybaritic guests of the *fin de siècle* did without such modern delights as the year-round swimming pool, the fully equipped sports center, and the 9-hole golf course. If the gabled roofs and romantic balconies look familiar, it's because you saw them in a James Bond film. Greater proof of glamour hath no hotel. There are two seasons — December to March (for Cortina's incomparable skiing) and June to September (for inspiring mountain rambling). Details: *Miramonti Majestic Grand Hotel,* Pezziè 103, 32043 Cortina d'Ampezzo (Belluno) (phone: 0436-4201).

CALA DI VOLPE, Costa Smeralda, Sardinia: The crown jewel of the complex that the young Aga Khan developed according to stringent aesthetic codes and then discreetly tucked into a vividly turquoise cove, just at the water's edge on the once-remote island of Sardinia, is grand in scale, deluxe in comfort and management, and rustic in style — a mixture of Moorish and medieval, farmhouse and Hollywood, full of arches, pillars, beams, stucco, and such. The sheer beauty of the place has made it a favorite shooting location for fashion photographers and filmmakers (*Diamonds Are Forever,* among others, was filmed here). Rooms come in all shapes and sizes, some with balconies. Tennis, boating, swimming in the sea or in an Olympic-sized pool, skin diving, golf on one of the country's best courses (described in *Great Italian Golf*), and one of the Mediterranean's most fascinating islands are just outside your door. Closed October through April. Details: *Hotel Cala di Volpe,* Cala di Volpe, 07020 Porto Cervo (Sassari); phone: 0789-96083.

HOTEL VILLA SAN MICHELE, Fiesole, Tuscany: Michelangelo designed the façade for a Spartan monastery, but this 28-room hostelry in the hills above Florence, under the same careful ownership as the *Cipriani* in Venice, is a place of aristocratic dinners by candlelight in an open-air restaurant, state-of-the-art Jacuzzis, manicured gardens, canopied beds and other antiques, and princely prices. A limousine is available to whisk guests back and forth to see Michelangelo's other creations in the museums and churches of Florence. Art critic Bernard Berenson's famed villa and painting collection, *I Tatti* — now the property of Harvard University — is only a Titian's throw away. Closed mid-November through February. Details: *Hotel Villa San Michele*, Via di Doccia, 50014 Fiesole (Firenze); phone: 055-59451.

SANTAVENERE HOTEL, Maratea, Basilicata: The Santavenere's white-arcaded façade, set in a verdant fabric of olive and pine trees, and its dramatic position between Saracen tower and turquoise Tyrrhenian would ensure a nomination for an Oscar among Mediterranean hostelries. So it's surprising that this structure, built when Maratea was an innocent fishing village and no one who counted vacationed in the tumbledown region, remained such a well-kept secret for so many years. The fact is that those who knew about it wouldn't tell even their best friends. Maratea's narrow streets, rising and falling over well-trod steps and twisting and turning under ancient arches, bustle nowadays, but the hotel is as pretty as ever — elegant but not stuffy, scattered with reproduction antiques, model sailboats, and other nautical touches, rather like a comfortable country home. The disco-and-boutique option is there when you want it. Closed from October to May. Details: *Santavenere Hotel,* 85040 Fiumicello di Santa Venere, Maratea (Potenza); phone: 0973-876160.

GRAND HOTEL DUOMO, Milan: If modern industrial Italy has a heart, you can watch it beating in this hotel right next to the cathedral, that mad Gothic confection at the center of Milan. It's here that the country's *pezzi grossi* (big businessmen) meet to make the country's biggest deals. The upwardly mobile rooms are arranged on two levels, with the lower living room section providing a suitable atmosphere for the signing of contracts. The furnishings are contemporary, but elegant notes of marble, Oriental carpeting, and burnished wood enliven the background. An added attraction is the companionable silence of the pedestrian zone outside the hotel — which also happens to be the most animated part of town. Details: *Grand Hotel Duomo,* Via San Raffaele 1, 20121 Milano; phone: 02-8833.

HOTEL SPLENDIDO, Portofino, Liguria: Since its transformation from private aristocratic residence at the turn of the century, this very special 67-room hotel has pampered both well-to-do and ne'er-do-well; and the view from its terraces and balconies — of many-colored cottages and bobbing boats in Portofino and its aquamarine port down below — has remained so miraculously unchanged that the late Duke and Duchess of Windsor would feel right at home, as they did long ago. The perfectly tended grounds, atwitter with birds and perpetually scented with mimosa and orange blossoms, modestly conceal tennis court and swimming pool. A romantic path leads down to town and the irresistible *aperitivo* hour at dockside, where ruddy fishermen mend their nets and bronzed gigolos cast theirs. Groucho Marx summed it up: "Wonderful place, wonderful people," he scrawled in the visitors' book. Closed January through mid-March. Details: *Hotel Splendido,* 16034 Portofino (Genova); phone: 0185-69551.

ALBERGO SAN PIETRO, Positano, Campania: Even the bathrooms in this stunning and supremely romantic hilltop hotel have views over the Amalfi Coast, so that not one moment of visual pleasure is wasted. The building seems tied to the cliff that plunges into the Bay of Salerno, its architecture and furnishings a colorful blend of the Italian and the Moorish. Rooms are tucked into the cliff, layer upon layer of them. Their walls are white and dazzling, their floors tiled and scattered with Oriental rugs, and each is embellished with antiques and sea-view balconies. And there are flowers at every turn, inside and out. The swimming pool is on top, with more of the stunning view, and an elevator that pierces the rock carries guests to the private beach and tennis courts below in style. Chic little Positano is a couple of kilometers away; visit it at the ice cream cone hour to browse through the shops brimming with kaleidoscopic summer cottons and to people-watch in streets teeming with Italian magazine cover folk. Film and opera director Franco Zeffirelli has his summer palace here and gives the town a kind of perpetual opening-night air when he and his retinue are in residence. Closed January through mid-March. Details: *Albergo San Pietro,* 84017 Positano (Salerno); phone: 089-875455.

HASSLER VILLA MEDICI, Rome: A German general once said, "Position is everything," and that is what the Hassler has. Perched atop the Spanish Steps and at the edge of the Villa Borghese and its gardens, it also has a famous roof garden, splendid sunset views over the glowing city, and an understated luxury that contrasts sharply with the raucous city all around. The impeccable bar makes a fine headquarters for planning the next day's strategy. The neighborhood's best-known targets — places like *Fendi* and *Ferragamo* and *Armani* — are within easy striking distance. Details: *Hassler Villa Medici,* Piazza Trinità dei Monti 6, 00187 Roma; phone: 06-6792651.

PALACE HOTEL SAN DOMENICO, Taormina, Sicily: Most people visit Taormina for the clear air, the ridiculously clear water, the good food, the strolling, the Greek theater, the haunting tour to the moonscape of Mount Etna, or the August film festival. If you can, knock all that off in an hour — and then never again set foot outside this house of gilded repute. In 1896, after 500 years as a Dominican monastery, this regal Renaissance construction, dramatically positioned high above the Mediterranean, was reborn as a singularly un-ascetic hotel and has been playing host to the famous ever since. Luminaries like John Steinbeck, Sophia Loren, and Marlene Dietrich have marveled at the spectacle of sunset from the terrace and inhaled the scents of lemon and jasmine in the garden overlooking the azure Ionian and nearby Etna. Elsewhere, shady cloisters, immense salons, tapestry-hung corridors, and sober bedrooms artfully mix the extravagant and the severe. Life at the arcaded edge of a heated pool is a side of earthly existence the friars never even imagined. Details: *Palace Hotel San Domenico,* Piazza San Domenico 5, 98039 Taormina (Messina); phone: 0942-23701.

VILLA SASSI, Turin, Piedmont: In the wooded hills just outside the city, where the local patrician industrialists have their homes — Italy's answer to "Dallas" and "Dynasty" country — it's fun to live the life of Agnelli at this noble and splendidly restored mansion set in an immense park. Then, amid marble floors and antique furnishings, wine and dine in the villa's eminent restaurant (with perhaps a bottle of heady, crimson Barbaresco to accompany the tender, truffled roast beef). The trip home afterward lasts only as long as it takes to climb the stairs. 12 rooms. Details: *Villa Sassi,* Strada Traforo del Pino 47, 10132 Torino; phone: 011-890556.

HOTEL CIPRIANI, Venice: On the serene Giudecca island, away from the hubbub of San Marco, the Cipriani is the ultimate posh country club. It exudes Venetian polish and poise, presenting a secluded paradise comprising a peaceful garden, spa, heated Olympic-sized saltwater swimming pool and tennis court (the only ones in Venice), and stunning views of the lagoon. The hotel's two restaurants, from the dynasty that brought you *Harry's Bar,* make it worthwhile to eat six or seven meals a day, not counting a buffet at poolside, a dazzling spread of shrimp, spiny lobsters, Adriatic crabs, desserts by the dozen — everything perfectly cooked and immaculately served. Some of the hundred-odd superbly decorated rooms have Jacuzzis of their own. Others offer gold-leaf-trimmed furniture, lace curtains, vast windows, circular bathtubs, and more. Some guests are relieved to discover that there's a private yacht harbor; if you're slumming, you will enjoy the free shuttle service by brass-fitted, lace-curtained, mahogany-hulled boats to St. Mark's Square, 5 minutes away. Closed December through February. Details: *Hotel Cipriani,* Giudecca 10, 30123 Venezia; phone: 041-707744.

GRITTI PALACE, Venice: Dramatically situated on the Grand Canal, this polished and sumptuous 99-room Renaissance *palazzo,* a compact version of the Doge's Palace, has been a favorite destination of Maria Callas, Charlie Chaplin, Charles de Gaulle, Paul Newman, and a procession of authors from Somerset Maugham to Ernest Hemingway. One of its most notable features is its greenery-edged dining terrace, which floats on the Grand Canal in the middle of the gondola traffic, just opposite the great Baroque church of Santa Maria della Salute — the perfect place to down quantities of beluga and drink museum-quality wines. The rooms have high ceilings, damask couches, Venetian mirrors, antique tables and chests, elaborate parquet floors, huge down pillows, and comfortable beds practically paved in crisp linen. No two are alike, and all are wonderful. Many overlook the canals, so just hang out your window to listen to the occasional tenor of a gondolier and watch most of Venice float by. Details: *Gritti Palace,* Campo Santa Maria del Giglio 2467, 30124 Venezia; phone: 041-794611.

HOTEL DUE TORRI, Verona, Venetia: A magnificent living museum fitted out entirely with antiques, this deluxe centuries-old inn, constructed as the official guesthouse for Verona's Scaligeri family, is *the* place to be during the summer opera festival at the Arena di Verona (described in *Theater, Music, and Opera*). The management and the mood are highly personal. There's a roomy lounge full of antiques on each floor, and each guestroom is furnished in a different style (Louis XVI, Greco-Roman, Charles X, Biedermeier) — the object being to re-create the hotel that Grand Touring Americans might have found at the turn of the century. Enrico Wallner, the man responsible for refitting the *palazzo,* not only knows his antiques but also exhibits exquisite good taste: Even his ashtrays are lovely. When the hotel isn't full, guests choose a room from a set of slides in the marbled, columned, and frescoed lobby. Music lovers will be gratified to note a plaque in the lobby commemorating the sojourn of "Wolfgango Amadeo Mozart" in 1770. Details: *Hotel Due Torri,* Piazza Sant'Anastasia 4, 37121 Verona; phone: 045-595044.

AGRITURISMO

When you've had your fill of marble bidets, Raphaels, and four-posters, try taking the cure under the auspices of the nonprofit purveyor of simple accommodations known as *Agriturist.* Spend a week tasting the wines of the Chianti region, walk in the mountains of Trentino, go cross-country skiing a half-hour drive from the Italian Riviera, canoe in Campania, or hunt in Tuscany — and return each night to a quiet place in the country.

Each year, Agriturist publishes an enthrallingly detailed index to hundreds of private farms, villas, even castles that accept paying guests. Some offer independent miniapartments, others room and homey country board. Still others will turn the whole house over to a traveler and ten friends for, say, Christmas week. Send for the catalogue, or abbreviate matters by writing your exact requirements, and the organization will send a short list of places to contact directly. You may never allow yourself to be snubbed by a frock-coated concierge again. Details: *Agriturist,* Corso Vittorio Emanuele 101, 00186 Roma; phone: 06-6512342.

Buon Appetito:
The Best Restaurants of Italy

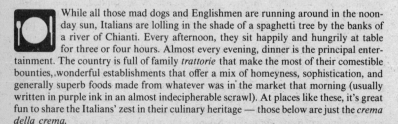

While all those mad dogs and Englishmen are running around in the noonday sun, Italians are lolling in the shade of a spaghetti tree by the banks of a river of Chianti. Every afternoon, they sit happily and hungrily at table for three or four hours. Almost every evening, dinner is the principal entertainment. The country is full of family *trattorie* that make the most of their comestible bounties, wonderful establishments that offer a mix of homeyness, sophistication, and generally superb foods made from whatever was in the market that morning (usually written in purple ink in an almost indecipherable scrawl). At places like these, it's great fun to share the Italians' zest in their culinary heritage — those below are just the *crema della crema.*

The *nuova cucina* — Italy's answer to the nouvelle cuisine of France — is firmly established. And unlike the food found at the United States of McDonald, Italian specialties change significantly from region to region. Just as you've memorized one menu, you're forced to master a whole new culinary vocabulary. Forge ahead. With 5,000 miles of coastline, there are plenty of fish in the Italian seas. There are more pasta dishes in Italy than there are forks. We suggest making an effort to try them all. (Be sure to phone ahead for reservations.) And if you overeat, a shot of the pungent little herbal horror known as Fernet-Branca, available in most bars and restaurants, will normally chase away all evil abdominal spirits. *Buon appetito.*

PARACUCCHI-LOCANDA DELL'ANGELO, Ameglia, Liguria: A modern, unprepossessing hotel near the buzzing beaches of Liguria's Riviera is the modest backdrop for Angelo Paracucchi's nationally acclaimed seafood workshop, one of the culinary landmarks of Italy. Traditional marine staples like clams, rock lobster, shrimp, and sea bass all appear here in enticing and original guises. The pasta is tossed with asparagus or seafood or the simplest tomato and olive oil sauces. Game in the fall and winter, raspberries and wild strawberries in early summer, and honey-and-vinegar-flavored duck for all seasons. Be sure to wait three days before going in the water. Details: *Paracucchi-Locanda dell'Angelo,* Via XXV Aprile, Ameglia, 19031 La Spezia; phone: 0187-64391.

CAVALLO BIANCO, Aosta, Valle d'Aosta: Coaches and carriages clattered up to the door of this wood-balconied restaurant for hundreds of years before cars ever whizzed through the nearby Alpine tunnels to France and Switzerland; the foundations go back to Roman times. The table decor is pure and perfect — linen cloths from Flanders, crocheted centerpieces, underplates of silver, porcelain covers. The six-page menu is as innovative as the setting is traditional. Make your own choices or simply nod and they'll be made for you. Selections cover terrine, quiche, *spuma di trota* (trout mousse), *sformato di verdura* (vegetable timbale), delicately sauced lamb, turkey, pheasant, and guinea hen. And accompanying each course are small loaves of home-baked breads chunked with olives, nuts, or herbs. Closed Sunday evenings, Mondays, and from mid-June to mid-July. Details: *Cavallo Bianco,* Via Aubert 15, 11100 Aosta; phone: 0165-362214.

DANTE, Bologna, Emilia-Romagna: In a city widely known as a destination of choice for the Italian *buongustaio* (gourmet), this restaurant on a quiet back street among Bologna's ochre porticos is *primo* among equals. Breaking with the weighty local traditions of lasagna, tortellini in cream sauce, and boiled meats by the platterful, proprietor Dante Cesari has invented his own feathery feasts, and in the bite-sized dining room diners nibble his light fantastic — weightless terrines of pheasant or duck, flaky *sfogliate* (whispers of pastry with salmon or asparagus). Watercress in the ravioli, eggplant on the tagliatelle, artichokes gathered around the lamb are the style here. And if you can't make up your mind, just order the taster's menu to sample a little bit of quite a lot. The perfect complement to Dantean delights is a bottle of the region's simple, sparkling Lambrusco. Closed Mondays and Tuesdays at lunch in winter, Saturdays and Sundays in summer, and most of August. Details: *Dante,* Via Belvedere 2 bis, 40121 Bologna; phone: 051-224464.

ANTICA OSTERIA DEL PONTE, Cassinetta di Lugagnano, Lombardy: When you're ready to take pastoral refuge from the clatter of brisk, commercial Milan, make the short drive to this fetching and photogenic *osteria* — an old country inn near a bridge and a bubbling stream, with a pretty landscape in the distance. The walls are white, the floors dark, the fire crackling, the flowers cheery, and the atmosphere decidedly warm and comfortable. Owners and kitchen-masters Ezio and Renata Santin create according to the calendar, and diners unswervingly trust the day's fixed-price selections. Highlights may include wild mushroom soup, lobster risotto, beef with artichoke mousse. Details: *Antica Osteria del Ponte,* Cassinetta di Lugagnano, 20081 Abbiategrasso (Milano); phone: 02-9420034.

LA FRASCA, Castrocaro Terme, Emilia-Romagna: That proprietor Gianfranco Bolognesi began life as a sommelier is evident here. The stone walls of the cozy dining room are upholstered with empty wine bottles, the cellars are pavement-to-beams with the best vintages from around the world, and Bolognesi himself still delights in helping guests match, say, a thickly perfumed Cannonau from Sardinia with the lobster ravioli in sweet pepper sauce; an ardent Aglianico del Vulture from Potenza to accompany the stuffed rabbit; a pale blond Müller Thurgau to honor the seafood-and-truffle salad. End the celebration with a grappa *digestivo* and stroll around this graceful spa town in the Apennine foothills. The air blowing in from the nearby Adriatic coast is as cool and tangy as a 1983 Colli Morenici Mantovani del Garda. Closed Tuesdays, 3 weeks in January, and 3 weeks in June. Details: *La Frasca,* Via Matteotti 4, 47011 Castrocaro Terme (Forli); phone: 0543-767471.

ENOTECA PINCHIORRI, Florence: Michelangelo, Botticelli, and the Enoteca Pinchiorri make a perfect Florentine day. The edible art here changes with the market's offerings but often exhibits such masterworks as *foie gras* with pomegranate salad, sole with onion-and-parsley purée, tiny *gnocchi* (potato dumplings) with basil, veal with caper-and-lime sauce, duck in red wine. The charming 15th-century-palace setting and the flawlessly appointed tables complete the picture. An *enoteca* is a kind of wine merchant's showroom — that's how the restaurant got its start — and red, white, and rosé are still its flying colors. Closed Sundays, Mondays at lunch, and August. Details: *Enoteca Pinchiorri,* Via Ghibellina 87, 50122 Firenze; phone: 055-242777.

TREDICI GOBBI, Florence: At this restaurant, whose name means "thirteen hunchbacks," a local good luck symbol, the cooking of Tuscany makes strange tablefellows with the classics from Hungary. Pass up the goulash and go straight to the *bistecca alla fiorentina,* which comes as a huge slab of meat that drapes over the edges of the plate and needs only a supporting cast of pungent Tuscan *fagioli* (beans) and dark, velvety Chianti. If you're here during the harvest, don't miss the *schiacciata di uva,* a rough-hewn grape tart that the Medicis munched. Otherwise, go for the strudel. Details: *Tredici Gobbi,* Via del Porcellana 9r, 50123 Firenze; phone: 055-298769.

SAN DOMENICO, Imola, Emilia-Romagna: Probably more superlatives have been slung at San Domenico than at any restaurant in Italy. Make the half-hour pilgrimage from Bologna to the shady, tree-lined square beneath the castle in Imola, and you, too, will want to coin a few "issimos" of your own. The ambience is refined without being precious, and every harmonious detail has been attended to, right down to the waiters' buttons. The warm and winning proprietor, Gianluigi Morini, makes guests feel as though all this luxury were their due. The chief pleasures: the *garganelli in salsa primavera* (twisted pasta in a fresh vegetable sauce), the green *gnocchi* adrift in sage-flavored cream, shrimp salad with truffle butter, trout mousse in shrimp sauce, stuffed chicken thighs, sole in mushroom-and-champagne sauce, beef with basil and white wine. Your just desserts: apples baked with almonds and cider, *zabaione* with vanilla and hazelnuts. For a postprandial, have a prowl through the wine cellar in the old convent tunnels beneath the restaurant. Closed Mondays. Details: *San Domenico,* Via Sacchi 1, 40026 Imola (Bologna); phone: 0542-29000.

IL SOLE, Maleo, Lombardy: This rustic converted farmhouse — in the same family for a century — rises among grapevines, birds' nests, and gentle church bells. The ceilings are wooden and the walls whitewashed, and the menu's offerings suit the setting. Minestrone precedes traditional Milanese *maccheroni alla verdura* (giant macaroni with vegetables), pheasant with apples, *ossobuco* with fresh peas — all country foods, urbanely prepared. Proprietor Colombani collects antique recipes and delights in researching and re-creating long-ignored regional dishes from other eras. In summer, you can drink your coffee and *grappa* on the shady loggia, watch the flight of the swallows, and breathe the herb-scented country air. Closed Sunday evenings, Mondays, and August. Details: *Il Sole,* Via Trabattoni 22, 20076, Maleo (Milano); phone: 0377-58142.

GIANNINO, Milan: The foods of Tuscany are featured here, despite a Lombard location, and the noted eatery first made its name in the 19th century with a simple plate of beans, and delicacies like *olivette di vitello tartufate* (slices of veal wrapped around ham and seasoned with truffles), *panzerotti* (mozzarella in grilled pasta), and *tortelloni al basilico* (tortelloni with basil) are still the most popular offerings. The fish is outstanding, whether it's crisply fried or served in salad and lightly dressed with olive oil and lemon. Visible from the foyer is the spectacular and spotlessly clean kitchen — so before the gastronomic performance, take a peek at the actors in the wings. Closed Sundays and August. Details: *Giannino,* Via Amatore Sciesa 8, 20135 Milano; phone: 02-5452948.

GUALTIERO MARCHESI, Milan: The quality of the meal guests enjoy in the domain of television idol and cookbook king Gualtiero Marchesi fully supports his reputation. Responsible for introducing notions of nouvelle cuisine to Italy a few years ago, he now demonstrates this inventive cooking at its unfussy best in Italy's one and only Michelin three-star establishment. Choose from a wide selection of seafoods, often joined with vegetables — lobster with peppers, shrimp with cucumbers, hake with potatoes. The meat dishes are more traditional; when thyme and rosemary work sorcery on rare roasted rack of lamb here, the result is enchanting. Sherbets of imaginative flavors are one closing note; or it's possible to depart with a mountain of white and dark chocolate mousse with chocolate sauce under your belt, or perhaps a dollop or two of Grand Marnier ice cream. Closed Sundays, Mondays at lunchtime, and August. Details: *Gualtiero Marchesi,* Via Bonvesin de la Riva 9, 20129 Milano; phone: 02-741246.

EL TOULÀ, Rome: Completely unlike the plain, brightly lit restaurants so typical of Rome, this one boasts decor that is at once plush and subtle, a clientele that is aristocratic and well traveled, a staff as warm and easygoing as the local *trattoria*'s, and a menu that takes diners through Paris, Vienna, and a score of other European capitals. Stick to the dishes of Venice, the restaurant's culinary starting place. Try the *radicchio di Treviso ai ferri,* a slightly bitter red lettuce served grilled. Go on to black *risotto,* a rice dish perfumed with squid and its ink. Try calves' liver with onions or sage butter. And finish up with *tiramisù,* a creamy coffee-and-chocolate-flavored confection whose name means "pick-me-up." Skiers and hikers headed for the Dolomites should look up the sister restaurant by the same name in Cortina d'Ampezzo. Closed Saturdays at lunchtime, Sundays, and August. Details: *El Toulà,* Via della Lupa 29b, 00186 Roma; phone: 06-6781196.

GIRARROSTO TOSCANO, Rome: The cramped staircase entrance to this popular restaurant (whose name means simply "Tuscan roast things") doesn't prepare first-time guests for the spacious, cavelike rooms around the corner. From Roman *haute bourgeoisie* and movie producers to Middle Eastern yuppies and American cardiologists on convention, the clientele waits patiently at the entrance and then sits down zestfully to enjoy the eavesdropping, the people-watching, and the bustle — and to dine excellently on Tuscan specialties. Waiters automatically serve platterfuls of well-aged hams, mortadella, salami, prosciutto, mozzarella, stuffed tomatoes, meatballs, baked eggplant, and other antipasti. Then, right after you've eaten enough to last at least a couple of days, dinner begins. Gigantic Florentine steaks grilled to perfection stand out in any season; spaghetti with fresh tomato and basil is a worthy summer offering. Menus with prices are sometime things at best, and if you don't want antipasto, which costs extra, say so as soon as you sit down. Closed Wednesdays and for 2 weeks between late July and early August. Details: *Girarrosto Toscano,* Via Campania 29, 00187 Roma; phone: 06-493759.

LE TRE VASELLE, Torgiano, Umbria: In the center of a quiet village rising gently above the soft, reassuring Umbrian countryside, this restaurant is the latest effort of the Lungarotti family, the area's most highly regarded wine producers, and their own home-bottled Torre di Giano, Rubesco, and San Giorgio grace tables full of rabbit with laurel, arugula-and-mushroom salad, zucchini with basil and parmesan, and more. Details: *Le Tre Vaselle,* Via Garibaldi 48, 06089 Torgiano (Perugia); phone: 075-982447. See also *Most Visitable Vineyards.*

Caffès

Perhaps no other institution reflects the relaxed Italian lifestyle as much as the ubiquitous caffè. From village emporia with three tin tables where the black-hatted pensioners perpetually argue the Sunday soccer results, to the sprawling outdoor drawing rooms of Venice's Piazza San Marco, life slows to a sit-and-sip. Italians order Campari or cappuccino and put the world on hold. Inside, Italian caffès are for receiving friends and suitors, reading the paper, and writing the great Calabrian novel. Some regulars even get their mail at their local caffè. Outside, in summer, the caffè is for appraising and supervising the spectacle. Puccini set a whole act of his opera *La Bohème* in a caffè.

When you visit those below — a few of the most evocative of the breed — remember that caffès are not necessarily inexpensive. Table prices are usually far higher than what you pay for the same items standing at the bar. So when you're charged $5 for an espresso, don't grumble — just think of it as rent.

GRAN CAFFÈ PEDROCCHI, Padua, Venetia: This sedate gathering place in the center of Padua, built in 1831 long before Italy became a unified state, once reverberated with revolutionary patriotic fervor, and its three rooms — open from dawn until after midnight — are still painted red, white, and green like the Italian flag. A bullet hole in the wall of the White is a cherished reminder of the 1848 student uprisings against the city's Austrian rulers. Earnest young people come to the Green to study, talk, and celebrate graduation from the nearby university. The Red? It's where local businessmen, intent on their double espresso, plot to preserve the status quo. Via 8 Febbraio.

RONEY, Palermo, Sicily: At one end of its immense bar, Roney serves the best stand-up food in Sicily; at the other, a hundred different sweets, including the island's special *cannoli.* In between is a coffee bar that serves a particularly black and potent espresso. In the spacious tentlike pavilion outdoors, patrons lean back in their wicker chairs, look out on the tree-lined avenue, and ponder the mystery of Palermo. How can a city whose per capita income is one of Italy's lowest be among the country's top ten consumers? The answer — the rumor is that it's hidden Mafia money — may give people-watching in this caffè an added dimension. 13 Viale della Libertà.

CAFFÈ GRECO, Rome: When this caffè was opened in 1760 by the Greek-born Nicola della Maddalena, its clients were local working people. Later, the tranquil little marble tables in the three back rooms were a place for Stendhal and Schopenhauer to pause and reflect. They prompted Hans Christian Andersen to characterize Rome as the only city in the world that made him feel instantly at home. Casanova mentioned the establishment in his memoirs, Mark Twain loved the place, Nicolai Gogol scribbled *Dead Souls* seated on its austere benches, and the painter Giorgio de Chirico said he couldn't paint without stopping here for his daily dose of the Italian drink Punt e Mes. After World War II, local intellectuals dubbed the narrow elongated room where John Keats, Washington Irving, and Oscar Wilde had taken coffee "The Omnibus." Today, the place is full of busts and statues of such famous habitués, and the front bar is jammed with expensive furs and suede slippers whose owners are catching their breath between jaunts to Fendi and Ferragamo. Couturier Valentino comes here, as do members of the Bulgari clan, whose shop is nearby. Caffè Greco has been declared a part of Italy's national patrimony, and even the waiters, who dress in tails, look as if they're being preserved for posterity. Via Condotti 86.

TRE SCALINI, Rome: Not surprisingly, this place is a favorite with foreigners, particularly in summer, when the cone-seekers are often three deep at the ice cream counter inside. The setting — right at the center of Rome's most beautiful and fume-free Piazza Navona, staring down the famous Bernini *Fountain of the Rivers* — is incomparable; the cast of characters colorful; and the ice cream the finest in Rome. The renowned specialty is *tartufo,* a kind of chocolate-covered chocolate with chocolate in the middle, under an avalanche of whipped cream, named for its resemblance to the knobby truffle. Piazza Navona 28.

CAFFÈ FIORIO, Turin, Piedmont: Only a few steps from Piazza Castello, tucked into the famous *portici* — those roofed-over sidewalks so welcome in intemperate northern Italian cities — this century-old caffè hums and clinks with top-drawer Torinese, from tailored Fiat executives to old Piedmont aristocrats and their well-groomed offspring just back from skiing in the mountains at the end of the street. No less than Friedrich Nietzsche was a habitué, and the *zabaione* with whipped cream that was a favorite in his day is still on the menu. Via Po 8.

CAFFÈ SAN MARCO, Trieste, Friuli–Venezia Giulia: With its newspapers on wooden poles, its card tables surrounded by intent retired government employees, its corners occupied by solitary readers and scribblers, this holdover of pre–World War I days, when Trieste had 56 coffee houses, is like something out of the late great Austro-Hungarian Empire. Its *fin de siècle* Viennese atmosphere is treasured by habitués, many of whom regularly meet and chat with friends here as if it were their own living room. Note the coffee-bean motif on the walls, the wrought-iron floor lamps, and the carnival masks dating from the 1930s. 18 Via Battisti.

Temporarily closed for restoration at press time is another Trieste landmark, the *Caffè Tommaseo,* on Riva 3 Novembre, along the blowy seafront. The marble tables, on their cast-iron bases, the ornate coat stands, the mirrors, and the cupids are all as they were when James Joyce was living in the city, hanging out at the Tommaseo, teaching at Berlitz, and trying to scrounge a few lire for a glass of *birra.*

CAFFÈ FLORIAN, Venice: The show first opened in 1720 and has been running here ever since — both outdoors, on the dizzyingly ornamental and people-packed Piazza San Marco, and indoors, among the salons full of red velvet, parquet, and intricate paneling and painting. To enjoy it all, order a *cappuccino* on an early April morning, when the pigeons and the first trans-Alpine backpackers herald Venice's spring opening. Or sip a cold white Soave on a balmy summer night when the crowds seem to sway in unison to the lilting rhythm of Strauss or Rossini or Offenbach, as interpreted by the Florian orchestra (or rock music as arranged for piano and accordion and clarinet). Or enjoy a rum punch on a windy November afternoon, standing shoulder to shoulder with soigné Venetians in the coffee-fragrant bar. Or experience the Florian with a Brandy Alexander in hand and a pale winter sun outside. Venice is for all seasons, and this favorite of Casanova and Madame de Staël is as important a stop on a Venice itinerary as the Doge's Palace, whose superb Gothic pastel façade is clearly visible from most tables. Piazza San Marco 57.

Shopping in Italy

In the beginning, Italians created marble statues, stone *palazzi,* and alabaster altarpieces. In our era, the national talent has turned from the eternal to the ephemeral, from the permanent to the portable. As a result, the descendants of Cellini and Michelangelo lavish their genius for design, their sure instinct for what is simply beautiful, on the creation of objects for daily use that delight the senses. The result has come to be known as "Italian style."

Most shops practice the Anglo-Saxon rite of *prezzi fissi* (fixed prices). Or at least they claim to. But it never hurts to try for the traditional *sconto* (discount) on the grounds that you're paying in cash, that you're buying in quantity, that the price is outrageous, or that you were sent by the owner's brother-in-law in Buffalo.

For information on the value added tax (VAT) refund scheme, see *Shopping,* GET-TING READY TO GO. For information about the best buys and where to find them, read on.

WHERE TO SHOP

CHAIN STORES: In a nation dedicated to the proposition that boutique is best, the department store and one-stop shopping site are only a minor part of the scene. *Coin* and *La Rinascente,* the nationwide major-leaguers, both sell middle-priced clothing and sporting goods of decent quality. The former has over two dozen shops all over the country, many in wonderful old palaces in the historic town centers. The latter is in major cities; the store in downtown Rome, on Via del Corso, is a comfortable place to begin conspicuous consuming within the city limits of the capital. *Standa* and *Upim* resemble glorified Woolworth's; one or the other (or both) is found in every important town or city. Clothing is a good buy, especially at *Upim;* prices are fair, and many items are pure cotton or all wool. Housewares are also attractive and inexpensive.

Since all four chains are self-service and have fitting rooms, they're convenient places to figure out your Italian size and get a feel for price or fit — without having to sign-language with salespeople.

STREET MARKETS: If shopping is entertainment, Italy's street markets are its best theater. Most of the country's most intriguing goods can be found here. High-quality shoes show up at Rome's *Porta Portese.* Top designers are remaindered on Turin's *Via della Crocetta.* Imitations of all the big names in leather will fool you in Florence. Forget the four walls and shop as the Italians do — *al fresco.*

Amantea, Calabria – A typical southern market heaped high with technicolor fruits and vegetables, this cheerful weekly happening shows off stands of therapeutic herbs, handmade baskets, embroidered fabrics, wooden sculpture, and mountains of hot red peppers. Sunday mornings.

Bari, Apulia – The flea market on Via Calfati offers antique beds, antebellum fur coats, old shoes, garish crockery, and the overflow from the nearby American navy base. Monday mornings.

Campobasso, Molise – Local handmade cheese, earthenware, and knives are the specialties of this traditional provincial market. Daily except Sundays.

Florence, Tuscany – Florence's two markets make an exhilarating contrast to the sober beauty of its narrow streets. Exuberant *San Lorenzo* teems with low-cost temptations: mohair and Shetland sweaters, prim and practical underwear, costume jewelry, brilliantly colored scarves. The *Straw Market,* also known as *Il Mercato Nuovo* or *Il Mercato del Porcellino* — centrally located on Via Calimata — is covered over and graced with a bronze wild-boar fountain. It's the world center for plastic Fendi, Gucci, and Gherardini handbags and other knockoffs, and there's a motley medley of straw hats, bags, and baskets. If only the best will do, this market is better for browsing than buying. Daily except Sundays and Mondays.

Forte dei Marmi, Tuscany – Everything for the beach life — wooden clogs, novelty T-shirts, and straw hats — plus the latest and glossiest Chinese trinkets. Wednesdays until 2 PM.

Isernia, Molise – Since the earthquake, the houses on the tiny streets of this town are shored up with posts, and the women sit outside on low chairs embroidering goods soon to appear in the market. These, together with rustic woolen stockings, wild camomile and oregano, and over two dozen different qualities of olives, impart a genuine country feeling. Saturday mornings.

L'Aquila, Abruzzo – Besides the usual fruits, vegetables, and inexpensive housewares, this 600-year-old market sells good-quality lace, ceramics, hand-worked leather, and metal goods. Look into the many little artisans' shops nearby for baskets, fabrics, wood sculpture, and wrought iron. Daily except Sundays.

Naples, Campania – Sicilian puppets, German shepherd puppies, wooden *polenta* plates, broken mandolins, tubes for wireless sets, shiny new electrical appliances: The old, the new, the borrowed, the blue, and the stolen enliven this chaotic conglomeration of hundreds of stands and thousands of voices that sprawls between Via del Vicinale and Santa Maria del Pianto. Sunday mornings.

Rimini, Emilia-Romagna – Dried mushrooms and freshly gathered wild salad greens flourish next to a colorful maritime assortment of sandals, sand toys, sun togs, and seashells by the seashore. In Piazza Cavour. Wednesday and Saturday mornings.

Rome – For every Roman who goes to mass on Sunday morning, a dozen go shopping with the masses at *Porta Portese.* To join them, stuff a little naked cash in a tight pocket, leave camera and purse at home, and prepare to shuffle through the packed streets. While searching for the perfect paperweight or the kitchiest ashtray, don't miss the Russian refugees selling caviar, cameras, amber, and nested wooden dolls; hundreds wait for visas in the towns around Rome and scrape together extra money by merchandising their native wares. Sundays until 1 PM.

The vast clothing market at *Via Sannio,* near San Giovanni, is the place for good buys and a wide assortment of rough stuff — army surplus, jeans, down jackets, mode-of-the-moment sweaters. Beware of imitation Levis, Wranglers, and such, and be sure to check out Rome's mini-Macy's across the street — the *Coin* department store.

San Remo, Liguria – *Piazza del Mercato* in this flower capital of the Riviera blooms with carnations, roses, gladioli, local herbs, and spices. Pungently overshadowing it all is the perfume of fragrant masses of *basilico* (basil): This is the region for pesto, the green, basil-based spaghetti sauce. Tuesday and Saturday mornings.

Turin, Piedmont – The flea market known as *Il Balon* is open at Porta Palazzo every morning, but the big day is Saturday, and the best time is dawn. The dealers' stock in trade ranges from furniture and prewar spark plugs to stamp collections, bicycles, and Mussolini relics. Tourists seldom visit.

In *Via della Crocetta,* right next to the fruit and vegetables, eagle-eyed shoppers can find model-sized cashmere, silk, and leather goods left over from last year's fashion shows — their labels neatly removed. Friday and Saturday mornings.

BEST BUYS

CERAMICS AND POTTERY: In the days when earthenware was made from local clay to stock local kitchens, towns in every corner of Italy created their own pottery designs and have continued the traditions down through the centuries. Consequently, the search for pottery and ceramics can lead a traveler to far-flung villages, and for those who see shopping as simply an excuse to explore, the search for ceramics and pottery is particularly gratifying.

Albisola, Liguria – Dozens of factories and workshops produce hundreds of windows full of the baroque blue style that has been traditional since the 17th century. Little figures for Christmas crèches are a specialty, and there's a museum at the Villa Faraggiana.

Deruta, Umbria – Lavishly supplied showrooms are scattered all along the main road. Look at the museum in town and at the church of Madonna dei Bagni a mile south of the city before making a selection.

Faenza, Emilia-Romagna – The French word *faïence* has come to signify any ceramic tableware. But the trademark of Faenza is a cheerful red, blue, and green flower pattern. The local museum has antique pottery from all regions of Italy.

Grottaglie, Apulia – In this town not far from Taranto, an entire quarter is dedicated to ceramics. You can find everything from doll-sized pitchers to gigantic urns with the local pattern of blue flowers on a beige background.

Fratte Rosa, Marches – Pots made of the iron-rich local clay, often painted a rich eggplant color, come in many sizes and shapes. Sturdy pots suitable for cooking are particularly attractive, albeit a challenge to carry home.

Terlizzi, Apulia – Royal blue and rust glazes characterize the ceramics of this town.

Vetralla, Latium – This tiny town near medieval Viterbo was once full of potters. Now, in a cave dug out of the tufa rock, a solitary remaining potter produces rustic, but satisfyingly sturdy, containers for cooking and ornamental use.

Vietri sul Mare, Campania – The last town (or the first, depending on direction) on the Amalfi Drive is still full of potters. Pass the picturesquely tiled food stores en route to the huddle of shops around the main square. Naively painted goats are one motif among the many on the plates, vases, and colorful whatnots for sale.

CLOTHING: The prospect of picking up an entire wardrobe in Italy is so tempting that some travelers dream of an airline losing their luggage permanently.

Giorgio Armani creates clothing for women in styles not unlike those he makes for men. The star of both shows has always been the broad-shouldered, loose-fitting jacket and slacks that manage to be at once comfortably baggy and elegant of line. The designer's Emporio models can be found in many outlets; his boutiques have exclusive models at triple the price. A shopper's prime destination is Via del Babuino 102 in Rome.

Fiorucci launched his colorful and eccentric clothes in a conventional and well-mannered Italy in the late 1960s, and brash has been beautiful ever since. The trendiest in day-glo colors, transparent bags and belts, and show-stopping hemlines should delight the rebellious teenager in every shopper. Piazza Strozzi 12–13r, Florence.

Missoni started with knitwear, but the unexpected patchworks can now be found as shirts, slacks, bathing suits, and even belts for men and women. The all-time classic is a heavy cardigan sweater for men, suitable as outerwear, in sophisticated color mixes. On a rainy day, it's cheering just to pop into a Missoni shop. You'll find them in Milan, Turin, Venice, and Rome.

Valentino has ready-to-wear for men and women with a sophisticated look that is both timeless and elegant. Women's dresses are slim and tailored or full and definitively romantic. If money doesn't matter, bypass the boutiques and go for the *alta moda* (haute couture). It's all under one roof at Via Santo Spirito 3 in Milan; there are also shops in Rome.

Luisa Spagnoli offers high-quality, moderately priced clothing for women in the purest cotton and wool — which is why this designer's more than 100 shops are popular in every corner of the country. In Florence, stop at Via Strozzi 20.

EMBROIDERY AND LACE: These are still produced and prized in Italy.

Isola Maggiore, Lake Trasimeno, Umbria – Fine handiwork is still practiced in a workshop on an island in the middle of Lake Trasimeno. A permanent exhibition and sale near the castle on the island is accessible by boat from the town of Passignano, and some items are on sale in *Spigo,* Piazza Mazzini, in Castiglione del Lago.

Offida, Marches – When the warm weather comes, the women of this town near Ascoli Piceno sit in their doorways and make lace, sometimes spending as much as a year on a single tablecloth. Meanwhile, local monasteries exhibit 500-year-old examples.

San Caterina Villermosa, Sicily – A thousand pairs of hands carry on old traditions in this small town near Caltanisetta, where the entire female population is employed in embroidering precious household linens. The customary purchasers, still-powerful aristocratic Sicilian families, may pay over $500 for a single magnificent heirloom sheet.

FABRICS: Italy is known around the world for its velvets, linens, silks, and other fabrics.

Città di Castello, Umbria – Tablecloths, towels, and sheets are worked on Renaissance looms in the *Laboratorio Tela Umbra* in this small city on the left bank of the Tiber.

Como, Lombardy – Como has always been *the* Italian silk center, and *I Centri della Seta* at Via Volta 64 or Via Bellinzona 3 stocks yard goods as well as scarves, ties, and classic shirts that demonstrate the range of the Italian imagination.

Rome – *Cesari* has a dizzying selection of upholstery material in its Via del Babuino building, as well as regally impractical lingerie and home linens at the branch on Via Barberini. Branches are in Florence, Milan, and Turin; all stores offer good prices during January white sales.

Sant'Arcangelo, Forlì (Emilia-Romagna) – Linen is still hand-printed here with great wooden blocks that have been used since the 17th century. The antique tools and techniques are still visible at *Alfonso Marchi,* the shop in Via Battisti.

Venice – *Rubelli* manufactures and markets its own elegant upholstery fabrics in Venice, Florence, and Rome.

FOOD: In Rome, there is a wide selection of Italy's finest food products in the shops along Via della Croce or at *Franchi,* Via Cola di Rienzo 204. And when Italians travel around their own country — and they rarely bother with any other — they pride themselves on knowing when and where to find each special food at its golden moment.

Asparagus – A tender white variety, delicately tipped with violet, is grown from March to May. Eat it raw, sliced into salad. The best place: Azienda Zuttioni, Nogaredo (Udine), Friuli–Venezia Giulia.

Cheese – Made of pure buffalo milk, fresh mozzarella is delicate and soft — not the rubbery square stuff seen in American supermarkets. Stands line the streets in Mondragone and Formia on the coast between Rome and Naples; sample before deciding.

Fruit – A sour cherry known as the *amarena* appears in Cantiano, near Pesaro in the Marches, in late spring. Out of season, buy the homemade jam. The year's first peaches ripen in Monte San Biagio, near Latina in Latium, in mid-May, and the town celebrates with a peach festival in late June. This is also the place to try white peaches, Italy's most succulent fruit. Nemi, near Rome, is known for its strawberries.

Grappa – In any season, the best of this powerful grape-based liquor is found in the north. Visit the *Distilleria Rossi d'Angera,* in Angera (Varese) in Lombardy, for a look at the venerable slow methods of maturing it in oak barrels.

Honey – There are more types than ever imagined at the *Cooperativa Montarlu* in Rovegno (Genoa) in Liguria. Most romantic of all is the one that's fragrant with lavender. Open in summer only.

Olive Oil – Balestrino (Savona) in Liguria grows 17 different types of olives. To compare the oil made from each type, visit in March, when samples are offered to the public for tasting. Bitonto, near Bari in Apulia, is another olive capital; the local oil can be bought in little shops all over town.

Pasta – It's available in every imaginable size, shape, and composition at *De Filippis* on Via Lagrange in Turin.

Pastries – In Assisi in Umbria, eat *mostaccioli di San Francesco,* a honey-and-almond cake that the saint is said to have requested on his deathbed. And especially on Sunday, all Palermo lines up in tiny Piazza Venezia, behind the Teatro Biondo, for cookies and cakes made by the cloistered nuns, who take orders and hand out sweets through a curtained, wrought-iron grating. Open daily, 9:30 AM to 7 PM (phone: 091-585299).

Truffles – Acqualagna, near Pesaro in the Marches, is fragrant with pungent truffles, especially at the end of October. The white truffles reign in the Thursday and Sunday markets in Piazza Mattei. To enjoy them in a meal, visit the *Ristorante Ginestra,* Passo del Furlo (phone: 0721-70013).

Vinegar – Balsamic vinegar is the champagne of its breed, and a tiny bottle of the real thing, a result of years of distillation, sells for over $10. The best is found at the San Giovanni fair, held in June in the Emilia-Romagna town of Spilamberto, near Modena (a community also known for its manufacture of roller coasters and Ferris wheels).

FURS: The youthful look of family-owned *Fendi* became famous around the world when the company introduced the fur-lined raincoat over 20 years ago. Since then, the five Fendi sisters have made squirrel and shearling as sexy as sable, and put their double-F symbol on leather goods of every description, from key chains to suitcases. There are 22 boutiques from Palermo to Venice, and the whole range of Fendi design can be seen in the firm's five separate shops on Rome's Via Borgognona, near the Spanish Steps.

JEWELRY: Italians have been working with precious stones and metals since the time of the Etruscans. So if you make only one Italian purchase, it ought to be a small (but fine) piece of jewelry. Your Gucci shoes may lose their charm, but gold never seems to go out of style.

Campoligure, Liguria – The score of family-run workshops in this tiny mountain town export almost all of their precious handmade filigree, a braid of two threads of gold or silver woven into delicate webs and then connected to make feathery jewelry and decorative objects. A show is held in September. Beware of factory-made imitations sold throughout the rest of the country.

Florence – A line of minuscule jewelry shops tempt strollers on the Ponte Vecchio, the oldest bridge across the Arno. Other outstanding jewelers are strategically stationed in the center of town: *Cartier* at Piazza Santa Trinità and *Torrini* on Piazza Duomo 10r.

Rome – A quarter of Via Condotti's windows glow with gold. Look for *Bulgari* and *Buccellati* (still reigning supreme), newly arrived *Cartier* and *Van Cleef,* and, nearby, newcomers like *Arte Orafa, Di Consiglio, Massano, Merli,* and *Rapi.* Knowledgeable buyers also seek out the exclusive shops tucked discreetly into corners of the neighboring Piazza di Spagna district: *Capuano,* inside the courtyard of the Palazzo Caffarelli, Via Condotti 61; *Vincenzo Arcesi,* whose contemporary designs are made on the premises at Via della Vite 86; and *Petochi,* which sells imaginative jewelry and lordly old clocks at Piazza di Spagna 23, above Babington's *Tea Room.* For irresistibly convincing costume jewelry, stop at *Bijoux de Paris,* Via Condotti 27.

Torre del Greco, Campania – The cameo and coral capital of Italy is just outside Naples. But unless your eye is infallible, trust only the best shops — *Donadio* and *Apa.*

Valenza Po, Piedmont – With more than 1,200 companies and studios, this one-industry town works (and then exports) almost all the gold that Italy imports. Professional jewelers and passionate amateurs should aim to visit during the annual October exhibition. Near Turin.

KNITWEAR: The knitted creations of Italian factories are famous for reasons that can be immediately seen in almost every clothing store all over the country.

Benetton is a prime destination for anyone who wants to take home an armload or two. In the last few years, the streets of Italy have sprouted hundreds of Benetton shops, and their windows are full of the informal, brilliantly colored, and inexpensive sweaters, shirts, pants, and accessories for men, women, and children.

Albertina hand-finishes glamorous knit clothes in a tiny workroom above the store at Via Lazio 20 in Rome. The best of her works are on exhibit in the Metropolitan Museum of Art; the merchandise is a paradigm of Italian craftsmanship.

LEATHER GOODS: Just as France's Louis Vuitton made his initials the hallmark of luxury luggage, Italy's big *G*'s — *Gherardini, Gucci,* and *Nazareno Gabrielli* — have become synonymous with Italian leather fashion. Each company makes and markets its own lines, emblazoning its initials on boots, briefcases, key rings, umbrellas, bags, and baggage. Since the quality is high (with prices to match), any one of these items is sure to impress. Shops are located in the major cities — on or near Via Condotti in Rome, Via Tornabuoni in Florence, and Piazza del Duomo in Milan.

Bottega Veneta's advertising suggests that your own initials are enough. But the firm's buttery soft, basket-weave leather is their own unmistakable statement, as you can see for yourself in the many company shops — most notably those on Piazza Ognissanti in Florence and Via San Sebastianello 18 in Rome. *Tanino Crisci*'s many outlets are our choice when searching for the finest, most fashionable men's and women's shoes and boots.

For less-expensive versions of Italy's luxury lines, visit *Pier Caranti* on Piazza di Spagna in Rome. *Enny* makes sporty, classic bags, and *Piero Guidi* at Piazza di Spagna 43 offers designs of woven leather in bright colors against a solid background.

MUSICAL INSTRUMENTS: The antique tradition of hand-crafted musical instruments is alive and well in a few renowned centers all over Italy.

Accordions – The first accordion was made in 1863 in Castelfidardo, near Ancona in the Marches, and the streets of the town still echo with the sounds of tuning and testing from a dozen workshops. Watch the 8,300 pieces being assembled at the *Brandoni* shop in Via Sauro 38 and see 100 vintage instruments from all over the world in a museum in Piazza della Repubblica.

Bagpipes – Simple bagpipes, fifes, drums, and other folk instruments have been made with the same techniques for some 2,000 years in the town of Scapoli, near Isernia in the Molise. Look for those made of cherry wood and goatskin by *Ettore di Fiore* and *Giovanni Gualtieri.*

Lutes and Violins – Cremona, a sizable town in Lombardy, was the home of *Antonio Stradivari,* the greatest violin maker of all time, and the art of creating stringed instruments has not been forgotten. On the Corso Garibaldi, look for the *Scuola Internazionale di Liuteria* and the workshops of a number of master lute makers and, at No. 95, the workshop of world-class violin maker *Istvan Konja,* a Hungarian.

Whistles – Comic terra cotta figures of priests, roosters, and puppets are made into whistles in Rutigliano, near Bari in Apulia. Vito Gara and the *Argilarte* studio create more surrealistic forms.

Wind Instruments – The traditional craft goes back to the 18th century in the small lakeside town of Quaina, near Novara in Piedmont, where 600 workers turn brass, silver, and ebony into clarinets, flutes, and saxophones in family-run workshops. A small museum shows off the town's historical best.

SHOES: You'll find a shoe shop on virtually every corner in Italy, but it's the rare Anglo-Saxon foot that matches an Italian last. Price is generally a clue to what you're getting — as usual, you get just what you pay for. When in doubt about the composition, just sniff. The aroma of real leather is inimitable.

Ferragamo made Italian shoes a byword of elegance in the US when its namesake and founder fitted John Barrymore, Mary Pickford, and Gloria Swanson in Hollywood in the 1920s. Still largely handmade today, the firm's shoes are available in various widths — which makes them a rarity in Italy. Soft and comfortable men's and women's loafers are top sellers despite prices that will take your breath away. Shops are found in the major Italian cities; the headquarters are at Via Tornabuoni 16r in Florence.

Raphael Salato offers sparkly sandals, glossy moccasins, and other attention-getters for men, women, and children at three shops in Rome. Best bets: Via Veneto 149 and 104.

Beltrami dresses its windows at Via Condotti 19 in Rome with a moneyed gleam every bit as splendid as those of the jeweler Bulgari down the street. Sleek and sophisticated women's clothing rounds out the picture. You can also shop in Florence, Milan, and Bologna.

TIES: Choose model, fabric, and color at *Marinella,* which still makes silk and wool ties to order as it did for the Duke of Windsor. All internationally important club, university, and association emblems are in stock. The shop is in Riviera di Chiaia 287 in Naples.

Spas

In Italy, real water-immersion addicts wouldn't even think about a trip to the Riviera or the Greek isles when they could wallow happily in the mud of Salsomaggiore. Consequently, Italy's water — and its mud — are the base of one of the country's most lucrative industries. There are *terme* (spas) all over the country. Some flourish on the sites of thermal springs first exploited by those imperial water-worshipers the ancient Romans, who built baths with great fervor. Others trace their origins to antique legends of healing streams spurting from the warm blood of slain princes and miraculous geysers that gushed forth from the tears of abandoned maidens.

Today, for those who are "taking the waters," there is a whole menu of steamrooms and saunas, sprays and whirlpools, mud tubs and honey rubs, paraffin packs and vapor inhalations, underwater gymnastics and regimens of just plain drinking. Every spa has its specialty, and things are so clinical that if a doctor prescribes the cure, the patient's health insurance plan may well cover it. In any event, checkups are generally required before any steam treatments or submersions can be undertaken.

As important to the cure as the sipping is what's done afterward. After all, who's to say whether the healing comes from the waters that bubble or from the diversions that have proliferated alongside the spas and springs — golf and tennis and horseback riding, casinos and discos and boutiques, not to mention abundant fine cuisine. Some of the most salutary of total vacation destinations — for whatever reason — are described below.

ABANO, Venetia: *Mud* is the magic word at this favorite of the ancient Roman aristocracy and military, whose name derives from the Greek for "pain remover." And after mud, which is mineral-enriched volcanic material at about 189°, comes massage — all available as part of the facilities of most hotels. Then the rest of the day is free for swimming in thermal waters or for golf, riding, tennis, or touring. Abano is a pretty, bustling town of tree-lined streets, just outside Padua and a half hour from Venice. The Brenta River is nearby, and a boat trip on *Il Burchiello* to see the more than 70 harmonious and gloriously frescoed villas built in the 17th and 18th centuries for the great Venetian families. The cities of Verona and Vicenza are within reach as well. In fact, with so much to see in the area, the distractions may leave only limited time for wallowing. Of the dozens of comfortable hotels, the *Grand Hotel Royal Orologio* and the *Quisisana Terme* have the best food and the most cosmopolitan clientele. Details: *Azienda Autonoma di Soggiorno,* Via Pietro d'Abano 16, 35031 Abano Terme (Padova); phone: 049-669455.

CHIANCIANA TERME, Tuscany: The origins of this red-roofed town can be traced to the Etruscans and a pre-Roman era, and, like many other Italian spas, its springs were much appreciated in ancient times. Today, the lure of the rich Tuscan and Umbrian countryside distracts some visitors from the venerated water regimen that proposes to return their livers to their original pristine state. Nearby is Arezzo, with its serene frescoes of Piero della Francesca and a lively, irresistible antiques market on the first Sunday of every month. Siena, home of the raucous, twice-yearly horse race known as the Palio (described in *Italy's Most Colorful Festas*), is an hour distant, as are the churches of Assisi and the towers of San Gimignano. Body and soul will both thrive in the unhurried atmosphere, the fine air, and the cypress- and pine-trimmed landscapes of this beautifully groomed region, whether or not guests decide to drink the waters with the clockwork regularity that a proper cure demands. The season runs from mid-April to mid-November. For low-key comfort, stay at the *Hotel Excelsior*. Details: *Azienda Autonoma di Cura,* Piazza Italia 67, 53042 Chianciano Terme (Siena); phone: 0578-63167.

FIUGGI, Latium: When Michelangelo felt the need to flee Rome and the rigors of painting the Sistine Ceiling — for a breath of clean air and a sip of purifying water — it was to this town (an hour south of Rome and 2,500 feet above sea level) that he came. Carried by papal couriers to Boniface VIII in Rome during the Middle Ages, this water is now bottled and sold all over Italy, but many Italians still consider a summer holiday at the source essential to year-round health. The two springs, each set in a lush garden, are known nationally as sure-fire cures for kidney disturbances; one is recommended for morning therapy, the other for postprandial. During the interval, leave the spa area and explore the old town with its high walls, stone staircases, and evocative aromas of wine cellars, wood fires, and grilled meat; one of its charming outdoor restaurants makes a pleasant stop before a tour of the surrounding Ciociara hills. Details: *Azienda Autonoma di Soggiorno,* Via Gorizia 4, 0315 Fiuggi (Frosinone); phone: 0775-55446.

GRADO, Friuli–Venezia Giulia: Up the coast from Trieste and the Yugoslav border, this island town, now linked to the mainland by a 3-mile causeway, has a great deal in common with many other Adriatic resorts. The beach is broad, sandy, and umbrella-gaudy; the old medieval mariners' quarters have been upstaged by spacious avenues, and sailboats and water skiers outnumber fishing craft offshore. What distinguishes it from the pack is its marine thermal establishment and the renowned *sabbiatura* treatments. Here's the place to get buried up to your neck in sun-warmed sand for relief from the aches and pains of arthritis and rheumatism, or simply for the pleasure of the immersion. There are also the classical warm seawater procedures — pool and tub soaks, inhalations, and the like. When all that palls, this far corner of Italy is also a good jumping-off point for visits to Trieste, the Roman ruins of Aquileia, or the unique Yugoslavian grottoes of Postojna. Details: *Azienda Autonoma di Soggiorno e Cura,* Viale Dante Alighieri 58, 34073 Grado (Gorizia); phone: 0431-80277.

ISCHIA, Campania: The largest island in the Bay of Naples is volcanic, and it bubbles with hot springs and naturally radioactive water. The steamy mud is good for aching bones, and the vapors do wonders for respiratory disorders. All the sloshing and sniffing can be done right in your hotel — and in some cases in your own room, if that's what you want. Of the four main thermal centers, Lacco Ameno is the best supplied with luxury hotels with their own thermal establishments: *San Montano,* whose furnishings re-create the atmosphere of a transatlantic ship; the new *Sheraton Ischia,* right by the sea, with giant American beds and its own private beach; and the outstanding *Regina Isabella,* which offers the most elaborate medical menu of all. Taking the cure at Ischia is a favorite activity of burghers from the north eager to bake the chill out of their bones, but the island attracts sun-seekers of every age and type, as well as those who come mainly for mud during its prime season, from April to October. Auto access is limited but not banned, and the peak summer months are peak indeed. Slip away to the promontory of Sant'Angelo, a tiny village on the far side of the island, and enjoy a tranquil, freshly fished meal on the square. Details: *Azienda Autonoma di Soggiorno,* Via Iasolino, 80077 Porto d'Ischia (Napoli); phone: 081-991146.

LEVICO TERME, Trentino–Alto Adige: Just 13 miles (21 km) from the mountain city of Trento, Levico Terme is set on an idyllic, tree-bordered lake at the foot of Monte

Fronte at an altitude of 1,800 feet; its sister town, Vetriolo Terme, is about 7 miles away (12 km) at about 4,900 feet. Both offer a wide variety of sports; sailing and windsurfing in summer at Levico and skiing in winter at Vetriolo are the main draws. The colonnaded thermal complex, set in a botanical park remarkable for its variety of exotic trees, dates from the turn of the century; the high arsenic and iron content of spring waters available here is reputed to benefit blood and nerves, cure skin diseases, and even resolve various ailments of the reproductive system. Details: *Azienda Autonoma di Cura e Soggiorno,* Via Dante 6, 38056 Levico Terme (Trento); phone: 0461-706101.

MERANO, Trentino–Alto Adige: Not far from the Brenner Pass and Austria, the mountain town of Merano glows with Tyrolean charms — steep-roofed houses with painted façades, oak-beamed wine cellars with wrought-iron signs, flower-bordered streets and balconies, *caffè*-lined promenades, 6,560-foot-high trails that can be reached by skiers or hikers by cable car in a few minutes. The spa is across the river from the tightly packed streets of the old town. Mud baths and masks, radioactive waters, vigorous rubdowns, and steamy saunas administered at the spacious, greenery-rimmed thermal center not only pamper those in good health but also bring relief to sufferers of arthritis, allergies, and asthma. The *Hotel Meranhof* is next to the thermal center and its lake and swimming pool; the *Castel Rundegg* has all the facilities of a health and beauty farm; and the *Villa Mozart,* newly renovated in perfect *jugendstil,* has an outstanding restaurant that makes no attempt to cure guests of anything. Details: *Azienda Autonoma di Soggiorno e Cura,* Corso Libertà 45, 39012 Merano (Bolzano); phone: 0473-35223.

MONTECATINI, Tuscany: Time passes with Olympian calm in this most celebrated of Italian spas, an elegant enclave that once belonged to the Medicis and that has hosted princes and pashas, dukes and duchesses, marquises and their betters since it became popular in the late 19th century. Giuseppe Verdi wrote the last act of *Otello* while taking the waters here, Samuel Barber readied his opera *Vanessa* for production between sips, and Kostelanetz, Cole Porter, and Von Karajan all found inspiration in the soothing routines. Visitors stop at the grandest of the grand spa pavilions, the Tettuccio Terme, all columns, caryatids, and ceramic tile murals, and then stroll for hours in the splendid and serendipitous gardens, sipping the medicinal waters before lunch as many a Henry Jamesian character has done on the pages of his period novels, and peregrinating past the nine other pavilions — they look more like castles, palaces, and monasteries. The straight, tree-lined streets are silent as a siesta for much of the afternoon. Only in the evening do the crowds emerge, glowing and rested — the provincial grocer's liver purified, the jet-lagged nerves of the overfed nobility untangled. The cultural calendar that attracts this cross section of Italian society is chock-a-block with theater, films, concerts, dance performances, and even auctions, after which the refreshed spa-goers find their way to little *caffès* where they sip an espresso to the waltzes of a local orchestra. Stay in the venerable *Grand Hotel e La Pace,* an establishment as regal as the town itself. The more energetic routinely travel to Arezzo, Florence, Pisa, Lucca, Pistoia, or Siena, all less than an hour away. Details: *Azienda Autonoma di Cura e Soggiorno,* Viale Verdi 66–68, 51016 Montecatini (Pistoia); phone: 0572-70109.

SAINT-VINCENT, Valle d'Aosta: All the deep relaxation of the day's thermal treatments can be cheerfully undone each evening in the gambling casino of this Alpine town. But if guests can resist the charm of chips and late nights around the wheel, they may discover the myriad benefits that Saint-Vincent's waters are said to offer the digestive system. These powers are put to the test with the ravioli and salmon mousse of the town's top restaurant, *Batezar da Renato.* The *Grand Hotel Billia,* set in its own pretty park, has a swimming pool and medical staff to advise guests on the optimal diet-dissolution ratio. There are footpaths for quiet post-sip rambles; high-altitude hiking trails are just a short drive away. Details: *Azienda Autonoma di Soggiorno e Turismo,* Via Roma 52, 11027 Saint-Vincent (Aosta); phone: 0166-2239.

SALSOMAGGIORE, Emilia-Romagna: When a local doctor named Lorenzo Berzieri successfully used the local warm salt springs to cure an ailing young patient in 1839, he little imagined the parade of screen folk, royalty, and Miss Italy candidates that would descend on this garden-greened town in the years to come. Equidistant from Milan and Bologna (in the hills between Lake Garda and the Italian Riviera), Salsomaggiore was where Italy's crowned heads of the 19th and early 20th centuries recovered from overdoses of champagne and rheumatism induced by damp palaces. (The *Grand Hotel des Thermes,* their destination, is now a convention hall.) Said to be efficacious in treating chronic inflammations of every sort, the local regimen of massages, baths, mud packs, and irrigations — which often attract singers looking after abused vocal chords — is administered at major hotels with their own thermal facilities. But most visitors patronize the huge Baroque spa center and splash along with the masses. More worldly than most Italian spas, Salsomaggiore brims with boutiques and discos, and *caffès* are shoulder to shoulder in the traffic-free town center. The busy morning market and the frequent evening auctions staged by one or the other of the numerous antiques shops give Salsomaggiore a cheerful animation missing at many other Italian health resorts. Details: *Azienda Autonoma di Cura e Soggiorno,* Viale Romagnosi 7, 43039 Salsomaggiore Terme (Parma); phone: 0524-78265.

SATURNIA, Tuscany: This tiny spot in the Tuscan hills between the Aurelia coast road and the Via Cassia, near a less tiny place named Manciano (at Rte. 74), is simply a warm thermal waterfall where 2,000 years of bathers have smoothed and hollowed out sitting places among the rocks. Swimming and soaking here can be done comfortably even on a crisp day in February by anyone brave enough to race from car to springs. If you prefer to soak in greater style, check into the only hotel — *Terme de Saturnia* — whose two grandiose sulphur-pungent pools are more elegantly accessible. The hot fumes float above the warm water, and, when the evening chill sets in, they swirl foggily above the grass-edged basins, mysteriously concealing, then revealing, their borders. Details: *Terme di Saturnia,* 58050 Saturnia (Grosseto); phone: 0564-601061.

The Most Visitable Vineyards

Italy has been producing wines since long before the ancient Greeks knew the local landscape as "Enotria" — the land of wines — and winemaking is still big business from the cool Alpine terraces of the South Tyrol to the sun-scorched Sicilian isles off the coast of North Africa. With 4 million acres planted in vineyards, 220 zones of controlled name and origin (known as *Denominazione di Origine Controllata* or, simply, DOC) established by law in 1963, and another five regions bearing the prestigious government guarantee (*Denominazione di Origine Controllata e Garantita* or DOCG), the nation produces more liters of wine than any other country in the world — and more varieties.

Touring Italy's countless wineries shows off this oenological spectacular in all its many facets. Visitors will encounter vast modern plants turning out tens of millions of bottles annually — as well as cramped cellars presided over by a farmer who puts out just a barrel or two in a good year. Signs reading *vendita diretta* (direct sales) invite visitors to stop, sample, and buy wine to take away. Wine shops or public displays denoted by the term *enoteca* (wine library) welcome browsers; in many cases tastings are offered by the glass for a nominal fee. And exceptional hospitality is everywhere.

Spring and fall are the most pleasant times to travel and taste, but winters are fine as well because winemakers may have more time to devote to visitors. Even in July or August, when urban Italy nearly closes down, there is always somebody on hand to look after a wine estate. Whenever you go, try to phone ahead to make sure there will be someone to show you around when you get there.

Unexpected treasures can be turned up in vineyards nearly everywhere in Italy; many very fine Italian bottlings are sold as simple *vini da tavola* (table wines) — perhaps because the wines are relatively new and a DOC standard has not yet been codified or because they don't fit an existing DOC statute and are depending on word of mouth and critical acclaim for their business. However, serious oenophiles may want to start in an area where the wines are of premium quality. So the following representative selection of visitable wineries is culled from a handful of top winemaking areas — Venetia, Friuli–Venezia Giulia, and Alto Adige in the northeast; Piedmont and Lombardy in the northwest; and Tuscany and Umbria in central Italy.

THE NORTHEAST

ALTO ADIGE: In the province of Bolzano, known as Bozen by the area's German-speakers and as the South Tyrol to the rest of the world, many wineries are located along the *Weinstrasse* (Wine Road) that runs from Bolzano south past Lago di Caldaro to Roverè della Luna. With the Dolomites towering over valleys of neatly kept apple orchards and vineyards, cozy guesthouses, and hearty Austrian food, the area presents an inviting contrast to Mediterranean Italy. It is also one of the few parts of the country where white wines are treated with as much care as reds. There are many fragrant and well-balanced Rieslings, Sylvaners, and Pinots; the Traminer Aromatico grape originated near Termino (Tramin to the Germans), and the best Italian Gewürztraminers still come from here — pale gold and spicily aromatic but more restrained than their Alsatian cousins. The area also makes, in fairly small quantities, Cabernets that are delightfully perfumed, clear-flavored, supremely fresh, and notably well balanced.

Schloss Turmhof, Entiklar, Bolzano – This winery run by Herbert Tiefenbrunner and his family occupies a shady glen with a castle that looks as if it belongs in the Viennese woods. The wines are first-rate — particularly the white Pinots, Chardonnays, Rieslings, Sylvaners, Gewürztraminers, and Goldenmuskatellers; the Müller Thurgau, which goes by the name of Feldmarschall and comes from 3,300-foot vineyards that are the highest in the South Tyrol, is exquisite. Plates of cold cuts, sausages, and sauerkraut are served with the wines in the gardens and the cozy, wood-paneled *weinstübe*. Details: *Schlosskellerei Turmhof,* Entiklar, 39040 Kurtatsch (Bolzano); phone: 0471-88122.

FRIULI–VENEZIA GIULIA: With Trentino–Alto Adige, this area of northeastern Italy is the center of Italy's white wine production. The hilly areas known as the Collio Goriziano and Colli Orientali del Friuli, near the Yugoslav border, produce some remarkably fruity and flowery whites that range from delicate to light to substantial and full-bodied and rich (depending on the producer). They are generally known by their varietal grape names — Pinot Bianco, Pinot Grigio, Riesling Renano. Charming, nicely rounded reds, simple and rather light because they are not wood-aged as in France and California, are made with Merlot and Cabernet grapes in these two areas and in the flatter districts known as Grave del Friuli and Isonzo. The *Enoteca La Serenissima* at Gradisca d'Isonzo, 7½ miles (12 km) southwest of Gorizia, was Italy's first public wine library and remains one of the most impressive.

Russiz Superiore, Capriva del Friuli, Gorizia – This estate founded just over a decade ago by Marco Felluga, in the Collio Goriziano just west of Gorizia, is a model of its genre in Italy. Everything about its manicured vineyards and up-to-the-minute cellars is designed to bring out the most from the local grapes. The white Tocai Friulano, Sauvignon, Pinot Bianco, and Pinot Grigio wines epitomize the finesse of the regional style, while the red Cabernet and Merlot are as elegant as they are easy to drink. Details: *Russiz Superiore,* 34070 Capriva del Friuli (Gorizia); phone: 0481-80328.

VENETIA: This pretty area of hills and villas produces more DOC wines than any other, and the bulk of them are the Veronese trio of Bardolino and Valpolicella (reds) and Soave (white). Known worldwide as everyday wines par excellence, they are never tastier than when drunk young and fresh at the vineyard in which their grapes were grown. Oeonological-minded visitors should make the pilgrimage to Verona in April, when the nation's most important wine fair, *VinItaly,* is in full swing. Above all, sample the costly, majestic Valpolicella known as Amarone. This deep garnet-red, almost portlike wine derives its intense fruity flavors (and an alcohol content of up to 17%) from grapes crushed only after weeks-long aging off the vine on straw pallets. Tourists in Venice may be tempted by a side trip to nearby Treviso province, where a number of Italy's best country restaurants serve good local Pinot, Cabernet, Merlot, and the fizzy white Prosecco di Conegliano–Valdobbiadene — dry but fruity and distinctively aromatic.

Masi, Gargagnago di Valpolicella, Verona, Venetia – In a zone dominated by the industrialized giants among wine producers, Masi treads a civilized middle ground and draws on choice vineyards of the area to produce highly individualistic wines — Soave Classico Col Baraca, Valpolicella Classico Serego Alighieri, sweet Recioto, and two unusual table wines known as Masianco and Campo Fiorin. The latter, a distinctive, dark red, is elegantly flavored and long-lived as a result of having been partly fermented on the skins of grapes pressed to make Amarone. The Amarones, made in several styles, rank among Italy's most distinguished red wines. Details: *Masi Agricola,* S.p.A., 37020 Gargagnago di Valpolicella (Verona); phone: 045-7701696.

Col Sandago, Pieve di Soligo, Treviso – The modern cellars in the town of Pieve di Soligo are used to transform grapes from 197 acres of estate vineyards in the nearby Marca Trevigiana hills into a wide range of wines — from bubbly Prosecco and Pinot Bianco to Chardonnay, Pinot Grigio, Cabernet, Merlot, and the unique red Wildbacher. Details: *Col Sandago,* Via Chisini 79, 31053 Pieve di Soligo (Treviso); phone: 0438-82029.

THE NORTHWEST

PIEDMONT: Well known for its robust, complex, dry reds — authoritative Barolo, Barbaresco, Gattinara, and others like them that develop greatness with aging — this area also makes two whites of renown, the sweetish and sparkling Asti Spumante and the bone-dry still wine called Gavi, as well as delightful lighter reds that are meant to be drunk young. These most notably include Barbera and Dolcetto. Far from being sweet (as its name might suggest), Dolcetto is a soft, intensely fruity, low-acid wine. Well-marked wine roads lead through major DOC zones, including Barolo, Barbaresco, and Asti Spumante, and there are impressive public *enoteche* at Barolo, Grinzane Cavour (near Alba), Costigliole d'Asti, and Vignale Monferrato.

Fontanafredda, Serralunga d'Alba, Cuneo – This handsome wine estate began its life in 1878 as the hunting lodge of Conte Emanuele Guerrieri, son of King Vittorio Emanuele II, and his wife, Contessa Rosa Mirafiori. Today it is a major producer of Barolo (with several single-vineyard bottlings), Barbaresco, Barbera d'Alba, the rugged and astringent Dolcetto d'Alba, Asti Spumante, and two impressive Champagne-style whites — Contessa Rosa and Brut Gattinera. Located near Alba, about 46½ miles (75 km) southeast of Turin. Details: *Fontanafredda,* 12050 Serralunga d'Alba (Cuneo); phone: 0173-53161.

Abbazia dell'Annunziata, La Morra, Cuneo – This 15th-century abbey, south of Alba in the heart of the Barolo zone, houses a wine museum organized by Renato Ratti, who is perhaps the leading authority on Piedmont's wine today. Author, lecturer, and a key member of the national DOC committee, Ratti also produces noteworthy Barolo, Barbaresco, Nebbiolo, Barbera, and Dolcetto at his cellars adjoining the museum. Details: *Renato Ratti,* Antiche Cantine dell'Annunziata, 12064 La Morra (Cuneo); phone: 0173-50185.

Martini & Rossi, Pessione, Turin – Among Piedmont's large wine and vermouth houses, Martini & Rossi is perhaps the most visitable. A wine museum on the premises has pieces that date to the times of the Etruscans and Greeks, and the hospitality is impeccable. Guided tours and tastings at the main cellars in Pessione, about 9 miles (15 km) southeast of Turin, may be arranged by appointment. Details: *Martini & Rossi,* S.p.A., Casella Postale 475, 10100 Torino; phone: 011-57451.

LOMBARDY: This area around Milan makes wine of virtually every style. There are dry spumantes and fruity whites, light rosés, and reds of all styles. Rugged and mountainous Valtellina to the north — a growing area praised by Pliny, Virgil, and Leonardo da Vinci, among others — starts with the hard-to-cultivate Nebbiolo grape, grown on south-facing vineyards. Then the pressings are wood-aged to produce a simple, substantial red with rich color and deep flavor that is less austere and more immediate than the Barolo, Barbaresco, and other Nebbiolo-based wines from Piedmont. Valtellina Sfursat is produced by methods similar to those used for Venetia's Amarone. Oltrepò Pavese, to the southwest, makes a number of full, grapey reds, plus clean, crisp, fruity whites that range stylistically from Müller Thurgaus to Pinots. Franciacorta to the east is the home of some of Italy's best sparkling wines. Some of these are dry, some sweet; those made by the *metodo champenois* (Champagne method) tend to be less yeasty than their French counterparts.

Guido Berlucchi, Borgonato di Cortefranca, Brescia – Some 12½ miles (about 20 km) northwest of Brescia, near Lake Iseo at the nation's largest producer of Champagne-style wines, visitors are welcome to witness the intricacies of the *metodo champenois* and sample the product — Berlucchi Cuvée Imperiale Brut, Brut Millesimata, Pas Dosé, Grand Cremant, and Max Rosé — all made from Pinot or Chardonnay grapes from Franciacorta, Oltrepò Pavese, and Trentino–Alto Adige. Nearby, the firm also has a small estate known as Antica Cantina Fratta. Details: *Guido Berlucchi & Compagnia,* S.p.A., Via Don Secondo Duranti 4, 25040 Borgonato di Cortefranca (Brescia); phone: 030-984381.

CENTRAL ITALY

TUSCANY: Tuscan winemakers have been building their reputations of late on the strength of imposing reds such as Brunello di Montalcino, Vino Nobile di Montepulciano, and a variety of new *vini da tavola.*

Still, Chianti remains the quintessential Italian wine, and Tuscany is its home. You'll find it here in all its many styles — from light and easy-drinking *Classicos* to spicy and assertive *Riservas.* Don't miss the vineyards of the Classico zone between Florence and Siena, some of the most picturesque in all of Italy, particularly the Castelnuovo Berardenga, Radda, and Gaiole townships. And be sure to stop at the towered town of San Gimignano, known for its white Vernaccia. The *Enoteca Italica Permanente* in the Fortezza Medicea in Siena displays and serves choice wines from all over Italy.

Badia a Coltibuono, Gaiole in Chianti, Siena – This ancient abbey, amid a forest of pine and fir overlooking the valley of the Arno, may have been the place where the first Chianti was made nearly 1,000 years ago. Today the Gaiole township is known for the delicacy of its Chianti Classicos, particularly in good years; the estate itself is noted for its stocks of fine Chianti Riserva, as well as good red and white table wines. The local Vin Santo Toscano, made of Trebbiano and Malvasia grapes that have been left to dry before pressing and then allowed to ferment in small oak barrels for three or four years, is especially interesting; it is dark gold, has a lively bouquet, a velvety texture, and more or less sweetness depending on the sugar content of the original grapes. The establishment also produces a delicious extra-virgin olive oil. Wines and oils can be tasted at a restaurant on the grounds; visits to the abbey and cellars are by appointment only. Details: *Badia a Coltibuono*, 53013 Gaiole in Chianti (Siena); phone: 0577-749498.

Ruffino, Pontassieve, Florence – A large but widely respected producer of Chianti and other wines, Ruffino welcomes visitors to its main cellars at Pontassieve, 10½ miles (17 km) east of Florence. There, and in the restaurant *Girarrosto* in Pontassieve, tasters may sample the white Galestro and Orvieto Classico, Chianti Classico Aziano, the aged Riserva Ducale, and Chianti Torgaio di San Salvatore, as well as a new line of premium table wines with the designation Alto Predicato. In a region whose wines usually vary radically from year to year, Ruffino Chianti has the distinction of maintaining its quality from one vintage to the next. Details: *Ruffino*, S.p.A., Via Aretina 42/44, 50065 Pontassieve (Firenze); phone: 055-8302307.

Villa Banfi, Sant'Angelo Scalo–Montalcino, Siena – This vast estate belonging to Villa Banfi, one of the leading US wine importers, is quickly taking shape as a major tourist attraction. The cellars, which California's Robert Mondavi described as "the world's most modern winery," are open to the public daily. Wines use the fruit of more than 2,000 acres of vines. Notable products include an austere and full Brunello di Montalcino, Rosso di Montalcino Centine, Santa Costanza, the bubbly-and-sweet Moscadello di Montalcino, and the California-style Chardonnay Fontanelle and Cabernet Sauvignon Tavarnelle. A medieval castle is being restored to house an ambitious restaurant and wine museum, with adjacent hotel, shops, and recreational facilities. Details: *Villa Banfi*, S.p.A., Piazza Mincio 3, 00198 Roma; phone: 06-421901.

UMBRIA: Known as "the green heart of Italy," this region was noted in the past for the sweet white wine from Orvieto. In the last few years its winemakers have experimented with non-Italian grapes like Chardonnay and Cabernet Sauvignon, with the result that Umbria promises to one day produce some of Italy's finest modern wines. The areas of special interest are Orvieto and the hills along the Tiber between Perugia and Todi.

Cantine Lungarotti, Torgiano, Perugia – This estate winery about 6 miles (10 km) south of Perugia has become something of a contemporary legend under the supervision of Giorgio Lungarotti, who made his name with the Torgiano DOC white and red wines (most notably the single-vineyard reserve Rubesco red). He has recently taken on prestigious Chardonnay, Cabernet Sauvignon, and San Giorgio wines — this last a blend of Cabernet and Sangiovese, the grape on which Chianti is based. The family also owns *Le Tre Vaselle* (described in *The Best Restaurants of Italy*). A major national wine competition known as the *Banco d'Assaggio* is held here each fall. Nearby are an attractive wine museum and a display of local ceramics. Details: *Cantine Lungarotti*, 06089 Torgiano (Perugia); phone: 075-982348.

Cooking Schools

Until recently, every Italian kitchen was a cooking school, *la professoressa* was Mama, and the student body was restricted to family members. However, Italians have discovered the pleasures of their own nation's regional cooking right along with the rest of the world: Neapolitans now eat Tuscan food at home and Venetians down Sicily's *cannoli* and *cannelloni* — foods which, as often as not, Mama's Mama told her nothing at all about. Enter the cooking school.

Some are taught by superstars of Italian cooking like Marcella Hazan and Giuliano Bugialli. One is given by a movie star, the perennially popular Ugo Tognazzi. Some are in Italian with translation on the spot. Others are in English. Most are staged in spring and summer, and early booking is a must. Some of the best include the following.

COOKING IN FLORENCE, Florence: Giuliano Bugialli is well known as the author of three definitive books on Italian cuisine. However, every year in Florence, he also offers a short hands-on course that covers the culinary delights of all Italy. Each of the five classes in each course involves supervised preparation of a complete meal planned by Bugialli — a different menu for each class. In English. Details: *Mrs. Bernard Berman,* 2830 Gordon St., Allentown, PA 18104; phone: 215-435-2451.

RUFFINO TUSCAN EXPERIENCE, near Florence: Chefs such as Annie Feolde Pinchiorri and Rosario Santoro who demonstrate their culinary expertise and a group of sommeliers that includes Ruffino Wine Company owner Ambrogio Folonari Ruffino are the lure of this adventure in the wine and food of Chianti country. Accommodations are in the *Grand Hotel Baglioni.* Details: *World of Oz, Ltd.,* 3 E 54th St., New York, NY 10022; phone: 212-751-3250 in New York State; 800-223-6626 elsewhere.

ITALIAN COUNTRY COOKING, Positano, Campania: In the classes of this 8-day full-participation course in fabled seaside Positano, on the Amalfi Coast, the emphasis is on country cooking with locally available ingredients. Each of the various spring, summer, and fall sessions emphasizes a specific area — pastas and other first courses, meat, fish, desserts. All instruction is in English in director Diana Folonari's cliffside home. Lodging is in nearby hotels. Details: *Folonari Country Cooking Classes,* c/o E&M Associates, 45 W 45th St., New York, NY 10036; phone: 212-719-4898 or 212-302-2508 in New York State; 800-223-9832 elsewhere.

CLUB NUOVA CUCINA, based in Rome: Actor Ugo Tognazzi directs this establishment dedicated to schooling Italians and foreigners in the best of Italian cooking. Each of the three separate weekend courses is taught in a different part of the country, each by a local master chef. Franco Paoli, who heads the Florentine restaurant *Coco Lezzone,* teaches Tuscan cooking in Florence. Fulvio Pierangeli holds classes in fish preparation at the restaurant *Gambero Rosso* in San Vincenzo, a pleasant little coastal town near Leghorn (Livorno). Tognazzi himself surveys Mediterranean cooking in Sorrento. Classes are limited to 12. Details: *Club Nuova Cucina,* Via Revere 16, 20123 Milano; phone: 02-4981341.

LO SCALDAVIVANDE COOKING SCHOOL, Rome: After Jo Bettoja, an American from Georgia, exhibited her good taste by marrying into a distinguished Italian family that still cures its own prosciutto and salami, she soon came to realize that other Italians were not learning what she had learned from her new Mama-in-law. So she began combing the countryside for great classic Italian recipes. With this knowledge under her belt, she wrote a cookbook and now is now sharing her culinary expertise at her Lo Scaldavivande Cooking School (the name means "the covered dish"). The 9-day course is held in a 17th-century Roman *palazzo,* with a farewell graduation luncheon at the family's 18th-century hunting villa outside the city and lodging in the first-class *Hotel Mediterraneo,* which her husband's family also owns. Details: *E&M Associates,* 45 W 45th St., New York, NY 10036; phone: 212-719-4898 or 212-302-2508 in New York State; 800-223-9832 elsewhere.

GRITTI PALACE COOKING COURSES, Venice: Every year in July or August, this splendid old hotel, once the palace of a Venetian doge, is home to a month of 5-day cooking courses. Each is taught by a different master chef invited for his or her knowledge of some regional cuisine — from Tuscany, Liguria, Emilia-Romagna, and other prime Italian gastronomic areas. The venue is the hotel's own ultra-professional kitchen, and the coordinator is American chef and author Julie Dannenbaum. Students may sign up for just one or stay for all four courses; it's not necessary to stay in the hotel to participate. In Italian with English translations. Details: *Mauro Scoccimarro, Gritti Palace Hotel,* San Marco 2467, Venezia; phone: 041-794611. See also *Italy's Most Memorable Hostelries.*

DIRECTIONS

The Italian Riviera

What is pine green and bay blue, has over 18 million wisteria petals, and collects 3,000 annual hours of sunlight — most of which seem to be crammed into any average August afternoon? Answer: The Italian Riviera. And as anyone who has spent a part of summer hereabouts will gladly agree, there is no satisfactory answer to the riddle of why this glorious arc of Mediterranean coast has remained so long in the shadow of its honky-tonk French cousin to the northwest.

Given a snorkel and a little wanderlust, it's really no trouble to polish off the itinerary offered below in less than a week — provided there's no dallying over lunch. But then, why *not* dally over lunch, letting your eye follow the frolicking gulls as they swoop among the yachts? With a little preplanning, the most strenuous afternoon activity could be ordering another bottle of chilled Vermentino or a slushy *granita di caffè*. Who needs Nice? (With no preplanning, however, it's likely that you'll spend much of your time seeking accommodations.)

The backdrop for this *dolce vita* is a 180-mile-long crescent drizzled along the Ligurian Sea and halved in the middle by the sprawling port city of Genoa. Everything to the west is known as the Riviera di Ponente; everything to the east and south, as the Riviera di Levante — referring to whether the sun will be setting or rising as you gaze from your seafront window. In midsummer, the resident population of Liguria is outnumbered four to one by beach umbrellas, and from the air the whole province appears to be a series of blue-and-white-striped bumps. However, there are hundreds of wild, craggy coves chopped into the wall of the coastline, and it takes only a 15-minute dinghy ride to be far from the paddling crowd.

Some of Italy's classiest vacationers indulge in cove hopping across the whole coast, from Ventimiglia to Lerici, via sleek sloops, eliminating the risk of being cast ashore at a five-star hotel. Mahogany-legged signorinas in wet bikinis share dry martinis with titled beachcombers — they're normally found on the wharf at Santa Margherita during the Allegro Hour, or at the roulette wheels in San Remo. But this is a secondary attraction.

The Italian Riviera has a lot more to offer than superb climate and beaches. The narrow coastline is protected by a semicircle of mountain ranges, the Alps to the north and the Apennines to the east, making Liguria one of Italy's most scenically variable regions. The terraced hills that look like giant staircases are devoted to growing grapes for the region's delicate wines or olives for the olive oil industry. The seafood here is some of the best served anywhere in Europe. The Ligurians themselves are proud and reserved, but they welcome visitors to their many ancient festivals and pageants, as well as to the modern-day boat shows, flower fairs, and song contests.

Liguria has always been a seafaring region. Even today, 70% of the population of 1.7 million lives on the coast. Many of these people work at the ports, especially Genoa, or in the production of slate, olive oil, or pasta, but most are involved in tourism or related industries. Liguria is famous for hand-crafted filigree, macramé, and ceramics, but even more famous for floricul-ture. As early as the sixteenth century, the Italian nobility of other regions sent to Liguria for fresh flowers — roses, carnations, strelitzias, gladioli, and daisies, to name only a few of the varieties grown here — to decorate wed-dings and festivals.

The most famous date in Ligurian history is the discovery of America in 1492 by the Genoese Christopher Columbus. But the oldest evidence of Ligurian citizenry comes from the Balzi Rossi caves of Ventimiglia, near the French and Italian border. Over 200,000 years ago, men and women took shelter in these caves. Other parts of the western coast are also rich with traces of prehistory: Neanderthal people (who existed from about 100,000 to 30,000 BC) lived in caves in the San Remo and Finale districts. Farther inland, Paleolithic people (about 30,000 to 10,000 BC) left burial mounds and funeral artifacts. Coastal and hill tribes developed separately; their innate differences in temperament — coastal folk tend to be outgoing, hill people more reticent — are noticeable even today.

The Romans made their appearance after the first Punic War (third century BC). The fierce Ligurian tribes fought savagely for independence, but by 14 BC Augustus Caesar had conquered the whole Alpine arc region, and Liguria became completely Romanized. Towns sprang up at Albingaunum (Albenga) and Albintimilium (Ventimiglia) in the west and at Luna (Luni) in the east. Archaeological remains of these Roman towns are still in existence, most notably in Luni.

Liguria was considerably larger during antiquity than it is in modern times; its western borders stretched well into what is now France. However, the unity and prosperity of the region under the Romans was undermined by the collapse of the empire and the barbarian invasions that followed. Alaric, king of the Visigoths, destroyed Albenga in AD 409. Other barbarian tribes con-tinued to wreak havoc in the area until the Lombards invaded in AD 568 and dominated for two hundred years. Liguria's Middle Ages properly began only toward the end of the eighth century, when the Franks established a Tuscan-Ligurian feudal mark.

The ports along the coast had been important as trading centers. Genoa, in particular, from as early as the fifth century BC, had been a firm ally of Rome. After the fall of the Roman Empire and throughout the Middle Ages, Saracens, highly organized plunderers from the south, repeatedly stormed the entire Ligurian coast. In AD 935 they sacked Genoa, and for the next two centuries, largely in response to the continuing Saracen threat, Genoa slowly built itself up as a powerful maritime center.

In the twelfth century, Genoa began its conquest of the rest of the Riviera, although other independent Ligurian cities, particularly Savona and Ven-timiglia, fought hard to retain their individual liberty. The conquest was completed by the end of the fourteenth century. Despite unification, however, trouble began to arise from within. Factions that supported the pope, the Guelphs, fought bitterly with those who supported the Holy Roman Empire, the Ghibellines, whether or not warring parties were members of the same city or even the same family. This, and the devastation caused by wars with Venice and Pisa, the two leading maritime centers on the Adriatic coast, so weakened the region that, between 1499 and 1522, Louis XII of France was able to impose his authority over the area. A few years later, the French were ousted by the great Ligurian leader Andrea Doria, with the help of the Spanish. Doria, a brilliant admiral as well as a politician, known as Father of the Country, also framed a constitution and helped to create a unified Republic of Genoa that remained intact for nearly two hundred years.

In 1746 the Austrians occupied the region and remained in control until the French Revolution. In 1797 the Ligurian Republic became a battleground for the Napoleonic Wars. For the first decade of the nineteenth century the region was annexed to France, but with Napoleon's defeat in 1815, the newly titled Duchy of Genoa became united to the Kingdom of Sardinia.

The decades that followed witnessed the struggle for Italian unification. Ligurians contributed to its realization in a decisive way. In 1831, Giuseppe Mazzini founded the Young Italy movement, which led to the growth of a national spirit otherwise known as the Risorgimento, the "revival" or "rebirth." Another Ligurian hero was Giuseppe Garibaldi, a charismatic military leader who was responsible for bringing Sicily and Naples into the growing union. Garibaldi achieved the liberation of the south with his famous "Thousand" red shirts, who were all fierce Ligurian sharpshooters.

Today's visitors to the Italian Riviera will see not the fierce and independent side of the Ligurians but only their hospitality, which, like the Ligurian sunshine, is rarely clouded over. All the towns and many of the villages have extremely efficient and friendly information offices that go under the lengthy name *Aziende Autonome di Soggiorno Cura e Turismo,* but just ask for *"informazione turistica"* and you can't go wrong. The offices will give advice on sights to see, hotels, tours, and festivals — also on where to find the best water-skiing instructor or the best local wine.

This route, starting in Ventimiglia (near the French border not far from Nice), winds along the arc-shaped coast, passing through such chic resorts as San Remo and ancient fishing villages like Noli. It is bisected by the city of Genoa, then continues south toward such internationally famous playgrounds as Rapallo. Halfway along the Riviera di Levante, the route turns slightly inland, skirting the insular Cinque Terre (Five Lands) to finish at Portovenere, on the peninsula just south of the port town of La Spezia.

Distances between towns are short — few are more than a 10-minute drive from one another. There are also a number of trains that stop at every village along the coast, and the energetic visitor could even cover some of the area on foot. There are two roads that traverse the Riviera, almost parallel to each other. Both have an average length of 164 miles (the coastline itself is closer to 200 miles). The autostrada (A10 west of Genoa and A12 east), which has some stunning views, generally runs inland and at a higher altitude. The older Via Aurelia (SS1) clings to the coast, running through all the towns and villages. The coast road can be congested with traffic, especially during the busy summer season, so unless you are a very patient driver, you probably should use the autostrada to make time, exiting to visit particular places.

Accommodations range from the height of Old World luxury and elegance at such hotels as the *Royal* in San Remo or the *Splendido* in Santa Margherita, where a double room with bath is from $120 to $210, to more moderately priced hotels from around $50 to $120, to inexpensive hotels under $50. (A warning here for visitors arriving during July and August: Sometimes as much as six months' advance booking is required by the more popular hotels, and that does not necessarily mean the most expensive.) At restaurants rated as expensive, dinner for two costs $70 or more; at moderate, about $40 to $70; and at inexpensive, less than $40. Prices include wine but not liquor.

En Route from the French Border – Coming from the French border, whether on A10 or SS1, stop at Mortola Inferiore, 3 miles before Ventimiglia, to visit the Hanbury Gardens. The gardens, which now have over 6,000 species of flora, were begun by the Englishman Sir Thomas Hanbury in 1867. They are regarded as one of the most important sites in Europe for the cultivation of exotic plants. The gardens are usually open daily, 9 AM to 6 PM, but call 0184-39507 to check the hours.

VENTIMIGLIA: The medieval section of Ventimiglia stands on a hill to the west of the River Roja, which divides this part of the town from the modern center below and to the east. This ancient port was independent until 180 BC, when it became subject to Rome. Invasions by Goths and other barbarians forced the citizens to move uphill from the coast, where some fine Roman archaeological sites, such as a well-preserved amphitheater, remain. The fortified hill city is very much as it was in the 13th century, when it was conquered by Genoa. The church of San Michele is a large, sober Romanesque building (11th to 13th century), with the original crypt incorporating Roman columns and milestones. The modern section of Ventimiglia is important principally as a center for the production and sale of flowers. Every year in mid-June a festival called *Battaglia di Fiori* (*Battle of Flowers*) features huge floats carrying sculptures made entirely from blossoms parading through the town. A yearly *Festival di Musica Antica* (*Festival of Ancient Music*) is held between July and August, and a colorful historical folk festival takes place around the middle of August. Tourist information is available at Via Verdi 15 (phone: 0184-352844).

CHECKING IN: *La Riserva* – Just on the outskirts of the medieval city, 1,300 feet (400 meters) above sea level, this secluded hotel offers a homey atmosphere, a superb restaurant next to a heated pool, and a wonderful panorama of the coast. Open March to October and 2 weeks at Christmas. (Castel d'Appio, Ventimiglia; phone: 0184-39533; moderate.)

Eden – A small, quiet hotel with a lovely garden and a good restaurant. Open April to mid-November. (Corso Montecarlo 68, Mortola Inferiore; phone: 0184-39431; inexpensive.)

EATING OUT: *La Mortola* – The cuisine is international with variations on scampi, the specialty, and delicious crêpes Suzette. Closed Monday evenings, Tuesdays, and November. (Opposite the Hanbury Gardens, Mortola Inferiore; phone: 0184-39432; expensive to moderate.)

En Route from Ventimiglia – Only a mile or so out of Ventimiglia on A10, the exit to Pigna leads to Dolceacqua (4 miles from the exit), which means "sweet water." In keeping with its name, the village produces some of the best wine in the region, a delicate, light red called Rossese. Perched on a hill, with houses seemingly carved into it, are the impressive 12th-century ruins of the Doria family castle. Many of the narrow alleyways that run up to the castle are completely cut off from daylight, as the buildings through which they run engulf them on all sides.

There are a number of traditional craft shops here, most notably that of Jean Perrino, who sculpts fantastic shapes from 300-year-old local wood (phone: 0184-36096).

Back on the autostrada, it is only 3 miles to Bordighera and another 7 miles to Ospedaletti. Both these small towns are popular winter resorts distinguished by their luxuriant vegetation and *fin de siècle* ambience. The British have been coming to Bordighera for over a century; Queen Margherita chose this palm-shaded resort as her principal residence. The Vatican gets its supplies of palms for Holy Week exclusively from this district. Ospedaletti has always been important as a health resort and gets its name from a hospital founded there in the 14th century by the Knights of Rhodes.

 CHECKING IN: *Grand Hotel del Mare* – A large modern complex about 1 mile outside the town center, including a pool, restaurant, and private beach. Closed mid-October to mid-December. (Via Porto della Punta 34, Bordighera; phone 0184-262201; expensive to moderate.)

Grand Hotel Capo Ampelio – Set in a park, this well-established, elegant hotel has over 100 recently modernized rooms as well as a pool and a good restaurant. Closed mid-October to mid-December. (Via Virgilio 5, Bordighera; phone: 0184-264333; moderate.)

SAN REMO: The capital of the Riviera di Fiori (Riviera of the Flowers), San Remo is an elegant Edwardian resort reminiscent of Cannes. It is devoted to pampering visitors. Popularized at the turn of the century by Russian and German aristocrats, it is still a favorite watering spot of today's rich and powerful, as is evident from the number of luxurious yachts moored in the harbor.

The origins of the town are Roman, but its most potent period took place during the Middle Ages, when the Genoese bishops resided here. San Remo was, in fact, named after the first of the bishops, San Romolo. Over the centuries, the town was heavily fortified, having to endure persistent invasion by the Genoese, the pirate Barbarossa (who sacked the town in 1543), and the English. The medieval nucleus of the town, known as Pigna ("pine cone") due to its shape, is perched on a hill. Its tall houses, between which run dark flights of steps and alleyways, are joined by small arches for reinforcement against earthquakes. Sitting on top of this ancient pile of stones is the Baroque church of Madonna della Costa, the origins of which go back to the 6th century, when there was a sanctuary on the site; the façade of the church is particularly graceful. Another noteworthy building is the Russian Orthodox church of Santa Maria degli Angeli; the building, on Corso Nuvoloni, is not often open to visitors, but the colorful exterior is delightful in itself.

A visit to the *Mercato dei Fiori* (*Flower Market*), open weekdays, October to June, from about midnight to 8 AM, will reveal an abundance of roses, jasmine, carnations, narcissi, tulips, and countless other varieties: 20,000 tons of blossoms are shipped from the Riviera each year. The *Municipal Casino* on Corso Inglesi is one of only four in Italy; players must have some form of identification, such as a passport, to get in. Winnings can be spent immediately at the fashionable boutiques on nearby Corso Matteotti, which is one of the most exclusive shopping areas in this part of the Riviera. An international song festival takes place here each year, usually between mid-January and mid-February. For a spectacular view of the coast, as well as Cannes on a clear day, which is nearly always, take the funicular (when it's working) from Via Isonzo up to Monte Bignone. The Tourist Office is at Corso Nuvoloni 1 (phone: 0184-85615).

 CHECKING IN: *Royal* – The most luxurious hotel on the Riviera di Ponente, with 140 rooms and everything a guest might possibly need, including a nightly dance orchestra and impeccable service. At least one member of European royalty or international celebrity is normally in residence. Although the hotel is located in the center of town, the surrounding parks, with rare species of plants, lend a secluded atmosphere. Closed mid-October to mid-December. (Corso Imperatrice 80, San Remo; phone: 0184-79991; expensive.)

Grand Hotel Londra – Dating from 1860, this large, elegant establishment was the first hotel to be built in San Remo, and it is still one of the great favorites. Closed October to mid-December. (Corso Matuzia 2, San Remo; phone: 0184-79961; expensive.)

Astoria West-End – Another large hotel, this one is considerably more modern than the two previously mentioned, but it has similar amenities and a high standard of service. (Corso Matuzia 8, San Remo; phone: 0184-70791; expensive.)

EATING OUT: Pesce d'Oro – Regarded as one of the best in Italy, for its pasta dishes with *pesto* (a sauce made with fresh basil, pine nuts, and garlic) and excellent fish. Try the *zuppa di frutti di mare* (seafood soup), with either the local Pigato or Rossese wine, for a particularly memorable experience. Closed Mondays and from mid-February to mid-March; reservations advisable. (Corso Cavallotti 272, San Remo; phone: 0184-66332; expensive.)

Ristorante Casino – Compared with that of other Italian restaurants, the atmosphere here is formal, but this does not deter the devoted. Both the kitchen and the service are excellent. (Corso Inglesi, San Remo; phone: 0184-79901; expensive.)

Da Giannino – A small, simple place particularly well known for its *tagliolini integrali al nero di seppia* (whole-wheat pasta in squid ink sauce). The *branzino in salsa di ribes* (sea bass with currant sauce) is another specialty. Closed Sundays and Monday midday. (Lungomare Trento e Trieste 23, San Remo; phone 0184-70843; expensive to moderate.)

En Route from San Remo – Take the short but worthwhile detour to Bussana Vecchia. Exit from A10 about 2 miles out of San Remo (if the exit is still under construction, use the Via Aurelia instead). This medieval village was leveled by an earthquake in 1887 and all its inhabitants were killed when the church, where they had taken refuge, collapsed. Recently a community of artists have started to work and live in the village; they have made charming homes and studios within the restored interiors of the old buildings without changing the exteriors. Beyond Bussana Vecchia, for the next 30 miles or so, the route is lined with industrial developments, but there is a fine strip of beach at Alassio. There are also two very good restaurants along this stretch.

EATING OUT: Lanterna Blu–da Tonino – This restaurant, with a friendly, relaxed atmosphere, is regarded as one of the best in Liguria. Its specialties are *scampi* (shrimp) and *bianchetti* (tiny anchovies and sardines). The building, one of the most attractive in an otherwise busy, modern harbor, dates from the 1700s. During the summer it's pleasant to eat outside and watch the fishing boats go by. Open daily in July and August, closed Wednesdays the rest of the year. (Borgo Marina, Porto Maurizio; phone: 0183-63859; expensive to moderate.)

Salvo-Cacciatori – Another great favorite with the Italians, this excellent restaurant is situated just to the east of Imperia. (The *Lanterna Blu* lies to the west. If you happen to be en route from one to the other and it's June 24, you will have to make a detour because the Via Aurelia is closed in Imperia for the feast of St. John the Baptist, when wild pigs are roasted in the street!) Fish is the thing to eat here, especially *bottarga* (fish eggs). Closed Mondays and the first half of November. (Via Vieusseux 14, Oneglia; phone: 0183-23763; moderate.)

ALBENGA: This small, flourishing market town, which lies just in from the sea on a fertile plain, is the most important historical site on the western Riviera. From the 6th century BC, Albenga was the seat of the Ingaunian tribes, until it was conquered by Rome in 181 BC. It then became a prosperous commercial center with territorial supremacy stretching from Finale in the east to San Remo in the west. The fortified walls of the historic center are still largely intact; the layout of the medieval buildings within reveals the early Roman influence. The most distinctive and evocative features of the town are the 50 brick tower houses, many still in excellent condition. Except for an early invasion by the Goths, the city enjoyed a long period of peace. This accounts for the preservation of the most important Christian monument extant in Liguria, the 5th-century cathedral baptistry, with its decagonal exterior and octagonal interior, and fine blue and white mosaic, *Christ Amidst Doves*. The cathedral, except for the baptistry, was reconstructed in the 13th century. With a somber and impressive interior and a graceful, rather than imposing, exterior, it has many little corners where architectural features have not changed for centuries, most notably the Piazzetta dei Leoni, which lies behind the apse. Although subject to Genoese authority since 1251, Albenga retained considerable independence; building continued here until the 15th century. Tickets to the baptistry are available at the civic museum in the cathedral square. The civic museum has a collection of prehistoric artifacts and Roman exhibits relating to the town. Open daily, except Mondays, 10 AM to noon and 3 to 6 PM; phone: 0182-51215. Tourist information on Albegna and nearby towns is available at Viale Martiri della Libertà (phone: 0182-50475).

    En Route from Albenga – About 7 miles from Albenga, take the exit for Borghetto. Just north of A10 is the village of Toirano, where at the prehistoric museum (open daily, 9:30 to 11:30 AM and 2:30 to 6 PM) visitors can get tickets for a guided tour of the nearby Basura grottoes, filled with stalagmites and stalactites in pastel shades of rose and green. Tourist information is available in Albenga (address above).

FINALE-LIGURE: Ten miles farther along the coast is the pleasant resort of Finale, which has a very good beach. On the west side of town is a charming historical section known as Finalborgo. The harshness of the surrounding countryside makes the ornate, colorful buildings, many with *trompe l'oeil* effects, all the more attractive. The Convent of Santa Caterina, with its serene inner courtyards, is in vivid architectural contrast to the ruins of the 12th-century Castel Gavone, which stands above the town in massive isolation. Tourist information is at Via San Pietro 14 (phone: 019-692581).

    CHECKING IN: *La Residenza Punta Est* – One of the region's most delightful small hotels is situated on the outskirts of Finale, in a shady hilltop garden. The elegant complex of buildings has been converted from a private residence, and its ambience is still more like that of a private villa than a hotel. Closed mid-September to mid-May. (Via Aurelia, Finale; phone: 019-600612; moderate.)

SAVONA: There are some attractive fishing villages, such as Noli and Spotorno, on the way to Savona, and nearby Garlenda has an excellent golf club (see *Great Italian Golf,* DIVERSIONS), but, for the most part, the coastline from here to Genoa is dominated by industry and shipping. Savona is the largest town on the Riviera di Ponente and is itself a large industrial complex. In its small historic center, however, is a civic gallery containing a rich collection of 14th- to 18th-century paintings that are well worth a visit. Most of the paintings are Lombard and Ligurian, including works by Foppa and Magnasco. Open daily, except Mondays, 9 AM to noon and 3 to 6 PM; Sundays, morning hours only. (Via Quarda Superiore 7; phone: 019-26201). Tourist information is at Via Paleocapa 7 (phone: 019-20522).

    EATING OUT: *Sodano* – In the middle of the medieval section of town is an attractive, spacious Renaissance eatery with a black and white decor that manages to be cool in summer and cozy in winter. *Cima,* the specialty here, is a veal joint stuffed with vegetables and eggs, served warm rather than hot; it is a traditional dish and one of the most popular in Liguria. Open evenings, also midday Sundays; closed Mondays. (Piazza della Maddalena 9, Savona; phone: 019-38446; moderate.)

La Farinata – In this very lively, crowded spot, frequented mainly by locals, any fish dish will be delicious and fresh and should be eaten with *farinata,* roasted flat cakes made from corn and chickpeas. From the street this restaurant looks like a bakery only, but don't be put off, for there are two large rooms behind the shopfront. Open for lunch and dinner, or take away a *farinata* any time of day; closed Sundays and Mondays. (Via Pia 15, Savona; very inexpensive.)

GENOA: This dynamic city, sprawling up the Ligurian hillsides and along the coastline for nearly 25 miles, is the principal Italian port as well as one of the most important maritime centers on the Mediterranean. Many visitors to Liguria, intent on sun and sea, bypass Genoa, but it is a city of vivid contrasts, and a little exploration will reveal that it has many hidden treasures and a beauty of its own.

From the 5th century BC, when it became a Roman center of considerable importance, Genoa expanded in size and wealth. Gradually, by the 14th century, it reigned supreme over the entire Riviera, a position which in many ways it has never relinquished. Known as La Superba, for the pride of its inhabitants, it also played a major role in Italian unification. The narrow alleys (*caruggi*) and small piazzas of the city's historic center contrast with the orderly layout of its modern sections. Besides containing a number of exceptionally important galleries, museums, and palaces, Genoa is a city where people have fun. For full details on sights, hotels, and restaurants, see *Genoa,* THE CITIES.

RAPALLO: Only 17 miles from the center of Genoa is one of Europe's most renowned resorts. Rapallo passed its peak before the last war, but the splendid yachts anchored in its perfect bay testify to the town's continuing, if largely nostalgic, popularity. Rapallo is a city of ancient origins. Hannibal is said to have passed through here after he crossed the Alps; the Roman single-span bridge on the east side of the bay has been named after him. The town was under the jurisdiction of the bishops of Milan until 644, after which Genoese influence prevailed. Its most notable monuments are from the 14th to the 15th century. Examples from this period are the Leper House of San Lazarus, which still bears the original frescoes on its exterior, and the cathedral of Saints Gervasio and Protasio. The cathedral was founded in the 6th century, reaching its present proportions only in 1606. Behind the modern, palm and orange tree–lined promenade lie the remains of the medieval quarters, where over 500 years ago the wives of sailors and fishermen developed a lacemaking technique still in use today. In the quaint shop of Emilio Gandolfi (Piazza Cavour 1, phone: 0185-50234), dedicated shoppers can still find exquisite lace, although extremely expensive, suitable to pass on as a family heirloom. Tourist information offices are at Via Diaz 9 (phone: 0185-51282).

CHECKING IN: *Bristol* – Now the only ultramodern building on the Riviera after recent extensive renovations. Besides seclusion, guests enjoy all the usual comforts in a luxurious and relaxing environment, as well as superb views of the bay. Closed December. (Via Aurelia Orientale 369, Rapallo; phone: 0185-273313; expensive.)

Eurotel – Well established but smaller than the *Bristol* and close to the harbor. It has a pool and a good restaurant. (Via Aurelia Occidentale 22, Rapallo; phone: 0185-60981; expensive to moderate.)

EATING OUT: *Da Ardito* – *Pansotti,* a pasta stuffed with walnut sauce, is just one of many appetizing options in this popular *trattoria.* Closed Tuesdays. (Via Canale 9, San Pietro di Novello; phone: 0185-51551; moderate to inexpensive.)

Savoia – A cut above the average pizzeria, this is a sunny, bright, friendly place with a view of the promenade. Features exceptionally good pizza, as well as seafood. Open daily. (Piazza IV Novembre 3, Rapallo; phone: 0185-274021; inexpensive.)

En Route from Rapallo – Penisola di Portofino (Portofino Peninsula) is a little off the beaten track, but far too good to miss. From Rapallo, detour onto south-bound SS227. Only 2 miles down the road is Santa Margherita Ligure, which is a more sedate, less developed version of Rapallo; many people prefer it to the busier town. Three miles away is the exquisite fishing village of Portofino. It's best to leave your car at Santa Margherita and take one of the frequent buses to Portofino. Not only are the roads narrow here, but parking is impossible, and Monte Portofino is now a national park with stringent regulations to protect its wildlife and lush vegetation.

A tiny place, Portofino is known as the Pearl of the Riviera for its unspoiled charm and romantic land- and seascapes. It has two castles: Castello Brown was renovated by an Englishman in the 19th century; Castello San Giorgio was completely rebuilt at the beginning of this century by an American millionaire. Each April, to commemorate St. George's feast day, Portofino residents burn a huge pine tree in the center of the village. Depending on whether the tree falls to the left or the right as it burns out, good luck will follow for one side of the town or the other. During the bonfire, villagers and visitors alike feast on wonderful food and delicious wines. The tourist information office for Portofino is at Via Roma 35 (phone: 0185-69024).

From Portofino, you might take one of the frequent boat excursions to San Fruttuoso, also on the peninsula, but accessible only by sea. It is an even smaller village, with an abbey in its center. The original monastery, built in 711, was destroyed in a Saracen raid and then rebuilt after the 10th century. The church beside it is a young relation, having been founded only in the 13th century.

The Penisola di Portofino has some delightful hiking routes. Detailed maps are available at various tourist information offices. But be aware that during the summer even a short walk (of an hour or so) can be fatiguing in the heat; good shoes and sensible planning are essential. (See *Camping and Caravanning, Biking, and Hiking* in GETTING READY TO GO and *Walking* in DIVERSIONS.)

CHECKING IN: *Splendido* – Regarded as supreme among the many wonderful hotels along the Riviera, perhaps because the building is situated in what can only be described as paradise, or because the standards of service (implemented by a huge and efficient staff) are simply the best. Whatever the cause, be prepared for the treat of a lifetime. Reservations are required at least 3 months in advance for July and August. (Portofino; phone: 0185-695151; very expensive.)

Imperial Palace – Set in a spacious park, this luxury hotel combines all the modern comforts (including a heated pool) with Old World elegance — the bedrooms and public spaces are furnished with antiques. Once a favorite retreat for members of the aristocracy, it also has a very good restaurant. Closed November to March. (Via Pagana 19, Santa Margherita Ligure; phone: 0185-88991; expensive.)

Grand Hotel Miramare – A more modern and lively but still very tasteful building overlooking the sea from tropical gardens. Open year-round. (Lungomare Ignoto 30, Santa Margherita Ligure; phone: 0185-87014; expensive.)

EATING OUT: *Il Pitosforo* – A very popular waterfront fish restaurant; reservations are essential. Closed Tuesdays, January, and February. (Portofino; phone: 0185-69020; expensive.)

La Trattoria Cesarina – There is a good cellar here — the Pegato wine is a favorite — and the specialties are regional fish and meat dishes. Closed Wednesdays and mid-February to mid-March. (Via Mameli 2, Santa Margherita Ligure; phone: 0185-86059; expensive to moderate.)

La Bassa Prora – This sunny, friendly, and relaxed Santa Margherita waterfront spot specializes in fresh fish. Closed Monday evenings, Tuesday middays, and mid-September to mid-October. (Via Garibaldi 7, Santa Margherita Ligure; phone: 0185-86586; moderate.)

LEVANTO: Back on A10 or the SS1, another 12 miles along the coast from Rapallo, the route turns inland, away from Sestri Levante (a tiny peninsula famous for its ceramics). Turn right at Passo del Bracco onto SS332 and drive 8 miles south to Levanto.

A small resort with the last good stretch of beach for the next 20 miles, Levanto has a delightful historic section with a number of interesting buildings. One is the 13th-century Town Hall, with five arcades gracefully adorning its exterior. Another is the 15th-century church of San Francesco, which contains an impressive painting of the miracle of San Diego by Bernardo Strozzi. There are also some very pleasant *trompe l'oeil* paintings on the exteriors of the townhouses. Levanto is the most convenient point — as an alternative to the larger town of La Spezia — to use as a base for touring the neighboring Cinque Terre. Tourist information is available at Piazza Colombo 12 (phone: 0187-808125).

CHECKING IN: *Stella d'Italia* – A well-run little hotel, the building itself is an elegant villa with a garden and a restaurant. Closed September to March; restaurant closed Mondays. (Corso Italia 26, Levanto; phone: 0187-808108; moderate to inexpensive.)

Stella Maris – All the rooms in this tiny *pensione* are painted in fresco and decorated with 18th-century furniture. The owners prepare all the delicious food themselves, including homemade ice cream. Reservations well in advance are essential for this Italian family experience. Closed November. (Via Marconi 4, Levanto; phone: 0187-808258; inexpensive.)

En Route from Levanto – The Cinque Terre is a string of five small fishing villages — nearly hidden between the mountains and the sea — that have changed very little over the centuries because, until recently, they were accessible only by donkey or by boat. Now the villages can be reached relatively easily by train or by road. Exit the Via Aurelia at the fork at Pian di Barca. This leads to the largest of the villages, Monterosso al Mare. We recommend parking your car here and walking to the other villages (you could also take the local trains). An experienced hiker could cover all five villages on one long day's march (of about 12 miles), but it is more enjoyable to take your time, strolling over the steeply terraced, vine-covered slopes. Vernazza is the most colorful of the five villages. Like Manarola and Riomaggiore, it sits on a tiny strip of coastline backed by a wall of sheer cliffs. Corniglia, in the center of the strip, is perched high on a hill, offering a fine view of the whole area. There are many little places in the Cinque Terre to take a break for a snack. Try a piece of the delicious *focaccia col formaggio* (a flat, savory cheesecake) and a glass of Sciacchetra, the region's celebrated white wine. Stay overnight only in Monterosso.

CHECKING IN/EATING OUT: *Porto Roca* – Perched on a cliff above Monterosso and surrounded by quiet, shady gardens, this modern hotel offers first-class service and cuisine. Closed November to March. (Monterosso; phone: 0187-817502; expensive to moderate.)

Il Gigante – Also in Monterosso, this restaurant specializes in shellfish soup and *risotto*. Closed October to March. (Monterosso; phone: 0187-817401; moderate.)

LA SPEZIA: Return to SS1 or A12 and drive another 8 miles or so to Italy's largest dockyard. The indented Golfo della Spezia is a natural safe harbor for the huge naval arsenal here, which can be visited only once a year — on the Sunday closest to March 19, the feast of the city's patron saint. La Spezia is a modern, highly industrialized city.

Consequently it is often able to offer accommodations on short notice when smaller nearby resorts are booked. The city has an interesting naval museum exhibiting relics from the Battle of Lepanto, as well as objects relating to sailing and steamships. Open 9 AM to noon and 3 to 6 PM Tuesdays, Thursdays, and Saturdays (Piazza Chiodo; phone: 0187-36151). The civic museum contains some remarkable statues from the Bronze and Iron ages and a collection of traditional costumes and household implements from the Cinque Terre. Open daily, except Monday afternoons and Sundays, 9 AM to 1 PM and 3 to 5 PM. (Via Curtatone 9; phone: 0187-37228). Tourist information and boat tours are both at Viale Mazzini 47 (phone: 0187-36000).

 CHECKING IN: *Jolly* – Not beautiful, but the service is dependable and good, and the facilities modern. (Via XX Settembre 2, La Spezia; phone: 0187-27200; expensive to moderate.)

Residence – Conveniently located on the edge of town, near the motorway, with comfortable, pleasant rooms. There is a bar but no restaurant. (Via Tino 62, La Spezia; phone: 0187-504141; moderate.)

 EATING OUT: *La Posta* – A traditional *trattoria,* serving good food in a convivial atmosphere. Try the *lattuga ripiena* (stuffed lettuce) and the *frittelle di baccalà* (stockfish in batter), both house specialties. Closed Saturdays, Sundays, and August. (Via Don Minzoni 24, La Spezia; phone: 0187-34419; moderate.)

Da Dino – A popular local restaurant specializing in seafood. Reservations are advisable, particularly for lunch. Closed Sunday evenings, Mondays, and late June to mid-July. (Via Da Passano 19, La Spezia; phone: 0187-509665; moderate.)

PORTOVENERE: A steeply pitched, pastel-colored little port town, 5 miles southwest of La Spezia, reachable on the SS530. Just opposite, across a narrow strait, is Isola Palmaria. Prehistoric man first settled the area, and then came the Romans (Petrarch refers to it in his poetry). In the 12th century Genoa came into power and began to give the little town the heavily fortified appearance it maintains today. Although isolated, many poets and writers have made their way to this idyllic place. Among the famous who have sought inspiration here were D. H. Lawrence, Percy Bysshe Shelley (who drowned nearby), and Lord Byron. At the extreme edge of the village, standing on a mass of rocks, is the church of San Pietro, a 13th-century Gothic construction with 6th-century interior elements still visible. Evidence suggests that the origins of the building were pagan and perhaps dedicated to the goddess of the sea. The town is dominated by the Genoese Castello, which offers a panoramic view of the surrounding area. Portovenere can also be reached by boat, and from here the trip can be extended to Isola Palmaria, with its famous blue grotto; Isola del Tino, where the ruins of the 11th-century abbey of San Venerio stand; and Isola Tinetto and its 6th-century monastery. Gold-veined black marble is quarried on these islands; marble items can be purchased in Portovenere.

CHECKING IN/EATING OUT: *Royal Sporting* – A stay at the Royal, with its lovely gardens and views, is a perfect alternative to the rush of nearby La Spezia. The pool and restaurant are very pleasantly situated. Closed October to April. (Portovenere; phone: 0187-900326; expensive to moderate.)

Locanda San Pietro – With fewer amenities than the *Royal,* this little hotel is nevertheless quite comfortable, and it has a very good restaurant. Closed January to mid-March. (Near the church of San Pietro, Portovenere; phone: 0187-900616; inexpensive.)

Piedmont and Valle d'Aosta

Tucked into northwestern Italy and dominated by the Alps, these two regions impress visitors not only with their unique topography but also with the hearty spirit of their people. *Piemonte* (meaning "at the foot of the mountains") borders France in the west and abuts the Valle d'Aosta, a tiny, semi-autonomous region of green valleys and glaciers wedged between Piedmont, Switzerland, and France.

There is no typical Piedmont landscape — the whole area is crisscrossed by rivers fed by sources high in the Alps traversing a landscape of mountains, plains, woodlands, and rolling hills. The Valle d'Aosta, on the other hand, is a perfect example of an alpine region, with farmlands in its deep valleys, pasture lands on the upper plateaus, and, higher, stately conifer forests and glittering glaciers overlooked by barren rocks and the snow-capped mountains.

The history of the two regions is linked, although not as closely as geography would suggest. The Valdostans — *valdostani* to the Italians — have always lived in a remote enclave, keeping themselves separate from the rest of Italy, both culturally and politically. They speak a patois closer to French than Italian, and their sense of their own national unity has generated a modest "independence movement," the intent of which is to loosen ties to the central Italian government. This separation movement does have an ancient historical precedent. Although both Piedmont and Valle d'Aosta were fiefs of the powerful house of Savoy, Piedmont was the personal possession of the Savoyard dukes, while Valle d'Aosta managed as early as the twelfth century to gain a constitution granting it a degree of freedom. That is not to say that the House of Savoy did not make its presence felt — Valle d'Aosta was a favorite Savoy playground, so the area is littered with hunting lodges, castles, and sanctuaries all built to serve the ruling family.

Valle d'Aosta's strategic position has made it a crossroads of history. Recent road construction has revealed evidence of the original inhabitants, the Salassi, a pre-Roman tribe that may have drifted in from France. In the third century BC Hannibal, with his troops and elephants, passed through the region. The Romans, heading in the other direction, entered Gaul through one of the numerous passes in the Valdostan Alps. Part of the Roman road to Gaul can still be seen at various points, and the regional capital at Aosta has extensive Roman remains. In 1800 Napoleon led his army through Valle d'Aosta on his way to conquer northern Italy.

For centuries pilgrims walked through Valle d'Aosta on their way to Rome. It was here that the famous St. Bernard dogs were trained to rescue travelers lost in the snow. St. Bernard himself was a canon of the Cathedral of Aosta charged with keeping the Alpine passes cleared of robbers and keeping track of the pilgrims intent on making their way south. The famous St. Bernard dogs — the little flagons of brandy tied under their necks — do come from this region and were used for tracking, but (disappointing to learn) St. Bernard didn't think up the plan himself. The dogs were bred here many years after his death and only named in his honor. St. Bernard is the patron saint of alpinists and mountain climbers. The dogs are still bred and kept at the hospice of the Great St. Bernard Pass (the hospice was founded by the saint), but these days German shepherd dogs are favored for rescue operations, as they are lighter and fit more easily into a helicopter (no brandy either).

Formed millennia ago by a vast glacier, the Valle d'Aosta is shaped much like an oak leaf, with a main valley as its spine. Running laterally like veins from this central valley are side valleys, usually not more than twenty-five miles of twisting road, most of which end in soaring mountains ten and twelve thousand feet high: Monte Bianco (Mont Blanc), the Matterhorn (Il Cervino in Italian), Monte Rosa (Mount Rosa), and the Gran Paradiso. Parco Nazionale del Gran Paradiso (the Gran Paradiso National Park) lies south of the central valley and runs over the mountains into Piedmont. The width of the central valley, the Vallata della Dora Baltea, varies in places, but wherever topography permits, local inhabitants make the best of a beautiful, if inhospitable, landscape. Where the valley is widest, there are vineyards and apple orchards.

The castles that dot the valley served for defense as well as for residences, as the Valle d'Aosta was the beginning of the main "highway" into central Italy. Watchmen at the castles kept a sharp lookout for invaders, but they also kept a close watch on ordinary travelers — they were a source of taxes, and the Savoyard and local rulers wanted their due. So meticulous were the customs agents back then that they even set a tax on the import of monkeys and elephants (one assumes the tax on the latter was not imposed when Hannibal passed through!).

The route for this tour runs from the Piedmont capital of Turin through the major provincial town of Ivrea and on into Valle d'Aosta. The distance from Turin to Aosta, the capital city of the Valle d'Aosta region, is just under eighty miles. This ancient and charming town makes a good base for trips throughout the region. This itinerary explores the "lateral" valleys of Gressoney and Valtournenche and visits the most interesting castles along the way. From Aosta, our route travels south to Cogne in the Gran Paradiso National Park. From there, a little doubling back leads to the ultra-chic ski resort of Courmayeur, near the French border, for an Italian-side view of Mont Blanc.

From June to October all but the highest roads can be negotiated without snow tires or chains, but these are essential from November to May. During the winter many of the passes are closed. The Great St. Bernard tunnel is open year-round. The autostrada (A5) runs direct from Turin to Aosta, but after Ivrea it might be best to take the state highway (SS26), which passes through many picturesque Valdostan towns and villages.

Those who are heading for Valle d'Aosta during prime ski season (advance booking essential from Christmas through March) might find themselves lucky enough to attend the thousand-year-old St. Orso fair. It is held in Aosta at the end of January, and its primary attraction is the array of fine local woodcarvings. Stone carving and lacemaking are also specialties of the region.

Expect to dine well and heartily in Valle d'Aosta. The climate encourages the stick-to-the-ribs sustenance of beef, game, and mountain trout. Also look forward to delicious dairy products, such as fondue of fontina cheese, *polenta,* and thick meat and vegetable soups. The best-known locally produced wine is the Sang des Salasses and that produced by the monks of the Great St. Bernard Abbey. In keeping with their appetites, *valdostani* drink from a giant beaker called *la grolla.*

The Valle d'Aosta region has both a winter and a summer season, the winter season lasting from Christmas to March and the summer from June to the end of August. During both, hotel reservations are necessary. Hotels rated as expensive charge $80 or more for a double; moderate, from $50 to $80; inexpensive, under $50. Expensive meals are $65 and up for two; moderate, between $40 and $65; inexpensive, under $40.

TURIN: For a detailed report on the city, its sights, hotels, and restaurants, see *Turin,* THE CITIES.

   En Route from Turin – Stop at Chivasso, Caluso, or Strambino to visit minor ruins. Otherwise, it is a quick drive north (about 35 miles) on A5 or SS26 through the Po Valley.

IVREA: This largely industrial city is considered the gateway to Valle d'Aosta, although still in the region of Piedmont. It has a fine castle, built by the Savoys in the 14th century, that is still largely intact. The true attraction of Ivrea is its unique two-week-long *carnevale,* usually held at the end of February. It seems that in the 12th century the local lord insisted on *droit de seigneur* (his rights) with a young miller's daughter. She pretended to agree to the Marquis's demands, but when the opportunity presented itself, she decapitated her would-be lover and set fire to his castle. Far from decrying her actions, the local *ivreasi* — presumably sick of this sort of thing — supported her and celebrated her freedom. This story, greatly embellished over the years, is reenacted each year in a parade in which, oddly enough, Napoleonic generals and officers appear, along with medieval pipers and squires. A feature of the *carnevale* is the battle of oranges, in which two teams — one on foot, the other mounted — pelt each other with fruit. If you are a spectator, be prepared to duck an unexpected dose of vitamin C.

 CHECKING IN: *Sirio* – A little over a mile north of Ivrea, overlooking a lake with the same name, this small, modern hotel offers its guests rowing, swimming, fishing, and sailing. In addition, it houses the town's finest restaurant. (Via Lago Sirio 85, Ivrea; phone: 0125-423646, -40862; expensive to moderate.)

   ***Moro* –** A small, homey downtown establishment that serves a good prix fixe dinner. (Corso Massimo D'Azeglio 41, Ivrea; phone: 0125-40170; inexpensive.)

 EATING OUT: *Ristorante Arancere* – For tasty local cuisine and attentive service, try this cozy, wood-paneled restaurant set under the arcades of a fine neoclassical square. Closed Sundays. (Piazza Ottinetti, Ivrea; phone: 0125-422443; moderate.)

PONT-ST.-MARTIN: The climb into the Valle d'Aosta proper begins at the tiny hamlet of Pont-St.-Martin, a pretty little town that seems more French than Italian. Here a Roman bridge of the 1st century BC still spans the river Lys.

CHECKING IN: *Ponte Romano* – A well-maintained and well-attended hostelry overlooking the Roman bridge, as the name suggests. (Piazza IV Novembre 10, Pont-St.-Martin; phone: 0125-82108, -84329; moderate.)

 EATING OUT: *Ristorante Dora* – Besides appetizing hot hors d'oeuvres and good game dishes, customers receive a painted ceramic plate as a souvenir of the meal. Near the railway station. Closed Mondays and the second half of September. (Via della Resistenza 10, Pont-St.-Martin; phone: 0125-82035; moderate.)

En Route from Pont-St.-Martin – Drive north into the beautiful Gressoney Valley on a winding 25-mile road that leads ever higher into the mountains and closer to the towering majesty of Monte Rosa, one of the principal peaks in this part of the country. The mountain takes its name from its deep, rose-red color at sunset, a sight worth seeing despite the drive down afterward in total darkness (caution is advised). More Swiss than Italian, valley inhabitants are descended from the Walser people who crossed over from Switzerland several centuries ago — and have clung tenaciously to their old customs.

GRESSONEY-ST.-JEAN: The largest town in the valley, where the former villa of Queen Margherita of the Italian royal family now houses the local tourist authority.

 CHECKING IN: *Lyskamm* – Quiet and clean, with magnificent views of the surrounding countryside. Like most hotels of its size and class, it is not open year-round. (Gressoney-St.-Jean; phone: 0125-355436; moderate.)

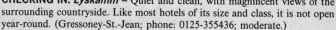 **EATING OUT: *Lo Stambecco*** – Named for the local mountain goat (*ibex* in English) and an excellent place to rest and "refuel" after a long drive in the mountains. The game dishes, open-fire roasted meats, and cornmeal *polenta* are guaranteed to revive the weariest traveler. Closed Wednesdays. (Via Deffeyes, Gressoney-St.-Jean; phone: 0125-355201; moderate to inexpensive.)

En Route from Gressoney-St.-Jean – To visit the next valley, which runs parallel to the Gressoney, retrace the route to Pont-St.-Martin and then follow signs for Aosta. Near Donnas, a yellow sign indicates the location of part of the Roman road to Gaul. (As there is a danger of falling rock, the section of ancient road is fenced off.) Just beyond Donnas is the great fortress of Bard. Built in the 10th century by Ottone of Bard, it commands the narrow gorge below. Napoleon led an entire army up this gorge at night without raising the alarm of the garrison.

ISSOGNE: Four miles along the road from Bard a signpost marks the turnoff to the Castle of Issogne. From the outside, the unprepossessing castle seems to be nothing more than the largest building in the village. Inside, it is fascinating, both historically and artistically. It was the residence of the Challont family, one of the most powerful in Valle d'Aosta, who in the 15th century created a cultured oasis here. The atrium and portico are decorated with frescoes which, because of the rarified climate, have remained remarkably intact. The pictures are a charming record of local life, with scenes of butcher shops, tailors, fruit and vegetable markets, and the local pharmacy. As the exterior walls of the castle tell much about the life of the common folk of the age, so the interior is a marvelous record of the lives of their "betters." The noble bedrooms have attached chapels; there is a room for storage of the carpets and thick wall coverings that helped retain precious heat in the winter. Even here, in the remoteness of the Alps, protocol had an important part to play in the life of the nobility — elaborate assembly halls and opulent rooms were kept just in case the family had to entertain a passing Savoy duke or French king. Open daily, 9:30 AM to noon and 2 to 4:30 PM March to November; 9:30 to 11:30 AM and 2 to 4 PM December to February. Closed Mondays. Admission fee.

VERRÈS: Immediately beyond Issogne on the main highway is the village of Verrès.

The castle here was built by the same Challont family who constructed the manor at Issogne. A much earlier structure, however, it was built for defense rather than gracious living. A huge cube measuring some 90 feet along each wall, it has a square courtyard and a number of large high-ceilinged rooms. Completed in 1390, it was designed to display the power of Ibleto di Challont, the duke of Savoy's regent in the district. It still makes a strong impression. Open daily, 9:30 AM to noon and 2 to 4:30 PM March to November; 9:30 to 11:30 AM and 2 to 4 PM December to February. Closed Wednesdays. Admission fee.

 CHECKING IN: *Evançon* – Pleasant and quiet, with a charming garden and a small restaurant. Rooms are spacious and bright, if a touch Spartan. (Via Circonvallazione 9, Verrès; phone: 0125-929035; inexpensive.)

 EATING OUT: *Da Pierre* – The chef makes the most of good local ingredients, with outstanding selections that include mushroom and game dishes in season; homemade pâtés; delicious *agnolotti* (large ravioli) stuffed with a variety of fillings; and trout with almonds. The homemade desserts are excellent, especially the *gelato di crema con zabaione caldo* (homemade vanilla ice cream with hot *zabaione*). Closed Mondays and Tuesdays. (Via Martorey 43, Verrès; phone: 0125-929376; expensive to moderate.)

SAINT-VINCENT: Before entering the Valtournenche, spend some time in Saint-Vincent, often called the Riviera of the Alps. Protected by the imposing bulk of Mount Zerbion, the town has a mild climate and Mediterranean vegetation. Its curative hot springs drew visitors as early as the 18th century. It is still one of the chic-est communities in Valle d'Aosta, home to Europe's largest casino (open year-round) as well as fine hotels and a wide range of shops and restaurants.

 CHECKING IN: *Grand Hotel Billia* – In addition to a lovely parkland setting, this large turn-of-the-century hotel has a heated swimming pool, tennis courts, and direct access to the hot springs. There is a fine restaurant and a passageway that leads from the hotel to a nightclub and the casino. The whole effect is not unlike discovering a miniature Palm Springs or Monte Carlo in the middle of the Alps. (Viale Piemonte 18, Saint-Vincent; phone: 0166-2011; expensive.)

***Elena* –** Small, extremely well run, and centrally located. Less magnificent than the *Billia,* but luxurious in its own way. (Piazza Zerbion, Saint-Vincent; phone: 0166-2140; moderate.)

***Posta* –** Efficiently managed and well staffed, with an inexpensive but well-recommended restaurant and a good location. (Piazza XXV Aprile, Saint-Vincent; phone: 0166-2250; inexpensive.)

 EATING OUT: *Batezar–Da Renato* – Small and elegant, with a limited but exquisite menu and the finest service. Specialties include *pazzarella* (a pizza garnished with mushrooms and truffles), cannelloni, and filet of lamb with mint. With only eight tables, reservations are essential. (Via Marconi 1, Saint-Vincent; phone: 0166-3164; expensive.)

***Le Grenier* –** After cocktails on the upper level, diners descend to the warm, rustic dining room for excellent fondues and trout. Closed Tuesdays. (Piazza Zerbion 1, Saint-Vincent; phone: 0166-2224; expensive.)

En Route from Saint-Vincent – The entrance to the long, deep Valtournenche is approached from Chatillon on SS406, a few miles north of Saint-Vincent. The Matterhorn, rising to 14,700 feet, stands at the head of this valley, with the town of Breuil-Cervinia just beneath it.

BREUIL-CERVINIA: Most attempts on the mountain have been made from this base. Until 1937 the town had little importance as a resort, but in that year it was linked to the outside by the first proper roadway and a cable car. Since then, intrepid climbers have had to share the neighborhood with skiers, who come in droves to enjoy the Matterhorn's long ski runs, and with nonskiers, who come merely to see the magnificent mountain and the surrounding scenery. Development of the little town, unfortunately, has been too rapid to be entirely tasteful.

CHECKING IN: *Cristallo* – Amid quiet luxury and unobstructed views of the Matterhorn and its surrounding mountains, guests are pampered by an extremely attentive staff. Other amenities include an indoor swimming pool, tennis courts, and a lovely garden where guests can admire the view and take the mountain air. Open December to May, July, and August. (Breuil-Cervinia; phone: 0166-948121; expensive.)

Hostelerie des Gardes – Opened to coincide with the 100th anniversary of the conquest of the Matterhorn, this establishment has the atmosphere of an English gentlemen's club. The lobby is a mini-museum to the feats of mountaineering; although emphasis is on the exploits of the Matterhorn guides (who have their office in the hotel), the museum also features mountaineering arcana from points as diverse as Canada and Nepal. There is a fine bar and billiard room. (Via J. A. Carrel, Breuil-Cervinia; phone: 0166-949473; moderate.)

Hermitage – The roaring fireplace in the lobby is indicative of the cozy and friendly mountain atmosphere throughout. The restaurant has giant windows looking out at the Matterhorn. It is not unusual to find the owner seated at one of the tables following with his binoculars the progress of a climb on the mountain. Open mid-November to mid-May and early July to mid-September. (Breuil-Cervinia; phone: 948434; moderate.)

EATING OUT: *Copa Pan* – Casual atmosphere and local Valdostan specialties; particularly good fondues. (Via Jumeaux, Breuil-Cervinia; phone: 0166-949140; moderate.)

Les Neiges d'Antan – About 2½ miles southwest of town, and one of those rare finds — a first-class restaurant at a moderate price. In addition to friendly, attentive service, this family-run restaurant/guesthouse features delicious local *antipasti*, particularly sausages and pâtés, as well as an excellent onion soup. Good second courses are trout grilled in butter and tiny quail with *polenta*. There is a huge selection of local cheeses and lots of homemade puddings and pies. Reservations suggested. (Strada Statale 406, Breuil-Cervinia; phone: 0166-949775; moderate.)

En Route from Breuil-Cervinia – On the state highway, just after the village of St. Denis, is the 14th-century castle of Fénis, one of the best-preserved and most picturesque in Europe. Its powerful double walls and jumble of squared and cylindrical towers make the castle look virtually impregnable. Within, surrounded by loggias and galleries, is a courtyard giving access to richly decorated rooms. The frescoes adorning the various apartments have been restored to some degree; in the State Room, a magnificent *St. George and the Dragon* is a first-class example of Gothic painting. Closed Tuesdays.

AOSTA: The capital of the region is an ancient settlement; the old town is still contained within the walls built by the Romans a hundred or so years before Christ. Among the many Roman remains are the Arch of Augustus, a fine theater with the cavea intact, the Porta Pretoria, and the single-arched bridge over the Buthier River. There are a number of imposing medieval sights as well. The Church of St. Orso has a magnificent cloister, although the interior of this 10th-century structure has suffered two overzealous restorations. The medieval towers set in the city walls look as strong today as they must have been when they were built between the 12th and 13th centuries. One such tower is, sadly, called the *Torre del Lebbroso,* commemorating the internment there of a lone leper for the greater part of his life. The part of the city enclosed by

Roman walls has been closed to motor traffic, making it an enjoyable area for strolling. Here there is a variety of shops stocking both Italian and French products, as well as typical Valdostan handicrafts — lace, wood and stone carvings, and such local delicacies as *tegole* (almond cookies) and, for those who fancy it, *mocetta* (dried reindeer meat) — which are featured at the Festival of St. Orso held at the end of January.

CHECKING IN: *Valle d'Aosta* – The best place to stay if you are traveling by car. Located about a kilometer out of town, it even has a heated garage. Accommodations are clean, quiet, and comfortable; restaurant and bar. (Corso Ivrea 146, Aosta; phone: 0165-41845; expensive to moderate.)

Turin – A modest but spotlessly clean and cheerfully run establishment in the middle of town. (Via Torino 14, Aosta; phone: 0165-44593; moderate.)

EATING OUT: *Cavallo Bianco* – Formerly the site of a 16th-century carriage stop and now one of the best restaurants in the entire province. A massive hearth in the middle of the room is the backdrop for excellent food, particularly the chamois ham, the fondue, and the vegetable pie. There is an extensive list of regional wines. Excellent service. Reservations suggested. Closed Sundays and for lunch Mondays. (Via Aubert 15, Aosta; phone: 0165-2214; expensive.)

Brasserie Valdôtaine – A typical mountain *birreria* with wood-paneled walls and a warm and inviting atmosphere, where local specialties such as good grilled meats and sausages and Valdostan fondue are featured. Closed Thursdays. (Via Xavier de Maistre, Aosta; phone: 0165-32076; moderate.)

Piemonte – The owner/chef plies his trade in the kitchen, turning out dishes that include various home-cured hams and fresh tagliatelle and peppers in a *bagna caôda*, a "hot bath" of anchovies, oil, and garlic. Closed Sundays. (Via Porte Pretoriane 13, Aosta; phone 0165-40111; moderate to inexpensive.)

En Route from Aosta – About four miles west of Aosta toward Mont Blanc is the sign for Cogne. Watch for the two magnificent castles visible from the turnoff. One, standing on an isolated rock, is St. Pierre, the most fairy tale–like of all the Valdostan castles. The locals claim that this is the one that Walt Disney must have had in mind when he built Disneyland. Unfortunately, it is open only sporadically (a good time to visit is the summer, when there are archaeological exhibitions). Above St. Pierre is the 13th-century fortress of Sarre. This imposing building was once used as a hunting lodge by the Savoy family, a fact attested to by the enormous number of hunting trophies on display. The castle of Sarre is open only in the summer. Nearby, also on the road to Cogne, is the four-towered castle of Aymaville, dating from the mid-15th century and only recently opened to visitors.

COGNE: A mountain village known for lacemaking and woodcarving, Cogne is the gateway to the Gran Paradiso National Park. Founded in 1922, the park is the best-preserved Alpine nature reserve in the world. Its flora and fauna are representative of the Alps in general: Edelweiss, gentian, artemisia, and juniper grow in profusion or can be seen at the Giardino Alpino in the park itself. Chamois and the ibex — once threatened by extinction — are now quite plentiful here, as are the fox, hare, marmot, and stoat. The rarest Alpine birds, notably the eagle, owl, and imperial raven, are occasionally visible. While hunting and scavenging are strictly forbidden in the park, hiking is encouraged and, in winter, there are some 40 miles of cross-country skiing trails around Cogne. The Gran Paradiso National Park is open year-round.

EATING OUT: *Lou Ressignon* – Just beyond Cogne on the main road is a family-run restaurant that dispenses good local food. Chamois, served either as an hors d'oeuvres or as a main course, delicious *polenta*, an extremely filling rice and bread soup (*soupe à la cogneintze*), and veal *carbonada* (marinated in red wine) are specialties of the house. (Via Bourgeois 81, Cogne; phone: 0165-74034; moderate.)

COURMAYEUR: Courmayeur was not popular as a resort until the British discovered it in the late 18th century. These prototypical alpinists came for the fine air, the beautiful views, and the excellent climbing and skiing on the slopes of Mont Blanc and environs. The town gained importance with the 1965 opening of the Mont Blanc tunnel, which brought many more visitors. Today it is an elegant resort, an Italian equivalent of Gstaad or Klosters in Switzerland. But it is much more than a winter vacation spot; the sheltering effect of Mont Blanc makes the summer climate far more agreeable than that of Chamonix on the other side of the border, so there is also an active season for walkers and hikers and those who just come to take the air, as well as for summer skiers. One of the most exciting cable-car journeys in the Alps is that from La Palud, just two miles away, over the Mont Blanc massif, with views of the "sea of glaciers" that wend their way down the sides of the mountain. The highest point of the ride is 12,400 feet, from which the entire Chamonix Valley is visible.

Courmayeur attracts the sort of vacationers that make it worthwhile for the best Roman, Milanese, and international retailers to keep permanent stores here, so the shopping is excellent. Especially on Via Roma, such names as *Cartier, Trussardi, Valentino, Fendi,* and *Armani* are easily found. In the center of town is the *Museo Duca degli Abruzzi,* one of the best mountaineering museums in Europe.

CHECKING IN: Most hotels close for some weeks from April to June and from September to December.

Pavillon – A member of the prestigious Relais et Châteaux association and the finest hotel in Courmayeur. All 40 rooms have balconies with stupendous views. Beautifully situated, it is only 2 minutes from a ski lift, and for those who find a few miles of skiing on Mont Blanc not enough exercise, there is a covered, heated swimming pool, complete with a lovely solarium and sauna. There is a relaxing bar for après-ski. (Strada Regionale 60–62, Courmayeur; phone: 0165-842420; expensive.)

Royal e Golf – A sleek, modern place set in a lovely garden with beautiful views of the mountains and glaciers. Guests can swim in the heated swimming pool and are also provided with ski lift passes. (Via Roma 81–83, Courmayeur; phone: 0165-843621; expensive.)

Dolonne – Housed in a tastefully remodeled 17th-century house, with spacious and comfortably furnished rooms. A nearby cableway gives immediate access to the ski slopes of Val Veny. Breakfast only. (Via delle Vittorie 62, Courmayeur; phone: 0165-841260; moderate.)

Lo Bouton d'Or – Small but clean, comfortable, and tastefully furnished rooms, some with views of Mont Blanc and others facing the valley and less majestic mountains. Breakfast only, but it's very near *Le Vieux Pommier* (see *Eating Out*). (Strada Statale 26, Courmayeur; phone: 0165-842380; inexpensive.)

EATING OUT: *Le Bistroquet* – Housed in the *Pavillon,* this is the grand restaurant of Courmayeur. In addition to delicious local delicacies, such as *bagna caôda,* a hot dipping sauce for vegetables that sometimes contains the local thistle, and a wide range of fondues, there are excellent pastas and *risotto,* as well as fine cuts of meat grilled to perfection. (Strada Regionale 60–62, Courmayeur; phone: 0165-842240; expensive.)

Le Vieux Pommier – An excellent family-run establishment, associated with *Lo Bouton d'Or* (see *Checking In*), featuring various preparations of dried Alpine beef, pasta, fondue, and homemade desserts. (Piazzale Monte Bianco 25, Courmayeur; phone: 0165-842241; moderate.)

Va Cherie – A few miles south, on the state highway between Morgex and Pré-Saint-Didier, this restaurant specializes in seafood, a nice change of pace for the region. The ground floor holds an expansive bar with an open fireplace, a charming place to sit before or after dinner. Closed Wednesdays. (Between Morgex and Pré-Saint-Didier; phone: 0165-80777; Moderate.)

La Maison de Filippe – The food is so good and the prices so low that even the grandees at the *Pavillon* and the *Royal* come here to eat. A prix fixe meal includes an incredible number of courses — dozens of appetizers which make up the bulk of the menu. The restaurant itself is rustic and intimate, with outdoor dining in the summer. (Just north of Courmayeur in Entrèves; phone: 0165-89968; inexpensive.)

LA THUILE: A small resort town, a few miles along SS26 toward the Little St. Bernard Pass, with ski lifts linking directly with the La Rosière–Montvalenza resort area in France.

CHECKING IN: *Planibel Hotel and Residence* – A vast complex that takes in the bulk of the skiers who come to La Thuile, it has a skating rink, squash courts, restaurants, pubs, pizzerias, and a complete range of shops, including a supermarket. (Some rooms have cooking facilities.) Very much a "fun for the whole family" kind of place. (La Thuile; phone: 0165-684541; expensive.)

En Route from La Thuile – In summer, drive through the Little St. Bernard Pass (which is closed in winter) to Bourg St. Maurice in France and then descend the beautiful Val d'Isère. Reenter Italy at the Colle di Liseran, in the Piedmont section of the Gran Paradiso National Park. At San Giorgio, just outside Ivrea, rejoin the Turin-Aosta autostrada (A5), which connects with highways leading to Milan and Genoa.

The Lombardy Lakes

The Italian lakes have been a playground since the Romans conquered Gaul and Cicero set up a summer house on Lake Como. They continue to get good press: Wordsworth, Stendhal, D. H. Lawrence, and Hemingway were all inspired by the spectacular and majestic beauty of this most romantic of landscapes. Rossini, Donizetti, and Liszt were moved to compose music in response to its spellbinding natural beauty. The lakes are in the far north of Italy, in the region of Lombardy, although they also touch the region of Piedmont to the west and the Veneto and Trentino–Alto Adige regions to the east. South of them is the rest of Lombardy, a good deal larger than just its lake district, and north is Switzerland, into whose territory the topmost segment of Lake Maggiore projects and whose border dips to surround a good chunk of Lake Lugano. The lakes were originally formed by the same glaciers that cut the peaks and valleys of the nearby Alps into such fine relief, and up here the towering Swiss Alps are constantly in view.

The intense natural splendor of the landscape is embellished by some of the finest examples of manmade beauty. The lakeshores are dotted with palatial villas, the grandeur and opulence of which sometimes defy belief. And the lakes themselves are far from alike in mood and character. There are marked contrasts between the fine aristocratic bearing of Stresa on Lake Maggiore, the dreaminess of Lake Como, the more rugged scenery around Lake Iseo, and the magnificent mountain countryside around the highly sophisticated and developed Lake Garda.

The 2,000-year history of Lombardy has been scarred by war and domination, but the turbulent past has left a splendid heritage of castles, fortresses, and towers in the ancient cities and hill towns throughout the region. The earliest known invaders were the Etruscans, who came north from Tuscany to settle in the fertile plain of Lombardy, south of the lake district. Later came the Romans, who included Lombardy in their province of Cisalpine Gaul. The barbarian Longobard tribe invaded in the sixth century and, in retrospect, left the region a name. After their departure, Charlemagne, bishops of Milan, the Holy Roman Emperor Otto I, sundry feudal lords, as well as some independent city-states, or communes, all had something to say about some part of Lombardy at some time. In the twelfth century, in an effort to resist the authority of another Holy Roman Emperor, Frederick I, or, as he is better known, Barbarossa, some of these communes joined forces by forming the Lombard League, and they did indeed defeat him at Legnano in 1176. But their newfound freedom was brief. Foreign domination was replaced by civil strife, and the territory was carved up between the powerful families whose names — Visconti, Sforza, Pallavicino, and Gonzaga, among others — are remembered today in the wealth of beautiful villas, castles, and works of art they built or acquired during this early Renaissance period.

At the beginning of the fifteenth century, the powerful Republic of Venice moved into the eastern part of the region, annexing Bergamo and Brescia, among other areas. The Venetians were followed by another wave of foreign invaders who penetrated farther afield: first the French, in the sixteenth century, then the Spanish, who stayed for 200 years, and finally the Austrian Hapsburgs. Apart from a brief hiatus under Napoleon in the early nineteenth century, Lombardy remained under Austrian control until 1859, when an allied French and Piedmontese victory finally ousted them. Lombardy thus became part of the independent kingdom of Italy just one year before Garibaldi and his thousand men achieved unification for most of the rest of the peninsula.

Perhaps because of their long history of domination, the people of Lombardy — the *lombardi* — are intensely proud of being Italian. Statues of Garibaldi are never more prominent than in the town squares of this region. Also very strong is a pride in the beauty of their homeland, which they are keen to show off to the visitor. Travelers who master even a few basic words of Italian will be rewarded by an extraordinary helpfulness and readiness to explain on the part of the people who live here.

Visitors to Italy and to Lombardy sometimes neglect the lakes in favor of towns with more established traditions as cultural and artistic capitals. But within the lake region itself are numerous fine cities whose architecture, museums, and monuments are wonderfully rich. The region has the bonus of a breathtaking natural landscape with clear air, piercingly blue water that is safe for swimming, and miles of glorious rolling hills, woods, and mountains to be explored or simply admired. This is an area endowed with all the natural beauty of Switzerland, combined with the unmistakable warmth of the Italian people.

Lombardy is also a fertile and very prosperous region, leagues apart from the poorer southern regions of the peninsula, and its cooking reflects the richness of the soil and the relative wealth of its people. The local cuisine is based on plentiful supplies of meat, game, and, naturally, lake fish, all prepared with skill and sophistication. Specialties include *polenta,* often inelegantly translated as cornmeal mush, plus venison and wild boar and other game, and fresh trout and the delicate *persico* (perch). The wines of the Franciacorta zone include a sparkling white the Italians claim rivals anything produced over the border in France.

Many of the fine villas around the lakes, especially those at Maggiore and Como, have magnificent gardens, so a visit in late April, May, or June will be rewarded with the spectacle of a riot of colors and scents. On Lake Garda, the peculiarly Mediterranean climate also makes spring a very attractive time of year. But to take advantage of all that the lakes have to offer — boat trips, swimming, water sports, evening strolls along the lakeshore, and dinners savored out of doors at the water's edge — the summer months are best. The majority of lakeside hotels and many restaurants close for the winter months from November to Easter.

The route outlined here heads northwest from Milan, the capital of Lombardy, to the attractive medieval town of Varese. It then proceeds west to Lake Maggiore, which is not the major lake of Lombardy, its name notwithstanding. After visiting both sides of Maggiore, it cuts east to explore Lake Lugano and a bit of its Swiss surroundings before arriving at Lake Como, of the distinctive upside-down Y shape. From here, the route continues eastward to the ancient hill town of Bergamo, to the smaller, lesser-known Lake Iseo, and to the historic city of Brescia. It ends still farther east, with a circle around the last, largest, and best known of the Lombardy lakes, Lake Garda.

A tour of the area would not be complete without the magical experience of spending at least one night in an aristocratic villa on the lakeshore, although travelers who savor the very grand will pay for it: Prices for a double room at the palatial *Grand Hotel Villa d'Este* in Cernobbio on Lake Como begin at $200 a night. But it is still perfectly possible to stay in hotels of great comfort, lakeside and otherwise, for far more reasonable rates. In the listings below, an expensive hotel is one charging $75 and up for a double room. A moderate one will cost between $40 and $70, and an inexpensive one will cost $35 or less. In the restaurant listings, the expensive category means dinner for two will come to more than $60; moderate means $25 to $60, and inexpensive, under $25. Prices do not include alcoholic drinks other than a basic house wine.

MILAN: For a detailed report on the city, its sights, hotels, and restaurants, see *Milan,* THE CITIES.

   En Route from Milan – Take SS233 northwest to Varese, 32 miles from Milan and 3 miles away from its own lake, Lago di Varese.
VARESE: An attractive market town of medieval origin, it is also a prosperous commercial center, known for its production of shoes. Like Rome, it is surrounded by seven hills. The town's most striking monument is the 254-foot-high bell tower of the *Basilica di San Vittore,* designed by Varese architect Giuseppe Bernascone in the early 17th century. At the foot of the tower stands Varese's most ancient building, the 12th-century *Battistero di San Giovanni,* which contains some interesting 14th- and 15th-century frescoes. Well worth a visit is the *Palazzo Estense,* built in the 18th century as the summer home of Francesco III d'Este, duke of Modena and lord of Varese. Today the palace is used as the Town Hall, but its splendid gardens are open to the public. The adjoining Villa Mirabello houses the *Museo Civico (Civic Museum)* and has impressive English-style gardens with good views of the Alps.

About 5 miles outside town is the Sacro Monte, or sacred mountain, for centuries a focal point for pilgrims. Follow the signs leading northwest out of Varese, passing the village of Sant'Ambrogio. At the Prima Cappella (First Chapel) begins a footpath that leads past 14 shrines to the Rococo Santa Maria del Monte sanctuary. The shrines, designed by Bernascone in the early 17th century, contain frescoes and life-size terra cotta statues depicting the mysteries of the rosary. (Those in the tenth chapel — representing the Crucifixion — are by Dionigi Bussola.)

CHECKING IN: *Palace* – Built at the beginning of this century in Art Nouveau style and magnificently set in its own parkland in the hills overlooking Varese. In addition to spectacular views of the lake and Monte Rosa, this 110-room hotel offers grand Old World comfort, one of the most highly regarded restaurants in the area, and tennis courts. Breakfasts are a real treat, with a vast array of fresh fruit, juices, cereals, and brioches. (Via Manara 11, Varese; phone: 0332-312600; expensive.)

EATING OUT: *Al Vecchio Convento* – Good country cooking at reasonable prices in an attractive, rustic setting. Closed Tuesday evenings and Wednesdays. (Via Borri 348, Varese; phone: 0332-261005; moderate.)

En Route from Varese – The road to Vergiate leads southwest out of Varese and passes through wooded scenery, with a view of Lake Varese to the right. Continue to the old Roman market town of Sesto Calende and pass over the bridge that spans the Ticino River. Ahead lies Lago Maggiore, with magnificent mountains in the background. Follow the road (SS33) up the western side (the Piedmont side) of the lake to Arona. Across the water on the eastern shore is the *Rocca di Angera,* a fortress owned by the noble Borromeo family. The road proceeds northward through some of the loveliest scenery on Lake Maggiore, with villa after villa perched up on the left, most with spectacular gardens. At La Sacca, just before Stresa, another glance across the water will be rewarded with a view of the remarkable *Santa Caterina del Sasso,* a 13th-century Carmelite convent built into the sheer cliff face.

STRESA: Flanked by a belt of woods, surrounded by mountains, and facing the three Isole Borromee (Borromean Islands), one of the area's main attractions, this town enjoys a superb position on Lake Maggiore. Despite its long tradition as a resort, it has remained pleasantly small, its streets full of elegant townhouses and fine villas. This is the town where Ernest Hemingway's protagonist stayed in *A Farewell to Arms* before escaping by rowboat on the lake into Switzerland. The *Grand Hotel des Îles Borromées,* described in the novel, still dominates the waterfront. At the entrance to Stresa (coming up from Arona) is the *Villa Pallavicino,* a privately owned villa whose splendid gardens are open to the public from March through October (admission fee).

Boats for the Borromean Islands — Isola Madre (Mother Island), Isola Bella (literally Beautiful Island, but also a variation of the name Isabella), and Isola dei Pescatori (Fishermen's Island) — leave at frequent intervals from the landing stage. The islands are named after the Borromeo family, one of the greatest of the Italian aristocracy, and except for the Isola dei Pescatori, they still belong to the family, as do the fishing rights to the lake. Isola Bella, the closest island to Stresa, is all but taken up by the 17th-century palace built by Count Charles III Borromeo for his wife Isabella (thus the name of the island). The terraced gardens of the palace are open from March through October and are worth a visit (admission fee). Try not to let the countless tacky souvenir stands discourage you; once you're inside the palace grounds, the view improves perceptibly. The next island, Isola dei Pescatori, is really a fishing village, full of narrow cobbled alleys and many contented cats. Isola Madre, the largest of the group, has the most spectacular gardens, especially in May, when the azaleas are in bloom. Both the gardens and the 18th-century palace are open to the public from May through October for an admission fee.

Each year, from late August to late September, Stresa holds an international music festival, the *Settimane Musicali di Stresa (Stresa Musical Weeks),* 3 to 4 weeks of symphony and chamber concerts with world-famous soloists, as well as performances by young winners of international competitions. The concerts regularly take place at the Palazzo Borromeo on Isola Bella, in addition to other locations.

CHECKING IN: *Grand Hotel des Îles Borromées* **–** This gracious, 19th-century Baroque villa on the lakefront is Stresa's most deluxe hotel. Part of the CIGA chain, it has 122 handsomely furnished rooms and suites, all with private baths. Along with superb gardens and an incomparable view of the Borromean Islands, there is a private beach on the lake, two heated outdoor swimming pools, tennis, a bar, and a restaurant. Open year-round. (Corso Umberto I 67, Stresa; phone: 0323-30431; very expensive.)

EATING OUT: *Delfino* **–** An excellent seafood restaurant in a hotel on the island of Isola Bella. A lunch eaten here is garnished with views of Stresa and the other islands — an unforgettable experience. (Albergo Delfino, Isola Bella; phone: 0323-30473; moderate.)

En Route from Stresa – The lakeside road running north from Stresa passes through Baveno, where Queen Victoria used to stay, and over the bridge to Verbania, which includes the two centers of Pallanza and Intra. (The Roman name for Lake Maggiore was *Lacus Verbanus*, from the plant that grows abundantly on its shores, and even today, the lake is sometimes called Lake Verbano.) From here, it is possible to follow the lakeside road (now SS34) all the way up to the Swiss town of Locarno and return via the lakeside road along the eastern shore. It is also possible to explore the upper part of the lake by boat. A steamer service from Arona to Locarno can be boarded at various interim points including Stresa and Intra (passports should be taken). A third option is to cross directly to the eastern shore of the lake, using the car ferry that leaves Intra every few minutes for the 10-minute ride to Laveno.

LAVENO: This picturesque port on the Lombardy side of Lake Maggiore has a harborfront of warm ocher buildings. A resort town, it is also known for its ceramics factories. Take the cable car that runs from Laveno almost to the summit of the Sasso del Ferro; it stops at Poggio Sant'Elsa and is worth the ride for the superb panorama over the lake and the mountains. Just short of 2 miles south of town, in the fishing village of Cerro, a ceramics museum is housed in the 15th-century Palazzo Guilizzoni-Perabò, the courtyard of which is used for concerts during the summer.

EATING OUT: *Hotel Ristorante Bellevue* – As its name suggests, this restaurant affords its guests splendid views of the lake and the little port of Laveno, with the car ferries plying from side to side in the foreground. The chef is a specialist in cooking lake fish and preparing sauces to bring out their flavor. Try the *antipasto del lago,* which is white *lavarello* fish served with a delicate tartar sauce. Also heavenly are the *ravioli ripieni di pesce del lago,* homemade ravioli stuffed with fish. The restaurant has a small number of hotel rooms, most with the same spectacular panorama. (Via Fortino 40, Laveno; phone: 0332-667257; moderate.)

En Route from Laveno – Luino is 10 miles north of Laveno along Lake Maggiore's eastern shore. For those with time to spare, however, it's a very pleasant drive south from Laveno along the lakeside, passing through Cerro and continuing to Ispra. After Ispra, take the right turn to the enchanting village of Ranco, an idyllic spot with the bonus of an excellent restaurant. Then return to Laveno and drive east along SS394 to Cittiglio. Turn left here into the hills toward Casalzuigno, and left again for Arcumeggia, an ancient village nestled in the woods and remarkable for the frescoes painted on the outside of its houses, all by contemporary artists. Continue through the hills to Sant'Antonio, where there is a marvelous view of Lake Maggiore and the Alps, and then down to Nasca. Once back on the lake, turn right to Castelveccana and follow the shore road north to Luino.

CHECKING IN/EATING OUT: *Il Sole* – A restaurant with a few rooms to rent — and such is the reputation of the restaurant that Milanese industrialists often fly in by private helicopter. Nevertheless, it is a haven of peace and tranquillity, with a vine-covered terrace for outdoor eating. The menu changes every month, but there are always carefully prepared dishes based on lake fish, rabbit, pigeon, and other local produce. The small hotel next to the restaurant, a recent addition, consists of just 8 rooms (really miniature apartments), each beautifully decorated in modern style. Restaurant closed Monday evenings and Tuesdays; hotel closed January. (Piazza Venezia 5, Ranco; phone: 0331-969507; expensive.)

LUINO: This attractive town at the mouth of the River Tresa, which connects Lake Maggiore to Lake Lugano, grew up as a fishing village but flourished in the 19th century as a textile manufacturing center, run mostly by Swiss proprietors — it's only a few miles from the Swiss border. Today most of the textile mills have closed, and many of the townspeople make the daily trip over the border to work in Swiss chocolate and watchmaking factories. The town has a long promenade along the lake, especially lovely in spring. Another attraction is its Wednesday market, which is 200 years old, has some 900 stalls, and draws bargain hunters from miles around.

CHECKING IN: *Camin* – A turn-of-the-century lakeside villa that has been converted with great taste and an eye to comfort into a very attractive hotel known for its exceptional service. There are only 13 rooms, so staying here is more like being a guest at a 19th-century nobleman's country residence than a customer. The restaurant, one of the finest in the area, offers specialties such as homemade pasta in salmon sauce and home-smoked trout from the lake, as well as a mouth-watering *carré d'agnello alle erbe aromatiche* (lamb roasted with herbs). Hotel closed mid-December to early March; restaurant closed Tuesdays. (Viale Dante 35, Luino; phone: 0332-530118; moderate.)

EATING OUT: *Le Due Scale* – On the lakefront, overlooking the harbor, with a cloistered courtyard for outdoor dining during the summer. The fixed-price menus are a very good value. (Piazza della Libertà 30, Luino; phone: 0332-530396; inexpensive.)

I Tre Re – Housed in an attractive old building with a pool in the center of Luino. Patrons are invited to select their own trout if they care to. If not, there are also local delicacies such as *prosciutto di cervo* (venison ham) and *salame di cinghiale* (salami made from wild boar). (Viale Manzoni 29, Luino; phone: 0332-531147; inexpensive.)

En Route from Luino – Take the road marked Fornasette. It climbs up out of the town through some lovely mountain pasture, crosses over the Swiss border, and leads into Ponte Tresa, a town at the Lago di Lugano end of the River Tresa and remarkable in that half of it is in Switzerland and half in Italy. Then turn northward along Strada Cantonale 23 toward Lugano.

LUGANO: The main city of Switzerland's Italian-speaking Canton Ticino, this is an elegant resort with a beautiful lakefront on the body of water from which it takes its name. Across the water lies the tiny enclave of Campione d'Italia, a bit of Italian soil entirely surrounded by Swiss territory — it even uses Swiss currency and the Swiss postal and telephone systems. Campione, best known for its casino, one of only four legal ones in Italy, can be reached by boat from Lugano or by road across the bridge at Melide, south of Lugano. A visit to *Villa Favorita,* on the outskirts of Lugano at Castagnola, is well worth the effort. The 17th-century villa is owned by Baron Thyssen-Bornemisza and contains his private art gallery with a collection including works from all the major European schools from the Middle Ages to the 19th century. It is regularly supplemented by major paintings borrowed from the world's leading museums. The villa can be reached by cab, bus, or by boat from the main landing stage at Lugano. While in Lugano, try to dine at the splendid *Da Bianchi* restaurant.

En Route from Lugano – The lakeside road leading northeast out of Lugano is one of the most spellbinding of the route, with calm blue water to the right and mountains and tiny perched villages to the left. It crosses the border back into Italy just before the town of Oria, which was the home of the Italian poet Antonio Fogazzáro, and continues to hug the shore as far as Porlezza, at the eastern end of the lake. Then it leaves Lake Lugano behind and crosses the Porlezza plain to Lake Como, entirely in the Lombardy region. The first glimpse of the lake, whose praises were sung as early as Virgil's time (he gave it its other name, Larius, now

Lario), comes as the road curves around above Menaggio, a little more than 7 miles from Porlezza.

CHECKING IN: *Stella d'Italia* – The village of San Mamete, between Oria and Porlezza, is worth an overnight stop for the sheer pleasure of staying in a family-run establishment in the most romantic of settings. It, too, has links with Fogazzaro. The poet used to stay here soon after the present Signor Ortelli's grandfather opened the hotel early in this century. There are 37 rooms, a very attractive terraced garden for outdoor eating, a private beach, and even a hotel rowboat. Closed in winter. (San Mamete; phone: 0344-68139; inexpensive.)

EATING OUT: *Regina* – A splendid position overlooking the lake in Porlezza is one reason to eat here. In addition, the owners — Franco Vurro, who is head chef, and his Parisian wife, Dominique — provide a very warm welcome and excellent food. The *antipasto Regina,* a selection of mouth-watering, piping-hot hors d'oeuvres, is particularly recommended. Closed Mondays. (Albergo Regina, Piazza Matteotti 11, Porlezza; phone: 0344-61526; moderate.)

MENAGGIO: This resort town is set on what many consider the most beautiful stretch of the Lago di Como. Just south of it, the lake splits into two, one branch pointing southwest, with Como itself at its southernmost tip, the other pointing southeast, with the town of Lecco at its tip. On a promontory across the water, in an angle between the two branches, is the picturesque town of Bellagio. Directly opposite, on the far shore, is the enchanting fishing village of Varenna. Menaggio, Varenna, and Bellagio are connected by car ferry.

CHECKING IN: *Grand Hotel Victoria* – A superbly situated lakeside property with spectacular views. The highly regarded hotel restaurant, *Le Tout Paris,* features classic French as well as Italian dishes. (Via Castelli 11, Menaggio; phone: 0344-32003; expensive.)

En Route from Menaggio – The lakeside road south to Como passes through the resorts of Cadenabbia and Tremezzo, between which is the exquisite Villa Carlotta. Built in the mid-18th century and further embellished into the 19th century, it is open to the public from March through October (admission fee). The villa's garden is a spectacle, especially in April and May when its world-famous azaleas and rhododendrons are in bloom. The little hill town of Mezzegra, up on the right, is where Mussolini and Clara Petacci were shot by partisans after they were captured farther north at Dongo as they were fleeing toward Switzerland. The lakeside road continues south to the town of Sala Comacina. Just offshore here is Lake Como's only island, Isola Comacina, reached by a traditional lake boat called a *Lucia,* the local equivalent of Venice's gondola (they're the ones with the oval hoops over the hull). Farther on, just 3 miles before it reaches Como, the road passes through another lake resort, Cernobbio, site of the exquisite *Villa d'Este,* built in the 16th century as a palace for Cardinal Tolomeo Gallio and now a fabulous (and fabulously expensive) hotel.

CHECKING IN: *Grand Hotel Villa d'Este* – The most elegant retreat in the lake district. Stay in the main building, the 16th-century cardinal's palace, awash in marble pillars, crystal chandeliers, and winged staircases, or in the more secluded "annex," a 19th-century villa. In either case, guests luxuriate in the midst of acres of park with superb formal gardens landscaped right to the edge of the lake. The 180 rooms and suites are opulently decorated with period furniture and 19th-century antiques. There are multiple restaurants (the *Grill/Sporting Club* is best), tennis courts, pools (an indoor pool plus an outdoor one that floats in the lake), and facilities for water sports. Open April through October. (Via Regina 40, Cernobbio; phone: 031-511471; very expensive.)

EATING OUT: *Locanda dell'Isola* – The menu in this rustic restaurant, a 5-minute boat ride from Sala Comacina, hasn't changed much in half a century. Be prepared for a unique dining experience as nonstop *antipasti*, trout smuggler's style (grilled and seasoned with salt, lemon juice, pepper, and olive oil), roast pressed chicken, salad, cheese, dessert, coffee — approximately 3 hours' worth of indulgence — are served outdoors on tree-shaded, rough-hewn wooden tables. Open March through October. (Isola Comacina; phone: 0344-55083; expensive.)

COMO: Twice a year, fashion buyers from all over the world flock to this bustling lakeside town to see what's new in silk fabrics. Como is not only one of the larger lake resorts — the largest on this lake — but also a famous silk-producing town, and has been since the 16th century. It enjoys a spectacular position at the southern end of the lake, with mountains all around and lovely villas scattered among the hills outside the city.

Como began as a Roman colony, and two famous Romans, Pliny the Elder and Pliny the Younger, were born here. In the medieval period, it was an independent commune. The old part of town is well preserved, despite a strife-torn history, with the three towers of the city walls still standing, several old churches, and a wealth of old cobbled streets and colonnades that house an array of irresistible shops. Piazza del Duomo is the heart of town. Here, side by side, are the black and white marble Broletto (the ancient Town Hall), built in 1215, with the Torre del Comune on one side and the Duomo on the other. Begun in 1396, the Duomo combines Gothic and Renaissance elements in its façade (the rose window is renowned) and interior, and it was finished in the 18th century with a Baroque cupola. Among Como's other notable churches are the 11th-century Sant'Abbondio, in the Lombard Romanesque style, the 12th-century San Fedele, and the 14th-century Sant'Agostino.

Como is an excellent starting point for boat trips — by far the best way to explore the lake. A fleet of 50 or so paddle steamers and motor boats plies the water from here to the northern point of the lake at Colico, crisscrossing from bank to bank and stopping at lakeside villages on the way. A pass granting unlimited travel for one or more days can be purchased. Tickets and timetables are available at the office by the landing stage in Piazza Cavour, where there is also an information office of the *Ente Provinciale per il Turismo* (Piazza Cavour 16; phone: 031-262491). It's also possible to enjoy the lake and eat at the same time by having lunch on board one of the boats that leave the landing stage twice daily, usually at 10:30 AM and at midday. The food is good, the scenery unparalleled, and the prices an extraordinarily good value. The boats go to the north of the lake, with stops en route, and return in the early evening.

 CHECKING IN: *Barchetta Excelsior* – Recently refurbished, with 54 rooms all attractively decorated in modern Italian style, and conveniently situated on Como's lakefront main square, just by the landing stage. It has a restaurant. (Piazza Cavour 1, Como; phone: 031-266531; moderate.)

Posta – Right in the heart of town, with 17 clean, comfortable rooms and a small dining room that dispenses hearty, well-prepared food. (Via Garibaldi 2, Como; phone: 031-266012; inexpensive.)

 EATING OUT: *Imbarcadero* – Good food in elegant surroundings, overlooking Lake Como. Closed the first week in January. (Piazza Cavour 20, Como; phone: 031-277341; expensive.)

Rino – One of the best of a number of good *trattorie* in town, serving local dishes and lake fish specialties. Closed Mondays and part of July. (Via Vitani 7, Como; phone: 031-273028; inexpensive.)

En Route from Como – The slow, winding road leading up the eastern shore (of the western branch) of the lake passes through some of the smaller lakeside towns and villages such as Blevio, Torno (just beyond which is Pliny's Villa or, rather, a 16th-century villa with an unusual intermittent waterfall on its grounds that was described by both Pliny the Elder and the Younger and Leonardo da Vinci), Riva, Nesso (which has a dramatic waterfall), and Lezzeno. Beyond this is Bellagio, about 19 miles from Como.

BELLAGIO: The town sits on a promontory at the inner angle of Lake Como's upside-down *Y*, right where the eastern branch of the lake, commonly called the Lago di Lecco, or Lake Lecco, takes leave of the main branch, which retains the Como name. No more than a small village, Bellagio rises sharply from the lake, so that streets behind the flat area right at the waterfront are actually more like stairs. The gorgeous gardens of the *Villa Serbelloni* occupy much of the promontory itself. Built in the 16th century and redone in the 17th century, it passed into the hands of the Serbelloni family in the 18th century and was donated to the Rockefeller Foundation in this century. The villa is not open to the public, but the gardens, fortunately, are open twice daily, for 2-hour guided morning and afternoon tours, from Easter to mid-October (admission fee). Nearby, the gardens of the *Villa Melzi* are also open to the public from mid-March to mid-October (admission fee), as is the early 19th-century palace they surround. This was built by Duke Francesco Melzi, vice president of the short-lived Italian Republic that was set up by Napoleon. The villa gardens are worth a visit, especially for the marvelous view across the lake toward Tremezzo, the same view Liszt had the year he spent here with his mistress, Countess Marie d'Agoult (one of their daughters, Cosima, who was to marry Wagner, was born here).

CHECKING IN: *Grand Hotel Villa Serbelloni* – This is not *the* Villa Serbelloni, but it is named for it, and it is *the* hotel to stay in in Bellagio. It's more than a century old, poised in a dramatic position on the headland. Public rooms, such as the dining room, have frescoed, vaulted ceilings, whereas the guestrooms, with garden or lake views, are more homey. There are tennis courts, a heated pool, and a private beach. Open from mid-April to mid-October. (Bellagio; phone: 031-950216; very expensive.)

En Route from Bellagio – Take the car ferry across the lake to Varenna, a colorful little marble-quarrying port with pink and red houses in the harbor and steep, narrow alleyways leading up to the main piazza. It has a lovely lakeside promenade, shaded with fragrant bougainvillea. Also in town and worth a visit is the *Villa Monastero,* founded as a monastery in 1208 and today serving as the International Center of Physics. Both house and gardens are open to the public.

The steep backdrop of the Grigna Mountains, home to one of the most famous climbing schools in Europe, accompanies the route south from Varenna along the eastern arm of Lake Como (Lake Lecco). The landscape here differs sharply from that of the western arm, and it fascinated Leonardo da Vinci — it is believed to be the background for his famous *Mona Lisa.* At the end of the lake is the town of Lecco, now an iron-manufacturing center but most notable as the setting for *I Promessi Sposi* (*The Betrothed*), the classic novel by the 19th-century author Alessandro Manzoni. Several places in and around Lecco are mentioned in the book, and the *Villa Manzoni,* where the author lived as a boy, houses the Manzoni museum. Continue south of Lecco and then turn east to Bergamo, 20 miles away from Lecco.

BERGAMO: The roads leading in and out of Bergamo may not be as beautiful as some of the lake routes, but this historic city is well worth a visit. From the 11th century to the 13th century Bergamo was a free commune but later came under the control of the squabbling noble families of Lombardy and later still belonged to Venice (from the early 15th to the late 18th century) and then to Austria. It is divided into a modern, busy Città Bassa, or Lower City, built largely during the Fascist period, and a quiet, medieval Città Alta, or Upper City, which stands majestically on a hill at the foot of the Bergamesque Alps. The *Accademia Carrara* (closed Tuesdays), one of the best art museums in the country, with works by Botticelli, Canaletto, Bellini, Tiepolo, and Carpaccio, is in the Città Bassa; otherwise, the Città Alta, with its well-preserved fortifications, cobbled streets, and tiny shops, is by far the most interesting part of the city.

The Città Alta is reached by a funicular that drops its passengers in Piazza Mercato delle Scarpe, inside the walls of the old city and not far from Piazza Vecchia, its heart. In or around this square is a breathtaking collection of buildings, including the severe, medieval *Palazzo della Ragione* and its massive tower. Built in the 12th century, the palace was damaged by fire and restored in the 16th century (note the lion of St. Mark on the façade, a relic of the city's centuries as a Venetian possession). Through the archways of the palace is Piazza del Duomo, with the 15th-century *Cappella Colleoni,* actually a funerary chapel housing the tomb of Bartolomeo Colleoni, the famous *condottiere* (or soldier of fortune), a native *bergamasco.* The chapel's façade, in Lombard Renaissance style, is a striking composition of colored marbles and delicate carving. Also on the square is the 12th-century Romanesque basilica of *Santa Maria Maggiore,* to which the chapel is attached; the small 14th-century baptistry, which was once inside the basilica but is now freestanding, behind the wrought-iron fence; and the Duomo, Bergamo's cathedral, which has a 19th-century façade. If you're an opera lover, be sure to go inside Santa Maria Maggiore to pay your respects at the tomb of Gaetano Donizetti, another native. It's covered with grieving cherubs looking for all the world as though they'd just seen Lucia unfold her wings to the sky.

Make your way back to Piazza Mercato delle Scarpe, from which Via Rocca leads off to the medieval lookout post, La Rocca, in the middle of a spacious park. From its height there's a glorious view of upper and lower Bergamo and over the surrounding mountains and plain.

EATING OUT: *Trattoria da Ornella* – A busy family-run restaurant in the heart of the old city, a stone's throw from Piazza Vecchia. Its fixed-price lunch is a good idea in the midst of sightseeing. Try the *casonsei bergamaschi,* homemade ravioli filled with meat and served with butter, cheese, and sage. (Via Gombito 15, Bergamo Alta; phone: 035-232736; inexpensive.)

En Route from Bergamo – Take SS42 east out of Bergamo through the suburb of Seriate and the hilly Val Cavallina, past the tiny Lago di Endine to Lovere, on the shores of Lago d'Iseo.

LAGO D'ISEO: This is the smallest and most rugged of the main Lombardy lakes, and although it does not have the range of sophisticated amenities found on the larger lakes, the beauty and peace of the surroundings make forgoing luxury for at least one night worthwhile. Driving clockwise around the lake, you'll pass through some attractive towns, notably Pisogne, the gateway to the beautiful Val Camonica, and the pleasant little port town of Iseo itself, with a 14th-century castle, Castello Oldofredi. But the main attraction of the lake is the beautiful island in it. At 2 square miles, Monte Isola is the largest of the Italian lake islands, but it is an oasis of peace, where only the local doctor, the veterinarian, and the priest are allowed cars. The island rises to a point, with four clustered fishing villages around its base and the sanctuary of the Madonna della Ceriola at the top. The islanders derive their income from fishing, tourism, and netmaking — some of the sports nets for the Los Angeles Olympic games were made here. Boats to the island leave daily from Iseo and Sulzano, traveling north along the lakeshore from Iseo.

CHECKING IN: *La Foresta* – If you don't mind leaving your car behind and taking your luggage over on the boat to the island, this charming, if very simple, hotel has only 10 rooms, good food, friendly service, and blissful peace. (Peschiera, Monte Isola; phone: 030-988210; inexpensive.)

La Posada – In a small town about halfway between Lovere and Iseo, set in a garden of olive trees overlooking the lake, this small, family-run hotel has 17 clean, comfortable rooms, all with shower or bath, and a well-known restaurant. Closed November. (Via Provinciale 1, Sale Marasino; phone: 030-986181; inexpensive.)

EATING OUT: *Osteria Gallo Rosso* – A warm, friendly restaurant loved by locals, who return time and again for the atmosphere, attractive rustic decor, and excellent cooking, supervised by two young brothers. Try the inviting array of *antipasti misti* and the remarkable *petto d'oca affumicato* (smoked goose breast). Meat is grilled over the open fire in the dining room, the salads are a work of art, and the wines are mostly from the family vineyard in the hills. Closed Thursdays. (Vicolo Nulli 11, Iseo; phone: 030-980505; inexpensive.)

Trattoria del Pesce – On Monte Isola, run by a very capable *signora*. Among the superb fish dishes are the *antipasto del lago,* which includes little *lavarello* fish in a sweet and sour sauce, and home-cured lake sardines served with *polenta.* Also try the *tinca al forno,* a white fish baked with butter and parsley. Closed Tuesdays. (Peschiera, Monte Isola; phone: 030-988137; inexpensive.)

En Route from Iseo – To the south of Iseo lies the small wine-producing area of Franciacorta, whose red, white, and sparkling wines are fast developing a well-deserved reputation. Don't miss a visit to one of the wine cellars. The largest is that of *Fratelli Berlucchi,* in the tiny village of Borgonato. The firm is family-run from a 16th-century farmhouse, where visitors are always welcome. Take the coast road westward from Iseo and turn left down through the village of Timoline to Borgonato, or call ahead (phone: 030-984381) for directions. Otherwise, drive southeast from Iseo to Brescia, about 15 miles away.

BRESCIA: This ancient city is an important industrial center of modern Lombardy, but it is still rich in architectural monuments from its earlier days, from the Roman period through the Middle Ages to the Renaissance. Right at the center of town is Piazza della Vittoria, a modern square dating from the Fascist era; Mussolini gave public addresses from the red marble Arengario, or public-speaking rostrum, here. Just north is another square, Piazza della Loggia, the heart of the city since the Renaissance, surrounded by Renaissance buildings largely in the Venetian style. (Brescia, like Bergamo, was Venetian for nearly 400 years.) One of these buildings, the *Palazzo del Comune,* also known as the *Loggia,* was begun in the late 15th century and finished in the late 16th century by numerous architects, sculptors, and painters, including Sansovino, Palladio, and Titian. In front of it is the exquisite *Torre dell'Orologio,* a clock tower designed on the model of the one in Piazza San Marco, Venice, with two statues striking the hours. Pass beyond the tower to Piazza del Duomo, which had been the civic as well as the religious center of town until it was superseded in the former capacity by Piazza della Loggia. Of interest here is the *Duomo Nuovo* (*New Cathedral*), whose huge cupola is the third largest in Italy. It was begun in the 17th century to replace the 11th-century Duomo Vecchio, the old cathedral next door, which is better known as the Rotonda because of its circular plan. Also in the square is the *Broletto,* a medieval town hall with an 11th-century tower, the Torre del Popolo.

The heart of Roman Brescia is Piazza del Foro, which covers part of the ancient forum and has the spectacular remains of the *Tempio Capitolino* (*Capitoline Temple*), built in AD 73, in the background. An archaeological museum, the *Museo Civico Età Romana* (closed Mondays), has been installed in part of the temple. Next to it is the vast *Teatro Romano,* which held an audience of 15,000. Brescia has other monuments of interest, particularly churches dating from various periods (in fact, it used to be known as the "city of 100 convents" before the anticlerical Napoleon closed most of them). For information, stop in at the provincial tourist office (EPT) at Corso Zanardelli 34 (phone: 030-43418).

EATING OUT: *Ristorante Raffa* – An elegant restaurant in the heart of the city, especially popular at lunchtime for its good Brescian cooking. Closed Sundays and August. (Corso Magenta 15, Brescia; phone: 030-49037; moderate.)

***Trattoria Pergolina* –** A comfortably furnished *trattoria* near the Capitoline Temple with good home cooking. (Via Musei 65, Brescia; phone: 030-46350; inexpensive.)

En Route from Brescia – The SS11 and the A4 lead to the southwestern corner of the Lago di Garda, the largest of all the Italian lakes. Its shores border the Lombardy, Veneto, and Trentino–Alto Adige regions and are dotted with cypresses, olive groves, vineyards, and flowering shrubs. Head first for Desenzano del Garda, which has an attractive harbor and old town center, and pick up SS572 north, the first leg of the Gardesana Occidentale (the road along the western shore). After passing through the Moniga area, known for its production of red Chiaretto wine, take the turnoff for Salò. This beautiful spot was the seat of Mussolini's puppet government, the Republic of Salò, set up in September 1943. It is also the birthplace of Gasparo Bertolotti, held by some to have been the inventor of the violin. Much of the town was destroyed by an earthquake in 1901, but the two ancient town gates remain, as does the 15th-century late-Gothic cathedral. On Saturday mornings, a large market stretches along the lakefront. The resort town of Gardone Riviera is just 3 miles north of Salò, but if you have time, leave the lake road at Barbarano, turning left into the Via Panoramica, which leads up into the hills, for a marvelous view over the lake and the tiny island Isola di Garda before winding down into Gardone.

CHECKING IN/EATING OUT: *Laurin* – An Art Nouveau villa used as Mussolini's Ministry of Foreign Affairs during World War II. Its owners have restored it beautifully, leaving many original features but furnishing the 36 large and airy guestrooms in a comfortable, modern style. The hotel restaurant, a wonderfully elegant, frescoed room, attracts customers from some distance, particularly for its exquisite fresh lake trout in a piquant wine sauce. The desserts are also very special. (Viale Landi 9, Salò; phone: 0365-22022; moderate.)

GARDONE RIVIERA: The main point of interest in this lakeside resort is the villa built by the flamboyant poet and novelist Gabriele d'Annunzio and occupied by him until his death in 1938. D'Annunzio was also a hero of World War I. After the Treaty of Versailles failed to recognize Italy's claim to the port city of Fiume, on the Dalmatian coast, D'Annunzio rounded up a band of volunteers, captured the city himself, and ruled it for 15 months, much to the embarrassment of the Italian government. The estate is in the upper part of town — Gardone di Sopra — and it reflects all of its creator's eccentricities, not to mention his delusions of grandeur. Called *Il Vittoriale degli Italiani*, it is actually a complex of gardens, monuments, and memorials to his wartime and postwar achievements, containing the mausoleum where he and his comrades in the march on Fiume are buried, the car and airplane used in various exploits, and even a ship stuck into the flank of a hill. Visitors can walk around the grounds and are led through the memorabilia-stuffed villa, where the poet's study and his bathroom, chock-full of *objets,* including a marvelous, deep-blue glazed tub, are most interesting. Closed Mondays; admission fee.

En Route from Gardone – Traveling north through the former Roman colony of Maderno, one comes to Gargnano, where Mussolini had his villa (Villa Feltrinelli — not open to the public) and where a series of tunnels begins. Continue all the way up the Gardesana Occidentale (now SS45 *bis*) to Limone sul Garda and Riva del Garda, or, if time is no object, take the turn left toward Tignale, about 2 miles beyond Gargnano. This winding mountain road is even more spectacular than the last, leading through magnificent scenery, with views of the lake stretching for 30 miles. (The sanctuary of the Madonna di Monte Castello is a superb panoramic point.) Following signs for Limone and Riva, the road eventually winds down through the pretty hill village of Tremosine into Limone sul Garda, an enchanting, old-fashioned town that was loved by Goethe and D. H. Lawrence, among others, and until a half century ago was accessible only by boat. Its steep mountain backdrop prevents it from expanding too much and also acts as a remarkable sun trap — which accounts for the lemons growing at this northerly point.

Continue north from Limone to Riva del Garda. A spectacular feat of engineering, the road passes through tunnel after tunnel hewn from the rock, with splendid vistas out over the lake. Riva itself has been Italian only since the defeat of the Austrians in World War I (you're now in the Trentino–Alto Adige region). At Riva, round the northern segment of the lake and turn southward along its eastern shore, most of which touches the Veneto region. The road (the Gardesana Orientale — SS249 the whole way) leads into Malcesine, which was a favorite holiday spot of Greta Garbo and has an impressive 13th-century castle housing a small museum. Another well-preserved castle is at Torri del Benaco, where the car ferry crosses over to Maderno. The road follows the outline of a lovely promontory — Punta di San Virgilio — where Winston Churchill painted just after the war and continues through the town of Garda and on to Bardolino, home of the delicious light, fruity wine of the same name. There are several wine cellars in the town where visitors are welcome. From here, drive south again, rounding the far end of the lake at Peschiera del Garda and into the spectacular walled town of Sirmione.

 EATING OUT: *Al Torcol* – Housed in a converted stable, this lively, attractive restaurant specializes in meat and fish grilled on an outdoor barbecue. (Via IV Novembre 44, Limone sul Garda; phone: 0365-954169; inexpensive.)

SIRMIONE: This resort town is dramatically set; it runs the length of a narrow, 2-mile-long peninsula that projects into Lake Garda from the middle of its southern shore, dividing the water into the two bays of Desenzano and Peschiera. It has been a favorite holiday spot since Roman times, largely because of its hot sulphur springs, which have given rise to numerous spa clinics treating a wide variety of ailments. The Roman poet Catullus loved the place and wrote about it, although the Roman villa that has been excavated here — and is named for him — was not necessarily his. In the 13th century, the town, heretofore independent, fell to the powerful Della Scala, or Scaligeri, family of Verona, who immediately put a wall around it and built a fortress to guard the gate. This well-preserved castle, the *Rocca Scaligera,* its towers and crenelations intact, still stands right at the entrance, surrounded by water — it's actually built out onto the lake (open to the public daily except Mondays). Beyond it are the narrow streets of the old town, a pedestrian island, and at the very tip of the peninsula is the archaeological zone, where the so-called *Grotte di Catullo* (*Grottoes of Catullus*), actually the remains of a large, imperial-era Roman villa, can be visited (closed Mondays; admission fee). Sirmione offers plenty of swimming and boating and other holiday activities, and there's a beautiful, well-posted walk, the Passeggiata Panoramica, that runs right around the headland.

CHECKING IN: *Villa Cortine Palace* – A league apart from the many other hotels in Sirmione, it is set in a cypress-studded park beyond the town on the way to the Grotte di Catullo, just where a nobleman would choose to put his summer residence. Beautifully converted into a hotel, it has 50-plus rooms, a garden restaurant, swimming pool, private beach, and peace and quiet. Open April through October. (Via Grotte 6, Sirmione; phone: 030-916021; expensive.)

Mon Repos – Set among the olive groves at the end of the promontory, this small hotel is a much more economical choice than the *Villa Cortine*. Most rooms have a balcony for sunbathing and eating breakfast. (Via Arici 2, Sirmione; phone: 030-916260; inexpensive.)

EATING OUT: *Ristorante Piccolo Castello* – Patrons enjoy a stunning location by the Scaligeri castle, just inside the ramparts of the town. (Via Dante 9, Sirmione; phone: 030-916138; moderate.)

Osteria al Pescatore – A popular restaurant specializing in carefully prepared fish dishes. (Via Piana 18, Sirmione; phone: 030-916216; inexpensive.)

The Dolomites

The Italian Dolomites are one of Europe's most beautiful and striking mountain ranges. Part of the eastern Alps, they extend from the region of Trentino–Alto Adige and the Adige River valley east to the Veneto region and the Piave River valley, both only a short distance from the Austrian border. To the south, they continue as far as the Brenta River valley. Named after Déodat Guy Silvani Tancrède Gratet de Dolomieu, an eighteenth-century French geologist who spent his life studying them, they are home to some of Italy's most popular ski resorts, including Cortina d'Ampezzo. Eighteen of the many Dolomite peaks rise above 10,000 feet. The highest, the Marmolada, "Queen of the Dolomites," a great glacier at its side, rises to 10,964 feet. The Marmolada range is one of the principal mountain groups of the Western Dolomites, which also include the Pale di San Martino, Cima d'Asta, Latemar, Catinaccio, Sassolungo, and Sella groups. The principal mountain groups of the Eastern Dolomites — the area around Cortina — are the Sorapis, Civetta, Pelmo, Antelao, Tofane, and Tre Cime di Lavaredo.

At certain times of the day, the majestic Dolomite peaks are definitely pink. According to legend, this is because they were once covered by pink and red roses. Here lived a king named Laurino who called his domain the Garden of Roses. He fell in love with the daughter of a king who ruled nearby and kidnapped her. The father soon found out where she was being kept — no mistaking such a rose-colored world — and rescued his beloved daughter, taking Laurino prisoner. Laurino escaped and returned to his home, but on seeing the roses that had betrayed him, he cursed them and turned them into stone so that no one would ever see them again, by day or by night. So it is that still today, they can be seen only at dawn and at sunset.

In geological terms, it is the mixture of dolomitic limestone and porphyry that transforms the Dolomites from a hundred shades of pink at dawn to an intense, almost inflamed red at sunset. In simpler terms, it is also the angle and intensity of the sun that breathes life into these massive and bizarre rocks. But the word "rock" doesn't really say it all. Pinnacles, towers and turrets, pyramids and columns, all pointing straight to the sky — they are truly a work of art sculpted by the forces of erosion.

Picture these bizarre rock formations surrounded by grassy pastures and plateaus, peaceful valleys, and dreamy mountain villages. It's an enchanted scenario, and part of the fascination these mountains hold for so many is that they are truly fabled. Legends linger everywhere. Today, as in the past, the children of the mountains love to sit by the fireplace in the evening to hear about Salvans and Ganes, the wild divinities who make their home in caves and appear only to protect the herds and the forests, or the Dragons of the Dolomites, who live at the bottom of mountain lakes, fighting other monsters for supremacy. The Gran Bracun, who saved the people of the valley by killing the evil dragon, is perhaps the noblest figure of all.

Historically, the Dolomite regions underwent countless vicissitudes. Stone weapons and utensils reveal that part of the area was inhabited as far back as the fifth millennium BC. Barbarian Celts then arrived, and at the end of the second century BC they fell under Roman domination. Next came invasions by the Huns, Ostrogoths, and, last but not least, the Lombards — a great deal of coming and going in a region where the mountains were insurmountable barriers. But credit must be given to the Romans, who as far back as 15 BC began opening roads in the Dolomites that were the forerunners of what is today considered one of the best networks of mountain highways in the world.

The invasions, lootings, and battles culminated when Charlemagne gained control, and then the ensuing events of several centuries eventually led to Austrian control. It wasn't until 1919 that the last of the area, now the autonomous region of Trentino–Alto Adige, returned to Italy.

The Dolomites remain a crossroads where different cultures, languages, and customs meet. En route, travelers come across Roman ruins, medieval castles, Baroque churches, and Tyrolean chalets. The Trentino — the province of Trento — is predominantly Italian speaking. But north of it, the Alto Adige — the province of Bolzano, which was until 1919 Austria's South Tyrol (the Italian name derives from the Adige River) — is predominantly German speaking. Newspapers, radio, and television are bilingual, as are most road signs. If you know some German, use it, and you will be better received than if you were to speak Italian. (Inhabitants of the Südtirol still remember Mussolini's attempts to Italianize the area, and not kindly.)

Another population in the Alto Adige speaks Ladin, a mixture of Celtic dialect and the vernacular Latin brought to the area by the Roman soldiers and colonizers in the first century BC. The Rhaeto-Roman descendants of this historical encounter still live in the Ladin valleys of Badia, Gardena, Fassa, and Ampezzo. Not quite 80,000, they are a proud people, currently engaged in a struggle to keep their heritage and national identity alive.

All of the mountain people, in fact, seem to have learned to benefit from the modern world while maintaining more than a fleeting attachment to centuries-old traditions. On holidays or even on Sundays, they don their ancient costumes and dance elaborately to the tune of yodled music. Their mountain folklore is a part of their lives, not something brought out for the sake of tourists. In short, the Dolomites are a way of life, not simply a region of natural beauty. So begin by exploring the villages, the museums of arts and crafts, and the local shops of the wood carvers and sculptors. Walk through the tiny farm settlements that dot the valleys and look for signs of the past in the decorations encircling the windows, the carved symbols over the doors, and the painted façades. The balconies of these rustic houses are usually framed by geraniums, and even the *baite,* typical Alpine wood structures used to stack hay and stable animals, have a special charm.

As to the natural beauty, keep in mind that the almost unreal peaks and bizarre massifs that are fascinating when seen from the valley become an unparalleled reality up close. If time allows, take some hikes up the mountains or ride the chair lifts and tramways. If possible, stop in at one of the many *rifugi,* or rustic lodges (at times little more than wood huts), scattered all over the mountains and at the base of the peaks. Some of them are repositories of another kind of mountain lore — that concerning the daring pioneer climbers who came from all over the world, especially England, in the mid-nineteenth century to scale the exhilarating Dolomites. Their pictures hang on the walls and their old-fashioned climbing equipment is proudly displayed. Moreover, a hike up to a *rifugio* (in many places, the chair lift or tramway will also get you there) will allow you to watch as the modern-day climbers start out on their ascents or to enjoy a hearty mountaineer meal, and rather inexpensively, too.

Not surprisingly, the main attractions of the Dolomites in winter are the ski slopes. The network of lifts is exceptional, providing access to hundreds and hundreds of miles of great skiing. In the summer, the villages and the valleys come to life with music, folk, and wine festivals and parades in ancient costumes. Hikers populate the mountains, and the climbers can be seen on just about every peak. The climate is generally mild. Winters are cold but not frigid; summers are pleasantly warm and sunny. Storms, especially in August, do have a way of sneaking up, so hikers should be prepared with lightweight waterproof jackets and the like. A word of warning: These splendid mountains can also be very treacherous. It's easy to get lost, and darkness descends quite rapidly. All excursions are marked by painted symbols on stones or tree trunks. Only an expert mountaineer, or someone familiar with the area, should stray from the marked trails.

The most scenic and most popular driving route through the Dolomites is the Grande Strada delle Dolomiti (Great Dolomite Highway), from Bolzano to Cortina d'Ampezzo, which leads across grassy meadows and valleys, over famous mountain passes, close to majestic peaks, and into lovely Alpine villages. For the most part, the route outlined here follows the highway, with some detours to the most important and beautiful valleys and resorts. After Cortina, the route circles north and west to take in Brunico and Bressanone on its way back to Bolzano. A side trip to Merano is suggested before proceeding from Bolzano to Trento, after which another side trip is possible, to Madonna di Campiglio. The Great Dolomite Highway is fairly wide but, as with all mountain driving, bends and hairpin turns are unavoidable. Take it slowly. Visitors planning to be in the Dolomites in the winter should keep in mind that some of the higher passes may be closed due to snow. Numerous alternative routes are available, so check before starting out.

There are literally hundreds of hotels all over the Dolomites, although there aren't many restaurants. Each hotel has its own dining facilities, and the food is generally quite good everywhere. The cuisine, mostly Austrian, includes specialties such as *gnocchi* (or *knödel* as they are called in Alto Adige and *canederli* in Trentino) and *polenta* (cornmeal mush), a good hearty dish served with assorted meats or mushrooms. *Speck* is an excellent smoked *prosciutto,* delicious in a sandwich. And last but not least, strudel — excellent all over. The most renowned wines are Teroldego Rotaliano, Pinot Nero dell'Alto Adige, Alto Adige Riesling Renano, and Merlot dell'Alto Adige.

Expect to pay approximately $70 and up (usually up to about $90, but more in places like Cortina) per night for a double room in those hotels listed as expensive. In the moderate category, a double room costs approximately $30 to $50. A meal for two in a restaurant listed as expensive will cost $60 and up, more than $100 in some cases; moderate means approximately $30 to $55 for two; and inexpensive, less than $30. The residents of the Dolomites usually take their vacations from early November to mid-December. Many hotels and restaurants close at this time, although one or two usually stay open in each village and resort.

BOLZANO (BOZEN): Capital of the Alto Adige, Bolzano (or *Bozen* in German) is an important industrial and commercial city, as well as a tourist center. Its position on the way to the Brenner Pass has made it a gateway to northern Europe since its earliest days; now it is also the holiday-maker's gateway to the Western Dolomites. While modern highways have made it unnecessary to go through the city, it is a colorful and charming place; so plan to visit before heading for the mountains. Don't be surprised to hear the Italians speak German here or to eat the kind of food more common in Austria. Until the end of World War I, Bolzano was capital of Austria's South Tyrol, and it is still bilingual and bicultural, predominantly Austrian in character and flavor, with interjections of contemporary Italian design. In fact, the sensation of being in two countries at once is one of its most distinctive (and attractive) features.

Life in Bolzano is pleasant and unhurried, as is immediately apparent while strolling through the old town. This district is set in an angle formed by the confluence of the Isarco and Talvera rivers (which then flow into the Adige south of town) and is entirely Tyrolean. Piazza Walther (Waltherplatz) is dominated by a splendid 14th- and 15th-century Gothic cathedral with a characteristic colored roof. Not far away is the 13th- and 14th-century Church of the Dominicans, also Gothic, containing a chapel with an important cycle of frescoes of the Giotto school. North of it is one of the main streets of old Bolzano, Via dei Portici (Laubengasse), narrow and flanked by medieval arcades along which more modern buildings — 16th and 17th century — house modern shops. The buildings, the carved wood doors, and the elaborate windows are uniquely Tyrolean. Via dei Portici leads into Piazza delle Erbe, where a very colorful outdoor fruit market is held each day. Nearby is the 14th-century Franciscan church, noted for its altarpiece. After Piazza delle Erbe, Via dei Portici becomes Via del Museo, named after the Civic Museum, which houses a vast archaeological and ethnographic collection as well as paintings and precious wood sculptures. Last, take a walk across the Talvera River past the newer sections of the city into picturesque, suburban Gries. Once a resort town of its own, now a part of Bolzano, Gries has an old parish church with a 15th-century carved wood altarpiece by Michael Pacher, one of the most famous Tyrolean painters and sculptors of his time, as well as the 18th-century Baroque church of the Benedictine monastery, noted for frescoes by Martin Knoller.

There are several interesting ancient castles in the immediate vicinity of Bolzano. One of the most famous is *Castel Roncolo* (*Schloss Runkelstein*), approximately 1½ miles north, along the road to the Val Sarentina. Built in 1237, it rises high on a steep cliff and dominates the valley below, looking typically medieval. The interior is notable for its 14th- and 15th-century frescoes depicting feudal and court life (open for guided visits 10 AM to noon and 3 to 5 PM Tuesdays through Saturdays). For information on the other castles in the vicinity, some of which have been turned into fine hotels and restaurants, contact the *Ufficio Provinciale del Turismo,* Piazza Walther 2 (phone: 0471-26991).

CHECKING IN: *Park Hotel Laurin* – Bolzano's most luxurious hotel offers excellent service and a very elegant ambience. Set in a park in the old center of town, it has 106 rooms, a restaurant, and a heated swimming pool. (Via Laurin 4, Bolzano; phone: 0471-47500; expensive.)

Grifone-Greif – On the main square, near the cathedral. Guests enjoy modern comforts in an atmosphere that is elegantly reminiscent of the past, plus a very good restaurant (see *Eating Out*). 131 rooms. (Piazza Walther 6, Bolzano; phone: 0471-977056; expensive to moderate.)

Luna-Mondschein – Somewhat less refined than the other hotels in its category, it is nonetheless very pleasant and rustic. There are 85 rooms, a garden, and a restaurant. (Via Piave 15, Bolzano; phone: 0471-25642; expensive to moderate.)

Herzog – An unpretentious, but typically Tyrolean, hotel where the emphasis is on coziness. There are 29 rooms; no restaurant. (Piazza del Grano 2, Bolzano; phone: 0471-26267; moderate.)

Scala-Stiegl – A very Tyrolean hotel on the edge of town. The service is extremely good, and in summer meals are served outside in a lovely garden. 60 rooms. (Via Brennero 11, Bolzano; phone: 0471-41111; moderate.)

EATING OUT: *Grifone* – Old-fashioned Tyrolean elegance characterizes this hotel–restaurant. The cuisine, both regional and Italian, and the local wines — Sylvaner, Santa Maddalena, and Lago di Caldaro — are of high quality. Closed Sundays. Reservations necessary. (Hotel Grifone-Greif, Piazza Walther 6, Bolzano; phone: 0471-27056; expensive to moderate.)

Da Abramo – In a building that was once the Town Hall of Gries, where the style is decidedly Liberty, enlivened by a multitude of flowers and plants. Traditional and Italian cuisine are served. Closed Sunday evenings and Mondays. (Piazza Gries 16, Bolzano; phone: 0471-30141; moderate.)

Chez Frederic – Currently the "in" place to eat, its ambience and style are French. The cuisine is a combination of the best French and the best Italian, and the wines are regional, Italian, and French. Closed Tuesdays. (Via Armando Diaz 12, Bolzano; phone: 0471-41411; moderate.)

En Route from Bolzano – Head northeast out of the city and pick up SS241 at Cardano (Kardaun), approximately 1¾ miles from Bolzano. For approximately 5 miles, SS241 leads eastward through a narrow, and somewhat frightening, gorge called Val d'Ega (Eggental), whose entrance is guarded by the Castle of Cornedo. Continue through Nova Levante, a pretty summer resort surrounded by pine forests. As the road climbs, look up through the treetops for a glimpse of two impressive Dolomite peaks — the highest peak (9,236 feet) of the Latemar group and the 9,756-foot Catinaccio, in whose German name, Rosengarten (Rose Garden), the legend of Laurino lives on. Farther up the road is a grand view of Lago di Carezza (Karersee), a typical Alpine lake whose emerald green waters mirror the Latemar peaks. SS241 continues up and over the 5,671-foot Passo di Costalunga, also known as the Passo di Carezza (Karerpass), which marks the boundary between the provinces of Bolzano and Trento. On the approach to the top of the pass, the view suddenly opens up: to the west, in the far distance, are the Ortles and Venosta Alps; to the east, beyond the Fiemme and Fassa Dolomites, the renowned Pale di San Martino.

After the pass, the road descends into the Val di Fassa, and the Marmolada, or Queen of the Dolomites, the most majestic of all the mountains, comes into view. At Vigo di Fassa, time permitting, take the tramway to Ciampedie, where there is a natural panoramic terrace at the foot of the Rosengarten. From Vigo, continue north to Canazei, now on SS48.

CANAZEI: This summer and winter resort in the Alta Val di Fassa (High Val di Fassa) is surrounded by the peaks of three Dolomite groups — Sassolungo, Sella, and Marmolada — and is also central to three Dolomite passes — Passo del Pordoi, Passo di Sella, and Passo di Fedaia. In the center of town is the delightful late-Gothic church of San Floriano, decorated with Baroque wood altars. A hike or the chair lift takes visitors to scenic high spots such as Pecol and Col dei Rossi.

CHECKING IN/EATING OUT: *Diana* – This very characteristic mountain lodge, paneled entirely in pine, is near a small pine forest. Restaurant; 28 rooms. (Via Roma 84, Canazei; phone: 0462-61477; moderate.)

Tyrol – A rather refined, chalet-like hotel near the center of town, on the edge of a pine forest. Restaurant; 36 rooms. (Viale alla Cascata 3, Canazei; phone: 0462-61156; moderate.)

En Route from Canazei – It would be a terrible mistake to leave Canazei without taking a side trip to Marmolada. Take SS641, a somewhat narrow but panoramic road, to the Fedaia Pass, which is also the boundary between the provinces of Trento and Belluno (the latter in the Veneto region), and continue on to Malga Ciapela. From here, catch the tramway that takes visitors as high up Marmolada as they can go short of mountain climbing for an unequaled view spanning the entire Dolomite range. The Marmolada glacier is also famous for some great summer skiing.

Return to Canazei and pick up SS48 northeast. Approximately 9 miles from town, to the left, detour onto SS242, which travels over the Sella Pass, with the mountains of the Sella group to the east and Sassolungo to the west. The road then descends into tiny Plan de Gralba and right into the heart of the Val Gardena — one of the most beautiful resort areas in the Dolomites, a skiers' paradise in winter and a favorite summer playground for mountain climbers and hikers. The valley is part of the Ladin-speaking region of Alto Adige, and its inhabitants still conserve their enthusiasm for mountain culture and folklore. Its craftsmen are renowned — expert woodcarvers who are especially famous for hand-carved furniture, statues, and toys. The route (SS242) traverses the entire valley, passing through its three most important villages: Selva di Val Gardena, Santa Cristina, and Ortisei, all within a few miles of each other.

SELVA DI VAL GARDENA and SANTA CRISTINA: Known in German as *Wolkenstein in Gröden* and *St. Christina,* these two villages are equally charming. A number of excursions begin in each town. The Passo di Gardena can be reached by tramway from Selva di Val Gardena. After the 20-minute ride, passengers are rewarded with an incomparable view of the Sella, Sassolungo, and Sciliar mountains, and as far as the Ortles in the west, as well as of the Alpe di Siusi, a high Alpine plain. From Santa Cristina, a chair lift ride of less than 10 minutes leads to Monte Pana, where weary visitors can relax at the *Sporthotel Monte Pana* and enjoy the magnificent view. For more altitude, another 10-minute chair ride carries visitors up to the Rifugio Mont de Soura at 6,565 feet, and a 3-hour hike reaches the top of the famed Sella Pass.

ORTISEI (ST. ULRICH): This summer and winter resort village is the chief town of Val Gardena. It lies at the foot of the Alpe di Siusi, the most extensive plateau in the Alps. Grassy and wildflower-strewn in summer and snow-covered in winter, it can be reached by tramway from Ortisei and offers wonderful views. Ortisei is another village with a Ladin heritage (as are Selva di Val Gardena and Santa Cristina), and Ortisei's Ladin museum is a good place to learn about the culture and folklore, as well as to see typical Gardena sculptures and paintings. Ortisei is also a village of woodcarvers, and shops selling carvings are everywhere.

 CHECKING IN/EATING OUT: *Aquila-Adler* – Undoubtedly the best hotel in Ortisei. It conserves a golden book of famous guests and offers a covered swimming pool, tennis, sauna, and solarium. Restaurant; 87 rooms. (Via Rezia 7, Ortisei; phone: 0471-76203; expensive.)

Angelo-Engel – A typical Alpine lodge, cozy and pleasant, with good service. Restaurant; 37 rooms. (Via Petlin 35, Ortisei; phone: 0471-76336; moderate.)

Hell – Don't be deceived by the name. This recently built hotel offers typical Tyrolean comfort in its 27 rooms, international cuisine, hearty breakfasts, a sauna, and a solarium. (Via Promenade, Ortisei; phone: 0471-76785; moderate.)

Ronce – A cozy family atmosphere, all wood decor, near the ski slopes. There are two dozen rooms and a restaurant. (Via Ronce 1, Ortisei; phone: 0471-76383; moderate.)

En Route from Ortisei – The next destination is Corvara in the Val Badia, but there are two ways to approach it. One way is to backtrack through Santa Cristina and Selva di Val Gardena to Plan de Gralba and pick up SS243 at the intersection. Travel north-northeast to the Gardena Pass (taking in yet another view of the Sella group as you climb) and into the village of Colfosco. To the right, after approximately 1¼ miles, is Corvara in Badia.

Unfortunately, this approach cuts out what some consider the most splendid Dolomite pass of all — the 7,692-foot Pordoi Pass, which affords an exhilarating view of the Marmolada, Catinaccio, Sassolungo, and the Sella mountains. One way to see the Pordoi Pass is to head for Corvara straight from Canazei. Take SS48 over the pass and on to SS244, which leads into the Val Badia and to Corvara in Badia. Since the Val Gardena is only a stone's throw from Val Badia, side trips from Corvara are easy (via the Gardena Pass), or stop there after having visited the Val Badia.

CORVARA IN BADIA: This dreamy mountain village is in the heart of the Alta Val Badia, another Ladin valley. On the approach to town, the sight of a massive rock that seems to rise out of the earth is dazzling. This is the Sassongher (8,668 feet), Corvara's pride and joy. The small town sits at the foot of this lone giant, content to be dominated by it. Like the rest of the Val Badia, Corvara holds a special kind of appeal. Not as fashionable as the other resort areas, it is genuine and friendly, and probably as authentic today as it was in 1880 when visitors began to discover it.

Before then, Corvara was a tiny settlement of a few farmhouses and perhaps one or two taverns. The first tourists were English climbers, who came not only because of the challenging mountain but also because of the reputation of a local Alpine guide, Franz Kostner, who had spent much of his life as a guide in the Himalayas and was the first to lead the English to the top of the Matterhorn. The village rapidly became the place to go, especially to avoid frivolity and to live close to nature. Corvara is still basically the same. The people in town and in all of the valley take pride in an old-fashioned hospitality. In return, they — Ladins, as they consider themselves — ask only that visitors respect their mountains and learn to know and love them — not too much to ask considering the Val Badia's fabled setting.

The valley can be explored using Corvara as a base. The tiny town of Colfosco is literally around the bend and within walking distance (1¼ miles). Other villages — Pedraces, La Villa, and San Cassiano — are only a few miles away. Short hikes into the mountains will turn up a variety of rustic farmhouses and barns or entire tiny settlements of mountain farmers — a very pretty sight, especially in summer when geraniums of all colors are in bloom. Some of the façades of the structures are frescoed, while the windows are framed by classic Ladin decorations. Look carefully for sundials or carved or painted flowers with six petals set inside a circle — the wheel of life, a Celtic symbol.

 CHECKING IN: *La Perla* – This 50-room hotel introduces a touch of sophistication into a typically Tyrolean atmosphere. Besides a restaurant, it has an indoor pool, a sauna and solarium, a boutique, and an art gallery. (Corvara in Badia; phone: 0471-83132; expensive.)

Posta-Zirm – Corvara's oldest and most prestigious hotel was opened in 1880 by the Alpine guide Franz Kostner after his return from the Himalayas. It has become an international gathering spot where friends meet again and again in a characteristically Ladin ambience. There are 74 rooms, a restaurant, indoor pool, sauna, and solarium. (Centro 16, Corvara in Badia; phone: 0471-83175; expensive.)

Sassongher – A 50-room hotel that combines rustic Tyrolean elegance and a cozy atmosphere. The finishing touches include locally produced antique furniture. Restaurant, indoor pool, sauna, solarium, hot tub, boutique. (Via Pescosta 29, Corvara in Badia; phone: 0471-83085; expensive.)

Tablè – Tastefully furnished according to the mountain tradition. This 30-room hotel organizes many special gastronomic evenings and candlelight dinners and is also renowned in the valley for its wonderful pastries. (Via Pescosta 127, Corvara in Badia; phone: 0471-83144; moderate.)

EATING OUT: La Tambra – A typical Alpine chalet, small but lively, this is where the natives go for a good mountain meal. The cuisine is regional, offering such dishes as barley soup, goulash, and game in season. (Via Pescosta 159, Corvara in Badia; phone: 0471-83281; moderate.)

En Route from Corvara – Head north to La Villa and then turn right into the Valle di San Cassiano. Travel through Armentarola to the Passo di Valparola (7,046 feet), past the foot of another mountain, Lagazuoi. The road then hooks into the Passo di Falzarego, a pass that is open only in summer. The next stop is Cortina d'Ampezzo, in the Eastern Dolomites, approximately 21 miles from Corvara.

CORTINA D'AMPEZZO: Of all the resorts in the Dolomites, Cortina is the only one that requires little introduction. The splendid town sits in a large basin called the Valle del Boite surrounded by majestic mountains. The Tofane, Pomagagnon, Cristallo, Tre Cime di Lavaredo, and many more gold-pink peaks frame it, making it picture-perfect. Cortina has been known as a mountaineers' paradise since the mid-19th century, although it wasn't until near the turn of this century that the first hotels were built. It then developed quickly, and even before World War I it was on the map as one of the best resorts in the Dolomites. The first ski competition in Italy took place here in 1902, and the Winter Olympics were held here in 1956. The town offers a huge variety of ski runs and facilities for all winter sports, including the Olympic Ice Stadium (Stadio Olimpico del Ghiaccio).

Much larger than other Dolomite villages, Cortina is actually a small but cosmopolitan city, with exclusive shops, luxury hotels, refined restaurants, nightclubs, and discos. Such glamorous and sophisticated accouterments have made it *the* place to be and ski in Italy, and at least once a year the jet-set crowds meet here to renew acquaintance. But Cortina is not glitter alone. It has a more rustic side sought by mountain climbers who test their courage on the high peaks and by hikers who pitch up at the quaint *rifugi,* small lone lodges, where the pioneer mountain spirit still lingers.

Corso Italia, the main avenue through the town, is largely a pedestrian island, where you'll find the *Ciasa de ra Regoles,* which houses an important museum of geology and mineralogy and the Rimoldi collection of modern art (Corso Italia 67). Stop in at the Artigianato Artistico Ampezzano, a permanent exhibit of the crafts of local artisans, also on Corso Italia, to see wood carvings with precious inlays of ivory and mother-of-pearl; wrought-iron, brass, and copper objects; and splendid filigree necklaces, clasps, and brooches.

But since Cortina's real wealth is the mountains, it would be a mistake not to take a few excursions to some of nature's best belvederes: The same mountains that are breathtaking when seen from the town will leave you absolutely speechless close up. There are tramways and chair lifts (not all of them depart from town, however) to some of the most scenic spots, such as the 10,673-foot summit of the Tofana di Mezzo or the foot of the Tofane group, west of Cortina, and the foot of the Cristallo group, east of town. The Rifugio Cinque Torri, the Rifugio Col Drusciè, and the Belvedere di Pocol shouldn't be missed. For more details about these and other excursions, contact the *Azienda Autonoma di Soggiorno e Turismo,* Piazzetta San Francesco 8, Cortina (phone: 0436-3231, 0436-2711).

CHECKING IN: *Cristallo* – One of the many fine CIGA hotels, it offers real mountain-style luxury on a slope above town. The decor is both classic and Alpine, with beautiful paintings decorating the walls. There are 90 rooms and suites, a restaurant serving regional specialties, more than one bar, an outdoor swimming pool, a skating rink, and tennis courts. Open June through September and December through March. (Via Menardi 42, Cortina d'Ampezzo; phone: 0436-4281; expensive.)

Miramonti Majestic Grand – Another of Cortina's finest, also set above the town, offering mountain-style elegance. It has 120 rooms, a restaurant serving regional specialties, a sports club and fitness center, as well as a 9-hole golf course, heated indoor pool, tennis, and its own ski lift to keep guests happy. Open June through August and December through March. (Pezziè 103, Cortina d'Ampezzo; phone: 0436-4201; expensive.)

Hotel de la Poste – Dating back to 1805, when the Manaigo family received permission to open an inn with only four bedrooms, this hotel has undergone many renovations over the years. It is elegant, sophisticated, and fashionable, and no newer hostelry has been able to replace it as the chic place to congregate. Closed mid-October to mid-December. (Piazza Roma 14, Cortina d'Ampezzo; phone: 0436-4271; expensive.)

Cortina – Rustic yet refined, with Persian rugs adorning the floors, bed headboards hand-sculpted in Val Gardena, and 48 rooms furnished with beautiful objects made by Cortina's artisans. Restaurant. Open mid-December to mid-April and mid-June to mid-September. (Corso Italia 94, Cortina d'Ampezzo; phone: 0436-4221; expensive to moderate.)

Europa – The very rustic, alpine atmosphere is complemented by several beautiful pieces of antique furniture. The restaurant's international cuisine is highly recommended; 52 rooms. (Corso Italia 207, Cortina d'Ampezzo; phone: 0436-3221; expensive to moderate.)

Menardi – On the outskirts of town, this small hotel was once a large, old farmhouse. Chalet-like furnishings give it a warm and cozy atmosphere. Open mid-December to mid-April and mid-June to mid-September. 41 rooms. (Via Majon 110, Cortina d'Ampezzo; phone: 0436-2400; moderate.)

EATING OUT: *El Toulà* – Housed in a former hayloft, which is what its name means in local dialect, this sister to *El Toulà* in Rome serves exceptional international cuisine. Reservations are a must. Closed Mondays. (Via Ronco 123, Cortina d'Ampezzo; phone: 0436-3339; expensive.)

Da Beppe Sello – Traditional but exquisite cuisine is served in a rustic and cozy atmosphere. Closed Tuesdays, mid-April to mid-May, and October. (Via Ronco 68, Cortina d'Ampezzo; phone: 0436-3236; moderate.)

Il Meloncino – Known for its remarkable grilled platters. Reservations suggested. Closed Tuesdays, June, and November. (Località Gillardon, Cortina d'Ampezzo; phone: 0436-61043; expensive to moderate.)

Rifugio Dibona – If the idea of going halfway up a mountain in the evening for a meal, of taking a Sno-Cat to get there, and returning on a small one- or two-seat sled intrigues you, then this is one dining experience not to miss. It's strictly for winter and not for the fainthearted. Before embarking, rent your own sled (at any ski rental shop in Cortina) and don't forget to take it up with you. The cuisine in this lodge is rustic, hearty, and excellent, served with an abundance of wine, which is needed to find the courage to ride back down the mountain. Along with the wine and the courage, hope for some moonlight because that is the only way to see where you're headed. The *Rifugio Dibona* is well known around town for this unique dining experience. Survivors report that it is great fun and not at all dangerous! For more information, contact Cortina's tourist office.

En Route from Cortina – Take SS48 east out of town through the Passo Tre Croci and enjoy an impressive view of Monte Cristallo. Continue on SS48 *bis* for Lago di Misurina. Although this lake is not as pretty as other, lesser-known Alpine lakes, it is famous for the way it mirrors the majestic 9,746-foot Tre Cime di Lavaredo (Drei Zinnen), a truly breathtaking visual effect. SS48 *bis* becomes SS51 and leads to the outskirts of Dobbiaco (Toblach), another lovely village in a very green valley, the Alta Val Pusteria. The parish church in Dobbiaco offers one of the best examples of Baroque art in the whole Alto Adige. Pick up SS49 westbound for Brunico and then turn south on SS49 *bis* to Bressanone. A stroll through the old centers of either town will reveal many old and elegant buildings, churches, porticoes, Baroque palaces, typical Tyrolean homes with bays and pinnacles, and colorful courtyards.

BRUNICO (BRUNECK): The capital of the Val Pusteria, it is famous for the spacious and gentle slopes that surround it. It is dominated by a 13th-century castle, but the area's greatest attraction is the panorama from the Plan de Corones, reached by cable car.

CHECKING IN/EATING OUT: *Andreas Hofer* – Pine-paneled walls and typical Tyrolean furniture are the most distinctive decorative features of this modern, 54-room hotel. The restaurant is cozy and friendly, and the Tyrolean cuisine is reputed to be the finest around (an entire dynasty of chefs comes from here). The specialty is game with *polenta,* Italy's signature cornmeal concoction. Restaurant closed Saturdays; hotel closed part of May and the first half of December. (Via Campo Tures 1, Brunico; phone: 0474-85469; moderate.)

BRESSANONE (BRIXEN): On the road to the Brenner Pass, this most charming Alto Adige town claims an eclectic combination of architecture and monuments from the medieval to the Baroque. From the 11th century to the first decade of the 19th century, it was ruled by prince-bishops, who also ruled much of the surrounding area. Its 13th-century cathedral, redone in the Baroque style in the 18th century, is imposing, and it has an adjoining cloister covered with 14th- and 15th-century frescoes, as well as an even older (begun in the 11th century) frescoed baptistry. The *Palazzo dei Principi Vescovi* (*Palace of the Prince-Bishops*) is also worth a visit, but even if you see nothing else in Bressanone, stop at the *Hotel Elefante,* a beautifully preserved 16th-century building with one of the best restaurants in the Dolomites.

CHECKING IN/EATING OUT: *Elefante* – In the mid-16th century, this old inn stabled an elephant the king of Portugal was sending over the Brenner Pass as a gift to the Hapsburg emperors in Vienna. A fresco still remains to commemorate the event, and the inn looks as it did then, except for essential modernization such as heating, hot water, and phones. The public rooms and some of the 40-plus guestrooms have antique furnishings; across the street is an annex and a heated swimming pool. The restaurant serves Tyrolean cuisine and homemade pastry, but no dish is as famous as its *elefantenplatte* (*piatto elefante*), or elephant platter — a mountainous heap of meat and vegetables served to no fewer than four diners. Reservations suggested. Restaurant closed Mondays; hotel closed mid-November through February. (Via Rio Bianco 4, Bressanone; phone: 0472-22288; expensive.)

En Route from Bressanone – Pick up A22 to return quickly to Bolzano. Before leaving the Alto Adige, however, a side trip to charming Merano, approximately 18 miles from Bolzano, is recommended for those who have the time. Take SS38 northwest.

MERANO (MERAN): This old-fashioned spa town has few major monuments but definite character. It is picturesque and quaint — see Via dei Portici in the old city center — as well as cosmopolitan. The town is also very lively, thanks to events such as summer evenings of folk dancing or the two concerts held each day from April to October along the Passeggiata Lungo Passirio (only one of Merano's promenades offering tranquillity or scenic views — others are the Passeggiata Tappeiner and the summer and winter promenades, the Passeggiata dell'Estate and the Passeggiata d'Inverno). Europeans also visit Merano for their health, since its mineral waters are supposed to be very beneficial, especially for digestive and circulatory problems as well as skin ailments. In the summer, the town draws walkers; in the winter, skiers; but spring and autumn are the spa seasons. In fall, too, the town, in the center of a grape-growing district, has been the traditional place to take the grape cure, although the distinction between grape cure and wine therapy is sometimes fuzzy.

CHECKING IN: *Castel Freiberg* – Once upon a time, this hotel was a castle. Built in the 14th century, it stands on a hill in total isolation a bit more than 4 miles southeast of Merano. Although reminiscent of very ancient times, the quality of service, the facilities, and the level of comfort in the 35 rooms are all up-to-date. Restaurant, sauna, solarium, indoor and outdoor pools, tennis. (Località Fragsburg, Merano; phone: 0473-44196; expensive.)

Kurhotel Palace – A majestic structure with 124 rooms set in a park and surrounded by exotic plants. It's furnished in the elegant Empire style and is both traditional and comfortable. Restaurant, spa, indoor and outdoor pools, sauna. (Via Cavour 2, Merano; phone: 0473-34734; expensive.)

Kurhotel Schloss Rundegg – Another castle that has been transformed into a hotel, and since this one was built in the year 1100, a stay in one of the 30 rooms is like taking a leap into the past. Restaurant, spa, indoor pool, sauna, solarium, tennis, garden. (Via Scena 2, Merano; phone: 0473-34364; expensive.)

Schloss Labers – This medieval castle became a hotel in 1885, and the interior is highly evocative. Outdoor restaurant in the warm months; typical Tyrolean bar. Heated pool. 32 rooms. (Via Labers 25, Merano; phone: 0473-34484; expensive to moderate.)

Augusta – A beautiful Liberty villa with some two dozen rooms and a restaurant. (Via Otto Huber 2, Merano; phone: 0473-49570; moderate.)

EATING OUT: *Andrea* – The tone of this highly recommended restaurant is traditional; the cuisine is regional but with a modern twist. Spinach *krapfen* and crêpes with Parmesan and beer are among the specialties, and there is a very refined selection of local and national wines. Closed Mondays. (Via Galilei 44, Merano; phone: 0473-37400; expensive.)

Villa Mozart – A very exclusive and refined restaurant in a small hotel decorated in authentic turn-of-the-century Viennese Jugendstil. Well-chosen regional and national wines accompany cuisine of very high quality. Reservations suggested. (Via San Marco 26, Merano; phone: 0473-30630; expensive.)

Naif – A classic Austrian beer hall serving regional food. Closed Mondays. (Via Val di Nova 35, Merano; phone: 0473-32216; moderate.)

Terlaner Weinstube – Typical ancient Tyrolean, located under the arches of a picturesque street. The furnishings are antique, and the food is regional and international. Reservations suggested. Closed Wednesdays. (Via dei Portici 231, Merano; phone: 0473-35571; moderate.)

En Route from Merano – Return to Bolzano on SS38 and switch there for the A22 southbound to Trento, only 18 miles away.

TRENTO: Trento is a noble, although somewhat austere, city on the Adige River, surrounded by mountains — the Dolomites to the east and the Brenta group, a prolongation of the Dolomites, to the west. Roman in origin, Trento became an important town on the way to the Brenner Pass for the same strategic reasons its northern neighbor, Bolzano, did. From the 11th century until 1803, it, along with the rest of the Trentino province, was ruled by prince-bishops of Trent, whose rule extended into Alto Adige for part of that time. The city gained lasting fame in the mid-16th century as the seat of the Council of Trent, which sat from 1545 to 1563 in an attempt to reform the church and curtail the spread of the Protestant Reformation. After a brief stint of Napoleonic rule, Trento became Austrian until the end of World War I although, unlike Bolzano, it has always been largely Italian-speaking and Italian in character. Today it is the capital of the Trentino–Alto Adige region.

Much remains in Trento from the medieval period and much also from the early 16th century, due to the influence of a particularly humanistic prince-bishop, Bernardo Clesio. Among the city's highlights is the Duomo, 12th- and 13th-century Lombard Romanesque to Gothic in style. Inside is the Cappella del Crocifisso (Crucifix Chapel), containing the crucifix before which the Council of Trent's decrees were proclaimed. From the Duomo, walk north along Via Belenzani, the city's most beautiful avenue, lined with Venetian-style Renaissance palaces, some with frescoed façades. Turn right onto Via Manci, another notable street, and follow it to Trento's most celebrated monument, the *Castello del Buonconsiglio (Castle of Good Counsel)*, the residence of the prince-bishops. It actually consists of several parts, including the 13th-century Castelvecchio, the oldest, and the 16th-century Palazzo Magno, a Renaissance addition by Bernardo Clesio.

 CHECKING IN: *Alessandro Vittoria* – Very modern but tasteful. No restaurant; 70 rooms. (Via Romagnosi 16, Trento; phone: 0461-980089; expensive to moderate.)

Grand Hotel Trento – Larger than the *Alessandro Vittoria,* with 94 rooms and a cozy atmosphere. Its restaurant, *Il Caminetto,* is a good dining spot. Private garden. (Via Alfieri 1, Trento; phone: 0461-981010; expensive to moderate.)

America – A very cordial family atmosphere is one of the plusses of this 43-room hotel. Restaurant. (Via Torre Verde 52, Trento; phone: 0461-983010; moderate.)

EATING OUT: *Chiesa* – Housed in a 16th-century palace, with the accent on sophistication. The cuisine is regional Trentino but very refined, and a very select range of Trentino wines is served. Closed Sunday evenings and Mondays. (Parco San Marco, Trento; phone: 0461-985577; moderate.)

Birreria Forst – Don't miss the chance to eat in this very popular beer hall. The cuisine is regional as are the wines. Closed Mondays. (Via Oss Mazzurana 38, Trento; phone: 0461-26399; inexpensive.)

En Route from Trento – One last side trip leads to the Dolomiti di Brenta and to the popular resort of Madonna di Campiglio. Take A22 north 9 miles to Mezzolombardo. Exit and follow SS43 northbound to Cles. If its name rings a bell, it's because this pretty medieval village was once the home of the Clesio family, one of whose members figured prominently in Trento's past and whose ancestral castle is outside of town. After Cles, at the intersection, take SS42 westbound, through Male. At Dimaro, pick up SS239 southbound into Madonna di Campiglio.

MADONNA DI CAMPIGLIO: If ever a resort came close to competing with Cortina, it's Madonna di Campiglio. It has all the ingredients: first-class hotels, excellent facilities, fashionable shops, and a marvelous setting at the bottom of a large valley, dominated to the east by the beautiful Brenta Dolomites and to the west by the magnificent Presanella and Adamello groups. Dense fir woods surround the village.

Although the first hotel was built in Madonna di Campiglio in 1872, the resort became known in the years between the two world wars. It owes its popularity above all to skiers, but the area is also a real paradise for mountain climbers — it has one of the best mountain climbing schools in the Alps. For the less ambitious, there are countless excursions and hikes to some of the most scenic spots, and tramways and chair lifts are available for many of these. The best, by far, are trips to the Grosté, to Monte Spinale, and to Pradalago.

CHECKING IN/EATING OUT: *Golf* – This very fashionable 124-room hotel is 1½ miles north of Madonna di Campiglio, in Campo Carlo Magno. A former summer residence of the Hapsburg family, it is both elegant and cozy, with an excellent restaurant, as well as a 9-hole golf course. Closed April through June and September through November. (Campo Carlo Magno; phone: 0465-41003; expensive.)

Carlo Magno Zeledria – A cozy Alpine lodge that was a tavern in the 18th century. Set in a lovely pine forest, it has 100 rooms and an indoor pool. Closed May, October to early December. (Passo di Campo Carlo Magno; phone: 0465-41010; expensive to moderate.)

Grifone – Modern yet cozy. The atmosphere of a mountain lodge prevails in this 38-room hotel, which also has a nursery for children. Closed May, June, October, and November. (Via Vallesinella 7, Madonna di Campiglio; phone: 0465-42002; expensive to moderate.)

Il Caminetto – Cozy and warm atmosphere, especially in the *caminetto* (fireplace) room. Wicker furniture is well blended with some antiques. (Via Adamello 17, Madonna di Campiglio; phone: 0465-41242; moderate.)

The Veneto

Ask a citizen of the Veneto to describe the area and, apart from showering the questioner with a well-used inventory of superlatives, the most likely reply would describe the region as having a little bit of everything. Such claims, far from being ill-founded boasts, are solidly rooted in the region's geography. Stretching from the soaring pink-hued peaks of the Dolomite Mountains to the flat, green plains of the Po River, the Veneto is one of the most diverse regions in all of Italy. Indeed, Truman Capote's description of Venice — "like eating an entire box of chocolate liqueurs in one go" — could equally apply to its namesake region.

Aside from the Dolomites and their rambling foothills, which define the Veneto's northern frontier with Austria, other highlands include the Asolan and Euganean hills, whose tranquil, vine-covered slopes have long been relished by writers, poets, painters, and others with a good excuse for escaping the often oppressive heat of the lowland summer. Even more typical of the region are the vast landscapes of its plains, ironed flat as a pizza by the sweeping maneuvers of mighty rivers like the Po, Italy's most important, the Adige, the country's third longest, the Brenta, Piave, Sile, and Livenza (all of which are touched and often intimately pursued by this itinerary).

The area is also abundantly rich in agriculture. Unlike the rural scenery found throughout much of Europe, the farms of the Veneto still retain a human scale, and many of the ingredients waiting to be savored on the local *trattoria* tables, including the wines, have been grown on a small holding, probably no more than a few minutes' drive from the kitchen.

Vacationers, after touring the hinterlands of the Veneto, will invariably — and loudly — sing the praises of its beaches. Or rather its beach, for almost all the coastline constitutes one continuous, fine sand ribbon, interrupted only by the mouths of rivers and lagoons. But the flavor of its many parts does vary, from the heavily trafficked resorts of Jesolo and the Lido of Venice to miles of deserted horizons which remain the exclusive territory of birds that thrive in a low-profile world of reed beds and tall grasses. Inland the Veneto offers its visitors another bonus shoreline — over thirty miles of beach on the eastern coast of Lake Garda, Italy's largest lake. Like the region's hillier retreats, the Riviera-like resorts of Garda have been popular since ancient times.

But the Veneto is more than a place of natural beauty. Historically and artistically it is the one region that reflects the Byzantine influences imported through Italy's eastern trading routes. Roman influence also left its mark, for the conquering legions of the emperor Augustus based themselves here to repulse the invading barbarian tribes of northeastern Europe. Later, during the Middle Ages, under the influence of rich local families who ruled the

Veneto cities (the Scaligeri of Verona, the Carraresi of Padua, the Camino of Treviso) the Veneto became, together with Tuscany, economically and artistically one of the richest areas of the peninsula.

The Veneto was also subject to the central government of Venice at the zenith of its career as a republic (during the fourteenth and fifteenth centuries). Venice's ascendancy resulted in the creation of some of the world's greatest works of art and supreme examples of serene architectural grandeur — most notably the magnificent Palladian villas, several of which still grace the Veneto landscape.

The rich, lively paintings and frescoes that adorn so many Venetian interiors are the work of such Renaissance greats as Giotto, Pisano, Andrea Mantegna, and Filippo Lippi in the fourteenth and fifteenth centuries, and the Tiepolo father and son Venetian painters of the seventeenth and eighteenth centuries, most of whom either lived or passed through the Veneto.

Venetian cuisine is as diverse as its geography. The hearty mountain fare, featuring dumplings, soups, rich desserts, and cakes, shows a strong Austrian influence. The fertile hills and plains around Verona, Vicenza, and Treviso offer magnificent veal and vegetable dishes. In the hilly forests around Belluno, there is a wealth of wild mushrooms and game, while *cucina casalinga* (home cooking) on the coast boasts the culinary delights of Adriatic fish and shellfish, such as tuna, sardines, and lobster. Venetian wines are world famous, from the dry white Pinot Bianco and Grigio to the red Cabernet and Merlot, not to mention the fiery, highly alcoholic *grappa* made from the final grape pressings and the rare and costly white Piccolit.

So, being a land for the art lover or architecture buff, the winter sports enthusiast or beach bum, the mountaineer or the gourmet, the wine taster or the health nut, the Veneto is built to satisfy the most conservative tastes and the wildest whims. From Venice, our route follows the Brenta Canal, and the magnificent country villas that overlook it, to Padua (with an optional detour to the Euganean Hills) and, by-passing Vicenza, heads for Verona. After a stop at Verona on the Adige River, the route returns via Vicenza — the city of Palladio — branches out to the Dolomite foothills and Bassano del Grappa on the Brenta Canal, and then continues on to the mountain town of Belluno by way of the delightful panoramic setting of Asolo, before detouring down through the mountains to the town of Treviso. Nine or ten days should be allowed for a leisurely drive since the countryside is as spectacular as the towns in this northeastern border region of Italy.

Prices in the Veneto vary greatly depending on whether an establishment is in the tourist honeypots like Venice and the historic centers like Padua, Verona, and Treviso, or slightly off the beaten track in Belluno, Bassano del Grappa, or the Euganean Hills. As a guideline, expect to pay from $90 to $130 for an expensive double room with breakfast, $50 to $90 for moderate, and under $45 for an inexpensive one. An expensive meal for two with wine should cost between $90 and $120; a moderate one, between $60 and $90; and an inexpensive one, under $35.

As in most regions, the Veneto has a network of efficient tourist information offices. Most towns and cities have either an *Azienda Autonoma di Soggiorno e Turismo* (local tourist board) or an *Ente Provinciale del Turismo* (provincial tourist board). The latter will have information not only on the town but also on the surrounding province.

En Route from Venice – Take the road for Porto Marghera and then follow signs for Malcontenta. Here the road follows the Brenta Canal, where, escaping the steamy heat of Venice, noble Venetian families took their ease in magnificent villas, some designed by seminal architect Andrea Palladio. It is still possible to travel by boat to Padua aboard *Il Burchiello,* which makes the journey from Venice on Tuesdays, Thursdays, and Saturdays, and the return trip on Wednesdays, Fridays, and Sundays, from the end of March to the end of October, stopping off at three villas. The price (90,000 lire, approximately $60) includes lunch in Oriago, a guide, entrance fees, and return bus fare. Details: *Siamic Express,* Padua (phone: 049-660944).

BRENTA RIVIERA: Villa La Malcontenta, the first of the grand villas, constructed by Andrea Palladio for the Foscari family in 1560, is a gracious masterpiece lying half hidden behind weeping willows. (Open 9 AM to noon, Tuesdays, Saturdays, and the first Sunday of the month from May to October.) The next villa worth stopping for is Widmann, an impressive house with French Baroque overtones to its original early-18th-century Venetian façade. Here the family portrait is a frescoed ceiling in the hall, and there are mythical frescoes by Giuseppe Angeli. The garden is a typical example of the Venetian mannerism of the 18th and 19th centuries, with its box hedges and statues. Open daily, except Mondays, 9 AM to noon and 3 to 6 PM. Admission fee.

DOLO: This town is dotted with 17th- and 18th-century family villas, many of them still inhabited, as well as the domed and pillared 18th-century parish church of San Rocco. Just beyond Dolo lies one of the Brenta's pièces de résistance, Villa Lazara Pisani, a romantic 18th-century construction, its creeper-covered façade facing the canal, its elegant porticoed back to the flat Veneto plains.

STRA: The climax of this canalside tour is reached at Stra, on the outskirts of Padua, where the Villa Pisani, now a national monument, dwarfs all other Brenta villas both in size and magnificence. Built in the mid-18th century for the Pisani family (who owned 50 villas in all), there are 164 rooms (only 8 of which are open to the public) bearing original frescoes, including the huge ballroom ceiling, a work by Giambattista Tiepolo that depicts the power and success of the Pisani family. As befits such a palatial residence, it was visited by several monarchs, grand dukes, and tsars traveling around Europe. In 1807, Napoleon bought it and gave it to his brother, the viceroy of Italy. Then, in 1934, it served as the first rendezvous for Hitler and Mussolini. The villa is open daily, except Mondays, 9 AM to 1:30 PM; the park is open 9 AM to 5 PM, to 6 PM in summer. Admission fee.

PADUA: Padua's frenetic, noisy, unattractive approaches are a poor indication of what lies ahead. The city's heart is, like all the Venetian towns on this route, a historic jewel, its buildings looking more like a brilliant stage setting for some Shakespearean performance (in which no expense has been spared!). With a history dating back to the Trojan War, Padua (or Patavium, as it was known in 10 BC — Padova in modern Italian) is today one of the most important industrial, commercial, and agricultural centers in northern Italy. In 1200 the first wall around Padua was built and its university founded — one of the earliest in Europe and in Italy second in age only to Bologna.

Feudal rule in the mid-14th century culminated in virtual ownership of the town by the Da Carrara family, until they met their end in a war with the Venetians, under whose rule Padua prospered until it underwent the vicissitudes common to the Veneto region when it was ceded to the Austrians. The artistic landmarks of Padua are relics of its dramatic history, and today some of the major treasures of art and architecture in this part of the world are housed here.

The Scrovegni Chapel was erected by the noble Paduan family of the same name alongside the Piovego Canal (which runs through the city center) and is entirely decorated with 14th-century frescoes by Giotto. Considered to be among the most striking examples of the Tuscan painter's later works, they depict 38 scenes from the lives of the Virgin Mary and Jesus Christ. Corso Garibaldi (phone: 049-650845). Open April 1 through September, 9 AM to 12:30 PM and 2:30 to 5:30 PM; October through March, 9:30 AM to 12:30 PM and 1:30 to 4:30 PM. Admission fee.

When Padua's patron, Saint Anthony, died just behind the present train station in 1231, a Gothic basilica was erected around his tomb in Piazza del Santo. Known simply as the *Santo,* it is a wonderful mixture of Romanesque Gothic and Byzantine architecture, with arched doorways and eight-tiered domes. The main altar, notable for its ornate gold bas-reliefs, is the work of Donatello, a leading Renaissance artist, as are the nine sculpted reliefs along the top of the saint's enormous tomb. Open daily, 6:30 AM to 7 PM October to March; to 7:45 PM April to September (phone: 049-663944). It is worth asking the sacristan for access to the cloisters, which were built between the 13th and the 16th century and which afford a fine view of the basilica.

Across the square from the Santo is the *Oratory of Saint George,* a family burial chapel of the Soragna family frescoed by Jacopo Avanzi and Altichieri. Next door, the *Scuola del Santo (School of Saint Anthony)* is lined with 16th-century frescoes, some by Titian. Both are open daily, 9 AM to noon and 2:30 to 6 PM; to 6:30 PM May to September. Closed April. Admission fee.

The neoclassical, "doorless" *Caffè Pedrocchi* is Padua's pride and joy and its principal 19th-century monument. Standing in Piazzetta Pedrocchi in the precincts of the university just off Piazza delle Erbe, it was bought by Antonio Pedrocchi in 1831. The ground floor is still used as a *caffè,* its outside seating a popular vantage point over the lively, cobbled Piazza delle Erbe (phone: 049-27397).

To stand in Piazza dei Signori, one of Padua's several historic squares, is to step back in time. It is surrounded by the one-time local government seat, the 14th-century *Palazzo del Capitanio,* the early-15th-century clock tower, and the Renaissance *Loggia del Consiglio.* In another of the city's beautiful squares, Prato della Valle, there is an open-air market every Saturday, selling, among other items, footwear manufactured along the Brenta River.

 CHECKING IN: *Grande Italia* – One of Padua's smartest hotels, opposite the main station. (Corso del Popolo 81, Padua; phone: 049-650877; expensive.) *Europa* – A large, centrally located, efficient establishment with all the modern amenities. (Largo Europa 9, Padua; phone: 049-661200; moderate.)

EATING OUT: *El Toulà* – One of the eclectic chain of restaurants that specialize in Venetian cuisine, housed in a delightful 16th-century palace. Fish dishes make up the most important segment of the menu, supplemented by grilled vegetables, including the Venetian specialty, grilled *radicchio* (red lettuce), fresh salmon in a peppery marinade, grilled lamb and veal, and a variety of creamy desserts. Try Padua's special wine, the crisp, white Moscato from Arqua Petrarca in the heart of the Euganean Hills, as an accompaniment. (Via Belle Parti 11, Padua; phone: 049-26649; expensive.)

Da Giovanni – A must for meat lovers, specializing in huge whole roasts or boiled meats (a specialty here) that are carved at the table and homemade pasta as a hearty first course. Vegetables and salads are fresh and dressed with pure olive oil. Wines, whether of the house or from local vineyards, are excellent. (Via Maroncelli 22, Padua; phone: 049-772620; moderate.)

En Route from Padua – Just south of Padua, in the middle of the plains, is an unexpected collection of small, cone-shaped, densely vegetated volcanic hills called the Colli Euganei (Euganean Hills). This is one of Italy's most romantic corners; its small villages, monasteries, vineyards, and villas have been visited by poets, writers, and artists over the centuries. From Padua's main station, follow the city's ancient walls to the turnoff for the airport (Via Sorio). First stop is the magnificent *Abbey of Praglia,* a Benedictine monastery founded in the 11th century set against a backdrop of sharply rising hills with a magnificent view over the surrounding plains. Facing the monastery is the *Chiesa dell'Assunta,* a church dedicated to the Madonna, reconstructed in the 15th century in Venetian Renaissance style. Ask one of the monks for permission to visit its art treasures and elegant cloisters.

From the abbey, return to the main road, turn right, and follow the signs to Torreglia, Galzignano, Valsanzibio (with an excellent 18-hole golf course and the beautiful gardens of the Villa Barbarigo), then on to Arqua Petrarca. The latter is one of the most picturesque medieval villages in the region and the former home of 14th-century poet Petrarch. Return to Padua by way of Montegrotto Terme and Abano Terme, both important spa towns, so-called cities of miracles, where hotels continue the tradition of mud baths and similar therapies that have been enjoyed since Roman days. Today the area boasts over 100 indoor/outdoor swimming pools. It is also well endowed with simple *trattorie* — many offering quail and meat grilled on an open fire as specialties — and inexpensive *alberghi.*

The 55 miles that separate Padua from Verona can be covered on either the state highway (SS11) or the autostrada (A4), which runs more or less parallel and gives splendid views of the luscious green vine-clad hills of one of the most fertile areas of the country.

VERONA: Verona, of *Romeo and Juliet* and *Two Gentlemen* fame, is one of Italy's oldest and most beautiful cities, already in existence when it was occupied by the pre-Roman Etruscans. By 89 BC it had become one of the most flourishing Roman colonies, strategically situated at the junction of three important roads on a U-bend of the Adige River.

Today the city, known as "little Rome," still stands in a historical time warp, or, rather, time *warps,* since there is a Roman, a medieval, and a "modern," or Renaissance, Verona to enjoy. Important Roman buildings and gateways are still visible, including the magnificent amphitheater dominating the heart of the city. The Roman walls surrounding Verona were added to and fortified through years of invasions and now offer splendid views of the old city and the Adige River. Later, in the Middle Ages, Verona became an important feudal city of the Venetian Republic, under the 14th-century Scaligeri family, whose richly carved stone tombs figure largely on most itineraries. Veronese churches and museums house numerous samples of works by the grand masters of the "Serenissima" — such as Paolo Veronese, Francesco Buonsignori, and Liberale da Verona. For a more detailed report on the city, its sights, hotels, and restaurants, see *Verona* in THE CITIES.

En Route from Verona – Before returning eastward to Vicenza, time permitting, take a brief 40-mile excursion to Lake Garda, visiting Peschiera and returning to Verona via the impressive *Gardens of Sigurta.* Open 9 AM to sunset, Thursdays, Saturdays, Sundays, and public holidays, March through September.

From the northern outskirts of Verona, either follow the green signs for A4 to Vicenza (about 32 miles in the direction of Padua) and exit at Vicenza Ovest (west) or, alternatively, drive almost parallel to it along SS11, following a more scenic, if slightly longer, route through vineyard country, passing through the home of Soave wine.

VICENZA: Beautiful enough to be dubbed "the Venice of terra firma," Vicenza is best known as the city of Palladio. Born in the city (though some experts contest this, maintaining his birthplace to be Padua), Palladio was to have a huge influence not only on Vicenza's architecture — hence its common name Città del Palladio — but also on the development of buildings in the rest of Europe and America.

The central hub of activity is Piazza dei Signori, no less busy now than in the heyday of Vicenza's civic life. Like other Venetian cities, Vicenza was first and foremost a Roman colony which, having then suffered tyrannic ecclesiastical rule in the 11th century and coming close to destruction in medieval wars with neighboring armies in Padua and Verona, eventually flourished under the Venetian Republic. By the end of the 16th century the city was resplendent with new buildings, many of them built by Palladio, that survive to this day.

Piazza dei Signori is flanked on one side by what many consider this remarkable architect's masterpiece, the *Basilica,* formerly the Gothic Palazzo della Ragione, which Palladio converted to High Renaissance style. The Basilica was once the town hall — Palladio simply enveloped the preexisting building with his classic columns on two levels, the ground level in Doric form, the upper level in Ionic, transforming it into one of the finest Renaissance buildings in the world. Open 9:30 AM to noon and 2:30 to 5 PM Tuesdays through Saturdays; 10 AM to noon Sundays. Closed Mondays. Admission fee.

In one corner the Basilica is flanked by a tall, elegant 14th-century clock tower, *Torre di Piazza.* Facing it is the *Loggia del Capitano,* the former residence of the Venetian local governor and one of Palladio's most imposing works, although he never completed it. The town's main shopping street, Corso Andrea Palladio, is a visual delight, with its pillar-fronted buildings on either side interspersed with Renaissance palaces.

Another of the architect's works of genius is the Olympic theater in Piazza Matteotti. Modeled on an ancient Roman theater, it was completed only a few months before he died in 1585. The theater is an elliptical, rather than round, hemisphere made of wood and stucco, and the stage is surrounded by Corinthian columns and niches between painted street scenes with a masterly *trompe l'oeil* effect. (Open to visitors daily, except Sunday afternoons. Admission fee.) Although theater and ballet performances were not being staged during recent renovation, several performances are planned for 1987. Tickets can be purchased from the Agenzia di Viaggi Palladio, Via Cavour 16 (phone: 0444-546111).

Palazzo Chiericati is yet another of Palladio's imaginative projects, with its entire façade, except for the doorway, composed of two tiers of columns. This is now the home of the municipal museum and a fine collection of Venetian paintings by such artists as Paolo Veneziano, Battista da Vicenza, Carpaccio, Paolo Veronese, and Giovanni Buonconsiglio. Open daily, except Saturday afternoons, 9 AM to 12:30 PM and 2 to 4 PM; 2:30 to 5:30 PM in summer. Admission fee.

Vicenza sits in the middle of a countryside peppered with Palladian villas — a total of 56 are included in a booklet *The Villas* produced by the regional tourist board, Piazza Duomo 5 (phone: 0444-544805). One of the closest and most important is *Villa Valmarana "ai Nani"* ("of the dwarfs" because of the tiny statues on the garden wall). Built in the 17th century by Mattoni, a follower of Palladio, it is decorated with frescoes by Giambattista Tiepolo and his son Domenico. Open 3 to 6:30 PM Mondays through Saturdays (to 6 PM from October to April); 10 AM to noon Thursdays, weekends, and holidays. Closed mid-November to mid-March. Admission fee. Another villa is *La Rotonda,* just beyond Villa Valmarana and visible only from the garden, but this view is enough to admire the mastery of this perfectly proportioned villa begun by Palladio in the 16th century. Its four pillar-fronted façades have been copied by numerous English and French architects.

CHECKING IN: *Palladio* – A small, elegant hotel on a quiet, peaceful side street off Piazza dei Signori. (Via Oratorio dei Servi, Vicenza; phone: 444-21072 or -547328; moderate.)

Campo Marzio – For modern but basic amenities, try this hostelry at the edge of the gardens of Campo Marzio and a short walk from the Duomo and Corso Andrea Palladio. (Viale Roma 21, Vicenza; phone: 0444-545700; moderate.)

EATING OUT: *Abbuffata 2* – The house specialty is Adriatic fish, prepared in inimitable Venetian dishes, such as pâté, *risotto,* or en casserole, and accompanied by excellent local white wines. On the eastern outskirts of Vicenza. (Contrà Porta Padova 65–67, Vicenza; phone: 444-505213; moderate.)

Scudo di Francia – Housed in one of the city's many delightful old *palazzi* and dispensing cuisine as authentically local as its antique furniture. This is a good place to try the traditional dish of the area, *baccalà* (cod fish with *polenta*), or pasta with white beans, as well as game or a flight of fancy such as turkey with pomegranates. The wine list has an excellent selection of local vintages. (Contrà Piancoli 4, Vicenza; phone: 444-28655; moderate.)

En Route from Vicenza – Take a northeasterly route for Bassano del Grappa by following SS53. At the first main intersection turn left on SS47, which leads past the Villa Trissino at Cricoli and the Villa Casarotto and Villa Del Conte, both at Dueville and open only on Sundays. A 20-mile drive, this road heads northward to the foothills of the Dolomites, which rise against the skyline, marking an abrupt boundary to the now familiar flat horizon. Before you reach Bassano del Grappa it is worth taking a slight detour to the splendid walled hill town of Marostica.

BASSANO DEL GRAPPA: On the banks of the Brenta River, Bassano del Grappa is a delightful little town filled with medieval and Renaissance streets, arcades, and houses and palaces with painted façades. From here, both the Venetian plains to the south and the mountains to the north, including Monte del Grappa, are visible. The town is famous for its 13th-century covered wooden bridge over the Brenta Canal. Designed to look like a ship moored between two quaysides, the bridge was immortalized in songs during World War I, when Bassano was at the center of fierce fighting between the Austrian and Italian armies (a war cemetery on Monte del Grappa holds the bodies of more than 20,000 victims). Bassano memorializes the war with Viale dei Martiri (Avenue of the Martyrs), which leads to the town's finest viewpoint, as well as with monuments to fallen soldiers. Bassano is also famous for its *grappa,* the fiery alcoholic drink made from the last grape pressings, as well as for its fine white sculpted pottery.

The *Museo Civico* (*Municipal Museum*), housed in an old convent behind the medieval Church of Saint Francis (Via Museo 4), includes works by Jacopo dal Ponte, a local 16th-century realist painter known simply as Bassano, who excelled in *trompe l'oeil* painting. Open daily, 10 AM to 12:30 PM and 3:30 to 6:30 PM; weekends, 10 AM to 12:30 PM. Admission fee.

EATING OUT: *Ca 7* – Housed in an 18th-century Venetian villa about one mile south of town on SS47. Enjoy selections from the fish-based menu either in the garden or in the gracious dining room, with a dry, sparkling, white Prosecco. (One mile north of Bassano; phone: 0424-25005; moderate.)

ASOLO: From Bassano it is a 9-mile drive eastward to Asolo through countryside dotted with villas and green hills but lined mostly with unsightly ceramics factories (their showrooms, open to the public, are more interesting).

Known as "the town of a hundred horizons" because of its immense panoramas, Asolo is a small farming market village. Perched on a hill and built around a small square filled with leafy horse-chestnut trees and 15th- to 17th-century buildings, it was much loved by Anglo-Saxon writers and painters in the last century. The local museum (irregular openings — inquire on the spot) has documents and manuscripts belonging to the English poet Robert Browning, who spent many years in Asolo (his son is buried here, as is the Italian actress Eleonora Duse), as well as works by the immensely successful 18th-century sculptor Antonio Canova (who was born 6 miles north of here in a village called Possagno).

CHECKING IN: *Villa Cipriani* – Among the green hills overlooking Asolo stands this 16th-century villa, embellished in the 18th century and now the epitome of rural romanticism and seclusion. It is a member of the luxury CIGA hotel chain. Today's guests enjoy the same suggestive surroundings that seduced Anglo-Saxon travelers a century ago. (Via Canova 298, Asolo; phone: 0423-55444; expensive.)

Bellavista – For classic views and accompanying birdsong, just on the outskirts of town. Closed mid-December to mid-January. (Via Collalto 8, Asolo; phone: 0423-52088; moderate.)

EATING OUT: *Charly's One* – Like the clientele, the menu is both local and foreign, with Scottish smoked salmon, onion soup, local smoked goose, Châteaubriand with tarragon and béarnaise sauce. Fresh fish served Tuesdays to Thursdays. Closed Fridays and November. (Via Roma 55, Asolo; phone: 0423-52201; moderate.)

Hostaria Ca Derton – Enjoy excellent local fare in this 16th-century house with a 19th-century wood interior. The menu offers such traditional dishes as pasta with beans, *risotto* with fresh mushrooms, asparagus or *radicchio* from Treviso, and, according to season, game, suckling pig, and rabbit accompanied by fresh artichokes or peppers. Desserts are homemade and vary with the whim of the proprietor. (Piazza D'Annunzio 11, Asolo; phone: 0423-52730; inexpensive.)

En Route from Asolo – Follow the minor road that leads eastward for five miles to Cornuda La Valle and the intersection of the main road to Belluno. Here turn left and head for the mountains. The road follows the Piave River of World War I fame and rises to fresher, purer mountain air. For some 30 miles, pastures, woods, and mountain peaks are occasionally interrupted by small villages of wooden chalets and smoking chimney pots.

BELLUNO: The approach to Belluno, as with a number of Italian towns, is a disappointing confusion of small industries and roadside billboards, with only glimpses of field and mountain between. Press on to the heart of the town, however, where its pretty *piazze* and cobbled streets, embodying the characteristic layout of a Roman city, lead to the market square and the 15th-century fountain with four water spouts. Some streets are still lined with shady, Renaissance porticoes.

Belluno's inhabitants, living so high, are blessed with magnificent views of the northeastern Dolomites. Nearer home, the skyline is dominated by the huge Baroque cathedral with its green, onion-shaped dome/bell tower, which still has its 14th-century crypt. The 15th-century *Palazzo dei Rettori* (*Rectors' Palace*), with its carved stone balconies and huge clock, retains its Venetian splendor but is now an administration center and, unfortunately, is no longer open to the public. The same applies to the *Bishops' Palace*, across the square, which, although largely rebuilt in the 17th century, is the only town building with medieval characteristics.

The town's museum is in the ancient Lawyers' College and contains works by both famous (such as Bartolomeo Montagna) and lesser-known local artists, plus archaeological remains dating from prehistoric, Roman, and medieval times that were found in the area. Open 10 AM to noon and 3 to 6 PM Tuesdays through Saturdays; mornings only on Sundays. Admission fee.

CHECKING IN: *Villa Carpenada* – Surrounded by a large garden and wood-land, this 18th-century villa is an ideal spot from which to enjoy mountain jaunts. (Via Mier 158, Belluno; phone: 0437-22078; moderate.)

Dolomiti – A neat, clean establishment tucked away down a side street off the main Piazza Vittorio Veneto and its arcaded shopping streets and cafés. (Via Carrera 5, Belluno; phone: 0437-27077; moderate.)

EATING OUT: *Al Borgo* – Veneto mountain cooking is at its best in this simple 19th-century villa. Features include soups, *gnocchi* (small dumpling-like pieces of pasta) mixed with meat or ricotta cheese or with local *radicchio,* and pancakes made with field herbs or mushrooms, as well as local venison or goat, roasted or cooked with fresh vegetables. The homemade desserts are often based on local fruit, such as mountain blueberries or wild strawberries. (Via Anconetta 8, Belluno; phone: 0437-24066; moderate.)

En Route from Belluno – For a taste of the Dolomites, head north along the Piave River to Ponte nelle Alpi, then turn right, leaving the river behind, onto the main Venice road, and almost immediately take the left turn marked Cansiglio. Here the villages, meadows, and pine- and chestnut-covered mountains, their summits often hidden by cloud, make a refreshing change from the sultry summer heat of the towns and lagoons. The road winds around the mountains past the red, overhanging eaves of tiny holdings, sudden *trattorie,* and the occasional *albergo.* Continue across the flatter, lush meadows of the Alto Piano before descending steadily to Vittorio Veneto (where there is an excellent 9-hole golf course) and then follow the signposts to the attractive 15th-century town of Treviso.

TREVISO: This walled city is approached by straight-as-a-die, tree-lined avenues. One of Italy's industrial and agricultural centers, it stands where two rivers emerge (having traveled underground from the mountains), meet, and then divide into fast-flowing canals, giving the city a mini-Venice stamp of design.

Treviso suffered extensive damage during World War I, and nearly half its buildings were destroyed in an air raid in 1944; hence the general lack of antiquity in a town that was founded during the Roman Empire. Nevertheless, narrow streets and old houses decorated with frescoes are still evident. The central Piazza dei Signori is flanked on one side by the Romanesque *Palazzo dei Trecento,* named after the city's 13th-century governing council of 300 citizens. One of the buildings that needed scrupulous reconstruction after the bombing, it is now used for town administration.

A short walk down the Calmaggiore, the main street with its elegant shops semihidden behind elegant 15th-century porticoes, leads to the *Duomo,* with its seven hemispherical domes in lead and copper, its Neoclassical façade a 17th-century addition to the original Romanesque design. Inside is an altar painting of the Annunciation by Titian.

The *Civic Museum* on Borgo Cavour contains frescoes and paintings by Venetian artists, including works by Cima da Conegliano, Titian, and Gino Rossi. Open daily, except Mondays, 9 AM to 12:30 PM and 2:30 to 6 PM; to 4:30 PM October to April. Admission fee.

CHECKING IN: *Villa Condulmer* – Ten miles south of Treviso in Zerman, on the outskirts of Mogliano Veneto, this 18th-century villa stands in its own parkland surrounded by such 20th-century luxuries as a swimming pool, golf course, riding stables, and tennis courts. For a final act of indulgence in Venetian hospitality, this hotel is hard to beat, with the added pleasure of an excellent restaurant. Closed November to mid-March. (Zerman; phone: 0422-457100; moderate.)

EATING OUT: *Alfredo El Toulà* – This is the original from which sprang the haute cuisine chain. The highest traditions of *mittel* European cuisine are respected and developed with local *trevigiano* flavor. Blinis with caviar, kidneys cooked with juniper berries, sirloin steaks with herbs, and veal with onions are just some of the culinary delights. Desserts include feather-light sorbets as well as more substantial creamy confections. (Via Collalto 26, Treviso; phone: 0422-540275; expensive to moderate.)

A l'Oca Bianca – A must for lovers of *cucina casalinga* (home cooking). Also near the central square. (Vicolo Bianchetti, Treviso; phone: 0422-541850; moderate.)

Le Beccherie – Tucked away behind Piazza dei Signori, this is both a hotel and an immensely popular, traditional, family-run restaurant. The menu changes with the seasons, so all ingredients, whether vegetable or game, are garden- or field-fresh and exquisitely cooked. The staff are extraordinarily fast and efficient as they steer between the tables at breakneck speed with steaks sizzling on marble slabs and with tempting dessert trolleys. (Piazza Ancilotto 11, Treviso; phone: 0422-540871; moderate.)

En Route from Treviso – Follow A27 due south for 19 miles to Venice.

Emilia-Romagna

The Emilia-Romagna region lies north of Tuscany and south of Lombardy and the Veneto, and from east to west it nearly stretches from sea to sea. Its eastern edge is on the Adriatic and its western tip reaches almost to the Ligurian coast, stopped short only by the Apennine range. Although part of the region is hill or mountain — a southerly strip that runs northwest to southeast along the Apennines — most of it is flat and low-lying, the fertile plain of the Po River, which forms the region's northern boundary. That geographical fact has made the region home to some of Italy's most abundant agriculture, which in turn has supported the rich and varied local cuisines. Bologna, the regional capital, fairly wallows in this abundance and revels in its nickname, *Bologna la Grassa* (Bologna the Fat).

The geographical reality of a low-lying wedge driven into an essentially mountainous country has also contributed to making Emilia-Romagna one of Italy's most prosperous commercial centers. The region takes its name in part from the Via Emilia, the ancient Roman road that runs, practically in a straight line, from Milan to the sea at Rimini. Laid out by Marcus Aemilius Lepidus in 187 BC to connect the Roman Empire with its newly acquired lands in northern Europe, the road proved to be the region's lifeblood, a communications link and a conduit for trade that played a role in virtually every social, political, and military development in the area from the days of the Roman Empire to World War II.

Despite the fact that modern Italy has made Emilia-Romagna one region, the area is, in fact, easily divided into two quite different sections. Emilia is the territory to the west, embracing the cities of Piacenza, Parma, Modena, and Bologna. Romagna is the smaller zone to the east, including Rimini and Ravenna. It is said in Italy that if you go to the house of an Emilian, he will offer you a glass of water; in Romagna, you will be offered wine. The gruffness inherent in the Emilian manner might have something to do with the fact that, until the unification of Italy in the nineteenth century, Emilia's cities and towns — first free communes, then medieval and Renaissance duchies or principalities — spent the greater part of their history fighting against outsiders and among themselves. The region that is today noted not only for its beautiful, flourishing cities but also for the small-town hospitality that prevails in them was not always so trusting of strangers.

The history of Romagna, on the other hand, tended toward internal cohesiveness and a wider identification with the world beyond its borders. The existence of the seaport at Rimini, once a major Western entrepôt for trade with the East, fostered a more cosmopolitan view of outsiders. That attitude lives on today: Rimini and the numerous seaside resorts nearby draw tens of thousands of holidaymakers from Britain, France, Germany, and Scandinavia, all anxious to play on the wide beaches and swim in the warm

Adriatic. At high season in Rimini it is rare to hear Italian spoken on the streets.

A more detailed account of the separate past of the two areas might begin with the period from the fifth to the eighth century, when Emilia was invaded repeatedly by wild and bloodthirsty barbarians — Goths, Lombards, and Franks. Three centuries of foreign domination left the region's cities in ruins and completely disunited, so that no sooner had they driven the invaders out than they began warring with their neighbors. With the outbreak of the struggle between the Guelphs and the Ghibellines, the bloody and largely pointless internecine warfare gradually became codified along political lines. By the thirteenth century, there was hardly a city on the entire Italian peninsula that hadn't been drawn into this seemingly interminable dispute between the forces of the pope and the Holy Roman Empire, and Emilia was no exception. Cities formed allegiances, betrayed them, were subjugated, and rebelled throughout the medieval period. It was only with the establishment of some of the great ruling families that a semblance of order was restored. Parma and Piacenza initially fell under the sway of the Visconti of Milan. Ferrara became the seat of the Este clan, which gradually extended its power to Modena and Reggio. The Pepoli and the Bentivoglio families dominated Bologna.

Although the brilliant, erratic, and ruthless Malatesta family seized Rimini and held it from the thirteenth to the sixteenth century, most of Romagna managed to stay aloof from the torment experienced by the Emilian cities. In 402, after the division of the Roman Empire into an Empire of the East and an Empire of the West, Honorius made Ravenna the capital of the latter. After the fall of Rome in the West (476), a short-lived kingdom of the Goths, under Odoacer and Theodoric, maintained Ravenna as a capital city. In the sixth century, however, the great emperor of the East, Justinian, defeated the Goths, and Ravenna became part of the Byzantine, or Eastern Roman, Empire, ruled by exarchs (civil governors), with an eye to what was going on back home in Constantinople.

The world-famous, Byzantine-inspired mosaics of Ravenna are a legacy of that far-off time when the city, in effect, turned its back on Italy and looked to Byzantium for culture and guidance. By the eighth century, however, the Lombards had established themselves in much of northern Italy. They even took Ravenna, but only briefly, and Romagna owes its name to the fact that it remained Roman while the Lombards prevailed in the region that bears their name. Then, in a rapid turn of events, the pope asked the help of the Frankish kings Pepin and Charlemagne in stemming the Lombard tide. Each proved willing and able, and Romagna came under papal domination, a condition that was to last until the nation of Italy was born in the nineteenth century.

Papal forces had, in the meantime, made some headway in Emilia, gaining a foothold in Bologna and its environs, but by and large this region remained fragmented and hard to handle. Then, in 1545, Pope Paul III, a member of the noble Farnese family, took control of Parma and Piacenza, creating a duchy for his illegitimate son to rule. By the seventeenth century, most of Emilia was in the hands of either the Farnese or the Este family, and the question of political power seemed more or less settled — until Napoleon invaded in the late eighteenth century, turning the balance of power upside down again. When the dust had settled, the empress Marie Louise of France had become duchess of Parma, and Austria had taken the rest of the province (along with Venice and a huge chunk of northern Italy). Romagna stayed safely in papal hands.

But it was not to last. By 1848, popular feeling for a united Italy, free of foreign occupiers, had become too great to suppress. Piacenza was the first city to throw in its lot with Piedmont (the birthplace of a unified Italy), and the rest of the region rapidly followed. In 1860, the area, now known as Emilia-Romagna, joined with Piedmont to form the nucleus of the modern Italian state.

Despite all the blood spilled in settling the fate of the region, Emilia-Romagna is today a peaceful, prosperous part of Italy. Some of the country's most famous exports originate here. Parma is the home of Parmesan cheese and Parma ham. From Modena come such great Italian automobile marques as Ferrari and Maserati. Bologna has given the world *spaghetti alla bolognese* and mortadella, the granddaddy of American "baloney"; Faenza is the home of faïence pottery. Perhaps the most enduring gift of all is the genius of composer Guiseppe Verdi, who was born in the tiny hamlet of Le Roncole, just outside Piacenza.

Piacenza, in the west and only 40 miles southeast of Milan, is the logical starting point for a tour of Emilia-Romagna. From here, following the ancient route — in some cases over the actual cobblestones — of the Via Emilia (SS9 on modern maps), our itinerary passes through Parma, Modena, Bologna, Imola, and Faenza to Rimini. From Rimini, it takes the coast road north to Ravenna and then turns inland to end in the majestic medieval town of Ferrara. Accommodations in the region range from expensive, as at the *Grand* in Rimini, where a night for two in high season can cost $100 and up, to many more moderate hotels ranging from $30 to $70. Inexpensive rooms are $20 and less. Expect to pay over $80 for a meal for two at those restaurants categorized as expensive; $30 to $50 at moderate ones; and under $25 at inexpensive places.

PIACENZA: Originally founded by the Romans, Piacenza is now a modern industrial city, but the medieval underpinnings of the old town remain largely intact. The city has always had considerable strategic value — it lies at the point where the Via Emilia touches the Po River — and in keeping with the history of settlements in this region, a great deal of blood was shed over the centuries to keep it in one camp or another. In 1545, Alessandro Farnese, otherwise known as Pope Paul III, created the duchy of Parma and Piacenza, which the Farnese family ruled until the early 18th century. Piacenza, however, has a history of independent thinking, a trait that showed itself on two notable occasions. In 1547, a group of Piacenza nobles tired of the tyranny and debauchery of their overlord, Pier Luigi Farnese, and murdered him. Since the Farnese family was extraordinarily powerful and Pier Luigi was the (illegitimate) son of the pope, the tyrannicide was an action requiring great courage. Three hundred years later, in 1848, Piacenza took another step into the unknown as the first Italian city to vote for annexation with Piedmont, the nucleus of the new unified Italian nation, and for this it became known as the *primogenita,* or firstborn.

The medieval heart of the town is Piazza dei Cavalli, so called because of the two massive 17th-century equestrian statues that dominate the square. These are two Farnese dukes, Alessandro and Ranuccio I, both descendants of the murdered Pier Luigi but obviously held in higher esteem. Facing them, looming over the piazza, is the graceful *Palazzo del Comune,* built in 1281 in Lombard-Gothic style and also known as the *Palazzo Gotico.* The Palazzo del Governatore, opposite, is a building of the late 18th century, and to one side of the square is the 13th-century Chiesa di San Francesco (Church of St. Francis), at the beginning of Via XX Settembre. Piacenza's *Duomo,* just down Via XX Settembre from Piazza dei Cavalli, is a towering Lombard-Romanesque building of the 12th and 13th centuries. It appears to have been built more for fortification than for worship, and its most curious feature is a thick-barred iron cage set in the masonry at a dizzying height on the side of the soaring bell tower. Miscreants of the town were tossed naked into this *gabbia* and forced to endure the jeers and mockery of the townspeople in the marketplace below. Inside, the cathedral shows evidence of the evolution from Romanesque to Gothic style, and there are frescoes by Guercino.

The *Museo Civico* (*Municipal Museum*), in Piazza Cittadella, is housed in the *Palazzo Farnese,* built in the latter part of the 16th century for that illustrious family. It contains paintings (especially of the 17th and 18th centuries) and a variety of archaeological specimens, one of which — the *fegato di Piacenza* — is a particularly odd relic of the days when Emilia was the land of the ancient Etruscans. This bronze cast of a liver inscribed with the names of various Etruscan deities is thought by archaeologists to have been a sort of religious road map, a guide to be consulted when Etruscan priests were called upon to read the entrails of a sacrificial beast.

If time permits, some other sights to see in Piacenza include two Renaissance churches, San Sisto and Santa Maria in Campagna, the latter with frescoes by Pordenone, and Sant'Antonino, an 11th-century Romanesque church with 14th-century Gothic additions. The tourist office (EPT) at Piazzetta dei Mercanti 10 (phone: 0523-29324) can provide further information.

CHECKING IN: *Grande Albergo Roma* – The best hotel in town, only a block from Piazza dei Cavalli, it has a restaurant with a good view of the city. This is a perfect location for exploring the city on foot, and there is ample parking for guests. (Via Cittadella 14, Piacenza; phone: 0523-23201; expensive to moderate.)

EATING OUT: *Antica Osteria del Teatro* – A quaintly elegant restaurant set in a narrow, picturesque street in the oldest part of town. It's famous for ravioli stuffed with duck and, in season, *flan di ortiche ai dadini di pomodoro,* a mousse made from local greens and tomatoes. There is also a wide array of other local delicacies, meats, and produce. Service and atmosphere are excellent. Closed Sundays and August. (Via Verdi 16, Piacenza; phone: 0523-23777; expensive.)

***Antico Caffè* –** As an alternative to a heavy lunch, try this beautifully decorated café, a few blocks from Piazza dei Cavalli. It serves good sandwiches on crusty bread, delicious pastries, and the best cappuccino in town. (Via Garibaldi 49, Piacenza; phone: 0523-24918; inexpensive.)

En Route from Piacenza – On the way to Parma (38 miles away by the direct route), a road running parallel to the Via Emilia travels through flat, bucolic countryside to the village of Busseto. The great opera composer Giuseppe Verdi was born in the tiny hamlet of Le Roncole (now known as Roncole-Verdi), about 3 miles southeast of Busseto, lived for a time in Busseto itself, and later built an estate at Sant'Agata, about 2 miles northwest of town. A ticket for admission to three Verdi landmarks can be bought at the Rocca (castle) of Busseto. It permits entry to the *Teatro Verdi,* a small opera house built by the town in honor of its famous son; to a museum in the Palazzo Pallavicino, where a few rooms are given over to Verdi memorabilia, including a piano he played as a child; and to the rough stone farmhouse where he was born and raised in the center of Le Roncole. Part of the Verdi villa at Sant'Agata, still a private home, is also open to the public from April through October. Visitors can see the composer's bedroom studio and a library, the bedroom of his second wife, singer Giuseppina Strepponi, a death chamber replicating the Milan hotel room where he died, and the surrounding gardens.

CHECKING IN: *I Due Foscari* – A small hotel owned by tenor Carlo Bergonzi and named after one of Verdi's operas, it offers 20 pleasant rooms near the center of town and has a restaurant with a terrace for outdoor dining in summer. Restaurant closed Mondays. (Piazza Carlo Rossi, Busseto; phone: 0524-92337; moderate.)

EATING OUT: *Guareschi* – Known for fabulous meals served with delightful informality. All of the vegetables, meat, poultry, butter, and bread are produced on the premises. Feast on the roast duck and *polenta,* the house specialty, but be sure to leave room for the coffee-flavored *zabaione* — you've never tasted anything quite like it. Open only for lunch. Closed Fridays and July. Reservations suggested. (Roncole-Verdi; phone: 0524-92495; expensive to moderate.)

PARMA: Despite heavy bombing during World War II, Parma retains the splendor it knew as the capital of the Farnese dukes from the mid-16th to the early 18th century. The French Bourbons succeeded the Farnese family, and then Napoleon annexed the duchy to France for a time. After his downfall, the Congress of Vienna awarded it to Marie Louise of Austria, Napoleon's second wife, who settled in for a long stay as duchess (1816–1847) and added her own touches to the city. Parma's elevated reputation among Italians is based largely on two factors. First, it is said to be one of Italy's most graceful and gracious towns, known not only for its architectural and artistic treasures but also for the courtly good manners of its people. Second, it has given Italy and the world *parmigiano* (Parmesan cheese) and *prosciutto di Parma* (Parma ham).

Two painters of the early 16th century are associated particularly closely with Parma: Antonio Allegri (known as Correggio because he was born in that nearby town), who worked extensively in Parma, and Il Parmigianino, who was born and worked here. In addition, Parma provides the setting for Stendhal's classic novel *The Charterhouse of Parma,* and it has quite a few musical associations besides its nearby links to Verdi. Arturo Toscanini was born in Parma; Nicolò Paganini, the virtuoso violinist, was born elsewhere but is buried here. The opera house built by Marie Louise, the Teatro Regio, is considered one of the most beautiful in Italy, and its audience is believed to be the toughest, perhaps in the world — the normal courtly good manners are nowhere in evidence if an operatic performance is merely mediocre.

The architectural beauty spots of the town are many, although the Duomo, the Baptistry, and the Chiesa di San Giovanni Evangelista (Church of St. John the Evangelist) — all part of the *centro episcopale,* on an ancient cobbled square in the historic heart of town — must have first claim to a visitor's attention. The Lombard-Romanesque *Duomo* was built in the 11th century, its campanile in the 13th century. Inside, the chief works of art are the *Deposition* bas-relief (on the west wall of the south transept) carved by sculptor Benedetto Antelami in 1178, the bishop's throne, which also has reliefs by Antelami, and Correggio's famous *Assumption of the Virgin* fresco on the ceiling of the dome, painted from 1526 to 1530. Recently restored, this swirling ascent of concentric circles of figures is a stunning sight, anticipating the Baroque in feeling, even though it was once unkindly described as a "hash of frogs' legs."

Building of the extraordinary, multitiered, octagonal *Baptistry* began in 1196, and when it was completed in the next century, Parma was graced by one of the finest ecclesiastical structures of the age. The work of Antelami adorns the doors, and the series of reliefs of the months and the seasons inside is also his, but the 13th-century ceiling frescoes are by an unknown hand. *San Giovanni Evangelista,* behind the Duomo, is noted for another ceiling fresco by Correggio, this time of St. John (the scene of St. John writing the Apocalypse over a doorway in the left transept is another Correggio), and for numerous frescoes by Parmigianino.

Not far from the *centro episcopale,* on the banks of the Parma River, is the giant and rather gloomy-looking *Palazzo della Pilotta,* begun by the Farnesi in the late 16th century but never finished. It is, however, big enough. The name derives from *pilotta,* a version of handball that was played in its vast, echoing chambers. Today the palace houses a complex of museums, including the Galleria Nazionale (National Gallery), the Museo Nazionale d'Antichità (National Museum of Antiquities), and the Biblioteca Palatina (Palatine Library), plus a theater, the Teatro Farnese. The *National Gallery* has some fine paintings by non-Emilian masters, such as Fra Angelico and da Vinci, as well as a variety of works by Correggio and Parmigianino. The *Palatine Library* incorporates a museum dedicated to Giambattista Bodoni, the 18th-century printer, who worked in Parma. The most extraordinary sight in the Palazzo della Pilotta, however, is the *Teatro Farnese.* Although the original was lost when the palace was bombed in World War II, the precise reconstruction that now stands is more than enough to give 20th-century visitors a sense of the lavish life lived at a ducal court. This giant Palladian folly held 4,500 spectators and was in use from 1628 to 1732. Made entirely of wood, it's too much of a fire hazard to be used today.

For more of Correggio's work, go to the *Camera del Correggio,* off Via Melloni, not far from Piazza Marconi. It's actually a room in the former convent of San Paolo decorated with the artist's earliest frescoes, the spirit and subject matter of which (mythological scenes, greenery, and *putti*) hardly seem monastic. Also worth a look is the majestic 16th-century *Chiesa della Madonna della Steccata,* damaged by bombs in the last war but admirably restored. It contains Parmigianino frescoes, tombs of the Farnese family, and the tomb of Field Marshal Count Neipperg, Marie Louise's second husband. Parma's tourist office (EPT), Piazza del Duomo (phone: 0521-34735), has information on still other sights.

 CHECKING IN: *Palace Hotel Maria Luigia* – Not far from the train station and within easy walking distance of the major sights, this modern, elegant hotel has 67 rooms and a well-regarded restaurant, *Maxim's* (no relation to the one in Paris). (Viale Mentana 140, Parma; phone: 0521-21032; expensive.)

Park Hotel Stendhal – Modern, comfortable, and well-run, in the center of town. There are 60 rooms, all with bath and air conditioning. (Piazzetta Bodoni 3, Parma; phone: 0521-208057; expensive.)

Savoy – A good choice for budget travelers, on a quiet side street in the center of town. The 21 rooms are good value for the money, and the service is also first rate. No restaurant. (Via XX Settembre 3, Parma; phone: 0521-21101; inexpensive.)

EATING OUT: *Angiol d'Or* – The specialties that made Parma famous are served here, and any pasta dish *alla parmigiana* is sure to be a winner. Follow with one of the excellent beef, veal, or pork dishes as a second course. Closed Sunday evenings, Mondays, and late August. (Via Scutellari 1, Parma; phone: 0521-22632; expensive to moderate.)

Parizzi – This is one of Parma's best known — and busiest — restaurants. The local specialties are best; particularly delicious are crêpes stuffed with Parmesan cheese. A good second is *stinco del santo,* a complicated pun (*stinco* is a cut of beef; in slang, a *stinco del santo* is someone who is too good to be true), but it adds up to a delicious beef casserole. Closed Mondays and most of August. Reservations required. (Strada della Repubblica 71, Parma; phone: 0521-25952; expensive to moderate.)

Vecchio Molinetto – A fine, old-fashioned, family-run restaurant, with rustic decor and a menu that falls squarely in the hearty-country category. There are excellent homemade pastas and veal dishes, and a delicious stuffed, boned chicken is the specialty of the house. All can be enjoyed in a nice little garden during the summer. Closed Fridays and August. (Viale Milazzo 39, Parma; phone: 0521-52672; moderate to inexpensive.)

MODENA: Bypass Reggio Emilia and continue on to this large industrial city, the next stop along the Via Emilia (SS9), 35 miles from Parma. The Este family brought it out of the bloody Middle Ages and conferred a long period of prosperity and prominence on it, through the Renaissance and beyond. The relative calm of the ducal period came to an abrupt end with the Napoleonic wars and subsequent Austrian domination, but the city rebelled twice and by the middle of the 19th century had dispatched the foreigners for good. Like Piacenza and Parma, it was an early member of the "new" Italy. Today, Modena is, above all, an automobile city. Three of the greatest names in Italian automobile design — Ferrari, Maserati, and De Tomaso — have their factories here. In addition, Modena is famous for its sparkling red Lambrusco wine, for the walnut liqueur Nocino, for *aceto balsamico* (balsamic vinegar), and for a local delicacy, *zampone* (stuffed pig's trotter), eaten all over Italy at New Year's Eve dinner. The great Italian opera singer Luciano Pavarotti is a local boy made good.

Today most of Modena is newly built, a large part of it dating from the postwar period. However, a kernel of the old town remains around the *Duomo*. Begun in 1099 and consecrated in 1184, it was designed by Lanfranco, an architect from Lombardy, and decorated by Wiligelmo, a master sculptor who did the four friezes on the façade. Dedicated to Modena's patron saint, St. Geminiano, it is one of Italy's best preserved Romanesque cathedrals. The *Torre Ghirlandina,* the tall, graceful Lombardian bell tower next to the cathedral, is one of the city's most conspicuous landmarks, completed in the early 14th century. Behind the cathedral is Modena's Piazza Grande, which has been the traditional marketplace of the city for centuries. Even today, on the last Sunday of every month, it is the focal point of a giant antiques market where it's fun to rummage through bric-a-brac, artwork, furniture, musical instruments, suits of armor, "genuine" religious relics, jewelry, and plain old junk, all available for prices far lower than those at comparable flea markets in Rome or Florence.

One additional worthwhile sight is the *Palazzo dei Musei,* along Via Emilia at Largo Porta Sant'Agostino. It contains various museums and picture galleries, but the most noteworthy installation is that of the *Biblioteca Estense* (*Este Library*), which houses thousands of books and illuminated manuscripts. Among the treasures on display is the 1,200-page Bible of Borso d'Este — a tour de force of 15th-century illumination. Modena's tourist information office is at Via Emilia Centro 179 (phone: 059-222482), not far from Piazza Grande.

CHECKING IN: *Fini* – Modena's best hotel has 93 attractively decorated rooms and all the modern amenities, even hair dryers in the bathrooms. It's on the outskirts of town, in the direction of Bologna and thus not near the restaurant under the same management (see *Eating Out*). But guests can be shuttled back and forth. Closed part of August and at Christmastime. (Via Emilia Est 441, Modena; phone: 059-238091; expensive.)

EATING OUT: *Fini* – The best restaurant in town, very elegant and quite expensive — the clientele tends to be Modena's first citizens or out-of-town sports dropping by to pick up their new Ferraris. The Fini company is one of the region's major producers of sausages, salamis, and other foods, so it's no surprise that the menu in the restaurant is virtually an encyclopedia of regional specialties. This is a good place to try *zampone* (stuffed pig's trotter) if you wish, or the rich selection of boiled meats known as *bollito misto.* Closed Mondays,

Tuesdays, and August. Reservations recommended. (Largo San Francesco, Modena; phone: 059-223314; expensive.)

Aurora – An intimate restaurant with good service and excellent food, very close to Piazza Grande. The roast veal is particularly good, as is the *pasta alla zucca* (pasta in pumpkin sauce). Closed Mondays. (Via Coltellini 24, Modena; phone: 059-225191; moderate to inexpensive.)

BOLOGNA: This historic city of red slate roofs, long arcades, and distinctive domes is roughly 24 miles down the Via Emilia from Modena. It is a hub of commerce and learning, renowned for its university — one of the oldest in Europe — and a gastronomic center of no small repute. For a detailed report of the city, its sights, hotels, and restaurants, see *Bologna,* THE CITIES.

En Route from Bologna – Continue southeast in the direction of Imola and Faenza, respectively 20 miles and 30 miles from Bologna via the Via Emilia (SS9). About halfway between Castel San Pietro Terme and Imola is the turnoff for Dozza, a charming hill town crowned by a majestic castle built between 1300 and 1600. In odd-numbered years, the outside walls of many of Dozza's houses are painted with frescoes, the work of artists taking part in the International Festival of the Painted Wall. The best frescoes are eventually removed and put on display in a gallery in the castle. The one-time castle dungeons have become the headquarters of the wine growers' guild of Emilia-Romagna, an *enoteca* (cellar) where their wines can be sampled and purchased. Imola itself doesn't have quite the charm of some of the other cities in the region, although it does have a 14th-century castle housing a good collection of arms and armor. For lovers of fine food, however, Imola is one of the most important stops in the entire Emilia-Romagna region, as it is the home of one of Italy's finest restaurants.

EATING OUT: San Domenico – Housed in a little cottage — part of a former convent — facing the castle, this delightful restaurant consistently serves some of the best food in the country. The cuisine is a blend of festive dishes that would have been served at the aristocratic tables of yesteryear and latter-day nouvelle cuisine, and everything is always expertly prepared and beautifully presented. The prix fixe menu of seven courses changes with the season. Reservations are a must. Closed Mondays. (Via Sacchi 1, Imola; phone: 0542-35830; expensive.)

Hotel Canè – A tiny hotel restaurant just down the street from the castle in Dozza. Its shaded terrace offers spectacular views of the fertile countryside. For the pasta course, try the handmade *garganelli.* Closed Mondays. (Via XX Settembre 27, Dozza; phone: 0542-88120; inexpensive.)

FAENZA: Faenza is a small town, most of it still encircled by its medieval walls. It is best known for the *maiolica* ceramics it has produced since the Middle Ages. Indeed, by the early Renaissance, Faentine potters enjoyed such wide renown that *maiolica* (the word refers to the Spanish island of Majorca, where the technique originated) became known to much of the world by another name: faïence. Today, some of the buildings in town are faced with ceramic tiles, and the street signs are ceramic plaques. Any number of artisans are at work in and around Faenza, and any number of shops offer vast assortments of their wares — among the best are *Bottega d'Arte Ceramica Gatti,* Via Pompignoli 4; *Morigi Mirta,* Via Barbavara 7; and *Geminiani Silvana,* Corso Mazzini 52. The industry that put Faenza on the map has also spawned a museum, the *Museo Internazionale delle Ceramiche* (*International Museum of Ceramics*), at Via Campidoro 2. Large and well designed, it covers the history, manufacture, and decoration of ceramics in every corner of the globe, from the dawn of time to the present, but the extensive collection of old Italian ceramics is particularly noteworthy. There is also a modern section, containing pieces by artists such as Matisse, Chagall, and Picasso.

En Route from Faenza – Keeping to the Via Emilia, the Adriatic coast at Rimini is now only 40 miles away. A few small towns, however, make interesting deviations from the straight and narrow. One is the spa town of Brisighella, just south of Faenza, on SS302. This beautiful little hill hamlet is dominated on one peak by a 14th-century castle and on another by a 13th-century clock tower. The whole town is extremely picturesque, particularly its central piazza, which is overlooked by a curious, arcaded main street, Via del Borgo. Another detour can be made for Predappio, just south of Forlì. This tiny village has earned an unenviable place in history as the birthplace, and resting place, of the dictator Benito Mussolini. The Mussolini crypt at the cemetery of San Cassiano in Appennino, containing the tomb of Il Duce, as well as other family members, is open to the public. A spotlighted bust of the dictator glowers down at visitors, and a guestbook set before his tomb is filled with messages from the unrepentant few who continue to make the pilgrimage to their leader. From Predappio, drive over some rolling hill country (via the town of Meldola, then back to the Via Emilia, turning south off it just past Forlimpopoli) to another quaint town, Bertinoro, which produces some of the region's best known wines. In its main square the village has a *colonna dell'ospitalità* (hospitality post), which is actually a tall stone column with wide metal rings in its sides, each ring corresponding to the home of a local family. Although it is a modern reconstruction, its site is that of a post set up in the 13th century to settle disputes among the townsfolk as to who would play host to travelers (everyone, it seems, was only too eager to oblige). The idea was that a traveler would tie his horse to a particular ring, and that family would welcome the traveler for the night.

Note that just before arrival in Rimini comes the epic crossing of the Rubicon. Travelers pass over the legendary river just as Julius Caesar did in 49 BC, except that Caesar was moving south from Gaul to Rome when he forded it. Regrettably, the event is hardly notable these days, for the river is now an uninspiring ditch at Savignano, between Cesena and Rimini.

■ **EATING OUT: *Antica Cantina Pasini*** – This ancient wine cellar perched on a hillside serves a hearty lunch of good cold cuts, sausages, and crusty bread. It's also pleasant to sample some of the local wines: the sweet, white Albana amabile, the drier Albana secco, the medium-dry white Pagadebit, and the full-bodied red Sangiovese. (Via Francesco Rossi 1, Bertinoro; phone: 0543-445667; inexpensive.)

La Grotta – An intimate, first-class eatery housed in a hollow scraped out of the giant rocks of the mountainside of Brisighella. The food is excellent, the service flawless, and the high overall quality of the place seems a bit out of synch with the modesty of the town (yet the prices are in keeping, because they're astonishingly reasonable). Three set menus are offered, ranging from a small sampling of one or two courses to a full four-course meal. (Via Metelli 2, Brisighella; phone: 0546-81829; inexpensive.)

RIMINI: The Via Emilia comes to an end at Rimini, at once an ancient town and the most popular holiday resort on the Adriatic. The Lido di Rimini is a long, wide stretch of beach lined with hotels, bars, restaurants, souvenir stands, and discos that can be, by turns, sleazy, ultra-chic, or fun for the whole family. Foreigners descend on it by the tens of thousands each summer; in fact, Rimini gets so crowded that spur-of-the-moment visits in high season are probably a mistake — always have a reservation in hand unless you enjoy cruising crowded streets in desperate quest of accommodation. Bear in mind, too, that although there is much beach in Rimini, there is not much *public* beach, so if the hotel you've selected has not staked a claim to its own portion of sand, there's a good chance you'll find yourself staring, hot and hostile, at all those tens of thousands of bathers enjoying beaches you can't visit.

Difficulties notwithstanding, Rimini is just the place for those who like a fun-in-the-sun, dance-until-dawn summer vacation. While totally nude sunbathing is a no-no, topless women are the norm rather than the exception. At night, the beachfront main drags — Lungomare Tintori, Lungomare Murri, and parallel Viale Vespucci — draw hordes of boys and girls on the make, some "professional" talent, and carousers of every nationality. It almost looks like a scene from Federico Fellini, Rimini's most famous son. Those who like the Rimini scene come back again and again, as witnessed by the graffito near the train station that reads, in English: "Ciao Rimini, see you next year."

The historic center of Rimini, about half a mile from the beachfront and separated from it by the railroad tracks, contains one sight of exceptional historic interest. This is the *Tempio Malatestiano,* a Gothic church converted in the 15th century into one of the most influential buildings of the Renaissance. Designed by the Florentine architect Leon Battista Alberti, who based the façade on Rimini's ancient Roman Arch of Augustus, it was one of the earliest Renaissance buildings to be based on an actual classical model. Alberti was in the employ of Sigismondo Malatesta, the tyrant of Rimini at the time but also a patron of the arts. Contemporaries have recorded that Malatesta was a brilliant man, with the ability to be very amiable when he chose, but it seems his wives saw little of that charm. He denounced one, poisoned the second, and strangled the third. Yet he was so full of love for his mistress Isotta that he raised the Tempio Malatestiano as a monument to her memory. The spacious interior is finely decorated with works of art and dotted here and there with the fanciful symbols of the Malatestas, the elephant and the rose. (The *S* superimposed by an *I* seen everywhere stands not for the dollar but for Sigismondo and Isotta.) The Tempio boasts, also, what must be the only souvenir stand in the world graced by a beautiful Piero della Francesca fresco.

The Arch of Augustus that inspired Alberti is the breach in the city wall at the end of Corso di Augusto. For other local sights, either the *Ente Provinciale per il Turismo* (*EPT*), at Piazzale Cesare Battisti (phone: 0541-27927), next to the train station, or the *Azienda Autonoma di Turismo* (phone: 0541-24511), at Piazzale Indipendenza, can provide information. Rimini is also one of the main jumping-off points for trips to the independent republic of San Marino, which is about 15 miles away and which maintains its own information office in Rimini at Piazzale Cesare Battisti (phone: 0541-56333), next to the EPT.

CHECKING IN: *Grand* – The grande dame of the Adriatic coast. Built in 1908, this giant Edwardian building still recalls the more opulent days of seaside resorts before World War I, even though it has recently been renovated from top to bottom. The entire hotel is decorated in lavish *fin de siècle* style, and the service is what would be expected of Rimini's premier hotel. As befits this premier position, the finest bit of Rimini seafront is reserved for its guests, but there is also a giant heated swimming pool on the extensive grounds for those who prefer fresh water. In addition, the *Grand* has tennis courts and a sauna. The more sedentary will enjoy the fine bar. The restaurant, facing the water, serves very good food. There are 119 rooms. Open year-round. (Piazzale Indipendenza 1, Rimini; phone: 0541-24211; expensive.)

The Club House – One of Rimini's newest hotels, it sits squarely on the beach. Each of its 28 rooms has a terrace, and the entire hotel is the last word in modern, high-tech convenience. From bed, guests can raise or lower the blinds, close the curtains, lock the door, and turn on a variety of gadgets, all at the touch of a button. Prices are reasonable, even in high season, and the service is good. No restaurant. (Viale Vespucci 52, Rimini; phone: 0541-52166; moderate.)

En Route from Rimini – Ravenna is 32 miles north of Rimini via SS16. The Adriatic coast is lined with seaside resorts the whole way, each one, unfortunately, more tawdry than the last. A great exception is Cesenatico, 14 miles north of Rimini. Today the town is a very pretty fishing village, but it was born in the early 14th century as a military port for the town of Cesena and can also claim to have been laid out in part by Leonardo da Vinci on behalf of Cesare Borgia. The central canal, dividing the town in two, is home to a permanently moored fleet of old fishing vessels and sailing barges. Just south of Ravenna, SS16 turns inland toward Ferrara, while the main coast road proceeds to Ravenna, passing the Chiesa di Sant'Apollinare in Classe, about 3 miles south of the city. Stop here for a first look at Ravenna's magnificent mosaics. This beautiful building, standing where the ancient Roman port of Classis once stood, is notable for the simplicity of its 6th- and 7th-century mosaics. Ravenna's first bishop and martyr, Saint Apollinaris, is shown with the faithful depicted as lambs; Christ is surrounded by Apostles depicted as lambs; there is a great Latin cross surrounded by stars; and trees, birds, and flowers are in abundance.

EATING OUT: Gambero Rosso – One of two restaurants in this seaside resort to have won a Michelin star. Fresh fish is the specialty. Closed November through February. (Molo Levante, Cesenatico; phone: 0547-81260; expensive.)

Al Trocadero da Vittorio – The other Michelin-starred restaurant in Cesenatico, also specializing in seafood. Closed Mondays. (Via Pasubio, Cesenatico; phone: 0547-81173; expensive.)

RAVENNA: Ravenna's position in the history of Western Europe is unique. It existed as a Roman city even before the emperor Augustus founded the port of Classis just to the south. In the 5th century, after the Roman Empire had split into an eastern and a western section, it became the capital of the Empire of the West. It then went through a short period as a kingdom of the Goths. But at the height of its splendor, from the 6th century to the 8th century, while the western portion of the empire fell into the hands of many chiefs, it was part of the Eastern Roman Empire — the Byzantine Empire — and its dominant influence came not from the Italian peninsula, or even the rest of Europe, but from Constantinople. This eastern-facing stance marked the art and architecture of the city with the indelible imprint of Byzantium, first and foremost in the mosaic masterpieces that are the chief glory of Ravenna's early Christian churches. The most famous are in the Chiesa di San Vitale and the adjacent Tomb of Galla Placidia, in the Orthodox Baptistry and the Arian Baptistry, and in the Chiesa di Sant'Apollinare Nuovo.

San Vitale is an octagonal church built between 526 and 547, and probably based on a much older church in Constantinople. The upper gallery, beneath the dome, is the *matroneae,* an area once reserved for female worshipers. While the church itself is quite beautiful, the variety and complexity of the mosaics in the apse make San Vitale world famous. On the outer walls of the chancel are Old Testament scenes: on the left, Abraham and the three angels and the sacrifice of Isaac, and on the right, the death of Abel and the offering of Melchizedek. However, it is the inner part of the apse that is best known. Here presides the very grave figure of Empress Theodora with her retainers. Dressed in the ornate robes of the East, she looks out solemnly at the world, holding in her hands the chalice containing the wine of the sacrifice of Christ. Facing her, on the opposite wall, is the emperor Justinian, her husband, with his court, and by his side stands the archbishop Maximian, who consecrated San Vitale, holding the Eucharist. Blues, golds, and greens predominate, and the effect of the tiny mosaic tesserae, angled irregularly to catch and hold the light, is astonishingly beautiful.

In the same complex as San Vitale is the exquisite Tomb of Galla Placidia, the sister of the emperor Honorius. It dates from the mid-5th century, and its mosaics are the oldest in Ravenna, still Roman rather than Byzantine in style. In some ways, the mosaics in this tiny, dark room are also more affecting than the ones in the main church, since they are closer to the eye and their symbolism is more personal, their execution more natural. The tomb is dominated by a tympanum mosaic of Christ the Good Shepherd and, facing that, one of St. Lawrence with the instrument of his martyrdom (a gridiron — he was roasted alive). In the transepts are some charming stags — representing souls — drinking from the Fountain of Life. The ceiling of the dome is deep blue, studded with countless stars. (*Note:* The coin box to light the tomb is outside, set in the wall facing the front door of the building.)

The *Battistero degli Ortodossi* (*Orthodox Baptistry*), also known as the *Battistero Neoniano,* adjoins the *Duomo of Ravenna,* which is largely an 18th-century Baroque building. Originally a Roman-era bathhouse, it was dedicated to Christianity in the mid-5th century and is thus contemporary with the Galla Placidia tomb. The centerpiece of the mosaics in the dome here — betraying telltale signs of 19th-century restoration — is the baptism of Christ, the figures surrounded by Apostles as by the spokes of a wheel. The other baptistry, the *Battistero degli Ariani* (*Arian Baptistry*), is on a quiet side street not far from the main square of Ravenna, Piazza del Popolo. This structure, thought to have been built by Theodoric in the early 6th century, houses another set of brilliant mosaics with the sacrament of Baptism as a major theme.

The *Basilica di Sant'Apollinare Nuovo* is the last great treasurehouse of mosaics in the city. It was erected by Theodoric in the early 6th century and adapted for Christian use toward the mid-6th century by Justinian. Most, but not all, of the mosaics are from Theodoric's time — in fact, the transition from a classical Roman style to pure Byzantine is evident here. The mosaics of the two upper registers on either side (scenes from the life of Christ and prophets or saints) are from the era of Theodoric, as are the two city scenes on the lower friezes: the port of Classis, with its two lighthouse towers on the left frieze, and the palace of Theodoric, with the city of Ravenna behind it on the right frieze. The two glorious processions on the lower friezes, however, are from the time of Justinian, fully Byzantine. On the left is a procession of 22 virgins, preceded by the Magi marching toward the enthroned Virgin and Child. On the right, a procession of 26 martyrs moves toward Christ enthroned. They are the largest mosaics in Ravenna and are absolutely stunning.

A monument of an entirely different era is near the restored church of San Francesco, not far from either Sant'Apollinare Nuovo or Piazza del Popolo. This is the *Tomb of Dante,* Italy's greatest poet. Exiled from his native Florence for political reasons, Dante spent his last years in Ravenna at the court of Guido da Polenta and finished his *Divine Comedy* here. He died on September 13, 1321, and is still in Ravenna — his tomb in Santa Croce in Florence is empty. The tomb seen here today dates from 1780, covering another of the late 15th century, beneath which is the actual resting place.

Ravenna has two tourist information offices close to its center: The *EPT* is at Piazza San Francesco 7 (phone: 0544-36129), south of Piazza del Popolo, and the *Azienda Autonoma di Turismo* is at Via Salara 8 (phone: 0544-35404), north of the piazza.

CHECKING IN: *Park* – Slightly out of the way, in Marina di Ravenna, this large (146-room) resort hotel is a perfect compromise for those who want to do a little sightseeing in town and then relax on the beach, by the pool, or at tennis. Open April through October. (Viale delle Nazioni 181, Marina di Ravenna; phone: 0544-431743; expensive.)

Centrale Byron – For location rather than spacious quarters, try this very well run, simple hotel, only a step or two from the central piazza and in the midst of Ravenna's very good shopping district. No restaurant. (Via IV Novembre 14, Ravenna; phone: 0544-22225; moderate to inexpensive.)

EATING OUT: *Tre Spade* – Considered the best restaurant in town. The menu is limited, but the food is well prepared and very good. Closed Mondays and late July to late August. (Via Rasponi 37, Ravenna; phone: 0544-32382; expensive.)

Ca' de Ven – This huge old *enoteca* (wine cellar) is one of the nicest dining spots in town. A Ravenna institution, it's famous for a local creation called *piadina:* a bready pancake fried on a griddle and brought to the table warm, along with a huge platter of hams, salami, mortadella, and cheese. The wines served here, as might be expected, are exquisite, particularly the local Pagadebit. Closed Mondays. (Via Ricci 5, Ravenna; no phone; inexpensive.)

En Route from Ravenna – Take SS16 north out of Ravenna to Ferrara, only 45 miles away.

FERRARA: Like Bologna, 30 miles to the south, Ferrara has — unjustly — been left off the itineraries of most foreign visitors to Italy, although it is familiar to some as the setting of Vittorio De Sica's *The Garden of the Finzi-Contini,* based on the book by Giorgio Bassani. While not a very large city, it has a colorful history and is rich in art and architecture, most of it in the beautiful, quaint medieval heart of town dominated by the giant *Castello Estense (Castle of the Este Dukes).* The size and prominence of the castle are telling reminders of the importance of the family in the history not only of the city but also well beyond its walls. Ferrara was the seat of the Este family from the 13th century to the very end of the 16th century, and during that time it was a cultural stronghold of the Renaissance in northern Italy. Few royal families lived with quite the splendor of the dukes and duchesses of Ferrara — they were famous for the luxury of the palaces they built, for the lavishness of their hospitality, and for the richness of their garb. They were also noted patrons of the arts, their court a meeting place for the most famous poets, painters, and philosophers of their age. Ludovico Ariosto and Torquato Tasso, writers of two of the great classics of Italian literature, were in the dukes' service.

The city flourished under Este patronage; in fact, at the end of the 15th century, Duke Ercole I embarked on a plan to double Ferrara's size by building a new urban quarter — the area known as the Herculean Addition — north of the castle. Later dukes consolidated the family's power and prestige. Ercole's son Alfonso I married Lucrezia Borgia; their son Ercole II married Renée, daughter of Louis XII of France (another son, an Este cardinal, built the Villa d'Este at Tivoli, near Rome). The marriage didn't work out, and Ercole exiled his royal wife. That the move was accomplished without any repercussion is a sign of just how powerful the Estes had become. The end came swiftly, however. In 1598, the duchy was annexed to the Papal States, because the Estes failed to produce a legitimate male heir. A branch of the family lived on in Modena and Reggio Emilia, but with the loss of Ferrara its glory days were gone.

Begin by visiting the castle, right in the center of town (and just opposite the tourist office, which is at Largo Castello 22; phone: 0532-35017). Protected by a moat and four drawbridges, this giant building was begun in 1385 and finished some two centuries later. It now houses provincial offices, but some of the rooms in which the Estes lived are open to the public. Among these are the large and small Games Rooms, so called because of the theme of the frescoes decorating the ceiling — athletic games — and the Aurora Room, decorated with four frescoes showing different hours of the day. Beyond is the tiny chapel of the unhappy princess Renée (Renata, in Italian), one of the few old Protestant places of worship in Italy. (Princess Renée, an ardent Protestant, sheltered John Calvin in the city during the 1550s.) The last act of a particularly sordid chapter in Este family history was played out in the dungeons beneath the northeast tower. A 15th-century duke, Niccolò d'Este, discovered that his wife, Parisina Malatesta, was having an affair with Ugo, his illegitimate son. Niccolò imprisoned the two lovers in the dungeons and had them decapitated in 1425. The dungeons were in use as late as World War II, when first the Fascists and later the Nazis held political prisoners and resistance fighters there.

A block from the castle is Ferrara's beautiful cathedral. Begun in 1135, it is remarkable for a wide marble triple façade, the upper portion of which is Gothic, the lower portion Romanesque. There is a stern Last Judgment over the main portal by a sculptor whose name has been lost to time. The cathedral museum inside contains two early-15th-century statues by the Sienese sculptor Jacopo della Quercia, late-15th-century works by Cosmè Tura, a master of the Ferrarese school of painting, as well as an unknown 12th-century master's sculptured reliefs of the months of the year that were part of a door on the south side of the cathedral. On the whole, the interior of the cathedral has been much altered, but outside, the cathedral itself, the beautiful and large adjacent piazza, and the towering campanile (a 15th-century addition) are so perfectly preserved they look as if they have been copied from a medieval painting illustrating the benefits of a just prince or good communal government. The façade of the Palazzo Comunale, however, is a 20th-century reproduction.

On the edge of the historic center, at Via Scandiana 23, is the *Palazzo Schifanoia,* a home away from home for the ruling family. This noble building, begun in 1385 for Alberto V and much modified by Borso d'Este (whose famous Bible is in the museum in Modena) and by Ercole I in the late 15th century, was used primarily for the Estes' extravagant entertainments — it was their pleasure palace. The frescoes in the Salone dei Mesi, by Francesco del Cossa, Ercole de' Roberti, and others of the Ferrarese school, make up one of the most important fresco cycles of the Renaissance with a profane theme. Zodiacal motifs and triumphs of the gods occupy the upper levels, but the lower levels, showing scenes of courtly life, with Borso d'Este figuring prominently in each one, are invaluable documents of the everyday existence of a great ducal family of the Renaissance. The palazzo now houses the numerous collections — illuminated manuscripts, ceramics, coins, medals, and so on — that make up the Museo Civico.

Still another Este palace, the *Palazzo dei Diamanti,* stands at the corner of Corso Ercole I d'Este and Corso Rossetti. Built in the late 15th century by Duke Ercole I as the centerpiece of his Herculean Addition, the new Renaissance quarter he built to the north of the medieval part of town, it takes its name from the thousands of diamond-shaped blocks of stone on its façade (the diamond was a symbol of the Este family). Inside the palace is the Pinacoteca Nazionale, the most important picture gallery in the city.

Other notable palaces built by members of the ruling family are not far from the Palazzo Schifanoia. The *Palazzo di Ludovico il Moro,* on Via XX Settembre, was built at the end of the 15th century by the Sforza husband of Beatrice d'Este. It is now the home of the *Museo Archeologico Nazionale* (*National Archaeological Museum*) and houses, among other curiosities, two Roman boats found in the region, each carved out of a single gigantic tree trunk. Also visit the *Palazzina di Marfisa d'Este,* at the far end of Corso della Giovecca, a small but beautiful 16th-century residence with elaborately painted ceilings, an outdoor theater, and a delightful garden.

CHECKING IN: *Ripagrande* – A restored 14th-century palazzo in the heart of the medieval section, it has 40 modern rooms, many with sitting rooms, kitchens, and second bathrooms. Ask for a room on the top floor — the rooms under the eaves have beautifully beamed ceilings and terraces with magnificent views. The attentive staff bends over backward to please. There is a good bar, quite a good restaurant, and a pleasant courtyard for al fresco breakfasts during the summertime. (Via Ripagrande 21, Ferrara; phone: 0532-34733; expensive to moderate.)

Europa – This eccentrically decorated hotel is on the main street of Ferrara, a stone's throw from the castle. The rooms are large, old-fashioned, and ornate. The staff is helpful, and there is ample parking in the courtyard behind the hotel. (Corso della Giovecca 49, Ferrara; phone: 0532-21438; moderate.)

EATING OUT: *Buca San Domenico* – The pizza here is the best in town, but there are many other good dishes as well. Closed Mondays and July. (Piazza Sacrati 22, Ferrara; phone: 0532-37006; moderate.)

Grotta Azzurra – A popular place specializing in northern Italian cuisine. Closed Sundays and part of July. (Piazza Sacrati 43, Ferrara; phone: 0532-37320; moderate.)

Vecchia Chitarra – For solid Ferrarese cooking, try this good, old-fashioned place on the other side of the river. Closed Mondays, Tuesdays, and mid-July to mid-August. (Via Ravenna 11, Ferrara, phone: 0532-62204; moderate.)

San Marino

Every year, more than three million tourists visit San Marino, the oldest and smallest republic in the world. The number is so high that it's easy to understand the feeling that this horde might overwhelm the entire country — considering that it has a population of only 22,000 and an area of only 23 square miles — and to a certain extent it does. At high noon on a balmy midsummer day, it can be hard to see San Marino's quaint charm beyond the droves of day-trippers and the gaudy displays of countless souvenir shops vying for their attention.

But if that day is a clear one, look again. From any number of points in San Marino, the panorama embraces not only the Apennines to the south, expansive plains and hills to the north, and the brilliant blue Adriatic to the east, but also the Yugoslav coast, 156 miles away. No doubt about it, San Marino's mountaintop setting is spectacular, and it is this, along with interesting historical sites and colorful remnants of the republic's long past, that makes a visit worthwhile.

San Marino lies 11 miles from the Adriatic coast of north central Italy, bordering the regions of Emilia-Romagna to the north and the Marche (Marches) to the south. Most visitors arrive from the coastal town of Rimini, and as you approach from this direction, the republic's distinctive "skyline" comes dramatically into view: Monte Titano (Mount Titanus), at a height of 2,470 feet, with its three fortified peaks. The territory of San Marino consists of this mountain, with the capital, San Marino City, on top, and the surrounding hills, scattered with eight small villages or *castelli* (castles). The climate is moderate, with summer temperatures rarely exceeding 80°F.

According to tradition, San Marino dates back almost 1,700 years, to AD 301 and the arrival of a Christian stone cutter from Dalmatia named Marinus. Fleeing the religious persecution of the Roman emperor Diocletian, Marinus sought the secluded safety of Monte Titano, where he built a chapel and began to live a saintly life. Other Christians soon followed him, giving rise to a free community that very early in its history developed the democratic institutions still governing it today.

San Marino's inaccessibility protected it throughout the downfall of the Roman Empire and the subsequent barbarian invasions. Later, when covetous neighbors did cast eyes in its direction, it struggled valiantly to remain independent. Only twice was it unsuccessful, once in the sixteenth century, when it was occupied by Cesare Borgia, and again in the eighteenth century, when Cardinal Giulio Alberoni, legate in Romagna, annexed it to the Papal States. In each case, the loss of liberty lasted only a few months.

Along with its freedom, the country prides itself on a long tradition as a place of asylum. The Italian patriot Giuseppe Garibaldi was one of the most famous figures to find refuge here, in 1849. During World War II, there were

100,000 refugees within the borders. Sadly, the republic was bombed in 1944, despite its proclaimed neutrality.

San Marino does have a small, picturesque volunteer army. The blue uniforms, blue and white plumed headgear, and old-fashioned muskets and sabers of the militia and the Guardia del Consiglio Grande e Generale (the latter serving as an honor guard to the country's rulers) can be seen on special occasions. Guardsmen of the Guardia di Rocca are on regular duty at the entrance to the government palace, and their green jackets, red trousers, red and white feathered caps, and vintage pistols are no less decorative.

The economy of the country is based on tourism, light industry, some farming, and the sale of postage stamps, which have considerable philatelic value. While the Italian lira is the local currency in common use, the minting of coins, mainly for collectors, is another source of revenue.

San Marino is accessible by bus, car, and even helicopter. The year-round bus service from Rimini leaves frequently from several stops, including the Rimini train station, and takes about 45 minutes. Buses arrive in San Marino at either Piazzale della Stazione or Piazzale Marino Calcigni, both within easy walking distance of the walls of the historic center. In summer, a helicopter service connects Rimini with Borgo Maggiore, one of San Marino's *castelli,* from where San Marino City is reachable via cable car. The nearest airports are at Miramare di Rimini (nine miles away) and Forlì (thirty-eight miles away). The nearest train station is in Rimini. Travel by car is scenic on the four-lane highway from Rimini, though the border can also be reached along other well-paved, but more sinuous, routes.

En Route from Rimini – The border is marked by a banner proclaiming, in Italian, "Welcome to the Ancient Land of Liberty." A passport is not needed to enter, and there is no customs control — despite the customs station.

Within minutes a visitor is in Serravalle, the most populous of the *castelli.* Here there is evidence of industrial growth alongside one of the country's oldest and best-kept castles. Since the cession of Serravalle to San Marino in 1463, the republic's territory has not grown by a single inch. Not even Napoleon's offer to extend its borders in 1797 was accepted.

Continue along the winding road to reach Domagnano, another of the castles, to the left before arriving at Borgo Maggiore.

BORGO MAGGIORE: Originally known as Mercatale, this market town, established in the 12th century, is worth a stop. Its weekly open-air market, held on Thursdays, has been taking place since 1244. The porticoed Piazza di Sopra remains practically unchanged. Just off the main square, Piazza Grande, is one of San Marino's most important museums, the *Museo Postale, Filatelico e Numismatico.* It contains examples of all stamps and coins issued by the republic, along with stamps from other countries. Nearby is the *Museo delle Armi da Fuoco* (*Firearms Museum*), whose collection spans the 14th to the 19th centuries and also includes a section dedicated to Garibaldi. Stop also for a look at the ultramodern *Santuario della Beata Vergine della Consolazione* (*Sanctuary of the Blessed Virgin of Consolation*), which was built in the 1960s and contrasts sharply with the town's medieval appearance.

En Route from Borgo Maggiore – San Marino can be reached by foot along the short cut called the Costa, by car, or by cable car.

SAN MARINO: Proceed along the highway toward San Marino City and leave the car in one of the several parking areas near the historic center. The old city within the walls is entered through the Porta di San Francesco (St. Francis' Gate), begun in the

14th century as the doorway to a convent. Once inside, to the right, is the convent and the small Chiesa di San Francesco, both founded in 1361. Though this is the oldest church in the republic, only its façade reveals its age; much of the original character of the interior was lost in 17th- and 18th-century restorations. The cloister next door houses a gallery of changing exhibitions and a museum with some noteworthy old paintings, including one of St. Francis by Guercino.

From the Porta di San Francesco, San Marino's narrow streets must be explored on foot, and the ascent can be quite steep at times. Via Basilicius leads upward to tiny Piazzetta del Titano, one of the social centers of the town. Not far off the square, on Contrada Omerelli, is the *Palazzo Valloni,* a structure partly of the 15th century and partly of the 18th century. It houses the state archives, with documents dating from 885, as well as the government library. Until recently, it also contained the Museo Pinacoteca di Stato, whose collection of paintings and objects of historical and archaeological interest now await a new home. In the meantime, some of the collection is temporarily displayed in the *Chiesa di Santa Chiara* (*Church of St. Clare*), farther along on Contrada Omerelli. The street ends with the Porta della Rupe, the gate through which visitors enter the city if they take the short cut from Borgo Maggiore.

To continue the ascent, return to Piazzetta del Titano and take the short walk up the hill to Piazza Garibaldi and the government stamp and coin office (*Azienda Autonoma di Stato Filatelica e Numismatica*). Then turn and follow Contrada del Collegio up to Piazza della Libertà, the largest and most elegant of San Marino's squares. It takes its name from the 19th-century statue of liberty in the middle, but it's also known as the *Pianello* ("little plane"), since it's one of the few flat spaces within the walls. Off to the left is the mountain shelf and a spectacular view, while directly in front, dominating the square, is the *Palazzo Pubblico* (*Government Palace*).

Although there has been a public building here since the early 14th century, today's Palazzo Pubblico dates only from the end of the 19th century, but it was built in an old-fashioned neo-Gothic style. Those who arrive for the changing of the guard should stop at the nearby tourist office on Contrada del Collegio for information on the time. (For a fee, this office will also stamp a traveler's passport with an unnecessary, but official, San Marino visa.)

San Marino is governed by two Captains Regent chosen twice a year for 6-month terms by the Great and General Council, whose 60 members, in turn, are elected by popular vote and hold office for five years. When parliament is in session, a tourist's visit to the palace will be limited; otherwise, it's possible to see its most important chamber, the richly decorated Sala del Consiglio, with the double throne of the two rulers at one end beneath a large allegorical painting featuring San Marino at its center. Two other rooms are usually on view, in addition to the atrium and the grand staircase, whose walls are covered with busts and inscriptions, works of art, as well as symbols of the republic's past. Among them is a bust of Abraham Lincoln, who was made an honorary citizen of San Marino in 1861. The *sammarinesi* are proud of the thank-you letter, preserved in the state archives, in which Lincoln said, "Although your dominion is small, nevertheless your State is one of the most honoured throughout history. . . ."

Beyond the Palazzo Pubblico, Contrada del Pianello leads to the cable-car station. En route, it passes the Cava dei Balestrieri, the field on which the Palio delle Balestre Grandi, a crossbow competition complete with Renaissance costumes, is held each year on September 3, in celebration of the saint's day of San Marino and the founding of the republic. Don't assume that this colorful event is put on only for tourists — it was mandated by law in the early 17th century, even as crossbows began to be superseded by more modern weapons. Exhibitions are held at other times of the year, but if you miss them, it's still possible to see one of San Marino's crack crossbowmen engaged in target practice.

From here, continue the climb by following Contrada Omagnano or by returning to

Piazza della Libertà. Either way, follow signs to the *Basilica di San Marino.* The mortal remains of the republic's founding saint are buried under the altar of this Neoclassical church, which was built in the 19th century to replace an older church that stood on the spot.

From the Basilica, more signs point through the oldest quarter of the city to the first of the three fortified towers that figure on the country's coat of arms. The tower, known as the *Rocca* or *Guaita,* dates back to the 11th century, although in its overall appearance it is of the 15th century. San Marino is 2,465 feet above sea level at this point. Climb to the top of the tower and enjoy the cool breezes blowing off the Adriatic as well as a splendid view.

The Rocca is joined by a watch path to the second tower, the *Fratta* or *Cesta,* on the highest point of Monte Titano (2,470 feet). This tower dates from the 13th century and contains a museum of early arms and armor through which visitors have access to lookouts affording more magnificent views.

The more hale and hardy may want to go along the less beaten path to the third tower, the *Montale,* although the tower itself is not open to the public. This narrow, graceful structure was in use from the 13th to the 16th century.

From the Montale tower, a path leads down the slope to the modern *Congress Palace.* Turn back toward the center along Viale J. F. Kennedy, Via Giacomo Matteotti, and Viale Antonio Onofri to see other modern buildings and, just up the hill, tennis facilities, all evidence of the present in this most ancient of states.

San Marino is at its traditional best during its holidays. Besides September 3, celebration of the saint's day and the founding of the republic, two choice days to be on hand are the first of April and October, when the elaborate investiture ceremony of the newly elected Captains Regent takes place.

A note to shoppers: Souvenirs of a very pedestrian nature are the most conspicuous items for sale in San Marino. Nevertheless, there are some legitimate buys. These include stamps and coins, of course, as well as local wines and liqueurs. For an idea of craft products available, go to the Mostra dell'Artigianato (Handicraft Exhibition) above the Piazzale Mario Giangi parking area, just off Viale Federico d'Urbino. If you've brought plenty of spending money, have a look at *G. Arzilli,* Via Donna Felicissima 1, a large and serious jewelry store, on a par with the best in Italy.

Expect to pay $50 or more per night for a double room in hotels rated as expensive; about $35 to $45 in those listed as moderate; and about $30 in inexpensive hotels. A meal for two will cost from $45 to $60 in expensive restaurants, and from $30 to $45 in moderate ones. All restaurants serve an economical tourist menu whose fixed price is prominently displayed. Most San Marino hotels and restaurants close for a month or two in winter.

CHECKING IN: *Grand Hotel San Marino* – Just outside the old city walls and probably the most comfortable hotel in San Marino. Each of the 54 rooms has a private bath or shower, and the front rooms all have a balcony with a beautiful view of the Apennines. There is a restaurant, the *Arengo,* and a parking garage. (Viale Antonio Onofri, San Marino; phone: 0541-992400; expensive.)

La Grotta – A charming hotel with 14 rooms, all with private bath or shower, and a pleasant restaurant. (Contrada Santa Croce, San Marino; phone: 0541-991214; moderate.)

Titano – Opened in the 1890s and San Marino's first hotel, it is just a few steps from Piazza della Libertà. It has 50 rooms, all with bath or shower and some with a view. The panoramic terrace restaurant is one of the loveliest spots in town. (Contrada del Collegio 21, San Marino; phone: 0541-991375; moderate.)

Tre Penne – A simple hostelry in the higher reaches of the old city. All of the 12 rooms have bath or shower, and there is a restaurant. (Via Lapicidi Marini, San Marino; phone: 0541-992437; inexpensive.)

EATING OUT: *Righi–La Taverna* – In summer, the tables right on Piazza della Libertà are filled with tourists feasting on one-dish platters and the grand view of the Palazzo Pubblico. But the local specialties also served at this two-story restaurant make it very popular with the *sammarinesi* year-round. Open every day in summer; closed Wednesdays in winter and from mid-December through January. (Piazza della Libertà, San Marino; phone: 0541-991196; expensive.)

Buca San Francesco – Straightforward cooking of San Marino and the neighboring Romagna region. Pasta dishes include *tagliatelle, tortellini,* and green *lasagne,* and second courses range from *scaloppine al formaggio e funghi* (with cheese and mushrooms) to grilled and mixed roast meats. Open daily March through October. (Piazzetta Placito Feretrano 3, San Marino; phone: 0541-991462; moderate.)

Diamond – Another of the better restaurants in town, with 7 inexpensive rooms for guests. The building is quite unusual in that it's been dug out of rock. Open daily mid-March to mid-October. (Contrada del Collegio, San Marino; phone: 0541-991003; moderate.)

Tuscany

Nature has bestowed great gifts on almost every area of Italy, but it is widely agreed that Tuscany must surely be the most richly endowed region of all, the preferred child. There is nothing predictable about Tuscany's character — the open, cattle-raising plains of the southern Maremma area are the perfect antithesis to the haughty grandeur of the Apennine mountains — but there is one constant: a remarkable wealth of beauty, mellowed by history and tempered, ever so gently, by the hand of man.

If the landscape evokes a peculiar sense of familiarity, it is because it is almost inevitable that you have seen it all before. These gently undulating hills, punctuated by lone, dark cypresses and pines, and crowned by hilltop bastions, are the bucolic backdrop of every Raphael Madonna and every Botticelli nymph. The Renaissance masters superimposed the image of the Holy Land itself onto the Tuscan landscape — the same landscape that has triggered the genius and fired the soul of its people since the very earliest days of the pre-Roman Etruscans.

The ancient race that D. H. Lawrence described as "the long nosed, sensitive footed, subtly smiling Etruscans," first "appeared" in Tuscany. They were one of the most sophisticated Mediterranean civilizations of all times, yet only recently have advanced studies helped dispel our ignorance of them and lift a corner of the veil of mystery surrounding their lives and times. For centuries, Tuscan peasants left their land untilled, lest they disturb the Etruscans' reposing souls. What's more, nothing is left of their civilization aboveground, a result of the ephemeral wood with which they built their homes. Still, numerous brightly painted necropoli have been excavated beneath innocent forest-covered hills — the Etruscans, fortunately, were avid believers in a happy afterlife and left elaborate provisions for it. They were wise in the ways of agriculture, mining, and goldsmithing — three Tuscan inclinations that have survived well across the millennia — and they were surprisingly advanced (and not just for their time) in the manufacture of arms, for which they were known throughout Europe. Only now is it understood that they did not merely fade into oblivion but were gradually and perfectly integrated into a new Roman society sometime by the first century BC.

The Roman Empire grew from the seed of Etruria, the land of the Etruscans, actually a loose federation of twelve city-states that extended down into present-day Umbria and northern Lazio as well. The Roman Emperor Augustus declared Etruria a region, and then Diocletian reorganized it as Tuscia. Many centuries later, the regional perimeters were established as those we know today. That the towns of the region built their medieval walls upon Roman fortifications covering Etruscan foundations illustrates a process of continuing civilization that impresses even those who are not history buffs.

In the Middle Ages, Tuscany, as it came to be known (*Toscana* in Italian), was a theater of constant warfare among the free communes of Lucca, Pisa, Florence, and Siena, with the continuing strife between the two medieval political factions — the pro-papal Guelphs and the pro-imperial Ghibellines — an added complication. Small, lofty hill towns, caught in the crossfire, fortified their naturally strategic positions with massive walls that became one with the hillside itself. Many of these towns never grew beyond their medieval walls or mentalities, having dreamed away the centuries. They tend to be tucked far back from the main arteries, but travelers who take the time to wend their way up to one of them are likely to find a one-tower, one-church settlement whose handful of families seem indifferent to the staggering view of mountains, valleys, and occasional plains that extend from their hushed *piazzetta*. Yet although their power and prestige are long gone, the Tuscans remain particularly proud of their resplendent patrimony. They are not entirely joking when they tell you that, while the Creator may be responsible for the beauty that is Tuscany, the designs were drawn up by Michelangelo.

Michelangelo and his contemporary Leonardo da Vinci were archetypal Tuscan and Renaissance men who headed an extensive roll call that was, without a doubt, the greatest company of genius ever assembled in one place at one time. It is difficult to circumscribe the Renaissance with actual dates. The fifteenth and sixteenth centuries were the indisputable apogee of this great period of art and thought. The fourteenth century, however, had already seen the arrival of the artist Giotto and three outstanding Florentine men of letters — Dante, Petrarch, and Boccaccio. They put the seal of approval on the Tuscan dialect by writing in the vernacular rather than in Latin, developed Italian literary style, and put Tuscan culture and manners on the map; they quite literally made Florence, and indeed all Tuscany, in D. H. Lawrence's words, "the perfect center of man's universe."

Florentine and other Italian artists, such as Donatello, Botticelli, and Raphael, later flourished under the tutelage of the Medici family, rulers of Florence and eventually grand dukes of Tuscany as well as insatiable patrons of the arts. The frescoes of Masaccio, Piero della Francesca, Fra Filippo Lippi, and Luca Signorelli can be found today in small country chapels or in the magnificent urban cathedrals that were the unprecedented engineering feats of architects such as Brunelleschi, the Pisano family, or Michelangelo (there was little he could *not* do).

For centuries, historians and curious travelers have marveled at the remarkable concentration of Renaissance genius that flowered within the confines of this small region. Why Tuscany? What was it about the Italian or Tuscan spirit that freed this avalanche of original thinking and artistic creativity and gave Western civilization its most fertile and exciting moment?

Italy had never completely forgotten its classical Roman heritage, whose rediscovery was the very essence of the Renaissance. Furthermore, the country had long been the crossroads for lucrative trade between the wealthy Orient and the merchants of the West, so that its cities grew rich financially as well as culturally. Tuscany, too, was the home of many prosperous monastic communities where advanced secular studies, such as the sciences and philosophy, were taken no less seriously than spiritual development. As a result, by the early fifteenth century, Florence had become an active and wealthy banking and commercial city whose political domain extended over most of the region. Florence's first family, the Medici, clever bankers themselves, even supplied the Vatican with a number of popes, and other family members soon assumed political positions. There is little doubt that the glorious period of the Renaissance was born as a result of the state of relative stability and unbounded prosperity the Medicis inspired and nurtured. The unusual enlightenment and enthusiastic support of Lorenzo de' Medici, called Lorenzo il Magnifico, and his personal attraction to the arts and humanities, assured that Florence would become a veritable hotbed of cultural innovation.

The sumptuous Medici courts rivaled those of Paris and Vienna; they were alive with theater, spectacle, banquets, salons, and important festivities such as weddings, baptisms, and celebrations of patron saints' feast days. To escape epidemics, summer heat, or urban ennui, the Medicis built regal country villas and hunting lodges in the cool, game-populated hills outside Florence. They elevated the garden to an art form that was soon imitated all over Europe as the "Renaissance garden" — embellished with geometric parterres and terraces, labyrinths, topiary hedges, Roman statues, pergolas, outdoor theaters, and manmade grottoes. Everywhere there were refreshing pools, fountains, and *giochi d'acqua* (practical jokes played with water) that revived the ancient Arab technique of tapping underground springs. Tuscany's aristocracy followed the new Medici mode, and the elite of Florence, Lucca, Siena, and other powerful Renaissance cities left their handsome *palazzi* within the protection of the fortified walls to carry rural villa life to the height of aristocratic refinement.

The Medici family ceased to exist with the death of Gian Gastone in 1737, and many of the aristocracy's country villas now stand empty, most Tuscans opting to live in the very cities their ancestors chose to leave behind. A more recent convergence on Tuscany of outstanding individuals in the arts, however, brought about a second and new kind of Renaissance. Goethe, Shelley, Stendhal, the Brownings, Dostoyevsky, Mark Twain, Gorky, Dylan Thomas — they all made Tuscany their home and escape, the goal of a spiritual pilgrimage that became a source of inspiration for some of their finest works. They spoke and wrote about art, history, love, God, and, always, the landscape. It is this same landscape that draws millions of lesser-known tourists who come to study the frescoes of Giotto or that treasure trove that is Florence's Uffizi and then return home remembering nothing but the gentle hills that the Tuscans call *dolci* (sweet).

More than 70 percent of Tuscany consists of these characteristic hills — only one-tenth of the region is flat plain, mostly in the Maremma, Pisa, and Lucca area — and entire tracts of land are works of art. They may not have been designed by Michelangelo, but human intervention and the farmer's resourcefulness are obvious everywhere. Slopes have been terraced to stop erosion, improve drainage, and increase the amount of arable land. Some forests have been cleared to provide more room for crops, while others have been planted in compensation. Mountains were (and still are) being carved away, their quarries supplying the needs of the world with the same white Carrara marble that supplied the geniuses of the Renaissance.

According to an ancient legend, the Etruscans introduced the one element that has come to be recognized as the most Tuscan of all: the cypress. Originally, the stately rows of these slender trees, so often seen in dark profile along the curve of a hill, had a specific function: They marked property boundaries and blocked the wind. Single, isolated cypresses that once stood as reference points to traveling pilgrims still play sentinel, marking forks in the road and turnoffs.

Since ancient times, their longevity (many trees thrive for well over 1,000 years) and ever-green nature have lent them a sacred aura, and they have always been used to flank churches and adorn cemeteries. Unfortunately, a recent widespread fungus has attacked this most recognizable feature of the Tuscan countryside, eating away at them from within and posing a serious threat. Unfortunately, too, tens of thousands of centuries-old olive trees, entire silvery groves of them, were destroyed by record-breaking cold temperatures in January 1986. The local farmers have left the gnarled stumps alongside new tender shoots that face long decades to maturation and have planted field after expansive field of *girasoli*. Although the oil from these armies of sunflowers will help soften the shortage of Tuscany's deep green, award-winning olive oil, they are a feeble, if colorful, substitute.

Besides the cypresses, the olive trees, the characteristic hills, and hilltop villages still peaked with fortified castles and church steeples — the two ever-contending symbols of power in medieval Italy — there are other characteristics of this very peaceful landscape, such as the vineyards. The heart of the region is braided with vines, row upon row of them, the only straight lines in what is otherwise a land of sinuous contour. Then there is the purest example of Romanesque art, the *pieve,* the country parish church, along with the cluster of buildings that served it. Often built on Etruscan or Roman foundations, they are today scattered across Tuscany like jewels, many still being used as religious seats.

The most indigenous architecture of all, however, is the *casa colonica,* or Tuscan farmhouse. Frequently set atop a hill, and built of whatever stone was immediately available, its style grew from a response to the simple needs of the *contadino* (peasant) into a natural, unpretentious elegance, its color and texture in rustic harmony with the tones and shapes of its surroundings. The extended family lived over the animal quarters for warmth, an outside staircase usually joining the two floors. For centuries, the farmers of the region had worked the land under a system known as *mezzadria,* where the laborers shared profits with the landowners. The practice finally died out in the early part of this century due to poor returns and a gradual exodus to the city, and the majority of these old country homes have been bought and restored by urbanites and foreigners who use them for weekend or summer homes.

It was from the economical hearth and frugal spirit of the Tuscan *contadino* that the regional cuisine evolved. Food was commonly cooked over a hearty fire, and today's high-quality Tuscan meats are cooked just that way, using only herbs (the frequent use of tarragon, sage, rosemary, and thyme came from the Etruscans) and a brushing of extra-virgin olive oil (unfiltered and from the first pressing). Long bouts of famine gave rise to *cucina povera* (poor cuisine), consisting of simple and unsophisticated dishes where everything was — and is — used. Stale bread thickens such winter soups as *pappa al pomodoro* (roughly, "tomato pap") and *ribollita* (literally, "reboiled"); chestnut flour is used for dessert breads such as *castagnaccio*. Game has always been important — the Tuscans are Italy's keenest hunters, and the region's thick woods are rich in wild boar (*cinghiale*), pheasant, wild pigeon, and hare — and the most beloved mushrooms of all are the *porcini* that grow wild, the size of T-bone steaks. With the discovery of America came white beans, an important source of protein in the peasant diet (Tuscans are insultingly called "bean eaters"). The favorite cheese, the pungent *pecorino,* originated in Roman times. Made from sheep's milk, it comes in over a hundred surprisingly different varieties.

As with all aspects of Italian life, Tuscan cooking underwent a great change during the Renaissance. The Medicis hosted marathon feasts for popes and kings. In 1533, Catherine de' Medici was sent off to uncivilized France to marry the future Henry II and took along retinues of chefs, provisions of olive oil, and *la forchetta* (the fork). Even the great Escoffier was later moved to admit, "The French cuisine is an enriched recapitulation of Tuscan cooking." Such conspicuous consumption and innovative license have diminished, and it is the simple cooking of the farmer that has reached us today. The olive oil from the Lucchese hills vies with that of the Chianti area as the world's best. Chianti wines, both red and white, cost a fraction of their price abroad; many of the finest reserve bottlings never leave the country. Most restaurants also offer Vin Santo, a dessert wine something like old sherry that is difficult to find elsewhere.

As in much of Europe, Tuscany's prime touring months are May, June, September, and October. But with the exception of erratic rains and not-so-central heating systems, there are very few months of the year that do not have a certain beauty of their own. August is particularly hot, but Tuscany has 330 kilometers of long, sandy beaches lined with pine groves that alternate with a dramatic, rocky coast, and the Tuscan archipelago's eight islands offer delightful respite. During high season, ferries leave frequently for the islands from Livorno and Piombino. Summer is also the time when Tuscany's medieval *feste* take place — jousts, crossbow contests, Siena's wild bareback horse race, and other events that date back to the volatile Middle Ages. They are re-created with an attention to authenticity and detail that is amazing: Gleaming armor, luxe velvets and brocades, and brilliant plumes bring history out of the museums and into the piazzas.

The following circular itinerary begins 12 miles northwest of Florence, in Prato, and continues west to Pistoia, Montecatini, and Lucca before almost touching the sea at Pisa. It then proceeds south and inland, to Volterra, and east to San Gimignano, Chianti country, and the glorious medieval city of Siena. From there it loops in a southeasterly direction, taking in several charming hill towns on its way up to Arezzo. At Arezzo, it's possible to return to Florence, to turn south into the neighboring region of Umbria (and pick up the *Umbria* route at Perugia), or to persevere and see the rarely visited northeastern corner of Tuscany, which offers cool mountains, monasteries, and solitude. The route is designed to be followed in full or sampled in bits and pieces, with optional detours for those who have the time or a particular interest. A detailed road map is necessary, but don't be inhibited for fear of getting lost — just follow your instincts and peek in the back door of Tuscany by following those turnoffs that appeal to your imagination.

Whenever possible, reserve both hotels and restaurants in advance. Hotels listed below as expensive will cost from about $85 to $150 for a double room; those listed as moderate, from about $35 to $75; and inexpensive, less than $35. A meal for two (with house wine) will cost $55 and up in restaurants listed as expensive, while moderate means from $35 to $55, and inexpensive, under $35.

PRATO: Much medieval and Renaissance wealth went into the embellishment of this very prosperous town, which has been known for its high-quality textiles, especially its wool, since before the 8th century. Like all modern cities with ancient origins, however, there is an old and a new Prato. By-pass all the lifeless apartment buildings, textile factories, and peripheral reminders of the 20th century and head right to the heart of the well-preserved historic center, following signs for the *centro storico.* The imposing 13th-century *Castello dell'Imperatore* (*Emperor's Castle*) is the principal landmark. Medieval Prato was a staunch supporter of the Ghibellines (those favoring the emperor and opposing the temporal power of the pope), and in thanks for its loyalty the flattered emperor Frederick II had this massive fortification with crenelated walls built, one of the very few examples of this type of architecture outside Sicily. A lofty view from any of its eight lookout towers is enchanting. Independent Prato eventually fell to the Florentine Guelphs (archenemies of the Ghibellines) in the 14th century, and the same Renaissance masters who lavished their arts on Florence were sent here to do the same. Witness the 15th-century *Santa Maria delle Carceri* (*St. Mary of the Prisons*), a fine Renaissance church by the noted Florentine architect Giuliano da Sangallo, just across the square from the castle. The magnificent interior is a study of harmonious proportions, highlighted with the beautiful white-on-blue glazed terra cottas by Andrea della Robbia.

Undoubtedly the most renowned of all the Renaissance artists to work in Prato was Fra Filippo Lippi, who was *pratese*-born. An orphan, he was put in a monastery at the age of 15, but, more suited to an unorthodox (and slightly licentious) life, he fled. He was captured by pirates, sold as a slave in Africa, and freed by the Saracens, who marveled at his artistic talents. Upon his return to Prato, he succumbed to the fair beauty of Lucrezia Buti, a young nun whose angelic face soon began appearing as that of the Madonna in most of his paintings. She gave birth to a little Filippino, who would also become a prominent figure in Renaissance art, and Cosimo de' Medici had Fra Filippo released from his vows, freeing him to cover Prato's fine Duomo, and much of the rest of Tuscany, with his delicate frescoes.

The Duomo stands in Piazza del Duomo, on a site originally occupied by the 10th-century *pieve* (parish church) of Santo Stefano. One of the best examples of Romanesque-Gothic architecture in Tuscany, it has the typical white and green marble stripes adorning its façade, with a Della Robbia lunette over the entrance. To the right is an exterior pulpit, the work of Donatello and Michelozzo (1428–1438); the *Dancing Putti* reliefs decorating it are copies of Donatello's originals, which are now in the *Museo dell'Opera del Duomo* (*Cathedral Museum*). Several times a year, on special occasions (including May 1, August 15, and September 8), the Holy Girdle of the Virgin Mary is put on display in the pulpit. Said to have been given to the ever-doubting Apostle Thomas upon the Virgin's ascension into heaven, this precious relic was brought to Prato in the Middle Ages by a Tuscan merchant who had a Palestinian wife. Ordinarily, it's kept in a chapel of the Duomo, where frescoes by Agnolo Gaddi tell the story. The frescoes in the chancel of the church — stories of the lives of St. John the Baptist and of St. Stephen — are of greater significance, however. These early

Renaissance masterpieces took Fra Filippo Lippi 14 years to finish and are considered his finest work. Frescoes by another master, Paolo Uccello, are in the Boccherini Chapel, to the right.

The old civil law court building, the 13th- and 14th-century *Palazzo Pretorio,* is in picturesque Piazza del Comune. It houses the Galleria Comunale (closed Mondays), one of the region's major collections of Renaissance, mainly Florentine, masters. Prato's tourist information office is at Via Cairoli 48 (phone: 0574-24112).

CHECKING IN: *Palace* – Well managed, with modern comforts — TV, air conditioning, and a pool — that are especially welcome after a day visiting the Middle Ages. The restaurant (closed August) is also highly regarded. (Via Piero della Francesca 71, Prato; phone: 0574-592841; expensive.)

Villa Santa Cristina – This 17th-century villa is a perfect introduction to Tuscan hospitality. It has a pool and gardens and modern features that only enhance its charm. Game, especially wild boar in season, is the specialty at the restaurant, which is closed Sunday evenings, Mondays, and August. (Via Poggio Secco 58, Prato; 0574-595951; moderate.)

EATING OUT: *Il Piraña* – A modern yet elegant restaurant that is especially well — and widely — known for its specialties of fresh fish from nearby Tyrrhenian waters. Closed Saturdays, Sundays in July, August, and from Christmas through Epiphany (January 6). (Via Valentini 110, Prato; phone: 0574-25746; expensive.)

Il Tonio – A rustic place, always busy and reliably good, in the *centro storico* on the picturesque piazza where Fra Filippo Lippi was born (in a building that is no longer standing). It includes fish specialties on its extensive menu of Tuscan dishes. Closed Sundays, Mondays, and August. (Piazza il Mercatale 161, Prato; phone: 0574-21266; expensive.)

En Route from Prato – Pistoia is due west, but about 10 miles directly south from Prato is the village of Poggio a Caiano and the delightful wine-producing zone of Carmignano. The village is the setting of one of the most splendid Medici summer villas, the *Villa Medicea a Poggio a Caiano,* which was originally a fortress but was transformed from 1480 to 1485 into a showplace for Lorenzo il Magnifico by the very busy Giuliano da Sangallo. Lorenzo's son, the future Pope Leo X, was mostly responsible for the villa's impressive art collection. (The gardens of the villa are open daily, except Mondays and Sunday afternoons. For information on visiting the interior, call 055-877012.) From the villa, follow signs for the village of Artimino and a twisting, hairpin road through lovely, rolling countryside to another Medici outpost, the *Villa di Artimino.* This magnificent 16th-century structure, sometimes called the Villa of the Hundred Chimneys (for obvious reasons) or La Ferdinanda, was designed by Buontalenti as a hunting lodge for Ferdinando I de' Medici. It sits atop a prominent hill overlooking elaborate gardens and olive groves, thick pine and ilex woods, and the vineyards that produce the famous red Conte di Carmignano wines, lauded since the days of the Medici connoisseurs. The grounds of the villa are open to the public, and it is possible to actually eat and spend the night here, though not in the villa itself (see *Checking In* and *Eating Out,* below).

From the Poggio a Caiano area, it's a 20-minute, approximately 15-mile ride (pick up SS66) to the important agricultural and commercial center of Pistoia.

CHECKING IN: *Albergo Paggeria Medicea* – A stay in the renovated page's quarters of the Medicis' Villa di Artimino comes close to fulfilling any fantasy of being a guest of that illustrious family. The 37-room hotel is less opulent than the villa next door, but the utter silence, the bucolic surroundings, and the modern decor steeped in historical ambience are a magic combination. The management is very apologetic for the lack of a swimming pool; it seems every time they break ground, they unearth another Etruscan ruin or Roman wall. But it does have tennis courts. (Via Papa Giovanni XXIII, Artimino; phone: 055-871-8081; moderate.)

EATING OUT: *Biagio Pignatta* – Just behind the *Paggeria,* in what were once the stables for the Medicis' steeds. Wild game from these very hills and recipes that purportedly pleased many a Medici palate are the specialties. Closed Wednesdays and at lunchtime on Thursdays. (Via Papa Giovanni XXIII, Artimino; phone: 055-8718086; moderate.)

Da Delfina – A rustic place within the medieval walls of the village of Artimino, a short walk down a tree-lined road from the *Paggeria,* where the local cuisine is at its very finest. There is also a wide selection of Carmignano wines. Closed Monday evenings, Tuesdays, early January, and August. (Via della Chiesa, Artimino; phone: 055-8718074; moderate.)

PISTOIA: The treasures of this town easily merit a day's visit, but since they were created by the roll call of artists who performed similar artistic feats in Prato and Florence, and because the creative inspiration is again equaled in the great city of Pisa farther west, most visitors give short shrift to Pistoia. That is a shame, because it is a town full of character, still girdled by a handsome set of 14th-century walls that were fortified by the Medicis and once accommodated over 60 lookout towers. Like its neighbor, Prato, Pistoia was a firm supporter of the Ghibellines, and it, too, eventually fell to that most puissant of rivals, Florence.

From a map of the city, it is possible to pick out a square plan (harking back to Pistoia's Roman origins) inside a trapezoid (the walls), right in the center of which is Piazza del Duomo. The *Duomo* itself was built on 5th-century foundations during the 12th and 13th centuries, Pistoia's wealthier days. The Pisan-style façade has three tiers of arcades (as does the slim, adjacent bell tower, which was transformed, in the 13th century, from a Lombard military guard tower) and terra cotta decorations by Andrea della Robbia around the central door. The simple interior sets off an ecclesiastical masterpiece, the famous silver altar of St. James, housed in the Cappella di San Jacopo. Begun in the late 13th century, the altar contains more than 600 silver figures created by numerous artists through the mid-15th century — a compendium of Tuscan sculpture from the Gothic to the Renaissance. The Duomo's Museo Capitolare (Chapter Museum) is worth a visit just for the dazzling array of antique gold plates, trays, chalices, and other objects. The 14th-century white and green marble *Baptistry,* across from the Duomo, was built according to the design of Andrea Pisano, a name behind much of northern Tuscany's finest architecture. Two other buildings in the same square are the austere 14th-century *Palazzo del Podestà,* adjoining the Baptistry, and the 13th- and 14th-century *Palazzo del Comune.*

Not far away from Piazza del Duomo is the 13th-century *Ospedale del Ceppo,* which takes its name from the *ceppo,* or box, in which offerings were once left. The hospital's most striking feature is the beautiful multicolored terra cotta frieze decorating the early-16th-century portico, a splendid work by Giovanni della Robbia and the Della Robbia workshop. Elsewhere among this labyrinth of medieval streets are the city's two oldest churches — the 12th-century Sant'Andrea and San Giovanni Fuorcivitas, which dates from the 8th century but was reconstructed from the 12th to the 14th centuries. Each is the proud possessor of an elaborate pulpit, the former a masterpiece carved from 1298 to 1301 by Giovanni Pisano (as with the Della Robbias, the skilled Pisano family of architect-sculptors spanned several generations — another pulpit by Giovanni is in the Duomo at Pisa and one by his father, Nicola, is in the Pisa Baptistry), and the latter by Fra Guglielmo da Pisa, a student of the Pisanos, finished in 1270.

It's hard to believe, but thousands of Pistoia's buildings were damaged during World

War II. The city's pride, and a timeless expertise, have re-created history, however. The tourist information office (EPT) in Piazza del Duomo (phone: 0573-21622) can tell you all about it.

 EATING OUT: *Cucciolo della Montagna* – Pistoians maintain that this is the city's finest restaurant. It's just a few medieval blocks from Piazza del Duomo. Closed Sunday evenings, Mondays, and mid-July to mid-August. (Via Panciatichi 4, Pistoia; phone: 0573-29733; moderate.)

En Route from Pistoia – Meticulously groomed *vivai,* extensive nurseries of fledgling trees, from exotic palms to the ubiquitous cypress and everything in between, compose the outskirts of Pistoia. Just beyond them, following SS435, lies the elegant spa town of Montecatini Terme, less than 10 miles from Pistoia.

MONTECATINI TERME: What Vichy is to France and Baden-Baden is to Germany, Montecatini is to Italy. The resort's heralded mineral waters have had a salutary effect on many a stomach, liver, and intestine — including those of Giuseppe Verdi, Arturo Toscanini, and La Loren. To "take the waters" in Montecatini means to settle into a hotel, undergo an obligatory clinical consultation with a hydro expert, and make tracks each day, almost always in the morning and on an empty stomach, to one or the other of the town's *stabilimenti termali* (thermal establishments) to down the prescribed measure from any of the five springs — Tamerici, Torretta, Regina, Tettuccio, Rinfresco — that are used for drinking. About 2,000 immaculately clean WCs stand by, blending discreetly with the surroundings. The waters of two other springs — Leopoldina and Giulia — are for mineral baths, and an eighth spring, Grocco, is expressly for mud baths. The *terme* were once the private property of the Medicis, who undoubtedly appreciated the restorative treatments for gout and an excess of *la dolce vita,* but it was not until the late 1800s that the waters' curative powers became well known. Early in this century, all the various springs were taken over by the state, a massive building program was undertaken, and fashionable hotels were constructed to accommodate shahs, bluebloods, and Milanese industrialists. Now numbering well over 400, the hotels operate from Easter to the end of November.

A serious treatment should really last 12 days, so if you're here just a day or two, don't expect miracles (although it's possible to buy the bottled waters and schlep them home). But even for those who don't take the cure, a peek at one of the *stabilimenti,* all laid out in a vast green park, is enlightening. The most beautiful is the *Stabilimento Tettuccio,* built in 1927 in a classical style. Here, from early morning until noon, an orchestra plays under a frescoed dome, attendants fill cups at fountains spouting from counters of inlaid marble set before scenes of youth and beauty painted on walls of ceramic tile, and patrons stroll through the colonnades, peruse newspapers, or chat. The entrance fee is stiff because it includes water for those who are taking the cure (most who do, however, have a subscription) as well as the otherworldly atmosphere, and there is a lovely, conventional coffee bar inside. Off-season, only the less-impressive *Stabilimento Excelsior,* built in 1915 and with an ultramodern wing, is open.

Montecatini also has expensive boutiques, sports facilities, and seemingly endless flower gardens and forests of centuries-old oaks, pines, palms, cedars, magnolias, and oleanders. The tourist information office at Viale Verdi 66 (phone: 0572-70109) has booklets on different walks through this luxurious vegetation as well as walks up into the nearby hills. Spa information can be found at Viale Verdi 41 (phone: 0572-75851). The old town of Montecatini, Montecatini Alto, is another excursion. Set on top of a hill that dominates the spa town, it is reached by funicular from Viale Diaz or by a road winding 3 miles through olive groves and orchards.

CHECKING IN: *Grand Hotel e La Pace* – Open since 1870, this classic and quintessentially elegant Old World hotel still has a grandiose period decor and a pampering staff that keeps the clientele all feeling like VIPs. There are 150

Solferino – Another comfirmation of Lucca's importance as a gastronomic center, this excellent, family-run establishment is 3 miles outside town, on the road to Viareggio. The fare is basically local, but originality flares in dishes such as baby water buffalo and duck in cream sauce. Closed Tuesday evenings, Wednesdays, a week in January, and 2 weeks in August. (San Macario in Piano; phone: 0583-59118; moderate.)

Da Giulio in Pelleria – A simple, informal *trattoria* that is surprisingly high quality for such a relaxed setting. Lucchese specialties are served; try the *agnello con olive nere* (lamb and black olive stew). Closed Sundays and Mondays. (Via San Tommaso 29, Lucca; phone: 0583-55948; inexpensive.)

En Route from Lucca – Take SS12R to Pisa, 14 miles to the southwest.

PISA: Visitors invariably rush to Piazza del Duomo, otherwise known as the Campo dei Miracoli (Field of Miracles), to see the Leaning Tower. Then what to their wondering eyes should appear on this spacious green lawn but three stunning white buildings — the *Leaning Tower,* the *Duomo,* and the *Baptistry* — flanked by a fourth structure, the white wall of the Camposanto. The Duomo, especially, which set the style known as Pisan Romanesque, or simply Pisan, was one of the most influential buildings of its time; regardless of whether a visitor appreciates the fine points of architecture, it's hard not to be impressed by the Pisan triumvirate.

This city on the Arno was a maritime power almost from the beginning. It was a naval base for the Romans, and during the darkest days of the Middle Ages it kept the Tyrrhenian coast free of Saracens. A fleet of Pisan ships sailed off to the First Crusade. By the 11th century, Pisa had developed into a maritime republic to rival Genoa and Venice. By the 12th century, it had reached the height of its supremacy — it defeated the maritime republic of Amalfi in 1135 — and also of artistic splendor, but the seeds of decline were already planted, in the form of internal rivalries and external strife with nearby Lucca, Genoa, and Florence (which was moving farther and farther along the Arno toward the sea). Pisa never fully recovered from a defeat by the Genoese in 1284, which decimated its fleet and aggravated its internal problems, and in 1406 it was defeated by the Florentines after a long siege. Although there was a period of well-being under the Medicis and even a brief period of independence at the turn of the century, from 1494 to 1509, from the early 1500s its history merges with that of Florence.

The Duomo was begun in 1064 and finished by the end of the 12th century. Its façade, consisting of four graceful galleries of columns, was much imitated (as visits to Lucca and Prato will attest). The bronze doors facing the Baptistry are from the 16th century, replacing originals lost in a fire, but the highly stylized bronze doors facing the Leaning Tower are by Bonanno Pisano and date from 1180. The interior is cavernous, close to 400 feet long and interrupted by 68 columns, but find the way to Giovanni Pisano's intricately carved pulpit (1302–1311), perhaps the cathedral's greatest treasure. The 16th-century bronze "Galileo lamp" that hangs opposite is of special interest, too. According to the story, Pisa-born Galileo came up with his theory of pendulum movement by studying the swinging of the lamp set in motion by a sympathetic sacristan.

The Baptistry, begun in 1152 but not finished until the end of the 14th century, is most famous for its pulpit, carved by Nicola Pisano in 1260. Not long after construction had begun on the Baptistry, ground was broken for the elegant cylindrical *campanile,* the bell tower standing (or leaning) behind the Duomo. The tower rose quickly, but at the third floor, the complication that's very evident today appeared, suspending work for a century. Complications notwithstanding, construction was resumed in 1275, and the finishing touches were made between 1350 and 1372. A few romantic historians contend that the leaning was purposefully brought on by the architect who sought to prove his inordinate skill. Most, however, attribute it to a shifting of soil that has been corrected somewhat by injections of concrete, although the tilt continues to increase by an average of about one millimeter a year. A walk up the tower's 294 steps produces a peculiar sensation but affords spectacular views of the city and the Arno River. From the top terrace Galileo dabbled in his experiments to establish the laws of gravity.

The long, low rectangular building running along the side of the Pisan Triumvirate, its absolute simplicity relieved only by a tiny Gothic tabernacle, is actually a cemetery, the Camposanto, begun in 1277. It is said that some of the earth enclosed inside was brought from the Holy Land aboard Pisan ships. Many of the frescoes that once decorated the interior of the Camposanto walls were destroyed or heavily damaged in World War II, but some by Benozzo Gozzoli remain and enough remains of the famous *Triumph of Death, Last Judgment,* and *Inferno,* by the so-called Master of the Triumph of Death, to suggest the uneasy turn of the 14th-century mind. Sinopias (preparatory designs, drawn directly on the walls) of the frescoes, uncovered during postwar restoration, have now been placed in the Museo delle Sinopie, across the street from the Duomo.

Note, if pressed for time in Pisa, that the Duomo, the Baptistry, and the museum all close at lunchtime, while the Leaning Tower and the Camposanto stay open. Even if pressed, make your way to the Arno for a look at *Santa Maria della Spina* (*St. Mary of the Thorn*), a little jewel of a church in Pisan Gothic style. It was built in the early 14th century to house a relic from Christ's crown of thorns (no longer kept here), and it once stood much closer to the river — in the late 19th century it was moved piece by piece to its present spot. Another stop should be the *Museo Nazionale di San Matteo* (*National Museum of St. Matthew*), which contains many works of 12th- and 13th-century sculpture (the Pisano family is well represented) as well as a Madonna and Child with Saints by Simone Martini. The feast day of the city's patron saint, San Ranieri, is celebrated on June 17 with a regatta on the Arno, and the Gioco del Ponte (Battle of the Bridge), played in medieval costume by two teams from opposite sides of the river, also takes place in June. Another regatta, the Regatta of the Four Ancient Maritime Republics, rotates among Pisa, Venice, Amalfi, and Genoa, so that once every four years it takes place in Pisa. The city's tourist information office is in Piazza del Duomo (phone: 050-501761).

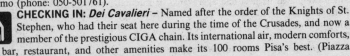

CHECKING IN: *Dei Cavalieri* – Named after the order of the Knights of St. Stephen, who had their seat here during the time of the Crusades, and now a member of the prestigious CIGA chain. Its international air, modern comforts, bar, restaurant, and other amenities make its 100 rooms Pisa's best. (Piazza Stazione 2, Pisa; phone: 050-43290; expensive.)

Grand Hotel Duomo – Large, busy, and only a minute's walk from the Campo dei Miracoli. (Via Santa Maria 94, Pisa; phone: 050-27141; expensive.)

EATING OUT: *Sergio* – A small, elegant, and welcoming restaurant on the banks of the Arno, long considered Pisa's best. If you find the thought of baby eels appealing, look for *cee* on the menu, or try the fish soup flavored with basil or the swordfish steak with herbs and mushrooms. Closed Sundays, Mondays at lunch, January, and the latter half of July. (Lungarno Pacinotti 1, Pisa; phone: 050-48245; expensive.)

Buzzino – Pisans are avid fish eaters, and this establishment keeps them happy with a fine selection of the day's freshest. The homemade pasta is also superb. Only a few blocks from the Campo dei Miracoli. Closed Tuesdays. (Via Cammeo 44, Pisa; phone: 050-27013; moderate.)

En Route from Pisa – Take SS67 for about 14 miles southeast to Pontedera, then turn south onto SS439, following signs to Volterra. Much of the fertile land along this route was once swampland. The blue-green Cecina hills on the right stretch for miles, and as Volterra (about 25 miles from Pontedera) comes closer, the countryside of green velvet hills turns lonely and scarred, with only an occasional flock of sheep to soften its appearance. The gashes marring the landscape are the alabaster quarries that have been Volterra's chief source of income since Etruscan days. More remarkable, however, are the yawning rifts, or *balze,* a peculiar earth flaw caused by intense erosion. The edges of the city have been eaten away by this unrestrainable and continuous movement, which has already consumed a portion of one-time Volterra — Etruscan and Roman temples and dwellings and the 7th-century church of San Giusto.

VOLTERRA: Seen from a distance, Volterra rises up from abandoned countryside — isolated, gaunt, aloof. It has been the site of 3,000 years of continuous civilization, and the walled medieval city still stands within the perimeter of another, larger set of walls — Etruscan. Ancient Velathri was the northernmost and strongest of the 12 city-states of the Etrurian federation, three times larger than Volterra is today. The medieval city dates mostly from the 12th and 13th centuries. Built largely of a gray stone, *panchina,* it has taken on something of a golden hue, but Volterra is still not flirtatious or charming like some other Italian hill towns. It is, however, fiercely proud of its seemingly immortal disposition.

The beautiful, central Piazza dei Priori is bounded by sober medieval palaces, of which the *Palazzo dei Priori (Town Hall),* built from 1208 to 1254, is the most prominent. It is the oldest town hall in Tuscany still used as such, and from the top of its tower an unrivaled panorama can reach as far as the Tuscan coast on a clear day. The church behind the Town Hall is the Duomo, a Romanesque edifice consecrated in 1120, with Pisan touches that were added in the 13th century. The Baptistry, too, dates from the 13th century. Close by is the Porta all'Arco, an original Etruscan gate to the city, from which there are still more extensive and breathtaking views. The *Museo Etrusco Guarnacci (Guarnacci Etruscan Museum),* Via Don Minzoni 15, has one of the best and largest collections of Etruscan objects in all Italy, including the famous elongated bronze figure known as the *Ombra della Sera (Evening Shadow)* and some 600 funerary urns of tufa, terra cotta, and alabaster that demonstrate that the Etruscans were already working the local alabaster in a skilled and imaginative way. (The alabaster industry still provides a third of Volterra's population with employment, and its myriad polychromatic products crowd most store windows.) The climb to Volterra's 14th- and 15th-century *Fortezza* begins not far away from the museum. Lorenzo de' Medici was largely responsible for this massive installation, which serves as a reminder that independent Volterra, like many other Tuscan towns, eventually fell to the superior force of Florence. Lorenzo modified an existing 14th-century fortress (the Rocca Vecchia, or Old Fortress, which has a tower referred to as the Torre Femmina, Female Tower) and added a Rocca Nuova (New Fortress) of five towers, one of which is known as the Torre Maschio, Male Tower. Only the park of the Fortezza is open to the public (the rest is used as a prison), but the whole is an impressive feature of Volterra's silhouette.

Volterra's tourist information office is at Via Giusto Turazza 2 (phone: 0588-86150), just off Piazza dei Priori.

CHECKING IN: *San Lino* – Named after a Volterrano, the first pope to succeed St. Peter, and formerly a cloistered convent built in the 17th century, this is now a modern establishment with wide arches, handsome beamed ceilings, and a delightful enclosed garden terrace. The restaurant comes highly recommended. (Via San Lino 26, Volterra; phone: 0588-85250; moderate.)

EATING OUT: *La Biscondala* – A rambling old farmhouse, recently renovated, just a few minutes' drive southwest of the city walls on the road to Saline (watch for the signs). The service is friendly and the food — dishes such as *pappardelle alla lepre* (broad, flat noodles with hare sauce) and grilled or roasted meats — is straightforward. Closed Wednesdays. (SS68; phone: 0588-85197; inexpensive.)

***Ombra della Sera* –** A new, but highly regarded, restaurant, just 100 yards from the Etruscan Museum. Game is the specialty in season, but the whole Tuscan menu is delicious. (Via Gramsci 70, Volterra; phone: 0588-86663; inexpensive.)

Il Porcellino – Tista, the gregarious owner, keeps the traditions of Tuscan home cooking vibrantly alive. Tables move outdoors during the spring, but the quaint pocket-size dining room inside is far more charming. Try the *piccata al funghetto* (roast lamb with mushroom sauce) or the *coniglio alla cacciatore* (rabbit with tomato sauce). Closed Tuesdays. (Canto delle Prigioni, Volterra; phone: 0588-86392; inexpensive.)

En Route from Volterra – Proceed east on SS68 in the direction of Colle di Val d'Elsa. At Castel San Gimignano turn north onto a less-frequented road and travel through incomparable Tuscan countryside, above which rises the characteristic skyline of the small hill town of San Gimignano.

SAN GIMIGNANO: Ringed by three sets of historic walls, San Gimignano bristles with 14 (or 13 or 15, depending on exactly what you count) of its original 72 medieval towers and thus is known as San Gimignano dalle Belle Torri — San Gimignano of the Beautiful Towers. Each tower was attached to the private palazzo of a patrician family and was used partly for defense against attack from without but also partly for defense against attack by feuding families from within the walls. As with today's skyscrapers, height was an indication of prestige, so "keeping up with the Joneses" is as old as the Tuscan hills.

The town's origins are Etruscan, but it takes its name from a bishop of Modena who died here in the 4th century. It became a free commune in the 12th century, and life would have been tranquil had it not been for the destructive conflict between two families in particular, the Guelph Ardinghelli and the Ghibelline Salvucci (the city was predominantly Ghibelline). In 1300, Guelph Florence sent Dante as ambassador to make peace between the warring factions, but he was unsuccessful; internal strife grew so volatile that 53 years later, an exasperated San Gimignano willingly surrendered to the Florentines it had resisted for so many centuries.

Dante wouldn't be too overwhelmed by a return to 20th-century San Gimignano, so little have things changed. The two main streets of this perfectly preserved town, Via San Giovanni and Via San Matteo, feed into two splendid squares, Piazza della Cisterna and Piazza del Duomo. At the center of Piazza della Cisterna is the 13th-century well from which it takes its name. The piazza is paved with bricks inlaid in a herringbone pattern and surrounded by an assortment of medieval *palazzi* and towers. In the adjoining Piazza del Duomo, the 12th-century cathedral, known as the *Collegiata,* is flanked by more stately *palazzi* and 7 towers. The *Palazzo del Popolo,* to one side of the cathedral, is the home of San Gimignano's small Museo Civico. It contains, besides paintings from the 14th and 15th centuries, the room from which Dante delivered his harangue in favor of the Guelphs, and it provides access to one of San Gimignano's towers, from which there is a view of the town and hills in all directions. The admission fee to the museum also permits entry to the Cappella di Santa Fina in the cathedral, a Renaissance addition that is decorated with Domenico Ghirlandaio's frescoes of the life of the saint, who was born here and died at the age of 15.

Stop in the 13th-century church of Sant'Agostino at the far end of town to see the frescoes by Benozzo Gozzoli, and for another view out over the surrounding countryside — or back toward the town and towers — climb to La Rocca, a one-time fortress, now a public park (good pictures of the towers can be taken from the battlements here, but try to arrive early in the day to avoid direct sunlight). While away an hour in one of the sidewalk cafés with a glass of local *vino bianco* — San Gimignano's famous Vernaccia is considered the finest white wine in the region and one of the finest whites in Italy.

CHECKING IN/EATING OUT: *La Cisterna* – A rustic 48-room hotel in a 13th-century *palazzo* in one of the central *piazze* of San Gimignano. The windows and large wooden balconies of some rooms overlook the surrounding valley and thus afford beautiful Tuscan views. The hotel's *Ristorante Le Terrazze* has kept its age-old ambience, and the kitchen is the domain of some very fine chefs. Closed mid-December to mid-February; restaurant closed Tuesdays, Wednesdays at lunch, and November to mid-March. (Piazza della Cisterna 23, San Gimignano; phone: 0577-940328; hotel, moderate; restaurant, moderate.)

Bel Soggiorno – The former 13th-century Convento di San Francesco, its façade is barely distinguishable from the other medieval buildings on the street. Somewhat smaller than *La Cisterna,* and with no shower or bath for some of its 27 rooms, it's still comfortable in a simple Tuscan fashion, and its back rooms afford a view of the morning mist swirling up over the fields. Even the restaurant has a view. Restaurant closed Mondays. (Via San Giovanni 41, San Gimignano; phone: 0577-940375; hotel, inexpensive; restaurant, moderate.)

En Route from San Gimignano – Siena is less than 25 miles from San Gimignano and can be reached directly by taking the picturesque road east to Poggibonsi and then turning south and taking the old Roman consular road, the Via Cassia (SS2). Avoid the Florence-Siena superstrada. Nine miles north of Siena is the tiny hill town of Monteriggioni, created by Siena as an elevated lookout fortress against the archenemy, Florence, in 1213. Ownership of Monteriggioni passed from one combatant to the other, and the town never grew beyond its original perimeters. Its walls have been left perfectly intact, although its 14 towers must have been considerably higher to have elicited Dante's likening them to looming giants.

A pleasant alternative to the direct route to Siena is to explore the Chianti Classico zone, driving east from Poggibonsi to Castellina in Chianti, there picking up the SS222, romantically referred to as La Chiantigiana because it cuts through the heart of Chianti country. The Chianti Classico zone is not very large, measuring only 30 miles in length between Florence and Siena and 20 miles at its widest point, but the landscape is considered one of the most Italian in all Italy, exemplifying a wonderful harmony of color and form between the land and its provincial architecture. From Castellina, one option is to follow SS222 up to Greve, the unofficial capital of the wine-producing region. Another is to simply zigzag through the network of country roads, visiting Radda in Chianti and Gaiole in Chianti, both east of Castellina, or any number of even more minor towns. The best way to explore this stretch is to drift from castle to roadside shrine, following the signs for *degustazione,* where producers at private, centuries-old *fattorie* (literally, "farmstead") invite travelers in for a taste (see *The Most Visitable Vineyards,* in DIVERSIONS). Afterward, take either the Chiantigiana or the Via Cassia south into Siena.

CHECKING IN: *Residence San Luigi* – Once a working *podere* (farm), this is 4 miles west of Monteriggioni, at Strove. The old farm buildings have been tastefully restored and turned into small apartments sleeping 2, 4, or 5 people, and they are surrounded by acres of peaceful grounds, with swimming pool, tennis and basketball courts, flowers, and trees. Rustic elegance best describes the whole, which includes a restaurant that excels in local cuisine. Although the apartments are rented weekly in high season (May through September), single-night stays can be arranged when there is availability, especially off-season or in the early spring or fall. (Strada della Cerreta 38, Strove; phone: 0577-301055; moderate.)

EATING OUT: *Il Pozzo* – A very highly regarded restaurant in an idyllic setting within the walls of Monteriggioni. Like most rustic Tuscan establishments, the menu turns to game specialties such as *cinghiale in dolce e forte* (wild boar in a kind of sweet and sour sauce, a Sienese specialty) in season. The pasta and earthy *zuppa di fagioli* (bean soup) are other favorites. Closed Sunday evenings, Mondays, most of January, and the first 2 weeks in August. (Piazza Roma 2, Monteriggioni; phone: 0577-304127; moderate.)

SIENA: A wonderfully well preserved medieval city laid out on three hilltops and surrounded by walls, Siena has an artistic heritage second only to that of Florence within Tuscany, and it is the site, twice each summer, of the running of the Palio, a famous bareback horse race that traces its origins to the Middle Ages. Siena is also a wine center, hardly remarkable considering its setting in the midst of Chianti country and its proximity to the Chianti Classico zone. For a detailed report of the city and its sights, see *Siena* in THE CITIES.

  En Route from Siena – To get to Montalcino, about 25 miles south, follow the Via Cassia (SS2) past Buonconvento and turn off (either at Torrenieri or before) to Montalcino. If there is time for a detour along the way, however, turn east at Buonconvento to visit the *Abbazia di Monte Oliveto Maggiore,* a famous abbey that was a major cultural center in the 15th and 16th centuries. The few miles to the cypress-sheltered motherhouse of the Olivetan monks, a congregation of the Benedictine Order founded in 1319, is a marvelous drive, and readers who found Umberto Eco's *The Name of the Rose* intriguing (or those who liked the recent film) will be fascinated by this extensive compound still known for its skilled restoration of ancient illuminated manuscripts. Of greatest interest is the Chiostro Grande (Great Cloister), decorated with splendid frescoes on the life of St. Benedict by Luca Signorelli (9 frescoes, done from 1497 to 1498) and Il Sodoma (the remainder, painted from 1505 on) that alone are worth the trip. The refectory and chapterhouse offer some faint indication of simple monastic life as it has always been, and there are beautifully manicured grounds, with gardens and meditation paths. The abbey is open daily, except at lunchtime.

 EATING OUT: *La Torre* – The restored medieval tower that houses this restaurant run by the monks goes back to the abbey's earliest days. The food is simple and good. Closed Tuesdays. (Monte Oliveto Maggiore; phone: 0577-707022; inexpensive.)

MONTALCINO: The hill town of Montalcino is extraordinarily perched in the midst of a pretty area known for its noble wines and subtle light. In its early days, the site belonged to an abbey, the Abbazia di Sant'Antimo, 7 miles to the south. Then Montalcino became a free commune — fought over by the Sienese and the Florentines, however, until the former defeated the latter in 1260 and the town became Sienese. When Siena fell to Medici Florence in 1555, Sienese patriots fled to Montalcino to form a short-lived Sienese republic-in-exile, until Montalcino itself was forced into submission by Cosimo I. In recognition of this hospitality, a delegation from Montalcino occupies a place of honor in the historical procession that precedes Siena's twice-yearly Palio race. Most of Montalcino's stately architecture shows medieval Sienese influence. Be sure to visit the 14th-century *Rocca,* the fortress from whose aerial lookouts the city kept its enemies at bay and whose main attraction these days is its informal *enoteca* (wine bar), serving thick *panini* sandwiches, cheese, and glasses of the local Brunello di Montalcino, one of the most celebrated (and costly) wines in all Italy. The other command post in town is the handsome 19th-century *Caffè Fiaschetteria Italiana,* in the central Piazza del Popolo, where the townsfolk converge to talk for hours, usually about the current status of the famous Brunello grape. The Sagra del

Tordo — part archery contest, part thrush festival — is held here on the last Sunday in October, when colorful medieval costumes — and rivers of wine — bring the town to life.

To visit the Abbazia di Sant'Antimo, just follow signs along the drive south from Montalcino. The abbey, one of the most noted examples of medieval monastic architecture, is visible from afar, isolated in an open expanse of olive groves. According to legend, Charlemagne founded it in the 9th century, but most of what is seen today dates from the 12th century. Best preserved of the buildings is the church, built of travertine now turned golden, with alabaster used for much of the trim, column capitals, and windows — at sunset there is nothing quite as beautiful. To visit the church, contact the custodian at Via del Centro 12, in Castelnuovo dell'Abate, at the top of the hill. And if at all possible, be on hand for early evening vespers (weekdays at 4 PM in winter; 5 PM in summer) when the monks walk down from their quarters in Castelnuovo for an hour of Gregorian chant that fills this sanctum sanctorum to its aged beams.

 CHECKING IN: *Giardino* – A dozen clean, modest rooms as well as a good restaurant stocked with the best Chianti and Brunello vintages. Restaurant closed Wednesdays. (Piazza Cavour 2, Montalcino; phone: 0577-848257; inexpensive.)

Giglio – A convenient, clean, and unpretentious hotel with about a dozen rooms, an interesting restaurant, and a well-stocked wine cellar. Restaurant closed Mondays. (Via Soccorso Saloni 49, Montalcino; phone: 0577-848167; inexpensive.)

EATING OUT: *La Cucina di Edgardo* – Just up the street from the *Giglio,* it is the best choice in town. Very good local cuisine. Closed Wednesdays and part of January. (Via Soccorso Saloni 33, Montalcino; phone: 0577-848232; moderate.)

En Route from Montalcino – Return to Torrenieri and the Via Cassia and follow it south to SS146, the turnoff for Pienza. After a visit, continue another 8 miles east on SS146 to Montepulciano.

PIENZA: This little town was once called Corsignano and once belonged to the powerful Piccolomini family, one of whose number, Aeneas Sylvius Piccolomini, was born here and grew to be an exceptionally clever Renaissance man and, eventually, in 1458, Pope Pius II. An acclaimed humanist, he dreamed of creating the perfect Renaissance city, executed to a precise urban plan, and so he commissioned a famous architect, Bernardo Rossellino, to create this small jewel. It became a papal annex and summer home for Pius, who officially changed its name to Pienza in 1462. Today this unusual miniature city is so pristinely preserved that when director Franco Zeffirelli chose to film his *Romeo and Juliet* here, every set was already in place. White lace curtains grace the windows, flowers bloom on sills, and streets are curiously named del Bacio (of the Kiss), dell'Amore, and della Fortuna. A simple Renaissance cathedral stands in Piazza Pio II, the center of town, and to the right of it is the Palazzo Piccolomini, where the Piccolomini family lived until just after World War II when the last family member died. Also in the square are the Palazzo Vescovile, the Palazzo Comunale, and a small cathedral museum. Be sure to walk behind the church for a sweeping view of the whole Val d'Orcia and Monte Amiata, a dormant volcano.

EATING OUT: *Dal Falco* – A simple, rustic place, in a shady square just outside the town gate, it's always busy. Try the *bici,* very tasty homemade pasta of flour and water (no eggs). Wednesday is the day for fish, not commonly served in this landlocked, game-loving part of Tuscany. Closed Fridays. (Piazza Dante Alighieri 7, Pienza; phone: 0578-748551; inexpensive.)

MONTEPULCIANO: Famous for its wine — Vino Nobile di Montepulciano — and several times larger than Pienza, it is still something of a perfect miniature Renaissance city, except that it owes its harmonious aspect more to the continuing patronage of the Medicis than to the utopian dream of one man. A major determinant of the Medicis' favor, no doubt, was Agnolo Ambrogini, one of the great Renaissance poets and a friend and protégé of Giuliano de' Medici and Lorenzo il Magnifico. Born in Montepulciano, he was better known as Il Poliziano, from the ancient name of the town, which was in existence in Etruscan times. Montepulciano sits 2,000 feet above sea level, with the spacious and grandiose Piazza Grande at its highest point. Its major claim to fame is the number of handsome *palazzi* lining that square as well as the two main arteries — Via Roma, which begins at Porta al Prato but leads to the other end of town under several different names, and Via Ricci. Various architectural styles are represented, but Montepulciano is most noted for its monuments of the 16th century, as well as its flourishes of the Baroque, and for the way these important buildings are superimposed on a town plan that goes back to the Middle Ages. There are few "must-see" attractions (discounting the view from the tower of the *Palazzo Comunale,* a 14th-century building with a 15th-century façade, possibly designed by Michelozzo, in Piazza Grande), but the town itself is a joy to discover, with its winding *vicoli* (alleys), majestic door knockers, window ironwork, and the aged clock tower with the masked Pulcinella striking the hours in front of the *Church of Sant'Agostino* (the Pulcinella is a 16th-century gift of a Neapolitan visitor, the church a definite Michelozzo design). Outside of town (a mile-long walk down the Strada di San Biagio) is the *Tempio di San Biagio,* a 16th-century church in pale gold travertine. A High Renaissance masterpiece by Antonio Sangallo the Elder, it sits in an open field, overlooking the whole valley.

CHECKING IN: *Panoramic* – A simple hostelry 1½ miles southeast of town, in the direction of Chianciano Terme. It has only 25 rooms but boasts the amenities — air conditioning, tennis courts, a fine restaurant — of a much larger establishment. In addition, it offers rural calm, pleasant gardens, and expansive views. (SS146; phone: 0578-53045; moderate.)

La Terrazza – This renovated 16th-century residence-turned-hotel is only a minute's walk from Piazza Grande. The name refers to two terraces that make it particularly enjoyable in warm weather. Each room is furnished differently, most rather handsomely, and there are mini-apartments with kitchenettes that sleep up to 5. (Via Piè al Sasso 16, Montepulciano; phone: 0578-757440; inexpensive.)

EATING OUT: *La Chiusa* – This farmhouse restaurant can be reached by backtracking a few miles west of Montepulciano on SS146 and then turning north to the town of Montefollonico (which is roughly equidistant from Pienza and Montepulciano, so a meal here can be combined with a visit to either one). If the drive through hilly vineyards seems too far to go, consider that some discriminating diners make the trip from Paris, so the inconvenience is worth the culinary reward. Rarely found Tuscan dishes, such as *gran farro* (a thick peasant soup of cracked wheat) and *piccione al vin santo* (wild pigeon in a sherry-like sauce), make it an effort to reach the heavenly *parfait al cioccolato.* Closed mid-January to mid-March and Tuesdays from October through June. (Montefollonico; phone: 0577-669668; expensive.)

Fattoria Pulcino – Out of town in the direction of Chianciano Terme, this is a medieval monastery–turned–farm that now also operates as a restaurant. Walk past the open wooden ovens and through a tempting maze of farm products (olive oil, wines, pecorino cheese, beans) before entering the large dining room, where meals are served at communal tables. The rustic menu is simple, and most of the choices are cooked on the grill. There are excellent steaks, sausages, and some very delicious first courses. (SS146; phone: 0578-757905; moderate.)

Trattoria Diva – A noisy, friendly, and unpretentious place right in town. The decor may be a little nondescript, but the local dishes that grace the table make it a memorable dining experience. Closed Tuesdays. (Via di Gracciano nel Corso 92, Montepulciano; phone: 0578-757951; moderate.)

En Route from Montepulciano – To reach Arezzo, take the winding, bucolic road to Nottola, and then head north toward Torrita di Siena and onward to Sinalunga. At Sinalunga, either head east and pick up the *autostrada nord* (A1) to the exit for Arezzo, or continue northward along minor roads to Monte San Savino and then to Arezzo. The latter route passes by (or near) two tiny walled hamlets left over from the Middle Ages and, in a certain sense, from feudal times, because both are private property. Both have a farm family or two still living within the walls, and both are primarily visited now for the restaurants and hotels operating in some of the estate buildings. The first hamlet, the Fattoria dell' Amorosa, is seen from a distance, gently elevated above its own rolling farmlands south of Sinalunga. The second is another 20 minutes north to Gargonza, just outside of Monte San Savino.

CHECKING IN/EATING OUT: *Locanda dell'Amorosa* – A regal sweep of cypress trees leads up to this unique establishment, a tiny 14th-century walled village–cum–farming enclave turned into a restaurant with rooms to rent. Those who are only passing through can sit in the small, airy *piazzetta* in the warm Tuscan sun, nursing a long lemonade. Those staying in any of the 8 light and spacious rooms (once farmworkers' quarters) are more able to partake of the gastronomic genius of the kitchen, which is built into the old oxen's stalls and has garnered high praise for its local cuisine with an imaginative nouvelle twist. All in all, it is just as quaint as its name — Lover's Inn — implies, and it is a paradisiacal spot to call home while jaunting off to nearby Siena, Arezzo, and other Tuscan towns. Restaurant closed Mondays, Tuesdays at lunch, and mid-January through February. (Località l'Amorosa; phone: 0577-679497; hotel, expensive to moderate; restaurant, expensive.)

Castello di Gargonza – A 13th-century walled hill town in miniature, Gargonza's claim to fame is that Dante used it as a refuge at some time during his exile from Florence. For over 400 years it has belonged to the noble Guicciardini family, which today runs it as a storybook hotel. There are spacious rooms in the simple, renovated *castello* (castle); otherwise, a score of skillfully renovated stone cottages, with kitchenettes and working fireplaces, sleep 2, 4, or 6 and can be rented weekly or nightly, depending on availability. Just beyond the town walls is the establishment's rustic restaurant, where tables are moved outside during the summer amid the fireflies and the scent of pine. Restaurant closed Mondays. (Castello di Gargonza, Monte San Savino; hotel phone: 0575-847021 or 055-241020; restaurant phone: 0575-847065; hotel, moderate to inexpensive; restaurant, inexpensive.)

AREZZO: A hill town set at the confluence of green valleys — the Valdarno, the Casentino (the upper valley of the Arno), the Valdichiana — ancient Arretium has been of strategic importance since its earliest Etruscan and Roman days. A free commune with Ghibelline leanings during the Middle Ages, it fell to Guelph Florence in 1289. Early in the next century, however, the short but decisive reign of Guido Tarlati, a bishop who ruled Arezzo from 1312 to 1327, lifted the city to prominence, and it is its early-14th-century character that remains most in evidence today. After Tarlati's death, Arezzo's fortunes waned, and in 1384 it fell once again, definitively this time, to Florence. Some very prominent Italians were born here: Guido d'Arezzo, the 11th-century Benedictine monk who invented the musical scale, the great Renaissance poet Petrarch, and Giorgio Vasari, Renaissance painter, architect, and historian. Piero della Francesca may have been born in nearby Sansepolcro, but Arezzo holds him as one of its dearest sons.

At the top of the series of terraces on which the town is built stretches a spacious public park — the Passeggio del Prato — that overlooks the surrounding farmland. Arezzo's Romanesque-Gothic Duomo stands to one side of the Prato. Begun in the late 13th century and not finished until the beginning of the 16th century, it is home to a host of artworks, from the stained glass windows of Guillaume de Marcillat (a 15th-century French artist) to a famous fresco of Mary Magdalene by Piero della Francesca and, to the left of that, the tomb of Guido Tarlati, completed in 1330 by Giovanni and Agnolo di Ventura, possibly according to a design by Giotto. A few blocks north of the Duomo, in Piazza Fossombroni, is the 13th-century church of San Domenico, which has a beautiful wooden crucifix, one of the earlier works of Cimabue. Not far away, at Via XX Settembre 55, is the house (open to the public) of Giorgio Vasari, who supervised the construction, took care of the furnishing, and decorated it himself with frescoes between 1540 and 1548.

Pace yourself, because Arezzo's main attractions are still to come. Piero della Francesca's remarkable fresco cycle illustrating the legend of the true cross, a mature work and the one on which most of his fame rests, is behind the high altar of the *Basilica di San Francesco,* a large, barren 14th-century church that is the spiritual nucleus and geographical center of the old town. And not far from that is the Piazza Grande, center of urban life for centuries. This sloping, rhomboid piazza is surrounded by *palazzi* reflecting the architectural styles of several centuries: Giorgio Vasari's 16th-century *Palazzo delle Logge* (*Loggia Palace*), with its open portico of shops, is on the north side, flanked by several handsome Renaissance *palazzi* and medieval homes; the *Palazzo della Fraternità dei Laici* (*Palace of the Lay Fraternity*) has a Gothic-Renaissance façade; and the magnificent *Pieve di Santa Maria,* a 12th-to-14th-century church with a Pisan-Lucchese Romanesque façade of the 13th century, backs into the square, with its tall campanile of "100 holes" (it actually has 40 mullioned windows) standing alongside it. The first weekend of every month, Piazza Grande and the surrounding streets become the site of an antiques fair, with hundreds of vendors — of inexpensive bric-a-brac, sublime *objets* and furniture, and just plain junk — in attendance. On the first Sunday in September, the market moves elsewhere to make room for the annual Giostra del Saracino, a re-creation of a medieval jousting tournament in which eight knights representing the town's four quarters attack an effigy of the Saracen. Accompanying the joust is a historical procession of lance-bearing knights on brilliantly caparisoned horses, a fitting spectacle for this evocative and picturesque old square.

Other places of interest in Arezzo include the remains of a Roman amphitheater and the nearby *Museo Archeologico Mecenate* (*Mecenate Archaeological Museum*), which contains a collection of the *corallini* vases made by Aretine artists from the 1st century BC to the 1st century AD. Arezzo's tourist information office, at Piazza Risorgimento 116 (phone: 0575-20839), can supply information on other attractions.

 CHECKING IN: *Continentale* – Large (78 rooms), modern, and only a few minutes' walk from the medieval quarter. It has a restaurant. (Piazza Guido Monaco 7, Arezzo; phone: 0575-20251; moderate.)

Minerva – Not as central as the *Continentale,* but modern, clean, and comfortable, with 100 rooms and a restaurant. (Via Fiorentina 6, Arezzo; phone: 0575-27891; moderate.)

 EATING OUT: *Buca di San Francesco* – The dining room is the frescoed former *cantina* (wine cellar) of a lovely 14th-century *palazzo,* and if that's not enough, the food here is some of the best in the region. In addition to thick, juicy steaks and roast lamb, there's a *timbale* of spinach and chicken livers, vegetable *sformati* (soufflés), and a hearty white bean soup. Closed Monday evenings, Tuesdays, and July. (Piazza San Francesco 1, Arezzo; phone: 0575-23271; moderate.)

Al Principe – Aretines love this warm and busy *trattoria,* one of the oldest still operating in the area. It's in the rural periphery, along SS71 northbound, a 5-

minute drive from the center, but the ride is more than compensated by the pleasant culinary experience in store. It offers the whole roster of unpretentious local goodness, plus a few house specialties such as lamb cooked in a crust or baby eels (*cee*) in terra cotta casseroles. Closed Mondays and mid-July to mid-August. (Località Giovi; phone: 0575-362046; inexpensive.)

En Route from Arezzo – To expedite the tour, hop on the A1, and be back in Florence in 45 minutes. Or, for those who intend to explore the neighboring region of Umbria, take SS71 south to Lake Trasimeno, then skirt the lake to Perugia, visiting a final Tuscan hill town, Cortona (18 miles from Arezzo), before reaching the lake. The birthplace of Luca Signorelli, Cortona has an Etruscan background and a medieval appearance, with steep, narrow streets, only one of which, Via Nazionale, the main street, is level. It leads into Piazza della Repubblica, with the *Palazzo Comunale* (Town Hall), and then on into the adjoining Piazza Signorelli, where the *Palazzo Pretorio* (or *Palazzo Casali*) houses the *Museo dell'Accademia Etrusca* (*Etruscan Academy Museum*), most famous for its 5th-century BC bronze Etruscan chandelier, the largest and most richly decorated of its kind. The *Museo Diocesano* (*Diocesan Museum*), in a former church in front of the Duomo, contains — besides several Signorellis — an especially beautiful Annunciation by Fra Angelico.

Otherwise, take SS71 north out of Arezzo to explore the northeastern corner of Tuscany. The road follows the Arno into a little-known, sparsely populated, forest-dense area known as the Casentino, site of powerful monastic developments in the late Middle Ages that were instrumental in paving the way for the Renaissance. The monasteries were usually set in inaccessible mountain sites along the backbone of the Apennines, and the overwhelming beauty of their natural surroundings predisposed residents to extraordinary meditational heights. Contact with the secular world was not totally severed, however, and artistic works and rich architecture are evident, if not abundant.

At Bibbiena, 20 miles north of Arezzo, turn onto SS208 and climb another 17 miles through pine and beech forests to the most famous of the Casentino monasteries, *La Verna*, at 3,500 feet. The noble Cattani family of Chiusi in Casentino donated this mountain to St. Francis in 1213, and it was here, in 1224, that the saint from Assisi received the stigmata. A cluster of churches sprang up in the century after his death (1226), many, as in the Chiesa Maggiore, filled with very beautiful terra cottas by Andrea della Robbia. A large community of Franciscans still lives in seclusion at La Verna, carrying on the 800-year-old tradition of the 3 PM procession and singing of vespers. The monks also maintain a modern but modest *foresteria* (quarters with accommodations for visitors); a few small, clean rooms are available, and the price includes three obligatory meals (good and honest fare, and there really is no other place to eat). To reserve a room, write to the *Santuario della Verna*, 52010 Chiusi della Verna (AR), or call 0575-599016.

Another monastery, Camaldoli, the oldest monastic center in all Tuscany, can be reached by a pine-shaded road from La Verna (about a 20-mile drive) or by returning to Bibbiena and there taking SS71 north (from Serravalle, follow signs to Camaldoli). What functions as the monastery today was founded in the 11th century as the *foresteria* for pilgrims visiting the renowned Eremo (Hermitage) of the Camaldolensian division of Benedictine monks, another mile up the road. Gradually it turned into a monastery itself and was a famed center of learning during the Renaissance — Giuliano and Lorenzo de' Medici used to meet here to discuss classical texts and philosophy with Marsilio Ficino, Leon Battista Alberti, and other 15th-century intellectuals. The monastery has an interesting 16th-century pharmacy with the original cabinets and ceramic containers, and still sells the herbal panaceas for which the monks have always been known. It also has its original 12th-century Hospitium Camalduli for receiving guests — simple, clean, renovated rooms, some with bath. (Unlike La Verna, there's no obligation to eat here because there are two other modest restaurants in the tiny town.) For reservations, write to *Monastero di Camaldoli,* Foresteria, 52101 Camaldoli (AR), or call 0575-556013. The Eremo, where the original monks lived in complete seclusion near the powers that be, is also open to the public. Founded in 1012 by St. Romualdo, it consists of 20 isolated, single cells, each with a sleeping area, study, and small outdoor garden.

Return to Bibbiena and take SS70 north to Poppi, where a quick slip through the old town will be of interest. Medieval home of the powerful Guidi counts, who ruled the Casentino from the 11th to the 14th century, Poppi has a superb castle (now the *Palazzo Pretorio*) with a small but elaborate courtyard and a tower offering sweeping views of all that was once the Guidi domain. From Poppi, bear west on SS70, up and over the Passo di Consuma, and then, after about 7 miles, turn left at the signs for Pelago and Vallombrosa. The latter, an ancient fir forest between the Casentino valley to the east and the Valdarno to the west, is a traditional summer escape for Florentines and the site of another ancient monastery, the seat of the Vallombrosian division of the Benedictines. The monastery dates from 1230, although the nucleus of monks founded by St. Giovanni Gualberto goes back to the year 1000. The body of buildings has undergone changes over time, but the 13th-century campanile and a 15th-century dungeon still exist. Nearby Saltino has a number of good restaurants and hotels, some with open vistas over the valley below.

To return to Florence, head south toward Reggello and then west to Leccio. Loop north onto SS69, stopping at Sammezzano, if desired, for a last, inimitable treat.

CHECKING IN/EATING OUT: *Castello di Sammezzano* – This amazing piece of architectural whimsy was originally a Roman fort, then a Renaissance abode of the Medici, then the property of a 17th-century Spanish grandee whose descendants turned it into a sort of mini-Alhambra. Moroccan, French, and Italian artists sculpted the inside into a gorgeous Moorish marble fantasy, with 14 vast hotel apartments decorated with Spanish furniture and painted ceilings. The park is filled with rare (for this part of the world) species of trees, including California redwoods and Atlantic cedars. The restaurant, built around a flood-lighted indoor Moorish fountain, serves delicious traditional Tuscan food. Restaurant closed Tuesdays in winter. (Località Leccio, Reggello; phone: 055-867911; expensive.)

Elba

Known for the popular palindrome "Able was I ere I saw Elba" and for Napoleon's brief residence, Isola d'Elba remains a relatively undeveloped vacation paradise, with more than fifty beaches along its ninety miles of coastline, fine local wine and cuisine, typically Tuscan hospitality, and great natural beauty. Five and a half miles from the mainland, Elba is just difficult enough to reach, and sufficiently out of the way, to deter hordes of package tourists. But those who do take the ferry from Piombino or the flight from Pisa find the extra leg of their journey well worth the effort. They tend to come back again and again, preferring Elba's quiet dignity to the more fashionable vacation spots along the frenetic Mediterranean-Ligurian coastline.

Despite its diminutive size, Elba has been known since the birth of history. Called *Ilva* by the Ligurians and *Aethalia* by the Greeks, it passed from the Etruscans and became part of the Roman Empire. It was ruled by the Pisans in the Middle Ages and served as a haven for the Barbary pirates in the sixteenth century. The Medicis, too, left their mark — their influence can be seen in the fortifications of Portoferraio.

The island was perhaps most influenced by Napoleon Bonaparte, whose first exile from France, and short reign of Elba, began in May 1814. Although he lived here less than a year, the emperor did much to improve the island, altering street plans and building new roads, modernizing agriculture, and developing iron mines. His summer home, the Villa di San Martino, can be visited and admired, and the hardy can climb the hillside beyond to the island's oldest fortress, Volterraio, where the local residents gathered to protect themselves from the notorious pirates Barbarossa and Dragut.

Iron ore is still mined in the hills above Rio Marina and then shipped from Portoferraio ("Port of Iron"). Garnet, beryl, marcasite, tourmaline, and pollucite are just a few of the other 150 minerals and semiprecious stones to be found in Elban soil, the result of the seismic turmoil that created the island, and there are more varieties of granite here than anywhere in Europe. Geologists and gemstone collectors can often be found happily chipping away at the rock ledges along many of the island's winding roads. The astonishing range of colors of the island's hydrangeas is the result of the soil's rich mineral composition.

Elba bathes in sunshine most of the year. Its mountains create an east-west wind break from the prevailing *scirocco,* which brings hot air and sometimes dust from Africa, and a *maestrale,* which blows cool air south from the Alps. As a result of its peculiar formation, some parts of the island are green and wooded, while others are buff and sandy.

The high season begins just before Easter, when the sea begins to warm and the island bursts into bloom — marguerites, broom, and other wildflowers cover the pine-forested hills, and potted geraniums and hydrangeas brighten every doorstep and windowsill. It ends in late September, when the smell of autumn is in the air and many hotels close for the winter. Sometimes the weather does become *brutto,* but the rain seldom lasts more than a day or two and provides a break from the normally hot and sunny weather.

Life here is governed by the seasons far more than by any other factor. For all the bustle of summer tourism, a largely agricultural existence creates a quiet atmosphere. Every town and village has its own well-cared-for *bocce* pitch, where the men (and more recently the women as well) play this traditional game almost every evening. The grass on the airport runway is kept trimmed by flocks of sheep and goats from a nearby farm that produces the extraordinary fresh ricotta cheese used in many of the island's dishes. At night, the lights of the island's fishing boats can be seen bobbing up and down at sea; in the morning, their catch — swordfish, cuttlefish, various white fish, clams and mussels, as well as prawns and small spiny lobsters — is displayed in ice-filled boxes on marble slabs at the market.

Whether a visitor chooses to relax on the island's wonderful beaches, to climb and picnic in the pine forests on the mountains, or to drive along the sometimes spectacular coastal roads, it's hard to miss Elba's natural charm, peaceful abundance, and timeless beauty.

TOURIST INFORMATION: Prices are generally higher from May to September, but tourist services are more plentiful during this time, too. Numerous free guides, including lists of hotels and restaurants, are available from the Azienda Autonoma di Cura Soggiorno e Turismo dell'Isola d'Elba, Calata Italia 26, Portoferraio (phone: 92671), which serves the entire island. In addition, information in Portoferraio and other towns is available from the following sources: *Portoferraio:* Agenzia Viaggi, Calata Italia (phone: 92386); *Marina di Campo:* Ufficio Turistico Cipat, Via Mascagni (phone: 97414); *Procchio:* Agenzia Viaggi Bruno, Via Provinciale (phone: 907716); *Marciana Marina:* Ufficio Turistico Brauntour, Via Mentana 2 (phone: 996874); *Porto Azzurro:* Ufficio Turistico La Pianotta, Lungomare A. De Gasperi (phone: 95105); *Rio Marina:* Ufficio Turistico Forte, Via Palestro 23 (phone: 962392); *Cavo:* Ufficio Turistico Estelba, Cavo (phone: 949934).

Telephone – The telephone code for the entire island is 0565.

FOOD AND WINE: Elba offers excellent Tuscan food. Particularly delicious are dishes composed of freshly caught seafood — for example, *cacciucco,* a form of fish soup or stew resembling bouillabaisse, and *gamberi* (prawns) or *polpi* (octopus), served in many ways, often together, dipped in batter and fried. Other fish offerings may include *dentice* (sea bream), *nasello* (whiting), and *triglia* (red mullet). There is a tradition of *cucina casalinga* (home cooking) with pasta, often handmade, combined with wonderful fish and shellfish — *alla margherita* (with spider crab), *all'aragosta* (with lobster), or *alle seppie* (with cuttlefish). More familiar is *spaghetti alle vongole* (with tiny clams) or *al pesto* (with fresh basil, oil, and Parmesan cheese).

Elban wine is of very high quality, even by Italian standards. The island produces a variety of table wines — white, red, rosé, and sparkling — and several sweet dessert wines. Of the former, the white is outstanding; try the Procanico and Elba Bianco. The Moscato and Aleatico dessert wines are delicious served with fresh fruits or with cookies called *crostate.* If you have a special interest in wines, drive to Marciana Marina and visit the bar–tasting platform at the end of the Lungo Mare. This is the place to sample locally made wines that complement Elban food. While on that side of the island, drive a little farther toward Poggio and taste the local brandy. The town is well marked and easy to find. Also the Elban white *grappa,* served very cold and drunk in modest amounts, is a bracing after-dinner drink.

GETTING AROUND: Traveling to and around Elba often sounds more difficult than it really is. Transportation and route depend only on personal preference and available time.

Air – San Giusto Airport in Pisa is the international airport nearest Elba. *Alitalia* operates daily flights to Pisa from Rome, Milan, Turin, Sicily, and Sardinia, and there are daily flights to Pisa from other European cities such as London, Frankfurt, and Paris. From Pisa, *Transavio* flies to Elba daily (except Saturdays and Sundays), one flight per day, from April to June, and four flights per day (except Sundays) from June to October. The flight takes half an hour and provides a panoramic view of the island.

Car Rental – Cars can be rented at the airport in Pisa: *Avis* (phone: 050-42028); *Hertz* (phone: 050-44426); or *Europcar* (phone: 050-41017). The drive from Pisa to Piombino takes about two hours. You *must* have reservations to put your car on any of the ferries (see *Ferry,* below); reservations can be obtained through most travel agents.

Cars also can be rented on Elba. The main rental agency on the island is *Maggiore Rent-A-Car;* offices are in Portoferraio (phone: 915368) and Marina di Campo (phone: 976988). *Taglioni Giovanni-Aeroporto* (phone: 977150) is at the Elba airport. You can arrange to have a car meet you at the ferry in Portoferraio or at the airport. However, renting on the island is considerably more expensive than on the mainland, where rates tend to be more competitive.

Train – There are no trains on Elba, but to reach Piombino (and ferries) by train, take the main rail line that runs along the west coast of Italy and get off at Campiglia Marittima (be sure to take a train that stops in Campiglia). From Campiglia Marittima, a branch line runs to Piombino Marittima, its quayside terminus. Be careful not to get off at two earlier stops in the town of Piombino. During the summer, there are several trains daily.

Ferry – There are ferries from Piombino to Portoferraio, and vice versa, about every 50 minutes from 5:15 AM to 9:30 PM during July and August. Departures during other months are less frequent and more variable; inquire directly from the ferry companies (listed below). All the ferries accept cars and caravans; the journey takes an hour. The hydrofoil is for foot passengers and takes half an hour. All ferries and hydrofoils operate between Piombino and Portoferraio. Some ferries go to Cavo, Rio Marino, and Porto Azzurro as well. There is also a direct ferry (*Toremar*) from Livorno once a day. This leaves from the Porto Mediceo and takes about three hours.

Toremar has offices at Via Calafati 4, Livorno (phone: 0586-24113); Calata Italia 22, Portoferraio (phone: 0565-918080); Piazzale Premuda 13/14, Piombino (phone: 0565-31100); and Via Palestro 23, Rio Marina (phone: 0565-95004). *Navarma* can be found at Piazzale Premuda 13, Piombino (phone: 0565-39775); and Viale Elba 4, Portoferraio (phone: 0565-92133).

Boat Excursions – Regular excursions around the island operate from Portoferraio throughout the summer; inquiries may be made at the main tourist agencies (see *Tourist Information,* above), your hotel, or the principal bar on the waterfront. A few excursions operate from Porto Azzurro as well. Small motor boats can be hired at Porto Azzurro and Marina di Campo.

Bus – Regular bus service on the island is designed to meet the requirements of the inhabitants rather than those of visitors. Bus runs start very early in the morning; their frequency is reduced on Sundays and holidays. The main station in Portoferraio is next to the *Grattacielo,* Elba's ten-story "skyscraper." Pick up a schedule at the *ACIT* office, Viale Elba 20, Portoferraio (phone: 92392).

Moped and Bike Rental – Either is a good alternative to a car for day trips on this small island. Contact *Alle Ghiaie,* Via Cairoli 25/27, Portoferraio (phone: 92666).

Guided Tours – The main travel agencies offer a number of half- and whole-day guided tours. Details may be obtained in Portoferraio from either *Aethaltour,* Viale Elba (phone: 915755), or *Intourelba,* Via Carducci 162 (phone: 916034).

SPECIAL EVENTS: Easter is a very special time on Elba, but tourist services are severely limited at that time of year. On Good Friday evening, villagers gather at the local churches to organize processions. Young men carry the cross and an effigy of Christ through village streets, while others in the procession sing Gregorian chants. Early on Easter morning, villagers from Sant'Ilario and San Piero, hill towns above Marina di Campo, meet in procession on the way to worship in each other's churches. On Easter Monday worshipers make a pilgrimage to the Shrine of the Madonna del Monte above Marciana and, on Ascension Thursday, to the Shrine of Santa Lucia outside Portoferraio.

On August 12 the island celebrates the feast of Santa Chiara, the patron saint of Marciana Marina, with a religious procession, dancing in the piazza, and fireworks. Celebrations start in the evening and go on until the early hours. Similar rites are held on August 7 for San Gaetano in Marina di Campo.

 SPORTS: During the summer, there are a multitude of friendly competitions, such as boat races, tennis matches, and water skiing and windsurfing championships, all with vacationers in mind. These tend to be very friendly affairs, not serious tournaments. In general, water sports are the most popular. Equipment can be rented at most of the large beaches.

Beaches – Elba has a variety of wonderful beaches, some sandy and safe for swimmers and waders, others rocky and suitable for deep diving. The following are the best sandy beaches: on the north coast — Spartaia, Procchio, Campo all'Aia, La Biodola, Scaglieri, and Cavo (a little rocky); on the south coast — Reale, Barbarossa, Naregno, Straccoligno, Calamita Peninsula, Pareti, and Morcone. Usually, hotels and bars near the beaches own concessions for such facilities as deck chairs, umbrellas, changing cabins, and toilets; charges are by the day or week. During the high season, deck chairs at popular beaches are reserved months in advance by regular summer residents.

Fishing – Both underwater and by boat, fishing is free except in the protected area between Le Ghiaie pebble beach at Portoferraio and the submarine nature reserve at Capo Bianco. Inquire at your hotel or at the waterfront. The village of Chiessi is a favorite base for spear fishers.

Golf – The *Acquabona Golf Hotel* has a beautifully situated, well-maintained 9-hole golf course inland on the main road between Portoferraio and Acquabona.

Sailing – Sailing clubs and schools are affiliated with hotels on Portoferraio Bay — the *Hotel Garden* in Schiopparello, *Villa Ottone* in Ottone, and *Grotte del Paradiso* in Le Grotte (near the Roman Villa).

Skin Diving – The waters around Elba are wonderful for skin diving, especially along the rocky northwest and west coasts and also along the east coast of the Calamita Peninsula, which is accessible only by boat. The fishing village of Chiessi is a favorite base.

Tennis – Many hotels have tennis courts or can arrange for tourists to play on the floodlit courts at public and private tennis clubs.

Windsurfing – This sport is taking hold on Elba, as elsewhere around the Mediterranean. The Elba Windsurfing School is headquartered at the *Hotel La Perla* in Procchio. *La Foce* campground in Marina di Campo also has a school.

 NIGHTCLUBS AND NIGHTLIFE: Discos and nightclubs dot the island, and almost every Friday, Saturday, and Sunday evening one village or another has dancing in the open air. However, the favorite Elban evening pursuit is definitely *bocce,* the Italian version of French *boule.* The game is played with great fun and seriousness. Each town has lighted courts; nearby bars do a good business.

TOURING ELBA

Elba is a tiny island and its roads are quite good, so it's easy to drive around it in just a day. With this in mind, choose accommodations from the variety of resorts listed below and explore from one base. For the sea lover, there is every kind of beach and aquatic facility. Inland, the mountains offer a completely different experience even though they are only a mile or two from the beaches.

In general, costs on the island are moderate compared to most mainland prices. Hotels rated as expensive charge from $75 to $100 for a double room; moderate, from $50 to $75; and inexpensive, less than $50. A meal for two, including drinks and tips, in a restaurant rated as expensive costs $50 or more; moderate, $25 to $50; and inexpensive, less than $25.

PORTOFERRAIO: The capital of Elba is well worth exploring but is not recommended as a base (except during the off-season, when the many resort hotels elsewhere on the island are closed). It lies on the northwest promontory at the entrance to Portoferraio Bay. Walk from the harbor through the walled arches (stopping for a treat at the *gelateria*) and continue onward and upward along beautiful, steep streets flanked by yellow houses. On Via Garibaldi, the main street, is the *Town Hall,* the boyhood home of Victor Hugo. To the northeast, on Via Napoleone, is the *Chiesa della Misericordia;* mass is said here every May 5 for Napoleon. Continue to the highest point in town, *Piazza Napoleone,* for spectacular views: To the west is the *Forte del Falcone;* to the east, above the lighthouse, *Forte della Stella.* Both were originally Medici fortresses, built in 1548 and later completed by Napoleon. On the ridge between the two fortresses lies the *Palazzina dei Mulini,* which was Napoleon's principal residence; it has a pretty garden and contains his library and other memorabilia. Open daily, except Tuesdays, 9 AM to 1:30 PM and 3 to 6 PM May to October; 9 AM to 2 PM in winter. Admission fee (can include admission to the Villa di San Martino; see *En Route from Portoferraio*). The covered market, *Galleaze,* in Piazza Cavour is open weekdays. The bustling open-air market in *Piazza della Repubblica* is open Friday mornings.

 CHECKING IN: *Albergo Ape Elbana* – This old villa, with a wide verandah, offers comfortable rooms and a homey restaurant. (Salita Cosimo de' Medici 1, Portoferraio; phone: 92245; moderate to inexpensive.)

 EATING OUT: *La Ferrigna* – The best restaurant in Portoferraio specializes in Elban cookery, especially seafood. Try the prawns, squid with *risotto,* or stuffed zucchini. Closed Tuesdays and December to March. (Piazza della Repubblica 22/23, Portoferraio; phone: 92129; inexpensive.)

En Route from Portoferraio – *Villa San Martino,* Napoleon's summer residence, lies south of Portoferraio on a hill overlooking the sea. Although Napoleon lived here only a few months before his departure for the Hundred Days, ending with the Battle of Waterloo, the villa is imbued with his mystique. The central room is decorated with *trompe l'oeil* paintings depicting the Egyptian campaign. On one wall the emperor's graffito "Napoleon is happy everywhere" is still readable. Open daily, except Mondays, 9 AM to 1 PM and 3 to 6 PM May to October; 9 AM to 2 PM in winter. Entrance fee (can include admission on the same day to the *Palazzina dei Mulini;* because the villa is closed on Mondays and the *palazzina* on Tuesdays, a combined visit cannot be made on either day).

BIODOLA: West of Portoferraio toward Procchio, Biodola is one of the most beautiful resort areas on Elba's north coast. It has a broad, sandy beach and is set well off the road.

CHECKING IN: *Hermitage* – An elegant, old luxury hotel, tucked into a corner of Biodola Bay. Accommodations include bedroom cottages on the steep, wooded slopes overlooking the bay, and there are two swimming pools, a private beach, garden, and tennis courts. Open April to October. (Golfo della Biodola; phone: 969932; expensive.)

La Biodola – This place has a loyal clientele. Its tastefully decorated rooms overlook the bay, and it has a seawater pool in a lovely, landscaped garden. Open April to October. (Golfo della Biodola; phone: 969966; expensive to moderate.)

En Route from Portoferraio Bay Area – Bordering the bay, southeast of Portoferraio, are the *Terme San Giovanni,* specializing in medicinal mud baths for the treatment of arthritis, cellulitis, rheumatism, and sinusitus (phone: 92266, 92680).

The wooded foothills in this area lead to the low mountain range of the central section of Elba. The road then climbs in sharp curves to the promontory of *Punta delle Grotte.* An open gateway to the left leads to the remains of the tremendous *Roman Villa,* thought to have been built during the reign of Emperor Augustus. The view across the bay to Portoferraio is lovely, and what has been excavated of the villa is easily explored.

Head inland toward the mountains and the *Volterraio fortress,* probably constructed in the 13th century by the Pisans. The fortress is perched high on the hillside dominating the skyline. Park halfway up the hill and take the footpath. It is a rugged climb that takes about 45 minutes, but the breathtaking views and the grandeur of the fortress, with its ruined walls and fig trees growing wild in the courtyards, make it well worth the effort.

 CHECKING IN: *Villa Ottone* – Less than two miles southeast of Portoferraio, on Portoferraio Bay, this resort is known for its sailing school. It also has a pool and tennis courts. Open April to October. (Ottone; phone: 966042; expensive.)

Garden – Overlooking the bay from pretty, pine-shaded grounds, the Garden, too, has a sailing school and its own sand and gravel beach. (Schiopparello; phone: 966043; expensive to moderate.)

Acquabona Golf Hotel – South of Schiopparello and inland on the road to Porto Azzurro, the Acquabona owns and adjoins Elba's only 9-hole golf course. (Acquabona; phone: 940064; moderate.)

RIO MARINA: There are many different minerals to be found on Elba — rock crystal, common white opal, white quartz, malachite, azurite, feldspar, and copper pyrite, to name only some — and it is easy to collect samples while exploring the island. For non–rock rappers, most indigenous minerals are for sale at the stalls in the open market in Rio Marina. (*Note:* The ropes of rock necklaces sold to tourists are usually made from gemstones imported from Africa. Most Elban rocks are too soft for polishing.) Rio also has a small mineral museum in the town hall in the Palazzo Comunale, Via Principe Amedeo. North of Rio Marina is Cavo and the mining district.

 CHECKING IN: *Rio* – A simple hotel with its own restaurant, overlooking the harbor. Open April to September. (Via Palestro, Rio Marina; phone: 962016; inexpensive.)

PORTO AZZURRO: Originally called Porto Longone, this is a small town, the southern terminus of the ferry lines. The main life revolves around the harbor, which is usually full of yachts and fishing boats. During high season, day-long excursions are operated to the island of Montecristo.

CHECKING IN: *Cala di Mola* – Overlooking the estuary just outside Porto Azzurro harbor, this attractive hotel has a well-appointed restaurant and public rooms, beautiful gardens, and a double swimming pool. (Mola; phone: 95225; moderate.)

Elba International – Large, modern, and built high on a wooded promontory, Capo della Tavola, across the bay from Porto Azzurro. (Naregno; phone: 968611; moderate.)

CAPOLIVERI: An ancient town dating from the Roman occupation, Capoliveri has a bloody history of vendettas, drinking, and fighting. Its position 500 feet above sea level affords spectacular views.

 EATING OUT: *Il Chiasso* – Typical Elban ambience. Limited seating; reservations advised. Open Easter to mid-October. Closed lunchtime and Tuesdays. (Via Nazario Sauro 20, Capoliveri; phone: 968709; moderate to inexpensive.)

En Route from Capoliveri – Follow the coastline along the low wooded cliffs down to the plain of Lacona. This leads to the principal bays of the south coast: *Golfo Stella* has two main sandy beaches, Lido and Margidore; *Golfo della Lacona,* a tremendous, wide, sandy beach, free to all, has very good, well-run campsites nestled among the trees.

Tourists heading through the mountains to Marina di Campo pass Elba's airport on the right. The airport has developed a great deal in the past decade; still it maintains only a single runway for light aircraft.

 CHECKING IN: *Antares* – Overlooking Stella Bay, on the south coast, with access to Lido beach. Open mid-March to September. (Lido di Capoliveri; phone: 940131; moderate.)

Hotel della Lacona – Large, modern, only 300 feet from the sea, with its own stretch of beach. (Lacona; phone: 964054; expensive to moderate.)

 EATING OUT: *Ristorante da Gianni* – One of the best restaurants on the island is near the airport, only a mile and a half from Marina di Campo. Gianni's great specialty is his seafood *risotto* of clams, mussels, and other shellfish in a rich wine-based stock, but some think his delectable baked mussels, served as an appetizer, are his real pièce de résistance. Open March to September; closed Fridays. (La Pila; phone: 976965; inexpensive.)

MARINA DI CAMPO: A lively, pretty town and a good base for expeditions. It is always fun to stroll here or to sit at the little bars watching the fishing boats in the harbor. Some Elban enthusiasts feel it is the best place to stay on the island. Accordingly, there are many good hotels along, or near, the excellent sandy beach. Market day is Wednesday.

 CHECKING IN: *Montecristo* – Named for the island due south, this is easily the best hotel in town. Situated on the beach, with its own pool. Excellent service. Open April to October. (Viale Nomellini 11, Marina di Campo; phone: 976861; expensive.)

Iselba Residence – Spacious stone buildings set among umbrella pines beyond the sandy beach east of Marina di Campo. (Via Etruschi 28, Marina di Campo; phone: 977124; expensive to moderate.)

Barcarola Seconda – Very comfortable, close to the beach, with a restaurant and a pretty garden. Open mid-April to October. (Località San Mamiliano, Marina di Campo; phone: 97255; moderate.)

Hotel dei Coralli – A comfortable hotel on the edge of town, it has a swimming pool and a restaurant with good food and service. Open June to September. (Via Etruschi, Marina di Campo; phone: 97336; moderate.)

Meridiana – A very pleasant hotel, close to the beach and pine belt on the edge of town. (Via Etruschi 69, Marina di Campo; phone: 97308; moderate.)

Villa Nettuno – Adjoining the beach on the edge of town, set in the pine belt. Good food and service. Open mid-April to October. (Via Etruschi 30, Marina di Campo; phone: 97028; moderate.)

Pensione Elba – A small family hotel with a homey atmosphere and excellent food. (Località San Mamiliano, Marina di Campo; phone: 97224; inexpensive.)

 EATING OUT: La Triglia – Authentic Elban cuisine. Very good fish. Open March to November; closed Thursdays. (Via Roma, Marina di Campo; phone: 97059; expensive.)

Bar Pizzeria Tre P – Beautifully situated, overlooking the beach and mountains, at the extreme eastern end of the beach. Good food from a large menu; charming service. (La Focè; phone: 976892; inexpensive.)

En Route from Marina di Campo – Follow the main road north from Marina di Campo to La Pila, then to Sant'Ilario. This beautiful little town was an ancient village fortified in the 12th century, probably by the Pisans. There is a lovely walk around the outer walls with spectacular views in every direction.

From Sant'Ilario take the main road out of the piazza towards San Piero. Bear right uphill to the ruins of the large Romanesque *Chiesa di San Giovanni.* Nearby is the impressive watchtower, *Torre di San Giovanni.* From the top, a sentry could see the whole of Campo Bay, and often as far as the island of Pianosa. Take the road up to the main ridge behind Monte Perone. There is a natural stopping place here with excellent picnic areas and fabulous views in all directions. There is also an abundance of wildflowers and beautiful butterflies.

Return to the main road and bear right for the village. San Piero is bigger than Sant'Ilario and even older, built on the site of a Roman colony. The parish church contains the remains of some 14th-century frescoes. Wonderful fruit ices and cappuccino are sold at the *caffè*-bar next to the butcher. Customers who get to the *panificio* (bakery) early can buy fresh *schiacciata,* flat salted bread perfect for homemade pizza or sandwiches.

 EATING OUT: La Cantina – On the main street in La Pila. Good food and eclectic, typically Elban menu. (Via Giovanni XXIII 21, La Pila; phone: 97041; expensive.)

MARCIANA: Also called *Marciana Alta,* this is one of the oldest and prettiest villages on the island, dating from Roman times. Like some other Elban towns, it was fortified in the 12th century by the Pisans. It is set high in the hills overlooking a steep valley full of vineyards and olive, chestnut, and fig trees.

Just south of Marciana are cable cars to the summit of *Monte Capanne,* the highest point on Elba. Park and follow a path through the trees to the terminal. The cable cars run from mid-May to mid-September; they are closed in cloudy or windy weather. Quite primitive-looking, they rather resemble bird cages. But bravery is rewarded by the view from the top, which includes all of Elba and the coasts of mainland Italy and the island of Corsica.

Fonte di Napoleone (Napoleon's Spring) lies just off the road between Marciana and Poggio. Towards Poggio is the small factory where Elba's own very good mineral water, Acqua di Napoleone, is bottled.

EATING OUT: Da Luigi – Beautifully set on the hillside outside Poggio; approached by an improbable track, but definitely worth the drama of getting there. Food and ambience are excellent. Pastas include fresh *gnocchi,* in addition to *pesto* and *carbonara.* Don't miss the heavenly fritters of zucchini and eggplant. Good grills of lamb, chicken, and steak. (Località Feno, Poggio; phone: 99413; moderate.)

Ristorante Publius – A magical night view from its terrace overlooking the valley and bay. Good food and service. Reservations necessary for a table outside. (Piazza XX Settembre, Poggio; phone: 99208; moderate.)

MARCIANA MARINA: This very pleasant seaside resort has an excellent harbor for yachts and small boats. Its wide waterfront promenade ends near the medieval watchtower, *Torre Saracena*.

 CHECKING IN: *Gabbiano Azzurro* – An inland establishment, nestled among the vineyards on the lower slopes of a hill near Poggio. (Viale Amedeo 48, Marciana Marina; phone: 99226; moderate.)

La Primula – The only first-class hotel in the town center, a short distance from the waterfront. (Viale Cerboni, Marciana Marina; phone: 99010; moderate.)

 EATING OUT: *Rendez-Vous da Marcello* – Dine on a variety of seafood — mussels, clams, crab, and lobster — on the terrace at the water's edge. Specialties are *spaghetti alla Margherita* (with crab) and *crème caramel.* Closed January and on Wednesdays. (Piazza della Vittoria, Marciana Marina; phone: 99251; expensive.)

Il Fosso – A must for marvelous pizza with very thin, light, crispy dough, laden with cheese, *prosciutto,* and local mushrooms. Also good are the spaghetti with zucchini and the seafood *risotto.* (Località San Giovanni, Marciana Marina; phone: 99233; moderate.)

En Route from Marciana Marina – To return to the Portoferraio Bay area, take the main road east out of Marciana Marina along the coast to Procchio (a seaside village where accommodations are quite good) and Bivio Boni.

 CHECKING IN: *Desirée* – On Spartaia cove, just west of Procchio. Has its own sandy beach and sheltered harbor. Secluded, comfortable bedrooms have private terraces. (Località Spartaia, Procchio; phone: 907502; expensive.)

Hotel del Golfo – At the western end of a long, sandy beach, it has gardens, a swimming pool, and tennis courts. (Procchio; phone: 907565; expensive to moderate.)

EATING OUT: *Lo Schioppo* – Pleasant restaurant off the main road on a quiet hillside. Outstanding fish and shellfish. (Località lo Schioppo, between Procchio and Marciana Marina; phone: 99038; moderate.)

Umbria

It is often said that Umbria, the small, landlocked region that lies at the heart of the Italian peninsula, takes its name from the Latin word for shade, *umbra*. In fact, these hills, pitted with caves and the mountain watersheds that give birth to the mighty Tiber River, are lush and verdant, particularly in contrast to the arid and stony Abruzzo next door. The more academic-minded may point out that three of the ruling families in Umbria's Etruscan past had names — Umria, Umruna, and Umrana — that may have been taken to identify the region. Still, even on a map, Umbria looks like a leaf from a shade tree, and how not to see its single lake, Trasimeno — where Hannibal routed 16,000 Roman soldiers in 217 BC — as a single drop of dew?

Indeed, there is something soothing about this quiet, pleasant, humble region, and it is entirely in keeping with its character that several of Christendom's most beloved saints were born here. Among them were St. Valentine, a third-century Bishop of Terni, which is today an Umbrian industrial town, and St. Clare, founder of the Order of Poor Clares. Foremost among all the region's saints was Clare's friend, gentle St. Francis of Assisi, founder of the Franciscans. Umbria's saints and their followers prayed in the mountain grottoes and preached in the cobbled streets and among the daisies and wild red poppies of the field. It is probably a sense of their spirit that still pervades the Umbrian atmosphere today, just as the graceful abbeys of the orders they founded crown the green hilltops. It goes without saying that Umbria's monastic orders have left an indelible mark not only on the region but on the entire Western world.

Monasticism came to Western Europe from the deserts of the Middle East. The two worlds met in Umbria when a large number of Syrians migrated to live as hermits in the hills, spreading the concept of monastic life. St. Benedict, born in the Umbrian town of Norcia around 480, gave a Western imprint to the tradition of hermit prayer by adding the concept of work. Hence the Umbrian monks prayed, but they also farmed, studied, and copied manuscripts, maintaining a wondrous intellectual and social order that can be seen even in the tidy ledgers of abbey farm and vineyard holdings and the monks' treatises on agriculture displayed in the fascinating Wine Museum at Torgiano, near Perugia. This Umbrian monasticism, with the work ethic it incorporated, spread throughout Italy and then throughout the West, carrying culture and stimulating commerce as it went.

This is not to portray Umbria as solely a clerical state. In fact, disobedience to the papacy became so serious at one point in sixteenth-century Perugia that Pope Paul III had to use troops to put down an uprising over a church-imposed salt tax (even today, the *perugini* use salt sparingly in cooking). And many of the region's festivals hark back to pagan rites. Most famous is the Calendimaggio Festival at Assisi, a romantic rite of spring. During the Middle

Ages, young minstrels sang ballads and love songs in the streets, and each April 29 to May 1, Assisi is still illuminated by torches, decked with medieval flags, and populated by damsels and knights in sumptuous costume. The fun is justified today by explanations that it reevokes St. Francis' youth, for as a boy he, too, participated in the revels.

Nor is Umbria locked into its past. Every June and July, Spoleto plays host to the Festival of Two Worlds, a panoply of the arts of Italy and the US. The well-established festival was created by the Italian-American composer Giancarlo Menotti, and some of Italy's foremost musicians, dancers, actors, directors, painters, and sculptors have taken part over its approximately three decades of existence.

In the beginning, the Umbri were a Villanovan tribe, believed by scholars to have reached Umbria from across the mountains around Bologna. Shepherds and farmers, these Umbri were soon pushed aside by the more sophisticated and aggressive Etruscans, who came as invaders from the Tyrrhenian coast. Perugia, for instance, a Villanovan settlement perched on a rocky stronghold that dominated the upper Tiber valley, had already fallen to the Etruscans by the fifth century BC. The Etruscans considerably improved the region. They taught the illiterate Umbri an 18-letter alphabet, and their ambitious public works can be seen in the city walls and mighty arched gate at Perugia. They also left beautiful painted tombs at Orvieto.

The Romans, in turn, overwhelmed the Etruscans and the Umbri in 310 BC. Quintessential builders, they bequeathed an amphitheater at Assisi; a temple, a theater, and a high, many-arched bridge at Spoleto; and a theater and another bridge at Gubbio. Hostile Lombards from the Po valley were next. With the fall of the Roman Empire, they won control over the region and set up the powerful Duchy of Spoleto, which ruled much of Umbria from the sixth to the eleventh century and became an important center for the arts. One Lombard monastery dating from the eighth century can still be seen at Ferentillo, in the valley of the Nera River between Spoleto and Terni.

In the eleventh and twelfth centuries, the age of communes began, a period when Italy's city-states experimented with a form of self-government. Umbria's chief communes — Perugia, Assisi, Foligno, Spoleto, Orvieto, Gubbio, and Città di Castello — are all fascinating to visit today for the rich evidence they still reveal about that era. True, they fought each other with dismaying regularity, allying themselves, as convenient, with one or another of the great powers, which in those days meant either Rome or Florence, pope or emperor. Geographically close to Rome, Umbria was perennially a tempting morsel for the papal powers, to which it would eventually fall in the sixteenth century.

In the meantime, however, the wars were not all negative, because the alliances that were formed stimulated trade and the arts, and Umbria felt the influence of Florentine culture. As the monastic movement inspired by St. Benedict and St. Francis spread throughout the region, Assisi, Italy's second spiritual capital, acquired an important role. The arts in Umbria naturally came to reflect the region's ardent religious life, and in the thirteenth century they began to evolve, for the first time in Europe, from the rigidity of icon-like Byzantine painting and sculpture toward the more lifelike and dramatic works that can be seen in the great cathedrals at Assisi and Orvieto and in the museums and churches of Perugia. Giotto's frescoes of the life of St. Francis in the cathedral at Assisi marked a point of departure for painting in the West.

During the late fourteenth and the fifteenth century, Umbria's cities were run by powerful noble families. In Perugia, these *signori,* or lords, included two bitter rivals, the Oddi and Baglioni. The Trinci ruled in Foligno, the Gabrielli and later the Montefeltro in Gubbio, the Vitelli in Città di Castello, and the Orsini in Terni. Flanking them in the latter part of the period were war leaders called *condottieri,* whose presence possibly reflected the warrior tradition of the old Lombard dukes. They organized mercenary armies and sometimes came into power on their own, and when their power bids in Umbria failed, they did not hesitate to put themselves at the service of foreign rulers. Nevertheless, local autonomy came to an end in the sixteenth century. Perugia's bitter revolt against the pope's salt tax in 1540 was the last gasp, and when its leading city finally fell to the troops of the pope's nephew, the region passed definitively into the papal empire. Umbria then remained part of the Papal States until the 1860s.

During the Renaissance, Umbria's painters came into their own. Pietro Vannucci, who grew to fame as "il Perugino," was born at Città del Pieve but worked in Perugia, where his lyrical works can be seen in the National Gallery of Umbria. He taught Raphael — Raffaello — to paint. Other great masters who worked in Umbria included Pinturicchio from Perugia, Piero della Francesca, and the architect Bramante. If, as in Tuscany, the landscape in Umbria has an awe-inspiring familiarity, it is because we have seen it before in the paintings in our museums: the flowers, cypress lanes, blue hills in the distance, the winding river. So, too, there is a sense of déjà vu when we view Perugia's bristling towers, city walls, gates, and tile roofs on the crest of a hill rising from the broad plain of the Tiber River basin.

Next to its artists worked exacting craftsmen. Italy sometimes seems one giant beehive of artisanry, but even in Italy, Umbria's artisans stand out. Besides weaving hand-loomed fabrics, embroidering, potting, and turning furniture, they are today celebrated for their fine wrought-iron work. For the value, prices of hand-spun linens and tablecloths, which can be ordered to measure, or of finely decorated ceramic ware, are reasonable, but visitors should not expect bargain-basement prices for articles that are often one of a kind or made with especially good raw materials. A bedspread woven on a hand loom can easily cost a million lire.

Umbrian food is more subtle than that of Rome and lighter than that of Tuscany, which makes it close to perfect. A taste for *nuova cucina* or anything fast will have to be satisfied elsewhere, because here one makes do — to take a sample menu — with a selection of antipasto hams and salamis from Norcia, served with pickled wild mushrooms; thin egg noodles tossed with grated black truffle and olive oil; fresh fish from a mountain stream or eel from Lake Trasimeno; a choice of wild game dishes; ewe's and goat's milk cheeses, delightfully unpasteurized; and fresh fruit or dried figs from the orchards that carpet the valleys. Dessert may include an almond torte in the form of a fat eel gaily decorated with sugar candies. This traditional Umbrian Easter cake

can be seen all year long in the pastry shop windows in, for one place, Perugia.
The olive is king in Umbrian cuisine. Some consider Umbrian olive oil,
especially that produced around Spoleto, to be Italy's very best. Soil conditions give it an especially low acid content, and Umbrians swear it is also
"lighter," less fatty, than other oils. It is never better than when eaten on slices
of crusty country bread toasted over an open fire, peppered, and drenched
with garlic — *la bruschetta.* Another very special Umbrian treat is the truffle.
Five varieties, in color from white through gray to black and resembling small
potatoes, grow wild in the woodlands, and local hound dogs, especially
around Assisi and Norcia, are trained to retrieve them with rewards of
chocolate. Three towns have truffle festivals: Terni, in June; Gubbio, in November; and, the most important, Norcia, in February. But other towns host
other festivals. Orvieto stages a wine show each May and June. A mushroom
festival takes place at San Leo, near Città di Castello, in September, and a
chestnut frolic, at which *marrons glacés* hold the place of honor, goes on at
Preggio di Umbertide in October. There is even an onion festival at Cannara,
near Assisi, in late September, when the village's best cooks show off their
recipes.

Especially in wintertime, menus may include the tiny, tasty lentils grown
in the high, wildflower-filled valley of Castelluccio, in the mountains above
Norcia. A prized local salami, *mazzafegato,* is made of pork liver, pine nuts,
raisins, sugar, and orange peel. *Castagnaccio* is a flat bread made of chestnut
flour, seasoned with pine nuts, raisins, and fresh rosemary and served with
a glass of dessert wine. Around the Christmas holidays comes *pan pepato*
— peppered bread — which is, in reality, a fruitcake of walnuts, almonds,
raisins, chocolate chunks, and candied fruit. The secret ingredient, however,
is *mosto* — the residue of the grape left after wine is pressed.

Pliny the Elder was among those who have rhapsodized over the wines of
Umbria. Well he might. Umbrian wines were so prized back in the fifteenth
century that Torgiano vintners pushed through laws severely punishing anyone doctoring Torgiano's own wine or improperly using the label. Today, the
region's wines include half a dozen fine DOC labels. Best known is the light,
straw-colored Orvieto; Orvieto Classico comes from grapes grown on the very
oldest wine estates, closest to the town of Orvieto. Torgiano comes both red
and white, as does the wine grown on the hills around Lake Trasimeno, Colli
del Trasimeno. Montefalco is an especially prized red wine. The name Colli
Altotiberini DOC specifies that these fine red, rosé, and white wines come
from grapes grown on the hillsides facing the upper Tiber River valley.
Perugia's red, rosé, and white DOC wines are named Colli Perugini.

Our circuit of Umbria begins at Perugia, its capital, and passes through
hilly, chestnut-wooded countryside interspersed with broad rolling valleys of
olive groves and vineyards to Assisi, a hill town with a soft, saintly aura. The
route loops southward to Spoleto, a jewel of a town, and then, rather than
continue south to Terni (an industrial center with some historical monuments), cuts west and north to Todi, another small hill town with fine art and
architecture. After Todi, a detour to Orvieto is strongly recommended; its
cathedral should not be missed by anyone coming this close. The route goes
to Deruta (for pottery browsing) and Torgiano (for the Wine Museum) on

its way back to Perugia and, at the end, a side trip to Gubbio is suggested for those who have the time.

Hotels listed below as expensive charge anywhere from $85 to $135 for a double room with bath; moderate means approximately $45 to $75 for a double room; and inexpensive means $40 or less. The very best restaurants may charge well over $100 for a meal for two served with a fine wine. In a restaurant listed below as expensive, expect to pay from $60 to $100 for a meal for two served with a local wine of good quality. Restaurants listed as moderate will charge from $35 to $60 including a bottle of wine, and those listed as inexpensive will charge from $20 to $35 including a carafe of house wine. But note that in an especially popular place such as Spoleto, where fashionability strikes quickly, prices in any establishment can rise fast from season to season.

PERUGIA: Umbria's regional capital is set on a hill, and the best way to see it is to leave the car at the public parking lot halfway up the road that winds to the top. From there, five escalators whisk visitors up 1,000 feet into the heart of town. Interestingly, the escalators tunnel straight through the Rocca Paolina, the fortress that Pope Paul III raised in the 16th century to show the *perugini* who was boss. The fort incorporated the mansion belonging to one of the leading rebel families, the Baglioni, and the surrounding neighborhood, including three churches and several streets from earlier centuries. The Rocca was largely destroyed in the 19th century, debris was dumped into it, and its upper walls were used as the foundations of nearby *palazzi*, sealing all previous layers into oblivion. Excavations began to uncover it all in the 1950s, and it is through this time-warped ghost city that the escalators climb to the top, even passing a tiny, Renaissance-era basketball court.

It becomes immediately obvious to a visitor that Perugia is a university town. International students taking Italian language and culture courses at the Università Italiana per Stranieri (Italian University for Foreigners) and Italian students from the nearly 700-year-old University of Perugia throng the main street, Corso Vannucci, a wide pedestrian island lined with outdoor cafés, hotels, and fine shops (as well as the tourist information office; phone: 075-23327). Just at the end of this thoroughfare is the main square, Piazza IV Novembre, with one of Perugia's most celebrated monuments, the 13th-century *Fontana Maggiore*, in the center. This notable achievement was built to celebrate the completion of an aqueduct bringing water to Perugia from Monte Paciano, 3 miles away as the crow flies. Designed and executed by Nicola and Giovanni Pisano, it consists of two marble basins and a bronze cup decorated with 24 relief sculptures and 24 statues. On the north side of the square is Perugia's *Duomo,* or, rather, its side, since it faces onto Piazza Danti. Begun in 1345 to replace an earlier building, it was finished in 1490 — finished, that is, except for the pink and white marble stripes that were to have covered it; only a patch has ever been completed.

On the south side of the square (at the corner of Piazza IV Novembre and Corso Vannucci) is the ancient *Palazzo dei Priori,* built from 1293 to 1443, for hundreds of years Perugia's Town Hall. The part facing the square, with the grand staircase and the doorway topped by the Perugian griffin and the Guelph lion in bronze, was completed by 1297 and is the oldest part of this fine example of medieval civic architecture. Inside the palace (entry from Corso Vannucci) are the frescoed Sala dei Notari (Notaries' Room) and the Collegio della Mercanzia, a sort of Renaissance chamber of commerce covered with 15th-century wood carvings and marquetry. Inside, also, is the Galleria Nazionale dell'Umbria (National Gallery of Umbria), where the entire development of Umbrian painting — from the stiff religious art of the 13th century to the breathtaking explosion of color and grace in Pinturicchio and Perugino — can be admired, in addition to works by Beato Angelico, Piero della Francesca, and others. Those interested mainly in Perugino, however, should stop in at the *Collegio del Cambio* next door. This was built for the use of money changers in the 15th century, and its most important chamber is filled with vibrant frescoes by Perugino and his pupils. On the middle pilaster is Perugino's self-portrait, and in the painting of the Prophets and the Sibyls, presumed to be by Perugino's pupil Raphael, then all of 17 years old, is that young painter's self-portrait as the prophet Daniel. The fine inlaid woodwork in the lobby is from the 17th century. Note the wonderfully carved furniture.

Going out the west end of Piazza IV Novembre, it's possible to approach Perugia's Etruscan Arch by way of a medieval street, Via delle Volte. This winding street with its lovely arches is also called Via Maestà delle Volte, for a 14th-century fresco in a small church at its end. Adjacent streets — Via Fratti, Via Ritorta — are well worth a detour. Via Maestà delle Volte leads to Piazza Morlacchi, from where Via Cesare Battisti leads along a wall built by the Etruscans and then, via a stairway, to Piazza Fortebraccio. Here, the 18th-century Baroque *Palazzo Gallenga-Stuart,* seat of the University for Foreigners, stands next to the Etruscan Arch, or the Arch of Augustus, as the Romans called it. Where Roman builders raised the wall higher is readily seen, but the arch itself is pure Etruscan. A delicate porch on top is from the Renaissance.

At the other end of town, taking Via Marzia out of the Giardini Carducci (public gardens), is the Porta Marzia, a 2nd- or 1st-century BC gate in the walls. It was moved 10 feet away and reconstructed by the architect (Antonio da Sangallo the Younger) working on the Rocca Paolina, and it gives access to the underground Via Bagliona, the subterranean world that was sealed off by the fortress and that can be visited. The *Museo Archeologico Nazionale dell'Umbria* is also at this end of the city, next to the Gothic Church of St. Domenic. It houses a collection of prehistoric, Etruscan, and Roman sarcophagi, vases, coins, and jewelry, but its greatest treasure is the Cippus, a marble slab inscribed with 151 words with the Etruscan language. Some urns in the collection are engraved in Etruscan with the translation into Umbria's Latin dialect.

The tradition of the *passeggiata* — the evening promenade — is very much alive in Perugia: On Corso Vannucci it seems that everyone who is ambulatory is out for a stroll. Do the same. Or, for an *aperitivo* at any time of the day, visit the *Enoteca Provinciale,* Via Ulisse Rocchi 16, which offers samplings of the 150 wines from the 60 vineyards in Umbria.

CHECKING IN: Brufani – An old favorite of travelers, this pleasantly old-fashioned grand hotel is the best in town. There are 22 rooms. (Piazza Italia 12, Perugia; phone: 075-62541; expensive.)

La Rosetta – In the same square as the *Brufani,* it has a graceful courtyard and a highly regarded restaurant to make up for the relatively small size of the 104 rooms. (Piazza Italia 19, Perugia; phone: 075-20841; moderate.)

Lo Spedalicchio – About 6 miles out of town in the direction of Assisi, in a village called Ospedalicchio. Off an unpretentious road, inside a gate, there stands an ancient castle that once guarded the approach to Perugia, now converted into a 28-room hotel. The furnishings are handsome, modern interpretations of traditional regional styles, including hand-loomed bedspreads in ancient Umbrian motifs. There is an elegant dining room; drinks are served in the garden. A warning: Those who have serious problems sleeping should go elsewhere. A venerable church bell tolls each quarter hour all through the night. (Piazza Bruno Buozzi 3, Ospedalicchio; phone: 075-809323; inexpensive.)

EATING OUT: Falchetto – With its 14th-century walls, it looks like a medieval tavern, and visitors interested in sampling authentic Umbrian cuisine should make this their first choice. Among the dishes to try are grilled trout from the Nera River, truffled veal, and delectable roast pheasant. Even snails sometimes appear on the menu of this temple to tradition. The wines are from Torgiano and other local vineyards. Closed Mondays. (Via Bartolo 20, Perugia; phone: 075-61875; moderate.)

Del Sole – The charming garden terrace, with its view over the green hills toward Assisi, is a major asset. The Umbrian specialties include *penne norcine* — pasta "quills" — and a stew of wild boar. Be sure to make reservations in summer. Closed Saturdays and at Christmastime. (Via Oberdan 28, Perugia; phone: 075-65031; moderate.)

En Route from Perugia – Take the SS75 *bis* southeast out of town in the direction of Foligno and Assisi. On the left, after about 3 miles, is the rocky *Ipogeo dei Volumni,* an Etruscan necropolis. The Volumni were an important Etruscan family in the 2nd century BC, and these are important excavations. The road crosses the Tiber River at Ponte San Giovanni, and then, at Ospedalicchio, SS147 branches off to Assisi, which is 16 miles from Perugia.

ASSISI: This delightful town is the goal of religious pilgrims and secular tourists alike. Set on the slopes of Monte Subasio, with panoramic views all around, and full of medieval houses of pink stone, it seems as gentle and charming as the saint who was born here (1182) and who lies buried in the crypt beneath its prime monument. Begun in 1228, two years after his death, the *Basilica of St. Francis* is a commanding structure whose unmistakable outline appears, from a distance, to be almost as large as the town itself. It is actually two churches, one on top of the other, and both are set over a huge monastery, the *Sacro Convento.* All together, the venerable walls and buttresses of this fine example of Umbrian Gothic architecture constitute a lesson in the history of art.

The realm below, the Chiesa Inferiore, is spacious, a place where legions of pilgrims could be welcomed, but dark — unfortunately, because the walls are covered with frescoes. Those in the nave are the oldest, by the 13th-century Maestro di San Francesco; others are by Giotto (the right, or south, transept and the third chapel on the right), Pietro Lorenzetti (left, or north, transept), Simone Martini (first chapel on the left), and Cimabue (his striking *Virgin and Child with Four Angels and St. Francis* is in the right transept, right wall). In the bright upper church, the Chiesa Superiore, there are frescoes by Cimabue, including a Crucifixion, and Giotto's famed frescoes of the life of St. Francis, 28 scenes running counterclockwise around the nave (the attribution of the last few scenes is in doubt). Painted almost 800 years ago, they are captivating for the views they offer of ordinary life — fabrics, weapons, faces, furniture, landscapes, homes, walls, towers — as well as for their narrative and inspirational content. As some critics have put it, art with a human dimension was born here, a far cry from the stylized rigidity that went before.

There are several other sites associated with St. Francis in and around Assisi. About 2½ miles east of town is the mountainside *Eremo delle Carceri* (*Hermitage of the Prisons*), to which St. Francis and his followers retreated to "imprison" themselves spiritually in prayer. A small Franciscan monastery soon developed, carved out of bedrock; adjacent is a tiny grotto in which St. Francis lived — his rude stone bed can still be seen. The setting is extraordinarily beautiful and imbued with an aura of holiness, much more in keeping with the spirit of St. Francis than is the huge basilica in town. The *Convento di San Damiano,* another of Italy's most revered shrines, is a bit more than a mile south of Assisi. St. Francis restored the little church here, and his friend St. Clare lived in the humble convent with her nuns, the Poor Clares, until her death in 1253. This is also the spot where St. Francis composed the *Cantico delle Creature* in praise of all creation including Brother Sun and Sister Moon. Almost 3 miles west of Assisi is the 16th-century *Basilica di Santa Maria degli Angeli,* really no more than a huge covering for an area where St. Francis spent much of his life, was joined by his first followers, and died. It contains several tiny shrines, including the

Porziuncola, an almost toylike chapel he restored and to which crowds of pilgrims arrive each August 1 and 2 for the Festa del Perdono (Pardon of Assisi), instituted by the saint in 1216.

If you have still more time to spend in Assisi, visit the *Chiesa di Santa Chiara* (Church of St. Clare), 13th-century Gothic, as well as the *Duomo,* begun in the 12th century and dedicated to San Rufino. Assisi also has Roman remains, including the *Temple of Minerva,* transformed into a Baroque church in Piazza del Comune, the medieval main square. Also medieval is the *Rocca Maggiore,* or fortress, set on a hill north of the center and reached by a stepped street leading out of the square in front of the Duomo; the view from the top is well worth the climb.

CHECKING IN: *Fontebella* – Only 37 quiet rooms, most overlooking the broad Umbrian valley, and its own renowned restaurant, *Il Frantoio* (see *Eating Out*). (Via Fontebella 25, Assisi; phone: 075-812883; moderate.)

Subasio – In the heart of Assisi adjacent to Piazza San Francesco, but some of its 66 rooms overlook the valley and, therefore, ensure quiet. Considerable charm and a restaurant known for good food. (Via Frate Elia 2, Assisi; phone: 075-816317; moderate.)

Giotto – Assisi's largest hotel, with 72 rooms and a restaurant. (Via Fontebella 41, Assisi; phone: 075-812209; inexpensive.)

Umbra – A small (20-room), romantic place, downtown on a narrow street away from the more noisy thoroughfares. A few of the rooms have a splendid view over the rooftops, and some rooms are furnished with real antiques. It has a garden restaurant (see *Eating Out*). (Via degli Archi 6, Assisi; phone: 075-812240; inexpensive.)

La Terrazza – The 50 rooms are spare, but most have showers or baths and they're in the spirit of Assisi, since the building was once a convent. There is a restaurant. (Piazzetta A. Luigi 1, Assisi; phone: 075-812368; very inexpensive.)

EATING OUT: *Il Frantoio* – Part of the *Fontebella* hotel, and one of the best restaurants in Umbria. It occupies what was, in the 17th century, an olive oil pressing room, and it has a garden terrace with a fine view of the valley. Among the specialties are *stringotti* (egg noodles) with artichoke sauce and *tortelloni* (big ravioli) stuffed with cream cheese. In season, truffles garnish nearly everything, and there is a choice selection of local wines. Closed Fridays. (Hotel Fontebella, Via Fontebella 25, Assisi; phone: 075-812977; expensive to moderate.)

Umbra – Another well-known hotel restaurant, which does not let its international clientele alter its Umbrian traditions. Depending on the season, the menu may feature such mouth-watering dishes as *crostini al tartufo* (truffled pâté on toast), lentil soup, *risotto* with white truffles from Gubbio, and roast game, rabbit, or duckling. In summer there's dining outdoors on the terrace. Closed Tuesdays and November. (Hotel Umbra, Via degli Archi 6, Assisi; phone: 075-812240; moderate.)

Il Medioevo – A highly recommended restaurant with an evocative decor. The mixed fry is a tempting abundance of stuffed olives and meats. Closed Wednesdays. (Via Arco dei Priori 4, Assisi; phone: 075-813068; moderate.)

En Route from Assisi – Drive south to Spoleto, part of the way on SS75 and the rest of the way on SS3, passing through picturesque hill country with olive groves everywhere. Just 8 miles from Assisi is the old town of Spello, whose stone houses cling to the terraced mountain slopes within ancient Roman walls. If you stop, visit the *Chiesa di Santa Maria Maggiore,* particularly its Cappella Baglioni, which has a 16th-century majolica floor from Deruta and frescoes by Pinturicchio, including an Annunciation with the self-portrait of the painter. Spoleto is 30 miles south of Assisi.

EATING OUT: *Il Molino* – Set up in a 700-year-old flour mill that was itself built in Roman ruins, it has a big fireplace turning out the grilled meats that are among its traditional Umbrian dishes. The house specialty, named after the painter Pinturicchio, translates as filet in puff pastry with a wild mushroom sauce. Closed Tuesdays. (Piazza Matteotti 6, Spello; phone: 0742-651305; moderate to inexpensive.)

SPOLETO: Success has not spoiled this ancient Roman town and former headquarters of the Lombard Duchy of Spoleto that ruled most of Umbria in the early Middle Ages. However, should you want to stay in Spoleto during its all-embracing festival of the performing arts, the *Festival of Two Worlds*, be sure to book both hotels and tickets to festival events as far in advance as possible. The festival runs for a month or so from mid-June to mid-July, but its finest hour is always the last evening, when a full orchestra and chorus perform in front of the 12th-century *Duomo*, whose stone façade glows pink in the twilight. Lovely frescoes by Fra Filippo Lippi and his school are inside the cathedral, as is the tomb of the master painter and defrocked monk. Portraits of Fra Filippo, his two assistants, and his son Filippino figure in the fresco of the *Death of the Virgin.*

No other sight in this hill town ranks with the Duomo, but it is filled with minor sights — including Roman remains such as a theater and amphitheater — and the effect of the medieval whole is fascinating. Stop at the tourist information office, Piazza della Libertà 7 (phone: 0743-49890), for information and brochures and then set out for a walking tour. During the festival, every alley and staircase is turned into a showroom for contemporary artists, some great names already, others still waiting for recognition. The late Alexander Calder, a festival regular, designed the huge sculpture that's installed permanently in front of the train station in the lower, modern part of town. Among the sights out of town is the 13th-century *Church of St. Peter,* 5 miles east. The road that winds upward past the church leads to the top of Monteluco, where St. Francis lived for a time at the monastery.

CHECKING IN: *Il Gattapone* – This miniature hotel has just 8 elegant rooms, a garden, and a restaurant. Reserve well in advance if you hope to be among the lucky guests. (Via del Ponte 6, Spoleto; phone: 0743-36417; moderate.)

Duchi – A modern, efficient, pleasant place. Some of the 50 rooms look out at the Teatro Romano, others onto the valley. There is a restaurant and a nice little bar. (Viale Matteotti 4, Spoleto; phone: 0743-44541; inexpensive.)

EATING OUT: *Il Tartufo* – A temple to the noble tuber, the place to dine on fresh truffles, though not, alas, during festival time — the truffle is an autumn and winter delicacy. Here, in what is considered the best of a not very crowded field, diners enjoy traditional dishes with gussied-up names such as prisoner's *rigatoni,* Spoleto-style rags (*stracci,* a type of pasta), and courtesan-style steak. Closed Wednesdays and mid-July to mid-August. (Piazza Garibaldi 24, Spoleto; phone: 0743-40236; expensive.)

Sabatini – In the former hotel of the same name, it has a pleasant atmosphere. Italian and traditional Umbrian dishes are prepared with style. Closed Mondays. (Corso Mazzini 52, Spoleto; phone: 0743-37233; moderate.)

En Route from Spoleto – Todi is about 28 miles to the northwest. Take SS418 west from Spoleto to Acquasparta and there pick up SS3 *bis* north.

TODI: Still another small hill town with an overall medieval aspect — and an especially beautiful setting — Todi lives around its main square, Piazza del Popolo, which is lined with 13th- and 14th-century palaces. The most important is the *Palazzo dei Priori,* standing alone at one end with its crenelations and tower. Facing it, at the other end, is the *Duomo,* fronted by a grand staircase, with a Renaissance rose window in its façade and a bell tower. On another side of the square, the *Palazzo del Popolo*, wearing a crenelated crown, and the *Palazzo del Capitano* stand as one, joined by a staircase that provides entry to both. Inside is a delightful museum, whose small and eclectic collection ranges from Etruscan artifacts to Umbrian religious art. The nearby Piazza Garibaldi is a rewarding stop — the view embraces the whole valley below — and two other churches are worth a visit. The *Chiesa di San Fortunato,* at Piazza della Repubblica, is a lovely 13th-century structure with an unfinished 15th-century façade set off by the green of the lawn and hedges in front. Its setting is not nearly as striking, however, as that of *Santa Maria della Consolazione,* reached by a brief walk (about half a mile) south of town. An exquisite white marble church set on a field of green, this Renaissance gem is thought to have been designed by Bramante.

CHECKING IN: *Bramante* – A lovely hotel in a woodsy setting just outside Todi. All 43 rooms have a bath or shower. (Via Orvietana, Todi; phone: 075-884033; moderate.)

EATING OUT: *Jacopone–da Peppino* – A relatively modest *osteria* (inn) whose kitchen is part of the rustic decor. Try the *pasticcio Jacopone,* a pasta specialty, the braised beef in a rich mushroom sauce, and the local wine. Closed Mondays and two weeks in July. (Piazza Jacopone 5, Todi; phone: 075-882366; moderate.)

Umbria – Good for local cuisine. It has a rustic decor, as well as a terrace for summer dining. Closed Tuesdays. (Via San Bonaventura 13, Todi; phone: 075-882737; moderate.)

En Route from Todi – The route continues north to return to Perugia along SS3 *bis,* stopping at Deruta, a town known the world over for its ceramics, and at the wine town of Torgiano. For travelers heading to Lazio or Rome, the recommended route is west to Orvieto, 25 miles away, and south from there. The cathedral at Orvieto is so spectacular, in fact, that even those ultimately headed northward should detour to Orvieto.

ORVIETO: This city clings, somewhat precariously (it has serious landslide problems), to a high, flat table of tufa stone rising up over the gentle, wide valley carved by the Paglia River. During the Middle Ages its name was Urbs Vetus, suggesting to modern historians that this was probably Volsinii, a large Etruscan city of many temples destroyed by Roman troops in 265 BC and then rebuilt in the vicinity. Two Etruscan necropoli, including several painted tombs, have been found nearby; from one of them came the archaic statue of Venus now in Orvieto's Palazzo Faina museum, facing the Duomo.

For most people, Orvieto's *Duomo* is what most impresses, no matter how many cathedrals they have seen before. From the gilded mosaics and dainty rose window of the façade to the fresco masterpieces inside, this is one of Italy's greatest treasures. It was begun in 1290 in Romanesque style, possibly according to a design by Arnolfo di Cambio, but in the first decade of the 14th century, after some difficulty with the construction, a master builder, architect, and sculptor from Siena — Lorenzo Maitani — was called to the rescue. The present church, including the design of the strikingly beautiful Gothic façade, is largely his, even though numerous other architects, as well as sculptors, painters, and mosaicists, succeeded him, and the project was not completed until the early 17th century. Stand back to study the overall effect of the façade and you'll probably agree that it looks something like a giant triptych altarpiece. At the lowest level, on the pilasters between the doors, are bas-reliefs carved in marble. They illustrate scenes from the Old and New Testaments and are thought to have been done (1320–30) by Maitani himself (the central bronze doors are modern).

On the next level, brilliantly colored mosaic scenes of the life of Mary point upward to still further mosaic scenes and to a large rose window (the work of Andrea Orcagna in the mid-14th century) surrounded by busts and statues of prophets and apostles. At the apex of the triptych is a Coronation of the Virgin in blue, red, and gold mosaic.

Walk up close to the façade and notice that even the parts that appear plain are actually exquisitely decorated — every graceful, slim column, twist, groove, and strip of surface is studded with color. Inside, however, the contrast is startling, because most of the interior — its walls of alternating stripes of green and white marble, its alabaster windows — is quite simple. Make a beeline to the Cappella Nuova (New Chapel, also known as the Cappella di San Brizio) to see the fresco cycle that influenced Michelangelo and made a name for Luca Signorelli. Fra Angelico began the decoration of the chapel in 1447, but completed only two sections of the ceiling; in 1499 Signorelli was commissioned to finish the work, which took him five years. Among the scenes of the *End of the World,* the *Coming and Fall of the Antichrist,* and the *Last Judgment* are two men dressed in black. The blond is a self-portrait of Signorelli, the other a portrait of Fra Angelico. Dante is pictured in one of the decorative squares of the wainscoting.

In the left transept is the Cappella del Corporale, housing a cloth on which the blood of Christ is supposed to have appeared miraculously in nearby Bolsena in 1263. The relic — its possession was the original impetus for building the Duomo — is carried through the streets of Orvieto on the Feast of Corpus Christi each spring, a holy day that originated in Orvieto in 1264.

The severe Gothic building to the right of the Duomo is the *Palazzo Soliano,* formerly the Palazzo dei Papi (Papal Palace). Commissioned by Pope Boniface VIII in 1297, it today houses the cathedral's collection of religious treasures, artworks, and historical bibelots. In front of the Duomo is the *Museo Claudio Faina,* an archaeological museum with, among other things, a collection of Greek vases. Elsewhere in Orvieto is its oldest building, the *Palazzo del Popolo,* begun in 1157, and not far from that is the *Chiesa di San Domenico,* begun in 1233; inside, the tomb of Cardinal Guglielmo de Braye is a masterpiece by Arnolfo di Cambio, who carved it in 1285. The *Pozzo di San Patrizio (St. Patrick's Well)* is at the far end of town, at an overlook called the Belvedere. Designed by Sangallo the Younger and built in 1528, the well is 200 feet deep and was meant to provide water for the city in case of a siege. Visitors walk to the bottom and back up via two separate spiral staircases of 248 steps each, one superimposed on the other so they never meet.

Orvieto is synonymous with fine white wine, either dry or *abboccato* (mellow). The wine is a blend of several grapes — Tuscan trebbiano, verdello, grechetto, and Tuscan malvasia — grown on local hillsides. Each May and June, the town sponsors a wine show.

CHECKING IN: *La Badia* – A beautifully restored and gracious ancient cloister, about 3 miles south of Orvieto. It has 22 rooms, tennis courts, a swimming pool, and an elegant dining room whose menu is as sophisticated as the setting warrants. (Località La Badia, Orvieto; phone: 0763-90359; expensive to moderate.)

Maitani – This hotel has 44 rooms, right in the heart of town. It vaunts a terrace with a superb view of the Duomo, as well as charming decor. (Via Maitani 5, Orvieto; phone: 0763-33001; moderate.)

EATING OUT: *Ristorante Morino* – Orvieto's most important restaurant is run by Dino Morino and his family. Sauces for the pastas tend to be rich, as in the *agnolotti* with fondue and black truffle, so those who like the lighter touch of *nuova cucina* might prefer the *trenette alla Morino.* Roast kid and stuffed capon are among the fine second-course selections. Closed Wednesdays and January. (Via Garibaldi 37, Orvieto; phone: 0763-41952: expensive.)

Dell'Ancora – Because of the splendid view of the Duomo, this restaurant tends to get crowded during tourist season. The cuisine blends Roman and Umbrian cooking: From Roman country kitchens come specialties like tripe, a fine dish visitors should not hesitate to try. Among the pastas, all homemade, the irregularly cut egg noodles with hare sauce — *pappardelle alla lepre* — are special. Closed January and Thursdays except in August and September. (Via di Piazza del Popolo 7, Orvieto; phone: 0763-35446; moderate.)

En Route from Orvieto – To resume the route, go back to Todi and proceed north on SS3 *bis.* Deruta, about 13 miles farther on, deserves a stop to browse through the multitude of workshops selling painted ceramic ware. The town's ceramics industry dates from the 14th century at least, and typical Deruta ware has arabesques, dragons, and grotesques harking back to that period. Reference to a shipment of vases and jugs for the Basilica of St. Francis in Assisi appears in a document of 1358; other documents refer to orders of ceramic tiles to pave Gothic churches in Perugia. The industry was at the height of its fame in the early 16th century; in fact, the Victoria and Albert Museum in London has a plate made at Deruta by Raphael. Other sites to see in Deruta include its 13th-century *Palazzetto Municipale,* the Town Hall. In the atrium is a headless Roman statue of a seated man holding a small boat. It is believed to represent the god of the Tiber River, Tiberino. Upstairs is a collection of 500 paintings by Umbrian masters.

Continue on SS3 *bis* for another 4 miles (watch for the turnoff) to reach Torgiano. A visit to the tastefully arranged *Museo del Vino* (*Wine Museum*) begins, as does local history, with the ancient Etruscans. On view are wine vases and jugs from an Etruscan funeral dowry and dozens of Roman amphoras. A photo exhibit of documents from Umbrian archives shows various contracts between vineyard tenants and the monasteries who owned the land. A monumental wine press from the 17th century occupies most of one room, and a series of gorgeously decorated antique plates shows versions of Dionysius and Bacchus. A head of Bacchus is by Giovanni della Robbia.

After Torgiano, follow signs back to Perugia, approximately 8 miles away. Our Umbria route terminates here, but it's possible to prolong the exploration of the region with a side trip to Gubbio, 24 miles northeast of Perugia via SS298.

CHECKING IN/EATING OUT: *Le Tre Vaselle* – The same vintner — Giorgio Lungarotti — who founded the Wine Museum established this luxury hotel with 48 rooms installed in a handsomely restored old country house. It has a restaurant that pleases some very sophisticated palates, who are also well pleased with the Torgiano wines — especially the Rubesco. A stay here is an alternative to staying in Perugia itself. (Via Garibaldi 48, Torgiano; phone: 075-982447; expensive.)

GUBBIO: On the slopes of Monte Ingino, reached by a winding road that twists and turns through chestnut woods, this town is just far enough off the beaten track to have a wondrous flavor of authenticity. Leave the car in the parking area next to Piazza Quaranta Martiri and look up to the Città Alta (Upper City) for an introduction to all its main buildings — especially the Gothic *Palazzo dei Consoli* — seen from here with the green mountain as backdrop. Then take the plunge, following Via della Repubblica inward and upward. The narrow streets, stone houses, and tiny churches give Gubbio a particular medieval charm, so even an aimless amble through town is rewarding (but try to include Via Galeotti, Via dei Consoli, Via Baldassini, and the banks of the Camignano in your route). Note the tiny door next to the main door in many buildings; this is the so-called *porta del morto,* the doorway for the dead. While such doors are seen elsewhere in Italian churches, only in Gubbio are they a typical feature of domestic architecture (supposedly, only coffins passed through them, but another explanation is that these were the doors to the medieval living quarters above, while the larger doorways led to ground-floor shops and workshops).

Via della Repubblica crosses Via Baldassini, above which a staircase leads to Via XX

Settembre. Suddenly, a vast square, Piazza Della Signoria, opens up, with a breathtaking vista out over the valley to one side. The facing *Palazzo dei Consoli* (or *Palazzo del Popolo*), constructed between 1332 and 1337, and the *Palazzo Pretorio* facing it, constructed in 1349, were conceived as one civic whole, along with the other buildings of the piazza, in Gubbio's most florid period. Today the Palazzo dei Consoli houses a small painting gallery and archaeological museum whose greatest treasures are the seven 3rd- to 1st-century BC bronze plaques known as the *Tavole Eugubine.* Discovered nearby in the 15th century, they are written in the ancient Umbrian language, some using an Etruscan-derived alphabet and others the Roman alphabet. They prescribe the omens for which priests should watch to divine the future and other rituals that shed light on the Etruscans' daily life. Before leaving the museum, go up to the loggia for a panoramic view of the whole red-roofed town.

Note that Gubbio is almost as well known for ceramics as Deruta. Here, too, the industry dates back at least as far as the 14th century and was at its height in the early 16th century, after a certain Mastro Giorgio developed a particularly intense, iridescent ruby red that allowed the Gubbians to subdue much of the nearby competition. Even today, workshops are everywhere, and lovely flowered plates line walls to the left and right of shop doorways.

Each year on May 15, the eve of the feast day of Sant'Ubaldo, Gubbio's patron saint, the town stages the *Corsa dei Ceri* (Race of the Candles), an event that's been going on since the Middle Ages (and probably since pagan days). The "candles" are three tall wooden "poles" (20 feet or so high, 700 pounds or so) topped by wee statues of saints and set on litters for carrying. Men in costume shoulder the contraptions and puff and pant their way up the mountain behind Gubbio to the church of Sant'Ubaldo, ordinarily an hour's walk. The saint, who is buried in the church, was a bishop of Gubbio and is credited with inspiring Gubbian troops to withstand an onslaught by their enemies in 1155. On the last Sunday in May, Piazza della Signoria is the scene of another medieval event, the colorful *Palio della Balestra,* a crossbow match pitting Gubbio against a team from nearby Sansepolcro (a return match is played in Sansepolcro in September). For details, see *Italy's Most Colorful Festas* in DIVERSIONS.

EATING OUT: *Taverna Del Lupo* – An authentically Umbrian restaurant in an authentically 14th-century setting. Its menu reflects Gubbio's proximity to mountain and forest: *risotto* with mushrooms or truffles, rabbit, broiled meats with polenta, duckling. Try the local *eugubini* (Gubbian) wines. Closed Mondays and January. (Via Ansidei 21, Gubbio; phone: 075-9274368; moderate.)

Lazio

If all roads lead to Rome, they lead away from it as well. And there are few better ways to discover Rome and its civilization than to explore, one by one, the ancient roads that radiate from the city the ancients knew as *Caput Mundi,* the center of the world. From Mediolanum in the north — today's Milan — to Brindisi and Taranto at the heel of the Italian boot, all the great cities of the Roman Empire were linked to the capital by roads so enduring that their engineering remains a benchmark for road builders into our own century. Financed by tribute, the 400 major Roman roads were built to last, with up to five feet of layered sand, lime, crushed rock, and, often, big flat paving stones of basalt. Down them rattled settlers in covered wagons off to found new Roman towns. Sandal-clad soldiers trudged to war, and tradesmen rode in horse carts to hustle everything from Greek pottery made in Naples to wool from the flocks the Sabines tended on the Apennine foothills around their capital, Rieti.

Beginning northwest of Rome and moving clockwise, the main roads were the Via Aurelia, which ran up the peninsula along the sea; the Via Cassia; the Via Flaminia; the Via Salaria, so named because it brought inlanders to the salt flats at the mouth of the Tiber River; the Via Praeneste, which led to one of antiquity's greatest shrines; and, heading due south, the great Appian Way.

Leaving the city today by any one of these ancient roadways is, at least initially, a painful trip through traffic jams and undiluted urban blight, relieved by occasional serendipitous glimpses of a section of Roman aqueduct, a stretch of ancient wall, or a tomb whose brickwork marks it as Roman. Surprisingly quickly, however, the city comes to an abrupt end. Just beyond a block of high-rise apartment buildings are rolling fields where a shepherd tends a flock grazing under a stately umbrella pine. Lazio, as the region around Rome is called from its ancient name, Latium, has only a limited industrial belt, mostly around the Via Pontina south of Rome and the Via Tiberina, which meanders along with the Tiber.

On a map, the region of Lazio resembles an ivy leaf. One of its trinity of lobes points north, into Tuscan Italy, where gently rolling countryside and neat olive orchards and vineyards suddenly alternate with lofty cliffs of ruddy brown tufa stone. Here, where the plain of Lazio begins to turn into the foothills of the Apennines, villages are typically perched on a hilltop and clustered around a castle. Many were founded by the Etruscans, who liked the safety of an acropolis.

The central lobe, surrounding Rome and pointing east into the rugged limestone fastnesses of the Apennines, borders the Umbria and Abruzzo regions. It has a harsher look, and its steep mountains and their springs provide the water for the cascades feeding, among others, the fountains at Tivoli.

The third and largest lobe sprawls southward. Its sand beaches, hopelessly crowded in July and August, form one border. Then flat, rich farmland stretches toward rocky hilltops ablaze with yellow broom in summer. This is a pious area, and these hills are often crowned with a monastery, perhaps built on the foundations of a pagan temple. Several, including the Abbey at Monte Cassino, were founded by St. Benedict.

The different landscapes of these three prongs coincide roughly with the equally distinct historical peoples who inhabited them and then gradually converged toward the cluster of seven hilltop settlements on the Tiber plain, which the Etruscans called *Ruma.* Together, the mingled tribes built Rome into a glorious capital whose population grew to nearly one million in the century after Christ was born.

The Etruscans were in the northern prong. Of uncertain origin, they were a ruling class of warrior sailors who quarreled constantly among themselves, except over their common religion, and dominated Italy from the Arno River to the Tiber — their ancient land, Etruria, extended into present-day Tuscany and Umbria, as well as northern Lazio. While Rome was still a shepherds' trading post, the Etruscans reigned in a federation of twelve city-states. One of these, Tarquinia, was important enough to give Rome three early kings, the Tarquins. The fascinating ruins of another two lie close to modern Rome: Cerveteri (ancient Caere) is close to the sea, off the Via Aurelia. Veii, just ten miles north of Rome, off the Via Cassia, is close to where contemporary Roman aristocrats tee off at the Olgiata golf course. Traditionally considered the greatest of the Etruscan city-states, Veii was the first to fall to the Romans, in the fourth century BC.

The central prong corresponds roughly with those hilltop Latin tribes that merged to conquer Rome and then Etruria and finally the Mediterranean, North Africa, northern Europe, and western Asia. Pliny the Elder explained that there were several score of these tribes, each on its own hilltop. They were rude farm folk, less cultivated (and less economically advanced) than the Etruscans. They dressed in leggings and sheepskins, and their descendants, wearing a fair approximation of their garb, can be seen in Rome at Christmastime today, playing carols on bagpipes. Although rough and ready, the Latin tribes were quick studies and dedicated pragmatists. They let the Etruscans teach them how to use an alphabet, how a priesthood should govern, how to read a sheep's liver to foretell the future (if you've ever had your own palm read, don't smile), and even how to dress elegantly — that is, in a toga.

According to tradition, Alba Longa, the earliest Latin town and head of a confederation of Latin towns, sat atop a crest on the horseshoe of volcanic mountains southeast of Rome — where today's Castel Gandolfo stands, above the shore of a volcanic lake. Another Latin town became today's Rocca di Papa, across the lake on the chestnut-wooded slopes of Monte Cavo. Each spring and fall, all the Latins came in procession to a great Temple of Jupiter Latialis on the top of the mountain to sacrifice a white bull. By 500 BC, they were already arriving from forty-seven different towns. Then, as today, they could look down from the 3,124-foot peak to see all of Lazio.

The southernmost prong of the Lazio leaf points downward into territory where the Greeks, allied to a powerful local tribe, the Samnites, ruled, including the city the Greeks founded, Neapolis (Naples). The area was inhabited far earlier, however. On Monte Circeo, which juts into the Tyhrennian Sea (from *Tyrrhenoi,* the Greek name for the Etruscans), the voyager Ulysses was seduced by a bewitching pig shepherdess named Circe. Long before that, a real Neanderthal tribesman killed a rival, broke a hole into his skull for magical purposes, and left the skull inside a ring of ritual stones in a cave on the Circeo. The skull was found there during the 1930s, 40,000 years later.

To travel throughout Lazio today, therefore, is, first, to travel through time, seeing traces of three distinct major cultures — Etruscan, Latin, Magna Graecian — that influenced Western civilization. Then there is Lazio's more modern aspect. Among its big cities are, in the north, the port of Civitavecchia (Rome's own port was silted over during ancient times) and, inland, Viterbo. Heading into the Latin towns there is the fairly large walled city of Rieti and, continuing to circle Rome clockwise, the volcanic horseshoe that includes the Alban Hills and two lakes, Albano and Nemi. The Alban Hills are home to thirteen small towns, known collectively as the Castelli Romani. They are cool and airy when Rome is not, so many Romans have weekend houses in the Castelli, and more and more are beginning to live there permanently and commute into Rome. The Castelli slopes quench Romans' thirst with an amber wine that is highly prized when it is the real thing, and wine buffs say the Castelli now produce an excellent red wine as well.

Also south and east of Rome, but farther afield, is the Ciociaria, a mountainous district between Rome and the relatively modern town of Frosinone. Fiuggi, an old-fashioned spa with waters that are reputed to help kidney sufferers, and a bracing hill climate in the summer, is in the province of Frosinone. Another modern town, Latina, the largest city in Lazio after Rome, is to the west of the Ciociaria, in the midst of the Pontine plain. Once a swampy area where malaria raged, the plain was drained, settlers were brought in to farm, and Latina was founded at the end of the project in 1932. Actually a rather dull industrial and agricultural center, it is surrounded by pastures much favored by the water buffalo imported centuries ago from India. Their milk makes Lazio's fresh mozzarella one of the world's finest cheeses. Various beach resorts bask in the sun of the coast west and south of Latina — they include Anzio, with its vast American military cemetery nearby, Terracina, and Sperlonga. And inland on a mountaintop is the Monte Cassino monastery, bombed by the Allies during World War II and meticulously rebuilt.

The food of the Roman countryside is, like the old Latins themselves, rustic rather than elegant. It is a fine cuisine, however, in the sense that it employs ingredients literally unavailable elsewhere, and in certain cases more flavorful than elsewhere because of the soil and climate. Beef was never a Lazio dish. The Lazio diet was (and is) made up of mozzarella or piquant *pecorino* (ewe's milk) cheese, baby lamb or roast kid for a feast day, and pork in all its forms, including a fennel-laced salami. With an abundance of imagination rather than a surfeit of raw ingredients, the cooks of Lazio learned to turn the poorer cuts of meat into dishes fit for a king, or pope. These included a shepherd's pie of lamb heart, potatoes, and onions; oxtail chunks stewed in wine, celery, and tomatoes; and tripe dressed in a sauce of tomatoes, grated cheese, and fresh mint. Count on a Lazio cook to insist on the best quality of tripe, the cut they call *millefoglie,* for this favorite dish.

Spaghetti alla carbonara — that is, with a sauce of creamy egg, bacon bits, cheese, and a dash of nutmeg — can be found everywhere. It was supposedly brought to Lazio by Umbrian coal peddlers. But the most authentic Lazio pasta variation is *all'amatriciana,* from the town of Amatrice, in the province of Rieti. In quarrels over how it is properly made, cooks will often toss pots at each other. Purists hold that the diced salt pork must come from Amatrice itself, that only the faintest dab of tomato sauce suffices, and that strong *pecorino,* and never Parmesan cheese, must be used.

The Roman countryside does produce an abundance of vegetables, whose consumption follows the seasons. On May 1, Italy's Labor Day, fava beans are served raw with chunks of pecorino and a robust red wine. Throughout spring, many restaurants offer a fresh vegetable compote called, appropriately, *primavera* (spring). A medley of fried foods may include batter-fried mozzarella chunks, codfish, zucchini, zucchini flowers with a cheese stuffing, and flattened artichokes. A special salad green, *puntarelle,* is invariably dressed in an anchovy and garlic vinaigrette. In late summer and autumn, when sun and rain come in just the right doses, the hills around Rome abound in wild mushrooms (note that all sold in shops and restaurants are checked rigorously by local health inspectors). They may appear on the menu as a raw mushroom salad; as a sauce with noodles, *polenta,* or *risotto;* or, when the giant *boletus edulis,* or *porcini,* are available, as a main course. Some Castelli restaurants offer an entire menu of different wild mushroom courses.

Lazio's desserts are generally uninspired, so fresh fruit is usually a wise choice, especially the tiny, woodland-scented strawberries that grow near Lake Nemi. Lazio cooks rinse them in aromatic Frascati wine rather than water. Cultivated strawberries grow in fields throughout Lazio and are harvested when they are perfectly ripe, never before, to be eaten with fresh orange or lemon juice.

Most travelers see some of the sights of the Lazio region on their way into or out of Rome. But since all of the sights of Lazio are within easy reach of the capital, they can also be seen in a series of day trips out of Rome — much as the Romans themselves usually see them. The six routes outlined below are for those who have already seen Rome's standard sights or for those who like to pack and unpack only once during a foreign jaunt. They presuppose a hotel base in Rome, so no hotels are listed, and a car is a must. A tip: The *Raccordo Anulare* is the ring road around Rome. It connects all the roads that lead to Rome — or from it. Another tip: "Never on Monday" should be a traveler's most vital motto. Most museums and many restaurants are closed. Each Friday, the Rome daily paper *Il Messaggero* carries a column reporting which Lazio town offers a festival, religious procession, parade, or even a demonstration by the *butteri,* Lazio's authentic cowboys. Lazio towns fete just about anything, in its season: the wine vintage, the artichoke crop, the chestnut harvest. A friendly hotel concierge might be coaxed into translating the relevant listings.

In the restaurant listings below, expensive means that a meal for two will cost from approximately $45 to $75 with a bottle of wine; moderate means from about $20 to $45. Generally, prices rise with the iodine content in the air — that is, higher near the seashore, lower inland. Regrettably, no inexpensive restaurants were worthy of listing.

DAY TRIP 1: TARQUINIA, TUSCANIA, VULCI

This route takes in Tarquinia, one of the 12 city-states of the Etruscan federation and one of the must-sees among Italian archaeological sites. Tarquinia is noted for the wall paintings found in its extensive necropolis, one of the main sources of our knowledge of Etruscan life. The walled medieval town of Tuscania is also on the route, as are the ruins of a second prominent Etruscan city, Vulci.

En Route from Rome – Leave town by the Rome-Fiumicino Airport Highway (from most places in Rome the Via Aurelia followed by the Raccordo Anulare is the best starting point), then turn north onto the toll highway (A12) toward Civitavecchia. Tarquinia is about 1¼ hours (63 miles) away.

TARQUINIA: Tarquinia dates back to the early Iron Age. It was one of the most powerful Etruscan cities from the 8th to the 4th century BC, and after the 6th century BC it was a far more important city than Rome, thanks to its powerful fleet. The huge underground necropolis, which extends east of the city along the road to Viterbo, contains approximately 200 excavated tombs, and aerial photos taken at dawn have shown that the hay fields and farms surrounding Tarquinia contain hundreds more still untouched by archaeologists or grave robbers. More than 60 of the excavated tombs are decorated with bright wall paintings documenting Etruscan life — its banquets, sports, dances, religious rites, furnishings, travel. The *Museo Nazionale Tarquiniese,* in the elegant 15th-century Palazzo Vitelleschi just inside the gate to Tarquinia's old town, makes a good first stop. Its collection of Etruscan artifacts, taken from the nearby tombs and from other sites in the area, is one of Italy's most important. Besides fine Greek and Greek-influenced pottery, gold jewelry, magical mirrors, and sarcophagi, its prized possessions are two winged horses that adorned a late-4th-century BC temple at Tarquinia's acropolis and several reconstructed tombs decorated with wall paintings detached from the actual site for safe keeping. Admission to the museum includes admission to the necropolis, about a mile away (the museum attendant can provide driving instructions). To conserve the frescoes, only four tombs are open to visitors on any given day, and exactly which four varies from day to day. Museum and necropolis are closed Mondays.

True enthusiasts may want to visit *Pian di Civita.* Take the road toward Viterbo; at km 3.5 turn left onto a dirt road and follow it for 2 km. It leads to the 4th-century BC Ara della Regina (Queen's Altar), the hilltop temple where the winged horses were found and where new archaeological excavations are under way.

 EATING OUT: *Antico Ristorante Giudizi* – Across the piazza from the museum, this establishment offers comfortable dining. Fresh seafood is featured, so try the *spaghetti alle vongole* (with clams) and the mixed fish fry. Closed Mondays. (Piazza Cavour 20, Tarquinia; phone: 0766-855061; expensive.)

En Route from Tarquinia – Take the main exit road. Just at the foot of the hill there's a country road (and a sign) for Tuscania; take the country road for 1½ km and then turn right onto the Tuscania road. The town is about 15 miles away.

TUSCANIA: This is a beautiful example of a southern Etrurian walled town. Built on a hill of tufa rock, it is surrounded by Etruscan burial mounds of the 5th century BC, including one belonging to a family named Vipinana, whose tombs were found with no fewer than 27 sarcophagi. Some 50 members of another Etruscan family, the Statlane, have been counted. After the city was conquered by Rome, it continued to prosper, becoming a bishop's seat in the Middle Ages. Just how wealthy it was then can be seen in the scores of medieval towers it retains; these fortunately survived the 1971 earthquake that sorely damaged much of Tuscania. The fine 11th-century *Chiesa di San Pietro* (*Church of St. Peter*), built on the site of an Etruscan acropolis, is just outside the present town. The crypt, with its myriad columns, is a study in architectural styles dating from the Roman era.

EATING OUT: *Al Gallo* – The best-known restaurant in town is a pleasant hotel dining room in the center near the Duomo. Frequent signs from the main gate in the city wall lead directly to it. Closed Tuesdays. (Via del Gallo 24, Tuscania; phone: 0761-435028; moderate.)

La Palombella – A popular restaurant, its *polenta* (cornmeal mush), served on the classic wooden platter, comes with a spicy sauce of mushrooms, sausage, and tomatoes. Chops and sausages are lovingly grilled over a wood fire, but the house specialty is game. Try the delectable stuffed pigeon. Closed Saturdays. (Via Canino 23, Tuscania; phone: 0761-435419; moderate.)

En Route from Tuscania – Follow the excellently marked, easy-to-drive country roads about 12 miles north to Canino, and after another 3 miles turn right to Vulci (watch for the yellow signs indicating tourist sights).

VULCI: The bare ruins of another of the 12 Etruscan city-states lie in an area of Maremma countryside — the Pian di Voce — where flat fields, poplar lanes, and Roman aqueducts stand out against the brilliant Mediterranean light. Here a Bronze Age town was located on the banks of the Fiora River. By the 9th and 8th centuries BC, its craftsmen's skill in making bronze daggers, helmets, and shields was already known. Relics from the excavation of the town and the four necropoli in the vicinity are found in the world's greatest museums — artifacts from the *Isis Tomb* in the Polledrara necropolis, for instance, are in the British Museum in London. The monumental *Cuccumella Tomb* is well worth seeing. Then see the *Museo Nazionale* at Castel di Badia, a short drive from the excavations. This beautifully arranged small museum is set up inside a restored 12th-century castle replete with a tiny moat. Next to the castle, a humpbacked bridge — its foundations Etruscan, the rest of the structure Roman — arches over the rushing Fiora River. As a fortified monastery at the edge of the Papal States, the castle once controlled a major north-south highway link between Etruria and Rome. Carts en route to market were stopped by customs collectors at the castle dooryard. Together, castle and bridge are among Italy's most romantic sights, and construction of a nuclear power plant at Montalto di Castro, 5 miles west as the crow flies, has alarmed Italian ecologists.

En Route from Vulci – Turn back toward the sea and the town of Montalto di Castro (8 miles by road) where the Via Aurelia (SS1) provides the best route for the return to Rome.

DAY TRIP 2: CERVETERI, BRACCIANO, VEII

This second tour through Etruscan Lazio is especially suited for families with children. It visits Cerveteri, another of the Etruscan city-states, with an important museum and tombs carved into the soft tufa stone to look for all the world like the interiors of Etruscan households. After Cerveteri, it proceeds to the town of Bracciano for lunch, perhaps a swim in the lake, and a visit to a magnificent castle. It finishes up with a visit to the excavations of Veii, the Etruscan city closest to Rome.

En Route from Rome – From the Via Aurelia, take the Raccordo Anulare to the Rome-Fiumicino Airport Highway and then the toll highway (A12) toward Civitavecchia. Exit at Cerveteri.

CERVETERI: Settled 900 years before Christ, Cerveteri (ancient Caere) lies on a small tufa plateau between two gorges carved by rivers. Its development lagged behind that of Tarquinia, Vulci, and Veii, but it made up for its slow start when the mines in the nearby Tolfa Mountains turned it into an Iron Age boom town. Cerveteri grew rich as its ships set out from the nearby port of Santa Severa (ancient Pyrgi). In the 6th and 5th centuries BC, it was a sea power with a fleet important enough to make common cause with the Carthaginians in fighting the Greek-dominated colonies of Magna Graecia, which ruled from Naples down through western Sicily. That trio — Carthage, Etruria, and Magna Graecia — continued to jockey for power until Rome emerged and settled the power struggle for good by conquering all three.

Of the hundreds of tombs from the 8th to the 1st century BC in the necropolis at Cerveteri, the most important concentration is at *Colle della Banditaccia,* about a mile outside the modern town. Many of the burial chambers have lost their paint, but their fascination lies in their furnishings and architectural details — ceiling beams, doorways, divans — all carved in soft tufa stone. The *Tomba dei Capitelli* (*Tomb of the Capitals*), in particular, built at the height of Caere's wealth and power, shows what the inside of an Etruscan home was like. The walls of the 4th- or 3rd-century BC *Tomba dei Rilievi* (*Tomb of the Reliefs*), which were the burial vaults of the rich Matuna family, are covered with charming painted stucco reliefs of household objects and scenes. They, too, show everyday life in Caere, right down to the Matunas' stew pots and the family mutt. The *Regolini Galassi Tomb,* in another location closer to town and dating from the late 7th century BC, is also famous. Its dowry of presents to accompany the dead on their voyage to the afterlife is now in the Etruscan collection at the Vatican. In Cerveteri itself, see the *Museo Nazionale Cerite* (closed Mondays), housed in the 16th-century Palazzo Ruspoli in Piazza Santa Maria. When it opened in the 1960s, it was widely praised for its particularly attractive and coherent displays of Etruscan and other ancient artifacts in its collection. At the museum, it's also possible to make arrangements to visit the Regolini Galassi Tomb.

En Route from Cerveteri – Proceed inland by country road to the town of Bracciano, on a volcanic lake, Lago di Bracciano. Or, for those with the time, continue up the coast to Civitavecchia, which became the port of Rome after the port at Ostia, built by the ancient Romans, silted up. Civitavecchia's *Forte Michelangelo,* a 16th-century structure for which Michelangelo designed the keep, its *Museo Nazionale Archeologico* (closed Mondays), and vestiges of an antique Roman port make the detour worthwhile. Then cut inland over country roads through the Tolfa Mountains toward Tolfa and then Manziana. At Manziana, a right turn leads to Bracciano, 35 miles from Civitavecchia.

BRACCIANO: The outstanding feature of this small resort town on the southwest side of Lake Bracciano is the *Castello degli Orsini.* It was the first sight Sir Walter Scott wanted to see in Rome, and children of all ages will understand why. This is a dream castle, in fine condition. In fact, it is still inhabited by the Odescalchi, a princely Roman family whose glittering parties and balls are Rome's grandest. Built between 1470 and 1485, the castle has five sides, with a crenelated tower at each juncture. Guided tours take place on Wednesdays, Thursdays, Saturdays, and Sundays at intervals all day, except during the long lunch break. While waiting for a tour, spend the time at any of the several summer dining rooms of the pleasant family-style *trattorie* that jut into the lake on wooden piers. Lake fish — grilled alone or in a fine *risotto* — are standard fare, but local enthusiasts order eel whenever it appears.

 EATING OUT: *Alfredo* – For an appetizing *risotto alle ortiche* (rice with wild nettles), as well as good fresh lake fish, try this charming lakeside restaurant. Closed Tuesdays. (Via Sposetta Nuova, Bracciano; phone: 06-9024130; moderate.)

En Route from Bracciano – Circle the lake to Trevignano, a sleepy lakeside town, ever more developed as Romans install weekend homes. The pretty *Chiesa*

dell'Assunta (*Church of the Assumption*) is worth a visit, and so are the *osterie* (wine shops), which sell local wine by the glass. From Trevignano, pick up the Via Cassia (SS2) to visit the ruins of *Veii* (*Veio* in Italian), near the town of Isola Farnese (watch for the yellow signs).

VEII: Ancient Veii, built on the right bank of the Tiber, was the largest of the dozen Etruscan city-states, with seven miles of walls. It grew rich because of its control of the road to the salt flats and depots at the mouth of the Tiber and because of the commercial and military importance of the river itself. Rome coveted Veii; in fact, it was the first of the Etruscan cities to fall to Roman domination, the beginning of the end for Etruria. This occurred in 396 BC, after a decade-long siege that was broken only when the slaves of Furius Camillus tunneled into the city through the tufa rock. The most famous find uncovered during the past century of excavations is the statue of Apollo, now in the Villa Giulia Museum in Rome. Today's visitors can see a pretty waterfall, the foundations of a 6th-century BC temple, its altar with drains for the blood of the sacrificed, and an adjacent pool for ritual dunkings. The same ticket permits entry to the site of a nearby Roman-era villa.

En Route from Veii – Continue down the Via Cassia (SS2) to head back to Rome.

DAY TRIP 3: BOMARZO, VITERBO

This tour continues the exploration of the northern tip of Lazio, this time the area around the largest of the region's three volcanic lakes, Lago di Bolsena. Children will love this drive because it visits Bomarzo, where stone monsters disport in a garden. From Bomarzo it goes to Viterbo, stopping to see the terraced gardens of the Villa Lante en route. After Viterbo, it heads north to the town of Montefiascone, from which various lakeside points can be visited.

En Route from Rome – Take the Via Salaria to the Raccordo Anulare and then the Autostrada del Sole (A1) north to the Attigliano exit. Follow signs to Bomarzo, about 4 miles from the exit.

BOMARZO: A Renaissance equivalent of Disneyland, inspired by Dante's *Inferno,* is the best description of Bomarzo's *Parco dei Mostri* (*Monster Park*). The park is actually a terraced, wooded slope strewn with carved stone animals and fantastical figures, from larger than life size to colossal. It was conceived and built by the 16th-century nobleman Vicino Orsini, an intrepid Renaissance traveler whose family palace is nearby. Among its huge carvings, all in *peperino,* a granulated form of tufa, are elephants and lions, dragons, giants, and nymphs, faces with mouths as big as doorways, and a leaning house, just like the fun house in a modern amusement park.

En Route from Bomarzo – Drop down to SS204 and follow it west toward Viterbo, 15 miles from Bomarzo. Stop just short of Viterbo, at Bagnaia, for the Villa Lante, then drive on to Viterbo.

VILLA LANTE: The small but elegant twin 16th-century villas, designed by Vignola, are not open to visitors (except by prior arrangement), but the spectacular surrounding garden is open daily, except Mondays. This wonderful example of a formal Renaissance garden is laid out on five terraces descending to a pond and decorated with fountains — some of which play tricks on the unwary!

VITERBO: Viterbo, the capital of *La Tuscia,* as northern Lazio is called, is an Etruscan city that became important under the Romans and remained so through the Middle Ages. In the 13th century — troubled times for the papacy, given the continual struggle between the Church and the Holy Roman Empire — several popes found it safer to live here than in Rome, so that by the middle of the century, the *Palazzo Papale* was built for their use. Several conclaves were held here, including the one that elected Gregory X, the longest conclave in the history of the Roman Catholic Church.

Supposedly, it ended after 33 months only because the cardinals' food supply was cut off.

The papal palace is still one of the major monuments of Viterbo, so head first to Piazza San Lorenzo, where the delicate Gothic palace stands right next to the *Duomo,* a 12th-century building with a Renaissance façade, and both stand right over the old Etruscan acropolis. Then turn back along Via San Lorenzo and stroll in the direction of Porta San Pietro. The walk leads through Viterbo's San Pellegrino quarter, one of Europe's most completely medieval cityscapes. Be sure to visit the tiny *Piazzetta San Pellegrino,* the hauntingly medieval heart of the quarter, and *Piazza Cappella,* another characteristic spot. The exterior stone stairways leading to second-story balconies and front doors, called *profferli,* are typically Viterbese. The quarter is not a museum, and some of its charm lies in the glimpses of craftsmen hard at work in their *botteghe* (workshops) off the narrow streets. Many shops sell pretty copies of black Etruscan-style terra cotta pots and vases.

Two very old fountains, the 13th-century *Fontana Grande,* in Piazza Fontana Grande, and the 14th-century *Fontana di Piano Scarano,* in Piazza Fontan di Piano, are of interest. The latter was at the center of a popular uprising in the 14th century when a member of the papal court of Urban V attempted to wash a puppy in the fountain, which the townspeople used for drinking water. The city's tourist office (*EPT*), Piazza dei Caduti (phone: 0761-226161), can provide information on other sights and on special events, such as the *Festa di Santa Rosa* (September 2–3), when a parade in historic costume takes place, followed the next day by a procession featuring a hundred men carrying a 4-ton, 90-foot tower through the streets.

EATING OUT: La Zaffera – This oasis of tasteful decor and service is in the heart of the San Pellegrino quarter. One of its charms is a small garden for the *aperitivo* hour. It's more expensive than most Lazio restaurants outside Rome, and it's best to reserve in advance. Closed Mondays. (Via San Pellegrino, Viterbo; phone: 0761-29777; expensive.)

Aquilanti – An old favorite, a scant 2 miles out of town in the direction of Bagnaia. Steaks, lamb, and pork chops are grilled on an open fire. Be sure to reserve on Sundays. Closed Tuesdays and July. (Via del Santuario 4, Madonna della Quercia; phone: 0761-31701; expensive.)

En Route from Viterbo – Head north to visit Montefiascone, which stands on the edge of the crater of an extinct volcano, now Lake Bolsena. Then drive westward to the edge of the lake.

MONTEFIASCONE: This small town on a hill overlooking Lake Bolsena is the home of the wine called *Est! Est!! Est!!!* Once upon a time, a cardinal's servant quenched his thirst so very well at Montefiascone that he left his master a sign outside the wine shop exclaiming, three times, "This is it!" The name stuck and, along with the wine of Frascati, this is considered Lazio's finest. Castle ruins in the town's upper reaches offer a fine view of the lake and of the mountains beyond.

LAGO DI BOLSENA: This largest of Italy's many volcanic lakes takes its name from an early Italian tribe, the Volsinienses, from the area around Orvieto, a short distance to the north. The lake is nearly a perfect circle averaging 8 miles in diameter, and it contains two small islands, Isola Bisentina and Isola Martina. The former has a chapel housing the bones of St. Christine; the latter, a horrific Gothic history: In the year 532, Queen Martana of the Ostrogoths was strangled on the islet by her cousin, Theodahad, to whom she was betrothed but who, alas, coveted her throne. The lake so abounds in eels that a particularly gluttonous pope, if Dante is to be believed, ate himself to death on them. On the western shore are ruins of what was first a Villanovan, then an Etruscan, and finally a Roman town, Visentium. For the Etruscans, the lake held special meaning, and scores of Etruscan tombs have been found nearby.

Drive as far as Capodimonte, a tiny summer resort with a sleepy old-fashioned air on the southwest shore of the lake. For a pleasant side trip, circle the lake to the town of Bolsena, on the northeast shore, to visit the Chiesa di Santa Cristina. On its portal is a terra cotta panel from the Della Robbia school, and a chapel inside contains a Della Robbia terra cotta portrait of the saint.

 EATING OUT: *Er Verace* – A pleasant and unpretentious restaurant on the street skirting the lake, specializing in *spaghetti alle vongole* (with clams), fresh lake fish, and eels. Closed Mondays. (Strada Verentana, Capodimonte; phone: 0761-80255; moderate.)

En Route from Lago di Bolsena – To return to Rome, two routes are available. Either cut seaward from Capodimonte to pick up the Via Aurelia (SS1) at Montalto di Castro and follow the coastal road south to Rome. Or return to Viterbo from either Capodimonte or Bolsena and take a leisurely ride on the Via Cimino through the hills and past a tiny volcanic lake, Lago di Vico. En route, there are towns with pleasant historic quarters to be visited, such as Ronciglione, just south of the lake, and Sutri, where Pontius Pilate was born. At Sutri, pick up the Via Cassia (SS2) south.

DAY TRIP 4: PALESTRINA, ANAGNI, SUBIACO, TIVOLI

This tour turns away from Etruscan Lazio toward areas where Latin tribes such as the Sabines, who conquered the Etruscans, lived before settling Rome. The area has suffered far more than Etruscan Lazio from the construction of tasteless modern buildings, but some extremely interesting sights, such as the ruins of the Roman temple at Palestrina, the medieval town of Anagni, and the monasteries of Subiaco, remain. On the way back, stop at Tivoli, if you haven't already seen it by public transport or guided tour from Rome.

En Route from Rome – Take Via Prenestina eastward out of Rome to Palestrina, 24 miles away.

PALESTRINA: This town, known to many because the 16th-century composer Pierluigi da Palestrina was born here, was known to the ancient world as Praeneste. It dates at least as far back as the 7th century BC, and even farther, according to the ancients, for whom it was said to have been founded by the son Circe bore to Ulysses. It passed to the Romans in 499 BC, and various Roman emperors, including Augustus, Tiberius, and Hadrian, later built pleasure palaces here. But the wonder of Palestrina was its shrine to the goddess of fortune, *Fortuna Primigenia,* so important to the Romans that they built the Via Praeneste (Via Prenestina now) to enable them to make the journey to consult the oracle more regularly. In 82 BC, the Roman statesman Sulla tore down the old buildings — which had been there for at least a century — and replaced them with a many-terraced majestic temple, the largest religious complex in the entire Roman world. It remained in use until the 4th century AD and then gradually became the foundation of a medieval city. In 1640, the Barberini family of Rome built a palace right in the sacred area, the same palace that today houses the *Museo Archeologico Prenestino* (closed Mondays).

Be sure to visit the museum before the excavations (same ticket). One of its treasures is a very large and beautiful 1st-century BC mosaic that once decorated a floor of the temple. Another is a scale model of the temple as it was in ancient times. It shows the shrine to the goddess, Jupiter's first daughter, laid out in a triangle on a hillside extending from the level of the present Piazza Regina Margherita, where the Duomo now stands, up to Piazza della Cortina, where the museum entrance is. Vast ramps and staircases adorned with elegant columns, colonnades, vaults, and arches lead toward a vast open terrace. At the top was a semicircular portico (the Barberini Palace now follows the same curve) in the center of which stood a gold statue of Primigenia, long since lost. The Romans were so proud of the monument, which must have bowled over the pilgrims who came from all around, that they lighted bonfires on the terraces so that sailors at sea could see the sanctuary at night. Even today, the ruins are highly evocative, and the windows of the museum offer a wonderful view.

EATING OUT: *Farina* – Near the Duomo, this restaurant is often recommended by the locals, and rightly so. Owner Mario Pinci serves homemade fettuccine with porcini mushrooms, cannelloni with either meat or ricotta and spinach filling, and roast or grilled lamb. Closed Wednesdays. (Piazza Garibaldi 16, Palestrina; phone: 06-9558916; moderate.)

Trattoria alla Pergola – Generous portions of simple, well-prepared food are served in a garden under a wisteria arbor. Closed Tuesdays. (Corso Pierluigi 61, Palestrina; phone: 06-9558204; moderate.)

En Route from Palestrina – Proceed south to Valmontone and pick up the Autostrada del Sole (A2) for about 10 miles southeast to the Anagni exit. From Anagni, follow signs to Fiuggi.

ANAGNI: Cicero had an estate in this hilltop town, and four popes, including Boniface VIII, were born here. It has a medieval quarter with a particularly harmonious aspect because almost all of its buildings are of the 13th century, and it has one of Lazio's more noteworthy cathedrals. This basically Romanesque structure, built in the 11th and 12th centuries atop a former Roman temple and then modified in the 13th century, stands on the highest point of the town. Inside, the loveliest sight is the crypt (open only in the early afternoon), whose walls are decorated with 13th-century frescoes (there is a painting of Hippocrates in one lunette). Anagni does not make news today, but it did in the past. In 1160, an archbishop announced the excommunication of Frederick Barbarossa from the cathedral. And in 1303, at the Palazzo di Bonifacio VIII, another of its old buildings, an emissary of French King Philip the Fair slapped the aged, frail Pope Boniface full in the face with his iron gauntlet, an episode that lives on in Dante.

FIUGGI: Fiuggi is a two-part town. There is Fiuggi Città, the actual town, and, a short distance away, Fiuggi Fonte, a spa whose *fonte* (spring) attracts health seekers, especially elderly ones. It bustles in summer, languishes in winter. Although the spa itself is of limited interest to tourists, its quaint, Victorian-era hotels have charm, its shops sell a fair sampling of the local products, from salami to cheese and honey, and its tea shops offer good pastries.

En Route from Fiuggi – Drive north to pick up SS411 in the direction of Subiaco. Just before the town, turn right onto the Vallepietra road where Subiaco's most famous sights are found.

SUBIACO: According to legend, workmen building a villa for Nero by a long-gone lake needed a place to stay. Their work camp of huts became the town of Sublaqueum, meaning "under the waters." The ruins of Nero's villa can still be visited, about a mile and a half out of town, but Subiaco — considered the birthplace of Benedictine monasticism — is best known for its monasteries. In the 6th century, St. Benedict came here from his native Norcia, in Umbria. Living as a hermit, he prayed in a cave for three years, and before leaving for Monte Cassino (see *Day Trip 6*) he had founded several monasteries. One of these original establishments is the *Monastero di Santa Scolastica* (she was Benedict's sister), which was especially influential from the 11th through the 13th century, but kept growing through the 16th century. The cave in which St. Benedict prayed (known as the *Sacro Speco*) is now part of the *Monastero di San Benedetto*, founded in the 12th century. Both monasteries are southeast of town on the road to Vallepietra, one just beyond the other, and both are open to visitors.

En Route from Subiaco – Circle north and west back to Rome, passing through villages such as Anticoli Corrado, which has a little medieval square, Vicovaro, and Tivoli, the last stop.

TIVOLI: Already a resort in Roman times, this hilltop town has very nearly become a worldwide household word because of the *Villa d'Este,* a 16th-century cardinal's palace with terraced gardens that contain some of the most famous fountains of Rome — and not merely one or two or a few squirts and sprays, but 500 of them. Nearby is the *Villa Gregoriana,* another park with waterworks (actually a waterfall), in addition to archaeological interest in its Corinthian-style Temple of Vesta, or Temple of Sibyl. But the *Villa Adriana* (*Hadrian's Villa*), 4 miles out of Tivoli in the direction of Rome, is by far Tivoli's greatest archaeological attraction. This was the summer estate Hadrian built for himself after the one he built at Palestrina, and to make it a showplace, as well as to remind him of his travels, he included on the grounds copies of some of the marvels he had seen around the empire. Set on a hillside studded with cypress trees and umbrella pines, the villa is still a showplace and a place for reverie, even in ruins.

Tivoli is certainly interesting enough to warrant a full day. It is easily reached by public transport, and it is included on many guided day tours out of Rome. Because of this, it is discussed more fully in *Rome,* THE CITIES. But if this will be your only chance to see the Villa d'Este and the Villa Adriana, stop now, leaving the Villa Gregoriana for last. The Villa d'Este and the Villa Gregoriana are open daily; the Villa Adriana is closed on Mondays.

En Route from Tivoli – Take Via Tiburtina (SS5) back to Rome, 19 miles away.

DAY TRIP 5: CASTELLI ROMANI

Southeast of Rome, in the lovely Colli Albani (Alban Hills) region, are 13 hill towns known collectively as the *Castelli Romani* (*Roman Castles*). The curious name derives from the castles, or fortresses, palaces, and villas built here over the centuries by various popes and patrician Roman families. This is also wine country, and our route goes directly to Rome's prime wine town, Frascati. It then explores a selection of other Castelli towns surrounding the two volcanic lakes of the region, Lago di Albano and Lago di Nemi.

En Route from Rome – Take the Via Tuscolana (SS215) southeast out of Rome and drive 13 miles to Frascati.

FRASCATI: An ancient Roman town, Frascati is famous both for its wine and for its patrician villas of the 16th and 17th centuries. Although heavily damaged during World War II, and much rebuilt, it is still one of the Romans' favorite Castelli destinations for an outing. Its main square, Piazza Marconi, affords a panoramic view over the Roman countryside and the gardens of the *Villa Torlonia,* open to the public. The 16th-century villa itself was bombed to smithereens during the war, but the remains of a water theater (a fancy arrangement of fountains) designed by Carlo Maderno, one of the architects of St. Peter's in Rome, are fascinating. Sitting on top of a hill and dominating another side of Piazza Marconi is the *Villa Aldobrandini,* built for a cardinal at the end of the 16th century by Giacomo della Porta. It is not open to the public, but its splendid gardens can be visited (with permission from the Azienda Autonoma di Turismo). Next to it is the privately owned *Villa Lancellotti,* also not visitable — but note its gate, by the architect Borromini, Bernini's great rival. Still another famous villa, *Villa Mondragone,* is about a mile east of town and is now a Jesuit seminary. Here Pope Gregory XIII issued a bull establishing a new calendar — the one we use today.

Frascati's well-known wine is mostly from white grapes and at its best should be amber in color. Wine consortiums sell the local product everywhere, and some wineries encourage visits. Another Frascati specialty — a bit peculiar — are the *pupazze,* honey cakes baked in animal or human forms. One favorite is a three-breasted fertility goddess who harks back to the area's pagan days.

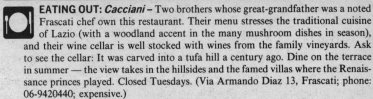

EATING OUT: *Cacciani* – Two brothers whose great-grandfather was a noted Frascati chef own this restaurant. Their menu stresses the traditional cuisine of Lazio (with a woodland accent in the many mushroom dishes in season), and their wine cellar is well stocked with wines from the family vineyards. Ask to see the cellar: It was carved into a tufa hill a century ago. Dine on the terrace in summer — the view takes in the hillsides and the famed villas where the Renaissance princes played. Closed Tuesdays. (Via Armando Diaz 13, Frascati; phone: 06-9420440; expensive.)

Spartaco – Near the railway station, this restaurant serves fettuccine with porcini mushroom sauce, in a garden setting. Closed Tuesdays. (Viale Letizia Bonaparte 1, Frascati; phone: 06-9420431; moderate.)

En Route from Frascati – Turning south, drive just short of 2 miles to Grottaferrata. After a visit, continue to Marino, about 4 miles away by SS216. Still farther along on SS216 is Castel Gandolfo, where the pope spends his summers in the cool, green hills. From Castel Gandolfo, proceed to Albano.

GROTTAFERRATA: Best known for its fortified abbey, a castle-like monastery that was founded in 1004 and is still inhabited by monks of the Greek Catholic rite. The abbey was built on top of the ruins of an ancient Roman summer villa, part of which became a chapel incorporated into the abbey's Church of St. Mary. In front of the church is a handsome fountain, and there is an adjacent shop where monks sell olive oil and wine.

MARINO: In summer, this favorite Castelli town is crowded with day-trippers from Rome. Like Frascati, Marino is famous for its wine, and each year on the first Sunday in October it holds a wine festival, the *Sagra dell'Uva* (see *Italy's Most Colorful Festas* in DIVERSIONS). The event begins with a religious procession, but after the solemnities are over, Marino puts itself entirely into the hands, or jug, of Bacchus, and wine really does flow from the fountain in the main square.

EATING OUT: *Al Vigneto* – Fish, polenta, and homemade *crostate* (tarts) are served here. The restaurant is a little less than 3 miles out of Marino on the Via dei Laghi in a woodland setting where children can romp while adults sample Marino's fine wines under a grape arbor. Closed Tuesdays. (Via dei Laghi, km 4.5; phone: 06-9387034; moderate.)

CASTEL GANDOLFO: A particularly lovely setting overlooking Lake Albano prompted the popes to select Castel Gandolfo for their summer residence. It is supposed to have been the site of Alba Longa, the most ancient city of Lazio, founded, according to legend, by the son of Aeneas and destroyed by the Romans in about 600 BC. Roman legend also speaks of a duel fought between the Horatii, male triplets of Rome, and the Curiatii, triplets of Alba Longa, in an attempt to resolve a tiresome war. Through a ruse, a Horatio won after his two brothers had been slain. When his sister, mourning one of the dead Curiatii, turned on him, he killed her as well. The tomb in which the Horatii and Curiatii were supposedly buried lies farther along the road on the way to Ariccia.

A Bernini fountain and the graceful *Chiesa di San Tommaso da Villanova,* also by Bernini, decorate Castel Gandolfo's main square. Also on the square is the entrance to the *Palazzo Papale* (papal residence), designed by Carlo Maderno and built from 1624 to 1629 on the site of a sprawling pleasure palace belonging to the emperor Domitian in the 1st century AD. The palace and its grounds, enlarged by the later addition of the grounds of the *Villa Barberini,* are all part of the Vatican city-state, and the complex is huge — extending all the way to the next Castelli town, Albano. The grounds house the famous Vatican Observatory and a modern hall used for general audiences on Wednesday mornings when the pope is in residence (attendance at the audience is the only way tourists can visit the property, which is closed to the public). When in residence, the pope also appears at a window in the inner of two courtyards at noon on Sundays and can then be seen from quite close.

ALBANO: In the 3rd century AD, the emperor Septimius Severus established a permanent garrison — the Castra Albana — for the Roman army here. The camp evidently took up the entire territory of the present town, although, covered by later construction, it was only bombed into view during World War II. Now the main gateway to the camp, the Porta Pretoria, can be seen, and a giant Roman cistern, carved out of the rock and still in use, as well as the ancient amphitheater, can be visited. The so-called tomb of the Horatii and Curiatii, but more probably the tomb of an unknown Roman from the time of the republic, sits by the side of the road on the way out of Albano.

   En Route from Albano – Take the Via Appia (SS7) to Genzano, and turn off toward Nemi.

   GENZANO DI ROMA: This Castelli town is noted for its *Corpus Domini* celebrations. Each year, on a Sunday in mid-June, the entire Via Italo Belardi (ex–Via Livia) leading up to the Chiesa di Santa Maria della Cima is covered with "paintings" made entirely of flowers. The subjects are religious scenes, historical scenes, copies of famous master-pieces, portraits, or abstract designs, intricately worked out in petals, pistils, stamens, and leaves — the townspeople have had more than 200 years to perfect their technique. The next morning, at 10 AM, the children of the town descend on the street like a swarm of locusts and wipe out all the artwork in a matter of minutes.

   NEMI: Set high above the lake from which it takes its name, Nemi is dominated by the *Ruspoli Palace* and is best known for its strawberries. When they're in season in early summer, Romans make pilgrimages here to eat them, and in June the town holds a strawberry festival. The ancient Romans referred to the lake as the Mirror of Diana because it reflected a nearby temple dedicated to the goddess of the hunt in an area called the Sacred Grove of Diana. Festivals in her honor took place here in ancient times, and in the 1930s part of the lake was drained to recover two Roman boats built by Caligula to take part in the celebrations. Unfortunately, the museum in which the boats were placed was bombed during World War II, and they were destroyed.

   En Route from Nemi – Pick up the Via dei Laghi (Lake Road, SS217) north-west, and turn right at the turnoff for Rocca di Papa.

   ROCCA DI PAPA: The highest of the Castelli clings to the side of Monte Cavo, at an altitude of 2,250 feet. It takes its name from a castle built here by the popes in the Middle Ages (and destroyed during the Renaissance) and consists of a higher, medieval quarter and a lower, modern town. In Roman times, a temple of Jupiter stood at the 3,124-foot top of Monte Cavo, which was approached by a Via Sacra over which the earliest Romans marched in solemn procession with sacrifices to dedicate to the one god they all worshiped. In the 18th century a monastery was built where the temple presumably stood. On a clear day, the view from the top of the mountain is immense, taking in the Castelli, the two lakes, and the surrounding countryside as far as the coast. Getting there, however, requires turning off before Rocca di Papa and following a winding road that eventually turns into a private road (the custodians charge a minimal fee).

   En Route from Rocca di Papa – Go back to Grottaferrate, then to Frascati, and from there take the Via Tuscolana back to Rome.

DAY TRIP 6: MONTE CASSINO, SPERLONGA, ANZIO

Southern Lazio has a flavor all its own, a mixture of pious abbeys and pagan temples, roadside stands selling delectable mozzarellas, beachheads whose names ring with the horrors of war, and chic beaches with frequently topless bathers. This tour leads south of Rome, through a part of Lazio known as the Ciociaria, to visit the Abbey of Monte

Cassino, a fascinating experience for people of all faiths. Then it cuts seaward to Gaeta and returns north along the coast via a number of seaside towns — Sperlonga for a swim and lunch, Terracina, Anzio (where the Allied landing took place during World War II), and Nettuno.

En Route from Rome – Take the Autostrada del Sole (A2) south 70 miles to the Cassino exit. The *Abbey of Monte Cassino* is 5½ miles west of the modern industrial town of Cassino, at the end of a winding mountain road.

ABBAZIA DI MONTE CASSINO: Most travelers racing down the autostrada from Rome to Naples only glimpse this historic monastery from afar, but it is open to visitors, provided they respect the sanctity of the place and dress appropriately. The imposing, medieval-style complex of buildings, set in a commanding position on a mountaintop, is headquarters for the Benedictine Order, founded by St. Benedict in 529 after, according to legend, three ravens led him from Subiaco to Cassino. He died in the new monastery 14 years later and was buried here, as was his sister, St. Scholastica. During the Dark Ages, following the fall of the Roman Empire, the abbey was not only one of the great European centers of Christian culture, but also one of the greatest repositories of ancient learning — it is thanks to the zealous preservation efforts of the monks of Monte Cassino that much of ancient Latin literature and thought survived. Destroyed several times in the distant past — by the Lombards in the 6th century, the Saracens in the 9th century, the Normans in the 11th century, and an earthquake in the 14th century — the abbey was always rebuilt. Then, in 1944, it was destroyed again, this time bombed by the Allies who suspected it was occupied by German troops (justification for the bombing is still a matter of controversy). Reconstruction began immediately after the war, and the library of medieval books and manuscripts that were spared by the bombing is still one of the greatest collections in the world. Besides breathtaking views from the abbey, visitors today can see the basilica, several cloisters, and a photo exhibition on the extent of the damage that is quite moving. The military cemetery seen on the way up contains the graves of 1,100 Polish soldiers who lost their lives in the final assault.

En Route from Monte Cassino – Cut seaward across the peninsula for a visit to Gaeta, and then turn north along the coast and stop at Sperlonga.

GAETA: A handsome fortress of ancient origin, but much transformed from the 13th through the 16th century, sits on a promontory jutting into the sea in this port and resort town. The 12th-century cathedral is interesting, but best of all is a stroll through the bazaar-like, crowded, narrow alleys parallel to the Lungomare Caboto. The pleasure yachts anchored in the basin are impressively posh.

SPERLONGA: This whitewashed town with a Moorish look has long sand beaches on either side of a rock spur into the sea. It is perhaps Lazio's loveliest summer resort and, accordingly, is overcrowded from mid-July through late August, but it is a delight in June and September. About a half mile south of the town is a small, fascinating archaeological museum (closed Mondays) with finds from the area, including from the Grotta di Tiberio, a great cave on the beach that the ancient Romans (traditionally, Tiberius) used for summer amusement. Various ancient statues were found in the cave, and some statues can still be seen there. Others, put together again from fragments, like Humpty Dumpty, are in the museum.

EATING OUT: *Laocoonte–Da Rocco* – The best of many pleasant restaurants in town serving fish. It has a covered terrace overlooking the sea. Closed Mondays and November. (Via Colombo 4, Sperlonga; phone: 0771-54122; moderate.)

Grotta di Tiberio – Near the cave and the beach, the attraction here is a charming garden in an old orchard. Specialties include classic fish dishes such as *risotto al pescatore* and spaghetti with clams. Try the delicate *pesce al cartoccio* (fish sealed in parchment). Closed Mondays and November and December. (Via Flacca 8, Sperlonga; phone: 0771-54027; moderate.)

En Route from Sperlonga – The next coastal town north of Sperlonga is Terracina, where fishing boats jam into a canal leading to the sea. Terracina is a traffic-clogged, colorful town that becomes tourist-clogged in midsummer. Serene on a high cliff above it, however, are the ruins of a famous temple of Jupiter dating from the 1st century BC. Beyond Terracina, the Via Pontina (SS148) turns north to Rome, while the coast road heads to San Felice Circeo, a bathing resort on the slopes of the 1,795-foot promontory of Monte Circeo, home to the Neanderthals, to Circe, and now to the very rich who populate the expensive resort hotels. The area is also home to a good deal of bird and animal life, since it is now a nature reserve, the *Parco Nazionale del Circeo,* which encloses four coastal lakes, dunes, forests of oak and brush, and a variety of archaeological remains. Among these are the ruins of a lavish summer residence and spa the emperor Domitian built here in the 1st century AD. Although the park is regularly open to the public (in fact, both San Felice Circeo and the next seaside resort north, Sabaudia, are in it, and visitors will be driving through it along a good stretch of the coast road), advance permission is necessary to visit the ruins of Domitian's villa, which is on one of the coastal lakes between the promontory and Sabaudia. Requests should be addressed to *Parco Nazionale del Circeo,* Via Carlo Alberto 6, 04016 Sabaudia (Latina) (phone: 0773-57251).

From Sabaudia, either return to SS148 and continue north to the turnoff for Nettuno and Anzio, or follow the coast road north. It's also possible to turn off SS148 at Campoverde and follow the well-marked road directly to the American Military Cemetery at Nettuno.

EATING OUT: *Miramare* – A seaside eatery with a garden, it offers *tagliolini* (fine noodles) with shrimp and *risotto* with *frutti di mare,* a mixture of seafoods. Closed Tuesdays. (Lungomare Circe 32, Terracina; phone: 0773-727332; moderate.)

Hostaria Porto Salvo – A spacious verandah overlooks the sea. The fish baked in parchment is special. Closed Mondays. (Via Appia, Terracina; phone: 0773-727551; moderate.)

NETTUNO and ANZIO: Modern history remembers the stretch of beach between these two resorts as the blood-drenched strand where American and British troops landed in the "soft underbelly of Europe" on January 22, 1944. The British came ashore at Anzio, the Americans, closer to Nettuno, and together they found that the underbelly was not at all soft: The Germans resisted the Allied onslaught for more than four months. Some 1,000 British soldiers are buried in the British Military Cemetery at Anzio (on SS207, about 2 miles north). Nearly 8,000 American soldiers lie in the American Military Cemetery, off the Via Santa Maria, about a half mile north of Nettuno. In the center of the cemetery, which is always open, is a chapel, and next to it a small museum illustrates Allied military operations from the invasion of Sicily to the end of the war.

Together, Anzio and Nettuno form almost one continuous town. Anzio was already a resort in Roman times: Cicero had a summer palace here, and both the emperors Caligula and Nero were born here — ruins of the latter's villa can be seen near the lighthouse. Not far away from the villa are the *Grotte di Nerone* (*Nero's Caves*), actually ruins of ancient Roman port warehouses. Some very famous statues have been found on Nero's property, including the *Apollo Belvedere* in the Vatican collection in Rome. Nettuno is known for its picturesque medieval quarter.

En Route from Anzio and Nettuno – The SS207 leads back to the Via Pontina (SS148) for the return to Rome.

Sardinia

Sardinia's beloved Grazia Deledda, an unschooled woman from the mountain town of Nuoro, won the Nobel Prize for Literature in 1926. Deledda was a prolific, lyric writer whose works reflect Sardinian peasant life in the early twentieth century. Then, as now, Sards were fiercely independent, proud, and wary of outsiders.

One of Deledda's novels, *Canne al vento* (*Reeds in the Wind*), immortalizes the heady Sardinian winds. They can turn ferocious in the north, where the seven-mile-wide Strait of Boniface separates the island (the second largest in the Mediterranean) from its geological kissing cousin, French-owned Corsica. Ancient settlers fleeing Crete and later Carthage in frail craft learned to steer clear of Sardinia's churning waters and treacherous winds. (Today's yachts-men, anchored at the posh playground inlets of the Costa Smeralda, enjoy the challenge.)

The first people known to have lived on the island were called the Nura-ghesi, believed to have sailed to Sardinia from the eastern Mediterranean by way of North Africa around 3000 BC. They left behind them about seven thousand towers called *nuraghi,* built of huge stones joined without mortar. Some are like medieval castles. They typically have a cone-shaped central tower of several stories and two or three rings of defensive walls. During an enemy attack the farm folk who lived in nearby huts sought shelter inside for their families and flocks.

Sardinia's location, 116 miles from the Italian mainland — about the same distance as from North Africa — puts it at the center of Mediterranean trade routes. Like the other islands, it was in constant danger of invasion, and in rather rapid succession it was occupied by Greeks, Romans, and Phoenicians. One of the delights of beach life in Sardinia is the occasional serendipitous discovery of reminders of those days. The traces of brickwork half buried in the sand at water's edge may have come from a fisherman's cottage built in Caesar's day. Remains of Carthaginian colonies can be seen half submerged in the sea near Nora, south of Cagliari, and on the western coast near Oristano.

Later, the coastal villages were looted and destroyed by Vandals, Byzan-tines, and Arabs. Retreating into the impervious — and, until the eighteenth century, heavily wooded — mountain interior, the refugees built the towns that survive to this day. During the Middle Ages, the maritime republics of Pisa and Genoa battled for supremacy in Sardinia, followed by the Spanish and Austrians. Each new occupier left a stamp — the Genoese and Spanish their towers and ramparts, the Pisans the elegant Romanesque churches that appear suddenly in lonely meadows.

With each successive invasion over the centuries, islanders retreated into the interior. This retreat, and its resulting insularity, helps explain another

Sardinian peculiarity — its language, Sardo, the romance language closest to spoken Latin. Utterly incomprehensible to most other Italians, its four dialectal variations borrow words from Arabic, Spanish, and Portuguese. The Spanish House of Aragon dominated Sardinia for four centuries, leaving its imprint especially on the western coastline, where the local dialect, one of the four variations, is called Catalan. The Spanish were ousted by the Piedmontese, blamed for deforesting the island to fuel the fledgling industrial revolution in northern Italy.

Despite unification with the new Italy in 1870, Sardinia remained undeveloped and malaria-ridden. It achieved limited political autonomy as an independent region after World War II. Progress came with somewhat jarring rapidity after the 1960s, so that these days the old and new sometimes seem incongruously juxtaposed: Country women still dress in traditional costume at outdoor markets, while nude sunbathers are frequently seen on the beaches.

With the arrival of spring, Sardinian winds turn warm. The beaches in the south near Cagliari, the capital, offer good swimming earlier than elsewhere in Italy, thanks to the balmy breezes from Africa. In summer the winds send shivers through the eucalyptus trees and flowering shrubs that line the roads winding through the broad valleys; they waft the unforgettable fragrance of *la macchia,* the shrub that covers most of Sardinia's 9,724 square miles of otherwise largely barren mountain peaks and endless rolling hills.

The coast is ringed by islets whose soft rock has been carved into monument-like structures by the elements. This is the easiest part of Sardinia for outsiders to get to know. One of the world's most spectacular coastlines, it was somewhat defaced by cement and stucco construction during the 1970s, but most of it is still undisturbed. So the eye can feast on breathtaking vistas as yet another hair-raising hairpin turn brings into view a beach with white sand, or a secluded cove, or a cliff dotted with grottoes and, atop, a millennium-old Saracen tower in ruins. The network of watchtowers was built on the coast, each within sight of another, to warn of the approach of pirates and other invaders.

Inland from the fabled coastline of granite cliffs and turquoise, iridescent sea is the rugged mountain interior, capped by 6,017-foot Punta La Marmora in the Gennargentu range at Sardinia's heart. Above terraced vineyards, rock-strewn plateaus are guarded by solitary shepherds tending their flocks as if in biblical times. Life here reflects centuries of isolation. Sardinian folk culture has been kept undiluted and genuine, especially in the Barbagia area. From foods to handicrafts, clothing, and home furnishings, the grazing economy affects traditional Sardinian life. A Sardinian might describe a childhood friend as a *compagno d'ovile* (sheep pen chum). This Sardinian interior, still authentic, takes a bit of work to get to know, but it's worth the effort.

As modernization efforts (such as the petrochemical industry centered at Porto Torres in the west) bring change, and as new roads break into the isolation of the mountain towns, some Sardinians protest the outside incursions. For instance, for a while a movement to promote Sardinian nationalism had airline pilots striking to protest that radio communications were not broadcast in Sardo.

Schools and folk dance clubs help retain traditional culture, and in summer many hotels schedule an evening of local culinary specialties, followed by folk dances to the music of a triple-piped flute called a *launeddas.* As in Greece, such dances, with their staccato rhythms and sometimes intricate footwork, are not solely for tourists' amusement. In the countryside after a family picnic, someone may produce an accordion, and the men — with as much dignity as they can muster after the big meal and abundant wine — will begin one of the solemn traditional dances right in the field.

Unlike Malta or Sicily, Sardinia was never a military or commercial crossroads. This helped to limit its population, today estimated at only 1.6 million, or 170 people per square mile (by contrast, Sicily has 490). But like some other Mediterranean islands, Sardinia suffers at times from its own success in today's tourism industry. In early August, especially in the coastal areas, the crowds of visitors may endure poor service and unfair prices. During the rest of the long season, however, from May to September, the swimming, sunning, and touring are delightful. Many resorts close in September, but some, especially in the cities, remain open year-round. Temperatures are comparatively warm and rainfall scanty, so that even in January visitors enjoy pleasant touring. At that time, the mean temperature in Sassari in the northeast is 47°F, and in Cagliari in the south, 49°F. Indeed, *cagliaritani* boast, exaggerating only a bit, that they can swim in January, when the almond trees are already in spectacular bloom.

TOURIST INFORMATION: The major tourist offices are in the following cities: *Alghero:* Piazza Portaterra 9 (phone: 079-979054); *Arzachena:* Via Risorgimento (phone: 0789-82624); *Cagliari:* Piazza Matteotti 9 (phone: 070-669255); *Nuoro:* Piazza Italia 19 (phone: 0784-30083); *Olbia:* Via Catello Piro 1 (phone: 0789-21453); *Oristano:* Via Cagliari 276 (phone: 0783-74191); *Santa Teresa di Gallura:* Piazza Vittorio Emanuele 24 (phone: 0789-754127). Most offices are closed from 1 to 4 PM during the summer. Brochures usually include the *Annuario Alberghi* (current hotel guide) and *Calendario Manifestazioni Turistiche* (festival calendar); they are not always translated into English. Good maps are available as well.

The *Italian Touring Club* maintains an office in Cagliari at Corso Vittorio Emanuele 30 (phone: 070-656345), as does the *Italian Automobile Club* at Via Carboni Boi 2 (phone: 070-492881).

FOOD AND WINE: Along the coast, Sardinia's specialties begin with the freshest fish and shellfish, including prawns, crabs, oysters, octopus, lobsters, sea bass, red snapper, and flounder. Any hors d'oeuvres platter is likely to include mixed shellfish salad or *moscardini,* fried baby octopus no bigger than a dime. The most popular first course is *su ziminu,* Sardinia's version of bouillabaisse, which always includes the homely little *scorfano* fish, small crabs, and often lobster claws in a broth rich with chopped, sun-dried tomatoes and white wine. Lobster and tomato sauce is popular as a midnight spaghetti snack. Fresh sea urchin caviar, most abundant in the winter, is also used to flavor spaghetti. Year-round, Sardinians grate salted, dried tuna caviar — or the far more costly mullet, *bottarga* — onto spaghetti tossed with olive oil.

Inland dinners may begin with *salumes de Berchidda,* variations on salami made from pigs that have foraged on the fragrant local heath. This leads to the *pièce de résistance* of all Sardinian cuisine, the *porceddu* — suckling pig slowly roasted on a bed of aromatic myrtle. Lamb is also sometimes roasted this way. Both pork and lamb are served with chunks of celery and radishes, *sa birdura croa.*

Pastas include *malloreddus,* tiny saffron-tinted shells served with tomato or meat sauce, and *culonzones,* big ravioli stuffed with spinach and ricotta cheese made from ewe's milk and sometimes flavored with fresh mint. Available everywhere in Sardinia is *carta da musica* (music paper) bread, which is named for the rustling sound it makes when eaten dry; moistened, it becomes as soft as fresh bread. Shepherds carry it with them on their long migrations into the mountains with their flocks.

Aged cheeses made from ewe's milk — *pecorino* — range in flavor from gentle to tangy. The most celebrated of all Sardinian cheeses, *casu beccio,* has a creamy center. A rarity, it is cured by worms. (Don't worry — it is too prized to appear on a restaurant menu.) More customary methods are employed for aging the cheeses that go into delectable honey-dipped fried pastries called *sabadas,* served for dessert. Some visitors may develop a taste for the dark, slightly bitter honey Sardinians like on bread. Honey is also used to coat suckling pigs and even lamb.

Sardinian wines are increasingly popular, even abroad: From the south comes the dry white Nuragus of Cagliari; from the north, the still white Aragosta (good with fish) and the sparkling white Vermentino di Gallura. Red wines include Cannonau, the most popular, and Rosso di Mamoiada. Meals may end with the mellow, sherry-like golden Vernaccia often used in sauces, with sweet Anghelu Ruju (red angel), or with a chilled thimbleful of the strong liqueur Filu di Ferru (wire string).

 GETTING AROUND: Airports – Cagliari, Alghero (which also serves Sassari), and Olbia, close to the Maddalena Archipelago, with its 14 islands, all have airports, with flights to the island from Rome, Milan, Pisa, and Bologna. In summer, additional flights depart from other Italian, and some European, cities as well.

On the Costa Smeralda at Porto Cervo a reservation center handles air and steamship arrangements (phone: 0789-9400).

Ferry – Frequent ferry service, especially in summer, links Olbia, Santa Teresa di Gallura, and Porto Torres in the north of Sardinia with the mainland cities of Civitavecchia (near Rome), Leghorn, and Genoa, as well as with the south of France and Corsica; except for Corsica, these crossings take from 7 to 12 hours. From Cagliari in the south, ferries connect with Civitavecchia, Genoa, Naples, Palermo, Trapani, and Tunisia; these crossings take from 14 to 23 hours. Book many weeks ahead in the summer, particularly if you are taking a car. On longer crossings, which can be monotonous and wearying, it is a good idea to book a cabin and travel overnight.

The chief companies running ferries are *Tirrenia,* whose US contact is *Extra Value Travel,* 437 Madison Ave., New York, NY 10022 (phone: 212-750-8800); *Trans Tirreno Express;* and *Traghetti Ferrovie dello Stato* (Italian State Railways) with offices at all railway stations in Italy. Any travel agency in Italy can make ferry bookings. Tirrenia's agencies in Sardinia are in Alghero (Via Vittorio Emanuele 27; phone: 079-979005); Cagliari (Piazza Deffenu 7; phone: 070-654644); and Olbia (Corso Umberto 17; phone: 0789-511221).

Bus – *PANI* is the main bus company connecting major cities; in Cagliari, its address is Piazza Darsena 4 (phone: 070-652326). Local buses are too crowded and slow to be recommended. Bus tours do not yet exist.

Car Rental – The major rental firms have offices at Sardinia's three airports. In summer, reserve in advance. *Alghero: Avis,* Piazza Sulis 7 (phone: 079-979577); *Hertz,* at the airport (phone: 079-935054); *Maggiore,* Piazza Sulis 1 (phone: 079-979375). *Cagliari: Autonoleggio Italia,* Via Sonnino 95 (phone: 070-664940); *Avis,* Via Sonnino 89 (phone: 070-668128); *Hertz,* Piazza Matteotti 8 (phone: 070-663457) and at the airport (phone: 070-240037); *Maggiore,* at the airport (phone: 070-240069). *Olbia: Autonoleggio Italia,* at the airport (phone: 0789-69501); *Avis,* at the airport (phone: 0789-22420); *Hertz,* Via Regina Elena 34 (phone: 0789-21274); *Maggiore,* Via Mameli 2 (phone: 0789-22131) and at the airport (phone: 0789-69457). *Porto Torres:*

Avis, Via Mazzini 2 (phone: 079-235547); *Hertz,* Piazza Italia (phone: 079-236261); *Maggiore,* Via Losto 18 (phone: 079-514652).

Train – Connections between the major cities — Olbia, Sassari, Oristano, and Cagliari — are tolerable. It takes about 3½ hours to travel from Cagliari to either Porto Torres in the northwest or Olbia in the northeast. Local trains creep at a snail's pace. In Cagliari, the *Italian State Railways (FS)* station is at Piazza Matteotti (phone: 070-656293).

 SPECIAL EVENTS: Sardinia sometimes resembles Scotland and, like the Scots, the Sards sometimes appear dour and solemn. This does not keep them from celebrating every possible feast day, however, and honoring more than 100 traditional festivals. All are religious/folkloric, involving feasting, pageantry, and general holiday merriment (see *Special Events* in GETTING READY TO GO and *Italy's Most Colorful Festas* in DIVERSIONS). The most important feasts are *Carnevale,* celebrated everywhere just before Lent; *Sa Sartiglia,* in Oristano the Sunday and Tuesday before Ash Wednesday; *Sos Mamuttones,* Shrove Tuesday at Mamoiada near Nuoro; the *Sagra di Sant'Efisio,* May 1–4 in Cagliari; *La Cavalcata,* the next-to-last Sunday in May at Sassari (commemorating the routing of the Moors in the year 1000); *Li Candelieri* (Feast of the Candlesticks), August 14 in Sassari; *Sagra del Redentore,* in Nuoro the last Sunday in August.

 SHOPPING: During the summer, resort hotels allow handicraft representatives to show their wares in the lobbies from time to time. By American standards, the hand-loomed, pure wool bedspreads and carpets, worked in traditional Sardinian motifs whose origins date back to earliest times, appear relatively expensive, but they are well worth the price, given their high quality. Other good buys: jewelry incorporating the local oxblood-colored (and even rarer) coral; the traditional Sardinian engagement ring, the *fede sarda,* in gold or silver filigree; shawls in black wool or silk, hand-embroidered in pastel hues and real gold; and pure white Sardinian pottery, worked into lacy patterns.

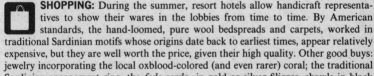 **SPORTS: Boating** – Boats — with or without diving equipment or crews for fishing or cruising — can be rented at the *Marinasarda* at Porto Cervo on the Costa Smeralda (phone: 0789-92475).

Fishing – Spearfishing — with or without air tanks — is popular but severely controlled by the authorities. Serious scuba and deep-sea divers should check with hotel officials about restrictions as well as available emergency care. All scuba divers, however experienced, should use balloon markers, as boaters like to creep into sea-level grottoes.

Golf – Sardinia has two 18-hole golf courses — at the Costa Smeralda in the northeast and near Cagliari in the south. The *Pevero Golf Club* (see also *Great Italian Golf* in DIVERSIONS), designed by Robert Trent Jones, is near the Cala di Volpe resort hotel. The course is open year-round; clubs and carts can be rented (Porto Cervo 07020, Sardinia; phone: 0789-96210). Near Cagliari is the *Is Molas Golf Club.* For information, contact *Is Molas Golf Hotel,* 09010 Santa Margherita di Pula, Cagliari (phone: 070-9209447).

Hunting – The highlands of the Barbagia are popular with hunters. For information, apply to *Board of Sardinian Regional Directors,* 69 Viale Trento, 09100 Cagliari.

Swimming – The water is very warm in the south, cooler but still pleasant in the north in midsummer. Everywhere away from big cities it is sparklingly clear and unpolluted. Many first-class hotels on the coast offer a full panoply of beach life, including windsurfing rentals and lessons, swimming pool for days of rough seas, tennis and *bocce* courts, water skiing, and scuba diving. Instruction is available. Water skiing within 500 meters of the coast is outlawed.

Tennis – Many resort hotels have courts. In particular, the *Baia di Conte* outside

Alghero runs camps for adults and children from June to September. For information, contact *Baia di Conte,* Alghero (phone: 079-952003, 079-951109).

TOURING SARDINIA

Vacationers can view Sardinia from either a rented car or a beach chair. During torrid late July and early August the latter is wiser. Stake out a beach and on the coolest days take short day trips. Few areas are better suited than Sardinia to a beach-centered vacation. Its rocky inlets are ideal for snorkeling. They alternate with secluded coves or, as at Stintino and Alghero, with mile-long stretches of sandy beaches. The very nicest beaches are often the private oases of hotels. Even hotels in the moderate price range may face their own uncrowded beaches.

In resort areas in high season — usually mid-June to mid-September — reservations are a must. During this time expect to pay $75 or more for a double room with bath in hotels listed as expensive; $45 to $75 in those listed as moderate; and under $45 in those listed as inexpensive. This includes Continental breakfast, service charge, and taxes. A meal for two, including service and taxes and sometimes beverage, will cost $40 or more in an expensive restaurant, $20 to $40 in a moderate one, and under $20 in an inexpensive one.

This driving tour of the island begins at Sardinia's prettiest town, Alghero, which has its own airport and is also a one-hour drive from Porto Torres, served by ferry boats to the mainland. From Alghero, the route goes to Sassari, then to tiny medieval Castelsardo. It dips inland through cork oak groves by Tempio Pausania, to rejoin the coast beginning at Palau, which faces the isle of La Maddalena with its necklace of islets. Proceeding to the swanky Costa Smeralda and its neighboring Golfo Aranci, it heads south down the coast past Olbia, another air and sea port, then turns inland to Nuoro in the mountainous Sardinian heartland. Here begins the Barbagia, a wooded highland of dramatic scenery, prehistoric monuments on a heath, cork oaks, and shepherds' villages where folk costumes are still everyday wear for many. Safe but winding, the slow roads twist through the interesting Gennargentu mountain hamlets before straightening out onto a plain where 600 tiny native ponies run free. Next comes Barumini, the island's largest ancient Nuraghesi castle-fortress. The Barumini road links with SS131, leading to the capital, Cagliari, founded on the Costa del Sud by Phoenicians and surrounded by breathtaking beaches. The northern return drive is on SS131 to Oristano and then on SS292 back to Alghero, taking in Tharros and Bosa.

ALGHERO: This town of 48,000 on the "Riviera of Coral" is coastal Sardinia at its loveliest. The great ramparts by the sea were begun by the Genoese and completed by the Spanish. Distrusting the hostile locals, the Spanish grandees shipped them inland and replaced them with Catalans. The Spanish flavor of the town is still so pronounced that it is sometimes called *Barcelonetta* (little Barcelona). Streets are *calles,* signs designate monuments in Spanish and Italian, and many of the natives, especially the older ones, still speak Catalan. The cloister of San Francesco, where Charles V of Spain once stayed, hosts a summer music festival. The remaining coral beds lie extremely deep in the ocean, so much of the coral seen in Alghero's goldsmith shops today is imported — although still imaginatively set in jewelry. Alghero has its own long sandy beach, but excellent and less crowded stretches are at Porto Conte and around Capo Caccia, with its dramatic cliffs and eerie grotto, about 11 miles away.

 CHECKING IN: *Villa Las Tronas* – On a promontory overlooking the sea, with its own fine restaurant, this was once a summer residence of the Italian royal family. Only 31 rooms — book ahead. Number 31 is tops. Hotel open year-round; restaurant closed Wednesdays and mid-September to mid-May. (Lungomare Valencia 1, Alghero; phone: 079-975390; expensive.)

Baia di Conte – For a beach vacation, this large hotel complex on a bay 8 miles northwest of Alghero offers 2 pools, horseback riding, disco dancing, and other amenities. Open April to October. (Porto Conte; phone: 079-952003, 079-951190; moderate.)

Calabona – On the seashore road to Bosa on the outskirts of town, it contains 113 rooms, a restaurant, pool, gym, and sauna. Open April to October. (Calabona; phone: 079-975728; moderate.)

EATING OUT: *Dieci Metri* – Fish is a must — fish ravioli, seafood *risotto,* grilled fresh catch from local waters — in this popular former inn. A bit noisy. Closed Mondays and January and February. (Vicolo Adami 37, Alghero; phone: 079-979023; moderate.)

La Fattoria – Good for Sardinian specialties, as well as grilled meat and fish. Closed Mondays from November to spring. (Via Olmeda, near Carboneddu; phone: 079-951165; moderate.)

La Lepanto – A terrace on the ramparts helps make this Alghero's favorite dining spot. Its full seafood menu ranges from humble anchovies to prized local lobster, including lobster in spaghetti sauce. Closed Wednesdays during winter. (Via Carlo Alberto 135, Alghero; phone: 079-979023; moderate.)

Il Pavone – Noted for seafood, spaghetti with rock lobster, and fine local Torbato wine. Open year-round; closed Wednesdays. (Piazza Sulis 3/4, Alghero; phone: 079-979584; moderate.)

Excursion from Alghero – *Neptune's Grotto,* a cave at water's edge with deep caverns and two lakes within, can be reached either by excursion boat from Alghero (3 hours round trip) or by car. The advantage of driving is the beauty of the views en route to *Capo Caccia* (*Hunter's Cape*). The disadvantage is the 670-step climb down to the grotto and then back up. Wear a sun hat. Open 9 AM to noon and 3 to 5 PM. Admission fee.

SASSARI: SS291 from Alghero ends up in Sardinia's second largest city (with 100,000 inhabitants), founded during medieval times when invaders drove the populace inland from Porto Torres. The ritual evening promenade focuses on Piazza Cavallino. The *Sanna Archaeological and Ethnographic Museum* at 64 Via Roma contains rare Sardinian artifacts, including some from the Bronze Age Anghelu Ruju tombs near Alghero, plus costumes richly adorned with gold filigree, and a collection of Renaissance paintings. Craftwork is on sale in a hall in the *Giardino Pubblico* (*Public Gardens*) with a good selection of cork, inlaid wood objects, baskets, and ceramics.

EATING OUT: *Tre Stelle* – A good modern restaurant, with good fish soup, oven-baked fish marinated in Vernaccia, and Alghero and Gallura wines. Closed Sundays and August 10–30. (Via Porcellana 6, Sassari; phone: 079-232431; moderate.)

Excursion from Sassari – The fishermen's cottages of the summer resort town of Stintino, facing the prison isle of Asinara, have a wind-swept look. The town is northwest of Sassari, on the tip of a long promontory, the Capo del Falcone, with a miles-long sand beach, the Spiaggia di Pelosa.

En Route from Sassari – Take SS200 to the charming old fort town of Castelsardo on the sea. Its 16th-century cathedral has traces of the original Gothic church. Turn inland on SS134, then onto SS127, passing cork oak groves and ancient *nuraghi.* At Tempio Pausania, an old Roman town famed for its wine, swing north on SS133 toward Palau and the island of La Maddalena. From Castelsardo the distance is just under 85 miles.

LA MADDALENA: The isles of Maddalena and, beyond, Caprera, part of an archipelago that shelters a US nuclear submarine base, are reached by ferry from Palau, a 20-minute trip with sometimes a long wait at peak season. The young Napoleon suffered the first defeat of his military career here after islanders withstood a three-day siege launched from Corsica. Caprera, where Giuseppe Garibaldi is buried, is connected to La Maddalena by causeway. The museum in Garibaldi's home is open daily, except Mondays, 9 AM to 1:30 PM and Sundays 9 AM to 12:30 PM.

 EATING OUT: *La Grotta* – Simple but delicious island fare: grilled fresh fish and spaghetti. Closed Sundays and October. (Via Principe di Napoli 1, La Maddalena; phone: 0789-737228; inexpensive.)

COSTA SMERALDA: Drive south from Palau on SS125 to the Emerald Coast, a stretch of yacht basins, adjacent shopping plazas and cafés, and secluded private homes and beach hotels. This 30-year-old, grandiose, 33-mile resort development is popular with the boating set; indeed the best show in town is at the Porto Cervo Marina, crammed buoy-to-buoy with million-dollar yachts. Before all that, nature lavished its best energies on the heavenly bays, overlooked by hills full of olive trees. As in all Sardinia, the brilliant light plays tricks with the water, making it appear dappled green and turquoise. The salt wind has carved giant boulders into eerie shapes. The Costa Smeralda's pink stucco heart is at Porto Cervo, a bayside town 45 minutes by car from both La Maddalena and Olbia. The café at its Piazzetta is the place to rubberneck. The surrounding mall's boutiques sell the world's priciest labels. The Pevero Golf Club is a 10-minute drive from Porto Cervo.

 CHECKING IN: Fuller information on the following development consortium–owned hotels is available by writing to the hotels by name, Porto Cervo 07020, Sardinia. All are opulent and expensive, and many require guests to pay for full board during high season. (Also see *Beaches* in DIVERSIONS.)

Cala di Volpe – Moorish-style cluster of white towers whose 125 rooms are furnished with antique reproductions and Sardinian crafts. Olympic-size saltwater pool and a boat that ferries guests to a very private beach. Succulent array of foods in a very elegant dining room. Open May to October. (Phone: 0789-96083.)

Pitrizza – Consisting of a handful of 4- to 6-room villas, each with a terrace or garden overlooking the rock-hewn pool. Private beach, terrace, and fine restaurant set on the beautiful Liscia di Vacca Bay. Clubhouse with piano bar. (Phone: 0789-92000.)

Cervo – Near the Piazzetta, with garden, pool, 95 rooms, and shuttle boat to a private beach. Its restaurant overlooks the Old Harbor. Cozy piano bar is a favorite meeting place. *Cervo Tennis Club* and *Pevero Golf Club* are nearby. Open March to October. (Phone: 0789-92003.)

Romazzino – For the sporty crowd and families, a large bougainvillea-festooned, Mediterranean-style hotel. Outdoor pizza oven, boats for hire, tennis, windsurfing, and dancing. Special events arranged for children. (Phone: 0789-96020.)

 EATING OUT: *Il Pescatore* – In the Old Port, just across the little wooden bridge from the Piazzetta. Try seafood delicacies such as *spigola al finocchietto* (fish grilled with fennel), grilled prawns, or *spaghetti alla bottarga* (with mullet roe). For a fine view of the port, reserve a table beside the water. Open evenings May to October. (Porto Cervo; phone: 0789-92296; expensive.)

Il Pomodoro – A chic *pizzeria-ristorante* just behind the *Hotel Cervo.* Excellent antipasto and mouth-watering pizzas in an attractive rustic setting indoors or outside under a grape arbor. Open all year. (Porto Cervo; phone: 0789-92207; expensive to moderate.)

La Fattoria – Rustic, with a huge indoor fireplace and outdoor dining under an olive tree. Typical Sardinian foods, including grilled lamb and sausage. Open March to late October. Closed Mondays. (Porto Cervo; phone: 0789-92214; moderate.)

 NIGHTCLUBS AND NIGHTLIFE: *Sotto Vento Club* – Disco spot, with restaurant and piano bar. (Porto Cervo, on the road to the *Cala di Volpe* hotel; phone: 0789-92443.)

Ritual Club – Same offerings as *Sotto Vento.* (Near the town of Baia Sardinia; phone: 0789-99032.)

PORTO ROTONDO: Nine miles from Porto Cervo, this yacht basin surrounded by sumptuous private summer houses is Sardinia's answer to fashionable American summer beach towns — and more exclusive than its neighbors.

CHECKING IN/EATING OUT: *Sporting Club* – A member of the Relais et Châteaux group, this deceptively simple retreat, which sprawls on a spit of land overlooking a magnificent bay, caters to the international yachting set. All 28 rooms have sea views. The restaurant, *Dell'Hotel Sporting,* is noted for grilled fresh fish, fine wines, and a very special evening buffet. Open mid-April to September. (Porto Rotondo; phone: 0789-34005; expensive.)

En Route from Porto Rotondo – The drive south toward Cagliari on SS125 (214 miles) via Olbia takes 5 hours without detours for sightseeing. But 35 miles after Orosei, at the village of Posada, amidst orange groves, for those desiring to visit the Barbagia, is the *Fava Castle.* Here the road cuts inland on a beautifully engineered new highway, SS131, to Nuoro (just under 30 miles), the first lap on an excursion through the wild, mountainous heart of Sardinia. It was named by Roman soldiers, who dubbed it "the place of the barbarians."

NUORO: Residents of this homey little town where Grazia Deledda was born, at the foot of rugged Monte Ortobene, consider themselves standard-bearers of the real Sardinia, and so they are. What that is can be seen in the *Museum of Sardinian Life and Traditions.* Open 9:30 AM to 1 PM; closed Mondays. (56 Via Mereu.)

CHECKING IN/EATING OUT: *Fratelli Sacchi* – This country inn 5 miles east of Nuoro offers spotless rooms and a garden; its restaurant serves genuine Sardinian hill country fare, such as trout *alla Vernaccia.* (Mount Ortobene, Nuoro; phone: 0784-31200; moderate.)

En Route from Nuoro – A good map and good weather are a must for this crossing of the Barbagia. From Nuoro, take SS389 through the hamlet of Mamoiada to Sardinia's highest village, Fonni (3,250 ft), on Monte Spada. Depending on your temperament, either continue on the main road, SS389D, or take the mountain road short cut to visit Desulo, a shepherd's village noted for its weavers, where men wear a distinctive wool jacket, the *orbace.* Pay careful attention to signs: Travelers skipping Desulo will turn right onto SS128 about 5 miles after Tiana; those visiting Desulo will continue past the village and turn right on the main road to Tonara; after 1.4 miles, turn left onto SS128. The next stop for either route is Sorgono, another typical craftwork village. From Sorgono drive through Laconi to tiny Nuralla, on a road traced during prehistoric times — count the roadside *nuraghi.* Turn right onto SS197 to cross the Campidano Plain through the Giara di Gesturi, the plateau where the tiny native ponies still range. They are not wild but are branded and belong to villagers.

BARUMINI: A haven for history buffs, Nuraghe Su Nuraxi is the largest of the *nuraghi* yet excavated. Its huge central tower dates from 1100 BC. Bronze Age excavations of a village are nearby. Open all day.

En Route from Barumini – The remaining 37 miles to Cagliari are an easy drive on SS197 and, bearing left just after Sanluri, on the broader SS131.

CAGLIARI: Founded by the Phoenicians, the Sardinian capital (population 250,000) is the main port-of-entry for Sardinia by both sea and air. Its hilltop old quarter, *Il Castello,* around the medieval castle, offers a spectacular view of the *Golfo degli Angeli* (*Gulf of the Angels*) and the outlying salt marshes. The quarter itself is an architectural and historical patchwork of ruins, including a Roman amphitheater (in which operas are performed in August), Pisan watchtowers, and Spanish townhouses with wrought-iron balconies. An old Spanish fort, the Belvedere, is now a park. The duomo, originally built in the 13th century, has become a mélange of styles, including a neo-Pisan façade, a fine Romanesque pulpit, a Gothic transept and apse, and a Baroque crypt.

The antiquities collection at the *National Archaeological Museum* includes hundreds of rare bronze miniatures showing Nuraghesi life 2,500 years ago. The tiny shepherds wear cloaks and caps similar to those in use today. Open Tuesdays through Saturdays 9 AM to 2 PM and Sundays 9 AM to 1 PM; closed Mondays. At the nearby Piazza Arsenale, modern museum rooms have been tucked into the ancient fortress walls, the windows of which overlook the Poetto Beach and salt marshes.

Cagliari's beaches have calmer and warmer water than those in the north. On the road hugging the coast toward Villa Simius are resort hotels suitable for family vacations.

CHECKING IN: *Cormoran* – The best beach in the vicinity is at the *Cormoran,* a 45-minute drive southeast of Cagliari, just past Capo Boi. Windsurfing, swimming pool, tennis courts, good food, and a view of the romantic islet, Isola dei Cavoli. (Capo Boi; phone: 070-791401; moderate.)

***Mediterraneo* –** A garden setting and a view of the bay make this large comfortable hotel near the air terminal and train station a good choice. Restaurant (closed Sunday evenings through Mondays). (Lungomare Cristoforo Colombo 46, Cagliari; phone: 070-301271; moderate.)

***Panorama* –** A modern hotel, with 97 air-conditioned rooms, swimming pool, conference rooms, and penthouse restaurant (closed Sunday evenings through Mondays). Near the city's sports complex. (Viale Armando Diaz 231, Cagliari; phone: 070-307691; moderate.)

EATING OUT: *Dal Corsaro* – A menu featuring spaghetti with rock lobster, crêpes stuffed with mussels, and other fine seafood dishes makes this a local and tourist favorite. Closed Tuesdays. (Viale Regina Margherita 28, Cagliari; phone: 070-664318; expensive to moderate.)

***Dal Corsaro al Poetto* –** From June through September the management of *Dal Corsaro* also runs this open-air seaside restaurant. About 3½ miles from downtown Cagliari, near the salt marshes where flamingos visit in the spring and autumn. (Viale Poetto, Marina Piccola, Poetto Beach; phone: 070-370295; expensive to moderate.)

***St. Remy* –** A very atmospheric restaurant with the vaulted ceilings and exposed stone walls of a 15th-century building: It was originally a pharmacy run by a friar's order. Tiny fried fish (*seadas*) for appetizers and the cheese-stuffed veal (*fagottini St. Remy*) are special. Good Sardinian desserts and wines. Closed Saturdays at lunchtime and Sundays. (Via Torino 16, Cagliari; phone: 070-657377; expensive to moderate.)

Excursion from Cagliari – Head due south on SS195 for 18 miles; bear left onto the side road to Nora, Sardinia's oldest city. Founded by Carthaginians and subsequently ruled by the Romans, ancient Nora is survived by its well-preserved amphitheater, baths, temples, and stunning mosaic floors. Consider combining this visit with a swim at an adjacent beach. The ruins are open daily, 9 AM to 8 PM. The admission ticket includes museum entry.

EATING OUT: *Sa Cardiga e su Schirone* – Before heading back to Cagliari, stop here for the *aragosta* (lobster), *gamberoni* (prawns), or *zuppa di pesce* (fish soup). Large selection of Sardinian wines. Piano bar and terrace overlooking the beach. Closed Mondays. (On the Pula road at the Capoterra intersection; phone: 070-71652; moderate.)

En Route from Cagliari – The 55-mile trip from Cagliari to Oristano on SS131 is very fast, about an hour, unless detouring to make a side trip to visit the "painted" villages of San Sperate or Serramanna (exit south at Monastir, just northeast of Cagliari). In these villages the art of mural painting is practiced on many outside walls. Techniques and themes, as well as degree of talent, may vary considerably from wall to wall and town to town, but this homespun art form can be quite interesting, especially when it expresses passionate religious feelings and political protests. The rest of the drive runs through the Campidano plain. Serious equestrians might make a detour to Arborea, where there is a hotel-equitation complex that specializes in expert instruction. (See *Horsing Around, Italian Style* in DIVERSIONS.)

ORISTANO: With a population of only 27,000, this is the smallest and newest of Sardinian provincial capitals. Its peaceful and serene aura belies the fact that it is the largest farming center on the island and a thriving commercial and industrial center and port. It was founded during the Middle Ages by the refugees of ancient Tharros, who fled when the Saracens sacked and destroyed their city. Oristano gave birth to Sardinia's 14th-century Joan of Arc, Princess Eleonora d'Arborea. Defying Spain, she ruled over this cathedral town and drafted a law code which became the basis for the island's laws. A small collection of archaeological artifacts is in the *Antiquarium Arborease.* Nearby is the Pisan Gothic Church of Santa Giusta.

 EATING OUT: *Il Faro* – Near Oristano's central market, with an excellent seafood menu. It has real cork on the walls and souvenir ceramic plates. Closed Sundays and July 1–16. (Via Bellini 25, Oristano; phone: 0783-70002; expensive to moderate.)

Da Giovanni – Near the lighthouse in the seaside resort of Marina di Torregrande, midway between Tharros and Oristano. Plain surroundings, but good fish soup and ravioli stuffed with lobster. Closed Mondays. (Via Colombo 8, Marina di Torregrande; phone: 0783-22051; moderate.)

THARROS: A Phoenician port founded in 800 BC, its remains — plus later Roman temples — can be seen at water's edge partly submerged on the southern tip of the Sinis Peninsula, 12.4 miles from Oristano. Today's archaeologists consider Tharros one of Sardinia's most fascinating sites. Also on the peninsula are a 15th-century Spanish tower and the remains of a Jewish temple. Nearby beaches are excellent.

En Route from Tharros or Oristano – Take the coastal road, SS292, through Bosa back to Alghero, a distance of about 70 winding miles. There are pleasant green valleys, picturesque towns, and smashing sea views along the way. The area is known for its cheeses, woolens, lace, figs, artichokes, and Malvasia wine.

Campania and the Amalfi Coast

Campania has long lured visitors with its spectacular natural scenery. It has two picturesque gulfs, or bays (the Bay of Naples and the Gulf of Salerno), enclosed by picturesque promontories, including the Sorrento Peninsula. It has a massive volcano (Vesuvius) as well as many more benign, forest-covered mountains that plunge into the Tyrrhenian Sea. There are 220 miles of coastline and several romantic islands (Capri, Ischia, and Procida). The natural endowments alone are sufficient reason to tour the region, but add to this plenitude one of the greatest concentrations of archaeological excavations in the world — Pompeii, Herculaneum, Paestum, and more — unforgettable towns of mythological and historical importance such as Sorrento, Positano, Amalfi, and Ravello (not to mention Naples), and, finally, the people themselves, who have cheered the world with their music and cuisine, and the region becomes a journey of compelling interest.

The Greeks came to Campania as early as the eleventh century BC, setting up colonies in Cumae and Pithecusae (present-day Ischia). The arts flourished, towns such as Paestum, with its impressive temples, were built, and olive trees and vineyards were introduced to local agriculture. The Romans gained the upper hand by 326 BC and forced the Greeks into an alliance that eventually became entirely to the Roman advantage. Under the emperors, Campania became a playground for the wealthy, who built villas along the coast for the same reason people do today. They liked the temperate climate, the dramatic scenery, and the proximity to the sea.

A period of Byzantine influence followed the disintegration of the Roman Empire, but the Byzantines always had to contend with rebellious tribes, outside invaders (most prominently the Lombards, who established themselves in the interior but also managed to take Salerno), and city-states with independent ambitions (Naples achieved autonomy by 763, and in 786 Amalfi did the same). By the following century, there were incursions of Saracen mercenaries. Often invited in by warring duchies, these Moslems from Sicily brought with them an Arabic influence that is still seen in Campanian architecture. During the eleventh century the Normans came. Thereafter, the south of Italy, including Campania, was dominated by a succession of French, Austrian, and Spanish kings and cross-fertilized with cultural influences from the north of Europe to the Mediterranean, from Vienna to Madrid, until it was annexed to the Kingdom of Italy in 1860.

Today Campania attracts visitors from even more diverse origins. But they arrive as tourists, not conquerors, and they come to admire the region's artistic heritage, not to carry it away. Dominated by the cities of Naples and

Salerno, the area consists primarily of three sections, each with a splendor of its own. There's the Bay of Naples in the north, a volcanic area with steaming natural hot springs first used by the ancient Romans as thermal spas. Vesuvius, still active, stands poised midway along the bay between Naples and Sorrento. The eruptions that buried Pompeii and Herculaneum in AD 79 have not occurred with force since 1944, but its twin peaks still periodically emit trails of smoke.

The three romantic islands off the coast of Naples are natural extensions of the tormented geophysical constitution of the mainland and they, too, attract the maximum number of visitors, especially the international resort of Capri, and Ischia, celebrated for its hot baths. Ischia and Procida share the same genes as the Phlegrean Fields — the crater-filled, sulfurous area west of Naples that the ancients believed was the gateway to the underworld.

The third section of Campania that draws visitors is the Amalfi Coast, which stretches from Sorrento to Salerno, along the Gulf of Salerno side of the Sorrento Peninsula. Although portions of it have been exploited over the years, much of it remains a prototype for paradise — sun-warmed rocks and terraced gardens, lemon and olive groves overlooking sparkling blue bays and coves, flowered promontories and secret beaches. In *The Immoralist,* André Gide says that the road from Sorrento to Ravello "was so beautiful that I had no desire . . . to see anything more beautiful on earth."

Famous resorts, geographical splendors, and historical sites do not exhaust the attractions of Campania. Although not as well known and not as chic as the Amalfi Coast, the Cilento Coast farther south — from Agropoli to Santa Maria di Castellabate, then south to Palinuro and Sapri — is less expensive, less crowded, and utterly charming. There are coves and beaches waiting to be discovered and transformed into this decade's Positano.

Inland, much of the countryside is mountainous and wild — and snow-covered for six months of the year. Near Matese, at Bocca della Selva, is a winter sports center with ski facilities. In summer, clear streams offer fishing, and deep woods beckon hikers. Laceno also has ski facilities.

Pompeii, Herculaneum, and Paestum are internationally renowned, but there are also important archaeological sites at Velia, Santa Maria Capua Vetere, and Benevento. While Ischia may be more celebrated for its hot baths, Campania has over 6,000 thermal springs, and there are spas at Castellammare di Stabia, Agnano, Montesano, and Telese.

The simple, wholesome cuisine of Campania emphasizes fresh local products, from the fields and the sea. Clams (*vongole*) are used with pasta and rice and in seafood soups and salads. Mozzarella cheese, produced from the buffaloes that graze in the region, is a staple. It is served *in carrozza* (batter-fried), as a topping on pizza, and with eggplant, which is sometimes used in a pasta sauce. But first and foremost, it is served in *insalata caprese,* a salad of sliced mozzarella and tomatoes garnished with basil. Squid and shrimp are delicious whether cooked in batter, served in seafood salads, or used in pasta sauces. The local meat and fish are best grilled over charcoal and lightly seasoned with lemon and salt. For dessert, there are typical pastries, nougats, and traditional Christmas and Easter sweets such as *zeppole, taralli,* and *struffoli.*

The best-known wines come from the slopes of Mount Vesuvius: white or red Lacryma Christi. The vineyards at Pozzuoli and Cumae yield Falerno. Good wines also include Greco di Tufo, Taurasi, Ravello, and Barbera di Castel San Lorenzo. The well-known and potent Strega (witch) liqueur is made in Benevento.

The tourist season at the major resorts of Campania runs from Easter until the end of October. July and August, since they are both warm and dry, are the most popular months. Consequently, they are also the most crowded, and beaches and hotels, not to mention the roads, are apt to be full. Make reservations well in advance for high season, and be prepared for long waits and heavy traffic even on the A3 autostrada, where bottlenecks tend to form at toll booths and exits. One solution is to avoid traveling on weekends, especially Sundays, and to try to move from town to town between 2 PM and 4 PM, when most Italians are eating or taking a siesta. Better yet, schedule a visit for May or early June, or September or early October, when the weather is warm and the hotels are open, but the crowds are much smaller.

Off-season visits offer splendid solitude, rare silence, and unobstructed views, but not a Caribbean or Florida climate. Capri and the Amalfi Coast can be quite cold in winter, even on sunny days. The average temperature at that time of year is 50°F — hardly swimming weather. And at night and on rainy days — lamentably frequent in winter — it is much colder. Be aware, too, that many hotels and restaurants are inadequately heated. During a winter vacation visit, come prepared with warm clothing and an umbrella, and don't bother bringing a bathing suit.

During high season, classical plays are performed in the ruins in Pompeii. There are Wagnerian concerts in the gardens of the Villa Rufolo in Ravello, film festivals in Sorrento and Salerno, and carnivals in Minori and Maiori on the Amalfi Coast. In fact, every feast day and holiday in the region is likely to take on the trappings of a carnival.

Our tour heads south from Naples and swings along the curve of the bay through Herculaneum and Pompeii. It turns almost directly west to Sorrento, then crosses the tip of the Sorrento Peninsula to the Amalfi Coast, driving eastward through Positano, Amalfi, Ravello, Maiori, and Vietri sul Mare. At Salerno, it heads south again to Paestum. Although not much more than ninety miles in length, the route passes through towns, historical sites, and resorts that are often crowded and are connected by narrow, tortuous roads. The region is also rich in attractions that cannot be sampled in a short time. So set aside a minimum of three days, preferably much longer.

In our accommodations listings, expensive means $70 and up for a double room, although there are super-luxurious hotels, such as the celebrated *San Pietro* in Positano, where rooms can run $200 a night for two, even off-season; moderate means from $30 to $60 double; and inexpensive means $25 or less. In the restaurant listings, a full dinner (not just pasta and salad) for two will come to more than $40 in the expensive category; a moderate meal for two will cost $25 to $35; and an inexpensive one, $20 or less. These prices include service and house wine, but not expensive bottled vintages or aperitifs or after-dinner drinks. Note that at the height of the season it is not uncommon for hotels at seaside resorts to require that a minimum of breakfast and one other meal per day be taken in house, and some may impose a minimum stay.

NAPLES: For a detailed report on the city, its sights, hotels, and restaurants, see *Naples,* THE CITIES.

En Route from Naples – Take the autostrada (A3) toward Salerno (avoid the cluttered and confusing coast road) and get off at the Ercolano exit, about 4½ miles from Naples.

HERCULANEUM: Although only about a quarter the size of Pompeii, Herculaneum (*Ercolano* in Italian) is an eminently important archaeological site; in fact, many visitors find it more interesting than Pompeii. Both cities were destroyed by the same volcanic eruption of Mount Vesuvius on August 24, AD 79, but while Pompeii was smothered by live cinders and ash, Herculaneum was inundated by something akin to a massive mud slide (technically, a pyroclastic flow of superheated gases and rock debris), in some places over 60 feet deep. The "mud" hardened, making excavation difficult. (The earliest diggers, in 1709, more interested in plunder than in history, simply burrowed tunnels and hauled out the loot.) But the volcanic blanket also preserved the houses, many of which were partly constructed of wood. Unlike Pompeii, where the wood went up in flames, the beams, staircases, doors, window frames, and even some furnishings of Herculaneum's houses are intact, and they give a far better idea of what daily life was like in that era than do the more fragmentary ruins in Pompeii. Furthermore, Herculaneum has a wider range of structures and building styles, from the elaborate villas of the patrician classes that stood on the edge of town with clear sea views (the bay is farther away now), to shops, multilevel apartment buildings, municipal baths, and a *palestra* (sports arena).

Many books have been written about Herculaneum, and scholars have spent years digging — some, quite literally — to gain a better understanding of the place, so it is foolish to claim that it can be seen in a few hours. But for those on a tight schedule, or with only a passing interest in antiquities, at least the high points can be touched. Don't miss the Terme (baths), built during the reign of Augustus and notable for the degree of practical planning they display as well as for their excellent state of preservation. Also be sure to see the Casa dell'Atrio a Mosaico (House with the Mosaic Atrium), where the black and white mosaic floor is wavy from the weight of the mud; the Casa a Graticcio (Wooden Trellis House), the only extant example of an ancient type of cost-cutting construction; the Casa del Tramezzo di Legno (House with the Wooden Partition), where the partition in question is carbonized; the Casa Sannitica (House of the Samnites), with an atrium surrounded by Ionic columns; the Casa del Mosaico di Nettuno e Anfitrite (House with the Neptune and Amphitrite Mosaic), which, in addition to its beautiful blue mosaics, offers an excellent example of a commercial establishment; and the Casa del Bicentenario (House of the Bicentenary), at first a patrician villa and subsequently transformed into a multifamily dwelling — in a room upstairs is a small cross and altar, evidence that a Christian lived here and that the cross was already a symbol of Christianity in the 1st century AD. Another interesting house is the Casa dei Cervi (House of the Stags), with its red and black frescoes and its sculpture of stags attacked by dogs.

Note that only the most important buildings in Herculaneum are open all the time; others are locked, but a guard stationed in the vicinity will gladly open them if tipped (each guard is responsible for 10 or so houses). Alternatively, be alert for any small group forming in front of a doorway because it means it's about to open. Note that one very important building in Herculaneum is never open to the public — or to anyone. This is the Villa dei Papiri (so called because of papyrus scrolls found there), a grandiose private house that was excavated in the mid-18th century and then sealed off when toxic gases made further work impossible. The famous bronze statues of water carriers (or dancers) in the National Archaeological Museum in Naples are part of the booty carried out of it, however, and the J. Paul Getty Museum at Malibu, California, is a reconstruction of it, based on plans made by Karl Weber, a Swiss engineer who participated in the 18th-century excavations. Herculaneum can be visited from 9 AM until an hour before sunset; it's closed Mondays and holidays, and there is an admission fee.

En Route from Herculaneum – To inspect the cause of all the destruction in Herculaneum up close, return to A3 and drive south to the Torre Annunziata turnoff. The brooding shape of Vesuvio (Mount Vesuvius) can be seen at a distance from almost anywhere in the vicinity of Naples, but it's also possible to climb or take a *seggiovia* (chair lift) to the summit. The volcano's name derives from two words meaning "the unextinguished," and Vesuvius is indeed a live one, the only active volcano in continental Europe (Mount Etna, also active, is on the island of Sicily). Vesuvius last erupted in 1944 and has given a few smoky belches and rumbles since then. All this adds a slight shiver of excitement — other shivers come from the cooler air at the 4,189-foot summit — as one skims along in the chair lift, passing vineyards that produce Lacryma Christi wine and then sailing up the steeper slopes of bare, windswept soil to the top. (Spartacus, the rebellious slave, is supposed to have hidden in the crater, but that was a century before its first eruption.) The views — either of sea and coast and countryside or down into the smoldering cone — are well worth the trip. The chair lift operates daily year-round except November, from 10 AM to 3, 4, or 5 PM depending on the season. More detailed information on Mount Vesuvius is given in *Naples,* THE CITIES.

Return to A3 and continue south a short distance to the Pompeii exit. Along the road, there are huge black volcanic rock formations, umbrella pines, and orange and lemon groves on the terraced hillsides. It doesn't take a large leap of the imagination to realize why the ancient Romans, and before them the Greeks, built villas and resort towns along the bay. The land is fertile, the light golden, the sea a deep blue, and the terrain spectacular as it buckles and breaks up into mountains just beyond the coast. But today, much of this stretch of shoreline between Naples and Castellammare di Stabia is dreary — overrun with traffic and overbuilt with tacky apartment houses, gas stations, discount stores, and snack bars, among which an occasional august old villa may still stand like a sad relative fallen on hard times.

POMPEII: Like Herculaneum, Pompeii is an archaeological treasure trove, an immense one; entire lives have been spent studying it or uncovering it, yet one-third of the town still remains to be excavated. It is possible to touch the high spots in a single visit, though a few words of advice can be valuable. In summer, especially on Sundays, tour buses and cars often stand idling from the A3 exit all the way to the parking lots around the ruins. So avoid visiting on Sundays and holidays, and try to arrive early on any day, between 9 and 10 AM, before the heaviest influx of sightseers. In addition, be prepared for the seedy modern town of Pompeii; it's not unusual for the immediate environs of the ruins — and sometimes even the site itself — to be swarming with hotel touts, dubious tour guides, and con men of all sorts. It's also wise to hold on to your camera and purse. While it's unlikely anyone will do more than importune you for a tip or try to hustle you off to his brother's shop, don't take chances. If you want a guide, hire one at the gate at the prescribed rate.

Before Vesuvius erupted, Pompeii was a thriving commercial and political center with 25,000 inhabitants. Originally a seaport — the eruption raised the land and left the ruined town far from the bay — it bustled with trade; witness the ruts ground into the cobblestone streets by passing chariots. On that fateful day in August, AD 79, Pliny the Younger watched the catastrophe from Cape Miseno, and in a letter known to generations of students laboring at their Latin lessons, he described the chaos, the rain of ashes and cinders, and the inhabitants' desperate attempt to escape the suffocating heat and fumes. Two thousand people perished, and the city was buried.

Although the excavation process began, at least in part, as soon as survivors returned to dig out their belongings, Pompeii is said to have been "rediscovered" in the 16th century by Domenico Fontana, an architect rebuilding roads. Systematic excavation didn't begin until the 18th century, and it still goes on, with the current emphasis less on carting artifacts off to museums than on restoring them on the spot. Be sure to see the Basilica, the largest and most important of Pompeii's public buildings, just off the Forum, the religious, civic, and business center of the city. Along the side and at the far end of the Forum are the temple of Apollo (which has a copy of the bronze statue of the god found here and moved to the National Archaeological Museum in Naples) and the temple of Giove, or Jupiter, with its triumphal arches and a view of Vesuvius in the background.

Walk out of the Forum along Via dell'Abbondanza to the Terme Stabiane (Stabian Baths), which are well preserved and contain a *palestra* (sports arena or gym), a swimming pool, and separate sections for men and women. Both the 5,000-seat Teatro Grande and the 1,000-seat Teatro Piccolo (which was covered) are not far from the baths. The Anfiteatro, the oldest Roman amphitheater in existence (ca. 80 BC), with a capacity of 12,000, is some distance away, next to the Grande Palestra, where athletes trained.

Of Pompeii's many interesting private houses, three stand out. The Casa del Menandro, named after a portrait of the Greek poet found there, is a huge villa highly decorated with paintings and mosaics. The Casa dei Vettii (House of the Vettii), which belonged to two rich merchants of the Vettio family, is a meticulously restored, sumptuously decorated villa with fine frescoes in the Fourth, or late, Pompeiian style, characterized by mythological and architectural scenes drawn in dizzying perspective. The Villa dei Misteri (Villa of the Mysteries) might be called an ancient suburban house, since it's actually outside the ruins (but visitable with the same admission ticket). Thought to have belonged to a woman initiate of the Dionysian cult, it contains a famous fresco depicting the initiation of young brides into the cult, painted on a background of Pompeiian red. The fresco (or cycle of frescoes) covers the walls of an entire room, the largest painting to have survived from antiquity.

The Pompeii site is open from 9 AM to 6 PM in summer; in other seasons its closing time seems to depend on the setting sun. There is an admission fee. The 1980 earthquake that devastated vast parts of the interior of Campania did some damage here, and some excavations are still closed.

CHECKING IN: *Villa dei Misteri* – This convenient, inexpensive motel is endowed with ample parking. Much favored by academics and archaeologists, it has a nice garden and a swimming pool for a cool dip after a day baking in the hot ruins. (Villa dei Misteri, Pompeii Scavi; phone: 081-8613593; inexpensive.)

EATING OUT: *Internazionale* – Inside the ruins, near the Forum. A simple place, its main virtue is its convenience for hungry and thirsty tourists. (Via del Foro, Pompeii Scavi; phone: 081-8610777; inexpensive.)

En Route from Pompeii – Returning to A3, drive to the Castellammare di Stabia exit and proceed slowly — there's little choice, given the chaotic traffic and potholed street — through the cluttered and rather ugly center of town. Then take a more scenic road, SS145, that swerves along the northern coast of the Penisola Sorrentina (Sorrento Peninsula) which holds the southern part of the Bay of Naples in its embrace. Suddenly, a traveler has the sensation of flying, of swooping birdlike along the sheer cliffs that drop to the sea. At Vico Equense and elsewhere by the roadside, signs point down to tiny beaches — or to pizza stands that sell their goods by the yard (or by the meter in this case). At every turn in the road there are marvelous views of Naples and Vesuvius.

SORRENTO: This small city of pastel houses, brilliant flowers, and sea-scented air has been the subject of song, story, and legend throughout the centuries. According to Greek mythology, as filtered through the Romans, Surrentum (now Sorrento) was home to the Sirens who sang out to seamen and tricked them into shipwreck against the stony shores. Ulysses was said to have outsmarted the Sirens by plugging his crew's ears with wax and having himself tied to the mast to resist their seductions. Most present-day travelers can whistle a bar or two of *Torna a Surriento* ("Come Back to Sorrento") and quite a few find the town seductive enough to take the words to heart.

The center of town is Piazza Tasso, named after Sorrento's most famous son, Torquato Tasso, the 16th-century author of *Jerusalem Delivered,* an epic poem that is one of the classics of Italian literature. The *Church of San Francesco,* the city's duomo, has a 13th-century cloister with distinctive pointed arches that reflect the Moorish influence. The *Museo di Correale* contains some rare editions of Tasso's work, as well as a small archaeological collection and fine examples of 17th- and 18th-century furniture, mostly Neapolitan. But the principal attraction of the city is its color, beauty, and carnival atmosphere, and its breathtaking setting atop 150-foot-high cliffs with views of the sea. Most beaches are reached by steep zigzag staircases or by elevators. Stop in at the tourist office (AAST) at Via Luigi de Maio 35 (phone: 081-8782104) for further information about the town and its environs. Sorrento is a popular starting point for trips to the islands of Capri and Ischia and tours of the Amalfi Coast. It is also known for its wonderful inlaid woodwork sold in shops on almost every street.

CHECKING IN: *Grand Hotel Excelsior Vittoria* – In 19th-century Belle Époque fashion, this 125-room hotel is full of potted palms and ferns, gilded ceilings, and chandeliers. It's surrounded by manicured gardens and terraces with splendid views, and it has a pool as well as direct access to the sea via elevators. Good service; restaurant; open all year. (Piazza Tasso 34, Sorrento; phone: 081-8781900; expensive.)

Parco dei Principi – Built around an 18th-century villa that belonged to Prince Leopold of Sicily, it, too, has a swimming pool and a private beach. Motorboating and water skiing can be arranged, and many special events, concerts, and receptions take place here. Restaurant; 173 rooms; open all year. (Via Rota 1, Sorrento; phone: 081-8712101; expensive to moderate.)

Imperial Tramontano – In the heart of town, surrounded by gardens. Many of the 104 rooms overlook the bay and a beach. There is a swimming pool and a restaurant. Closed December through March. (Via Vittorio Veneto 1, Sorrento; phone: 081-8781940; moderate.)

President – Set high on a bluff outside Sorrento amid a pine grove overlooking the bay, this 82-room hotel has a swimming pool, gardens, and restaurant. Closed November through March. (Via Nastro Verde Colle Parise, Sorrento; phone: 081-8782262; moderate.)

Loreley – Clean and unpretentious, with an impressive position and a view fully as good as the much more expensive places nearby. It has about two dozen rooms and an excellent restaurant. Closed in winter. (Via Califano 2, Sorrento; phone: 081-8781508; inexpensive.)

La Minerva – Somewhat out of the way, but worth considering because of its lovely location on the sea. With only 50 rooms, this family-style *pensione* has charm and a good restaurant. Closed in winter. (Via Capo 30, Sorrento; phone: 081-8781011; inexpensive.)

EATING OUT: *La Favorita O'Parrucchiano* – On the busiest street in town, offering authentic Campanian cuisine, much of it made with fresh local cheeses, wine, oil, and vegetables produced by the owners, the Maniello family.

The *gnocchi* are especially recommended. The terrace garden is delightful in warm weather. Closed Wednesdays in winter and spring. (Corso Italia 71–73, Sorrento; phone: 081-8781321; moderate.)

La Pentolaccia – A pleasant restaurant in the heart of Old Sorrento, it's renowned for its seafood and Neapolitan background music. Closed Tuesdays. (Via Fuorimura 8, Sorrento; phone: 081-8785077; moderate to inexpensive.)

Mayflower – Just off Corso Italia, this combination bar and restaurant is clean and modern and is managed by cheerful, friendly people who turn out wonderfully good food. The specialty is grilled fish. (Piazza Angelina Lauro 210, Sorrento; phone: 081-8771719; inexpensive.)

En Route from Sorrento – A narrow, twisting road leads around the entire peninsula to Positano. But it is far less nerve-racking to turn back on SS145 toward Naples, drive a few miles to the tiny town of Meta, and then take SS163, which cuts south across mountainous terrain to the Costa Amalfitana (Amalfi Coast) on the other side of the peninsula. From there, SS163 continues on its sinuous course all the way to Salerno. This route, known as the Amalfi Drive, is scarcely a superhighway. In fact, it can be hair-raising and treacherous, especially on weekends, when trucks, buses, and cars jockey for position even on the sharpest turns. But much as the drive may tax nerves and patience, it's a memorable, not-to-be-missed experience. If one picture is worth a thousand words, then one glimpse of the Amalfi Coast must be worth a thousand pictures. Literature, art, and photographs all fail to convey the full measure of its magic — it has to be seen firsthand.

The crumbling Lattari Mountains come plunging down to the Mediterranean, and whitewashed houses cling to the cliffs like barnacles. Most buildings show the full extent of the Saracen influence on the architecture of the area. There are church domes covered with gleaming *maiolica* tiles and barrel-vaulted ceilings to keep houses cool during the sun-dazzled summers. There is also a string of towers left along the coast by the Saracens, some of them now renovated and transformed into hotels, bars, and private homes. In many places the mountains have been terraced and planted with olive trees and citrus groves, carefully protected against hail by tentlike canopies of loose-woven mesh. At the foot of the mountains, the sea has worked at the limestone for centuries, creating caves and grottoes and an occasional miniature beach.

POSITANO: John Steinbeck, like many other artistic people, was transported by Positano and wrote that it "bites deep. It is a dream place that isn't quite real when you are there and becomes beckoningly real after you have gone." As the steep hills drop almost vertically to the sea, the houses of Positano appear to hang like a canvas of cubistic shapes in a broad spectrum of earth tones and pastels, the green and gold tiled cupola of Santa Maria Assunta — the Chiesa Madre — presiding over the point where the hills flatten out to a small sand-and-pebble beach. Only one road passes through town; the rest of the streets run downhill in a series of switchbacks that reach a dead end a few hundred yards from the shore. All cars must be left in parking lots and garages. After that, the going is by foot, so the streets are blessedly free of traffic.

For decades, the peacefulness and picturesqueness of Positano have attracted artists, especially painters, many of whom came for a visit and stayed indefinitely — or a lifetime. More recently, roughly since the arrival of director Franco Zeffirelli (who owns a villa here), it has attracted more and more celebrities and movie stars, now rivaling Capri. For six months of the year, life focuses on the beach (called the Spiaggia Grande, even though few beaches along this coast are large) and the half dozen restaurants just behind it. Boutiques abound, selling beachwear and loungewear made in Positano — the clothing hangs outdoors, the bright materials flapping in the wind. When travelers weary of swimming, shopping, or simply killing time at a restaurant or café, there is also tennis. The town court is cleverly tucked away atop a large garage, framed by cacti, cliffs, and clouds. If you need help or further information, Positano's tourist office (AAST) is at Via del Saracino 2 (phone: 089-875067).

CHECKING IN: *San Pietro* – This is one mile east of town, on the road toward Amalfi. There is nothing so crass as a sign to identify it, only a 15th-century chapel. The hotel itself is strewn down the side of the cliff, with the reception area, restaurant, rooms, swimming pool, and beach all on different levels, reached by elevator. The 55 rooms, actually more nearly suites, are furnished with antiques, each in a distinctive style. Bougainvillea has overgrown much of the exterior, and it has also sent branches inside some of the rooms, so that they resemble arbors. An authentic gem. Closed January to mid-March. Reservations necessary in all seasons. (Località San Pietro, Positano; phone: 089-875455; very expensive.)

Le Sirenuse – With its Pompeiian red exterior, this stands out even amid the splendors of Positano. Once a private villa, it was turned into a hotel by the Sersale family, which still runs it and has, over the years, added modern rooms (more than 60 total), a heated swimming pool, and three terraces on which to dine overlooking the beach and the yellow and green tiled dome of the church. Open all year. (Via Colombo 30, Positano; phone: 089-875066; expensive.)

Palazzo Murat – The 18th-century palace of Gioacchino Murat (a king of Naples and Napoleon's brother-in-law) has been tastefully restored with some period furniture and wood-beamed ceilings. The best of the 30 or so rooms are those in the L-shaped *palazzo*, looking out onto the courtyard where guests can have breakfast surrounded by bougainvillea and lemon trees. There is also a modern wing. Open all year. (Via dei Mulini 9, Positano; phone: 089-875177; moderate.)

Casa Albertina – A small (20-room), family-run hotel with personal service, this is a minor jewel, with gilt mirrors and bronze lamps, dramatic sea views, and rooms done in soothing shades of mauve and blue. Open all year; restaurant. (Via Tavolozza 4, Positano; phone: 089-875143; moderate to inexpensive.)

Casa Maresca – White as sugar, this cozy, comfortable hotel has 19 rooms, most with private bath and a sea view. There's also a good restaurant where guests can dine *al fresco* and gaze out at a floodlit Saracen tower. Closed mid-November to mid-March. (Viale Pasitea, Positano; phone: 089-875140; moderate to inexpensive.)

EATING OUT: *Buca di Bacco* – Conveniently just off the beach, this is a favorite restaurant of the yachting crowd. It rightly claims that it has "the largest and most comfortable terrace." Tempting *antipasti*, a fine seafood salad, and eggplant pasta are among its other claims to fame. Closed from mid-October through March. (Via Marina, Positano; phone: 089-875004; moderate.)

La Cambusa – It, too, is set just beyond the beach and it, too, has a verandah with a lovely view. It serves excellent fish soup, spaghetti *alle vongole* (with clam sauce), and *risotto* with squid. Try washing down a seafood meal with a local white wine, Greco di Tufo. Open all year. (Via Marina, Positano; phone: 089-875432; moderate.)

Chez Black – A favorite of bathers, especially the younger crowd taking a lunch break. Try the spaghetti with clam sauce or the mixed fried fish. Closed in winter. (Via del Brigantino 19, Positano; phone: 089-875036; moderate.)

Da Vincenzo – Away from the congestion of the beach and the crush of tourists, this is a genial place on a quiet street where the clientele is likely to consist of more local people than vacationers. The vegetables are fresh and the zucchini with Parmesan is very good. (There is no phone and the only address is "at the Casa Soriana curve." Ask anyone. Inexpensive.)

En Route from Positano – The road narrows, winding and twisting toward Amalfi. A 10-mile drive can easily take half an hour or even much longer — not simply because of the road, but because there are constant diversions. The villages of Vettica Maggiore and Praiano are worth more than a quick look. Then, between two tunnels, the cliffside corniche passes over the gorges of the Vallone di Furore (Valley of the Furies). A finger of the sea, no wider than a river, presses deep into the gorge, and a tiny fishing village hangs on to the rock like a swallow's nest. Farther on, there are signs for the Grotta di Smeraldo (Green Grotto), only a shade less famous than the Blue Grotto on Capri. It can be reached by a steep staircase, by elevator, or by boat from Positano.

AMALFI: Although not as preciously picturesque as Positano and Ravello, Amalfi was once much larger (almost 70,000 inhabitants; now it's down to fewer than 7,000) and much more important. During the 6th century, it developed considerable trade with the Byzantine Empire, and by the 9th century it was already a maritime republic, Italy's oldest, ruled first by prefects and judges and then by a doge. In the 11th century, it was a mercantile and maritime power to rival Pisa, Genoa, and Venice. Amalfi's domain on land extended at one time from Sorrento to Salerno and back to the Lattari Mountains; its influence by sea was felt all along the southern Italian coasts, where it fought the Saracens, and as far as Jerusalem, where it built churches and hospitals for pilgrims of the First Crusade. In fact, the rules by which the republic governed all its maritime activity, the Tavole Amalfitane (Amalfi Tables), became the maritime code for all the Mediterranean and remained in force until 1570, long after Amalfi had lost its primacy. This happened rather quickly, in the 12th century, after it was captured by the Normans and sacked by the Pisans and suffered its share of natural disasters, including devastating floods. Still, something of the old splendor returns once every four years, when it is Amalfi's turn to host the Regatta of the Four Ancient Maritime Republics, a race and a colorful parade of boats that rotates annually among Amalfi and the other one-time rulers of the sea (Genoa, Pisa, and Venice).

Apart from its lovely seaside setting, the town's greatest pride is its Duomo, dedicated to St. Andrew. Dating from the 10th century, restored and expanded on subsequent occasions as recently as 1894, it sits at the top of a broad, tall staircase, somewhat as on a pedestal, its lively façade displaying stylistic influences that range from Moorish to Norman to early Gothic. A Romanesque bell tower next to it, begun in the 12th century, is crowned with green and yellow glazed tiles. The cathedral's bronze entrance doors were cast in Constantinople in 1066. There is also a beautiful cloister, the Chiostro del Paradiso, built in the 13th century and distinguished by lacy Arabic arches.

Heading inland and farther into town from Piazza Duomo, Via Genova and Via Capuano lead eventually to the Valle dei Mulini (Valley of the Mills), where ancient paper mills stand. Amalfi's tourist office (AAST) is at Corso Roma 19 (phone: 089-871107).

CHECKING IN: *Santa Caterina* – Right at the water's edge, with an elevator that drops down to the swimming pool and the rock beach level. There are terraces and gardens for *al fresco* dining and lounging, and most of the 54 rooms have balconies. Open all year. Less expensive rooms are available in an annex. (Via Nazionale 9, Amalfi; phone: 089-871012; expensive.)

Excelsior Grand – About 3 miles outside Amalfi, on the way to Pogerola, this modern 85-room hotel has access to a private beach, a 100-foot swimming pool with cool spring water, a garden, restaurant, and smashing views. Unconventional in design, it takes excellent advantage of its setting, with many large windows and balconies. Closed from mid-October to mid-April. (Via Pogerola, Amalfi; phone: 089-871344; expensive to moderate.)

Belvedere – This quiet place is about 3 miles west of Amalfi in the tiny hamlet of Conca dei Marini. Cut into a cliff, its 36 rooms and terraces are well shielded from the sound of passing traffic. It has wonderful views and a swimming pool. Restaurant. Closed from November through March. (SS163, Conca dei Marini; phone: 089-871266; moderate.)

Cappuccini Convento – A 13th-century monastery, one of the landmarks of Amalfi, has been transformed into a splendid 41-room hotel. High on a cliff, it's reached by an elevator that burrows through rock to daylight; various terraces offer views of the coast, and the air is fragrant with the scent of citrus groves. Rooms are enlarged monks' cells (two cells for each room). The hotel has a private beach and a restaurant. Open all year. (Via Annunziatella 46, Amalfi; phone: 089-871008; moderate.)

Luna Convento – Ibsen wrote *A Doll's House* here, and St. Francis of Assisi is supposed to have slept here. This landmark 13th-century monastery turned hotel reposes on a panoramic rocky point where the Amalfi Drive turns a bend toward the next town. A charming cloister makes up the lobby; a glorious dining room with high arched windows faces the sea. There is a swimming pool and a private "beach" of rock flattened out by concrete across the road; 50 rooms. Open all year. (19 Via Amendola, Amalfi; phone: 089-871002; moderate.)

Bellevue – It opens onto the sea and, although it has no garden, it is clean, cheerful, and moderate. Open all year; 23 rooms. (Via Nazionale, Amalfi; phone: 089-871846; inexpensive.)

EATING OUT: *Da Gemma* – A short walk from the Duomo, this homey *trattoria* with a terrace for outdoor dining offers authentic local cuisine — spaghetti with clams, *linguine* with shrimp, simply prepared meat dishes, fresh fish with lemon, and good local wines. Closed Thursdays. (Via Cavalieri di Malta, Amalfi; phone: 089-871345; moderate.)

La Caravella – Since it's close to the beach, some diners are apt to show up in their bathing suits. The place serves genuine southern Italian specialties such as fish soup, fried shrimp, and squid — all at bargain prices. Closed Tuesdays and November. (Via Camera 12, Amalfi; phone: 089-871029; inexpensive.)

En Route from Amalfi – Head east, passing through Atrani, which is virtually an extension of Amalfi. To reach Ravello, turn inland and uphill onto a well-marked road that swerves through the ominously named Valle del Dragone (Dragon Valley). After dozens of hairpin curves, the road rises to over 1,000 feet above the coast and reaches the main square of the most gloriously positioned town on the Gulf of Salerno.

RAVELLO: The spectacular panorama visible from so many spots in this tiny town, its narrow step streets, and the profusion of flowers and greenery gracing every nook and cranny make it a place of incomparable beauty. Frequented by the talented and the famous, among them Richard Wagner, Jacqueline Kennedy Onassis, Princess Margaret, and William Styron — who set a novel, *Set This House on Fire,* here — Ravello is now the part-time home of Gore Vidal.

Leave the car in the square — Piazza Vescovado, which is Ravello's main square and as far as the car can go — and walk over to the *Duomo,* dedicated to the patron saint of Ravello, San Pantaleone. Begun in 1086 but finished in the 12th century, it has magnificent paneled bronze doors by Barisano da Trani (1179). Inside are two impressive pulpits. The older (1130), less intricate one features two large mosaics of Jonah being eaten and regurgitated by a dragonlike green whale (symbolizing the death and resurrection of Christ). The other, by Nicola di Bartolomeo da Foggia (1272), rests on six columns supported on the backs of lions and is covered with mosaic medallions of fantastic animals and birds. It was paid for by Nicola Rufolo, a member of one of

Ravello's rich merchant families, at a time when the town had more than 30,000 inhabitants (now it has fewer than 3,000) and was every bit as active in commerce as was Amalfi, to which it belonged at one time.

Nearby, the Villa Rufolo, built by the same family, also in the 13th century, looks unprepossessing from the outside, but at closer inspection it is easy to understand why Wagner was inspired to use it as a model for the magic garden of Klingsor in *Parsifal.* Except for the Cortile Moresco (Moorish Courtyard), little remains to be visited of the actual villa. The gardens, however, merit superlatives. Terraced on several levels and planted with beds of bright marigolds, red salvia, pink and white phlox, and many other flowers, they are surrounded by umbrella pines and cypresses and open out to a stunning view of mountains and sea, and the town of Maiori below. The villa is open daily, with a lunchtime closing; there is an admission fee.

It's a 10-minute hike to Ravello's second most famous site, Villa Cimbrone, also open daily, with an admission fee. Built in 1904 by Lord Grimthorpe, an Englishman searching for peace of mind, it has a lovely cloister where, at the entrance, marble faces on the far wall represent the seven deadly sins. A cypress-shaded path leads through the extensive garden to the Belvedere, a ledge that seems to lean out over the Gulf of Salerno. It almost does because it's set at the very point of the spur of mountain that holds Ravello. On a clear day, you can see as far as Paestum, 30 miles south.

Ravello's tourist office is at Piazza Vescovado (phone: 089-857096).

CHECKING IN: Palumbo – An exquisite small hotel in the higher reaches of town, this is *the* place to stay. Once a private villa, built on the ruins of the 12th-century Palazzo Confalone, it is stylish and charming, with beautiful *maiolica* floors, a lovely interior courtyard from the original building, a restaurant, a grassy garden terrace and a dining terrace with gorgeous views, and some rooms looking out to the sea. The menu features specialties such as *fusilli al gorgonzola,* spaghetti *alla puttanesca,* and tasty apple pie, all washed down by the hotel's own red and white Episcopio wines. Open all year. (Via San Giovanni del Toro 28, Ravello; phone: 089-857244; expensive.)

Marmorata – If all the rooms in Ravello are full, return to the coast road, SS163, and drive east a short distance to this delightful hotel. Overlooking the sea, it has a terrace restaurant, a swimming pool, and rocky access to the water. Small (40 rooms) and family-run, it's been in business only a few years. Reserve well in advance. Closed November through March. (Località Marmorata, Ravello; phone: 089-877777; expensive to moderate.)

Caruso Belvedere – Just up the street from the *Palumbo,* here is another old building — the 11th-century Palazzo d'Afflitto — converted into a delightful hotel with charm, character, and beautiful views. Some of the 26 rooms face the garden, some face out to mountains and sea. This hotel has a good restaurant, famed for its *cannelloni,* its *crespini* (a kind of cheese and ham crêpe), and its delicious, light lemon chocolate soufflé, all of which go well with the house wine, Gran Caruso. Open all year. (Via San Giovanni del Toro 52, Ravello; phone: 089-857111; moderate.)

Rufolo – This 29-room hotel is on the way to Villa Cimbrone. All rooms face a marvelous view toward Villa Rufolo and the mountains in the direction of Maiori, and the hotel also has a swimming pool. Restaurant. Open all year. (Via San Francesco 2, Ravello; 089-857133; moderate.)

Parsifal – A tasteful, 20-room hotel, incorporating parts of a 13th-century Augustinian monastery. Some rooms have private baths. There's a cloister, a charming garden with a reflecting pool, and a seductive view of the coast. In warm weather, meals are served on the trellis-covered, flower-scented terrace. Closed October through March. (Piazza Fontana, Ravello; phone 857-144; moderate to inexpensive.)

EATING OUT: *Compa' Cosimo* – Home cooking, Ravello style — fresh fish and vegetables. Specialties include minestrone and bean soup, served with the usual fine local wines. Closed Mondays in winter. (Via Roma 48, Ravello; phone: 089-857156; moderate to inexpensive.)

En Route from Ravello – The road toward Salerno swings down to sea level, running through two delightful towns, Minori and Maiori. When the chic hotels and pricey resort towns elsewhere along the coast are crowded, these two, with their broad sandy beaches and palm-lined boulevards, are attractive alternatives.

After Maiori, the road begins to climb and grows narrow and winding again. The landscape still shows some of the damage caused by floods and landslides decades ago, as well as the damage of repeated brush fires in the recent past. Around Capo d'Orso, the countryside becomes wilder and less heavily populated, and the small, colorful fishing village of Cetara is the only real town until Vietri sul Mare, where the Amalfi Drive comes to an end. Vietri is famed for its ceramics, and around the main square of the upper city, shop after shop spills over with colorful plates, pots, jugs, and other pottery pieces for sale. Even shops selling other types of wares, such as the fish store and the greengrocer, have storefronts decorated with images of their produce in ceramic tiles. A brief stretch of SS18 leads around a bend in the coastline from Vietri straight into Salerno.

SALERNO: Sorrento, Positano, Amalfi, and Ravello are tough acts to follow and, quite frankly, Salerno, a city of some 200,000, cannot really compare with the elegance and unearthly beauty of the Amalfi Coast. Yet is is not without interest and attractions. A seaport, slightly seedy and raffish — imagine a miniature Naples or Genoa — it's a city with a long and dramatic history. In the 12th and 13th centuries, its most prosperous period, much of its fame was due to its School of Medicine, the oldest in the Western world, possibly begun in the 9th century (and closed in the 19th century). Just as Paris was preeminent in science and Bologna in law, Salerno became so renowned in the field of medicine that it was called the Hippocratic city. On September 9, 1943, it became famous for a far different reason. The Allies launched their invasion of mainland Europe from here, landing south of the city after an aerial bombardment. They encountered heavy resistance from a German Panzer division, and when the Americans entered the town the next day, much of the waterfront was destroyed. Now the area has been rebuilt, and broad walkways curve along the waterfront, shaded by palms and scattered here and there with playgrounds, small amusement parks, and sidewalk cafés. In the evening, it seems the entire town takes a *passeggiata,* or walk, by the sea.

Uphill from the port and the modern part of town, the old quarter is well worth a visit, especially the *Duomo di San Matteo* (*Cathedral of St. Matthew*). Built in 845 and rebuilt from 1076 to 1085 by Robert Guiscard, it was heavily redone during the 18th century, but more recent restoration is uncovering its earlier forms. It has a Romanesque doorway, guarded by statues of lions, leading to a beautiful atrium surrounded by 28 columns that came from the Greek ruins down the coast at Paestum. A freestanding *campanile* (bell tower) looms above the atrium. Inside the church are two highly decorated pulpits and a pascal candlestick in a mixture of Saracen and Byzantine styles, full of mosaic ornamentation. A stroll through the old town along Via dei Mercanti passes elegant shops as well as the poorest street vendors. It's very lively and colorful, crowded and loud. The tourist information office (EPT) at Piazza Ferrovia 1 (phone: 089-231432), by the train station, can provide information on Salerno and its province, which includes most of the towns on the Amalfi Drive; in addition, there's another tourist office (AAST) at Piazza Amendola 8 (phone: 089-224744).

CHECKING IN: Lloyd's Baia – Outside Salerno on the drive in from the Amalfi Coast and Vietri, it stands on a bluff overlooking the sea, but it's surrounded by gardens and adequately screened off from traffic. The 120 rooms are open year-round, there is a restaurant, a pool, and a private beach reachable by elevators. (On SS18, Salerno; phone: 089-210145; expensive to moderate.)

Jolly delle Palme – At the northern end of the waterfront, looking out over a playground and a public beach, this is a modern, comfortable member of the Jolly chain. Its aim is less charm than efficiency, and on its own terms the 105-room hotel is quite satisfactory. It's easy to find in the broader, better-marked streets of the modern town, yet it's a short walk from the old quarter. Open year-round; restaurant. (Lungomare Trieste 1, Salerno; phone: 089-225222; moderate.)

EATING OUT: Nave Ristorante al Concord – For a change of pace, try this restaurant aboard a ship permanently moored on the waterfront in the center of Salerno. It features, naturally, a variety of seafood salads, seafood pastas, and seafood main courses. It also makes pizza and has a reasonably priced fixed menu. (Piazza della Concordia, Salerno; phone: 089-226856; expensive to moderate.)

Alla Brace – Just across from the *Jolly*, this is both a restaurant and pizzeria. As its name suggests, it specializes in meat and fresh fish cooked over a charcoal grill. The *linguine* dishes are also quite good, and try the Gragnano wines. (Lungomare Trieste 11, Salerno; phone: 089-225159; moderate to inexpensive.)

En Route from Salerno – It is possible to reach Paestum via the coast, but the first half of the drive is made terribly unattractive by construction sites and industrial zones. It's far better to take A3 out of Salerno, get off at the Battipaglia exit, and follow SS18 to Paestum.

PAESTUM: Called Poseidonia (City of Neptune) by the Greeks who colonized it at the end of the 7th century BC, the city was taken over by a local tribe, the Lucanians, about 400 BC. A hundred and fifty years later it fell to the Romans. But its low-lying position near the sea made it vulnerable to malaria; it gradually lost population and was sacked by the Saracens in AD 877. Crumbling and overgrown with vegetation, it wasn't rediscovered until the 18th century.

Arriving from the north, drive past the first two entrances, park, and enter through the Porta della Giustizia, near the *Albergo Nettuno*. The grounds are beautiful and pastoral; cypresses, oleander, pines, and rose bushes flourish. Lizards scuttle over the ruins, the most prominent of which are three temples, all amazingly well preserved. The *Basilica,* the oldest temple in Paestum, was constructed in the mid-6th century BC and dedicated to the goddess Hera (it was mislabeled by Christians in the 18th century AD). Facing east, it has 50 fairly bulbous Doric columns that taper dramatically at the top, creating the optical illusion that the temple pitches outward. The Greek builders' grasp of column shape and placement improved considerably by the time the temple next to it was built in the mid-5th century BC. Known as the *Temple of Neptune* (and also as the Temple of Poseidon, but also misnamed because it, too, was dedicated to Hera), this is considered to be perfectly proportioned, one of the most beautiful Doric temples in Italy or Greece as well as one of the best preserved (along with the Temple of Theseus in Athens and the Temple of Concord at Agrigento in Sicily). It is also the largest (200 feet by 80 feet) and best-preserved temple in Paestum. Both temples to Hera are at the southern end of the Via Sacra. At its northern end is the so-called *Temple of Ceres,* built in approximately 500 BC to honor the goddess Athena. The smallest of the temples of Paestum, it once had, in addition to its Doric exterior columns, Ionic interior columns (whose scant remains are in the museum). It still contains three medieval tombs dating from a time when the temple was used as a Christian church.

Paestum's museum is across the street from the archaeological zone. Among its most interesting exhibits are wall paintings from the Tomba del Tuffatore (Diver's Tomb), found about a half mile away. Dating from the late 5th century BC, they are the only paintings of figures to have been found in Magna Graecia. Also noteworthy are the 34 metopes from the Temple of Hera Argiva at the mouth of the Sele River, 8 miles north of Paestum. In addition, reproductions of various cornices in the museum show how richly colored the temples across the street once were. The museum in Paestum is open mornings only and closed Mondays, whereas the archaeological zone is open daily, except for a few holidays, from 9 AM to an hour before sunset (last tickets are sold two hours before sunset). A single admission ticket is good for the museum and the archaeological zone.

 CHECKING IN: *Strand Hotel Schuhmann* – One of many hotels on the sea outside Paestum, it is clean and up-to-date and often frequented by German tourists. Restaurant and 27 rooms. (Via Laura Mare, Paestum; phone: 0828-851151; moderate.)

Martini Gardens – A modern, clean, pleasant place, across from the Porta della Giustizia. It consists of whitewashed cottages set in a beautiful garden, with a restaurant, bar, and dance floor in the main building. Closed November to April. (Zona Archeologica, Paestum; phone: 0828-811020; moderate to inexpensive.)

EATING OUT: *Nettuno* – Just beyond the Porta della Giustizia, it serves fine food in the rustic dining room and on the trellis-shaded terrace. It offers a good selection of local wines, as well as more celebrated vintages from other parts of the country. (Zona Archeologica, Paestum; phone: 0828-811028; inexpensive).

Capri

Capri (pronounced *kah*-pree, not kah-*pree*) is a tiny jewel sparkling in the Bay of Naples. Although only four miles long and two miles wide, the island has almost as many identities as it does visitors. An estimated two million tourists make the short trip over from the mainland every year and what they find usually depends on what they are looking for.

Wealthy jet-setters discover kindred spirits, not to mention a multitude of elegant shops, chic cafés and restaurants, and plush hotels and private villas. On summer evenings, Piazza Umberto I looks less like a public square than an exclusive cocktail party with guests attired in the colorful clothes they had made to measure earlier that day. Noel Coward rightly called the island "the most beautiful operetta stage in the world." Yet for those who want privacy and tranquillity, even solitude, the island has a surprising number of out-of-the-way corners, quiet wooded paths, and isolated gorges. One of its enduring charms is that its craggy, mountainous landscape leaves much of it inaccessible to cars and buses, and anyone willing to wander a bit can soon be on his or her own. For the young and the energetic, Capri offers hiking — a long walk to Villa Jovis or to the summit of Monte Solaro will hone anyone's appetite and tone up the muscles for an evening of dancing — as well as the obvious water sports — swimming, skin diving, water skiing — and tennis.

A map shows that the island is nothing more than a geographical continuation of the Sorrento Peninsula, a large chunk of limestone that rises from the deep — precipitously in most places — and comes to two points. The west side of the island culminates in Monte Solaro, altitude 1,923 feet, the highest spot on the island. The east side peaks in the somewhat lower (1,100 feet) Monte Tiberio — but here, nevertheless, is the island's highest cliff, from which, according to Suetonius, the emperor Tiberius threw his enemies into oblivion. In a saddle between the two mountains, but hardly at sea level, is Capri's main town, Capri. Its other town, Anacapri, is twice as high, on a plateau at the base of Monte Solaro. Visitors to the island disembark at Marina Grande, the port, and make the ascent to either town by road (or to Capri, directly by funicular). The ancients reached Anacapri by a staircase of 881 steps, built by the first Greek colonizers, restored by the Romans, and still in use as late as the nineteenth century.

Over the centuries, writers, artists, and eccentrics have found a welcome home here. Hedonists as different as arms dealer Baron Von Krupp and the acerbic Oscar Wilde were drawn as much by the island's live-and-let-live attitude as by the cerulean sea and subtropical vegetation. Strange as it is to imagine, Maxim Gorky settled on Capri from 1907 to 1913 and ran a school for revolutionaries that was attended by Lenin and Stalin. Graham Greene still returns to his house in the Caprile district when he wants to work uninterrupted.

The common denominator among all visitors to Capri seems to be the desire for an intensification of life. Whether it's Tiberius spending the last decade of his licentious rule building sumptuous villas or budget-conscious travelers just over from Naples or Sorrento for the afternoon, people come looking for the ultimate resort, a place where the sun, the sea, the fine wine and food, the seductiveness and sensuality of the entire Italian peninsula are compressed into one tiny spot. That the island's permanent population of 12,000 works so hard to welcome foreigners and expatriates is no doubt part of the reason visitors return again and again.

 TOURIST INFORMATION: The high-season months in Capri are June through September, in addition to the period around Easter. Given the island's popularity, it's best to visit in May and September, when the weather is warm and the island less crowded (although September is still officially high season as far as prices are concerned). Winter, especially around Christmas, can also be an enticing time if — and it's a large *if* — the sun is shining. Visitors in winter must expect to find more than half the hotels and restaurants closed, and despite the drastic differences in climate and attractions between summer and winter, the hotels that remain open year-round do not reduce their rates commensurately. A meager 10% off-season discount is the general rule. The *Ente Provinciale per il Turismo* in Naples, Via Partenope 10/A (phone: 081-406289), can provide information about Capri. On the island, local tourist offices (*AAST*) are at the dock at Marina Grande (phone: 081-8370634), at Piazzetta Ignazio Cerio 11 (phone: 081-8370918), and at Piazza Umberto I (phone: 081-8370686) in the town of Capri, and at Via G. Orlandi 19/A (phone: 081-8371524) in Anacapri. Off-season, the tourist office on Piazza Umberto I posts the names, addresses, and phone numbers of hotels and restaurants that remain open year-round.

Many free guides are available in English from travel agencies and hotels, which can also arrange short tours of the island. An excellent free guide is *Isola di Capri,* an illustrated index of hotels and *pensioni,* and *L'Isola,* which contains a long list of addresses and telephone numbers of hotels, restaurants, bars, and sports facilities, as well as schedules for buses, taxis, and boats to and from the mainland.

Telephone – The prefix for the entire island is 081, the same as for Naples, Sorrento, and Ischia.

 FOOD AND WINE: While some Capri restaurants offer standard Italian fare and the ubiquitous international cuisine, the food on Capri generally shows the influence of nearby Naples, and the sea. There are pasta dishes with tomato or eggplant, or with olive or clam sauces. Pizzas have thicker crusts than elsewhere in Italy and are topped with sliced tomatoes and slabs of *mozzarella di bufalo.* The seafood is marvelous, especially the *scampi, gamberoni,* and *calamari,* which may be batter-fried or served in a salad or pasta sauce. An *insalata caprese* (sliced tomato and mozzarella, seasoned with fresh basil) makes an excellent start for any meal, and the traditional chocolate almond cake (*torta di mandorle*) is a tasty dessert.

Local wines are simple, of limited production, and make no extravagant claims to merit. But the *bianco* from Falanghina and Greco does go down well with seafood.

GETTING AROUND: Visitors are *not* allowed to bring cars to the island between June 1 and September 30, but it doesn't make sense to drive at any time of the year because the roads are narrow, crooked, and already crowded with local traffic. Places of interest are all within easy walking distance, or else they are well connected by bus, taxi, or funicular. Taxis and buses meet boats and hydrofoils arriving in Marina Grande and transport passengers to Piazza Martiri d'Ungheria in the town of Capri, a few steps from the main square, Piazza Umberto I, or to Piazza della Vittoria in Anacapri.

Bus – In general, buses leave Marina Grande every 15 minutes for Capri and Anacapri. Buses also leave Marina Piccola, the little port on the other side of the island, every 15 minutes (every 30 minutes in winter) for Capri and Anacapri. For additional bus information, call 8370420.

Ferry – There is frequent ferryboat and hydrofoil (*aliscafo*) service between Capri and the mainland. From Naples (1¼-hour trip), one of the most reasonable and dependable ferry services is provided by *Caremar,* which also operates out of Sorrento (45 minutes). Hydrofoil service is provided by both Caremar and *Aliscafi SNAV* (approximately 40 minutes from Naples). In summer, ferries and hydrofoils for Capri are regularly scheduled from additional points such as Salerno, Amalfi, Positano, and Ischia. For times and prices, check at local tourist information offices. In high season, book passage well in advance; off-season, be sure to get precise information — boats may be canceled. Generally, in winter, there is regularly scheduled service to Capri only from Naples and Sorrento, but it is possible to make private arrangements on small boats. Caremar's phone number on Capri is 8370700; Aliscafi SNAV's number on Capri is 8377577.

Funicular – The way to go from Marina Grande to Capri town; a *seggiovia* (chair lift) operates from Anacapri to the top of Monte Solaro.

Helicopter – Service to and from Capodichino Airport in Naples can be arranged (phone: 081-446762).

Taxi – For a taxi in Capri, call 8370543; in Anacapri, call 8371175.

SPECIAL EVENTS: Religious festivals and celebrations have a way of taking on a pagan guise on Capri, and fireworks are set off on any pretext — a saint's day, Christmas, or a baptism. On May 14, the island celebrates the Festa di San Costanzo, the feast day of its patron saint, and on June 13, Anacapri celebrates the feast of Sant'Antonio. On September 7 and 8, on Monte Tiberio and Monte Solaro, the Festival of the Madonna is held. Later in September, a more secular celebration, the annual grape harvest, generates hundreds of impromptu parties.

SPORTS: Boating – One way to see Capri and gain a different and dramatic perspective on its sheer limestone cliffs is to circle it in a boat; indeed, some parts of the island are accessible only by sea. Trips around the island can be arranged through *Gruppo Motoscafisti* (phone: 8370286, 8377714). A tour takes about 2½ hours and can be combined with tours to the famous Grotta Azzurra (Blue Grotto) and the less well known Grotta Spumante, Grotta Corale, and Grotta Bianca, as well as the Bagni di Tiberio. If no one answers the phone, go down to Marina Grande and ask for information at the stand marked *Gite dell'Isola.* On many off-season days, local boatmen decide there aren't enough customers or the sea is too rough, and they close up shop.

Boats can be rented by the hour or the day, with or without guides, through *Capri Mare Club* (phone: 8370021) at Marina Piccola. The same establishment runs a windsurfing and sailing school and can arrange water skiing.

Skin Diving and Snorkeling – Although there is no reef around Capri, and the fish can sometimes be few and far between, the clear water and the abundance of caves and grottoes make the area interesting for divers. Gennarino Alberino and his American wife, Cindy, run the *Gennarino and Cindy Sub* shop at Marina Grande 17, right next to the funicular (phone: 8379191 at the shop; 8377118 at home). They rent snorkeling equipment and can arrange for scuba diving and instruction.

Swimming – Capri is not a swimmer's paradise, since there are only a few small, stony beaches on the island's craggy coast. The best swimming is probably at Marina Piccola, where concrete platforms have been built over the water's edge. Many hotels, however, have pools.

Tennis – The *Tennis Yacht Club,* Via Camerelle 41 (phone: 8370261, 8377980), across from the swank *Quisisana e Grand Hotel,* has three clay courts, a clubhouse, bar, and shower rooms. The club pro, Giuseppe de Stefano, well known on the Grand Prix circuit as an umpire, speaks English and gives lessons at reasonable prices, with court fees included. Make reservations at least a week in advance in high season.

THE ISLAND OF CAPRI

Since there are essentially just two towns on the island — Capri and Anacapri — it is wise to settle in one and make forays from it, heading downhill on foot and returning uphill by taxi or bus. Distances are quite short, and no trip will take more than a few hours.

Prices tend to be a bit higher on Capri than on the mainland. Expect to pay $80 and up for a double room in hotels listed as expensive; $40 to $75 in those listed as moderate; and less than $30 at the inexpensive ones. These prices do not take into account any minimum half-board requirements that may be in effect in some hotels in high season. The price of meals here, as in so many spots in Italy, depends in large measure on the fish or meat ordered (pasta is reasonable almost everywhere) and the wine drunk — bottled or house wine served in a carafe. Generally, a full meal for two will cost $40 and up in an expensive restaurant; $25 to $35 in a moderate establishment; and less than $20 in an inexpensive one. These prices include service and in some cases a local wine. The seafood on Capri is delicious but by no means inexpensive.

CAPRI: This whitewashed town has the look and feel of a North African *medina*. Many of the streets that radiate from tiny Piazza Umberto I, the main square, are as narrow as hallways, as steep as staircases, as dim and cool as tunnels. Occasionally, the cramped passageways open onto small roomlike *piazzette* where people sit eating, drinking, and chatting, creating the impression that the town is one immense, rambling house. As Eleanor Clark has written about the streets of Italy, they "constitute a great withinness . . . Even a tourist can tell . . . he is *in* something and not outside something as he would be in most cities . . . To go out is to go home."

But the lively, enfolding labyrinth of streets is only one of Capri's charms. There is color and excitement, and at every turn, through every open window, there are breathcatching views of the sea, of Monte Tiberio to the east and Monte Solaro to the west, and of villas strewn across terraced hillsides shaded by cypress trees, palms, and citrus groves. Capri's greatest attractions are almost all present-day and physical — the play of sunlight and shadow, the smell of jasmine, the sound of the sea against the rocks — rather than monuments of historic or artistic importance. This is not to say that the island has not preserved its past. *Santo Stefano,* the church on Piazza Umberto I, dates from the 17th century, and the adjacent *Palazzo Cerio* contains a small, private museum of antiquities and fossils found on the island. Leaving the piazza by its south corner and descending Via Vittorio Emanuele III leads to Via Federico Serena, which curves down to the *Certosa di San Giacomo (Carthusian Monastery of St. James),* open mornings until 2 PM and closed Mondays. Built in the late 14th century, it has barrelvaulted ceilings and domes, making it appear slightly Byzantine. It now houses a school and the town library, as well as some Roman statues removed from the Blue Grotto.

Roman ruins supply the major part of Capri's historical heritage. In 29 BC, the emperor Augustus visited the island, which then belonged to Naples, and was struck enough by its beauty to trade an island already in his possession (Ischia) for it. He built roads, aqueducts, and villas. His successor, Tiberius, came here in AD 27 and for the last 10 years of his life ruled the Roman Empire from here. He erected more villas on prominent points throughout the island, dedicating them to various Roman deities. All together, there are supposed to have been a dozen imperial villas on Capri, but among the various Roman ruins on the island, only the Villa Jovis, built by Tiberius and dedicated to Jupiter, amounts to anything today. This he set at the top of what is now called Monte Tiberio.

To reach *Villa Jovis* (also called *Villa Tiberius*), leave Piazza Umberto I by Via Le

Botteghe, which becomes Via Fuorlovado and then Via Croce. From Via Croce take Via Tiberio uphill, following the signs. (The hike takes about an hour.) Just beyond the entrance to the villa is the Salto di Tiberio, the dizzyingly high precipice from which, as the story goes, Tiberius tossed his unfortunate victims to the stony shore of the sea. The villa itself, up a flight of steps, has been stripped of most of its mosaic pavements and decorative devices, but even in its reduced state, the ruins show extensive evidence of size and structural complexity. Incongruously, the very highest point of the pagan emperor's estate is crowned by a chapel and an immense, modern bronze statue of the Madonna that was blessed by Pope John Paul II and flown to this site by a US navy helicopter. Villa Jovis is open daily, except Mondays and holidays, from 9 AM to one hour before sunset; there is an admission fee.

Other spots well worth a visit include *Punta di Tragara,* which offers a good view of the Faraglioni, twin rock islands that stand needlelike offshore and have become one of the symbols of Capri, and the *Giardini di Augusto (Gardens of Augustus),* a public park that offers another good view of the Faraglioni, Punta di Tragara, and Marina Piccola. From the gardens, walk down to Marina Piccola by Via Krupp, officially closed because of falling rocks but still passable. The *Arco Naturale (Natural Arch),* which is just that — a rock eroded to the shape of an archway — and the *Grotta di Matromania,* a cave in which the ancient Romans possibly worshiped Cybele, the Mater Magna, are not far from Villa Jovis.

The *Blue Grotto* has been incessantly described, rendered in paintings, and pictured on postcards, but it should be seen firsthand — although the process of doing so feels something like riding on an assembly line. The discovery of this cave on the north side of the island in 1826 put Capri on the modern tourist map. Visitors are taken by motorboat to the cave entrance — a mere 2-meter-wide hole in the rock, 1 meter high when the sea is normal — and then transfer to a small rowboat to be taken inside, where sunlight refracting through water makes the walls of the cave appear blue and gives submerged objects a silvery phosphorescence.

CHECKING IN: *Quisisana e Grand* – A sumptuous white wedding cake of a building, in a central location, but spacious and well screened from noisy or nosy passersby. Its 142 elegant rooms, swimming pool, tennis courts, popular bar, restaurant, and courtyard for dining all attract a well-heeled clientele. Closed November through March. (Via Camerelle 2, Capri; phone: 8370788; very expensive.)

***Punta Tragara* –** A 10-minute walk from the main square, this 33-room hotel is beautifully set with a splendid view of the Faraglioni. Its spa, hydromassage, and other luxurious facilities appeal to those looking for relaxation and privacy, but it also has a pool and a beach for more active guests. Terrace restaurant. Closed mid-October to mid-April. (Via Tragara 57, Capri; phone: 8370844; expensive.)

***Scalinatella* –** A small hotel about midway between the *Quisisana* and Punta di Tragara, it has an understated elegance and a soothing view of the sea. No restaurant. Closed November to mid-March. (Via Tragara 8, Capri; phone: 8370633; expensive.)

***Gatto Bianco* –** Its rooms are convenient, and it compensates for its lack of a view with the warmth of its welcome. Restaurant. Closed November through March. (Via Vittorio Emanuele 32, Capri; phone: 8370203; moderate.)

***Villa Krupp* –** A favorite of academics and budget-conscious travelers, this is set apart from the clamor and conspicuous consumption that dominate much of Capri. It has a beautiful view, but only 15 rooms. No restaurant. Open year-round. (Via Matteotti 12, Capri; phone: 837-0362; inexpensive.)

EATING OUT: *La Canzone del Mare* – A Capri social institution, as well as an excellent restaurant, not to mention a bathing establishment, this place attracts a large daily clientele that comes to soak in the sun, to see and be seen, and to eat lunch (the restaurant closes at dusk). The specialty of the house is fresh fish, and desserts are excellent, particularly the orange *pastiera*. Reservations suggested. Closed October to Easter, as are all other restaurants in Marina Piccola. (Marina Piccola; phone: 837-0104; expensive.)

La Capannina – Unprepossessing in appearance, this restaurant serves food as straightforward, unpretentious, and fresh as its decor. As a result, it is patronized by everybody from movie stars to day-trippers to royalty. *Penne alla siciliana,* a type of pasta with an eggplant and mozzarella sauce, makes a fine first course. The fish here is simply seasoned and always fresh. Closed Wednesdays, except in August, and November through March. (Via Le Botteghe 14, Capri; phone: 8370732; expensive to moderate.)

La Cisterna – This restaurant serves tasty pizza with thick crust, sliced tomatoes, and mounds of mozzarella. Its menu also features the largest, most succulent *gamberoni* you're likely to see and a light red local wine bottled by the owner. Open in winter. (Via Madre Serafina, Capri; phone: 8377236; moderate to inexpensive.)

Settanni – A few steps off Piazza Umberto I, it features good, reasonably priced food and friendly service. In winter, when fresh basil is hard to find, *Settanni* serves its *insalata caprese* with arugula. Try it. Open all year. (Via Longano 5, Capri; phone: 8370105; moderate to inexpensive.)

La Savardina (da Eduardo) – In the countryside, halfway to Villa Jovis, this simple *trattoria* offers excellent ravioli in butter and sage, fresh fish, and grilled sausage seasoned with fennel. Open in winter. (Via Lo Capo 8, Capri; phone: 8376300; inexpensive.)

ANACAPRI: Actually the upper town of Marina Grande, Anacapri can be reached by a hair-raising bus or taxi trip. Horns blaring, tires squealing, the traffic careens around hairpin turns with little hesitation. Even so, the *Scala Fenicia (Phoenician Staircase),* the 881 steps used by the Greeks (who carved them out of the rock), the Romans, and everyone else until 1887 (when the road to Anacapri was built), is not a recommended alternative.

Less claustrophobic and more secluded than the town of Capri, Anacapri offers more in the unending series of spectacular views of the Bay of Naples and the mainland. One magnificent view is from the garden of the *Villa San Michele,* built in the 1880s by the Swedish doctor and writer Axel Munthe, who lived here until 1910 and often wrote about the island, most notably in *The Story of San Michele.* Constructed on the site of one of the villas of Tiberius, the house contains some Roman antiquities but is furnished mostly in 17th- and 18th-century style. The villa is open daily for a fee. For an even more awe-inspiring view, take the chair lift from Anacapri to the top of Monte Solaro. Airborne, riders float over citrus groves and tropical gardens to a summit from which the entire island and, in the distance, the Apennine Mountains running down Italy's spine are visible. The chair lift operates daily, except Wednesdays, 9 AM to 5 PM June through September, with slightly shorter hours the rest of the year.

CHECKING IN: *Europe Palace* – A spacious, contemporary hotel built on three levels, it has large terraces, broad expanses of glass, a swimming pool, a good restaurant, and other modern amenities. Closed November through March. (Via Axel Munthe 104, Anacapri; phone: 8370955; expensive.)

San Michele di Anacapri – Close to Axel Munthe's villa, it has the look and feel of a private house, with traditional furnishings and modern amenities. Large gardens provide shady nooks for daydreaming and other spots for unobstructed views. Restaurant. Open all year. (Via G. Orlandi 14, Anacapri; phone: 8371427; moderate.)

Loreley – Economical, clean, cozy, and convivial, it looks out on lemon groves and is flower- and fruit-scented. The rooms are large and well furnished and some have a private bath and balcony. No restaurant. Open all year. (Via G. Orlandi 16, Anacapri; phone: 8371440; inexpensive.)

Ischia

It is difficult to say when, much less why, Ischia began getting second billing to nearby Capri. Perhaps it goes back to the emperor Augustus, who gave the island to the Neapolitans in a trade for Capri, an island half its size (Ischia measures about six miles east to west and four miles north to south). Today Ischia is too often overlooked by American travelers, who would be wiser to have a firsthand look. Many Italians prefer it to Capri, which they consider too crowded, and many Germans have also discovered it, returning again and again. They love its clear sparkling waters, its sandy beaches (a marked contrast to the dearth of them on Capri), its extensive pine forests, vineyards, and citrus groves — all the green scenery that has caused it to be known as the Emerald Isle. A good many visitors also come for the hot mineral waters, to "detox," and perhaps lose a kilo or two.

Just as Capri is a continuation of the Sorrento Peninsula, the southern shore of the Bay of Naples, Ischia is a continuation of the Campi Flegrei (Phlegrean Fields) of the northern shore. This, in fact, was where the "fiery fields" finally got down to business, because Ischia is a volcanic island of craters and lava beds, with the cone-shaped, 2,590-foot Monte Epomeo, the crux of it all, standing nearly dead center. Monte Epomeo hasn't erupted since the early fourteenth century, and its slopes are now covered with vines that produce the well-known Epomeo wine. The mineral springs, whose beneficial effects were known to the ancients, do endure, however, continuing to issue forth at varying temperatures. Here, the waters are not used for drinking (as in Montecatini and many other Italian spas), but for hydromassage, inhalation, and thermal mineral baths — and for mud baths above all.

The island has had a turbulent history. Beginning with the ancient Greeks, it has been colonized, occupied, ruled, or sacked by a succession of invaders, among them the Neapolitans, the Romans, the Goths, the Saracens, the Normans, the Pisans, the Angevins, the Aragonese, the pirate Barbarossa, the duke of Guise, and Admiral Nelson. And from time to time, islanders and invaders alike found it necessary to surrender to the superior force of the island's volcanic nature and evacuate completely. Today the island shows few signs of this tumult except in the variety of its architectural styles and in the accretion of history surrounding, for instance, the *isolotto,* the little island that sits just offshore of the town of Ischia, connected to it by a pedestrian bridge. The Greeks built a fortress here in the fifth century BC, although the Castello d'Ischia — a collection of walls, fortifications, and other buildings — seen today was built by the Aragonese in the fifteenth century. In the meantime, the *ischitani* sought refuge here over the centuries, from invaders and forces of nature alike. In fact, when the last volcanic eruption occurred (1301 or 1302), and the original town of Ischia was buried in lava (it was farther northwest than the town is today), the inhabitants took cover here and didn't begin to build the new town until the sixteenth century.

The town they built, on the island's northeast corner, has now become the island capital and has grown enough to consist of two settlements: Ischia Porto, where most visitors arrive, and Ischia Ponte, the older nucleus, connected by bridge to the *isolotto*. Circling the island counterclockwise are the other main centers of resort activity, which coincide with the location of the most important springs: Casamicciola Terme, on the north shore, reborn after destruction by an earthquake in 1883; Lacco Ameno, at the northwest corner, a fishing village grown fashionable; and Forio, on the west coast, a picturesque wine-producing village. Sant'Angelo, on the southern shore, is a tiny fishing village, linked, as is Ischia Ponte, to a tiny islet offshore, and it has a beach with fumaroles, the Lido dei Maronti, stretching east of it. Sant'Angelo is somewhat off the beaten track; even more so are mountain villages of the interior whose position has kept them relatively untouched by the tourist activity of the coastline.

Accommodations on Ischia can be luxurious or humble — and mineral baths, mud baths, and other such ministrations are given in many hotels with their own thermal facilities, as well as in the communal bathing establishments. Dining on the island can be in simple *trattorie* or in first-class restaurants. In season, expect to pay $80 and up for a double room in hotels listed as expensive; $40 to $75 in those listed as moderate; and less than $30 in the inexpensive ones. (As on Capri and the Amalfi Coast, compulsory meal plans may be in effect in some hotels in some seasons, causing higher prices.) A full meal for two in an expensive restaurant will run $40 and up; $25 to $35 in a moderate establishment; and $20 or less in one listed as inexpensive.

 TOURIST INFORMATION: The official high season on Ischia runs from July through September, although unofficially it begins about Easter. In winter, many of the tourist facilities are closed, but with a permanent population of almost 40,000 people, the island never has the bleak shuttered look of some resorts off-season. The *Ente Provinciale per il Turismo* in Naples, Via Partenope 10/A (phone: 081-406289), is a source of information about Ischia. In addition, local tourist offices on the island itself are at Corso Vittoria Colonna 126 (phone: 081-991464, -983066) and at Via Iasolino (phone: 081-991146), both in Ischia Porto. Many free guides and maps are available in hotels and travel agencies.

Telephone – The prefix for the entire island is 081, the same as for Capri, Naples, and Sorrento.

 FOOD AND WINE: Like Capri, Ischia is influenced by Naples and the sea. The cuisine features fresh fish, lobster, mussels and clams, pizza, and various pastas with sauces of mozzarella and eggplant, or tomatoes, olives, and capers. Inland *trattorie* frequently serve rabbit. Local wines include the well-respected Biancolella and red and white Monte Epomeo.

 GETTING AROUND: Ischia does not, like Capri, prohibit tourists from bringing cars to the island in summer; although there are limitations to keep traffic manageable, they affect only residents of the region of Campania.

Bus – There is regular and inexpensive bus service to most villages; in fact, it's possible to do a complete circuit of the island by public transportation in about 2½ hours. Check at the tourist office for details and times of departure.

Ferry – Ferries and hydrofoils (*aliscafi*) run frequently between Ischia and the mainland. From Naples, *Caremar* provides dependable service from Molo Beverello, near Castel Nuovo, and there is also service from Mergellina (Molo Ovest) and, slightly north of Naples, from Pozzuoli. In summer, ferries and hydrofoils run to Ischia from Sorrento and Capri. The ferry trip between Naples and Ischia takes approximately 1 to 1½ hours. By hydrofoil, the same trip takes 40 to 45 minutes.

Taxi – Taxis are plentiful, and some hang around the port offering tours of the island. Before taking such a tour, be absolutely certain of what it will cost, and if in doubt about the price or the itinerary, don't do it.

SPORTS: Swimming, skin diving, snorkeling, tennis, and hiking can be easily arranged in season. Be sure to visit the beach at Sant'Angelo.

ISCHIA: The town of Ischia consists of two settlements, Porto d'Ischia and Ponte d'Ischia (or Ischia Porto and Ischia Ponte). They are separated by a *pineta* (pine woods) and connected by a main street that is called Via Roma at its north end and then becomes Corso Vittoria Colonna; it runs parallel to a sandy beach and is lined with cafés, restaurants, and shops. Most boats from the mainland dock at Porto d'Ischia, a harbor formed by an extinct volcano. Once an interior lake, it was opened to the sea in 1854 with the construction of a canal through the rim of the crater. Not far from the port, on Piazza del Redentore, are the *Terme Comunali* (*Communal Baths*). Ponte d'Ischia is the older part of town, named for the 15th-century pedestrian bridge — Ponte Aragonese — that links it with the *isolotto,* the cluster of buildings, churches, and 15th-century castle that is the oldest part of all. In the early 16th century, Vittoria Colonna, whose name lives on in Ischia's main street, spent part of her life in the castle. A member of a famous Italian family, with her own reputation as one of the great poets of her time (and as the object of love sonnets written by her friend Michelangelo), she is credited with polishing Ischia's cultural image so that it outshone Naples for a while.

CHECKING IN: *Excelsior* – This extravagantly decorated and furnished building has 67 rooms and is famed for its fine service and comfortable accommodations. The rooms tend to be less ornate, less inclined toward fantasy, than the lounge, which has a raised fireplace, an intricately carved bar, and black beams radiating against a white ceiling. The hotel is set amid pine trees and gardens; it has a swimming pool and newly built thermal facilities; a beach is nearby. Closed mid-October to mid-April. (Via Emanuele Gianturco 19, Ischia Porto; phone: 991020; expensive.)

Jolly Grande Albergo delle Terme – A member of the Jolly chain, it has 208 comfortable rooms, 2 swimming pools in a tree-shaded garden (a third pool for children), an excellent restaurant, and its own thermal facilities. Closed January and February. (Via de Luca 42, Ischia Porto; phone: 991744; expensive.)

Moresco – An old Spanish-style structure, smothered in bougainvillea, with 63 rooms, tennis courts, a solarium, game rooms, gardens equipped with lounge chairs, and a swimming pool with a bridge across its narrowest point. The rooms have beamed or vaulted ceilings, tile floors, and ornately carved dressers and beds, the brilliant color scheme contrasting dramatically with the whitewashed walls. Closed November through March. (Via Emanuele Gianturco 16, Ischia Porto; phone: 991122; expensive to moderate.)

La Villarosa – The best *pensione* in Ischia, it is set in lush subtropical gardens and furnished with a variety of antiques that range from chic to kitsch. It is known for friendly, personal service and the fine local specialties of its kitchen. Thermal facilities. Closed November through March. (Via Giacinto Gigante 13, Ischia Porto; phone: 992425; inexpensive.)

EATING OUT: *Da Ugo Giardini Eden* – Set in a paradisiacal location among black lava formations created centuries ago. The service is excellent and so are the salads, the lobster, the charcoal-grilled fish, and the house white wine. (Via Nuova Cartaromana 40, Ischia Ponte; phone: 993909; expensive.)

Damiano – Fish is the specialty of this modern-looking restaurant with a glass-enclosed terrace. Reservations recommended. Closed October through March. (Via Nuova Circonvallazione, Ischia Porto; phone: 983032; expensive to moderate.)

Massa – Specializes in straightforward dishes such as fresh fish and rabbit (*coniglio*). Closed Tuesdays and in winter. (Via Seminario 29, Ischia Ponte; phone: 991402; moderate.)

LACCO AMENO: On the northern coast, a short bus ride or taxi trip from the port, Lacco Ameno has some of the best hotels on Ischia, which in turn contain some of the island's best restaurants. Just off shore, the town's landmark, an outcropping of rock called *il fungo* (mushroom), juts out of the sea. The center of this one-time fishing village is Piazza Santa Restituta, with a sanctuary dedicated to the island's patron saint (the oldest part of the church dates back to the 11th century, but most of it is modern). The mineral springs at Lacco Ameno are said to be radioactive, and the remains of ancient baths dating back to the 8th century BC have been found here. Victorian baths were built over the Greco-Roman remains in the 19th century, but they were torn down in the 1950s to make way for Lacco Ameno's modern thermal baths — Terme Regina Isabella e Santa Restituta — and a connecting luxury hotel. Other hotels followed, many equipped to offer thermal treatments in house, and Lacco Ameno soon became a resort town with an international clientele. The mineral baths, mud baths, inhalations, and beauty treatments claim to cure all ailments known to man, but the town's setting has curative powers of its own.

CHECKING IN: *Regina Isabella e Royal Sporting* – An ultra-deluxe hotel in the grand Continental tradition. At the water's edge in the center of Lacco Ameno, it has 135 comfortable rooms, most with sea-view balconies (other rooms have a village view), 2 seaside restaurants, terraces, 2 swimming pools (one saltwater, one hot thermal water), a private beach, a tennis court, and a beautiful garden. Water sports and diet, exercise, yoga, dance, and aerobic programs are offered; a full roster of spa treatments is available at the connecting *Regina Isabella e Santa Restituta* baths. The atmosphere of a private club prevails — especially in the Royal Sporting section, which has super-luxury suites only. Closed November through March. (Piazza Santa Restituta, Lacco Ameno; phone: 994322; expensive.)

San Montano – Outside Lacco Ameno, on a hill above the tiny bay and beach of San Montano, with lovely views of the coast and town. It has 65 rooms with all amenities, indoor and outdoor dining, a thermal pool and a seawater pool, a tennis court and a *bocce* court, a large garden, a reserved beach, plus baths and beauty treatments in its own thermal establishment. Closed November through March. (Via Monte Vico, Lacco Ameno; phone: 994033; expensive.)

Sheraton Ischia – Centrally located, the newest, most modern hotel in Lacco Ameno. It has 119 rooms and suites, all with balconies, 2 restaurants, an indoor pool with thermal water, an outdoor pool, a private beach, tennis courts, and a fully equipped thermal establishment. Closed November through March. (Viale Campo 128, Lacco Ameno; phone: 994944; expensive.)

La Reginella – Across from the *Regina Isabella* and under the same ownership, it is a less expensive alternative. Its 50 rooms are in a large villa with graceful terraces and French doors leading onto balconies. Guests may use some of the facilities of the more celebrated establishment, including the 2 pools. Closed November through March. (Piazza Santa Restituta, Lacco Ameno; phone: 994304; moderate.)

Puglia

Italy's southeasternmost region, Puglia — or Apulia, as it is known in English — constitutes the "heel" of the "boot," nearly a spike heel equipped with a spur. Most of the region is flat, covered with fruit and olive trees, tomatoes, grain, and grapes. But it has one of the longest coastlines of any Italian region, the Adriatic bathing it on the eastern upper ankle and the heel dipping down into the Ionian Sea. Although many Italians come to Puglia for its beaches, the region is hardly a fashionable vacation spot overrun with tourists. It is a little-known, developing region rich in history, culture, and traditions that have been influenced over the centuries by Greeks, Romans, Goths, Lombards, Byzantines, Normans, Swabians, Angevins, Aragonese, Spanish, Bourbons, and French.

The region can be divided into four geographic areas. In the north is the Tavoliere di Puglia, a vast, flat, fertile, wheat-producing zone that has been growing grain since ancient times — its name derives from *tabulae censuariae,* Roman for "record books." The area is also known as Capitanata, and the main reason visitors venture into it is the Gargano, the dramatic, jagged promontory that juts forty miles out from its eastern edge into the Adriatic. The Gargano, both peninsula and mountain, Puglia's only mountainous zone, is the spur of Italy's boot, known for its outstanding beaches, limpid sea, romantic grottoes, and tall rock formations. At the center of the region is Bari and its surrounding province, Puglia's richest agricultural area, with its greatest concentration of historic and cultural sights. Often called Terra di Bari, it corresponds topographically with an area of low hills and stretches of stony ground known as the Murge (Murges). Southward is the Salento Peninsula, or simply the Salento, which forms the high heel of the boot and offers visitors the chance to easily explore both the Adriatic and the Ionian shores.

Puglia's succession of rulers and invasions is reflected in its cities and ancient villages, each with its own character and charm, as well as in its impressive monuments incorporating a variety of architectural styles. The influence of the Greeks — especially apparent in Taranto, Gallipoli, Otranto, and Bari — dates from the period when Puglia was part of Magna Graecia, the early Greek colonization of southern Italy that began in the eighth century BC. Remnants of Magna Graecia and evidence of its tremendous impact on the Puglian people and culture can be found in the art and artifacts in the region's archaeological museums as well as in many of its customs, dialects, and even cuisine.

Under the Normans, in the eleventh and twelfth centuries, many churches were built, and the Puglian-Romanesque style of architecture originated, incorporating Norman, northern Italian, and Oriental motifs. Solid, massive structures with rounded arches are typical of this style; the Basilica di San

Nicola in Bari is considered its prototype. The thirteenth century was Puglia's happiest moment, especially the few decades under the rule of Holy Roman Emperor Frederick II of Swabia (1220–1250), who encouraged the building of splendid castles as well as extraordinary Romanesque cathedrals, and the region flourished economically, culturally, and artistically.

By the fourteenth century, the region had already begun to decline: Venetians took its trade; the Turks raided its coasts; famine, plague, malaria, and the insidious effects of the feudal system all played a part in the demise. Not much of the Renaissance is visible in Puglia, although the Baroque did have a great, grand flowering in seventeenth-century Lecce.

Puglia's unique architectural form is the *trullo.* At its most authentic, this is a cylindrical limestone hut, whitewashed to a fare-thee-well and topped with a conical stone roof. In the *trulli* district, centered in the town of Alberobello and the Valle d'Itria south of the town, from Locorotondo to Martina Franca, they are huddled together in villages or scattered about the landscape, gleaming against the red clay earth. Such houses are of ancient origin, although the examples seen today are at most a few hundred years old, and many are even brand-new (these exhibit variations on the structural theme). Some are still inhabited, some are used as shops and storehouses, and some are rented as summer cottages. Indeed, at Alberobello, it is possible to stay in a hotel made entirely of modern *trulli.*

Elsewhere there are numerous towns that, although without *trulli,* still have a bleached, whitewashed look about them, as though they belong in Greece or in North Africa. They can be found in the Gargano, in such towns as Rodi Garganico and Peschici, and in the Salento; perhaps the most picturesque is Ostuni, in the province of Brindisi.

Puglia has busy commercial ports, beautiful stretches of uncrowded beach, and clear azure waters. Its wonderful regional cooking is based largely on an abundance of squid, octopus, mussels, clams, and a variety of fish (red mullet, spiny lobster, dentex, fresh sardines, and eels) found in its two seas. Specialties include *ciambotto,* a fish sauce for spaghetti, native to Bari; the Spanish-inspired *tiella* (baked layers of potatoes, rice, mussels, clams, or other seafood); *spaghetti alle cozze* (with mussels) or *alle vongole* (with clams); *zuppa di pesce* (fish soup); and seafood salad with squid, octopus, and cuttlefish.

Regional dishes also use products from the countryside's wheat fields, olive groves, fig trees, and fragrant almond trees — as well as endless vineyards. Local pasta includes the ear-shaped *orecchiette,* served with a variety of sauces, and *maccheroni al forno* (a kind of pie with pasta, sausage, meatballs, and cheese); other specialties are *cicoria con fave* (purée of dandelion greens and fava beans) and *bruschetta* (toasted crusty country bread brushed with olive oil and topped with tomatoes or arugula). Puglian breads, olive oil, and cheese are superb. Bread is always served along with *taralli,* small yeast-dough rings made with flour, olive oil, and white wine, and sometimes flavored with fennel or pepper (sweeter versions of *taralli,* frosted with sugar icing, are served for dessert). The fruit course is customarily served with vegetables such as fennel and cucumbers.

Puglia's dessert grapes are the best in Italy, but the region is also one of the country's largest producers of wine. Excellent local wines, once used chiefly for blending with those from the north and from France, are now available everywhere. Among those recommended are Castel del Monte, Copertino, Locorotondo, and Salice Salentino.

The best times for a visit are spring and fall, when the mild Mediterranean climate is ideal. From the rest of Italy the region is easy to reach by plane (flights to Bari or Brindisi from Milan and Rome), train (roughly 13 hours from Milan, 7 hours from Rome), or car. Once there, however, seeing Puglia by car is a must — and a pleasure, as the roads and highways are in excellent condition.

The route outlined here begins in Bari and forms two loops, one leading north and the other south. The northern loop follows the Adriatic coast for a stretch, detours inland to a 13th-century castle, Castel del Monte, and returns to the coast to visit Trani and Barletta before continuing north to the promontory of Gargano and its resorts. Then it turns inland to the Capitanata area and returns to Bari after a visit to Foggia. The southern loop also follows the coast for a stretch, then heads inland to visit Alberobello and the *trulli* district. It returns to the Adriatic via Ostuni and passes through Brindisi on the way to Lecce, a lovely Baroque city in the middle of the Salento. Otranto, on the Adriatic side of the peninsula, and Gallipoli, on the Ionian side, are visited before the route winds up at Taranto and returns to Bari.

A double room in a hotel listed as expensive will cost $70 or more; in a hotel listed as moderate, prices will range from approximately $45 to $60; an inexpensive hotel will cost less than $30. Dining in Puglia — three courses plus wine and service — will run from $60 and up for two in an expensive restaurant, from $30 to $50 in a moderate restaurant, and less than $30 in an inexpensive one.

BARI: The region's capital city is a metropolis of close to 500,000 people, an important trade center, and, with Brindisi, one of the two most important commercial ports on the lower Adriatic. Because of its enviable coastal position, it was subjected to countless invasions and periods of foreign domination throughout history. Possibly of Illyrian origin, it was colonized by the Greeks, then by the Romans (who called it Barium), and later ruled by Goths, Lombards, Byzantines, and Normans. Today it consists of two distinct parts. In its attractive and sophisticated modern section, built from the early 19th century on, streets follow a grid pattern. There are broad, palm-lined boulevards, fashionable shops (in the vicinity of Via Sparano), good hotels, and excellent restaurants. The contrast with its old section, Bari Vecchia, on a promontory between the old and new ports, is striking. In Bari Vecchia, narrow stone streets and tiny arched alleyways wind around pastel buildings, ancient churches, bountiful produce stands, and scenes of bustling local life. Newly washed laundry hangs above the streets, and elderly women dressed in black still scrub the steps in front of their homes.

In the heart of the old town stands the *Basilica di San Nicola* (*Basilica of St. Nicholas*), the first Norman church in Puglia and an outstanding example of Puglian-Romanesque architecture. It was built between 1087 and 1197 (on the site of the city's previous Byzantine governor's palace, of which some parts remain) to house the bones of San Nicola, the city's patron saint, stolen from Asia Minor by a group of Barese sailors. Bari's San Nicola is the very same St. Nicholas, a 4th-century bishop of Myra (now in Turkey) who was known for his good deeds on behalf of children and who eventually evolved into Santa Claus. (The bones are underneath the altar in the crypt.) The church is also known for its 12th-century bishop's throne. Still in the old city and not far away is the 12th-century *Cathedral,* also Puglian-Romanesque, and the *Castello Svevo* (*Swabian Castle*), which was begun by the Byzantines and Normans but was significantly redesigned by Frederick II in the 13th century and later inhabited by Duchess Isabella of Aragon. The castle is open daily, except Mondays; there is an admission fee.

Bari has an art museum, the *Pinacoteca Provinciale,* in the Palazzo della Provincia, along Lungomare Nazario Sauro, the seaside promenade east of the center. Each September, the city hosts the *Fiera del Levante* (*Levant Fair*), southern Italy's most important trade fair (and one of Europe's most important commercial events), to encourage trade between East and West. More traditional events include the *Sagra di San Nicola* (feast of St. Nicholas) on May 7, when a parade in historical costume relives the arrival of the saint's bones in the city. The next day a statue of the saint is put on a boat and sent out to bless the sea (San Nicola is also the patron saint of sailors).

Bari is an important departure point for car ferries to Yugoslavia; some for Greece also leave from here, although most leave from Brindisi, farther south along the coast.

For more information about sights in Bari, stop at the tourist information office (EPT) at Via Melo 253 (phone: 080-225327), near the train station.

CHECKING IN: *Palace* – One of the city's finest hotels, with 210 rooms, a restaurant, and first-class facilities. It's within easy walking distance of both Bari Vecchia and the shops in the modern part of town. (Via Lombardi 13, Bari; phone: 080-216551; expensive.)

EATING OUT: *Ai 2 Ghiottoni* – Very good seafood and Puglian specialties are served in attractive, modern surroundings. Closed Sundays and most of August. (Via Putignani 11, Bari; phone: 080-232240; expensive to moderate.)

La Pignata – The atmosphere is elegant, the food superb. Seafood *risotto,* spaghetti *alle vongole* (with clams), and regional favorites such as *orecchiette con cime di rape* (pasta with green tops of turnips) and *tiella* (a seafood-potato-rice casserole) are among the choices. Closed Wednesdays and August. (Via Melo 9, Bari; phone: 080-232481; expensive to moderate.)

Sorso Preferito – A restaurant known for its seafood specialties, its wide variety of *antipasti,* and its rustic charm. Closed Sundays. (Via Vito Nicola de Nicolò 46, Bari; phone: 080-235747; expensive to moderate.)

En Route from Bari – Drive northwest along SS16 (commonly known as the Adriatica Highway) past silvery green olive groves and a succession of vineyards; at Molfetta turn inland and continue through Terlizzi and Ruvo di Puglia. Here the landscape is made up mostly of low hills, typical of the Murge of central Puglia, and vast fields of golden wheat. At Ruvo di Puglia, pick up SS170, which leads in about 11 miles, to Masseria Castello, where there is a turnoff (marked SS179 dir) for Castel del Monte, one of the region's primary landmarks.

CASTEL DEL MONTE: This striking castle, in an isolated position on the top of a hill, is one of Puglia's architectural masterpieces and one of the finest castles in Italy. It was built by Frederick II of Swabia between 1240 and 1250, probably as a hunting lodge, and was later used as a prison. It is a perfect octagon, with eight corner towers, also octagonal, and eight trapezoidal rooms on each floor. The pale, champagne-colored structure — one of the earliest and purest Gothic buildings in southern Italy — was once full of sculpture, its walls faced with marble, but much of its decoration was lost by the 18th century, when the building was more or less abandoned, left to house the occasional shepherd. The windows of the castle afford a good view of the Tavoliere and surrounding Murge hills. Open daily, except Mondays.

EATING OUT: *Vecchia Masseria* – Housed in an ancient farmhouse a mile south of the castle (back at the turnoff for Minervino), it provides delightful ambience — high ceilings supported by dark wooden beams and white stucco walls adorned with rich paintings. Order a sampling of several kinds of pasta, followed by *spiedini misto carne* (a shish kebab of lamb, veal, sausage, and pork). Castel del Monte (white, red, or rosé) is the appropriate wine. (Km-22, SS170, Castel del Monte; phone: 0880-81529; moderate.)

En Route from Castel del Monte – Return to the coast on SS170 dir north to Andria, and then detour northeast to Trani, a 45-minute drive from Castel del Monte. After the visit, continue to Barletta, 8 miles west of Trani along the coast road (SS16).

TRANI: The approach to this coastal town runs through vineyard after vineyard of the Moscato (Muscat) grape that is used to make the sweet dessert wine for which Trani is famous. Also famous is Trani's exquisite 11th- to 13th-century Puglian-Romanesque cathedral, built of the very pale stone called Trani marble. The cathedral, dedicated to San Nicola Pellegrino, stands at the edge of the sea, a splendidly off-white building against a backdrop of glistening deep blue. Its bell tower is set on an arch, with the number of windows increasing as it rises. The cathedral's extraordinary bronze doors (ca. 1180), reflecting Byzantine influence, are by Barisano da Trani (who also did the doors of the Duomo at Ravello and the one at Monreale). Inside, this remarkable church is actually three churches on separate levels: The much older (perhaps 7th-century) Chiesa di Santa Maria, on which the main church was built, is reached through the crypt, and under it is the still older Ipogeo di San Leucio. Trani's surrounding medieval quarter is also of interest.

BARLETTA: Only a short ride from Trani, this port city is best known for the famous *Disfida di Barletta* (*Challenge of Barletta*), a bloody battle between 13 Frenchmen and 13 Italians that took place on February 13, 1503. The context of the challenge was the struggle between the French and the Spanish for hegemony of the region (the Spanish won), and its immediate provocation was a disparaging remark made by a Frenchman regarding Italian courage. The Italians won the challenge. Barletta's main attraction, however, the *Colosso* (*Colossus*), predates this incident. It is a massive bronze statue of a Byzantine emperor (exactly which one is not certain), 16 feet tall, cast in the 4th century AD. It once stood in Constantinople and was part of the booty the Venetians took from the sack of the city in the early 13th century, along with the famous four bronze horses now in Venice. Due to a shipwreck, the Colossus was abandoned on the shores of Barletta and now stands at the corner of Corso Vittorio Emanuele and Corso Garibaldi, next to the 13th-century Church of San Sepolcro. The city also has a lovely Romanesque cathedral and an impressive 13th-century castle. Each year, on the last Sunday in July, a historical reenactment of the Disfida takes place. A small museum, the Cantina della Disfida, displays objects of the period.

EATING OUT: *Il Brigantino* – A rustic place offering typical Puglian *antipasti*, such as delicious olives; a salad of squid, octopus, and cuttlefish; *focaccia molle* (a soft pizza bread stuffed with onions and anchovies); *cavatelli con fagioli* (cavatelli pasta with beans); *fichi e prosciutto* (large, moist figs with prosciutto); and *scamorza alla griglia* (grilled scamorza cheese). Closed January. (Litoranea di Levante, Barletta; phone: 0883-33345; moderate to inexpensive.)

En Route from Barletta – Continue northwestward, first on SS16 and then on SS159, through Margherita di Savoia and beyond, past mounds of sparkling salt beds and geometric patches of farmland. Stay on the coast road, and as it approaches Manfredonia, the strikingly beautiful and rugged promontory of Gargano appears. A winding road (SS89, also known as the Garganica) climbs high into the coastal mountains — which eventually soar to over 3,000 feet — affording dazzling panoramas of the dramatic blue-green Adriatic and its craggy, white-rock outline. The road descends to the sea at the ancient town of Vieste.

VIESTE: This one-time fishing village, on a rocky outcropping at the far end of the

Gargano, has become the chief resort town of the area. Its old quarter, a spill of whitewashed houses and narrow step streets, reaches out along a small peninsula, with an old cathedral and a Swabian castle (built by Frederick II) perched on a cliff overlooking the sea. Although Vieste is surrounded by beaches, its southern (or eastern) side is especially favored. Just at the edge of town, marked by the giant rock called the Pizzomunno, the long, wide Castello beach begins, and some 14 miles along the coast on this same side is the huge resort complex of Pugnochiuso, set on a small, picturesque bay.

Either Vieste or Pugnochiuso can be used as a base for exploring the Gargano area. Not to be missed is the spectacular coastal drive north and west around the promontory to the villages of Peschici and Rodi Garganico, considered one of the most scenic drives in all of Italy. From Rodi Garganico, as well as from Vieste and Pugnochiuso, ferries travel to the Isole Tremiti, a trio of rocky islands (San Domino, San Nicola, and Capraia) with beaches, historic ruins, and gorgeous views, off the northern coast of Gargano (a 3- to 4-hour trip from Vieste or Pugnochiuso, shorter from Rodi). In the Gargano interior, the shady, tranquil Foresta Umbra stretches for thousands of acres.

CHECKING IN/EATING OUT: *Pizzomunno Vieste Palace* – A 183-room, full-service resort, with luxurious accommodations, a stretch of private sandy beach, and facilities for a full range of water sports and other activities. Its dining room serves excellent regional specialties — try the *agnello al forno* (roast lamb) or any kind of seafood. Open late March to mid-October. (Spiaggia di Pizzomunno, Vieste del Gargano; phone: 0884-78741; expensive.)

Pugnochiuso – This resort complex, along the coast south of Vieste, is a village unto itself, containing two beachfront hotels — *Albergo del Faro* and *Albergo degli Ulivi* — with more than 400 rooms, as well as bungalows and cottages. Guests may limit themselves to communing with the sand, sea, and surrounding pine woods, or make maximum use of the resort facilities: two swimming pools (one Olympic-size), tennis courts, gym, horseback riding, sailing, and water skiing facilities, a theater, a nightclub, and even a commercial center with a bank, boutiques, travel agency, and more. All told, there are five restaurants. Minimum stay required; full board obligatory. Usually open April through October. (Centro Vacanze di Pugnochiuso; phone: 0884-79011; expensive.)

En Route from Vieste – Take SS89 west out of Vieste for several miles and pick up SS528 inland (alternatively, pick up SS528 by turning off the coastal drive at Valazzo, between Peschici and Rodi Garganico, and driving inland past Vico del Gargano). The road leads through the Foresta Umbra to SS272, where a turn to the east leads to Monte Sant'Angelo and a turn to the west to San Giovanni Rotondo.

MONTE SANT'ANGELO: This is the highest town of the Gargano and an important place for pilgrimages. According to tradition, the Archangel Michael appeared here more than once in the late 5th century (to a bishop according to one story, to shepherds according to another), leaving behind either a footprint or a red cloak (again, depending on the legend), but certainly enough of an impression to cause a shrine to be built. The resulting *Santuario di San Michele* (*Sanctuary of St. Michael*) was especially well known during the Crusades, when the Gargano was a way station en route to the Holy Land. The sanctuary is at the edge of town, entered through impressive bronze doors with 24 illustrated panels cast in Constantinople in 1076. Across from it is the so-called *Tomba di Rotari* (*Tomb of Rotharis*), which was built in the 12th century, but most likely as a baptistry. Nearby, the town also has a castle, originally Norman, that was enlarged by the Swabians and the Aragonese.

SAN GIOVANNI ROTONDO: Inland from Monte Sant'Angelo, this town is another popular place of pilgrimage, but it gained its status only in the 20th century as the result of its association with Padre Pio. The Capuchin monk, who received the stigmata and who performed miracles for the sick, lived in a convent and is now buried here. The town has a modern church and hospital dedicated to him that is supported by his followers, many of them American.

En Route from San Giovanni Rotondo – Leave Gargano by taking SS273 south and turning onto SS89 to Foggia.

FOGGIA: Capitanata's capital city, in the center of the Tavoliere, was chosen by Frederick II as his residence and was also a favorite of the Angevins and the Aragoneans. The city suffered an earthquake in 1731 and was heavily bombed during World War II, but its beautiful 12th-century cathedral (largely rebuilt in the 18th century), largest in the province, is worth a visit. The *Museo Civico,* Via Nigri 2, is housed in a building sporting an arch that is the only remnant of Frederick's 13th-century palace; it contains fascinating artifacts and archaeological background on the area. Open Wednesdays and Fridays only.

Lucera, 12 miles west of Foggia, makes an interesting excursion. On one side of this pre-Roman village is one of the oldest known Roman amphitheaters, dating from the 1st century BC. On the other side, on a hill at the edge of the Tavoliere, is a superb castle, consisting of a fortress built by Frederick II in 1233 and a surrounding pentagonal wall built by Charles I of Anjou in the late 13th century. The Swabian structure is virtually dwarfed by the Angevin wall, which is nearly a kilometer in circumference and is articulated with 24 defensive towers. The town's *Duomo,* in a strikingly simple Gothic style, is another Angevin monument, from the early 14th century.

CHECKING IN/EATING OUT: *Cicolella* – The best rooms and the best food in town can both be had at this 125-room hotel in the center of Foggia. The restaurant serves regional specialties (try *troccoli,* a local pasta) as well as wines, such as Torre Quarto Rosso, a fine red. Restaurant closed Friday evenings, Sundays, 2 weeks in August, and 2 weeks at Christmastime. (Viale XXIV Maggio 60, Foggia; phone: 0881-3890; expensive.)

En Route from Foggia – Return to Bari by A14 (80 miles) and proceed beyond the city to visit the *trulli* district and the Salento. Mola di Bari, a lovely fishing village with both an ancient town and a modern quarter, a Romanesque cathedral, and an Angevin castle, is 13 miles south of Bari along the coastal SS16. The highlight of its 3-day *sagra del polpo* (octopus festival), held each July, is octopus prepared a hundred different ways! Continue on the coastal road to Monopoli and turn inland on SS377 to Castellana Grotte, famous for its caves, the most spectacular in Italy. These are a little over a mile southwest of town, and their fantastic stalactite, stalagmite, and alabaster flower formations can be visited in 1- or 2-hour (partial or complete) guided tours. The *pièce de résistance,* the Caverna Bianca, figures only on the complete tour. Tours offered daily, mornings and afternoons in summer, mornings only off-season; there is an admission fee.

After Castellana, continue to Putignano and there turn east along SS172 to Alberobello, the center of the *trulli* district.

EATING OUT: *Grotta Palazzese* – Along the coast between Mola di Bari and Monopoli. There are a few rooms for rent here, but the real treat is the summer dining — in a cave carved out of the rock above the beach, overlooking the water. Good, fresh seafood. (Via Narciso 59, Polignano a Mare; phone: 080-740261; expensive to moderate.)

ALBEROBELLO: This unique village has over a thousand of the whitewashed conical stone huts — *trulli* — that are characteristic of this part of Puglia. These curious examples of domestic architecture are of ancient origin, although most of those seen today are no more than a few hundred years old, and the *trullo* design is also used for modern variations on the theme. Alberobello has an entire zone, the all-white *zona monumentale,* of old "urban" *trulli* — attached and semidetached in clusters or lining the narrow streets. Many are still inhabited, while others serve as shops selling local crafts, handwoven items, regional wines, and foods. The most famous is the 50-foot-high, 2-story *trullo sovrano,* but the town also has a modern *trullo* church, San Antonio, and a *trullo* hotel.

CHECKING IN: *Albergo dei Trulli* – This establishment consists not of rooms, but of entire individual *trulli* of modern construction, each of which has its own bath and sitting room. Restaurant, swimming pool, verdant grounds. (Via Cadore 28, Alberobello; phone: 080-721130; expensive.)

EATING OUT: *Trullo d'Oro* – The next best thing to staying in a *trullo* is having a meal in one. The Puglian dishes served here may include *calzone di cipolla* (yeast bread stuffed with a sauce of onions, tomatoes, and capers), *orecchiette con ciceri* (ear-shaped pasta with chickpeas in broth), various eggplant entrées, *fave e cicoria* (fava beans and chicory), and fresh mozzarella cheese. Closed Mondays. (Via Cavallotti 29, Alberobello; phone: 080-721820; moderate.)

En Route from Alberobello – Head southeast to Locorotondo, a delightful village built on a circular plan, as its name suggests. Then drop south to Martina Franca. The route passes through the Valle d'Itria, where isolated rural *trulli* dot the landscape.

MARTINA FRANCA: Halfway between the Adriatic and Ionian coasts and on the highest point of the Murge, this enchanting town is built in an almost perfect circle. Its historic center has an overall 17th- and 18th-century look, and a walk along its narrow streets reveals Baroque and Rococo mansions and balconies, sculpted festoons of flowers, little squares, and whitewashed cottages. The 17th-century *Palazzo Ducale,* now the Town Hall, was designed by Bernini (his only work in the south); its walls and ceilings were frescoed by a local painter, Domenico Carella, and its terrace has views of the Itria Valley.

En Route from Martina Franca – It's only 6 miles north to Cisternino, a charming, chalk-white medieval hill town that is worth a stop. From there it is another 9 miles east to Ostuni.

OSTUNI: Probably the most remarkable town in Puglia; from a distance across the plain, it appears as a mirage of bleached-white buildings covering three hills, with a 15th-century Gothic cathedral at the highest point. Close up, the intricately detailed rose window over the church's central door comes into view, followed by the town's narrow streets spanned by graceful archways, its black wrought-iron balconies and lanterns, and its sparkling white buildings with green or turquoise shutters, all reminiscent of a Greek village. The main square, Piazza della Libertà, has the Baroque obelisk of Sant'Oronzo (who rescued Ostuni from a plague in the 17th century), a church, a bookstore, a small *caffè,* and a *gelateria* turning out fresh *granita di limone* (lemon ice). From Ostuni, it is 4 miles to the coast and a beachfront zone, Marina di Ostuni, that extends for several kilometers.

CHECKING IN/EATING OUT: *Grand Hotel Rosa Marina* – An outstanding, attractive, modern resort on the coast northwest of Ostuni proper. Its architecture is in the pure-white Moorish vein, and many of the 240 rooms open onto gardens. Tennis courts, an inviting pool, access to a private beach, and a restaurant serving fine regional specialties and local wines. Minimum-stay and meal requirements. Open mid-May to early October. (Centro Vacanze Rosa Marina; phone: 0831-970061; moderate.)

En Route from Ostuni – Take SS379 as far as Brindisi (20 miles from Marina di Ostuni) and from there take SS16 or the Superstrada Brindisi-Lecce another 25 miles to Lecce. Brindisi is a major port and departure point for ferries to Greece, but the city is largely modern, with little of interest to visitors. One of the two ancient Roman columns that marked the end of the Via Appia Antica (Appian Way) stands overlooking the port, near the house where Virgil died. The other column fell down during the 16th century and is reputed to be in Lecce.

LECCE: In the center of the Salento Peninsula and known as the Florence of the South, Lecce was first a Greek and then a Roman town, but it reached its height of cultural and architectural development between the 16th and 18th centuries. It is virtually brimming with fine examples of *barocco leccese*, a particularly exuberant version of Baroque architecture made possible not only by the local temperament but also by the soft local stone, which can be easily worked but hardens on exposure to air, taking on a warm golden tone. The city's most striking church, the *Basilica di Santa Croce*, built from the mid-16th to the mid-17th century, has a glorious façade exploding with Baroque detail — flora and fauna, monsters and angels. The interior, by contrast, is in the more restrained style of the Renaissance. The artist responsible for the most ornate parts of the Santa Croce façade, Giuseppe Zimbalo (one of the most spirited practitioners of the local Baroque), was also responsible for the lower levels of the Palazzo del Governo next door, while his pupil, Giuseppe Cino, did the upper levels. Several blocks away, in Piazza del Duomo, is a wonderful Baroque ensemble consisting of the cathedral, rebuilt by Zimbalo in the mid-17th century, its 210-foot bell tower, a seminary (more of Cino's work), and, in the seminary courtyard, a fantastic Baroque well embellished with rich clusters of fruit, garlands, flowers, and little *putti*.

At Piazza Sant'Oronzo, roughly equidistant from Santa Croce and Piazza del Duomo, are the most noteworthy of Lecce's Roman remains: a Roman ampitheater from the 1st century BC and the (alleged) remaining Roman column that marked the end of the Appian Way in Brindisi. Here it's called the *Colonna di Sant'Oronzo* and is topped with a statue of Lecce's patron saint. The 16th-century *Palazzo del Sedile*, in the same square, houses Lecce's tourist information office (phone: 0832-24443).

CHECKING IN: President – The most luxurious rooms in the city, although in the newer section of town, about a 10-minute walk from the old center. Restaurant; 150 rooms. (Via Salandra 6, Lecce; phone: 0832-51881; expensive.)

Risorgimento – Local politicians frequent this atmospheric hotel in a 19th-century *palazzo* near Piazza Sant'Oronzo. Roof garden restaurant; 57 rooms. (Via Augusto Imperatore 19, Lecce; phone: 0832-42125; moderate.)

EATING OUT: Ristorante da Totò – A pleasant restaurant serving lean prosciutto, excellent buffalo milk mozzarella, a good mushroom *risotto*, and rolled veal stuffed with cheese and parsley. Good local wines are Donna Marzia, Salice Salentino, and Locorotondo. In the newer section of town. (Viale Lo Re 7, Lecce; phone: 0832-21000; moderate.)

En Route from Lecce – Otranto and Gallipoli are south of Lecce on opposite coasts. Take SS543 to the Adriatic and then the coast road, SS611, southeast to Otranto; afterward, cut directly across the Salento Peninsula via SS16 and SS549 to Gallipoli, on the Ionian coast. Alternatively, either city can be explored from Lecce — Otranto is 27 miles away, and Gallipoli is 23 miles (take SS101 south out of Lecce).

OTRANTO: Italy's easternmost town is quite attractive, some of it still enclosed in its old walls. An important town during Puglia's Byzantine era, it was later ruled by the Normans and was sacked by the Turks in 1480. An amazing mosaic covering the entire floor of Otranto's 11th-century cathedral is especially worth the trip. The work of a monk, Pantaleone, from 1163 to 1166, it features a tree of life with vivid depictions of biblical, mythological, and secular scenes, months of the year, animals, and more.

Also fascinating are the 42 columns (no two alike) in the crypt of the cathedral and the *Cappella dei Martiri* (*Chapel of the Martyrs*), which houses the bones of 560 martyrs slaughtered by the Turks (they may be viewed by permission only). Otranto also has a famous castle, begun by the Aragonese in 1485, after they ousted the Turks. The writer Horace Walpole set his novel *The Castle of Otranto* here, although he never actually saw the castle.

 EATING OUT: *Albania* – A small, charming restaurant in the center of town serving seafood specialties and offering al fresco dining in summer. (Via San Francesco di Paola, Otranto; phone: 0836-81183; moderate.)

GALLIPOLI: This busy port on the Ionian Sea was justly named Kallipolis (beautiful city) by the Greeks. It consists of a modern city on a spit of land pointing toward a little island, on which lies the medieval quarter, with an ancient bridge connecting the two. The medieval quarter has narrow winding streets and white houses, giving it a Greek look even today, and it's circled by a panoramic road on the site of the old walls. Gallipoli has a castle on the island at the bridge. Begun by the Angevins (but altered in the 16th century), its ramparts seem to emerge directly from the sea. At the opposite end of the bridge is another of the town's main attractions, the *Fontana Ellenistica,* a fountain dating from the town's Greek days, although it was rebuilt in the 16th century. Gallipoli's old harbor, at one time occupied by Spanish and Turkish galleons, is now crowded with fishing boats.

 CHECKING IN: *Grand Hotel Costa Brada* – Out of town, 4 miles south along the coast, but well worth the drive. It has 64 pleasant, modern rooms, a restaurant, a pool, and its own sandy beach. (Lungomare Costa Brada, Gallipoli; phone: 0833-22551; expensive to moderate.)

 EATING OUT: *Marechiaro* – Wonderful seafood is served in a rustic setting along the Ionian's white rocky coast and deep blue sea. Try the *zuppa di pesce alla gallipolina* (fish soup Gallipoli style). Closed Tuesdays from October to May. (Lungomare Marconi, Gallipoli; phone: 0833-476143; moderate.)

En Route from Gallipoli – Follow the coast road north along the Gulf of Taranto. In and around Porto Cesareo are some of Puglia's loveliest beaches and coves, where the clear water of the Ionian Sea ranges in hue from jade green to lapis blue. Not all of the beaches are open to the public, but those that are make wonderful summer rest or relaxation stops en route to Taranto.

TARANTO: A city of very ancient origins, Taranto was founded by the Spartans in 708 BC. Called Taras by the Greeks, it was a major center of Magna Graecia, and its importance endured long after other Greek colonies had declined — it was not conquered by the Romans until the 3rd century BC. Ancient remains are sparse in today's Taranto, however; this is largely a modern, industrial city and a naval base. But its *Museo Nazionale* (*National Museum*), containing superb Greek statuary, pottery, and jewelry, is an archaeological museum of prime importance (closed Mondays; admission fee).

Taranto does have an old, medieval city, which, as in Gallipoli, is on an island joined to the new city by a bridge. Both the old and new town are sandwiched between an internal sea, the Mar Piccolo, and the larger Mar Grande, which is an extra scallop in the edge of the greater Gulf of Taranto. Given its special geography, it's hardly surprising that mussels, oysters, and other seafood are cultivated with great success. The city is also known for its waterside promenades and parks — such as the Lungomare Vittorio Emanuele III along the Mar Grande and the Villa Peripato, with a terrace overlooking the Mar Piccolo (both in the new city).

The *Duomo* in the old city, built from the 10th to the 12th century, was redone again and again; its façade is Baroque, although traces of its original form remain in Byzantine-style mosaics and frescoes. Some renowned Holy Week events take place in Taranto: On Holy Thursday, a procession of hooded penitents takes place, and during Good Friday's Procession of the Mysteries, groups of statues depicting the Passion of Christ are paraded through the streets.

EATING OUT: *La Barcaccia* – In the new city, on the waterfront facing the old city and the sea, serving excellent seafood and local specialties. Closed Mondays. (Corso Due Mari 22, Taranto; phone: 099-26461; moderate.)

Milan Bar – A casual *ristorante/pizzeria* in the heart of the new city, with colorful soccer pennants decorating its walls. Specialties include mussel dishes, known as *mitili* rather than *cozze* to local patrons. Try them with spaghetti or stuffed and baked, or try the *fritto misto di mare* (lightly fried squid, octopus, cuttlefish, and shrimp). (Corso Umberto 25, Taranto; phone: 099-28123; moderate to inexpensive.)

En Route from Taranto – If time is short, pick up the autostrada (A14) to return to Bari, where connections can be made to various Italian cities. Otherwise take SS7 to Castellaneta, and then the A14 to Bari.

CASTELLANETA: A visit to Puglia would not be complete without a stop in this village, the birthplace of Rudolph Valentino. Castellaneta is set dramatically high on a ravine, and it has a late-Gothic cathedral (in the center of the divided old quarter) that was completely rebuilt in 18th-century Baroque style. The house where the actor was born is at Via Roma 114.

Calabria

Calabria, the "toe" of the Italian boot, has had an infamous reputation. For centuries, its mountains have been home to bandit bands, and its cities and villages have been prey to corrupt government and bloody personal feuds. As recently as 1912, Herr Baedeker warned his guidebook readers not to venture here unless they could stay with the local gentry because the hotels, available only in the larger towns, were "of the most squalid description." The region still remains an economic backwater, overlooked by the broad sweep of industrialization that seems to have lost its momentum just south of Naples. But it also has been neglected by the hordes of tourists that have made the rest of Italy one of Europe's star attractions. As a consequence, the air is clean, the richly forested mountains preserved, and the 450 miles of coastline some of the least developed along the Mediterranean. Government and tourism have intruded just enough in the last decade to make Calabria a safe, hospitable place to visit.

The stretches of uncluttered sands, blessed by a summer sun from April to October, are a temptation, but the "impressive and mystic" Calabria about which Stendhal wrote lies in the higher hinterlands. The Apennines, the chain of mountains that forms the backbone of the entire country, dominate Calabria. There are four main mountain groupings within the region: the Pollino, the Sila plateau, the Serre, and the Aspromonte — the last being the southernmost and the highest, touching 6,000 feet and blanketed by beech, pine, oak, chestnut, and ash.

Even though three-quarters of Calabria is officially classified as "nonviable," its soils too thin or its slopes too steep for farming, the land is still the essential provider. The villages are populated by peasant families, the *contadini,* who intensively cultivate their small holdings, rows of narrow terraces that have been etched from the gentler hillsides. The land provides sustenance in the form of vegetables (eggplant, zucchini, peppers), fruit (melons, cherries, figs, and grapes for the area's wonderful wine), and grain for bread and pasta. On the more fertile coastal plain are orange groves, almond trees, and rows of gnarled olive trees that look as if they date from the times when ancient Greeks occupied this land. Since most of the cultivated land is terraced (it's too restricted for open grazing), all the animals live close to, and sometimes within, the family *casetta,* usually a collection of ramshackle shelters that have been fashioned out of timber scraps and corrugated iron sheeting. They are accessible only by foot or hoof (usually a donkey's). Mornings are announced by the rooster and are soon followed by a Noah's ark in quadraphonics. There is mooing, bleating, oinking, clucking, high-pitched squeaking, and even a little billing and cooing.

While the men work on the terraces, the women wash clothes in the rivers, bake bread or pizza in the mud ovens, make pasta by hand, or preserve harvested crops for the winter, perhaps filling empty beer bottles with tomato sauce, including a sprig of homegrown basil sealed in each. Depending on the time of year, there is also food to gather — wild strawberries, blackberries, snails, nuts, herbs, and weirdly shaped mushrooms. The main event of the day is the noon meal, inevitably a gigantic mound of pasta, boiled in a bath-size pan over an open fire, followed by whatever is ripe or freshly slaughtered. The women ask, "Is it good?" in a tone that is hardly a question, but rather a statement of fact. There is no room for disagreement, only superlatives. After the meal, any leftovers are scraped into a bucket to be fed to the family pig, next year's salami. Calabrians seldom waste.

Calabria's economic problems have been much greater than those of other regions of Italy. Despite government attempts since World War II to entice industry here, subsistence has been a struggle for its people, who are very different from the excitable, smiling image many foreigners have of southern Italians. Yet their misfortunes have done nothing to dampen their quiet dignity and the hospitality of which they are justly proud.

Thousands of years ago, the area that is now Calabria prospered as part of the expansion and surge of art and civilization known as Magna Graecia, but since that time of glory it has been plagued by a succession of natural disasters and unhappy dominations. It is one of the most seismic zones in the Mediterranean, and earthquakes have consistently wiped out whole towns and most vestiges of the past. Slowly, dedicated archaeologists, backed by the Italian government, have begun to exume fragments of Calabria's rich antiquity. Hardly a place exists that doesn't have its archaeological treasure — a Greek temple, a Byzantine fresco, or a terra cotta masterpiece. The entire region is sometimes referred to as an "open-air museum." Particularly exciting, in 1972, was the discovery of two fifth-century Greek statues — magnificent six-foot bronze warriors, trimmed with silver and copper — in coastal waters near Riace. (They are now on permanent display at the National Museum of Magna Graecia Culture in Reggio Calabria.) More recently the remains of what might well be the oldest synagogue in Europe, thought to have been built during the Roman Empire, were found in the tiny town of Bova Marina.

When the Romans took control of this region, they created problems from which it has never fully recovered. In search of food and wood for ships and other domestic needs, they ravaged the forests of the high valley. Lack of protective trees meant accelerated erosion, which affects agriculture in some parts of Calabria to this day. In medieval times, Christianity developed along the internal routes carved out by the Romans. Around 476, when the region fell under Byzantine rule, there was a revival of Hellenic traditions. The Byzantine influence was reflected in religious rites, architecture, and language. There are still mountain villages that conserve Graecanic traditions and speak a language closely resembling Greek. When the Byzantine domination collapsed under the Norman penetration, Calabria enjoyed a long period of peace and tranquillity. Subsequent Anjou, Aragonese, and Spanish rule, however, marked the beginning of a long, painful period in Calabrian history. Essentially feudal and exploitive governments existed, even under the later Bourbons and Bonapartes, until Italian unity in 1861.

At first, political unity did little to alleviate the problems of the deep south. Thousands of years of neglect and continual wars and upheavals inhibited agricultural productivity. The poor Calabrian peasants could not compete with rich northern Italy, from which they were cut off by a vast mountain range. The government responded to peasant unrest and brigandage by cracking down fiercely. Instead of trying to improve the productive state of the land and the social conditions of the peasants, officials were intent on creating infrastructures mostly for military needs. Many peasants found the only solution to their problems in emigration: Between 1882 and 1902 more than 300,000 people left Calabria, most for the US.

In the first half of this century, a series of devastating earthquakes, one of which leveled Reggio, followed by World War I, a worldwide depression, and then World War II, precluded any aid for Calabria. Finally, in 1950, the Cassa del Mezzogiorno, an investment organization, was established to introduce industry to the south on a grand scale. Unfortunately, many of the projects were white elephants, and by the 1960s emigration had started again — this time to Turin, Milan, Switzerland, and Germany. One successful project, however, was the building of the Autostrada del Sole, which has at last connected Calabria with the rest of Italy and made the region accessible to tourists. This in turn has helped stabilize the economy. Many émigrés have returned home, believing that the development of their coastal resources for tourism is the key to future prosperity.

The region is divided into three provinces named after their capital cities: Cosenza, the inland section in the north; Catanzaro, farther south, near the Ionian coast; and Reggio di Calabria, at the tip of the toe, separated by only a narrow strait from Sicily.

If this is a first visit to Calabria, we suggest driving from central Italy. Although it's possible to fly to Lamezia Terme or Reggio di Calabria and rent a car there, the drive south from Salerno along the Autostrada del Sole (A3) is worth the time. Despite the increasing number of tourist resorts popping up indiscriminately along the coast, the 248-mile drive from Salerno to Reggio can be breathtaking. An alternative to A3 is SS18, which follows the coast more closely and is a little rougher and more winding than the newer autostrada.

Leave the autostrada at Lagonegro for Praia a Mare and follow SS18 down the coast, passing Diamante, Belvedere Marittimo, Terme Luigiane, and Paola. From Terme Luigiane, take a breathtakingly beautiful drive into the mountains to eventually reconnect with the autostrada and speed down to Cosenza. After seeing Cosenza, get back to Paola via SS107, a half-hour journey over a good road, and rejoin SS18; alternatively, continue along the autostrada to Pizzo. (Another option is to leave our route and head east toward the Sila Massif and Crotone or southeast toward Catanzaro; our preference is to continue south toward Sicily.) From Pizzo, travel down to Vibo Valentia, detouring for Tropea and Nicotera if desired. The route then proceeds down the Costa Viola (Violet Coast). This is a strip of small towns and sandy beaches lapped by a sea of violet and turquoise and stretching 31 miles from Gioia Tauro to Santa Trada Cannitello just north of the provincial capital of Reggio di Calabria. From Reggio, the most modern city of the region, continue around the Ionic Coast to the site of the ancient Greek city of Locri. From here it is a 15-minute drive up the mountain road to Gerace and, if the weather conditions are right and you feel a little adventurous, drive slowly back across the mountains to Gioia Tauro.

Driving is difficult in Calabria and distances between points of interest are quite long — so it's a good idea to carefully consult a topographical map before plotting the journey. In winter there is often snow on the roads; it's a good idea to ask if they are passable before setting off.

Hotels in Calabria have improved considerably over the past few years. Travelers do not have to fight off brigands or search long for comfortable accommodations in the bigger towns. There aren't many luxurious hotels, however. Expect to pay $65 or more for those categorized as expensive, between $35 and $65 for moderate, and under $35 for inexpensive. Restaurants serve generous portions of southern Italian cooking. Expect to pay $50 or more for a meal for two at those restaurants categorized as expensive, between $30 and $50 for moderate, and under $30 for inexpensive. Prices do not include drinks and tips.

En Route from Salerno – Make the first stop in Calabria at Praia a Mare. The sandy beach here faces the Isola di Dino, a tiny island where legend says Ulysses landed long ago. This is the part of the coast that has been most developed for tourism; for a more peaceful coastal town, try Diamante a bit farther along. Both towns provide a fine introduction to the province of Cosenza, with its wooded plains and rocky beaches.

On the way to Diamante, make a detour at Scalea to see the caves with paleolithic drawings at Papasidero. At Scalea turn off onto SS504 toward Mormanno and travel 14 miles to Papasidero. This will be your first encounter with the winding roads so typical of the Calabrian inland. The route passes through forests, vineyards, and orchards, with frequent glimpses of the coast. In Papasidero, visit the ruins of the Byzantine castle and the fourteenth-century frescoes of the Sanctuary of Santa Maria di Costantinopoli. It's a bit of a walk to the Grotta del Romito. In one of the caves, there is a paleolithic drawing of two oxen; it is believed to be one of the oldest manifestations of art in Italy. Excavations inside the caves have revealed human skeletons — one with his breast pierced by a stone arrowhead. To get to the caves, continue along SS504 toward the Lao River to the village of Montagna. From here, walk along a mule track for about 40 minutes toward the Lao Valley.

Beyond Papasidero and Montagna, at the town of Mormanno, those in a hurry can pick up A3 and speed down to Cosenza (after the visit, return to the route via SS107, a fast, modern road that goes back up to Paola). Otherwise, retrace the path from Papasidero back to SS18, the coast road, and continue the journey down to Diamante and a few more beach towns before turning inland to Cosenza.

 CHECKING IN/EATING OUT: *Sant'Elena* – This comfortable, rustic hotel has an excellent restaurant. (Via Salviera, Mormanno; phone: 0981-81052; inexpensive.)

DIAMANTE: This pretty resort town, in addition to its wide beach of yellow sand, has a 16th-century watchtower.

 CHECKING IN/EATING OUT: *Ferretti* – From the terraces of this romantic hotel, built in Mediterranean style, visitors can get a spectacular view (and a suntan) without even going down to the private beach. The hotel also has a swimming pool, tennis court, and its own excellent restaurant, *La Pagoda,* which offers a delicious introduction to traditional Calabrian cooking. Try *maccheroni alla pastora con ricotta, sagne chine* (lasagna stuffed with mushrooms, bay leaves, celery, artichokes, peas, eggs, and cheese), *crespolini al formaggio* (thin pancakes rolled around cheese), or *pasta al forno* (baked pasta). Open April through September. (Via Lungomare, Diamante; phone: 0985-81428; moderate.)

En Route from Diamante – The stretch of road from Diamante down through Belvedere offers lovely views of mountain slopes covered with olive trees, where peasant folk can often be seen at work in the fields. The colors are reminiscent of the rich greens and browns used in traditional glazes on Calabrian pottery. Beyond the pleasant beach town of Cetraro, turn off onto SS283 at the sign for Terme Luigiane.

CHECKING IN: *Grand Hotel San Michele* – This clifftop hostelry in Cetraro is one of the few in Calabria awarded four stars by the Touring Club Italiano. It is a beautifully renovated old villa set in a park of grape vines, oleander, bougainvillea, and geraniums. An elevator takes guests down to the "secret" beach below. The hotel has its own swimming pool and restaurant, and in the summer visitors can listen to a concert while dining on the terrace. Closed in November. (SS18, Tirrena Superiore, Cetraro; phone: 0982-91012; expensive.)

TERME LUIGIANE: Just after the turn onto SS283 are the *terme* (thermal baths) themselves, famous since ancient times for their alleged healing powers. They are named after the Bourbon Louis, count of Acquila, who frequented the springs. The waters are said to be particularly good for arthritis, rheumatism, and respiratory and gynecological disorders. Mudbaths, massages, and postsurgical treatments can be had at the two well-equipped baths of San Francesco and Thermae Nova.

CHECKING IN: *Grand Hotel delle Terme* – A large, modern hotel with a swimming pool. Connected to the baths, it provides physiotherapy and beauty treatments. Open late May to early October. (Via delle Terme, Terme Luigiane; phone: 0982-94052; moderate.)

Parco delle Rose – Surrounded by mountains and not far from the sea. A small hotel with comfortable rooms and a restaurant. Open June through November. (Via delle Terme, Terme Luigiane; phone: 0982-94090; inexpensive.)

En Route from Terme Luigiane – East of Terme Luigiane, SS283 continues to offer excellent scenery — the Italians call it a "superstrada" — and although the drive through the hills can be quite lonely, it is highly recommended. The rural communities along the route provide a real flavor of peasant life in Calabria. Rejoin A3 at Spezzano and drive south to Cosenza. Watch carefully for signs; at certain crossroads in Calabria, they can be enigmatic, so it is well to study a map beforehand.

COSENZA: The old town, dominated by its Norman castle, is built on a hill above the confluence of the Crati and Busento rivers. The modern city sprawls north of the Busento. In the part of the river that divides the old from the new, according to legend, Alaric the Visigoth was buried with his treasure in AD 412. The waters were supposedly diverted for the burial and then restored to their natural course. For years, archaeological teams have searched the riverbed at various points but have failed to find any evidence to support the legend.

Cosenza was part of Magna Graecia and later part of the Roman Empire. The imperial road Via Pompilia passed through the town, linking Rome with Reggio Calabria. Cosenza was twice destroyed by the Saracens before it was conquered by the Norman Robert Guiscard in the 11th century. It was later ruled by his half brother Roger. Under subsequent Aragonese, Angevin, and Spanish rule, it was the most important town in Calabria and has always had strong links with Naples and the other major cities of Italy. Today it is an important commercial and agricultural center. The University of Calabria — Italy's newest and most modern — was recently built on the outskirts of the city.

Visitors arriving in Cosenza between 7 and 8 PM will find minor chaos. This is "passeggiata" time, when the whole town empties into the main thoroughfare to stroll and greet each other. Piazza Kennedy seems to be the favorite meeting place for students, who stand in the middle of the road in groups earnestly chatting, making pedestrian traffic impossible. Only a few blocks away, the streets are virtually deserted. The people of Cosenza are animated but very different from the image of southern Italians described in most guidebooks. They have fine, chiseled profiles, like the Greek faces in archaeological museums; they are often fair and solemn-faced.

For the visitor, the most interesting part of Cosenza is the old city, and the most romantic point of entry is along the road that skirts the castle and leads straight into Piazza XV Marzo, where the town museum is located. Corso Telesio leads from the square into the heart of the old city, passing the duomo. This Gothic building was rebuilt after the 1184 earthquake and adjoins the archbishop's palace, which contains one of Calabria's most precious treasures — a Byzantine reliquary cross, said to have been the gift of Frederick II. The reliquary is made of gold filigree and is encrusted with jewels. There are many other art treasures in the churches of old Cosenza. A visit to the Chiesa di San Domenico is especially rewarding.

 CHECKING IN: *Agip* – A large hotel with good views of the countryside, about 4 miles out of town. Like all of the Agip chain, it is modern and functional. (SS19, Cosenza; phone: 0984-839101; moderate.)

Centrale – Centrally located near the station and well marked on the road into Cosenza. The hotel garage is useful, since parking is difficult in Cosenza. Service is efficient and polite; the restaurant is good. (Via del Tigrai, Cosenza; phone: 0984-73681; moderate.)

EATING OUT: *La Calavrisella* – In its own garden, about a 15-minute walk from the *Centrale,* this attractive restaurant offers traditional Calabrian cooking at very reasonable prices. Try *rigatoni con le melanzane* (with eggplant) and *fusilli alla Calavrisella* or *capretto alle frasche d'origano* (kid cooked with oregano). Closed Saturdays and Sundays. (Via Gerolamo de Rada 11a, Cosenza; phone: 0984-28012; inexpensive.)

En Route from Cosenza – The fast, modern SS107 links Cosenza and Paola. The road climbs through vineyards, orchards, and forests of oak, chestnut, and beech, with occasional glimpses of the sea nearer the coast. Take A3 out of Cosenza north toward Salerno, then turn off for Paola onto SS107. Alternatively, take A3 south toward Reggio and get back onto SS18 at Pizzo.

PAOLA: Paola is the most important commercial and agricultural center on the Tyrrhenian coast, but it is more famous for being the birthplace (in 1416) of San Francesco di Paola, the saint of humble charity who founded the Minim order of the Franciscan brotherhood. Every May, pilgrims come from all over southern Italy to pay tribute to the saint; ceremonies include a procession into the sea. The *Sanctuary of San Francesco* is on a hill behind the town, on the spot where the saint built a convent in 1435 to commemorate St. Francis of Assisi. Unwary motorists may find themselves going uphill and then down again without having seen the sanctuary — signs are a little confusing. At the basilica there is an awe-inspiring collection of cast-off crutches, splints, trusses, and other gruesome body cages strung from the ceiling or draped across the stone walls of the rooms below. When leaving Paola, don't be misled by the signs for Reggio. It's easier to go back to A3 than to take the coast road, which is very pretty but potholed and tortuous.

PIZZO: Pizzo is a picturesque fishing town that looks down from a cliff onto a beautiful sea with white sandy beaches. It is famous for the castle where Napoleon's brother-in-law Joachim Murat, ex-king of Naples, was imprisoned and shot in 1815, five days after he had landed in an attempt to recover his throne. Part of the castle is now used as a youth hostel. All that remains of the original structure is an archway and towers. In the spring, when the tuna boats are blessed before setting out with their nets, the church bells peal across the water. (In Calabria there are different bell tones for different occasions.)

 CHECKING IN: *Grillo* – A comfortable hotel with a holiday atmosphere, right on the sea, less than 2 miles from the town. (Via Prangi, Pizzo; phone: 0963-231632; inexpensive.)

Sonia – Smallish but comfortable family-run hotel. (Via Prangi 110, Pizzo; phone 0963-231315; inexpensive.)

 EATING OUT: *La Medusa* – As popular with the locals as with visitors, this restaurant is in the heart of Pizzo. Try the fish *risotto,* especially the *risotto ai gamberi* (rice with prawns) or the delicious stewlike fish soup. Closed Mondays in winter. (Via Salomone, Pizzo; phone 0963-231203; inexpensive.)

VIBO VALENTIA: From Pizzo to Vibo Valentia, SS18 winds around the hills; silver-gray olives and prickly-pear cacti tumble down the steep slopes. About 1¼ miles north of Vibo, stop to see the remains of an ancient Greek temple and an imposing wall with a view of the Tyrrhenian coast. As with most towns on the Calabrian coast, Vibo Valentia is divided into two — the hill town and the beach town, or marina. The hill town is dominated by a Norman castle under renovation; the marina has been developed so tourists can take advantage of its beautiful beaches. Now a large commercial city, most of Vibo is not particularly attractive, but its past is rich. It was always a strategic center for the possession of central Calabria, hosting Greeks, Romans, Byzantines, Normans, and Bourbons. It was an important intellectual center in the 18th century and a provincial capital under Murat.

 CHECKING IN/EATING OUT: *501* – A large, modern hotel on the slope leading up to town, it has an excellent view of the Gulf of Tropea. There are 2 restaurants: At the main restaurant inside, the emphasis is on fish, and the *antipasti* are free; open all year. Outside, diners can dawdle over puddings and local wines at the poolside restaurant; open summers only from sunset to the small hours of the morning. (A3 turnoff for Vibo Valentia; phone: 0963-43951; hotel, moderate; restaurants, inexpensive.)

En Route from Vibo Valentia – Before going to Gioia Tauro, which is the beginning of the Costa Viola, make a detour toward the coast to Tropea and Nicotera. Follow SS522 from Vibo Marina to Tropea.

TROPEA: Crouched on a cliff above the sea, Tropea is one of the few old towns that have remained virtually intact in earthquake-prone Calabria. It is one of the most picturesque fishing villages on this part of the coast. Many of its 5th- and 6th-century buildings are still standing, though the origins of the town go back even farther. On a clear day, it's possible to see as far as the Lipari Islands.

 CHECKING IN: *La Pineta* – A modern, comfortable seaside hotel with restaurant catering to conventioneers and holiday celebrants. All rooms are double. (Via Marina 150, Tropea; phone: 0963-61700; expensive to moderate.)

Virgilio – A comfortable 48-room hotel near the center of town. (Via Tondo, Tropea; phone: 0963-61778; moderate.)

NICOTERA: It's sensible to study directions in this area well before arriving. As the excellent Italian guidebook to Calabria *Incontro con la Calabria,* by Domenico Laruffa, points out, the access roads to Nicotera are "quite accidental." But Calabrians will always try to be helpful, so if in doubt, stop a passing motor scooter and ask. SS522 winds along the coast for another 25 miles beyond Tropea to Nicotera, and the view is particularly stunning, passing lush fields of olives, wheat, and onions, for which the area is famous. The old town clings to the hill above. Drive to the top — the modern part of Nicotera — and if it's Sunday morning, join the market throng surveying the many excellent food stalls stuffed with local sausage, pecorino cheese, fresh almonds, and the traditional honey bread — formed into animal shapes or musical instruments. Walk down into the old part of the town and wander along the winding little streets. An agricultural and fishing village, Nicotera also is home to many artisans. A few miles down the road at Badia di Nicotera, master ceramist Giuseppe Cocciolo works in his *laboratorio* at Piazza Fontana. He makes wonderful terra cotta masks which, according to tradition, keep away evil spirits.

 CHECKING IN: *Miragolfo* – Just on the outskirts of town, its balconied rooms overlook the sea in front and the countryside in back. (Via Corta 68, Nicotera; phone: 0963-81470; moderate.)

GIOIA TAURO: SS522 continues down the coast to Gioia Tauro, the first town on the Costa Viola. The olive trees on the Plain of Gioia are said to be the oldest and largest in Europe, dating from the time of Christ.

 CHECKING IN: *Euromotel* – About 1¼ miles southeast of the city, this is adequate for a short stay. Air conditioning and a garden. (SS111, Gioia Tauro; phone: 0966-52083; moderate.)

Park – A simple place with air conditioning, a garden, and a restaurant. (Via Nazionale 18, Gioia Tauro; phone: 0966-51159; moderate.)

 EATING OUT: *Il Buco* – Northern Italian dishes primarily from Emilia share the menu with local cuisine. (Via Lomoro, Gioia Tauro; phone: 0966-51512; moderate to inexpensive.)

PALMI: On the drive south from Gioia Tauro, the road suddenly opens out to the largest of Palmi's sandy beaches, La Tonnara. Lush subtropical plants and uncultivated flora — jasmine, bougainvillea, prickly-pear, and bergamot — fill the air with a sweet fragrance. The view from Mount St. Elia, "the balcony over Tyrrhenia," just south of the city, includes Mount Etna and Messina in Sicily, the Lipari Islands, and the Calabrian coast as far north as Capo Vaticano.

The *Calabrian Folklore Museum* is housed in the Casa della Cultura, a modern cultural center on the road leading out of Palmi to Mount St. Elia. The museum has a wonderful collection of old and new terra cotta masks and water vessels, Greek-style ceramics from the Ionian coast, hand-carved wooden utensils from the Aspromonte Mountains, a number of religious and pagan objects, and examples of traditional costumes. Closed Mondays.

 CHECKING IN: *Arcobaleno* – This small hotel on the road between Palmi and the Taureana beach (about 4 miles north of the town proper) has a restaurant, swimming pool, and tennis courts. (Contrada Taureana; phone: 0966-46315; moderate.)

Costa Viola – The rooms have a lovely sea view in this quiet countryside hotel set among olive groves. Open in summer only. (Località Torre; phone: 0966-46278; moderate.)

Garden – Palmi's first hotel is quite pretty, in an old-fashioned way, but to enjoy it you must have an appreciation for history. (Piazza Lo Sardo 9, Palmi; phone: 0966-46343; inexpensive.)

Miami – Not as sophisticated as its name suggests, but good because of its location on the beach, almost 4 miles north of Palmi. (Lido Tonnara; phone: 0966-46296; inexpensive.)

Oscar – In the heart of town, this place offers a more modern alternative to the *Garden.* (Via Roma 85, Palmi; phone: 0966-23293; inexpensive.)

EATING OUT: *La Lampara* – A rustic restaurant serving excellent fish dishes, especially *involtini di pescespada* (swordfish) in season. Closed November and December. (Lido Tonnara, Palmi vicinity; phone: 0966-46332; moderate to inexpensive.)

Pizzeria La Margherita – Specialties are *pizza alla pioggia* and *la struncatura* (homemade whole-wheat pasta in anchovy sauce). (Across the road from the northern end of Lido Tonnara; no phone; moderate to inexpensive.)

La Marinella – Pasta with tomato sauce, local pecorino, and good fresh fish are the best culinary bets here. (Marinella cove; no phone; moderate to inexpensive.)

La Pineta – Pizza is served under pine trees. (Monte Sant'Elia; phone: 0966-22926; inexpensive.)

En Route from Palmi – To learn more about the ceramic pots and masks at the Folklore Museum, take a side trip to a little town less than 2 miles southeast of Palmi. The artisans of Seminara make the traditional green and yellow pottery according to ancient methods passed on from generation to generation. Their wares are sold in shops in the town's main piazza. Stop at 30 Corso Barlaam and see the work of master potter *Il Mago* (the magician), as Paolo Condurso is called. His ceramics have been exhibited throughout Europe; even Picasso was enchanted by them. He is one of the craftsmen teaching at the School of Ceramics founded by the Reggio di Calabria local government.

BAGNARA CALABRA: South of Palmi, beyond the famous Zibibbo vineyards, is the swordfishing center of the Costa Viola. Between April and late July or August, when the *pescespade* (swordfish) come to the coastal waters here to spawn, life in Bagnara Calabra centers around their capture, sale, and preparation. This activity hasn't changed since the days of the early Greeks; fishermen still harpoon the swordfish by hand. The *bagnarote* (women of Bagnara) are legendary. While the men are at sea (for superstitious reasons, the women are not allowed to go), the town operates under a matriarchy; when the men return with the catch, the women prepare the fish in an infinite variety of ways — most often grilled and then dowsed with *salmoriglio,* a tasty sauce of garlic, oregano, and olive oil. A *bagnarota* walking around with a *pescespada* on her head is a typical sight. While in Bagnara, look for the locally made glassware and *torrone* (nougat made with almonds and honey).

EATING OUT: *Ristorante Greco* – The Greek woman who runs this restaurant, the best in town, brought her favorite recipes for swordfish from Corfu. (Just ask for directions; moderate.)

SCILLA: The legendary rock of Scilla is where a six-headed monster lay in wait for sailors who had escaped the equally terrifying ogre of Charybdis, who swallowed and then regurgitated the waters of the sea several times a day. These legends are based on real natural phenomena: High winds often break on the cliffs of the Calabrian coast, including the rock of Scilla, and strong alternating currents create whirlpools at 6-hour intervals in the Strait of Messina. Sailing is treacherous.

Near Scilla's picturesque fishermen's quarters, known as La Chianalea, is an impressive medieval castle, seemingly sculpted out of the rock of Scilla itself. Its ruins now house a youth hostel — one of the best — and a discotheque. This, as well as the grand terrace of the main town square, is worth a visit. Now a favorite promenade for residents and visitors, the terrace overlooks the rooftops of the old town and the beautiful sandy Sirens Beach.

CHECKING IN: *Le Sirene* – This 7-room *pensione* on the beach also has a restaurant where diners feast al fresco on fresh fish. (Via Nazionale 57, Scilla; phone: 0965-764019; inexpensive.)

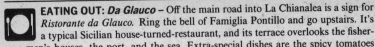

EATING OUT: _Da Glauco_ – Off the main road into La Chianalea is a sign for _Ristorante da Glauco_. Ring the bell of Famiglia Pontillo and go upstairs. It's a typical Sicilian house-turned-restaurant, and its terrace overlooks the fishermen's houses, the port, and the sea. Extra-special dishes are the spicy tomatoes and pickled eggplant _antipasto_. (Via Chianalea, Scilla; no phone; moderate to inexpensive.)

Alla Pescatora – Run by a former fisherman, this restaurant serves especially good seafood, specializing in lobster in season. Closed Tuesdays and from mid-October to March. (Via Colombo, Scilla; phone: 0965-754147; inexpensive.)

SANTA TRADA CANNITELLO: The Costa Viola ends with this town, the peninsula's closest point (about 2 miles) to Sicily. There has been talk for the last hundred years of joining the mainland and the island. Parliament passed a law authorizing the building of a link, but commercial and political conflicts have held up construction until at least 1988, and it will probably be the year 2000 before vehicles will make the trip from Calabria to Sicily under their own power. Rejoin A3 here and continue to Reggio. Alternatively, stay on SS18 for Villa San Giovanni.

VILLA SAN GIOVANNI: If the glimpses of Sicily are tempting, take one of the regular car ferries or a hydrofoil across the Strait of Messina. Similar transport to Messina is also available from Reggio, making a day trip to Taormina (only 31 miles from Messina) almost irresistible. At the gas station on A3, just before the turnoff for Villa San Giovanni, an information office has up-to-date information on schedules.

EATING OUT: _Restaurant Piccolo Hotel_ – While waiting for the ferry, have a meal here in front of the docks. Try the _involtini di pescespada_ (swordfish rolls) or the _saltimbocca al Piccolo Hotel_ (thin slices of veal in a subtle light sauce). The wine is good, as are the homemade sweets and ice cream. (Piazza della Stazione, Villa San Giovanni; phone: 0965-751153; inexpensive.)

REGGIO DI CALABRIA: Founded in the 8th century BC by the Greeks, Reggio is one of the biggest cities in Calabria. It certainly had the most splendid past, particularly in the Greek, Roman, and Byzantine periods. Unfortunately, visitors will find few remains of ancient Rhegion, as the Greeks called it. Virtually no building dates before 1908, the year a massive earthquake devastated the entire area. Much of the city has been rebuilt in a pleasant, romantic, turn-of-the-century style. It's a pretty, quiet, tranquil place, particularly between 2 and 4 PM on a weekday or Saturday. This is lunchtime, when government offices close for the day and shops pull down their shutters for a few hours' rest.

Like most southern Italian towns, Reggio was not designed with the automobile in mind, so it is difficult to pass through the narrow streets and impossible to park. Avoid spots marked _Zona Auto Rimozione_ — they're tow-away zones, and the process of retrieving a towed car is quite complex.

Wander along the elegant and typically Mediterranean boardwalk, called the Lungomare Marina, with its central strip of grass, enormous fig trees, and majestic palms. At the north end of the Lungomare, turn right for Piazza De Nava, where the _Museo Nazionale_ (_National Museum_) has an interesting collection of antiquities from archaeological excavations of the ancient towns of Magna Graecia — Sibari, Locri, Medma — and artifacts from later Roman civilizations. This museum is particularly well known for its Bronzi, the bronze warriors of Riace, accidentally discovered in 1972 by a diver in only 8 meters of water off the Ionian coast. The two statues, thought to be the most interesting examples in existence of the great Greek Bronze Age, have become symbols of the city — images and reproductions of them appear throughout Reggio. Open 9 AM to 1 PM and 2 to 7 PM Tuesdays through Saturdays; 9 AM to 12:30 PM Sundays; 9 AM to 1 PM Mondays; admission fee.

An excellent selection of local arts and crafts is on sale at controlled prices at the local government's *Centro di Documentazione per le Arti Popolari Calabresi* on Corso Garibaldi, the town's main thoroughfare. The tourist office is next door at No. 329. If sore feet are a problem by this time, drop into the bar next to the tourist office to rest and sample the famous *granita di caffè con panna e brioche* (coffee-flavored ice with cream and sweet pastry), a Calabrian summer specialty.

CHECKING IN: *Grande Hotel Excelsior* – One of the deluxe Excelsior chain, this is the best hotel in Reggio. Right behind the Museo Nazionale, it has traditional elegance and has been renovated to provide modern comforts. (Via Vittorio Veneto 66, Reggio di Calabria; phone: 0965-25801; expensive.)

Grand Hotel Miramare – Old World feeling is imparted by the spaciousness of the rooms and the old-fashioned salons; service and facilities are likewise a little old-fashioned. (Via Fata Morgana 1, Reggio di Calabria; phone: 0965-91881; moderate.)

Palace Hotel Masoanris – Less elegant than its sister hotel the *Excelsior*, but nonetheless very comfortable. (Via Vittorio Veneto 95, Reggio di Calabria; phone: 0965-26433; moderate.)

Primavera – This simple but comfortable hotel in suburban Pentimele overlooks the Strait of Messina. (Via Nazionale 177, Reggio di Calabria; phone: 0965-47081; moderate.)

EATING OUT: *Baylik* – Sample traditional raw fish dishes of the Ionian coast. Closed Thursdays and July. (Via Leone 1, Reggio di Calabria; phone: 0965-48624; expensive to moderate.)

Hotel Miramare Restaurant – Chef Francesco Pellegrino's specialty is swordfish, which he serves in many different ways, and in season he also prepares excellent game. Closed Sundays. (Via Fata Morgana 1, Reggio di Calabria; phone: 0965-91881; expensive to moderate.)

Bonaccorso – Generally recognized as one of the finest restaurants in Calabria, serving fine pasta and local specialties, as well as excellent traditional Italian dishes. Closed Mondays. (Via Battisti 18, Reggio di Calabria; phone: 0965-96048; moderate.)

Collina dello Scoiattolo – Classic Calabrian dishes are served with art and tradition. Meat is cooked over a wood fire, and *antipasti* are served in infinite varieties. Try the *penne alla brigante* (pasta favored by one of the last of Calabria's brigands, Giuseppe Musolino.) Closed Wednesdays. (Via Provinciale 34, Reggio di Calabria; phone: 0965-382047; moderate.)

Conti – An elegant restaurant close to the Museo Nazionale, it serves traditional Calabrian dishes and is always adding new items to the menu. Pastas are particularly recommended. Closed Mondays except in August and part of September. (Via Giulia 2, Reggio di Calabria; phone: 0965-29043; moderate.)

Da Pepe – An excellent restaurant serving traditional and cosmopolitan food in generous portions. The lobster in Cognac is well worth the extra cost. Closed Mondays. (Via Bligny 11, Reggio di Calabria; phone: 0965-44044; moderate.)

En Route from Reggio di Calabria – Whether you have detoured to Sicily or have been able to resist, continue south on SS106 along the Costa dei Gelsomini. On this gorgeous coastal route, long stretches of bright blue water and green fields and the odd goatherd and shepherd are still visible, despite considerable recent urban development. Behind many of the little towns on the coast are mountain villages bearing the same names. Because of their position and the difficulty of access, many have remained unchanged for centuries. The nearest and most accessible is Bova. The people here, numbering about 1,000, trace their ancestry back to Magna Graecia and speak a language similar to modern Greek. Each year in June or July, they host a festival with costumes and music for all members of Calabria's Graecanic community. The view from the Norman castle at the summit of the village is well worth the rather frightening trip up; going down is much easier.

LOCRI: Farther along SS106 are the remains of the Hellenic city of Locri Epizephyri, from which modern Locri has borrowed its name. The new city is a lively commercial town, flat and modern and little resembling its predecessor. Locri is noted for the manufacture of mattresses, bitumen, and garden ornaments. The gnomes and plaster effigies of Snow White and her companions bear little in common with the treasures for which the older city is famous.

The ruins of ancient Locri, buried in an olive grove, are spread out like a relief map among the grasses and shrubs. From the road the remains of a temple and a wall are visible. A little farther on at Portigliola are a Greek-Roman theater and a Doric temple. Beyond those is the celebrated sanctuary of Persephone, where ancient Locri's religious life centered. The area has not been fully excavated, but much of what has been found is now in the Museo Nazionale in Reggio. The small, modern antiquarium beside the ruins has clear plans and photos of the history and artistic development of the city, as well as bronzes and some pottery and votive statues. Local craftsmen still make terra cotta pots closely resembling some of those seen in the antiquarium. Open daily, 9 AM to 1 PM, with additional afternoon hours in the summer. Admission free.

CHECKING IN: Demaco – The seaside rooms are preferred in this modern hotel in the main town. Open year-round; restaurant in the summer only. (Via Lungomare 28, Locri; phone: 0964-20247; moderate.)

Faro – Conviently located for exploring the Greek-Roman theater of Locri. It has sports facilities, children's play area, a restaurant, and access to a private beach. Open all year. (SS106, Portigliola; phone: 0964-361015; inexpensive.)

EATING OUT: Trattoria Rocco Simone – Rocco Simone used to work in the fields, but he now serves his wife's excellent cooking, with the greatest courtesy, to anyone who cares to drop in to his little *trattoria* just behind the Greek theater. Although the atmosphere is far from luxurious, the food is outstanding and the cost low. (Piazza Contrada Moschetta, Locri; phone: 0964-20384; inexpensive.)

Da Umberto – For less than $7, diners here can sample small portions of all the local specialties. Near the ruins. Open all year. (Contrada Caruso; phone: 0964-29794; very inexpensive.)

GERACE: About a 15-minute drive from Locri up SS111, an excellent mountain road, is a picturesque medieval town with art treasures unequaled in the region. Its position has helped protect it from modern spoiling. Founded in the 9th century BC by Greek refugees from Saracen raids, it later became one of the strongest Byzantine fortresses in the south. Gerace's Norman Gothic cathedral is the largest sacred building in Calabria. Built in 1045 and later altered and restored, its supporting columns are believed to have come from the temples of ancient Locri. Gerace is a timeless place. The *botteghe artigiane di vasai* (shops of local craftsmen) turn out *amphora*-type pots from the local clay, using the same methods their predecessors used centuries ago.

EATING OUT: Fagiano Bianco – Unless traveling with a group that has made advance reservations, visitors may find this lovely cantina closed, but the same food is served at the bar on the main square, where a few tables are set outdoors in fine weather. *Antipasto della casa* and the wine are excellent. (Piazza Centrale, Gerace; no phone; inexpensive.)

En Route from Gerace – Rather than retrace the route back to Reggio di Calabria, head northwest on SS111 toward Gioia Tauro on the Tyrrhenian coast. The 28-mile drive curves upward behind Gerace into the hills of Aspromonte, an area once as famous for its outlaws as for the beauty of its scenery. It's still very beautiful.

Sicily (and the Lipari Islands)

To many Americans, the mention of Sicily conjures up visions of black-clad elderly women, grizzled peasants, barefoot children, and ominous-looking Mafia dons. But this island, the largest in the Mediterranean (almost 26,000 square kilometers), possesses a rich natural beauty and a unique artistic patrimony that reflects its tumultuous history and curious mix of cultures. Centuries of occupation by invaders from both East and West have left a legacy of Baroque churches, Norman castles, Moorish domes and arches, as well as an exotic cuisine. Sicily's spectacular Greek temples and amphitheaters are the best-preserved Hellenic sites outside Greece.

Located off the "toe" of the Italian peninsula, from which it is separated by the narrow Strait of Messina, Sicily has a remarkably varied landscape. Believed to be a natural continuation of the Apennine chain of mountains that runs down the Italian peninsula, the island is mountainous in the north and east, with a vast central plateau that slopes down to its fertile coastline. Mount Etna, Europe's largest active volcano, dominates the eastern region.

Like much of Italy's south, Sicily still lags behind the north in economic development. There are fewer industries here, and unemployment is high. But the island remains an important agricultural center, producing — among other things — citrus fruit, olive oil, wine, and the most luscious tomatoes, eggplants, zucchini, and other vegetables.

Much of Sicily's history has been shaped by its position in the center of the Mediterranean, enabling successive waves of conquerors to fight for and possess it. Sicily's name comes from its earliest inhabitants, the Siculi, an ancient tribe that occupied the western part of the island. Sicily was known to Phoenician traders as far back as the tenth century BC. Greek colonization, which began in the eighth century BC, brought a long period of growth, prosperity, and cultural development. Powerful city-states such as Syracuse, Agrigento, and Selinunte competed to construct the most spectacular Doric temples and theaters. The well-preserved remains of these monuments can be visited today. In the third century BC Rome took control of the island, and Sicily gradually declined. Subsequent invasions by Ostrogoths and Byzantines led to the Saracen conquest in AD 878. Under Arab domination, Sicily's influence in both trade and culture expanded, making it attractive to other groups. In 1072 the Norman king Roger I conquered the island. French rule eventually was replaced by Spanish and Bourbon domination, which ended when Sicily became part of the united Italy in 1860.

For decades, however, the Italian central government pursued a policy of benign neglect in Sicily, causing massive numbers of emigrants to leave in search of better economic opportunities. Today the island — with a population of five million — is a semi-autonomous region, and there are some small signs of social and economic progress.

The Mafia continues to be powerful — some say it dominates — in Sicily, although lately the Italian government has been taking strong measures to overcome the organization's influence. Despite the fact that the Mafia represents a real social and economic problem, it would be misleading to assert that it colors every aspect of Sicilian life — or that it represents any special danger for the casual visitor. In general, the island's calm Mediterranean rhythm is extremely appealing and restful. Sicilians still savor simple pleasures — an unhurried *aperitivo,* a predinner stroll, a pleasant visit to a favorite *caffè.*

 TOURIST INFORMATION: Spring and fall are the best times for a visit; summer can be hot and crowded, though the beaches are beautiful. Winters are mild, with occasional rain.

As in the rest of Italy, most stores close for a 3-hour lunch break, generally from 1 to 4 PM, and remain open until 8 PM. Many churches also close between noon and 4 PM; museums usually close at 2 PM and do not have regular afternoon hours. In general, expect to find variations in official hours. Many archaeological sites, for example, remain open "until sunset," a time open to diverse interpretation.

Local tourist information offices are located throughout the island and will provide brochures on sights, hotels, and restaurants. Major tourist offices are in the following Sicilian cities: *Agrigento:* Piazzale Roma 1 (phone: 0922-21050); *Catania:* Stazione Centrale (phone: 095-228440); *Cefalù:* Corso Ruggero 114 (phone: 0921-21050); *Enna:* Piazza Garibaldi 1 (phone: 0935-21184); *Erice:* Viale Conte Pepoli (phone: 0923-29701); *Lipari:* Corso Vittorio Emanuele 239 (phone: 090-9811410); *Messina:* Piazza Stazione (phone: 090-775335); *Palermo:* Piazza Castelnuovo 34 (phone: 091-583847); *Sciacca:* Corso Vittorio Emanuele 84 (phone: 0925-22744); *Syracuse:* Via Maestranza 33 (phone: 0931-66932); *Taormina:* Palazzo Corvaia (phone: 0942-23243).

 FOOD AND WINE: Given the lushness of Sicilian fruits and vegetables and the rich-tasting local meats and fish, it is not surprising that the pleasures of the palate play such an important role in Sicilian life. Though Americans tend to confuse it with the garlic and tomato sauces of Naples, Sicilian cuisine stands apart from other Italian food in the noticeable Arab influence left by three centuries of Saracen domination. The sweet-and-sour contrasts that are minimal in most other Italian cooking are all-important to Sicilian cooks, who frequently use raisins and pine nuts or almonds, and who liberally spice their super-sweet desserts with cinnamon, sesame, almond, and pumpkin. The French and Spanish made their own culinary contributions. Gastronomic traditions vary from city to city, although hardly so radically as in the past when communications and transportation were more difficult. Travelers are advised, therefore, to intersperse visits to local monuments with samplings from area restaurants and *trattorie.* Both aspects of Sicilian life — culture and cuisine — combine to form an unforgettable experience. (For further discussion of Sicilian food, see *Palermo,* THE CITIES.)

 GETTING AROUND: Air – Italian domestic airlines operate regular daily connecting flights from all major Italian cities to Palermo, Catania, and Messina. In addition, during the summer only, there are a few regularly scheduled direct flights to Sicily from abroad.

Train – Along with direct trains from the mainland across the Strait of Messina, Italian State Railways (FS) operates several Sicilian lines; the two main lines are Palermo–Messina and Messina–Catania–Syracuse. The fastest trains are generally the TEE and *rapido* express trains originating on the mainland; nevertheless, delays along the way are almost inevitable. Advance reservations are recommended. The *rapidi* require supplementary payment (*supplemento*). Local trains are slow and crowded.

Ferry – Italian State Railways also operates a car ferry across the Strait of Messina. The trip takes 20 minutes from Villa San Giovanni or Reggio Calabria. *Tirrenia,* Italy's largest privately operated ferry service, offers service across the strait as well as daily and overnight service from Naples to Palermo and, less frequently, from Naples to Messina, Catania, and Syracuse; advance reservations are advisable (Rione Sirignano 2, Naples; phone: 081-7201111; and Via Bissolati 41, Rome; phone: 06-4742041). Two other private companies, *Caronte* (phone: 090-45183) and *Tourist Ferry* (phone: 090-55903), offer runs across the strait. There is occasional service from Genoa and Livorno. Regular service operates between the Lipari Islands and Milazzo, Messina, and Palermo (see *Lipari Islands* below).

Car Rental – Once in Sicily, there is no doubt that the best way to see the island is by car. The roads skirting the coast, where most of the important cities and sights are located, are all good. Roads into the interior are generally good but are winding and, therefore, slower in mountainous areas. Gas stations are located throughout the island; most close during the 3-hour lunch break.

Major car rental firms have offices in the principal Sicilian cities; some offer special low rates for non-Italian visitors, generally by the week. *Palermo: Avis,* Via Principe Scordia 12/14 (phone: 091-333806) and at the airport, international terminal (phone: 091-591684); *Hertz,* Via Messina 7C (phone: 091-323439) and at the airport, international terminal (phone: 091-591682); *Maggiore,* Via Agrigento 27 (phone: 091-291297) and at the airport (phone: 091-591681); *InterRent,* Via Cavour 61 (phone: 091-328631) and at the airport (phone: 091-591683). *Catania: Avis,* Via San Giuseppe La Rena 87 (phone: 095-347116); *Hertz,* Via Toselli 45 (phone: 095-322560) and at the Fontanarossa airport (phone: 095-341595); *InterRent,* Via Firenze 104 (phone: 095-444063). *Messina: Avis,* Via Vittorio Emanuele 35 (Cortina del Porto) (phone: 090-58404); *Maggiore,* Via T. Cannizzaro 46 (phone: 090-775476); *InterRent,* Via Garibaldi 209 (phone: 090-47852). In Rome, the central reservations number for *Avis* is 06-47011, for *Hertz,* 06-547991, and for *Maggiore,* 06-851620.

Buses – Many cross-Sicily routes are covered by Sicilian bus companies, the largest of which are ATS (Azienda Trasporti Sicilia) and SAIS. Regular bus service runs between Palermo and Catania (about 2 hours) as well as between most other Sicilian cities and towns.

Tours – Local travel agencies can arrange 5- to 8-day tours originating in Palermo, Catania, or Taormina.

 SPECIAL EVENTS: Film, theater, music, and dance performances are combined in an entertainment festival in Taormina in late July and August (see *Taormina,* THE CITIES). A close second to the Taormina festival is the Greek theater festival in Syracuse held in May and June of even-numbered years; tickets are available from May 5 at the *Istituto Nazionale del Dramma Antico,* Corso Matteotti 29 (phone: 0931-65373). The town of Erice holds a program of theater, music, and dance each summer and a review of Mediterranean folk music instruments in December; contact *Ufficio Informazioni,* Viale Conte Pepoli 11 (phone: 0923-869388). The marionette festival in Palermo in November features Sicilian *pupi,* but guest puppets from elsewhere in Europe perform, too (see *Palermo,* THE CITIES).

Colorful religious events take place during Lent, culminating in numerous Easter celebrations. The *Carnevale* festivals at Acireale, Sciacca, and Termini Imerese usher in the Lenten season. At Prizzi, near Palermo, Easter revelers drink and frolick at the *Abballu delli diavuli,* a festival in which costumed devils take over the city for a day until the Madonna and her angels arrive to drive them out. Residents of Piana degli Albanesi, also near Palermo, parade in Albanian Byzantine costume on Easter Sunday. Worshipers at Caltanissetta participate in six Holy Week processions that are basically unchanged from the Middle Ages, with groups of "living statues" and a Black Christ. The most moving Easter pageantry is at Trapani, where *I Misteri* (The Mysteries) — twenty groups of statues depicting the crucial moments in Christ's life — wind through the old city in magnificent procession.

SPORTS: Deep-Sea Fishing – Offshore waters teem with many species of fish. The best angling, especially for tuna, is near the port of Milazzo and off the Lipari Islands. With a little Italian and some inquiries at port cafés, an enterprising visitor can probably find a boat and a fisherman-guide. An alternative is to contact the Azienda Autonoma di Soggiorno e Turismo in Lipari.

Tennis – Many hotels have courts or access to them. The *Valtur* vacation village in Brucoli, near Augusta, operates a tennis clinic from May through August. Contact Valtur, Via Milano 42 (phone: 06-4706238, 06-4706239).

Water Sports – Sicily has countless beautiful beaches for swimming and sunning. Many resort hotels have facilities (and larger cities have clubs and schools) for sailing, water skiing, and windsurfing. Contact the local Azienda Autonoma di Soggiorno e Turismo.

TOURING SICILY

Hotels on Sicily and in the Lipari Islands are rated as expensive if they charge from $100 to $150 for a double room; moderate, from $50 to $100; and inexpensive, below $50. A meal for two, including drinks and tips, in a restaurant rated as expensive costs $60 or more; moderate, $40 to $60; and inexpensive, below $40. Many small hotels, *pensioni,* and *trattorie* in small towns, especially inland, are well below this range.

MESSINA: Located on the strait separating Sicily from the Italian mainland, Messina is the third largest city in Sicily (262,000 inhabitants). Almost totally destroyed in the earthquake of 1908 in which 84,000 people (two-thirds of its population) perished, Messina has been rebuilt with broad streets and low buildings. Called Zancle by the Greeks because of the sickle-shaped peninsula enclosing the port, Messina was a major settlement in ancient times. During the Middle Ages, it was an important departure point for the Crusades — a stronghold of the Plantagenets and a wintering place for Richard the Lion-Hearted and his troops. It was the birthplace of the Renaissance painter Antonello da Messina and the setting of Shakespeare's *Much Ado About Nothing.*

As a result of various disasters over the centuries — from plagues and earthquakes to wartime bombardments — few of the city's most important monuments have survived intact. The Orion Fountain (first built in 1547) and the twice-destroyed duomo have been restored along original lines. The Museo Nazionale (Viale della Libertà) houses some ancient artworks and a good collection of Renaissance paintings. Open daily, except Mondays and holidays, 9 AM to 2 PM; to 1 PM on Sundays. Admission fee.

CHECKING IN: *Jolly Hotel dello Stretto* – This centrally located modern hotel looks out over the Strait of Messina. Its rooms are comfortable, the roof garden pleasant. (Corso Garibaldi 126, Messina; phone: 090-43401; expensive to moderate.)

EATING OUT: *Alberto* – An elegant downtown place with a quiet, refined decor, offering a choice of no less than 48 *antipasti.* Good fish and meat, delicate desserts, and excellent wines. For an entrée, try the *spaghetti en papillote* or the *pescestocco alla messinese* (cod with tomato sauce, onion, celery, olives, and capers). Reservations advised. Closed Sundays and August. (Via Ghibellina 95, Messina; phone: 090-710711; expensive.)

Pippo Nunnari – An airy, modern restaurant decorated with Sicilian artifacts has made its reputation with excellent and original *pastasciuttas,* such as cannellini with zucchini, ravioli with octopus ink, and macaroni with ricotta, basil, eggplant, and tomato. The fresh fish, especially the swordfish, is delicious. Closed Thursdays and the first two weeks of July. (Via Ugo Bassi 157, Messina; phone: 090-2938584; moderate.)

En Route from Messina – It is a quick drive (about 30 miles) down the coast on either the autostrada (A18) or the state highway (SS114) to Taormina, the beautiful and balmy cliffside resort that first put Sicily on the international tourist map.

TAORMINA: Set on Mount Tauro within sight of both the blue Ionian Sea and majestic Mount Etna, Taormina has been known since antiquity for its fine climate and calm beauty. Also well known for its Greco-Roman theater and other ruins, it has been a resort town since the second half of the 19th century. It offers more than 70 hotels and *pensioni,* as well as excellent dining and shopping. (For complete coverage, see *Taormina,* THE CITIES.)

En Route from Taormina – Both A18 and SS114 continue south to Catania. Just north of Acireale, a town built on seven conjoining streams of lava, begins a stretch of rocky seacoast known as the Riviera dei Ciclopi (Coast of the Cyclops). This area is known for its charming small bays, grottoes, and fishing villages. The rock formations in the harbor at Aci Trezza were hurled there, according to mythology, by Polyphemus, the Cyclops, after Ulysses blinded him by thrusting a burning stake into his eye. Aci Castello is dominated by an 11th-century black rock castle.

 EATING OUT: *Da Federico* – Somehow fish always tastes better in a fishing village. Try the sumptuous *zuppa di pesce.* Closed Mondays. (Piazza Verga 115, Aci Trezza; phone: 095-636364; inexpensive.)

CATANIA: Sicily's second largest city and the undisputed capital of the eastern part of the island, the busy seaport of Catania has a long and tormented history of conquests by Romans, Vandal and Goth barbarians, Swabian and Angevin kings, Aragonese nobility, and marauding Barbary pirates. But even more calamitous for Catania were the forces of nature. Destroyed by a massive earthquake in 1169, the city was rebuilt, only to be razed again and again by earthquake or by eruption of its powerful, menacing neighbor, Mount Etna.

Modern Catania, a city of some 383,000 people, has a well-laid-out, spacious center. Many of its buildings are made of the same black lava rock that, in its molten form, has so often submerged its roads, homes, and inhabitants. Some traces of the classical past remain — for instance, the Roman theater and a smaller odeon — but far more impressive are the medieval and Baroque palaces and churches that give the city its air of 18th-century well-being. At the center of the old town is Piazza del Duomo, at the center of which stands a lava elephant–obelisk statue that has become the symbol of the city. The duomo — *Chiesa di Sant'Agata* (*Church of Saint Agatha*) — was built by the Norman king Roger in 1094 and rebuilt after the 1693 quake. Its Baroque façade includes granite columns from the Roman theater. *Chiesa di San Niccolò* (*Church of Saint Nicholas*) in Piazza Dante is the largest church in Sicily (open daily, except Saturdays, 8 AM to noon). Also of note is the monumental Swabian *Castello Ursino* in Piazza Federico di Svevia; it now houses the *Museo Civico* (*Civic Museum*). Open 9 AM to 2 PM except Sundays and holidays, when it closes at noon.

The city's Baroque flavor is best expressed by Via dei Crociferi, which starts at Piazza San Francesco and is lined with palaces, churches, and monasteries. The two-mile-long Via Etnea is the most important thoroughfare, running north and south through the city and on toward the volcano. Catania is also known for its beaches, particularly the wide, sandy La Plaja on the city's southern coast, where there are plenty of bathing establishments and restaurants.

 CHECKING IN: *Excelsior* – The best hotel in Catania is a modern establishment with large, comfortable rooms, a rooftop garden, and a restaurant. (Piazza Verga, Catania; phone: 095-325733; expensive to moderate.)

Central Palace – Simple, comfortable, and quiet, unobtrusively tucked away. Modern rooms, most of which overlook the hanging garden. (Via Etnea 218, Catania; phone: 095-325344; moderate.)

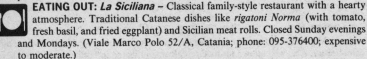 **EATING OUT:** *La Siciliana* – Classical family-style restaurant with a hearty atmosphere. Traditional Catanese dishes like *rigatoni Norma* (with tomato, fresh basil, and fried eggplant) and Sicilian meat rolls. Closed Sunday evenings and Mondays. (Viale Marco Polo 52/A, Catania; phone: 095-376400; expensive to moderate.)

Pagano – Centrally located, serving excellent pasta, fish, and wines in a pleasant setting. Try the pasta with octopus ink and black broccoli. Closed Sundays and August. (Via De Roberto 37, Catania; phone: 095-322720; moderate.)

Costa Azzurra – About 2½ miles from the city center, on the Gulf of Ognina, with huge glass windows and a terrace overlooking the sea. Good seafood and local wines. Closed Mondays and August. (Via De Cristofaro 4, Ognina; phone: 095-494920; moderate.)

Excursion from Catania to Mount Etna – Etna dominates the life and landscape of eastern Sicily. The very configuration of the land is the result of the volcano's eruptions and accompanying earthquakes. Some towns and roads are actually built of lava rock. Elsewhere the remains of flows have cut black swaths through the valleys. A day trip to the great mountain is not only beguiling but easy. Leave Catania by the Via Etnea. (It is also possible to take a tour bus or train from Stazione Centrale at Piazza Stazione; both depart daily at about 8 AM.) From Nicolosi, the main town on the southern slope (about 10 miles from Catania), drive to the Sapienza refuge; from here, in good weather, visitors can make Jeep and cable car excursions to the summit. The road leads around the mountain to other towns such as Zafferano and Linguaglossa in the midst of lovely pine woods. (For more information on the volcano, see *Taormina,* THE CITIES.)

En Route from Catania – South of Augusta, SS114 passes several minor archaeological sites. Shortly after Faro, a dirt road leads to the few remains of Megara Hyblaea, a colony founded by Greeks from Megara in the 8th century BC. It crosses the Magnisi peninsula site of the ancient port of Thapsos, where the Athenian fleet anchored before the siege of Syracuse in 415 BC. Finally, just before Syracuse stands the ruin of the 4th-century BC *Castello Eurialo* (*Castle of Euryalus*), Sicily's most complete Greek military fortification.

SYRACUSE: Situated on the Ionian Sea in southeastern Sicily, 36 miles from Catania, Syracuse (*Siracusa* in Italian) is now a small, sun-bleached provincial capital. But in ancient times it was the western capital of Magna Graecia and one of the greatest cities in the world. Founded in 732 BC by settlers from Corinth, Syracuse gradually grew to rival Athens in military and commercial importance. The Greek mathematician Archimedes and the poet Theocritus were both from Syracuse.

Fortunately, many of the buildings from this ancient period have survived. Most are in the "archaeological zone," which corresponds to ancient Neapolis (Naples) on the mainland. The Greek theater — in a natural, wooded bowl — is one of the best preserved and largest in the world; in late May and June of even-numbered years (as was the practice in ancient times) theater festivals are produced here (for details, see *When to Go,* GETTING READY TO GO). The Altar of Hieron II, once used for public sacrifices, is now the setting for concerts and ballets. The Latomia del Paradiso is a steep-walled quarry that, with much of its roof collapsed, has been taken over by flourishing semitropical vegetation. In one corner of the quarry is the famous Ear of Dionysius, a huge artificial cavern with impressive acoustics. Legend has it that slaves worked in this cave, hewing stone, and that Dionysius eavesdropped on them through a crack in the ceiling. (The name was coined in 1586 by the painter Caravaggio, who was referring to the shape of the entrance to this cave.) Sites are open daily, 9 AM to twilight. Small admission fee. Parco Monumentale della Neapoli, Viale Rizzo.

The small offshore island of Ortygia, which is connected to mainland Syracuse by a bridge, is the site of the medieval "old town." Ortygia is one of the most charming places in Sicily. A network of narrow, intersecting crossways, its faded, balconied houses near the Maniace Castle (at Piazza Federico di Svevia) appear unrelated to the 20th century. In the center of the island is Piazza del Duomo, with its cathedral (Chiesa di Santa Maria del Piliero), the Baroque city hall, and the National Archaeological Museum. The museum (open daily 9 AM to 2 PM; to 1 PM on Sundays and holidays) has an impressive collection that chronicles eastern Sicily's Greek past. Nearby is the Fountain of Arethusa, supposedly the spot where the nymph reemerged from the sea after hiding from her impetuous suitor, the river god Alpheus.

CHECKING IN: *Grand Hotel–Villa Politi* – Said to have been Winston Churchill's favorite, this hotel is hardly "grand," but it is still very nice and a good value. (Via M. Politi Laudien 2, Syracuse; phone: 0931-32100; moderate.)

***Jolly* –** Part of the well-known chain, it is slightly more modern, slightly more expensive than the *Grand.* Comfortable, functional, in a central location. (Corso Gelone 45, Syracuse; phone: 0931-64744; moderate.)

EATING OUT: *Arlecchino* – Traditional, family-style, with seafood specialties. Closed Sunday evenings, Mondays, and August. Reservations suggested. (Largo Empedocle 8, Syracuse; phone: 0931-66386; moderate.)

***Fratelli Bandiera* –** Bright and spacious, near the Ortygia outdoor market, with an enormous array of fish, vegetable *antipasti,* and excellent pastas (try the *fusilli en papillote*). Closed Mondays and July. (Via Perno 6, Syracuse; phone: 0931-65021; moderate.)

***Jonico-a Rutta e Ciauli* –** Housed in a small villa in a garden overlooking the Ionian and the best in town. Try the spaghetti with anchovies or tuna, Sicilian style. Closed Tuesdays. (Riviera Dionisio il Grande 194, Syracuse; phone: 0931-65540; moderate.)

En Route from Syracuse – The area around Syracuse is dotted with archaeological sites. SS124 leads to the Pantelica necropolis, 34 miles from Syracuse by way of Floridia, the largest and best-preserved prehistoric necropolis in Sicily. Rocky walls near the ruins of the ancient town of Hybla are honeycombed by 5,000 cave-tombs. The road continues to Palazzolo Acreide and the remains of Akrai, a military colony founded by the Syracusans in 664 BC. SS287 rejoins the main route. Alternatively, proceed straight from Syracuse to Noto, about 20 miles, on SS115.

NOTO: The second largest town in Syracuse province is considered the best example of Sicilian Baroque. Noto's major monuments are located in three groups along the main street, Corso Vittorio Emanuele. Beyond the entrance to the town through the Porta Reale, the *corso* widens first into a square framed by the Chiesa di San Francesco (also called L'Immacolata), the Chiesa di Santa Chiara, and the San Salvatore convent, the first two floors of which now house the Museo Civico (Civic Museum). Next it leads into a square dominated by the Municipio (City Hall), the Chiesa di San Nicola, the

Chiesa di San Salvatore, and the Palazzo di Landolina di Sant'Alfano. A third square contains the theater and the Chiesa di San Domenico. Parallel streets are joined by broad stone staircases.

 EATING OUT: *Trieste* – The best place for lunch. Try the *pasta al forno* and veal stew. Closed Mondays and the last two weeks of October. (Via Napoli 17/21, Noto; phone: 0931-835495; inexpensive.)

En Route from Noto – SS115 leads through Rosolini and Ispica to Modica, 25 miles away, and then on to Ragusa. The Cava d'Ispica, a deep chalk gorge whose walls are dotted with medieval cave dwellings and prehistoric tombs, can be reached by a turnoff after Ispica at the junction for Bettola del Capitano. Modica, built on two sides of a gorge, is noted for its palm trees and interesting medieval and Baroque monuments.

RAGUSA: The outskirts of Ragusa are neither attractive nor appealing because of the huge chemical plants surrounding this city of 65,000. But the old part of town, Ragusa Ibla — originally a Byzantine settlement and then an important Norman stronghold — is extremely picturesque. The new town has a small but well-organized museum — *Museo Archeologico.* Open daily, except Mondays, 9 AM to 2 PM; Sundays to 1 PM.

 CHECKING IN: *Montreal* – Small and simple, perfectly adequate for a short stay. (Via San Giuseppe 6, Ragusa; phone: 0932-21133; inexpensive.)

 EATING OUT: *'U Saracinu* – The Saracen serves a variety of local pasta dishes, such as *maccarruni al ragù di maiale* (macaroni with pork ragù) and lamb pot pie. Ragusa Caciocavallo, the local sharp cheese, is a favorite in these parts. Closed Fridays. (Via del Convento 9, Ragusa; phone: 0932-46976; moderate.)

CALTAGIRONE: Follow SS514 north and then SS124 west to the Queen of the Hills, Caltagirone, one of the most flourishing communities in the Sicilian interior. Its position on three hillsides gives the town its winding streets and irregularly shaped piazzas. For centuries Caltagirone has been known as a center for pottery and ceramics. Local shops sell today's wares. Of even more interest, however, is the lovely *Museo della Ceramica,* which exhibits pottery from prehistoric times through the 19th century. Off Via Roma in the public garden. Open daily, except Mondays, 9 AM to 2 PM; Sundays to 1 PM.

 CHECKING IN: *Grand Hotel Villa San Mauro* – New and supermodern, with comforts that make up for the surliness of its personnel. Garden and swimming pool. (Via Portosalvo 18, Caltagirone; phone: 0933-26500; moderate.)

PIAZZA ARMERINA: This small town northwest of Caltagirone has an impressive duomo with a fine 15th-century Gothic-Catalan campanile. Piazza is also known for its colorful August 15 celebration of the feast of the Assumption, in which the Byzantine *Madonna of Victory,* said to have been given by Pope Nicholas II to the Norman king Roger, is carried through the streets in medieval procession.

Four miles south of town is the ruin of the *Villa Romana del Casale* (a Roman imperial villa) considered to be the most important Roman construction in Sicily. Built in the 3rd or 4th century AD at the foot of Mount Mangone, the sprawling villa probably was the country or summer residence of the emperor Maximian Herculius. Archaeologists and historians believe that the villa was inhabited throughout the Byzantine-Islamic period, destroyed during the barbarian invasions, restored to glory by the Normans after the year 1000, and razed by William the Bad in the 12th century. It was gradually buried by repeated flooding and soil erosion; its modern excavation began in 1928. The building is organized in four large groups of rooms linked by corridors, peristyles, and galleries. It had cold- and hot-water baths, gymnasiums, gardens, and halls, the dimensions of which alone testify to their original grandeur. But most remarkable is the delightful quality, color, design, and notable state of preservation of the mosaic floors that run through most of the villa. These may well be among the most important historical documents of antiquity. The best known decorate the *Room of the Lesser Hunt,* the *Room of the Cupid Fishermen,* the *Ambulatory of the Great Hunt,* and the *Room of the Ten Maidens.*

 EATING OUT: *Ritrovo* – Here the *ragù* is as hearty as in days of old, and the charcoal-broiled lamb chops are delicious. Closed Tuesdays. (SS117B, Piazza Armerina; phone: 0935-85282; inexpensive.)

ENNA: Its commanding position on a steep hill made Enna an impregnable stronghold in ancient times and earned it the nickname Belvedere of Sicily. The town is built on the site of ancient Henna, which was founded by the Siculi tribe and, according to mythology, was the site of the rape of Persephone by Pluto. It became the center of the cult of Demeter, or Ceres, Persephone's mother.

An agricultural center today, Enna has several major monuments. The 14th-century duomo, founded by Eleonora, wife of Frederick II of Aragon, is a strange mixture of Gothic and Baroque with interesting carved black alabaster columns in the nave. The massive *Castello di Lombardia* at the end of Via Roma is one of the most important medieval castles in Sicily, although only 6 of the original 20 towers survive (open mornings and from 3 to 5 PM). On the other side of the old city is the octagonal *Tower of Frederick II of Swabia.* Enter from the Giardino Pubblico (Public Garden); open 9 AM to sunset.

 EATING OUT: *Centrale* – Delicious Sicilian and Ennese specialties. Try a slice of *pani cunzatu* (baked bread and bacon slices), homemade *maccarruni* with fresh local vegetables, or *coppole di cacchio* (roast peppers with pasta). Closed Saturdays. (Via 6 Dicembre 9, Enna; phone: 0935-21025; moderate.)

La Fontana – Near the center of town, not far from a belvedere that overlooks the valley below, this *trattoria* offers typical Sicilian fare such as *risotto* with herbs, *cavatelli,* and grilled lamb. Closed Sundays except in the summer. (Via Volturno 6, Enna; phone: 0935-25465; inexpensive.)

Excursion from Enna – The red-hued medieval town of Calascibetta, on a peak 4 miles north of Enna, got its name from the Arabs, who called it Kalat-Scibet. A walk around town is a stroll into the past. There are splendid views from the Calascibetta belvedere.

CALTANISSETTA: Southwest of Enna is Caltanissetta, a largely modern town built on the site of the ancient city of Nissa. The duomo (*Chiesa di Santa Maria la Nova e San Michele*) has two *campanili* and, inside, some interesting paintings. A street running alongside the duomo, Via San Domenico, leads through an old quarter with narrow, winding streets. The *Museo Civico* (*Civic Museum*), Via Colajanni 3, has a small archaeological collection.

 EATING OUT: *Cortese* – Although some critics feel the recent move to larger, more modern quarters has meant a loss of ambience, the food is still as good as ever. The *cavatelli al ragù* is excellent for a pasta course, the *involtini* (veal rolls) as a main dish. (Viale Sicilia 166, Caltanissetta; phone: 0934-31686; moderate.)

En Route from Caltanissetta – SS122, one of two routes to Agrigento, 36 miles away, passes through picturesque towns like Naro, with its crenelated city walls and Baroque churches and convents, and Favara, a Norman town that grew up around the 1275 Chiaramonte Castle that stands in Piazza Cavour.

AGRIGENTO: In ancient times, Agrigento — known to the Greeks as Akragas — was one of the most prosperous cities in ancient Sicily — and probably one of the most beautiful — with its location in a vast natural amphitheater between the mountains and the sea. Modern Agrigento is overbuilt and unattractive, but the surviving Doric temples of the ancient city — unequaled outside Greece itself — the excellent archaeological museum, and parts of the old medieval and Baroque town make it an essential part of any Sicilian visit.

The ruins in the Valley of Temples are built in a more or less straight line running parallel to the sea. They are interesting in any light but are hauntingly beautiful at dawn, twilight, or at night when illuminated by floodlights. The most intact is the Temple of Concord, built in 450 BC and possibly the best-preserved Greek temple in the world except for the Theseion in Athens. Its 34 exterior columns are still standing. To the east is the imposing Temple of Juno, built 20 years later but with only 25 columns intact. To the west, separated by the 6th-century early Christian burial ground, stand the remains of the Temple of Hercules, built in 520 BC, and the oldest monument here; it may originally have been as large as the Parthenon in Athens. Farther west and on the other side of the Via dei Templi, the road running through the archaeological zone, are the widely scattered remains of the mammoth Temple of Olympian Jove, the roof of which was originally supported by 38 telamoni (stone giants). Stretched out on the ground is a reassembly of one of the giants; another is in the nearby archaeological museum (see below). Of the Temple of Castor and Pollux, only the four columns of the northwest corner survive. The Tomb of Theron is believed to hold the remains of the Greek Tyrant who once ruled Akragas. Other monuments include the Temples of Dioscuri (Jove's sons), of Aesculapius, and of Vulcan. There are also the remains of the ancient Hellenic and Roman quarter.

Across the road from the Hellenic-Roman quarter is the 20-year-old *Museo Archeologico* (*Archaeological Museum*), a small, recently built, pleasantly appointed museum. The collection includes vases and amphorae from the 6th to the 3rd century BC, some magnificent Attic pottery, early and later Bronze Age material, architectural fragments from the temples, and Greek and Roman sarcophagi, helmets, and other artifacts.

Next door is a 3rd-century BC Ekklesiasterion (meeting hall). Adjoining it is the 12th-century church of St. Nicholas, with its Romanesque-Gothic façade and, inside, 15th- and 16th-century paintings and frescoes and the Phaedra Sarcophagus.

Agrigento's medieval old town also has appeal. Via Atenea, the main street, leads into the Salita Santo Spirito and on to the Cistercian convent where the nuns still produce and sell *frutta della martorana* (marzipan fruits) and other sweets. The church has a Gothic portal and 17th-century stucco decorations. A cloister and refectory hall house the public library. Santa Maria dei Greci is a small church built on the site of a Doric temple; it can be viewed on request to the custodian. Nearby is the 14th-century duomo and the Teatro Luigi Pirandello, named after the Italian playwright, who was born in the simple village of Caos nearby; the village has a museum (open daily; closed 12:30 to 2:30 PM).

CHECKING IN: *Villa Athena* – A small, exquisitely comfortable 18th-century villa set amid the olive and almond trees that surround the Valley of Temples. The hotel's terraces and balconies and many of its 41 rooms overlook the three principal temples. The best rooms are the few with private patios. Swimming pool and restaurant. Reservations advisable. (Via dei Templi, Agrigento; phone: 0992-23833, -23834, -56288; moderate.)

Jolly dei Templi – Less attractive than the *Villa Athena* but also comfortable and near the archaeological sites. Its facilities include a swimming pool. The hotel restaurant, *Pirandello,* is one of the most elegant in the area. (Parco Angeli, Villaggio Mosè, Agrigento; phone: 0922-76144; moderate.)

EATING OUT: *Trattoria del Vigneto* – Set in a vineyard overlooking the temple area. The menu offers good, if rustic, regional fare. Closed Tuesdays and October. (Via Magazzeni Cavaleri 11, Agrigento; phone: 0922-44319; inexpensive.)

En Route from Agrigento – The coast road west (SS115) to Sciacca passes a turnoff for the excavation site of Eraclea Minoa, a Minoan colony located in an isolated position at the far point of a rocky cape. The site is open all day.

SCIACCA: This fishing village is known today for its thermal baths and its ceramics industry, but it also has some interesting medieval monuments. An important trading center since the Roman domination 2,000 years ago, Sciacca became a major harbor during the Arab domination. The local pottery shows definite Arab influences. Significant building and fortification took place under the Normans and Spaniards. Of particular note are the richly decorated 16th-century Porta di San Salvatore, the 14th-century Chiesa di Santa Margherita, and the 15th-century Palazzo Steripinto.

CHECKING IN: *Grande Albergo Terme* – A pleasant establishment on the sea road just out of town, near one of the principal spas. (Lungomare Nuove Terme, Sciacca; phone: 0925-23133; moderate.)

EATING OUT: *La Ferla* – Fresh fish is the specialty at this seashore restaurant. Try the linguine with fish sauce and the mixed fry. Ignore the so-called international offerings. Closed Mondays and September 1–15. (Via al Lido 26, Sciacca; phone: 0925-23621; moderate.)

SELINUNTE: The ancient town of Selinus was founded in 682 BC by settlers from Megara Hyblaea, a Greek colony near Syracuse. It was most prosperous and powerful in the 5th and 6th centuries BC when most of its temples were built. Selinunte is today one of Sicily's most important archaeological sites. The disarray of the ruins — crumbled walls, toppled columns — is believed to have been caused more by earthquakes than by enemies.

Selinunte occupies three hills close to the sea and is divided into two distinct groups of ruins. The eastern group includes the remains of three large temples believed to have been dedicated to Hera, Athena, and Apollo. The western group, across a gorge (Gorgo di Cottone) that may have been one of the town's ancient harbors, includes the massive walls of the Acropolis, five more temples, and several lesser buildings. The now famous metopes (Doric temple carvings) excavated from this complex are now housed in the Museo Nazionale Archeologico in Palermo.

MARSALA: SS115 leads north to Castelvetrano and then west toward Marsala, the city that produces the sweet, musky wine of the same name. Known to the Arabs as Mars-al-Allah (harbor of God), its history is closely linked with the sea. Founded by the Phoenicians in the 8th century BC, it later became a military garrison for the armies of the Syracuse tyrant Dionysius I, who used it as a base for his war against the Carthaginians. Ancient remains include the Carthaginian city of Lilybaeum (396 BC) on the Cape Boeo headland, a Roman bath, a Punic-Roman necropolis, and 6th-century fortifications. Wine merchants who started businesses here in the 18th and 19th centuries brought a decidedly English influence; the city's Baroque cathedral, in Piazza della Repubblica, is dedicated to Saint Thomas of Canterbury. Garibaldi and his Thousand landed in Marsala in 1860, commencing the movement for Italian unification.

EATING OUT: *Delfino* – An excellent seaside restaurant specializing in shellfish salad, fish soup, pasta with shrimp, and grilled fish. Closed Tuesdays and January. (Lungomare Mediterraneo, Marsala; phone: 0923-969565; moderate.)

En Route from Marsala – SS115 continues another 19 miles to Trapani, a large modern city with only a few interesting monuments and churches. Trapani is the departure point for the three Egadi islands, Favignana, Levanzo, and Marettimo. Ferries leave regularly year-round from the maritime station. Erice is less than 9 miles northeast of the city.

ERICE: Ancient Eryx — founded, like nearby Segesta, by the Elymnians, another ancient tribe — was famous for its temple to the goddess of fertility, Venus Erycina. The town was mentioned in Virgil's *Aeneid.* Despite its mythological and ancient origins, Erice primarily bears the stamp of its Norman rulers. Its stone houses and fortified castles have retained, almost intact, a medieval aura. The streets are paved with stone blocks; the tiny balconies are filled with songbirds and flowerpots; and hidden behind austere doorways are charming courtyards that belong to another century. The duomo has an elaborate interior. The *castello* is built over what are believed to be remains of the temple of Venus. The views are stunning. (See also *Palermo,* THE CITIES.)

CHECKING IN/EATING OUT: *Ermione* – A bit drafty but otherwise pleasantly appointed, with a good restaurant. The cook turns out an excellent Trapani seafood *couscous,* another example of the adaptation of Arab cuisine to Sicilian ingredients. (Via Pineta Comunale, Erice; phone: 0923-869138; moderate.)

Taverna di Re Aceste – The walls of this tavern are decorated with scenes from the *Aeneid* in which King Acestus, according to legend the first king of Erice, offers a funeral banquet to Aeneas to console him for the death of his father, Anchise. Try the pasta with Erice pesto, followed by fish or meat and local desserts. Closed Wednesdays and November. (Viale Conte Pepoli, Erice; phone: 0923-869084; moderate.)

Moderno – A cozy, whitewashed hotel near the duomo. It has a pleasant restaurant that can turn out a fine regional meal. (Via Vittorio Emanuele 63, Erice; phone: 0923-869300; moderate to inexpensive.)

En Route from Erice – The seacoast route toward Palermo meanders around Capo San Vito (look in on the charming San Vito lo Capo resort where many Trapani residents have summer homes) and runs along the coast to the lovely Golfo di Castellammare, rimmed with orange groves. From here pick up SS113 at Alcamo. Alternatively, take SS113 directly from Erice east to Segesta.

SEGESTA: The ancient rival of Selinunte is believed to have been founded as long ago as the 12th century BC by the Elymni, a people possibly descended from Greek-Trojan stock. Although its cavea apparently was never completed, the huge Doric temple at Segesta is one of the most impressive ancient monuments outside Greece. Nearby is a well-preserved theater and an Elymnian sanctuary believed to date from the 8th century BC. (See also *Palermo,* THE CITIES.)

ALCAMO: Named for the Arab fort Alkamuk, once situated on top of Mount Bonifato, the town was rebuilt by Frederick II of Swabia in the 13th century. The 14th-century Basilica di Santa Maria Assunta, which has frescoes by Borremans, was restored in the 17th century; its campanile is the original.

CHECKING IN/EATING OUT: *La Funtanazza* – On a hill overlooking Alcamo and the Golfo di Castellammare, this simple restaurant offers good local and traditional Italian dishes. A few guestrooms are available. Closed Fridays. (Località Monte Bonifato; phone: 0924-25314; inexpensive.)

En Route from Alcamo – A few miles south of the junction of SS113 and SS186 is a small village well worth visiting. Piana degli Albanesi is an Albanian community dating from the 15th century. On important holidays, such as Easter and Epiphany, the people dress in traditional costumes. (See also *Palermo,* THE CITIES.)

MONREALE: Rejoin SS186 and continue east. Five miles from the Sicilian capital is the small hilltop town of Monreale, which over the centuries has grown up in the shadow of its magnificent cathedral, Santa Maria la Nuova. (For a complete discussion, see *Palermo,* THE CITIES.) The road out of Monreale leads directly into downtown Palermo.

PALERMO: Sicily's capital retains few vestiges of its Greek past, but it does have some of the island's most impressive Norman-Arab and Baroque monuments. Arab-style outdoor markets coexist with medieval churches and monasteries. The climate is mild, the people generous, and the food delicious. (For complete coverage, see *Palermo,* THE CITIES.)

BAGHERIA: This small town east of Palermo originally was set in the midst of orange groves, but with the capital's expansion it has become almost a suburb. Part of the "triangle of death" in the Mafia gang wars that raged from 1980 to 1983, it is better known for its lovely 18th-century villas. A few of these are open to the public. For example, the *Villa dei Principi di Cattolica* is a conspicuous landmark on the Palermo road; it now houses the local museum (generally open until 1 PM), which has a large collection of works by Renato Guttuso, a well-known contemporary painter from Bagheria. The *Villa Palagonia* in Piazza Garibaldi was built in 1705 by the prince of Palagonia; an eccentric grandson later added dozens of statues of grotesque figures to the garden wall (open mornings to 12:30 PM and after 5 PM in winter and 3 PM in summer).

SOLUNTO: Solunto is 5 miles from Bagheria by way of a picturesque coastal road. In an isolated position on the slopes of Mount Catalfano overlooking the sea, Solus was an important 4th-century BC Greek settlement. The entrance to the complex of ruins is through a small museum, leading to an *agora* (marketplace), a gymnasium, and a cistern (reservoir).

TERMINI IMERESE: Originally this town was settled by inhabitants from the neighboring Greek towns of Thermae and Himera. Conquered by Carthage after the destruction of Himera by Hannibal in 409 BC, it later fell to Syracuse and eventually to Rome. The modern town has some ancient ruins and an antiquities museum.

En Route from Termini Imerese – Continuing eastward along the coast, the road passes near the ruins of Himera, founded by settlers of ancient Zancle (Messina) in 648 BC and destroyed two centuries later by Hannibal. The birthplace of the 7th-century BC poet Stesichorus, Himera was also the site of Carthage's defeat by Gelon of Syracuse. Excavations have unearthed a large Doric temple built in 480 BC to celebrate Gelon's victory. There are also three small 6th-century temples and a necropolis with 22 tombs.

CEFALÙ: An ancient Greek seaport, Cefalù is now known mostly for its lovely beaches and delicious seafood. It also has one of the most beautiful Norman cathedrals in Sicily. Built by Roger II in the 12th century, the duomo stands against a massive cliff. Inside are an unusual triple apse and well-preserved Byzantine-style mosaics to rival those of Palermo and Monreale. The nearby Palazzo Paraino and the Palazzo Martino contain fine examples of late Renaissance–style decoration. Also in the old town is the medieval public bathhouse (*Lavatoio Pubblico*), originally an Arab bath (Via Vittorio Emanuele). The *Museo Mandralisca* (Via Mandralisca) has an interesting collection of ancient coins and other artifacts and some Renaissance paintings (closed daily from noon to 3:30 PM and afternoons on Sundays and holidays). On the *rocca* (promontory) overlooking Cefalù are the ruins of a feudal castle, a 6th-century BC cistern, and an ancient temple to the goddess Diana. (See also *Palermo,* THE CITIES.)

CHECKING IN: *Carlton Riviera* – Three miles out of Cefalù. Very comfortable, with pool, private beach, and tennis courts. (Località Capo Plaia, Cefalù; phone: 0921-20304; moderate.)

Le Calette – About a mile out of Cefalù. Very pleasant, with pool and private beach. (Località Caldura, Cefalù; phone: 0921-24144; moderate.)

Tourist – On the shore road. Comfortable, with both a pool and a private beach. (Lungomare G. Giardina, Cefalù; phone: 0921-21750; moderate to inexpensive.)

EATING OUT: *Da Nino* – Indulge on the vast spread of fresh, enticing *antipasti* (served on colorful ceramic dishes made in the area), followed by typical Sicilian *pastasciuttas,* and then fresh fish or seafood. Good selection of wine. Closed Tuesdays and November. (Via Lungomare 11, Cefalù; phone: 0921-22582; moderate to inexpensive.)

Al Gabbiano–da Saro – Comparable to *Da Nino* in quality and ambience. (Via Lungomare 17, Cefalù; phone: 0921-21495; moderate to inexpensive.)

En Route from Cefalù – The 110-mile drive to Messina is dotted with picturesque places. On the stretch of road leading from Cefalù to Santo Stefano di Camastro, a local pottery center, there are side roads inland to Castelbuono (a good starting point for a drive through the Madonie mountains), Pollina, San Mauro Castelverde, and Tusa, all of which have interesting minor churches. SS117 from Santo Stefano leads inland to the charming medieval town of Mistretta. SS113 and A20 continue along the coast to Capo d'Orlando, from which SS116 leads to Naso in the Nebrodi mountains, and on to the ruins of Tyndaris (Tindari), originally a colony of Syracuse.

MILAZZO: Ancient Mylae was founded by settlers from the Greek city-state of Zancle (Messina) in the 8th century BC. The second largest harbor in Sicily, it is the point of departure for the Lipari (Aeolian) Islands (see below). The town's most important monuments — the Duomo Vecchio, the castle, and the ancient city walls — are in the Città Alta (Upper City). Colorful folk processions are held on the second Tuesday after Easter (Sacred Feast of the Sea) and on the first Sunday of September (feast of Santo Stefano).

CHECKING IN: *Eolian Inn Park* – Very pleasant, with a swimming pool and tennis courts, set in its own park. Open April through September. (Via San Guiseppe, Milazzo; phone: 090-926133; moderate.)

Silvanetta Palace – Large and pleasant, with nicely appointed rooms, tennis courts, private beach, and restaurant. It's about a mile out of town, in the direction of Messina. Closed Mondays. (Contrada Mangiavacca, Milazzo; phone: 090-921638; moderate.)

EATING OUT: *Al Gambero* – Decorated with traditional Sicilian artifacts and handicrafts, including some Sicilian puppets, this centrally located restaurant serves good pasta and seafood. Closed Mondays and the last three weeks of January. Reservations advised. (Via Luigi Rizzo 5/6, Milazzo; phone: 090-921783; moderate.)

TOURING THE LIPARI (AEOLIAN) ISLANDS

These islands, off the northeastern coast of Sicily, are considered by many to be the most beautiful in Sicilian waters. Originally named after Aeolus, the mythical god of the wind, whom the ancients believed made his home in a cave here, they have recently been renamed after the largest, Lipari. There are seven major islands — Lipari, Vulcano, Salina, Panarea, Stromboli, Filicudi, and Alicudi — and numerous minor islets and outcroppings. Created by volcanic eruptions many thousands of years ago in this deepest part of the Tyrrhenian Sea, they have a primitive, rocky beauty, softened here and there by typically Mediterranean greenery — acanthus, broom, rosemary, and caper. The natural beauty of the islands, combined with the simple lifestyle of their inhabitants, has made them an attractive vacation spot for travelers weary of modern life. Electricity does not exist here except in homes and establishments that have their own generators. Cars, especially for nonresidents, are prohibited or discouraged. Many of the most beautiful and secluded beaches and the best diving or fishing spots are accessible only by boat, which for the tourist means hiring a local fisherman on a daily or hourly basis. Most visitors hardly seem to mind these inconveniences, for the volcanic sand beaches and crystal-clear, aqua blue waters are among the most inviting in Italy. Not surprisingly, with fish and shellfish in abundance, there are some particularly fine restaurants on the larger islands and numerous pleasant, if simple, *trattorie* throughout the archipelago. Price ranges are comparable to those for Sicily (see *Touring Sicily*).

Although it is possible to get to the Lipari Islands from other ports — there is overnight ferry service from Naples year-round and ferry and hydrofoil service from Naples, Palermo, Cefalù, Messina, Reggio Calabria, Vibo Valentia, and Maratea in summer — Milazzo is the major departure point for most visitors to the islands. Certainly, the trip from Milazzo is the quickest from Sicily. There is service daily to Vulcano, Lipari, and Salina; three or four times a week to Panarea and Stromboli; less frequently to Filicudi and Alicudi. The seven islands are also connected to one another by ferry, hydrofoil, and private boat. Departure times vary according to season and weather; it is best to inquire about timetables locally and, in summer, to make reservations in advance. In Milazzo, book through *Agenzia Eolian Tours,* Via Amendola (phone: 090-9811312); on Lipari Island, through *Azienda Autonoma di Soggiorno e Turismo* (*AAST*), 253 Corso Vittorio Emanuele, Lipari (phone: 090-9811410). AAST also has information on accommodations other than those recommended below.

LIPARI: The ancient Meligunis probably was settled in the 6th century BC, as is indicated by traces found on the promontory overlooking the town of Lipari and the harbor. Artifacts found at the site are displayed at the island's small but well-known *Museo Archeologico,* housed in a 16th-century Spanish castle that incorporates fragments of an ancient acropolis (hours variable; closed midday). Since Lipari has good roads, it is possible to tour the entire island by rental car. Other towns include Terme San Calogero, where vacationers can bathe in hot water springs as the ancient Romans did; Acquacalda, with its pumice quarries; and Rocche Rosse and its obsidian beds, which first made Lipari an ancient trading base. From the port in Lipari, it is possible to book day trips by boat around this island or to any of the others in the archipelago.

CHECKING IN: *Carasco –* The best hotel on Lipari offers quiet, comfortable rooms with particularly attractive views of the sea and coastline, a pool, and private beach facilities. Closed November to March. (Porto delle Genti, Lipari; phone: 090-9811605; moderate.)

Giardino sul Mare – Beautiful garden as well as a pool. (Via Maddalena 65, Lipari; phone: 090-9811004; inexpensive.)

EATING OUT: *Filippino –* Situated at the foot of the castle, this restaurant offers homemade macaroni, black *risotto,* fish soup, and Chinese-style lobster, as well as good wines such as Salina Malvasia. Open daily June through September; closed November and December and on Mondays from October to May. Reservations advised. (Piazza Municipio, Lipari; phone: 090-9811002; inexpensive.)

E' Pulera – Lovely garden with secluded tables and hearty meals in the island style. Open June through October. Reservations advisable. (Via Diana 51, Lipari; phone: 090-9811158; inexpensive.)

VULCANO: Only a short distance from Lipari, Vulcano is the most tourist-oriented of all the islands, largely because of its four volcanic craters, one of which, Vulcano della Fossa, is still slightly active. The crater has a circumference of roughly 1,650 feet that can be covered on foot in about an hour. Another seismic site is at Porto di Levante. Only a few yards from the sea lies a lake of thermal mud, reportedly with vast healing powers.

 EATING OUT: *Trattoria del Cratere* – On days that the fishing boats have been out, order fish. Otherwise, there are plenty of well-prepared meats, as well as pasta and eggplant and zucchini dishes. Open year-round. (Via Provinciale, Porto del Levante, Vulcano; phone: 090-9852045; inexpensive.)

SALINA: On the other side of Lipari, Salina has only two visible volcanic craters but far more vegetation than the other islands, probably because of the presence of underground springs. It also has extensive vineyards that produce the excellent local Malvasia wine. The coastline is rocky, with high cliffs and only a scattering of accessible beaches. It is a good place for a tranquil, utterly secluded holiday.

PANAREA: Many Italians consider Panarea, the smallest of the islands, the most beautiful, its cliffs of dark volcanic rock a dramatic background for the whitewashed fishing villages. There is little electricity and no paved roads, but the food is excellent and the scenery breathtaking. The ancestors of today's Panareans settled here thousands of years ago. At Capo Milazzese lie the remains of a prehistoric village with as many as 23 huts. The site is an hour's walk from the town of San Pietro or a short boat ride to Cala Junco. The ocean floor here is a vast underwater platform, so the sea is dotted with shoals and small islets. The largest of these, Basiluzzo, has rosemary and caper plants growing amid the traces of ancient Roman villas. Panarea is a favorite with scuba divers.

 CHECKING IN: *Lisca Bianca* – Offers a lovely view of the sea and dozens of tiny islets. (Via San Pietro, Panarea; phone: 090-9812422; inexpensive.)
La Piazza – The most comfortable hotel on the island. (Contrada San Pietro, Panarea; phone: 090-9811190; inexpensive.)

 EATING OUT: *Locanda del Sole* – Succulent meals — from oysters and seafood salad, to spaghetti with creamed fish and fennel, to baked grouper with capers and hard-boiled eggs — served on a picturesque terrace. Excellent wines and sherbets. Open evenings only from mid-June to mid-September. (Strada Communale del Porto, Panarea; phone: 090-9812558; moderate.)

STROMBOLI: The god Vulcan is said to have made his home in the mountain here; hence the slow-burning fire of this constantly (though not violently) active volcano. In modern times, it gained short-lived notoriety when it served as the trysting spot (and movie title) for the then scandalous liaison between Ingrid Bergman and Roberto Rossellini. Sometimes glowing streams of lava can be seen at night by ships passing by the northwest side. Clusters of white houses nestle at the foot of the volcano. The view from its slopes is awesome. The ascent from Ficogrande, by foot, is strenuous in its final portion along precipitous pathways. The crater, Sciara del Fuoco, emits plumes of volcanic ash and fumes of sulfurous gas. The Serra Vancora observation point at the summit above provides an excellent vantage point. All around the island are beaches of black volcanic sand bordering the cool, aqua sea. The fishing around Stromboli is excellent.

 CHECKING IN: *La Sciara Residence* – Quiet, with a pool, beach, tennis courts, and a lovely park. Management prefers that guests take board as well as room. Open April to mid-October. (Piscità, Stromboli; phone: 090-98604; moderate.)

EATING OUT: *Puntazzo* – Excellent fresh fish and lobster, as well as wild rabbit. Open May through September. (In Ginostra, on the opposite side of the island from Stromboli; boat transportation is available; phone: 090-981176; inexpensive.)

ALICUDI AND FILICUDI: These two small islands in the western part of the archipelago are well off the tourist track and are a favorite with underwater sports enthusiasts. Not surprisingly, accommodations are scarce and many who visit here come in private boats.

En Route from the Lipari Islands – Check ferry and hydrofoil timetables for departures to Sicily and the mainland.

Index